# THE
# HOODED
# GUNMAN

*An Illustrated History of*
## COLLINS CRIME CLUB

## JOHN CURRAN

THE SIGN OF A
CRIME CLUB BOOK.

# The CRIME CLUB

## FOR LOVERS OF DETECTIVE FICTION

### MEMBERSHIP IS FREE

THE CRIME CLUB has been formed so that readers of Detective Fiction may, at no cost to themselves, be regularly advised of the best Detective Novels before publication.

## HOW TO JOIN THE CRIME CLUB

Send a postcard to CRIME CLUB Headquarters, 48 Pall Mall, London, S.W.1., and your name will be entered on the Directory of Members.

You will be advised, before publication, of the Crime Club's selected book, chosen by a Panel of 5 Judges from the Crime Club List. THE CRIME CLUB MONTHLY BULLETIN brings news of forthcoming publications, enabling you to obtain, on publication day, the best detective novels through your local Bookseller or Circulating Library.

### ARE YOU A LIBRARY SUBSCRIBER?

Crime Club Books are available to all Circulating Library Subscribers **at no extra charge.**

### YOUR BOOKSELLER
### OR CIRCULATING LIBRARY

is your local agent for THE CRIME CLUB. Secure first editions of Crime Club Books.

We invite Authors throughout the world to submit their Detective Manuscripts for the consideration of the Crime Club Panel.

The CRIME CLUB

COLLINS

LONDON. S.V

# ACKNOWLEDGEMENTS

I would like to offer my thanks to Mark Terry of Facsimile Dustjackets for providing many dust jackets and for showing the tenacity of Inspector French in tracking down elusive titles. Most of the covers featured in this book can be found on his website of more than thirteen thousand vintage dust jackets – www.dustjackets.com

To Dawn Sinclair, Archivist at HarperCollins, Glasgow for invaluable and cheerful assistance on my many visits, and for always being willing to trawl through dusty record stores in search of answers to obscure queries.

To Cecil Jenkins and Colin Thomas for sharing their personal Crime Club memories.

And to many partners in crime for providing encouragement, images, information, and proof-reading expertise during the writing process: Sean Bourke, Geoff Bradley, Pete Coleman, Brendan Curran, Martin Edwards, Tony Medawar, Nigel Moss, Carmel O'Neill, John Perry, Barry Pike, Jamie Sturgeon.

Above all to my editor David Brawn who championed *The Hooded Gunman* from the moment I first tentatively suggested it. And Terence Caven for producing such stunning artwork to complement – and probably overshadow! – my text.

COLLINS CRIME CLUB
An imprint of HarperCollins*Publishers*
1 London Bridge Street
London SE1 9GF
www.harpercollins.co.uk

First edition 2019

# CONTENTS

**INTRODUCTION** • 7
The History of Collins • 8

**COLLINS AND CRIME FICTION** • 11
The Dawn of a Golden Age • 12
The Key to Success • 15
The Detective Story Club • 19
The Crime Club • 21
The Crime Club Cover Story • 25

**FIRST DECADE – THE 1930S** • 30

**SECOND DECADE – THE 1940S** • 62

**THIRD DECADE – THE 1950S** • 86

**FOURTH DECADE – THE 1960S** • 110

**FIFTH DECADE – THE 1970S** • 132

**SIXTH DECADE – THE 1980S** • 160

**SEVENTH DECADE – THE 1990S** • 94

**POSTSCRIPT – 65 YEARS OF BRILLIANT CRIME** • 210
The End of an Era • 212
'Phantom' Titles • 213
The White Circle • 214
Anniversary Volumes • 216
The Crime Club Card Games • 20
'Only for Dons' Crime Novel Competition • 222

**MURDER THEY WROTE** • 225
The Descriptive Blurbs • 226
Short Story Collections • 386
Omnibuses • 387
Duplicate Titles • 388
Abroad in Crime Club • 388
Topics in Crime Club • 389
White Circle Paperbacks • 390
Select References • 391
Index of Authors • 392
Index of Titles • 394

SIGN OF A GOOD
DETECTIVE NOVEL

# INTRODUCTION

IN LATE 1929 a club was founded in London; and from the beginning, and throughout its long existence, it remained a club with no premises, no annual subscription and no Board of Officers or secretary. There was no AGM, no proposals, no elections and no voting; in fact, there were no rules. The only condition of membership was a proficiency in literacy; and to join the only fee payable was the cost of a postage stamp.

Not surprisingly, within two years of its foundation this club boasted a membership of over 25,000. More surprisingly perhaps, this impressive figure represented all walks of life: doctors, clergymen, businessmen, lawyers, teachers and civil servants rubbed metaphorical shoulders with University Dons, millionaires, statesmen, peers, princes, princesses and knights. And yet none of these 25,000 ever met each other. To ensure that such a discerning clientèle remained happy, a carefully chosen Panel of Experts advised those running the club. And increasing membership proved that this Panel was indeed expert in this very particular sphere.

From its inception and throughout its existence the club was run from London by faceless and anonymous men – and, at a later point, one very influential woman – whose only contact with the membership was via an informative but attractive newsletter. The men were, in essence, businessmen capitalising on an interest shared by all members; an interest which could be enjoyed 'in [one's] favourite armchair' and from which enjoyment one arose 'refreshed and invigorated, with worries forgotten'. This absorbing pastime was described variously as 'fascinating, exhilarating, entertaining and thrilling', with benefits, members were confidently assured, 'as good as a holiday [and] better than a play…'. As endorsement, members were also assured that their interest was shared by 'Cabinet Ministers, Business Magnates, Harley Street Specialists, Famous Judges, Bishops and Leaders of Religion, Teachers, and men and women in every sphere of life'.

This interest was the reading of Detective Fiction. The club was Collins Crime Club.

# THE HISTORY OF COLLINS

WILLIAM COLLINS (1789-1853), the founder of Collins, Sons & Co. Ltd, was born in 1789 and after some years as a teacher went into partnership with Charles Chalmers in 1819 to establish a printing and publishing business. William Collins & Co. handled the publishing and printing side of the business while Chalmers & Collins dealt with bookselling and stationery. In 1826, Collins brought out Chalmers but retained the copyright of books already published.

William Collins (II) (1817-1895) joined his father's business and in 1848 was admitted as a partner, coinciding with a general expansion of the business. The growth in the number of churches following a major schism in the Church of Scotland, in 1843, and the church extension scheme created an increased demand for Bibles and religious literature. The advent of compulsory education combined with a general increase in literacy meant that there was an increased demand for published material.

William Collins (I) died in 1853 and William Collins (II) continued the business alone until 1865, when he took his two assistants into partnership, followed, three years later, by his two eldest sons, William Collins (III) and Alexander Collins, and the company became known as William Collins, Sons & Co. Alexander concentrated on extending the Bible sales. In 1880, the company acquired limited liability, becoming William Collins, Sons & Co. Ltd. By the time that William Collins (II) died in 1895 the business had greatly expanded and as he had also taken great interest in his workers' welfare and in 1887 the Collins Institute opened near the business' works in Glasgow, catering for the workers' educational, social and cultural needs.

In 1900, William Collins (III) began to publish, very successfully, children's literature and in 1903, he launched the Collins Handy Illustrated Pocket Novels, although the name was soon changed to Collins Illustrated Pocket Novels. In 1904, he founded Collins Brothers & Co. to operate in Australia and New Zealand and, in 1905, William Collins & Co., New York. He also improved and extended the company's printing works. He died in 1906 leaving no heirs.

William Collins (IV) (1873-1945), son of Alexander Collins, succeeded his uncle as Chairman in 1906. He

*L to R: William Collins 1789-1853; Book production in the 1930s: William Collins (III) 1846-1906; William Hope Collins (IV) 1873-1945; W. A. R. Collins (V) 1900-1976.*

had been elected to the board in 1897, followed by his brother Godfrey Collins and his cousin William Collins Dickson, both of whom became directors in 1899. William (IV) took over the supervision of the home and overseas offices, and the manufacture and sale of stationery while Godfrey was responsible for publications. In 1907, they introduced the 'Sevenpennies' series of cheap copyright novels by living authors.

The company continued to expand, and James Paterson, Ebenezer Dow and Alec B. Glen joined the board of directors while Godfrey Collins began to follow a career in politics. With the advent of the World War I, both Collins brothers enlisted for military service leaving the business in the hands of James Paterson. The company also began to seek out original fiction, history, biographies and poetry, a venture which continued to grow over following decades.

In 1919, Godfrey Collins was knighted and appointed Junior Lord of the Treasury. In 1924, he became the Chief Liberal Whip before being appointed to the Cabinet in 1932. He was made a Privy Councillor and became the Secretary of State for Scotland. He died in 1936.

The 1930s saw the next generation of Collins entering the company. Ian G. Collins, the second son of William (IV), began to learn the technicalities of book production as well as the export trade. William Hope Collins, the son of Sir Godfrey, and William Collins (V) also entered the company. During the 1930s the company continued to

flourish, embracing American as well as British fiction. William Hope Collins' visit to America in 1932 to inspect printing equipment resulted in the introduction of new printing presses and binding machines. In 1938, William Hope Collins became president of the Stationers Co. of Glasgow and, ten years later, president of the British Federation of Master Printers.

When William (IV) died in 1945 William (V) took over as chairman and managing director, with Ian G. Collins as vice chairman and managing director, and William Hope Collins as joint managing director. The company's output increased in terms of both book and stationery production, and printing and warehouse capacity was extended, most notably with the opening of the Montgomery Building in 1953. William Hope Collins continued the company's reputation for caring for their workers by developing the pension and profit sharing schemes and by the creation of a health and welfare department in the 1950s. William Hope Collins died in 1967.

In the 1970s, the company moved out of its central Glasgow offices in the Cathedral Street area to Bishopbriggs in the north of the city. In 1983, the company acquired the publishing interests of the media company, Granada Group Ltd, including Granada Publishing Ltd and its subsidiaries. In 1989, William Collins Sons & Co. Ltd merged with Harper & Row, publishers, New York United States, to form HarperCollins Publishers Ltd with head offices at Bishopbriggs, Glasgow.

# COLLINS AND CRIME FICTION

Between the beginning of the 20th century and the establishment 30 years later of Collins Crime Club, crime fiction in general, and detective fiction in particular, had developed into a hugely popular genre. The generally accepted 'date of birth' of detective fiction is 1841, the year that Edgar Allan Poe published the seminal short story 'The Murders in the Rue Morgue'. Over the following 60 years the seed planted by Poe was cultivated by myriad writers – some famous, many forgotten – into a bloom that attained its Golden Age around 1920 and was in full flower by the time the first Crime Club titles appeared in May 1930.

# THE DAWN OF A GOLDEN AGE

IN THE 90 YEARS between the initial contribution of Poe and arrival of the Hooded Gunman hundreds of writers produced thousands of stories of dark deeds and daring detectives, but only a fraction of them can be considered significant. The following are landmark titles in the development of crime fiction between 1841 and the dawn, 80 years later, of the Golden Age; and the innovations they presented are reflected throughout the 64 years of the Crime Club.

## 1841: The Amateur Detective

In 'The Murders in the Rue Morgue' Edgar Allan Poe (1809-1849) introduced most of the elements of what would become known as 'detective fiction'. In fact, no other writer established so many influential factors: the brilliant amateur detective and his less-than-gifted associate (known, from the most famous example, as the 'Watson'), murder in a locked room, the uneasy relationship between the official and unofficial investigators, the wrongly arrested suspect, the interpretation of overlooked clues ('ratiocination', as Poe called it), and, finally, the surprise solution and the unexpected murderer.

**Crime Club examples of detective and 'Watson':**
- Agatha Christie: Hercule Poirot and Captain Hastings
- Rex Stout: Nero Wolfe and Archie Goodwin
- Lionel Black: Husband-and-wife team Kate and Henry Theobold
- Lilian Jackson Braun: Jim Qwilleran and the Siamese cat Koko
- Harry Carmichael: John Piper and Quinn (but which is the detective and which the 'Watson'?)
- Sarah Caudwell: Hilary Tamar and a group of 'Watsons'
- Anthony Abbot: the author is narrator and 'Watson' to Thatcher Colt

## 1853: The Police Detective

The post-Bow Street Runners police force had its beginnings in the Metropolitan Police Act 1829, later augmented by the 1843 foundation of the Detective Department, a direct forerunner of Scotland Yard's C.I.D. A decade later Charles Dickens (1812-1870) featured the first police detective, Inspector Bucket in *Bleak House*.

**Crime Club examples of police detective:**
- Historical: Keith Heller's trilogy beginning with *Man's Illegal Life: A Story of London's Parish Watch* 1722
- Genteel: Carol Carnac's Julian Rivers; Ngaio Marsh's Roderick Alleyn; Patricia Moyes' Henry Tibbett
- Realistic: Novels of Roger Busby; John Wainwright
- Disreputable: Reginald Hill's Andy Dalziel; Jack Scott's Alf Rosher

## 1868: The Country House Mystery

*The Moonstone* by Wilkie Collins (1824-1889) is considered the first detective novel, containing many of the elements that would become almost standard through the Golden Age: a crime – usually a murder, but in this novel the disappearance of the fabulous Moonstone jewel; a confined setting containing a 'closed circle' of suspects with suspicion falling on each; a local policeman acting as foil to a brilliant detective, who notices, and correctly interprets, clues; a re-enactment of the crime and final gathering of the suspects to hear the explanation. (Wilkie Collins' earlier novel, 1860's *The Woman in White*, is frequently bracketed with *The Moonstone* but is more Gothic thriller than detective story.)

**Crime Club examples of the country house mystery:**
- Agatha Christie: *The Hollow*
- Ngaio Marsh: *Tied up in Tinsel*
- Rupert Penny: *Policeman's Evidence*
- Ellis Peters: *Black is the Colour of my True Love's Heart*
- Patricia Moyes: *Who Saw Her Die?*

## 1870: The 'Reader as Detective'

Charles Dickens' *The Mystery of Edwin Drood* remains the ultimate mystery as the author died before he wrote the final instalments of his serial novel, leaving forever unanswered questions: Was Edwin Drood murdered? By whom? Where is his body? And who is Dick Datchery? While this literary mystery has provided sufficient material to become a mini-industry, it is not entirely clear if Dickens intended the novel as a true detective story, with properly presented clues for the reader to notice and interpret.

**Crime Club examples of 'reader as detective':**
The 'Challenge to the Reader' ploy in:
- C Daly King: *Obelists En Route*
- Philip MacDonald: *The Maze*
- Rupert Penny: *Policeman's Holiday*

## 1878: A Legal Background

Anna Katharine Green (1846-1935) – the first woman to write a detective novel – published *The Leavenworth Case*. An immediate critical and commercial success, it featured a body in the library, a victim on the point of changing his will, a closed circle of suspects, an inquest, forensic evidence, a diagram of the murder scene, a subsequent death, and a dramatic final revelation. In fact, most of the elements that are to be found in many Golden Age novels half a century later. *The Leavenworth Case* is subtitled 'A Lawyer's Story' and unsurprisingly the law and lawyers have been central elements of crime fiction since its beginnings.

**Crime Club examples with a legal background:**
- Dominic Devine: *The Sleeping Tiger*
- Roy Lewis: *A Fool for a Client*
- Raymond Postgate: *Verdict of Twelve*
- The novels of Sarah Caudwell, Sara Woods and Roderic Jeffries

## 1887: The Great Detective

Arthur Conan Doyle (1859-1930) introduced Sherlock Holmes in *A Study in Scarlet* and the character became not only the most famous literary detective but probably the most famous literary creation of all time. His second full-length case, *The Sign of Four*, was published three years later but it was not until his short-story appearances, in the *Strand Magazine*, that the immortality of both creator and creation was assured.

**Crime Club examples of The Great Detective:**
- Nicholas Blake: *A Question of Proof* (Nigel Strangeways)
- Agatha Christie: *The A B C Murders* (Hercule Poirot)
- Rex Stout: *Some Buried Caesar* (Nero Wolfe)
- Ngaio Marsh: *Overture to Death* (Roderick Alleyn)

## 1891: Short Story Collections

Sherlock Holmes appears in 'A Scandal in Bohemia', the first of 56 short story appearances in the *Strand Magazine*. And the world of crime fiction was never the same again. This series, published over the following 36 years (24 stories between 1891 and 1893; 13 between 1903 and 1904; and the final 19 published sporadically between 1908 and 1927) was largely responsible for the enormous public appetite for detective fiction, especially in its shorter form. Dozens of imitators copied the central format of the Holmes stories: a detective figure and a 'Watson' investigating cases – not always a murder – brought to their attention by clients.

**Crime Club examples of short story collections:**
- Agatha Christie: *The Labours of Hercules*
- Elizabeth Ferrars: *Designs on Life*
- C. Daly King: *The Curious Mr. Tarrant*
- Martin Russell: *The Darker Side of Death*

## 1892: The Locked Room Mystery

Israel Zangwill (1864-1926) published *The Big Bow Mystery*, the first 'locked room' novel – where interest is equally divided between the identity of the villain and how that villain managed to leave a crime scene with all doors and windows locked from the inside – featuring a clever solution utilising both physical and psychological sleight-of-hand to fool the detective and the reader.

**Crime Club examples of 'the locked room':**
- Catherine Aird: *His Burial Too*
- Agatha Christie: *Hercule Poirot's Christmas*
- Rupert Penny: *Sealed Room Murder*
- Clayton Rawson: *Death from a Top Hat*

## 1897: The Spinster Detective

Anna Katharine Green's *That Affair Next Door* introduced Amelia Butterworth, the much-copied model of the inquisitive spinster detective.

**Crime Club examples of the 'spinster' detective:**
- Agatha Christie: *The Mirror Crack'd from Side to Side*
- M. G. Eberhart: *Wolf in Man's Clothing*
- Stuart Palmer: *Miss Withers Regrets*

## 1903: The Spy-Adventure Story

Erskine Childers's (1870-1922) *The Riddle of the Sands* and, a dozen years later, John Buchan's (1875-1940) *The Thirty-Nine Steps*, each the best-known work of their respective authors, still remain prime examples of the spy-adventure story.

**Crime Club examples of the spy-adventure story:**
- Kenneth Benton: *Sole Agent*
- Michael Butterworth: *Remains to be Seen*
- Agatha Christie: *N or M?*
- M. G. Eberhart: *The Man Next Door*
- Patricia McGerr: *Is There a Traitor in the House?*

## 1905: The Armchair Detective

The concept of the 'armchair detective', pioneered in Poe's 'The Mystery of Marie Roget' (1842), was consolidated by Baroness Orczy (1865-1947) with her 'Old Man in the Corner' creation, an elderly and enigmatic man who solves mysteries, details of which are brought to him by reporter Polly Burton, without ever (well, hardly ever) leaving his seat in an ABC tea-shop.

**Crime Club examples of the armchair detective:**
- Agatha Christie: *The Thirteen Problems*
- John Rhode: *Death at Breakfast*
- Rex Stout: *Murder by the Book*

## 1907: The Forensic Detective

R. Austin Freeman (1862-1943) introduced the best, and best-known, forensic detective, Dr. John Thorndyke, by training a doctor and a lawyer, in *The Red Thumb-Mark*, the first of 20 novels and 40 short stories over the following 35 years.

**Crime Club examples of the forensic detective:**
- Anthony Abbott: *About the Murder of a Startled Lady*
- Aaron Elkins: *Icy Clutches*

## 1909: Novels In Translation

The influential *The Mystery of the Yellow Room* by Gaston Leroux (1868-1927), creator of *The Phantom of the Opera*, was published in English, having appeared in French two years earlier. It featured seemingly inexplicable attempted murder and disappearances in a country house in the French countryside, a brilliant young reporter-detective and a dramatic courtroom denouement.

**Crime Club examples of novels in translation:**
- Catherine Arley: *Woman of Straw*
- Sergio Donati: *The Paper Tomb*
- Auguste Le Breton: *The Law of the Streets*
- Torben Nielsen: *Nineteen Red Roses*

## 1910: A Religious Background

G. K. Chesterton's Catholic priest-detective Father Brown debuted in 'The Blue Cross', the first of 53 short stories (Father Brown appears only in short story form) over the following quarter century.

**Crime Club examples with a religious background:**
- Robert Barnard: *Blood Brotherhood*
- Agatha Christie: *The Murder at the Vicarage*
- A. Fielding: *Mystery at the Rectory*
- Joseph Telushkin: *The Unorthodox Murder of Rabbi Moss*

## 1912: The 'Inverted' Detective Story

The Austin Freeman collection *The Singing Bone* pioneered the 'inverted detective story', in which the reader watches the planning and commission of the crime and subsequently the progress of the investigation. Rather than a question of 'whodunit' the reader's curiosity is focused on trying to spot the fatal flaw which will lead to the criminal's downfall.

**Crime Club examples of the 'inverted' story:**
- Catherine Arley: *Ready Revenge*
- Nicholas Blake: *The Beast Must Die*
- Andrew Garve: *The Long Short Cut*
- Malcolm Forsythe: *A Cousin Removed*

## 1913: The Deliberate Pastiche

E. C. Bentley (1875-1956) wrote *Trent's Last Case* to highlight the literary limitations of detective fiction but, ironically, the novel became one of the genre's immortal country-house titles.

**Crime Club examples of country-house pastiche:**
- Marian Babson: *Weekend for Murder*
- Reginald Hill: *An April Shroud*
- H. R. F. Keating: *The Murder of the Maharajah*
- Patricia Moyes: *A Six-Letter Word for Death*

# THE KEY TO SUCCESS

LISTS OF INFLUENTIAL contributions to the development of crime fiction do not normally include *The Skeleton Key* (1919) by Bernard Capes (1854-1918). Indeed Collins, whose first crime fiction title it was, could not have known that its appearance would lead directly, within the decade, to the emergence of the Crime Club. The blurb-writer certainly did not undersell the novel, describing it as 'a clever crime problem and plenty of thrills, a sensible love story, humour, excellent characterisation and strong human interest'. The 'crime problem' concerns the body discovered in the grounds of a country-house during a shooting party and its investigation by young Sergeant Ridgway and Baron Le Sage. Somewhat unusually the body is that of one of the housemaids. Like *The Mystery of the Yellow Room*, *The Skeleton Key* contains chapters of courtroom cross-examination, a 'foreign' detective, a country-house setting and a surprise solution. Barzun and Taylor in their *Catalogue of Crime* consider 'the forepart of the tale written with care and art' and Julian Symons in his *Bloody Murder* calls the book 'a tour-de-force'. G. K. Chesterton provided an introduction to the first edition in which he praised Capes' fertile mind and the 'touch of distinction' he brought to the detective story. Sadly, neither Chesterton's contribution nor the published book was ever seen by Capes, who died in the flu epidemic that followed in the aftermath of WWI. The book, however, enjoyed six reprints before being reissued – with the slightly altered title of *The Mystery of the Skeleton Key* – as one of the earliest volumes in Collins' Detective Story Club (see below).

Because of the success of *The Skeleton Key* the Pall Mall offices of Collins received a 'flood of unsolicited crime-story manuscripts'. One of these was a detective story by a railway engineer who, during a long illness, had amused himself by writing a story of crime detection. That writer was Freeman Wills Crofts (1879-1957) and the book was *The Cask*.

When the eponymous cask is being unloaded at the docks it leaks not wine, its legitimate cargo, but sawdust and gold coins; and closer examination reveals the fingers of a corpse. By the time that Inspector Burnley arrives both the cask and its guardian have disappeared. A meticulously detailed investigation, moving between France and the UK, follows in this landmark of detective fiction. Writing a quarter-century after the publication of *The Cask* (1920), Crofts noted that the book was 'written at least five times before the final draft was reached', adding ruefully, that, in his literary naïvety, he added an unnecessary 40,000 words; unnecessary in the sense that the same royalties were payable on an 80,000 as on a 120,000-word count! He also considered that his account of 'the journeying of the cask through London' was 'irrelevant padding'. In its original incarnation the denouement of *The Cask* featured a courtroom scene, but Crofts was advised that 'no trial like that described has ever taken place, either in this or any other country', and, with the promise of publication in the offing, Crofts was happy to rewrite his original Part III. Despite retrospective self-criticism, *The Cask* has been a steady seller ever since, rarely out of print.

Within the decade Collins was publishing, alongside Freeman Wills Crofts, some of the most influential (many now long-forgotten) names in the development of detective fiction. Of the following list of Collins authors all but Anthony Berkeley would appear in the Crime Club:

 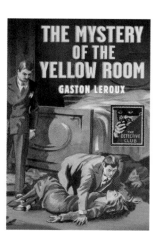

*The current Detective Club editions of* The Skeleton Key *and* The Mystery of the Yellow Room, *both reusing cover art from the late 1920s. The Capes cover is surprisingly violent, while Leroux's room seems to have been redecorated!*

The early 1940s saw a brief flirtation with the inclusion of an author photograph on the cover: a genial John Rhode appeared as 'A famous Crime Club author' on the covers of *Death on the Boat-Train* (April '40) and *Murder at Lilac Cottage* (September '40) and with the same photograph, though without the soubriquet, on *Death at the Helm* (April '41). A solemn Leslie Ford was dubbed 'A Crime Club Star Author' on *Snow-White Murder* (May '40) and *Road to Folly* (February '41); and Rupert Penny's impressive profile, while, presumably, hard at work on his next masterpiece, appears with the slogan 'A 'PENNY' FOR YOUR THOUGHTS' on the cover of *Sealed Room Murder* (May '41).

The 1950s saw the appearance of the iconic black covers with the title in a variety of strong, single colours and author's name, for the most part, in white; the words 'Crime Club Choice' was emblazoned across the top of the jacket. This was the distinction given to books which the mythical Selection Committee considered particularly worthy of readers' attention. The first such was Nigel Fitzgerald's *The Rosy Pastor* in January 1954 and the final title was Sara Woods' *And Shame the Devil* (November '67).

Alongside these, the pictorial covers continued, the majority of which were visually attractive. The only writer to suffer from consistently dull covers was, ironically, Agatha Christie; although Ngaio Marsh fared little better, *Opening Night* (April '51) being an exception. This was, presumably on the basis that their books – Christie's in particular – would sell even if wrapped in newspaper. It was not until the 1970s that Marsh's books showed any improvement, but Christie's remained disappointing until the end of her career. Two proposed covers aroused Christie's ire. Sadly, an early design for *The Labours of Hercules* has not survived: according to a 1947 letter she was appalled at the 'rough [sketch] for the wrapper…of Poirot going naked to the bath!', adding that 'all sorts of obscene suggestions' were forthcoming from her family. Likewise she was unimpressed with the 'pinky colour' on the cover of *N or M?*, finding it 'more sentimental than murderous'.

From the mid-'50s onwards covers became generally duller and darker, with little or no colour. The early years of the decade featured many visually attractive covers – *Save the Witness* (May '50), *Milk of Human Kindness* (July '50), *The House over the Tunnel* (May '51), *Murder, Repeat Murder* (September '52), *Murder as a Fine Art* (March '53), *Shroud of Darkness*

*An advertisement on a Crime Club stand at a 1964 book trade exhibition pulled no punches about the quality of its titles.*

(March '54) – but these disappeared almost completely after *The Odd Flamingo* (April '54).

Two new designs were introduced in the 1960s, each relatively short-lived. In April 1965 *Call after Midnight* pioneered the first of these. The book title, in black capitals, appeared on a single-colour rectangle at the top of the cover above a contrasting colour with a diagrammatic image on the lower half; the author's name appeared on a dividing white line between the two. The words 'Crime Club' appeared in white on the illustration. These continued until *Web of Silence* (February '68). Interspersed with these, pictorial covers continued, although in muted colours for the most part. Notable exceptions included *The Seeds of Hate* (January '60), *Gambit* (April '63) and *The Morning after Death* (October '66). And collectors of Tom Adams, noted artist of the famous series of Christie Fontana paperbacks, should note his cover for Martin Russell's *No Return Ticket* (September '66).

An even more short-lived design appeared between 1967 – as soon as the black 'Choice' covers ceased – and

# CRIME CLUB TITLES

January-June 1976

**All at £2.95**

## JANUARY

**THE MODIGLIANI SCANDAL**
ZACHARY STONE

This suspenseful and ironic story of three rivals on the track of a hitherto unknown Modigliani lays bare the skulduggery and wheeler-dealering within the international art world when masterpiece hunters, forgers and thieves collide.

**FALSE EVIDENCE** HARRY CARMICHAEL

George Ainsworth disappeared from the Dublin-Liverpool ferry and everyone, including the police, believed he had gone overboard. Only Quinn of the *Morning Post* had doubts, and doubt resolved itself into a double tragedy before the truth was revealed.

**REMAINS TO BE SEEN**
MICHAEL BUTTERWORTH

The remains were to be seen in Bernard Davis's car—dumped there when he left it in a London street. When Bernard realized there was international espionage interest in the undertaking Davis (formerly Davydov) family from Scunthorpe, something vital was obviously at stake. *Crime Club Choice*

## FEBRUARY

**NEW FACE IN HELL** ROGER BUSBY

An armed killer on the run in the West Country is the quarry in this gripping police procedural in which the action swings between the men on the trail and the men at headquarters as conflict develops and the killer strikes again.

**CRISSCROSS  PAT FLOWER**

Edward Piper, an accountant, had dreams of being creative, but his conflicting emotions towards those who were and towards his wife, who was so understanding, led him ever further from reality and ever nearer to crime.

**LEGACY OF EVIL  ANNA CLARKE**

Herbert Bullen was a vicious and cruel man, but when his downtrodden wife helped him out of life she tasted evil for herself and this grimly enthralling novel becomes the story of an obsessional killer and her victims.

## MARCH

**HOME TO ROOST**  ANDREW GARVE

Can a man break a perfect alibi? Mystery writer Walter Haines had to try when he confessed to a murder he couldn't in theory have committed. But was it a genuine alibi?

**THE MATTER OF PARADISE**
BROWN MEGGS

Music critic Hobie Milne didn't care what happened to his old classmates from The Mather School Class of 1950—until they began to die one by one. For 25 years later what had they in common? Nothing but Mather, sudden death—and the 'matter of Paradise'. *Crime Club Choice*

**A HEALTHY WAY TO DIE** LIONEL BLACK

Reporter Kate Theobald looked forward to slimming at one of England's best-known health farms. But when a man died violently in these healthy surroundings, she had a newspaper scoop on her hands, a farm full of suspects, and an intriguing mystery.

## APRIL

**DOUBLE DEAL  MARTIN RUSSELL**

Peter Connors was approached separately by a husband and wife, each anxious to secure his aid in disposing of the other. Two attempts later, he began to wonder if he had been had—but by then it was too late: he was a murderer.

**WITNESS MY DEATH  ROY LEWIS**

The Welsh mining valleys, Roy Lewis's own background, are the setting for an unusual story of a local doctor's involvement in murder, corruption and the scandal of a dangerous slag heap.

**A LITTLE LOCAL MURDER**
ROBERT BARNARD

The decision to send a radio team to Twytching to record some of its inhabitants for the benefit of its American twin town resulted in high comedy and also in murder. Wit is not the least leathal of the weapons employed.

## MAY

**BLOOD FLIES UPWARDS**
ELIZABETH FERRARS

The young woman who took the post of cook-housekeeper at the wealthy Eckersalls' weekend retreat was not all she seemed—but neither were the Eckersalls. Alison was there to try to discover what had happened to her sister who had mysteriously disappeared. What the Eckersalls had to hide was not without bearing on that disappearance.

**ANOTHER DEATH IN VENICE**
REGINALD HILL

Three married couples on holiday in Italy become involved among themselves, in the death of an unknown young man, and in the lives of another very enigmatic couple—with unexpected consequences all round. *Crime Club Choice*

**ONE GOOD DEATH DESERVES
ANOTHER** RITCHIE PERRY

Back in Brazil, the setting of his first adventure, Philis finds a number of people want him dead. What has he done to become so immediate a target? Or is it what Pawson has done—behind the scenes?

## JUNE

**A FAMILY AFFAIR** REX STOUT

What could make Nero Wolfe so determined to solve a crime that he would work without fee or client? Never before has Rex Stout shown us the extremes to which his great detective can be pushed. The last Nero Wolfe novel is one of the best. *Crime Club Choice*

**PAYOFF** HARTLEY HOWARD

Dr Wolf Neustadt had an attractive wife, a lucrative practice and an office on Madison Avenue. He also had a problem: he was being followed. Yet the New York police could find no evidence. So Neustadt hired Glenn Bowman, who was soon on the trail of Neustadt's past.

**END OF A GOOD WOMAN**
MARGARET HINXMAN

Who could want to kill a good woman like Ruth Brenner—loving mother, kind neighbour, loyal friend? Yet when Ruth was found mysteriously dead, the police were dissatisfied, and several people proved to have reason to regret her existence. Was she a good woman? And what was her real end?

| UK | Australia* | New Zealand* | South Africa |
|---|---|---|---|
| £2.95 | $7.15 | $7.00 | R6.95 |

* recommended price

*In the 1970s the Crime Club Newsletter changed format, appearing twice a year and listing all titles for the coming six-month period, complete with colour illustrations.*

1969: predominantly black-with-coloured-wording which began with *The Cat Who Ate Danish Modern* (March '68) through to *Of Malicious Intent* (November '69). These all included 'A Crime Club Recommendation' above the two-coloured title and although not visually exciting, they did make the books instantly recognisable.

The 1970s led off with one of the most unattractive covers of the entire series: *Young Man, I Think You're Dying* by Joan Fleming (January 1972). Despite the merits of the book, which won the Gold Dagger Award, and the cover's attempt to reflect 'Youth Underworld' subject matter, the jacket remains jarringly unappealing. For the first few years there was little consistency, with oddities like the provocative *The Thrill Machine* (January '72) and *Blood on a Harvest Moon* (October '72), and the stark simplicity of *Most Deadly Hate* (June '71) and *El Rancho Rio* (August '71). From 1973 onwards there was uniformity as regards title and author fonts, mainly white for author and a variety of colour for title. In 1977 the design on the spine was regularised with 'Collins Crime Club' circled at the head and the Hooded Gunman circled at the foot of each spine. A wide variety of colours was used on the spine itself. With very few exceptions – *Miss Marple's Final Cases* (October '76) and the Ngaio Marsh titles – this design continued until the end of 1988, the longest period of design consistency. Covers throughout were photographic. From 1989 onwards the size of books increased and the spine (title, author, Hooded Gunman and Collins Crime Club) wording was re-arranged, on a variety of colours like the previous decade.

From January 1990 the Diamond Anniversary was celebrated with the Hooded Gunman now enclosed in a diamond shape with the addition of the wording '1930-90' for the anniversary year itself. And this design remained for most of the Club's remaining years, with some exceptions for Reginald Hill, Gwendoline Butler and David Williams *inter alia*. Possibly as a prelude to many writers moving to Collins Crime, the final titles retained little Crime Club outward identity.

Over the decades identification of cover artists remained elusive. It was not until the photographic covers of the 1980s that the name of the artist-photographer appeared regularly on book-flaps.

Of those identified, two of the most prolific were William Randell and Kenneth Farnhill, with over 150 covers between them. Of the two, Randell is the most identifiable, with covers frequently featuring a figure, usually male, who could be either victim or villain: *And Death Came Too* (April '56), *The Narrow Search* (March '57), *Sapphires on Wednesday* (May '57), *Shadow on the House* (January '58). Farnhill is more unpredictable with covers ranging from *And Shame the Devil* (November '67) and *Hand in Glove* (September '62) to *A Charitable End* (April '71) and *Photographs Have Been Sent to Your Wife* (February '71).

When covers became exclusively photographic – intermittently from the late 1960s and almost exclusively from the 1970s onwards – the names of the photographers were more readily identified and three names dominated: Margaret Murray, Colin Thomas and Howard Bartrop. These three were responsible for almost 600 covers between them. Colin Thomas told me:

'I used to work for the art director [who would] give me a manuscript to read, and I would come up with ideas for the cover in the form of a rough scribble…my art school training in drawing came in handy! [The art-director] then got one of my rough ideas approved by Elizabeth [Walter] and then I would go away and shoot it. I had to be very careful to make sure that I could get the necessary props and "models" for virtually nothing, as that was the fee that they paid! When [a new art director] took over she used to come up with the ideas, and I shot the pictures with her at my studio.

'I remember that Elizabeth Walter had a very literary attitude to cover images, in the sense that she would always respond positively if there was some sort of text visible in the cover image, for example the writing on a letter, or a will, a name carved into a tree trunk or written in blood. It's not surprising I guess as she made her living with words!

'I think we were generally working about six months in advance. They used to keep me well away from authors, who as far as I know were not given any sort of cover approval.'

Crime Club covers rarely featured anything explicitly violent, *Fell of Dark* (May '75), *Cold Light of Day* (November '83) and *The Bilbao Looking-Glass* (October '83) being notable exceptions. However, skulls/skeletons – *Dial Death* (July '77), *The Corpse Now Arriving* (May '83), *Once Dying Twice Dead* (May '84) – weapons – *Two-Faced Death* (September '76), *To Kill a Coconut* (January '77), *This Is Your Death* (October '81) – and, less often, blood – *The Pretty Pink Shroud* (April '77), *Life Cycle* (July '78), *The Sweet Short Grass* (September '82) – did feature. But never in an overtly gruesome fashion; less was always more. The power of the covers lies in their juxtaposition of the mundane and the menacing: *Candles for the Dead* (October '73), *The Eve of the Wedding* (June '80), *A Six-Letter Word for Death* (May '83), *Natural Causes* (January '84), *Murder for Lunch* (Octtober '86), *Passing Strange* (October '80). All feature everyday objects subtly incorporating a hint of something darker…

My own Desert Island covers would include: *Murder Gone Mad* and *Bats in the Belfry* (1930s); *Murder at the Munition Works* and *Situation Vacant* (1940s); *Murder as Fine Art* and *Crossed Skis* (1950s); *Falling Star* and *Gambit* (1960s); *Slight Mourning* and *Two Little Rich Girls* (1970s); *Trio in Three Flats* and *Welcome to the Grave* (1980); *The Company She Kept* (1990s). And if I could take just one? That has to be the cover for Ellis Peters' *Funeral of Figaro* (November '62). Eye-catchingly stark, its simplicity is deceptive. What is recognisably a face is composed of two quaver notes – the setting is an opera house – and the tear from one eye proves, on closer examination, to be a noose.

# THE SIGN OF A GOOD CRIME STORY

## THE CRIME CLUB

BETWEEN MAY 1930 and November 1939, the Crime Club issued 346 titles. In theory three titles were issued on the first Monday of every month but, as will be seen, this was more aspirational than realistic. The writers, and settings, were for the most part British and American but more exotic locales were found in Greece (G. D. H. and M. Cole), India (Lawrence Blochman), Russia (Ethel Lina White), Mexico (Stuart Palmer), the West Indies (Hulbert Footner) and the various Middle Eastern settings of Agatha Christie. The titles were a mixture of every type of crime fiction; clearly many of them were 'pure' detective fiction and, in fact, the slogan of the Crime Club was to become 'Sign of a Good Detective Novel'. Exponents of this type of crime novel from that first decade included Anthony Abbot, Nicholas Blake, Lynn Brock, Miles Burton/John Rhode, Agatha Christie, G. D. H. and M. Cole, Freeman Wills Crofts, C. Daly King, E. C. R. Lorac, Philip MacDonald, Rupert Penny, and as the decade ended, Ngaio Marsh. Others, writing to a less rigid whodunit formula, included Herbert Adams, Anthony Gilbert, A. E. Fielding and Ethel Lina White, while M. G. Eberhart, Leslie Ford and Mabel Seeley explored the 'Had I But Known' school, characterised by a (usually) female narrator enmeshed in a mysterious and threatening situation, with the added complication of a romantic dilemma. Thrillers, with the emphasis on the physical rather than the cerebral, were published by J. Jefferson Farjeon, Hulbert Footner, and Henry Holt.

## JOIN NOW!

## IT COSTS YOU NOTHING TO JOIN

# FIRST DECADE

# THE
# 1930s

# THE CRIME CLUB

**MILES BURTON/JOHN RHODE**, the pen-names of Cecil John Charles Street (1884-1964), had already published nine crime titles by the time Crime Club issued *The Hardway Diamonds Mystery* in 1930. Dubbed by the *Manchester Guardian* 'Public Brainteaser No. 1', he was to become the Club's most prolific writer, producing 150 books over the next 30 years. All 63 Burton titles appeared under the Crime Club imprint; from 1946, after 32 titles, he moved his Rhode output to Geoffrey Bles publishers (Bles was bought by Collins in 1953). Between 1930 and 1939 Street published a staggering 43 titles; 22 Burtons, all but two featuring his detective duo Inspector Arnold and Desmond Merrion, and 21 Rhodes, all with his detective Dr. Lancelot Priestley, appeared with the Hooded Gunman on the title page. In 1936 Rhode explained how he set about plotting his novels: 'My own method is first to complete the crime as though I were myself the criminal, trying to think of every possible precaution. This done, I next take the opposite point of view, that of the investigator charged with inquiring into the death of the victim.'

***Burglars in Bucks*** (1930)
**G. D. H. and M. Cole**

Told in epistolary style – letters, notes, newspaper reports, telegrams – this novel is also notable for the absence of a body.

***The Folded Paper Mystery*** (1930)
**Hulbert Footner**

This book features real-life journalist, novelist and personal friend – and founder-member of the Baker Street Irregulars – Christopher Morley, who was Footner's editor at Doubleday in the early 1910s.

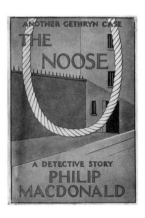

***The Murder at the Vicarage* (1930)**
**Agatha Christie**

This is the first Miss Marple novel, although not the first appearance of the detective of St Mary Mead. She made her debut in a series of short stories, later collected in *The Thirteen Problems* (1932), beginning in December 1928. The Miss Marple of this novel is markedly different from later appearances; she is described, in Chapter 1, by the vicar's wife as 'the worst cat in the village'.

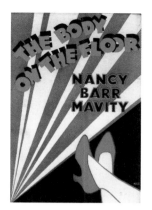

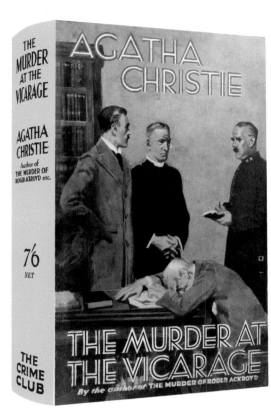

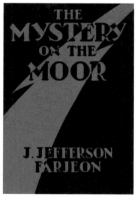

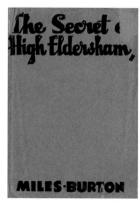

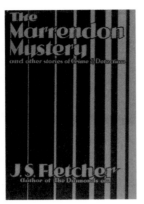

**Murder Gone Mad** (1931) Philip MacDonald

This is an early example of the 'serial killer' novel as 'The Butcher' goes about his deadly work in Holmdale, challenging the police in a series of taunting letters. Strictly speaking, it is not a detective novel, and is surprisingly gory – it includes two murders of children, one an infant in a pram – but wonderfully exciting.

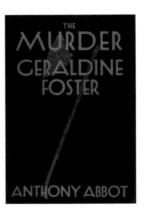

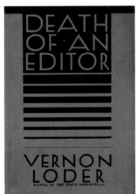

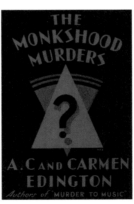

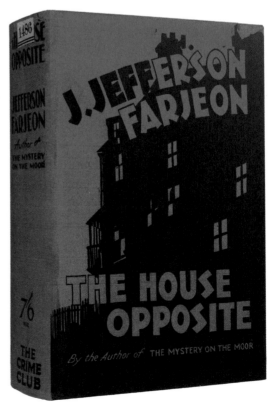

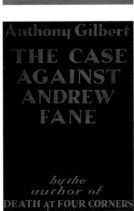
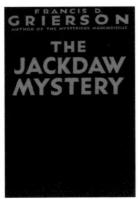

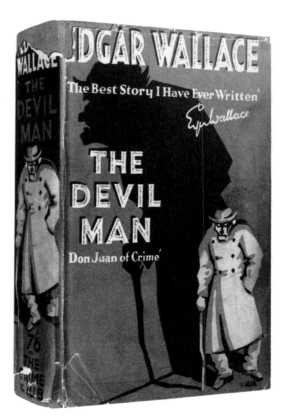

**The Devil Man (1931) Edgar Wallace**

A title notable for two reasons: the only Crime Club book from the vastly prolific Edgar Wallace (although he had many books published in the 'Collins Mystery' list), it is also an example of 'faction' – a novelisation of the life of Charlie Peace, the notorious nineteenth-century burglar and murderer. Wallace wrote the entire book in 60 hours, between Friday night and Monday morning, and earned £4,000 for the serial rights. The dust wrapper includes Wallace's modest claim, complete with 'signature': 'The best story I have ever written'.

**The Crime of the Century (1931) Anthony Abbot**

This Thatcher Colt investigation is based, in part, on the infamous Halls-Mills murder case in 1926 America, the headline-grabbing murder of a clergyman and his mistress.

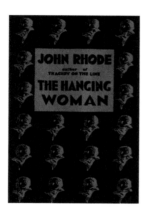

MILES BURTON
AUTHOR OF DEATH AT THE CROSS ROADS ETC.
TO CATCH A THIEF
The Sign of a CRIME CLUB Book

HULBERT FOOTNER
AUTHOR OF MURDER RUNS IN THE FAMILY, Etc.
DANGEROUS CARGO
The Sign of a CRIME CLUB Book

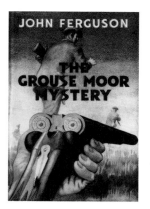

JOHN FERGUSON
THE GROUSE MOOR MYSTERY

MURDER AT THE BOOKSTALL
by HENRY HOLT
THE CRIME CLUB
MURDER AT THE BOOKSTALL
HENRY HOLT

VERNON LODER
AUTHOR OF MURDER FROM THREE ANGLES, Etc.
TWO DEAD
The Sign of a CRIME CLUB Book

SHOT AT DAWN
JOHN RHODE

ANTHONY GILBERT
AUTHOR OF AN OLD LADY DIES, ETC.
THE MAN IN BUTTON BOOTS
The Sign of a CRIME CLUB Book

A. FIELDING
AUTHOR OF THE CAUTLEY CONUNDRUM, ETC.
THE PAPER CHASE
The Sign of a CRIME CLUB Book

THE DIAMOND RANSOM MURDERS
NELLISE CHILD
author of MURDER COMES HOME

57
THREE ACT TRAGEDY
A New Poirot Story
AGATHA CHRISTIE
AGATHA CHRISTIE featuring HERCULE POIROT in THREE ACT TRAGEDY
7/6 NET
THE CRIME CLUB

G. D. H. AND M. COLE
AUTHOR OF END OF AN ANCIENT MARINER, ETC.
BIG BUSINESS MURDER
The Sign of a CRIME CLUB Book

The PUZZLE of the SILVER PERSIAN
by STUART PALMER

OBELISTS Fly High
C. Daly King
Author of Obelists en Route, etc.

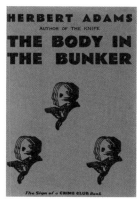

HERBERT ADAMS
AUTHOR OF THE KNIFE
THE BODY IN THE BUNKER
The Sign of a CRIME CLUB Book

Poet (later Poet Laureate) Cecil Day Lewis (1904-1972) wrote his first detective story, *A Question of Proof*, to pay for a glass-house roof; and he published it under the pseudonym **NICHOLAS BLAKE**, in order not to jeopardise his day job as a schoolteacher. All of his crime fiction was published by Collins, all but *A Tangled Web* (1956) in the Crime Club. However standard-seeming the setting – the country-house of *Thou Shell of Death* and *The Case of the Abominable Snowman*, the office of *Minute for Murder* and *End of Chapter*, the country village of *The Deadly Joker* and *The Dreadful Hollow* – all his work is distinguished by exceptional characterisation and writing. For him 'the classic qualities of the detective novel proper are bafflement and suspense', although he did wonder if 'people who read detective stories do not like the detective novelist to be anything like a serious poet'.

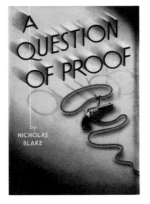

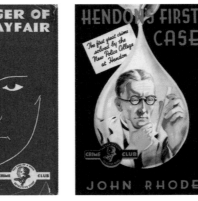

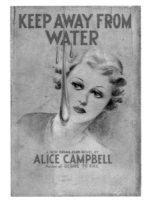

The writer with the longest association with Crime Club was **MIGNON GOOD (M. G.) EBERHART** (1899-1996); she published with the imprint for over 50 years and 50 books, from 1935 to 1988. Sometimes called (very inaccurately) 'the American Agatha Christie', she wrote in the Had-I-But-Known school of crime writing, eschewing classical detection in favour of female-centred suspense and romance. Glamorous backgrounds, frequently in exotic locales – France, Bermuda, the Caribbean, Mexico – and experimentation with period settings ensured a large and loyal readership, despite the lack of a series character. For Eberhart '…the starting point is, as a rule, the indescribably, pleasantly chilling certainty that this house or that garden, has fatefully known and will fatefully know again, romance, hazard, danger; the entanglement of lives within its boundaries.'

*The Curious Mr. Tarrant* (1935) C. Daly King

The Holy Grail for Crime Club collectors, this impossible-to-find volume is a collection of stories featuring the one-off eponymous character rather than King's usual detective Michael Lord. This collection was not published in King's native America until a paperback edition in 1977.

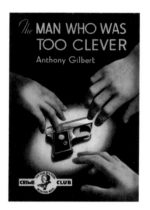

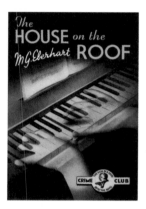
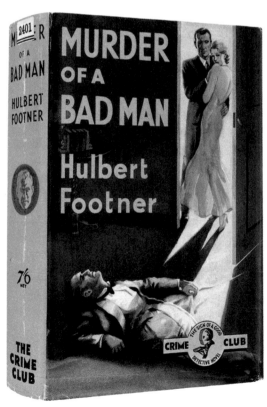
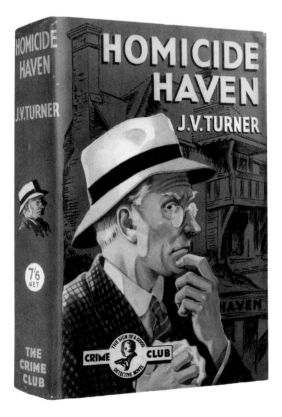

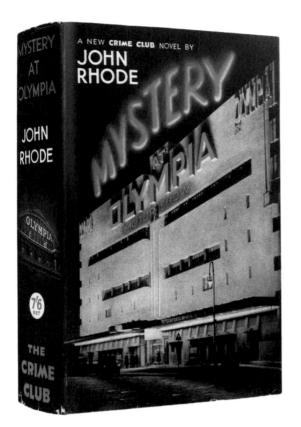

After publishing nine novels with publisher Sampson Low, **E. C. R. LORAC** moved to the Crime Club in 1936. Edith Caroline Rivett (1894-1958) published a further 39 books as Lorac and, beginning in 1953, eleven Crime Club titles as **CAROL CARNAC**. Her Lorac pen-name is composed of her initials and the first five letters of her middle name reversed. Her ever-reliable output under both names was impressive if unremarkable; there is little, apart from the series characters – Scotland Yard detectives Chief-Inspector Rivers (Carnac) and Inspector/Superintendent MacDonald (Lorac) – to distinguish one series from the other. She is, however, one of the best-served of all Crime Club authors by her cover designers.

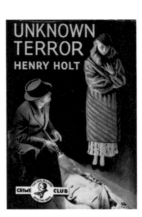

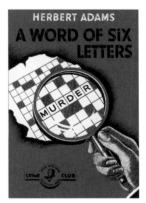

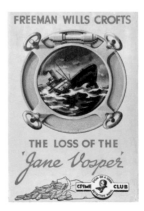

**ETHEL LINA WHITE** (1876-1944) published three 'straight' novels and four crime novels before she appeared in the Crime Club series in 1936 with *The Wheel Spins*. More Gothic 'Had-I-But-Known' than detection, her output specialised in an atmosphere of mounting fear and suspicion centring on a female protagonist. Of her childhood she wrote: 'We had Welsh nursemaids whose lurid stories probably were excellent training for a future thrill writer'. Her final novel, *They See in Darkness* (1944) was published posthumously.

### *The Wheel Spins* (1936) Ethel Lina White

Why does no-one believe Iris Carr when she claims that an elderly fellow-passenger on the continental express train has disappeared? Destined to achieve lasting fame as Hitchcock's *The Lady Vanishes* (1938), this is White's best-remembered story, although Robert Siodmak created another classic film noir, *The Spiral Staircase* (1946), from *Some Must Watch* (1933), a non-Crime Club title.

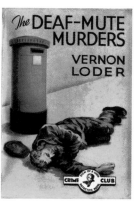

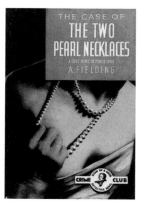

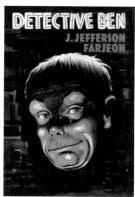

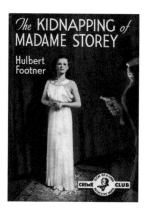

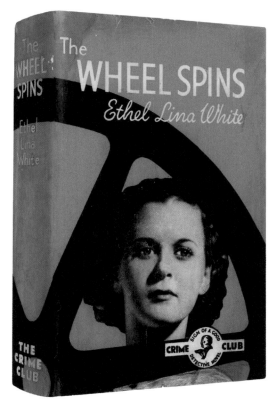

Between 1935 and 1941 **RUPERT PENNY** (Ernest Basil Charles Thornett 1909-1970), who worked in Bletchley Park during WWII, published eight unapologetically brain-boggling detective stories, all featuring the duo of Inspector Beale and Jerry Purdon. Their pages are littered with diagrams, floor-plans, ciphers and timetables, culminating in a penultimate Challenge-to-the-Reader. While sometimes dark – the insane asylum background of *The Lucky Policeman* and the dismembered corpse of *She Had to Have Gas* – the books are frequently witty. In the 'Foreword' to *The Talkative Policeman* (1936) Penny claimed: 'The detective story is no self-supporting form of literature. It is not…destined for the future equally with the past. By its nature it is for today, and possibly for tomorrow.'

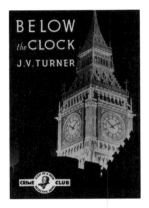

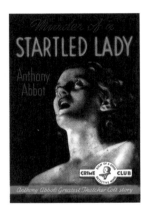

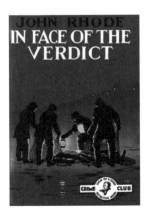

As with all publishing, Crime Club books contain their fair share of errors, inconsistencies and peculiarities. Oddities in the 1930s run of titles include:

- *Burglars in Bucks* (1930) lists *The Person Called 'Z'* and *The Shop Windows Murders* on the flap – neither is a Crime Club title.
- The dedication in Anthony Gilbert's *The Long Shadow* (1932) is to Scott Egerton, Gilbert's fictional detective.
- *Murder Gone Mad* (1931) lists Inspector Pyke in the blurb, rather than Pike.
- E. C. R. Lorac is referred to as 'Mr.' in reviews on the cover of *These Names Make Clues* (1937) and the blurb of *John Brown's Body* (1939).

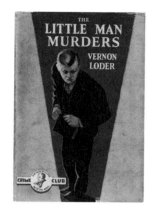

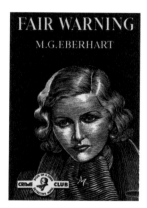

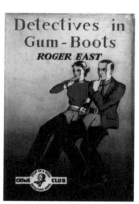

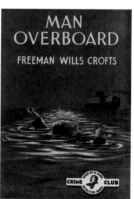

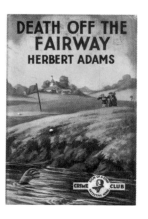

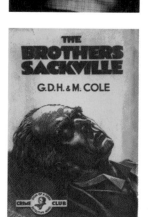

## *Death in the Hopfields* (1937) John Rhode

The cover of *Death in the Hopfields* shows actual oast houses belonging to the Whitbread Company at Beltring Hop Farm at Paddock Wood in Kent.

**JOHN STEPHEN STRANGE** (Dorothy Stockbridge Tillett 1896-1983), another example of a female writer adopting a male pseudonym, published 22 crime novels, joining Crime Club with her third novel, although both of her earlier titles were issued by Collins. Almost completely forgotten today, she was very popular in the 30s and 40s, although her plots rarely rose above the pedestrian.

**STUART PALMER** (1905-1968) published five crime novels before his 1934 Crime Club appearance with *The Riddle of the Silver Persian* (1935). His series detective, elderly school-teacher Hildegarde Withers, appeared in all but one of his Crime Club books, *Death in Grease-Paint* (1956). The Withers series is notable for the amusing badinage between the elderly teacher and Inspector Oscar Piper, a New York policeman.

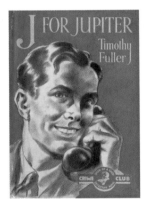

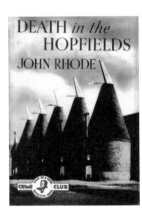
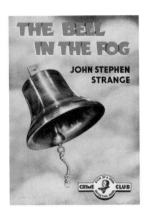
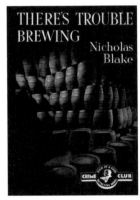
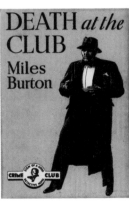

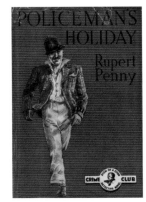

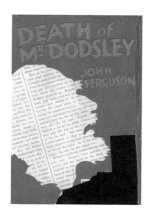

**LESLIE FORD** (1898-1983), the pseudonym for Mrs Zenith Brown, also wrote crime fiction as David Frome. After publishing six titles, she debuted in Crime Club in 1937 and over the following quarter-century published two dozen books for the imprint. Most of these titles feature her detective duo of attractive widow Grace Latham and Colonel Primrose, late US army. Their relationship is platonic and their cases are closer to 'Had-I-But-Known', rather than Golden Age, detection. Interviewed in 1977 Ford admitted: 'I don't even like detective stories in which the corpse appears on the first page. I like to know who the corpse was, and why it was tremendously important for somebody – who I never want to know until the last page – to see the corpse become a corpse.'

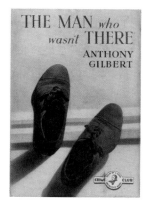

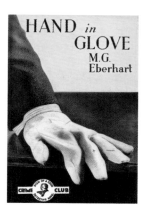

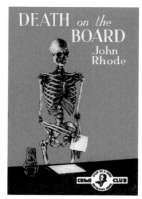

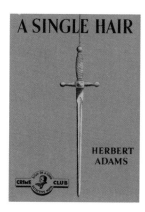

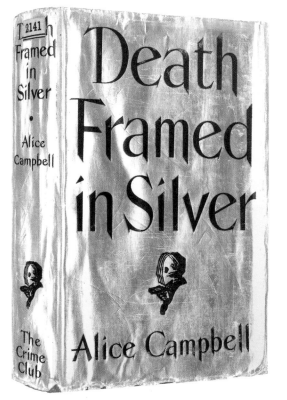

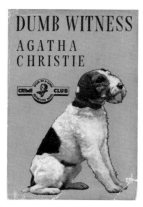

Also a Collins author before the launch of the Crime Club, **ANTHONY GILBERT**'s 43-year career with the imprint began in 1931 with *The Case Against Andrew Fane*. Lucy Beatrice Malleson (1899-1973) recalled in her autobiography that, inspired by *The Cat and the Canary*, 'she wrote her first novel [*The Man Who Was London*] and Collins accepted it, after some alterations, paying her a £40 advance, instead of the £200 she had expected, adding ruefully that "the book failed to earn even this sum, being a complete flop"'. She also wrote as J. Kilmeny Smith and Anne Meredith, but it was as Anthony Gilbert that she was most successful. Her detective Scott Egerton, who had first appeared in *The Tragedy at Freyne* (1927) continued to detect alongside, briefly, a Monsieur Dupuy, but these were both replaced by the disreputable lawyer Arthur Crook from 1936 onwards. Gilbert was, with two exceptions, a Collins author from 1925 until her final novel, *A Nice Little Killing* (1974), published posthumously.

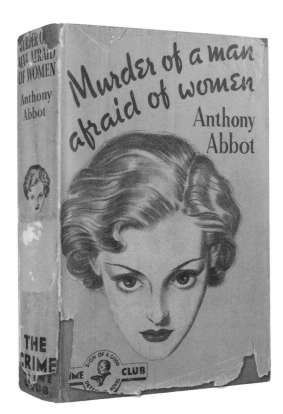

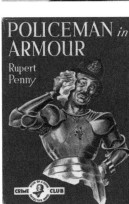

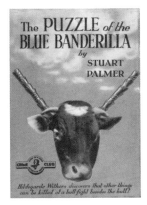

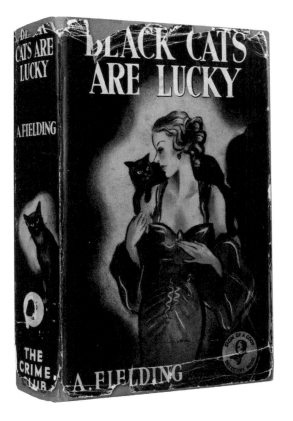

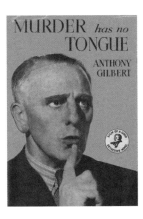

**PHILIP MACDONALD** (1899-1981) published 13 books in the Club's first three years, three of them under the pseudonym of Martin Porlock; but only three more over the following 23 years. This fitful output was explained by his departure in 1931 for Hollywood and a screen-writing career. His final Crime Club novel, *The Dark Wheel*, was a collaboration and his last two novels and two short story collections were not published by Crime Club. His initial fertility was matched by originality of plot, strict adherence to the 'fair-play' rule and a penchant for experimentation: his pre-Crime Club *Rynox* begins with an Epilogue and finishes with a Prologue; and *Murder Gone Mad* is an early example of the 'serial killer' novel. Writing in 1963 of the former, MacDonald called it 'a light-hearted thriller' and 'one of those razzle-dazzle, now-you-see-it-now-you-don't affairs' and the latter as 'an attempt to break away from the then accepted, and terribly confining, limits of the pure Whodunit…suggested by the macabre but very real-life exploits of the greatest mass murderer of the century, the monster of Düsseldorf.'

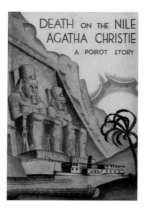

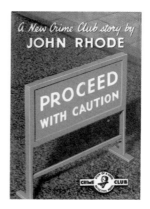

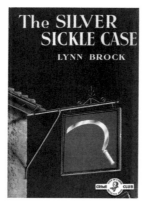

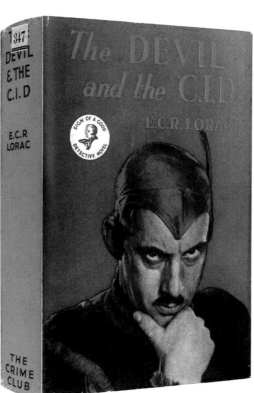

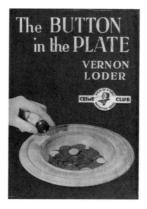

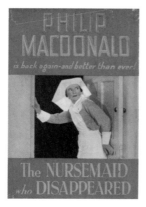

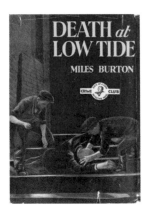

### *The Beast Must Die* (1938) Nicholas Blake

From its opening line – 'I am going to kill a man' – this ingenious novel toys with the reader's emotions and intellect as we follow the plan of detective novelist 'Felix Lane' to avenge the hit-and-run death of his small son. The plot was inspired by Blake's witnessing a near fatal road accident involving his son, Sean.

### *Appointment with Death* (1938) Agatha Christie

This was the last of the eye-catchingly attractive covers that graced Agatha Christie's 'foreign travel' titles of the 1930s, starting with *Murder in Mesopotamia* (1936) and *Death on the Nile* (1937), as well as the more domestic *Murder in the Mews* (1937). All were painted by Robin McCartney, a young architect and amateur painter who worked with Max Mallowan, Christie's archaeologist husband, on his 'digs'.

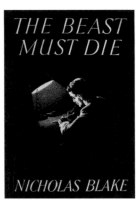

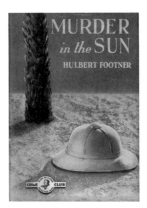

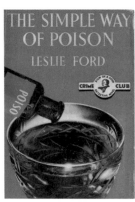

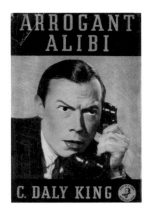

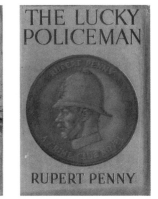

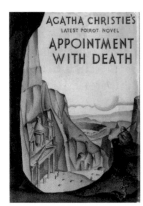

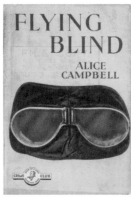

Already the author of nine detective novels before her first Crime Club appearance, *Figure Away* (1937), **PHOEBE ATWOOD TAYLOR** (1909-1976) penned two distinct series for Crime Club: the Cape-Cod based Asey Mayo series appeared under her own name, and as Alice Tilton she created Leonidas Witherall. Both series depend largely on humour for their impact and in all cases this humour takes precedence over plot. Taylor wrote no fiction for the last 20 years of her life.

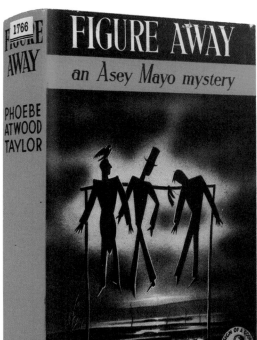

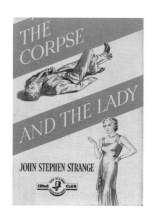

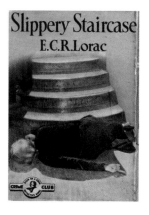

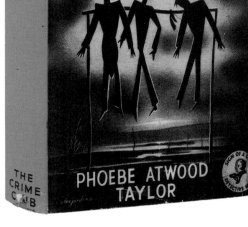

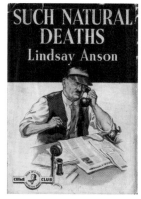

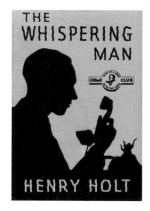

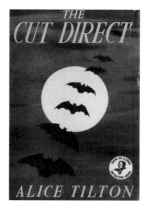

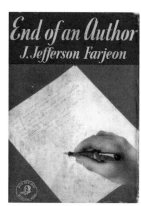

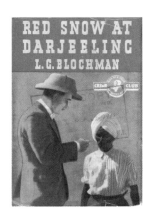

**CLAYTON RAWSON** (1906-1971) published only three novels with Crime Club, although he also wrote a series of short stories and novelettes, and one non-Crime Club novel, not published in the UK until 1972. Nevertheless, his reputation remains high, particularly among fans of the 'impossible' crime novel. By profession a magician, he brought many of the 'tricks of the trade' from that world to his detective fiction. As he put it himself: 'The magician tries to conceal his clues completely; the writer can't. He must explain all at the end. This is why writers have to write new stories, but magicians continue to repeat the same tricks.'

 *Kill in the Ring* by Vernon Loder is the second novel of the decade with a background of boxing. Philip MacDonald's *Death on My Left* (January 1933) also features the unexpected death of a pugilist.

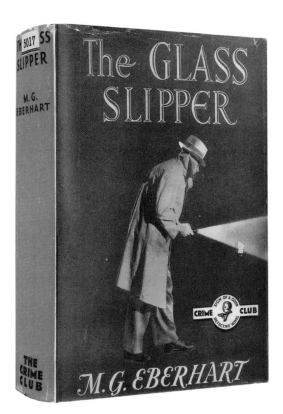

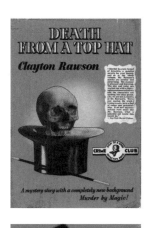

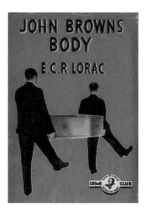

**NGAIO MARSH** (1895-1982) had already introduced Inspector Roderick Alleyn in seven novels published by Geoffrey Bles but *Overture to Death* (1939), her first for the Crime Club, was her longest and most ambitious novel to that point. Throughout her career she remained faithful to the model of classical detection and, although not an experimenter or pioneer, Marsh wrote another two dozen novels, all with a keen eye for the dramatic, many of them set in the world of theatre, her first love. In a talk, 'Our Particular Job', broadcast on Radio New Zealand in 1957, she said: 'The truth about professional writers is this. We worry and fumble and rehash…We do not wait for inspiration…but when all is said and done we toil at this particular job because it's turned out to *be* our particular job and in a weird sort of way I suppose we may be said to like it.'

**CYRIL ALINGTON** (1872-1955) published only one novel with Crime Club but he deserves mention as he *was* the much-vaunted 'committee of experts' who allegedly chose which novels would appear with the Hooded Gunman logo. In reality it would seem that he was paid solely for his co-operation in the use of his name – he was Headmaster of Eton College – although he published over 50 novels throughout his life.

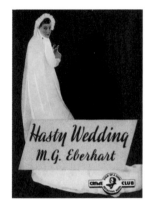

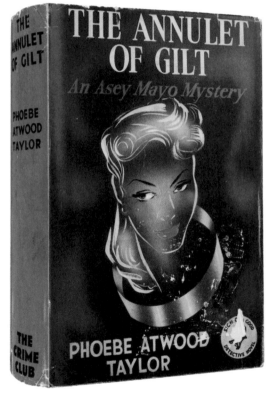

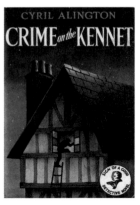

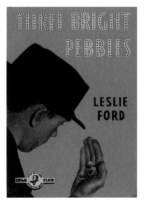

Arguably, the best work of **RICHARD HULL** (Richard Henry Sampson 1896-1973) had appeared before he joined Crime Club in 1939. His debut novel, the classic *Murder of my Aunt* (1934), is narrated by an odious nephew who is attempting to kill his aunt, and *Excellent Intentions* (1938) was a courtroom drama in which we discover the identity of the accused only in the novel's final chapters. Both culminate in sublimely ironic twists. But despite experiments such as beginning with the last chapter in *Last First* (1947) and the diary of an unnamed murderer in *A Matter of Nerves* (1950), his Crime Club books rarely fulfilled their intriguing premise.

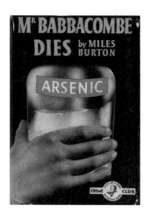

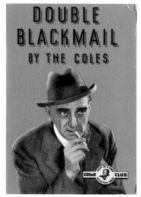

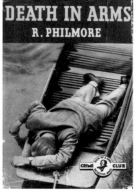

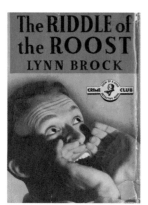

When, in March 1938, **REX STOUT** (1866-1975) received confirmation that Collins would publish his next book, *Too Many Cooks*, he wrote to his US publisher: 'Of course I am pleased – though a close observer might have perceived on my lips a bitter smile, with a lurking hint of pathos, as I read of the royalty provision after 10,000 copies are sold.' In subsequent decades Stout was to become one of the most popular Crime Club writers, selling over two million books. Even though they had been appearing since 1934, only two Nero Wolfe novels appeared in the Crime Club's first decade. 1939 saw the appearance of another detective creation, Dol Bonner, and her only solo investigation, *The Hand in the Glove*. In their Autumn 1938 newsletter Crime Club claimed that Stout was the first Crime Club writer to have a beard!

### *Ten Little Niggers* (1939) Agatha Christie

Christie's greatest technical achievement, this is the best-selling crime novel of all time. Prophetically, the July 1939 Crime Club newsletter had little hesitation in describing it as 'the greatest story Agatha Christie has ever written' and 'certainly the greatest detective story that the Crime Club has ever published and probably, we believe, the world will declare it the greatest detective story ever written'. It was eventually retitled *And Then There Were None* in 1986.

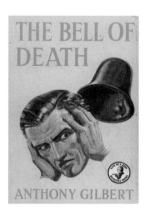

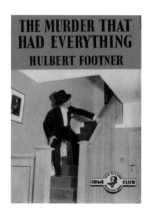

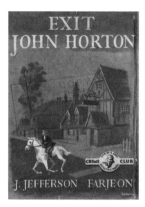

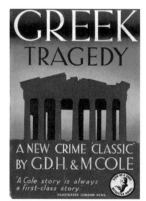

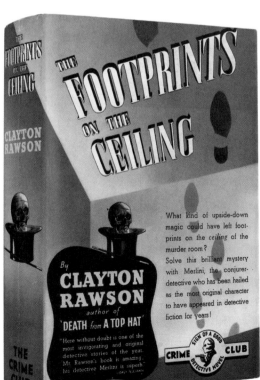

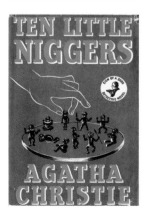

DUE TO SECOND WORLD WAR paper shortages only 243 Crime Club books were published during the 1940s, a reduction of almost 100 on the previous decade, with 1946 seeing an all-time low of only 16 new titles appearing. Furthermore it is noticeable that many of the books of the early part of the decade had fewer pages – down from the standard 256, 272 or 288 pages to 160, 176 or 192 – with smaller print on inferior paper. From 1942, it was announced on many dust-wrappers that the quarterly newsletters would cease.

DUE IN LARGE PART to this situation, this decade saw very few new authors enter the list, although some – Elizabeth Ferrars, Shelley Smith, Conyth Little – did move to Crime Club from other publishers. But many of the established names continued, despite the exigencies of war, to be as prolific as before: Miles Burton/John Rhode published 30 titles, Anthony Gilbert 15, Agatha Christie 14, Rex Stout and M. G. Eberhart 13, and J. Jefferson Farjeon and Leslie Ford 12 each. Unlike his productivity in the 1930s, when he published 11 Crime Club titles, Philip MacDonald issued only one – a non-typical collaboration – explained by his departure for Hollywood as a screenwriter for, among others, *Love from a Stranger*, an adaptation of Christie's 1924 short story 'Philomel Cottage', and *Rebecca*, the Hitchcock-directed version of Daphne Du Maurier's famous 1938 novel.

# Second Decade

# The
# 1940s

THE CRIME CLUB

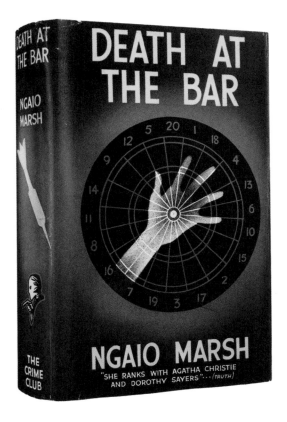

### *Verdict of Twelve* (1940) Raymond Postgate

One of only three crime novels by Raymond Postgate (1896-1971) and the only one for Crime Club, this absorbing novel uses the backdrop of a murder trial to examine in detail the background of each juror and show how it colours their reactions to the trial. Postgate was brother of author Margaret Cole and father of the children's writer and animator Oliver Postgate.

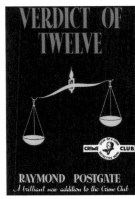

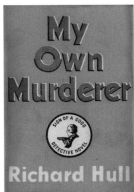

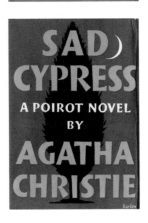

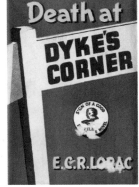

Note the short-lived idea of including an author photograph on the cover – as distinct from the flap or back cover – of *Death on the Boat Train* and the next two John Rhode books. Leslie Ford's photo graced two covers but the idea was abandoned after Rupert Penny's *Sealed Room Murder* (1941)

Despite the success of her first book, *The Listening House* (1939), and Howard Haycraft's prediction in *Murder for Pleasure: The Life and Times of the Detective Story* (1941) that **MABEL SEELEY** (1903-1991) was 'the White Hope who will pilot the American-feminine detective story out of the doldrums', she failed to fulfil her initial promise. Her novels, five more of which were published by the Crime Club, veered towards the darker side of 'Had-I-But-Known' and eschewed formal detection. She published her last crime fiction in 1954, almost 40 years before her death.

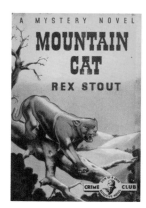

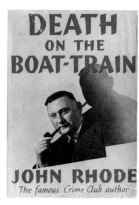

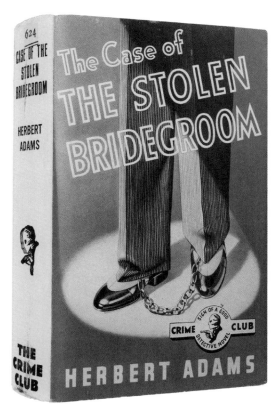

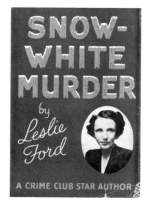

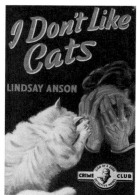

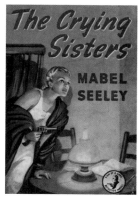

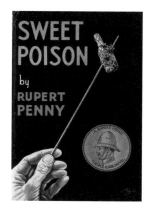

### *Malice in Wonderland* (1940) Nicholas Blake

Capitalising on the popularity of the 'holiday camp' – 200 such existed in the UK prior to WWII – Nigel Strangeways investigates the sinister activities of a 'Mad Hatter' practical joker wreaking havoc among happy holiday-makers. But can he prevent the jokes from becoming deadly before he hosts the Mad Hatter's Tea-Party?

The blurb of *Murder at Buzzards Bay* includes an endorsement from F.B.I. Chief J. Edgar Hoover, praising Thatcher Colt's logical approach.

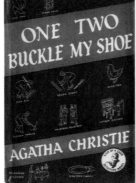

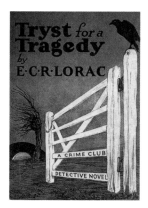

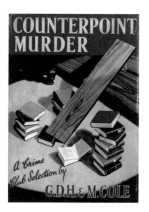

### *Surfeit of Lampreys* (1941) Ngaio Marsh

In her autobiography, *Black Beech and Honeydew*, Ngaio Marsh writes: 'In writing detective stories I have only once, with intention, based a complete family upon people I actually know...Although the ages, sex, circumstances and behaviour of my imaginary family were not precisely those of its prototypes, its members were, in their I hope inoffensive way, portraits. I shall therefore make no bones about calling their dear originators "The Lampreys".' The eponymous Lampreys were based on the Rhodes family.

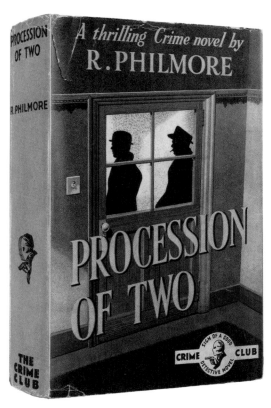

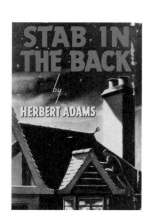

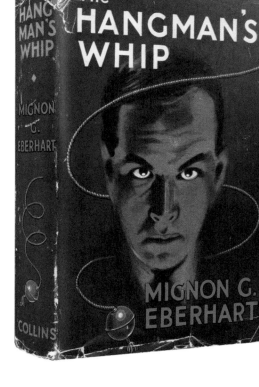

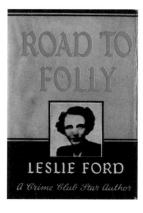

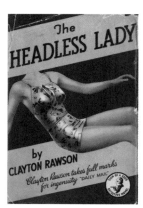

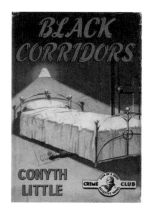

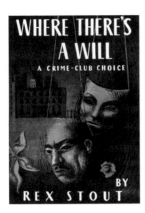

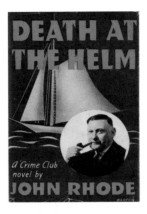

 Can it be coincidence that so many E. C. R. Lorac titles are alliterative?

- 1930s: *Crime Counter Crime, Post after Post-Mortem, A Pall for a Painter, Bats in the Belfry, Slippery Staircase, Black Beadle.*
- 1940s: *Tryst for a Tragedy, Case in the Clinic, The Sixteenth Stair, Murder by Matchlight, Death before Dinner, Part for a Poisoner, Policemen in the Precinct.*
- 1950s: *Murder of a Martinet, Murder in the Mill-Race, Dangerous Domicile, Murder on a Monument.*

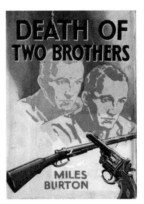

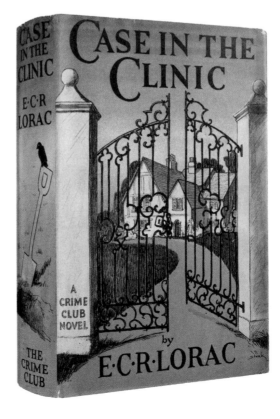

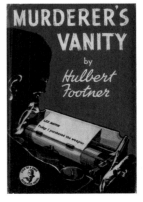

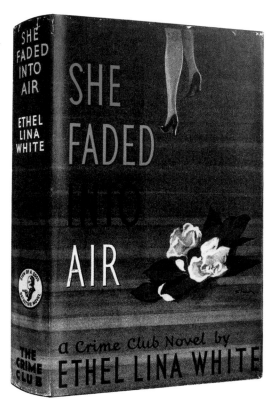

More light-hearted than most were the novels of **CONYTH LITTLE**, all but two of which were issued by Crime Club between 1940 and 1953, thirteen of them in the 1940s. The pseudonym was an amalgamation of the names of two Australian sisters, Constance (1899-1980) and Gwenyth (1906-1985). The books, written without a series character, all had titles containing the word 'black'.

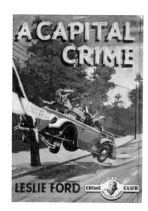

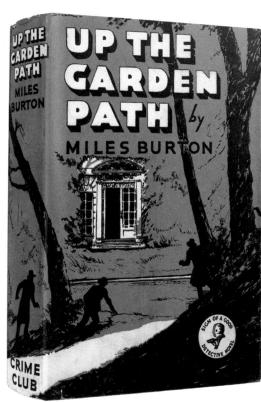

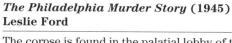

### *The Philadelphia Murder Story* (1945)
### Leslie Ford

The corpse is found in the palatial lobby of the real-life Curtis Publishing Company building on the intersection of South 6th and Walnut Street, Philadelphia. They published *The Saturday Evening Post*, which serialised many of Ford's novels, and it was at their request that she deposited her murder victim there.

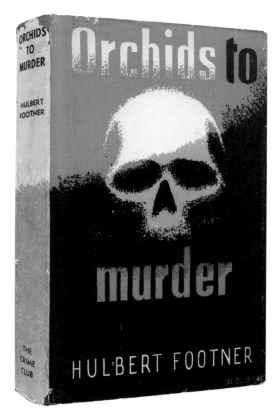

 Although not identified, it is reasonable to assume that the same Edward Hopper-influenced artist designed the covers for:

- *Bad for Business*: Rex Stout (previous page)
- *The Black Eye*: Conyth Little
- *Wings of Fear*: M. G. Eberhart

### *Fire in the Thatch* (1946) E. C. R. Lorac

Set in Devon at the end of WWII, *Fire in the Thatch* is notable for misspelling the author's name on the jacket!

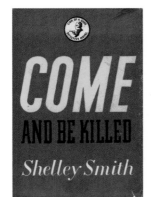

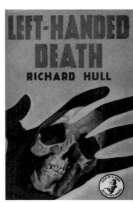

***Murder Among Friends*** **(1946)**
**Elizabeth Ferrars**

This was the first Elizabeth Ferrars title for Crime Club, heralding a career of over 50 years and titles, and with all the merits – civilised people, conversation and settings – and many of the weaknesses – arbitrary solutions and little solid detection – that were to become her trademark.

 There were notable 'odd' titles on some of the books in this decade, including:

- *The Case of the Tea-Cosy's Aunt* (1942) Anthony Gilbert
- *Death and the Dancing Footman* (1942) Ngaio Marsh
- *The Mouse Who Wouldn't Play Ball* (1943) Anthony Gilbert
- *Vegetable Duck* (1944) John Rhode
- *The Cockroach Sings* (1946) Alice Campbell

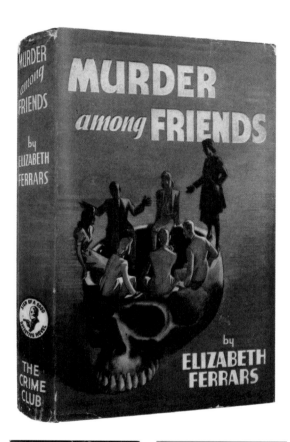

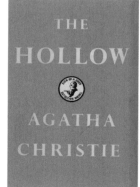

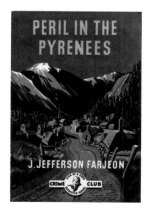

### *Last First* (1947) Richard Hull

Adopting a ploy somewhat similar to C. Daly King's in *Obelists Fly High* (1935) and Philip MacDonald's pre-Crime Club *Rynox*, both of which began with an Epilogue, Richard Hull here presents the last chapter first. Although the mystery remains, this bold experiment is not totally successful.

The use of thallium as a poison in Agatha Christie's *The Pale Horse* (1961) garnered unwanted publicity during the trial of the serial poisoner Graham Young in 1972. But thallium made its Crime Club debut fourteen years earlier in Ngaio Marsh's *Final Curtain*.

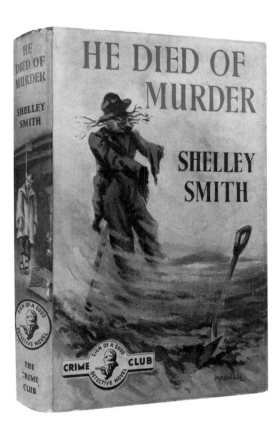

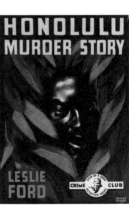

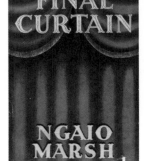

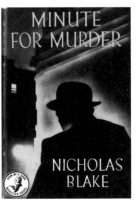

A forgotten writer who genuinely expanded the parameters of the detective story published her first book in this decade. **PAT (PATRICIA) MCGERR** (1917-1985) experimented with the usual whodunit element by challenging the reader to identify not the killer but the victim in *Pick Your Victim* (1947), both victim and killer in *The Seven Deadly Sisters* (1948), the detective in *Catch Me if You Can* (1949) and the witness in *Save the Witness* (1950). Although Anthony Berkeley's non-Crime Club novel *Murder in the Basement* (1932) had kept the reader in suspense about the identity of the victim, and Richard Hull's *Excellent Intentions* (1938) did not identify the person in the dock throughout the novel's trial, McGerr's quartet of novels represents a sustained effort at ringing the changes on the usual formula. In 1984 she recalled: '…when I began to assign roles [in my first novel], it was obvious that only one of them could commit the murder, whereas any of the other ten could be his victim…In my next book I carried that idea a little farther by asking the reader to discover both murder and victim…'

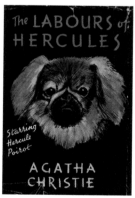

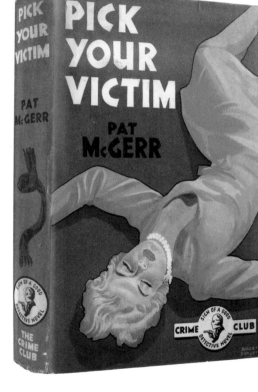

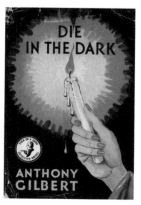

A writer destined to become one of the Crime Club's most productive contributors published her first Crime Club title in 1946. **ELIZABETH FERRARS** (1907-1995) was already the author of six crime novels, published between 1940 and 1945 by Hodder and Stoughton, five of them featuring a series character, Toby Dyke. She remained with Collins from 1946 to the end of her career, eventually publishing 63 books and receiving a special award from the Crime Writers' Association in 1981 to mark her 50th title. She recalled in 1977 that while still with Hodder she 'wrote one more which went a little more deeply into character, called *Murder among Friends* (1946). So [my agent] told me, "Don't worry about this; we'll get you a much better contract with somebody else." And that's when I went to Collins. And I've been there ever since'. Throughout her career she remained true to her belief that the detective story should contain 'a good puzzle, good writing and original characterisation' and admitted that 'Descriptions of violence have always repelled me and I do not think there is scope within the limits of the detective story to explore the mind of the criminal with any seriousness'.

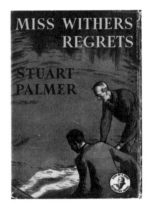

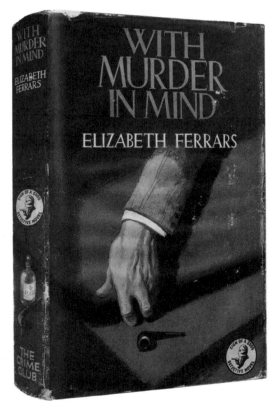

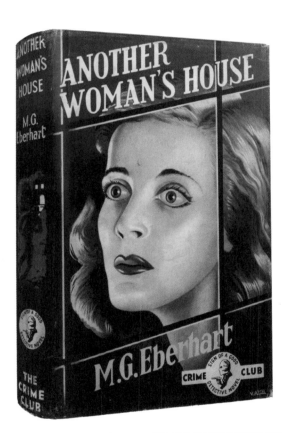

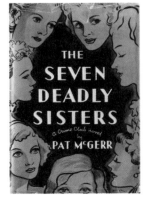

### *The Woman in the Sea* (1948) Shelley Smith

A somewhat disingenuous 'Author's Note' disowns any connection between the plot of this novel and a 'famous case of domestic murder', in all likelihood the 1935 case of Alma Rattenbury and her lover George Stonor, who stood trial for the murder of Alma's husband, Francis. The similarities between the novel and the case are certainly remarkable.

### *The Black Piano* (1948) Conyth Little

Notable for the 'gimmick' of the heroine investigating her own murder and coming under suspicion of having committed the crime.

### *The Dark Wheel* (1948)
### Philip MacDonald and A. Boyd Correll

An example of an acknowledged Crime Club collaboration, this was, unlike most of MacDonald's detective output, a suspense novel. The shadowy Correll wrote at least one further crime novel and some short stories

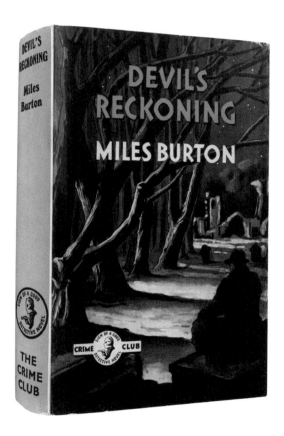

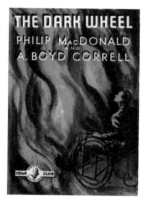
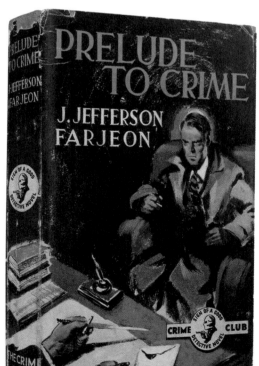

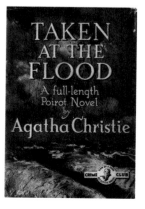

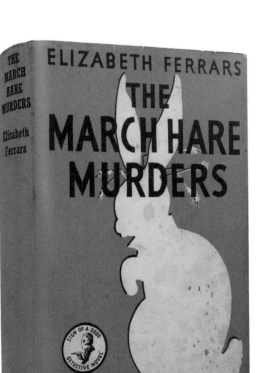

Some writers ceased Crime Club production during this decade: C. Daly King ended his short (6 book) Crime Club career in 1940; Rupert Penny's last Crime Club novel appeared in 1941 (that same year he published a final crime novel, *Cut and Run,* under the name Martin Tanner); and Clayton Rawson also ceased Crime Club publication that year. G.D.H. and M. Cole published their final Crime Club novel in 1942, although they continued to write short stories; Henry Holt moved publisher after 1940; and the prolific Herbert Adams followed suit five years later.

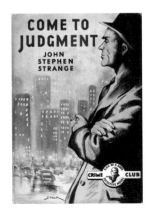

John Rhode's final book for Crime Club appeared in 1945 thereafter moving to Bles publishers, although his output as Miles Burton remained. Alice Tilton stopped in 1947, although her *alter ego* Phoebe Atwood Taylor issued one more in 1951. After a gap of six years A. Fielding published her final book in 1944 and that same year Ethel Lina White's *They See in Darkness* appeared posthumously. Lynn Brock died in 1943, followed by Hulbert Footner in 1944.

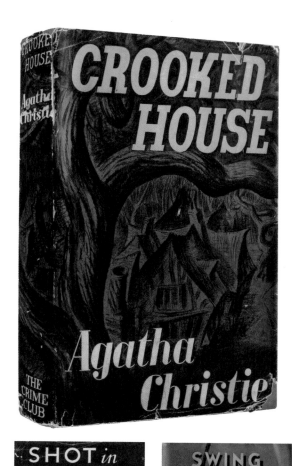

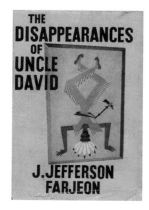

**SIGN OF A GOOD** · **DETECTIVE NOVEL**

**CRIME** **CLUB**

ALTHOUGH THE NUMBER of books published during the 1950s increased only slightly over the previous decade – 249 compared to 243 – a number of writers who were to become constants on the list first appeared: Harry Carmichael and his alter ego Hartley Howard in 1952 and 1951 respectively; Julian Symons in 1956 and Joan Fleming in 1957 and Patricia Moyes in 1959; Andrew Garve – and his alter ego, Paul Somers – also debuted during the decade.

AGATHA CHRISTIE CELEBRATED the new decade with the appearance of her 50th title, *A Murder is Announced*, the first of a dozen titles during the 1950s, although it was during this period that she ceased producing more than one title per year. Ngaio Marsh and Nicholas Blake each published a further five novels and Collins also published Blake's *A Tangled Web* (1956), but not as a Crime Club title. Miles Burton published a staggering 19 titles during the 1950s while the ever-reliable M. G. Eberhart and Elizabeth Ferrars produced seven and twelve titles respectively. Of Rex Stout's 17 titles seven of them were collections of novelettes and Anthony Gilbert added 13 cases to the career of Arthur Crook. J. Jefferson Farjeon ended his Crime Club career in 1954 and E. C. R. Lorac published her final 14 titles; she also moved the output of her other pen-name, Carol Carnac, to Crime Club in 1951, publishing eleven titles, the last, *Death of a Lady Killer* (1959), posthumously.

CRIME CLUB WRITERS who stopped writing during this decade included Alice Campbell and Richard Hull; Mabel Seeley, Conyth Little, Shelley Smith and Stuart Palmer continued their crime-writing careers but with other publishers.

# THIRD DECADE

# The 1950s

SIGN OF A GOOD
CRIME CLUB
DETECTIVE NOVEL

**ANDREW GARVE** (Paul Winterton 1908-2001) published 30 books – plus two under his Paul Somers pseudonym – in the Crime Club and two further Somers titles in Collins Mystery series. Eschewing a series character, Garve's output was ingeniously unpredictable, writing thrillers, adventure stories, spy stories, 'scam' stories, mystery stories. His best books are those which centre on the protagonist undertaking, against all the odds, to clear someone arrested for – or even convicted of – murder. His first Crime Club novel, *No Tears for Hilda* (1950), featured this ploy, as did *The Cuckoo Line Affair* (1953), *The Galloway Case* (1958), *The Far Sands* (1961) and *Prisoner's Friend* (1962). He is also one of the few Crime Club authors (Ethel Lina White was another) to set a book, *Murder in Moscow* (1951), in Russia, a country he knew well from his days as the Moscow correspondent of the *London News Chronicle*. Notably, and exceptionally, his next-to-last book, *Home to Roost* (1976) is one of his best. Andrew Garve had always had 'a built-in urge' to write, and what appealed to him 'were tales with intricate plots and plenty of action and drama'. His job as reporter for the *London News Chronicle* gave him 'a lot of useful background material about crime, criminals and police procedure'.

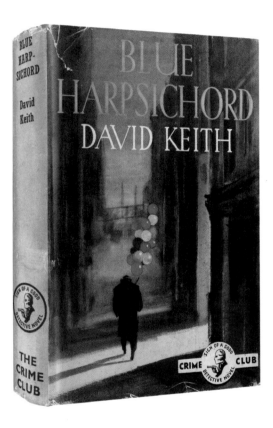

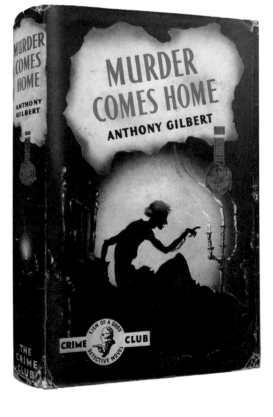

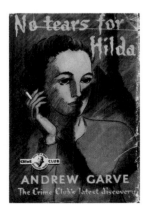

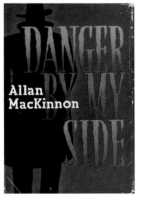

### Spot the Lady (1950) Lester Powell

*Spot the Lady* is unique in having a Crime Club dust-jacket only; the binding and title-page showing Collins Mystery series. It was the third of five novels based on Powell's popular BBC radio series starring Robert Beatty as Philip Odell.

### A Murder is Announced (1950) Agatha Christie

Agatha Christie's 50th book: one of her best; and Miss Marple's finest hour. Thirty years into her career the Queen of Crime was still able to bring something new to the traditional village mystery. Strictly speaking, the significant figure of 50 is arrived at only if some US-only short story collections are included. But the coincidence of 50th book and 50th year of the century was too good for Collins to overlook.

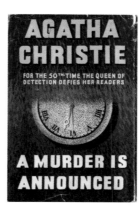

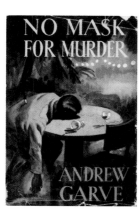

From *They Came to Baghdad* onwards the Christie dust-jackets are notable only for their dullness. For most of the decade, presumably on the basis that her popularity did not need elaborate artwork to attract readers, her titles are surrounded by the colourful and eye-catching jackets of her fellow-writers. Ngaio Marsh and Nicholas Blake fared only slightly better.

INVITATION TO AN INQUEST
by RICHARD HULL

WHICH I NEVER
L.A.G. STRONG

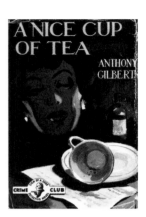

A NICE CUP OF TEA
ANTHONY GILBERT

THE LAST APPOINTMENT
HARTLEY HOWARD

MAN WITH A CALICO FACE
SHELLEY SMITH

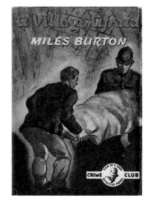

a Village Afraid
MILES BURTON

HUNT WITH THE HOUNDS
M.G. EBERHART

PAT McGERR
YOUR LOVING VICTIM

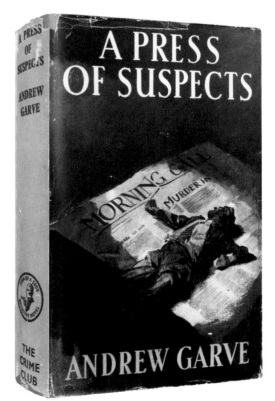

A PRESS OF SUSPECTS
ANDREW GARVE
THE CRIME CLUB

A Miss Withers Mystery
AT ONE FELL SWOOP
STUART PALMER

AGATHA CHRISTIE
THEY CAME TO BAGHDAD
AGATHA CHRISTIE

Even in the Best Families
A Nero Wolfe Story by REX STOUT

### *Opening Night* (1951) Ngaio Marsh

This Marsh title, the best of her 'theatre' novels, was chosen to represent the 21st anniversary of Crime Club. And four years later Ngaio Marsh's *Scales of Justice* was the choice to celebrate the silver anniversary. This double accolade is a measure of the high regard in which the writer was held.

Between 1950 and 1959 Rex Stout's Crime Club titles included no fewer than seven short story/novella collections; and a further three followed in the next decade. Editors were creative at inventing titles featuring variations on Three: *Three Doors/Men/Witnesses/for the Chair* as well as *Triple Jeopardy* and *Curtains for Three*. 1959's *Crime and Again*, containing four stories, is an improvement on the US title of *And Four to Go*.

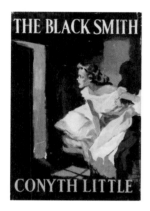

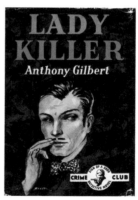

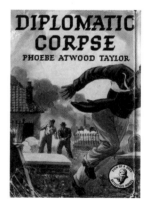

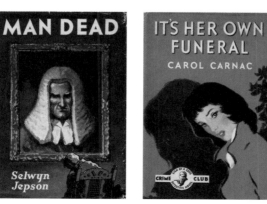

The 1956 appearance of **JULIAN SYMONS** (1912-1994) on the Crime Club list was important not only for the intrinsic quality of his books – he had already published half-a-dozen novels – but also because of his growing reputation as a crime fiction reviewer, commentator and historian. His second Crime Club novel, *The Colour of Murder* (1957) won a CWA Gold Dagger. Symons' output was varied and, in some cases, ground-breaking. Never formulaic, he pushed boundaries, experimenting with detective fiction, historical mysteries, 'faction' and psychological explorations of crime and criminals, and of the sociological pressures that can impel people to crime. Symons believed that 'the crime novel at its best is something more serious and more interesting than a parlour game…and that the author's business shall be to investigate, with all the freedom that the medium permits him, the springs of violence'.

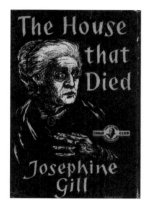

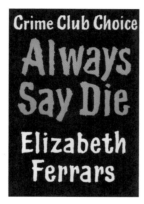

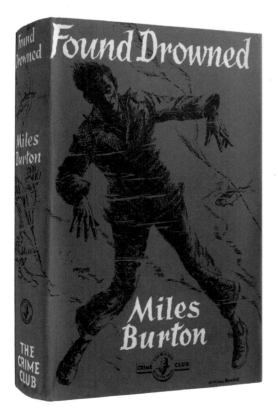

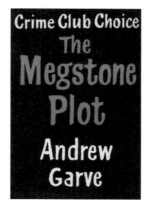

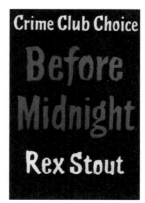

### *CAT* (1956) Val Gielgud

The shortest title in the entire Crime Club history. Close runners-up include *R.I.P.*, *X v. Rex* and *N or M?* Gielgud's title is derived from the initials of the novel's protagonist Charles Adolphus Trent, so '*Cat*' should have been in capitals, as indeed it was on the title-page.

Note the similarity of the cover design on *Murder Comes to Eden* and *Ellery Queen's Awards Tenth Series*. Each features a figure dressed, for some reason, in pyjamas and brandishing a gun!

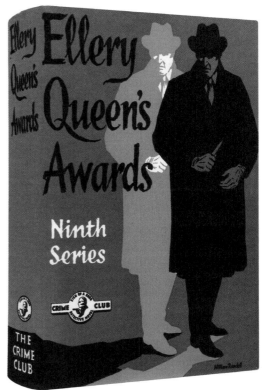

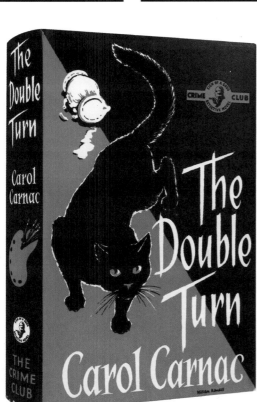

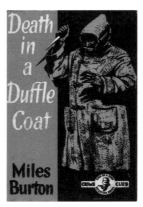

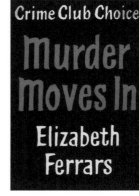

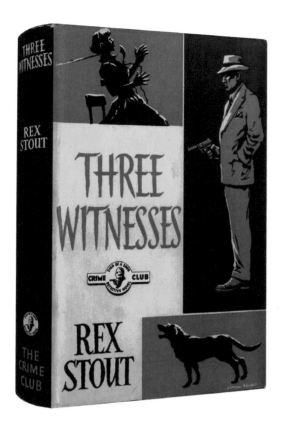

Although compared, inaccurately, with Edgar Allan Poe, **CATHERINE ARLEY**'s (Pierrette Pernot b.1924) tense thrillers, all translated from the French, were minor best-sellers for the Crime Club. They issued only three of her 20+ books and, ironically, she was not published in her native France until 1972. Her most famous title, *Woman of Straw* (1957), was filmed in 1964 with Sean Connery and Gina Lollobrigida.

Harry Carmichael's *Put Out That Star* features an 'impossible crime': the disappearance of a glamorous actress from a hotel under constant observation.

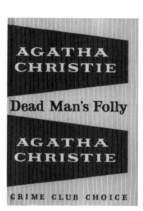

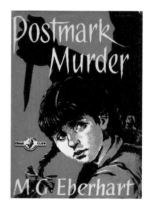

**JOAN FLEMING** (1908-1980), one of few writers to win the CWA's Gold Dagger twice, had already published seven novels before moving to Crime Club with *You Can't Believe Your Eyes* (1957), a multi-narrator account of a mysterious death in a London boarding house. Utterly unpredictable and enviably original, Fleming mined Ruth Rendell territory – the *folie à deux* of *Hell's Belle* (1968), the mild bank clerk on a guilty spree in *In the Red* (1961), the entertaining but ultimately appalling account of the Borgan family of *No Bones about It* (1967) – probing the darker, and sometimes the lighter, heart of remarkable and unforgettable characters and situations. When writing she began work as soon as she woke up, believing that 'the best time to work is when you feel fresh'. She never worried about running out of ideas: 'A chance remark, a photograph in a newspaper, or just somebody sitting opposite me in the Underground can start me off'.

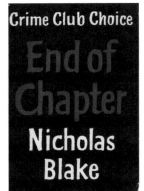

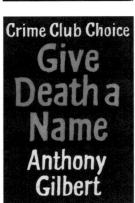

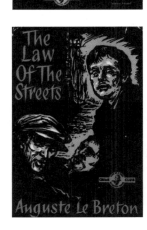

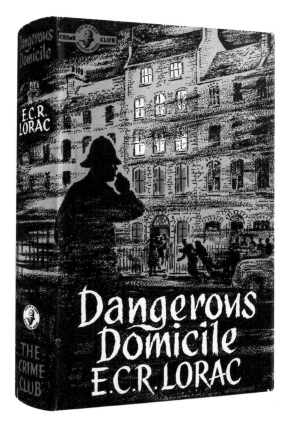

### *4.50 from Paddington* (1957) Agatha Christie

4.15, 4.30 and 4.54 were all under consideration as train times before Agatha Christie and her agent settled on *4.50 from Paddington*. Their main concern was to avoid inadvertently choosing a real train time.

Paul Mansfield's *Final Exposure* and Florence Ford's *Shadow on the House* were advertised as 'New discoveries of outstanding merit'.

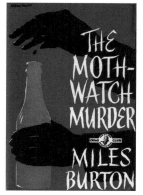

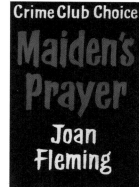

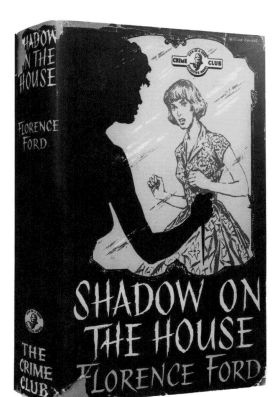

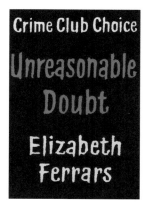

**Beginner's Luck** (1958) Paul Somers

This was the first of two Crime Club books published by Andrew Garve under the pseudonym Paul Somers. In truth, they are little different to his Garve output, apart from the fact that they feature a series character, newspaperman Hugh Curtis, a concept that the Garve output avoided. Note that two Somers and a Garve appeared in this six-month period.

Nigel Fitzgerald's *Suffer a Witch* features a young girl who is convinced that she is a witch; author Stewart Farrar (*The Snake on 99*) was a witch who, with his wife, founded his own coven.

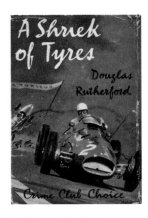

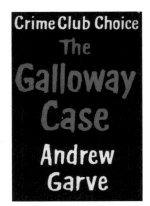

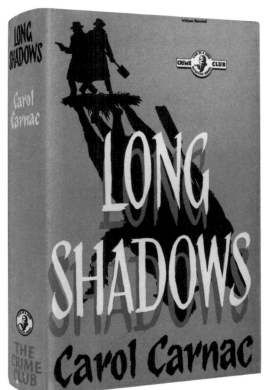

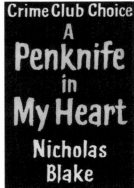

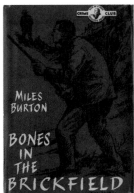

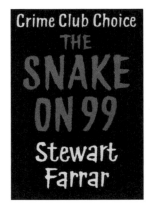

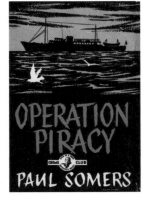

Australian **CHARLOTTE JAY** (1919-1996) was one of the most original suspense writers to appear this decade. Only three of her books appeared under the Crime Club imprint, although her Edgar-winning *Beat Not the Bones*, was published by Collins in 1952, preceding her 1955 Crime Club debut. Her peripatetic life provided then-exotic backgrounds – Pakistan, New Guinea, Lebanon – for many of her titles.

**VAL GIELGUD** (1900-1981) published the first of eight Crime Club novels in 1956, all but the first featuring his main series characters, Inspector Pellew and Viscount Clymping. Gielgud worked in radio and, subsequently, television drama for almost 25 years and *The Goggle-Box Affair* (1963) provided an inside look at the then innovative world of commercial television. For Gielgud: 'Authenticity of background, coupled, of course, with the creation of characters that have some relation to flesh and blood, seem to me to be the most essential ingredients of the modern detective story'.

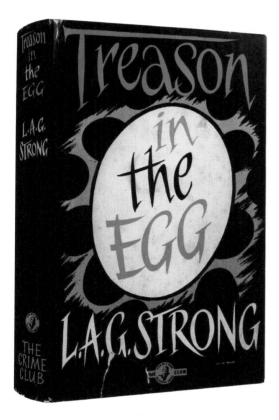

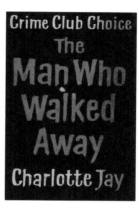

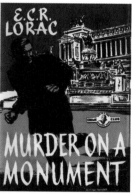

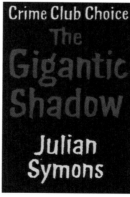

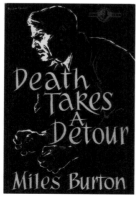

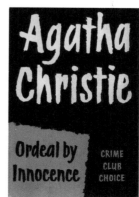

### *Singing in the Shrouds* (1959) Ngaio Marsh

This was Marsh's venture into 'serial killer' territory. The murderer strangles victims at regular intervals, leaving flowers scattered on the corpse, and is immediately dubbed 'The Flower Killer' by the press. After the first chapter, the novel is set entirely aboard a ship, reflecting the surroundings in which Ngaio Marsh began writing it.

### *This Won't Hurt You* (1959) Nigel Fitzgerald

This novel – Fitzgerald's only one not set in Ireland – wins the prize for the most appalling murder in Crime Club, if not the entire genre of crime fiction: an injection of phenol into the gum of a patient in the dentist's chair causes his jaw to disintegrate.

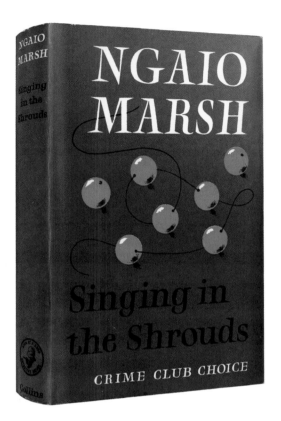

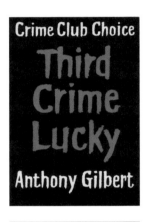

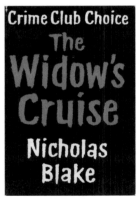

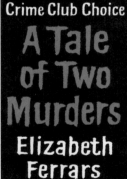

Although **ELLIS PETERS** (Edith Pargeter 1913-1995) first published crime fiction in 1938 (*Murder in the Dispensary* as by Jolyon Carr) her first Crime Club novel was *Death Mask* (1959), and a further nine followed before she moved to Macmillan, with whom she published her famous Cadfael Chronicles for the following quarter-century. Peters considered that: '…the thriller is a paradox…it must be a mystery. And it must be a novel. And it is virtually schizophrenia to aim at both. But for the dedicated author nothing less is conceivable'. Seven of her ten Crime Club novels feature various members of the Felse family.

A writer who came to be regarded as a Crime Queen began her career as the decade was closing. **PATRICIA MOYES** (1923-2000) and her detective, Scotland Yard Inspector Henry Tibbett (and wife Emmy), debuted with *Dead Men Don't Ski* (1959). This was followed over the following 23 years by a further eighteen Crime Club books, all featuring Henry and Emmy. Most were in the Golden Age tradition and, as well as clever plots, were noted for their varied settings and backgrounds: the fashion industry and the world of film-making in the UK, skiing in Italy, the UN in Switzerland, diplomatic life in Washington, and drug-running in the Caribbean. Patricia Moyes wished that she 'could simply recommend that every writer had the good luck I had – the chance to spend years working in the theatre before I ever came to novel writing.' She further credits her 'eight years as an aide to Peter Ustinov' with 'any expertise [she] may have in writing'; from him she learned 'how to write dialogue and the value of humour'. Boredom, the result of a dislocated foot during a skiing holiday, forced her 'to turn to crime' when she decided that, as her ski hotel had no novels in English, 'If I can't read a mystery, why don't I write one?'

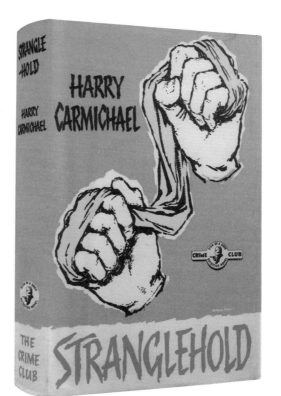

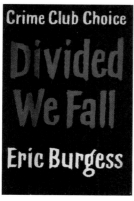

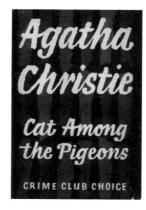

**the sign of a good crime novel . . .**

**the Crime Club gunman is always
on  target with the best in crime fiction**

---

There were 248 titles issued with the Hooded Gunman
logo in the 1960s. The first year of the decade saw
the exit of one of Crime Club's most prolific authors.
In November 1960 Miles Burton published his last
novel, *Death Paints a Picture*. This was his 63rd book
since *The Hardway Diamonds Mystery* in June 1930.
In those 30 years he rarely, if ever, deviated from
the novel of detection and although his characters
were little more than cardboard, his plots showed
resourceful ingenuity, particularly with murder
methods. All but two – his first and *Murder at the
Moorings* (1932) – featured his detective combination
of Desmond Merrion and Inspector Arnold. The final
John Rhode book appeared from Bles in June 1961.
Cecil John Street died in 1964.

---

# Fourth Decade

# THE 1960s

## The Crime Club

### *Zero in the Gate* (1960) Stewart Farrar

A setting which, even in 1960, was nearing extinction is found in Farrar's *Zero in the Gate*. The detailed behind-the-scenes of a newsreel company, *Headline Gazette*, is evocatively portrayed from first-hand knowledge; Farrar worked at one point for *Associated British Pathé*. The title is newsreel jargon for identifying the same starting-point on film-reel and soundtrack to ensure synchronisation.

Despite being hailed by the Crime Club as a 'remarkable and original master of atmosphere and suspense', **FLORENCE FORD** (d. 1975) published only two books for the series. And the 'remarkable originality' is difficult to discern in this largely Gothic tale. A further three titles for other publishers followed.

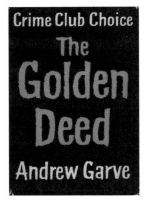

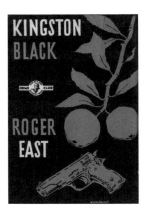

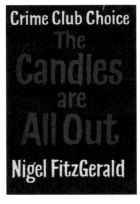

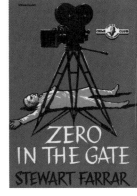

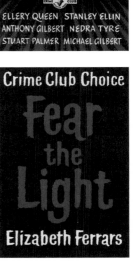

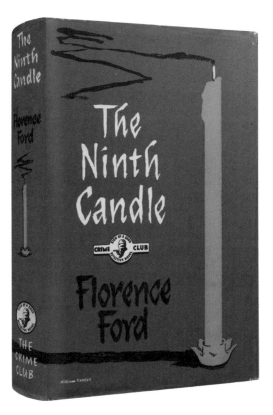

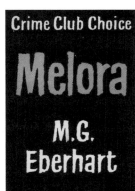

### False Scent (1960) Ngaio Marsh

For the third time a Ngaio Marsh novel was selected to celebrate a Crime Club anniversary, this time the 30th, with an elegantly written novel of classical detection with a theatrical background.

### The Adventure of the Christmas Pudding (1960) Agatha Christie

Even though Miss Marple was one of the first detective characters to appear in Crime Club she is mis-named on the flap of this short story collection as Miss Marples!

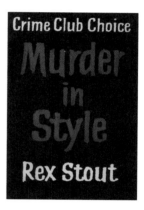

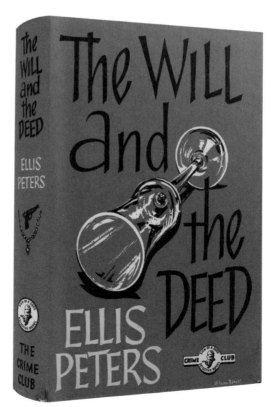

### *Death Paints a Picture* (1960) Miles Burton

*Death Paints a Picture* was the 63rd and final Miles Burton novel since *The Hardway Diamonds Mystery* in June 1930. In those 30 years he rarely, if ever, deviated from the novel of detection and although his characters were little more than cardboard, his plots showed resourceful ingenuity, particularly with murder methods. Cecil John Street died in 1964.

### *Message from Sirius* (1961) Cecil Jenkins

Described as 'exciting and original' (Christie), 'a truly original crime novel' (Symons) and 'a really intelligent and thrilling thriller' (Blake), this joint winner of the Don's Crime Novel Competition was Jenkins' only crime novel. He was, at the time, a lecturer in French at the University of Exeter.

### *The Smartest Grave* (1961) R. J. White

Joint winner of the Don's Crime Novel Competition, White's novel was described as 'a crime story for all connoisseurs' (Symons), 'a most distinguished and unusual crime novel' (Blake) and 'a good period story of crime' (Christie). White was a lecturer in History at the University of Cambridge and published two more crime novels in 1969 and 1971, the year he died.

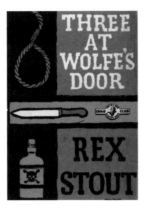

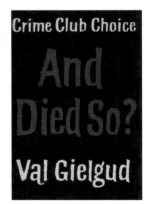

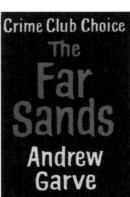

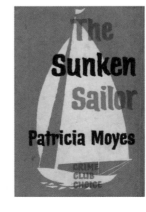

1961 saw the Crime Club debut of **ROSS MACDONALD** (1915-1983) – considered by many to be a novelist first and a crime writer second – who had previously published over a dozen novels under his real name, Kenneth Millar, as well as Ross and John Ross Macdonald. His second Crime Club novel, *The Wycherley Woman* (1962), featured his main character, private eye Lew Archer, modelled on Chandler's laconic Philip Marlowe: 'The work of Hammett and Chandler and their fellow writers seemed to constitute a popular and democratic literature.' And 'while the essential features of its plot are a crime and its solution, there is room in the form for complexities of meaning which can match those of the traditional novel'.

*A Tapping on the Wall* (1961) Helen Hull

Winner of the $3,000 Dodd-Mead Award for a crime novel written by a University professor, this was Helen Hull's (1888-1971) only appearance in Crime Club.

*The White Shroud* (1961) Robert Nicholas

It is very possible that *The White Shroud*, appearing in the same year as the prize-winning titles (across), was also an entrant in the Only for Dons Competition. The only book by Robert Nicholas, it is set – as the cover suggests – against a closely observed (fictional) university background.

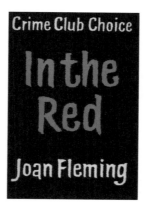

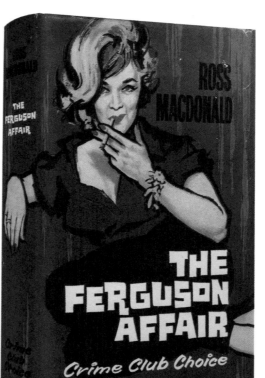

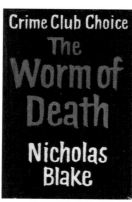

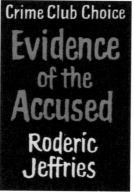

### *My Brother's Killer* (1961) D. M. Devine

A splendid example of latter-day Golden Age detection, complete with suspects, clues, alibis, misdirection and a wonderfully surprising killer. Devine's original title – *Murder off the Record* – was a clue in itself…

### *Trial from Ambush* (1962) Leslie Ford

Although Ford had been writing for the Crime Club since the 1930s, the last of her 24 titles was something of a shock. The crime around which it is built is not murder, but rape. Not the usual Crime Club subject or, indeed, a common theme for crime fiction at all at that point in the genre's development. Discreetly done, it was a brave experiment.

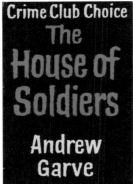

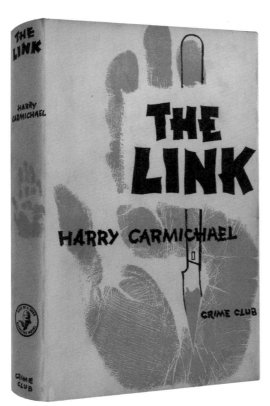

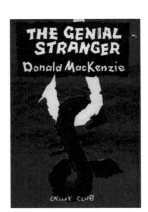

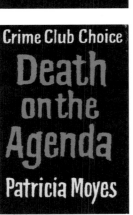

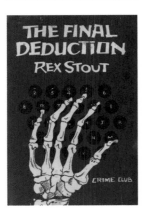

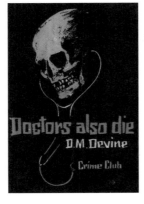

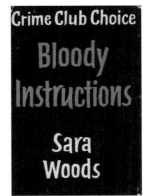

**SARA WOODS**' (Sarah Bowen-Judd 1929-1985) *Bloody Instructions* (1964) was the debut of a writer who went on to publish 48 further titles – 18 of them with Crime Club – and 10 more under three pen-names. Antony Maitland, her gentleman barrister, is the series character throughout the Woods *oeuvre*. As she explains: 'I write crime novels with a legal background because the law has always interested me.' The dust-jacket of *Bloody Instructions* 'confidently introduced a new writer and new fictional detective of whom we believe a lot more will be heard' and went on to name 'with pride and enthusiasm' the next four further titles that would appear in the series. Presumably, Sara Woods had been writing for quite a few years before securing a contract. A decade later she commented: 'I concentrate mostly on murders because they are the kind of crime that anybody can commit. But, in fact, I am not very interested in the murder – it's just a peg.' Her titles are all quotations from Shakespeare.

### *The Lethal Sex* (1964) John Macdonald (Ed.)

A collection of short stories by women crime writers including Margaret Millar, Christianna Brand, Ursula Curtiss and Anthony Gilbert, the only Crime Club author in the compilation. Originally published three years earlier in the US as a Mystery Writers of America anthology, the Crime Club volume contained only 10 of the 14 stories included in the original edition.

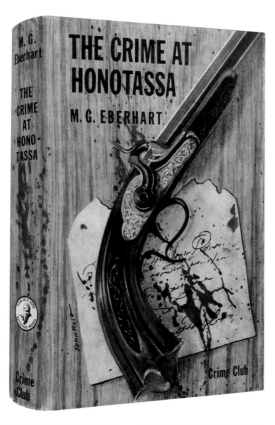

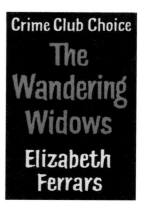

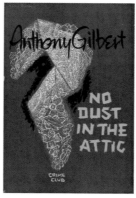

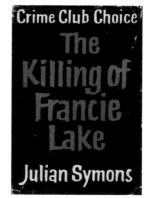

### Funeral of Figaro (1962) Ellis Peters

Surely the most creative, less-is-more jacket design of 2,012 covers is *Funeral of Figaro*. The opera background is perfectly captured in the music-notation quavers of the mournful face. And what looks like a tear is, on closer inspection, a noose…

**LAURENCE MEYNELL** (1899-1989) was already an established writer before his first Crime Club book, *Virgin Luck* (1963). His first novel was published in 1928 and by the time of his death he had over 150 books to his credit. Although only eight of his titles appeared under the Crime Club imprint, many of his other titles appeared in the Collins Thriller series. Meynell admitted: '…there is more perspiration than inspiration in writing a thriller. Four hours steady writing a day is my method of getting the work done'.

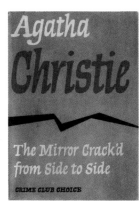

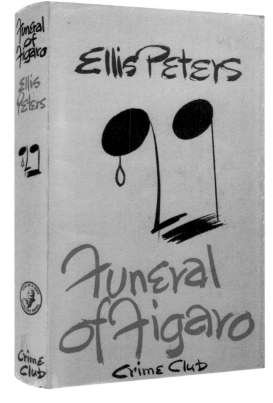

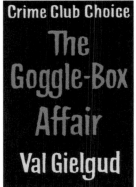

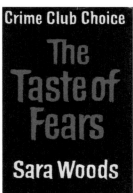

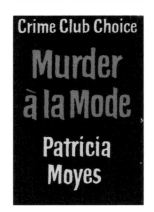

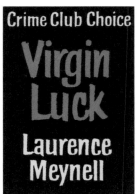

Although published first by Gollancz, **H. R. F. KEATING** (1926-2011) moved to Crime Club in 1963 and stayed for 20 years, before moving again to Macmillan. His famous character, Inspector Ganesh Ghote, first appeared in the Gold Dagger-winning *The Perfect Murder* (1964) and went on to feature in two dozen titles. Keating observed: 'Like Ghote, I am reasonably shy and diffident myself, and though we both do manage to overcome it, I like to think that the shy get their rewards. Ghote gets his reward by discovering things that brasher policemen do not'. The series is set, for the most part, in India, a country Keating had never visited until ten years after Ghote's debut. Ghote was originally to be named Ghosh until Keating learned from a friend, recently returned from Bombay, that Ghosh is a Bengali name and, therefore, unsuitable for a Bombay detective. Ghote, a Maharashtrian name, was the compromise solution. As a commentator on crime fiction Keating asked: 'Is there anything, when life get a little much, as comforting as a detective story? … For many of us the quintessential detective story does have a warm inward spreading cosiness that can expel any number of everyday horrors'

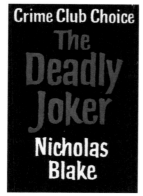

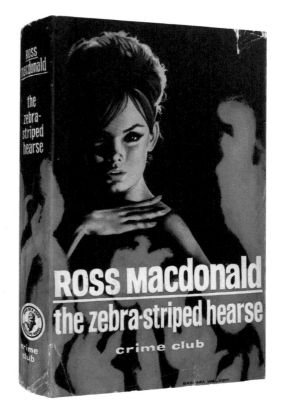

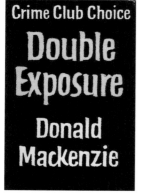

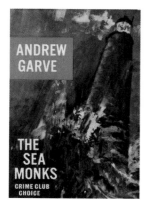

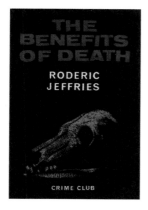

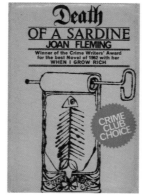

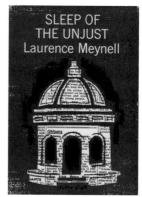

### *The Late Clara Beame* (1964) Taylor Caldwell

The multi-million selling American novelist experimented with the crime genre just this once and chose the 'suspects isolated by a snowstorm' ploy in a tale of familial murder in rural America. Though suspenseful, there is no detection.

**DONALD MACKENZIE** (1908-1993) has the distinction of being the only Crime Club author to begin his writing career while in jail. He served time, mainly for robbery, in both the UK and US with, in his own words, 'depressing regularity'. Crime Club published only three of his 30+ books.

### *Frame-up* (1965) Andrew Garve

A throw-back, in many ways, to the Golden Age of unbreakable alibis, this novel poses the question: Which of two cousins has faked his alibi for the murder of his wealthy uncle? Agatha Christie's *Cards on the Table* presented readers with only four suspects but Garve halves that suspect list, and still manages to keep the reader in suspense.

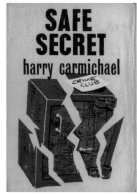

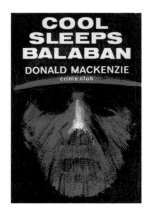

 During the 1960s Crime Club authors garnered five major awards for crime-writing:

- The British Crime Writers' Association gave their Gold Dagger Award to *The Perfect Murder* (H. R. F. Keating), *When I Grow Rich* (Joan Fleming) and *The Far Side of the Dollar* (Ross Macdonald)
- The Edgar Award for Best Novel from the Mystery Writers of America was presented to *Death and the Joyful Woman* (Ellis Peters) and *The Progress of a Crime* (Julian Symons)

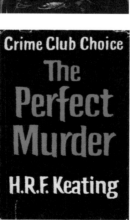

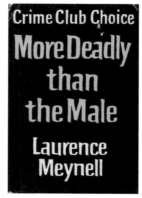

The year following his debut in print, *Death in a Sleeping City* (1965), **JOHN WAINWRIGHT** (1921-1995) left his job as a policeman to devote himself to writing, eventually producing over 80 titles, all but the first nine for Macmillan (when George Hardinge left Collins for Macmillan in 1968 he 'took' Wainwright with him). His personal knowledge of the day-to-day life of 'a copper' was reflected in his writing. His novels were, for their day, tough and uncompromising and his policemen very different from Ngaio Marsh's Roderick Alleyn or Patricia Moyes' Henry Tibbett.

### *Is Skin-Deep, Is Fatal* (1965) H. R. F. Keating

Although this could be an entry in the 'Odd Titles' category, it is notable for a curious reason: its similarity to a famous, and erstwhile controversial, novel of detection from 40 years earlier. Although the setting of the 1965 book, a sleazy beauty contest in a Soho nightclub, is far removed from its more illustrious predecessor, the plot bears remarkably close similarities to events in the village King's Abbot surrounding the death of the eponymous Roger Ackroyd…

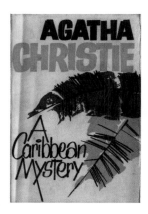

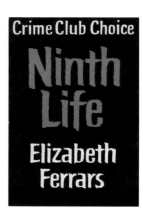
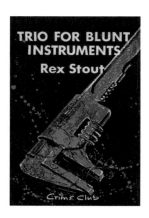

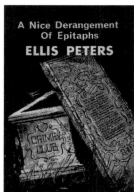

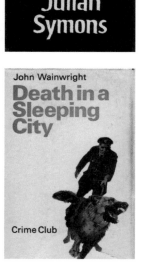

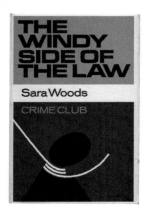

**MICHAEL KENYON** (1931-2005) published a dozen humorous crime novels in the Crime Club imprint, beginning with *May You Die in Ireland* (1965). He maintained two series characters: Superintendent O'Malley, who investigated crimes in Ireland, and Inspector Henry Peckover, and unusually brought them together in *Zigzag* (1981). The humorous crime novel is a difficult literary balancing-act but Kenyon's infectious humour often camouflaged an ingenious plot. His *The Rapist* (1977) is an indication of how far crime fiction has come since an earlier Crime Club novel on the same subject, Leslie Ford's *Trial from Ambush* (1962); a later Crime Club book, Sheila Johnson's *Goldilocks* (1983), examines society's attitude to this crime while Faye Kellerman's *A Ritual Bath* (1987) is unflinchingly realistic. That said, both the jacket and the blurb of the Kenyon novel are shockingly casual and comical for so serious a subject. 'Biggles, Buchan and Graham Greene' were Kenyon's only acquaintance with suspense fiction when he embarked on his first crime novel. Writing of *May You Die in Ireland* 15 years after publication he labelled it 'spy entertainment'.

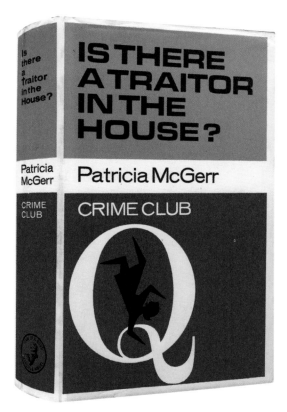

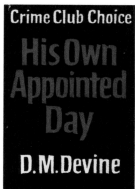

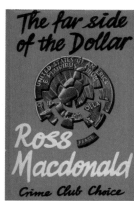

Mid-way through the decade **MARTIN RUSSELL** (b. 1934) published *No Through Road* (1965), the first of 34 Crime Club books. Rather like Andrew Garve, Russell's strength was the resourcefulness of his plotting. He rarely repeated a plot and, although avoiding the pure whodunit, Russell was as unpredictable in his twists and turns as the best Golden Age authors: the hotel with no guests and no staff (*Phantom Holiday*), the man who returns home to discover that no one recognises him (*Mr. T*), the deserted airport (*Touchdown*), the couple who each approach the same man to kill their spouse (*Double Deal*). Russell explained: 'The people I like to think I write for are those who want a reasonably well-written story with a few shocks and surprises, reasonably believable characters, and not necessarily a happy ending (although in this respect I'm mellowing)'.

### *Johnny Under Ground* (1965) Patricia Moyes

*Johnny Under Ground* shares a connection with Stephen Murray's *Fetch Out No Shroud* (1990). Both quote John Pudney's poem 'For Johnny' and both explore the setting of a wartime airfield as a background to murder.

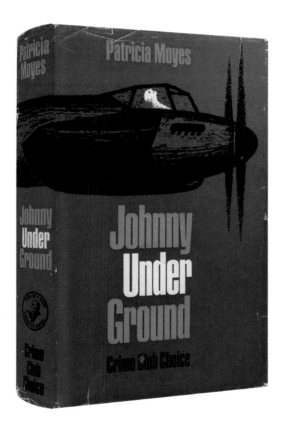

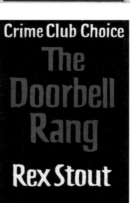

Although *My Brother's Killer* (1961) by **D. M.** (later **DOMINIC DEVINE**) was the first of thirteen meticulously plotted titles, *Devil at Your Elbow* reflected his own career background; he worked at St Andrew's University from 1964 – as Assistant Secretary, Deputy Secretary and then as Registrar – until his death. Collins' readers were so impressed with the technical skill of *My Brother's Killer* that they initially doubted its claim to be a 'first novel'. His second book was completed before his first was published and his final novel, *This Is Your Death*, was found among his papers after his death. The enigmatic 'D. M.' was adopted to avoid confusion with the established writer David Divine.

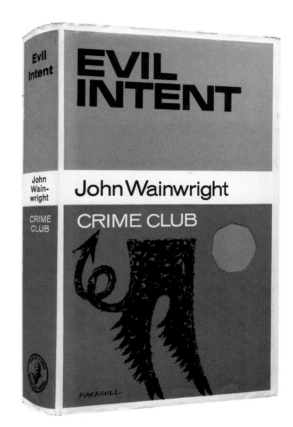

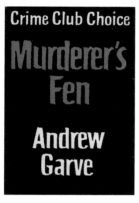

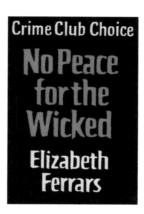

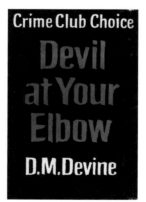

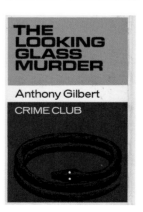

Odd titles 1960-1969:

- *Cool Sleeps Balaban* (1964) Donald Mackenzie
- *Crystallised Carbon Pig* (1965) John Wainwright
- *The Cat Who Could Read Backwards* (1967) Lilian Jackson Braun
- *Zero at the Bone* (1967) Elizabeth Ferrars

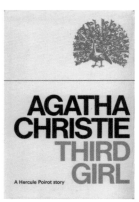

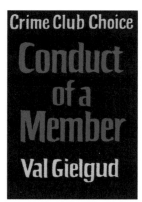

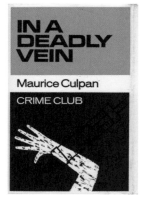

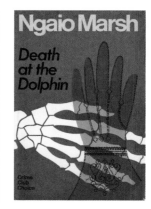

After publishing three Crime Club *The Cat Who…* books, **LILIAN JACKSON BRAUN** (1913-2011) abandoned writing for almost 20 years, before returning in 1986 and adding a further 27 titles to the series, though none of these appeared under the Crime Club imprint. Her Siamese cat detectives Koko and Yum Yum were certainly original, although ailurophilia is a prerequisite to enjoyment. She explained her absence: '[My publisher] declined to publish a fourth book, which was already written and titled *The Cat Who Ordered Caviar*…so I put the manuscript away in a trunk and forgot all about it for sixteen years.' Commenting on a pre-publication reading of *The Cat Who Could Read Backwards*, Val Gielgud gave a glowing endorsement, finding it 'enchanting', with 'one of the best double twists' he could remember.

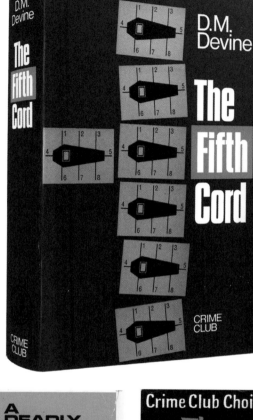

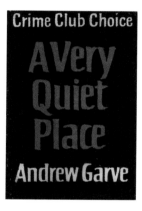

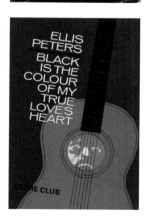

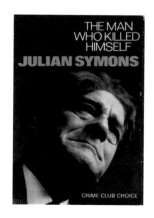

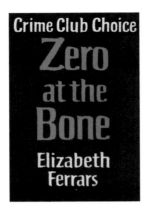

### *Endless Night* (1967) Agatha Christie

Easily the best book of Christie's last 20 years. In many ways an atypical offering – working class narrator marries fabulously rich American – until the Agatha Christie magic takes over in the final chapter. As Edmund Crispin said in his review for *The Sunday Times*, '…one of the best things Mrs Christie has ever done.'

In February/March 1968 Crime Club books changed from the original size to a slightly larger format and the price increased to 18 shillings (90p). H. R. F. Keating's *Inspector Ghote Hunts the Peacock*, D. M. Devine's *The Sleeping Tiger* and Lilian Jackson Braun's *The Cat Who Ate Danish Modern* were the first books to be issued in this new size.

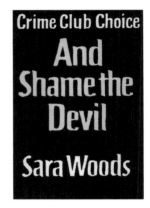

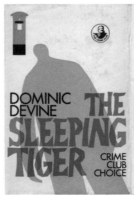
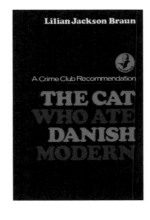
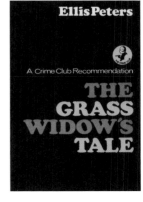

The Editor of The Crime Club, George Hardinge, was the dedicatee of three books in the months leading up to his departure from Collins:

- *Death of a Philanderer*: Lawrence Meynell
- *Web of Silence*: John Wainwright
- *The Man Who Killed Himself*: Julian Symons

Nicholas Blake ended his crime-writing career in May 1968 with a novel set in 1930s Ireland, six months after his fellow-Irishman Nigel Fitzgerald published the last of his dozen novels. After a 30-year association John Stephen Strange published her last Crime Club title in 1962. Val Gielgud and Ellis Peters both moved to Macmillan in 1970.

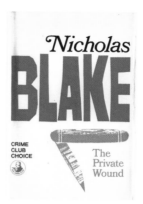

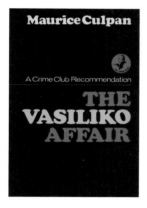

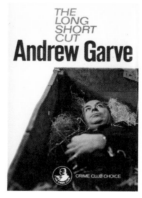

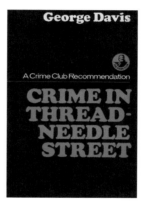

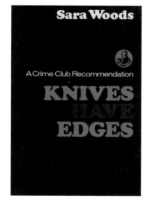

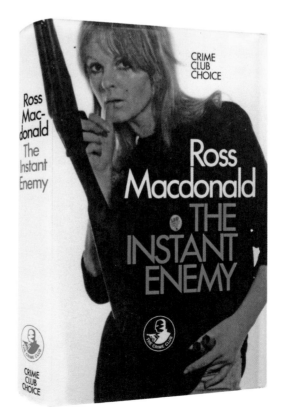

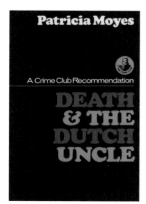

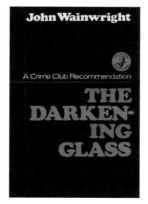

## A Necessary End (1969) Val Gielgud

This book mentions 'the Crime Club' twice. The stock of the ship's library is described as containing 'a peculiar selection of volumes, ranging from the products of the Crime Club…to a number of Victorian memoirs'. Later, one of the suspects, providing an alibi, says that he '…found one of those Crime Club books. It promised to be absorbing. But promise out-ran performance.'

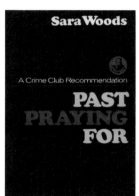

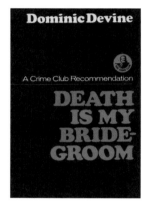

**ROY LEWIS** (b.1933) began his 30-novel Crime Club career in 1969 and, after the dissolution of Crime Club in 1994, published the same number again. Stories featuring his two series characters, Eric Ward and Inspector Crow, appeared alongside standalone novels, notable for their characters and settings rather than their whodunit elements. In 2012 Lewis said: 'I was very fortunate. The first one I wrote [*A Lover Too Many*] was accepted by Collins in the Crime Club series, which was then the biggest publisher of crime. Having got that first one sold, it moved on from there. The difficulty has always been to get your first novel published but, once the firm has made an investment in you, so to speak, they are more inclined to help you. My second and third novels had to be rewritten because they were not good enough, but at least I was getting the assistance. After that, it got into a pattern and I would do a book every eight to ten months, something like that, and that's continued now since 1968.'

**ROGER BUSBY** (b. 1941) made his Crime Club debut in 1969 with *Robbery Blue*, the first of 'police stories through which [he tries] to give an authentic flavour of criminal investigation'. Reversing to some extent the usual pattern, Busby subsequently joined the police force in 1973 as Force Information Officer, Devon and Cornwall Constabulary, after an earlier career as a journalist and five of his eleven Crime Club novels.

### *Of Malicious Intent* (1969) Laurence Meynell

This entertaining novel has the 'distinction' of being the first Crime Club title to include a (then) notorious four-letter word. In Chapter IV in a discussion on censorship, during a literary festival, the word is used freely and frequently.

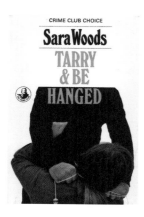

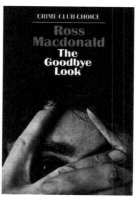

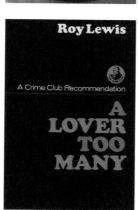

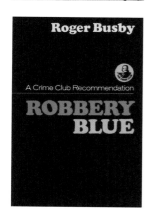

# The sign of a good crime story

## The 1970s

There were 330 books issued this decade, which was an increase on the previous three decades, and only slightly fewer than the initial 1930s total of 346 . But the decade also saw the most seismic changes in the roster of authors.

Agatha Christie celebrated her 80th birthday in September 1970 with the publication of what Collins chose to count as her 80th book, the atypical and disappointing Passenger to Frankfurt. This occasion was marked by extensive publicity – an aspect of publishing that was anathema to the author – followed by a six-month presence on the best-seller lists. The following January, in the New Year Honours List, the Queen of Crime became Dame Agatha Christie. Five years later, on 12 January 1976, her reign would come to an end...

# CRIME CLUB

# FIFTH DECADE

# The 1970s

COLLINS CRIME CLUB

### *Who Saw Her Die?* (1970) Patricia Moyes

This Edgar-nominated novel by a writer hailed as a new Queen of Crime was a return to the house-party murder mystery of the 1930s. As a family gathers from various parts of the world to celebrate a milestone birthday one of the guests contrives a murder with a highly original method from, as the *TLS* put it, 'the great Sayers days of cunning devices.' In an 'Afterword' Moyes explains that the device derived from a real-life incident some years earlier, in which an Italian woman, inexplicably, almost died. Medical detection followed and arrived at a startling explanation...

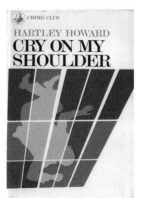

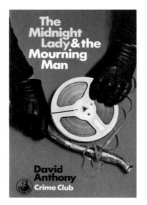

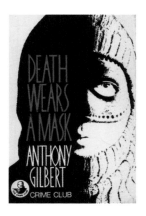

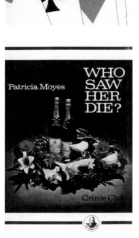

Unsure whether she is 'a poacher turned gamekeeper or a gamekeeper turned poacher', **CATHERINE AIRD** (Kinn Hamilton McIntosh b.1930) 'took to crime when I realised that I was reading more works of detective fiction that any other form of literature'. A writer very much in the Golden Age tradition, she began her crime-writing career in 1966 and four novels later joined the Crime Club with *A Late Phoenix*. Her detective duo of policemen Crosby and Sloan appeared in most titles and the books are all characterised by gentle wit and unobtrusive erudition. Although only nine of her novels appeared under the Crime Club imprint she has gone on to produce over twenty novels.

The illustrious career of **REGINALD HILL** (1936-2012) began with *A Clubbable Woman* (1970), in which his series characters, the outrageously unorthodox Inspector Andy Dalziel and the more traditional Sergeant Peter Pascoe, made their debut. The following year he published one of his darkest non-series books, *Fell of Dark*, although as Hill recalled in 1992: '*Fell of Dark* was the first completed book, which got an encouraging rejection from Constable and by the time I'd finished with them…I'd finished *A Clubbable Woman* and Collins took both'. An alternating pattern of Dalziel/Pascoe and standalone continued through much of his career. But there is little doubt that the duo of contrasting Yorkshire policemen remains Reginald Hill's most significant legacy. By the time of his later Crime Club novels he was regarded as one of the best crime writers in the UK, if not the world.

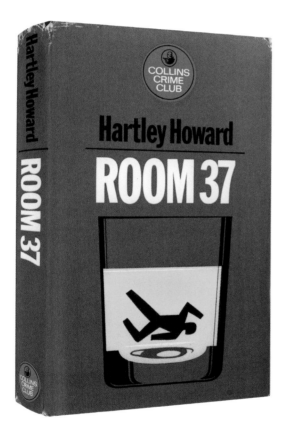

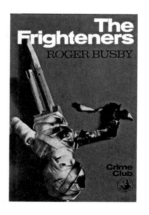

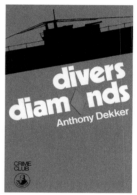

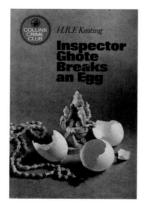

### *The Protégé* (1970) Charlotte Armstrong

Edgar-winning American crime novelist Charlotte Armstrong (1905-1969) issued just this one, posthumous, Crime Club title, although she had previously published seven titles in the Collins Mystery list, one of which, *Lemon in the Basket* (1968), was also nominated for an Edgar Award. Undeservedly forgotten nowadays, her novels are nearer in style to Patricia Highsmith or Margaret Millar than Agatha Christie.

Novelist and biographer Dudley Barker (1910-1980), writing as **LIONEL BLACK**, published the first of ten Crime Club novels, *Breakaway*, in 1970. This account of the attempts of a gang of bank-robbers to escape both police and a rival gang, all battling the worst floods ever experienced in the UK, was not typical of his later output. Subsequent novels ranged from the old-fashioned whodunit, *Death Has Green Fingers* (1971) and *A Healthy Way to Die* (1976), a locked-room problem in *The Penny Murders* (1979) and the psychopath hoaxer of *Death by Hoax* (1974).

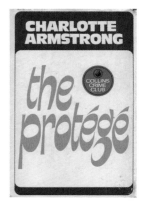

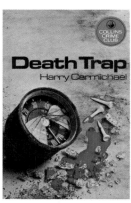

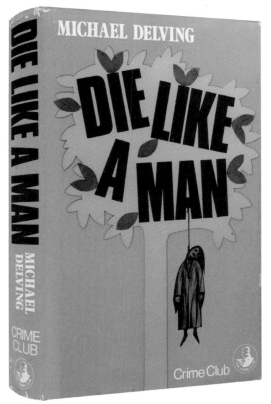

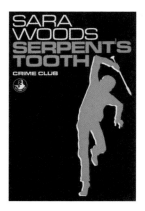

Already the author of 15 novels, **PHILIP LORAINE**'s (Robin Estridge 1920-2002) first Crime Club novel was the eye-catchingly titled *Photographs Have Been Sent to Your Wife* (1971). Seven more followed, notable for their unpredictability: the hijacked hotel of *Lion's Ransom* (1980), the occult theme of *Voices in an Empty Room* (1973) and culminating in the unnamed serial killer narrator of *Crackpot* (1993).

### *Come Out, Come Out, Whoever You Are* (1971) Thomas McCann

It seems highly likely that Thomas McCann was the pen-name of Thomas Campbell Black/Campbell Armstrong (1944-2013). The biographical notes included on his Crime Club title – which admits that he has written under a different name – and Campbell Black's *Death's Head* (Collins 1972) are remarkably similar on most points.

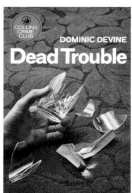

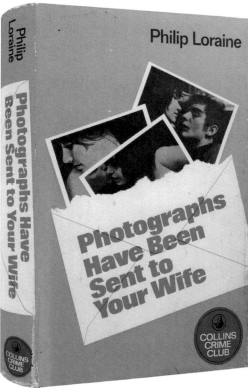

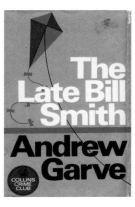

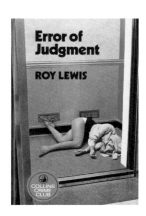

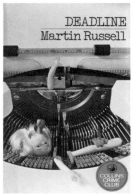

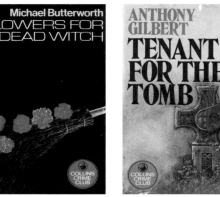

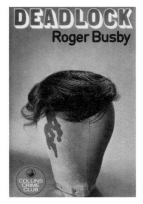

US-born **MARIAN BABSON** (Ruth Stenstreem 1929-2017) spent most of her life in London where her prolific output of light-hearted thrillers began in July 1971 with *Cover-Up Story*. All but four of her 22 novels avoided a series character and were remarkable both for the diversity of the backgrounds – cat shows, the PR business (in which Babson had worked), murder mystery weekends, the worlds of catering, fashion or film – and their twice-a-year appearance.

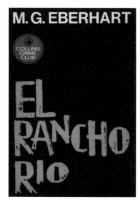

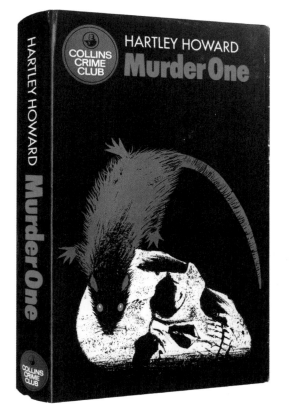

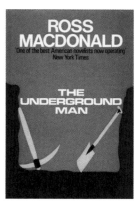

### *Inspector Ghote Goes by Train* (1971)
### H. R. F. Keating

Who can resist a train-set crime story? Ghote undertakes a trans-India journey and the ensuing battle-of-wits with a master criminal climaxes in an unlikely undertaking, hinted at by the jacket illustration…

Three of **DIANA RAMSAY**'s (Rhoda Brandes 1934-2014) six Crime Club novels have backgrounds of dance and music: *A Little Murder Music, Deadly Discretion* and *Four Steps to Death*. Startlingly different, *Descent into the Dark* is a disturbing exploration of one woman's solution to a major urban problem.

### *The Thrill Machine* (1972) Ian Hamilton

This novel about murder and corruption is set in the world of Australian television. Various aspects of the television industry also provide backgrounds for:

- *Cover-Up Story*: Marian Babson
- *The House That Jack Built*: Eileen Dewhurst
- *The Goggle-Box Affair*: Val Gielgud
- *The Night They Murdered Chelsea*: Margaret Hinxman
- *Die Laughing*: Patricia McGerr
- *The Renewable Virgin*: Barbara Paul
- *Natural Causes*: Jonathan Valin

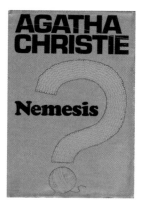

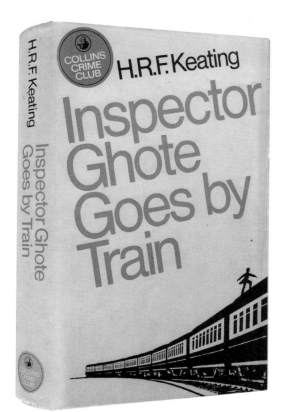

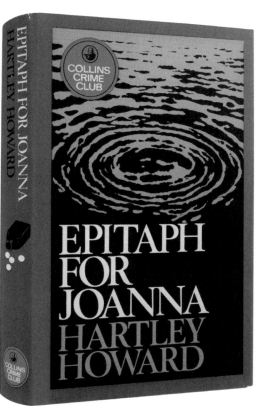

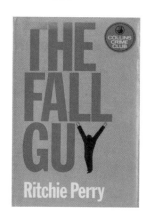

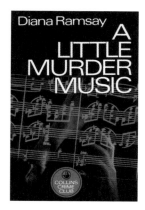

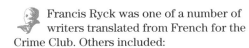

Francis Ryck was one of a number of writers translated from French for the Crime Club. Others included:

French:
- Auguste Le Breton: *The Law of the Streets*
- Catherine Arley: *Woman of Straw, Dead Man's Bay* and *Ready Revenge*
- Yves Jacquemard and Jean-Michel Sénécal: *The Eleventh Little Nigger*

Italian:
- Sergio Donati: *The Paper Tomb*

Danish:
- Torben Nielsen: *A Gallowbird's Song* and *Nineteen Red Roses*

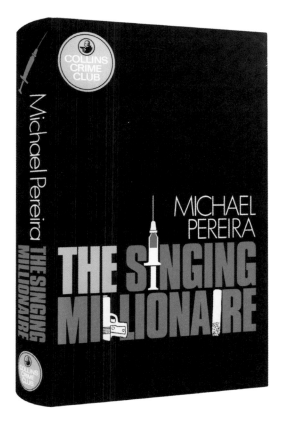

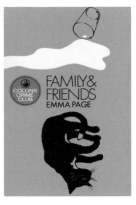

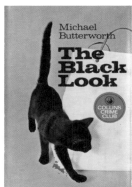

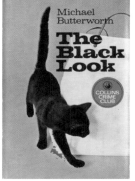

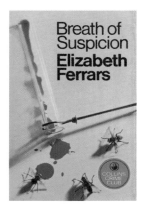

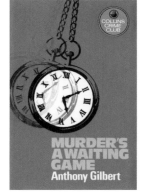

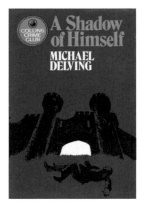

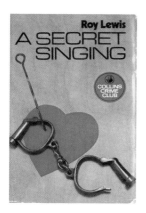

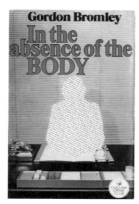

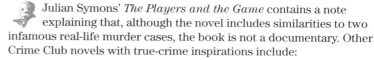 Julian Symons' *The Players and the Game* contains a note explaining that, although the novel includes similarities to two infamous real-life murder cases, the book is not a documentary. Other Crime Club novels with true-crime inspirations include:

- *The Crime of the Century*: Anthony Abbot
- *Midnight Hag*: Joan Fleming
- *Inspector Ghote Trusts the Heart*: H. R F. Keating
- *Miss Lizzie*: Walter Satterthwait
- *The Woman in the Sea*: Shelley Smith
- *Sweet Adelaide*: Julian Symons
- *The Smartest Grave*: Reginald James White

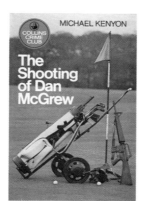

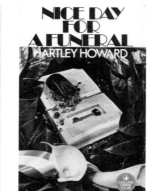

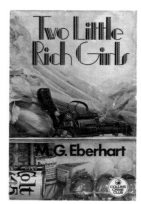

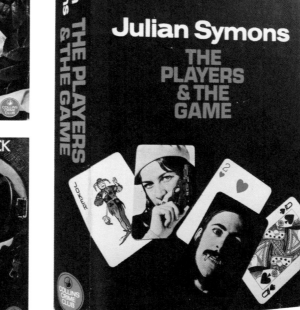

'There's an old saying that the lawyer who defends himself has a fool for a client' is the opening line of the blurb of *A Fool for a Client*; Roy Lewis' *A Wolf by the Ears* also has a strong legal emphasis. Legal backgrounds featured regularly in the Crime Club, most notably in the first half-dozen titles from Roderic Jeffries and the entire output of Sara Woods. Other titles with legal emphasis include:

- Harry Carmichael: *Confession*
- Dominic Devine: *The Sleeping Tiger*
- Hamilton Jobson: *The Evidence You Will Hear*
- Nancy Barr Mavity: *He Didn't Mind Hanging*
- Haughton Murphy: *Murder for Lunch*
- Raymond Postgate: *Verdict of Twelve*
- John Stephen Strange: *Dead End* and *Reasonable Doubt*

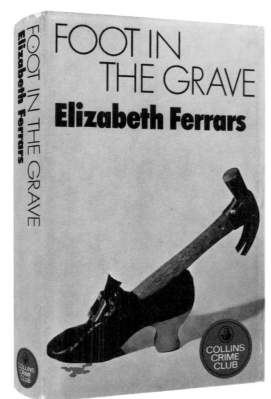

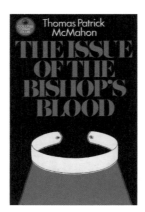

Crime Club continued to publish books with intriguing titles in the 1970s, including:

- *A Very Good Hater*
- *Grim Death and the Barrow Boys*
- *The Man in the Sopwith Camel*
- *The Issue of the Bishop's Blood*
- *Blood on a Harvest Moon*
- *The Thrill Machine*
- *The Curious Affair of the Third Dog*

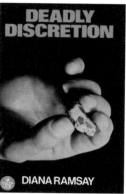

DEADLY DISCRETION — DIANA RAMSAY

Gordon Bromley — THE CHANCE TO POISON

RULING PASSION — Reginald Hill

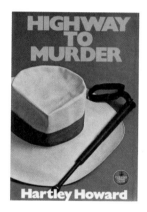

HIGHWAY TO MURDER — Hartley Howard

BLOOD MONEY — Roy Lewis

Pat Flower — CAT'S CRADLE

HIS BURIAL TOO — Catherine Aird

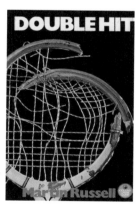

DOUBLE HIT — Martin Russell

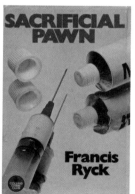

SACRIFICIAL PAWN — Francis Ryck

PATTERN OF VIOLENCE — Roger Busby

THE SMALL WORLD OF MURDER — Elizabeth Ferrars

THE 95 FILE — James Martin

THE PLOT AGAINST ROGER RIDER — Julian Symons

Joan Fleming

THE CURIOUS AFFAIR OF THE THIRD DOG — Patricia Moyes

The first four of the eleven Crime Club novels of **MICHAEL BUTTERWORTH** (1924-1986) were dark thrillers with a strong whodunit element, beginning with *Vanishing Act* in July 1970 to *Villa on the Shore* (1973). He then opted, with erratic degrees of success, for what his blurbs describe variously as 'hilarious romps' and 'felicitous black comedies' or the 'funniest criminal farce of the year'.

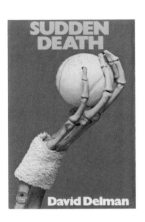

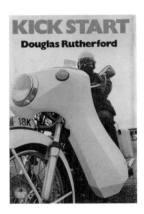

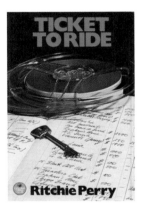

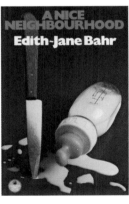

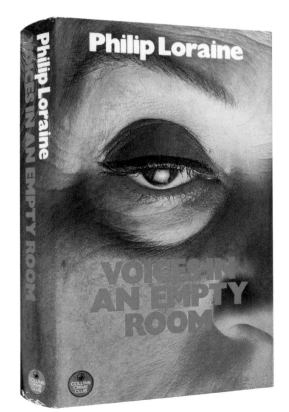

### The File on Lester (1973) Andrew Garve

Further evidence of Andrew Garve's plot-resourcefulness, this is an epistolary novel – the first such since the G. D. H. and M. Cole's *Burglars in Bucks* (1930) – of a cleverly constructed and seemingly fool-proof allegation of sexual assault levelled against an MP. Like many Garve novels - *The Cuckoo-Line Affair, The Megstone Plot, The Narrow Search, A Hero for Leanda, The Far Sands, The Sea Monks, A Very Quiet Place, Home to Roost* – boats and boating are a feature.

By her own admission **ANNA CLARKE** (1919-2004) 'only started writing late in life and should never have done so if a very long and severe illness [agoraphobia] had not destroyed my chosen career [in mathematics]'. Her Crime Club output is a series of ten civilised crime novels, some of them whodunits, all featuring family situations which threaten to get out of control. After 1980 Clarke published a further ten crime novels with other publishers. *Plot Counter-Plot* concerns a battle of wits between two writers, one of them a successful suspense novelist.

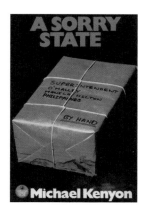

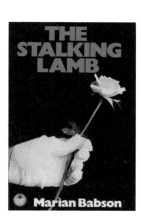

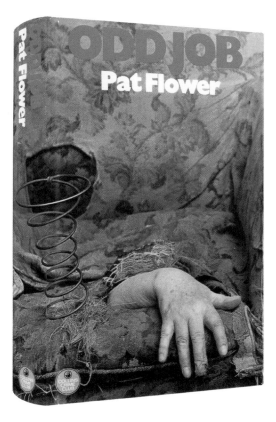

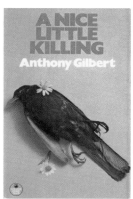

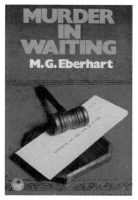

### *Poirot's Early Cases* (1974) Agatha Christie

After the 1973 publication of *Postern of Fate*, Agatha Christie wrote no new material. 1974's 'Christie for Christmas' was a nostalgic collection of 18 of the little Belgian's early short stories, not previously published in the UK. And within a year Crime Club issued his final investigation, *Curtain*, written 35 years earlier when the Queen of Crime was at her peak. It appeared on the best-seller lists worldwide, remaining there for months, and Hercule Poirot received a front-page obituary in the *New York Times*, the only fictional character ever accorded this honour.

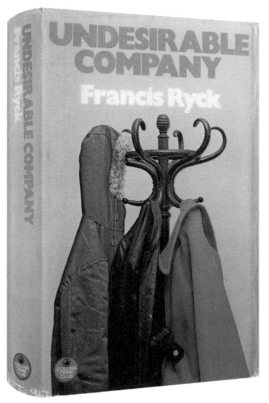

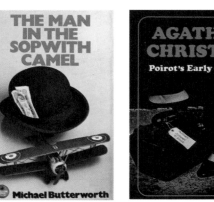

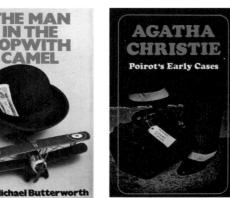

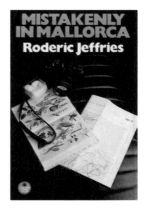

ROBERT BARNARD (1926-2013) began his Crime Club career in November 1974 with *Death of an Old Goat*, based, to some extent, on his experiences while teaching in an Australian University. Twenty years later he admitted: 'I never expected it to be published; I was writing the book for myself, for my wife, and a few friends.' His novels were characterised by an acute wit and keen social observation, fused with a Golden Age-type plot. For him 'the formula [of the classic whodunit] is adaptable...it will take more realism, more humour, a wider class range, more psychological depth than the Golden Age writers used. But the basic formula is still very much alive and useful. The whodunit is not dead. It is hardly even dozing'. He published 22 Crime Club novels, as well as a perceptive analysis of the Christie phenomenon, *A Talent To Deceive* (1980).

***A Three-Pipe Problem* (1975) Julian Symons**

The intriguing title is from the Sherlock Holmes short story 'The Red-Headed League' (1891), a case which was, according to the great detective, 'a three-pipe problem'. During a book tour she shared with Symons in May 1974 Ngaio Marsh suggested the title for the novel, thereby earning the book's dedication. It is the only Sherlock Holmes-themed book in the Crime Club catalogue.

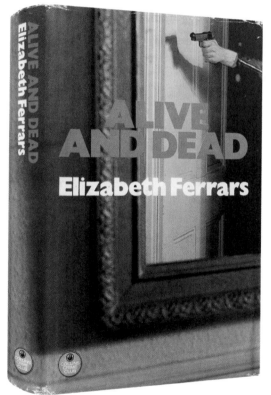

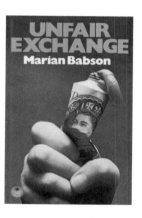

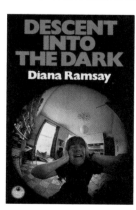

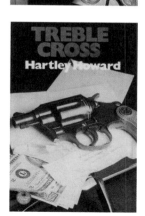

### *The Evidence You Will Hear* (1975)
### Hamilton Jobson

Already the author of eight crime novels before joining Crime Club Jobson (1914-1981) had had 30 years' experience as a police officer, eventually as Divisional Inspector, before writing his first book. His series character is, not surprisingly, an Inspector Anders.

For a brief period Crime Club Choice titles were indicated by the appearance of a handcuff logo extending from the bottom of the spine and on to the cover of the dust-jacket, each bracelet encircling 'Crime Club Choice'. The first such titles were Patricia Moyes' *Black Widower* and Reginald Hill's *An April Shroud* in July 1975. Over the following 18 months this design was repeated on another Hill, as well as titles from Agatha Christie, Catherine Aird, Rex Stout, Michael Butterworth, Ross Macdonald and H. R. F. Keating.

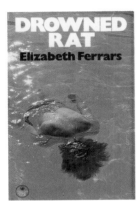

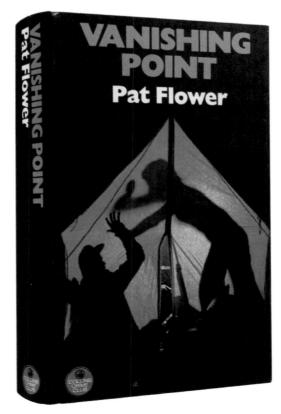

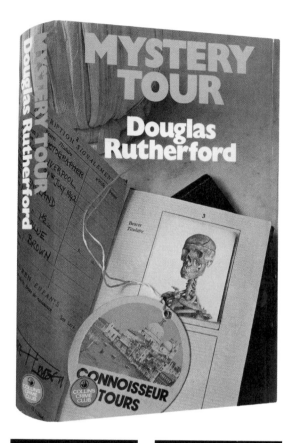

### Saturday Games (1975) Brown Meggs

Brown Meggs' (1930-1997) debut was Edgar-nominated in the Best First Novel category by Mystery Writers of America. A second novel, *The Matter of Paradise* (1976) concerns the and-then-there-were-none nightmare of a group of classmates. More importantly (possibly...) when Meggs worked for Capitol Records in the 1960s he was responsible for signing The Beatles.

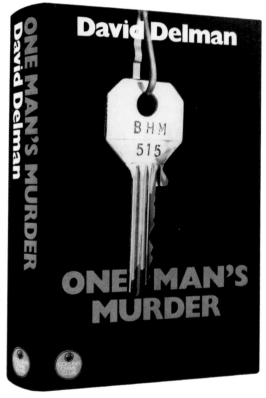

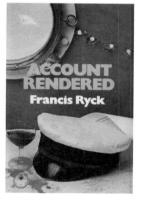

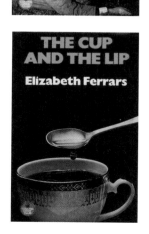

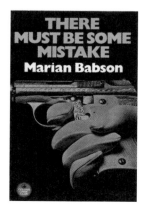

*The Modigliani Scandal* (1976) Zachary Stone

This thriller set in the art-world was the first of two Crime Club novels by Zachary Stone, the third pseudonym used by the later best-selling Ken Follett. Immediately after the second Stone title, *Paper Money*, he published the award-winning spy thriller *Eye of the Needle* aka *Storm Island* (1978).

British-born **PAT FLOWER** (1914-1977) emigrated with her family to Australia in 1928. A prolific script-writer, her crime-writing career began in 1958 but she abandoned her Inspector Swinton character and concentrated on dark psychological thrillers, publishing seven Crime Club titles in four years.

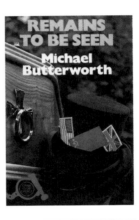

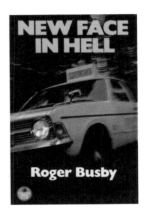

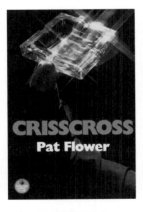

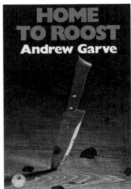

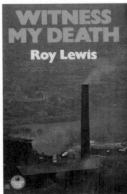

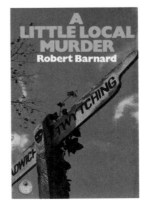

MARGARET HINXMAN's (1924-2018) first Crime Club book, *End of a Good Woman* (1976), was a traditional village mystery, a milieu repeated in half of her Crime Club output. Her remaining titles reflected, to a greater or lesser degree, her real-life job as a film critic, featuring backgrounds of TV in *The Night They Murdered Chelsea* and *A Suitable Day for Dying*, the Austrian background of *The Sound of Music* in the appropriately titled *The Sound of Murder* and *Nightmare in Dreamland* is set in the 'garish and sinister' world of Hollywood.

When **DAVID WILLIAMS** (1926-2003) suffered a stroke in his early 50s he abandoned his career in advertising and turned to crime fiction. His detective, Mark Treasure, appears in all nine Crime Club titles. Unusually, Williams published seven Crime Club titles, moved to Macmillan for eight books and returned to Crime Club for the final two in the series. Williams admitted that he 'rarely knew the identity of the murderer before the penultimate chapter', a technique which was 'stimulating if often taxing'. And he believed that 'the specialist, informed amateur can be as believable as the trained professional. Both principal performers have the satisfaction of solving their puzzles and bringing the criminal to justice…'

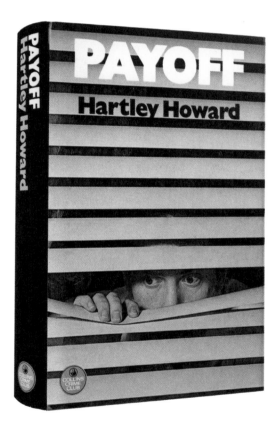

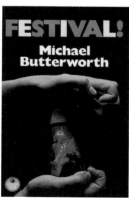

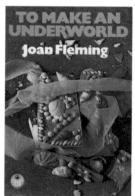

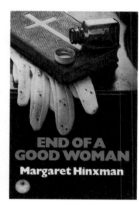

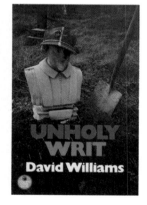

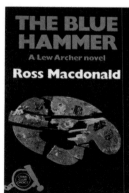

 The international scope of the Crime Club at this time is well illustrated by some of the titles on this page with settings such as:

- Australia: *Shadow Show*
- Africa: *The Heat of the Sun*
- India: *Filmi, Filmi, Inspector Ghote*
- Denmark: *A Gallowsbird's Song*
- Caribbean: *To Kill a Coconut*
- Channel Islands: *Last Ditch*
- Europe: *Return Load; Dead End*
- New Zealand: *Hot Pursuit*
- Ireland: *The Rapist*
- USA: *Stud Game; You Can't Call It Murder*

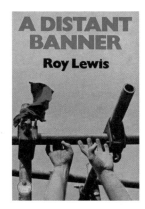

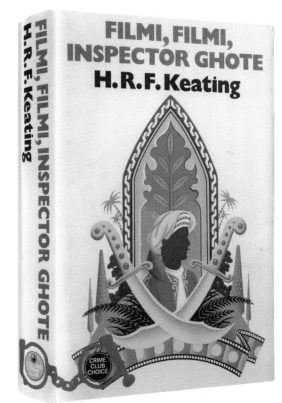

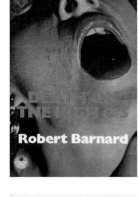

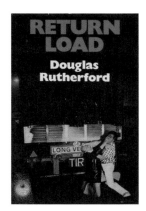

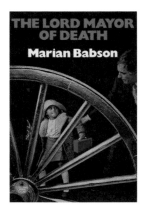

### *Hot Pursuit* (1977) Gavin Scott

Novelist and broadcaster Gavin Scott's single Crime Club title is set in New Zealand. That country is also the setting for Ngaio Marsh's *Colour Scheme*, *Died in the Wool* and *Photo-Finish*, as well as Simon Jay's *Death of a Skin-Diver*.

### *Every Inch a Lady* (1977) Joan Fleming

The ever-inventive Joan Fleming pens a 1950s-set murder mystery, rich in period detail, with a wonderfully resourceful anti-heroine.

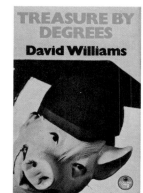

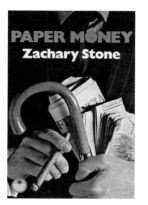

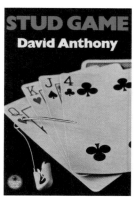

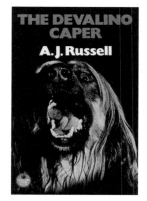

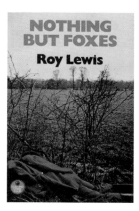

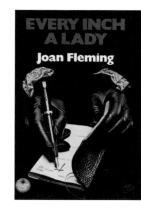

The Judas Pair (1977) introduced readers
to the Robin Hood-type antique 'dealer' Lovejoy,
created by **JONATHAN GASH** (John Grant
b. 1933), and over the following twelve years
a dozen further titles appeared. His fame was
consolidated by a hugely popular TV series with
71 episodes between 1986 and 1994. Intriguingly,
Gash also wrote a one-off Crime Club novel, The
Incomer, issued under a different name, Graham
Gaunt, in 1981.

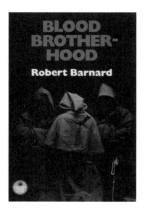

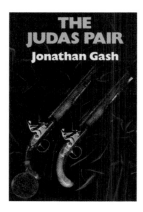

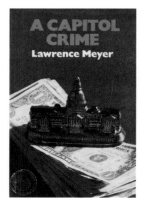

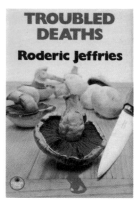

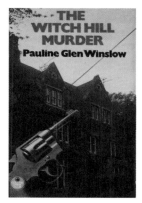

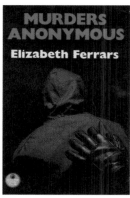

**A PINCH OF SNUFF**
Reginald Hill

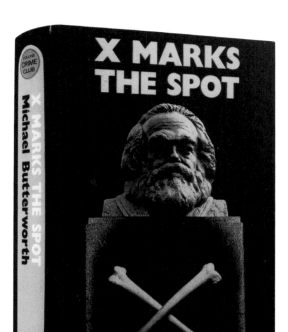

**X MARKS THE SPOT**
Michael Butterworth

*Unruly Son* (1978) Robert Barnard

In a return to Golden Age detection, best-selling detective novelist Sir Oliver Fairleigh-Stubbs of Wycherley Court collapses and dies during his birthday party. Whodunit? More importantly, how many titles, derived from Golden Age novels, can you recognise in the chapter titles?

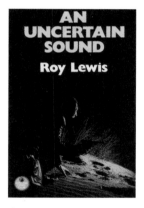

**AN UNCERTAIN SOUND**
Roy Lewis

**THE FOURSOME**
Lionel Black

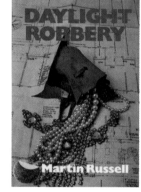

**DAYLIGHT ROBBERY**
Martin Russell

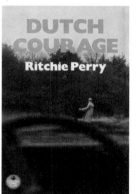

**DUTCH COURAGE**
Ritchie Perry

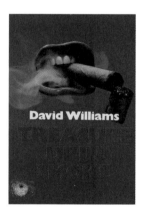

David Williams

**UNRULY SON**
Robert Barnard

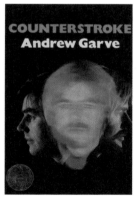

**COUNTERSTROKE**
Andrew Garve

**ONE OF US MUST DIE**
Anna Clarke

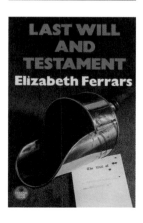

**LAST WILL AND TESTAMENT**
Elizabeth Ferrars

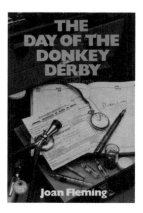

**THE DAY OF THE DONKEY DERBY**
Joan Fleming

**SLEEP IN A DITCH**
Maisie Birmingham

**GARVEY'S CODE**
Roger Busby

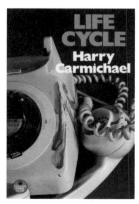

**LIFE CYCLE**
Harry Carmichael

The plot of *Who is Simon Warwick?* is built around establishing the true identity of a claimant to an inheritance. Other Crime Club titles with a similar theme include: *The Belting Inheritance* (Julian Symons), *Child's Play* (Reginald Hill), *A Painted Devil* (John Welcome); and Sara Woods' *Trusted Like the Fox* features a 'Tichborne claimant in reverse', while Agatha Christie's *Taken at the Flood* plays variations on similar themes of identity and inheritance.

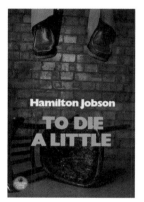

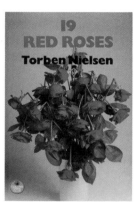

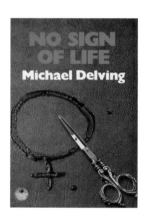

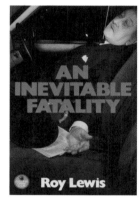

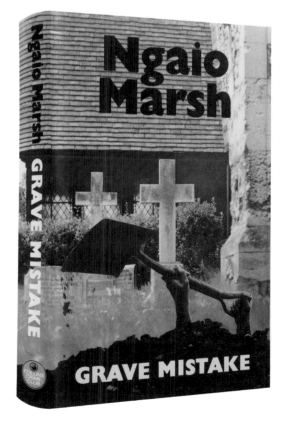

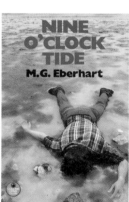

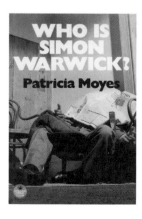

***The Eleventh Little Nigger*** (1979)
**Yves Jacquemard and Jean-Michel Sénécal**

This ingenious and affectionate homage – complete with detailed floor-plan and a split-page timetable of suspects' movements – is dedicated to Agatha Christie. It was published in French in 1977. Crime Club later published the authors' previous book, *The Body Vanishes*, which had won the *Prix du Quai des Orfèvres* (the French equivalent of the Gold Dagger) in 1976.

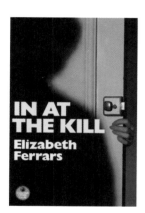

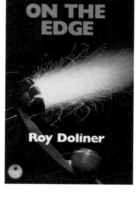

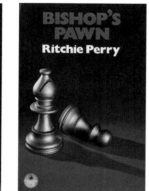

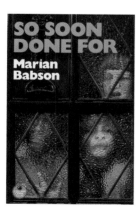

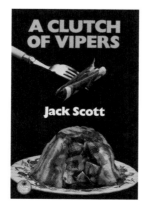

Agatha Christie died in January 1976; and this followed on from the death of Rex Stout, four months earlier. Thus, two long-standing stalwarts of the Club's list – 45 years (Christie) and 35 years (Stout) – bowed out almost simultaneously, although in each case there were posthumous books for their devotees to relish. The final Poirot, Miss Marple and Nero Wolfe novels were all issued before the end of 1976. Neither writer could be replaced in the affections of their immeasurable worldwide audience; and few matched them in terms of frequency and dependability of output.

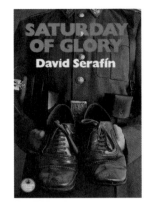
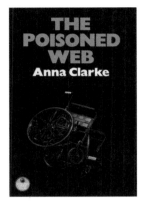

### *The Sealed Envelope* (1979) Hartley Howard

The dedication reads: 'This, Hartley Howard's last book, is dedicated to the memory of Leo Ognall by his loved ones.' Leo Ognall was the real name of Hartley Howard/Harry Carmichael.

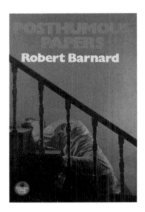
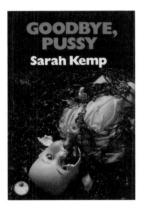

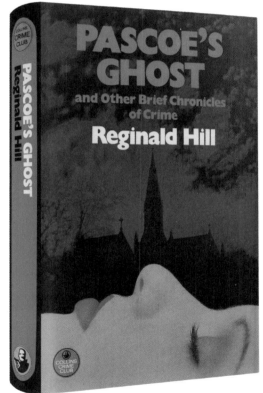

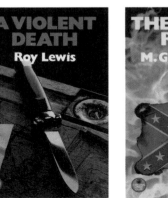
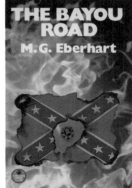

Other names – less prolific, less long-lasting, less famous – also made final appearances in the 1970s. Sara Woods moved to Macmillan in 1972 and Anthony Gilbert's final novel, *A Nice Little Killing,* was issued posthumously in 1974. The last Ross Macdonald novel was published in 1976, and the last Douglas Rutherford the following year. Joan Fleming, Andrew Garve and Harry Carmichael all published their final novels in a three-month period in 1978, although Carmichael's alter ego, Hartley Howard, issued one final title, *The Sealed Envelope,* in 1979, the year of Harry Carmichael's death.

Before her 1979 appearance in Crime Club, **CHARLOTTE MACLEOD** (1922-2005) was already the author of ten novels – some for children – and a book of short stories. And then: 'I'd done a little story about a college professor who'd tried to sabotage the college's Grand Illumination. It had been returned to me with the speed of light and I'd forgotten about it until suddenly it clicked that here was the plot I'd been waiting for. So, I wrote *Rest You Merry…*' Her 19 titles are divided between her two series detectives, Sarah Kelling and Peter Shandy. On her death her sister wrote: '[Charlotte] wrote specifically for people who did not want blood and guts, at least not a whole lot of it anyway. Everybody drank tea and ate molasses cookies. It was that kind of thing.'

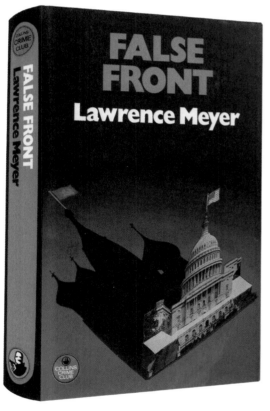

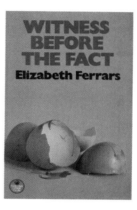
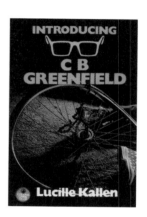

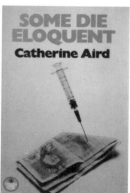
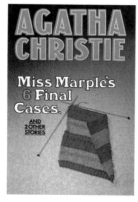

# All the best from
# Collins Crime Club

With the appearance of 407 titles, the 1980s was the Crime Club's most prolific decade; and appropriately so, as in May 1980 the Club celebrated its Golden Anniversary. This remarkable milestone was achieved despite the intervention of a World War; consequent paper shortages and distribution difficulties, the disappearance of the Circulating Library, and despite inevitable changes in reading tastes. For half a century the Club maintained its avowed aim of 'supplying the reading public with a continual supply of first-rate books by the finest writers'. Tastes and trends in crime fiction inevitably changed over the years and detective fiction, once the mainstay of the list, now formed only part of it.

### *Designs on Life* (1980) Elizabeth Ferrars

After 35 years of novels, this collection of short stories came as a surprise to Elizabeth Ferrars' many fans. The nine short stories – or, more accurately, eight stories and a novelette – were written over a 40-year period and includes her first ever short fiction and earliest flirtation with literary crime, 'After Death the Deluge'.

### *Sweet Adelaide: A Victorian Puzzle Solved* (1980) Julian Symons

As well as his selection of, and introductions to, the Golden Anniversary Crime Club Collection, Julian Symons published one of his most original novels in 1980. A 'faction' account of the still unsolved 1886 poisoning of Thomas Adelaide Bartlett, for which his wife, Adelaide, stood trial and was acquitted.

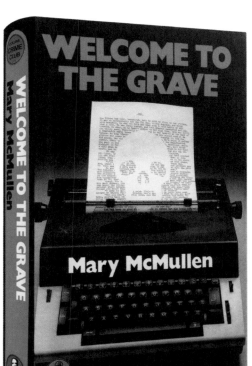

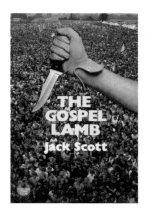

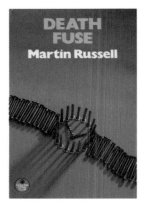

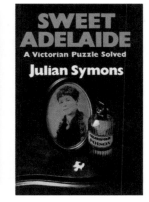

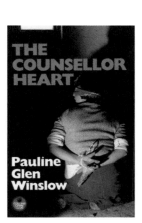

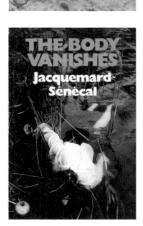

### *The Murder of the Maharajah* (1980) H. R. F. Keating

This Golden Age-style whodunit set in 1930s India was part of the 50th anniversary celebrations. In keeping with the traditions of that era the book introduces a variety of guests, all journeying to a house-party at the fabulous palace of the eponymous Maharajah. A closed circle of suspects, an unusual murder method, an unlikely detective and a last-line surprise all combine to re-create a forgotten time and place. The book won that year's CWA Gold Dagger Award.

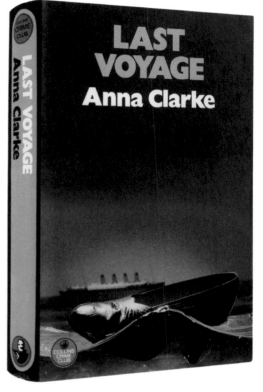

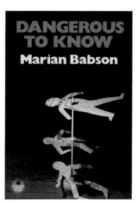

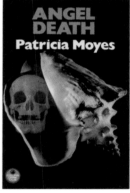

LIZA CODY (b. 1944) had major success with her first novel *Dupe* (1980), the first of six Anna Lee cases, five of which appeared in the Crime Club. *Dupe* won the CWA John Creasey Award for Best First Novel of the year, as well as an Edgar nomination. Cody's final Crime Club title was the stand-alone *Rift*, set in Ethiopia.

Despite an output of only three titles – a fourth non-Crime Club novel appeared posthumously – SARAH CAUDWELL (1939-2000) established her place in crime fiction history by achieving something new. Her titles all feature a group of legal professionals – Caudwell was a barrister – and their involvement, with various crimes, for the most part from a distance. Sarah Caudwell's wit, erudition and good writing would have always gained attention but what set her books apart was the question that has bedevilled readers ever since: is her narrator, Professor Hilary Tamar, male or female? The Professor's exact relationship with the group is never specified and even his/her age is debatable. Caudwell remembered finishing *Thus Was Adonis Murdered* 'just before going on holiday to the US and showed it to an agent there. She said she thought it was too wordy and too mannered for an American audience. Then I was advised to send it to Elizabeth Walter at Collins, who accepted it'.

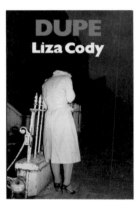

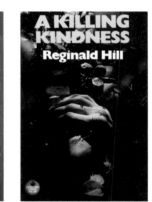

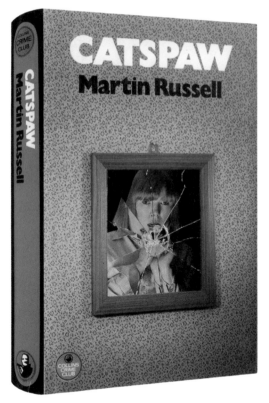

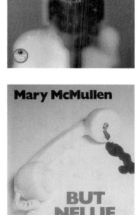

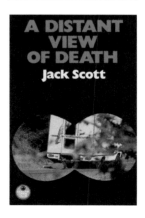

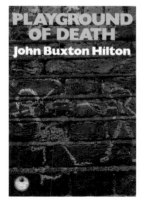

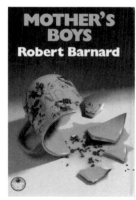

### *Deep and Crisp and Even* (1981) Peter Turnbull

Like all eight of former social-worker Peter Turnbull's (b. 1950) Crime Club output, this novel revolves around the police of Glasgow's P Division. The series, which features every stratum of Glasgow society, has been compared to Ed McBain's 87th Precinct novels.

### *The Incomer* (1981) Graham Gaunt

In the middle of producing his Lovejoy books Jonathan Gash, writing as Graham Gaunt, published this non-series novel, a village mystery with a dark centre. Crime Club issued 13 Lovejoy novels and the series continued with a different publisher, eventually reaching 24 titles.

### *Go West, Inspector Ghote* (1981) H. R. F. Keating

Ghote in California! What reader could resist that fish-out-of-water situation, especially when combined with a 'locked house' problem into the bargain? It is described in the blurb by Len Deighton as 'Wonderful'.

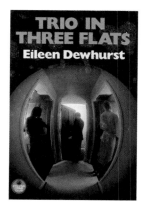

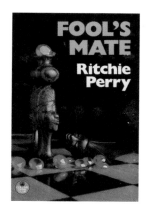

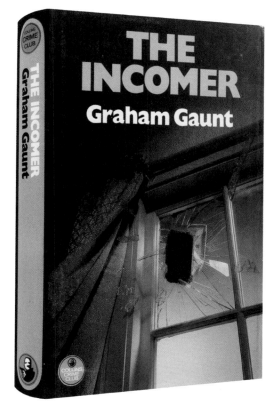

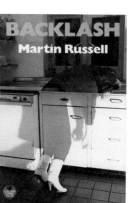

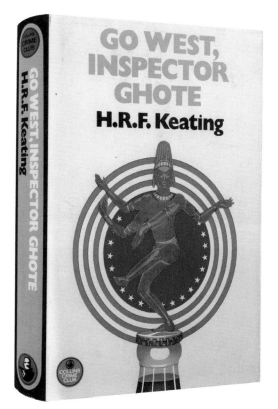

### *The Loss of the Culion* (1981)
### Jeffrey Ashford

Roderic Jeffries (1926-2017), whose first Crime Club novel appeared in 1961, had also written since 1960 as Jeffrey Ashford, and this parallel strand joined Crime Club in 1981 with *The Loss of the Culion*. He continued his impressive output under these two names – as well as three others with different publishers – for another 30+ years.

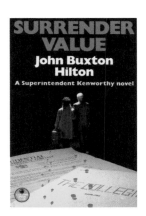

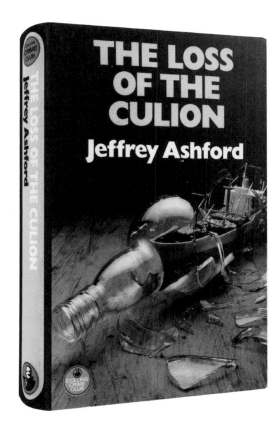

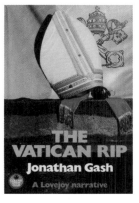

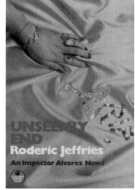

### *This Is Your Death* (1981) Dominic Devine

Dominic Devine, discovered 20 years earlier by Crime Club, published a thirteenth novel in October 1981, a posthumous book, found among his papers after his death in 1980.

Likewise, Lionel Black's *The Rumanian Circle* (see across) was also his final, posthumous novel. He also died in 1980.

### *Crime Wave: World's Winning Crime Short Stories 1981* (1981) selected by an international jury and with an introduction by Desmond Bagley

More than 400 stories were submitted to a competition held in conjunction with the 3rd Crime Writers' International Congress in Stockholm in June 1981. First prize, a Saab Turbo, was awarded to the American short story writer Frank Sisk. One of the International Jury was one-time Crime Club editor George Hardinge, but there were no Crime Club alumni in the collection.

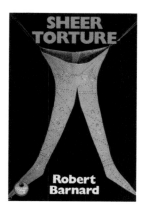
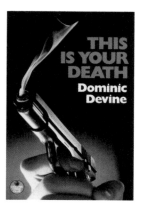

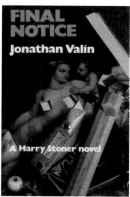

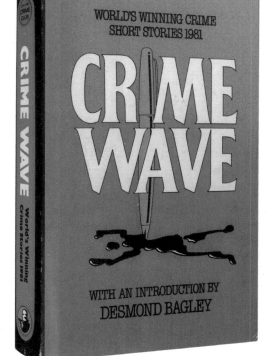
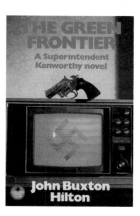
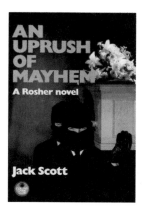
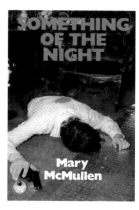

Kensington Palace and a (fictitious) member of the Royal Family appear in Robert Barnard's *Death and the Princess* and similarly in Robert Tine's *Uneasy Likes the Head*. Other high-profile settings are also exploited in these Crime Club novels:

- The Vatican: *The Vatican Rip* (Jonathan Gash) and *State of Grace* (Robert Tine)
- The House of Commons: *Beneath the Clock* (J. V. Turner) and *Murder among Members* (Carol Carnac)
- Capitol Hill: *Is There a Traitor on the House?* (Patricia McGerr) and *A Capitol Crime* (Lawrence Meyer)
- Canterbury Cathedral: *The Becket Factor* (Michael David Anthony)

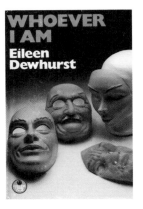

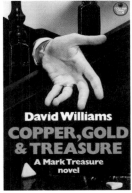
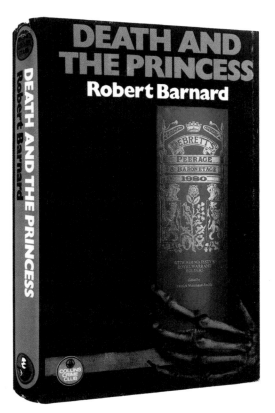
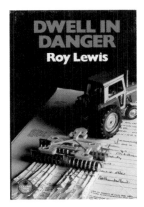

The intriguingly titled *Your Eyelids Are Growing Heavy* by Barbara Paul explores, in a highly original manner, the condition of amnesia. Other Crime Club titles with this plot device include:

- *Give Death a Name*: Anthony Gilbert
- *The Blackout*: Conyth Little
- *No Return Ticket*: Martin Russell
- *The Windy Side of the Law*: Sara Woods:

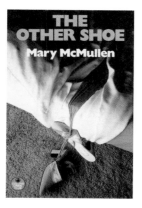

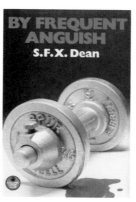

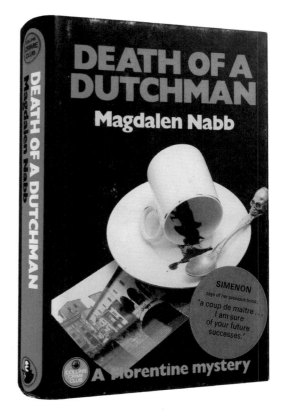

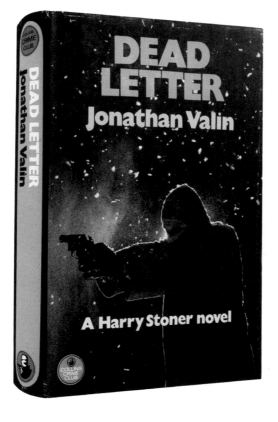

### *Light Thickens* (1982) Ngaio Marsh

The typescript for *Light Thickens* arrived at Collins on the day Ngaio Marsh died in February 1982. Even though this was one of her weakest novels, necessitating a lot of work by editor Elizabeth Walter, reviews and sales were excellent. It can be considered a 'follow-on' to *Death at the Dolphin* (1967), as they are both set in the same theatre with the same main protagonist, Peregrine Jay. The title is a quotation from Act III of *Macbeth* and the novel is set during a spectacularly ill-fated production of that 'Scottish play'. The long-delayed murder facilitates a detailed account, written from personal experience, of the play's production.

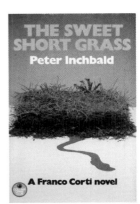

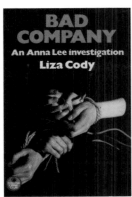

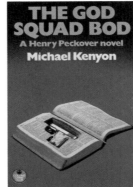

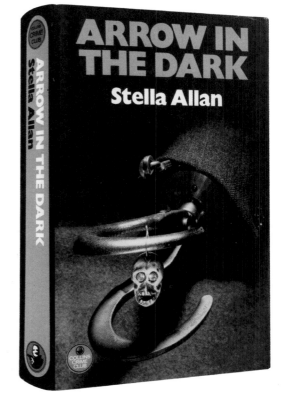

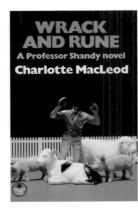

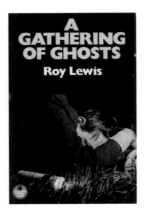

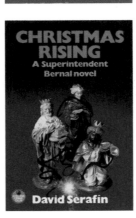

### *The Local Lads* (1983) Jack Scott

Detective-Inspector Rosher appeared in all but one (*A Little Darling, Dead*) of Jack Scott's (Jonathan Escott 1922-1987) nine Crime Club books, described as 'exuberant', 'irreverent' and 'sardonic'.

### *The Ariadne Clue* (1983) Carol Clemeau

This one-off novel won the John Creasey Award for the year's best first novel, earning a glowing endorsement from P. D. James: 'Civilised and literate…an impressive debut.' It seems to be Clemeau's only fiction.

### *Such Pretty Toys* (1983) S. F. X. Dean

The second of three Crime Club investigations by American professor Neil Kelly. Like his creation, the author, college professor Francis Smith, hides behind a formidable array of initials.

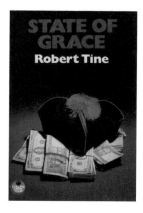

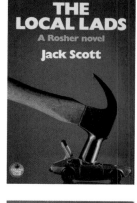

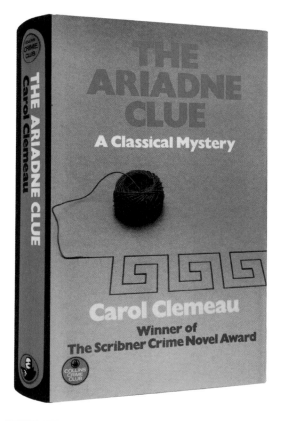

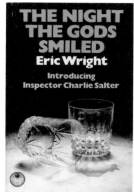

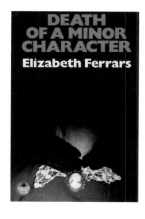

### *A Six-Letter Word for Death* (1983) Patricia Moyes

Incorporating two crossword grids, *A Six-Letter Word for Death* revolves around a weekend house-party for pseudonymous crime-writers. An unexpected death during the gathering uncovers a 20-year-old crime. Herbert Adams' *A Word of Six Letters* (1936) also features a crossword grid on the cover. Patricia Moyes was a fan of the more abstruse crosswords, as were fellow-Crime Club authors Sarah Caudwell and Agatha Christie. And Nero Wolfe enjoys solving the *New York Times's* Double-Crostic puzzle, the Ximenes in *The Observer*, as well as *The Times*.

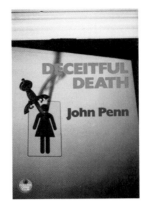

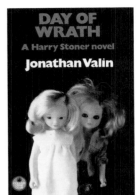

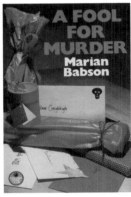

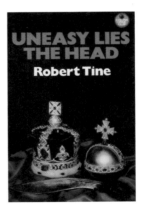

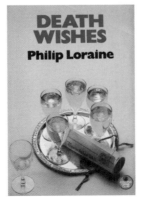

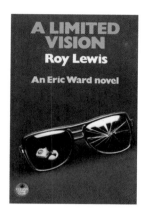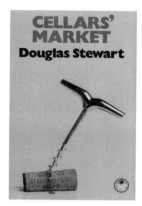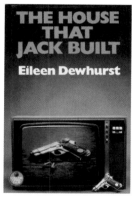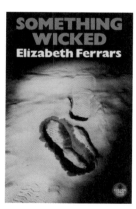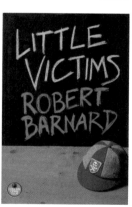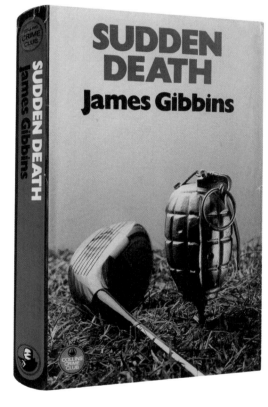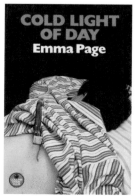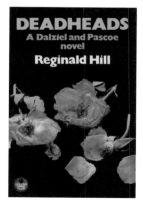

### Cold Light of Day (1983) Emma Page

One of the most explicitly disturbing covers of the entire Crime Club series is *Cold Light of Day*. The usual 'less is more' approach to representations of violent death seems to have been abandoned here. It was published the month following Charlotte Macleod's bloody-jacketed *The Bilbao Looking-Glass*, although neither author can, in any sense, be considered a 'dark' writer. Crime Club's design strength had always been its ability to suggest violence in subtle, understated ways. See examples in this decade alone:

- *The Sweet Short Grass*: Peter Inchbaid (1982)
- *The Corpse Now Arriving*: Margaret Hinxman (1983)
- *Death in Fashion*: Marian Babson (1985)
- *Dead Heat*: Martin Russell (1986)
- *The Skeleton in the Grass*: Robert Barnard (1987)

***Dead in the Water*** **(1983) Ted Wood**

This was the first case for Ontario policeman Reid Bennet and his Alsation dog, Sam. Other dog-related mysteries include Agatha Christie's *Dumb Witness* and *Postern of Fate*, Francis Ryck's *Loaded Gun*, Patricia Moyes' *The Curious Affair of the Third Dog*, A. J. Orde's *Death and the Dogwalker*, Elizabeth Ferrars' *Beware of the Dog*, Michael Pearce's *Mamur Zapt and the Night of the Dog*, and the novels of Janet Edmonds.

 And cat-lovers should check out:

- Charlotte Macleod: *Something the Cat Dragged In*
- Lilian Jackson Braun: *The Cat Who...* series
- Marion Babson: *Murder on Show* and *Nine Lives to Murder*
- Nicholas Blake: *The Case of the Abominable Snowman*
- Miles Burton: *The Cat Jumps*
- Mike Ripley: *Angel* series features Springsteen, a 'cynical black cat'.

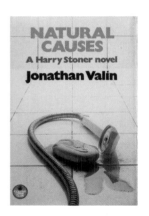

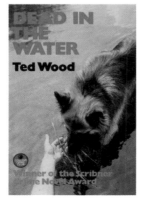

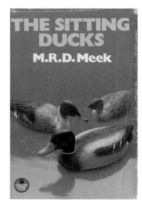

Crime writers adopting names with initials only have always been found in the world of crime fiction: G. K. Chesterton, E. C. Bentley, H. C. Bailey, S. S. Van Dine, A. A. Milne, J. J. Connington, and, more recently, P. D. James.

The Crime Club was not without similar examples: M. G. Eberhart, L. R. Wright, A. J. Orde, J. V. Turner. And some of the Club's writers added an extra letter: E. C. R. Lorac, M. R. D. Meek, S. F. X. Dean, H. R. F. Keating, L. A. G. Strong, G. D. H. Cole.

If mysterious anonymity was the desired effect it often worked: in the case of E. C. R. Lorac, she was referred to as 'he' for many years.

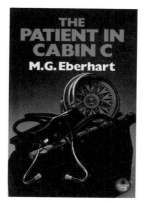

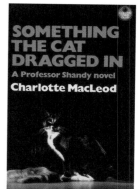

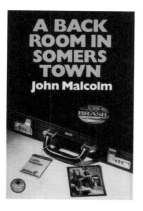

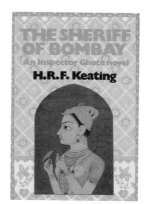

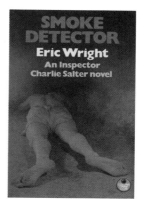

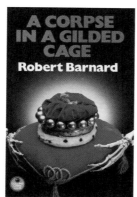

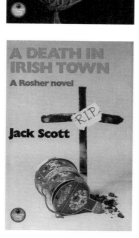

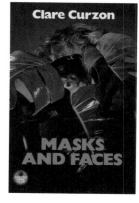

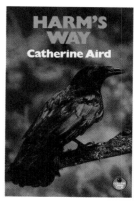

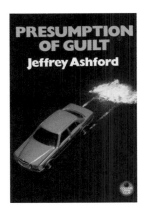

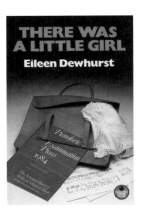

Some sources claim that Alison Cairns q. v. was a pen-name for Scottish author **M. R. D. (MARGARET REID DUNCAN) MEEK** (1918-2009). An examination of the Crime Club contracts for each writer does not bear out this claim, even though the short biographical notes on the flap of each writer's first novel share similarities.

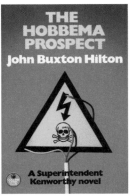

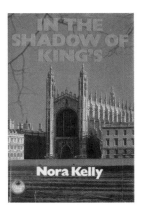

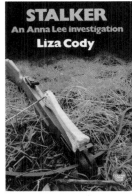

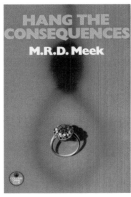

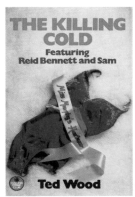

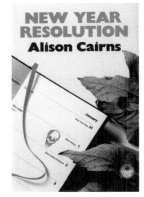

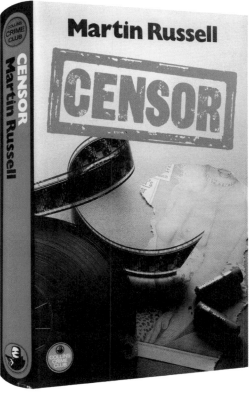

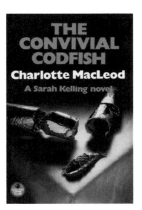

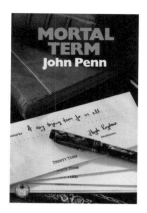

***Mortal Term*** (1984) John Penn

John Penn concealed the names of husband-and-wife Palma Harcourt (1917-1999) and Jack Trotman. In her own right Harcourt was a suspense novelist prior to, and during, her Penn output. Their 16 Crime Club novels are, for the most part, traditional.

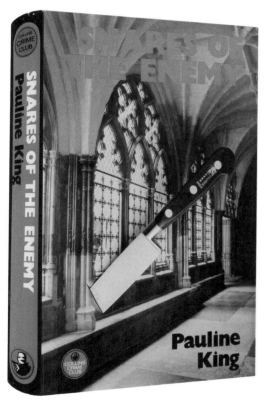

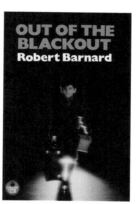

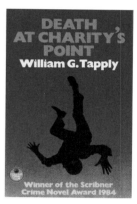

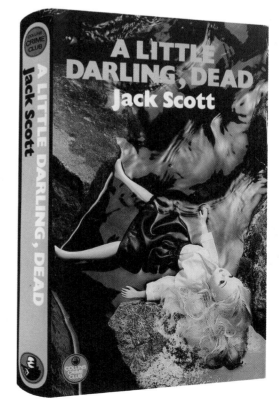

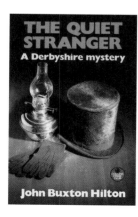

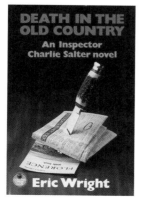

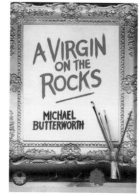

The first of **KEITH HELLER**'s (b. 1949) short-lived historical series, *Man's Illegal Life*, appeared in April 1984. Set in Restoration London, all three novels featured George Man, a watchman of the city. In a prefatory note Heller explains that 'in the first half of the eighteenth-century London was probably the most dangerous city on earth', and that 'the watchmen patrolled the streets from sunset to sunrise' in a futile effort to overcome lawlessness.

Various aspects of the 'rag trade' feature in Marion Babson's *Death in Fashion*, Michael Butterworth's *The Black Look*, Gwendoline Butler's *Coffin in Fashion*, Patricia McGerr's *Fatal in my Fashion* and Patricia Moyes' *Murder à la Mode*.

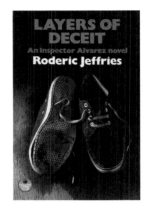

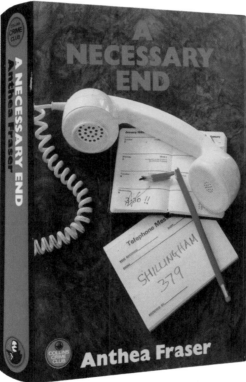

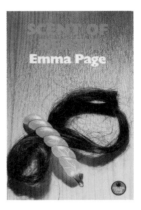

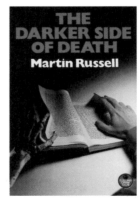

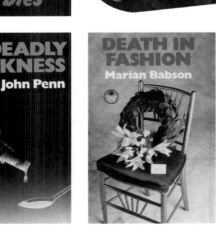

### *The Disposal of the Living* (1985) Robert Barnard

One of Barnard's best books is also notable because of its very clever title. The phrase 'disposal of the living' has obvious criminous connotations but it also refers to the action of an archbishop in allocating a parish (known as 'a living') to a new priest, the situation at the heart of this novel. Barnard's wit is very much in evidence in this village mystery, although the dust-jacket is in danger of giving too much away.

### *The Dutch Blue Error* (1985) William G. Tapply

This intriguingly-jacketed novel was William G. Tapply's (1940-2009) second case for Boston attorney Brady Coyne, who had eleven Crime Club appearances and eventually featured in 25 books.

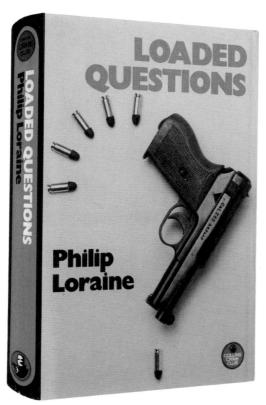

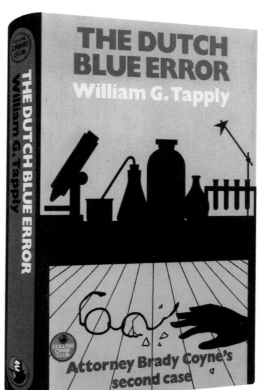

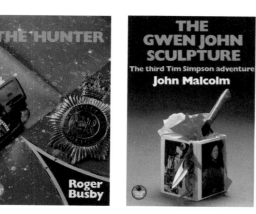

### *The Dorothy Parker Murder Case* (1985)
**George Baxt**

Only this volume of George Baxt's (1923-2003) hugely enjoyable 12-volume period murder mystery series set in 1930s Hollywood featuring real-life characters – Greta Garbo, Mae West, Alfred Hitchcock *inter alia* – appeared in the Crime Club list. The cover cleverly shows, within the circle of a magnifying-glass, the table of the famous *Algonquin Round Table* literary salon in 1920s New York; and all is clearly not well...

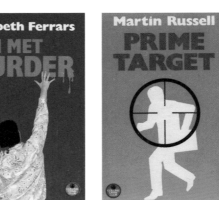

Although she had published her first novel in 1956 **GWENDOLINE BUTLER** (1922-2013) did not appear under the Crime Club banner until thirty years later, with *Coffin on the Water*. Her eight Crime Club titles all feature her series character, Inspector John Coffin, who had first appeared in 1957, and investigated over a dozen cases before his Crime Club debut. She won a Silver Dagger from CWA for her 1973 novel *A Coffin for Pandora* (which despite its title is not a Coffin novel) as well as a Romantic Novelists Association Award for her 1981 novel, *The Red Staircase*.

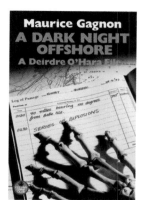

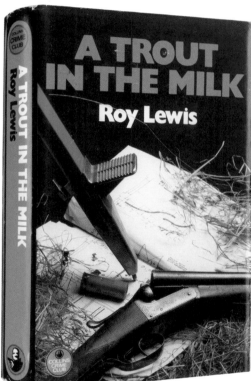

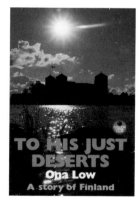

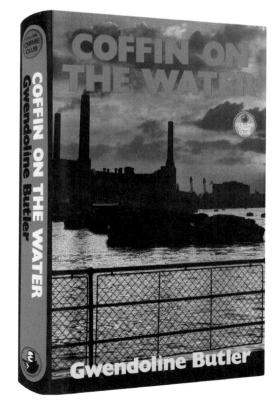

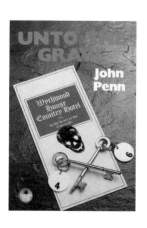

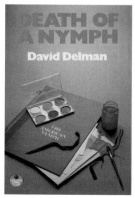

### *Bodies* (1986) Robert Barnard

As hinted by the cover, *Bodies* concerns the use of pornographic photographs, a theme also found in John Penn's *Outrageous Exposure* and Philip Loraine's *Photographs Have Been Sent to Your Wife*. Ian Hamilton's *The Thrill Machine* features 'blue movies', while Reginald Hill's *A Pinch of Snuff* explores, as its title suggests, a more gruesome aspect of the industry: so-called 'snuff movies'.

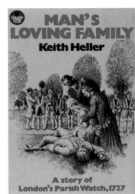

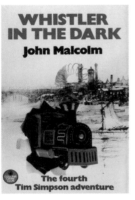

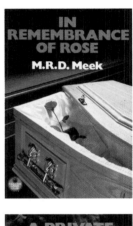

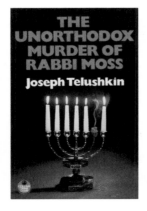

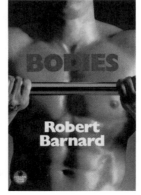

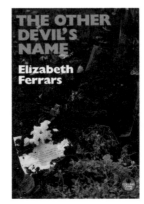

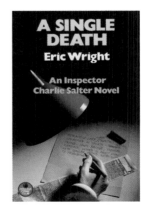

### *Riot* (1986) Roger Parkes

As evidenced by the emblazoned cover, *Riot* received a glowing endorsement from then-famous politician Robert Kilroy-Silk: 'A dramatic story full of pace and suspense…so true to life.' Other novels of the decade with recommendations from well-known people included Magdalen Nabb's *Death in Springtime*, with a front-cover 'Bravissimo!' and a page-long introduction from Georges Simenon; and Jeanne Hart's *A Personal Possession* boasted a positive review from Ruth Rendell.

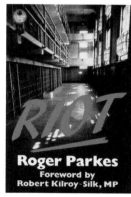

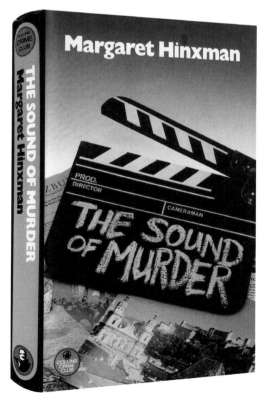

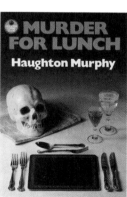

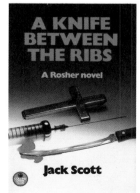

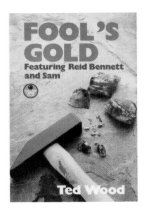

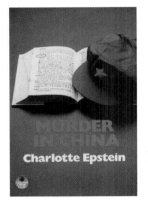

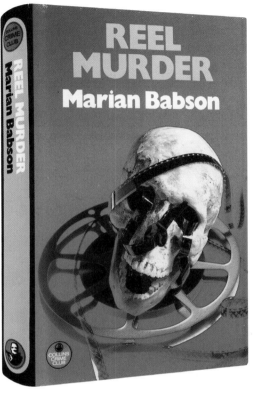

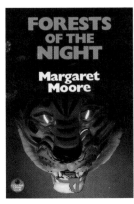

### *Fool's Gold* (1986) Ted Wood

In 1954 UK-born Wood (1931-2019) moved to Canada, where all the adventures of policeman Reid Bennett – and his Alsatian, Sam – are set. His first case, *Dead in the Water*, was written 12 years before it was published. Nine more followed, all but the last appearing in Crime Club.

### *Murder in China* (1986) Charlotte Epstein

This novel is notable as no other Crime Club novel is set exclusively in China. The book afforded a fascinating insight into life and law in the country at that time. Sadly, the insight does not compensate for the mediocre plot.

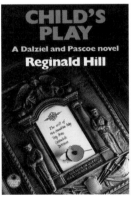

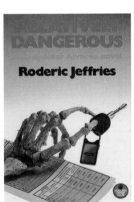

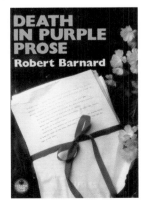

The first in a series of 'new' Nero Wolfe novels, authorised by the Rex Stout estate, from life-long fan **ROBERT GOLDSBOROUGH** (b. 1937) appeared in 1987. *Murder in E Minor* was so well received there were seven titles in eight years, although only three were published by the Crime Club. The second and third books contain forewords by noted Stout expert John McAleer and Rebecca Stout Bradbury (Rex Stout's daughter) respectively. Goldsborough resumed the series in 2012 after a gap of 18 years.

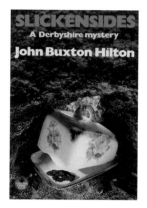

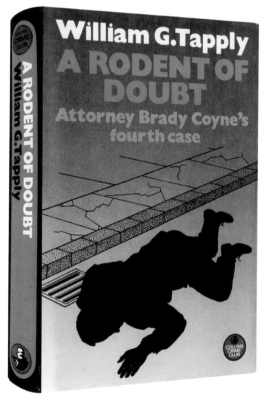

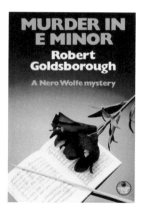

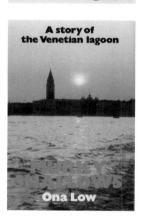

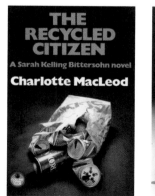

### *Miss Melville Regrets* (1987) Evelyn E. Smith

Unlike other elderly ladies who devote their declining years to the elucidation of crime – Jane Marple and Hildegarde Withers, for instance – Miss Susan Melville has a different agenda. She undertakes, for a fee, to eliminate unpleasant persons from society. And gets to like it. The first three of Miss Melville's four novels appeared in the Crime Club.

### *Bloodstains* (1987) Andrew Puckett

Andrew Puckett's *Bloodstains* (across) contains a very elaborate floor-plan, reminiscent of the Golden Age, of the blood transfusion laboratory which is the setting for the novel.

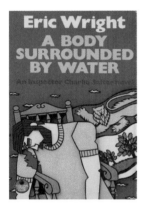

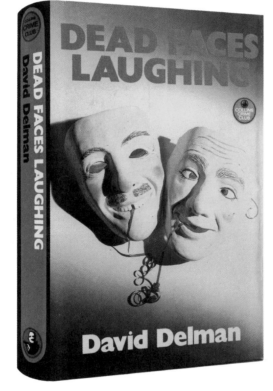

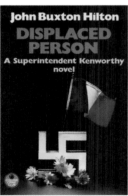

### There Are No Ghosts in the Soviet Union (1987) Reginald Hill

Better known as a novelist, Reginald Hill published his second volume of short stories with the intriguing title taken from the name of a novella in the book.

### The Nine Bright Shiners (1987) Anthea Fraser

This began a seven-book series, the titles of which were all taken from the rhyme 'Green Grow the Rushes-O'. Six appeared in Crime Club, the final one, *The Gospel Makers*, in Collins Crime in 1994.

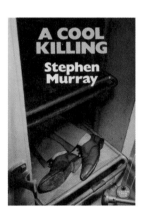

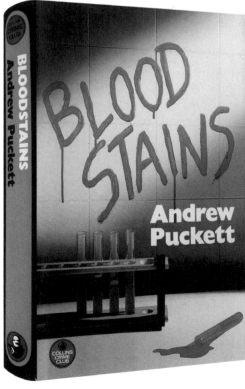

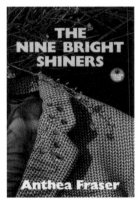

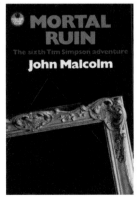

In 1988 **MICHAEL PEARCE** (b. 1933) began his series of novels set in turn-of-the-century Cairo with *The Mamur Zapt and the Return of the Carpet*. Pearce had grown up, and later taught, in Anglo-Egyptian Sudan. The series continued after the demise of Crime Club, under the Collins Crime banner. The Mamur Zapt is the British Head of Cairo's Political CID, the Secret Police.

**Death and the Trumpets of Tuscany (1988) Hazel Wynn Jones**

Italy, during its 1950s heyday as a film-making hub, is the background to this whodunit, written from first-hand experience by a former 'continuity girl'.

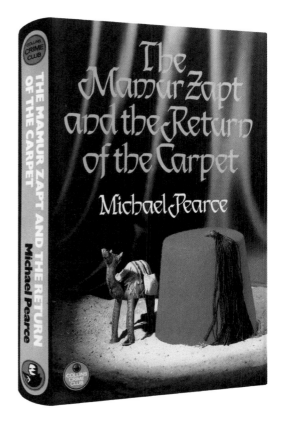

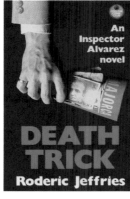

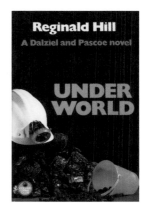

### *Rift* (1988) Liza Cody

*Rift* was Liza Cody's only standalone novel for the Crime Club after five series novels featuring private detective Anna Lee. It was set in Africa, also the setting for three other Crime Club novels:

- *The Heat of the Sun*: Maisie Birmingham
- *The House of Shadows*: J. Jefferson Farjeon
- *The Swaying Pillars*: Elizabeth Ferrars

M. G. Eberhart, first published by Crime Club in September 1935, published her 51st and final novel, *Three Days for Emeralds*, in June 1988, ending a 53-year association with the Crime Club. Thus Eberhart was the longest-serving writer, even if others – Miles Burton/John Rhode, Agatha Christie, Elizabeth Ferrars – published a greater number of books.

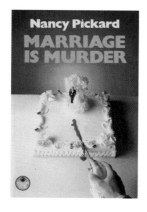

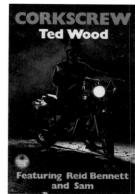

### *Just Another Angel* (1988) Mike Ripley

Fitzroy Maclean Angel, a trumpet-playing black cab driver who lives with a psychotic cat called Springsteen, first appeared in this book. Laugh-out-loud funny, his second case – if that's the appropriate word – *Angel Touch* won the Crime Writers' Association Last Laugh Award. The first four (of 15) Angel novels appeared in Crime Club.

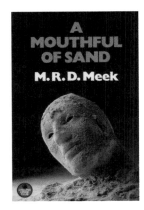

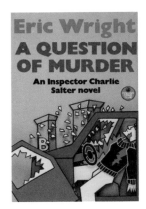

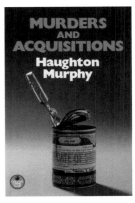

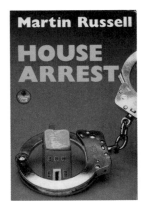

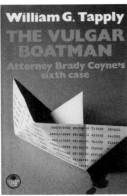

**Marian Babson**
**GUILTY PARTY**

**A VIOLENT END**
**Emma Page**

**ELIZABETH FERRARS**
**TRIAL BY FURY**

Pat Burden's *Screaming Bones* was the first of the new-size Crime Club books, adopting the new demy octavo format favoured by libraries at that time. Taller than before, the spine colour matched that of the front-cover title with the author's name usually in white. Covers were, for the most part, photographic.

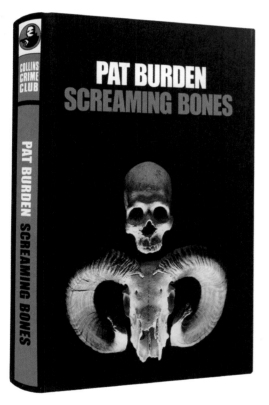

**PAT BURDEN**
**SCREAMING BONES**

COLLINS CRIME CLUB

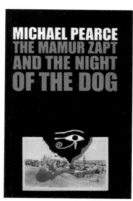

**MICHAEL PEARCE**
**THE MAMUR ZAPT AND THE NIGHT OF THE DOG**

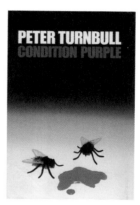

**PETER TURNBULL**
**CONDITION PURPLE**

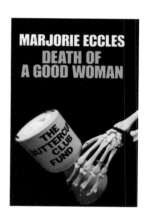

**MARJORIE ECCLES**
**DEATH OF A GOOD WOMAN**

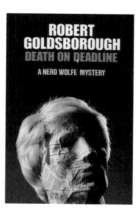

**ROBERT GOLDSBOROUGH**
**DEATH ON DEADLINE**
A NERO WOLFE MYSTERY

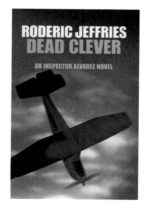

**RODERIC JEFFRIES**
**DEAD CLEVER**
AN INSPECTOR ALVAREZ NOVEL

**ROBERT BARNARD**
**DEATH OF A SALESPERSON**

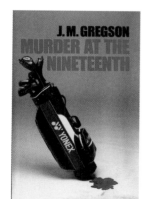

**J. M. GREGSON**
**MURDER AT THE NINETEENTH**

**HAZEL WYNN JONES**
**MURDER IN A MANNER OF SPEAKING**

**ANDREW PUCKETT**
**BED OF NAILS**

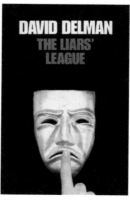

**DAVID DELMAN**
**THE LIARS' LEAGUE**

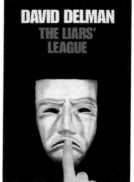

**M. R. D. MEEK**
**A LOOSE CONNECTION**

'Odd' titles in this decade include:

- *The Deep Blue Seize*
- *Frog in the Throat*
- *But Nellie Was So Nice*
- *A Virgin on the Rocks*
- *The God Squad Bod*
- *The Night They Murdered Chelsea*
- *The Convivial Codfish*
- *Slickensides: A Derbyshire Mystery*
- *But He Was Already Dead When I Got There*
- *Death and the Chaste Apprentice*

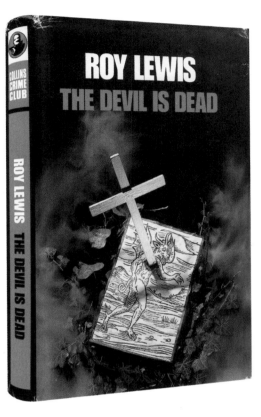

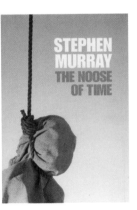

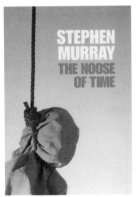

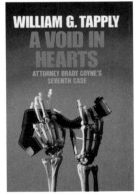

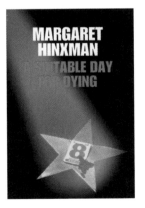

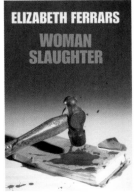

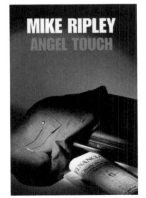

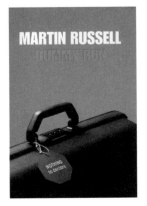

### *The Very Last Gambado* (1989) Jonathan Gash

This was, appropriately, the last Lovejoy title to appear in Crime Club. Although another Lovejoy novel, *The Great California Game* was advertised in Collins' 1990 catalogue, it was published by Random Century.

Several Crime Club authors moved publisher in this decade: Anna Clarke and Michael Kenyon to Hale and Hodder respectively. And, possibly following the lead of Crime Club editor George Hardinge, Julian Symons, H. R. F. Keating, Robert Barnard and Catherine Aird all moved to Macmillan.

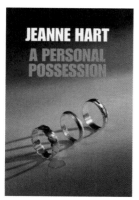

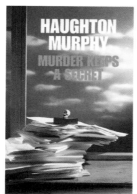

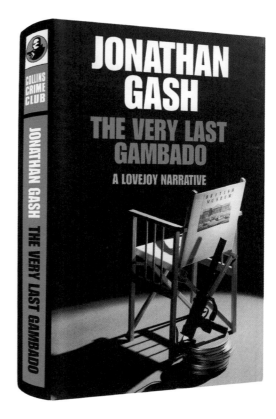

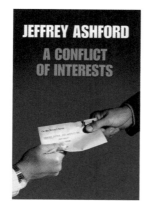

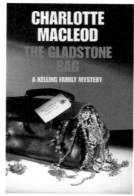

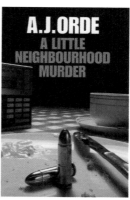

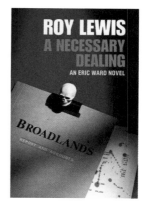

# COLLINS CRIME CLUB
## SIXTY BRILLIANT YEARS OF CRIME

The last five years (January 1990-March 1994) saw the publication of 189 books, which was relatively in keeping with previous years. The ending of the Crime Club in March looks, at first, more like abandonment rather than a considered cessation, as HarperCollins' crime output continued under a new logo, Collins Crime; but the first title had appeared in May 1930, so an March closing date conveniently rounded off the timespan at 64 years.

Many 'old favourites' continued to appear with the Hooded Gunman and thence, with the exception of Patricia Moyes and Martin Russell, into the Collins Crime list: Marian Babson, Reginald Hill, Roderic Jeffries, Martin Russell, Elizabeth Ferrars, Charlotte MacLeod, Patricia Moyes, Emma Page, Roy Lewis and David Williams (who published two further 'Treasure' books, in 1992 and '94, after an absence of eight years). The Diamond Anniversary was celebrated with a re-imagined Gunman logo, a 12-volume collection of reprints, an anthology called, appropriately, *A Suit of Diamonds* and a one-off special, September 1990 from one of the Club's biggest names, Reginald Hill: *One Small Step...*

# SEVENTH DECADE

# THE
# 1990s

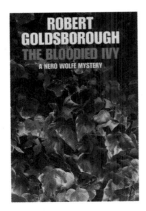

ROBERT GOLDSBOROUGH
THE BLOODIED IVY
A NERO WOLFE MYSTERY

JOHN MALCOLM
THE WRONG IMPRESSION
THE SEVENTH TIM SIMPSON ADVENTURE

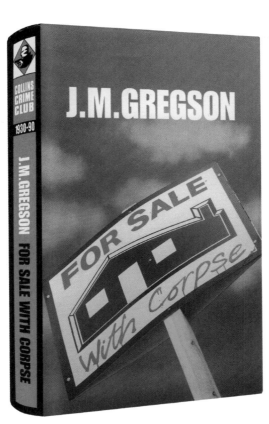

J.M.GREGSON

COLLINS CRIME CLUB
1930-90

J.M.GREGSON FOR SALE WITH CORPSE

FOR SALE with Corpse

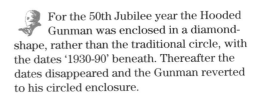 For the 50th Jubilee year the Hooded Gunman was enclosed in a diamond-shape, rather than the traditional circle, with the dates '1930-90' beneath. Thereafter the dates disappeared and the Gunman reverted to his circled enclosure.

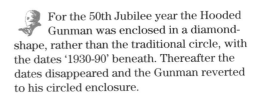 The blurb of Moyes' *Black Girl White Girl* gives the wrong date of her first novel as 1958; *Dead Men Don't Ski* was published in October 1959.

ERIC WRIGHT
A SENSITIVE CASE
AN INSPECTOR CHARLIE SALTER NOVEL

COLLINS CRIME CLUB
1930-90

ERIC WRIGHT A SENSITIVE CASE

RODERIC JEFFRIES
TOO CLEVER BY HALF
AN INSPECTOR ALVAREZ NOVEL

STEPHEN MURRAY
FETCH OUT NO SHROUD

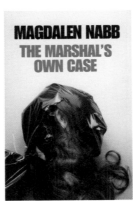

MAGDALEN NABB
THE MARSHAL'S OWN CASE

JOHN PENN
A KILLING TO HIDE

A SUIT OF DIAMONDS

Crime Club Diamond Jubilee Commemorative volume

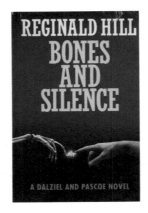

REGINALD HILL
BONES AND SILENCE
A DALZIEL AND PASCOE NOVEL

PATRICIA MOYES
BLACK GIRL WHITE GIRL

MICHAEL PEARCE
THE MAMUR ZAPT AND THE DONKEY-VOUS

### *Miss Lizzie* (1990) Walter Satterthwait

The murders of Andrew and Abby Borden in Fall River Massachusetts in 1892, for which Andrew's daughter, Lizzie, stood trial and was acquitted, are among the most notorious and controversial in criminal history. Satterthwait's book is not an exploration of these crimes but of a similar killing in the same place in 1921, seen through the eyes of a young girl who has befriended the 60-year-old Lizzie. The events of thirty years earlier haunt the investigation and the relationship between Lizzie and young Amanda is both touching and enigmatic, and the atmosphere of the small town is evocatively captured.

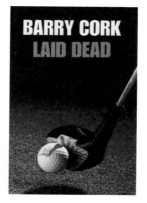

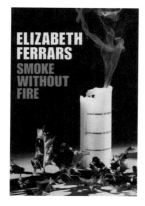
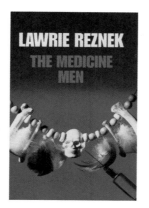

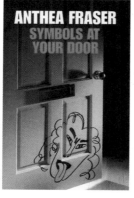

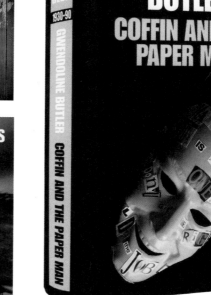

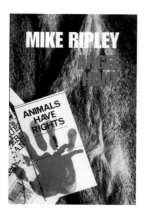
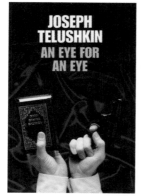

### *One Small Step* (1990) Reginald Hill

In its entire 65-year history there is no more unusual entry in the Crime Club list. Described on the cover as 'A Dalziel and Pascoe novella', it is the shortest book, at just under 100 pages. It is the only title with (uncredited) line drawings of the characters, the only title in which the author discusses in a lengthy and characteristically witty foreword the development of his series characters; and the only title set in the then future, the year 2010. Investigating a murder on the moon, Andy Dalziel is no more politically correct than in his heyday. Even the dedication is unusual: 'TO YOU DEAR READERS without whom the writing would be in vain and TO YOU EVEN DEARER PURCHASERS without whom the eating would be infrequent.'

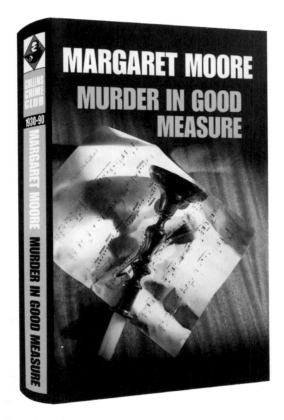

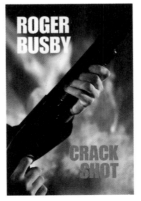

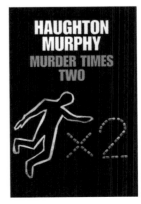

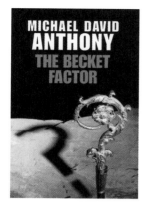

David Delman's *The Last Gambit* is one of only two Crime Club books centring on the game of chess. Rex Stout's *Gambit* also concerns a chess tournament. E. C. R. Lorac's *Checkmate to Murder* and Ritchie Perry's *Bishop's Pawn* do not, despite their titles, feature chess.

### *Murder in the Queen's Armes* (1990) Aaron Elkins

Aaron Elkins (b. 1935) published only three titles with Crime Club but he continues to publish, his latest appearing in 2018. Many of them feature his forensic anthropologist creation Gideon Oliver. His final Crime Club title, *Make No Bones*, won an Edgar Award in 1988.

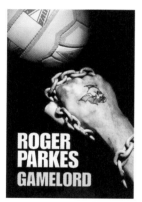

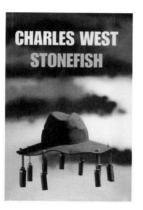

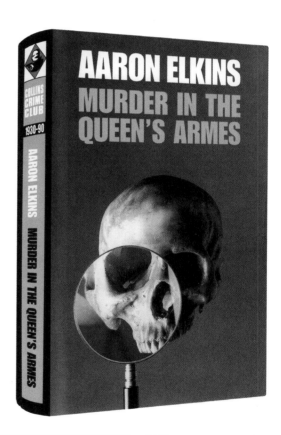

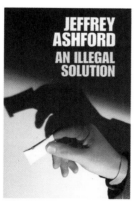

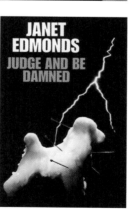

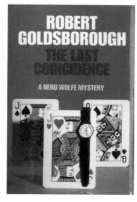

### *Sheep, Goats and Soap* (1991) John Malcolm

The world of antiques is the overall theme of the Tim Simpson novels of John Malcolm Andrews (b. 1936), who prided himself on the accuracy of the art history in the novels. As Andrews he is the author of a number of books on antiques. Other novels with a similar background include:

* *Ransom for a Nude*: Lional Black
* *The Cat Who Turned On and Off*: Lilian Jackson Braun
* *The Five Million Dollar Prince*: Michael Butterworth
* *The China Expert*: Michael Delving
* *The Modigliani Scandal*: Zachary Stone
* *A Painted Devil*: John Welcome
* *Tondo for Short, Short Break in Venice* and *The Sweet Short Grass*: Peter Inchbald

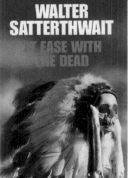

Australia-born Anne Infante set her five Crime Club novels in her native country; as does Charles West his four. All but their debut novels were published in the final decade of Crime Club. Ian Hamilton's sole Crime Club entry, *The Thrill Machine* (1972), is also set in his native Australia, as are Pat Flower's.

Crime Club veterans who were not Australian also used 'Down Under' as background: Robert Barnard's debut, *Death of an Old Goat*, utilises his teaching experience in the early 1960s at the University of New England in Australia. Elizabeth Ferrars uses Australia as background in three of her novels: *Come and Be Killed*, *The Crime and the Crystal* and *The Small World of Murder*, and Andrew Garve brilliantly uses the Australian outback as both setting and plot device in *Boomerang*.

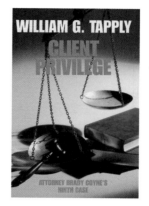

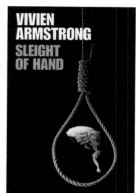

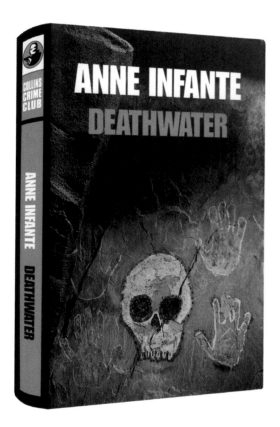

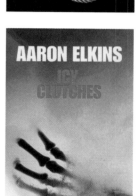

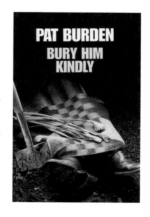

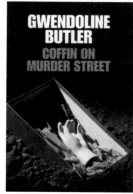

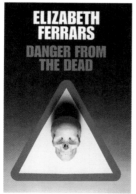

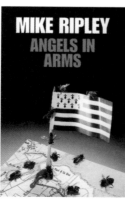

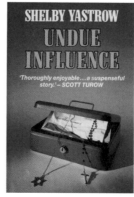

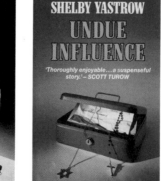

Stephen Murray's *Fatal Opinions* has as background a medical research laboratory. Andrew Puckett's *Bloodstains* and *Bloodhound* (see across) also feature a blood laboratory. Nurses, doctors and hospitals of various types have provided characters and settings for many Crime Club novels:

- Doctors: *Doctors Also Die* (Devine) *Murder M. D.* (Burton), *Death Comes to Perigord* (Ferguson), *Shot in the Dark* (Ford), *The Link* (Carmichael)
- Nurses: *Murder in Mesopotamia* (Christie), *Wolf in Man's Clothing* (Eberhart), *Passing Strange* (Aird), *Scales of Justice* (Marsh)
- Hospitals: *The Black Thumb, Black Corridors, The Black Stocking* (Little), *No Mask for Murder* (Garve), *You Can't Call It Murder* (Ramsay), *Playing Safe* (Dewhurst), *A Cool Killing* (Murray), *The Medicine Men* (Reznek)

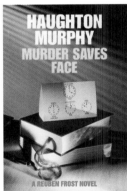

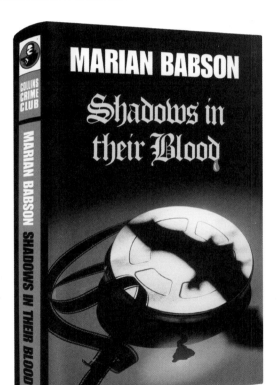

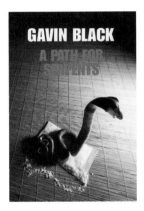

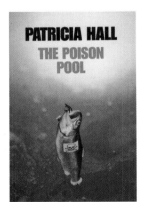

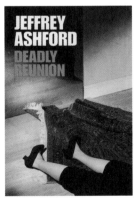

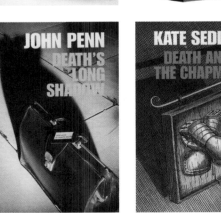

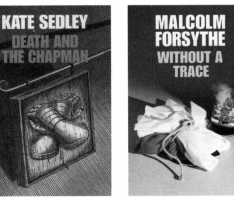

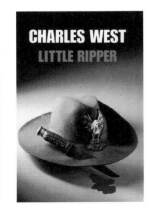

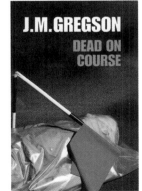

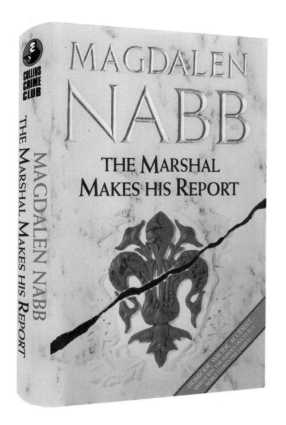

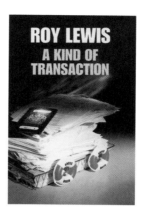

ROY LEWIS
A KIND OF TRANSACTION

Gregson's *Dead on Course* (see across) and his earlier *Murder at the Nineteenth* both feature a background of golf. Other golf mysteries include:

- Herbert Adams: *The Body in the Bunker, Death Off the Fairway* and *The Nineteenth Hole Mystery*
- Miles Burton: *Tragedy at the Thirteenth Hole*
- Barry Cork: *Dead Ball, Laid Dead* and *Unnatural Hazard*
- James Gibbins: *Sudden Death*

ANDREW PUCKETT
BLOODHOUND

MARGARET HAFFNER
A MURDER OF CROWS

A. J. ORDE
DEATH FOR OLD TIME'S SAKE

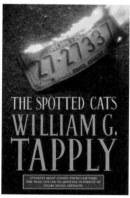

THE SPOTTED CATS
WILLIAM G. TAPPLY

Michael Pearce
THE MAMUR ZAPT AND THE GIRL IN THE NILE

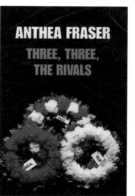

ANTHEA FRASER
THREE, THREE, THE RIVALS

RODERIC JEFFRIES
A FATAL FLEECE
AN INSPECTOR ALVAREZ NOVEL

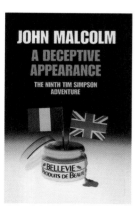

JOHN MALCOLM
A DECEPTIVE APPEARANCE
THE NINTH TIM SIMPSON ADVENTURE

WALTER SATTERTHWAIT
WILDE WEST

ELIZABETH FERRARS
BEWARE OF THE DOG

### *Planning on Murder* (1992) David Williams

This was was David Williams' return to the ranks of Crime Club after an absence of eight years, during which time he was published by Macmillan. One more Mark Treasure novel, *Banking on Murder*, followed in 1993.

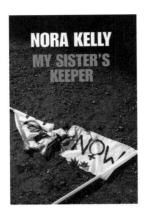

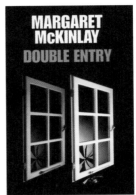

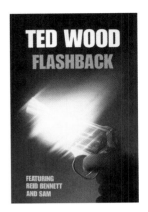

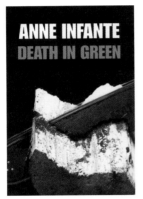

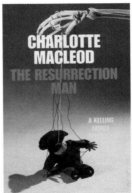

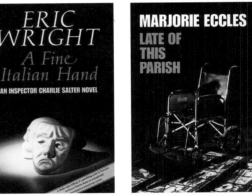

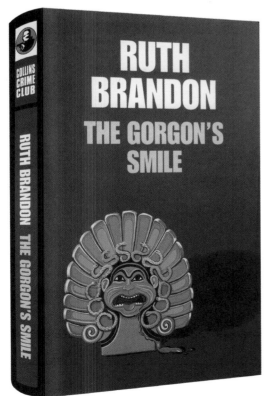

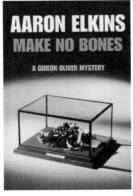

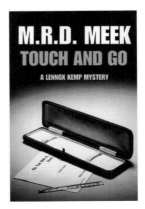

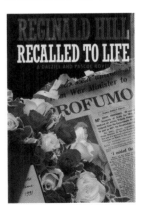

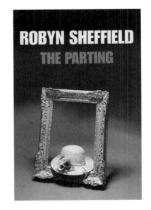

The 'Body in the Library' has long been considered a cliché of detective fiction. Agatha Christie herself mentions this in the foreword to a 1953 Penguin reprint of her 1942 novel of that name. And corpses do turn up in Crime Club libraries: *Mystery in Kensington Gore* (Martin Porlock), *The Black Stage* (Anthony Gilbert) and *The Simple Way of Poison* (Florence Ford).

And other libraries can also be scenes of crime:

- *Sleep of the Unjust*: Lawrence Meynell
- *Final Notice*: Johnathan Valin
- *By Frequent Anguish*: S. F. X. Dean
- *Murder Saves Face*: Haughton Murphy
- *The Caravaggio Books*: Bernard Peterson
- *The Book Lady*: Malcolm Forsythe

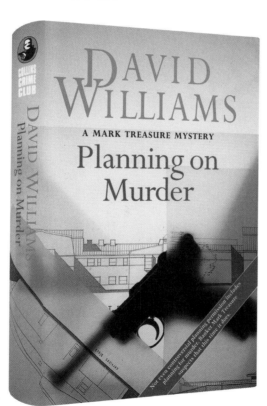

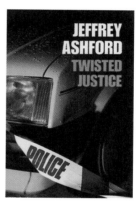

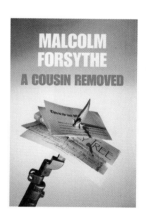

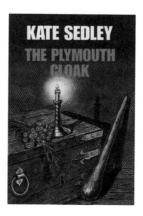

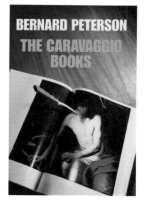

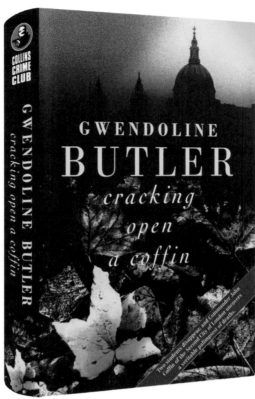

### Endangered Species (1992) Barry Cork

Together with Stephen Murray's *Fetch Out No Shroud*, this shares a common background with Patricia Moyes' *Johnny Under Ground* from almost 30 years earlier. They are all centred on abandoned WWII airfields and dark deeds committed there during the war. The Moyes and Murray titles both quote in full the poem from which they derive their titles: John Pudney's 'For Johnny'.

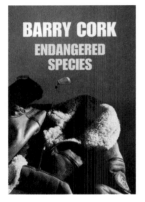

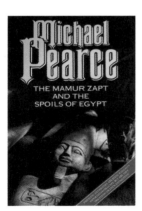

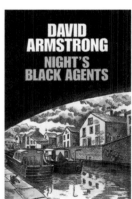

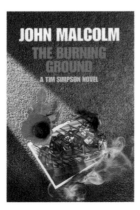

### *Blood Sympathy* (1993) Reginald Hill

Although only this one Joe Sixsmith title appeared in Crime Club, Reginald Hill produced a further quartet of books featuring the most unlikely Private Investigator in crime fiction history: 'a balding, middle-aged redundant lathe-operator from a high rise in Luton'.

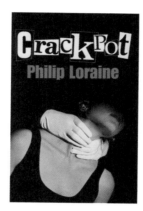

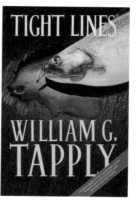

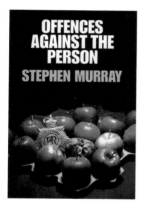

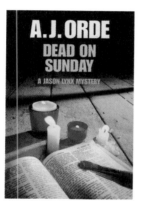

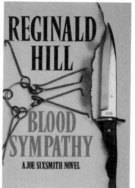

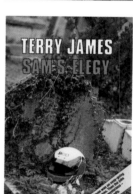

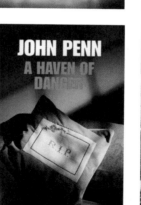

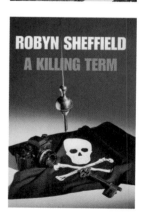

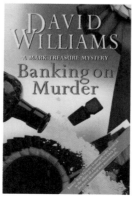

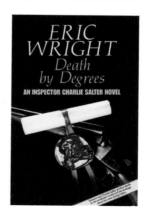

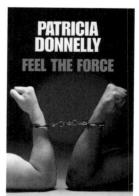

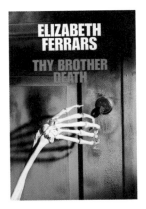

Appropriately, the writing career of two longstanding Crime Club stalwarts, Patricia Moyes (first appearance 1959) and Martin Russell (1965), drew to a close as the Club itself rang down its criminal curtain. The creatively unpredictable Russell and the more traditional Moyes entertained readers for 30 and 35 years, respectively.

Elizabeth Ferrars contInued to publish with HarperCollins for some more years; as did Jeffrey Ashford and Gwendoline Butler with other publishers.

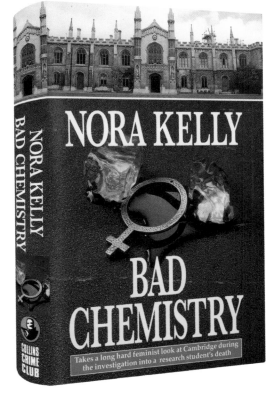

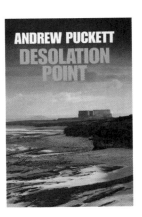

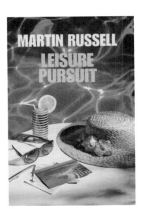

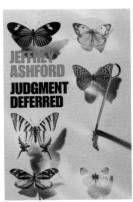

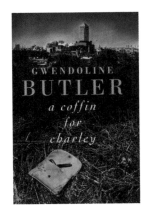

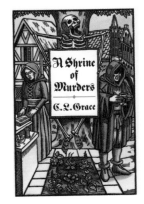

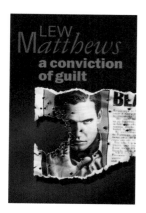

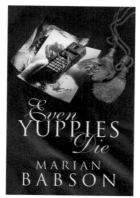

### Pictures of Perfection (1994) Reginald Hill

Reginald Hill dedicated his last Crime Club book to the imprint's editor, Elizabeth Walter:

*'To the Queen of crime editors, Elizabeth Walter, this work is, with her gracious permission, most affectionately dedicated, by her admiring and grateful friend, The Author. Nullum quod tetigit non ornavit.' [She touched nothing which she did not adorn]*

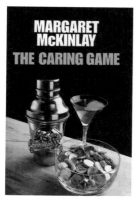

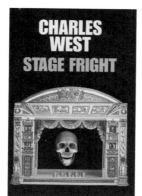

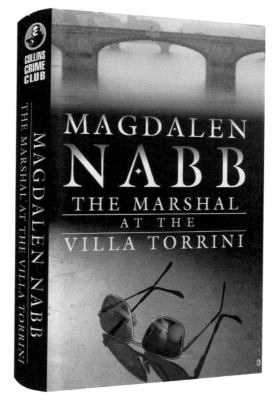

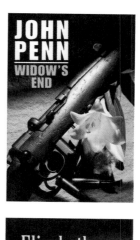

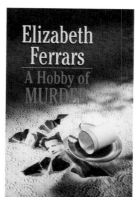

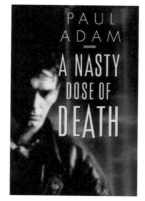

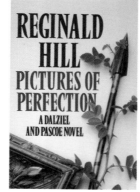

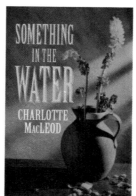

The termination of Crime Club coincided with the retirement of its guiding light, Elizabeth Walter. In May 1993 the HarperCollins house magazine, HarperCollins*Life*, contained the following item:

'Elizabeth Walter, the doyenne of Collins Crime Club has, after 32 years, decided to give up "crime", and take up retirement. She joined the company in January 1961 and retired for the first time in 1982, having been involved with major authors such as Victoria Holt and Winston Graham. However, she was asked by Mark Collins to become the editorial consultant for Crime Club where she has worked for the last ten years with authors such as Magdalen Nabb, Elizabeth Ferrars and Reginald Hill.'

Walter had discussed her editorial philosophy in a short essay in 1977. Of the 36 books that Crime Club published a year during her reign, three or four would be by new authors. And 'in any given month we try to offer three different kinds of mystery. If one has a village setting, another might be American or have an exotic locale, and another might be a police procedural. There should be something for everybody each month.' The only subject she refused to consider was anything 'explicitly sadistic'. And because she had no specialised background she tended to pick a book 'on the basis of its appeal to me as a general reader'. Her droll opinion of 'difficult' writers was simple: 'No temperament below a sale of fifteen thousand'!

# POSTSCRIPT

# 65 YEARS OF BRILLIANT CRIME

THE CRIME CLUB

# THE END OF AN ERA

AND SO, IN its 65th year, the final Crime Club book, Walter Satterthwait's *The Death Card*, was published in March 1994; and the most influential UK crime publishing venture of the century ended. So, how did Collins Crime Club survive – and thrive – through an economic depression, a World War, the atom bomb, the Swinging Sixties, flower power, the Common Market, gay rights, MTV and glasnost; almost, in fact, into the 21st century?

First and foremost, it was dependable, in terms of both quantity and quality. The appearance of three or four titles every month meant that readers – whether purchasers or borrowers – were assured of a regular supply of their favourite type of reading. Most Crime Club authors published at least one book per year and in the case of some writers – Agatha Christie, Rex Stout, M. G. Eberhart, Elizabeth Ferrars, Anthony Gilbert, E. C. R. Lorac – readers could count on more than one.

The type of book was also assured: no explicit sex or violence or sadism; even after the arrival of the Swinging '60s and its so-called 'sexual revolution', no Crime Club book ever reached the heights – or, more accurately, plumbed the depths – of sexual frankness found in, for instance, the output of Mickey Spillane. A Crime Club book was a 'safe' read; one could, with peace of mind, automatically request or borrow each new title. And in catering for all tastes – from the University Dons to the housewives of its early publicity – titles covered the entire spectrum of the crime novel: whodunit, thriller, adventure, suspense, private eye, legal, police procedural, historical. And, despite inevitable changes in size, price and jacket design, every title was instantly recognisable on the shelf of either library or bookshop by the presence of the iconic Hooded Gunman.

Founded at the height of detective fiction's Golden Age, the Crime Club did not just reflect that genre but helped to create it by publishing the cream of detective fiction. The influence of Agatha Christie is incontrovertible – she is the biggest-selling writer in history – but many other Crime Club authors contributed to a lesser, though still significant, extent, to the development and acceptance of that genre: Nicholas Blake, G. D. H. and M. Cole, Freeman Wills Crofts, Miles Burton/John Rhode, E. C. R. Lorac/Carol Carnac, Philip MacDonald, Ngaio Marsh, Rupert Penny.

And as the years progressed so did Crime Club. As the Golden Age began to lose its lustre, a Silver version of it – with less rigid adherence to clues, alibis, timetables, cigarette ash and adenoidal housemaids – was easily accommodated into the lists in the output of, *inter alia*, Catherine Aird, Robert Barnard, Dominic Devine, Elizabeth Ferrars, Nigel Fitzgerald and Patricia Moyes. They continued the tradition of providing, as the original 1940s advertisement claimed, '…a clean and intriguing example of…works in which there is a definite crime problem, an honest detective process, with a credible and logical solution.'

Crime Club statistics are eloquent:

- 2,012 titles
- 263 writers
- 15 Edgar Nominations
- 11 anthologies
- 7 Gold Dagger Winners
- 3 games
- 3 Detection Club Presidents
- 2 Edgar Winners
- 2 Dames of the British Empire
- 1 Poet Laureate

Writers who enjoyed career-long associations with Crime Club included M. G. Eberhart, Elizabeth Ferrars, Anthony Gilbert, Rex Stout, Miles Burton, Harry Carmichael/Hartley Howard and Anthony Gilbert, all of whom provided long-lasting, dependable entertainment over half a century. And reliable, though less Golden Age-focused, authors Harry Carmichael, Joan Fleming, Andrew Garve, Reginald Hill, Roderic Jeffries, Roy Lewis and Martin Russell stayed with Crime Club throughout long and prolific careers.

The Crime Club also 'imported' from the US many writers and introduced them for the first time to British readers. Authors who became staples of the list included Anthony Abbot, C. Daly King, Stuart Palmer, Clayton Rawson, Mabel Seeley, Leslie Ford, Conyth Little, Patricia

McGerr, Charlotte MacLeod, John Stephen Strange and Phoebe Atwood Taylor; as well as the much-lauded and internationally admired Ross MacDonald.

As testament to the enduring appeal of the Crime Club many of these writers – Nicholas Blake, Philip Mac-Donald, Andrew Garve, Ngaio Marsh, Elizabeth Ferrars and Miles Burton/John Rhode – are enjoying a publishing renaissance for a new generation of crime fans. And the original novels are eagerly sought, commanding high prices in First Edition; and even early paperback reprints, whether Penguin, White Circle or Fontana, change hands for multiples of their original cover price.

As with the 'Cabinet Ministers, Business Magnates, Harley Street Specialists, Famous Judges, Bishops and Leaders of Religion, Teachers, and men and women in every sphere of life' of the 1930s, readers of this 21st century continue to find fascinating that iconic guarantee of a Good Detective Story: The Hooded Gunman.

# 'PHANTOM' TITLES

SO-CALLED 'PHANTOM' TITLES are books that were advertised – usually in the Crime Club section of Collins' biannual catalogue – but, for some reason, never appeared in print. They have been a sporadic feature of the Crime Club from its earliest days. Some can be explained as being title changes between cataloguing and publication:

Henry Holt's *There Has Been a Murder* (1936) was originally titled *Murder Next Tuesday* as per the 1936 catalogue, and H. Russell Wakefield's *Inquest Adjourned* appears to have become *Hostess to Death* (1938). Further confusion arises from some inexplicable delays. For example, Farjeon's *Room No. 6* (1941) and Ferrars' *Skeleton in Search of a Cupboard* (1982) were advertised in catalogues for 1938 and 1978, respectively. But some phantom titles remain:

### 1930:
Winifred Greenleaves published *The Trout Inn Tragedy* in 1929 and the 1930 Crime Club catalogue advertises a 'New Title' which never materialised.

### 1931:
Emlyn Williams – presumably the playwright (1905-1987) who wrote *The Corn Is Green* and *Night Must Fall* – was listed as publishing a 'New Book' in 1931. Collins did publish a novelisation of Williams' 1930 play, *A Murder Has Been Arranged*, in 1931 but not as a Crime Club title.

### 1932:
*The Weane Way Murder* by Lynn Brock is listed for 1932. Brock's 1932 novel was *Nightmare*, a non-Crime Club title with no connection with a 'Weane Way', and he did not have another Crime Club title until 1938.

### 1935:
*Much Ado about Murder*, by one-time Crime Club author Colin Ward, is listed in the 1935 catalogue. The British Library has no record of this and, in fact, *House Party Murder* (1932) seems to be Ward's sole contribution to the genre.

### 1941:
Cyril Alington's *The Crowded Hour* was advertised in the 1941 catalogue. Was it actually his 1944 novel *Ten Crowded Hours*, published by Macdonald?

### 1942:
The flap of Richard Hull's *The Unfortunate Murderer* (1942) advertises a title, *Murder in Dorset*, for established Crime Club author Vernon Loder. Not only did Loder, who died in 1938, never publish a book with this title but the British Library catalogue has no such listing. Is it possible that Loder supplied a typescript which was destroyed when Collins London offices were bombed in December 1940?

### 1961:
A 'New Novel' is listed for Miles Burton for June 1961, although his final Crime Club novel *Death Paints a Picture*, appeared in November 1960. An unfinished 48-page manuscript of what would, presumably, have been this 'New Novel', exists. Burton died in 1964.

**1970:**

Martin Russell had published four Crime Club books when a listing of *The Phillison Process* appeared in the 1970 catalogue. It remains a listing only, although, coincidentally or otherwise, 1970 is the only year between 1965 and 1989 in which at least one Russell title did not appear.

**APPEARED ELSEWHERE:**

In the final years of Crime Club five established authors appeared in catalogues with new titles. All subsequently appeared either in Collins Crime or from another publisher:

- Catherine Aird's *The Body Politic* appeared in the 1989 catalogue but was published by Macmillan in 1990.
- Jonathan Gash's *The Great California Game* was published by Century in 1991, despite its appearance in the Collins 1990 catalogue.
- Anthea Fraser's *The Gospel Makers*, Philip Loraine's *In the Blood* and J. M. Gregson's *Watermarked* were issued in Collins Crime although they appeared in the Crime Club 1994 listing in the catalogue.

**APPEARED AGAIN:**

When *The Julian Symons Omnibus* and *The Nicholas Blake Omnibus* were published in 1966 and 1967 respectively, each contained a non-Crime Club title:

- Blake's only non-Crime Club title, A *Tangled Web* (1956), was included in his *Omnibus*, complete with Hooded Gunman on the title page. In fact, the dust-jacket boasts: 'Containing three famous Crime Club novels'.
- Symons' *The 31st of February* (1950) preceded his joining the Crime Club list. And although his *Omnibus* does not include the Hooded Gunman, the title page reads: 'Published for The Crime Club'.

**WILL NEVER APPEAR...?**

As well as Miles Burton's 1961 phantom title, above, there are also in verified existence unfinished typescripts of 'final' novels from some other Crime Club authors:

- Elizabeth Ferrars left 'a few chapters' of manuscript on her death in March 1995.
- Nicholas Blake, in 1969, abandoned a final novel, *Bang, Bang, You're Dead* after 10 chapters.
- Two crime novels by E. C. R. Lorac, *Two-Way Murder* and an untitled novel, exist in unpublished, soft-cover format, as advertised by a bookseller in 2013. The untitled is dated 7 May 1958, the year of Lorac's death.
- A 'New Fiction' title *Nailchurch Walk* by Philip MacDonald is listed on the flap of Christie's *The Mysterious Mr. Quin* (1930). However, the British Library catalogue does not include a work of this title.

# THE WHITE CIRCLE

THE INTRODUCTION, BY Allen Lane in 1935, of Penguin paperbacks revolutionised mass-market availability of quality books, both fiction and non-fiction. Their colour-coded covers were eye-catching and could be found not only in bookshops and railway stations but also in many other retail outlets. Their crime novels were green-banded and would eventually boast a strong list of authors – Sayers, Carr, Queen, Marsh, Simenon – and Christie's *The Mysterious Affair at Styles* was one of the first ten titles.

It would be naïve to ignore the launch of Penguin paperbacks as coincidental in Collins's decision to issue similar paperback series the following year. Allen Lane's pioneering vision of making paperbacks as ubiquitous as newspapers was too good to remain unique. Even before Collins launched their brand, Hutchinson's Pocket Library appeared, also in 1935, and their Pocket Library Crime Book Society – with a design suspiciously like the subsequent White Circle series – was launched in 1936. And while green Penguins published many well-known and popular crime authors, Collins' Crime Club had a ready-made back catalogue of excellent authors from which to choose.

In April 1936 Collins issued the first paperback edition of a Crime Club title in the now-iconic White Circle series. Over the following 23 years a further 296 titles were

  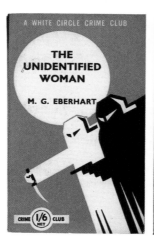  

issued, each with the distinctive cover design which was, in effect, an elaboration of the Club's original Hooded Gunman logo: actually two gunmen, a white one wielding a dagger and a green one brandishing a gun. This design, and variations thereof, appeared on every paperback and from 1954 onwards the covers were glossy.

Not surprisingly, the first title was a Christie: *Murder on the Orient Express*, which was, at that point, the best-selling title the Crime Club had published. Two more Christies, three MacDonalds (one as Martin Porlock), two Rhodes and one each from Crofts, Cole and Edgar Wallace made up the first ten titles. While Christie, Rhode/Burton, Cole, Farjeon and others continued to appear, as the Crime Club list of authors expanded so, too, did that of the White Circle. By the mid-1930s Eberhart, Gilbert, Lorac and Stout were also appearing in the distinctive covers, while the earlier authors were regularly reprinted.

White Circle also published Christie titles originally published by Collins before the launch of the Crime Club imprint: *The Murder of Roger Ackroyd* 19, *The Mystery of the Blue Train* 132c, *The Seven Dials Mystery* 47, *Partners in Crime* 231c, *The Mysterious Mr Quin* 286c; as well as *The Listerdale Mystery* 271c and *Parker Pyne Investigates* 292c, published originally in the Collins Mystery series.

Similar situations obtained with:

- Brock: (*The Kink* 31, *The Dagwort Combe Murder* 40, *The Mendip Mystery* 48, *The Slip Carriage Mystery* 91, *Colonel Gore's Second Case* 92, *Two of Diamonds* 126c (as by Anthony Wharton) were all pre-Crime Club)
- Cole: (*Poison in the Garden Suburb* 79 ditto)

- Crofts: (*The Cask* 25 ditto)
- Footner: (*The Owl Taxi* 72 and *The Substitute Millionaire* 103c ditto)
- Loder: (*The Shop Window Murders* 71 ditto)
- Strange: (*The Clue of the Second Murder* 70 ditto)
- Farjeon: (*Thirteen Guests* 58; *Mountain Mystery* 68, both post-1930 Collins but not Crime Club)
- MacDonald: (*The Rynox Mystery – Rynox*, a non-Crime Club title – appeared as 29 and 86)
- Crime Club authors Rhode (*The Venner Crime* 78, Odhams 1933) and Eberhart (*Murder of my Patient* 136c, John Lane 1934) also appeared, although these were not Collins titles originally. More inexplicably, non-Crime Club author Glynn Carr's Death on *Milestone Buttress* 246c was originally published by Bles in 1951; the 1954 purchase of Bles by Collins does not adequately explain this.

On the back cover of *Shot at Dawn* (White Circle No. 5, April 1936), above a listing of the first 15 titles, we read:

For six years the CRIME CLUB, now almost a national institution, has been sifting out the best detective stories for the delectation of an insatiable public; indeed, it is due to the high standard maintained by the CRIME CLUB that the public taste for detective stories has grown more and more keen. The CRIME CLUB has made a selection of the most successful detective novels published under its imprint and is issuing a new series, at a low price, which contains only the cream of its recent selections; each title was a best-seller in the original edition.

# MURDER THEY WROTE
## The Descriptive Blurbs

THIS SECTION OF *The Hooded Gunman* reprints the descriptive blurb for every Crime Club title as it appeared on the front flap of the book's dust wrapper. This copy was usually repeated inside, on the leaf preceding the title page. In most cases the interior text is identical; but sometimes it is different. The difference may be only the addition or omission of a sentence, and such cases are not noted here. But sometimes – for no apparent reason – it is radically different, and in these instances I have included both, with an 'OR' between the two versions. (See, for example, Henry Holt's *The Mystery of the Smiling Doll.*)

I have let stand interesting mistakes or oddities of spelling and/or grammar appearing in the blurbs, indicating these by '[sic]'. They may simply have been misprints, of course, but some seem unforgivable, not least 'Miss Marples' on the flap of *The Adventure of the Christmas Pudding*, 30 years after Miss Marple's first Crime Club appearance.

Note also that in the case of some early titles, such as Lindsay Anson's *Hung by an Eyelash* or Phoebe Atwood Taylor's *Criminal C. O. D.*, the blurb writer manages to engage reader interest without saying anything definite about the novel. More frustratingly, the opposite can also be the case. The blurbs for Martin Russell's *Advisory Service* and *The Search for Sara*, for example, give away far too much plot. Agatha Christie had this argument with the publisher during the summer of 1939 with the proposed blurb for *Ten Little Niggers*, pointing out that 'any book is ruined when you know what exactly is going to happen all the way along'.

Book titles appear on the front of the dust-wrapper, the spine and the title-page, but there can be inconsistencies. For instance, Joan Fleming's *Alas Poor Father* appears with an exclamation mark on both spine and dust-wrapper but without the exclamation mark on the title page. Conversely, Shelley Smith's *Come and Be Killed!* and *This is the House!* both include exclamation marks on their title pages but not on either the wrapper or spine. In such cases, I have adopted the title page version. The titles of the short story collections edited by Ellery Queen have all been regularised: *Ellery Queen Awards Eighth, Ninth, Tenth Series* etc.

Finally, it should be remembered that these blurbs are presented here as a matter of historical record and were written long before the days of political correctness, something to bear in mind when reading, for instance, the description of Michael Kenyon's *The Rapist*.

For ease of reference, the blurbs are arranged here alphabetically, first by author, and then by title. The month of publication is also given, to help locate the original jacket design within the chronological contents of the book.

## ABBOT, ANTHONY
### Crime of the Century, The
October 1931

This, the second of the secret chronicles of the New York Police Headquarters, revealed by Commissioner Thatcher Colt, concerns the strange mystery surrounding the deaths of Rev. Timothy Beazeley and Evelyn Saunders. The bodies were found in a small open boat adrift on the waters of New York Harbour, and the circumstances left no doubt that their deaths were due to violence. This singular crime was accomplished with such subtlety and in so strange a setting of melodrama and intrigue that the newspapers immediately styled it 'The Crime of the Century'.

### Deadly Secret
November 1943

Thatcher Colt, Police Commissioner of New York, makes a welcome return in this new story, told by his friend and assistant, Anthony Abbot. Colt has just been responsible for the conviction of Jeremy Taylor, who murdered, for the sake of a fortune of two million dollars, the man to whom he was secretary. Colt is not satisfied with the case because though Jeremy Taylor is to pay the penalty for the crime of murder no one has succeeded in tracing the stolen two million dollars. Just before Taylor is to go to the chair he asks to see Colt, and from the condemned cell Colt sets out to face the toughest job of his career. *Deadly Secret* is a story of crime so sinister and undetectable that it will keep you guessing to the very last page.

### Murder at Buzzards Bay
October 1940

Murder strikes swiftly on an isolated cliff overlooking Buzzard's Bay while Thatcher Colt and Anthony Abbot and a party of guests are visiting the seaside home of the wealthy Fortescue Baxter. Thatcher Colt, retired Police Commissioner, can no longer rely on his old force of 19,000 policemen of the City of New York. He has no laboratory, no scientific assistance, no trained helpers. He is pitted against a malevolent antagonist and triumphantly solves, at the risk of his life, not one murder but three, and one of them twelve years old. The book is more than a mere contest of wits; it is an adventure which the reader seems personally to share. Moreover, it has called forth a striking tribute from Mr. J. Edgar Hoover, celebrated chief of the G-Men, who writes: 'It is a most amazing story and is indeed a great innovation. I was particularly thrilled at the manner in which Anthony Abbot, himself a man well versed in scientific methods of law enforcement, related in detail the method utilised by Thatcher Colt in bringing his case to a logical solution.'

### Murder of a Man Afraid of Women
July 1937

Suave, debonair, and as astute as ever, Thatcher Colt, Police Commissioner of New York City, faces the most subtle and intricate problem of his career. The body of Peter Slade, with two bullet holes in it, is found hanging out the front window of his Greenwich village apartment – and Peter Slade was a man with an odd way of life, and very little past that could be discovered.

Every one connected with the case – from the lovely Carol Burgess to the curious man who came to Slade's apartment and took all his papers – seems to be concealing something. Colt is working under great pressure, for the case must be cleared up before his own wedding which is imminent. How he deals with Eleanor Foxhall and Norma Sutton, two women who had meant much in Slade's life, and the part played by Pittsburgh

Red and Tad Wing, make up a first-rate crime story.

Anthony Abbot's tales are always authoritative, based soundly upon real police procedure, and full of tension and humour. This is one of Thatcher Colt's best cases and most exciting adventures.

### Murder of a Startled Lady
May 1936

We have waited a long time (three years, in fact) for Anthony Abbot's new detective story. But as readers of *The Murder of the Circus Queen* and *The Murder of the Night Club Lady* will realise, it is worth waiting for. Thatcher Colt, Mr. Abbot's famous Commissioner of Police, is here faced with a seemingly impossible problem. The bones of a girl are found in a box brought up from the sea, but the police can find no unsolved murder on their records that fits the case. Who was she? What did she look like? Then comes a brilliant piece of work, when an expert remoulds on her skull the face of the girl as she must have appeared alive. That is the first step in a case in which, as the police explore and eliminate clue after clue, the excitement is almost unbearable.

Believe it or not, this process of reconstructing a case from a skull has been successfully applied (see back flap).

### Murder of Geraldine Foster, The
March 1931

This is one of the secret chronicles of Headquarters in New York City, the first of a series of adventures of Thatcher Colt, Police Commissioner of New York City. Mr. Abbot was Mr. Colt's friend and secretary, and tells here the baffling case of a beautiful girl, found hacked with an axe and buried nude in a shallow grave behind a bungalow in the woods. Nearby was a stream where pigeons came to drink and seven pigeons were found dead, with red stains on their white breasts. They had drunk from the brook that ran red with the blood of Geraldine Foster. The Medical Examiner said the girl had been killed only two days – but the pigeons had been dead two weeks. That was what Thatcher Colt started with in his strange quest for the murderer.

### Murder of the Circus Queen, The
March 1933

Madison Square Garden was packed to capacity. Seventeen thousand people thronged the long tiers of seats. The Garden was gay with lights and coloured bunting, for it was the opening night of the Greatest Show on Earth – the Grand Circus that was at once the pride and joy of its proprietor, Colonel Robinson. Seventeen thousand people watched with bated breath the girlish figure of Josie LaTour, the world's greatest trapeze artiste, as with the grace of a swan, the strength of a tiger, she swung dizzily high above their heads in precise rhythm. Then all at once the acrobatics were ended. The woman seemed struggling to keep her grip on the ring. The little body was shaking visibly. The next instant she uttered a cry of anguish and fell. Police Commissioner Thatcher Colt turned to his friend the District Attorney: 'Dougherty', he said, 'I think you had better go back to the dressing-room with me. What we saw was not an accident, it was murder.' Mr. Anthony Abbot in his new novel *The Murder of the Circus Queen* tells the story of what was perhaps the most baffling of all crimes investigated by Mr. Thatcher Colt while he was Police Commissioner of New York City.

### Murder of the Night Club Lady, The
April 1932

Mr. Anthony Abbot follows up his recent sensational successes, *The Murder of Geraldine*

*Foster* and *The Crime of the Century* with what is undoubtedly the most exciting crime story he has written. A beautiful unknown woman warns Police Commissioner Thatcher Colt that she expects to be murdered. Thatcher Colt is on the scene of the crime before it occurs, and despite the warning he has been given, a murder is committed according to schedule practically before his eyes. The murderer leaves no clue and the lady shows no trace of violence. Another life is claimed by the same mysterious agent before Colt discovers the means of death, and still another victim is added to the list before he can prevent his doom. Thatcher Colt's solution to the all but impenetrable mystery surrounding the deaths of Lola Carewe, 'the Night Club Lady', and two of her intimates, is another triumph of his legal procedure and brilliant detective work.

## ADAM, PAUL
### Exceptional Corpse, An
February 1993

A Rolls-Royce careers off the road on the Derbyshire moors, killing the driver, millionaire Sheffield business-man, Richard Sutton, pillar of the community and the force behind a huge local industrial development. Freelance journalist Mike McLean is the first reporter on the scene and recognises the man.

A post-mortem reveals a high blood-alcohol content and the police dismiss the crash as another drink-drive accident, but McLean starts to wonder when he discovers Sutton was a strict teetotaller. There was also a suspicious fire at the businessman's office on the night he died. Was there a connection? And why was Sutton's secretary so scared?

Before he can question the girl she is found dead in the canal and McLean himself is beaten up and warned off. Stubbornly he persists in his inquiries, while still finding time to hold off Inland Revenue queries about his own dodgy tax affairs, annoy the police and attempt to bed his alluring accountant, Maria.

Gradually, he uncovers a trail of fraud, murder and blackmail which takes him from the derelict East End of Sheffield to the bleak hills of the Peak District and a desperate stand in the Iron Age fortress of Carl Wark.

### Nasty Dose of Death, A
February 1994

A stormy winter night on the seamier side of Sheffield. Freelance journalist Mike McLean receives a mysterious phone-call from small-time burglar Andy Peters. They arrange to meet at Peters' flat but when McLean arrives he finds the burglar dead, his neck broken.

Then next morning, ex-con scrap metal dealer James Silvester escapes death by inches when an unknown gunman puts three bullets through the windscreen of his Mercedes.

Are the two incidents linked? McLean starts to ask questions but is discouraged by Silvester's fifteen-stone wife, Pinky, a professional wrestler with nineteen-inch biceps and a taste for blood and pink lycra leotards.

Undeterred, McLean continues to probe the underside of Silvester's business activities, pausing only to visit a massage parlour, take tea with a gay one-armed hitman and pursue his so-far unrequited passion for his beautiful accountant Maria.

But when a second man dies and McLean himself gets pulled in for questioning, he begins to realize that something more than simple murder is at the heart of the mystery.

## ADAMS, HERBERT
### Araway Oath, The
February 1942

Each of the young Araways received a letter

from their stepmother, who had most of the family money, inviting them to her home to hear 'wonderful news'. Being for various reasons hard up, they all eagerly accepted – Dot and Carrie, twins in the W. A. A. F.; Lawrence, Infantry Lieutenant; Irene, whose husband drew only a Private's pay; Leonard in the Secret Service; Dick at the War Office, with a beautiful and selfish wife, Juliet. When the stepmother was found dead in bed, Roger Bennion, that very experienced investigator, was faced with a two-fold mystery. His successful solution makes very agreeable reading. Mr. Adams' characters are particularly well-drawn and interesting portraits.

### Black Death
April 1939

'War 'planes will be toys; battle-ships scrap-iron'. Such was Professor Donachies's claim. Roger Bennion was sent to Bacton Manor ostensibly to play in a tennis tournament but actually to find out the truth. And when he learns it – and its simple but inhuman possibilities – the Professor is murdered and his secret stolen. So the quest, more urgent than before, starts again. This latest book of Herbert Adams is of great topical interest, and is full of the thrills and humour for which this author is justly renowned.

### Bluff, The
January 1938

A stirring and exciting plot, vivid characterisation and a welcome touch of humour have ensured success for Mr. Herbert Adams's detective stories. This story of the murder of an artist, is exceptionally ingenious. It features Roger Bennion, Mr. Adams' popular investigator, and through the story runs the influence of The Bluff, a sea-bound house on the coast of Kent.

### Body in the Bunker, The
February 1935

Mr. Herbert Adams, 'that great writer of thrills', as *The Daily Telegraph* calls him, begins his latest mystery with a surprising discovery on a golf-course. One of the players is bunkered and finds his ball resting against an obstruction that ought not to be found in any bunker – a human body. That discovery leads, of course, to an intricate and exciting mystery, which Mr. Adams elucidates with extreme ingenuity. This is a story full of golfing interest and therefore specially attractive to golfers – whatever their handicap – although it should be very popular with all classes of readers.

### Case of the Stolen Bridegroom, The
April 1940

When on his wedding night Matt Pender, popular night-club violinist, disappeared, his distracted bride sought the assistance of her old friend Roger Bennion to elucidate the mystery. Together with Roger's racing-motorist friend, Ian Stewart, they set out to find Matt. It was no case for the police, for Matt's reputation as a well-known musician must be cleared without public scandal. A complicated series of events, including deeds of desperate daring, a big-scale robbery, and even murder, makes this a tremendously exciting, fast-moving story that will more than enhance the reputation of its very popular author.

### Chief Witness, The
September 1940

It was mere chance that Inspector Goff left his well-bitten briar pipe in Roger Bennion's flat, but had he remembered to take it, a curious crime would never have been cleared up and an innocent man might have hanged. The death of two brothers in similar circumstances at the same moment, though in different places, indicated a suicide pact, but Roger Bennion's innate curiosity brought him to a different conclusion and, incidentally, as near to death as doesn't matter. Written by Herbert Adams with his customary brilliance and top-speed narrative, it is a story that will more than enhance the popularity of this already popular author.

### *Damned Spot, The*
July 1938

*'Out, damned spot! Out, I say'* – You will remember Lady Macbeth's words as she tried in her sleep to wash the guilty blood from her hands. But guilt, as Lady Macbeth found to her cost, has a way of sticking.

Read in this new Herbert Adams' thriller how the guilt was brought home to the man who murdered Harold Grove-Sutton, and how one spot of blood – 'damned spot' indeed – put Roger Bennion on the right trail.

### *Death off the Fairway*
November 1936

There two points to note about Mr. Herbert Adams's new story. The first is that it is a detective story with a golfing background and that, as readers of *The Body in the Bunker* will remember, is Mr. Adams's speciality. The second point is that it is a murder story from a new angle. The reader sees the deed done. The reader sees each cunning step that is to make it appear an unquestionable suicide. *But does the reader see the murderer's one mistake?* Inspector Ripley did not – and he was a smart man. But Roger Bennion did. Yet who among the light-hearted golfers on the Burlesford links would kill Basil Shelton, a harmless newcomer seeking rest and quiet in peaceful Devon? Little by little the method is revealed – but who did it?

### *Fate Laughs*
August 1935

'Fate laughs,' they say, 'at probabilities,' and in this book Fate has a merry time of it. Jim Flower, broke to the wide, is looking for a job. After an unsuccessful day he jumps into a first-class carriage as his train is steaming out of the station. There is only one other man in the carriage—and that man is his double! 'To settle a bet' he undertakes to impersonate his double for three-quarters of an hour, and during that time one of the most sensational murders London has known for years is committed. You think you've spotted the murderer? Well, Fate and the author are still laughing, and this time at you! But you'll forgive them for leading you such a dance when you remember all the thrills (spiced with humour and romance) they've given you on the way. Mr. Herbert Adams, 'the great thrill-writer,' caters joyfully for the holiday spirit.

### *Four Winds*
April 1944

'There is no room for sentiment in our job,' Roger Bennion said to his assistant big Bill Leicester. But was Bill to be blamed if he fell for so lovely a girl as Ruth Millican? Roger and Bill had gone to Four Winds, a lonely house on the Cornish coast exposed to the full fury of the Atlantic gales, to discover why…and if… its owner Frank Elsworth had shot himself. On the night of their arrival things began to happen. And they went on happening – things queer, exciting, almost incredible. Tense human drama is unfolded. Murder, mystery and espionage are skilfully blended with more than a little humour by the expert hand of Herbert Adams.

### *Nineteenth Hole Mystery, The*
July 1939

It was at the 'nineteenth hole' at Allingham, a quiet but tricky links in Dorset, that Roger Bennion first met the four crack players from London. He could hold his own with them at golf, and at cards, though they did then not realise that criminal investigation was his strong suit. Then came Hugh Denton. This caused a sensation. It was obvious that the four men knew him – and hated him. Anyhow, the next day he was found shot through the head. A second murder in the 'nineteenth' further complicates matters, and for a while the police are stymied. But Roger Bennion gets to work and the grim match is soon moving swiftly to a tense and unexpected conclusion. *The Nineteenth Hole Mystery* is a perfect example of Mr. Herbert Adams' clever work as a detective story writer, and provides really enjoyable entertainment.

### *Old Jew Mystery, The*
May 1936

Roger Bennion was enjoying a country ramble; even the fact that he had lost his way and was a considerable distance from his destination did not worry him unduly. He was pretty certain to get a lift, if necessary, from a passing motorist. And there, by Jove, was a car standing in the roadway – and a pair of legs protruding from underneath the car showed obviously that the motorist was engaged in minor repairs. But when Roger, eager to help, queried if anything was wrong, he soon perceived that something certainly *was*. A few moments convinced him that the motorist was dead. It was the start of an extraordinary mystery, one of the most original and exciting stories that Mr. Herbert Adams has written.

### *Roger Bennion's Double*
September 1941

When Mrs.Horton was fatally poisoned by a pill containing cyanide, her distracted son Kenneth seeks the help of that famous investigator Roger Bennion, for suspicion has fallen on his fiancée who was nursing his mother during her fatal illness. It is a grand murder mystery with some excellent characters and much really good drama. The best story that Mr. Herbert Adams has written.

### *Signal for Invasion*
November 1942

Captain Roger Bennion, whose war-time job is to keep an eye on subversive activities, plays for tremendously high stakes in *Signal for Invasion*. The signal was to be the simultaneous assassination of six of the leading public men of Britain. Our leaders do not travel in armoured cars. They are not surrounded by bodyguards. If in one fell moment six of the most eminent of them were struck down and at the same time a colossal enemy onslaught by land, sea or air were begun – how would the island fortress stand? This story show how Roger Bennion, investigating an apparently ordinary crime, gradually discovers what is behind it. With the aid of a daughter of the people capable of sublime heroism, the direst catastrophe is narrowly averted.

### *Single Hair, A*
May 1937

Herbert Adams consistently gives us good novels with a welcome dash of humour to lighten the business of crime. This new novel is perhaps the most intriguing that he has done. Roger Bennion again strays into the think of the trouble. He goes to inspect an old country house that looks the ideal place to convert into a country hotel. But while he is there a dastardly crime is committed, and only his powers of observations – and a single hair – save it from complete success.

### *Stab in the Back*
January 1941

Who was talking too much? Not only did the egregious Haw Haw know of the petrol dump at Calcaster but someone had told of the new depth charges being prepared there. Lady Penelope Gwynn had a house in the neighbourhood where officers and their wives, A. R. P. workers, local worthies and local beauties were accustomed to meet. Roger Bennion was sent to investigate. The 'Penguin' was his aunt, and her home seemed the right place at which to start. Some words in the dark and a whiff of scent provided a clue, but a double murder – or was it suicide? – wiped it out. Yet, if it was murder, was the murderer the spy? Another clue – some cigarette ash – led to discoveries that in the very nick of time told the whole story and averted a direful catastrophe. This is Herbert Adams at his best. A 'detective-thriller' you won't put down, even to listen to the News!

### *Victory Song*
October 1943

In Mr. Herbert Adams' latest novel, Roger Bennion of the Secret Service is called in to investigate the mysterious disappearance of Edward Dalton from a village near a big South Coast naval base. Dalton is a curious character, an American revivalist who has associated himself with an English clergyman, a Padre of the last war, who is conducting a Prayer for Victory campaign throughout Britain. Against the strangely emotional background of impassioned preaching and fervent hymn-singing, Bennion begins the unravelling of a most intricate and baffling case, full of excitement and surprise.

### *Word of Six Letters, A*
January 1936

Rich old Barty Blount, squire of Wintle Harford in Dorset, had gone for his usual afternoon ride. No one actually saw quite how it happened, but apparently the old man was thrown from his horse and broke his neck. The facts seemed straightforward enough; just an unfortunate accident. But a young and astute doctor on examining the body discovered signs of sulphonal, that invidious drug that sooner or later induces a deadly sleep. The mystery deepens, and it is found that 'a word of six letters' does in fact spell MURDER. Mr. Herbert Adams certainly presents an ingenious and fascinating problem.

### *Writing on the Wall, The*
March 1945

Sir James Norland, wealthy newspaper magnate, had summoned his newspaper editors to a week-end conference at his country house, The Brambles. Alcott, Balmain, Steel, Wetherall, Chappell – pressmen all, and hardboiled if men ever were. Tragedies and crises were their daily fare. Yet not one of them had ever actually come into personal contact with the horrors they recorded so frequently and with such an eye for effective detail, until that tense moment when a gong beating wildly through the house awoke them to the awful awareness of a murder in the night. Yesterday Sir James Norland, vigorous and overbearing, carried their fates in his hand. Now he lay dead, and they were shaken by the grim reality of murder. The love of Norland's son for a pretty actress and the views of his editors on current affairs, all play a part in the theme. Mr. Herbert Adams is a practised hand at a tale of mystery, and his readers will thoroughly enjoy his accomplished storytelling.

## AIRD, CATHERINE

### *Dead Liberty, A*
May 1986

Lucy Durmast, arraigned on a charge of murder, chose to remain obstinately silent. This was no help at all to those investigating the mysterious death of young Kenneth Carline, an employee in her father's civil engineering firm, soon after the disrupted opening ceremony of a new tunnel under the River Calle. The involvement of Lucy's absent father in the politics of the African kingdom of Dlasa contributed further to the puzzling situation, and so did the sudden disappearance from the University of Calleshire of the King of Dlasa's son.

Detective-Inspector C.D. Sloan came to the case too late in the day to save an innocent victim from paying the penalty of knowing too much, but he was still in time to see that justice was done in this thirteenth Calleshire chronicle from Catherine Aird's erudite and lively pen.

### *Harm's Way*
July 1984

It was the task of the reconnaissance party of the Berebury Footpaths Society to see that the path was clear. And so it was until a passing crow dropped something exceedingly sinister before their very eyes. From this small beginning developed a murder hunt that cast its net over the trail of a missing financier, someone's ne'er-do-well son, and a man whose facial bruises certainly needed accounting for. No little part was played in confusing the matter – or perhaps compounding it – by the village Fire Brigade, always ready to turn out at the first hint of smoke…

Detective-Inspector Sloan and his assistant Detective-Constable Crosby, were called in to help the policeman on the spot, an elderly constable whose motto was 'Anything for a quiet life' but knew the village of Great Rooden like the back of his hand. They were all too late, though, to forestall an attack on one of those involved in this bizarre case set deep in the heart of rural Calleshire.

### *His Burial Too*
April 1973

The Fitton Bequest was made of marble and weighed several tons. It had been moved safely into the belfry while reconstruction work was carried out in a local church. Yet there it was lying in pieces on top of the body of Richard Mallory Tindall, head of a scientific testing firm, who had been reported missing from his home.

Inspector Sloan of the Berebury CID had a problem on his hands. Several problems – especially when he realized that the Fitton Bequest had fallen while the belfry was locked and apparently empty. This posed a classic old-fashioned 'locked room mystery' for the Inspector. Hampered by his superintendent and hindered by his constable, he set about unravelling the case. And it was no help at all that Tindall's firm did highly secret work for all manner of people...

In the space of one hot July day Inspector Sloan uncovers all the answers. Catherine Aird's readers are invited to watch him at work, to be beguiled by her gift for humour and characterization, and to revel once again in the annals of Calleshire and one of her most skilfully plotted mysteries.

### *Last Respects*
September 1982

When Horace Boller, fisherman, found the badly decomposed body of a man in the waters of the estuary of the river Calle he thought he knew what to do for the best. The best, that is, from the point of view of Horace Boller.

What he did not know was where the finding of the body would lead. Nor did Inspector C. D. Sloan and his irreverent assistant Detective-Constable Crosby when they embarked on a diverse trail that ends in an exciting chase through the county of Calleshire.

Before that, though, there was to be unravelled as complex a puzzle as has ever come from the pen of Catherine Aird. The mystery is deepened by events offshore and in Collerton house which overlooks the estuary. Nor in this latest chronicle of Calleshire is the man in the water the only person to die…

### Late Phoenix, A
October 1970

The skeleton unearthed by a bulldozer on a bombsite scheduled for rebuilding appeared to be that of a blitz victim. And she was pregnant. Decent reburial might have covered everything, if medical examination hadn't disclosed a bullet in her spine.

Patiently, Inspector Sloan, aided by Detective- (or defective-) Constable Crosby, set to work to trace the unknown victim and investigate a murder at least twenty-five years old. Digging up the past proved unexpectedly rewarding; all sorts of fascinating details of life in wartime England came to light. It also proved highly dangerous to at least one of Sloan's informants. And for Dr William Latimer, just setting up in his first medical practice, the investigation cast some interesting sidelights on his elderly predecessor, and cleared up yet another mysterious death.

### Parting Breath
November 1977

The University of Calleshire was experiencing another student sit-in. As often happens, the cause was obscured by the effect, though the unlikely alliance of the Dean and the college porter ensured that matters did not get too much out of hand. There was no need to call in the police – everyone was agreed on that point – until one of the students was found dying in a College quad to a background of Elizabethan madrigals.

Inspector Sloan found his investigation hampered by the eccentricities of both the academic and student bodies, and by the predictable and often-voiced opinion of Superintendent Leeyes. Moreover, in the few days since term commenced the dead student had behaved very strangely, even down to his cryptic last utterance which defied all Sloan's attempts to discover why time was of the essence of the case.

In the circumstances the Inspector might have been forgiven for thinking that Miss Hilda Linaker's researches into Jane Austen's love-life (hers was to be the definitive biography) had little to so with his own researches into who and what had killed a boy of nineteen. How wrong he was became clear when there was a second murder.

### Passing Strange
October 1980

Things had gone wrong from the very beginning of this year's Almstone Flower Show. There had been a mistake over the judging of the tomatoes. There was a queue to see the gipsy Fortune Teller (who looked suspiciously like the District Nurse), though the Fortune Teller was nowhere to be seen, and a car had been parked where no car should have been – a car, moreover, hired by a girl whose past, present and future were all set about with mystery.

Detective-Inspector C. D. Sloan of the Berebury CID wasn't called in until the Fortune Teller was found, then he and his assistant, Detective-Constable Crosby, made

their way out to the heart of rural Calleshire very quickly indeed, and discovered a murder in which there seems to be a total absence of means motive and opportunity.

But of course all three were present, and Catherine Aird's many admirers will be delighted once again by the ingeniousness of her solution.

### Slight Mourning
November 1975

Bill Fent, one of the Fents of Strontfield Park in the country of Calleshire, died in a car crash and post-mortem revealed a ruptured aorta as the cause of death. It also revealed that Bill had recently ingested a lethal dose of barbiturate which, but for an unlucky chance, would have made him die seemingly naturally in his bed. And the poison must have been administered at his own table, for Bill and his wife had just given a dinner-party for twelve. All the guests were relatives, friend or near neighbours, and one of them was a murderer.

Inspector C. D. Sloan ('Seedy' to his friends), with the doubtful assistance of Detective Constable Crosby, found himself with a delicate investigation on his hands, for Bill Fent, a prominent local landowner, was at the heart of a development controversy which had split the peaceful village of Constance Parva in two. And representatives of both sides had been gathered around his table. What with those who wanted him to sell his land and those who wanted to prevent him, Sloan was not short of a suspect. Or two. Or three…

### Some Die Eloquent
October 1979

People were mildly sorry when Miss Beatrice Wansdyke was found dead alone at home – but not unbearably surprised. After all, she'd been known for years to suffer from diabetes. The only strange thing was the state of her bank account. That didn't fit in at all with everyone's idea of the quiet chemistry mistress and her modest way of life. Somehow, not long before she died Miss Wansdyke had acquired a very great deal of money…

This solitary clue was all there was to lead Inspector Sloan of the Berebury CID on to find that Miss Wansdyke's death had been far from natural. In fact she had been murdered in a particularly cunning way. Where there's a Will – and Miss Wansdyke's will was quite specific – there's usually a relative. Here there were several relatives and one beneficiary outside the family. Their reactions were just some of the many things that Inspector Sloan had to take into consideration in solving a very neat little problem.

The latest and liveliest in the criminous chronicles of Calleshire displays Catherine Aird's knowledge of medicine, forensic pathology, the police, and expectant fatherhood.

### ALINGTON, CYRIL
#### Crime on the Kennet
April 1939

Dr. Cyril Alington, Dean of Durham, needs no introduction to detective-story readers, for as a member of the Crime Club panel he has been responsible for a great deal of the pleasure they have had in their reading, and for the maintenance of the Crime Club's high standards in detective fiction. Modesty forbids that his own novel, with which he breaks a long silence in this field of writing, should be a Selection. But the Crime Club recommend it to everyone's notice as a detective story distinguished by a keen sense of humour and the culture of its writing. The setting is an old

manor house. A most delightful vicar is one of its chief attractions, and when will one get a better vicar portrayed than when a dean turns author!

### ALLAN, STELLA
#### Arrow in the Dark
November 1982

The Rev. Martin Dearsley is a decorated hero. In 1957 when he was a regular soldier serving in the Army in Cyprus, he had suffered the trauma of losing an arm and a brother officer and friend in the troubles there. The same incident had bereaved Sylvia Stanton of her lover. Its repercussions brought Martin and Sylvia together and soon after their first meeting they married, still strangers. Both had their reasons. Sylvia's were obvious; Martin's more devious.

Bound together by gratitude and guilt, they had fashioned a superficially satisfactory marriage until the unexpected arrival in their lives of Stuart Balfour with disturbing news concerning their daughter Marian. Stuart's advent and Marian's plight involve Martin and Sylvia in a web of suspicion and intrigue that finally forces Martin to face the past, his own nature, and inevitably the effect that the revelation of both will have upon Sylvia and their relationship.

This is a story of remorse, vengeance, desire and sudden death, but most of all of a marriage brought to a watershed through vicious circumstances.

### Dead Giveaway, A
November 1980

When Julia Sturgis emerged from the theatre where her latest play was enjoying a successful run and encountered her brother-in-law, now head of a vast business empire, she took an unhappy step back into the past. Richard Newton had twice ruined her life: once by marrying money instead of her, and again, after she had found happiness with his brother, by withdrawing his investment in their small firm, thereby hastening his brother's death.

Julia detested him. She would never have accepted an invitation to spend a weekend with him and his wife at their luxurious country home had it not been for the eagerness to go shown by the wealthy businessman who had backed her play and was now her lover – and her affection for the Newtons' unloved teenage son.

Suddenly Julia was at the heart of a drama more suspenseful for any she might have written for the stage: one involving kidnapping, murder, high-level financial chicanery, with an ironic, unexpected ending which readers of her two previous crime novels will recognise as distinctly Stella Allan's own.

### Inside Job, An
November 1978

When Sheila Pettit saw Braggart's Mill for the first time she felt as if she were watching the beginning of a film before the credit titles appeared, and though what was happening on the screen was ordinary enough, its normality was given the lie by staccato modern incidental music suggesting the macabre.

Braggart's Mill was the new home of a wealthy school friend, of whom Sheila had always felt a nagging jealousy. Now she was suddenly in a position to do her a favour, for Margaret's husband needed a job, and Sheila, very much the cool, competent London business executive, was able to suggest him to her boss.

Her boss was an old family friend, to whom Sheila had always been totally loyal, just as she had always considered herself

above such weakness as falling in love. Now she encountered in Margaret's husband an attractive man who deliberately set out to seduce her, and she succumbed completely to his charms. Before long, she was agreeing to his scheme to swindle the company out of a million dollars and flee with him to South America. Murder was no part of their plan, but a strange accident caused the conspirators on the eve of their flight to find themselves with a corpse on their hands and a situation far more macabre than that suggested by the first glimpse of Braggart's Mill.

Stella Allan's first crime novel is a swift-moving story of seduction, swindling and murder, packed with ironic surprises and carrying the unmistakable stamp of success.

### Mortal Affair, A
June 1979

Frances Parry was a woman to be envied. Married to a Harley Street consultant, with a beautiful home, wealthy friends, including the fascinating Bernard, her husband's friend since undergraduate days, and with a creative job to plug what otherwise might have been a gap in her childless existence, she seemed to have it made. Crime was totally outside her experience – something indulged in only by people one didn't know.

Suddenly Frances's world was turned upside down. Her home was sold, her sideline job became a vital means of livelihood, and Bernard the suave, the successful, gallantly burdened with a guilt that wasn't his – Bernard, who had become her lover, was exposed as a criminal.

Even so, Frances was unable to end their association. It was left to a third party to do that. And then Frances found that she herself was indulging in criminal activities in a deadly duel with the law.

Stella Allan's second crime novel has all the poise and expertise of her first. Once again the ending is unexpected and brilliantly ironic. A Stella Allan novel has a flavour all its own.

### ANONYMOUS
#### Crime Wave: World's Winning Crime Stories 1981
December 1981

'Here are the world's crime writers saying, "This is what crime writing is about" ', says Desmond Bagley in his Introduction to this superb collection of stories.

Authors from all over the world submitted more than 400 stories to the first ever international crime short story competition, held in connection with the 3rd Crime Writers International Congress, which took place in Stockholm in June 1981. In this volume the Crime Club is proud to publish the eighteen best stories, chosen by the Swedish Academy of Detection, organizers of the Congress, in conjunction with an international jury.

The range is wide – from New York's urban jungle to a Navajo Indian Reservation; from contemporary Amsterdam to Paris of the Belle Epoque; from domestic drama to what really happened in *Hamlet*, and the true identity of Jack the Ripper. Nor have the literary antecedents of the detective story been forgotten, and Shakespeare, Poe, Dostoievsky and Conan Doyle all receive due tribute.

In this volume lovers of guile, suspense, excitement, whodunits, psychological drama, will all find something to their taste, from the pens of some of the best-known crime writers and from several newcomers.

## Suit of Diamonds, A: Crime Club Diamond Jubilee Commemorative Volume
March 1990

Thirteen superb original short stories by leading Crime Club authors in a specially bound volume – what better way to commemorate the sixty years of crime represented by the Crime Club's Diamond Jubilee!

The stores range from a tongue-in-cheek, twist-in-the-tail Perry Trethowan narrative by Robert Barnard to the chilling resonance of Reginald Hill's account of an eighteenth-century shipwreck and its aftermath; from Sarah Caudwell's Professor Hilary Tamar inimitably chronicling a lethal legal quirk to John Malcolm's art expert Tim Simpson stumbling unwillingly on murder; from the graceful wit of Michael Pearce's story of a British policeman in Edwardian Egypt to the equally distinctive voice of Mike Ripley's streetwise Angel, up to the neck willy-nilly in the latest London scam. And that is to leave out queens of crime like Elizabeth Ferrars and Patricia Moyes, skilled craftsmen of the stamp of Eric Wright and Martin Russell, purveyors of pleasure like Anthea Fraser and Charlotte MacLeod, and Gwendoline Butler, so at home with evil that she can fool the reader into thinking it the most natural thing in the world.

For those who already know the works of these authors, here is renewed delight. For those who don't, here is an array of cunningly varied delicacies to tempt the appetite.

## ANSON, LINDSAY
### Hung by an Eyelash
May 1939

Mr. Lindsay Anson scored a hit with his extraordinarily good first detective story, *Such Natural Deaths*. His second book, *Hung by an Eyelash*, will bring joy to all those who like their mysteries spiced with wit. There is a refreshing originality about Mr. Anson's writing. His story is full of verve and point, with plenty of humour and a thoroughly modern atmosphere. There is excitement and suspense, and some good twists at the end of the tale. *Hung by an Eyelash* is a detective story definitely to read and recommend.

### I Don't Like Cats
May 1940

When Peter Allen, ambling through the Severn country, comes across the unconscious form of an attractive woman, he thought the circumstances were somewhat odd. But he soon discovered that the matter of the drugged lady was about the most normal affair to be found in that quiet countryside. With feelings of misgivings, he was inveigled into the most amazing household a country mansion ever held. He found people living in a world of fear, living in a weird world of their own in which murder, attempted murder, intellectualism gone mad, made normal life appear ridiculous. Mr. Anson has collected a gallery of characters which the reader will not readily forget. His touch is sure, the portraits are vivid, even the most staggering events seem to take their place among the commonplace. From the startling start to the macabre conclusion, Mr. Anson has spun a pattern with uncanny insight and dexterity, a pattern which flies miles above the ways of ordinary crime stories to achieve memorable atmosphere, sparking dialogue, a bewildering plot, and terrifying tension.

### Such Natural Deaths
September 1938

There are three murders in this story – each made so plausible that it seems like a natural death. A man catches his foot in a rabbit snare in the woods and falls to his death in a gully. Another slips on some marbles on a kerbstone and is run over by a bus. A girl takes too much of her usual sleeping draught and dies. The planning and unmasking of these three murders is one of the most ingenious pieces of work that we have ever read.

## ANTHONY, DAVID
### Blood on a Harvest Moon
October 1972

Lured from his dangerous career as a top private investigator by the promise of a leisured life as gentleman farmer, Morgan Butler, ex-Marine captain, is in the midst of harvesting when an unexpected visitor summons him from the fields. Concerned about the uncharacteristic and mysterious disappearance of her second husband, a successful business-man named Ralph Maynard, Butler's still-beautiful ex-wife has come to enlist his aid. Will he track down the missing Maynard.

Routine work for an old pro – until a string of brutal and baffling murders obscures Maynard's trail. Will Maynard be the next victim in this series of ingeniously executed slayings? Or is the threat to Maynard's life an artful deception designed to conceal Maynard's own guilt? Drawn into a subtle and ever-widening circle of deceit and death, Butler himself becomes the prey of a ruthless assassin determined to preserve the bloody secret of a wartime plot in this superbly crafted, high-tension novel of suspense.

### Long Hard Cure, The
May 1979

Three attractive young women in a small Southern town are bizarrely attacked. It seems the work of a madman, and, with an expensive private mental hospital on the town's outskirts, there is no shortage of suspects. The editor of a local paper has no doubt where the guilt lies, especially when his niece is one of the victims. Feeling between town and hospital runs high.

Into this tense situation comes Morgan Butler, ex- US marine turned farmer (and formerly detective), who is asked by the doctor who once treated him to investigate on the hospital's behalf. He finds an immediate ally in the local sheriff, who is well aware that the obvious and the right solution are not necessarily one and the same. The suicide of the most likely suspect merely fans their suspicions, when they discover someone with a very good reason for wanting this rich young man out of the way. Yet even here the obvious solution seems almost too pat to be convincing. A dangerous and subtle mind is at work. But is it sane or insane? And wherein lies the difference? David Anthony's absorbing whodunit casts a searching light on our assumptions about sanity and madness, and poses questions which every reader must answer for himself.

### Midnight Lady and the Mourning Man, The
March 1970

Take a not-so-ordinary detective – Morgan Butler, ex-Marine turned gentleman farmer – confront him with the not-so-ordinary murder of a beautiful frosty co-ed found dead in her quiet Midwestern college dormitory – and you have the ingredients of an extraordinary mystery. What is the significance of the copy of *The Brothers Karamazov* clutched in the dead girl's hand? Who stole the tapes recorded by students to recount their personal problems? In the search for the girl's killer, Butler plunges into a thick web of local intrigue. This is a stark, taut, up-tempo mystery novel, developed with unusual thrust and accented by exceptional characterization.

## Organisation, The
September 1971

For his second novel, David Anthony, author of the widely-acclaimed *The Midnight Lady and the Mourning Man*, takes the reader inside the world of organized crime in the USA, and provides a skilful guide through the intricacies of the Mafia hierarchy with its complex code of ethics.

Stanley Bass, free-lance investigator, poker-player, lone wolf, lover, fighter, is the star performer. He meets beautiful Brandy Kirkpatrick, who is seeking revenge for her sister's death at the hands of an Organization man, and they team up in an intricate plot of robbery and revenge, designed to relieve a gambling syndicate of $200,000 in 'skim money' from the tables of Las Vegas and pin the crime firmly on Brandy's victim. But something goes wrong, and just when the reader settles down for the expected routine chase story, the author begins to shuffle his cards and deals out surprise after surprise in a fast-moving story that crackles with excitement and suspense as it unfolds against the full panorama of California, from the hills of San Francisco to the beaches of San Diego.

### Stud Game
May 1977

Stanley Bass, tough, poker-playing, free-lance investigator who made his bow in David Anthony's *The Organization*, was approached by a retired judge, father of an old school friend, to conduct a delicate investigation on the family's behalf. Grant Hunter, architect, and the judge's elder son, had recently died in a car crash. Now his widow was confronted by an unknown girl demanding a large sum of money because she claimed Grant was the father of her unborn child.

The girl's story was circumstantially convincing, but Bass set to work undeterred to investigate Grant's friends and business associates, and every aspect of his life. Before long he was convinced of two things: whatever his widow might believe, Grant had a mistress; and the blackmail stake was high enough for murder to be part of the game.

Was Grant murdered? Bass believed so, but he had no clue to the killer's identity. Nor was he helped by the discovery that some years earlier a similar trick had been played on a grief-stricken widow, for everyone who might have been involved in Grant Hunter's death had a watertight alibi. Then from the depths of someone else's private tragedy, came the evidence Bass needed to make an accusation. That accusation put him next in line for death.

Set in California, where David Anthony lives, this tightly constructed story exerts a stronger grip on the reader with each fresh and unexpected twist of its skilful plot.

## ANTHONY, MICHAEL DAVID
### Becket Factor, The
October 1990

The Archbishop of Canterbury announces he is to retire. A sequence of bizarre and apparently inexplicable events follows and disturbs the usual calm of the cathedral precincts. The sudden death of one of the canons [sic] prompts uneasy suspicions on the part of a retired intelligence officer; the unearthing of an ancient coffin re-stirs the religious fervour surrounding Tomas Becket; and growing controversy surrounds the favoured candidate for the Primacy.

Goaded by the guilt of his past in the murky world of Intelligence, Richard Harrison, Diocesan Dilapidations Officer, is reluctantly drawn into a web of intrigue and enters a shadowy world where Church and national politics overlap. Prejudice and intolerance, both ancient and modern, alternately obscure and illuminate the past career of Bishop Maurice Campion who seems likely to succeed to the Augustine Throne. But who does Campion really serve? God – or the KGB?

This unusual, timely and utterly engrossing first novel demonstrates once again how far removed is the best of modern crime fiction from the narrow confines of the old-style detective story.

## ARLEY, CATHERINE
### Dead Man's Bay
June 1959

She was utterly alone. She turned back from the darkness and already the tentacles of fear had reached out and were entangling her as she felt again the isolation of the house high on the cliff, back by the bleak, deserted landscape of the Breton coast. She had forty-eight hours to endure before Andre returned. Two days in which, step by step, by day and by night, small, unexplained events occurred which drove her steadily away from the frontiers of reason. She discovered s cuff link on the floor; the kettle was found boiling on the stove; there was the weird episode of the knocking in the night and the grotesque death of the cat. Was there a pattern to these subtly malignant incidents? Was there a human agent conducting this gradual crescendo of terror?

Catherine Arley, in this brilliant and chilling successor to *Woman of Straw*, has allied a gripping study of terror with an ingenious and original plot. *Dead Man's Bay* bids fair to rank with Poe's *The Black Cat* and *The Tell-Tale Heart* in the field of the macabre.

### Ready Revenge
November 1960

When Daphne de Ferlac learned that the wealth and security provided by her husband had reached vanishing point she hardly hesitated: a few weeks later Alain de Ferlac was apparently the victim of a fatal and tragic accident. Not long after that Daphne married the bumbling newly-rich Marcel Blancard. It was a convenient equation – the death of Alain gave security to Daphne and married bliss to the amiable Marcel. But to Marcel's sister, Marthe, the marriage brought an anxiety and disquiet which rose to horror as events came to a dreadful climax in the warm seas of the Mediterranean, and a subtle and terrifying revenge was planned.

In *Ready Revenge* Catherine Arley has achieved levels of suspense and drama which surpass even the heights which she achieved in *Woman of Straw* and *Dead Man's Bay*.

### Woman of Straw
February 1957

*Crime Story?*
*Grand Guignol?*
*Psychological Thriller?*
*Nightmare?*

It is not easy to classify Mlle. Catherine Arley's second novel, the first to be translated into English.

Undoubtedly Hildegarde's motives were acquisitive in scanning the matrimonial advertisements so assiduously. Undoubtedly she was thinking of endowing herself with a quantity of this world's goods when she answered an advertisement inserted by a millionaire. Hildegarde was not so stupid that she did not ask herself why on earth a millionaire had to *advertise* for a wife.

From then on Hildegarde's life was transformed. It *might* have turned out alright, of course, if… But there are a myriad 'ifs' in this very ingenious and macabre story which Mlle. Arley relates in her ruthless, detached and casual manner.

Anyone who wants a vicarious thrill of a powerful order is strongly recommended to try *Woman of Straw*. Those who prefer to take it quietly and sunnily are warned; *Woman of Straw* is like the scenic railway – a rough ride and once on you can't' get off.

## ARMSTRONG, CHARLOTTE
*Protégé,The*
October 1970
Mrs. Moffat, a widow, lives in peaceful seclusion. At church one Sunday a bearded young stranger inexplicably joins her in her pew. He tells her he is Simon Warren, who lived next door to her as a child and has returned for a look at the old place.

Grateful for company, Mrs Moffat invites Simon home. They chat away the afternoon – but the visitor displays no eagerness to be gone. The afternoon becomes a day, the day a week, and the weeks turn into months. Having insinuated himself as a companion, gardener, and Jack-of-all-trades, Simon settles down with the old woman for an indefinite period.

When Mrs Moffat's granddaughter arrives from New York for a short visit, she immediately expresses concern over the peculiar relationship between Mrs Moffat and her protégé. What does the young man called Simon Warren hope to gain? Was he really a neighbour of Mrs Moffat's? Is there a connection between him and the prowler seen stalking the vicinity? And what is his interest in the sundial?

This nerve-jangling story again demonstrates why its author is known as 'America's Queen of suspense'.

## ARMSTRONG, DAVID
*Less than Kind*
January 1994
It is 1968, and Charles Somerville, son of impoverished landowner Philip Somerville, is on the run from London drug dealers in the Welsh Borders.

In nearby Llantrisillio, newly arrived James and Suzy's sylvan idyll is suddenly and brutally shattered by the voyeuristic behaviour of their farming neighbour.

Also in the Border country is Birmingham policeman, John Munro, who is liaising with his Welsh colleagues on a routine enquiry. But when there is an unexplained death in the area, he finds himself inexorably drawn into the investigation…one which is to uncover a tangle of dangerous passions and tensions running beneath the calm rural scene.

*Less Than Kind* is a gripping story of psychological menace which offers a penetrating insight into the darkest recesses of the mind. A remarkable follow-up to David Armstrong's first novel, *Night's Black Agents*.

*Night's Black Agents*
January 1993
Clifford Benyon, landlord of the grandiosely named Belle Vue Hotel in the Birmingham district of Ladywood, is tortured by his wife's flagrant affair with Thomas Beech, a traveller in surgical supplies and one of the hotel's regular and free-spending customers.

In despair, Benyon contracts with the brutal canal boatman, Ezra Talbot, to kill his rival.

The deed is duly done, but its results are far from what Benyon had hoped. Not only does his wife retreat ever further from him, but it brings Detective-Inspector J Hammond

on the scene. And Hammond has an intuitive grasp of the truth of the affair. The only problem is: can he prove it?

As events unfold, Benyon is horrified to find that the crime he has initiated is developing its own terrifying momentum.

Set on the canals of the Midlands and North-West during the 1930s, David Armstrong's first novel is an atmospheric, character-based mystery which intrigues as much by its unusual background as by the cat-and-mouse game played out between police and murderer.

## ARMSTRONG, VIVIEN
*Honey Trap, The*
April 1992
Rowan Morley, big and beautiful, made quite a splash when she went overboard from a pleasure launch into the Thames. Fortunately help was at hand but Rowan's rescuers were bewildered when she insisted on denying the existence of what seemed to them a clearly murderous attack.

Even when she was whisked away to an Oxfordshire village to act as housekeeper to two helpless males, Rowan remained a focus of mystery. Meanwhile Aran Hunter, art restorer, chafed at his inability to protect her; Frederick Flowers, retired civil servant, feared for her; Wayne Denny, general factotum of a fleet of Thames houseboats, lusted after her; and Inspector Laurence Erskine of Special Branch, now working with Interpol, found himself involved willy-nilly when he learned that Rowan's previous employers were connected with a case he had been working on for months.

None of them, except perhaps Erskine, could believe this glorious girl was involved in international crime, but when murder struck close to home it became a matter of life and death to discover what Rowan Morley, willingly or unwittingly, knew or possessed.

*Sleight of Hand*
May 1991
To Chief Inspector Ralph Arnott the bizarre death of Francis Quayne, QC, was the beginning of the end. Infuriated by what he saw as the unwarranted intervention of Special Branch in a routine investigation, he resigned early from the force.

But his young sergeant Judy Pullen knew the tough Yorkshireman too well to believe he could ever abandon interest in a case which had developed intriguing features. Encouraged by her, Arnott began investigating on his own and was soon drawn willy-nilly into the world of academic fraud which had blighted the careers and lives of several of those associated with Swayne, in particular his younger sister Sabina, now seemingly cocooned in a wealthy if difficult marriage.

The action shifts between London and Yorkshire, between the world of scientific research and glittering London lifestyles. Both seem alien to Arnott, but he finds himself drawn to the young woman whose promising career never got off the ground and to her brilliant but discredited professor, as he perceives in their distress at a life's work interrupted a curious parallel to his own. He also perceives that nothing about Swayne's death is as it seems…

## ASHFORD, JEFFREY
(*see also* **Jeffries, Roderic**)
*Conflict of Interests, A*
December 1989
The three men's lives had touched once before. Sanderson, the idealist, had joined an animal liberation group whose activities had

fallen foul of the law; the police officer, King, had arrested Sanderson; Bowles had been in charge of Hanburrey Manor, a centre where men and women useful to the police were given new identities and to which Sanderson had gone as a prelude to embarking on a new life. Their lives touched a second time when it became known that the animal liberation group were preparing to commit an outrageous act of terrorism to further their aims, and the former Sanderson was the one man able to pinpoint those responsible. Each of the three men fervently believed in certain standards; each was forced to make the bitter discovery that there were circumstances in which such standards could no longer be held inviolable. Their conflicting interests and ideals form the warp and woof of this memorable novel.

*Crime Remembered, A*
December 1987
For generations the Tourkville family had owned Highland Place and it was love for his inheritance which had made the present owner, Edward Pierre Darcy Tourkville, dedicate his life to rebuilding the estate which his father had almost lost through bad management. Success seemed to be within his grasp when suddenly he was brought face to face with the past, a brutal, murderous, wartime past, which threatened to destroy all his work and put not only the survival of the estate once more at risk, but his own survival as well…

Relentlessly the past caught up with him in the person of Detective-Sergeant Noyes. But did Noyes represent Nemesis or salvation? Were there ever circumstances in which murder could be justified? The reader must find his own answer to that question as Jeffrey Ashford probes deeply into men's actions under intolerable stress.

*Deadly Reunion*
October 1991
Gary Weston was amused to meet Jason Farley again after several years, and despite the fact that Farley had been expelled from school for breaking every rule in the book—and some that weren't—it didn't occur to him that their meeting in the south of Spain could have disastrous consequences. Not even when Farley organized a party with two very attractive and obviously willing women did he become apprehensive. That only happened after he awoke with a monumental hangover and found that his senses, or what remained of them, kept trying to tell him that he was not in his hotel bed, but in a bunk, at sea …

It was a voyage that was to lead to murder back in England; a murder that taught Gary Weston the bitter lesson that innocence is not always a sufficient defence when the odds are stacked against you in the form of circumstantial evidence.

*Guilt with Honour*
June 1982
As the four men and one woman stood in a small group in the shooting field, they heard confused shouting. But only Bob Howe, his reactions honed on the racing circuits of the world, immediately realised that the man running towards them was a would-be assassin and that one of the group was his obvious target. He knocked the intended victim to the ground and saved a life.

The police made it clear that so far as they were concerned the case was an open and shut one; a man, in popular terms mad, had attempted to murder the imagined instigator of his ills. The episode was to be hushed up. Unfortunately, Howe had already noticed one or two facts which seemed to cast doubts

on the police's conclusions, and though they asked him to keep his doubts to himself, he had already mentioned them to Moller, a reporter on a national newspaper who knew a good story when he saw one, especially when it might uncover some scandal.

Howe had direct and strongly held beliefs concerning truth and justice, but as the violence unleashed by Moller's story spread, he was forced to realise that the truth and justice were not immutable, nor guilt and honour incompatible…

*Honourable Detective, The*
December 1988
Two men witnessed the hit-and-run accident but neither of them had the slightest idea how his life would be affected by what he had seen. From the beginning, Mike Ansell cooperated with the police, but his fellow witness, who never acted against his own interests, did not. Then each received a thousand pounds in the post together with a cryptic message advising him to remember the three monkeys. It was not advice Ansell was prepared to take. As the pressure on them not to cooperate with the police mounted, the two men continued to react in character. And when the police failed him, Mike Ansell discovered unsuspected depths in his own character, just as Detective-Constable Brice did in his.

*Ideal Crime, An*
October 1985
To pay his way through law school, Jim Thorpe, a young man of old-fashioned ideals on such subjects as love, duty, honesty and integrity, took a job as night watchman in security vaults. Life might have seemed all solid slog had it not been for his employer's daughter, who never lost an opportunity of pointing out that all work and no play made for a very dull life indeed…

Then there was a robbery at the vaults and the guard who had changed shifts with Thorpe was killed. It soon became clear that someone had given details of the security arrangements to the robbers, and suspicion fell heavily on the conveniently absent Thorpe. Faced with the need to clear himself, Thorpe fought a long and bitter battle which took him to Spain and then to France. In the course of it, he was forced to abjure almost all his ideals.

*Illegal Solution, An*
December 1990
They made a good team, perhaps because their characters were so different; Detective-Sergeant O'Connor lived for tomorrow, Detective-Constable Brent only for today. O'Connor was a family man; Brent took his pleasures where he found them. So when the incidence of drug-related crimes showed a disturbing rise, their reactions to the fact were not at all the same; while Brent merely regretted it, O'Connor saw it as a direct threat to all the things in life he most valued, and believed he was called upon to take whatever measures were necessary to counter such a threat. It was a mistake that was to lead to an act of folly which put his career on the line. And when Brent, with typical, carefree indifference to the consequences, rushed in to help, he ran head first into murderous danger and not just his career but his life was at stake.

*Judgement Deferred*
September 1993
Despite their every effort, the police of two counties had been unable to gain any lead on the murderer; eight-year-old Vicky was his seventh victim. But her body was found more quickly than those of the other victims

in the form of a riot for unallotted seats or the sudden rush on stage of frenzied fans.

But what if the violence is in the form of a hidden enemy who seeks to destroy the star without apparent reason; a nameless dot in a human sea of thirty thousand faces; whose methods are hidden; who has all the advantages; what the police call 'a nutter', in short?

Despite tight security and a massive audience more interested in his music that in mobbing him, retiring, Oxford-educated Allen 'Bohny' Oppen has just such a one.

Oppen's lifestyle is publicized as quietly flamboyant, he doesn't need to outrage or arrest attention – his international fame has reached beyond all that. Yet among his vast following is the one person all rock musicians live in fear of: someone as personal to Bohny as his stage manager or his lawyer, his record producer or his bass player. As close as his girl-friend.

And just as dedicated…

This outstanding novel of suspense is also an inside look at the world of the rock-star by an author who is a rock music critic, a poetry critic, and a poet in his own right.

*Note: Owing to the feasibility of the technology used in this book, certain technical details have been deliberately misrepresented or falsified.*

## BRANDON, RUTH
### Gorgon's Smile, The
May 1992

Andrew Taggart and Rose O'Faolain have come to visit their old friend Maggy Hodge at her house in the Tuscan hills. The country is idyllic, the weather is perfect, and the three, all distinctly battered by recent misfortunes, look forward to a relaxing holiday.

Then a friend of Maggy's arrives with a mysterious package, and invites Taggart to join him on a wild boar poaching expedition. Taggart can't resist opening the package, and Maggy won't let him refuse the invitation.

The consequences are more than anyone bargained for. They find themselves enmeshed in a network of Etruscan tomb-robbing, antiquities-smuggling, and – it turns out – a great deal more besides. Under the sinister glare of the Gorgon mask friendships dissolve, certainties vanish, and the inhabitants of the calm hills of Etruria, both ancient and modern, become a great deal less bucolic and more menacing than anyone might have imagined…

### Left, Right and Centre
January 1986

Someone had leaked a top secret Pentagon document to the *Monitor* paper in London. Who is the mole? Just the sort of person Defence Through Strength would like to see put behind bars, and their spokesman Paul Silverlight says as much in his regular column in *The World* next day. In the bastions of the New Right, and the committee rooms of the Peace Movement, rumour buzzes. Will the leak set off the final holocaust? It seems as though it may…but by then, Silverlight is past caring. And in Fleet Street and Scotland Yard business is as usual, whatever the international situation. It is when Inspector Brian King of the Special Branch, rather than a CID officer, is given the Silverlight case, that Andrew Taggart of *New Politics* smells some fishy and decides to do a little investigating on his own account.

From Cambridge, England to Princeton, New Jersey, King finds he has to do without very much help from his friends. And Taggart had better keep well away from *his*…

Ruth Brandon's first novel looks shrewdly at the Left, Right and Centre of British politics and deals with a number of controversial issues in an entertaining and suspenseful way.

### Mind Out
February 1991

What do you do when your scientist husband, having disappeared on a visit to the States, returns home with his own mind, memory, personality, even voice but a different body? Belinda Watson soon found the change lent a certain piquancy to marriage, After all, she and Charles had been getting a tiny bit bored...

As for Andrew Taggart, the journalist who had been investigating her husband's disappearance (and incidentally consoling her), she didn't mind kissing him goodbye.

Then the new 'Charles Watson' is murdered and the innocent Taggart is arrested and charged. Taggart had learned too much about the way in which the original Charles Watson had been lured to the States to feel easy about it, and a visit to the Prospect Psychodynamics Clinic in New York, where Watson was last seen, had added to his anxiety. Nor was he the only one to suspect those activities at the Clinic which appeared to involve a senior British civil servant and a distinguished American academic.

Can Taggart prove his innocence? Who has framed him, and why? This brilliantly ironic crime novel poses the usual who-dunit questions, but goes further as it probes human credulity and the ultimate responsibility at the highest levels of our society.

## BRAUN, LILIAN JACKSON
### Cat Who Ate Danish Modern, The
March 1968

Newspaper reporter Qwilleran and Siamese cat Koko are again at work together on matters of robbery and murder – this time the sophisticated world of interior decoration. For Qwilleran it all began as a change of assignment when his paper starts a Sunday supplement on interior decoration and decides it should be written from a male point of view – Qwilleran's.

Interior decoration is far from Quilleran's metier, and his first issue is eminently successful – except that the house he uses for his subject is robbed of its owner's jade collection. He picks wrong the second time round too, and learns to be wary of the word professional. But when a friend of his becomes a victim, Qwilleran takes over as unofficial detective – a role he fulfils only with the help of the imperious, self-motivated Koko.

Here is a delightful, ingenious tale of unconventional happenings dealt with by a most unorthodox pair – a worthy successor to the highly acclaimed first novel *The Cat Who Could Read Backwards*. It is for anyone looking for a fresh approach to a mystery. Cat-lovers will be intrigued, and cat-haters may be won over.

### Cat Who Could Read Backwards, The
July 1967

For Jim Qwilleran, former crime reporter now on the comeback trail, an assignment to the art department of a newspaper is challenge enough – since he knows nothing about art. But then he finds that his job is meant to counteract the reader reactions caused by the real critic, George Bromfield Mountclemens III, a man who delights in destroying artists with a review. He is a gourmet who caters to his tastes by being his own chef and he is a brilliant conversationalist. He has a cat as aristocratic and talented as he, a Siamese, Ko Ko Kung – Koko to Qwilleran – who has

one special talent: he reads newspaper headlines carefully, from right to left.

Qwilleran finds his seemingly peaceful beat involves him in three deaths. And it is only with Koko's help that he can discover the reasons for the artistic demises.

Here in her debut as a novelist Lilian Jackson Braun shows the skill that made Anthony Boucher pick her twice for inclusion in *Best Detective Stories of the Year* because, as he put it, 'no one else has so successfully combined the crime story and the cat story.'

### Cat Who Turned On and Off, The
July 1969

The team of Koko, the Siamese cat detective, and Qwilleran, the reporter with the perceptive moustache, is back in action – with a female Siamese, Yum Yum, added to the household.

Feature-writer Qwilleran decides to do a series of articles on the part of the city called Junktown. By the time he learns that the junk in question is not dope but antiques, he is stuck with the assignment, While Qwilleran is learning the strange practices of dealers and collectors, he is also learning about the strange fall that ended the career of one of Junktown's leading citizens. Qwilleran is convinced it was no accident, but it takes Koko to help him prove it.

Lilian Jackson Braun is noted for her ingenuity, humour and bright writing as well as for her way with cats. She shows why, in a mystery in which the setting is as colourful as the story.

## BRINGLE, MARY
### Death of an Unknown Man
July 1987

In a village seven miles north of Dublin, a group of children find the body of an unknown man concealed in the ramshackle grandstand of a derelict racecourse. He is without identification. Dublin Garda Sergeant Sean Lynch has no more clue to the dead man's identity than the children have – and speculation among the residents of Balgriffin runs from the personal to the political: was he a drug dealer, a gangster? Or is this a crime linked to the troubles in Northern Ireland and to a family who have recently moved to the village from Belfast?

The murder takes on a distinctly international flavour, with links to the United Arab Emirates and a disturbing rumoured connection to the British Secret Service. As the lives of the people in Balgriffin are disrupted by a tragedy so remote that they have no way of comprehending it as yet, the children decide that the level of chaos has become intolerable. They make plans to deal with the police in an unusual way, with remarkable results.

Told with warmth, humour, and an unerring ear for the rhythms of Irish speech, Mary Bringle's novel about the death of an unknown man in a small corner of Ireland will intrigue and delight readers everywhere.

## BROCK, LYNN
### Fourfingers
January 1939

Marton Common, a purple-brown expanse of moorland in the South West corner of the New Forest, peaceful, swept by sea-winds, became suddenly news. Carla Waterlow, the beautiful green-eyed authoress of *Purple Parade*, was found shot through the heart in a car on a lonely stretch of road… and later, in the bracken nearby, another two bodies were discovered. 'Magnificent air, magnificent scenery,' said Chief Detective-Inspector Granley as he despatched Venn and Kither to

the scene of action. But mystery deepened on Marton Common when evidence from a gipsy caravan and a country house had been heard. When it was found that Carla's lunatic husband had escaped from his asylum shortly before the murder, and when suddenly an eminent M. P. disappeared, Venn and Kither (the tortoise and the hare) got going. But one thing eluded them – 'Fourfingers', a mysterious stranger who left his fingerprints on a gold cigarette-case in Carla's car. Lynn Brock's latest story is a kaleidoscope of brilliantly drawn characters against a background of moorland woods and sea-air, and, furthermore, it's the same county and the same Yard combination that made his last book, *The Silver Sickle Case*, such a tremendous success.

### Q. E. D.
July 1930

The celebrated Suspension Bridge which spans Linwood Gorge – its chains once spanned the Thames – has seen many tragedies in its seventy years, but none more sinister than that with which this latest of Colonel Gore's cases concerns itself. Staggering in the simplicity of its achievement, incredible in the selection of its victim, the murder of Dr. Sidney Melhurst presents itself to the reader, as it did to the police and to Gore himself – an apparently unsolveable mystery. Baffled for space by a parallel trail, in the end, inch by inch, and at grave personal risk, he drags the truth to light. The two trails converge, and meet in the certainty which, in some measure, explains the title, Q. E. D. – a certainty as agreeable to the reader as to Colonel Gore.

### Riddle of the Roost, The
September 1939

The setting of the crime in Lynn Brock's brilliantly ingenious new story is Pinehills, a seaside resort on the South coast. The 'roost' round which the riddle turns is the wing that Hector Dorbin occupies in his brother's house. Two brothers, middle-aged, close friends, both fond of golf, wine and women. Two brothers found lying dead, their heads battered in by a hammer, near a staircase in the 'roost'. Here is a case to hold the attention of every reader.

### Silver Sickle Case, The
January 1938

Lynn Brock's brilliant detective novels, although he writes too rarely, rank among the best crime fiction of our time. Famous literary critics have praised them. Mr. Frank Swinnerton has praised his 'fine sense of character and the power to excite'. Rose Macaulay says 'Lynn Brock is a very clever writer; he has an agreeable literary style, a gift for drawing lifelike people, and a lively sense of dramatic incident.' *The Silver Sickle Case* is something more than an intellectual puzzle; it is a long gripping novel with plenty of action, surprise and suspense; the characters are vividly drawn, the style lively and stimulating. Mr. Lynn Brock is to be congratulated on a splendid achievement in detective fiction.

### Stoat, The: Colonel Gore's Queerest Case
August 1940

Great news for Crime Club members! Colonel Gore, generally considered one of the great detectives of fiction, makes a spectacular return, after too long an absence, in *The Stoat*. Old admirers of the Colonel will find that his brain is still as nimble, his brilliant deductions still as devastatingly sound. *The Stoat* is an exceptionally fine detective story with really 'live' characters and vigorous dialogue written with an infectious exuberance of style. There is no break in the succession of thrills, and altogether Mr. Lynn Brock is to be congratulated on a most satisfying detective story.

## BROMLEY, GORDON

### *Chance to Poison, The*

April 1973

Troughton, headmaster of a private boarding school and chairman of the local preservation society, was not entirely a popular figure in the Devonshire village where he lived. Tensions in the school, within the headmaster's family, and on the committee left their mark on all involved. One of them hated Troughton enough to poison him. Inspector Severn, gently probing the motives, backgrounds and opportunities of a group of disparate residents, finds the viewpoint shifting constantly as new and sometimes surprising facts emerge.

Gordon Bromley plants his clues fairly and invites the reader to follow Severn through the series of interviews which eventually results in an arrest. As in his first crime story, *In the Absence of the Body*, he is primarily concerned with character and motive, and with the effect they have on events.

### *In the Absence of the Body*

July 1972

Jeremy Gaywood, an up-and-coming account executive in a Mayfair advertising agency, suddenly disappears one Friday evening, last seen in a pub after leaving work. Has he been kidnapped? Or murdered? Or is there some other mysterious reason? Inspector Severn is called in.

Severn's investigations reveal some surprising facts about the inner workings and staff of the agency, and about Jeremy Gaywood himself. Vain, wealthy and none too popular, Jeremy was nevertheless an immensely valuable employee for his successful handling of an important soft drinks account. Does jealousy on the part of a colleague or a rival agency lie behind his disappearance? Or has it to do with his love-life? Or his family? Severn tries to determine what crime, if any, has been committed, by seeking the motive that may have triggered it off.

*In the Absence of the Body* is an unusually intriguing story about people and their motives. The author – who was himself a copy director of a large agency – writes with wit and style. He presents a fascinating group of characters and gives an amusingly satirical picture of the advertising business. 'The people,' he says, 'are entirely fictitious, but the world in which they live is real enough.' He certainly makes it seem so.

## BURDEN, PAT

### *Bury Him Kindly*

June 1991

An abandoned Datsun found near the woodland home of recluse Alice Meddlar and her simpleton son Robby, followed by an alarmed newcomer's remark that Alice ran unwanted visitors off her property at the end of a shotgun, takes Ex-Detective Chief Superintendent Henry Bassett away from his chickens and into an investigation to find a missing person.

When a corpse is discovered in a lonely grave on Robby's territory, suspicion automatically falls on him. It is enhanced by rumours about Robby's father, a mystery character; and murmurings of 'Like father, like son'.

But what appeared to have been a motive for the murder quickly fades, and Bassett's thoughts turn to newcomers in Robby's village. Who among them had recognized the murdered man? Which of them might have had cause to fear him… .?

### *Father, Forgive Me*

August 1993

*Rebel Priest and Teenager in Death Tryst*, the headline read.

The evidence seemed to bear out that a double suicide had actually occurred, but when an appeal for help brought ex-Detective Chief Superintendent Harry Bassett on to the scene his friends Inspector Bob Greenaway and Sergeant Andy Miller weren't complaining. Once they put their three heads together, the evidence soon began to look flimsy.

Who was the dead girl's mystery boyfriend whom she claimed she could never marry, if he was not the priest? Who was the father of her unborn child? Were they one and the same?

Bassett uncovers the tale of a love that is anything but life-enhancing and pits his wits against a clever murderer, who isn't quite clever enough.

### *Screaming Bones*

January 1989

'Once a copper, allus a copper', local gloom-and-doom merchant Tod Arkwright warned the villagers when retired Detective Chief Superintendent Henry Bassett moved to a country cottage in Herefordshire. But good-natured Bassett soon settled in, pigs, chickens and all; and it was to him that the villagers turned when rumours of sheep-rustling turned into a murder inquiry.

A mummified body, so called; the demolition of a cottage with a history of a grisly murder and the rebuilding of another; then a dead man sitting on a tombstone in the local churchyard…they were all connected somehow. But how?

The dead man, Derek Wilson, was a newcomer to the village. All was peace until he came and began knocking down the cottage on Top Hill. What had he done, or seen, to upset someone enough to kill him?

Bassett's investigations take him back to the turn of the century and on to wartime and two boys and a girl and a permanent summer, before returning him to the present day, when the puzzle pieces begin to fit into place.

Pat Burden is a skilful and talented newcomer to the Crime Club. Her first novel, set deep in rural Herefordshire, is both a cunningly unfolded double mystery and a delightful depiction of country folk and their ways.

### *Wreath of Honesty*

June 1990

Murderers are supposed to lie. Why was it that everyone that Bassett questioned about this murder appeared to tell the truth?

Of course he wasn't questioning the same suspects as his friend, Inspector Bob Greenaway; Bob was ruled by events of eighteen months previously, when the victim disappeared. Bassett had his own ideas, based almost entirely on what he saw of the corpse. A corpse that didn't shriek murder but only whispered.

Embarking on a stone-cold trail – where on earth was he to start? – Bassett puts a theory to the test; and little by little unravels the mystery of who killed Hugh Jeffries; unwittingly helped by those seeking desperately to preserve their secret. For it was often what they omitted to say that gave Bassett his clues.

## BURGESS, ERIC

### *Divided We Fall*

July 1959

Here is a detective story which is right out of the rut. Two hundred and twenty-six people saw James Roylake die. The General Secretary of the National Association of Technical Workers and Allied Technicians collapsed on the platform at the Union's annual conference minutes before the decisive session at which he would have defended his challenged leadership. Ruthless and dictatorial, Roylake had always dealt with the legion of his public and personal enemies with derision and contempt. Now it seemed he had scorned one once too often.

Eric Burgess, making a brilliant return to the field of Crime Fiction, has evoked the atmosphere of the conference through the eyes of the diffident and inexperienced Martin Carter who found himself plunged into a world of intrigue, ambition, lobbying and, ultimately, murder. *Divided We Fall* has a highly original setting, characters who have their roots in real life, and presents a case of murder which is baffling and full of suspense. It measures up to the highest standards of crime fiction.

### *Killing Frost, A*

February 1961

The body twisted and turned in the icy waters of the Thames until it was discovered by the night watchman of Dackson's Wharf. Alive, and moving among the inhabitants of the small world-within-a-world which is London's dockland, the man had been many things to different people: a rival, a lover, a son, and a potential partner. Dead, his frozen corpse with a knife in its neck was a menace to everyone who had known him.

Eric Burgess, whose *Divided We Fall* intrigued and entertained a big public, has drawn on his own firsthand and intimate knowledge of the docks and its people whose lives are bound up in them, to write a crime novel which in background, characters and plot is a worthy successor to his earlier book and an enthralling story.

## BURTON, MILES

(*see also* **Rhode, John**)

### *Beware Your Neighbour*

June 1951

Murderers are not in the habit of advertising their intentions in advance, but the outbreak of anonymous letters in the little country district of Hallows Green seemed to warn the inhabitants that a killer was about to strike. There were only ten houses in Hallows Green, but each save two had received a mysterious communication. All were anonymous and difficult to trace, but all bore the same message – that Death was on its way. Into this atmosphere of mutual suspicion and mistrust comes Desmond Merrion, followed closely by Inspector Arnold of Scotland Yard – good friends among bad neighbours.

### *Bones in the Brickfield*

June 1958

If the peaceful villagers of Downfold were shocked when the body of that quiet widower, Mr. Reeve, was found in the old brickfield, they were horrified when the coroner's jury brought in a verdict of murder.

When Inspector Arnold and his friend Merrion started to investigate, a number of happenings were recalled which had passed unremarked at the time; but then the excavation of a bone from a prehistoric monster, just where Mr. Reeve's body had been found, created such an excitement in the village that people almost forgot about the tragedy.

But not for long. After the bone had come to light a sinister and deadly chain of events began, which presented Arnold and Merrion with as difficult a case as they have ever tackled.

Miles Burton gives his many admirers an ingenious and fascinating story which will keep them guessing to the last pages.

### *Cat Jumps, The*

February 1946

Sergeant Neatshead of the Aldershire Constabulary, stationed at the little village of Oswaldby, had been having rather a worrying week. As a rule crime in his province was limited to cyclists riding without lights after lighting-up time and an occasional family squabble. But during the previous week-end an unusual incident had occurred and seemed likely to remain unexplained. Farmer Britton of Gables Farm had turned his three horses out into a meadow some distance from the farmhouse. On the Sunday morning his waggoner had found a horse lying on the ground with a knife driven up to the hilt in its body. The knife was of curious make; the blade, a strip of steel, had been brazed into a massive and heavy handle of polished brass on which had been stamped irregularly the letters MORT. The horse had recovered from its wound, but the incident was puzzling. And worse is to follow, for on the following Saturday the Hon. Mrs. Gwendolyn Cottington, a wealthy widow of sixty-five, is found dead in her own dining-room at the Vintage, stabbed in the same manner and with a similar knife. Inspector Arnold and his friend Desmond Merrion take a hand in the case, but it is through a clue provided by that very fine and feline character Belisarius that at last they get on the right track.

### *Charabanc Mystery, The*

March 1934

Mr. Miles Burton finds his mysteries in quiet country places. His characters are the rustic types that congregate in village tap-rooms to discuss the vagaries of the weather and the price of beer and to exhibit their powers at the truly national game of darts. But even in such a community, as readers of newspapers well know, murder may rear its ugly head. So it happened that the little village of Wroughton in Brookshire found itself in the news, and the flaming headlines of The Charabanc Mystery told the world of the strange death of a rustic found dead in a charabanc returning from a village outing. The story, for all its simplicity of setting, provides a particularly ingenious problem.

### *Chinese Puzzle, The*

April 1957

In Miles Burton's new detective story a Chinaman is arrested for an attack on a fellow-countryman in a sleezy [sic] lodging-house in West London, and the police soon learn that the assailant has been trying to cash a Savings Bank account deposited in the name of Ah Lock. Their interest is intensified when the body of Ah Lock is found murdered in a seaport town where there is a colony of inscrutable, opium-smoking Chinese. Their investigations are pursued with the relentless precision which this author knows so well how to describe, and in due course they are satisfied that they can name the murderer. So far as they are concerned the case is closed. But for Desmond Merrion, whom they have invited to assist them, the case is not to be so easily disposed of. His knowledge of the Chinese mind leads him to feel doubts which for a long time he cannot persuade the police to share. He quietly follows his own line of reasoning, and comes at last to a dramatic and surprising conclusion.

Miles Burton has told an exciting tale of oriental ingenuity and revenge.

### Crime in Time, A
October 1955
Sir Phineas Bransdale was that extraordinary being, an inventor who had made money: and it was his money that killed him. If he had not had a penny to bless himself with he would never have met with that fatal injury from a blow on the head with an iron bar. The broad motives for the crime seemed evident from the first; it was the question of who had the opportunity and, more important, the *time*, that was to vex the minds of Inspector Arnold of Scotland Yard and his talented friend Desmond Merrion. 'Time is of the essence' – and never is the phrase proved more a truism than in this ingenious detective story, where a sense of timing, and a meticulous regard for time itself, play such important parts.

### Dead Stop
March 1943
Captain Desmond Merrion R. N., goes to the little village of Brightwood for a secret interview with Wilfred Louth, a scientist who has made a discovery which may be of great importance in the successful prosecution of the war. Mr. Louth demonstrates the invention to Merrion, who promises to arrange for a more elaborate demonstration before Admiralty experts. Soon after, Louth is killed by a mysterious explosion in his laboratory. Merrion joins forces with Inspector Arnold in investigating the explosion, which has certain odd factors. In *Dead Stop* Miles Burton has given us one of his finest stories, a mystery that certainly succeeds in mystifying.

### Death at Low Tide
February 1938
The old ferryman had caught many strange fish in his time, but none so strange as the body he fished out of the harbour one summer evening as the tide was on the turn. To his horror he saw at once that it was Captain Stanlake, the local harbour-master. In the few months that Captain Stanlake had been harbour-master at Brenthithe he had made himself a confounded nuisance to every one. That was perhaps not his fault, but was mainly due to his keen desire to make Brenthithe an industrial port rather than a seaside resort. He had made many enemies in this local feud, but would any one go as far as murder – for foul play it certainly was. *Death at Low Tide* is an enthralling mystery with an attractive setting and an absorbing plot.

### Death at the Club
February 1937
The distinguished members of the Witchcraft Club were greatly concerned when the secretary, Mr. Brockman, failed to arrive for the usual first-Friday-in-the-month meeting. So unusual were the circumstances that the Assistant Commissioner of Police (one of the Witchcraft Club's thirteen members) went into an adjoining room to telephone Scotland Yard. In doing so his foot struck some soft but unyielding object – the body of Mr. Brockman. This must indeed have been Inspector Arnold's most embarrassing case, for even his chief, the Assistant Commissioner, was not above suspicion. If it hadn't been for Desmond Merrion (who is no respecter of persons when it comes to crime) perhaps the mystery would never have been solved. Once again Mr. Burton gives his readers an unusual and interesting problem.

### Death at the Cross-Roads
November 1933
A collision occurs at Five Mile Cross, near Dormington, in the middle of a dark December night. Oscar Stalliford, the driver of one of the cars involved, is found dead, but there is no trace of the occupants of the second car, which belongs to a prominent citizen of Dormington, and has apparently been stolen from a parking-place that evening. Stalliford's death brings to light his discreditable past, and it is found that several persons are relieved at his disappearance from the scene. Some days later Stalliford's son is shot under mysterious circumstances. Inspector Arnold is summoned to Dormington, and with the assistance of his friend Desmond Merrion is enabled to unravel the double mystery.

### Death in a Duffle Coat
September 1956
Two old ladies, Miss Price and Miss Marsland, lived together in the Lodge Cottage. Old Miss Price's death looked like a tragic accident: she must have slipped and fallen in the icy yard of the cottage when, wearing a duffle coat against the cold, she went to fetch a bucket of coal. But it transpired that Miss Price had been murdered. Indeed, the cottage was empty, for Miss Marsland too had mysteriously disappeared, though in her case no body was found…Desmond Merrion and Inspector Arnold soon find themselves in a case of great complexity. There are more murders and discoveries, inexplicable and macabre. Merrion slowly moves towards a solution, impeded and baffled, as we believe the reader will be too, by the prevalent fashion for wearing duffle coats. Miles Burton has excelled himself in this most ingenious and exciting detective story.

### Death in Shallow Water
March 1948
Three deaths by drowning within the space of a few weeks in one small English parish where nothing untoward has happened for many years are bound to set tongues wagging. One drowned body *could* have been an accident; two drowned bodies *might* have been coincidence; but when it came to a third corpse found in shallow water, even the cautious village policeman began to think it was a bit of a rum go. Soon the experts are called in, and we meet again Inspector Arnold of Scotland Yard, and, inevitably, Desmond Merrion, his complement and friend in an investigation that gets 'curiouser and curiouser' as accident begins to look more and more like Murder.

### Death in the Tunnel
January 1936
The train in which Sir Wilfred Saxonby was travelling had slowed down in Blackdown Tunnel, but gathered speed again as the red signal light changed to green. In that brief interval, however, Sir Wilfred had been done to death – a mystery that presented Inspector Arnold and his friend Desmond Merrion with their most baffling case. *Death in the Tunnel* has a most ingenious plot and provides a glorious treat of thrills.

### Death Leaves No Card
February 1939
When Death pays a call he generally leaves a card behind…even if it sometimes takes a pathologist to find it. But on the morning that he visited the bathroom at Forstal Farm, he did it incognito. It took a man with a crowbar to break down the bathroom door, and there, on the floor, was Basil Maplewood, naked, with one foot still hanging over the edge of the bath. Basil was only twenty-one, and in the very pink of health, but the post-mortem didn't help much… no violence, no sign of poison. Here is a mystery in a thousand, and one that almost – but not quite – threw dust in the eyes of Inspector Arnold and his colleagues.

### Death of Mr. Gantley
February 1932
Mr. Gantley, owner of the Downhamshire Courier, is found dead in his car one Monday morning not far from his native town of Carnford. He had been shot through the head. Lady Gantley, Gantley's sister-in-law, had died suddenly from a heart attack on the Saturday evening, and from her will it appeared that in the event of her death preceding that of Gantley, her fortune shall go to her niece and nephew, Charles and Myrtle Harrington. If Gantley died first, then her fortune should go to her companion, Sylvia Chadwick, and her brother Percy. Both Inspector Driffield, who is a local man, and Inspector Arnold of Scotland Yard are baffled by the crime. A lucky meeting with Desmond Merrion brings that skilled investigator into the case, to which he eventually succeeds in supplying a brilliant and surprising solution.

### Death of Two Brothers
May 1941
Miss Baydon, as one of her nephews was fond of saying, was as hard as nails – a believer in plenty of exercise, which she obtained by going for long walks. The village of Lillingford seemed to her an ideal holiday centre for this purpose. On the second day of her stay there Miss Baydon was exploring the country lanes and bridle paths. It was then that she made her startling discovery. Although never before had Miss Baydon come upon a dead man lying at the bottom of a chalk pit, her habitual restraint did not fail her. She did most of the right things, with the result that Inspector Arnold of Scotland Yard was handed a first-class mystery to solve. Mr. Miles Burton's story has an attractive country setting, a war-time village, complete with Home Guard, wardens and special constabulary.

### Death Paints a Picture
November 1960
After the corpse of George Hawken had been found on the rocks near his Cornish home the coroner's jury brought in an open verdict. Hawken had been a respected but financially unsuccessful artist whose death benefited no one except one of his nephews, who inherited a modest cottage. Yet that nephew had mysteriously disappeared. There was no doubt about the death of Hawken's brother, Sir Matthew, which followed not long afterwards: five grains of potassium cyanide had killed him instantly. Inspector Arnold and his friend Desmond Merrion were faced with a paradox: those who had had an opportunity to commit both crimes had no motive; no one with a motive had had the opportunity.

Once more Miles Burton has succeeded in posing an intriguing problem whose solution will keep his readers guessing until Arnold finally arrests the triple murderer.

### Death Takes a Detour
October 1958
Inspector Arnold and Desmond Merrion have tackled many curious and difficult cases in their time but never one which led them on a longer and more puzzling trail than the death of Donald Carswell. It began when a sudden summer flood swept down on Brensford and marooned visitors and inhabitants alike in the attics and top floors of their houses. Before the waters had gone down a killer had struck. It was the odd behaviour of so many of the suspects which first began to puzzle the man from the Yard and his friend. Each theory they tested seemed to point to a criminal activity – but none of them seemed to point to a murderer.

Arnold's steady determination and Merrion's fertile imagination make the two a formidable team. But in *Death Takes a Detour* they need to use all their ingenuity and resource to untangle an absorbing and complex case of the sort for which Miles Burton is famous.

### Death Takes a Flat
November 1940
When Major Pontefract retired from the Indian Army he dreamt of the blissful tranquillity of English country life, enjoyed wistful pipe dreams not perhaps of three acres and a cow but at any rate of one acre and a score or more of fine Buff Orpingtons. Mrs. Pontefract's thoughts, on the other hand, had run to a nice flat in town. 'Besides, dear, think how you'd enjoy being close to your club,' was the final argument that tipped the scale. And so the gallant major lost his last campaign, and exchanged hunting the wild boar from the tamer pursuit of flat hunting in Kensington. A suitably obsequious agent conducted him to his prize flat, to find to their horrified surprise that it already had a tenant, for Death had staked out a very definite claim – a prior claim to that very desirable flat. Mr. Miles Burton is to be congratulated on a splendidly told detective story.

### Death Takes the Living
January 1949
The Rev. Jonathan Denby, a young clergyman with influential connections but humble aspirations, secures the quiet country parish of Clynde as his first living. On the night of his arrival at the ramshackle old Rectory he mysteriously disappears. Scotland Yard is called in and Inspector Arnold has a thorny time, even though supported by his old friend Desmond Merrion, as he is constantly being worried by his superiors, who are in turn being pressed by the missing parson's relations. An ingenious how-who-and-why murder story, skilfully told by an expert.

### Devereux Court Mystery, The
March 1935
A police whistle re-echoed shrill and insistent through the night. There followed a tense silence, soon to be disturbed by the sound of scurrying foot-steps. A policeman swung his light over a huddled object lying in the shadow. It was the body of a man in evening dress. His opera hat had fallen off and lay ridiculously on the ground a few yards away. Still clutched in the man's right hand was a leather attaché case. And inside the case was a remarkably complete set of house-breaking implements. Inspector Arnold of Scotland Yard smiled grimly. The crime promised to be full of interest; but neither he nor his friend Desmond Merrion could quite foresee the amazing development of what was to prove one of the most extraordinary cases they had ever investigated.

### Devil's Reckoning
July 1948
It was the custom and time-honoured privilege of Mrs. Bale, a cottager in the remote English village of Dellmead, to decorate the church for Sunday worship. One Saturday afternoon when busying herself with her flowers and water-can she is shocked to see revealed by the mellow October sunshine the figure of a strange woman reclining on the slab of a canopied tomb where, according to tradition, had once laid a carved effigy. Boiling with indignation at this desecration, Mrs. Bale advances and shakes the recumbent figure, only to realise with horror that the woman is dead. But that is only the first of many tragic happenings in a case that runs curiously parallel to an old local legend;

a case that is to baffle even the brain of Desmond Merrion and sorely try the patience of the unimaginative Inspector Arnold before it reaches a satisfactory conclusion.

### Early Morning Murder
August 1945
Life in the sleepy village of Swinbury Mordayne was tranquil and undisturbed. Folk lived there only to provide epitaphs on their own grave stones, yet this was the place that the novelist Aylmer Flotman had decided to visit in order to seek inspiration for a book. As it happened something did happen, and it started with the death of Lord Barromer, squire of the village, while out riding. That mishap was followed rapidly by even more inexplicable events. In *Early Morning Murder* Miles Burton tells an excellent story of detection, featuring, of course, Desmond Merrion and Inspector Arnold.

### Fate at the Fair
February 1933
George's Fair, in the county town of Middleford … Brightly lit roundabouts grinding out a raucous tune … the shrill cries of cheap-jacks, the laughter of rustic maidens making merry carnival. And then a police whistle sounding loud and clear above the din. … Two Red Cross men elbowing their way through the crowd. In the midst of gaiety Death has struck mercilessly. Mr. Miles Burton has selected a novel setting for *Fate at the Fair*. One of his best stories.

### Found Drowned
March 1956
This skilful detective story is set in Greycliffe-on-Sea, a holiday resort in the north of England. Mr. Merrion revisits his old preparatory school in Greycliffe and while reminiscing with the headmaster recalls the school doctor of his own day, a Dr. Harpole – he learns that Harpole's two sons are still living in Greycliffe. Charles, the eldest, is a master at the school, but Arthur, his youngest brother, is a waster, always out of work. One morning Arthur is found drowned and investigation reveals all too many reasons why it should not have been an accident. A marriage, a legacy, old scores and new, provide a tangle of motives, for the police and Merrion to unravel. The seaside town is an effective background for Miles Burton's cunningly told novel.

### Four-Ply Yarn
February 1944
St. Orran Cove, five miles from Penmouth Harbour, had the reputation of being one of the quietest and most restful villages in the West Country. But that night when Valetta Hosking arrived on leave from the W.R.N.S. it was as eventful as a peace-time New Year's Eve in Piccadilly! It was Valetta who first discovered the body of Hella Gruber, the flighty wife of a Penmouth photographer, lying on Tregeagle's Bed, a flat, bracken-covered stone near her home; a sensation to be followed by the finding of a drowned body, later identified by the proprietor of the local inn as one of his late guests. The mystery of St. Orran's Cove is investigated by Inspector Arnold of Scotland Yard and his old friend Desmond Merrion, now head of a section of Naval Intelligence. *Four-Ply Yarn* is a particularly striking detective story in which the various strands are dexterously woven into a first-class yarn by the able hand of that ingenious storyteller, Mr. Miles Burton.

### Ground for Suspicion
February 1950
To give crime a rest was the good intention of Desmond Merrion when he took himself and

his wife for an early holiday to a quiet seaside resort. Before a few days had passed, however, three inexplicable deaths had occurred in Shellmouth. The last to die was the first to be proved beyond doubt the victim of murder, though Merrion had already had his suspicions about old Colonel Delabole and the wealthy Mrs. Worthing. The odd thing was that while each suspect might have had a good motive for murdering *one* person, the deaths of the other two were distinctly to his disadvantage, and it seemed unlikely that there were three murderers operating independently in so small a community. Scotland Yard is called in, and Inspector Arnold finds his old friend Merrion a great help.

### Hardway Diamonds Mystery, The
June 1930
On a night of fog Pussy Herridge stole the Hardway diamonds – and on the same night they were re-stolen. It was a grim trail that Dick Penhampton followed which led him to discover one of them on a dead man in the marshes. Who was the Funny Toff, the terror alike of police and criminals, the unknown man with such amazing resource and ingenuity, a devilish, perverted sense of humour, and a lunatic laugh that few heard twice? Death was the answer meted out to all who tried to solve the riddle – to all except Penhampton. Why was he spared so often by his unknown adversary in that ghastly game of cat-and-mouse played out in the dark? Was Inspector Pollard entirely deluded when he turned his attention to trailing the trailer? Or was Alison Weatherleigh's faith in her lover justified? In *The Hardway Diamonds Mystery* we get a story packed with legitimate thrills quick-moving and logical which proves yet again that ultimately the criminal *cannot* win against the law. Miles Burton is a Collins discovery and himself a man of mystery. *He knows what he is writing about!*

### Heir to Lucifer
February 1947
Desmond Merrion, late of Naval Intelligence, and his wife Mavis go to the little seaside town of Croylehaven to spend a holiday. The place is practically owned by the wealthy Croyle family, who live in the large, ugly Castle Croyle. The present head of the family, Lord Croyle, an old gentleman of eighty, generally known as Lucifer, is surrounded by a large number of more or less expectant heirs. It is peculiarly fitting, therefore, that Desmond Merrion, expert investigator, should be at hand when death enters the grim Victorian mansion and tragedy descends on the Croyle family.

### Heir to Murder
May 1953
The fishing port of Carmouth was a health resort on the South-West coast, but for two of the inhabitants at least it was to prove the opposite of healthy. First Dr. Murford, then his partner, Nurse Penruddock, fall victims to fatal accidents of a highly suspicious nature. Desmond Merrion, who has brought his wife Mavis to Carmouth for a rest cure, has ample time and more than enough inclination to interest himself in the double tragedy. It becomes increasingly obvious that if it was murder no stranger to Carmouth could have possessed the necessary local knowledge that could give the deaths the aspect of accident. With Inspector Arnold of Scotland Yard to put a rein on his fertile imagination, and to keep a watchful eye on his sometimes unorthodox methods, Merrion succeeds not only in solving a tricky puzzle but in preventing further murders.

### Legacy of Death
June 1960
It was not often that anything disturbed the quiet routine of Forest House Nursing Home. But the morning of the sixth of July found the coroner holding an inquest in the dining-room on the late Mary Grace Tarrant, a widow, aged sixty-three. Verdict: Accidental death caused by an overdose of drugs taken by mistake. Mary Tarrant was a rich woman when she died but her will came as a rude shock to her son and his feckless wife. Her entire fortune, some one hundred thousand pounds, was left to the mild and kindly Henry Corfe, her greatest friend at the Nursing Home, who overnight found himself a wealthy man. But death came again to Forest House in a more violent form and in circumstances which made the local police call in Scotland Yard. Inspector Arnold and his friend Desmond Merrion faced a tough problem. Was the second death murder? If it was then could there be a connection between the two tragedies? Miles Burton has once again given his multitude of readers a typical and satisfying story full of mystery and suspense.

### Look Alive
July 1949
It was a lovely hot summer afternoon and old Mrs. Lavant had retired as usual to the hammock in her garden for her customary after-luncheon nap. There her great niece Annabel finds her when she calls with a friend David Wiston, but to her horror the old lady appears to be dead, a fact which David, a budding doctor, duly confirms. Yet within an hour the corpse is sitting up and taking notice! When is a corpse not a corpse? That is the question for you to answer, with the accomplished assistance of Inspector Arnold of Scotland Yard and his friend Desmond Merrion.

### Menace on the Downs, The
July 1931
Mr. Miles Burton, as readers of his previous stories, *The Secret of High Eldersham* and *The Three Crimes*, know, prefers a quiet country village as the setting for his thrilling mysteries. In *The Menace on the Downs* Mr. Burton describes anther village tragedy. Sydney Harper, the errand boy at the village store, is found dead by the roadside with his throat cut. The local police are unable to decide whether it is a case of accident, suicide, or murder. A broken bottle covered with blood, found on the spot, points to either of the former. The absence of the boy's bicycle points to murder. The case is further complicated when, six months later, a second boy is found murdered on the railway line. Mr. Burton arrives at a solution with his customary skill, and his readers will agree that this is one of the most satisfying mysteries that the author has yet written.

### Milk-Churn Murder, The
October 1935
The little village of Tolsham was surprised one day by a most extraordinary looking stranger. Clearly a foreigner, he had a full black beard, wore the oddest of old clothes, and from his mouth protruded a large cigar. 'Must be one of them Bolsheviks,' remarked the villagers, and left it at that. But with the stranger's disappearance came the discovery of a dismembered corpse in the milk-churn of a local dairy. Had the mysterious 'foreigner' anything to do with the crime? Inspector Arnold of the Yard and his friend Desmond Merrion think so at any rate. Soon they are up to their necks in the most baffling case of the century, a mystery that is remarkable for its intricacy and really clever detection.

### Moth-Watch Murder, The
October 1957
When a party of schoolboys assembles for a moth-watching party, the occasion turns out to be fatal not only to the moths. What is the explanation of the ruthless and deliberate killing of a normal, cheerful schoolboy whom everyone liked? Inspector Ferriby realises that in this unusual puzzle he will need the help of Scotland Yard and he is additionally pleased when Desmond Merrion turns up to assist in the investigation. Before long the police find themselves with a further mystery on their hands, when the body of a woman is found floating in the river. All the clues in the possession of the police only seem to deepen the mystery. The investigation is about to be abandoned when a third death, more dramatic and startling even than the others, opens the way to a surprising solution.

No writer can weave a mystery more neatly than Miles Burton, and only a reader with an unusually keen eye for the hidden clues will succeed in unravelling this one before the author is ready with the exciting revelations that fit everything into its appropriate place. Mr. Burton's ingenuity is as subtle and satisfying as ever.

### Mr Babbacombe Dies
June 1939
When Mr. Babbacombe, having made his pile, retired, it was unfortunate that his quiet bachelor existence should be marred by attacks of gastritis. It was fortunate that before succumbing to a particularly bad attack, he expressed a wish to be cremated. The stringent formalities necessary for cremation require the calling in of another doctor, who in this case happened to be a police surgeon. He suspected arsenic, and Inspector Arnold of Scotland Yard is summoned. *Mr. Babbacombe Dies* is a very ingenious mystery, which is solved by the admirable use of sheer common sense.

### Mr. Westerby Missing
July 1940
Mr. Westerby was keen on birds – sparrows and that sort of thing; he was, in fact, an inoffensive ornithologist and the last man in the world to have been involved in a mystery. For mystery certainly surrounded his disappearance at ten o'clock on a November evening with a considerable sum of money in his possession. Inspector Arnold found it a puzzling case. A straightforward murder was all right. But the case of Mr. Westerby was different. He might have been murdered; he might have met with an accident; he might have committed suicide; or he might be still alive. And so, without clues, Arnold gets to work on this amazing case.

### Murder at the Moorings
July 1932
Huddled on the carpet of the dining-room at 'The Moorings' lay the body of old Mr. Gregory. There was no sign of foul play, no trace of blood – just a tiny cut on the dead man's cheek. In the recess of the bow-window an old-fashioned sporting gun was found, one barrel recently discharged. Superintendent Yardley and Inspector Caldwell hold entirely different theories regarding the problem. You, the reader will of course form your own opinion. You are assured, in any case, of a mystery of sterling worth, a mystery of the excellent quality that one naturally associates with the name of Miles Burton.

### Murder in Absence
February 1954
First, there was a murder in Hembury in the Home Counties, then Desmond and Mavis

Merrion went on a cruise – two events with no apparent connection between them. But as the freighter *Ballerina*, with her small complement of passengers, steams between the ports of the Eastern Mediterranean, Beirut, Famagusta, Istanbul, and then remote Fetiyeh, it becomes clear that Merrion is once more faced with mystery. Tensions rise aboard the *Ballerina* as the odious Mr. Wilberton takes increasingly to drink, the sprightly Mr. Pulham to women, and Mrs. Stewart-Patterson, the formidable Scotswoman, resolutely continues her sketching, once again Merrion solves a multiple crime in a story of extraordinary ingenuity and suspense.

### Murder in Crown Passage
September 1937

It was a great shock for poor Mrs. Binsted when she stumbled over the dead body of her lodger. The word 'murder' ran through the little town of Faston Bishop and very soon a crowd collected at the end of the 'haunted' Crown Passage. How the dead man had been murdered was obvious, but why he had been murdered was quite another matter. Inspector Arnold was on the case, and Desmond Merrion was also very interested in it. Mr. Burton draws a vivid pen picture of country-town life, and his characters are all true to type. *Murder in Crown Passage* is one of the most skilful mystery stories that this admirable writer has given us.

### Murder in the Coalhole
January 1940

When Mr. Polesworth, the unpleasantly efficient school manager, was found dead in a gas-filled coalhole, Inspector Arnold was convinced that the explanation was a practical joke gone wrong. But the nimble mind of Desmond Merrion soon proves that this simple theory is not the correct one, and from the slenderest clues he relentlessly builds up a case that sends a very clever murderer to the gallows. Miles Burton is recognised as one of our most ingenious writers of detective stories, and in *Murder in the Coalhole* he gives us one of his best stories.

### Murder M. D.
August 1943

When the village doctor at Exton Forcett went off to the war his place was taken by Dr. Wiegler, an Austrian, and certainly a most skilful doctor, but unfortunately lacking in that very considerable asset – a good bedside manner. The *locum tenens* wasn't exactly popular in the village. There was even talk that he might be a spy of sorts. Such were the prejudices, but none in their wildest surmises could anticipate the strange drama that was to be enacted in their village, or the sensation that the sudden appearance of C. I. D. men was to cause.

### Murder of a Chemist
March 1936

Mr. Josiah Elvidge, by profession a chemist, in his spare time a member of the Downchester Bowling Association and by local repute an annoying man, reached for his lemonade. He drank, gulped, twitched and a moment later lay crumpled up in his chair, the victim of a deadly poison. A worried hotel manager hastily summoned Inspector Arnold of the Yard, who was partaking of an excellent lunch in the dining-room. Arnold, at first annoyed at being disturbed, soon found the extreme interest in the case arousing in him all his powers of observation. Was it Murder or Suicide? Why were crystals of the poison found in so many unlikely places? Which of the members of the ridiculous Bowling Club would it be possible to suspect? Arnold's

old friend, Desmond Merrion, arrives opportunely on the scene, and together they come to a conclusion both startling and complex. Mr. Burton goes to the country for his stories. And finds there, amid the quiet serenity of ancient hamlets and market towns, astounding mysteries, violent passions and calculated enmities.

### Murder on Duty
May 1952

Martyr's Mount, a rocky little island just off the harbour bar at Welmouth, was owned by Carlotta Castlehill, widow of a rich financier. Carlotta had at one time been on the stage and was still, in her fifties, a colourful personality. Found drowned near her house on the island, the manner of her passing was as sensational as any of her theatrical triumphs while alive, for her death had been violent. It was a case for Inspector Arnold and his friend Desmond Merrion, and between the two an amazing plot is revealed.

### Murder Out of School
November 1951

The first Sunday of term at Castle Court, a preparatory school for boys, began as every other Sunday – breakfast, then free time for the boys until half-past ten, when they were due to assemble for the mile-long walk to church at the small town of Roserhaven nearby. But this particular Sunday was to be talked about for many years to come, for on that memorable morning one of the boys discovered the body of a man lying in a disused trench in the school grounds. The stranger, who had been battered to death, is identified as a guest at a party given the night before by the new headmaster and his wife. The reason for his murder will puzzle the reader as much as it puzzles those well-known partners in crime detection, Desmond Merrion and Inspector Arnold of Scotland Yard.

### Murder Unrecognised
February 1955

Twice running the coroner said 'Accidental Death'. Each death had been caused by a hand grenade apparently left lying about by the military. Desmond Merrion, holidaying with his wife, Mavis, at a nearby seaside town, had his own doubts about the accidents on the remote heights of Westonbury and Sheepe Cliffe. But it is one thing to suspect foul play and quite another to discover a motive. What was the truth about farmer Joe Ling and his racehorses? And for whom was the first grenade really meant? Before the truth was pieced together poor Superintendent Flixworth found himself sweating up and down the steep hillsides; and Merrion, who was as partial to walking as detection, had plenty of exercise. Miles Burton again offers his readers a fascinating jigsaw which looks as though it will never come out, but into which everything fits smoothly and satisfactorily at the end. From first to last, their curiosity will never be allowed to slacken – and even Merrion finds more excitement than he bargained for.

### Not a Leg to Stand on
January 1945

If Mr. Methwold had been the sort of man given to flights of fancy Superintendent Guntly would have been inclined to dismiss his story as fantastic. But Mr. Methwold enjoyed a sober, well-earned reputation as a solicitor in the little market town of Raynethorpe and when he claimed that his young friend and client Edmund Coulston, had disappeared after telling Mr. Methwold that he was afraid of being robbed, the Superintendent is obliged to take action.

Edmund Coulston had been staying with Mr. Methwold for a few days before sailing for America, and Mr. Methwold had last seen him the evening before he had reported his disappearance to the police, when he left him at the gates of Orinoco, a neighbours house. And there, just inside the gates, the Superintendent finds sufficient evidence to justify calling in the Yard. Inspector Arnold, accompanied by his friend Desmond Merrion, comes down to take charge, and an excellent job they make of it.

### Platinum Cat, The
July 1938

The Reverend Peter Bordesley, Rector of Pascombe, had found in the study of astronomy not only an entrancing hobby but a relief from the torture of insomnia. What more natural for a clergyman than to turn his gaze heavenwards and survey the spacious firmament on high. And so it came to pass on a certain November night, when most people were sound asleep, the Rector noticed a cottage on fire and gave the alarm. When the flames were subdued, a startling discovery was made. The charred body of a man lay in the debris. Near the body were found a pair of gold cuff-links and a small piece of platinum bearing the figure of a cat. Slender clues indeed, but sufficient to start Inspector Arnold on a trail of brilliant investigation.

### Return from the Dead
June 1959

'A clear case of murder,' said the police surgeon. Beatrice Datchet had been stabbed, her body lay huddled on the office floor in a pool of blood. Inspector Arnold could find no trace of a weapon nor uncover any motive for her death. But when, not long afterwards the faceless corpse of a man was found in the country village which had been the girl's home Arnold and his friend Desmond Merrion began to realise that the two deaths might not only be linked but could both be strangely related to a mystery of twenty years ago: the fate of a famous explorer who had failed to return from an expedition to South America.

*Return from the Dead* ranges from sudden death in the present to distant places far in the past and confronts Arnold and Merrion with another baffling case. Miles Burton's many readers have here one of this popular author's most entertaining and intriguing stories.

### Secret of High Eldersham, The
December 1930

Constable Viney of High Eldersham in East Anglia was cycling home on the last night of March. He stopped at the Rose and Crown inn for a chat with Whitehead, the landlord, and found the latter a blood-soaked corpse. Detective Inspector Young was sent from Scotland Yard to help the local police. He soon realised the queerness of East Anglian folk in general and those of High Eldersham in particular. It was Viney who told him "Strangers don't never prosper in High Eldersham" and Whitehead had been a "stranger." Desmond Merrion, a rich bachelor, comes to be Young's unofficial assistant. In the cottage of Mrs. Portch he finds – a *mommet*! And this tells him that High Eldersham is a place of hateful mysteries. The gentry and peasantry of the place are all involved. Sir William and Mavis Overton, Doctor Padfield, Laurence Hollesley – what parts can these possibly have played in the murder of a publican? People who read of the old witch-trials would be horrified to come upon the witch-cult persisting in modern England. But there are queer survivals of ancient rites in rural

England, and there is not a little foundation in fact for the sinister Secret of High Eldersham which Merrion tracked down to the altar on the island.

### Situation Vacant
July 1946

Mr. Green was seriously put out. His daughter Iris had left home at half-past four to fetch her handbag, which she had left at Mrs. Whyttington's where she did part-time secretarial work, and here it was past six and she had not yet returned. Who was to get his tea he'd like to know. But Iris would never get him a meal again, nor give reluctant help again behind the counter in her father's chemist's shop, for Iris was dead. Her body is found the next day floating in a sluice not far from her employer's house. It seems that in the October dusk she must have lost her footing on the narrow planking which bridged the sluice and 'accidental death' is the official verdict at the inquest. But when three months later Iris's successor as secretary to Mrs. Whyttington is found dead in most suspicious circumstances, and once again the situation becomes vacant, things begin to take on rather a different complexion and Scotland Yard is called in. It needs all Inspector Arnold's talent for patient, plodding inquiry, assisted by the lively imagination and brilliant powers of deduction of his friend Desmond Merrion to solve a mystery that must be surely one of the most ingenious that Miles Burton has ever evolved for our entertainment.

### Smell of Smoke, A
November 1959

When the body of Horace Ingrave was taken from the stream at Moat House no one in Lamsford was very disturbed – except Matthew Calder, who had been in the vicinity when the ne'er-do-well had drowned. He had been aware of a strange smell of smoke, and it was this one fact that roused his suspicions about his nephew and heir, Philip [should be Ronald]. But even when Matthew realised that the younger man might have a motive for Ingrave's death, he kept silent.

A second violent death in the village was clearly a case of murder, and it brought Inspector Arnold and Desmond Merrion on to the scene to unravel a case which the silence of Matthew Calder was to become a vital factor in the fate of the suspects whose lives and happiness were in jeopardy.

*A Smell of Smoke* fully maintains the qualities of suspense and ingenuity for which Miles Burton is so widely popular.

### Something to Hide
January 1953

The White House was more than a home for convalescents, it was a home of mysteries. Everyone, it seemed, had something to hide. Why, for instance, did the Jurbys keep it going when it obviously did not pay? Why was Mr. Foster so shy of strangers? Was Anastasia Penkevil really the victim of secret poison administered by her relatives? And why was George Yarpole so interested in the accident Roy Dysart had met with on Colonel Granby's boat, hinting mysteriously that it was not genuine? All these secrets become the business – and the headache – of the police when Freda Malin, a young maid-of-all-work at the home, is found murdered. As Inspector Arnold of Scotland Yard says to his friend Desmond Merrion, 'In trying to follow one crime, we're perpetually being side-tracked by half a dozen others!' This is a particularly ingenious detective story, skilfully narrated.

### *This Undesirable Residence*
May 1942
Ash House stood empty and deserted just off the main road between the small country town of Wraynesford and the village of Betherston, an attractive looking house that certainly ought to have appealed to anyone seeking a desirable country residence. But for over a year Ash House had for some inexplicable reason sought a tenant in vain. And then one morning the gardener was surprised to see a car drawn up at the door and went to welcome the visitor. But the contents of the car provided him with a disagreeable shock. The occupant was dead. And so began the tremendous hue and cry which was to engage the attention of Inspector Arnold for many days.

### *Three Corpse Trick, The*
August 1944
On the afternoon of Wednesday, June 197th, Wendy Burge takes the bus from the county town of Deaning in Deanshire to the outlying village of Goose Common, where until recently she lived with her husband Peter, to make her usual collection for the Deanshire County Hospital. From this journey she never returns. Her body is found the next day floating in the River Lure by a market-gardener of the name of Ezra Robbins. The local police call in the Yard, and Inspector Arnold, accompanied by his friend Desmond Merrion, go down to investigate. *The Three Corpse Trick* is a first-rate detective story with a really mystifying plot, some excellent character studies and a highly satisfying solution.

### *Three Crimes, The*
March 1931
Here we have Miles Burton at his best. For sheer ingenuity, *The Three Crimes* would be hard to beat. And it is all so appallingly possible! Murderers are generally traced by motives and by previous association with their victims. But here is a story of cold-blooded, subtle, carefully-planned crimes executed in the most business-like manner by those whose profession was – murder! Detective-Inspector Young is detailed to investigate the mysterious death of the not very popular Sir Charles Formby in the cross-channel steamer *Isle of Sheppey*. He is helped by his old friend Merrion and by his new friends, May and Frederick Brunton, the charming brother and sister who run the antique shop called Vallingfields. With Formby's death still unsolved, Young is switched on to the strange disappearance of the rather unprepossessing Mr. Pilkington, and finds that a lady of title is discreditably involved. Pilkington reappears – not to the best advantage – and Merrion promptly disappears. Squinter Garway bears unwilling witness in the matter of the attempted murder of the distinctly unloveable Mr. Fortescue. Young discovers Merrion, and for reason of his own, retires from his profession.

### *To Catch a Thief*
September 1934
Excellent detective work on the part of Inspector Arnold and Desmond Merrion is the outstanding feature of this first-rate story. The plot centres round what at first seems an obvious case of suicide, a man dead in a chair with the room full of gas – but a post-mortem proves that death was due to an injection of strychnine. The police discover that a jewel robbery has been carried out at Lord Lutterworth's house where Pewlett, the dead man, had been formerly employed as butler. Could there be any connection between the two crimes? And if so, what motive could have instigated the murder of Pewlett? The detectives eventually solve the mystery by putting to the test the old adage: 'Set a thief to catch a thief'.

### *Tragedy at the Thirteenth Hole*
May 1933
Mr. Burnside, a wealthy manufacturer, was playing a round of golf with his nephew on the links at Heavenbeach. He played the approach to the thirteenth, then walked with his caddie towards the green. He disappeared into the dip in which the hole lay. A few moments later he fell dead, struck on the temple with a golf ball. Well, accidents, of course, will happen on even the best regulated golf courses, but...Inspector Arnold had chosen Heavenbeach as a suitable spot for a quiet holiday and he was mildly puzzled by the apparently insignificant fact that *three golf balls were found on the green*. The Inspector invites his old friend, Desmond Merrion, to join him and together they investigate the *Tragedy at the Thirteenth Hole*, which is certainly one of the most ingenious problems that the fertile imagination of Mr. Miles Burton has devised.

### *Unwanted Corpse, The*
August 1954
How to dispose of the corpse? In Miles Burton's new story the corpse of a young woman, shot through the head, turns up in a place where no corpse could possibly be. And the series of crimes, from jewel-robberies to car-thefts, into which Inspector Arnold and Desmond Merrion are plunged once they start their enquiries, become more and more baffling as time goes on. A deserted railway line from which weird shrieks have been heard at night, and which is thought to be haunted, adds to their bewilderment. Theories begin to form at last, Merion's appearing wilder even than Arnold's until the truth is at last revealed in a very surprising denouement. Miles Burton has written one more gripping story which will carry the reader along all the more happily because he knows all the mysterious events related will in the end will be ingeniously and convincingly accounted for.

### *Up the Garden Path*
October 1941
In the blackout of a January night in the little village of Downspring the body of a man is found on the garden path of 3 Woodland Villas, home of the village police sergeant. Later, the body is identified as Philip Noakes, the butler at Valley View, a large mansion in the neighbourhood. It is a prelude to a magnificent tale of crime, secret service and espionage in which Desmond Merrion, now of the Admiralty Intelligence, plays a prominent part. Mr. Miles Burton has never written a more exciting story.

### *Village Afraid, A*
January 1951
Five men were gathered together one August evening in the bar of an old coaching inn, The Swan, in the little village of Michelgreen. They were representative of any small country community in England; a farmer, a doctor, a retired colonel, a prosperous business man, and an old sea captain. It was an ordinary enough occasion, a quick drink after the council meeting, but it was the prelude to strange happenings in Michelgreen. On that very night one of the five was to die mysteriously, and later another became the victim of a curious accident. Inspector Arnold of Scotland Yard and Desmond Merrion, his friend, find a village afraid when they come at the request of the local police to investigate the untimely end of a leading citizen.

### *Where is Barbara Prentice?*
October 1936
The *CRIME CLUB* wishes to draw the attention of all detective 'fans' to the brilliance of Miles Burton's new story.

Detective-story connoisseurs have had their eyes on Miles Burton for several years, during which time he has been steadily building up a reputation as one of the best writers of the Freeman Wills Crofts school. Now in *Where Is Barbara Prentice?* he has given us that little extra 'something' which justifies The Crime Club Panel in making it a 'Selection'. It is a book that no serious detective-story reader can afford to miss.

OR

'I'm going out', Barbara Prentice had informed her cook, Mrs. Chester, 'and I might not be back tonight. If the doctor asks any questions, tell him I've gone to London.' And from that evening Mrs. Prentice was not seen or heard of again. Part of her fur coat had been found on the buffer of an engine and from time to time other of her belongings came to light, but where was Mrs. Prentice herself? Was she dead? If so, where was the body? Was she hiding? If so, for what reason? Had she been kidnapped? What were the circumstances? These weighty problems confronted Superintendent Rowley, Inspector Arnold and his friend Desmond Merrion. Not an easy job investigating a disappearance in a small provincial town – people did gossip so. But the problem of Mrs. Prentice was eventually solved and it turned out the most puzzling mystery they had ever had to tackle.

### *Will in the Way, A*
October 1947
It was Esther Kesgrave, maid in the service of the Botesdale family for many years, who found the second Mrs. Botesdale lying dead at the foot of the basement stairs. She made the discovery on her return from a visit to her master, the dead woman's husband, who was a certified lunatic confined in a mental home. The tragedy seems to have been accidental, but as the lady was alone when she fell police investigations and an inquest are inevitable and Inspector Arnold of Scotland Yard is called in. The Inspector's keen eye for detail soon picks out some interesting and highly suspicious facts connected with a tea-caddy and the incalculable lack of fingerprints on the china set out on a tea-tray. Ably aided and abetted by his old friend Desmond, Inspector Arnold is soon immersed in as baffling a murder case as any in his career.

## BUSBY, ROGER
### *Crackshot*
September 1990
Detective Vince Walker of Manhattan's Midtown South Precinct and Sergeant Tony Rowley from Scotland Yard, in New York on a manhunt mission, are two tough street cops fighting crime in the sewers of their respective cities.

Then the villain known as the Brown Bag Bandit robs a Broadway bank and comes out shooting. The difference is that this time he's caught. Jubilation – until the two detectives find themselves trapped in a web of police politics and manipulated by government agencies on both sides of the Atlantic as they infiltrate the highest echelons of organized crime.

For back in Britain, Special Branch and M15 are on the trail of a shadowy assassin and when a multi-million drugs hi-jack ends in a siege inside London's most famous store and the SAS move in for the kill, nothing is really what it seems. Especially when Rowley and Walker decide to exchange frustration for action ...

Have the street cops finally beaten the system and turned the tables on their scheming chiefs? Can they get away with murder ... in the name of the law?

### *Deadlock*
June 1971
The girl's home was in a Midland city, but her body lay outside the city limits, in the territory of the county police. To find who had brutally raped and strangled her, the two forces were obliged to co-operate. And because the county police, unlike their city counterparts, felt the investigation was too big for them to handle, Detective-Sergeant Leric, who has already figured in Roger Busby's two previous crime novels, found himself collaborating with his opposite (and very different) number, Dave Kynacc from Scotland Yard.

Despite a number of leads and much hard-slogging police work, the murder enquiry bogged down. Even the Yard was forced to admit deadlock. Kynacc's chief prepared reluctantly to pull out.

Leric, for whom the case had meant big things personally as well as professionally, was bitterly frustrated, until an apparently routine safe-breaking job turned up. His trained mind noted certain anomalies and he set to work to unearth a vital clue.

As the police close in on their man, the action erupts with shocking and unexpected violence, precipitating a dramatic denouement to what is undoubtedly Roger Busby's best and most exciting book.

### *Frighteners, The*
August 1970
The underworld of a big Midland city is badly frightened. Tough as its members are, they are not tough enough to stand up to the agents of the big boys from 'the smoke', who are seeking to extend their field of operations – especially when those agents employ against them a silent, deadly weapon which can reduce a man's hand to nothing or leave his body one vast burn.

The police are keenly aware of the new and dangerous threat posed by the London gang. Under the leadership of the Assistant Chief Constable, co-ordination is established between the city and regional crime squads, which include several police characters who figured in Roger Busby's widely acclaimed previous novel, *Robbery Blue*. Bit by bit the police piece together the evidence and identify the secret weapon, but they lack the cogent proof that would stand up in court. The working together of the different branches of the police force, their rivalries, jealousies and ultimate dedication are as graphically portrayed as are the tactics of the local underworld, for once on the same side as the police.

The unexpected and ironical means by which the London gang are finally brought to a rough justice reveal Roger Busby's realistic appraisal of both underworld organizations and of the methods by which the police are occasionally forced to proceed.

### *Garvey's Code*
June 1978
At 38, Detective Mick Garvey was dogged by disaster: his police career damned by a sexual indiscretion; a job he didn't understand any more when computers took precedence over fundamental police work.

Then there was Frank Cooper, just out of uniform, still green and impressionable, to be taught the age-old skills of the detective, that sixth sense of intuition, to carry on the tradition before it was too late.

At times like this, Mick Garvey could have used a breathing-space, but then came the murder at Blackenstone, the bungled investigation and the savage killings which were to follow.

As the two detectives were drawn deeper into a web of police politics, intrigue and power struggles set against brutal crime in the wilds of Dartmoor, only Garvey's stubborn streak and acid wit saved them from being thrown to the wolves.

And in the final desperate moves with everything at stake, there was only one code to cling to – Garvey's code.

### *High Jump*
September 1992

The girl got out of the yellow sports Jag and walked towards the Arrow Bridge.

Walked straight into the messed-up lives of Bogan, the maverick street cop who bends the law to suit himself; Nigel, his new partner, an eager young graduate – and Vicky Rivers, a firebrand internal police investigator out to prove herself in a man's world.

As the girl climbs the bridge, a tense police drama unfolds. Can the officers involved come to terms with their own frailties as they race against time to unlock the mystery of the girl on the bridge and solve the hide-and-seek riddle of her disappearing Jaguar?

Or, on that fateful day when the city holds its breath, are they all for the high jump?

Roger Busby succeeds brilliantly in building the tension while revealing the multi-faceted nature of police work – and of policemen's lives.

### *Hunter, The*
September 1985

Teetering in his temporary rank, Crime Squad DI Tony Rowley gambles his Metropolitan Police career on a supergrass who alone can clinch a case against two of London's most vicious criminals.

But a brutal double killing on a desolate Cornish clifftop plunges Rowley into a riddle he knows he must solve if he is to survive.

Alone in an alien landscape, the London detective pits his wits against a cast-iron murder case in a race against time as the police hierarchy conspires to throw him to the wolves.

Caught in a maelstrom of fast cars, whirling helicopter rotors, greed, lust, and the cold silent world of the stars, Rowley finally uncovers the awful truth...too late. For already the hunter has become the hunted!

### *New Face in Hell*
January 1976

Roger Busby, whose half-dozen police procedurals set in a Midland city have won him high praise, sets his latest in the quiet countryside of Devon and Cornwall, where he claims that crime, when it occurs, is more violent.

It is certainly a scene of carnage which confronts the CID late at night in a local casino where three people have been gunned down, several others wounded, and an armed killer is on the run. The story is concentrated into the hours that follow as the killer twists and turns and kills again in his efforts to get away.

The action swings between the police cars on the trail of the killer, gathering evidence of his every move, and the sifting of that evidence at headquarters, piecing together its significance. Also playing a vital role in events are the characters of the senior police officers and their different approaches to the crime, seen for the most part through the eyes of DCI Quick, and a sergeant who has recently transferred from the Midlands and now finds crime as ugly in the sticks as ever it was in the smoke.

In a finale of great power when the killer is cornered, Quick and his sergeant have to decide whether to go it alone, regardless of risk, or whether to abide by orders whose purpose is showmanship.

Roger Busby has never portrayed so vividly the crises and split-second decisions which police officers are obliged to face in the course of their day-to-day duties – duties which may at any time put their lives at risk.

### *Pattern of Violence*
June 1973

Since the publication of his first crime novel, *Robbery Blue*, in 1969, Roger Busby has established himself as the foremost English exponent of the police procedural novel.

*Pattern of Violence*, like his previous books, is set in a Midlands city, and deals with one of the most urgent and frightening problems of our time: armed violence, whether on the part of organized gangs or psychopathic loners, and the pitting against it of unarmed police. [Flap only]

The series of forged cheques uttered in jewellers' shops by a young man and his girlfriend did not seem unduly dangerous. But when a clumsy police officer attempted to arrest the young man and he escaped, he turned out to be a violent psychopath, and one who was armed with a gun.

At the same time, Detective-Inspector Leric is tipped off that there is to be an armed raid on a branch bank in the suburbs. But which branch? One by one the possibilities are eliminated in a desperate race against time, yet with the constant nagging possibility that the whole set-up may be a hoax.

Then, as the two situations mesh, the whole city is brought to a standstill by violence. Before it ends, the conflicting attitudes to it within the police force have been dramatically illustrated, and one police officer has paid for them with his life.

### *Reasonable Man, A*
May 1972

*'Mr Busby always did tell a good story, but he is now beginning to do more than this ... The story-teller is becoming a novelist,'* said F. E. Pardoe, reviewing *Deadlock* in the *Birmingham Post*. This felicitous development is brilliantly exemplified in Roger Busby's latest book.

The magistrates' court in the Midland city was much as usual on a Monday morning – mostly prostitutes and Saturday-night drunks. The cases droned on until a woman on the public benches glanced down at a carrier bag beside her, and shattered the somnolence with a scream.

The bag contained a man's leg, neatly severed, and left under the very noses of the police. The other leg turned up in a train, and the trunk in a decidedly bizarre situation. Obviously the murderer was a cool hand.

This is a story of police procedure with a difference. As Detective-Inspector Leric goes to work on the case he is himself presented in depth, as a man with a life often at variance with his uniformed existence and as a human being with a complex of talents and faults. And parallel with Leric, Mr Busby develops the character of the murderer intent for his own reasons both on revenge against his victim and on making the police look fools. Step by step, the moves of the police and those of the murderer are unfolded, with the murderer keeping just one jump ahead.

But in this duel between two men well matched in temperament and abilities there are many imponderables, including high-ups in the CID itself. When one of these flies back from holiday because results are not forthcoming fast enough for his liking, events really start to move. But in what direction are they moving? Mr Busby has his own surprises in store.

### *Robbery Blue*
October 1969

A tip-off to the police results in their attempting to forestall a wages grab. The elaborate plan misfires and a young detective is shot dead. The robbers get clear away with £250,000. From then on the suspense never lets up.

As all available police resources are mobilised and the smallest clue is followed up, as reporters and photographers converge on the scene like flies on carrion, the four criminals escape to a remote hide-out and lie low. Their plans are meticulously laid, and in the background the big bosses take care of everything; they even take care of the man who fired the gun. It looks as though the gang will succeed in making their escape to Ireland. And then chance intervenes.

A routine police check in a matter unconnected with crime flushes the robbers. The hunt is up and this time there are no mistakes, as the police, furious at the murder of one of their own and desperate to smash an organised crime ring, engage in a battle in which the law is quite prepared to bend the law ...

Roger Busby, a crime reporter on a Midland paper, knows police procedure intimately. He portrays convincingly both the vast organisation of the police and the characters of the men who operate it.

### *Snow Man*
October 1987

Three detectives trapped in nightmares from the past.

The Englishman: Scotland Yard crime intelligence sergeant Tony Rowley sentenced to death by London gangsters.

The American: Federal narcotics agent Jack Monroe reliving flashback horrors of the Vietnam war.

The German: Kriminal Hauptkommissar Rainer Wolfe haunted by the Munich Olympics massacre.

When an undercover policewoman dies in a booby-trapped Devon farmhouse their paths cross on the trail of a shadowy international crime cartel bent on flooding Britain with the angel dust of crack, rock and free-base cocaine.

The hunt takes them to Hitler's Eagle's Nest high in the Bavarian Alps as police chiefs of three nations scheme to grab the glory of the biggest drugs bust in the history of law enforcement.

Ensnared in a web of top-level police intrigue, the trio plan to trap the drug-runners, but when they learn the secret of the Snow Man their nightmares suddenly explode into frightening reality.

Roger Busby, PRO to the Devon and Cornwall Police, has never used his inside knowledge of police work to better effect than in this masterly thriller which transcends international boundaries as easily as it does the limits of the police procedural.

## BUTLER, GWENDOLINE

### *Coffin and the Paper Man*
June 1990

During his long career John Coffin, now Chief Commander of the Second City of London, had encountered many tragic and violent cases, but a series of deaths in the new Docklands represented one of the toughest and most painful he had ever faced.

The case began with the discovery of a young girl's body in an alleyway near the river. In some ways it looked like a simple crime, but soon other disturbing deaths followed. And the police began getting messages from the mysterious Paper Man promising yet more.

Who was the Paper Man, and what connection had the murder of the girl in Rope Alley with the deaths of a group of friends and neighbours in Feather Street, a crescent of prosperous homes in this changing part of London? Who would be the next victim?

Unease spreads through the whole district causing public disturbances between two rival gangs. Stella Pinero, the actress, is caught in this uproar and finds herself in great danger.

Of the characters who people *Coffin and the Paper Man* some, like Mimsie Marker who sells newspapers by the Tube Station, are old friends. Permanents of the district. Others, like the mongrel dog Bob, are new. All of them spring to vivid life, sometimes disturbing life, in Gwendoline Butler's expert hands.

### *Coffin for Charley, A*
September 1993

A young woman, Annie Briggs, who as a child had seen her two neighbours murdered and had identified the killers, becomes obsessed with the idea that she is being watched. When she learns that the murderers, a brother and sister, are being released from prison, she is terrified, fearing they will want revenge. Perhaps they do. One of them, now old and sad but unrepentant, returns to live close to Annie Briggs.

But another killer is already walking the streets, cunning and inventive, adept at disguise and at attracting chosen victims. It looks as though the Second City of London may harbour a serial killer. The police think this killer may be called Charley.

Is Charley the killer? Who is Charley? What is Charley?

John Coffin is responsible for finding who is behind these killings and what is their true motive, and soon discovers that in this case nothing is straightforward.

At the same time his own life has its problems. He is married now to Sheila Pinero, the actress. He loves her dearly but it is not an easy marriage. In addition, his sister and her beautiful daughter are causing trouble, for the girl has disappeared. Is she one of the killer's victims?

In tracing her, Coffin discovers the truth behind this series of murders in a case that will affect the lives of those involved for ever and ever.

### *Coffin in Fashion*
July 1987

More than a decade has passed since the Greenwich murders which launched the young John Coffin on his career as a policeman. Now a sergeant, he had bought a house in Mouncy Street, South-East London. And not only a house: with the house he has bought a body. In fact, more than one body, and the district of small rundown streets, including the locally infamous Paradise Street soon exercises its own influence both on the case and upon his imagination.

During the investigation, though it is not 'his' case, only his house, he makes contact with the world of fashion at the Belmodes clothing factory owned by the fascinating but troubled Rose Hilaire. Rose has problems with her difficult son and with her ambitious assistant, Gabriel. Coffin finds the two women attractive and is inclined to believe he is in love with both of them. Also in the case are Charley Moon, a young photographer, and – very much an active factor, although dead – Rose Hilaire's old Uncle Mosse.

This investigation is set at the beginning of the Swinging Sixties and enters the world of drugs and confused sex. All the characters, even Coffin himself, are in different ways touched by this world. At the same time Coffin continues his search for his lost sibling, and here he finds more than he expects. It helps to support him after the terrible climax to the murders in Mouncy Street, the full truth of which the reader learns only on the very last page.

### *Coffin in the Black Museum*
July 1989

That long-serving and ever-hopeful policeman, John Coffin, has now received well-deserved promotion, and has command of his own force in the newly created Second City of London, established on the old Docklands.

He knows he will face problems in a force put together out of several old Metropolitan police districts, but he does not expect all he gets. Some of it is personal. To his surprise he finds that his sister Letty has set up a Theatre Workshop in an old church, St Lukes, where he comes across an old love, Sheila Pinero, a celebrated actress now turned producer. He knows from experience that both ladies can bring trouble with them. And they do.

This time it is a double murder. In the course of investigating this crime, Coffin uncovers a multiple murder in the past. At first there seem too many bodies, too many suspects and too few clues, but in the famous Black Museum of his force he finds the essential evidence which leads to the unwinding of this most savage case.

With a theatrical background and a new city, a fascinating world opens up for John Coffin to walk in. He means to go on walking there.

### *Coffin on Murder Street*
July 1991

Regina Street in the Second City of London in which John Coffin is responsible for keeping the peace, was nicknamed Murder Street, for it had known more than its fair share of murders and violent deaths. One inhabitant predicted that worse was yet to come. A mass murder would soon happen, he claimed, if the police did not listen to him. But the local police dismissed him as an eccentric.

Was it the malign influence of Regina Street (or Murder Street) that operated upon the owner of a coach business called Terror Tours as a result of which he and his coachload of tourists disappeared?

But the loss of the Terror Tour was only the background to the more terrible story of the disappearance of a small boy at a time when a circle of pederasts was moving into Coffin's territory. The boy is the child of a young actress, herself something of an enigma, working in the St Luke's Theatre close to where John Coffin lives.

Once again, John Coffin and actress Stella Pinero are closely involved in murder, as the story behind the boy's disappearance unfolds into a history of jealousy and love.

### *Coffin on the Water*
March 1986

'A present for my mother', said the card, apparently sent by a boy who had been missing for years and whom everyone except his mother, the famous actress Rachel Esthart, believed to be long dead.

But the card was only the beginning.

The bodies came later. Presents delivered by the River Thames.

The year was 1946, and a bombed, rationed, but optimistic South London district by the river was recovering from the war and looking forward to a royal visit. In this context a triple murderer is on the loose.

The young detective, John Coffin, full of hope for his own future now the war is over, finds that his career has started with a multiple murder case that stretches his mind and his loyalties further than he could have imagined. While investigating the murder case, not always according to his superior's desires, he is also pursuing a private investigation of his own, and falling in love.

The river and the docks, Greenwich with its parks, palaces, and local theatre, form the backdrop against which this story is played out.

### *Coffin Underground*
July 1988

The year is 1978, the place South London, the area that by the river at Greenwich which has been the scene of earlier investigations by detective John Coffin. Now he is back, a senior and much respected police officer, called home in charge of his own small team of detectives. He has been handed the task of overseeing the local detective branch and of bringing it up to maximum efficiency. Like all men of strong character, he has his critics and his enemies, and he knows that this job will arouse hostility. It may lead to yet higher promotion, but for the time being he must work underground.

But even as he embarks on the job, he is involved in a series of violent happenings which have their roots in the past but take their terrible form from an early manifestation of a very contemporary phenomenon.

The brutality of the crimes which follow springs from a fantasy world of games. But these games are deadly, played out according to rules by masters, acolytes – and victims, and Coffin finds himself caught up in one for whose climax he is totally unprepared.

### *Cracking Open a Coffin*
October 1992

*Cracking Open a Coffin* is an important case in the history of the Second City of London and in the life of John Coffin, Chief Commander of its police force.

For him, the case brings more than an investigation into a terrible series of deaths; it arouses sharp doubts about his own career and painful reflections on the ambitions, loves and betrayals in his past, together with the recognition of a thread of violence in his own character. All this at a time when his very position as Chief Commander is under threat.

The story begins in the present with two missing students, one of whom is later found dead, but it soon probes deep into the past, laying bare a veritable palimpsest of deaths in scenes that range from the university to a refuge for battered women and to St Luke's Theatre, presided over by the actress Sheila Pinero, where an ambitious performance of excerpts from *The Ring* is being launched.

By the end, with the killer still spitting defiance in the bitter last act, Coffin has been forced to face his own nature and his love for Sheila.

As well as being a profound study of murder, Gwendoline Butler's latest novel of the Second City of London is also a love story.

## BUTTERWORTH, MICHAEL
*(see also* **Kemp, Sarah***)*

### *Black Look, The*
April 1972

'Anything to declare?' The last thing the Customs officer and beautiful model Candid Jeans expected to find in her luggage was a man's severed hand. Yet the grisly object lay there like a token of her forthcoming photographic assignment in Paris, where, against the marble background of the cemeteries of the French capital, she was to model the all-black outfits of the new Black Look.

For Candida, the assignment becomes a nightmare when the second hand turns up. All at once she is overwhelmed by memories of the traumatic events of her childhood and by the unexpected antagonism of the magazine fashion editor which she now has to face. Her photographer is the only person she can turn to, but his friendship and sympathy seem insufficient to save her from herself.

And all the time she is being closely watched by the French police – in particular by Superintendent Haquin, whose instinct tells him that there is more to Candida than meets the eye. Is this disturbed, beautiful girl, this persecuted victim, in fact a murderess?

Michael Butterworth, who has so adeptly portrayed the landscape of nightmare, in *Vanishing Act*, and *Flowers for a Dead Witch*, succeeds in conveying it once again in his latest crime story, with its background of magazine fashion photography which he knows intimately.

### *Festival!*
August 1976

August Bank Holiday, and in the grounds of a stately home 10,000 pop fans gather for the Great Funky Free Rock'n'Roll Festival. Among them is a former Broadmoor inmate with a supply of cholera germs which he plans to release into the water supply – a thought to make the blood run cold.

But something even more sinister is at work, for the killer is the unwitting tool of an international organization whose ramifications stretch from East to West, and whose aim is to crush subversive elements, especially in the Third World. Moreover, it has effectively penetrated many areas of life in England, as journalist Arnold Carradine soon discovers when he learns of the plot and tries to raise the alarm. All he succeeds in raising are the hackles of the influential and highly-placed. Despite the seeming protection of a seething crowd of youngsters, Carradine is suddenly in mortal danger, unless he can find allies – fast.

Those who already delight in Michael Butterworth's black comedies will know better than to expect a conventional tale. Soon the Prime Minister and Home Secretary, the vicar and the village policeman, and one of the world's most famous pop groups are all inextricably involved. How a potentially disastrous situation is resolved with minimum loss of life or face shows yet another aspect of the versatility of this author, who says he has no 'message' but merely rates himself an observer and recorder of the human comedy – high, low or medium, as you wish.

### *Five Million Dollar Prince, The*
April 1986

The Albert Memorial, that apogee of mid-Victorian Art and Architecture, has stood four-square in Kensington Gardens since 1872, and until an American multi-millionaire indicated that he'd like to buy it, no one had ever thought it would do otherwise. But when Horace Bunbury, BA (failed) Oxon, and ex-Guards officer Thomas Aquinas O'Leary learned of the American's interest in presenting it to his seventh bride as a wedding gift, they thought they perceived an easy way to acquire five million dollars for themselves, while leaving London's architectural heritage intact.

Of course the Albert Con, as it came to be known, required a deal of planning, but they were prepared for that. What they were not prepared for were the complications that ensued. These included the disposal of one or two bodies, the avoidance of one or two bullets, the laundering of a large cheque, the commission of a small – well, relatively small – fraud, and the total loss of one heart, formerly the property of that same Horace Bunbury BA (failed) Oxon.

From first to last, this hilarious romp zips along at Michael Butterworth's usual cracking pace, with enough comic situations and surprising twists of plot to keep the reader chuckling all the way.

### *Flowers for a Dead Witch*
May 1971

Polly Lestrange, arriving from Canada to visit her great-aunt in a Suffolk village, is bewildered to find the sick woman inaccessible, closely guarded by her housekeeper in the beautiful, crumbling mansion; the Rector denouncing from the pulpit the evil rampant among his flock; and the tomb of the local witch, Polly's sixteenth-century ancestress, mysteriously decorated with flowers.

Small happenings conspire to increase Polly's uneasiness, but it is not until she visits the ancient churchyard, which is slowly crumbling into the sea, and makes a macabre discovery in the witch's tomb, that she realizes the danger she is in.

Police enquiries are concentrated on the leader of the local drop-outs, who Polly unexpectedly befriends. But only when she forces her way in to her great-aunt's presence does the mystery begin to be dispelled, to make way for a terrifying denouement in which Michael Butterworth's talent for the unexpected reveals itself to the full.

### *Man in the Sopwith Camel, The*
September 1974

Ernest Kitteridge was one of life's non-starters, except when fantasy took over. Then he took hold of the joystick of his Sopwith Camel and became in imagination an air ace of World War I. By day he worked in a bank under Braithwaite, school bully turned manager. By night he dreamed of a fuller life on a Pacific isle.

Then Kitteridge found himself with three days in which to impersonate the late Braithwaite at the branch to which the manager had been transferred. With the access that this gave him to branch funds and his knowledge of banking procedure, Kitteridge's dreams were suddenly within his grasp.

Unfortunately news of Braithwaite's out-of-office proclivities had preceded him, and Kitteridge soon found himself taking part in what is surely the most decorous orgy ever chronicled while he racked his brains what to do.

Then another fold of Braithwaite's mantle descended upon him in the person of Gladys Grubb, a member of the oldest profession who turned out to be a blessing heavily disguised. For Gladys was more than equal to what the situation demanded of a woman – and it sometimes demanded a good deal. Pretty soon Kitteridge and Gladys were en route from England to Ireland to Mexico, though by first-class jet, not Sopwith Camel now. And with them went not only a large sum in Irish banknotes, but Gladys's sleeping tablets, of which an overdose had somehow to be contrived…

It would be a shame to say more, except that here is one of the most delightful and dottiest crime stories ever. You can start banking on Butterworth now!

### *Man Who Broke the Bank at Monte Carlo, The*
May 1983

Ernest Rowbotham was doing what many a young man dreamed of doing: he was travelling Europe in the luxury of the 1920s with all expenses paid by his wealthy Uncle Luigi. The comfort of the de luxe Blue Train, the heady delights of Monte Carlo, were lavished on him – nay, he was instructed to enjoy them. And at the end of the tour the prospect of fabulous wealth awaited him.

But of course there was a snag. Several.

The first was the presence of Uncle Luigi, which was something of an embarrassment. The second was a gimlet-eyed young woman who, on the Blue Train and later at Monte, watched Ernest's every move. The third was a pantechnicon transporting a group of Chicago musicians who were inseparable from their cased instruments yet were never known to play. The fourth was the arrival, by air from Le Bourget, of an intrepid widow with good cause to hate Luigi's guts.

And the fifth was that someone – perhaps even one of the above – was exceedingly anxious that Ernest Rowbotham shouldn't finish his tour alive.

Michael Butterworth's felicitous black comedies are all too rare a joy. Anyone who has revelled in *The Man with the Sopwith Camel*, *Remains to be Seen*, and *X Marks the Spot* will need no urging to embark on his latest with its splendidly researched background. New readers have a treat in store.

### *Remains to be Seen*
January 1976

The remains – those of a lecherous Armenian whom he had met precisely once in unforgettable circumstances – were to be seen in the back of Bernard Davis's car, where they had been dumped when Bernard left it parked in a London street on one of his trips to the capital to dispose of the jewels his father so mysteriously produced from time to time.

Of course his father, head of the family undertaking firm of Fitch, Davis in Scunthorpe, had escaped from Russia after the Revolution with the title of Prince Davydov, but that hardly explained why Soviet agents should be interested in him now, especially as the tyrannical old patriarch was dying. But when Bernard realized he was being followed and that there was a positively international concentration of interest in the Davis-Davydov family, it was obvious as glad rags at a funeral that there had to be something at stake.

There was. By the time Bernard learnt that his father had left Russia with something more potent than a title, the precious object, of interest to four Intelligence services, had gone almost beyond recall; that it was saved was due solely to English wind and weather, aided in some measure by Bernard himself. And by the time that Bernard, the only non-undertaker in the family, had outwitted all comers and ensured it a safe resting-place, not to mention disposing of the Armenian's remains, that unsuccessful poet and unexpected man of action was well on the way to discovering his true self.

*The Man with the Sopwith Camel* was described by Matthew Coady in the *Guardian* as 'the funniest criminal farce of the year'. As his next offering, Michael Butterworth gives us such a send-up of the spy thriller that it will be difficult to read one 'straight' again.

### *Vanishing Act*
July 1970

The holiday on Malta to which Deborah Tarrant had so eagerly looked forward seemed doomed to disaster when bereavement compelled her to go alone. Weighed down by guilt, bored, lonely, Deborah made friends with someone in similar plight: six-year-old Alec, only child of a widowed father, on holiday with his indifferent nurse. When, overnight, the child and his nursemaid vanish and the hotel attempts to cover up the fact, it is Deborah who informs the police.

Alec had confided to Deborah that he had found a dead body – but the body has mysteriously disappeared. And the one which turns up some days later makes it all too probable that Alec is no longer alive. The holiday island and its warm-hearted inhabitants become the background to a nightmare of increasing tensions as the Maltese police, led by Inspector Borg, organize a massive search for the missing child and uncover another murder, and as Deborah's unexpected intervention brings her face to face with death.

*Vanishing Act* will not disappoint the many readers of Michael Butterworth's two previous thrillers, *The Soundless Scream*, which Peter Phillips in the *Sun* described as 'a fine whodunit, written with sense and subtlety', and *Walk Softly, in Fear*, which possesses 'a quality of writing and a creation of situations well above the average' (*Nottingham Guardian Journal*).

### *Villa on the Shore*
September 1973

Natasha Collingwood thought it was too good to be true when she landed the job of secretary to Nathan Yardley, best-selling novelist, at his villa in Italy. And so it was, for when she arrived it was to learn that her predecessor had died mysteriously as a result of falling from a window. Almost at once, Natasha stumbles on her desecrated grave.

Several people thought they had good reason to hate the girl. Was her death really an accident? There are other macabre discoveries as Natasha learns of the widowed novelist's problems: with his late wife, with his stepchildren, with a jealous servant, with his secretary. She learns, too, that she is herself in danger, and that at the villa all things are not what they seem. But is it the truth she has discovered, or a clever novelist's presentation of it? Who is her enemy and who her friend?

When a murder takes place, Natasha is forced to recognize that evil stalks in this idyllic setting. But its source is as unexpected as is the source of her rescue. Once again, Michael Butterworth spins a skilful web of horror and intrigue.

### *Virgin on the Rocks, A: Variations on a Theme in the Black Manner*
March 1985

In 1933 Bernard Fosdyke, aspiring novelist, believing in common with others of his ilk and generation that Berlin was where the action was, squandered his patrimony in getting there and ended up on the rocks. But Berlin in 1933 had just become the headquarters of a new and ugly political movement, as a result of which, and of a fortuitously Semitic appearance, Bernard had to leave hastily for Paris, inseparably accompanied by an iron grating with *Berliner Stadwerke* neatly inscribed upon it in raised letters.

Which is how he came to meet Harold Hiram Levy, master forger, late of the Bronx, and Levy – 'Call me Hal' – was quick to detect a latent in Bernard: he had a genuinely criminal mind.

Hal did not believe in talents lying idle. Especially when he had need of them. In this case to devise a scheme whereby the Louvre's version of one of Leonardo da Vinci's masterpieces could be exchanged for his handmade copy.

Bernard was perfectly willing to help – especially for a cool half-million – but his heart wasn't in it, being in thrall to an enchanting young woman who, alas, was known to accept lifts from importuning gentlemen in limousines.

Nevertheless, with the unwitting assistance of Gertrude Stein*, Ernest Hemingway, Henry Miller, Pablo Picasso, and Jean Cocteau, not to mention the Temporary Acting Director of the Louvre, the night of the switch dawned. And with it, trouble...

*A Virgin on the Rocks* is in the same vein as Michael Butterworth's delightful *The Man Who Broke the Bank at Monte Carlo*. And even funnier.

*And Alice B Toklas, of course.

### *X Marks the Spot*
February 1978

For nearly a hundred years the bones of Karl Marx, founder of modern Communism, have reposed in Highgate Cemetery. But are they Marx's bones? This delicious extravaganza by Michael Butterworth, author of the much-praised *Remains to Be Seen* and *The Man in the Sopwith Camel*, postulates a skeleton snatch by one Edgar Fenworthy, art collector by inclination and pickpocket by profession, who has recently lost his working hand.

Reduced to Social Security and the company of a muscle-bound American, Fenworthy becomes involved in a plan to lift the father of Communism's remains and dispose of them piecemeal to those most likely to want them, in exchange for cash in a Swiss numbered banking account.

The skeleton snatch proves successful, thanks to British bureaucracy. Then the action gets out of Fenworthy's hand, despite the expertise of the charming advertising executive Angela Carruthers, a recent graduate of Holloway. There is nothing for it but to accept professional assistance – of a kind no one bargained for. Never in Fenworthy's life had he envisaged becoming involved with violence, any more than he expected to fall victim to a tenderer passion and try his hand – his only hand – at murder.

The outcome of this blackly comic crime novel lives up to what has gone before, for it so happens that the Vatican has been conducting discreet negotiations of its own behind the Iron Curtain which become inextricably mixed up with those of Fenworthy and his friends. Not one of them felt in their own or Marx's bones the significance of that remarkable coincidence. It is left to Michael Butterworth to point it out.

## CAIRNS, ALISON

### *New Year Resolution*
November 1984

On the Redlands estate preparations for Christmas were well under way. Redlands House was now a residential home for the elderly, but six houses had been built on the adjoining land and in each of them a drama was taking place.

The matron of the home and her teenage son were struggling to adjust to a figure from the past, as were the two unmarried sisters at No. 3 whose lives seemed so circumscribed; at No. 6 the retired Merchant Navy captain had just discovered the identity of the man who had fathered his beloved granddaughter's child; the young wife at No. 4, torn between her husband and her aging father, was beginning to realize just how worthless that husband really was; while the little family at No. 5 were devastated by the consequences of an accident for which a drunken driver was to blame. Only at No. 2 did the elderly former owner of Redlands House seem free from the troubles besetting her neighbours.

One person on the estate had consistently alienated all the others and several of them had made New Year resolutions to avoid him in future. So his suicide at first was almost a relief. Only when the police decided it was murder did his death begin to cause the same disquiet and suspicion as his life.

Alison Cairns, whose searching examination of a family under stress made her first novel, *Strained Relations*, an auspicious debut, here turns her attentions to a group of families, with the same engaging and suspenseful result.

### *Strained Relations*
July 1983

In the close-knit Cornish village of Treskellan no family was more close-knit that the Quinns: Russell, a local businessman with a motherly wife, bright teenage daughter, and spanking modern house; Christopher, a London schoolteacher married to glamorous Caroline and owner of a holiday cottage; and Alexis, their much younger sister, glorying in the solitude of her own small home.

It is to see Alexis that Toby Wilde, a young solicitor, comes to Treskellan, and it is through his eyes that the Quinns are first portrayed when Caroline Quinn mysteriously disappears. An interesting family, he thinks. Very close to one another but emotionally controlled, according to Geoffrey Taverner, the lonely man who has his own reasons for returning to the village year after year. Always friendly and helpful, agree Stan and Susanne Hyson, the affluent newcomers who have recently bought the Quinns' old family home. Highly respected, says Detective-Sergeant Golspie after the first of the terrible events which will strain family loyalty to the limit in the week ahead.

All these views of the Quinns are accurate, yet neither in whole nor in part do they reflect the truth. That is left for Toby to discover. And even then the picture is not complete.

## CALDWELL, TAYLOR

### *Late Clara Beame, The*
February 1964

The famous author of *Dynasty of Death*, *Prologue to Love* and *Dear and Glorious Physician* here brings her superb skill to the construction of a crime novel.

The remote farmhouse in Connecticut and the three million dollars that went with it under the will of Aunt Clara ('the late Clara Beame') had been inherited by Laura, who was not in fact her niece; Alice, who was not her niece either but who had equal place in Clara's affections and (Alice thought) an equal right to the great inheritance, had been left virtually nothing.

The action of the story takes place one Christmas in the Connecticut house, a festivity to which Laura had invited Alice, and Alice's brother; and the small party is joined by a mysterious young man who seems to have been invited more or less by accident...

When a snow hurricane cuts off the electricity and the telephone from the isolated house there comes an outbreak of violence in the tiny stranded community. Taylor Caldwell's skill makes the most of every possibility of surprise and suspense that arises from the ensuing dangerous situation.

## CAMPBELL, ALICE

### *Bloodstained Toy, The*
November 1948

Laurine Brace, a wealthy young American living in England, had already rid herself of two husbands and has recently announced her engagement to a possible third, Sir Luke

Pendry; but sudden and sinister tragedy at Wycherley Manor, her lovely village home, sets in motion a train of events that gathers in speed and complexity to a breath-taking conclusion. Every person involved – and there are many – has some urgent reason for concealing the truth. For sheer ingenuity and pace, for originality and tension, *The Bloodstained Toy* must rank among the best of Alice Campbell's achievements.

### Child's Play
August 1947

Alice Campbell, author of *The Cockroach Sings* and other top rank detective stories, has written another gripping tale, full of incident and the particular dramatic and macabre quality for which her stories are noted. It may have been child's play for the killer, but it certainly wasn't child's play for Hugh Mortray, K. C., when he found that he had secured the acquittal of a guilty man and it was up to him to forestall further havoc. This grim theme provides Alice Campbell with material for one of her best stories.

### Click of the Gate, The
April 1932

Alan Charnwood had reached the middle thirties without losing his heart, when he met Iris de Bertincourt at Goodwood. Since then he had paid frequent visits to Paris. There was a husband, worse luck, from whom Iris had not yet got a divorce, but that now seemed but a matter of time. Alan, meanwhile, must return to his engineering in Africa, while Madame de Bertincourt worked for that break with the degenerate Marcel which was to mean their happiness. But Alan was not destined to leave Paris yet awhile. Like a sudden cloud in a blue sky came the disappearance of Claire, Iris's beautiful child of fifteen. The police were beaten; she was gone without a trace. White-slave traffic? A homicidal maniac? Or was Clare [sic] merely the temporary prisoner of the old Comtesse, Iris's aunt, who was so anxious to bring her niece and her husband together again, or even of the impecunious De Bertincourt himself, to whom his marriage to Iris meant so much? For Iris's sake Charnwood must find Clare. Slowly the mystery implicated him in its doubts and horrors till not only the happiness of the woman he loved, but his own life, was threatened. This is an enthralling tale most enthrallingly told.

### Cockroach Sings, The
September 1946

In *The Cockroach Sings* Alice Campbell has written an exceptionally gripping story with plenty of incident and well sustained suspense. To Turrets, a lonely country house, hugged by dark cedars, ivy-clad and damp, comes a young American girl, Avis Marriott. She has been engaged as a kind of companion-housekeeper to two wealthy English spinsters, the autocratic Maud Bolles and her more than eccentric sister Erica, who spends most of her time shut in her room with her pet rabbit. The sinister and breath-taking happenings at the mansion provide Alice Campbell with rare material for what is undoubtedly one of her best stories.

### Corpse Had Red Hair, The
July 1950

John Guild was the Son in the publishing firm of Guild and Son, but that particular afternoon he would have readily changed places with the office boy. To him had fallen the singularly unpleasant task of telling Cora Forbes that her work was no longer wanted, and Cora was old and poor. To his relief, when he reaches Cora's flat he finds a tea-party in

progress, which certainly puts paid to any business talk. Instead, it precipitates him into an extraordinary murder mystery, involving Cora's red-headed daughter, Crystal and her husband; a rich and disagreeable neighbour, Lady Bantling, and her ne'er-do-well brother; not to mention the young and attractive Hope Fenning. An ingenious crime story with a dashing solution.

### Death Framed in Silver
July 1937

Margaret Fairlamb, celebrated actress, had been a popular and genuinely loved figure in the world of the theatre. Her death at the hands of an unknown, brutal assailant was a calamity fraught with horror not only to her family and friends but to a wider public as well. Every known fact pointed to robbery as the motive. What other belief was possible when the victim had not an enemy in the world, and when the handbag taken from her had contained close on £100 pounds in addition to valuable jewellery? Her death, following as it did, the equally mysterious demise of her friend and fellow actress Rose Walsh, was a first-class sensation, but it was only the prelude to a story that for sheer drama outclassed any of the pieces that had made her famous. Alice Campbell, the well-known author of *Juggernaut* and many other successes, has written a magnificent story of mystery and intrigue.

### Desire to Kill
July 1934

Dodo Quarles had been going the pace. Her parties at her Paris apartment were nights to be remembered. Dodo, not yet twenty-one but full-blooded and sensuous, could always be trusted to supply a new thrill for her jaded guests. On this occasion she had surpassed herself. Each guest had partaken of a new dish – an Indian sweet which contained a drug calculated to induce slumber and pleasant dreams. Later that evening into that strange circle of sleepers death walked...and Dodo was stabbed to death. In *Desire to Kill* Alice Campbell has written a brilliant mystery story, a fitting successor to that outstanding thriller *The Murder of Caroline Bundy*.

### Door Closed Softly, A
July 1939

It was purely by chance that David Beddoes and Alison Young stumbled on the strange house in Hampstead – a thick fog made it easy to mistake their destination – and thus set in motion the extraordinary train of events that was to end so sensationally. The house itself was peculiar, but it was the ghastly scream that rang out from upstairs just as they were leaving that crystallised their suspicions. Alice Campbell is an expert at keeping us on tenterhooks of suspense, and in this dramatic story she is admirably successful.

### Flying Blind
May 1938

*Flying Blind* has nothing to do with aviation. The title is used metaphorically to describe a situation in which daily, even hourly, calamity threatens through a fog of mystery. The fog enfolds the characters in the story; blinding them to their position; blotting out the truth; making every move a danger; effacing, with terrifying completeness, the ordinary facts of everyday existence. Through this fog Tommy Rostetter, free-lance journalist, gropes his way. It leads him from a smart amateur hat-shop in Mayfair to a sleepy Sussex village, and finally, after a night race with death, to a dark, lonely waste of Wiltshire downland. And not until the very last moment are the factors in the series of murders sorted out.

'Here is', as a critic has written of Alice Campbell's work, 'detective writing *par excellence*.'

### Keep Away From Water
July 1935

Miss Venables, a rich and kindly old lady, is the recipient of several threatening letters. Her companion, Sarah MacNeil, wonders who can possibly bear a grudge against her employer, but she courageously endeavours to find out who is threatening her. Together they set out for France, but on the point of departure they receive a mysterious communication which reads: '*Go to France if you like; but once there keep away from water*'. In this clever detective story Mrs. Campbell once more proves herself an expert purveyor of thrills.

### Murder of Caroline Bundy, The
January 1933

'*Murder at Bristol. Well-Known Somerset Woman found dead in Ditch.*'

These staring headlines first announced to a startled public the murder of Caroline Bundy, one of the most sensational crimes of recent years. The brutal circumstances of the murder aroused profound feeling, and when, in May, 193-, the niece of the murdered woman was tried at the Bristol Assizes, the resulting verdict divided opinion into two warring camps. Alice Campbell now presents the facts of the case as seen through the eyes of a character in the drama. This thrilling mystery novel is certainly the finest book that its talented author has yet written.

### No Light Came On
January 1943

Alice Campbell in *No Light Came On* writes a fast-moving story set in a Paris that it is pleasant to remember – the happy Paris of fashionable hotels, smart shops and chic well-dressed women. Gay Ripley, who tells the story, is staying in Paris with her cousin Mrs. Lou Renfrew, a wealthy American widow. One evening, Cousin Lou is poisoned at supper by some criminal hand. Gay, aided by Miles Dorsey, a young English lawyer, does some worthwhile detection with surprising results, finally elucidating an exceptionally interesting and baffling mystery.

### No Murder of Mine
April 1941

The cottage in Dorset had been lent to Rowan Wilde by her friends – a lovely little place with thatched roof and roses round the door. Lonesome, yes, but after London how soul-soothing! Or so the new tenant thought as she prepared to settle down for her first evening there. The evening then drew on to nightfall and then in the darkness Rowan Wilde made that terrible, terrifying discovery, and screamed aloud – a scream that echoed through the cottage and rang mockingly again in her own ears... Alice Campbell knows well how to pile up suspense, but she is also a first-rate hand at a detective story, and fully lives up to her reputation with this book.

### Ringed With Fire
September 1943

It all started when inoffensive little Mr. Kilmacross was found dead in the attic of a Bayswater boarding house. At first it looked like a simple case of a burglar murdering a bungling snooper; but that was before Miss Grant, a young secretary employed at one of the Ministries, began hearing suspicious noises on the blacked-out stairs, and before her chief, the lean and attractive Mark Chantrey, began turning up in places where he had no particular reason to be. To mix things up

still more there were two other murders, as well as several anonymous notes that arrived at the Ministry hinting at fifth column work, and even implicating Miss Grant herself. In this tale of spies and treason in high places, Miss Campbell has a timely and thrilling story to tell.

### They Hunted a Fox
February 1940

It was perhaps only a vague suspicion in the minds of one or two people that Tom Boldre, red-face fox-hunting squire had not died a natural death; a suspicion created by a crazy wager after a rowdy hunt-ball that he would not ride a horse up a steep and slippery staircase. It seemed to Alison Young that one of the dishevelled party standing in the hall beneath had waited with cold purpose for the truth that never came, and later had tried again and this time made sure. *They Hunted A Fox* is told with Alice Campbell's customary skill and ingenuity.

### Travelling Butcher
May 1944

Lady Hyacinth Gloam is an astute business woman who was attempting to cash in on the money-making possibilities of exporting antiques to America. During the London blitz she decides to evacuate her treasures to a cottage in the country, Foxgloves Cottage at Monkspond. Tragedy stark and macabre surrounds that extraordinary journey which started amid bombs and was accompanied by death – and murder. *Travelling Butcher* is a really gripping, fast-moving detective story, full of well-sustained suspense, and must rank as one of Alice Campbell's best.

## CAMPBELL, HARRIETTE
### Three Names for Murder
April 1940

*Three Names for Murder* is perfect fare for all who like detective stories. It is a highly ingenious and well-told mystery with some exceptionally attractive characters. One meets again the diverting Simon Brade, famous authority on art, a connoisseur not only of Chinese porcelain and jade but of crime, for much to his own annoyance, and certainly much to his inconvenience, Simon Brade shines at crime. He can detect a false piece of evidence as surely as a minute flaw in the firing of a piece of porcelain. The present case, which adds a gem to his collection, opens with the sensational murder of Professor Hammerd, eminent scientist, but before it ends the reader has been caught up in an amazing web of mystery.

## CARMICHAEL, HARRY
(*see also* **Howard, Hartley**)
### Alibi
March 1961

It was Mrs. Tadfield who said '...there's something bad about that place, something I never felt before she ... she went away...'

The disappearance of beautiful Patricia Warren presents John Piper with a problem to which there can only be one answer. No one can be in two places at the same time.

Piper's investigation inevitably leads him to a terrible discovery. From then on events move swiftly, tension grows with every step of the way towards a startling denouement.

*Alibi* is another gripping story written in Harry Carmichael's familiar blend of ingenuity and excitement. His previous novels have been translated into almost every European language and this, his nineteenth, is a spellbinder from start to finish.

### *Candles for the Dead*
October 1973
For Quinn of the *Morning Post* it all began when he heard about a man called David Breame and what had happened to him at Heathrow Airport on his return from Sweden. The story had promise…and it fitted neatly into a series Quinn was currently featuring in his Column of Crime.

But from then on nothing fitted. There was a motiveless killing…an attack on Quinn for no apparent reason…a wild search of a flat from which nothing was stolen. And behind the string of unconnected events loomed an unseen menace.

John Piper, assurance assessor and old friend, finds a bizarre explanation and then discards it. From the bits and pieces, Quinn creates a theory that is equally grotesque.

Somewhere in the maze of doubt and speculation lies the answer. It some out into the open only when a second death sheds light in dark places.

*Candles for the Dead* is a tangle of treachery that has the compulsive hold that one has come to expect from Harry Carmichael, acknowledged master of the surprise ending.

### *Condemned, The*
October 1967
Beneath the surface of respectable society there is an underworld of those who prey on their fellows – those who are known to the police as villains. This is an account of four such men.

It is with good reason that Harry Carmichael chose for his latest novel the title: *The Condemned.*

In every crime both the law-abiding and the criminal, the innocent and the guilty, suffer. Perhaps they are separated by only a thin dividing line. For a man called Terence Alexander Millward that line was the width of a lifetime.

*The Condemned* is his story.

### *Confession*
August 1961
This is the story of a betrayal that breeds hatred, a love that ends in death. Three people form the nucleus of tragedy: one dies, one faces trial for murder, the third is confronted with an inescapable decision.

The tension of the courtroom scenes is matched only by the drama of the fight waged outside the court by those who believe the accused to be innocent. As the inevitability of conviction grows, the search for a way of escape becomes ever more desperate.

In *Confession*, Harry Carmichael has written a novel that surpasses his many earlier successes – a story of love, murder and the terrifying power of misleading evidence.

### *Dead of the Night, The*
February 1956
A rich old man, an attractive wife, an enigmatic daughter – and a suspicion of attempted murder. John Piper investigates. The deaths which take place could be accidental or coincidental: but Piper does not think so. In an atmosphere of growing tension, he reaches the heart of a fantastic secret…and death passes from the house called Summerhill. With these ingredients, and his mastery of plot and characterisation, Harry Carmichael gives you *The Dead of the Night* – another fascinating study in crime and detection.

### *Deadly Night-Cap*
February 1953
Mrs. Esther Payne was a very unpopular lady – right up to the night when she took two sleeping tablets and died. Sleeping tablets don't kill, nor does hate – even so much of it, but when traces of strychnine were discovered in the tube of pills that lured her to her last long sleep, it seemed that hate had found a way. Of motive there was plenty, but four people only had the opportunity to obtain the poison for Esther's nightcap. John Piper, investigating for the insurance company that held her two-year-old policy for £10,000, finds himself caught up in a tangle of lies, baffled by so many people who have something they want desperately to hide. Who was the tormented soul who couldn't sleep at night for the sweating fear of some forgotten trifle that might betray the hidden guilt? What terrible compulsion had driven someone to destroy? Do you jump at a footfall; start at the sound of a creaking door? Do you fear to look behind you? We did after reading *Deadly Nightcap* – and *you will!*

### *Death Counts Three*
July 1954
The business which took John Piper to novelist Edith Ellerby's country house, Sicklehurst, had nothing to do with murder. The shot that Piper heard soon after his arrival had apparently nothing to do with murder either; he was told that Edith's secretary, Walter Parr, much enjoyed killing rabbits. Parr proved an elusive character. And Piper soon realised that there was more hatred than enjoyment in Ellerby's home. It was an uneasy party which gathered there that day – a party made scarcely more agreeable by the arrival of her publicity agent, Ambrose Durbin, accompanied by an uninvited guest, Lucille Lynton, the best 'bad' girl in British films. Lucille would have made trouble anywhere; her presence at Sicklehurst very quickly brought matters to a head. And Piper was landed with one of the trickiest problems he had every encountered – a problem which leads to a terrifying conclusion. *Death Counts Three* has vivid characterisation, a pace that travels non-stop to an unexpected denouement, and the excellent detection we have come to expect from Harry Carmichael.

### *Death Leaves a Diary*
February 1952
John Piper was late and he wanted to get home. It was with positive irritation that he stopped to listen to a frightened little man's tale of an intruder in his ground-floor flat. Piper wasn't interested in real or imaginary burglars – except in the course of business since he was an enquiry agent employed by insurance assessors – but he agreed to search Edmund Fligg's flat. He found no one. Next morning he read that Fligg had hanged himself. Partly through curiosity and partly through an uneasy feeling of responsibility, he decided to make a few inquiries; and at once he found himself mixed up in an exceedingly nasty case of murder. In *Death Leaves a Diary* a logical sequence of thrilling events is narrated at high speed and with deadly effect by a new and exciting writer.

### *Death Trap*
November 1970
Few novels of detection can fairly claim to be based on an original concept. The classic problem is all too rare – the kind of problem set out by Harry Carmichael in *Death Trap.* It is a puzzle wrapped in a mystery enclosed in an enigma. Each answer poses a new question, nothing is what it seems.

John Piper, insurance assessor, is intimately involved. So is Quinn, crime reporter extraordinary. But it is the puzzle that matters in this story of an everyday event woven with deceptive simplicity by Harry Carmichael.

As the pieces are taken apart there is an answer…and then another answer…and beyond that yet another. Somewhere just out of sight lies the ultimate truth. Harry Carmichael employs no tricks, no sleight-of-hand in his latest novel. *Death Trap* is an exercise in flawless deduction.

### *Emergency Exit*
August 1957
*Emergency Exit* is one of the most smoothly convincing novels that has yet come from the pen of Harry Carmichael. Here is a story of greed. Here are people who do not hesitate to kill when the need and the opportunity arise. Here is all the tension and excitement of a manhunt. Every step of the way is logically followed by insurance assessor John Piper; and there is a remorseless logic about the solution. *Emergency Exit* will add greatly to Mr. Carmichael's already considerable reputation.

### *False Evidence*
January 1976
When George Ainsworth drove from London to Liverpool on Friday evening, August 23, he left a twisted trail that others tried in vain to follow. No one knew why he took the Irish ferry to Dublin instead of returning home during the weekend. No one knew what happened to him aboard the MV *Glendowan* during the voyage back to Liverpool on Saturday night, August 24.

Quinn of the *Morning Post* picked up the story from the paper's northern office. When he began his enquiries he soon learned that everybody – including the police – believed that Ainsworth had been dumped overboard to drown.

There were many factors to support that belief. But the time came when belief changed to doubt…and doubt resolved itself in double tragedy before the truth was at last revealed.

*False Evidence* deals with tangled motives which concealed the betrayal of a man who sought to betray. It is a classic example of deduction from simple beginnings. This latest novel by Harry Carmichael has all the tension and tantalizing ingredients his readers have come to expect from an acknowledged master of the detective story.

### *Flashback*
November 1964
*Flashback* tells the story of an ordinary family who become involved in a mystery which proves to be complete and inexplicable. Gossip provides many answers but none of them is the right one.

Then John Piper is commissioned to find out what really happened on that October day in the home of the Kilmuir family in a quiet suburban street. Assisted by Quinn of the *Morning Post*, he goes back in time, step by step, to reveal that the life of Mrs. Janet Kilmuir was neither simple nor placid.

Harry Carmichael's tense new novel provides a tragic and startling answer to what can truly be described as a classic puzzle.

### *Grave for Two, A*
May 1977
An unexpected phone-call, the renewal of a long-forgotten association, involvement in the breakdown of a marriage – these formed the start of a series of events which immersed John Piper, assurance assessor, in the violent end to a life of betrayal.

By chance, Quinn of the *Morning Post* became interested in the same complex web of deceit. Together, he and Piper followed a road leading back into the past where the tragedy of a woman called Natalie Maynard had begun.

Then comes the time when Quinn has to decide that fantasy and reality are merely opposite sides of the same coin. Along with that thought he has a macabre notion that perhaps the dead do have a power over the living.

*A Grave for Two* illustrates the art of deductive reasoning which creates order out of confusion. Once again Harry Carmichael makes use of simple props to demonstrate his mastery of the sleight-of-hand.

### *James Knowland: Deceased*
March 1958
Shortly before ten o'clock on the night of October 30th, James Knowland, retired furrier, telephoned his lawyer to say that he wished to alter his will. Shortly after ten o'clock, James Knowland was dead. In the eyes of John Piper, commissioned by an insurance company to make inquiries, Knowland's death was just too opportune; his doctor's verdict of 'Death from Natural Causes' left too many questions unanswered.

Piper's investigations followed a twisted trail from sleazy lodging houses to slum apartments in the back streets of London before they produce an unexpected and disturbing conclusion. Once again we meet Quinn, the cynical chain-smoking journalist. Once again we are caught up in a baffling problem which grips from first page to last.

With *James Knowland: Deceased*, Harry Carmichael adds another tour-de-force to his long list of successes.

### *Justice Enough*
September 1956
*Justice Enough* is the story of a honeymoon on which death rode with the newly-weds. Behind the tangled events of the night when tragedy struck at Mr. and Mrs. David Eastwood, there lies a stolen formula and a life insurance policy...either of which might have represented the price of murder. John Piper's investigations lead him from the squalor of London's East End to the coast of Spain and the sinister streets of Monteciera... Against a strange and exciting background he finally unravels the truth. Harry Carmichael sets a baffling problem involving the tense situations and vividly-drawn characters on which his reputation has been so securely established.

### *Life Cycle*
July 1978
On an overcast evening in June, Dr Andrew Wingate finished his surgery somewhat earlier than usual. With only three calls to make on his way home, he was looking forward to some hours of relaxation.

The time was then seven o'clock. He had no presentment that in less than an hour he would be dead.

For Quinn of the *Morning Post* it was a routine assignment. He could not guess how murder would feed on murder in a killer's frantic pursuit of self-preservation.

*Life Cycle* weaves a complex pattern of human relationships in which ordinary people find themselves totally enmeshed. Harry Carmichael's latest novel is based on a typically impenetrable plot handled with the art that conceals art.

### *Link, The*
January 1962
When Quinn of the *Morning Post* deputises for a colleague he gets himself involved in the affairs of Dr. Christopher Healey, arraigned before the Disciplinary Committee of the General Medical Council on a charge of having had improper relations with a married woman patient. As the public hearing

proceeds, Quinn begins to ask himself questions to which there appear to be no answers.

In the desire to see that justice is done, he prevails upon John Piper to take an interest in the case. It is not long afterwards that sudden death intervenes – death that could have been accident, suicide or murder.

This is a novel of vengeance and ruthless self-interest, of people who are the victims of desire. In the practice of psycho-therapy a doctor is sometimes referred to as 'the link', and it is against a background of the manipulation of the unconscious mind that Harry Carmichael, with consummate skill, tells his ingenious and absorbing story.

### Money for Murder
January 1955

At the inquest on Raymond Barrett, an antique dealer insured for twenty thousand pounds, a verdict of suicide was returned. But one person refused to believe that Barrett had taken his own life. What happened to that person – and to others – makes an absorbing tale of intrigue and sudden death. In *Money for Murder*, Harry Carmichael has again written a first-rate story of crime, suspense and deduction.

### Most Deadly Hate
June 1971

If Quinn of the *Morning Post* had not been in the Three Feathers that night he would not have met a man called Leslie Chandler. It was a chance meeting – nothing more.

But chance played no part in the other events of the night of February 10th – events fostered by greed and betrayal. What happened in the home of Mr and Mrs Chandler was only the beginning.

When Quinn becomes involved, John Piper, friend of many years, offers to help. Soon they realize that there is more at stake than the life of a lonely woman. Soon they learn that it is the betrayer that has been betrayed, that death must be the price of silence.

This is a tense and gripping story in which too many know too much – but only one knows the truth. And there comes a time when Piper says: 'Hatred is a disease. It changes normal people into monsters.'

In *Most Deadly Hate* Harry Carmichael has woven a tale of suspense with his usual skill. It is storytelling at its very best.

### Motive, The
October 1974

The disappearance of Robert Q. Heseltine FRCS, consultant surgeon to the Brompton Clinic in London, aroused only moderate interest. All the indications were that he had drowned when he jumped off a cliff on the Dorset coast.

Quinn, crime reporter of the *Morning Post*, takes a different view. His friend, John Piper, insurance assessor, who had been on social terms with the missing surgeon, agrees that it may be worth while to probe into the background of a man who had no motive for suicide.

Then a woman known to Heseltine meets death by violence. From that moment his disappearance takes on a new and terrible significance.

This is a tightly-knit story of human relationships, as Harry Carmichael demonstrates once again his rare gift of deceptive simplicity that baffles even the most astute.

### Murder by Proxy
April 1967

Richard Stuart Armstrong, convicted of fraud, is sentenced to twelve months' imprisonment: Quinn of the *Morning Post* wins a

small bet: an undertaker finds he has been part of a macabre practical joke: John Piper, insurance assessor, meets two women – one nearly causes his death, the other changes his whole life.

There are the oddly-assorted threads with which Harry Carmichael weaves his story of corruption and conspiracy – the story of what happened to Richard Stuart Armstrong following his release from prison. When he went to gaol the wheels had been set in motion. When he came out they began gathering speed. By then only he could have stopped them. But by then he had gone too far.

*Murder by Proxy* is a compulsive tale, an exercise in sleight-of-hand, it is tense, exciting and smoothly deceptive. It is vintage Carmichael.

### Naked to the Grave
June 1972

When John Piper, insurance assessor, called at the Davey's flat in Hampstead he had no idea that his visit would be anything but an ordinary professional appointment. But before long he discovered that someone else had visited Flat 2A at Denholme Court that Saturday afternoon: someone who changed the fate of many people.

It began with Pauline Davey who wanted more than looks and money and the things most women desire. She could not have known that others would pay with their lives for what she wanted.

Quinn of the *Morning Post* becomes involved when he offers Piper his help. As the days pass, death strikes again…and again.

To many problems there would seem to be no answer. To this one there are too many – until the tangle of Pauline Davey's life is resolved.

*Naked to the Grave* is a story of everyday people in everyday surroundings, told with the cunning of simplicity which readers have come to expect of Harry Carmichael.

### Noose for a Lady
July 1955

Here is the story of an island with a secret – a secret which spreads its tentacles across the sunlit streets and brings menace with the night. To John Piper on holiday, danger came from the moment he stepped ashore. And violence struck wantonly as the days went by until murder settled an old account. Harry Carmichael's gift for vivid portrayal of people and places, combined with excellent detection, makes *Noose for a Lady* another swift-moving tale of suspense in the grand tradition.

### Of Unsound Mind
July 1962

'I don't believe,' Piper said, 'that anyone's discovered a way of making ordinary people commit suicide…'

Yet the Cresset Insurance Company was very interested in a number of suicides that had taken place in the London area: seven tragic deaths, all with one feature in common, but without a link which would connect any case with another. They had taken their own lives: of that there could hardly be any doubt. The question was – why?

John Piper, insurance assessor, and Quinn, crime reporter for the *Morning Post*, undertake a task that seems destined to end in failure. As their enquiries probe deeper and deeper still, it becomes obvious that each of the seven deaths has its own explanation: they were people who had died because death was preferable to the exposure of their private lives.

This is an original novel of exceptional ingenuity. Seven human documents have

been woven into one to create *Of Unsound Mind*. It is a story that grips and never lets go, a story which displays Harry Carmichael's rare talent for mystery at its best.

### ...Or Be He Dead
April 1959

Paul Craven was a peculiar young man; peculiar, too, was what happened to him one night when he left the 50-50 Club after drinking heavily in an attempt to rid himself of a nightmare which gave him no rest. The secret locked up in Paul's mind is the secret that John Piper, insurance assessor, is called upon to unravel. At the outset he has no inkling that events are about to take place which will alter the course of his own life – events which will, at the same time, put an end to the lives of others.

The greed of two people leads remorselessly to murder. It is greed which enmeshes the guilty and the innocent alike in a web from which, in the end, there is no escape.

Swift and tremendously exciting, ingenious but always perfectly logical, *Or Be He Dead* is the work of a craftsman. It has all the qualities that the public have come to expect from the pen of Harry Carmichael.

### Post Mortem
September 1965

When Evelyn Bailey, 28 years of age and partner in a successful T.V. singing act, died suddenly while taking a bath, her death aroused widespread comment but no suspicion. There was nothing to indicate that she had not died from natural causes.

At the inquest, a pathologist gave evidence that he had found no signs of physical injury, no trace of poison or organic disease. In his opinion, death had been due to vagal inhibition.

There the matter would have rested but for one thing – Evelyn Bailey had been heavily insured. The Cresset Assurance Company thought it might be worthwhile to ask John Piper to make a few inquiries.

Piper enrolled the help of Quinn of the *Morning Post*. And Quinn soon discovered that others had died from vagal inhibition – others who seemed to have had no possible connection with talented and glamorous Evelyn Bailey.

This is a most ingenious story, told with skill and excitement. It possesses all Harry Carmichael's well-known power of taut suspense.

### Put Out That Star
March 1957

*Put Out That Star* is a story of suspense of the Carmichael tradition – a story that will grip you from first page to last. It starts on the morning of Monday, February the twenty-seventh, when a young and beautiful woman with a secret arrives at a famous London hotel. From her secret springs a chain of strange events, and a menace that reaches out and beyond the confines of Suite No. 15… until death strikes twice…and poises again… Once more we have Harry Carmichael using his gift for graphic description and characterisation to the full. In *Put Out That Star* he weaves another of the baffling problems at which he excels.

### Question of Time, A
November 1958

Martin Kennedy was forced to realise that he was in a dangerous and frightening predicament. By calling at the Campbell's flat between five and five-forty on one particular evening he had sprung a trap on himself. Had anyone recognised him as the man who had frequently visited Felicity Campbell?

Had her husband ever suspected the intrigue that had gone on while he had been out of town? How great was the risk that clever, neurotic Kate Fenton would betray him if her attempt at emotional blackmail failed? Caught in the net of jealousy, hate and suspicion which lay just below the surface of the literary circle in which he lived and worked, he soon discovered that his desperate plight was not due to blind chance or his own criminal folly: the lengthening shadow of malice grew steadily darker as events moved against him. *A Question of Time* is Harry Carmichael at his best. It is an ingenious story of conflicting characters caught in a web of circumstances – a story of mounting tension that will keep the reader guessing up to the exciting finish.

### Quiet Woman, The
November 1971

The story of *The Quiet Woman* begins when two people conspire to steal a fortune in cash. It ends in double murder.

For crime reporter Quinn, the robbery at Jauncey Engineering was just another payroll theft. He checked the insurance angle with insurance assessor John Piper and then went around asking questions. At the time all he wanted was human background material for his column in the *Morning Post*.

As the days went by he found himself becoming more deeply, more personally, involved. And then came the phone call which led him to the place where death had been a silent visitor.

Here is a story of everyday people engulfed in frightening events. As an exercise in deductive reasoning it will challenge even the most astute.

### Remote Control
February 1970

On a bitterly cold night in January, Quinn of the *Morning Post* had a drink in the Three Feathers with a man called Hugh Melville. An hour later someone of whom Quinn had never heard took his dog for a walk along a quiet country road near the village of Suttondale.

That is how it all began. Two seemingly unconnected events – a man knocked down and killed: a woman dies in a gas-filled room – and Quinn finds himself one of the central figures in a case of suspected murder.

There appears to be only one solution to the problem – a solution that is obviously impossible. Then John Piper, insurance assessor and friend in time of trouble, offers to lend a hand.

As Piper says: '…Maybe the answer is so simple that we can't see it…or maybe we've been looking in the wrong place.' *Remote Control* is a novel of first-class detection – a story told with deceptive simplicity by a master of his craft.

### Requiem for Charles
July 1960

The day on which Charles Graham disappeared began very much like any other business day. Yet within a few hours events had led to what the newspapers called: 'The Knightsbridge Murder'.

Quinn of the *Morning Post* became involved when Annette Lindon asked him to fabricate an alibi for her – an alibi which was her only hope of escaping from a web of circumstance. His refusal was automatic. But the very fact that she had asked him to lie became the cornerstone of the case against her. But Quinn was not convinced of her guilt. He began asking questions. With each answer the affair took on a new significance – and then there came the ultimate answer which led Quinn into the shadow of death.

*Requiem for Charles* is a tense and absorbing story from the pen of a master-craftsman. It will undoubtedly enhance Harry Carmichael's very considerable reputation.

### *Safe Secret*
March 1964
Dick Thornton was an honest man; everybody said so. Employer, wife, colleagues, acquaintances – all described him as a quiet, respectable sort of fellow. Yet when he disappeared on the night of November twenty-fourth, £35,000 in cash disappeared at the same time.

Instructed by the insurance company to investigate, John Piper finds himself following a very elusive trail – a trail beset by lies and treachery. Nothing is what it seems. And along that twisted road, murder is done.

Harry Carmichael's latest novel grips the imagination. Based on a plot of exceptional ingenuity and told with characteristic punch, it builds up tension page by page until it reaches its climax with a startling revelation.

### *School for Murder*
August 1953
When John Piper was invited to the wedding of Adele Vincent, daughter of an influential client, he expected to rub shoulders with a vast number of guests – but not with murder. And it all began with a shot that no one heard, a shot that linked Adele with the death of a man whom no one knew. Surprising how often John Piper's work as an insurance investigator involves him in violence and murder – surprising too the places that it takes him. In this exciting and fast-moving story of strange happenings, his investigations lead from luxury hotel to sordid bed-sitter, and, in the end, to a college for girls in a secluded part of Devon.

### *Seeds of Hate, The*
January 1960
On a warm August evening Frank Mitchell took his customary walk with his dog along the banks of the Thames at Teddington. How did he get into the river where he was last seen struggling so desperately? Who had reason to wish him dead?

To insurance assessor John Piper, and to Superintendent Mullett of Scotland Yard, it seemed obvious that money was the key to the case. But the more they probed into the outwardly humdrum affairs of the Mitchell family the more puzzled they became.

When Piper eventually uncovers the secret behind the dead man's last hours he is torn between duty and compassion – for the seeds of hate in Frank Mitchell's life had yielded a strange and macabre harvest. Once again Harry Carmichael has achieved those high standards of suspense and ingenuity for which he is now famous.

### *Slightly Bitter Taste, A*
October 1968
On the night when Quinn of the *Morning Post* began his holiday he strayed into a late party where he had too much to drink. There was nothing unusual in that. What made this occasion different was that if he hadn't got drunk, a girl called Carole wouldn't have chosen to make herself responsible for him. Next day when he had pulled himself together she took him off for a quiet weekend with friends to Castle Lammering in Dorset.

Carole's friends turned out to be very strange people. Within only a few hours of Quinn's arrival death joins the guests at Elm Lodge. Although Quin protests that he is on holiday and the affair is not his concern, inevitably he gets caught up in the smouldering passions that govern this house of secrets.

*A Slightly Bitter Taste* is a gripping story of murder in the classical tradition – a story where the clues are fairly placed and yet the solution will elude all but those with the sharpest wits. It is one of Harry Carmichael's most ingenious exercises in deduction.

### *Stranglehold*
July 1959
If Quinn, cynical crime reporter for the *Morning Post*, had not missed the bus from Herngate he would not have visited the village pub. It was in the bar of the Kentish Arms that he met Dr. Charles Mason's attractive red-haired wife. That chance meeting on a bitterly cold night in January was the prelude to murder. Before the night was over Quinn found himself in a situation fraught with terrible danger – a situation from which he could see no way out. In despair he turned for help to John Piper, an old friend whose abilities and experience in criminal investigation are cloaked under the ambiguous title of insurance assessor. Piper agreed to make enquiries. He was not to know that those inquiries would eventually lead him to the point where his own life would be in jeopardy – the point of no return. *Stranglehold* is a fast, taut story of suspense. It has all the qualities that have made Harry Carmichael's name a guarantee of first-class detection.

### *Suicide Clause*
October 1966
Pauline Mason was a beautiful woman with a problem. When she died from strychnine poisoning it would have been all too easy to assume that she had solved her problem by committing suicide.

John Piper investigates on behalf of the Cresset Assurance Company and very soon realises that it is the insurance policy that stands in the way of a simple solution. Looking elsewhere, he comes up against a question to which there appears to be no answer.

As he tells Quinn of the *Morning Post*: 'For the moment I'm not very interested in why or who. What I want to know is – how?'

*Suicide Clause* weaves an ingenious web of intrigue and death around a group of guilty people who are afraid of the truth. It is a story that grips tighter with every page and culminates in the type of denouement for which Harry Carmichael is so well-known.

With *Suicide Clause* Mr. Carmichael enhances his very considerable reputation.

### *Too Late for Tears*
February 1973
On Tuesday, March 27, Gregory Whittle left his home in London before six o'clock in the evening. By eight-thirty he had not returned.

Meantime his wife had received two phone calls. The second one was sufficient to arouse alarm. That was the beginning. In the events which follow, death plays an inevitable part.

John Piper, insurance assessor, is engaged by the Cresset Insurance Company to hold a watching brief. When Quinn, crime columnist of the *Morning* Post, learns the circumstances, he suggests that things may not be quite what they seem.

Harry Carmichael's *Too Late for Tears* is another classic example of detection by an acknowledged master of the surprise ending.

### *Vanishing Trick, The*
August 1952
Jobs that pay good money don't grow on trees. John Piper was quite aware of that. But he had his personal integrity as an enquiry agent to consider, and there was something shady about this one *and* about the so-called solicitor who offered it. He didn't like Jacob Rawson or his dirty-looking office; he didn't like the idea of being paid in cash. And he thought the amount offered was far too much for the seemingly routine job of finding Godfrey Allen, partner in a firm of pottery manufacturers, who had disappeared three weeks before. Rawson's anonymous client would not go to the police, but when Piper threatened to call them in if he thought his preliminary investigations warranted it, Rawson still insisted on his taking the case. It just didn't add up! This is a fast and truly tricky story, with sharp characterisation and excellent dialogue.

### *Vendetta*
January 1963
John Piper's diary for Saturday 11th December read:

*Fritz Hauptmann. Call 2.30 re factory insurance with Cresset.*

When Piper arrived at the house and saw his client lounging in an armchair listening to Mozart, he had no reason to think that this was one day he would never forget. It was not Hauptmann's premonitions of disaster that so impressed themselves on Piper, nor even the startling beauty of Gizelle Hauptmann...

Disregarding the warnings Hauptmann had been given at séances held by a London spiritualist association, Piper endorsed the additional insurance that Hauptmann asked for. No sooner were the policies issued than it became apparent that something more tangible than ghostly spirits was bent on injuring Hauptmann. Somebody hated him: somebody was prepared to conduct a ruthless vendetta against him and all he held dear.

Harry Carmichael's latest novel builds up by way of numerous adroit twists, shifts of suspicion and rising excitement to a sensational climax.

### *Why Kill Johnny?*
January 1954
The death of Joseph Pulleyn, partner in Pulleyn, Leigh and McLaren, Chemical Engineers, was apparently due to 'natural causes'. As Pulleyn had been buried without fuss or comment, there didn't seem much sense in the threatening and anonymous letters which began to reach his colleagues and relatives. Why should a murderer draw attention to a killing which had gone off so smoothly? Quinn, a down-at-heel reporter, met Joseph's son, Johnny Pulleyn, when the latter got drunk in a pub through celebrating his father's death. Johnny told Quinn some disturbing facts. Quinn contacted Piper, but by the time the two of them had begun investigating in earnest other crimes had been committed: the fact that a murderer was at large was by then beyond doubt. This really gripping story, in which the murderer acts with such speed and initiative that even Piper is hard pressed to keep pace, ends in a dramatic and astonishing climax.

## CARNAC, CAROL
*(see also* **Lorac, E.C.R.***)*

### *Burning Question, The*
July 1957
P. C. Boyle was reluctant to leave his wife, his home and his supper on a night of thick fog in the steep moorland country. Yet the anonymous voice had been very definite that there was a dead body, killed by a motor vehicle, on a hill road a few miles away. If the body was there at all it was a dead one – wouldn't it keep till daylight? But Boyle was conscientious and went off to investigate.

It seemed straightforward enough. But that same night the little derelict church, near where the body was found, was burnt down. This could have happened by accident, and yet…the police began to investigate, and throughout the neighbourhood talk was about the gutted church, 'the burning question'.

In this book Carol Carnac introduces a new police detective, young Sergeant Kit Riddle of the C. I. D. He and his friend Robert Thorpe find themselves investigating a very much more complicated and sinister situation than they had anticipated. Because there *had* been a crime all right and only one of the local people, mostly farmers, could have committed it.

Some fine detection is needed to identify the criminal, for he had acted with ingenuity and daring. The detectives are not quick enough to prevent a second murder, but in a thrilling and surprising denouement they foil the murderer before he can commit a third.

### *Crossed Skis*
July 1952
It's a far cry from the slush of London's streets to the crisp, dry, shining snow of the Austrian mountains. Yet there was a direct trail leading from the decayed Bloomsbury boarding-house where a man's body was found, burnt beyond recognition, to a gay party of sixteen young ski-ing enthusiasts enjoying a holiday at Lech am Arlberg. The trail took Inspector Julian Rivers of Scotland Yard in search of a murderer of whom he knew only that he was well-educated, of great personal charm, probably Irish, a good climber and an expert ski-er. An exciting chase ends in dramatic fashion with a ski-run in a blinding snowstorm. Carol Carnac has never given us a better story than this one.

### *Death of a Lady Killer*
October 1959
The flirtation between the rich and handsome Brigadier Fotheringay and Mrs. Delancie (known to the younger guests as 'the widow de luxe') was appreciated by everyone at the comfortable and expensive Spa Hotel, Bourne Regis as a diversion and a splendid display of practiced, if dated, gallantry. The discovery of the Brigadier's body at the foot of the cliffs, the complete disappearance of the widow, and the savage attack on the night porter at the hotel plunged the residents of the Spa into a melodrama which become more ugly and more puzzling as Inspector Strang uncovered layer after layer of evidence each more baffling than the last.

Carol Carnac's many admirers will find *Death of a Lady Killer* an enthralling and entertaining mystery; a worthy successor to books like *The Burning Question* and *The Double Turn*.

### *Double Turn, The*
July 1956
What had become of old Adrian Delafield, who had once made a fortune and a reputation by painting vast canvases for municipal centres and boardrooms? This question came up when Susan Truby and her uncle, Jocelyn Truby, were talking with friends at an exhibition of Victorian paintings. It transpired that Delafield was still alive, but that the strangest rumours were current about his household in St. John's Wood. Soon they were to learn more about that household and the fierce jealousy that raged within it; they were to grow apprehensive of the threat of tragedy. Yet when murder *did* occur it was inexplicable as regards both motive and method.

Carol Carnac's new detective story is another fine example of that craft. The reader is not likely to be able to succeed in naming the murderer ahead of Chief Inspector Rivers, yet he is likely, on the way, to share and enjoy the excitement and the twists that precede the climax.

### Impact of Evidence
September 1954

Among the hills of the Welsh borders a little group of farmsteads is isolated by snow and ice, then floods. Late one afternoon there is a terrible car smash on a cross-roads in these hills. Old Dr Robinson is found dead in his big saloon, which, thrown off the road by the violent impact, has crashed down onto the steep hillside, now sodden with deep flood-waters. That was no surprise – the old man should long before have been prevented from driving, he was a menace on the roads. But why was there a second body in the back of Dr. Robinson's car? Who was the man who was found there, how had he reached these isolated hills? The local police Inspector, Welby, also has an accident; Rivers and Lancing have to come from Scotland Yard, cross the floods, and pick up the trail of events. They are soon involved in strange and mysterious happenings, which are made frighteningly real by the authentic picture of the isolation of the district, the daily struggle for survival of small farmers in hard conditions. In a night of dramatic events high in the lonely hills, Rivers discovers the identity of the murderer. Carol Carnac is at the top of her form in this thrilling story.

### It's Her Own Funeral
September 1951

Carol Carnac, an author well known to detective story devotees, joins the Crime Club list with a new novel of first-rate quality. Her special appeal is to those readers who like to be set a knotty problem with a fair chance of themselves unravelling it. In the untimely death of the well-to-do spinster Anne Tempest, Carol Carnac not only presents us with as ingenious a murder as we could wish, but she challenges us to find, on equal terms with Chief Inspector Rivers of the C. I. D., the answers to those three basic questions: What was the motive? How was the murder contrived? Who had the opportunity?

### Long Shadows
May 1958

Why were the journalists at Priscilla Sowerby's party so interested in Helen's Court?

It was certainly an interesting place: 'an ultra-modern house built mainly of glass in the U. S. idiom, set in an ancestral park'; 'it wasn't only a nursing home – it was a recuperation centre for jaded financiers.' It was the sort of place where death from natural causes was to be expected from time to time…

But when Burton Latimer died there it was clearly murder. There was the question as to who had killed him, and there was another question: who, in fact, *was* Burton Latimer?

Chief Inspector Rivers found himself launched into a case of phenomenal complexity and fascination, a maze that had alleys reaching back to a sensational crime in the past; Rivers found that many of his 'suspects' had been oddly associated with that crime.

This is the classic detective story at its best – fair, lucid, well-presented and well-reasoned. All the way to its exciting climax and astonishing denouement, it demonstrates the outstanding qualities of Carol Carnac's inventive writing.

### Murder Among Members
March 1955

In *Murder Among Members* Carol Carnac has invented an institution more fabulous even than her Ministry of Fine Arts: a Parliament Hostel, in Parliament Square, at which Members of the House of Commons can lodge cheaply and conveniently in London.

The scene is set a fortnight before the new session; only a few members are in Parliament Hostel – the great majority of its five hundred odd rooms are empty. It is Charles Crummock, MP for Blennerhasset, who, returning late to the hostel, sees two bodies lying motionless – and apparently lifeless – in Stationery Court, alongside the tall Hostel building. Chief Inspector Rivers and Inspector Lancing are soon plunged into a case of extraordinary difficulty and complexity; a case which may cost either of them their jobs if a false step is made, for their every move may be scrutinised in the Mother of Parliaments. As the case develops Rivers is obliged – against his usual instincts of meticulous care and logic – to follow what is little more than a hunch; it takes him into the East End and Dockland; into a nest of wrongdoing such as even he has rarely encountered. *Murder Among Members* is among the most ingenious and exciting of Carol Carnac's fine crime stories.

### Murder as a Fine Art
March 1953

The Ministry of Fine Arts had come into being during the short era of optimism following World War Two. Since its inception it had suffered from what might be called infant mortality. The first Minister died after six months in office, the second just before the General Election. Death claimed its third victim when Edwin Pomfret, deputy Permanent Secretary, was crushed to death at the head of a flight of stairs. Pomfret was murdered. By whom? That is the natural question in detective stories. But in Carol Carnac's latest novel an equally important question is How? Here is the crime of murder carried out with an artistic touch, which evokes the reluctant admiration of Inspector Rivers of Scotland Yard.

### Policeman at the Door, A
November 1953

Derek Thorpe worked in his father's office, trying hard to become the respectable, black-coated worker Mr. Thorpe expected his son to be. From a sense of duty and affection for his father, he kept secret his passion for painting: his sketches, done in what spare time he could snatch, were meticulously hidden. But Mr. Thorpe's fanatical hatred of all things artistic had a firmer foundation than his son realised. Rosamond, Derek's mother, had been an artist, and her marriage to the uncompromising Mr. Thorpe had ended in great bitterness. When Thorpe discovered the nude studies so carefully concealed by Derek, he at once suspected the worst – and the row between them was the first episode in a situation which led very quickly to murder. Besides presenting a fascinating problem this is a story of real people in the grip of a terrifying situation, resolved only in the nick of time by Chief Inspector Rivers in an astonishing climax.

### Rigging the Evidence
November 1955

In *Rigging the Evidence*, the Bough family, peacefully farming among the hills, suddenly find themselves at the centre of unpleasant events. During the busy routine of haymaking they are helped by a wandering artist who turns out to be as proficient with a pitchfork as with a paint-brush. However, the black sheep of the family, who has taken an instant dislike to the newcomer, disappears and the next day one of his friends is discovered murdered in a local railway tunnel. The case is not as straightforward as it appears to be, and the police find the trail leads them high up over the hills before they eventually run their quarry to earth. This is an exciting story of detection told with Carol Carnac's familiar skill and feeling for the countryside.

## CAUDWELL, SARAH
### Shortest Way to Hades, The
October 1984

'What is the duty of a barrister who suspects that her client has been murdered on Boat Race Day? Julia, as always, was anxious to do the right thing; but she and her friends at the Chancery Bar – Selena, Timothy, Ragwort and Cantrip – were far too busy with Opinions and Affidavits to deal with the problem themselves. In the best traditions of Lincoln's Inn they found someone else to do it; *videlicet* myself.

'Though I consented to investigate, laying aside my own trifling responsibilities as Tutor in Legal History at St George's College, Oxford, I did not in truth believe there was anything in it. Despite what Julia had discovered when imperfectly disguised as a schoolgirl in the flat of the dubious financier; despite the rather sinister charm of the beautiful Greek boy; despite what I should have inferred from the conduct of the temporary typist – I still did not think it was a question of murder.

'Only when Selena, sailing the Ionian Sea with my young colleague Sebastian, renewed her acquaintance with the dead girl's relatives; only then – even to the Scholar the Truth is sometimes obscure – did I begin to perceive the true significance of the events set forth in these pages; and to fear that my friends were sailing by the shortest way to Hades.'

### Sirens Sang of Murder, The
June 1989

Not even Cantrip's best friends – that is to say, the other members of his Chambers in Lincoln's Inn – would have claimed that he was an expert on international tax planning. Why then did his instructing solicitor require his presence in the Channel Islands? Did she merely have designs on his virtue, or was there some more sinister reason?

My responsibilities as Tutor in Legal History at St. George's College, Oxford, were, happily, not of immediate urgency: when the fatal accident rate among those whom Cantrip was advising became higher than seemed statistically probable, I was available to investigate.

I learnt, in the course of my inquiry, the details of Julia's romantic adventures in the Cayman Islands; I discovered in Monaco the true reason for the interest shown by the Chancery judge in the charming and enigmatic Contessa; and I at last established the identity of the white-robed figure seen on Walpurgis Night on the cliff-tops of Sark.

By the time, however, that by applying to the evidence the methods of Scholarship I was able to reveal the Truth, it was too late to keep Cantrip from his dangerous rendezvous at the place where the witches danced and the sirens sang...of murder.

### Thus Was Adonis Murdered
March 1981

'If the events in which Julia Larwood, one of the more susceptible and accident-prone members of the Chancery Bar, became involved while on holiday last September had not been subject to the scrutiny of the trained scholar – that is to say, my own – well, I do not say that Julia would even now be languishing in a Venetian prison, but I do say that it was only as a result of my own investigation that her innocence on a charge of murder was conclusively proved.

'As an instance of what the methods of Scholarship may achieve, the affair seems not unworthy of written record, and my readers may think that those friends of Julia's in Lincoln's Inn who had been privileged to observe the reasoning of Professor Hilary Tamar of St George's College, Oxford, would have competed in eagerness to describe how, by applying to Julia's letters the stringent principle of textual criticism, I was able to perceive the true significance of the curious incident in Verona, the nervousness of the man from the Revenue, and the presence of Julia's copy of the Finance Act at the bedside of the corpse.

'Alas, the Chancery Bar being what it is, I am obliged to do the thing myself, for mere personal delicacy must not deprive the public of an instructive chronicle. I have set down what happened, as it happened, in the belief that the discerning will perceive the true nature of my achievement, and that all is explained except the spider episode and Schedule 7 of Finance Act.'

## CHILD, NELLISE
### Diamond Ransom Murders, The
December 1934

Nellise Child's first novel, *Murder Comes Home*, was one of the outstanding successes of the Crime Club's list last year. In the successor to that splendid story, Detective-Lieutenant Jerry Irish makes a welcome reappearance. It is an extremely exciting story, exposing the nefarious activities of the American kidnapping racket, which recently has assumed a nationwide importance. As one prominent person after another disappears and is added to the list of victims compiled by the Missing Persons Bureau, the excitement grows. From kidnapping it is an easy stage to murder, and in the elucidation of what became known as the Diamond Ransom Murders, Jerry Irish plays a prominent part.

### Murder Comes Home
August 1933

Douglas Varding, middle-aged, eccentric millionaire and famous connoisseur of art, fears death. Nevertheless, death comes, and Varding is murdered in a room almost as impregnable as a fortress, with bars outside its locked windows and a door heavily bolted from the inside. The question is, first – how was the crime committed? And second, not who could have wished Varding dead, but which one of the many people who hated him had the courage and resource to commit the crime? Varding's beautiful young wife would profit from his death, so would his brother, and anyone of a half-dozen other people. There is more than one sinister influence at work in this strange household. To tell more of the story would be to spoil the suspense. The experienced reader of detective stories will find *Murder Comes Home* as different as it is exciting.

## CHRISTIE, AGATHA
### A B C Murders, The
January 1936

Agatha Christie, 'the best of all crime novelists', has, as one critic truly says, 'set herself such a standard that even she will scarcely excel it'. Yet, year by year, book by book, her power as a novelist develops, and her wit becomes keener. Now, with *The A B C Murders*, her own greatest triumph and a classic of crime fiction, she sets a new high-water mark in the history of the detective story.

The idea of the story is as brilliant as its execution. The murderer in this case is evidently a maniac, for he seems bent on working his way through a whole alphabet of victims. Beginning with A, he murders a Mrs.

Ascher at Andover. Proceeding to B he strangles Betty Barnard on the beach at Bexhill. For C, he chooses as his victim Sir Carmichael Clarke of Churston. And as a sign of his method he leaves beside the corpse on each occasion a railway ABC open at the name of the place where the murder has taken place. ABC...how far through the alphabet will he get. It seemed that nobody would be able to catch him. But he made the mistake – the one mistake that every murderer makes – when, out of sheer vanity, he challenged Poirot to frustrate his plans.

In recommending this story to your friends, please do not hint at anything that might spoil their pleasure in reading it.

### *Adventure of the Christmas Pudding and A Selection of Entrees, The*

October 1960

The proof of the pudding is in the eating. The six stories in this book are further proof, if it were needed, that as hostess and chef Agatha Christie can serve up a banquet which will satisfy gourmets of the detective story. In five of them Hercule Poirot is seen at the top of his incomparable form – whether he is involved in the ominous affair of 'The Dream' or in 'The Mystery of the Spanish Chest', a matter which, strictly speaking, was no business of his. He was introduced to the case of 'The Under Dog' by a girl whose calm and unemotional voice belied the tale of violence and tragedy she told, but in 'Four-and-Twenty Blackbirds' the little Belgian diagnosed murder whilst enjoying a quiet dinner with a friend in a Chelsea restaurant. In 'The Adventure of the Christmas Pudding' he is again involved with food, but, this time, accompanied by unseasonable deeds of ill-will which beset his first experience of the traditional English Christmas. In the sixth story, 'Greenshaw's Folly', Miss Marples [sic], calmly and characteristically, finds and solves a murder on her doorstop and provides a story which adds further variety to the menu of a feast fit for a king – prepared and served by the Queen of Crime.

### *After the Funeral*

May 1953

Richard Abernethie died a very wealthy man. All the relatives who attended his funeral benefited by his death. Although the newspaper announcements of his death said: *suddenly at his residence*, there was no reason to suspect that his death was anything but a natural one – or was there? One person certainly thought so, and old Mr. Entwhistle, the family lawyer, was made uneasy. He began to consider the various members of the Abernethie family. Though outwardly prosperous, how badly did they need the money old Richard's death brought them? Succeeding events deepened Mr. Entwhistle's uneasiness into active alarm. How best could he serve the interests of the Abernethie family, and what would his dead friend Richard Abernethie wish him to do?

Entwhistle goes for help to Hercule Poirot, an old friend of his, and the little Belgian solves things in his own inimitable way; making sense out of apparent nonsense; piecing things together from such widely different clues as a piece of wedding cake and a bouquet of wax flowers.

If there was one thing better than an Agatha Christie without Poirot, it is an Agatha Christie *with* Poirot. *After the Funeral* shows this happy partnership at its unbeatable best.

### *Appointment With Death*

May 1938

*'You do see, don't you, that she's got to be killed?'* Strange words to float in through a hotel window. Stranger still that Hercule Poirot is the man who overhears them. Later Poirot identifies the voice and his attention is drawn to the Boynton family. Even then he appreciates the psychological forces at work and the terrible emotional strain the Boyntons are undergoing.

We go with them on their journey – from Jerusalem to the Dead Sea, and onward into the desert. And there, in the rose red city of Petra, the appointment is kept – with Death...

A perfectly natural death, so it would seem, but Colonel Carbury is worried. He appeals to Poirot, who promises him the truth within twenty-four hours. Poirot keeps his word.

### *At Bertram's Hotel*

November 1965

If you turn off an unpretentious street from the Park and continue a little way down a quiet street you will find Bertram's Hotel on the right hand side. Bertram's Hotel has been there a long time – dignified, unostentatious, and quietly expensive. It has been patronised be the higher echelons of the clergy, dowager ladies of the aristocracy up from the country, girls on their way home for the holidays from expensive finishing schools.

Bertram's in fact, is the very height of respectability. Is it a little bit too good to be true? That is what Miss Jane Marple soon begins to wonder… Miss Marple as is well known, always suspects the worst – and, she claims, she is usually right.

It is Miss Marple's destiny to stumble across violence and mystery. Her brief London holiday at Bertram's Hotel soon presents her with a most complex and baffling puzzle.

In the pleasure she gives to readers of all ages, in the lustre and popularity she has given to the crime novel in our time, Agatha Christie stands alone. Here, as skilful, tricky, and compulsively readable as ever, is the latest full length novel from the most outstanding crime novelist of all.

### *Body in the Library, The*

May 1942

Colonel and Mrs. Bantry had always believed that 'a body in the library' only happened in books – until the day when a body was found in their own library! Whose body was it? Why should it be found in the library of Gossington Hall? That gentle elderly spinster, Miss Marple (whom readers of Agatha Christie will remember) was faced with all these questions. Following the trail from the quiet village of St. Mary Mead to a fashionable seaside hotel, she eventually found the answer. How did she manage it? Well, in her own words: 'It reminded me of Tommy Bond and our new schoolmistress, she went to wind up the clock and a frog jumped out!'

### *By the Pricking of My Thumbs*

November 1968

Tommy and Tuppence Beresford, once the *Young Adventurers*, later functioning as *Blunt's Brilliant Detectives*, finally active in the Second War tracking down that notorious spy *N or M*, are now living in peaceful retirement – they lead a happy life…

What more can they want?

Well -?

They go to visit an elderly relative, Tommy's Aunt Ada who is established in Sunny Ridge, well-run Home for Elderly ladies – on the surface it appears to be a model of its kind. *But is it?*

Aunt Ada dies peacefully in her bed, but another old lady leaves very suddenly in the care of somewhat mysterious relatives.

Tuppence has her misgivings – Tommy starts by pooh-poohing them. But Tuppence makes up her own mind that she will discover what has really happened to old Mrs. Lancaster.

The hunt involves an oil painting of a house by a canal, a peaceful village where nothing ever happens (?), a character whom Tuppence christens 'the friendly witch', a hunt through old tombstones in a churchyard, and, when Tommy returns from a hush-hush conference, he finds that Tuppence has failed to return from her quest.

Brilliantly sustained mystery is always to be found in a novel by Agatha Christie, but her latest story contains an extra element, and might equally well have been entitled *By the Chilling of Your Spine*.

### *Cards on the Table*

November 1936

'This case, to my mind,' says Poirot, 'has been one of the most interesting cases I have ever come across. There was *nothing*, you see, to go upon. There were four people, one of whom *must* have committed the crime, but which of the four? Was there anything to tell one? In the material sense – no. There were no tangible clues – no fingerprints – no incriminating papers or documents, there were only the people themselves.'

In fact, this is the 'closed' crime *par excellence*, the type of problem in which Mrs. Christie has always been most interested and which, by its very nature, is the fairest test of the reader's perspicacity. Four people are playing bridge, and in the course of the game their host, who has been sitting out, is murdered. He can only have been murdered by one of the players while dummy. Now any of the four, given the right circumstances, might have committed the crime, for each of them is known to have committed at any rate one murder and is quite capable of committing another. As Mrs. Christie writes in her preface, 'They are four widely divergent types, the motive that drives each of them is peculiar to that person, and each would employ a different method. The deduction must, therefore, be entirely *psychological* and when all is said and done, it is the *mind* of the murderer that is of supreme interest.'

No wonder Poirot called it one of his most interesting cases. All Mrs. Christie's readers will emphatically agree.

### *Caribbean Mystery, A*

November 1964

Miss Marple is on holiday at the Golden Palm Hotel in the island of St. Honore. She is enjoying herself, yet there is something lacking. At home in St. Mary Mead there was always something going on, something one could get one's teeth into.

Miss Marple listens politely to Major Palgrave's boring stories of his early life in Kenya – or at any rate pretends to listen. She is not paying all that much attention when he starts telling her about a murderer he has known; and when he reaches in his wallet to show Miss Marple a snapshot of that murderer, he is suddenly interrupted. Murder follows.

In this new full length novel the clues and keys to the murder's identity are fairly – one might even say ostentatiously – paraded in front of the reader. Yet we believe it will be a very perceptive reader who observes and interprets them correctly. Most of the large number of readers of *A Caribbean Mystery* will in the end ask themselves how they could have been so stupid – or how Mrs. Christie could have fooled them once again.

This is yet another dazzling tour-de-force from the greatest crime novelist of our time.

### *Cat Among the Pigeons*

November 1959

Meadowbank is one of the most exclusive girls' schools in England. Unthinkable that there should be a murder at Meadowbank. But a train of violence, starting in the Middle East and involving jewels, intrigues and secret agents, did in fact reach its deadly climax within the distinguished precincts of the school itself. Worse still, it became clear that the culprits must actually be among the staff or the pupils. There was a cat among the pigeons.

It was that intelligent schoolgirl Julia Upjohn who finally went to consult Hercule Poirot. 'It's very urgent,' she said. 'It's about some murders and a robbery and things like that.' Unruffled and retaining every bit of his customary and engaging aplomb, the incomparable Belgian set about unravelling a case which, he was forced to agree, was as devious and complicated as a snarl of tangled wool. Agatha Christie has once again succeeded brilliantly in blending entertainment, detection and suspense to give her vast number of admirers a book which fully maintains the unique and enviable Christie tradition.

### *Clocks, The*

November 1963

The whole thing was fantastic! A blind woman – a dead man whom no one could identify – four strange clocks all showing the same time – *thirteen minutes past four*. Who had brought them there? What did they mean? And who was the dead man?

It all has Detective Inspector Hardcastle badly worried – especially when a second murder follows. But his friend, Colin Lamb, who has come to Crowdean on a security matter, is so intrigued by these bizarre happenings, that he thinks of his father's old friend, Hercule Poirot. How Poirot would enjoy this! And Poirot does enjoy it.

'This crime is so complicated that it must be quite simple,' he declares

But is it so simple?

As a crime novelist Agatha Christie stands alone. Fashions change, new approaches to the crime novel come and go – but it is the 'Christie for Christmas' that readers of all ages are waiting for. Here is a new and most dazzling specimen; a perfectly fair detective novel of superb expertise which shows very clearly and enjoyably that the years have had no effect whatever on the ingenuity of Hercule Poirot.

### *Crooked House*

May 1949

This is Agatha Christie's 49th detective story. It is 29 years since her first was published, yet custom cannot stale her infinite variety, and we have little hesitation in asserting that if this new story is not the best she has ever done, then it is second only to that classic of detection, *The Murder of Roger Ackroyd*. It is certainly a remarkable witness to her unfailing verve, that when she is nearing her half-century she should still be able to knock one over the top of the pavilion to the fervent applause of admirers.

The old jingle 'all lived together in a little crooked house' here applies to the three generations of Leonides who lived together under the sheltering roof of Three Gables – a large household over whom the very old and very rich Aristide Leonides had long presided; not that there was anything about the very respectable Leonides that was crooked in the dishonest sense, but nevertheless all its members had grown up a little bit twisted in their outlook on life. But even now in death, that little old man with the dark velvet skull-cap and the head sunken in his shoulders, seemed to live on – a very real presence in that house of tragedy. A poisoner's hand had struck him down, but it was the old Greek himself who had supplied the blueprint for his own murder, actually suggesting the very method to be used – by the right person. The murderer must have been one of the family, but who was capable of this cold-blooded and calculated poisoning? Who was the *right* person?

Agatha Christie shows herself to be still the master of her medium, the incomparable queen of mystery, and *Crooked House* adds another jewel to her crown.

### Curtain: Poirot's Last Case
September 1975

This, the final volume in a series that has been delighting the world since 1920, will be acclaimed by Hercule Poirot's legion of fans as probably the best of all, even while saddening them because it is to be his last appearance.

In *Curtain* the wheel has come full circle, and the little Belgian detective is back once more at the country house where he made his bow in Agatha Christie's first detective story, *The Mysterious Affair at Styles*.

Styles is now a guest house and Poirot one of the guests. He invites his old friend Hastings to join him there, and confides the professional reason for this ultimate reunion. Among those at Styles is someone responsible for several murders, yet someone the law cannot touch. Poirot is reluctant to name his suspect.

But soon there is another death at Styles – and this time, with Hastings's daughter among the guests and suspects, even he contemplates murder!

Written over thirty years ago, but held back until now, this novel is a triumphant climax to the sequence, as Poirot solves his last case in a fashion characteristically brilliant and unorthodox.

### Dead Man's Folly
November 1956

Nasse House – and a fete in progress including, not a Treasure Hunt, but a Murder Hunt – devised by that well-known detective novelist, Mrs. Ariadne Oliver; the prizes to be given away by the celebrated M. Hercule Poirot.

That was how it appeared to the public. But what lay behind it? What was the summons that brought Hercule Poirot at a moment's notice from London to Devonshire – to meet there the bluff Sir George Stubbs, his beautiful exotic wife, old Mrs. Folliatt whose ancestors had lived at Nasse for generations, and all the other people who were helping to make the Fete a success? And what part did the little white 'Folly', set high in the woods above the river, have to play?

Once again, and with her habitual ingenuity, Agatha Christie presents a baffling story of murder and suspicion. Even Poirot is bewildered by a misleading tangle of evidence – even more than by Mrs. Oliver's confused exposition of her own plots.

An unlikely victim, an incredible disappearance, an impossible murder...so it seems. But in the end it all makes sense to Hercule Poirot.

This book follows *Hickory Dickory Dock* from the pen of the writer who is universally acknowledged as being the supreme practitioner of the complex and fascinating art of the detective story.

### Death Comes as the End
March 1945

As the wife of an eminent archaeologist, Agatha Christie has taken part in several expeditions to the Near East. Drawing upon this experience, she gives us, in *Death Comes as the End*, a murder mystery laid in Ancient Egypt 4000 years ago.

Into the household of Imhotep, the Mortuary Priest, comes the beautiful Nofret. The household, outwardly at peace, has at its core, in the words of the thoughtful scribe Hori, a rottenness that breeds from within. With Nofret comes anger, jealousy, quarrels and finally death.

Human passions were the same in 2000 B.C. as they are to-day. The fussy and pompous Imhotep, the timid Yahmose, and the quarrelsome Sobek, and the malicious 'poor relation' Henet – all are types to be met with in our present world.

Christie's latest experiment is as ingenious and baffling as always, and ends with a climax which few would anticipate.

### Death in the Clouds
July 1935

Out of the blue of a September sky the great cross-Channel airliner *Prometheus* appeared true to time and circled round gracefully to make a perfect landing at Croydon. A plain-clothes inspector accompanied by a uniformed policeman came hurriedly across the aerodrome and climbed into the 'plane. 'Will you please follow me, ladies and gentlemen?' The disconcerted passengers were escorted, not into the usual Customs department, but into a small private room. For high over the Channel, death, quick and mysterious, had struck at one of their number. The investigation had begun into what was to prove one of Hercule Poirot's most baffling mysteries. Once again we marvel at the wonderful deductive powers of the little Belgian, perhaps the favourite character in present-day detective fiction.

### Death on the Nile
November 1937

Mrs. Christie in her new long novel takes us for a journey down the Nile and adds one more to the mysteries of Egypt. She has never collected together a more variegated and interesting group of characters than for this journey during which murder is committed, and with her own knowledge of the Near East she creates the atmosphere so perfectly that one cannot believe, on finishing the book, that one has not made that self-same journey.

Coming events cast their shadows before them. We feel the death on the Nile long before it occurs. The victim, a girl who has everything – beauty, wealth, love – moves onward to death. We see danger slowly converging upon her from different quarters of the world. Hercule Poirot has been a spectator of the drama from an early moment. He foresees the inevitable end, but is powerless – his advice is disregarded. The murderer is among a little group of people isolated on a steamer far from civilisation. The facts seem to point overwhelmingly to one person – but Poirot is doubtful. He studies the psychology of the crime – bold, audacious, brilliant – and is thereby led to the surprising truth.

### Destination Unknown
November 1954

In this, her new and brilliant book, Agatha Christie has departed from the canons of classical detection, as she did in *They Came to Baghdad*.

The problem here is to trace the means by which a famous scientist, discoverer of ZE Fission, has been wafted away. The direction in which he has disappeared may be guessed at, but the tracks have been covered; suspect reports of the sighting of the missing man come in from all over Europe, then his wife asks permission to go away and rest – to take a holiday in Morocco.

Is it nothing but holiday she is going to look for? A plan is formed to keep watch on her journeyings, but some very surprising things then begin to happen.

The authentic Moroccan setting of this book and its exciting and surprising narrative will hold every reader enthralled. It is full of those sudden, ingenious twists and that brilliant though seemingly casual power of characterisation for which Agatha Christie is so justly renowned.

### Dumb Witness
July 1937

The death of Miss Emily Arundell, a rich, elderly spinster, surprised no one in the small town of Market Basing. But her will did. Autocratic and yet warm-hearted, Miss Arundell was reticent about her affairs. Even to her lawyer she had said nothing of the motives behind her startling will. Shortly before her death, however, she had written to Poirot, and although through some mischance her letter was delayed, the little detective did think it worthwhile paying a visit to Market Basing. The amazing ramifications of a superlatively ingenious plot, in which, by the way, a dog was to play a not inconsiderable part, were sufficient to keep Poirot busy investigating this mysterious affair of a lady lately deceased.

### Elephants Can Remember
November 1972

Hercule Poirot was expecting a visit from his friend Mrs Ariadne Oliver, the novelist. There was something, it seemed, that she wanted to ask him. He wondered why she sounded so doubtful about what she was doing. Was she bringing him some difficult problem? Or was she acquainting him with a crime? As Poirot knew well, it could be anything with Mrs Oliver! The most commonplace things or the most extraordinary things were all alike to her.

His mind ran back over the years – the various happenings in which she had embroiled him. A murder hunt for a charity which had unexpectedly included a real murder (*Dead Man's Folly*). A girl who had once interrupted his breakfast to tell him that she thought she had committed a murder but wasn't quite sure about it (*Third Girl*). Mrs Oliver had identified the girl, but had then managed to get herself knocked on the head with a near escape from getting killed.

Would this visit entail danger – or merely a dilemma? He had no idea that what was going to be laid before him would be a double suicide that had taken place twelve years ago and been satisfactorily dealt with by the Police Force of Great Britain.

He did not foresee that, at first unwillingly, he would become enmeshed – not in crime as crime – but because of two young people who loved each other and wanted to marry. He was not to suspect that this girl and boy would matter to him. The places he would go, the questions he would ask, the activities in which he would engage, the pity he would feel, the depths of tragedy he would plumb...

None of these things did he foresee as he replaced the receiver on the telephone. All that was in his mind was that Mrs Oliver was coming to see him after dinner and that she had a problem of some kind – about which she wanted his advice. Oh well, he didn't expect there would be any difficulty about that.

So little do the most intelligent of human beings foresee what is coming towards them in the immediate future.

### Endless Night
October 1967

The site of the house called The Towers had once been known as Gypsy's Acre. When it was sold Michael Rogers went to the auction, though he hadn't any money. His dream was of a new house on the old site, to be built by his brilliant young architect friend.

It was at Gypsy's Acre that Michael first saw the girl he was to marry; the account of Michael's courting of Ellie, their growing attraction for each other, is the starting point of the drama that begins and ends at Gypsy's Acre.

The story ends in the revelation of a monstrous crime, complete with all the paraphernalia that had been required to effect it.

A new novel by Agatha Christie is always a momentous event in the calendar of crime novel publishing. In this doom-laden story, different in kind from the experiences of Hercule Poirot and Miss Marple, all the author's great gifts of subtlety and interpretation are on full display. Here, from the master of crime story-telling, is something new and different – something extraordinarily exciting.

### Evil Under the Sun
June 1941

Hercule Poirot, resplendent in a white duck suit, with a panama tilted over his eyes, his moustaches magnificently befurled, lay back in a deck chair on a sunny terrace overlooking the bathing beach. Casually his fellow guests at the luxury hotel moved around him, talking, knitting, drying from their bathes, anointing themselves with oil. It was August and the holiday mood ran high; there was laughter among the crowds on the sands, children's voices from the surf, gay couples climbed on the cliff paths. But, as Agatha Christie's famous detective says, 'there is evil everywhere under the sun' and before long his languid holiday is disturbed by a more than usually urgent call for his professional help. No reader can help being fascinated by Poirot's manner and methods.

### Five Little Pigs
January 1943

How to find out the truth about a crime that was committed sixteen years ago is indeed a problem. No wonder Carla Lemarchant sought the best help available, and it was fortunate for her that she found Hercule Poirot, for as he said himself, 'Rest assured – I am the best.' Faced with the question: Did Carla's mother, Caroline Crale, really commit the murder for which she was sentenced? he began to reconstruct in his mind events long past. She was an enigmatic character, this Caroline Crale, who had pleaded innocent yet had not fought to prove it. Her life with Amyas Crale had been difficult, certainly. He was selfish, quarrelsome, inconsiderate and unfaithful, even though he was a great painter as some said. Approaching deftly and tactfully the other five people involved with the case, Poirot unravels bit by bit the true story of that summer day sixteen years ago. It is a fascinating story which leaves the reader to marvel more than ever at Poirot's performance, and to acclaim Mrs. Christie for yet another brilliant landmark in the history of detective fiction.

### 4.50 from Paddington
November 1957

Having done her Christmas shopping, Mrs. McGillicuddy relaxes happily in a train. Then another train, going in the same direction, draws abreast and for some minutes the two trains proceed side by side. That has happened to all of us. But in a first-class carriage of the second train, Mrs. McGillicuddy sees, to her horror, a man strangling a woman... then the second train gathers speed and vanishes into the night.

Who was the woman? Who was the man

strangling her? And why is the body not found for so long?

As Mrs. McGillicuddy is going to stay with her old friend Miss Marple, you may be sure that these questions all get answered – in the end.

Once again Agatha Christie demonstrates the ingenuity and mastery which have made her the most famous of crime writers. Once again she presents a story that will grip every reader from its exciting and unusual opening to the convincing solution at the end.

### *Hallowe'en Party*
November 1969

Hercule Poirot is spending an unexpectedly lonely evening, when he is rung up by his friend, Mrs Ariadne Oliver, who calls upon him in a state of agitation.

She has been to a Hallowe'en Party given for children and teenagers. The party has a tragic outcome, and she prevails upon Poirot to come to Woodleigh Common to sort out matters. Since Poirot finds that he already has an old friend living there, he accepts, and is plunged into a medley of conflicting statements, some interesting past history, an au pair girl who has mysteriously disappeared, and sundry deaths that are not, perhaps, quite what they seemed.

Woodleigh Common seems a peaceful respectable residential area – but is it really? In the end Poirot's painstaking gathering of evidence, and careful study of psychological possibilities, enables him to solve one of Mrs. Christie's most remarkable crimes.

Mrs. Oliver helps by switching from eating apples to dates at a psychological moment. In fact, another dazzling performance by the greatest crime novelist of our time.

### *Hercule Poirot's Christmas*
December 1938

Hercule Poirot spends a busy Christmas on a most amazing case. Agatha Christie's book is a seasonable offering for, as Poirot says, Christmas is a season of good cheer; that means a lot of eating, then comes the over-eating, and then the indigestion, then the irritability, and then the quarrel...and then the murder. Poirot is as amusing and yet as logical as ever.

### *Hickory Dickory Dock*
October 1955

Hercule Poirot frowned.

'Miss Lemon,' he said.

'Yes, M. Poirot?'

'There are three mistakes in this letter.'

His voice held incredulity. For Miss Lemon, that hideous and efficient woman, never made mistakes.

And so Hercule Poirot launched into another of his memorable cases to extricate Miss Lemon's sister, who ran a student's hostel in Hickory Road, from her troubles. The series of thefts there which had so upset Miss Lemon intrigues M. Poirot because of the complete incongruity of the missing articles; he was fascinated and uneasy. Unfortunately his worst fears were fulfilled.

By putting first things first and by peeling off layers of irrelevance one by one, Poirot was able to perceive, when it occurred, the inevitable mistake that betrays a murderer. At one point Inspector Sharp was inclined to apply to him the dictum 'No one is as clever as they think they are' but generalisations do not apply to the master mind, and Hercule Poirot – and Agatha Christie – has achieved another masterpiece of detection.

### *Hollow, The*
November 1946

The Hollow is the home of Sir Henry and Lady Angkatell. Here, for a week-end, come a Harley Street doctor, his devoted wife, a sculptress, a girl who works in a cheap dress shop, a disgruntled undergraduate, and the dilettante Edward Angkatell, owner of Ainswick, the lovely country house which secretly means so much to most of these people.

For one of the guests there is no return journey. Murder takes place at the Hollow. But there is an expert in murder close at hand. Hercule Poirot is trying the experiment of having a week-end country cottage. He comes to Sunday lunch, and finds a problem in crime that nearly succeeds in baffling him – until one simple sentence clears away the mists and shows him the truth.

This is a human story about human people, as Poirot himself is the first to admit.

### *Labours of Hercules, The*
September 1947

Nobody would say that Hercule Poirot bore the slightest resemblance to his mythological namesake. But with his usual disarming vanity the little Belgian detective whimsically decides that before he retires – 'to grow the vegetable marrow' – he will undertake twelve more cases, choosing each because of its resemblance to one of the twelve labours of Hercules. From the affair of the Nemean lion, to the capture of Cerberus literally from Hell, he carries out his task. There fortunately the analogy ceases, for the famous little detective does not die from wearing a poisoned shirt, but lives to labour for our enjoyment another day. Each of these twelve episodes is a perfect gem, varied in subject and setting, but all finely polished examples of the unrivalled craftsmanship of Agatha Christie.

### *Lord Edgware Dies*
September 1933

Supper at the Savoy! Hercule Poirot, the famous little detective, was enjoying a pleasant little supper party there as the guest of Lady Edgware, formerly Jane Wilkinson, a beautiful young American actress. During the conversation Lady Edgware speaks of the desirability of getting rid of her husband, Lord Edgware, since he refuses to divorce her, and she wants to marry the Duke of Merton. M. Poirot jocularly replies that getting rid of husbands is not his speciality. Within twenty-four hours, however, *Lord Edgware Dies*. This amazing story once more reveals Agatha Christie as the perfect teller of Detective stories. It will be difficult indeed to lay down the book until one learns the true solution of the mystery.

### *Mirror Crack'd from Side to Side, The*
November 1962

What was it that Marina Gregg, the famous film actress, saw just before a murder was committed in her house? What or who caused her expression to change so violently that one observer was reminded of Alfred Tennyson:-

*Out flew the web and floated wide*
*The mirror crack'd from side to side*
*'The curse is upon me,' cried*
*The Lady of Shalott.*

A few minutes later a body lay dead in Marina's large house – the second time a victim of wilful murder has been discovered there.

In this new full-length Agatha Christie novel Miss Marple, whose house in St. Mary Mead is close to the scene of the murder, finds a perfect opportunity to indulge in the particular kind of "unravelling" at which she is adept. Agatha Christie's millions of fans will enjoy the humour and characterisation of this ingenious and exciting story.

Yet again Agatha Christie demonstrates that in the field of the crime novel her achievement is unique and distinguished.

### *Miss Marple's Final Cases*
October 1979

Agatha Christie always claimed that she herself preferred Miss Marple, who made her bow in 1930, by which time her creator was established as the all-time Queen of Crime, to Hercule Poirot, who had appeared in her very first book. Many Christie fans will undoubtedly agree with her.

In the course of her long writing life Agatha Christie wrote a number of short stories featuring St. Mary Mead's best-known inhabitant, which were published in English magazines. However, not all of these stories have appeared in volume form on this side of the Atlantic, and the six which form the greater part of the present collection now do so for the first time.

*Sanctuary*, *Strange Jest*, *Tape-Measure Murder*, *The Case of the Caretaker*, *The Case of the Perfect Maid*, and *Miss Marple Tells a Story* will delight Miss Jane Marple's millions of admirers, and provide a delightful and unexpected postscript to Agatha Christie's crime-writing career.

For good measure, the volume also includes two additional stories, *The Dressmaker's Doll* and *In a Glass Darkly*, which display to the full the incomparable Christie talent for creating suspense.

### *Moving Finger, The*
June 1943

As a place to convalesce after a bad flying crash, Lymstock sounded ideal. So thought Jerry Burton when he took a house there for himself and his sister Joanna. But they soon discovered that the undercurrents of this placid backwater were both swift and dangerous. A poison pen was hard at work sending letters which were usually as ridiculous as they were unpleasant, until one day – the shaft struck home and death resulted. Who could it be in this peaceful, old world village who was bent on creating chaos? The police found many suspects and their investigations revealed some surprising facts, but they didn't find the criminal and the letters went on circulating. It needed an expert in human wickedness to solve the mystery of the moving finger. Here is Mrs. Christie at her most subtle and her most entertaining.

### *Mrs McGinty's Dead*
March 1952

Mrs. McGinty's was dead. She was hit on the back of the head with some sharp, heavy implement, and her pitifully small savings were taken. Her lodger was hard-up and had lost his job; his coat sleeve had blood on it. In due course he was arrested and tried, found guilty and condemned to death. Yet Superintendent Spence of the Kilchester Police, who had been instrumental in bringing about James Bentley's conviction, did not believe the man was guilty – for no tangible reason other than he did not think Bentley to be the *type*. Rather shamefacedly he took his problem to his old friend Hercule Poirot; and Poirot did not laugh – instead, he said he would help.

If Mrs. McGinty was not killed by Bentley for her savings, why *did* she die? She was, it seemed, just an ordinary char-woman, with no secrets and no coveted possessions; she minded her own business and nobody else's. Impossible, one would think, to get a lead; but 'somewhere', said Poirot to himself, indulging in an absolute riot of missed metaphor, 'there is in the hay a needle, and among the sleeping dogs there is one on whom I shall put my foot, and by shooting arrows into the air, one will come down and hit a glass house!'

The inimitable Poirot, with his slightly comical aspect, his 'little grey cells' and his genuinely warm heart, returns in an ingenious detective novel that once again earns for Agatha Christie the justifiable epithet of 'incomparable'.

### *Murder at the Vicarage, The*
October 1930

In the peaceful village of St. Mary Mead nothing ever happens. So it seems almost incredible when Colonel Protheroe, the churchwarden, is discovered, shot through the head, in the Vicarage study. Everybody thinks they know who has done it – including Miss Marple, the real old maid of the village who knows everything and sees everything and hears everything! She declares that at least *seven* people have reasons for wishing Colonel Protheroe out of the way! Excitement dies down when somebody confesses to having committed the crime. But that is not the end, for almost immediately someone quite different also confesses! And there is a third confession through the telephone! But who *really* killed Colonel Protheroe?

### *Murder in Mesopotamia*
July 1936

Agatha Christie and Hercule Poirot – 'the best combination in modern detective literature' – bring all their wit and wits to bear on the solution of another remarkable case.

This time the murder takes place among the members of an expedition which has gone to Mesopotamia to excavate the ruins of an ancient city. As to the murderer, he was so diabolically clever that he would certainly have gone undetected if Poirot had not been providentially passing through on his way to Bagdad [sic]. And never, perhaps, has that keen brain been put to a greater test. The story is told by a hospital nurse attached to the expedition, and to have kept the whole tale in character as it would appear to her commonsense mind and professional eye is not the least of Mrs. Christie's achievements.

The unusual setting is not only vividly but authentically described, for Agatha Christie is the wife of an eminent archaeologist and she actually wrote this story while accompanying him on one of his expeditions to Mesopotamia.

### *Murder in the Mews*
March 1937

The four long-short Poirot stories in this volume are absolutely first-class. Agatha Christie is just as good in a shorter story as she is in a full-length novel, and in these four tales she has devised four more cases to tantalise and entertain us. Or shall we borrow one of Torquemada's witticisms and call them four more 'little grey cells!'

### *Murder is Announced, A*
June 1950

With this outstanding detective story, Agatha Christie celebrates her jubilee as a writer. For the fiftieth time she leaves us breathless with admiration for her incomparable adroitness and ingenuity. It is this fertile imagination which has won her unstinted praise throughout her career.

Every Friday morning to practically ever house in the village of Chipping Cleghorn a copy of the *North Benham News and Chipping Cleghorn Gazette* was delivered by Johnny Butt from Mr. Totman, stationer, of the High Street. On Friday, October 29th, in the 'Personal' column, among the Articles for Sale or Wanted and the frenzied appeals for domestic help, was the following singular announcement: *A murder is announced and will take place on Friday, October 29ᵗʰ, at Little Paddocks at 6.30pm. Friends please accept this, the only intimation.* A joke, of course; probably perpetrated by Miss Blacklock's nephew Patrick; but nevertheless nothing would have deterred anyone who had the slightest excuse from calling on the owner of Little Paddocks at the appointed time. One by one, shortly after six, they began to arrive – Colonel and Mrs. Easterbrook, Miss Hinchcliffe and Miss Murgatroyd, Mrs. Swettenham and her son Edmund, Mrs. Harmon, the vicar's wife. Conversation was general; the chrysanthemums were admired, the central heating commented on; the only subject that was *not* mentioned was the newspaper announcement. Then at 6.30 precisely the lights went out...

In this latest crime story Miss Agatha Christie re-introduces Miss Marple, that benign old lady with a mind like a gimlet. Once more a murder is announced for the benefit and enjoyment of countless readers, and we on our part on this happy occasion sound a fanfare.

### Murder is Easy
June 1939
'Yes, murder,' the elderly lady in the railway carriage was saying. 'You're surprised, I can see. I was myself, at first. I really couldn't believe it, I thought I must be imagining things. I might have been the first time. But not the second, or the third, or the fourth. After that, one knows.'

'So many murders!' murmured the other occupant of the railway carriage. (Probably Scotland Yard got half a dozen old ladies a week coming in burbling about the amount of murders committed in their nice country villages. There might be a special department for dealing with the old dears!) 'So many murders! Rather hard to do a lot of murders and get away with it, eh?' Miss Pinkerton shook her head. 'No, no, my boy, that's where you're wrong. It's very easy to kill – so long as no-one suspects you. And, you see, the person in question is just that last person one *would* suspect...'

But is it the last person *you* would suspect? Surely you won't let Agatha Christie fox you again. It would be 'again', wouldn't it?

### Murder on the Orient Express
January 1934
The famous Orient Express, thundering along on its three days' journey across Europe, came to a sudden stop in the night. Snow drifts blocked the line at a desolate spot somewhere in the Balkans. Everything was deathly quiet. 'Decidedly I suffer from nerves', murmured Hercule Poirot, and fell asleep again. He awoke to find himself very much wanted. For in the night murder had been committed. Mr. Ratchett, an American millionaire, was found lying dead in his berth – stabbed. The untrodden snow proved that the murderer was still on board. Poirot investigates. He lies back and thinks – with his little grey cells... *Murder on the Orient Express* must rank as one of the most ingenious stories ever devised. The solution is brilliant. One can but admire again the amazing resource of Agatha Christie.

### N or M?
November 1941
Here's great news! A new story about that famous pair of sleuths, Tommy and Tuppence Beresford, who successfully solved the ticklish problems described by Mrs. Christie in *Partners in Crime*. Tommy and Tuppence have a grown-up family now, and are feeling a bit out of things until Tommy

is given a special assignment to investigate fifth column activities. His whereabouts is supposed to be a secret, even from Tuppence, but it isn't so easy to keep Tuppence and danger apart, and so they embark together on a very difficult and exciting job. The action takes place in or near a seaside boarding house, and Agatha Christie portrays in her own vivid style the inhabitants and their daily lives, and keeps us all on tenterhooks until the last thrilling episode is finished.

### Nemesis
October 1971
'Our code word my dear lady, is **Nemesis**.'

Miss Jane Marple sat in the armchair by the fireplace in her house at St. Mary Mead, and repeated the sentence softly under her breath.

It was part of a letter – an unusual letter from an unusual man. The man who had written the letter was dead. She had read the announcement of his death more than a week ago.

**Nemesis**... The word brought a picture before her eyes. Tropical palms – a blue Caribbean sea – and herself running through the warm fragrant night on the island of St Honore to ask for help. To get help in time so that a life could be saved. She had insisted – had demanded – help, and the word that had come to her lips that night had been **Nemesis**.

Now she herself was being asked for help – for a reason she did not know – in a matter of which she was ignorant! The whole thing was impossible, quite impossible – and yet…

What possible qualifications could she have – ? Again a certain sentence came back: 'You, my dear, have a natural flair for justice. I want you to investigate a crime. I see you in my mind's eye as I saw you once one night as I rose from sleep disturbed by your urgency enveloped in a cloud of pink knitting wool!' Miss Marple looked down at her knitting.

The letter had ended with a quotation from the Book of Amos:
*Let justice roll down like waters
And Righteousness like an everlasting stream.*
'It doesn't sound at all like *me*,' said Miss Marple doubtfully.

The latest Miss Marple story is a sequel to Agatha Christie's famous best-seller, *A Caribbean Mystery*.

### One, Two, Buckle My Shoe
November 1940
It has been said that no man is a hero to his valet. To that may be added that few men are heroes to themselves at the moment of visiting their dentist. Hercule Poirot was, says Mrs. Christie, 'morbidly conscious of this' as he entered his dentist's room in Queen Charlotte Street. 'His morale was down to zero. He was just that ordinary, that craven figure, a man afraid of the dentist's chair.'

For the reader it is a very pleasant turning of the tables to see the great Poirot at such a disadvantage, his mouth stuffed with cotton wool, hot air puffing down the cavity, unable to speak for himself! At half-past eleven Poirot stepped out, a free man. But before lunch-time, sudden death had claimed a victim at the dentist's. Soon Poirot was probing into the integrity of his fellow patients of that morning. The problem into which he is led provides him with one of his best cases.

### Ordeal by Innocence
November 1958
Agatha Christie, acknowledged and unrivalled Queen of Crime, goes from strength to strength. She reached a new peak with *4.50 from Paddington*. And in the present book

she has triumphantly succeeded with a new and ambitious theme.

Young Jacko Argyle had died in a prison hospital after serving only six months of a life sentence for the murder of his mother. There had been no room for argument or doubt about his guilt and not even his family could regret his passing. But now, more than two years afterwards, a stranger climbed the hill up from the ferry with news which ripped the peace of the household into shreds. Could Jacko's alibi have been proved after all? If it could, then a terrifying situation existed for the handful of people who fulfilled the classic formula: Motive, Means and Opportunity. Fear and suspicion spread among them like a disease as they were subjected to the agony of doubt and suspense.

*Ordeal by Innocence* combines another dazzling demonstration of the Christie guile and skill with a convincing and brilliant study of a family who found that they were living with murder.

### Pale Horse, The
November 1961
'As the priest ended his ministry, the dying woman spoke again.

"Stopped...It must be stopped...You will..."
The priest spoke with reassuring authority.
"I will do what is necessary. You can trust me"
A doctor and an ambulance arrived simultaneously a little later. Mrs Coppins received them with gloomy relish.
"Too late as usual!" she said...'

Father Gorman did his best, but on the way home he was killed; on his body was discovered a list of names, mysterious in that the people listed had *nothing in common*; yet, when Mark Easterbrook came to enquire onto the circumstances of the people named, he began to descry a connection between them, and an ominous pattern...

Agatha Christie's readers are legion and they await each new novel of hers with high expectations. No one is going to be disappointed by *The Pale Horse*, a crime story not one jot less convincing, ingenious, exciting and sinister than the best of its predecessors, which have made Mrs. Christie famous.

### Passenger to Frankfurt
September 1970
There were two passengers in the transit lounge at Frankfurt Airport whose lives were to depend on what took place in the next thirty minutes.

Sir Stafford Nye was a diplomat returning to London after attending a Commission in Malaya. Fog had caused his plane to be diverted to Frankfurt. He would arrive in London two hours late at least.

He sighed, yawned, and wished something would happen. He pushed aside the folds of the cloak it was his affectation to wear when travelling – a kind of Bandit's Cloak, concealing the face, which he had once purchased in Corsica. It was a noticeable garment – but Stafford Nye had a liking for the bizarre.

A young woman sat down beside him. Her face was vaguely familiar. Someone he had once met, he supposed. She held a magazine but was not reading. She was staring at him.

Then suddenly she spoke she spoke – a deep contralto voice, with a slight foreign accent.

'May I speak to you?'
'Why not?' Stafford Nye said lightly. 'It seems we have time to waste.'

This casual encounter on a Trans-European passenger flight to London was to lead them to strange and unexpected places, to encounters with people as yet unknown to

them, into a maze of conspiracy and plotting and danger.

Twenty minutes later Trans-European Airlines announced the departure of their flight 309 for London.

And in a corner of the Transit Lounge in Frankfurt a man in a dark suit lay slumped against the back of his seat, apparently asleep. On the table in front of him was an empty beer glass.

### Peril at End House
February 1932
Three near escapes from death in three days! Is it accident or design? And then a fourth mysterious incident happens, leaving no doubt that some sinister hand is striking at Miss Buckley, the charming young owner of the mysterious End House. The fourth attempt, unfortunately for the would-be murderer, is made in the garden of a Cornish Riviera hotel where Hercule Poirot, the famous little Belgian detective, is staying. Poirot immediately investigates the case and relentlessly unravels a murder mystery that must rank as one of the most brilliant that Agatha Christie has yet written.

### Pocket Full of Rye, A
November 1953
*'Inspector Neale [Neele] was thinking to himself that Miss Marple was very unlike the popular idea of an Avenging Fury. And yet, he thought, that was perhaps exactly what she was..?*

Miss Marple came to Yew Tree Lodge because she considered it her duty to do so. Nobody knew what that benevolent old lady was thinking as she sat knitting and listening to what the various occupants of Yew Tree Lodge had to say to her.

The facts were certainly mystifying. There was the strange behaviour of Rex Fortescue before his death, the grains of cereal found in his pocket, the unexpected return of the prodigal son, and the cryptic pronouncement of old Aunt Effie: 'Old sins have long shadows.'

In her mastery of the detective novel Agatha Christie has no rival. Once again she has written an exciting, baffling story, full of incident and mystery, and peopled by queer and interesting characters. Once again her many readers have the chance to disentangle a series of crimes in a story which shows Agatha Christie at her incomparable best.

### Poirot's Early Cases
September 1974
Eighteen short stories by Agatha Christie, with one exception never previously published in England in book form, add up to a treasure trove for the Queen of Crime's millions of admirers all over the world.

All the stories feature Hercule Poirot and the cases which helped to establish the little Belgian detective's professional reputation in this country when he first came over at the end of the First World War and became involved in the scandalous affair at the Victory Ball.

The majority of the stories are narrated by the friend who in those early days played Watson to Poirot's Holmes and afford fascinating glimpses of Poirot grappling with English problems even while grappling – sometimes less successfully – with the English language.

Here then are a dozen and a half new stories about one of the best-loved detectives in fiction. The stories are vintage Christie. There is no need to say more.

### Postern of Fate
October 1973
Tommy and Tuppence, now retired, move into a house in Devonshire. In an old children's

book left in the attic, Tuppence finds cryptic clues to a murder which took place in the village during the First World War. The girl who died was mixed up in an old scandal to do with the passing on of naval secrets. But was she innocent or guilty?

Intrigued, Tommy and Tuppence investigate. But few of those in the village at the time are left alive. And their memories are confused or failing. It was such a long time ago. For the rest, it is all hearsay – often contradictory hearsay at that. Yet from these disconnected items of information, a pattern slowly begins to emerge.

Tommy and Tuppence are on surer ground after Tommy's visit to a Mr Robinson in London. Then Colonel Pikeway of MI5 takes a hand. Although the murder is such an old one, there are signs that someone is anxious it should not be revived. Suddenly Tommy and Tuppence are in danger, though no one can guess from what source, nor why their raking up of the past should be so bitterly resented. What can it matter now?

Agatha Christie weaves a spellbinding mystery strung between past and present, in which the dog Hannibal plays a considerable part.

### *Sad Cypress*
March 1940

The young and beautiful Elinor Carlisle stands in the dock charged with the murder of Mary Gerrard. Before her misty blue eyes stretches a court packed with people, all watching and wondering...*Who murdered Mary Gerrard?* Faces! Rows and rows of faces! One particular face with a big black moustache and shrewd eyes. Hercule Poirot, his head a little on one side, his eyes thoughtful, sat watching the woman in the dock. Who *did* murder Mary Gerrard? *'C'est difficile,'* murmurs the famous detective. It *is* a difficult case, one of the most difficult in his vast experience. The incomparable Agatha Christie brings all her great talents to bear on this grimly fascinating poison drama.

### *Sittaford Mystery, The*
September 1931

It was a typical Dickens Christmas: deep snow everywhere, and down in the little village of Sittaford on the fringe of Dartmoor, probably deeper than anywhere. Mrs. Willett, the winter tenant in Captain Trevelyan's country house, was, with her daughter Violet, giving a party. Finally they decided to do a little table rapping and after the usual number of inconsequential messages from the 'other side', suddenly the table announced that Captain Trevelyan was dead. His oldest friend, Captain Burnaby, was disturbed. He quickly left the house and tramped ten miles of snowy roads to Exhampton. There was no sign of life in Trevelyan's house. A back window was broken in and the light was burning – and there, on the floor, was the body of Trevelyan. Inspector Narracott took the case in hand, and after wandering through a maze of false clues and suspects, he ultimately discovered the murderer of Captain Trevelyan. Mrs. Christie has never formulated a more ingenious or enthralling plot, and her characterisation is of the vivid type which marked *The Murder at the Vicarage* and *The Murder of Roger Ackroyd*.

### *Sleeping Murder: Miss Marple's Last Case*
October 1976

A vintage Christie, written – like *Curtain* – some thirty years ago, and alas, her last.

Pretty Gwenda Reed, twenty-one and newly married, had come from New Zealand to search for a home in England for herself and her husband, Giles. She settled on a small South Coast town, Dillmouth, and almost immediately fell in love with a delightful house where she at once felt strangely at home. But it was something more than a comfortable feeling of familiarity. Gwenda felt she actually *remembered* the house.

And then, on a visit to friends in London, a theatre party and a line from Webster's *Duchess of Malfi* brought back to her the terrifying vision of a woman's body lying in the hall. It also brought another member of the theatre party into the picture: Miss Marple. And at that point Giles Reed arrived.

I don't know whether you realize it, Miss Marple,' said Giles, 'but what it amounts to is, that we've got a first-class murder mystery on our hands. Actually on our very doorstep – or more accurately, in our front hall.'

'I *had* thought of that, yes,' said Miss Marple slowly.

'And Giles simply loves detective stories,' said Gwenda.

'Well, I mean, it *is* a detective story. Body in the hall of a beautiful strangled woman. Nothing known of her but her Christian name. Of course I know it's nearly twenty years ago. There can't be any clues after all this time, but one can at least cast about, and try to pick up some of the threads. Oh, I dare say one won't succeed in solving the riddle'

'I think you might,' said Miss Marple. 'Even after eighteen years. Yes, I think you might.'

### *Sparkling Cyanide*
December 1945

Rosemary Barton is dead nearly a year before the story opens. But she lives on in the minds of six people. Six people who cannot forget. Iris, her sister; Ruth, her husband's secretary; Stephen Faraday, her lover; Sandra Faraday, his wife; and Anthony Browne, her mysterious friend. Each of them has a special and secret reason for remembering….

Was her death suicide? Or was it murder?

Rosemary died at an evening party at one of London's most luxurious restaurants. A year later a second party takes place. There is a bowl of rosemary in the centre of the table, and round it sit the same six people who sat there the year before – with an empty chair to mark Rosemary's place.

Every one is on edge, nervous, afraid, waiting for something to happen. And something does happen.

*Sparkling Cyanide* is an altogether admirable example of Agatha Christie's virtuosity, of her skill in construction, plot and characterisation.

### *Taken at the Flood*
November 1948

A man calling himself Enoch Arden comes to Warmsley Vale on a Saturday, and is killed in his room at the local inn on the following Tuesday. Upon the identity of this man hang the fortunes of the Cloade family. There were sinister motives for his death – not the least of which was a sizeable fortune – but which of the suspects had taken the golden tide at its flood? Poirot thought he knew. 'In Agatha Christie's work,' writes Ellery Queen, 'the unusual is usually the usual.' Here she has given a new dramatic twist to the legend of a man who returns home after a long absence to find a strange welcome. Hercule Poirot's solution of the mystery is completely unusual.

### *Ten Little Niggers*
November 1939

This book is certainly the greatest story that the Crime Club has ever published. We believe it may come to be considered the greatest crime problem ever devised in fiction.

Agatha Christie has always shown her preference for the 'closed' murder problem, in which the possible suspects are limited to a small and definite group of persons. In the present case, ten people are invited to a lonely mansion off the coast of Devon by a host who fails to appear. They are completely cut off from civilisation – cut off from everything but each other and the inescapable shadows of their own past lives...

If any further proof is needed of Agatha Christie's genius, here it is. This book is outstandingly clever.

### *They Came to Baghdad*
March 1951

Victoria Jones was a shorthand typist, although she was actually out of a job more often than she was in one. Not only was she an indifferent typist, but she had an insatiable craving for excitement which often led her to choose drama at the expense of truth, a tendency which did not actually fit her for office life. Owing to a slight difference of opinion with her latest employer, Victoria is again unemployed when fate quietly steps in. A chance encounter in some London gardens sets her off in pursuit – as she hopes – of glorious adventure. Baghdad by air, a post with a mysterious organisation called the Olive Branch, which exists for the betterment of world relations, three words uttered by a dying man, and Victoria is caught in the relentless toils of international intrigue, with evil, violence and deadly peril as her close companions.

*They Came to Baghdad* is Mrs. Christie's gayest novel, and has all the well-known characteristics, plus a more than usually exciting background of mystery and intrigue.

### *They Do it with Mirrors*
November 1952

A conjuring trick has a fascination all its own, a magic that survives from childhood days, when one saw with open-eyed awe one's first rabbit emerging from a top hat. The basic principle of the magician's art is, or course, to rivet the attention of the audience on detail so as to distract attention from the essential; to create the illusion of doing one thing while actually employed with something else. In her new novel *They Do It With Mirrors* Agatha Christie successfully demonstrates how a clever criminal can employ such tactics to get away with murder. Miss Marple, that deceptively meek-and-mild spinster lady, is staying with her old friend, Carrie Louise Serrocold, at Stonygates, a country house turned into a college for juvenile delinquents. The college is run by her husband Lewis Serrocold, an energetic idealist with a passion for reforming young criminals. When Christian Gulbrandsen, Carrie Louise's stepson, comes to see Lewis Serrocold and is shot dead soon after his arrival, it seems impossible that anyone in the household could have had the opportunity to commit the crime. Yet it is only one amongst them who could possibly have any plausible motive. In a succession of dramatic situations the clear-thinking, far-seeing Miss Marple penetrates an artfully contrived smokescreen and exposes a totally unexpected murderer.

### *Third Girl*
November 1966

'Then what do you mean by saying she is the third girl?'

Mrs. Ariadne Oliver snatched up *The Times* and brought it to Poirot.

'Here you are – look. *"THIRD GIRL for comfortable second floor flat, own room, central heating, Earls Court." "Third Girl wanted to share flat. 5 gns. Own room." "4th girl wanted. Regents Park. Own room."* It's the way girls like living now. Better than P.G.s or a hostel.'

It is the 'third girl', Norma Restarick, who is the subject of the new and complex mystery that here engages Hercule Poirot. What is wrong with Norma? She walks in on Poirot at the breakfast table and announces that she 'may have committed a murder' and then walks out again, leaving Poirot to battle his way to the truth.

*Has* there been a murder? It would seem *not.* But Poirot repeats patiently and with increasing pressure: *'I want a murder.'* In time the pattern fits together; many random and intriguing events become logical once the underlying design has been understood. Though the clues are there, it will be a very perceptive reader who detects the truth before Poirot reveals it.

Agatha Christie stands alone among crime novelists; millions of readers from every age and country are addicts to the work of this most absorbing and distinguished of storytellers. Not one of those addicts will care to miss this brilliant new story, in which Hercule Poirot plays a full and dazzling role in the 'swinging London' of young people today.

### *Thirteen Problems, The*
June 1932

The appearance of Miss Marple in *Murder at the Vicarage* provided detective fiction with a new and distinctive character. Miss Marple, that delightfully clever village spinster who solves the most amazing mysteries quietly and unobtrusively from her chair by the fireside, appears in each of the stories comprising *The Thirteen Problems*. Each story is a little masterpiece of detection, clever and ingenious with that added twist that only Agatha Christie can give.

### *Three Act Tragedy*
January 1935

Should clergymen drink cocktails? Well, after all...The Reverend Stephen Babbington decided to try – that is, if his wife would allow him. He laughed a little gentle clerical laugh – and accepted. He took a sip. Ugh! Still, he must be polite. He took another mouthful with a slightly wry face. Suddenly his hand went to his throat. He rose to his feet, swayed to and fro, and collapsed – dead. This was only the first act in the drama – a three-act tragedy with a mysterious death in every act, and it was Hercule Poirot's keen mind alone that presented the reasonable commonsense that linked the crimes together.

### *Towards Zero*
July 1944

"Murder begins before the actual deed…" said Mr. Treeves, a distinguished barrister, at the last dinner party which Lady Tressilian ever gave. The next morning she was found dead. With consummate skill, Mrs. Christie draws a series of cameos introducing the leading characters who take part in the ensuing drama. There was Nevil Strange, Lady Tressilian's ward and heir, his wife Kay, his former wife Audrey, Mary Aldin, a distant cousin and Lady Tressilian's companion for many years, and Thomas Royde, who was in love with Audrey. The evidence points first to one person and then to another, or so it seems until the very end. As the *New Statesman* said, 'there is no hocus pocus with Mrs. Christie. Nothing but straightforward bamboozling from start to finish.'

### *Why Didn't They Ask Evans?*
September 1934

Believe it or not Bobby Jones had topped his drive! He was badly bunkered. There were no eager crowds to groan with dismay. That is easily explained – for Bobby was merely the fourth son of the Vicar of Marchbolt, a small golfing resort on the Welsh coast. And Bobby, in spite of his name, was not much of a golfer. Still, that game was destined to be a memorable one. On going to play his ball, Bobby suddenly came upon the body of a man. He bent over him. The man was not yet dead. 'Why didn't they ask Evans?' he said, and then the eyelids drooped...

It was the beginning of a most baffling mystery. That strange question of the dying man is the recurring theme of Agatha Christie's magnificent story. Read it and enjoy.

## CLARKE, ANNA

### *Deathless and the Dead, The*

October 1976

Quizzy the tabby-cat had a luxurious home with everything a cat could desire. But the human inhabitants of Sir Roderick Heron's big Victorian villa in North Oxford were less contented. Was the tough old baronet really plotting to be rid of his quarrelsome, crippled wife? And was Letty, the sly, downtrodden companion-help, also trying to poison the old lady and step into her place?

Into this tense and secretive household their great-niece Alice brings John Broome, a young scholar who is writing a book about a Victorian lady poet who died in a bicycling accident on Boars Hill many years before. Sir Roderick in his youth had known the young poet Emily: surely he would be willing to talk to John about her?

Full of love for Alice and dreams of literary fame, John meets the Herons. Before long he is appalled to see his academic researches turning into a criminal investigation that could lead to his losing Alice, his future career, and even his life. But he can no more constrain his curiosity than can Quizzy the cat. He has stirred up a hornet's nest and there is no turning back.

Set in the early nineteen-sixties, *The Deathless and the Dead* contains much of the feeling for place and time that was so notable a feature of Anna Clarke's earlier Oxford novel *My Search for Ruth*. The portraits of the old people are convincing, even touching, and the ding-dong battle between Sir Roderick and John assumes heroic proportions as the one seeks to evade and the other to uncover the truth.

Anna Clarke's crime novels are always strikingly original and well written. Her latest is no exception.

### *Lady in Black, The*

March 1977

Mr George Meredith was worried. Not only was the distinguished Victorian novelist in difficulties with his *Diana of the Crossways*; he was also in difficulties in his other unpublicized capacity as reader for a firm of publishers. On his desk was that prized rarity, an eminently publishable manuscript. But the author's unusual reticence, coupled with the mature and circumstantial details of the story and some rather strange coincidences, led Mr Meredith to fear that what lay before him was nothing less than the true story of a crime.

He consulted Mr. Frederic Chapman, head of the firm of Chapman and Hall, Dickens's publishers, who suggested that the mysterious author be asked to call. Which the lady in black did, with results which left the two distinguished gentlemen even more uneasy – as well they might be, since their efforts to resolve their publishing dilemma were to spark off a fatal chain of events.

The time is 1882, and Chapman and Hall really did (and still do) exist. Mr Chapman was indeed a sporting and eccentric gentleman who hung venison on the office cellar, much to the olfactory distress of his staff. And Mr Meredith's reports on the manuscripts submitted to him really did have the office in fits. The other details of Victorian London are equally well researched in this delightful and unusual crime novel, in which a young woman's burning ambition to be a writer leads her into dark and dangerous ways.

### *Last Voyage*

June 1980

Sally Livingstone, aboard the *SS Rutlandshire* as she steamed into Southampton Docks in September 1939, gripped the rail with both hands and stared into the calm water many feet below. It hypnotised her, as water looked on from a great height always did. Ever since, on her first voyage from South Africa eleven years earlier, she had seen a man thrust a woman's body through a porthole.

Now, in a London trying hastily to adjust to war and the threat of air attack, Sally came face to face for the first time with her sister's fiancé – and knew that this was the murderer she had seen. But whom could she tell? No one had been reported missing on that voyage and Sally had been eleven years old and desperately sea-sick. What she saw could be dismissed as a sick child's imagination, except perhaps by Christian Hofmeyer, the sympathetic doctor she had met on board the *Rutlandshire*.

Determined to save her sister by identifying the man who for so long had haunted her imagination. Sally went to the shipping line and managed to obtain a list of passengers and crew on that far-off voyage. One in particular she set out to trace, and her search took her to London's East End. There, in a tiny terraced home soon to be obliterated by Nazi bombers, she became party to a closely guarded secret which suddenly, terrifyingly, put her life at risk.

### *Legacy of Evil*

February 1976

Herbert Bullan was a vicious and cruel man, who had caused much suffering to animals, to his subordinates, and above all to his wife Elsie. It was perhaps not altogether surprising that when he lay paralysed after a stroke she decided to free herself by hastening on his end.

If only it had really been the end! But 'the evil that men do lives after them', and now that Elsie had tasted evil for herself, there was no holding her. One after another the members of the ordinary, harmless family who lived opposite succumbed to the intoxicating power that Elsie felt within her, until at last there was only one young girl left to resist.

*Legacy of Evil* is a grimly enthralling story about an obsessional killer, played out against the ordinary background of a seaside bungalow colony on the cliffs. In the hands of Anna Clarke, already an acknowledged mistress of the psychological crime story, the suspense mounts at times to the verge of horror, and the tension is maintained right up to the great life and death struggle which effectively climaxes the book.

### *Letter From the Dead*

October 1977

The letter that Maureen Myrtle left to be opened by her son after her death was duly delivered by hand on the day of her funeral. A solicitor's clerk brought it and saw it placed on the hall table at the Manor. After that it disappeared.

Maureen had been the third wife of the wealthy and disagreeable novelist Reginald Myrtle, who was already eyeing his prospective fourth. She had not been happy with Reginald, nor had Clive, her son. It was because Clive had taken refuge at the Vicarage that he was not at home when the letter arrived, though the house was full of people, for with typical insensitivity Reginald had turned the mourning gathering into a festive wake. Perhaps he wanted to forget his stepson's accusations at the graveside that he was responsible for Maureen's death.

Any of those present at the Manor might have taken the letter. Several of them had contrived – not always honourably – to see its contents, which were enough to disrupt three or four lives in the quiet Sussex village in which Maureen had been born and to which fate had brought her back to die. So when an opportune death occurred which was certainly not from natural causes, suspects were hardly in short supply.

Out of a tangle of motives and personalities, all affected by skeletons now rising from the past, Anna Clarke has fashioned a convincing human drama and a novel of considerable suspense.

### *My Search for Ruth*

February 1975

Who was she? What was she? Why was she so different from everyone else? They called her Ruth, but nobody ever told her that she had another name. And when she asked about her parents, everyone looked frightened, and talked of something else.

*My Search for Ruth* tells of a young girl's quest for the truth about herself. Starting with nothing but her own determination and a few meagre clues, she plays detective in the mystery of her own life and comes triumphantly through to a solution of the crime by which she nearly perished.

This is a story of hope and courage and love, a tale of suspense with a strong appeal to the heart; and the setting – an Oxford village in the nineteen-twenties – gives it the additional attraction of nostalgia.

### *One of Us Must Die*

May 1978

Dr Dorothy Laver and her husband lived together in great unhappiness in their beautiful Hampshire home. Their lives were bedevilled by the loss of their baby daughter fifteen years earlier. One of them was guilty of giving the child an accidental overdose, but both had been attending to her and it was impossible to say which one of them was to blame. The tension between them, heightened by Gerry's carefully staged suicide attempts and Dorothy's guilt feelings, had risen to breaking point. One of them must push the other over the edge of sanity, one of them must die.

Into this tense and claustrophobic situation new elements intrude: a girl about the age their daughter would have been who takes up residence in the house; Dorothy's wise, serene clergyman father, who may or may not be guilty of ending a human life; and the young electrician who falls in love with Dorothy and to whom she turns more and more for support.

When death does indeed occur, it is as innocent-seeming as the baby's death years before. But a new and horrible question-mark hangs over the survivors as the past tangle of guilt and suspicion is unravelled. One of them is guilty of murder. Once again, one of them must die.

### *Plot Counter-Plot*

May 1974

Gifted, rich, successful – that was how Helen Mitchell appeared to those who read her suspense novels, including Brent Ashwood, an unsuccessful young author who was desperate for fame. Why, then, was Helen writing her new novel in fear and in secret? Why had the pen become more dangerous than the sword?

This taut, economical story gives the answer, as Helen narrates her involvement with Brent from their first casual encounter at a party to the ultimate deadlock from which there seems only one escape. Both are accustomed to plotting, to manipulating characters and events. Now, imperceptibly, each has become a character in the other's story. Whose pen will write the final word?

This is a tense, unusual crime novel of a deadly battle of wits between two ingenious minds, written with insight and compassion, and skilfully interweaving past and present, fantasy and reality.

### *Poison Parsley*

November 1979

Bernard Goodwin was well known as a writer and lecturer on herbal remedies. Rosalind Bannister was a gifted artist. When they both came to live in the same Sussex village, it seemed only natural that Rosalind should be asked to illustrate Bernard's new book.

But Bernard and Rosalind had a closer bond than their common interest in plants, or even the attraction that quickly sprang up between them. Both had a partner who had died in suspicious circumstances, even though, in Rosalind's case, she had been tried and acquitted of her drunken husband's murder. As for Bernard, he alone knew the extent of his own guilt where the death of his first wife was concerned, but his unhappy, neurotic second wife made no secret of her conviction that he was subtly plotting hers. And Rosalind's teenage son was soon violently jealous of the association between his mother and Bernard. It was a situation ripe for murder, and the means grew in every local hedge ...

Anna Clarke's understanding of the complexities of human nature, the tortuous situations it creates, and their often violent resolutions have won a wide and growing public for her cunningly plotted stories, which are in the truest sense 'novels of crime'.

### *Poisoned Web, The*

April 1979

Patience Merriman was old, frail and frustrated. She had once reigned over the Oxford salon in the days when her professor husband was alive. Now the love of power and talent for intrigue which had made her a force in Oxford society were expended on her own household: on the two young students occupying the top floor whose relationship she aimed to destroy; on her only child, whom she had never forgiven for being a daughter, and who she alleged was seeking her death.

Romola Merriman certainly had every provocation to matricide, but was the old woman telling the truth, or was it one more of the malicious rumours she loved to circulate – a rumour which might this time come true? For Patience did not care if she caused a death, directly or indirectly, and others were soon tempted to cause hers – to save themselves or to save Romola. Who would win the battle of wits and wills?

Anna Clarke's skill at creating tension in a domestic setting has won her a wide readership. Here she tackles an all too common situation: a household in the monstrous grip of a powerful personality that refuses to accept the limitations of age.

## CLEMEAU, CAROL

### *Ariadne Clue, The: A Classical Mystery*

January 1983

As classics professor Antonia Nielsen entered the faculty lounge one spring morning, she was blissfully unaware that her peaceful academic world was about to be violated by crime.

Instead of the usual faculty lounge chit-chat, Antonia found her colleagues agog with talk of a major art theft. Someone had broken into the university museum and stolen invaluable Greek artefacts. And Ariadne Pappas, Antonia's prize student of Greek, had vanished. Could the simultaneous disappearance of Ariadne and the gold be mere coincidence?

Adopting some of her academic research techniques to the real world of detection, Antonia fought to stay one step ahead of the police as she searched for the missing graduate student. But as the days passed and Ariadne and the gold remained missing, Antonia began to fear the worst. Was there a murderer on campus? Only by using her knowledge of the classics, by unravelling the Ariadne 'clew' of Greek mythology, could Antonia hope to find the present-day clue that would lead to Ariadne's whereabouts.

Written with inside knowledge of the passions and frustration of academe and with delightfully erudite allusions to the classics, Carol Clemeau's first novel, which won the Scribner Crime Novel Award, establishes her as a gifted writer of crime fiction.

## CODY, LIZA

### *Bad Company*

October 1982

Mr Fourie wants custody of his teenage daughter, Claire, so Anna Lee and her colleagues from Brierly Security set out to gather evidence that Claire's mother is a corrupting influence.

Things are soon found to be not quite what they seem: Mr Fourie is the kind of client that Brierly Security likes to avoid and Claire is not the sweet innocent girl she pretends to be.

But this is nothing to what happens when Anna follows Claire and her friend to a swimming pool one sunny afternoon. She finds out that only fools try to be heroes. And some heroes can get into dire trouble.

With Anna missing, one case turned rapidly into another, so Anna's friend and mentor, Bernie Schiller, begins to investigate. The problem is the younger generation. Anna and Bernie, separately, stuck in the rift between generations, a frustrating place where every effort seems hopeless and which Liza Cody charts with a novelist's skill.

### *Dupe*

October 1980

Fobbed off with all the routine jobs that come to a London detective agency, Anna Lee, a former policewoman, could sleep through most of them. The patronising attitude of her boss and colleagues had become as irksome to her as the work was uninspiring.

Then Tom Jackson blustered into Brierly Security's sedate Kensington office looking for 'Satisfaction. And if we can't get it from the police we're prepared to pay for it. Look, my daughter is dead, and we didn't expect to come to the police with our reasonable doubts and be treated like country bumpkins who didn't know an apple from Adam…'

Jackson's spoiled daughter had died in a car accident near Heathrow Airport on an icy December night. The wrecked car had a disturbing smell, but there were no signs of foul play. To Martin Brierly business was business and he accepted the job. To Anna it meant just another dead-end investigation.

But Deirdre had left home in search of a glamorous career, and, in following her ghost, Anna was led to the seedy fringes of the film world, where she found that fraud, failure and violence, not glamour, marked Deirdre's path to a lonely death.

### *Head Case*

November 1985

Sixteen-year-old Thea Hahn is exceptional 'What on earth can I talk about to a kid gifted in mathematics and astrophysics?' wonders Anna Lee. But Anna, Brierly Security's youngest agent, has another problem – this daughter of strangely cold and withdrawn parents is missing and Anna is searching London for her.

To all appearances Thea Hahn is a model teenager. 'Brilliant,' says her economics tutor. 'No trouble at all,' says the cousin who should have kept a closer eye on her. But beneath the flawless surface Thea conceals painful secrets. And what Anna is looking for is not at all what she eventually finds.

Liza Cody, one of the best of the Crime Club's younger authors, once again creates a perfect vehicle for her heroine Anna Lee, 'the gutsily natural-acting investigator for Brierly Security' (*Sunday Times*)

### *Rift*

June 1988

'The most difficult thing to face is your own stupidity,' says Fay Jassahn at the beginning of a trip through Kenya and Ethiopia. She had just finished work on a film and is eager to see more of Africa by following the Rift Valley north. But it is 1974, and revolution is brewing, and Ethiopia is the wrong place to be young, naïve and alone.

One by one, travellers arrive in the border town of Moyale. Fay, Graham, Mel and Dutch Peter are all on their way to Addis Ababa. And by chance, it seems, they are following a mysterious American woman who went the same way only a week earlier. Everyone has a different purpose, disclosed or otherwise. But all their plans are upset by the chaos and violence they find, as Ethiopia overwhelms good and bad alike.

Fay learns painfully that ides of crime are bound up with ideas of civilization. When civilization crumbles, what is crime? And who are the criminals? The lessons she learns are as much about herself and her companions are they are about the unwelcoming terrain. Her ultimate discovery – that crime is indeed at the heart of this testing journey – will shock the reader as much as it does Fay.

### *Stalker*

October 1984

One Wednesday morning Anna Lee, Brierly Security's youngest agent met a new client. Mr Thurman appeared to be a helpless man who needed a solicitor to talk for him and Brierly Security to trace a bad debtor. Anna wondered how anyone so ineffectual could possibly survive as a money-lender. She should have given the question more than a passing thought.

The search for Ed Marshall, the defaulting carpenter, whom Mr Thurman was anxious to trace, took Anna first to a seedy district of London, where his wife was distinctly unwelcoming and the gentleman with whom she was associating even more so, and then to Exmoor, where urban Anna found herself in an unfamiliar world – a strange and dangerous one where love and death seemed disturbingly mixed.

The third Anna Lee investigation is every bit as good as its predecessors.

### *Under Contract*

October 1986

An up-and-coming rock star embarking on her first major tour provides Anna Lee, Brierly Security's only female agent, with one of her most frustrating cases.

Anna is on attachment to a larger, flashier firm which specializes in the protection of celebrities and who see her as Tiddler of Small Fry Security. Being patronized by her new colleagues, all men, is bad enough but the client, Shona Una, and her band make her even less welcome – she is the butt of cruel jokes and referred to as Snoopy.

Few people on the tour take security seriously, but to Anna it is more than just a PR exercise, especially when she discovers that her client needs greater protection than anyone imagined.

The rock world teems with odd people and strange relationships but, as Mr Brierly points out, events that would be taken as bizarre in normal society may have no significance at all here.

Anna, struggling to make sense of a chaotic scene, is met with hostile silence – even from Shona herself. So what can she do when her own client treats her as an enemy until it is far too late?

## COLE, G. D. H. and M.

### *Affair at Aliquid, The*

September 1933

David Rogers, after failing rapidly and romantically in several enterprises more adventurous than sound, secures – by false pretences be it whispered – an invitation to stay with the Duke of Aliquid at Aliquid Castle in the West Highlands. He arrives in the guise of an African missionary and is soon involved in a mysterious jewel robbery, for soon after his arrival Lady Snodgrass is robbed, a case that causes much consternation to the local police in the person of Inspector Bulkhead. *The Affair at Aliquid* may rightly be claimed to be the gayest mystery story of the year. G. D. H. and M. Cole possess just the right touch for their theme. Not since they wrote *Burglars in Bucks* have these delightful collaborators written so entertaining a book.

### *Big Business Murder*

January 1935

In the palatial city offices of Arrow Investments Ltd., Kingsley Manson, the suave, handsome, perfectly-dressed genius of the financial world, faced an angry meeting of his fellow directors. Wilfred Gathorne, who had always been a thorn in his flesh, was asking some deucedly awkward questions. Well, he would let them have it. Calmly he told them the brutal truth. The Arrow was, and had been for quite a long time, a fraudulent concern. After the bombshell burst confusion reigned, and the meeting was adjourned until the afternoon. But before it resumed Gathorne was murdered. In *Big Business Murder* G. D. H. and M. Cole have written an exceptionally clever detective story and one which certainly provided Superintendent Wilson with one of his most baffling cases.

### *Brothers Sackville, The*

December 1936

Here are two households – the Sackvilles of Birmingham and the Sackvilles of Brondesbury. How do they fit in to the puzzle which is set to the police by the sudden death – by accident or by murder – of John Ainsworth, who is Bertha Sackville's brother? There seems no doubt that Alfred Sackvillle was at hand when Ainsworth died. But did he kill him, and if so why – for he appears to have no motive? The solution, simple as it is when it is known, will surprise most readers, even in these days when readers have become far more sophisticated than they used to be. And, apart from the mystery, Mr. and Mrs. Cole have tried, as usual, to give us a somewhat satirical glimpse of life as it is lived in a high-class quarter of Birmingham and in a shabby-genteel house in a respectable London suburb.

### *Burglars in Bucks*

June 1930

The connoisseur of detective stories, wearying of the conventional, will delight in the originality of this book. Here is no elaborate narrative, concealing vital clues beneath the guise of frankness, and allowing the detective to ponder in the dark solutions which he never discloses until the last chapter. On the contrary, every clue and every incident – letters, telegrams, conversations, warrants, newspaper reports – is set down faithfully exactly as and when it occurred, and the reader can follow the strange story of the spook and the stolen jewels just as though he were participating in a real mystery. Even Superintendent Wilson's note-book is thrown open to inspection so that the reader can see at each stage of the story exactly how far the Superintendent's inquiries have got, and can pit his own wits against those of Scotland Yard.

### *Corpse in Canonicals*

November 1930

Superintendent Wilson thought he was in a *cul de sac*! Having been called to Middlebury to investigate the disappearance of Elinor Symonds' necklace, he arrives only to find that it had been returned as mysteriously as it went. He goes back to Scotland Yard, but in a few days he sees that his *cul de sac* is rather an avenue leading to one of the most amazing murders in his career. The body of a clergyman is found in the garden of the Chief Constable's house, and the police are faced not with the problem of finding a clue, so much as with finding the right clue out of the many provided – a revolver with all its chambers full, a small bottle of poison, a chloroform-soaked handkerchief, a cigar stump and a visiting card! *Corpse in Canonicals* is a most ingenious piece of crime fiction with that grip on the reader that ingenuity of plot alone cannot produce. G. D. H. and M. Cole are adding to that power which made successes of *Poison in the Garden Suburb* and *Burglars in Bucks*.

### *Counterpoint Murder*

December 1940

In Bradshaw's Club in Pall Mall, a timber merchant was found with his head smashed in, the apparent weapon being a heavy oak bookshelf. Inspector Doolittle found a number of people who had good motives for eliminating the timber merchant, but all of them had absolutely watertight alibis. Not long afterwards an old lady was poisoned in Kensington, and Inspector Mugge, to whom the job was entrusted, met with equal ill-success. Was a lunatic killer abroad in wartime London? It seemed a plausible explanation. But Superintendent Wilson, to whom fell the work of finally disentangling these mysteries, reached a solution which it is safe to say will baffle nine out of ten readers. This is one of the most ingenious plots the Coles have yet produced.

### *Dead Man's Watch*

December 1931

Few of us would care to share the experience of Ronald Bittaford, who, when on a holiday with his fiancée, found in a creek the drowned body of his uncle, whom he had not seen for a year and a half. And yet – was it his uncle or his uncle's brother, or an unknown stranger from Teignmouth? And how had he come to be there? Was he drowned, or strangled? and by whom? These, and other questions together, make one of the prettiest problems ever set before the great Superintendent Wilson; but in the end, with the aid of a watch, a boarding-house, a street betting-tout, and the congregation of a strange dissenting chapel, he brings it to a triumphant conclusion. *Dead Man's Watch* is one of the most amusing and vigorous tales which Mr. and Mrs. Cole have given us.

### *Death in the Quarry*
May 1934

A distinguished Visitor, visiting the Marlock Works, pressed a button which he had been assured was harmless – and immediately there was an explosion in the quarry. It was a Saturday afternoon, so all should have been well; but when the debris was cleared the body of the works manager was found beneath it. A regrettable accident? Perhaps; but how did he come to be there on a Saturday afternoon? And who put the shots in? And why? And what was the treasure of which the old man had been talking such a lot? And why wouldn't he sell that useless bit of field to the magnate next door? Dennis Blaney and Everard Blatchington, going for a walking week-end to the Gloucestershire Cotswolds, ran right into the heart of these perplexing problems, and had to go far and enlist further help before they got to the bottom of them.

### *Death of a Star*
December 1932

Outside a party on a summer's night, just by the wall of London River, a taximan stopped his taxi and asked a policeman to take charge of a curious bag which he had found in it. Revellers from the party rushed the constable, tore the bag open and disclosed – the severed head of a film artiste. How did the head come there? Where was the body? Why and how was she murdered? Who did it? The lover she was going to marry? Or the lovers she had discarded? The citizen with the Gladstone bag, who had lost his sweep ticket? Or the burglar who had no luck? Or the soldier boy whom nobody had seen for years, or the too cautious solicitor? Or —? It is safe to say that no reader of Mr. and Mrs. Cole's latest mystery will be able to guess the answer.

### *Double Blackmail*
July 1939

In *Double Blackmail* the Crime Club presents one of the finest detective novels of the year. It has, like every novel by the Coles, first-class detection and first-class characterisation. And in this tale of blackmail they have excelled themselves.

Amelia Selvidge, in her own opinion, had only made one mistake in her life, and that was in marrying Hugo. But he was banished from mind in Australia; her son was a respected Dean well on the high road towards a bishopric; Amelia herself was well known for her devotion to good causes. Everything, in fact, was going well – until the blackmail started. And even the sudden death of the blackmailer did not put an end to her troubles. Superintendent Wilson has an exceptionally hard problem to solve. Test your own wits on it!

### *Dr. Tancred Begins*
May 1935

The narrative of *Doctor Tancred Begins* is related by Ben Tancred's close friend, Paul Graham, who, convalescing in the village of Polruan, in Cornwall, stumbles at once into a love affair and a crime mystery, and calls upon Dr. Tancred for help. The tracking of old Simon Pendexter's murderer brings onto the scene not only Dr. Tancred but also our old acquaintance, Henry Wilson, not yet a Superintendent, but a plain Detective-Sergeant, from Scotland Yard. Simon and his sister, Sarah Pendexter, are rare 'characters', and the interest of the story turns largely on Simon's two stepchildren, Helen and Rupert.

### *End of an Ancient Mariner*
December 1933

It is said that dead men tell no tales, but sometimes a sudden death is the means of bringing well-hidden tales to life. It is so in this story; for out of the seemingly accidental death of the unknown old man who called on Philip Blakeway at Hampstead comes the clearing-up of an old crime. How Captain John Jay really died, how Ann Burton set out to look for her missing father, and how Superintendent Wilson unravelled the tangle, you will read in this book, in which you will find not only a detective story in Mr. and Mrs. Cole's best manner, but also another example of their habit of writing about people who behave like real men and women, and not merely figures whom the author moves about at his pleasure.

### *Great Southern Mystery, The*
March 1931

*The Great Southern Mystery* is one of the cleverest stories that these talented authors have yet given us. In accordance with the mode of this moment a great hotel provides the action for this most baffling mystery. When Rose Chapman, chambermaid at the Great Southern Hotel, enters Room 49 she discovers the body of the occupant stretched dead on the bed. Yet only a few minutes before the 'boots' had seen number Forty-nine in the lounge, in conversation with a young lady!... The dead man's hands had been tied tightly together and between them was a piece of paper on which was written the one word – 'QUITS' – a truly dramatic opening to a most exciting story.

### *Greek Tragedy*
November 1939

The Isles of Greece where burning Sappho loved and sang form an original and attractive setting for modern murder as devised by the Coles. The tragedy happens while a party of young and old, politicians and non-politicians, distinguished men and freaks, are enjoying an educational holiday cruise around the islands. Superintendent Wilson, what with coping with a foreign language and with the reticences of the Greek secret police, had one of his toughest jobs on hand before he found the solution. The vivid characterisation of the members of the party, and the unusual character of the setting, no less than the crime itself, make this one of the most delightful and entertaining stories which the Coles have yet given us.

### *Knife in the Dark*
December 1941

Who murdered the hostess of an undergraduates' dance, held by special permission in the ancient university of Stamford? No one knew until Mrs. Warrender, a harmless old lady with a logical mind, discovered the truth. Both in plot and technique the Coles are superb.

### *Last Will and Testament*
July 1936

This story reintroduces the Coles' readers to several familiar characters. Here is the detective, Dr. Benjamin Tancred, twenty-five years older than when we met him in *Dr. Tancred Begins*. Here is that extraordinary religious fanatic, Sarah Pendexter, and her nephew, Rupert Pendexter, who so narrowly escaped hanging in the earlier story. Here is his sister, Helen Pendexter, now Viscountess St. Blaizey, deeply involved in the mystery surrounding old Lord St. Blaizey's death. That is only one of the three mysteries that go to make up this tangled tale. Together with two no less intricate – Was the St. Blaizey will a forgery? and who killed Sidney Galloway? – it is resolved at last by Dr. Tancred's unflagging persistence and insight, and his greatest case is brought to a triumphant end in which the claims of justice are finally satisfied.

### *Lesson in Crime and other stories, A*
June 1933

The brilliant partnership of G. D. H. and M. Cole has been responsible for some of the most successful detective stories of recent years. The present volume contains a varied selection of mystery stories, each presenting a particular problem, and once again the authors prove themselves adepts at the entrancing game of keeping one guessing. Superintendent Wilson, that very likeable detective, figures prominently throughout, and admirers of his skilful sleuthing will have no cause to complain of the fare provided.

### *Missing Aunt, The*
December 1937

The Dower House of Gracechurch Abbey, ordinarily so calm and peaceful in its quiet country setting, is plunged into a hubbub of excitement when the shadow of tragedy falls across its well-kept lawns. Mary Anne Latchmere, an elderly spinster lady, disappears in most mysterious circumstances. Her disappearance is followed swiftly by another tragedy, which results in Scotland Yard being summoned, and with our old friend Superintendent Wilson in charge of the case one is assured of first-rate sleuthing until the final kill.

### *Mrs Warrender's Profession*
July 1938

Famous detectives, like poets, are born, not made, and as there's something in heredity, the mother of James Warrender, the well-known private detective, is a character of some importance in this book. Mrs. Warrender was a little old lady who lived a very pleasant life in a quaint house in Hampstead. She was not at all interested in crime, but she was very interested in James, her son, and she saw that he was right – or at least told him when he was wrong! 'You know a great deal about criminals, James, and how they behave', she used to say, 'but you don't know at all about ordinary people.' That deficiency in her son's make-up she did her best to remedy, as the stories in the Coles' latest volume amply show.

### *Murder at the Munition Works*
August 1940

The Coles here give us a war-time setting. A bomb explosion in a big mention works in Bullbridge kills the wife of the manager, and the local police suspect the leading Trade Unionist in the factory of the murder. His dismissal provokes a strike, and we are given a glimpse of strike meetings, shop-stewards' committees, and the industrial life of the country under war conditions. The reader is given, against this background, the opportunity of solving an exceptionally intricate puzzle, which leads our old friend Superintendent Wilson up a number of blind alleys before he finds his way to the correct solution.

### *Off With Her Head!*
December 1938

A well-known 'don' run down by a car in Oxford – just afterwards, the head of a young woman found in the room of an undergraduate – on the wall of the same room, a caricature of the dead woman sitting on the knee of one of the College tutors – a small boy flinging a cricket ball through a window and so discovering the rest of the body. The Yard is called upon in the person of Inspector Fairford, whom the Coles' readers have met before in *The Brothers Sackville*; and there is an amateur detective, Ann Maitland, to compete and to co-operate with the police. In short, a crime story set against the background of University life, with a wealth of 'characters' and suspects, and an exciting chase at the end.

### *Scandal at School*
December 1935

'For some reason,' writes Dorothy L. Sayers, 'nearly all school murder stories are good ones.' We certainly had a great success in the spring with Nicholas Blake's *A Question of Proof*, which dealt with murder in a preparatory school, and we expect to repeat this success with the Coles' new story, *Scandal at School*. The very 'advanced' school they have chosen as a setting is no doubt a curious school according to ordinary standards, but not so curious that when an unpopular girl dies suddenly in her sleep in can be taken as a matter of course. Was she poisoned? And if so, by whom? And what was really the truth about the school and its patrons? So much for the setting of this intriguing story. As to its quality, we quote the *Illustrated London News*: 'A Cole story is always a first-class story.'

### *Topers' End*
August 1942

Dr. Sambourne, a wealthy and eccentric scientist, had the benevolent idea of running a hostel for refugees from Nazi and Fascist oppression. Excalibur House was the resplendent title of the Home, which was quickly filled with, to quote Mrs. Mudge, servant at the home, 'outlandish aliens what ought to be shot out of hand and then locked up.' In this little community of brilliant men, G. D. H. and Margaret Cole stage one of their most absorbing murder mysteries, full of human interest, deft characterisation, and brightened with the added quality of a lively wit.

### *Wilson and Some Others*
April 1940

The Coles have long been known as expert purveyors of first-rate detective stories, which have made their name known far and wide. In what is perhaps the most difficult field of the short story they still succeed in baffling the reader with superb skill. That clever creation Superintendent Henry Wilson of Scotland Yard, appears in many of these stories, and whether it is a case of investigating the drugs in the dregs of a tankard, or the circumstances surrounding a curious catastrophe in church, the Superintendent always shows his customary acumen. *Wilson and Some Others* is an enjoyable book of many and varied mysteries.

## COLLINS, NORMAN

### *Bat That Flits, The*
May 1952

Deep in the heart of the West Country, only to be reached by crossing a desolate stretch of moor, was a Government Station for research in bacteriological warfare. To the newly arrived young scientist, James Hudson, the outlook was bleak. He was seeking quietude but not isolation – particularly not isolation from the village pub, for life, he contended, looked rosier through gin-coloured spectacles. Taking a swift look round his fellow-workers, he could spot no kindred spirit. He had met them all before in other laboratories: the German refugee with the persecution mania; the intense young man with tiresomely obtrusive leanings towards the U. S. S. R.; the ex-lab. boy suffering from an inferiority complex because he had no degree; the Institute's robot-minded statistician; the demure female research worker. Then on his first night Hudson found on his pillow a note reading: *'Don't interfere. Everything is under control.'* At the time the warning meant nothing to him. But piece by piece there emerged a pattern superimposed upon the natural fabric of Institute life – a pattern of theft and sabotage, attempted murder and eventual suicide. M. 1. 5. is called in. And gradually as the accident rate in the laboratory spirals upwards it becomes apparent that among the eight research workers, isolated from the outside world by the Cornish moors and the West Country mists, one of their number was working for the Other Side.

Mr. Norman Collins brings to his first thriller in addition to his exceptional powers as a novelist an unsuspected talent for making the blood run cold. Beneath the surface lightness imparted by the cynical, irrepressible humour of its narrator, James Hudson, lurks grim reality. Overt acts gradually reveal the existence of a hidden, bitter dedication to a creed which does not recognise the rights of the individual and denies all the secret tenderness of the human heart. *The Bat That Flits* is a notable crime story and a memorable novel.

## CORK, BARRY

### *Dead Ball*

April 1988

When someone ploughed up the eighteenth green at the Royal West Wessex Golf Club only days before a major tournament, Inspector Angus Straun seemed the ideal man to uncover the vandal. To his masters, he was something of an embarrassment – a bright officer confined to a desk by the effects of a bank robber's shotgun blast, a middle-ranking policeman who ran expensive cars from the proceeds of best-selling historical novels. But at least he was a golfer, and it seemed that even an office-bound copper couldn't do much harm sorting out the problems at the local golf club. So Angus returned to detection and found that in hosting the Tamworth Trophy the Royal West Wessex seemed to have incurred more than its fair share of problems. A ruined green was bad, but a body in a bunker was worse. And was there any real link between exploding golf balls and visitors from Outer Space? Angus Straun's escape from office routine threatens to become a nightmare played out against the background of a major golf tournament.

### *Endangered Species*

November 1992

When Inspector Angus Straun's car breaks down in a remote corner of the Lincolnshire fens, he finds himself drawn into a circle of men and women held hostage by their own pasts. At first he finds them no more than eccentric; the farmer obsessed with his Saxon forebears; a wealthy air enthusiast dedicated to restoring a B-24 bomber; an American war veteran reliving his brief triumph as a champion golfer. Then death strikes amid the ruins of a World War Two airfield, and Straun realizes that behind these lifestyles are people with accounts to settle and that the only acceptable currency is blood.

Trapped amid a hostile countryside, he pits his wits against the shadows of old wrongs and bizarre vengeance.

### *Laid Dead*

April 1990

Deep in stockbroker country Thetfield was not on Inspector Straun's list of golf clubs where the unusual might be expected to happen, so when on the 10th tee a player is killed by his opponent at first it seems no more than a tragic accident. But Straun is not convinced and probes suburban Thetfield's darker side. Why does a Dutch business tycoon choose a notorious confidence trickster as a playing partner? What prompts the thieves who raid the Pro's shop to take everything – including the waste paper? And how do golf balls come to be floating on the waters of a disused gravel pit? None of it makes sense until the scene widens to London and Angus Straun finds himself faced not only with murder but with what might well prove to be the most bizarre crime in the city's history.

### *Unnatural Hazard*

May 1989

When Inspector Angus Straun accepts and invitation to play in a Pro Celebrity golf match to mark the opening of a remote Scottish hotel he finds himself in a world that seems to have taken leave of its senses. What possible reason can there be for a complete stranger to push him out of the night express? Why should a respected antique dealer be guilty of shoplifting cannonballs? And what has prompted an elderly cleric to found a community of misfits who rule the countryside through fear? Above all, why are visitors so prone to fatal accidents on the lovely island of Sarne? Angus Straun's efforts to find out lead him to a deadly secret, long locked in the island's dark past.

### *Winter Rules*

August 1991

Had the thief who stole the red Maserati known that it belonged to Inspector Straun he might well have taken it back rather than driving it into a brick wall. Or would he? Straun's outraged inquiries are cut short by a special assignment to act as personal bodyguard to a Third World head of state, a politician whose passions are divided equally between his beautiful mistress and the ancient game of golf. At the mercy of diplomatic pressures, Angus finds himself accompanying his charge back to Africa, where the construction of a country's first golf course clashes murderously with a ruthless struggle for political power and a sophisticated trade in smuggled cars. At first only a reluctant spectator, Straun finds himself increasingly involved in a bizarre duel of wits in which all rules are suspended and the loser pays with his life.

## CRAIG, MARY

### *Were He a Stranger*

February 1979

That morning, like all other mornings, Sydney Fast wakened to the sound of her husband, John, getting into this jogging clothes. Without opening her eyes, she knew what clothes he would wear and what five miles he would jog along the cliff above the Pacific Ocean at Big Sur. And when he would return.

But John Fast never returned, victim of a hit-and-run driver who sent his body plunging from the cliff into the surf.

And in due course Sydney had to identify the body drawn from the sea – the body of a man John's age and size, wearing the clothes she had described, and with a scar like John's.

But the neatly lettered card beside the corpse read 'Graham Hastings'. And Sydney Fast had never heard the name Graham Hastings in her life.

Here is a compelling story of a young woman confronted with the unbelievable – the college professor she had loved and married had been a stranger. And the police believed she had murdered him.

## CROFTS, FREEMAN WILLS

### *Crime at Guildford*

May 1935

The accountant of a firm of jewellers arrives on a Saturday evening at his managing director's house near Guildford to attend an unofficial weekend meeting of his directors. Next morning he is found dead in bed. On the Monday morning it is learned that the safe of the office of the firm in Kingsway has been opened and half a million pounds' worth of jewels have been stolen. Investigation by the local police shows that the accountant has been murdered. Chief Inspector French meanwhile is inquiring into the sensational theft of the jewels. He ultimately discovers that the two crimes are connected and by brilliant detection succeeds in solving the mysterious crime at Guilford.

### *Death on the Way*

September 1932

The fireman suddenly stiffened, for a fraction of a second peered earnestly ahead and then swung round to the driver with a warning shout, 'There's something on the road!' With one hand the driver threw over the regulator, while with the other he clashed the brake handle full on. The engine gave a little shudder as it hit the body of Roger Ackerely. The tragedy deepened into mystery dark and sinister at the inquest when one witness swore that he had seen a man hastening away from the scene of the accident – a statement which caused Inspector French to be called in to investigate the greatest problem that he had ever encountered. Mr. Crofts is an acknowledged master of detection, and his treatment of his theme is at once clear, reasonable and realistic.

### *Loss of the 'Jane Vosper', The*

February 1936

*The Loss of the Jane Vosper* is magnificent drama, told quietly yet impressively, with no deliberate straining after effect. It must inevitably rank as one of the finest stories that Mr. Freeman Wills Crofts has written, comparable to that classic of detection, *The Cask*. From the moment that the *Jane Vosper*, rent by mysterious explosions, plunges to her doom in the Atlantic, the story grips us in a spell and we follow the unravelling of the intricate plot, including, of course, a first-rate murder mystery, until the patient, persevering Inspector French triumphs. The story is excellent, the characters well drawn, and the problem worthy of Mr. Freeman Wills Crofts' world-wide reputation.

### *Man Overboard*

October 1936

Freeman Wills Crofts describes this book as a companion, though in no sense a sequel, to *Sir John Magill's Last Journey*, for it is largely set in Northern Ireland and Chief-Inspector French finds himself once more co-operating with Superintendent Rainey and Sergeant McClung. In the course of the passage from Belfast to Liverpool a man disappears. Later his body is picked up by a fisherman off the Irish coast. Was his death due to accident, murder, or suicide? Accident seemed impossible, for no man surely would fall overboard on a calm day. Murder seemed equally impossible, since the body showed no trace of violence. And as to suicide, which was the verdict of the coroner's jury, no motive could be found. Mr. Crofts makes fine play between these equally unacceptable explanations of the man's death and then, of course, works out a brilliant and entirely satisfactory explanation.

### *Mystery in the Channel*

April 1931

The cross-channel steamer *Chichester* suddenly stopped half-way to France. Right in her course lay a yacht, motionless and apparently crewless. A boat was lowered and drew alongside the derelict, while a party from the *Chichester* climbed aboard. On the deck was a trail of blood and at its end the body of a man. Down below, in a wildly disordered cabin lay another man with a bullet-hole in his forehead; and not a living soul was aboard. MacIntosh, the *Chichester*'s third officer, and two men navigated the *Nymph* back to Newhaven, where Chief Constable Turnbull took charge. But there was more in this baffling mystery than he cared to tackle. Fortunately, like everyone who has met him, Turnbull remembered Inspector French. He took the mystery to him. Needless to say, French solved it; and in what brilliant manner every experienced reader of detective fiction must already anticipate. *Mystery in the Channel* more than justifies our confidence in the Inspector, and in his creator, Mr. Freeman Wills Crofts.

### *Sir John Magill's Last Journey*

September 1930

Sir John Magill, a well-known figure in the public life of Ulster, is coming to Ireland via the Stranraer-Larne route. He never reaches his destination. No trace of the missing man can be discovered. What strange fate has befallen Sir John Magill? Inspector French is called in, and admits that it is his most baffling case. With that admission we feel sure all admirers of Inspector French will agree, and they will follow eagerly the various stages, in the unravelling of this the greatest of Inspector French's mysteries.

### *Sudden Death*

January 1932

Mr. Freeman Wills Crofts has constructed his new mystery on novel and interesting lines. The action of the book is seen alternately through the eyes of two persons, Anne Day and the celebrated detective, Inspector French. Anne Day has secured an appointment as housekeeper at Frayle, the house of Mr. Grinsmead and his semi-invalid wife. She soon finds that something is wrong in the household, and to her horror this tension culminates in tragedy – the mysterious death of Mrs. Grinsmead. All is described as Anne sees it, including the incomprehensible suspicions of the police and the arrival of French to investigate. The viewpoint then alters and through French's eyes are described the police activities behind the scenes. Once again tragedy visits Frayle, the narrative being completed from Anne's and French's viewpoints, giving alternately the inner and outer history of a crime that is as ingenious and elaborate as any yet devised by Mr. Crofts.

## CULPAN, MAURICE

### *Bloody Success*

April 1969

Here is a story of such pace and ingenuity as to remind the reader of classics in this field, such as *Witness for the Prosecution*.

It begins with an account of some minor victims of the London protection racket, who incur the wrath of the Big Boss of the racket himself. There follow a crime and a prison sentence; three years later the prisoner emerges, bent on a furious double vengeance.

It is the story of how this vengeance is planned and attempted that makes the core of this thrilling novel: that takes Chief Inspector Bill Houghton (of the C.I.D.) on a very tricky assignment of impersonation in France: that adds fantastic complications to Houghton's already dangerous plight; and that leads to a denouement that is brilliantly exciting, baffling, and finally satisfying.

Bill Houghton has been the hero of Maurice Culpan's previous stories, such as *A Nice Place to Die* and *The Vasiliko Affair*. He is here involved in events much more extraordinary, and Maurice Culpan displays a craftsmanship of the mystery narrative that far transcends the high accomplishment of the earlier books.

### In a Deadly Vein
March 1967

There seemed no reason in the world why anyone should have needed to kill the veterinary surgeon called Hallam. The discovery of dog's hair on the clothing of the dead man didn't appear to offer much in the way of a clue. And yet Inspector Houghton, thorough and obstinate as ever, was determined to discover which dog those hairs had come from, and where the dog was now.

Houghton traced the dog, which had also died – and in very puzzling circumstances. The first unpromising clue of the dog's hairs introduces Houghton to a far-ranging conspiracy and a complex mystery. Increasingly at odds with his superiors, obstinately and doggedly pursuing his own way, Houghton uncovers the startling truth and nearly loses his own life in the process.

Following the success of *A Nice Place to Die* and *The Minister of Injustice*, Maurice Culpan's report of Houghton's latest case takes the Inspector among an intriguing group of characters, and ends in a series of revelations each more startling and exciting than its predecessors.

### Minister of Injustice, The
May 1966

Chief Inspector Houghton's most important case had a disquieting start. Gunshots had been heard in a London flat – the local police station was informed – and Houghton considered that the response had been perfunctory in the extreme. Had the local Inspector received orders from above to make light of the incident? If so, why? Houghton wanted to know.

But when Houghton began asking questions he was quickly transferred to another case. Despite the mounting evidence that those shots had killed someone, he was ordered to mind his own business.

Before long Houghton finds himself involved in a multiple crime that is dramatic and complex. A foreign country and huge vested interests have designed the London killing. And someone in the official hierarchy is determined to prevent Houghton from pursuing the investigation. But Houghton is resolute that crime shall be discovered and the law prevail.

Maurice Culpan's second novel is an unusual and exciting detective story. The conspirators whom Houghton eventually uncovers work for high stakes – their methods are ruthless and coldly ingenious. Houghton's second reported case is much more far-reaching and bizarre than was the first – the successful novel, *A Nice Place to Die*.

### Nice Place to Die, A
July 1965

It was the first murder in the Cornish village of Penruthan for 24 years. And it was just the luck of Houghton, Chief Detective Inspector, C.I.D., to find himself on holiday in the village – away from his job, his wife and his children for a solitary rest.

Houghton liked Penruthan, but took a somewhat disenchanted view of the locals and visitors who came within the scope of his investigation. Worse still, he made no progress. It looked as though the person who had knifed Mrs. Pascoe had devised a neat but complicated trail to thwart Inspector Houghton.

Who killed Mrs. Pascoe? Houghton found the answer in the end, but before he reached the end he came across the corpse of another murdered woman.

This whodunit is a first novel by a new writer. Against the background of a Cornish village a drama and mystery develop; in an exciting denouement the dogged Houghton discloses the surprising identity of the murderer.

### Vasiliko Affair, The
May 1968

The original murder was committed in November. The trial took place at the Central Criminal Court the following February. No appeal was lodged. Officially the final curtain descended on the scene of the tragedy. It became known as The Vasiliko Affair. The title, probably concocted in Fleet Street, was intended to convey that the episode was mysterious, dramatic, sinister, and disreputable. Certainly it was mysterious. Murders are often mysterious. Dramatic? Far too dramatic for the taste of Chief Inspector Houghton. It was macabre rather than sinister – and as for its being disreputable, it depends how you look at it.

Vasiliko, the young virtuoso musician, had come into possession of a fantastic historic document reputed to be the original score of a Bach clavier concerto never before sighted or played. The music was brought to England to be financially exploited, and at once Vasiliko was trapped in the intrigues of London's musical society. The mysterious concerto seemed to exert a malignant influence on all concerned in the negotiations. Threats are made. Quarrels break out. Murder follows.

Inspector Houghton, tormented and obstructed as usual by his senior officer, Superintendent Blake, finds his way to a solution that is exciting and surprising. But this story is more than a whodunit, and is more than a why-done-it; it is a story that goes beyond the police investigation and beyond the trial to a bitter sequel that brings Houghton's reputation into grave jeopardy.

## CURZON, CLARE
### Blue-Eyed Boy, The
May 1990

Who would kill a handsome, attractive young man like Joel Sefton, apparently mugged and dumped behind supermarket trash bins? But evil can wear a fair face and there were many who had good cause to hate this blue-eyed boy.

Joel was the youngest of ex-ballerina Harriet Sefton's five adult children, and in her eyes the most talented and charming. It was the less admirable traits underlying his charisma, patiently unearthed by Detective –Inspector Mike Yeadings and his team, that they believed had led to his violent end. And it was a secret in the past of WPC Rosemary Zyczynski, on loan to the Thames Valley Serious Crimes Squad for the case and given a mixed welcome by them, that proves vital in penetrating the blue-eyed boy's activities and their labyrinthine effects.

Clare Curzon ('a prime puzzler – *Sunday Times*) has won high praise for her 'devious, gripping and meticulously plotted novels' – *Scotland on Sunday*. Here she is at her best.

### Cat's Cradle
April 1992

Old Lorely Pelling was an eccentric. Raised under the British Raj in India, and caring for her retired Brigadier father until his death at their family home in Berkshire, she was variously regarded in the nearby village as 'queer as two left boots', someone to mind one's Ps and Qs with, a sometime wanton, and a local witch.

Detective-Superintendent Mike Yeadings of Thames Valley Police Force investigating her mysterious death from gunshot wounds, preferred to see her likeness to Kipling's *Cat That Walked by Himself*. But it was his young Down's Syndrome daughter who unknowingly led him to the right viewpoint to penetrate the maze of circumstances which led to her violent end.

### Face in the Stone, The
September 1989

Ex-Warrant Officer Class 1 Edward Mather died in his luxury Cyprus villa from asthma. That had also been the medical reason for his army discharge two years before. But his wasn't a serious case and some thought he shouldn't have died. Two months later an exhumation and post-mortem laid suspicion of murder on his widow.

An efficient Signalman, he was also a rogue adventurer with an eye to making his fortune. So where was his fortune, who were his associates and what had he been involved in?

Police investigation takes time, and the mystery man from Athens looked likely to get the answers first – until the widow took an active interest and the case blew wide open.

### I Give You Five Days
May 1983

Gillian was the accomplished and beautiful teenage daughter of a successful barrister with political ambitions. She was also so sharp that she ended up strangled beside the boating lake of a public park.

Clues were hard to come by. One, a taped message in a disguised voice, threatening her with 'only five days', proved almost totally misleading. Yet Detective-Superintendent Mike Yeadings used it to find the murderer. 'Look back and remember,' he told the individual and complex family, 'Relive everything in the five days of grace she was given.'

But all of them – father, stepmother, brother, grandmother – had secret lives they were unwilling to reveal. To solve the mystery of Gillian's death, all these must be laid bare, and when the murderer is brought to book, one wonders who truly killed Gillian Morton-Hayes.

### Leaven of Malice, A
September 1979

In the everyday world of Fulham's bedsitter-land a crime of possibly supernatural malevolence begins to emerge when three lives interlock: those of a girl escaping from a self-centred lover; a middle-aged ex-nun; and a part-time funeral director who has been under police surveillance ever since his wife unaccountably disappeared. Each life holds a private mystery; each character pairs in experience with one of the others; and where all overlap, as in the intersecting circles of a Venn diagram, a terrifying drama begins to build.

It is connected with the death on the other side of London of a former school-friend of one of the three. It might have been suicide, but the police believe it was murder, and each of the three in the Fulham house comes under suspicion – and under a strange influence. For the victim had grown up in a world where the paranormal was normal and had displayed unusual power. Was victim the word? Or was diabolical manipulator a better description? Could such a person really reach out and commit a vengeful murder, even from beyond the grave?

### Masks and Faces
June 1984

Julian Tawney, thirteen-year-old loner, deeply resents his parents' separation. His father, Vernon, with whom he lives, is an aging Classics master and autocrat, soured by guilt from some secret in his past. His mother, Caroline, still young and attractive, is now peripheral to their existence, wholly preoccupied with her new life. Father and son are increasingly locked in an unhappy bondage which an understanding housekeeper can do nothing to relieve. It ends when Vernon Tawney meets a violent death.

But who among his estranged family, his opportunist neighbours, Caroline's new intimates, his baleful colleagues hated him enough to kill? Finding out is the task of Superintendent Mike Yeadings of the Thames Valley Police, who must sift the true from the false, strip the masks from the faces.

Told mainly from Julian's viewpoint, this strong and sombre story of a tormented relationship and its outcome turns the screws of tension ever tighter as those concerned learn the truth about others – and about themselves.

### Quest for K, The
March 1986

Paula Musto had long promised herself a special holiday on Crete. Sharing her dead father's fascination with the Minoan past, she was forced back into the present by her package holiday companions, some of whom proved to be more than they at first seemed. And one at least was deadly. Unaware of their designs, she became dangerously enmeshed, and when their party returned to Heathrow Paula was not in it.

Angus Mott of Thames Valley police, seeking his lost girlfriend abroad, encountered his own profession from the opposite side of the desk and found the experience shattering. Barred from an official part in the search, he rooted among the remaining members of her tour party, some watchful locals and the sad descendants of the once-thriving hippy communes, in a quest for the mysterious 'K' of her final diary entry. Finally, assisted by Foden, one of society's middle-aged casualties, Angus reached journey's end to discover a tragedy no less poignant for involving others than himself.

### Shot Bolt
January 1988

Andreas Vassilakis, appointed to the World Health Organization and summoned in mid-honeymoon to Geneva on the sudden death of his predecessor, was plunged into unfinished business of a very doubtful mature. New contacts had sinister undertones, and apparently innocent acquaintances lived under threat of violence which gradually encroached on his own life and that of his English bride Sian. The background of greed, foreign intrigue and scandal merged into nightmare with the discovery of a dismembered body at the sluice gates to the Rhone. The related disappearance of a dinghy and a murderous crossbow left in their charge cast suspicion over a wide area which included them both, members of foreign delegations and a Genevese family locked in bitter dispute over inheritance and recent divorce.

Within this framework of suspense and murder runs the story of a new marriage being painfully forged in ironic parallel with the ruin of another.

Clare Curzon lived in Geneva for several years and both setting and human drama show her at the top of her very considerable form.

### *Special Occasion*
April 1981

The glittering reception at the Indonesian Embassy in London was a very special occasion for Veronica Holman and her Australian husband. They had married in Singapore and honeymooned idyllically in Bali. Now the reception promised to revive their happiest memories.

Instead it was marred by the theft of the Ambassadress's emeralds, and when, after inevitable delays, the Holmans returned to their Putney home, it was to find a special occasion of a very different kind awaiting them. Veronica's small son, his invalid grandfather and the teenage babysitter were being held hostage by a group of terrorists, and the roots of this outrage lay deep in her new husband's past.

The tension of the siege mounts steadily: among the terrorists themselves, among their helpless but ever resourceful victims, and among the police officers who watch and wait and plan outside the house. The gripping interplay of characters under stress and the climactic action scenes develop that skill in characterization and the creation of suspense so adroitly manifested in Clare Curzon's first crime novel, *A Leaven of Malice.*

### *Three-Core Lead*
November 1988

Howard Swaffam was a discreet and devious man, as befitted a government official concerned with Security. He was also a man of conscience, balancing loyalty against principle.

The Press notice mentioning Prague as his place of death startled his old acquaintance Superintendent Yeadings. Then receipt of a posthumous letter seemed to lay a moral charge on him to unravel some implied mystery, using a 'three core lead' devised by Swaffam.

Fully occupied with crime-busting in the Thames Valley, Yeadings deployed personal contacts to shake out the Swaffam puzzle, until suddenly it was no longer an unofficial matter but a case on his own doorstep…and triply enigmatic. Was Swaffam's letter a disguised confession to murder, a justification for some spanner thrown in the secret intelligence workings of his own side, or a prod to make his sometime ally search below the surface of what at first appeared a purely criminal case?

Walking a fine line between his police function and the forbidden territory of secret agencies, Yeadings found each question gave rise to another.

### *Trail of Fire*
February 1987

Sian Westbury, on a sketching holiday in Greece, slipped easily into a camping partnership with handsome Scandinavian Per, and was content to follow where his archaeological interests led – until a car plunged in flames down a mountainside. There were curious details about the dead man thrown clear of the wreckage. Was there also something curious about Per's reaction? But in a matter of days the arrogant young Anglo-Swede was also to die mysteriously when leaked camping gas exploded at an isolated farm.

As his family gathered and the police stepped in, it was Sian who came under suspicion. Yet as she learned more and more about the Wennbergs, she grew convinced that the trail led back far beyond her meeting with Per; back to an earlier death when a Youth Hostel burned down in Cumbria – and there too Per had been on holiday…

### *Trojan Hearse, The*
July 1985

The fatal collapse of an unknown man during a University ceremony at the Royal Albert Hall seems the sinister echo of an earlier international crime with political motives. Special Branch are concerned because Princess Anne was present; so was Detective-Superintendent Mike Yeadings and newly promoted Inspector Angus Mott of the Thames Valley Police, as witnesses to part of the action. On loan to Scotland Yard they unravel knot by knot a web of intrigue which stretches from the Balkans to the western seaboard of the USA.

Identification of the corpse brings to light in London a ring of enemies poised to fall like vultures on the rich empire of Loukas Antoniades, millionaire Greek shipowner and exporter. Their benefits from his death are various but the new freedom it offers is beset with traps – a proverbial Greek gift.

Moving among his urbane business associates, his seemingly loyal subordinates, the student friends of his beautiful and impetuous daughter Dimitra, the two policemen pick their way through a labyrinth of deception, to prove that Antoniades himself was no stranger to intrigue and had made plans of his own.

## DAVIS, GEORGE

### *Crime in Threadneedle Street*
July 1968

Roag's Syndicate, little heard of since the events recorded in *Friday Before Bank Holiday*, is here involved in events of even greater magnitude and complexity. Once again the Syndicate is well and truly ahead of the game.

Banks and other offices where money is dealt in have been broken into but nothing has been taken. Phineas Quine, in his Swiss millionaire's hideout, is tempted by a beautiful young woman – but again the objective is far from clear. Someone is trying to involve Roag's Syndicate in a plot, cast as villains; and they themselves are personally handicapped by a personal swindle run privately by Charles Hammersley, one of their members; Hammersley has thought out a way of making some loose cash on the side out of a Pluvius insurance policy, normally a device for insuring against holiday rainfall.

Ingenious, elaborate and civilised, *Crime in Threadneedle Street* is more light-hearted than much contemporary crime fiction. In the splendour of its criminal objectives, in its criminal invention, and in the knowledge of the shadier and neater possibilities of the insurance business, it is a connoisseur's taste. And it *does* have a perfectly good murder, though somewhat incidentally….

### *Death of a Fire-Raiser*
May 1974

At the end of the Second World War a certain Major Meek crawled out of a shell-hole with a few companions and the real conviction that Meek should inherit the earth. As a first step, he and his companions formed Roag's Syndicate. As a second, he changed his name to Good.

Since then, Simon Good, the Syndicate and their desire to get rich quick have figured in all George Davis's light hearted crime novels, and their expertise in banking and insurance has figured too – not surprisingly, since George Davis is himself an underwriter. In *Death of a Fire-Raiser* he puts his professional knowledge to good use.

This time, Good, made redundant by a firm of insurers, becomes involved with someone else's desire to get rich quick. This is Lenox, the owner of a plastics factory, who is anxious for early retirement and even earlier enjoyment of the luscious Frenetta. All Simon has to do is collect some diamonds from a Swiss bank for him. But Simon is wary – all the more so when Lennox's factory conveniently burns down and a body is found in the ruins. Murder is something at which the Syndicate has always jibbed.

### *Friday Before Bank Holiday*
September 1964

Two preordained events, which cost the insurance companies a lot of money, took place on the Friday before Bank Holiday. Charles Hammersley had a horse-riding accident in Knightsbridge; and the Continental Diamond Exchange in Hatton Garden were relieved of the Yellow Fire Diamonds.

The threads of these unconnected events came together to lead to Operation Safe-Deposit. Looking back, Charles Hammersley was inclined to believe that the proximate cause of the trouble was his chance meeting with Tim Tweedy in the White Hart at Esher. For if that meeting had not taken place Simon Good, Chairman of Roag's Syndicate, would not have been suspected of being behind the diamond robbery.

In its efforts to restore order, establish innocence and guilt etc., Roag's Syndicate was obliged to swing deviously into action in Belgium, Holland and the West country….

From Charles Hammersley's horse-riding accident to the bizarre show-down there is not a dull moment in George Davis's witty new novel of theft, murder, arson, fraud and double-cross.

### *Killer Grew Tired, The*
February 1971

Only Roag's Syndicate could have thought up that particular method of smuggling gold ingots into Britain, Superintendent Lingard recognized ruefully as he stood with a Customs officer beside the gleamingly elegant Mercado-Suisse.

The remarkable Syndicate which was first formed in a tight corner during the war by a certain Major Meek,who subsequently found it expedient to become Good, has been little heard of since George Davis's last chronicle of their activities, *Crime in Threadneedle Street*, but that is not to say that they have not been gainfully employed. Their operations, though still centred on the City, now extend from Holland where a certain Mr Hammersley manages to slip on his hotel steps just after taking out an accident insurance policy, to Cornwall and treasures from a wreck. The Rev. Magnus Carter has providentially already retired to the Cornish village of St Merrion, and he is instrumental in bringing the Syndicate's arch rival, Lady Veronica Tuke, on the scene.

But these are only peripheral pieces in this intricate crime jigsaw which George Davis fashions so lightheartedly. Readers who enjoy pitting their wits against those of some of the smoothest, most endearing operators in crime fiction must be prepared for a few surprises, as the picture builds up around the tree-planting activities of a young man from Ealing and the plans for a daring, ingenious and profitable crime.

## DEAN, S. F. X.

### *By Frequent Anguish*
July 1982

Neil Kelly, middle-aged Professor of English literature in a New England college and a settled widower, could not possibly be deeply in love with one of his students. But he was. More astonishing still, beautiful, intelligent Priscilla Lacey was in love with him.

Any qualms Neil might have had about their future together were abruptly obliterated when Pril was found murdered in the college library. Dazed by grief, Neil yielded to her parent's plea to find the murderer. 'Let the police go round knocking on doors,' insisted Morgan Lacey. 'I want to have a complete piece of research done.'

There was no better researcher than Neil Kelly, and no one better able to note any breaks in the pattern of Pril's life, to judge the reactions of her classmates and friends, to spot the one incongruity, the one unanswered question that would lead to her killer. His quest among the eccentrics and centrics of Old Hampton College makes an intriguing journey for the reader, for the author of this first crime novel, which he calls 'a love-story interrupted by a murder', offers them a many-faceted pleasure: an intricate and compelling plot, a wonderful variety of three-dimensional characters, and a style that never fails to entertain.

### *It Can't be My Grave*
November 1983

In London for the publication of his book on Donne, American professor Neil Kelly, who had already been dogged by murder in *By Frequent Anguish* and *Such Pretty Toys*, finds that his fate pursued him across the Atlantic. Through theatrical friends he becomes involved with Gordon Fairly, a vastly wealthy tycoon whose private interest – perhaps even his King Charles's Head – lies in identifying the author of an anonymous sixteenth-century tragedy about which he has a theory of his own. Kelly is engaged to investigate Fairly's theory, but before he can begin the tycoon is killed; blown up by letter-bomb in his own very personalized Daimler.

Kelly immediately encounters an array of suspects, including several among his own publishers, for the once independent firm is now one of Fairly's companies and many of the senior staff are unhappy at the changes he plans to introduce. Then there is Fairly's enigmatic and disaffected daughter, making one of her rare visits to London; and, of course, all those nameless, faceless, business rivals dismayed by the prosperity and growth of Fairly's empire.

Neil Kelly picks his way adroitly through the minefields of the English theatre, publishing, the media and big business to come up with a solution as brilliant as it is satisfying, which makes sense of Gordon Fairly's death by neatly tying in the disparate elements of his life.

### *Such Pretty Toys*
February 1983

Just as Professor Neil Kelly, first encountered in *By Frequent Anguish*, is about to depart for a sabbatical in England, he receives word that a bomb explosion has killed his close friend Morgan Lacey, and injured Morgan's wife, Barbara. From her hospital bed, Barbara prevails on Neil to fly to Santa Fe and try to find out who had hidden the tiny, lethal explosive in the jack-in-the-box she had sent her husband for an April Fool joke.

At the start of his search, Neil is amazed to learn that the wealthy over-achieving Laceys are involved in the activities of the CIA. And 'The Firm' is not his only companion – or rival? – in the search for the killer. The FBI also has some unexpected agents in the area, who appear to be working against the CIA operatives.

At the heart of the mystery is Barbara's beautiful niece, Linn, who runs the computer system at her father's successful construction company and is engaged to a brilliant engineer of shadowy background. Linn's family nickname has inadvertently supplied the code word for a treasonable computer organisation. How much is she involved in what is going on?

Before Neil can unravel this grim puzzle he has to augment his expert knowledge of 17th century English literature with a crash course in computer technology.

S. F. X. Dean once again demonstrates the delightful wit, deft characterization and graceful prose that marked his debut in crime fiction.

## DEKKER, ANTHONY
### Divers Diamonds
August 1970

In these days of escalation and inflation on all fronts, the criminal world is vying with Big Business to set new records.

Here now is the story of the most spectacular hold-up of all time, by the most daring criminals in the annals of organized crime.

It all started on Christmas Eve with the theft in Portsmouth of a newly refitted submarine awaiting delivery to the Israeli Navy. This bold coup and the subsequent complete disappearance of the submarine were not at first connected with some letters received at No. 10 Downing Street, demanding no less than £100 million, with threats to blow up every nuclear installation in the country if the demand was not complied with. This gigantic sum was to be paid in assorted diamonds and dropped by parachute at a pre-arranged point in the South Atlantic.

The Government wasted precious time debating whether the whole thing was a hoax, but the first explosion settled the argument. The deadline was approaching. A disaster of unprecedented magnitude faced the nation. Fortunately, an ingenious – albeit exceedingly dangerous – plan was set on foot which would comply with the criminals' demand, yet foil their ultimate victory.

Here is action all the way, in one of the most original crime stories of recent years.

## DELMAN, DAVID
### Bye-Bye Baby
November 1992

'Oh God, Bry, you honestly do think you're going to live forever.'

The speaker is Baby Robin Cantrell, the most famous female tennis player in the world. The person addressed is Bryant Gilchrist, her divorced husband. The occasion: an outrageous seduction attempt, by the former of the latter.

Baby is a terror, no question. And a charmer. And Bry is only one of a sizeable number with severely mixed feelings about her – a number that includes the well known detecting team of Helen and Jacob Horowitz.

For the Tri-Town Invitational, the midpoint of Baby's farewell tour, an all-star international cast (with a lot of secret agendas) has assembled. Violence erupts. Helen and Jacob, smack in the middle of it all, find their lives intensified in a way that shakes them both.

Is *their* marriage as vulnerable as *ordinary* marriages when they had blithely assumed it wasn't?

Witty as always, a shade darker than usual, David Delman offers the Horowitzes in an absorbing and complex murder mystery, with an ending that may shock you.

### Dead Faces Laughing
August 1987

Charley (the Elf) Elfenbein...from the streets of New York to the hearts of America. Described by some as 'the funniest man who ever lived'. By others – particularly whose women he stole – in a variety of harsher terms. And now dead – murdered.

A tremendously successful stand-up comic, Charley earned a six-figure income for making people laugh. And yet none who knew him well could take him lightly.

Not his vengeful son.

Not his betrayed brother.

Not his disillusioned agent.

Not his closest friend.

Not his discarded mistress.

Not any of that colourful cross-section who shared the 'old neighbourhood' with him, among them Homicide Lieutenant Jacob Horowitz, who, as a boy, had joined the Marwood Place discipleship.

Now the Horowitzes – Jacob and his beloved Helen – find themselves, in the aftermath of cataclysm, sorting out who did what to whom. And why.

*Dead Faces Laughing* is Jacob and Helen at their best. Warm, funny, and, as ever, markedly human as they sort out their own problems while sorting through the tangled clues – and even more tangled relationships – in the world of Charley the Elf.

### Death of a Nymph
April 1986

The Byrd School was established, its founder stated, because 'the world needs gracious women'. But that was over a hundred years ago, and times have changed. How much is underscored by a typical Byrd School joke, which specifies as requirements for graduation two years of maths, two years of a foreign language, and one year of nervous breakdown.

Into this elite but fevered grove of academe comes murder. Also the Horowitzes, Helen and Jacob, police officers, who for a while find themselves hunted as well as hunting. Among their enemies is a psychopathic killer and – almost as ferocious and no less implacable – a career-building fellow officer.

What is a 'nymph'? More to the point, what are American nymphs and why do they constitute an endangered species? The answers are contained in this droll but deadly story that moves swiftly and wittily to a spine-tingling climax. The Horowitzes, delightful as ever, have a hard time throughout. The reader is assured of a good one.

### Last Gambit, The
November 1990

Dmitri Kaganovich is an internationally ranked chess player. He is also something of a ladies' man. And something of a rogue. In a career that has featured multiple lifestyles in diverse countries he has made his share of enemies, one of whom is now threatening him.

The scene is Philadelphia where the annual Capa Open is about to get under way and chess-playing greats from all over the world are gathering. Homicide Lieutenant Jacob Horowitz has also gathered to compete in one of the tournament's lower sections, and it is to him that Kaganovich turns for help.

Meantime Jacob's wife Helen, now a full-fledged private-eye, is in Chicago tracking down the missing daughter of a successful venture capitalist. But why should that

generate twinges of Horowitzian jealousy? And is there a possibility that two such dissimilar cases could connect?

As always when David Delman chronicles the adventures of Helen and Jacob, the pace is swift, the tone wry, and the cast highly coloured. There's Lanie, Kaganovich's rich, repressed but fiercely possessive new wife. There's Buddy, the sad-eyed female newspaper columnist with a special connection to Jacob. There's Barney, the legendary baseball star with a special connection to Buddy. And there's Gregorin, the charmingly cynical chess teacher/manager with a special connection to the KGB...

In the rip-snorting world of power chess surprises, twists, and gambits proliferate – until the last of these unlocks the puzzle.

### Liars' League, The
April 1989

Take three star-crossed Duncannons. Examine only their shiny surfaces, and it's easy to place them among fortune's favoured. Pierce the veneer, however, and not many would find them enviable. Consider:

Alec – once a legendary football player and now the CEO of as high-powered advertising agency. A workaholic, because his life has an emptiness at its core that demands distraction.

Ellie: his sister, driving, ambitious. Today, the leading light of the local bench; tomorrow the Supreme Court. But she, too, has a secret emptiness.

Neil: the youngest, the least successful, but in many ways the most attractive Duncannon. Except that he once beat a man so savagely it landed him in prison.

The stage is set. Unexpected events begin to exert pressure, and what follows is an explosive chain reaction: first the lies, next the rage, and finally the murder.

And now here come the Horowitzes – Homicide Lieutenant Jacob and Private Investigator Helen – plunged by duty *and* friendship smack in the middle of their fastest-paced and most engrossing adventure to date.

As they struggle to discover what's meant by a liars' league they ride an emotional roller-coaster to a surprising and shocking end. And when they do find out, it's the hard way.

### Nice Murderers, The
November 1977

Everybody hated Piggy Ott – his two sons, his wife, his friends, if you could call them that, and William and Lizzie Winter. Piggy was a thoroughly disliked man.

Everybody – except Piggy Ott – loved William Winter. He and the beautiful Lizzie were a charming couple. All agreed. Even Jacob Horowitz, who suspected the Winters of murder. And Jacob was the detective who had to prove they'd killed Piggy Ott.

William and Lizzie had not wanted to commit murder. All they had in mind was a little larceny – that cache of diamonds, sapphires and emeralds Piggy had made so clear to them was sitting in his safe. Jacob and his policewoman wife, Helen, had not wanted to believe that such a lovable pair could be involved in murder – or that a friend like William could have shot a man in the back. Yet the evidence seemed to point straight in William's direction.

Two couples who should have been the best of friends were now poised as almost enemies: William and Lizzie with a taste for gems, Jacob and Helen with a taste for law. What happens as Jacob goes after William and William goes after the others – and Jacob unearths a stunning secret – makes a witty and suspenseful yarn, with the most

intriguing cops and robbers anyone's seen in many a caper.

### One Man's Murder
September 1975

Sully Byrnes was Target of the Year for Murder One, the kind of man you love to hate. President, or more accurately tyrant, of a major advertising agency, he ran the business on a Byzantine basis of internecine hatred, suspicion, and degrading fear. When he suddenly announced that he was relinquishing the job, the stage was set for a grim battle between the possible inheritors – all of whom it pleasured Sully to sweat.

Of his victims, Tom Odum had most to lose since he was the son of the agency's co-founder and Sully's chief whipping boy. Yet, much as he longed to see Sully go, it was Tom who got landed with staging a surprise birthday party for the old man at the palatial, almost medieval Odum estate on Long Island.

There were certainly surprises at that party, one of which involved Lt Jacob Horowitz of the Nassau County Homicide Squad, and what involved Horowitz also involved Helen, his bride. Soon, Jacob's headaches included a rotten cold, a list of prime suspects that goes awry in a hurry, an all-out war of nerves in the executive suite, and – worst of all – Helen's decision to liberate herself and return to being a cop like Jacob, thus opening the battle on a second front.

David Delman is vice-president and copy-chief of one of the largest advertising agencies in Philadelphia. He puts his inside knowledge of advertising to as good use in this book as he put his knowledge of tennis (he describes himself as 'an obsessive tennis-player') in his last.

### Sudden Death
August 1973

The professional rivalry of the international tennis circuit blends with the quieter but far more lethal play of private antagonisms in this intriguing mystery set amid the drama of the US Open at Forest Hills.

Everyone agreed that Cole Cooper, the top-seeded contender, was the man to beat at Forest Hills. There was agreement also that he was a man one might easily want to kill. When someone did just that, the job of finding his murderer fell to detective Jacob Horowitz.

As a man who knows a lot more about people than he does about tennis, Horowitz soon finds himself with a whole houseful of suspects, including a former champion with more than one reason to finish Cole off on the tennis courts; the champion's ex-wife who is now Cole's ex-girl; Cole's wife, who'd had a lot to put up with; and a black player who hated Cole for his racialist views.

Before the final ploy in his investigation is over, the persistent Horowitz has learned just how quickly the phenomenon known in tennis circles as Sudden Death can turn victory into defeat – in police work as well as on the courts.

## DELVING, MICHAEL
### China Expert, The
August 1976

End of June, and a bright, clear, cloudless sky of the sort which in New York would be thought of as mildly cool but which was received by Londoners as a heat wave. Marius Kagan, New York oriental art dealer and an expert in Chinese porcelain, in London to bid for a couple of items, is suddenly asked for help by no less an outfit than the British Secret Service. A priceless Sung vase, the gem of the collection, has been stolen in broad daylight from the new Museum of the East, the richly endowed foundation of an Arabian oil king, which is due to open its doors to the public in less than two weeks' time. Worse, the vase has been specially loaned by the Chinese People's Republic – and neither the Chinese not the British like losing face. Unless the vase can be recovered by the time the Museum opens, its theft will become a political matter, exactly as the thieves – whoever they may be – hope.

Marius's task is to pronounce on the authenticity of any vases which ill-wishers may try to palm off as the genuine Sung. He could scarcely have foreseen that so innocent an assignment would involve him with the agents of rival powers, with cloak-and-dagger activities in London's Chinatown, with violence and love and death.

Michael Delving skilfully deploys a knowledge of oriental art and oriental ways in this original and fast-paced thriller, with its neatly ironical end.

### *Devil Finds Work, The*

April 1970

Dave Cannon, amiable young American dealer in rare books and manuscripts, comes to the serene village of Bartonbury with his partner, Bob Eddison, only to be drawn into a strange, baffling mystery which begins with the theft of a famous silver cup and is followed by a murder in the village church.

A special kind of darkness hangs over the crimes because of the presence in the village of Tristram Vail, a notorious Satanist, once called 'the wickedest man in the world'. His frightening, inexplicable power brings a note of menace to the investigation. Other characters figure prominently in the story: Anthony Gaunt, Vail's ambiguous friend and defender; the cheerful, absent-minded Miss Trout, and the pretty niece, Jill.

Michael Delving writes knowingly and with relish of pubs and police procedure and satanism, deftly fusing them all into an original and spellbinding story.

### *Die Like a Man*

November 1970

Returning from a fruitless trip to South Wales in search of rare books and manuscripts, Dave Cannon, American antiquarian bookseller, whose visits to England have proved so unexpectedly eventful in *Smiling, the Boy Fell Dead* and *The Devil Finds Work*, is stranded overnight in the border town of Corbridge. In mysterious circumstances he is handed a dish, claimed to be none other than the Holy Grail. Next morning the owner is found hanged.

Immediate efforts are made to recover the dish. When Cannon insists on keeping it, those anxious to secure the prize employ first guile, then violence and conspiracy against him. A foreigner alone in a countryside turned suddenly hostile, Cannon seeks the help of the only persons who have befriended him: Ivor Howell, a retired lawyer, and Eileen Truce, sculptress. The violent death of one of them, and Cannon's own researches into the legend and mystery surrounding the Holy Grail prepare the way for a finale of terrifying power in the ruined castle of Corbridge, and the unmasking of a villainous plot.

Michael Delving's urbane style, his personal experience of the South Wales border, and his intimate knowledge of the Grail story, are brilliantly displayed in this unusual and arresting novel, which combines historical deduction with detection in crime.

### *No Sign of Life*

September 1978

There are number of reason why Americans visiting Britain flock to Walcombe, one of the prettiest villages in the Cotswolds. Murder is not one of them.

Yet when Cyril Lake, a dealer in antiquities with a slightly tarnished reputation, was found stabbed at his desk, a party of visiting Americans constituted the majority of the suspects. Another American visiting independently – Dave Cannon, the rare book dealer who has appeared in a number of Michael Delving's previous crime novels – had to turn detective once again.

Cyril Lake had recently organized a tour for a select group of American visitors with a particular interest in antiquities – Roman, Hellenic or prehistoric artifacts [sic]. He had also acquired a commission to sell a gold torc which couldn't be offered openly abroad. Very privately it was now offered to members of the party, some of whom were prepared to go to almost any lengths to possess it. Did those lengths include murder?

And what about the two fiancées Cyril had also acquired, one English and one American? Each had discovered the other's existence, and the sign scrawled crudely on the desk in Cyril's own heart's blood was the ancient Egyptian symbol for the feminine.

As usual, Michael Delving excels at characterization, at skilful plotting, a Gloucestershire setting, and a considerable knowledge of treasures from the past.

### *Shadow of Himself, A*

June 1972

Robert Eddison, a principal character in *The Devil Finds Work*, is the central figure in Michael Delving's fourth crime novel, which, like its predecessors, deals with the adventures in England of an American antiquarian bookseller.

Eddison's business trip this time has also a personal motive. He hopes to persuade the girl he met in England to marry him. He therefore returns to Gloucestershire, and while waiting for Jill to reach a decision, attends a local auction and buys a small nineteenth-century copy of a Dutch landscape.

The picture was formerly owned by an estate developer, a man who has left his mark on the picturesque village of Chaworth and recently met a violent end. Mystery still surrounds his death, alone at night in a ruined castle. Now one man in particular shows himself unreasonably anxious to gain possession of the picture for which Eddison has already been forced to overbid.

Unexpectedly, Eddison is drawn into the cross-currents of English village life. Beneath the surface he finds violence, loyalty, eccentricity and history, all of which he views with a tolerant but candid eye. By the time he and Jill have worked out their problems, and Eddison has had a brush with death, Michael Delving has peeled back layers of ambiguity to expose not only a murderer, but the seamier side of the art world and some of the mainsprings of the English way of life.

### *Wave of Fatalities, A*

June 1975

Dave Cannon, the American antiquarian bookseller who has figured in Michael Delving's previous crime novels, makes a welcome return in this his latest, which brings Dave and his English wife Lucy on a visit to her Gloucestershire home.

Interest immediately centres on a medieval silver-gilt box with a mysterious history which is furtively offered to Dave for sale. Next day the would-be vendor is found in the river, murdered, and the box has disappeared.

But the district is rich in modern poets as well as in antiques, and against the exotic alien who has settled there local feelings run high as a Severn tide. Dave himself in not exempt form it when he be-friends the unpopular poet, and is suddenly made aware that he too is a foreigner , even in this beloved corner of England with which he thought he had close ties. The local police seem less than impartial in their attitude, and Dave is virtually dragooned into assisting them. And then a series of dramatic revelations shatters still further the assumption which underlie the security of village life.

Michael Delving writes as entertainingly as always on places and people and the business world of antiques, and provides a sharp yet sympathetic view of English attitudes to the outsider from the point of view of one who has for over twenty years made his home alternately in England and Connecticut.

## DEVINE, D. M.
(*see also* **Devine, Dominic**)

### *Devil at Your Elbow*

June 1966

A lobby is active to oust Dr. Haxton from his job at Hardgate University. He is said to have cooked the accounts of the summer school to his own advantage. The beautiful Lucille Provan is a principal in the movement to get rid of him.

Haxton defends himself with threats: he will expose the real truth of a University scandal some years earlier when a young girl had died as the result of an abortion.

It is Haxton's threat which re-creates the tension and drama of an old crisis, and leads to murder.

This is a classical detective story set in a modern redbrick university. The customs and traditions of university life are cunningly interwoven into an exciting narrative that leads to a revelation which – though perfectly fair – will surprise many readers.

D. M. Devine is already widely respected and read as the author of detective novels set convincingly in contemporary life. Great critical acclaim greeted his last book, *His Own Appointed Day*, of which Julian Symons said in the *Sunday Times*: *'his book really does fill one with that almost anguished but pleasurable desire to reach the solution that is the hallmark of a good detective novel.'*

### *Doctors Also Die*

May 1962

The doctor's death had been accepted as an accident. The police may have felt a little suspicious, but they had nothing to go on. The fact that the doctor's young partner was fond of the doctor's young widow indicated that the doctor's death might be someone's gain; but it did not constitute grounds for suspecting – or investigating – murder.

It is the young partner who is the central character of this story; and who becomes damagingly suspect when the older man's death is attributed to murder. His reputation and his practice are at stake, as well as his liberty and life. But there are other suspects, too, in the Scottish of Silbridge – politicians, tradesmen, professional men and their wives and sweethearts.

This successful second novel (it follows *My Brother's Killer*) sets a very clever detective puzzle firmly in a credible contemporary setting: the lives and work of professional people in a modern Scottish town are portrayed in solid detail; the daily problems that beset them in a competitive world form part of the background of an ingenious and thrilling murder mystery.

### *Fifth Cord, The*

May 1967

*Eight people will die at my hand, the first within a week from now. No, I am not insane. My motives are rational and, I believe, compelling.*

It is an extract from the 'Confessions' of an unknown murderer that heralds a series of gruesome murders in the town of Kenburgh in Northern Britain.

The young narrator of the story, a gifted journalist whom bad luck has brought to the local paper (and also close to alcoholism), finds himself professionally engaged in the sensational 'Cord' murders; and he soon finds too that he himself is one of the small group of people which must include the murderer.

As a craftsman of the classical detective story in a contemporary setting, this author's stature has grown with every book, and has been acknowledged by critics. This story, grimly ornamented with the theme of the Cords that hang from coffins, brilliantly manipulates the ingredients of a modern detective mystery; and succeeds in combining these with serious characterisation and a satisfying revelation at the end.

### *His Own Appointed Day*

August 1965

'Each man has his own appointed day; the span of life is short and cannot be retraced.' Thus Ian Pratt translated in school – the fair-haired boy who himself planned a great appointment; who had written in his diary: 'I wonder what Mother will do. To hell with her! To hell with them all, the lousy rotten…'

Ian Pratt disappeared, and in time his sister Eileen reported his absence to the police of Silbridge. Detective-Inspector Nicolson and his colleagues began to probe Ian's movements, and the past secrets of the Pratt family. They found a number of trails, one of which showed clearly and strongly what had become of the clever, sensitive boy who had vanished.

In the small community of the policemen and schoolmasters of Silbridge, doubts and suspicions multiplied. The death of a girl killed by a 'hit and run' motorist was seen to be linked with young Pratt's disappearance.

This is a true detective story which has for its setting a modern, provincial, Scottish industrial town, where busy men and women work and face their daily problems. It is a whodunit of impressive craftsmanship. The solution is fair, though it will come as a shock to most readers.

### *My Brother's Killer*

November 1961

What sort of man had he been? Was he as his brother saw him – boisterous, sensual, flamboyant, weak? Or was he a cynical and ruthless blackmailer? At any rate it was worth somebody's while to kill him, and to arrange the killing so carefully that every circumstance of it was capable of misinterpretation. The mystery of the murder of Oliver Barnett is seen from the point of view of his brother, Simon. It is Simon who sets out to clear his brother's name, to disentangle the aftermath and to demonstrate the innocence of a woman of whom he himself had once been fond...

This first novel offers a fully worked-out detective story with a cast of credible suspects and a revelation at the end that comes as a powerful surprise – though the alert reader has the opportunity to foretell it.

*'A most enjoyable crime story which I enjoyed reading down to the last moment'*
AGATHA CHRISTIE

### *Royston Affair, The*

July 1964

Mark Lovell had been virtually outlawed from his home town of Riverhead since the day he gave evidence in the Royston Case. His father, his stepmother, his stepbrother and his partners in the office of family solicitors where he had worked – all regarded him as a perjurer.

But Mark had told the truth. And when a summons came from his father to return home Mark had some reason to suppose that the old man had at last discovered the true facts of the Royston Case, this supposition was backed by events; before Mark could have a word with him, his father was brutally and fatally knifed.

These events introduce a story of great complexity, ingenuity and excitement. In it the professional men of Riverhead, including the solicitors, are meticulously drawn – as is the social and moral climate of the world. This is a clever and exciting whodunit, which will please and satisfy the many readers of the author's earlier books, *My Brother's Killer* and *Doctors Also Die*.

## DEVINE, DOMINIC
### (*see also* Devine, D.M.)

### *Dead Trouble*
February 1971

She was young, attractive, on the rebound from a broken engagement, and alone in Paris. He was young, attractive and alone in Paris too. But the casual pick-up was more carefully planned that he was willing for her to discover. After all, Alma Vallance was the daughter of a very wealthy man.

Back in England, the affair continued on the lines he had always intended. Before long, another engagement was announced. And then, having milked her father of several thousands, Alma's fiancé disappeared. Good riddance, said the family, trying to console her for this second disappointment. But the young man made a reappearance, as totally unexpected as it was undesired.

The Vallance family find themselves involved in a murder investigation. There is no shortage of suspects in the case. But it is increasingly clear that there is a connection between the crime and a guilty secret which, years before, had caused Alma's best-selling novelist father to give up writing and quarrel with the family who were his closest friends.

Patiently the police investigate. Alma's elder married sister does some retracing of her father's past on her own. But they are none of them prepared for the final bizarre twist which Dominic Devine reserves to end this absorbing study of a scheming young man and an old one with something to hide.

### *Death is My Bridegroom*
January 1969

'It's about Denton. I've had a complaint.' Michael Denton was an assistant lecturer in the department.

'About his work?'

'No – his morals.'

'That doesn't surprise me.'

Michael Denton had lately been sharing house with Barbara Letchworth, a student at Branchfield University where he was teaching. And Barbara was dynamite in more ways than one, for she was the only daughter of Lord Letchworth, millionaire benefactor of the University.

A silly university 'rag' was used as the cover for something much more sinister. A brutal murder followed, and the investigations soon showed where the guilt must lie.

But the 'guilty party' was lucky in discovering a champion who would not accept the incontrovertible facts. Gradually there came to light details of a different motive and background, a whole long-planned and cold-blooded plot to achieve one single ruthless objective.

Dominic Devine is the author of a number of novels that are in the classical 'whodunit' tradition as well as being genuinely contemporary in setting and sentiment. He writes of university life today, and of professional men within the framework of their working and private lives; he combines a strong story with a mystery, and invents characters that are true to both.

### *Illegal Tender*
May 1970

In his latest novel Dominic Devine, already well established as a writer of classical whodunits, lays bare the bones – not to say the skeletons in the cupboard – of a Scottish town council.

A junior clerk, who has indiscreetly let it be known that she has discovered an irregularity, is murdered before she can reveal what she knows to the police. Inspector Hemmings investigates, and discovers that the number of possible irregularities in Kilcrannon is unexpectedly large. The Town Clerk is indulging in an affair with the only woman among his four Senior Deputes, while at the same time fighting to prevent the appointment over his head of his greatest rival on the council – an appointment sponsored by the dead girl's Councillor father. The woman Senior Depute, though unquestionably able, finds her promotion blocked by the antiquated prejudice of this same Councillor. And a local firm, whose tenders are always submitted at the last minute, has been having a remarkable run of luck in undercutting its rivals.

When a second murder takes place at the staff dance, all evidence points in one direction. But Inspector Hemmings is not satisfied. Any one of numerous Councillors, secretaries, deputes, even perhaps the Chamberlain, had motives and opportunity to dispose of those who knew too much.

Anyone who dismisses local government as boring is in for an exciting surprise. The ingenuity of plot and solid characterization which have distinguished all Dominic Devine's stories of detection find a setting worthy of them in the municipal buildings of Kilcrannon.

### *Sleeping Tiger, The*
March 1968

Charged with two murders, John Prescott, who had once himself been a solicitor, had become apathetic. The evidence, as everyone could see, was overwhelming. The tiger in Prescott's nature had, it seemed, gone to sleep, leaving him to drift towards any destiny, however catastrophic. Counsel said:

'These were not, members of the jury, crimes of passion, committed when the blood was hot. On the contrary, each was planned to the last inhuman detail many weeks in advance.'

The history Counsel presented went back five years into the past: to fateful meetings with Norah Browne, and Harriet Reece…the women in Prescott's life; to the disruption of friendships and relationships in a small society that had been shattered by violent death. The case against Prescott was overwhelming – and yet *someone else*, one of the others, must have been the killer: one of the witnesses – but which one?

In several books Dominic Devine has shown himself a brilliant craftsman of the contemporary whodunit. In stories ingeniously designed and precisely written he has presented problems which could be solved by reading the clues, but which were still baffling; stories in which characterisation was both serious and true even when the truth was revealed and guilt attributed. In *The Sleeping Tiger* he takes another step forward in a crime novel that is a tour-de-force of characterisation, plotting and excitement.

### *Sunk Without Trace*
February 1978

Illegitimate Ruth Kellaway returns to Silbridge, one of the new enlarged Scottish burghs created in 1974, to seek revenge on her father, a prominent local councillor. Her mother had been for many years assistant to the town clerk of Silbridge, and discoveries among her mother's papers have led Ruth to suspect that corruption was involved in the 1974 elections, and that proof of it might prove more damaging to her father's career in local politics than his siring of a bastard, which she had originally intended to expose. She therefore conceals her identity and takes a job in City Hall, where she will have access to municipal records. This brings her in contact with her unsuspecting half-sister, Judy, a senior City Hall employee, and with Judy's ex-fiancé, now living with a slatternly woman who unexpectedly poses a threat to Ruth's plans.

But it is Judy who is at the heart of the drama when the woman is murdered, for all the men in her life – father, brother, fiancé, and ex-fiancé – are under suspicion, and Ruth Kellaway even more so, for she was known to have quarrelled with the victim, and now she has vanished. Sunk without trace.

The complexities of human relationships and the ins and outs of local government combine skilfully in Dominic Devine's long-awaited new novel, his first since 1972.

### *This is Your Death*
October 1981

Geoffrey Wallis, bestselling novelist ad TV personality, had something on his mind – something apparently connected with the reappearance on his life of his pharmacist brother Lionel, whom he had reluctantly installed in a cottage close to his country home. His family feared he was being blackmailed – and he was not the man to be docile under threats. In the event it was Geoffrey who was murdered and his brother who was accused of the crime.

Asked to undertake a biography of Geoffrey, historian Maurice Slater is unwillingly drawn in. He had grown up in the novelist's shadow, and the engagement of his son to Geoffrey's daughter had involved him with the Wallis family once again. In an effort to fill in the missing years in his subject's voluminous diaries, he probes deep into the past, only to discover that any investigation of Geoffrey's life must involve him in an investigation of Geoffrey's death, for Lionel Wallis was not the only member of his family with a motive for murdering him.

Dominic Devine's crime novels have always delighted lovers of a cleverly crafted plot. The present one, found among his papers after his death in 1980, is a fitting coda to his work.

### *Three Green Bottles*
January 1972

With more than a dozen titles to his credit, Dominic Devine has established an enviable reputation among connoisseurs of the detective story for sound plotting and characterization. *Three Green Bottles* will pleasantly enhance it.

When a pretty schoolgirl is found strangled on the golf-links, and shortly afterwards the junior doctor in a local partnership, a young man with a history of nervous instability, is found dead at the foot of a cliff, the police are satisfied that they know the identity of the murderer. Only two people are not: the dead man's brother, and the writer of an anonymous letter which asserts that the young doctor was pushed.

In an effort to clear his brother's name, Dr Mark Kendall takes his brother's place in the partnership, and is soon drawn into the social circle of the senior doctor. This includes the doctor's much younger second wife; their retarded daughter; Dr. Ben Radford, the family's close friend; the earnest daughter of the doctor's first marriage, at odds with her stepmother; and the attractive schoolteacher to whom Mark's brother had been engaged. Yet when a second schoolgirl dies and it is obvious that Terry Kendall was not a murderer, all these people react in unexpected ways.

Through the skilfully interwoven narratives of various characters, the reader follows events, until the death of a third girl brings into the open a bold and cunning murderer.

## DEWHURST, EILEEN

### *Drink This*
January 1980

Following the disappearance of a big-time bank robber, Detective-Inspector Neil Carter of Scotland Yard is sent unofficially by his Chief to question the man's lovely, enigmatic wife in the idyllic village where she has retired hurt to her father's house.

Ostensibly a holiday-maker, dallying with the lady, and striking up friendship with her perceptive 12-year-old brother, Neil soon decides he is on 'a delightful wild goose chase'. But his cover is blown when he is forced to take action in the face of another and far more horrible crime.

Although he has no official role in its investigation, Neil has never felt so personally involved in a crime, finding himself strangely troubled at the possibility that a clergyman could be guilty of murder and sacrilege.

The inhabitants of the village are brought vividly alive through the eyes of Neil and young Tony, and in their reactions to the outrage in their midst. Neil's part in the two investigations ends only on his final return to London, with the sharpest shock of his whole extraordinary 'holiday'.

### *House That Jack Built, The*
September 1983

Sue Halliday was two weeks old when she first appeared in Festival TV's *The House That Jack Built* and has spent the whole of her sixteen years in the cast of the long-running serial. Known and adored nationwide she has all before her – until she becomes infatuated with a fellow actor and somebody steals the notebook in which she has confessed her feelings. Not much of a crime, but it leads from blackmail to murder in a macabre series of parallels of accidents to characters in the serial and accidents in real life to the people who play them.

Helpless in the power of the inhuman voice on the telephone which tells her what she must do, Sue watches aghast as events move relentlessly towards violent death. Unable to identify the voice, she is unable to trust anyone around her: friendly Meg who plays her mother in the serial, her own cold, clever mother; her boyfriend Jimmy; beloved Lloyd, the programme's producer; each of them could be the sinister voice making her pay so dearly for her indiscretion – dearly enough to find herself charged with the final, fearful crime.

As fascinating for its revelation of the behind-the-scenes world of a long-running serial as for its insight into a young girl's heart and mind, Eileen Dewhurst's latest crime novel offers all the originality, perceptiveness and mystification which her increasing readership has come to expect.

### *Playing Safe*
August 1985

Actress Helen Johnson, recently married to an officer in British Intelligence with whom she once worked, feels she lacks the nerve to join him in a further life-and-death assignment such as that she undertook in *Whoever I Am*, but still wants to exercise her unusual talents. It is after light-heartedly offering 'a unique service' through the advertisement columns of some magazines that she finds herself playing three such diverse parts as the bridegroom's only relative at a suburban wedding, the girlfriend paraded for the approval of Mama, and the wife of a would-be business executive who must be assessed along with her husband – not on the stage but in real life. She also finds herself innocently in trouble on a scale to send her back after all, and without choice, into another role where not only is her life at stake but her husband's life also and the safety of their home.

In the psychiatric clinic where Helen must anonymously go both to hide and to seek, can it really be that someone is trying to poison her? Can an internationally sinister development really be taking place alongside the innocent life of the hospital? This is horror enough, but it is when a very special patient is admitted that Helen's ordeal turns into a nightmare and she is forced to use her talents, her courage and a desperate ruthlessness in an effort to protect all she holds dear.

### *Private Prosecution, A*
July 1986

Autumn in a seaside town and four young girls are found strangled. Each body bears the 'signature' of a killer whom the media soon dub the Monster, and Detective Chief Superintendent Maurice Kendrick is driven by his sense of outrage into obsessive pursuit of the murderer.

A fifth killing, gruesomely different from the others, drives his friend Humphrey Barnes into an obsession, too – to disprove his fear that a beloved member of the victim's family may know something about the murders.

Another death, and the ordeal of a girl who escapes, solve the riddle of the Monster, but this is just the beginning of the separate efforts of the two friends to get to the truth of the fifth murder – Kendrick through orthodox police methods, Humphrey through his tortured contacts with the victim's unhappy family. Since Kendrick's wife left him Humphrey has become his confidant, but he keeps his unofficial ideas to himself as he listens reluctantly to the progress of the Chief Superintendent's official investigations. This time his intuition is not at the service of the police.

It is a race for the truth which only Humphrey knows they are running, and for one of them the final grim revelation represents a hollow victory.

### *Sleeper, The*
March 1988

Ten years have passed since Olga Lubimova married Englishman Henry Trent and left her native Russia. Her marriage is happy and she has two children, so why is she still unable to take her freedom for granted?

The answer comes anonymously by telephone the morning after a dinner party given by the fashionable photographer Hugo Stratton, where Olga and Henry witness his mischievous enjoyment of the encounter between his current girlfriend and another woman who arrives uninvited with an angry boyfriend in pursuit.

The cold voice on the telephone interrupts Olga's uneasy thoughts on the confrontation and plunges her into nightmare. There is no hiding place from those that threaten her children – until Hugo's lifestyle catches up with him and Olga can run headlong into the custody awaiting his murderer.

It seems she has presented the police with an open-and-shut case, but senior officers are bewildered when orders are given for a secret murder hunt, together with particulars of the three young people who went to Hugo's flat on the night of his party.

The hunt finds its quarry; hope of asylum seems dashed; but further revelations are in store, to keep Olga – and the reader – on edge.

### *There Was a Little Girl*
August 1984

'There was a little girl'... and her name was Juliet Payne. When she was good she lived in the New Forest with her widowed father, principal of an educational establishment, and once a month she spent a weekend in London taking piano lessons.

When she was bad, which was on those same seemingly innocent weekends, she became a teenage whore. And as such she was found strangled in a London flat.

Which brought Detective-inspector Neil Carter on the scene, for although it seemed an open and shut case with the girl's last client charged with the crime. Neil had once given her his name and rank in a sleazy London bar, and she had appealed to him for help a bare hour before she died. He had a painful sense of personal involvement in the death of this girl with two faces.

Both faces were hidden. To find them, Neil and his bride Cathy spend their honeymoon anonymously in the New Forest, asking questions in pubs and hotels and at the college which was the murdered girl's home. Their discoveries increase Neil's uneasy conviction that the wrong man has been arrested.

### *Trio in Three Flats*
February 1981

'Antique dealer by the name of Peter Shaw,' said the chief. 'Found dead this morning.' From a heart attack, or from the manual strangulation which had accompanied it? A complex problem, especially when Shaw's estranged love Hilary is Detective-Inspector Neil Carter's mysterious and beautiful neighbour. Whom Neil has begun to console...

His Chief doesn't know this – or does he? – but the fact of being neighbours is coincidence enough, and Neil is expected to play a subtle unofficial role in the investigation of a death which could have been from natural causes or murder.

At once other problems confront him. Has Hilary been back to Shaw's house since she left it three months earlier? And what of the antique dealer's new love? His cold brother and warm sister-in-law? Hilary's boss who changes so interestingly after Shaw's death?

There is also the problem of Neil's other neighbour Cathy, who helps him with his investigations and tries not to mind about his relationship with Hilary...

Finally, there is the problem of the antique dealer's priceless early copy of the Wedgwood Portland Vase, missing from the room in which he died. Hilary maintains the vase is the answer to the riddle of Shaw's death. But is it?

### *Whoever I Am*
February 1982

Hill House private nursing-home, attractively sited above Bournemouth shore, cares most competently for the sick. But two convalescent patients suddenly die, and actress Helen Markham leaves the stage and totters into the nursing-home as the weak-minded Miss Jones.

For there is already a patient at Hill House who is not who he or she seems. It could be the boring and amiable Mr Thomas. Courteous Mr Corlett or wild-eyed Miss Welch. Mrs Anthony always smiling, or Mrs Stoddart forever anticipating tea. Any one of the patients could be matching the quick mind of Helen Markham behind Miss Jones's blank stare. And who is the young man who haunts the corridors and cruelly tests all Helen's courage and acting skill?

There are no answers at the Laurels, the mock-Tudor pile where Helen's mysterious mentor lives with his daughter and where Helen learns her most difficult role. But here at least she can be herself – until a discovery which makes it seem there is no one in either house whom she can trust.

And when her job is done she must face the most terrible ordeal of all, the danger of death in the night against which she has been instructed not to defend herself.

## DOLINER, ROY

### *On the Edge*
January 1979

To those who ran the corrupt business empire faced with investigation by the Justice Department, Sullivan was the obvious scapegoat. They could get him on several counts. Unfortunately he had safeguarded himself by getting hold of some very sensitive documents, which made him the only link between the corrupt tycoon who employed him and a US Senator, and led to the highest government circles. Sullivan had to be made to face reality.

Reality meant several years in jail, against a fortune at the end of it. Otherwise he was a dangerous man. He knew where too many bodies were buried. And that, as his masters pointed out to him, was a nice way to get himself killed.

But the ex-CIA man prized his freedom. Luckily for him, he knew every trick of the trade, and he had to use them all against the best that government and big business could muster – and their best was very good indeed. It even included his old friend, security expert Alfi Morgan. The stakes were enormous – and murderous.

## DONATI, SERGIO

### *Paper Tomb, The*
June 1958

'The girl was standing motionless two steps from the desk, her back to the door. Her right arm was held slightly away from her body, and in her hand she was clutching a heavy bronze figure, bloodstained.'

There was a dead body on the floor, its head smashed in.

'You did a nice job,' Gianni said to Marina. 'One blow'. Thus they were introduced.

From its exciting and mysterious opening, this tale of violence moves fast. Set in Rome, it touches on the life of wealthy society there, conjures up an underworld of drug-traffic with the gangsters that inhabit it, and describes amusingly and sympathetically the tribulations of Italian journalists and policemen. The story is fast-paced, its background wittily imagined.

Isabel Quigly has made an admirable translation of Sergio Donati's second crime novel, his first to be translated into English.

## DONNELLY, PATRICIA

### *Feel the Force*
June 1993

The inner-city borough of Wallsden was in turmoil, and as usual the trouble seemed to emanate from the Fleetway housing estate. Somebody was going to get killed one of these days, they said.

Only the first death wasn't a Fleetway rioter but a friendly boy from the High Street. It could have passed for an accident if only Detective Chief Inspector Shields had kept his ill-conceived notions to himself.

Policing the sprawling estate meant keeping everything quiet and calm – to initiate a murder investigation among the hostile residents was to poke a wasp's nest with a stick. Somebody could get badly stung.

## DU BOIS, THEODORA

### *Seeing Red*
September 1955

It was a Saturday in August and the McNeills were enjoying their favourite recreation, sailing. With their two sons, Michael and Martin, and a friend, Pauline Dunbar, they manoeuvred their small cutter *Thetis* down New York's lower harbour, and sailed right into trouble. A day that started in peace and sunshine ended in the shadow of violent death. The discovery of the body of an unknown on Swinburne Island should have had nothing to do with the Jeffrey McNeills – but it had; and Theodora DuBois makes a breath-taking tale of it.

## EAST, ROGER

### *Bell is Answered, The*
July 1934

An old windmill, a lake, a church tower and a villa aping the country mansion – this is the setting for mysteries which would be fantastic, even, sometimes, grimly laughable, if they were not also horrible. It falls to a passée but still gaily adventurous ex-actress to solve the mysteries in which she is involved from the moment when, believing herself to be alone in a borrowed house, she idly presses the bathroom bell – and the bell is answered by an immaculately dressed and handsome young footman. This ringing of the bathroom bell begins and ends a story bizarre and romantic yet admitting of a solution logically deducted.

### *Candidate for Lilies*
January 1934

Four days before he was murdered, old Arnold Burgoyne wrote four letters summoning his lawyer, his niece and his two nephews to his country house with the thinly-disguised purpose of altering his will. With his heirs gathered round him at the dinner table, the old man explained what changes he intended to make in the disposal of his property if – The result was disturbing to some of his hearers. But that same night old Uncle Arnold was murdered at his desk. Mr. Roger East, the clever young author of *Murder Rehearsal*, amply fulfils the outstanding promise of that brilliant detective story, and in *Candidate for Lilies* has written a most fascinating story that from the very first page will grip the attention of the reader.

### *Detectives in Gum Boots*
September 1936

Roger East's detective stories are always among the liveliest of the year. There's drollery in them, a subtle and delightful humour, and what has been aptly called 'a flavour of exquisite intelligence'. Connoisseurs make a note of them, and critics give them a place in the headlines. The announcement of 'A new Roger East', in fact, is 'news'. So we present *Detectives in Gum Boots* in the certainty that it will be welcome. And if you are curious about the 'gum boots' we can only remark that they are, to say the least of it, noticeable as a form of footwear, and rather hampering!

OR

It all started when Lord Thurscaston suddenly vanished. Of course he might have been taking a very private holiday, but there was the anonymous letter that hinted that he was dead, the mysterious and guilty actions of his wife, his son and even his butler, and the fact that not a few political personages stood to gain by his removal. There was also the question of the pacifist; would a man who had devoted his life to the prevention of war and violence, remove, by one act of violence, an avowed militarist at the moment when England's attitude to world peace might sway the future of mankind? That charming couple, Colin Knowles and his wife Louie, reappear in this entertaining detective story, and squabble their way to a solution less highly coloured than Louie's alarmist imagination but eminently satisfactory.

### *Kingston Black*
February 1960

Robin Talliby gave up his job and came home from Teheran when Nigel Standing, brother of his fiancée Fleur, was openly suspected of murdering his neighbour's glamorous wife, Greta Bewley. She had been found shot in her husband's cider house. Fleur refused to involve Robin and his parents in the ensuing trouble, broke off their engagement and went abroad. Robin refused to give up the girl he loved and managed to trace her. In France, chance led them to Jack Mors, a man with supreme confidence in his strange theories of bio-typology, who declared flatly that a man of Nigel's type could never have committed the murder. Mors's friend Virginia Maye, a barrister, had sufficient faith in his judgment to go over all the evidence again. Heartened by the confidence of Mors and prompted by Virginia to probe aspects of the case which had apparently been overlooked, Robin went to Somerset and began to ask questions. The results were sudden and dangerous. The murderer was fighting back.

*Kingston Black*, Roger East's seventh crime novel, is a fascinating combination of ingenuity, imagination, and excitement.

### *Murder Rehearsal*
July 1933

The engagement between Colin Knowles, writer of detective stories, and Andria, a promising young actress has been broken off, and he is in the right mood for planning three safe and cunning methods of murder for his new book. Parallel with the writing of the book occur three mysterious deaths, which start with the discovery of the body of Andria's father at the foot of a Sussex cliff. Superintendent Simmonds suspects murder, but it is left to Louie, Colin's secretary – a young woman whom nobody takes very seriously – to link together the three murders, and then to connect them with Colin's book – *which is not yet completed.* Here is a brilliant and strikingly original idea for a mystery story, and Roger East skilfully handles the novel theme. *Murder Rehearsal* is an extremely clever story which will establish the reputation of its talented author.

### *Pearl Choker*
October 1954

Roger East, who has written several crime novels, including one with an unforgettable title, *Twenty-Five Sanitary Inspectors*, makes a spectacular return to the Crime Club with this new, exciting story. For this is much more than a murder, and a mystery. Its action takes place in Venezuela where, in the company of his endearing "dutch uncle," Don Xavier, and the redoubtable Eileen, Anthony Grimes, the narrator, finds himself in the towns and villages, in the plains and forests, even among the pearl fisheries of that fascinating and fantastic country. Anthony, sent to Caracas on a mission for his London firm, is soon caught up in the intrigues of financiers whose operations are widespread and secret, who think nothing of murder. He is uncertain even of his allies, and his concentration is dangerously diverted by other young ladies besides Eileen. Into this authentic, detailed and affectionate description of Venezuela is woven an exciting and complex story of murder, fraud and escape.

### *Twenty-Five Sanitary Inspectors*
May 1935

The setting of this novel is the remote and delectable island of San Rocco, a tiny West Indian Republic, which Pero Zaragoza, cosmopolitan financier, plans to make into a playground for millionaires; but strange happenings cross his plans—murder, fire and sabotage. As no police force is handy a force of twenty-five sanitary inspectors is recruited to investigate the mystery.

## EBERHART, M. G.

### *Alpine Condo Crossfire*
July 1985

Emmy Brace, researcher for a large TV news department in New York City, is summarily ordered to dance attendance on her guardian/uncle, a retired judge. Emmy arrives at his elegant suburban condominium in Alpine Village with mixed feelings about her visit to the domineering old man and his young wife, who had been Emmy's best friend during their schooldays. But at least she can stay with her elder sister, rather than with her uncle and his wife.

Alas for Emmy's plans. Her sister's guest room is not available and she is forced to accept hospitality from a former admirer. Worse still, she discovers that the Judge has been covertly interfering in her career and is adamant that she give it up. When two strange murders occur at Alpine Village, and these deaths are followed by a rash of baffling, ominous incidents that raise a number of disturbing questions, Emmy is forced to ask herself if there is a connection, as the Judge insists, between these killings and the news story she is researching.

Caught in the crossfire of mysterious events and conflicting emotions, to say nothing of a blizzard and a media blitz, Emmy fights for her life and, with the help of a rediscovered old love and an indefatigable colleague, searches for clues to unmask a killer and a villain.

Once again, in her fifty-seventh novel, M.G. Eberhart proves why the American Mystery Writers Association honoured her with the title of Grand Master.

### *Another Man's Murder*
August 1958

Murder and violence strike without warning in the deceptively idyllic Florida lake country when Cayce Clary returns to his childhood home to have it out with his uncle. There was one obvious witness – and possibly another hidden one – to the violent quarrel that erupted during their meeting. But there were no witnesses to the murder of his uncle, who was found shot to death near the lake shortly after.

Before long Cayce found himself fighting for his life, charged with the killing, and at the same time fighting for his land. Although there were many who hated the old man, motive and opportunity pointed to Cayce alone.

This taut story of a killer on the loose – a killer determined to murder again to hide his first crime – is played out against the exotic background of the orange groves and swamp lands of Florida. A master of atmosphere and suspense, M. G. Eberhart is writing at the top of her form in *Another Man's Murder*.

### *Another Woman's House*
February 1948

It stood on a point above the Sound, a perfect picture of a house surrounded by lovely gardens and lawns which sloped down to the sea. Nothing apparently had changed since the war and since that June night when Alice Thorne, or so the law had said, had taken a revolver in her beautiful hands and shot a man dead. It was still Alice's house, in the bitter thoughts of Myra, who had fallen in love with Richard Thorne, Alice's husband, even although fighting it fiercely. M. G. Eberhart skilfully unfolds the absorbing story of a deep and touching love affair complicated by murder, mystery and a strange quirk of fate.

### *Bayou Road, The*
August 1979

New Orleans in 1863 was a conquered city. In her once-luxurious home where the only remaining black servant battled alongside her young mistress to keep the family from want, Marcy Chastain, beautiful half American, half Creole daughter of a New Orleans family, fought a different, more frightening battle: against a sense of menacing surveillance, an unaccountable awareness of personal danger which she could not define. It was an additional, terrible burden for the girl. Ever since her brother had been killed and her father marched off by the Yankees to an unknown destination for refusing to take the oath of allegiance to the new United States, Marcy had had to assume responsibility for the others in the family: her impractical aunt, her dead mother's elderly cousin, her exquisite but useless sister-in-law, and her brother's illegitimate child.

Rescue seemed to be provided by the Unionist major billeted on the Chastains, especially since Marcy had met him briefly and romantically in Washington before the War. Now she found she was expected to prise Yankee secrets out of him, while murder crept steadily closer to the Chastain home.

Escape might lie in the old plantation along the Bayou Road, but what Marcy found there was greater danger as the menace was finally revealed. As in her immensely successful *Family Fortune*, M. G. Eberhart uses Civil War history as the background to a suspenseful and unusual story of crime.

### *Brief Return*
July 1939

The quiet afternoon drifted into the hush of evening and three women sat in the comforting twilight; Alice, happy now after years of sorrow, happy in her husband and her coming child; Jenny, her sister, grateful, adoring, content that peace had come at last; Cousin Mary Chace, come home after years of poverty and heartbreak. But that peace was shattered. A man stepped from the shadows – really from the shadows, for that man was Basil Hoult, Alice's first husband, dead – so every one believed and hoped – since a year. They had to tell him, these three, of the past year and its happenings. They were forced to throw themselves on his mercy, knowing that he would show them none. For everything was his – the house, the money – and Alice. With superb skill M. G. Eberhart has made the most of these dramatic circumstances – circumstances that lead to murder, and murder that leads to suspicion falling on a young girl's head.

### *Call after Midnight*
March 1965

The call after midnight that wakes Jenny Vleedman is from her former husband Peter. She hasn't seen him since their divorce but he now begs her to come to his house as he is afraid of being accused of trying to murder his present wife, Fiora.

Jenny, who still loves him, is unable to resist his pleas. She arrives at his house to find Fiora has been only slightly injured. But the murderer returns that same night to claim a victim…and later his attention turns to Jenny herself.

Family tensions and mistrust intertwined with office jealousies and friendships make murder inevitable, though its effect is startlingly different from what the murderer expected. None of M. G. Eberhart's many admirers will be disappointed in this exciting and spine-chilling suspense novel.

### *Casa Madrone*
September 1980

New York, 1906, and debutante Mallory Bookever and her widowed aunt were entertaining an unexpected caller: the young man sent to escort them to San Francisco for Mallory's wedding, because her fiancé was unable to come to New York to marry her as arranged.

Mallory had been lucky to capture the fabulously wealthy Richard Welbeck, for ever since her uncle's death she and her aunt has been living on credit and the proceeds of the Bookever art collection. As she prepared for her journey in Richard's splendidly furnished private railway car, attended by Chinese servants, Mallory had no inkling of the perils that lay ahead.

Barely had she arrived, after a journey that had had its fair share of dangers, than the city of San Francisco was engulfed by earthquake and fire. While the cataclysm raged around Richard's sumptuous residence, there was a death that appeared suspiciously like murder, and Mallory herself had had another near-fatal accident. Was it coincidence or was she in mortal danger? Why was her aunt so antagonistic towards the Welbeck family lawyer whom she had apparently never met before? Was Mallory's escort on the journey as sincerely attracted to her as she was to him? Why was Richard's cousin so possessive, almost ignoring her own husband? There were many mysteries to be explained.

As she glanced round the group of people huddled in the house for protection against the natural disasters that encircled them, Mallory was forced to wonder if one of them was a murderer, And if so, who?

### *Chiffon Scarf, The*
February 1940

To superb skill with the mystery plot, Mrs. Eberhart adds the qualification of the accomplished novelist – a gift for telling characterisation and a polished, ingratiating style. In *The Chiffon Scarf* she creates an atmosphere tense and electric with the quality of eeriness for which her novels are famous. A test flight to determine the value of a new airplane engine results in two apparently accidental deaths, but when the fateful chiffon scarf is found cruelly knotted about the throat of a third victim there can be no doubt that murder stalks the company gathered together at P. H. Sloan's grim house-party. Only after another murder does Sloan discover the significance of the chiffon scarf and the identity of the criminal – solving the series of murders and at the same time bringing a brilliant story to a satisfactory conclusion.

### *Crime at Honotassa, The*
July 1962

It was 1863. Sarah Hugot, a Northern heiress with loyalties to the Union cause, found herself in New Orleans on a hazardous assignment; burdened with contraband, gold and drugs, she was to make her way to Honotassa, the Southern plantation belonging to her husband Lucien, whom she had impulsively married in Cuba and about whom she knew very little. She was in enemy territory. She knew nothing of the big house of which she was to be mistress – and almost nothing about her husband Lucien.

Sarah reached Honotassa and found it beautiful. But Lucien had disappeared and the Hugot relatives staying in the house had many reasons not to welcome the newcomer who now possessed and controlled the estate. She was surrounded by enemies. And she was learning that Lucien had given her information about Honotassa and its inmates some of which was untrue...

When a member of the household is shot it looks as though murder has come to Honotassa – and worse is to follow. This historical novel marks a departure for M. G. Eberhart, author of *Melora* and *Another Man's Murder*, and a new milestone in the achievement of a celebrated crime novelist; the story has a powerful romantic appeal besides being utterly absorbing.

### *Danger Money*
September 1975

'Money is a danger,' said the Great Man wearily, and he, if anyone, should know. He was Gilbert Manders, financier and something of a man of mystery, known as the Great Man, or GM. 'You think when you're earning it,' he told Susan Beach, the young secretary who was half in love with him, 'that it's a way to make yourself safe. But a great deal of money is – well, call it danger money. It invites some really ugly things – blackmail, threats, even murder.'

His wealth did indeed seem to have extended an invitation to murder when Rose, his blowsy wife, was found dead – not in the beautiful Fifth Avenue apartment which he visited so rarely, but at his secret hideout in the country, where he entertained only his financial associates, the other Big League tycoons.

The Great Man had married Rose when he was very young and she was very rich, and had used his financial genius to get fantastically richer, but though they had drifted apart he had never abandoned Rose and had supported her drunken relatives, the Clansers, even finding them jobs in his entourage.

Now Rose's death had put the Great Man as well as the Clansers under suspicion, and Susan, who had arrived at the scene of the crime just in time to see a man running away, was certain of one thing only: it was not the Great Man she had seen.

M. G. Eberhart is the doyenne of American suspense novelists and the author of more than fifty books. In 1971 the Mystery Writers of America gave her their Grand Master Award in recognition of her sustained excellence.

### *Dead Men's Plans*
April 1953

Chicago's fashionable Lake Shore district is the setting, and the colourful Minary family the players, in this newest murder mystery in the best Eberhart tradition. Julius Minary, Great Lakes shipping tycoon, had been dead two months when his son Reg came home from abroad with his French bride, Zelie. When Reg was found shot, the trouble brewing in the Minary mansion boiled over. No one liked greedy, ambitious Zelie, and with reason. She was a threat to a good many people. It was obvious from the moment a gun was discovered in a desk drawer that someone in the Minary circle was poised for murder, but a whirlpool of horror was to engulf them all when the killer struck again.

### *El Rancho Rio*
August 1971

Why did a total stranger pretend that he knew Mady intimately and attempt to compromise her before witnesses? And what made her pick up the murder weapon and return it to its place at El Rancho Rio when she found the man murdered a few hours later on a riding trail near the ranch?

El Rancho Rio, the setting of this absorbing mystery, is a large, rich, working ranch in California owned by Craig Wilson, Mady's former employer, now her husband. Craig has been on a business trip, but because he has returned unexpectedly, his alibi at the time of the murder is shaky. Among the other characters are Susan, Craig's daughter by his first marriage; Mirabel, his aunt; Boyce and Edith, his brother and sister-in-law; Indian Joe, the family's major-domo; Rhoda, Craig's former wife, who knew the dead man; and Jim, Mady's ex-fiancé, who has accompanied Rhoda for purposes of his own. Then there is the mysterious Mr Banner, whose car has supposedly broken down in the raging blizzard which isolates the ranch and its occupants from civilization.

During the storm another murder occurs, and clearly, the killer – whose motives are obscure and who can only be one of them – will strike again unless caught.

With the terrifying climax of *El Rancho Rio*, M.G. Eberhart once again demonstrates why she is one of the best-selling practitioners of the novel of suspense.

### *Enemy in the House*
June 1963

The action in this historical crime novel takes place during the American War of Independence.

Amity Mallam, a young American heiress, is a Loyalist, faithful to the British King and the British cause; around her estate in Savannah the troops of the Continental army (Washington's army) are gathering; her father has departed to his estate in Jamaica (under British rule); besides the problem of trying to save her American inheritance from confiscation, Amity discovers she has treacherous enemies among the family group that surround her.

Amity goes to Jamaica. In the great lonely house of Mallam Penn, surrounded by its rich plantations, there unfolds a ruthless struggle so fierce that even murder counts for little.

M. G. Eberhart again triumphs in the difficult art of setting a crime novel in a historical background; *Enemy in the House* will bring delight to the thousands of readers who enjoyed *The Crime at Honotassa*.

### *Escape the Night*
July 1945

Serena March was returning to her old home on the enchanted coast of California, partly because she had a holiday from her New York job, partly because Leda Blagden had urged her to, 'because something is going to happen,' and chiefly because Leda told her that Jeremy Daly was there – the Jem Daly with whom she had fallen in love as a girl of nineteen the day her sister Amanda was married. She was returning to the old crowd with whom she and her sister had grown up. Her old home, the Casa Madrone, was closed now, and Amanda lived at the Condit ranch across the valley. Back to the old life of leisure, parties at Pebble Beach, trips to the one and only San Francisco, back to Jem – and what? What she met on the day after her return was murder, which struck suddenly, silently and again, involving the whole group of old friends in a web of suspicion and danger. The popular M. G. Eberhart's latest story is a subtle and sophisticated novel of character and suspense in which murder plays its overpowering motif.

### *Fair Warning*
September 1936

'If Mr. Crofts is the Alibi King, then M. G. Eberhart is the Atmosphere Queen,' the *Morning Post* has said. Read Miss Eberhart's description of the storm that is raging on the night of the murder and you will feel the air grown cooler around you, and if you should have to interrupt your reading to go out of the house, you will instinctively don your mackintosh and thrust your head down into the storm – even if the sun is shining from a clear blue sky. That is the sort of thing Miss Eberhart does superbly well, and when these unique powers of description are used to tell a story of a diabolically clever murder among a set of absolutely living characters, we have a book of most unusual quality. For, in spite of her gift for the sinister, Miss Eberhart s never fantastic, and it is her very naturalness and reasonableness that enhance the power of her drama.

### *Family Affair*
October 1981

Sarah Favor was frightened, more frightened than she had ever been. Engaged to her handsome cousin Fitz, she had been absorbed in wedding plans and was looking forward to joining Fitz on his first consular assignment when he was suddenly shipped off abroad on a hush-hush mission, replacing a friend who had been mysteriously shot. The marriage was postponed indefinitely.

Confused and sad, Sarah returned to the Favor home from seeing Fitz off at the airport – and discovered the body of her stepcousin, Forte.

The Favor household had evolved from the coming together of assorted relatives and was presided over by best-selling novelist Corinna Favor, who had taken charge of the house after Fitz's mother died. To motherless Sarah, whose father was often abroad, she was a surrogate parent. Everyone had accepted Corinna's mean, petty stepson Forte as the one flaw in their otherwise comfortable existence. But it was hard to imagine anyone hating him enough to kill him.

Now, to Sarah's horror, the family were determined to conceal the murder. Forte's body vanished, and they seemed intent on continuing with their lives as if nothing had happened. Worse still they watched her curiously when they thought she wasn't looking. After all, she was the only one to have heard the fatal shot; she was the one who had found the body…

As ominous signs multiplied around her, Sarah had cause to realize that her secret knowledge of two men who had been shot within days of each other was highly dangerous – and that the danger came from within the family.

### *Family Fortune*
July 1977

The time is the American Civil War, and the house is Bel Chance, a great Southern mansion located in West Virginia, not yet a state. The Chance family, as in most border states, is divided against itself. One brother is in the Confederate Army, but the two others are on the Union side, although the eldest does no fighting.

As the novel opens, the family have assembled for the reading of their father's will. Pendelton Chance had had three sons by his first marriage, and a daughter, Lucinda, by his second. Now half his estate was left to Lucinda, but her half-brother Jeff, the eldest son, was made her guardian until she was eighteen – almost a year away – or married. Jeff was determined that Lucinda should not inherit.

When a distant relative, serving with the Confederates, whom Lucinda had never met before, arrived wounded at Bel Chance, she enlisted the help of a faithful servant to carry him to her room and tend him. How she used him to help her thwart her brother's evil schemes, and what happened to the Chance family and its various fascinating members, makes an enthralling story of murder and suspense with an unusual historical background.

### *Fighting Chance, A*
January 1987

Julie Farnham's life was shattered when her fiancé, Jim Wingate, facing certain arrest for murder, vanished on the eve of their wedding.

In the ensuing five years Julie has become a modestly successful author when suddenly, inspired by an obscure law that seems to promise him immunity, Jim returns. He is determined to establish his innocence and re-establish his relationship with Julie.

But the murder is as insoluble as ever, and another suspicious death, an attempt on Julie's life, mysterious accidents, and the reappearance of a woman believed long dead combine to cast the terrible shadow of the past across the present. Without a fighting chance, Jim must solve the mystery or lose his freedom and Julie.

M. G. Eberhart is as suspenseful and romantic as ever in her latest novel about love and death in a small Connecticut town.

### *Five Passengers from Lisbon*
October 1946

Five passengers, two seamen and an officer from the wrecked Portuguese steamer *Lerida* are picked up by the U. S. Hospital Ship *Magnolia*. When they are hoisted aboard the *Magnolia*, the Portuguese mate is found murdered – stabbed in the back. After two more attempts at murder, everyone on the ship is engulfed in a wave of suspicion, and the trip home becomes a voyage through terror. A fascinating new romantic thriller by one of the Crime Club's favourite authors.

### *Glass Slipper, The*
November 1938

Crystal Hatterick, wife of one of the most distinguished surgeons in Chicago, was seriously ill. Under the care of Dr. Andrew Crittenden she was well on the road to recovery, when to everyone's amazement, she suddenly died. A few months later, Dr. Hatterick married the girl who had nursed his first wife. But it is one thing to be the second Mrs. Hatterick with the world at your feet – wealth, position, beauty – and quite another to be suspected of murdering the first Mrs Hatterick. Blended with the suspense of the investigation is a love story of really exceptional charm. *The Glass Slipper* makes splendid reading, and is certain to enhance M. G. Eberhart's reputation as one of the finest mystery writers of the day.

### *Hand in Glove*
May 1937

M. G. Eberhart is, beyond all 'probable, possible shadow of doubt', one of the best mystery writers of the day. For, in the first place, she can create character. Secondly, she can construct a really sound detective story. And above all, of course, she can fill her pages with an atmosphere of terror and suspense that distinguishes her work from that of any other writer. *Hand in Glove* is the story of a girl who fled from a party given in her honour before her marriage, to keep a tryst with a former lover – a girl who fled from a man she didn't love but was going to marry, to a final meeting with a man she loved but was never going to see again – a girl who ran through the wind and snow to meet love, and found murder.

### Hangman's Whip, The
February 1941
Search Abbot thought she had been successful in stifling her feelings about Richard Bohan since the day three years back before when he had walked down the aisle with another woman as his bride. She realised she was wrong when she saw Richard again, at the home where they had both lived as children. She had her brief time of knowing that Richard had always loved her, of thinking that divorce would free him to marry her; and then his wife, Eve, blandly announced that she had changed her mind about a divorce. Search showed her frustration so obviously that when death intervened to remove Eve, she and Richard naturally became suspects in the eyes of the law. M. G. Eberhart develops suspense and emotional tenseness to a point that she has never reached before, and *The Hangman's Whip* is a high-spot among her excellent books.

### Hasty Wedding
February 1939
Dorcas Whipple, Chicago heiress, on the eve of her wedding to steady Jevan Locke, and still infatuated with ne'er-do-well Ronald Drew, kept a final rendezvous with him and agreed to go to his apartment to say farewell. The next morning, her wedding day, the papers carried news of his suicide. Dorcas blindly went through the ceremony. As they left the church a newsboy flashed a paper, "RONALD DREW MURDERED." And her husband of five minutes was saying: 'Now listen, Dorcas, I know you killed Ronald. I don't blame you; he was a scoundrel... .' In her new book, M. G. Eberhart has outdone herself in the field which she has made pre-eminently her own. She has skilfully blended the elements of mystery, detection, love and intrigue. As a detective thriller, *Hasty Wedding* holds the suspense to the very last page for a smashingly unexpected, yet completely convincing climax.

### House of Storm
November 1949
To a green and lovely island in the blue and golden Caribbean comes an unwelcome visitor, treading his dark and invisible way between the two vast sugar plantations, Middle Road and Beadon Gates. The visitor has an ugly name, and it is – Murder. Hermione Shaw, owner of Middle Road, is shot dead and Nonie Hovenden, who though engaged to Roy Beadon, is secretly in love with Jim Shaw, Hermione's nephew, guesses with frightening accuracy that Jim will be suspected, because he had only that afternoon openly and irrevocably quarrelled with his aunt. Against the attractive background of this beautiful Caribbean island, in the eerie atmosphere of the lovely old plantation house shuttered and barred against the sudden violence of a tropical storm, M. G. Eberhart unfolds a gripping story of murder.

### House on the Roof, The
September 1935
The scene is Chicago – a Chicago as beautiful as Paris, as thrilling as New York, and as mysterious as London. The story opens in a small room in that strange little house on the roof – a perfectly appointed penthouse hidden upon the roof of an apartment building. Deborah Cavert was playing Massenet's "Elegie" as Mary Monroe, formerly an opera singer and now a woman of mystery, was singing the haunting words. Suddenly Mary paused in her singing, a crash of sound filled the room, and the air became faintly tinged with smoke. When the reverberations of the shot died away, Mary Monroe was only a crumpled velvet heap on the floor. In *The House on the Roof* M. G. Eberhart has written a story of crime and detection, a mystery that is truly great in its setting, its plot and its characters.

### Hunt With the Hounds
February 1951
In *Hunt with the Hounds* M. G. Eberhart again proves herself a master of suspense and romance, creating, against the lovely background of the Virginia fox-hunting country, an atmosphere of terror and intrigue which lasts up to the breath-taking climax. It had never occurred to Sue Poore that, when Jed Baily was acquitted for the murder of his wife, suspicion would turn on Sue herself. She had come forward and given Jed his alibi, thus placing herself at the scene of the crime. But the prosecution had suggested a motive at Jed's trial: that she and Jed were in love. Indeed, they artfully suggested that she was 'the other woman', and Sue's defence of Jed tragically lent colour to the accusation. Against this innuendo and against the killer who stalked her from the woods at dusk, Sue was suddenly terribly defenceless. For the police had decided she was a murderess, and not even a bullet scarring the wall beside her could convince them she was in danger.

### Jury of One
June 1961
Three days before her wedding to a rich, dynamic friend of her childhood, Maggy Warren was told, 'You can't marry Kirk. He's not the man for you.' Josh Mason gave no reason for his statement, but the events which followed it brought Maggy to an agony of doubt. Sudden death struck twice. Accident? Natural causes? ...or murder? The loyalties and hatreds of the small New England town in which almost everyone depended on the success of Kirk Beall's family business make an intriguing background to M. G. Eberhart's new book. It has all the ingredients of romance, the conflict of strong personalities, and the atmosphere of lurking evil which has won the author success as one of America's most popular crime writers.

### Man Missing
November 1954
In the shadowy, white-walled corridors of the sleeping hospital Nurse Sarah Keate caught sight of a khaki-clad figure. She saw the flash of three stripes of gold on an epaulette. She was not to know the vital significance of that one quick glimpse until one of her patients was found dead – murdered. Sarah Keate is well-known to M. G. Eberhart's many readers. In this book she makes a come-back to crime in a murder story set in the American western desert. The scene is a base where many thousand tons of naval ammunition are stored; where the sun beats down fiercely every day on a small and isolated community; where nerves are never easy in the proximity of the stores of high explosive; and where murder

stalks abroad. There is more at the base than danger – there is a problem. Who left the silent hospital so swiftly after the patient had been knifed? Who struck the second time? What made the pretty Sally Wilson so fatally reticent and frightened? We believe that readers, like the investigators at the base, will be distracted from spotting the murderer by the authoress's extraordinary ingenuity. In this thrilling and brilliantly constructed story M. G. Eberhart once more succeeds in a tour-de-force of detection.

### Man Next Door, The
January 1944
In this novel of wartime Washington, the popular M. G. Eberhart throws a dramatic spotlight on the spies and saboteurs who infest the American capital. For in this exciting mystery we see Maida Lovell, beautiful young Washington confidential secretary, enmeshed in a web of spying and intrigue and given the difficult choice of seeing the man she loved framed on a murder charge or of revealing to an enemy agent vital information regarding aircraft. *The Man Next Door* is excellent entertainment in the true Eberhart tradition.

### Melora
April 1960
'I am going to kill you'. That was the message that Anne found in her typewriter on that fateful day. Was it a prank, was it written out of pique by Brent's teen-age niece, or was it a serious threat?

Anne's marriage to wealthy New York socialite lawyer Brent Wystan had been shadowed by the menacing memory of his divorced wife, Melora. Hated by Brent's widowed sister-in-law Cassie, Melora had been adored by Cassie's children. Cassie, who continued to run Brent's home so smoothly, in her feline way made Anne feel useless and a trespasser. Other ominous notes follow the first one. An intruder, the threatening reappearance of Melora herself, and, finally, murder, all contribute to the mounting atmosphere of terror. The tension grows as the finger of suspicion points first to one and then to another. *Melora* displays the storytelling skill and the combination of action and excitement with suspense for which M. G. Eberhart is famous.

### Message From Hong Kong
September 1969
What did the cryptic message from Hong Kong mean? To Marci Lowry's father-in-law, who has never given up hope, it indicates that his ne'er-do-well son Dino is still alive three years after he has inexplicably vanished. But Mr. Lowry is an invalid, and since Marcia wishes to marry Richard Burke and begin a new life, it is up to her to try to track down the wayward husband she no longer wants.

In Hong Kong, Marcia finds the dead body of a man who had sent the message, and in an anonymous letter of warning she receives an apparently meaningless list of names, numbers and American cities. In their attempt to unravel the secret of the list, Marcia and Richard encounter a hurricane in Florida, another murder and a series of menacing intruders. The problem of outwitting this murderous gang and of solving Dino's disappearance and the secret of the list form the climax of this absorbing mystery. In the final confrontation in a quiet New York suburb Mrs. Eberhart demonstrates again her talent as a writer of tales of terror and suspense.

### Murder in Waiting
April 1974
The burglar alarm shrilled on as Bea groped through the dark garden, and when she

finally stumbled across the body of the judge, she was able to hear only a few muttered words before he died. In that instant the secure world of wealth and privilege she had enjoyed all her life in a small Connecticut town began to crumble into a nightmare of suspicion.

A number of people might have wished the judge dead. Among these is the family doctor, who is also the father of Rufe, Bea's fiancé; Senator Seth Hobson, who also serves as the family lawyer; a neighbour who has a shameful secret; and the paroled convict the judge had sent to jail. Even Captain Obrian, [sic] the chief of police, seems to be hiding something.

Into this community comes Lorraine – like Bea, also a ward of the judge and his wife. Lorraine seems to enjoy her scandalous reputation, and on her heels appears her gigolo husband, both intent on using the confusion and disruption caused by the murder for their own purposes. Bea soon finds herself in danger of losing Rufe to her beautiful, scheming cousin.

The tension mounts as inexplicable events multiply and the list of suspects lengthens. Finally, in a shocking confrontation that could only be staged by a master suspense writer, the identity of the killer is revealed.

### Never Look Back
August 1951
When Maggy Brooke returned from London to her aunt's apartment in New York, she was almost immediately made aware of the sinister influences that were dogging her footsteps. Yet she couldn't really believe that someone was trying to take her life until the mounting series of strange occurrences could no longer be argued away: a burning cigarette in the presumably vacant apartment, someone whose dark shadow she saw when she searched the terrace, someone who tried to lure Maggy to the balcony – the odour of cyanide in her bedside thermos. M. G. Eberhart, always a master of atmosphere and suspense, has done some of her most fascinating work in this book; conveying with consummate skill the heroine's almost excruciating sense of terror.

### Next of Kin
January 1983
Mady Smith may be a rich young woman, but she wants to do something worthwhile with the secretarial course she has just taken – like working for her best friend Lettie's husband, ex-senator Stuart Charming, who has just been offered a prestigious appointment in the President's Cabinet. And if a job in Washington will bring Mady closer to Stuart's younger brother, a distinguished physics professor, so much the better. Mady plans to put her best foot forward with the ex-senator when she sees him at the Valentine's Day party Lettie is giving at their New York apartment. With young Professor Charming as her escort, Mady has happy expectations.

But a snowstorm delays their arrival until after the other guests have left. Worse still, Stuart Charming has been closeted all afternoon and evening in his study making important confidential phone calls. When, after prolonged silence from the locked study, the Professor opens the door with his own key, he finds his brother shot dead at his desk.

Is it suicide or murder? The media have a field day speculating about possible personal or political reasons for the senator's Valentine's Day death. The case generates more and more questions but almost no answers, and the police seem as mystified as the Charming family in this novel of love, intrigue and murder by a mistress of suspense.

### Nine o'Clock Tide
October 1978

One evening, surrounded by family, friends and servants, wealthy Sam Havlock disappeared mysteriously from the terrace of his summer home. He had plunged soundlessly and abruptly over the balustrade to his death in the waters below, and his young wife was the major suspect for his murder.

Meade Havlock had married Sam three years earlier, for reasons which did not include love. Nevertheless, it had been a satisfactory marriage, for Sam was kind and generous even if she did not always know what he was thinking and planning, and Meade fitted fairly happily into her role of pampered, sheltered bride.

Suddenly everything was changed by Sam's murder, for Meade had the perfect opportunity and two powerful motives besides. Not only did she stand to inherit an incredible fortune, but her former fiancé, who had broken their engagement and disappeared to parts unknown, had returned to beg her to divorce Sam and marry him only a few hours before Sam's death.

With Meade the perfect suspect, would Chief Haggerty and the local police look further? Which of those surrounding Meade – her own family, Sam's friends, the servants he had capriciously appointed – was trying to frame her for Sam's death?

Man and nature combine to create suspense and terror before Meade is saved from both the law and the murderer in the latest novel by an author whose name has become a guarantee of excellence.

### Patient in Cabin C, The
March 1984

A luxurious private yacht is about to leave a Connecticut port on a pleasure cruise with a group of carefully selected passengers. Attractive young nurse Sewall 'Sue' Gates and her Aunt Addie are convinced that their host, a wealthy self-made businessman, has planned the trip as an engagement cruise for himself and Sue. Aunt Addie, old school despite her mild drinking problem, believes it is as easy to fall in love with an appropriate rich man as an inappropriate poor one. Her niece reluctantly agrees that the possible proposal would be the answer to their financial difficulties. She even likes the bluff, handsome entrepreneur…

But the trip begins to go wrong almost at once when Sue and her host each find someone aboard that they could well do without. The beautiful yacht also proves to have disadvantages, and her antique equipment is inadequate for the unseasonable fog that sends her disastrously off course.

Calamities mount; there is a mysterious disappearance; and then – accident or sabotage? – the engines stop.

When murder irrupts into this rarefied atmosphere of wealth and privilege the terrified passengers are forced to recognize that there is a killer on board. Amid the nightmare of fear and death that has overtaken them all, Sue searches for explanations and a resolution to her own personal uncertainties.

### Pattern, The
October 1937

In *The Pattern*, M. G. Eberhart gives us another fascinating murder mystery which will thrill Crime Club readers with its eerie atmosphere and its ingenious cold-blooded murder. The story takes place at a lakeside summer colony where the sense of pleasant leisure and happiness is rudely shattered by the discovery of the dead body of Celia Cable lying in a canoe drifting aimlessly on the lake. The tragedy brings mounting horror and a

foreknowledge of doom in its wake. Here are all the elements of the perfect mystery story, plus a love story of touching poignancy, done with the finish of a master craftsman.

### Postmark Murder
November 1956

Lots of people were interested in the 'Stanislowski' Fund of the late Conrad Stanley's will. There was the nebulous Stanislowski himself, who might still be alive in Poland; the eight-year-old girl refugee, Jonny, now safe in Chicago in the care of Laura March, herself a trustee of the fund; the beautiful Doris, Stanley's widow and others…

In the rush and bustle of Chicago in the weeks before Christmas Laura March received a strange telephone call from an unknown woman.

'Please, come! Hurry! Bring a doctor.'

When Laura reached the address she found a man she had seen only once before lying stabbed: murdered.

Thus Laura and Jonny are precipitated into a situation laden with terror and nightmare. Any one of the visitors that come openly or secretly to Laura's flat may be a murderer…

Once again M. G. Eberhart, the creator of Nurse Keate, provides a story as exciting in itself and as startling in its solution as she achieved in her last book, *Man Missing*.

### R.S.V.P. Murder
June 1966

Richard Amberly's wife had been brutally murdered two years before in the New York house where he still lives with his mother and sister-in-law. The murderer had never been caught, and slowly the memories of that dreadful night receded.

But Fran Hilliard's arrival in the household vividly recalls the agony of suspicions and fears that had followed the murder. Although Fran does everything she can she is unable to prevent her friends once more becoming the centre of sensational and unwelcome publicity.

*R.S.V.P. Murder* is an exciting and moving story told with all the skill and sympathetic understanding that has given so much pleasure to the many readers of M. G. Eberhart's earlier books. It describes a dying man's last crazy effort to provide security for his only daughter – and the appalling events that result from his actions.

### Run Scared
June 1964

Martha married Lem Bascom just before he started his campaign for election as Governor of the State; all eyes were on Bascom – if he made out well he might later succeed in running for President.

A few days before the ballot Martha was involved in a motoring incident. There was only one way of describing her part in it; she had 'hit and run'.

Martha was persuaded that the course of loyalty to Lem lay in saying nothing; she couldn't, after all, be really *sure* she'd hit anything… but then the body of the man in the incident turned up very dead in the lake of Bascom's big house. Police and Pressmen swarmed, scandal proliferated, yet it was too late in law for Lem to withdraw his candidature. It was his fate, instead, to 'run scared' in an election that he must surely lose after his wife's publicised, ignoble crime.

Against the detailed and fascinating background of an American gubernatorial election, amid the ballyhoo and telephones and television cameras, Martha wrestles with a personal crisis that holds within it the potential of private and public catastrophe.

M. G. Eberhart is famous for many gripping crime novels, none of which excel *Run Scared*.

### Speak No Evil
August 1941

In this fascinating novel, destiny carries several people to their deaths and several others to the shadow of the gallows. Critics have often commented on the high quality of Mrs. Eberhart's character drawing, and her uncanny skill in creating eerie suspense, but she has outdone herself in this book. The events take place in and about a villa on an estate at Montego Bay on the beautiful island of Jamaica. The author makes full use of the colourful background, the velvety black night and the occasional fogs drifting in from the bay to throw a pall over creeping terror and deeds of violence. Against this scene unfolds the story of Elizabeth Dakin, who is married to a millionaire dipsomaniac, and who is preparing her escape when he is shot. Suspicion immediately falls on her, but there are others in the tangled affairs of the Dakin household. This is more than a mystery story. It is a novel of great emotional intensity and Mrs. Eberhart's best to date.

### Three Days for Emeralds
June 1988

When Lacy Wales receives a frantic letter from a long-lost friend, Rose Murphy Mendez, she hesitates only briefly before showing it to her lawyer boss, Hiram Bascom, and asking his advice. Against Bascom's better judgement, Lacy drives to the village in upstate New York where Rose is hiding out. At her distraught friend's request, Lacy pours her a whisky, and before her horrified eyes, Rose drops dead. Wandering about the house in confusion, Lacy finds a snapshot in Rose's bedroom with an astonishing inscription by Lacy's own fiancé, Richard Blake, who is away on one of his frequent hush-hush assignments for the government agency where he works.

These are the opening moves in a story that becomes more and more complex. Is Rose's death an accident or murder? How will Lacy cope with her growing and disturbing attraction to Hi Bascom? And why does the subject of emeralds keep coming up?

These and other frightening questions must be answered before the end of M. G. Eberhart's new novel of romance and suspense.

### Two Little Rich Girls
September 1972

The milieu of M. G. Eberhart's forty-seventh novel of suspense is East Side Manhattan's snug, conservative world of inherited wealth, of 'old money'. In temperament and character Emmy Van Seidem fits comfortably into this world; her tempestuous, spendthrift older sister, Diana Ward, does not. Neither do Doug, Diana's husband, whose first play is about to open on Broadway, nor Gil Sangford, her constant companion in the last few months during the play's out-of-town tryouts.

When Gil is inexplicably murdered in Diana's Murray Hill town house one afternoon, all the evidence that slowly accumulates points to her. But Emmy, who arrived on the scene only moments after the killing, is convinced of her sister's innocence, even after Diana has been tried, convicted and sentenced to life imprisonment in Auburn. Sandy Putman, too, Diana's lawyer and a friend of Emmy's, knows that the real killer is still at large, and certainly there is no lack of suspects. Among them are the little man with glasses who seems to be following Emmy; Justin, Emmy's charming, parasitical

stepfather who is in financial straits; and even the actress who stars in Doug's play and who once was married to Gil.

In the next months the tension mounts as mysterious events multiply and Emmy's life is threatened again and again, but it is only in the hair-raising climax that the identity of the murderer is revealed.

In *Two Little Rich Girls*, M. G. Eberhart once again proves herself one of the masters of her craft.

### Unidentified Woman
February 1945

M. G. Eberhart has never written a more fascinating or more baffling mystery story than this tale of murder among the residents of a picturesque mansion close by a big army training camp. Mrs. Eberhart combines astonishing skill at weaving an intricate plot with the born novelist's sense of style and characterisation. As we learn more of the tangled affairs of the heiress, Victoria Stean, we find our emotions tied up with her uncertain fate. Not without reason does the yellow-eyed District Attorney fix upon her as the guilty party in the murders of the 'unidentified woman' and Clistie Forbes, friend of Victoria's dead mother. Somewhere, somehow, Vicky knew that there was one master key to the murders but it was not until still another death that it all became clear.

### Unknown Quantity, The
November 1953

In this highly original murder mystery, M. G. Eberhart leads her readers through an engrossing maze of intrigue and sudden death. Things are not what they seem, and we race from one crisis to the next with the harassed characters, always in search always in search of that unknown element which is at the centre of these fateful events. Arthur Travers, a wealthy oil magnate, arranges for a young lawyer, Jake Dixon, who resembles him in appearance, to impersonate him while he goes off on a mysterious mission, hinted to be government 'top secret'. On Travers' instructions Dixon and Arthur's young wife Sarah go to the Travers' country place near New York; and are immediately plunged into a maelstrom of murder and suspicion. This is one of M. G. Eberhart's best novels of suspense, of crime and punishment.

### White Dress, The
May 1947

Stepping from the plane at Miami, Marny Sanderson had a frightening sense of impending danger. For one moment she paused, almost tempted to turn around, re-enter the plane, go back to New York, anywhere. Recovering, she followed her employer Tim Wales, President of the Wales Airlines, down the runway, little knowing the drama, or rather the tragedy, in which she was about to play a leading part. M. G. Eberhart has never written a crime story more packed with action and sustained interest. As always, her subtle use of atmosphere and background – this time the tropical, sun-drenched, pleasure-loving Miami – lend intensity and conviction to a thrilling mystery.

### Wings of Fear
March 1946

'I am in a dreadful jam. Monica, come to me. Help me. Linda'. This was the message from Monica Blaine's one-time best friend that started the chain of events which led to the murder of Eric Weller in Monica's New York apartment and sent her with a packet containing ten thousand dollars to Mexico City to John Basevi, the man she loved but had not seen for five years. Monica had seen death and fled, but death flew at her heels, faceless and terrifying. Here against a background of Mexico City, with all its rich colour and strangeness, M. G. Eberhart gives us a crime story full of excitement and suspense.

### *With This Ring*
June 1942
*With This Ring* is set attractively in the sun drenched countryside near New Orleans where the wealthy family of the Chatoniers had their lovely house, Belle Fleur, surrounded by the old sugar plantations which had been the basis of their fortune. 'Nothing ever happens in the afternoon', Eric Chatonier had said once in describing the gracious, slow tempo of life at Belle Fleur. But on that sunny afternoon of September 17th much did happen. For out there where the small yacht *Catherine* lay, as sluggish and still upon the water as a painted boat upon a painted river, something terrible had happened. On board the yacht, old Judge Henry Yarrow, who had sent so many murderers to their death, now had met his own Fate, and lay face downwards in a welter of blood. This is a story in which the interplay of character and human emotion is equally as important as the murder mystery, for M. G. Eberhart is an accomplished writer, whose consummate skill keeps the reader enthralled throughout this extremely fascinating and satisfying novel.

### *Witness at Large*
September 1967
Had it not been for the proposed sale of the family publishing Company, it would have been a typical summer weekend on Mr. Esseven's private island on Long Island Sound. He was a shrewd, dominating and beloved old man, who had run the company for many years and had recently passed on both its management and ownership to his two adopted sons.

The two Esseven brothers were bitterly opposed over the sale but Boyd had the final vote and, egged on by his shrewish wife, he was determined to carry it through.

The horrifying events that take place upon the fog-shrouded island, and that change the normally idyllic holiday retreat into a claustrophobic nightmare, are narrated by Sister, Mr. Esseven's adopted daughter. The family close their ranks when one of the party on the island is murdered and attempt to pass it off as an accident. But despite the united front they present to the police and the limitless lengths they are prepared to go to preserve it, they are unable to stifle their own inevitable doubts and suspicions: nor are they able to prevent further tragedy.

The shivering climax is a murderous game of hide and seek which takes place in the marsh and woods of the island. As always in a suspense story by this distinguished American writer the killer is unsuspected by her readers and the tangled but convincing plot, skilful characterisation and realistic atmosphere of *Witness at Large* explain why she is acknowledged to be one of the great practitioners of the tale of terror.

### *Wolf in Man's Clothing*
May 1943
From the time that M. G. Eberhart first introduced the capable and peppery nurse Sarah Keate in *The Patient in Room 18*, readers have clamoured for more stories featuring this indomitable nurse. Well, Sarah is back again in her grandest case. From the moment the door of the Brent's country house opened to admit two nurses urgently summoned by the doctor to attend young Craig Brent, the story holds the reader spellbound and moves through a maze of clues and family intrigue to a climax as thrilling as anything even this master has ever accomplished.

### *Woman on the Roof*
May 1968
Murder on the roof garden has a nasty habit of repeating itself in M. G. Eberhart's new book. Sue Desart, who married the older Marcus after the assumed death of her fiancé, Jim, shot down over Vietnam, lives in the shadow of her predecessor.

Marcus now decides to enter politics again, with and against the advice of close friends. Whereupon the missing Jim turns up, very much alive, and claiming Sue, who still loves him. The implications, tragedy and fear that follow involve them all and make Jim number one suspect.

Those who like their excitement concentrated will enjoy the boxed-in tension played out in a luxurious New York penthouse, service by an elevator from which there is finally no escape.

## ECCLES, MARJORIE

### *Company She Kept, The*
May 1993
When the half-dressed body of Angie Robinson is found strangled in a lay-by on a lonely moorland road, it seems that her murder is the result of a meaningless and unprovoked sex attack. For Angie has led a blameless life, with no interests other than her untiring support for the campaign to keep open the local Women's Hospital.

But there are too many apparently unrelated elements in the case for DCI Gil Mayo to be satisfied with that explanation. For one thing, an anonymous letter has been sent to the police with hints of a long gone murder and ancient sacrificial rites. Then there is the old house, Flowerdew, which exerts a strange but compelling fascination. And what of Flowerdew's eccentric but endearing owner, the aged Kitty Wilbraham, a former archaeologist who had worked on the ruins of ancient Carthage and who has now disappeared?

It is not until another body is discovered that Mayo, with his new Sergeant, Abigail Moon, is finally able to link the two murders together and arrive at a solution which is as unexpected and bizarre as any in his career.

### *Death of a Good Woman*
February 1989
Fleur Saville, successful novelist and devoted to good works, disappears suddenly just before Christmas, at the beginning of a period of heavy snow. A fortnight later her friend Nell Fennimore, who cannot believe Fleur's husband when he insists she is spending Christmas alone in their country cottage to finish her latest book, asks Detective Chief Inspector Gil Mayo of the Lavenstock CID for help.

Mayo suspects a marital dispute, but agrees to make inquiries and soon learns that Edwin Saville had lied. He now admits that there had been a quarrel and says he believes Fleur has left him; her wedding and engagement rings abandoned on the dressing-table would seem to indicate this.

However, when the thaw begins and Fleur's body is discovered buried in a snowdrift, Saville falls under suspicion of murdering his wife. Not only does he inherit all her money, but there is also a young and attractive woman with whom he has formed a friendship, and though he has what appears to be an unshakable alibi, Mayo is sure he is lying.

As Mayo investigates deeper, he uncovers aspects of Fleur's character not in keeping with her public image. She was far from universally beloved, and Edwin is not the only person who might have had reason for killing her.

Marjorie Eccles spins the suspense neatly, and soon enmeshes the reader in her toils.

### *Late of This Parish*
May 1992
The Reverend Cecil Willard was not one of those born to be loved. A scholarly and austere man, ex-headmaster of the local boy's school, his stern moral principles and diehard opinions had never endeared him to either those close to him or to his neighbours in the village when he had lived and worked. The discovery of his murdered body at the foot of the altar steps in the church, however, shocks the whole community.

But as DCI Gil Mayo finds out when he begins his investigations into the murder, although there were plenty of people in Castel Wyvering who had cause to resent the old man, and one at least with reason to fear him for the knowledge he held, the question remains: why had he been killed? And what was the power-struggle for the Headship of the school, or the shooting of three badgers, to do with his murder? And who is the mysterious Sara mentioned in Willard's diary?

The answers, and the final solution to the murder, only become apparent after Mayo's far-reaching inquiries, and not before the killer has struck once more.

### *More Deaths Than One*
March 1991
Who was Rupert Fleming, found shot dead in his Porsche, apparently by his own hand? Was he what he first appeared to be, a young man who should have everything to live for? Or a character with dubious morals who relied on women to fund his expensive tastes and bolster his ego? For his cool and self-sufficient wife Georgina, who runs her own successful business, is not apparently the only woman in his life. Nor is Bryony, seemingly innocent, trusting and unworldly ...

During his life, Fleming had made enemies more easily than most people, but did any of them have reason to kill him? Detective Chief Inspector Gil Mayo's inquiries into his death converge on the local theatre, where a production of a Jacobean tragedy is being rehearsed under the direction of the local Arts Director, Ashleigh Cockayne, and where he at last begins to find the final solution to his investigation – though not before being confronted with the horror of more unexplained deaths.

### *Requiem for a Dove*
April 1990
Marion Dove had always been something of an enigma, even to her family. No one really understood why she chose to live a simple, uneventful life in a lonely lock-keeper's cottage by the side of the canal. But when her body is discovered in the canal and Detective-Inspector Gil Mayo begins his search for her murderer, he learns that she is the wealthy widow of a local glass manufacturer, and that the contents of her will might well have given several people a motive to kill her, not least Ken Dainty, Marion Dove's son-in-law and heir-apparent and his wife Shirley, with her expensive tastes, or young Paul Fish who has unaccountably disappeared.

As Mayo presses on with the investigation, however, he uncovers disturbing and surprising echoes from Marion's past, and becomes convinced that the answer lies within the closed circle of the family and the secrets they hold – in the dark, self-absorbed character of Wesley, her late husband, and the inheritance he had passed on to his daughters, and in the character and the past of Marion Dove herself.

## EDINGTON, A. C. and CARMEN

### *Murder to Music*
October 1930
This story has for its background a weird and mysterious turreted house, a house which does in actual fact exist in Hollywood. To this house one night the director and leading man of Superior Films' Special Productions Unit go on a voyage of exploration during the filming of a War Epic. The next morning they are both found dead in separate rooms, while near the director is lying the unconscious figure of a stranger who has been shot about the head. This is the murder problem which Detective Smith, who solved *The Studio Murder Mystery*, sets out to solve. The authors know all there is to know about Hollywood and the studio scenes have the authentic touch. The mystery is unfolded with consummate skill and reaches a dramatic denouement.

### *The Monkshood Murders*
May 1931
An editor is found dead in his office. No one is really sorry, and a dozen people are almost glad that Fate has done this thing for them. So much so, that, in spite of the coroner's verdict and the police surgeon's report, one man refuses to believe that it *was* Fate. Relentlessly he ravages the secrets of the dead man's life, until the whole mystery is before him, stripped of its complication of intrigues, religious fervours and black magic. The diabolical cunning that planned Josiah Wardock's death is beaten by some of the most painstaking and breathless detection in the world of crime fiction – but not before another meets the same uncanny death.

## EDMONDS, JANET

### *Dead Spit*
July 1989
When government vet Linus Rintoul bumps into an old friend of his mother's, she is unusually relieved at being recognized and he learns that she has recently returned to Britain after many years abroad, only to find someone else with her name, her address and her reputation as a breeder of Antiguan Truffle Dogs.

Linus's attempts to help her get to the bottom of the mystery take him into the esoteric world of pedigree dogs, where it is soon made abundantly clear to him that his incursion is resented. The imposter is determined not to be exposed. But with murder and terrorism becoming unexpected accompaniments to an otherwise harmless activity, Linus can no longer stand aside, and the prestigious Crufts Dog Show proves to be far more exciting than he had bargained for...

### *Death Has a Cold Nose*
June 1993
When Linus Rintoul's current girlfriend ditches him very publicly indeed, he is grateful for the tactful intervention of Maud Egremont, an elderly, eccentric and very wealthy widow who is particularly pleased to make the acquaintance of a government vet because she breeds and exhibits Korean Palace Dogs.

Linus gradually realizes that Mrs Egremont makes great demands on her friends, but his efforts to distance himself are only partially successful due to the fact that so many of her fellow dog-fanciers meet untimely ends.

Or is it just coincidence that they all sold Mrs Egremont a dog? His own position isn't much helped by the suspicions of George Upperby, Mrs Egremont's son-in-law, who tells the police that Linus is after both Mrs Egremont's money and her daughter, George's wife.

Again and again, Linus is drawn back into the net on one pretext or another, until Mrs Egremont asks him to meet her at the neolithic flint mines known as Grimes Graves. He soon discovers that they are all too aptly named …

### *Dog's Body*
November 1988

When Oxford-based Government vet Linus Rintoul learns that a kennelmaid at a local quarantine kennel has developed rabies, he anticipates nothing more exciting than a variation in his daily routine. Instead, he finds himself being drawn into a world of crime, corruption and brutality that reaches across the Atlantic and into the upper echelons of British society. Why should one quarantine kennel house so many of the notorious American Pit Bull Terriers and who is importing them?

The unexplained death of car dealer Henry Lewdown leads Linus to Portsmouth and the gradual realization that corruption has been so insidious that he dare trust nobody as he ventures deeper into the world of organized dog fights and what is behind them. As events reach their bloody climax he discovers just how dangerous this world he has so rashly entered can be to a vet with an inquisitive disposition. He will be lucky to escape alive …

### *Judge and Be Damned*
December 1990

The discovery of a dead judge in bizarre circumstances is thought by the police to be connected with a recent trial at which he presided, but when Linus Rintoul, a government vet, becomes involved with an attractive dog-breeder, he learns that there are unexpected connections between the judge and the breeder. His new friendship leads him into the show ring, where he finds that some people will go to extraordinary lengths both to win and to keep other competitors – like Linus – out. Linus refuses to bow to pressure, but he does not realize what he is up against, nor the lengths to which some people will go…

### *Let Sleeping Dogs Lie*
July 1992

When Linus Rintoul is asked to look into the alleged age of a Kennel Club member – a point which calls in question the man's integrity – he refuses, but when he buys an appealing watercolour of a cow he finds himself drawn into an extraordinary imbroglio concerning change of identities, Nazi war-loot – and murder. It's an imbroglio in which the age of dog-breeding art-dealer Raymond March is crucial – but who is John Smith? And why does an attractive woman engaged in tracking down missing works of art lack even the most basic knowledge of her subject?

The trail leads the government vet from his Oxfordshire base to a fort in the Solent, where not everything proves to be quite what it seems…

## ELKINS, AARON

### *Icy Clutches*
June 1991

Anthropology professor Gideon Oliver thought that accompanying his wife, Julie, to a forest rangers' conference in Glacier Bay, Alaska, would make for a restful vacation. But he hadn't counted on the presence of M. Audley Tremaine, TV's most popular science personality. Tremaine has just completed his memoirs of a geological expedition of thirty years earlier, when three people were killed in an avalanche – and Tremaine himself barely escaped with his life. Now he and the other survivors – as well as their late colleagues' heirs – have gathered to review and memorialise the victims.

When human bones turn up at the avalanche site and the FBI quickly needs expert analysis, everyone agrees how fortunate it is that Gideon Oliver, the Skeleton Detective, is on the scene. Everyone except for the person who wants ancient history to stay that way. Everyone but the person who thinks that murder is the best way to cover up the past.

In *Icy Clutches* the Edgar Award-winning Elkins and his detective hero reach even loftier heights with their special combination of new crimes and old bones.

### *Make No Bones*
May 1992

Albert Evan Jasper, 'dean of American forensic anthropologists', was a man who lived up to his eccentric reputation well beyond the grave: he willed his skeleton to science. Sadly, science had no place to put it and for ten years the bones lay in a drawer.

Now the problem is solved with the opening of an exhibition at a Museum of Natural History in Oregon. As part of a forensic anthropologists' conference, Jasper's remains are to be installed on permanent display.

Among the conference delegates is Gideon Oliver, looking forward to a stimulating and educational week. The stimulation begins when Jasper's bones are stolen from their case. Then the skeleton of a murdered man is discovered in a shallow grave in the grounds of the conference location: a scenic but decaying resort. While this is being investigated by local police, there is another killing – of a scientist connected with the conference, and Gideon, forced to the unwelcome conclusion that the murderer must be one of his own colleagues, narrowly escapes an attempt on his own life.

Aided by his wife and an old friend from the FBI, Gideon faces his most difficult challenge to date: unmasking a clever, dangerous killer who knows every bit as much about forensic science as he does.

### *Murder in the Queen's Armes*
November 1990

Gideon Oliver, the physical anthropologist known as the Skeleton Detective, is in England on his honeymoon. He and his wife, Ju1ie, find themselves in Wessex near a dig being run by a former classmate of Gideon's, and Gideon stops by to say hello. When he arrives, he discovers not only that the always-abrasive Nate Marcus is in serious trouble and about to be investigated by the foundations financing the dig, but that the local paper has mysteriously learned of Gideon's presence and linked it with the investigation.

The atmosphere at the dig is unpleasant; there is suspicion, professional and personal rivalry, and distrust among the archaeologists and graduate students working there. Nate claims to have found proof of a theory that is disputed – indeed, scoffed at – by almost the entire profession, and his refusal to reveal it to Gideon disturbs his friend. Then one of the students disappears, and when a body is found, Gideon is called upon to play Skeleton Detective once more. Before long his activities lead to another murder and put not only Gideon himself, but Julie as well, in mortal danger.

## EPSTEIN, CHARLOTTE

### *Murder in China*
December 1986

Comrade Li, honoured cadre of the Foreign Students Building, has been murdered, and the officer of the People's Liberation Army waits patiently for her murderer to confess. American professor Janet Eldine is less patient because she is one of the suspects. Others include the hardworking – and hard playing – Frenchwoman who battled Mrs Li for the right to live as she pleased. The young American student, afraid Mrs Li will have her shipped home, who wanders the streets of Peking and disappears, the African students who speak Chinese fluently and resent the way they are ostracized by the Chinese people, and the Chinese students and faculty, many of them victims of the cultural revolution in which Mrs Li played an active role. One such victim (and suspect) is now her attractive husband. Janet devoutly hopes he isn't the murderer.

Through Janet's analysis of characters and motives Chinese people from all walks come alive. The campus of Beijing Xue Yuan is a microcosm of Peking life, where frantic modernization and ancient conservatism are in constant conflict. The contrasts make any visitor's stay in China fascinating. Janet Eldine, one of the few foreigners working in China, invited to the homes of friends, touring the gorgeous temples and palaces, is enthralled by it all. Even as she realizes that people – and murder – are universally the same.

## EVERTON, FRANCIS

### *Insoluble*
March 1934

Cecil Manning, the managing director of the Ruston branch of British Industrial Chemicals, Ltd., is found dead in his bed one Sunday morning with a bottle of Perronal tablets on a table nearby. The door is locked on the inside. The circumstances, Cecil's character, and his prospects, all make suicide seem unlikely. A mistake, however, is equally improbable, for Cecil was a trained chemist. There remains that ugly third possibility – *murder*. But at the adjourned inquest, the jury did return a verdict of death by misadventure. Even so, after an inquest, 'It is well for one's peace of mind that the police, the coroner, the jury, and every one else concerned, should be completely satisfied and free from doubt. But after the inquest on Cecil Manning, whilst some of us were highly satisfied, there were others who were not. And I think we all had doubts – all, that is, excepting the one who poisoned Cecil.' That was his opinion, and there were others who shared it. Three people certainly had excellent motives for the murder of Cecil Manning. In addition, they each had the opportunity, being in his house the night before the murder, when, by sheer chance, hot whisky and lemon was drunk. And, by sheer chance again, of course, Perronal, which is *insoluble in water*, dissolves most readily in alcohol – especially when warm.

### *Murder May Pass Unpunished*
October 1936

If ever a murderer got away with it by sheer impertinence, it was the man who perpetrated the crime of Francis Everton's new story! Imagine the nerve of the man: to hold a party, explaining how he *could* have done the murder, but choosing his words so carefully that not one could be construed as a confession, and leaving the police, without a shred of material evidence against him, fuming at their impotence to lay the murder at his feet. It isn't often that murder passes unpunished in a detective story, but it does in this case; and what is more, the murderer, as he goes away scot-free, takes with him, to his bravado, the sneaking sympathy of the reader.

### *Young Vanish, The*
May 1932

Was it chance and nothing but chance that half-a-dozen prominent trade union officials had been killed in one form of accident or another in the short space of a few weeks? Pure chance or systematic murder? Russia's Five Year Plan is nearing its completion when this extraordinary sequence of fatal accidents aroused the suspicion of the authorities and the matter is handed over to Sir Victor Grahame's department, the Special Investigation Department of Scotland Yard, to which Detective-Inspector Allport is transferred from the C. I. D. Allport discovers his first clue in Bermondsey. It leads him to John Kisney's unusual offices in a lonely inn on the Yorkshire moors, and to Professor Lynde's laboratory at Upper-Inglemoreton Grange. It involves Mary Mace, Kisney's clever typist, Paul Stapleton, the Liberal M. P., and Sonia Lynde, the professor's Socialist daughter. Yet another successful case is added to the ugly little detective's list. *The Young Vanish* is an excellent story, well written, clever, and really exciting, in every way worthy of the author of *The Dalehouse Murder*, of which Mr. Arnold Bennett wrote, 'It is at least as good as any detective story I have read since Conan Doyle and Gaston Leroux.'

## FARJEON, J. JEFFERSON

### *Aunt Sunday Sees it Through*
June 1940

Mr. Jefferson Farjeon here presents a new character, Aunt Sunday, who we think will equal that great character "Ben" in popular appeal. After fifty years in a little country village from which she has never strayed farther than ten miles, Aunt Sunday comes to London with her two sisters – two other aunts of equal interest – and failing to connect with the niece who was to have met their motor coach, they are met by somebody else instead, and are taken to the wrong house. What happens in that house – the strange and dubious people they encounter there – the gradual realisation that they are being taken for dubious people themselves – the transformation of Aunt Sunday from a simple soul into a subtle sleuth – form the theme of a story which must rank as one of Mr. Farjeon's best yarns, if not indeed his best. The tale is told with a humour and charm which lift it, from the first page, above the range of the ordinary thriller.

### *Ben on the Job*
January 1952

This new and gripping story by J. Jefferson Farjeon sees the welcome return of his famous character Ben. Ben has a genius for trouble. Whenever his thumbs itch he knows that 'something 'orrible is going to happen. His thumbs had itched on that never-to-be-forgotten foggy afternoon when he had stumbled into a house numbered 'Seventeen'; they had itched before a peculiarly unpleasant meeting with an Indian. Now here they were itching again. And when the mist came up Ben was doubly sure of trouble, for that was the second infallible sign. So the discovery of the body of a well-dressed man in the basement of a deserted house came as less of a shock than it might have done, yet the subsequent hair-raising events are charged with all the mounting excitement that has made J. Jefferson Farjeon peerless as a story-teller.

### *Ben Sees It Through*
December 1932
Jefferson Farjeon's famous character "Ben" has become one of the most popular characters in present-day fiction. His recent appearance on the stage and on the silver screen has added tremendously to the already large number of his admirers, who will eagerly await his latest adventure in *Ben Sees It Through*, Ben is a complete success, a real character who makes this thriller thoroughly human. This poor chump, who gets himself into scrape after scrape, is full of humorous and pathetic appeal. He is the personification of the Cockney type – a real creation in detective fiction. In his new adventure Ben meets a mysterious stranger on a cross-Channel steamer and is promised a job. On arrival at Southampton they take a taxi. Ben alights to post a letter and on his return to the cab finds the stranger has been murdered. Ben bolts, is pursued by a mysterious foreigner, escapes from his clutches only to find the police are after him. The hunt is up, the mystery deepens. Jefferson Farjeon packs unexpected twists and turns into his story until we arrive breathlessly at a most exciting finish.

### *Black Castle*
January 1945
Hugh Donovan was a schoolmaster with a long summer vacation still six weeks away – and no plans yet made for his holiday. It was a trifling incident on the school cricket ground that decided that six weeks later Donovan should be travelling across Europe for that never-failing source of adventure, the Balkans. How he reached the grimly picturesque castle at Holz, and how he became involved in as extraordinary an adventure as any yet conceived by this resourceful and imaginative writer, is told with all Mr. Farjeon's customary skill.

### *Castle of Fear*
November 1954
Everything happened to Grace Jamieson. Her life had been full of incident and tragedy even before the moment when Paul Kennet saved her life by pulling her from in front of a fast-travelling motor car. Then a lot more things began to happen. She found herself attracted to Paul, who had mysterious troubles of his own. Soon they were on the train to Lenwick together, Grace to claim her inheritance, lonely and rugged Burncliffe Castle, Paul to escort and help her. Burncliffe Castle turned out to be a very sinister place, and its tenants people whose claim was less good than Grace's but whose possession was undeniable. What happened to Grace and Paul in this Castle of Fear, and the terrible predicament from which they at last escaped, make the story of this new, thrilling novel by that master of crime fiction, J. Jefferson Farjeon.

### *Cause Unknown*
September 1950
The spot that Brian Elton chose to end his walk that Monday afternoon in late summer was a part of Hampstead Heath that seemed specially designed in its seclusion and sequestered beauty for the assignations of lovers. But if the man Brian saw in front of him had any such rendezvous in mind it was ended before it began, for he suddenly dropped dead in his tracks. This was the third mysterious death in a week to puzzle both doctors and police, and Brian finds himself caught up in an absorbing mystery. *Cause Unknown* is an unusual crime story, possessing that strange and haunting quality which distinguishes all Mr. Jefferson Farjeon's work.

### *Dark Lady*
May 1938
"Use the spare-room," said Lena to her husband, after their quarrel. But he did not use the spare-room, and when she descended later to find out why … Well, the reason ends the first chapter of one of Mr. Farjeon's most thrilling novels. After that, the adventures of the Dark Lady proceed at Mr. Farjeon's usual dizzy pace, unless in this story he has exceeded even his own speed limit. His heroine moves perilously between the devil and the deep sea, and because she is a very human heroine, the reader who is hardened to literary beauty will not escape anxiety for her welfare. This would not be a Farjeon story if it did not contain humour and romance as well as thrills. All three qualities will be found in the packed pages of *Dark Lady*.

### *Dead Man's Heath*
September 1933
The blindness of a bat and its erratic behaviour in the glare of a head-lamp contrived to land Lionel North and his motor-cycle in the ditch – at the most desolate part of the blasted heath. Painfully he made his way to a lonely cottage, where he found a damsel in evident distress – and a corpse… . The curtain has risen on a typical Farjeon mystery, entertaining as well as thrilling, for in the deft blending of these qualities Mr. Jefferson Farjeon is pre-eminent. *Dead Man's Heath* provides most excellent fare for the ever-growing number of Farjeon 'fans.'

### *Detective Ben*
May 1936
It is good news for all Farjeon fans that Ben reappears in his latest story, *Detective Ben*. That 'awkward little bloke called Ben' is one of the favourites of present-day fiction. His half humorous, half-pathetic philosophy, and the persistence with which he runs into all sorts of adventures, though, as he ruefully reflects, he 'fair 'ates blood', have endeared him to thousands. In the very first chapter Ben finds a dead man on a bridge and is soon after whisked away from the scene of an obvious crime by a lady in a limousine. It is a startling prelude to a glorious tale, told with that creepy skill in which Miss Dorothy L. Sayers has asserted Mr. Farjeon is quite unsurpassed.

### *Disappearances of Uncle David, The*
December 1949
Some people are ever-present. Uncle David was ever-absent. And yet to the small nephew who had never seen him and who was forbidden to talk of him he was ever-present as a mental companion, residing in his thoughts, flitting through his dreams, haunting the cobwebby attic. Why was Uncle David a barred topic in his house? Where had he gone? Would he ever return? Uncle David became a legend. Then one day out of the blue came an invitation to a lonely house in Yorkshire, but when the invited guest arrived—Uncle David had disappeared again! Did nephew and uncle ever meet? You must read Mr. Farjeon's absorbing story for the answer to that question and for what befell Alan Parrish and three young friends when chance led him for a second time to his uncle's house.

### *Double Crime, The*
October 1953
Jim Tate was a reformed character – almost. He had run straight since his one conviction for robbery, but honesty had not paid; he hadn't even enough cash for the rent. So when, trying to sell toothbrushes and scissors at the back door of Greystones – that strange secretive house with it uneasy occupants – he met the butler who had been responsible for his first conviction, he became an easy prey to the latter's proposals. Jim was to return again later to rob the house, and with the butler's connivance. But he was an incompetent thief at best, and when a shot rang out and a body fell at his feet while he was actually on the job, he lost his head very completely. Jefferson Farjeon's skill as a weaver of mysteries is well-known and in *The Double Crime* he holds the reader in baffled suspense until the thrilling denouement.

### *End of an Author*
October 1938
When Peter Hanby advertised for a secretary and took her to an isolated cottage in the sea marshes to write his fiftieth novel, he hadn't an idea in his head. Poison, kidnapping, torture, cheating, blackmail, the duchess's diamonds – Hanby had drained them all. They had nothing fresh to offer his spinning brain … But while desperately searching for some new mystery he himself became the mystery that he sought, and it was his secretary who was set the job of solving it. This is not Mr. Farjeon's fiftieth novel. It is only his fortieth, and he thus has ten novels to go before reaching Peter Hanby's unenviable plight! Meanwhile, in this story, he once more proves that his own inventive faculty is still running strong. The mystery in *End of an Author* is probably the best he has ever evolved, and he has never given us a more intriguing or more diversified set of characters.

### *Exit John Horton*
October 1939
Nothing exciting ever happened to John Horton. He dreamed of adventure and romance while he dictated letters to his pretty secretary at the office, while he sat with his unresponsive wife at home, and while he pedalled through country lanes on his annual solitary cycle tour. But the dreams never materialised… Until one August, when he cycled north-west and never came back again. A few days later his wife was found dead in her bed. Then the hunt for John Horton began in earnest… An absolutely first-rate Farjeon novel, specially recommended.

### *Greenmask*
June 1944
John Letherton had led a singularly uneventful life, but he never ceased to have that happy feeling that Adventure was just round the corner. When one summer morning he set off for a walking tour in North Wales, he had this special feeling more strongly than ever. And this time he was right. When he sought accommodation for the night at a wayside inn called The White Lion the landlord was so reluctant to give him a room, and the other guests were so sinister, that he at once scented a mystery; and mystery indeed there was, linked up with a sensational double murder. *Greenmask* is a first-rate thriller, and is narrated with all Jefferson Farjeon's superb story-telling power.

### *Holiday at Half-Mast*
September 1937
Wellington Pryce returns from a trip round the world to find his brother Frank dead. What should have been a glad reunion is transformed to tragedy in which there is a strong element of mystery. A letter that Wellington subsequently receives convinces him that his brother was murdered, and that he must seek for a solution of the mystery at Rossiter Hall, a country house in Devonshire. He goes there and encounters more strange and tragic happenings, which Mr. Jefferson Farjeon weaves together to make an exciting and baffling story. Wellington Pryce is an excellent sleuth, whose gay humour and disarming personality conceal an exceptionally shrewd mind.

### *House of Shadows, The*
May 1943
It was a strange whim of a very fickle fortune that brought about the meeting of Morley Styles, a mining engineer, and Rhoda Alcott, newly arrived from England, at Kwama, an isolated spot in Rhodesia. Fantastic indeed that, twenty-four hours after Morley's arrival, the one train a day should deposit the dark-haired Rhoda at the lonely station. Rhoda had come out from England at the request of her father, who, after a twenty years' silence, had written to say that he needed her. Rhoda's arrival was too late. John Alcott was dead. His daughter's first glimpse of that strangely forbidding house, with its haunting, eerie atmosphere, not simply of neglect, but of evil, chilled her heart. In *The House of Shadows* Mr. Farjeon shows once again what a superb storyteller he is.

### *House Opposite, The*
May 1931
Mr. Farjeon was never more delightfully amusing or more genuinely uncanny than in the new exploit of Ben, the now famous tramp of *No. 17*, the play that made all London laugh. He was wise in bringing Ben back again into a novel, and his many admirers will find this prince of tramps, with his rich Cockney humour and naïve philosophies, more droll than ever. Ben, as usual, is in the thick of it. Strange things are happening in the untenanted houses of Jowle Street. There are unaccountable creakings and weird knockings on the door of No. 26, where Ben has taken up residence. But there are stranger things happening in The House Opposite. Ben has a visitor, a beautiful woman in an evening gown – the *dernier cri* in Jowle Street! Is she the one he saw earlier at the door of the house opposite? She gives him a cigarette and a taxi-ride which Ben never sees the end of. He sleeps strangely. Mr Farjeon's plot is as good as his characterisation, which is saying a lot. He knows how to cast the spell of all great mysteries.

### *House Over the Tunnel, The*
May 1951
The doctor's advice to Peter Bruce, who was suffering from overwork, had been to stop thinking, to stop imagining, and to get among lively, practical people who dealt with facts, not fancies. A gay seaside resort was just the place, he said. Such a holiday was far from Peter's taste, and it seemed as if fate agreed, for the express on which he was reluctantly travelling stopped by accident at the small country station of Belmor. Pete thankfully grasped the opportunity to escape and jumped the train. And so he came to the queer, solitary old house overlooking Belmor Tunnel, and found himself caught up in an old but unforgettable tragedy. It is partly due to his highly developed imagination, and his sensitivity to atmosphere, that the mystery of a sixteen-year-old murder is solved. J. Jefferson Farjeon's gift for the macabre has never been seen to greater effect than in this latest novel, *The House Over the Tunnel*.

### *Judge Sums Up, The*
July 1942
Peter Gaskell is on trial for his life, accused of the murder of Walter Drage. They had both been staying in the same golf hotel at East Malling, where they had made the acquaintance of Jean Yates, with whom Peter quickly fell in love, only to discover that she

preferred Walter's company. When Drage's body was found, battered to pieces, at the foot of a cliff in Westmoreland, suspicion naturally pointed to Peter. As Mr. Justice Unwin patiently and skilfully guides the jury through the mass of evidence, the reader shares the tense dramatic atmosphere of that crowded court during the closing stages of a most remarkable trial.

### *Murderer's Trail*
November 1931
Ben, the tramp, is one of those rare fictional characters whose familiar figure we expect to see round some corner of our work-a-day world any day. The fact that we do not, does not make us doubt his existence. It is merely our bad luck. But Ben is growing 'range-y'. Our chances are less, for Mr. Farjeon has taken him to Spain for his latest adventure. Ben, wandering hungry through the back alleys of Limehouse, found his imagination a mixed blessing. He could scent a perfect paradise of cheese where there was none, but he had to face ghosts that were only 'shadders', corpses that the fog half shrouded, and bills on every hoarding – 'Old Man Murdered in Hammersmith.' Ben got the wind up! He ran! He crossed a plank, slipped through a little iron door, and went to sea with the coal! But so did the man who did the murder in Hammersmith, and a very pretty lady who did not. The *Atlanta* sailed on, but she lost a stowaway, a pickpocket, a murderer, a super-crook, the daughter of her wealthiest passenger, her third officer, and a lifeboat in the night. And that is how Ben got to Spain.

### *Mystery in White*
December 1937
'Jefferson Farjeon is quite unsurpassed for creepy skill in mysterious adventures,' says Miss Dorothy L. Sayers. And *Mystery in White* is a splendid example of Mr. Farjeon's great gift as a writer. From the excellent opening, in which certain passengers, isolated in a snow-bound train at Christmas, make a bid for liberty with surprising results, the story holds us in its grip. For death strikes relentlessly again and yet again. Here is a murder story that every one will enjoy.

### *Mystery of the Creek, The*
March 1933
Once a year Henry Moyle sought adventure. He sought it consistently; and just as consistently missed it. This year Henry, a sedate middle-aged bachelor, started on his yearly holiday… . He awoke from oblivion after a motoring accident to find an unconscious girl beside him; a few yards farther on a dead man; and his cottage, which was not far away, broken into. To this cottage he carried the girl. The next surprise was the appearance of a strange young man who told a queer story of entering the house and seeing a black man from whom he ran away. From this startling opening Mr.. Jefferson Farjeon builds up one of his most exciting mystery stories, packed as usual with plenty of action and thrills.

### *Mystery on the Moor, The*
November 1930
Mist and mystery, and not a little romance—that is Mr. Farjeon's new novel in a nutshell. Some instinct took Dennis Shale from the fireside of his holiday inn out on to the moors, against his own better judgment and the advice of his landlord. Perhaps it was just the knowledge that Angela Weston was out there alone, snapping her fingers at the lowering clouds. His instinct was indeed a good one, for the girl needed help badly just then. She lay with a broken ankle, unable to move, and not likely to be found in the thickening mist. Dennis succeeded in getting her to the shelter of a barn, and then went in search of a house he had caught a momentary glimpse of through the grey. He reached the gate only to be met by an old man with a revolver—a lunatic or a criminal, or perhaps merely an eccentric—Dennis could not say. But the old man's bark was decidedly worse than his bite, and he agreed that Miss Weston be brought to his home till assistance could be found. Dennis returned to the barn—but Angela was gone!

### *Number Nineteen*
November 1952
On a certain grey afternoon he was destined never to forget, Ben sat down on a park seat and proceeded to think, not of cabbages and kings, but of numbers, lucky and unlucky. It certainly wasn't his lucky day! A man – a nondescript looking stranger sitting at the other end of the bench – was murdered before his very eyes. That was the prelude to the most uncomfortable and eventful twenty-four hours Ben had ever spent in an uncomfortable and eventful life. Mr. Jefferson Farjeon's famous cockney character Ben, who has appeared in *Ben on the Job*, *Number 17*, and other novels, has never been so richly humorous, so absurdly heroic, as in this latest hair-raising adventure taking place at Number Nineteen, Billiter Road.

### *Old Man Mystery*
December 1933
Two old septuagenarian clubmen decide to have one more adventure before they die, and disappear into Devonshire to see whether they can beat Scotland Yard in elucidating a mystery – a little girl who went out to post a letter in Torquay has disappeared. The venerable sleuths do not realise that their own disappearance will eventually involve a second search for them. In the end, after various encounters with crooks, they prove victorious – and return to their club window with plenty of fresh reminiscences to inflict on their fellow members. Mr. Jefferson Farjeon's customary humorous touch is much in evidence in this entertaining story, but while he amuses, he also mystifies his readers.

### *Oval Table, The*
March 1946
It was grimly appropriate that thirteen should sit down to dine on the night John Coleby ate his last meal on earth. But it was Coleby himself who had arranged the details of that dinner party. Even the name cards set carefully to indicate the chair of each guest took the form of tiny skulls mounted on slender ebony pedestals, and the white lilies in the centrepiece gave a funereal air to what surely was intended as a festive board. A grim joke with a grimmer ending! Mr. Farjeon is an acknowledged master of mystery and he packs his story with a full load of excitement.

### *Peril in the Pyrenees*
January 1947
While holidaying in the Pyrenees, David Rorke makes three interesting acquaintances – a young couple Celia Etherton and her slightly neurotic brother John, and a middle-aged Frenchman, Monsieur Paul Leroux. He discovers they are to be fellow-travellers on the same motor coach, but little guesses what a tale of hectic excitement and horror is to be played out before they reach their destination. Against the grim, majestic beauty of the towering Pyrenees, J. Jefferson Farjeon tells a breath-taking story of mystery and adventure.

### *Prelude to Crime*
October 1948
Crime, it is said, springs in the beginning from dark and evil thoughts, growing secretly like noxious weeds. Young Hugh Dexter had cause to fear his dreams, for in his dreams his subconscious mind seemed to be urging him irresistibly towards the most dreadful crime of all – Murder. In an attempt to rid himself of the obsession that he is going to kill someone – whom, he does not know – he enters the rest home of a famous psychiatrist, and there in that peaceful Hampshire retreat, in the midst of a group of strange and sinister characters, he lives out a nightmare week, moving inexorably towards a startling and inevitable climax. This is J. Jefferson Farjeon in his best imaginative vein – a crime novel of rare and macabre quality.

### *Room Number Six*
May 1941
Simon Smith was down on his luck – in fact, unemployed, and willing to try anything. He optimistically answered an advertisement – 'Man wanted immediately for confidential job, experience unnecessary, honesty essential.' When he interviewed his prospective employer, Mr. Henry Mildenhall, he was perhaps a little dashed to find that the confidential job was rather an ordinary one – a traveller in gum. Perhaps Simon's thoughts were too romantically inclined at the time, for he had just met for the first time Millie Brown. But Simon was not to be disappointed over his job. It was not all it seemed, and in fact as a traveller for Mr. Mildenhall he found life was one terrific adventure. Mr. Jefferson Farjeon is, as every one knows, a born story-teller. Seldom has he written a more enjoyable thriller than *Room Number Six*.

### *Seven Dead*
March 1939
Seven dead people, six men and one woman, in a locked and shuttered drawing-room – that was what Ted Lyte found when he climbed through a back window of Haven Lodge on his first housebreaking job. But this is not Ted's story. The Mystery of the Seven Dead, as it was called in the headlines, soon passed into the hands of Detective-Inspector Kendall, to become one of his most famous and bewildering cases. How far Kendall was assisted by the yachtsman-journalist who gave him unofficial aid may remain a moot point, but Tom Hazeldean introduced romance which was absent from the detective's cool and calculating brain, and was the first to track that romance across the water to a secluded, gloomy house on the ramparts of Boulogne. Mr. Jefferson Farjeon's brilliant story will appeal to both the lover of romance and the student of detection.

### *Shadow of Thirteen, The*
June 1949
The shadow of thirteen loomed darkly over Gatleigh Hall. On the thirteenth of October thirteen years ago there had been a death and a disappearance within its gates. For thirteen years, on the fatal anniversary, Lady Chelwyn had returned, in response to some mysterious inner compulsion, to her neglected home. Is the past really dead? Will the present provide an explanation of the past? Mr. Jefferson Farjeon is an accomplished master of the macabre, and yet he does not exaggerate his effects. Just what happened in the lodge at gloomy Gatleigh Hall makes a story frightening in its reality, breathtaking in its suspense.

### *Sinister Inn*
June 1934
Two men in a boat – to say nothing of the girl, even although she is young and attractive – take the leading parts in J. Jefferson Farjeon's exciting new story. It all starts with a summer holiday in Devon – the peaceful quiet of Dartmouth, slowly moving boats, gulls floating on lazy wings, the Channel calling. A boating excursion is planned and nearly ends in disaster. Caught in a storm, our three adventurers are blown towards France, finally landing on a desolate part of the coast of Brittany. They succeed in getting shelter for the night in an old inn. Thrill follows thrill as the castaways find that their presence is not welcomed by the strange old innkeeper. Evidently the man holds a secret at once sinister and mysterious. Mr. Jefferson Farjeon keeps us on tenterhooks of excitement as he narrates his amazing story, once again proving that he is not only a master of the macabre, but is an exceptionally entertaining storyteller.

### *Third Victim, The*
November 1941
This is the tale of a crime uncovered by strange methods.

Sir George Lyster returns to his ancestral home after an absence of twenty-six years, to find a strange story and strange characters awaiting him. He learns that his brother had fallen to his death from the high gallery in the great hall; that on the same day his niece Ursula had eloped with a scoundrel; that his brother's adopted son had fallen from the identical spot years before; that his mother lived alone in the great house, completely paralyzed; that there were only two servants, a butler and a housekeeper of whom the dowager Lady Lyster was frankly terrified. Mystery clung to the walls of the ancient house and George was determined to solve it. He invites to the house all the members of the house party who were there on the day of his brother's death but his carefully staged reconstruction had unexpected results...

### *Trunk Call*
September 1932
Tom Everard, a busy young novelist, was on holiday – a fortnight in Torquay. He had locked up his home, said *au revoir* to his desk and his hardworked 'phone – Hampstead 0077 – his weeks of glorious freedom from Gerrard, Central and Hop, Tru, Tol and Tel. He was gaily signing the register at the poshest hotel in Torquay when from the adjacent call-box came a voice, "Is that Hampstead 0077?" His own telephone number! A pause and then "Oh – you are Hampstead 0077. Good!" Someone answering from his own empty house! An unsettling accident at the start of one's holiday. Tom decided to return to London to investigate and then things happen, mystery follows mystery. The baffling situations are handled with J. Jefferson Farjeon's usual deft skill.

### *Windmill Mystery, The*
February 1934
The windmill stood out dark and sinister against a background of angry cloud-castles that foretold the coming storm. Lionel Savage, pack on back, and all set for a week-end hike, glimpsed it from the little wayside railway station and decided it might prove a suitable objective. Crossing the heath, he met a charming girl, and when the storm broke they raced to the mill for shelter. It was the start of an amazing adventure which rapidly developed into a crescendo of excitement, until as one hair-raising incident succeeded another, the two hikers found themselves involved in a sort of non-stop Grand Guignol of thrills.

### *'Z' Murders, The*
May 1932
While life reigned, the hotel smoking-room had been a dead place. Now DEATH had come it suddenly grew ALIVE. Figures flitted

about…voices exclaimed or whispered. The elderly man in the armchair by the window was dead – shot dead with a bullet through the heart. Suddenly Temperley remembered the lady…her subtle fragrance…the glimpse of a beautiful face no less beautiful for the vague trouble in it. Could she have – ? And then the voice of the inspector: 'What do you make of this?' He held out a small crimson object cut in the shape of the letter Z. That was the first murder! There were more, equally diabolical, equally mystifying, making as exciting a story as this talented author has ever written.

## FARRAR, STEWART

### *Death in the Wrong Bed*

October 1963

Kay Decker found pleasure in teasing and torturing her husband, while she herself carried on an ostentatious affair with a young man who took her fancy. Kay was beautiful and seductive, but also cold and ruthless, and it was not surprising that her husband should be driven into the arms of a sympathetic girl who worked at his studio.

Hugh Decker was a commercial artist, and it is among the artists, editors, and financiers of the world of glossy and trade magazines that this story is set.

When the victim of a murder was discovered in mysterious circumstances, Detective Inspector Morgan quickly reached the scene. The subsequent investigation and its denouement are baffling and exciting; a strong plot and a fascinating background give Stewart Farrar's new novel greater conviction even than his earlier crime novels, *The Snake on 99* and *Zero in the Gate*.

### *Snake on 99, The*

July 1958

*'You know', said Inspector Morgan, 'catching a criminal's like a game of Snakes and Ladders. You plod ahead, square by square; sometimes a Ladder takes you up a row or two. Sometimes you slide down a Snake. It's the same for the criminal. But for him there's nearly always the final pitfall – the dirty great Snake on 99 – waiting to drop him into our arms.'*

Morgan came to Dextergate Rise because, when Frank Branson fell to his death from the roof-garden of the hotel, one man actually saw him fall – and Joe Archer was certain that Branson had been pushed.

The residents of the hotel were all apparently friendly; as unlikely a group of people to contain a murderer as could be found. But it has been said that everyone has a secret which he or she would risk a lot to keep hidden. When Morgan, in his own (sometimes unorthodox) way began to investigate his mixed bag of suspects, some startling and unexpected features came to light. He found himself forced to rake over the ashes of old tragedies and follow clues which led him far back into the past. Only then does he see the pattern which made sense out of the violent death of a young and brilliant journalist in the present.

*The Snake on 99* is Stewart Farrar's first book and is a striking start in the field of the classic detective novel. Life-like and convincing, the inhabitants of 7 Dextergate Rise are lively and real; and in the very human Elwyn Morgan, Stewart Farrar brings a promising and likeable new recruit to that distinguished body, the Detective Inspectors of fiction.

### *Zero in the Gate*

March 1960

The headquarters of Headline Gazette, the 'Stop Press of the Screen', was a friendly place. Friction among the executives, cameramen, secretaries and technicians seldom seemed more than mild exasperation. When the dead victim of a poisoner was found in the office the shock was great enough, but worse was to come when Elwyn Morgan confirmed what some had feared: the murderer could only be among the handful of people who had stayed late one night to finish work on the newsreel of the Wimbledon Finals.

The shrewd, likeable Welsh policeman soon realised that motive was the only thing which could give him a lead; in the jargon of the newsreels he had to get 'zero in the gate', to search out and identify the right starting point, the point where the seeds of murder had first been planted. Stewart Farrar here maintains the high standards which distinguished his first book, *The Snake on 99*, and introduces the reader to a lively and believable cast of characters moving against a fascinating background and struggling to come to terms with a grim and dangerous situation.

## FARRER, KATHARINE

### *Cretan Counterfeit, The*

February 1954

Here is a crime story with exotic characters, an unusual and fascinating background of archaeological research, a baffling mystery, and a surprising climax. Sir Alban Worral's obituary notice was worded in the usual flattering language, but Clare and Richard Ringwood, reading between the lines, saw that its subtle intention was to denigrate the famous archaeologist. Sure enough, the notice drew a reply the next day, an impassioned attempt to restore the dead man's reputation. The reply was signed 'Janet Coltman'. Shortly after a girl of that name was knifed, and Detective Inspector Ringwood was put in charge of the case. Ringwood found that archaeology offers its own opportunities for crime!

## FERGUSON, JOHN

### *Death Comes to Perigord*

November 1931

*Death Comes to Perigord* is a detective story concerned with the disappearance and subsequent death of a man while under the care of a young doctor in the absence of the usual medical attendant. The story is set in the Channel Islands, among a mixed population of French and English, but its interest first lies in the discovery by the young *locum* of certain peculiarities in the dead body which flatly contradict each other. And the doubts thus raised are reinforced by the detective's discovery of a small peculiarity about the dead man's watch. Subsequent clues include a ship's figurehead, a perfumed handkerchief, a knife blade, a barking dog, a scrap of seaweed and a tennis ball that had been gilded, and these apparently disconnected objects Detective McNab, with the help of Dr. Dunn, builds up into a connected and coherent sequence which, step by step, reveals the part played by each article in the murder and leads to the identification of the real criminal.

### *Death of Mr Dodsley*

April 1937

Mr. John Ferguson's latest detective story centres round the murder of a Charing Cross Road bookseller whose body is found in the shop by a police officer in the early hours of the morning. As clues, all the police have to work on are three cigarette ends and two spent wooden matches found on the shop floor, and the fact that several books are out of position on the shelves. But although Mallet and Crabb of Scotland Yard deduce an astonishing amount from these clues it is when MacNab is called in to clear the first suspect that the case takes a new and unexpected turn. All the characters involved, from Members of Parliament to the bookshop's charwoman, are vividly presented, and as all the clues are fairly given, *Death of Mr. Dodsley* belongs to the type of story which offers the detective fan the opportunity of seeing just when and why the clues were misread. Mr. John Ferguson has written a particularly ingenious story, which poses a pretty problem for the reader.

### *Grouse Moor Mystery, The*

October 1934

A shooting accident on Keppoch Moor which was followed a few days later by the victim's death while alone, quickly resolves itself into what Francis McNab, the detective, found to be the stiffest problem he had ever faced. For the criminal had made none of those mistakes which are so helpful to a detective, and the detective is unaided by any of the intuitions or coincidences which are so helpful to an author. This story is, in consequence, a study in pure detection.

John Ferguson has written several mystery stories which have passed into numerous editions, but we believe it will be agreed that *The Grouse Moor Mystery* is the best detective story he has yet done.

### *Night in Glengyle*

October 1933

Alec Maitland returns from abroad down and out, till he meets a friend of his who happens to be an official in one of the chief Government offices and in need of a secret agent whose connection with the Ministry would not be suspected. Maitland accepts from him a commission to investigate certain strange happenings which threaten the safety of a British Crown Colony in Africa and to regain possession of certain papers which are found to be missing. Through an unfortunate incident arising out of his efforts to get on the track of these papers, he becomes the object of a hue and cry on the part of the police, who want him in connection with a sensational murder. His attempt to do his country an honourable service is made a great deal more difficult by having the minions of the law so close at his heels! A story of wits pitted against wits, of bloodshed, of hair-breadth escapes, of flight and pursuit, finishing with a piece of neat detection and a surprise both for the guileless Maitland and the reader.

### *Terror on the Island*

February 1942

Stories from the pen of this classic detective writer are all too rare. Many brilliant books have earned him wide popularity. *Terror on the Island* is a very gripping mystery, set first of all in Germany and later on the German-occupied island of Guernsey in the present war. The chief character is Allan Stewart, a British agent, and a rival to the famous Pimpernel himself. His duel with the Gestapo makes this one of the grandest and most exciting stories of the war.

OR

It is good to welcome again an exceptionally fine story by John Ferguson. Stories from the pen of this classic detective writer are all too rare. Such brilliant novels as *Stealthy Terror*, *The Man in the Dark* and *Death Comes to Perigord* have earned him wide popularity. *Terror on the Island* is an exceedingly gripping and well-told mystery, set first of all in Germany and later on the German-occupied island of Guernsey in the present war. We do not forget that one summer day in 1940, over one small portion of the British Empire the Swastika was hoisted. The symbol of all evil fluttered over those Channel Island beaches that once were crowded with carefree holidaymakers. It is a marvellous setting for a really hair-raising adventure; the chief character, Allan Stewart, a British agent, is a rival to the famous Pimpernel himself. His duel with the Gestapo makes this one of the grandest and most exciting novels of the war.

## FERRARS, ELIZABETH

### *Alibi for a Witch*

September 1952

If Lester Ballard had had any say in the matter he wouldn't have been seen dead in the cheap gabardine suit, the green cotton shirt, and the pointed brown suede shoes. But as he was dead, he had no control over such sartorial lapses. Ruth Seabright, governess to Lester's son Nicky, found his murdered body, and was as baffled by the incongruous attire as by the fact of murder itself. But that is only the first of many puzzles. Where, for instance, is Nicky? Who has been searching Ruth's bedroom? How can a corpse be in two places at once? Set beneath the dazzling azure skies and brilliant sun of a small seaside resort in Southern Italy, this exciting crime story is as baffling as it is entertaining.

### *Alive and Dead*

October 1974

Elizabeth Ferrars's fortieth crime novel is an occasion for rejoicing among her ever-growing readership, for it not only confirms her as one of the most skilled practitioners of the genre, but as one of fiction's most gifted and subtle portrayers of human relationships. The general reader will delight in her characters as much as the detective story addict will enjoy unravelling the situation in which they find themselves.

Martha Crayle worked for an association for unmarried mothers and thought she knew all their problems. But the blonde girl who strayed into her office one wet November afternoon posed a new one, for Amanda was pregnant but she was not unmarried. Therein lay the germ of a situation which was to involve Martha in a new and frightening world of crime.

Amanda's husband has been dead three years, or so everyone but Amanda insisted. But how could the same man be alive and dead? And what about the body recently discovered in the hotel opposite Martha's office? Were the police right in believing it was Amanda's husband and that she was a murderess? Or were others who knew Amanda right when they claimed quite sincerely that the girl was out of her mind? Only Martha seemed determined to befriend her, and Martha's devoted friend, Mr Syme. And Martha was soon in grave danger, for the truth behind Amanda's astonishing assertions was more bizarre than anyone could have guessed, and was to lead Martha to make a number of unexpected discoveries; not least discoveries about herself.

### *Always Say Die*

February 1956

Successful as her previous novels have been, Elizabeth Ferrars achieves a new level of mastery in *Always Say Die*. The story turns round the mysterious disappearance of Violet Gamlen who has inherited a house and fortune from her employer, Laurence Delborne, an elderly author. Why should she wish to leave the house? Could she have been removed against her will? Is she alive even? Both her own and Laurence Delborne's family have reasons for investigating her disappearance.

The excitement and suspense are such that the element of romance, although it quickens rather than relaxes the pace, is in striking contrast to the chilling creepiness that prevails through the rest of the story.

### Answer Came There None
November 1992

Sara Marriott was bewildered to return one day to the flat she had recently rented in the village of Edgewater and find a message on her answerphone which purported to be one half of a conversation. Not only did the woman's voice mean nothing to her, but how could this conversation about attending a party, trivial though it was, have taken place when an answerphone is unable to answer back?

Then, unexpectedly, Sara was invited by her landlady's son to a surprise party to celebrate his mother's eightieth birthday, and the telephone conversation acquired a curious significance when the old lady failed to appear for her party and was found dead in bed. But although a question-mark hung over her death, particularly in view of her announced intention to change her will in favour of her niece rather than her son, it was not until Sara discovered that the tape recording of the one-sided conversation had been removed from her answerphone that she became convinced of its sinister import.

Another death, this time indisputably murder, shocked the entire village. And even that was not the end …

### Beware of the Dog
March 1992

The dog was old and unappealing – which may have been why Virginia Freer decided to adopt him. That and the fact that he had belonged to her mother's old friend Helen Lovelock who had recently died.

The tensions evident among the mourners at Helen's funeral soon erupted, and before long one of them was dead, and so was the dog. The death was so convenient for the obvious suspect that the police could hardly be blamed for taking him into custody, but to Virginia it was all too pat, and when Mrs Lovelock's housekeeper begged her to call in Felix, her semi-detached husband who had a knack of sorting out such problems, she was only too glad to oblige. Between them, the Freers discovered that the death was convenient for several others who had been present at the funeral, but why should any of them poison the old dog?

Yet someone had – and therein lay the solution to the murder.

### Blood Flies Upwards
May 1976

The young woman who took the post of cook-housekeeper at the wealthy Eckersalls' weekend retreat was not all she appeared to be by any means. She was not separated from her husband, as she claimed, and desperate to earn her living; she was the sister of the previous cook-housekeeper who had allegedly run off with a boy-friend – a story Alison Goodrich found it hard to believe. She believed still less when she discovered that the boy-friend was still around appearing to be as worried as she was about Sally. There were other disquieting discoveries too. Gradually it emerged that the Eckersalls, their gardener and their secretary were no more what they seemed than Alison was herself. The more she probed, the more Alison became convinced that there was something sinister about Sally's disappearance, and the more impossible of solution the mystery seemed. Only when murder was committed did Alison at last discover with a vengeance the strange truth about her younger sister's fate.

Elizabeth Ferrars's widely acclaimed talent for mystery and penetrating characterization has never been better displayed than in this story of the loves, hates, jealousies and tensions within a tightly-know group of people caught in the toils of the past.

### Breath of Suspicion
May 1972

'I do like you,' the girl said. 'I like you enormously. We've never had anyone else come in here and tell us anything like this.'

The story that Richard Hedon had told her and the man who was calling himself Gavin Chilmark concerned a man named Paul Clyro, a scientist who had worked with another called Wolsingham at a research station in Sutherland, where they had been doing very secret work on viruses. But the security people had been closing in on Wolsingham, and he had known it, and one day he had taken his life in his laboratory by swallowing potassium cyanide.

'All that,' Richard said, 'got into the newspapers.'

Was it imagination that the face of the man before him had grown a little tauter than before?

Richard went on, 'Paul Clyro found the body. It must have been a fearful shock. Not just the shock of walking in on a corpse, but of discovering the kind of man he'd venerated, and being questioned and investigated and suspected himself. So it would seem he was driven half-mad, because one day he walked out of his house, leaving his wife expecting him home to lunch, and he's never been seen from that day to this.'

'But what put you on to the idea that I might be Clyro ?' asked the man known as Gavin Chilmark, whose two-year-old trail Richard had followed to a sunny village in Madeira, where the man was living a comfortable and contented life, free of any breath of suspicion …

### Busy Body, The
February 1962

Anne Lindsay knew very little about the man she had married; and now, only a week after the wedding, there came out of the past, and in a very curious guise, some frightening questions – what *was* he really? Had he in fact passed the years before his marriage only in the humdrum ways he claimed? What was his relationship to the dubious young man who looked so like him? Did they know as little about each other as appeared?

Anne's predicament was to become more menacing, the sequence of events more bewildering and ominous, before she discovered the truth.

This is a most satisfying crime novel, which moves at a great pace and is a fine successor to *The Sleeping Dogs*, maintaining the high reputation of Elizabeth Ferrars's most recent books for swift narrative and an agreeably challenging, mystifying plot.

### Clock That Wouldn't Stop, The
March 1952

Alex Summerill was the confidante of thousands of readers of the daily newspaper to which she contributed a weekly advice column. Her warm-hearted counsel went out all over England, to distracted lovers, women with faithless husbands, men with faithless wives, parents with difficult children, children with unaccommodating parents, young men wanting to find the perfect woman. Occasionally she received letters confessing to quite serious crimes. Realising what a perfect goldmine her correspondence could be for anyone with a slight leaning to blackmail, Alex took exceptional care of the letters

sent her by readers. But it was a letter which *didn't* reach her that precipitated murder. This is a blackmail story with a difference, told in inimitable fashion by the gifted Elizabeth Ferrars.

### Come and be Killed
June 1987

There was no one to meet Rachel Gairdner at Adelaide airport. Having inherited money she had come to Australia to visit her brother, her only surviving relative, but not only was he not at the airport, he was not at his lodgings either and his Greek landlord was evasive about his whereabouts. Accepting that her best course was to sleep off her jet-lag and wait for his return, Rachel woke to find she was alone in the house. Ian's landlord had also disappeared.

It was the beginning of a frightening series of events for Rachel, which soon included the knowledge that someone wanted her dead. Inexorably, she was drawn into the unhappy lives of her brother's employers, where the family was riven by suddenly discovered deceptions and a mysterious death occurred.

Alone in an alien environment, Rachel needed all her sharp wits, not to mention the support of the young doctor who had a habit of surfacing whenever she need him most.

Elizabeth Ferrars's sixtieth crime novel is sure to please her wide readership. She is a past mistress of the unobtrusive vital detail that surprises and delights.

### Crime and the Crystal, The
May 1985

Andrew Basnett, that endearing professor of botany who has discovered in retirement a talent for solving crime, decides to accept an invitation from a former student, Tony Gardiner, to spend Christmas with him and his newly wedded wife in Adelaide, where, so Andrew observes, he has heard more bizarre murders have happened than anywhere else in Australia. The remark provokes from Tony an uncharacteristically aggressive response.

Andrew could not have known that Jan Gardiner's first husband was the victim of such a crime, that the case is still unsolved, and that Jan is still a suspect. But when in the midst of celebrating Christmas on the beach someone else closely connected with Jan is murdered by identical means, Andrew cannot avoid being drawn into the little circle of family and close friends, among whom the police are convinced the murderer will be found.

And of course Andrew cannot avoid making his own observations and drawing certain conclusions which once again lead to the solving of the crimes.

Not since *The Small World of Murder* has Elizabeth Ferrars set a crime novel in Australia. Readers worldwide will welcome Andrew Basnett's foray into another continent, where his sharp eye for human foibles finds as much to occupy it as it has done nearer home in *Something Wicked* and *Root of All Evil*.

### Cup and the Lip, The
October 1975

For some men violence has a fascination. Max Rowley, a quiet solicitor, was one such, and he freely admitted to his school-friend, Peter Harkness, that he would like to associate with someone who had committed a violent crime. Harkness, a journalist and author, was not much interested. Neither man could have foreseen the effects of that conversation when they became involved in the mystery surrounding the distinguished novelist Daniel Braile.

The aged author was the head of a strange

household, consisting of wife, stepdaughter, and assorted literary hangers-on, among them Max Rowley's wife, a fellow novelist. Braile was also a very sick man who believed he was being poisoned. An invalid's fancy or the truth? And then, while most members of his household were attending a literary brains trust at which Peter Harkness was taking his place, Braile apparently sallied forth in pouring rain from his sick-bed and disappeared without trace.

### Danger From the Dead
July 1991

Wealthy novelist Annabel Astor lay dead in her drawing-room. She had suffered a stroke two years earlier and her death was not unexpected. But a gun lay near her hand, and in an adjoining room her younger half-sister, who had given up her acting career to help look after Annabel, sat bowed over the kitchen table, fatally shot through the head.

It seemed that Annabel had killed her sister and then collapsed from shock. Yet why were there no fingerprints on the gun? Who was the man seen driving off in a grey Mercedes about the time the sisters died? Why had Annabel's recent will specifically excluded her sister? Why had her brother-in-law Gavin been pleased to occupy their guest cottage for his summer holidays when he and his brother had never been close – certainly not as close as Gavin had once been to the dead actress? What is the role of their two quarrelsome sisters, who arrive unexpectedly?

These questions troubled Gavin. They troubled Inspector Frost too. The answers to them revealed complexities no one had suspected, and exposed a murderer.

Elizabeth Ferrars has published more than sixty crime novels. The craftsmanship of her latest shows why her popularity endures.

### Death of a Minor Character
April 1983

Virginia and Felix Freer, the separated but still semi-detached couple who have figured in several of Elizabeth Ferrars's recent novels, are both present at a party – Virginia because the hostess is an Australian friend returning home, Felix because he happens to live in the flat below hers. Among the guests are two or three connected with an antique-dealer and his wife who live near Virginia and whom she has come to know.

Within a couple of days both Virginia and Felix are involved with murder: Virginia in the small town in which she lives, Felix in London, when an insignificant fellow guest unconnected with anyone else at the party is found dead in an adjoining flat.

With his inclination to make mysteries about himself (what exactly is the nature of the new job he is so coy about?) and to unravel them when they concern other people, Felix is convinced that the murders must be linked. Before long Virginia's shifty, charming, light-fingered husband is caught up in something highly dangerous, and Elizabeth Ferrars is once again spinning a plot as inventive and ingenious as ever.

In 1981 Elizabeth Ferrars was honoured by the Crime Writers' Association with a Silver Dagger for her sustained excellence over fifty books.

### Designs on Life
January 1980

Elizabeth Ferrars is known to a wide public for her crime novels. She has written nearly fifty of them, they are translated into many languages, and their popularity has been further enhanced by frequent book club and paperback editions. What few of her readers realize is that Elizabeth Ferrars is also an accomplished short-story writer. *Designs on Life* provides the Crime Club with its first opportunity to make known this other aspect of her skill, and is a fitting tribute to its Golden Jubilee year.

The first story, 'The Dreadful Bell', is set in Edinburgh, where the author lives, and is published here for the first time. The remaining eight stories have appeared in magazines and anthologies, though most of them have been unavailable for many years. All of them have the freshness and originality which is the hall-mark of the classic short story. They are chilling, often grim, intricately plotted, and very, very good.

### Doubly Dead, The
May 1963

Margot Dalziel, successful journalist, was due at London Airport on Friday, returning from a conference abroad. On Saturday she was expected at her cottage in the country. But what really happened on Saturday? By Sunday it had become apparent that something had gone wrong. For some incomprehensible reason, the lady had vanished.

Margot's neighbours are soon swept into a web of mystery and suspicion. A violent – and apparently wanton – murder acts as a catalyst on people already taut with suspicion; although the villagers themselves are in no doubt who is the culprit.

The classical detective story provides an enthralling play of relationships between well-observed characters and a most ingenious device by which the murder *may* be detected.

### Drowned Rat
March 1975

*'It happened so fast, the cry, the splash, the flailing of strong arms across the still water to what lay sprawled at the bottom of the pool that Catherine Gifford was afterwards never certain that she answered as truthfully as she might the questions that were put to her. Had she or had she not seen anyone among the trees?'*

It mattered because it seemed clear that someone was out to kill Douglas Cable, recently returned from Australia to inherit Havershaw and its newly built pool. His return had meant that his cousin's wife and her daughter were no longer in charge of the beautiful house they loved. It also brought into their lives, and into the life of local doctor's daughter Catherine Gifford, two more Australians, one an artist of talent, one an enigmatic character who asked questions about the others that kept the village guessing.

Catherine unwittingly acts as a catalyst in this situation, which a sense of responsibility leads her to try and resolve, not least a sense of responsibility towards Frances Knox, the elderly eccentric whom many in the village dismiss as insignificant, but whose insight is sharper than others' logic and proves unexpectedly dangerous.

Elizabeth Ferrars is one of the leading names in crime fiction and her popularity grows with every book. Readers all over the world will enjoy her latest, which once again demonstrates her interest in 'the small world of murder' – a phrase she used as the title of a recent and highly successful book.

### Enough to Kill a Horse
July 1955

Fanny Lynam's party was awkward to arrange. Her old friend, Clare Forwood, wasn't eager to come, although she had particularly asked to meet Sir Peter Poulter, the newspaper tycoon, who had already accepted. Then there was the risk that Tom Mordue would quarrel with everyone. And

worst of all, Fanny was very nervous of the smart young widow, Laura Greenslade, who had just become engaged to her half-brother, Kit Raven. What did Laura want with Kit, Fanny wondered? Was it true that there was something mysterious about Laura – something peculiar? At any rate, Fanny knew that her speciality – lobster patties– would help to make the party a success. But in Elizabeth Ferrars's new detective story an ingenious plot is based on the actions of a small group of characters one can believe in, and the story, intriguing, exciting, and cunningly told, is as gripping as its predecessors.

### Experiment With Death
June 1981

The apples studied at the Institute of Pomology at King's Weltham did not normally include the Apple of Discord. But Sam Partlett seemed to have brought it with him when he joined the staff. Apart from the noses he put out of joint, there was the matter of his unfortunate personality. And his even more unfortunate treatment of his wife, who seemed afraid of him. Dr Emma Ritchie, also on on the staff of the Institute, soon had reason to regret allowing herself to be manipulated into giving the Partletts a home in her vacant flat.

But it was not Sam Partlett who was found dead at the Institute, throat slashed with one of the lab razors, while an unknown woman screamed in the doorway and a bloodstained colleague stood by, weapon in hand.

The small, close-knit scientific community was suddenly opened up as neatly as the victim's throat to the scrutiny of Inspector Day, who quietly set to work to probe the secrets of people who were, as one of them put it, 'as busy as bees with every sort of experiment, yet the one thing we don't think of investigating is the ultimate question.'

Had someone at last carried out an experiment with death?

### Fear the Light
May 1960

Alice Robinson was now too old and frail to cope with the stairs. But when Charles Robertson, paying a long overdue visit to his aunt, returned from an evening stroll he found that something had made her tackle them once more. The result had not only been tragic; after one look Charles sent for the police. There were very few people who could have had a motive for the old lady's death and Inspector Long was openly sceptical of the idea of murder. But then a rumour spread that in the house, forgotten for generations, were objects which had belonged to the first James Robertson. After two hundred years, it seemed, someone had rediscovered them; someone had recognised their value; someone had been prepared to kill to get them.

*Fear the Light* is a gripping and believable story which fully maintains the position which Elizabeth Ferrars occupies in the front rank of detective story writers.

### Foot in the Grave
January 1973

Life for Henry and Christine Findon was quiet, comfortable and uneventful. There were just the two of them and their housekeeper, Mrs Heacham, in the large house they had bought with a legacy from Henry's father. Then suddenly they were invaded by visitors: the two children of Christine's sister, plus an au pair to look after them; Mrs Heacham's long-lost son Lew, who received a far from joyous welcome from his mother; and an old school friend of Christine's, Vivien Richmond, an expert on historical footwear, who had come to address a local cultural society on this subject.

With such a houseful of people, Christine had the feeling that something was bound to go wrong. And sure enough, it did: as they were all preparing to leave for the talk and the dinner preceding it, Vivien announced that someone had taken the left shoe of every pair she had brought with her. It had all the makings of a practical joke, and the children seemed the natural suspects. Yet they hotly denied Vivien's accusations. If they were telling the truth, then who was the culprit?

Next morning there was more than just a practical joke to be answered for. One of the household was found in the storeroom – murdered. And that's when the suspicions and accusations really began.

According to the *Sunday Times*, 'there are few detective story writers as consistently good as Miss Ferrars.' This guarantee of satisfaction is amply fulfilled by her latest.

### Frog in the Throat
November 1980

When Virginia Freer went to spend a weekend with her friends the Boscotts the last person she expected to meet was the lying, light-fingered charmer who was her husband. She and Felix had been separated for several years.

And the last thing she expected to encounter was murder. Yet within a few hours of the party given to celebrate the engagement of a local poet and best-selling historical novelist, the novelist's sister arrived distraught on the Boscotts' doorstep to announce that she had found her shot dead in their bungalow next door.

But when Virginia, Felix and the Boscotts reached the scene they found that something very strange had happened to the corpse…

So begins a deftly-plotted mystery involving a group of people whose relationships reach far back into the past. It is Felix, with his intuitive perception of human frailties heightened by his wry awareness of his own, who eventually uncovers the motive and the murderer, with the same adroitness that he displayed in *Last Will and Testament*, in which he made his debut.

### Furnished for Murder
July 1957

Meg Jeacock wanted to let the furnished cottage next to her house – wanted, too, to show her husband Marcus, who was opposed to the whole idea, that she could do so profitably. So she did not care to face the fact that her new tenant had certain rather sinister characteristics.

When Marcus heard of him he said that any man who would pay three months in advance for the cottage was a crook… And when the stranger showed an inexplicable interest in Shandon Priory, the big house nearby, whose owner, an old lady, had recently died, it became clear to others besides Marcus that there was trouble brewing. When it came it took the form of a double murder.

Once again Elizabeth Ferrars demonstrates her mastery of the craft of the detective story in a book that is exciting, ingenious and above all convincing; the characters are real and interesting people.

### Hanged Man's House
January 1974

Dr Charles Gair was found hanged, but that was not what had killed him. This was the first of the bizarre surprises awaiting those who penetrated the home of the head of the Martindale research establishment on a Sunday morning to see what was amiss. Even more startling was the discovery in the house of a second body – perfectly mummified.

When the mummy was identified, the

mystery deepened. What has this foreign visitor, missing for more than a year, to do with the Martindale? Unless he had some connection with the attractive wife of the administrative officer who, like Gair's wife, had left her husband but still wrote occasionally from distant corners of the world.

Dr Gair travelled frequently, yet his passport was missing. This was only one of the problems Superintendent Patrick Dunn has to face as he delved deeper into the lives of those connected with the Martindale – and found himself with another body on his hands.

### Hobby of Murder, A
January 1994

When retired Botany professor, Andrew Basnett, goes to stay with old friends in a sleepy English village, his biggest problem seems to be what to do with the time he now finds on his hands; for Andrew has just finished the book he has been working on for many years. Everyone else seems to have a hobby of some kind – perhaps he should acquire one too.

But Andrew is soon faced with more pressing worries as he discovers that things are not what they seem: his hosts' once happy marriage now seems to be on the verge of collapse; a quaint local dinner party with a theme goes horribly wrong when one of the guests dies at the table. It doesn't look like natural causes, and there are no shortage of suspects, some of whom have motives more obscure than others…

As suspicion shifts, and Andrew finds himself discussing the case with the police, an already complicated situation starts to spiral out of control as the first death is followed by a second, and then a third… Every time Andrew feels he is starting to get an insight into the murders, the pattern changes, until he finally begins to unravel the dark secret at the heart of it all, and realizes why someone has made a hobby of murder.

### Hunt the Tortoise
January 1950

La Marette seemed just as Celia Kent remembered it, allowing for the inevitable changes made by the war – an unfashionable little seaside village in the South of France basking in the brilliant Mediterranean sunshine, depending for its existence on the swarm of little boats that bobbed on the blue waters of the harbour in the bay. But there were subtle changes apparent at the Hotel Bienvenu. In spite of its summer visitors, the holiday spirit was conspicuously absent, in its place a feeling of unease, an atmosphere of tension that mounted rapidly, and culminated, almost inevitably it seemed, in murder. Against the fragrant background of pine, tamarisk and rosemary, Elizabeth Ferrars has written a crime story of distinction, peopled with characters that really live.

### I Met Murder
December 1985

Whenever Felix, the light-fingered husband from whom Virginia Freer was semi-detached, reappeared in her life, it seemed that murder did too. Even when temporarily incapacitated by a pavement encounter with a child cyclist, Felix brought mystery with him. This time it concerned Holly, orphaned daughter of a famous actress, who had come from Rome to stay with Virginia's friends, the Brightwells. For Holly disappeared, believed kidnapped, and distraught Ann Brightwell was prepared to sell her valuables to meet the ransom demand.

But there was something odd about the kidnapping and Felix was convinced the ransom should not be paid. The discovery of a girl's body served only to deepen the mystery, as Virginia sadly accepted that she was once again involved with murder.

It was Felix who discerned what had really been going on in quiet Allingford, identified the guilty, and taught a famous crime novelist that fact and fiction are two very different things.

Elizabeth Ferrars's many readers will need no encouragement to embark on her latest novel which lives up to the standard they have rightly come to expect from an author awarded the Silver Dagger of the Crime Writers' Association for her continued excellence.

### *In at the Kill*
November 1978

Charlotte had her own good reasons for taking the furnished cottage on Edgar Frensham's estate. She wanted to be alone, and she was not prepared to be responsive to the young man who tried to engage her in conversation on the train. But she was only too anxious to see again the man who had rented her the cottage, and on that first evening she called at Edgar Frensham's house. His housekeeper, very different from what Charlotte had expected, let her in, but she did not see her landlord. He was out, the scared-looking housekeeper said. Half an hour later Charlotte learned to her horror that Edgar Frensham was dead.

He must have been shot dead in his drawing-room at just about the time that Charlotte had been ringing at the front door, and the 'housekeeper', now revealed as someone very different, had vanished without trace. As the only person to have seen her at the scene of the crime, or even to have been at the house, apart from old Mrs Frensham, who was incapacitated after a stroke, Charlotte was an object of interest to the police – perhaps to others. Certainly to the enigmatic young man she had met so fortuitously, who now turned out to be making enquiries of his own.

Whom could Charlotte trust among her strange assortment of fellow tenants? What motive lay behind Frensham's murder and a second, subsequent death? Elizabeth Ferrars knows better than anyone how to spin out suspense by means of skilful characterization while keeping the reader guessing till the end.

### *Last Will and Testament*
May 1978

As soon as Virginia Freer opened her front door and caught a whiff of cigarette smoke, she knew who was in the house: Felix, the charming, lying, light-fingered con-man husband whom she never mentioned. They have lived apart for five years.

He had come, as usual, for money, but Virginia was too preoccupied to mind. The death of an elderly friend was posing problems, for there was something suspicious about her will. She had had a penchant for changing wills, and the bequests in her last one were surprising – but was it actually her last? The question became acute when Virginia learned that the money bequeathed to her was non-existent. And then the most valuable remaining legacy vanished. And three people died violently.

The relationships of those connected with the testator were complicated, their motives equally so. Any one of them might have committed the first murder, but why had two other people died? In the midst of so much that was unexpected, Virginia found it easy to accept that Felix could be unusually astute. She even began to find it easy to accept Felix…

The tensions of a personal relationship are cleverly interwoven with the suspense of a crime novel in this latest example of Elizabeth Ferrars's skill.

### *Legal Fiction, A*
January 1964

When they were children together they had derisively called the painting the 'Decayed Gentlewoman'. Later the memory of it remained vivid, a childhood recollection. The picture itself had meanwhile disappeared, an event to which no one attached any special importance.

But the 'Decayed Gentlewoman' re-entered their gown-up lives with a bang. The manner of its reappearance sparked a train of suspicion about the true nature of past events, sharply confronting young Dr. Colin Locke with the question: Who could be trusted? Could he trust even the girl he had known and played with when they were children? Unless the 'Decayed Gentlewoman' was a great deal more valuable than anyone had ever supposed, what was all the fuss about?

The painting is the cause of a murder, and also of research into a question of ownership, made bizarre and intricate by an archaic law. The pronouncements of various solicitors on this question provide a kind of humorous, light accompaniment to the very gripping and unusual narrative.

Elizabeth Ferrars is at the top of her form with a story as ingenious and thrilling as *The Sleeping Dogs*.

### *Lying Voices, The*
June 1954

The Lying Voices were the clocks: the clocks that filled the room where Arnold Thaine was killed; that 'ticked in a hundred different rhythms, loudly and softly, on high or low notes...one thing all the clocks had in common. Every single one in that room, big or little, shabby or splendid, grotesque or beautiful, was wrong.' So the fact that a bullet from the gun that killed Thaine had broken and stopped a clock gave no pointer to the time of his murder. Justin Emery had come to Archersfield on the day of Thaine's death to visit a very old friend, Grace Delong. Grace, he found, knew the Thaines well, and had been to visit Thaine that morning – and perhaps also later, during the afternoon when Thaine was killed. Had Grace been the woman in the brown mackintosh who had been seen to enter Thaine's study near the time of his death? Who were the other two visitors? Was anything to be learnt from the broken clock? And how had Lewis Brillhart's dog come to be shut into Thaine's house that very afternoon? These are only some of the puzzling questions to which Elizabeth Ferrars produces brilliantly satisfactory answers in this entertaining and ingenious story.

### *March Hare Murders, The*
March 1949

An Elizabeth Ferrars novel is always particularly satisfying and stimulating. This clever writer is not primarily concerned with presenting the reader with a pretty problem, although her plot is ingeniously worked out. She is more interested in the 'why and wherefore' than the 'how'. To-day, so many seemingly ordinary people have been unbalanced by war and its aftermath and have lost their normal standards of behaviour. They have become unstable, losing all feelings of security. From their sick minds spring strange fantasies and irresistible desires, sometimes even the desire to kill. It is of such people that Miss Ferrars writes, plumbing their minds with an uncanny precision that lifts her story to heights far above the ordinary murder mystery.

### *Milk of Human Kindness*
July 1950

There is a peculiar insistence about the ringing of a door-bell that few people can resist. Say to yourself that it is only a crashing bore from the next flat, nevertheless some inner compulsion in the end will bring your unwilling feet to the door. So it was with Marabelle that September Sunday morning. It *might* be Peter Frere, and he could help her with the decorating she was trying to do while John was in Holland. But it was her sister, the beautiful, immaculate, and entirely self-centred Susan, who had come to command a favour. Marabelle thought afterwards if only she had not gone to the door that morning it would have saved a great deal of trouble and disturbance – and perhaps might have saved a life. Ingenious, intriguing and utterly absorbing in its revelation of human weaknesses and passions, *Milk of Human Kindness* is a first-rate crime story.

### *Murder Among Friends*
May 1946

Cecily Lightwood was giving a party to her friends, mainly drawn from the literary and artistic world in which the clever and talented Cecily moved. That night she was looking particularly radiant as she received her guests. But somehow the party didn't seem complete. It was in danger indeed of falling rather flat. And all because of the absence of one man. Aubrey Ritter, the playwright, was Cecily's nearest neighbour, actually occupying the flat above. Where was Aubrey, who should have been the lion of the evening? *Murder Among Friends* is a distinguished mystery story excellently told by Miss Elizabeth Ferrars, whose previous successes have earned her a deservedly high reputation. She excels in the portrayal of her carefully observed characters, her racy dialogue, and not least in the ingenuity of her solution.

### *Murder in Time*
May 1953

Nothing could sound more innocently gay – or fantastically extravagant – than a flight on a specially chartered plane for a week-end in Nice. But most of the nine people whom Mark Auty invited suspected some sinister intention. Why, then, did they accept? For accept they did, coming from such far-removed places as a pub on the edge of Dartmoor, a Bloomsbury hotel, a quiet Oxfordshire village, a Soho night-club, to gather for the journey in Mark's Surrey home. Why Mark really asked them and why they accepted are questions that are only answered in full after murder has intervened. *Murder in Time* has that touch of the bizarre which characterizes all Miss Ferrars' work. This is one of her most successful and intriguing stories.

### *Murder Moves In*
October 1956

Moving house is always an exasperating business, especially as everything usually seems to go wrong. But Robina Melanby was perfectly able to cope, in her cheerful and slapdash way, with the ordinary exigencies of the move. Her real anxieties were rooted much deeper; it might prove to be folly to have moved so near to the home of Martha Birch, with whom Sam Melanby had once been in love; Martha's husband, at least, seemed very uneasy about it. Robina found out, too, that there had been a good deal of gossip about an old man who had been run down and killed nearby by a car that did not stop…

When another victim dies in circumstances that left no doubt that this time it was murder, the move to a new house became a transposition into a world of nightmare. For in the aftermath of murder, Robina found the whole structure of her existence threatened.

In this masterly story of great subtlety, Elizabeth Ferrars has once again created a plot that will baffle by its ingenuity and will hold the reader to its exciting climax.

### *Murder Too Many, A*
July 1988

Andrew Basnett hadn't wanted to go back to Knotlington where he had once been a young assistant lecturer. The retired, distinguished Professor of Botany was only attending a conference there because an old friend had urged him to do so and had hinted that he needed advice. It turned out that what perturbed him was a past scandal, for two years earlier a member of the Fine Arts Department had been murdered. Yet his killer had been caught and sentenced, so why should Andrew's friend need advice?

The murdered man's interest in other people's wives was well known and several people had motives, including Stephen Sharland, now serving a life sentence for his death. The trouble was that there were those, including Andrew's friend and the murdered man's widow, who believed Sharland innocent. Perhaps Andrew, who had been involved with murder on other occasions, could help them?

Before Andrew could begin making enquiries there was another murder, the victim a key witness in the earlier case. Soon Andrew was drawn into a web of complex emotions and struggling to sift truth from lies.

Elizabeth Ferrars's skill in depicting human relationships has delighted her readers for more than sixty books. Here she is at her best in the small, closed world of academics which she knows well at first hand.

### *Murders Anonymous*
October 1977

Professor Matthew Tierney had a perfect alibi for the time of his young wife's murder: he was lunching in a pub with his brother-ion-law. It was when he received an anonymous telephone call suggesting that the alibi had been bought and paid for, that his troubles really began.

For Matthew had a motive for murder: he believed his wife was having an affair. Although the police were apparently satisfied that he could not help them with their enquiries, it seemed a good idea to take refuge with his sister and her husband in their cottage on the south coast. But it was while staying with them that his wife had met the man Matthew suspected of being her lover, and he still lived near by, one thread in a complex web of human relationships in which Matthew was rapidly enmeshed. Yet he never suspected the identity or motives of the web-spinner until one dark night on the cliffs…

Elizabeth Ferrars's acute psychological perception and intricate plotting once again combine in a crime novel of highest quality.

### *Ninth Life*
January 1965

When Caroline left hospital her sister Fenella insisted that she must convalesce in Fenella's house in the West Country. It would be a chance, as Fenella emphasised, to get to know the husband Fenella had recently married. And it would be restful in the old house at Dexter Abbas.

But in the event Caroline's visit was far from restful. Fenella's husband was moody, excitable, reckless in talk and inexplicably affluent. He was a surprising man for Fenella to have married.

The brooding atmosphere explodes into violence and death. Miss Ferrars achieves a high suspense, not by fireworks or bloodbaths, but by the precise observation of character and mood, and by her skill in surprising the reader at the climax.

## No Peace for the Wicked
May 1966

'It's the same man,' Antonia said to herself. 'I'm sure it is – or am I going mad?' The young man was down at heel and looked rather shoddy. And *unless* Antonia was going mad there could be no doubt that he was following her on her harmless chores round London.

Antonia had a clear conscience. So *why* should anyone follow her? Could he be a sex maniac? At any rate she would be off in two days for her annual holiday on a remote Greek island. There she would find absolute peace and quiet.

In the event things were to turn out quite differently from what Antonia had expected. She reached her warm and scented island – but what she found there was far from peace and quiet.

Elizabeth Ferrars has repeatedly shown herself to be a master of the novel of suspense that is based on good writing, precise observation of character, and ingenious plotting. She has written nothing better than *No Peace for the Wicked*. From the fear that first grips Antonia when she notices the man following her, to the astounding and bloody developments on her Greek island, the novel grips, intrigues and thrills the reader.

## Other Devil's Name, The
August 1986

It was with a sense of resignation that Andrew Basnett, retired botany professor, accompanied an old friend to her home in a Berkshire village because her sister has received a blackmail letter. The letter had obviously been put in the wrong envelope, but it seemed to indicate that a murder had been committed in Lindleham, where, strangely, several people were missing from their homes.

Had the old man really gone to visit his son in Australia? Was the little boy who had run away still alive? Had the doctor's wife walked out on him, as he reported? What had happened to the businessman who failed to return from his mysterious work in the City and whom his wife believed to be working for MI5?

Quietly Andrew investigates his friends' neighbours and discovers situations of deepening complexity. Not the least disconcerting is the dawning realization that his friends too have something to hide.

Elizabeth Ferrars is a mistress of mystification and shrewd observation. Both talents are employed with her usual skill in this latest addition to her considerable oeuvre.

## Pretty Pink Shroud, The
April 1977

The pretty pink Edwardian dress that Leila Guest had worn to a fancy-dress ball turned up next morning, blood-stained and bullet-torn, in a bundle of clothes for the local charity shop. And Leila herself, young and pretty second wife of Sir Edward Guest, the retired vice-chancellor of a university, was mysteriously missing from her home.

But Elizabeth Ferrars is far too wily to disappoint her readers with so obvious a solution. Awkward questions soon arose. How did the pink dress come to be included with Leila's cast-off clothing which had been collected the day before the ball? Where was Sir Edward's ex-brother-in-law, who had apparently disappeared at the same time as Leila? Were the two disappearances connected? Who was responsible for the petty thefts from the Guests' bungalow which had been puzzling them for months?

There can be few less likely sleuths than middle-aged Ruth Winter, laid low with a bout of 'flu. Yet even though she had the assistance of her daughter and her daughter's fiancé, a

detective inspector, it was Ruth's knowledge of character and her careful deductions that brought a murderer to book.

Elizabeth Ferrars has once again produced a skilfully plotted story guaranteed to baffle and intrigue.

## Root of All Evil
August 1984

Andrew Basnett, retired professor of botany, never supposed that accepting aged Cousin Felicity's invitation to stay with her in her Berkshire home over Easter would force him to turn detective.

But the reappearance of a former housekeeper in Felicity's vicinity (and her equally sudden disappearance from it) create a mystery which intrigues Basnett, even though it is dismissed by Felicity's relatives when they arrive for a family party. In any case, events at that party soon give them other things to think about – as they do Basnett, who now finds himself investigating a murder with all too many suspects and apparently just one motive: money.

Andrew Basnett's last sojourn in Berkshire, chronicled in *Something Wicked*, established him as a character whom Elizabeth Ferrars's vast and growing readership will be delighted to meet again.

## Seven Sleepers, The
May 1970

If evidence seems about to come to light that the late Professor Garvie-Brown of Edinburgh University had murdered seven wives, four of whom he had married bigamously, enriching himself by each marriage and dying regarded by his colleagues as a wonderful old man, what ought his descendants to do about it? What, particularly, ought they to do when the professor's eighth wife, who, astonishingly survived him, shows signs of developing a conscience and of feeling that they should all do something for an obscure young man in London called Luke Latimer, who, she has discovered, is the sole surviving grandson of one of the bigamous wives?

Luke himself wants nobody to do anything for him. He is in a job that he likes and he wants to be left in peace to get on with it. He has not the slightest inclination to blackmail or in any way to bother his wealthy relations, among whom are a High Court judge, a doctor and another professor. But how are they to be sure of that? They only know that if the truth were to become publicly known, they would all be ruined.

Their fears of this, their fears of what Luke perhaps might do to them, together with the devious activities of a certain private detective, Gilbert Arne, draw Luke helplessly to Edinburgh, into their lives and their problems, and to the scene of an eighth murder.

Elizabeth Ferrars has never displayed to better effect her well-known skill in characterisation and suspense.

## Skeleton in Search of a Cupboard
August 1982

The luncheon-party in honour of Henrietta Cosgrove's eightieth birthday had gone very well. Her five stepchildren had gathered to celebrate in her lovely old thatched house and to enjoy the food prepared by Freda, the narrator/wife of one of them. Suddenly Henrietta dropped a bombshell.

To shore up her dwindling income, she proposed to have valued, with a view to selling, two landscapes by a painter whose work had recently appreciated. The more practical suggestion that she should sell the over-large house instead threw the Cosgroves into confusion, for it was a suggestion to which several of them were violently opposed.

That night the house burned down. Henrietta was rescued, but it was clear that an arsonist had been at work. When the pictures were found to be missing, it looked as though the fire was intended to cover the theft.

But what the fire uncovered was far more dramatic, for some at least of the Cosgroves were aware of what the cottage walls concealed. Riven by the pull of old loyalties and new alliances, they have soon to contend with murder in their midst as Elizabeth Ferrars unravels her skilfully twisted tale.

## Skeleton Staff
September 1969

*Skeleton Staff* is set in Madeira, where wealthy Roberta Ellison and her husband had settled after Roberta had been crippled in a motor accident. The attractions of the island were its beauty, its climate and the ease with which domestic help could be found. But when Roberta is suddenly left widowed, she finds that her staff problems have only just begun. She longs for the company of another Englishwoman and her young half-sister, Camilla, comes out to help find her a companion. But Camilla brings problems of her own with her, problems which at first seem trivial, but which soon involve the sisters in violent and mystifying events which lead up to murder.

When it comes to creating a good crime novel, few authors can beat Miss Ferrars. Plot, background, characterization and suspense are blended here in expert fashion to make this one of the most satisfying of her books.

## Sleep of the Unjust
August 1990

The marriage table looked like furnishing the funeral baked meats when Hollywood actor Andrew Appleyard, in England for the wedding of his cousin and former fiancée, inexplicably committed suicide. More inexplicably still, he left two conflicting suicide notes and the fragment of a third in another hand. In the confusion, an unknown woman walked in and stole a valuable wedding gift.

Virginia Freer, one of the wedding guests together with her semi-detached husband Felix, had seldom been faced with a more distressing puzzle, particularly when it appeared that the dead Andrew might himself have been murderously included. But it took Felix to work out that the roots of the tragedy lay deep in the past and that an exceptionally calculating and cold-blooded killer was at work.

## Sleeping Dogs, The
September 1960

The acquittal of Teresa Swale from a charge of murder had been a nine-day wonder. Elspeth Marris's brother-in-law had been commissioned to 'ghost' the Swale story for the Press. The typescript was completed and only needed Teresa's signature of approval when Bernard went down with pneumonia. That was why Elspeth found herself on the doorstep of a squalid boarding house in Bloomsbury enquiring for the whereabouts of a woman with doubtful morals and a sensational past, and who turned out to be oddly elusive. In the search for her that followed, Elspeth was soon to learn that she was not the only one who was in a hurry to find the elusive Teresa and that it could be a dangerous and frightening thing to become involved in the aftermath of an unsolved murder.

Elizabeth Ferrars, acknowledged as one of the best of to-day's crime writers, has given *The Sleeping Dogs* a fascinating cast of acutely observed and believable characters, a fast-moving and exciting plot and a mystery which will keep the most experienced reader of crime guessing to the last pages.

## Small World of Murder, The
July 1973

It was not the happiest of journeys to the other side of the world for a family Christmas. Nina Hemslow knew that when she accepted the invitation to join her wealthy friends Nicola and Jocelyn Foley, for the Foleys had recently lost their only child – a daughter who vanished without trace from her pram outside a supermarket, and whom police and parents were convinced was dead.

Moreover the Foley's marriage was on the rocks, and Nina was reluctantly drawn into their mutual suspicions and recriminations, with each accusing the other of desiring the partner's death. And at the winery, where they stayed with Jocelyn's brother and his employer's family, things were also difficult, not least when Nina found her own emotions becoming involved.

Yet when sudden death occurred in the midst of an Australian Christmas, with turkey and plum pudding in a temperature of ninety degrees, it posed some very curious problems. Their unravelling, and the dramatic solution in London show Elizabeth Ferrars at her best.

## Smoke Without Fire
April 1990

Andrew Basnett, retired Professor of Botany, did not care for Christmas, not for him the holly and the ivy, the turkey and trimmings. He preferred to spend it with like-minded friends, the Cahills, in the peace of their country home.

But peace and goodwill were not to be. The day before Christmas Eve their neighbour, Sir Lucas Dearden, QC (retired), was blown up by a bomb. There were many who had it in for him, and one suspicious character had even enquired at the Cahills'. But Sir Lucas had intended spending Christmas with his married daughter in London and had changed his plans at the last minute only because she had been involved in an accident; no one knew he was returning to Berkshire. Had the bomb been meant for someone else?

Andrew found himself caught up in the complex relationships of the QC's family and Jonathan Cahill. When one of them was also murdered, it posed a number of questions. Whose account of their relationships was to be believed? And why had Sir Lucas so carefully destroyed one page of his memoirs?

By the time Andrew returned thankfully to London, he had the answers to all his questions – and rather wished that he hadn't.

## Something Wicked
October 1983

When Andrew Basnett, retired professor of botany, took his nephew's cottage in a quiet Oxfordshire village for the winter, he didn't expect to find himself living opposite a woman locally reputed to have killed her husband, even though an unbreakable alibi meant she had never been brought to trial. Nor did he expect to find himself cut off from all mains services as the result of a blizzard. And he certainly didn't expect to discover in his cold, dark living-room the body of the village's second murder victim.

Naturally suspicion centred on the 'murderess', and the police investigation, though hampered by snow, leaned heavily in her direction. But there were so many factors still unexplained about the first murder, so many dark secrets, such an atmosphere of evil within the village community, that Andrew Basnett was soon well on the way to becoming a detective. And that was something he hadn't expected either.

Few crime writers know better than Elizabeth Ferrars how to tell a tale guaranteed to keep the reader intrigued throughout and satisfactorily surprised at the end.

### *Stranger and Afraid, A*
April 1971
Holly Dunthorne remembers Marcus Meriden, brother of her best friend Kate, as a nice child, not at all likely to grow up to be the sort of young man who would beat up a harmless old man. Yet when Holly returns to the village of Roydon Saint Agnes, which had once been her home and where the Meridens live, she finds that this is the crime with which Marcus has been charged. There are witnesses to say they saw it happen, and the only witness who might possibly clear him stays stubbornly silent. The Meridens, who had always seemed to Holly the most united of families, are sharply divided as to Marcus's guilt.

When murder happens, understanding of his character, with his record of violence, is vital to the solution of the puzzle. So is that of a newcomer to the village, the controversial Lisa Chard, a successful dramatist whose influence seems to be affecting everyone there. Whatever the truth, Holly finds everything in the village changed, not least her old friends, the Meridens, among whom she feels herself a stranger – and afraid.

### *Swaying Pillars, The*
September 1968
The merest chance presented Helena Sebright with a three-month job in the newly independent African state of Uyowa. She was to escort a seven-year-old girl on the journey to stay with her grandparents who lived there; and to bring her back to her parents in England at the end.

It seemed a lucky break. Helena was not to know that she would become involved in a criminal enterprise. And this dangerous game was to be played against the background of a disintegrating state, with guns on the streets and bloody revolution imminent.

This well written novel gives us a beautifully observed and exciting picture of Africa as Helena sees it: an account of events both thrilling and ominous; a very acute involvement with the catastrophe that is swaying the pillars of authority and order in the new state; several gruesome deaths; and the fine standard of detailed characterisation for which Elizabeth Ferrars is celebrated, all dovetailing into an enthralling whole.

### *Tale of Two Murders, A*
April 1959
Hilda Gazeley was set in her humdrum existence as housekeeper to her solicitor brother Stephen and thought she was satisfied with it. She liked the attractive, inconvenient house. She was fond of Katherine, her niece, to whom she had acted as mother. It entertained her to sit in the garden and speculate about the strange woman who walked the river bank at sunset. But murder and the facts which came to light afterwards, changed everything that she had accepted for years, and made her ask herself desperately how she could have been so complacently blind to what had been happening around her.

Miss Gazeley didn't much care for Inspector Crankshaw, who was in charge of the case, but she was unusually impressed by him and told him all she could – and then conscientiously worried because she felt that somehow, somewhere she had misled him. She was sure that something she had seen, or done, or said was virtually wrong. But what? In *A Tale of Two Murders* Elizabeth Ferrars has combined a baffling problem with a setting which seems absolutely real and convincing and has again achieved the high standard which, after books like *Enough to Kill a Horse* and *Unreasonable Doubt*, her readers have come to expect.

### *Thinner Than Water*
December 1981
Virginia Freer and her husband Felix had been witnesses at Gavin Brownlow's wedding. Both marriages had since foundered, and now Gavin was marrying again. He had left London, joined his father in his architectural practice in the Midlands, and his new bride was the girl next door. At his request, Virginia and Felix agreed to witness the second ceremony also, even though they were now living apart. It was perhaps unconventional, but it was nothing to the startling developments that were to come.

The Freers returned from the reception to find themselves involved in murder, not to mention corruption in local government and burglary. A seemingly simple case revealed layer upon layer of complexity, and before long there was another death. Virginia's narrative and Felix's intuitive investigation take the reader into the darker recesses of two families, to reach a conclusion as ironic as it is unexpected.

Elizabeth Ferrars was recently given a special Silver Dagger by the Crime Writers Association in recognition of her continued excellence over more than fifty books.

### *Thy Brother Death*
June 1993
The letter from a woman in Aberdeen demanding maintenance from her husband and threatening court action if it was not forthcoming was simply addressed to 'Professor Carey, Knotlington University.' To the snide amusement of his colleagues, it ended on the desk of Dr. Patrick Casey, senior lecturer in Biochemistry, and a happily married man.

Patrick's first thought was that it must have something to do with his unstable brother, David, and he feared trouble.

Trouble duly arrived when the woman turned up on his doorstep. Someone in the department must have given her his address. But who disliked him and his wife enough to cause such embarrassment? And who hated this mystery woman so much that she died in a locked room in a house that had been deliberately fired?

Suspicion swirled around Patrick, for his colleagues and the police were beginning to question the existence of this convenient brother whom no one but Patrick and his wife have ever seen. They were also beginning to question whether the mystery woman was the arsonist's intended victim.

### *Trial by Fury*
January 1989
Widowed Constance Lawley rather enjoyed taking occasional domestic jobs to help out in other people's family crises. She enjoyed the beginning of the week she spent with Colonel Barrow, whose wife was recovering from an operation, and she was intrigued by their grandson, a strange brilliant, unpredictable teenager. But she had not bargained for the dramatic increase which occurred in the family's crises, nor that these would end in bloodshed.

The police regarded it as an open-and-shut case – until another body turned up to invalidate all their theories. In spite of herself Constance began to probe a little more deeply into the Barrow's relationships and those of others in the village where they lived. What she uncovered was as unexpected as the extra body, but with her daughter's help she began to make sense of it and to realize that the crime was far more complex than anyone had thought.

### *Unreasonable Doubt*
February 1958
Professor Alistair Dirke thought himself a reasonable man. He could scarcely acknowledge the suspicion that was beginning to grow in his mind every time he saw his wife Rose with his friend Paul Eckleston. Paul seemed to be there often these days…

Then a still more terrible suspicion was to grow and spread through the little community of Rollway, where the Dirkes had hitherto lived in peace with their neighbours. A man was murdered and a valuable collection of coins disappeared.

Once again, Elizabeth Ferrars has created a realistic world of interesting ordinary people whose lives are disrupted by events that are violent yet credible. She has posed a problem that is original and fascinating.

### *Wandering Widows, The*
July 1962
At London Airport, in Glasgow and in Oban, Robin Nicholl, a young man holidaying between jobs, finds his curiosity aroused by four cheerful middle-aged women who describe themselves as widows and whose trail, as he travels northward, he seems fated to cross. At last, on the island of Mull in the Hebrides, he discovers what has brought them together to that particular unlikely spot. He also discovers what the solitary fair-haired girl in the hotel is supposed to be doing there, and later, when tragedy has struck, that widows sometimes have husbands… . This is a most gripping story, cleverly written and excitingly plotted. The reader is baffled and intrigued as effectively as in Miss Ferrars's recent successful crime novels, *The Sleeping Dogs* and *The Busy Body*. *The Wandering Widows* is a *tour de force* that will keep every keen crime reader thinking hard.

### *With Murder in Mind*
February 1948
Something on her mind, something that burned in her brain every waking minute, had driven Andrea Stone to consult Dr. Fromhold, the eminent psychiatrist. And in the cloistered quiet of his consulting room, where the secrets of many distracted minds had been laid bare, Andrea Stone tells her extraordinary story. She is married to a murderer, a man whom she still loves deeply, and she is frightened, for murder is a frightening thing. Elizabeth Ferrars immediately captures the interest and sympathy of the reader and unfolds an absorbing story, told from an unusual angle.

### *Witness Before the Fact*
September 1979
'You can't make an omelette without breaking eggs.' It was the fact that Alec Methven had apparently done so that first made the police on the island of Madeira suspicious of his suicide. Despite all the indications to the contrary, he had not eaten his last meal in solitude, and someone was very anxious to conceal that fact.

Luckily for Peter Corey, who found his body, he had still been in the plane on his way to Madeira at the time his host died. The purpose of his visit was unusual, but his alibi was impeccable. It gave Peter the chance to ask some awkward questions, such as how, in the fifteen years since he had last seen him, had Methven become so rich? It also gave him the opportunity to get to know Methven's friends and neighbours: the arthritic colonel, his tense wife, and the spoilt teenager who was staying with them, to whom the murdered man had been so kind. Which of them had a motive for murder? And was there a connection between it and the second killing which so inexplicably occurred?

Elizabeth Ferrars weaves her customary skilful story, with the added bonus of interesting characters and a delightfully exotic locale.

### *Woman Slaughter*
August 1989
When a neighbour was knocked down and killed in a hit-and- run accident outside her house Virginia Freer was not displeased to have the company of Felix, the husband from whom she had been semi-detached for the past seven years. Felix, though not quite trustworthy, had a knack of solving problems, and the seemingly simple death of the accident victim proved to be only the beginning of a whole series of them.

Although it suited him to conceal his knowledge from the police, Felix had seen enough to make a tentative identification of the car concerned and which house it had been parked outside, and he couldn't resist dabbling unofficially in the investigation. The result of his intervention appeared to be a second brutal murder, and one which Virginia found unpleasantly close to home.

Fortunately Felix was once again able to use his talents to uncover a killer, but not before a third murder had taken place.

### *Zero at the Bone*
October 1967
'The police,' said Susan Lyne, 'seem to be taking an interest in your undesirable neighbours.'

'Quite time too.'

Fiona Laslett joined her sister at the bedroom window. For a moment or two both watched the policeman in the road talking to the man from the cottage at the corner.

But the police weren't interested in their neighbour – at least not yet. Later they would return in numbers, to investigate the inescapable fact of violent death. But at present they were only enquiring, rather quietly and casually, about a domestic python that had strayed from nearby Bright's Farm, where a number of rare animals, including an eagle owl, a goshawk and a peregrine falcon were among the household satellites.

Elizabeth Ferrars's new novel has pace and excitement, the characters are studied and true, and the background is colourful. The training of a falcon is described in some detail. But the story is also a classical puzzle with an extraordinarily ingenious mystery. The reader is fooled by a very simple trick, and will look back with admiration at the clue which disguises the final revelation.

## FIELDING, A.

### *Black Cats Are Lucky*
October 1937
Sir Henry Batchelor was found dead in his room, his fingers clasped tightly round a bottle marked POISON. *But it was not the contents of the bottle that had killed him.* This was the problem that confronted Chief Inspector Pointer and the members of Sir Henry's family. Only after the greatest difficulty was it solved, and Pointer pays handsome tribute to a four-legged assistant. *Black Cats are Lucky* is full of surprises to the very last page.

### *Case of the Missing Diary, The*
November 1935
The victim of the murder in this case is a man of orderly mind who had formed the habit of entering in his diary not only business appointments and family engagements, but the smallest thing that would require his attention. One day he makes an appointment

with a solicitor acquaintance of his, but the solicitor arrives at his pleasant house in St. John's Wood to find his client lying dead in the summer house. His diary has disappeared, and in its place is another of the same pattern but filled with entries in cipher. The problem which Chief-Inspector Pointer of Scotland Yard is called upon to face is strange and complicated – a problem deserving of his quite exceptional talents.

### Case of the Two Pearl Necklaces, The
March 1936

Arthur Walsh, son and heir of a very wealthy father, Colonel Walsh, shatters the complacent lives of his parents by his declared intention of marrying Violet Finch, daughter of 'the notorious Mr. Finch', owner of several night-clubs. Arthur's wedding gift to Violet is two strings of very valuable pearls, said to have belonged to Queen Charlotte of Mexico, and to have been sold because they brought bad luck to their owner. The pearls fully justify their evil reputation, for they bring sudden death; and present Chief-Inspector Pointer of Scotland Yard with one of the most baffling murder mysteries of his eminently successful career.

### Cautley Conundrum, The
February 1934

Major Cautley went out to shoot wood pigeons and was found later lying across a stile, with his head shattered by a shot which might possibly have come from his own gun. The local police, however, came to the conclusion that he had been murdered. At the same time a valuable pearl necklace – a treasured heirloom of the Cautley family, had mysteriously disappeared. Could there possibly be any connection between the loss of the necklace and the shooting of Major Cautley? Chief Inspector Pointer is called in, and by means of some very clever detective work scores a very striking personal triumph. The problem posed by the author is a real brain-teaser, the type of problem on which Crime Club members like to sharpen their wits.

### Craig Poisoning Mystery, The
July 1930

The case arising out of the death of Ronald Craig was one of the most perplexing that Chief Inspector Pointer ever had to solve. No clue, recognised as such, was left behind either as to the motive for the crime, the criminal, or the way in which the crime was carried out. Pointer has to hunt for each in turn. Though the circle is narrowed down to a handful of the dead man's intimates yet it turns and re-turns in a very baffling manner.

### Death of John Tait
June 1932

John Tait is murdered on the eve of his marriage to Mrs. Lucy Burnham, a young widow. Investigation shows that he was being blackmailed, but there are so many angles, each of which suggests a different motive and therefore a different criminal, that Chief Inspector Pointer finds the mystery extremely difficult to solve. A young girl who intrudes into Tait's family circle just after the suicide of a friend of his, and just before his own death, is evidently connected with both—so thinks Pointer—but just what that connection is he finds it by no means easy to establish. The solution of the very tangled web is well concealed, but is elucidated with A. Fielding's customary skill.

### Murder in Suffolk
May 1938

It was at the personal request of Scotland Yard that Hugh Duncan travelled down to Suffolk.

The Yard had been puzzled by the sudden cessation of reports from one of their plain-clothes men who had been detailed to keep an unobtrusive watch over a patient in a sanatorium. The Foreign Office took a particular interest in the patient, who was the son of an Arab sheikh. How Duncan got on the track of, and succeeded in unravelling, a most amazing mystery is the theme of this popular author's latest story, *Murder in Suffolk*.

### Mystery at the Rectory
September 1936

Women adored Anthony Revell, an attractive, wealthy young man, whose unfortunate death caused many a heart to sadden. There was no evidence of foul play – he had been careless whilst cleaning his revolver which went off suddenly and shot him in the head. A month later the rector of the parish preached one of the finest sermons of his life. It was his last, for that same evening he was found dead in his study – poisoned. Quite by chance Chief-Inspector Pointer heard that sermon (he was down on another matter), and after the rectory mysteries had been solved he observed: 'It's the only time I ever remember a sermon acting as a fingerpost to the right path in an inquiry.' It was a path with many turnings. Somehow Anthony Revell's death and the rector's were linked, and in solving the problem Pointer achieved his greatest feat of detection.

### Paper Chase, The
November 1934

A group of English people meet at a little place off the Brenner Pass for the winter sports. One of them enters an English bob for the Giovo Pass Cup. He saves a very pretty English girl from what might have been a fatal accident, and they form one of those swift friendships which may, or may not, grow into something deeper. On the return of the party to England, one of them is found shot dead in the flat of another member, who is missing. Scotland Yard is called in, and to Chief Inspector Pointer is given the task of elucidating the mystery. It is a complicated problem. The Chief Inspector considers it unique, because he was right and yet he was wrong, or, as the Yard put it, he was wrong, and yet he was right!

### Pointer to a Crime
February 1944

Good news for detective story readers! Inspector Pointer, hero of many excellent stories, returns after too long an absence in this highly ingenious and baffling mystery. The setting for the untimely and violent decease of Annabelle Robson is a house called The Clearing in a quiet Lincolnshire village. The murder of Annabelle Robson causes a widespread sensation, but Chief Inspector Pointer brilliantly solves a singularly intricate case and succeeds in bringing a particularly cold-blooded murderer to justice.

### Scarecrow
March 1937

The white cliffs of Dover … various reasons brought four men from Provence across the channel one evening to find mystery and death awaiting them above those white cliffs. Chief-Inspector Pointer has first to tackle a judgment of Solomon. Then, seeing further than the local police, he finds a cleverly carried-out crime, whose unravelling takes him to the farm of the Golden Goat high up on the hills behind Mentone.

### Tall House Mystery, The
May 1933

The Tall House in Chelsea was said to be

haunted – and therefore it was natural that talk at the house-party should turn on ghosts. Gilmour, one of the party, warns the others that he had once been frightened by a so-called ghost as a child, and will shoot at any apparition that he sees. The same night Moy is awakened by the sound of a shot. He rushes into the passage and finds the dead body of young Ingram wrapped in a white sheet – a bullet-hole through his forehead. An extremely unfortunate practical joke! Or was it something more sinister? Chief Inspector Pointer evolves a theory and patiently begins to unravel the many intricacies of this baffling mystery.

### Tragedy at Beechcroft
April 1935

It happened at a series of *tableaux vivants* at Beechcroft, the usual charitable and rather fatuous entertainment provided for the amusement of Major and Mrs. Moncrieff's guests. One of the items on the programme was a conjuring trick which necessitated a little knife play. Unfortunately on this occasion an error occurred – a fatal error. It might have been dismissed as such, but Chief Inspector Pointer of Scotland Yard was struck by something in the newspaper narrative of the tragedy and went down to see whether there was any evidence to substantiate a query which had occurred to him. The resulting problem challenges all his wits to solve.

### Upfold Farm Mystery, The
June 1931

This clever Inspector Pointer novel deals with two strange murders which follow each other at Upfold Farm. A little brass box with a damaged St. Mark's lion on the lid mysteriously appears and disappears as each murder is committed. The box is of no value, contains nothing of value and is not used as a message, but its position is directly responsible for the second death. It presents a perplexing problem to Inspector Pointer, but by skilful reasoning he discovers its meaning, and forms his theory. The Upfold Farm mystery is one of his most baffling cases, and the manner in which he builds up his theory from the slender evidence at his disposal is a perfect example of detective skill.

### Wedding-Chest Mystery, The
November 1930

What purports to be a Chinese wedding chest is given by Major Hardy to a Mr. and Mrs. Armstrong for their Chinese suite. A private inquiry agent has been requested to meet Mr. Armstrong at his house at an afternoon reception given on the day on which the chest arrives, and the place where the latter stands has been appointed for the rendezvous. When opened, the chest contains, instead of some dwarf trees which were to be distributed among the guests, the dead body of Mr. Armstrong. How it came to be there, what really happened to Armstrong, and why it happened, form the puzzle which Chief Inspector Pointer of Scotland Yard and the private inquiry agent solve together.

### Westwood Mystery, The
November 1932

Sir Adam Youdale, a prominent member of the Bar, is murdered at Westwood, his house in Wimbledon, by being smothered with a pillow. His death was a timely occurrence for several people, including Lady Youdale, his wife; the financier, Sturge, whose criminal activities are on the point of being discovered by Sir Adam; the mysterious Monsieur Gaudet, who is a friend of Youdale's French secretary, Mlle. Le Brun. Chief Inspector Pointer of Scotland Yard is sent to investigate, but is

baffled by the disappearance of a most important clue. He sticks pertinaciously to his task, however, and his solution is brilliant and unexpected.

## FITZGERALD, NIGEL
### Affairs of Death
October 1967

At Dublin Airport Standish Wyse meets his pretty young cousin Juliet Carr; together they go bumping by bus across the Irish Midlands to the village of Rossderg. Wyse, an actor, is to holiday with friends including Stella Hazard – an old flame of whom he is still very fond.

An accident on a bicycle results in Wyse attending a curious party before he reaches his destination. At the party a harmless game gets out of hand, an attempt is made to cast a spell in an amateurish imitation of a black magic ritual. Soon after it looks as though the spell may actually have operated: two bloody and savage murders occur.

Superintendent Duffy, polite and cool as ever, comes to investigate, but it is Wyse himself who detects the workings of the ruthless mind behind the murders, and the identity of its owner.

With consummate craftsmanship and persuasive characterisation Nigel Fitzgerald here constructs a fine cotemporary puzzle; set in a seaside village in the West of Ireland, the story ends with a startling revelation, and a narrow escape.

### Black Welcome
June 1961

The stiffened body of the red-haired girl provided a macabre welcome for Hector O'Brien Moore when he arrived from America at the home of his ancestors in Ireland. She had been doing research into the Moore family history and had been waiting to interview Hector. Did the reason for her death lie here? Or among the tangled and complicated relationships of the present-day family who still lived scattered around the bay and were ruled by the matriarch of Moore Court? Or among the neighbours who resented the feudal attitude which the family assumed as of right? Superintendent Duffy was called in to handle a case which was to prove the most complex, delicate and difficult of his career.

*Black Welcome* gives Nigel Fitzgerald a magnificent opportunity to write a story with all those qualities of wit, ingenuity and characterisation for which he is so well known. He succeeds triumphantly.

### Candles Are All Out, The
March 1960

There had been a muddle over the hotel bookings and the presence of the Circuit Court had filled all the accommodation in Invermore. Alan Russell, the actor-manager, was more than glad to accept the Standish's offer of hospitality – even though it meant struggling to their island home through the worst storm Ireland had known for a hundred years. By morning he had cause to regret the visit. The bridge to the mainland had collapsed into the flood and the body of one of his fellow guests, horribly battered, was taken from the river. It was obviously a case of murder and the killer could only be one of the six people who had spent the night marooned at Inishlahan. No help would reach the island for at least twenty-four hours so Alan, in his own inimitable way, took matters into his own hands and began an investigation which was to lead him into a tangled and dangerous situation.

A light touch and the creation of vivid characters and intriguing plots have always been the hallmarks of Nigel Fitzgerald's crime stories. *The Candles Are All Out* finds him at the top of his form.

### Day of the Adder, The
November 1963

The O'Corrams had had to sell the castle at Torcleeve, but in the village by the lake – where they still owned property – their name was held in almost feudal respect. After his mother's death the heir, John, returned there, seeking peace and possibly also the company of a young woman whom he had known before his marriage.

John's return appeared to act as a catalyst on the inhabitants of the peaceful Irish village of Torcleeve; among the consequences is a murder in bizarre and bewildering circumstances. Superintendent Duffy comes to investigate; on him falls the onerous task of separating fact from the fiction of which there is a plentiful supply in Torcleeve.

Nigel Fitzgerald writes with his usual humour and discovers in the Irish scene happenings that are by turn exotic, comic, gruesome, violent and exciting. The discovery of the murderer's identity will come as a surprise, and the narrative leading up to it is continuously gripping.

### Ghost in the Making
August 1960

The Mannion Crowes gave their latest party in an empty, haunted house in the country beyond Dublin. It was a typically impractical and uninhibited affair and Alan Russell enjoyed it wholeheartedly. But it had a strange aftermath. The night had produced its usual quota of quarrels and incidents but little to suggest that it was to be the grotesque final crisis in the life of one of the guests. Alan himself had no hint that in the next few days he would become so deeply involved with many of the guests or that he was to conduct a search for a missing woman which would rise to a crescendo of horror.

Nigel Fitzgerald, one of the liveliest and most accomplished writers of unusual crime stories, has given *Ghost in the Making* all the verve and suspense for which he has become famous.

### House Is Falling, The
January 1955

When, after many years' absence, Hugh Barry returned to his childhood home, the party he found there was a strange one, but it included two very attractive young women. He fell instantly in love with both of them, only partially dismayed by the fact that Hilary Blake took a poor view of the goings-on of her rival, the siren, Consuelo Cavan. The sun shone on the Atlantic beyond Cooline House, and on the Irish countryside; it was race week; Hugh's circumstances were agreeable and romantic – until murder intervened. That shrewd and taciturn man, Superintendent Duffy of the Irish Civic Guards, was called to examine a dead body inside Cooline House.

Readers of *Midsummer Malice* and *The Rosy Pastor* will know that they can expect interesting amusing and living characters from Nigel Fitzgerald, that they will be borne into the heart of Ireland and involved in a mystery which is baffling and exciting. *The House Is Falling* is an achievement in classical detection: from the time of the murder until the solution the reader is diverted by scenes that are in turn funny, moving, thrilling and horrifyingly macabre; yet throughout these scenes he can feel the atmosphere tautening – leading to an exciting and wholly astonishing climax.

### Imagine a Man
October 1956

'…if the author doesn't give you enough to go on, you've got to imagine a man for yourself. Imagine a man – yes that's it'. Mr. J. D'arcy Strutt was on the train for Cahirmore to adjudicate in the Amateur Drama Festival; when he spoke thus to Guy Morrough he presumably knew what he was talking about.

But the next thing Mr. Strutt did was to vanish off the face of the earth. When the train arrived he had apparently dissolved into thin air.

Guy was plunged into a sequence of violent occurrences, one of which was unmistakeably murder. Many of the actors at the Drama Festival were to fly immediately to play in a film that was being shot in Italy – among them the beautiful Annabelle Ashe. Soon Guy found himself in Italy, in the company of such diverse characters as the film's director, Basil Clare, and the voluptuous Italian film star Toni Gualia; it soon became evident that the murderer was one of those who had arrived in Italy from Ireland.

This new murder story by the author of *Midsummer Malice*, *The Rosy Pastor* and *The House Is Falling*, combines the virtues of a detective mystery, a high-paced thriller and the exotic background of Italy in the spring.

### Midsummer Malice
July 1953

Little ever happened in Cahirmore. It was a peaceful Irish town, made prosperous by the cattle that fed lushly on the rich surrounding grasslands. Fat Stock prices were the only source of excitement until the summer when, in a heatwave of almost tropical intensity, Murder stalked the soft-faced hills. The unclothed body of a young girl, the daughter of a widowed English baronet, is found in a wood. It appears to be the act of a maniac; the motive simply the all-embracing hate of the paranoic. But Superintendent Duffy suspects there is a cold and calculating purpose behind the seemingly wanton crime. Nigel Fitzgerald is a new-comer to the field of detective fiction, but so sure is his touch that it is difficult to believe this is his first novel. He has an Irish wit, which is delightfully evident in the many amusing characters and the entertaining dialogue.

### Rosy Pastor, The
January 1954

'I should hate to commit a murder in Bru-na-vera…the whole population would be witnesses', said Denis O'Rourke, when he came it settle in that delightful village spread round a bay in Ireland.

The first victim was a rare bird, the rose starling (*Pastor Roseus*), commonly referred to by the inhabitants as the 'Rosy Pastor'. But no one came forward to explain the death of this beautiful, harmless visitor. There were no witnesses, it seemed, any more than there were to the subsequent disappearance of the much-loved Professor Janeson.

Superintendent Duffy started his investigation, impeded as much as helped by the irrepressible actor-manager, Alan Russell. Janeson's body was found, and the evidence began to suggest that the killer was one of the four beautiful women who lived round the bay.

This, Nigel Fitzgerald's second novel, presents characters as amusing and individual and a problem as exciting as did *Midsummer Malice*, his first.

### Student Body, The
October 1958

It seems a far cry from the assassination of a Hungarian Countess in a London church to a date which two young repertory actresses make with some undergraduates in Dublin. But the girls had been in the church when the murder took place and so had the small, insignificant man whom they spotted again at the bar of the Dolphin.

Youth and Irish blood, sparked by alcohol, make an explosive mixture. Jer Milne and Don Carton took a course of action which began partly as a rag and partly in earnest. It led to a night which proves half farce and half nightmare. Dawn found two very shaken young men and their friends, involved in a situation which set the charming but shrewd Inspector Duffy on their trail, and in addition the nameless, elusive and deadly organisation whose path they had crossed and whose plans they had upset.

'Off we went with the body in the bag,' quotes Mr. Fitzgerald blithely at the head of Chapter Six, and his readers follow willingly, knowing that the author of *Suffer a Witch*, *Midsummer Malice* and *The House is Falling* can be relied upon to spin them a unique and intriguing tale, which switches from the lighthearted to the macabre, even while the author produces a plot full of shocks and surprises.

### Suffer a Witch
March 1958

'The girl seemed to be about fifteen, and was wearing a grey-green school uniform, and her fair hair was pillowed against the shoulder of the enormous black Great Dane…'

Somehow Vanessa had come to believe herself to be a witch; Hamlet, the black dog, went about with her as though he were her familiar, and so reinforced the impression.

Nigel Fitzgerald's new novel hinges round a hideous and brutal murder in the town of Dun Moher, in Western Ireland. Superintendent Duffy finds himself investigating the gruesome circumstances behind which there seems to lie the general suspicion of witchcraft. Many local characters are excellently portrayed; among them are some who might, for one reason or another, have benefited from the crime and its repercussions. The story moves to an exciting climax and a surprising solution.

Nigel Fitzgerald is already well known for such excellent detective stories as *Midsummer Malice* and *The House is Falling*. A similar blend of good writing, humour, good characterisation and ingenuity is here augmented by the macabre implications of witchcraft.

### This Won't Hurt You
June 1959

Larry Brerton was killed in the presence of two representatives of Scotland Yard. Superintendent Laud and Sergeant Benson had come to the dentist's surgery on a routine matter and had waited while Brerton was treated by one of his partners. They found themselves involved in a case of murder which was not only bizarre and macabre but which bristled with motives in spite of a baffling lack of evidence. Brerton had taken over an appointment originally booked for one of the fabulous Altonian brothers, joint rulers of the empire of Armenian International Oil. Could the murderer have killed the wrong man? There were too many others with a motive to be certain, and in a curious way every likely person was not only connected with the surgery but also with the questionable theatre club, chez Venus, whose star performer, the provocative Prudence Peel, had once worked as a dental assistant.

Nigel Fitzgerald has once again provided his unique blend of wit and ingenuity and set a fascinating problem to make his new book a worthy successor to *Suffer a Witch* and *The Student Body*.

## FLEMING, ANNE
### There Goes Charlie: A Rural Murder
October 1990

A Master of Foxhounds is murdered mid Hunt. Detective Chief Superintendent John Charter from Penfoldshire Area Headquarters takes on the case with the help of the highly intelligent local rural Sergeant who is knowledgeable about Hunt customs, rivalries and politics. Together they question the victim's beautiful young Irish wife, his university lecturer brother, and the Hunt members and servants, and the Hunt saboteurs.

The Chief Superintendent is unfamiliar with hunting and he experiences several moments of severe anxiety on horseback, not to mention a narrow escape form a nasty and deliberately planned death, as he pursues his inquiries from Hunt Kennels to farmhouse, from manor to market town and a run-down Irish estate, and of course to the chase itself.

Much fascinating country lore and a fair picture of the controversial subject of fox-hunting are among the incidental pleasures of this first crime novel, in which the solution is cunningly delayed till the very last page.

## FLEMING, JOAN
### Alas Poor Father
July 1972

Brigadier Patricott, a soldier first and foremost, put duty before pleasure as a matter of course. When his young wife died, leaving him with two young boys, he retired from his job as British Agent in a Persian Gulf Sheikdom and returned home to live with his boys on his pension in a rented gate-house. He tried hard to please his sons, but never quite succeeded. The boys greatly preferred the company of Con O'Duff, the eccentric Irish owner of the big house, who had a charming line in pigeon-fancying and other activities of more sinister portent.

Retirement was decidedly difficult for Brigadier Patricott. And nothing could have been more propitious than the sudden arrival of the man from the Foreign Office requesting him (as a special favour to the Sheik he had once served) to return to the Middle East on a brief special mission, for on that very morning a rich local widow, whom Patricott had visited the night before, had been found, shot dead and sitting bolt upright, at her luxurious home.

With her usual narrative skill and gift of characterization Joan Fleming tells the story of how this self-assured and competent soldier finds himself nearly defeated as he bungles a situation on his own home front, while performing a magnificent act of bravery which goes almost unnoticed by anyone but one small dog.

### Chill and the Kill, The
May 1964

Who can say what particular occurrence is most likely to stimulate the gift of clairvoyance (or second-sight or extra-sensory perception)? In the case of Rita Side the stimulus was inadvertently supplied by the vicar of Marklane, who knocked her over with his old Bentley.

Rita's attack of second-sight was spectacular: she could foretell the future with special reference to approaching death, and at moments she could read a stranger's whole past and future from just one glance. At once she was in demand as a seer, a fortune-teller, a social entertainer, a money-spinner and a popular freak. Journalists and crowds swarmed round the erstwhile tranquil village. Rita's mother was in despair although her grandfather, old Trinity Bend, rather enjoyed the hubbub.

Of the many deaths foreseen by Rita one took place in Marklane itself, and it was undoubtedly murder. The search for, and discovery of the murderer's identity provide an exciting conclusion to a series of bizarre and fascinating events.

Joan Fleming is among the most original and successful crime novelists writing today. Her *When I Grow Rich* received the Crime Writers Association Award for the best novel published in 1962. *The Chill and the Kill* will reach and delight an even larger number of readers.

### *Day of the Donkey Derby, The*
June 1978

The day of the Donkey Derby dawned bright and clear: a perfect June day. When the telephone rang at seven o'clock in the morning, Dr. Tom Lavenham, GP in a quiet market town, had no idea that it was to be a day he would remember all his life.

The telephone call was from his son, announcing the imminent arrival, alone, of the young woman who was to be the Lavenham's daughter-in-law. Such a situation can often be taxing to parents, but this one was doubly so, for not only had the Lavenhams never met Juniper, who was a paediatrician doing a course in London, but she happened to be Chinese. As he made plans to meet her off the two-fifteen train and his wife's mind turned to a suitable variety of fatted calf (did the Chinese have dietary taboos?), Tom Lavenham had no idea that he would shortly be confronted with the body of a beautiful girl, mysteriously dead in the home of a tricycle-riding eccentric; that he would be kept prisoner at the wrong end of a loaded gun from eight-thirty a.m. to half-past eleven at night; that a house known locally as Dedend would very nearly become one; and certainly no idea of the circumstances in which he would first encounter his future daughter-in-law.

Joan Fleming recounts with her usual charm and skill the events of a day which will be as suspenseful and memorable to the reader as it was to Tom Lavenham, and perhaps more enjoyably so.

### *Death of a Sardine*
October 1963

Brigadier Warrington built himself a palatial villa above the sea in Portugal. Very rich, widowed and retired, his main wish was to please his son Tom and his main diversion was the pursuit – idealistic, expensive and almost always vain – of unsuitable women. At the start of this story he is in the clutches of a very young and mysterious German adventuress called Irma, and because he's fond of his father, Tom is worried.

He arrives at the villa fresh from his finals at Oxford and takes an immediate dislike to Irma. Soon there looms, out of Irma's past, the threatened vengeful appearance of her husband, a German draper. The anticipated materialisation of Herr Gantzenhausen hangs like thunder round the villa and reduces its inhabitants to a virtual state of siege.

In due course murder (the death of a sardine – sardines are most interesting when dead) breaks the siege and wrecks the ambience of the luxurious villa. The mystery is not susceptible to the customary examination of alibis and clues since at the moment when it was committed the principal suspects were all blind drunk on local hooch.

Once again Joan Fleming has written a completely original story. This one is even more amusing and moving than the highly successful *When I Grow Rich* and it sustains a thrilling mystery to the end.

### *Every Inch a Lady: A Murder of the Fifties*
August 1977

York Cragg, young, wealthy, handsome, and just six months married, was found brutally murdered in his home, for no apparent motive, while his wife was spending the evening at the theatre with friends. Everyone, not least her father-in-law, a shipping magnate, was sorry for the tragic widow, especially when it became known that she had been cruelly deceived.

But her husband's death was not the last of the little woman's troubles. Soon she was called upon to show her pluck again, and to withstand the attentions of the 007-type agent who was investigating her husband's death. Alone in the world with no one to turn to, the young widow who was every inch a lady took matters into her small but unexpectedly determined hands, with results no one could have foreseen, though perhaps someone should have…

Joan Fleming's stylish, circumstantially detailed novel is a delightful evocation of the world as it was some twenty-odd years ago.

### *Grim Death and the Barrow Boys*
June 1971

An involuntary shout of boyish delight as Gideon escaped from Towser gave away the scene of his future activities to his overbearing partner. These two were not exactly criminals nor yet true wide-boys, but of both of them it could be said that you had to count your fingers after shaking hands. Towser was a cradle-coster-monger [sic] and Gideon, assisting him at the old clothes barrow, buying and selling what is often described as 'drag', absorbed all the tricks of the trade he learned from Towser.

Gideon was a truly deprived child; in early youth turned out of the room he shared with his unmarried mother in order that she might earn her living, he was also slightly crippled. Some have greatness thrust upon them but Gideon had merit, and lots of it, thrust upon him by kind people to whom his limp seemed pathetic. So when both young men were implicated in murder most foul at the seaside Towser was obviously guilty and Gideon clearly innocent...or was he?

Once again, Joan Fleming displays that talent for characterizing young people in highly original crime situations which has won such acclaim for her previous novels, *Hell's Belle* and *Young Man, I Think You're Dying*. The last-named won the Golden Dagger Award of the Crime Writers' Association for 1970.

### *Hell's Belle*
October 1968

She was sitting in a cafe in Paris, showing nearly all of her lovely legs; in grave trouble, she was drinking her sixth green Chartreuse and wishing she knew someone who would kill her stepmother for her. She was just eighteen, a child emotionally but old in experience and duplicity.

The man with the umbrella who sat down at her table seemed exactly the one for whom she was searching and to hook him she jumped over the parapet of a bridge into the Seine. He was hooked all right; he had finished with his own unsuccessful life but suddenly, at the last minute, he began to know how to live it with this catastrophic, Rolls Royce girl – or thought he had. They were both fundamentally lonely and each found in the other the playmate for which they had longed, but all the time she pressed subtly and cleverly for action. He was a mini-man caught in a monster man-trap; it was murder she wanted and murder she got.

'I say my prayers every night,' she announced.

'Oh, please God, kill my stepmother for me, is that it?'

It is funny and sad and unique, a *tour de force* featuring virtually two characters only; a study of reckless indulgence and demoralisation. It is an extraordinary and most compelling development in a writer whose brilliant stories have all presented something new and strange.

### *How to Live Dangerously*
July 1974

A splendid war record in Naval Intelligence and a disastrous marriage left Martin Pendle Hill alone, leading a reasonably contented and uneventful life in a pleasant Oxford upper maisonette. He had a good friend with whom he spent long holidays, and a black Labrador as a companion. But both these died of a ripe old age within a short time of one another and in his distress Pendle Hill accidentally fell and broke his thigh. That was what started it. 'After sixty-five years of age … live dangerously,' the Oxford Regius Professor of Medicine had publicly advised, and Pendle Hill, smiling at his own plan and without permission from his stern little landlady in the beautiful flat downstairs, decided to do just that: he would fill his life with bright young people by taking in lodgers, accommodating them on his top floor.

Meanwhile, his landlady had embarked upon a plan for her old age, which had within it the seeds of disaster …

### *In the Red*
July 1961

After twenty years as a bank clerk Leslie Williams can stand the daily round no longer. He plans a crime – but nothing very heinous, nothing more than a little dishonesty and a lot of unkindness. Yet once he has made the first fatal move he finds himself gathered into a fantastic web, part illusory, part real, of adventure, mischance and danger; the terrifying circumstances that eventually overtake him are very real.

The whole of this story takes place in London; the seedy hotel in the Cromwell Road, the open air market where he finds work as a salesman, are vividly seen through the eyes of Leslie Williams – the man who has broken loose, who doesn't know quite what dangers are hunting him from the past, or what sort of sense can be made of the present or the future: the man on a guilty spree.

Joan Fleming is a most intelligent and ingenious writer, as readers of *The Man From Nowhere* and her other novels will know. *In the Red* will delight and baffle the reader until the author chooses to reveal the true origins and facts of Leslie Williams's extraordinary adventures.

### *Kill or Cure*
January 1968

Jeremy Fisher is a smart doctor in what he calls the 'Jag belt, south of London'; the community are rich, talk with Harrods' accents, drink too much and call one another Bunny. When a young unmarried girl has to have an abortion it is done smoothly, without anybody knowing anything about it; unless the girl, hoping to save money for a boy-friend, has one at cut-rates and dies.

Jeremy Fisher, to oblige a friend, quickly hustles it all up under the carpet but a blackmailer gets to work and the girl's father an Irish baron and a thriller-writer comes upon the scene to investigate and uncovers Jeremy's unsatisfactory private life, peeling layer after layer, exposing him as a victim of malicious revenge.

With her usual quick humour, and brilliant off-beat characterisation, Joan Fleming tells a fascinating story full of strange possibilities and realities. The many addicts of this author's work (which includes *When I Grow Rich* and *No Bones About It*) will be delighted with this gay and gruesome story, set among the doctors.

### *Maiden's Prayer*
October 1957

Miss Maiden was no longer young by the time her mother died, but she was still full of enthusiasm and hope. 'And life's so short,' she said, 'There are such a lot of lovely things to be done.'

To Miss Maiden the mysterious Mr. Aladdin, with his Persian origins, his charm and his flavour of the exotic East, appeared like the answer to a prayer. He began to help her in the management of her business affairs.

It was perhaps a trifle odd that anybody should be called Mr. Aladdin. But lots of other odd things were to happen before the unfortunate Miss Maiden's fate was decided. Joan Fleming's exciting new novel culminates in a macabre situation and a surprise ending.

### *Malice Matrimonial*
February 1959

Love at first sight, caught on the rebound, whatever it was, young Henry Ormskirk – mild, kindly and unemployed – found that he had married the desirable Pia Palomi almost before he had time to think about it, and had landed himself a job in her mother's slick, exclusive dress business. For Henry it was the beginning of a time of progressive misery which even an unexpected financial windfall didn't improve. But for Pia and her glamorous and sophisticated mother it had been an audacious and successful manoeuvre. If Henry had been consistently weak or reliably strong all might have been well, but he vacillated from strength to weakness and as a result blundered further and further into a lethal situation which led finally to murder.

In this book, as in *Maiden's Prayer* and *You Can't Believe Your Eyes*, Joan Fleming has created lively characters and, with a light touch and humour, she involves them in situations which are as full of suspense and ingenuity as they are true to life.

### *Man From Nowhere, The*
August 1960

He came to Stargill one blustery afternoon in October. He was wearing a raincoat like any other and carrying a shabby canvas grip. The Man from Nowhere settled in the village, got work in the saw-mill and was gradually accepted by the inhabitants as a friend. But it was this man who was to discover the battered body of old Ma Perkins lying in the stream, and, when it became obvious that the murderer could only be someone from the village, the ranks began to close up. He was, after all, a stranger in Stargill. Kind, good company and likeable but, for all that, a 'foreigner'. When the murder was followed by another violent and bloody death the village became frightened, suspicious and cruel. The urge to protect, at all costs, its own security and peace of mind became imperative.

Joan Fleming has already been acclaimed as one of the outstanding Crime novelists of recent years. With *The Man from Nowhere* she has not only written a Crime novel which actually breaks new ground but told a haunting, powerful story with deceptive simplicity and great skill. This is a book you will remember.

### *Midnight Hag*
July 1966

There was no nonsense about old Mr.

Cumlock in that when he decided to die, he died, maliciously, leaving his fortune to a son, as an act of revenge.

'I can't live without a woman...and I can't live with one,' his heir, Valentine Belmont, an artist, was to complain and it was this complication that had dogged him throughout his life and was to bring everything tumbling about him in a blaze of disorder and misrule.

The events in his life had a fearful symmetry, enacted by falling starlight.

The story is full of movement and excitement. Joan Fleming is famous for her fluent and witty prose, and for the oddity of her characters, who are both surprising and convincing. She is at the top of her form here in this enthralling new novel.

### Miss Bones
October 1959

Mr. Walpurgis, art dealer of Shepherd's Market, London, was repulsive. Yet once young Thomas Melsonby had got over the first shock of meeting his new employer, and had begun work as resident picture restorer his natural good humour came back completely. Then, when his employer failed to return after a week-end holiday and the days slipped by without any word from him, Thomas began to wonder about some of those curious episodes which had occurred in the previous weeks, then to begin to put them together, and finally to probe into the movements of the mysterious and elusive man. The circumstances surrounding Mr. Walpurgis's eventual reappearance were sinister and macabre and Thomas found himself entangled in a puzzling and dangerous situation which Joan Fleming discloses with the skill, wit and reality which her many readers have come to expect from the author of *Malice Matrimonial* and *Maiden's Prayer*.

### No Bones About It
February 1967

The Borgan family had always been pressed for money. Parsimony had been the rule among them in their large house in Bedfordshire.

Wealth burst upon them suddenly in the form of huge presents of banknotes from Grandad, an octogenarian, resident relative. Grandad's banknotes made dreams come true for each member of the family. From thrift they were suddenly and mysteriously transported into a period that came to be known amongst them as 'The Affluence'.

But where did Grandad get the money from? And what use did the beneficiaries actually make of it?

To the first question the only answer was highly unsatisfactory. The answer to the second was to be revealed in the destiny of the Borgans. For the whole family eventually found itself in the dock on a charge so hideous that they became known in the national press as the 'Borgias'. Grandad's banknotes had come home to roost.

*No Bones About It* is made extraordinarily exciting by the fact that the nature of the appalling charge against the Borgan family is not revealed until near the end (though it may be guessed). Until that ghoulish climax the reader will be absorbed by the fascinating moral dilemma imposed on each Borgan relative by the sudden windfall of unearned and unexplained banknotes.

### Nothing Is the Number When You Die
February 1965

In Joan Fleming's *When I Grow Rich* there appeared a detective/hero unlike any other: Nuri bey, an impoverished Turkish scholar/philosopher who lives in Istanbul, was

described by Julian Symons in his review in *The Sunday Times* as 'the most unlikely, and the most likeable, detective hero of the year.' *When I Grow Rich* was chosen by a panel of critics for the Award of the Crime Writers Association for the best novel published in 1962.

In this new story Nuri bey is again involved in dramas of violence and murder. It is the science of detection rather than his scholarly pursuits that takes him at last to Oxford, to the 'dreaming spires' which in reality fall somewhat short of the city of learning he has conceived in his imagination.

A murder in Istanbul sends Nuri to Oxford. An explosion in a cottage in an English garden sends him back home. On the Black Sea coast he witnesses a macabre act of vengeance.

Witty and unconventional, this new crime novel will again increase the large numbers of readers who are already addicted to the work of this sparkling novelist.

### To Make an Underworld
July 1976

Robert Escrick was a good name. It was even Sir Robert Escrick Cravenhead's own – or part of it. So when the former chairman of the family firm ('Cravenhead's means machine tools') decided to disappear, because the firm had been taken over, he was retiring early, and his wife was abroad and no longer noticed whether he was around or not, it seemed to him entirely natural to adjust his name and set off for Cornwall, accompanied only by Banjo, his dog.

There was a house waiting for him in Cornwall – one he had had built in readiness. There was also a strange young woman waiting for him, locked in the bathroom and claiming to have been raped. Admittedly she was feeble-minded, but the locals took her part against a newcomer, and Robert found himself an object of suspicion from the start. Of course there were compensations: freedom to read and go [for] long walks with Banjo; the charming artist Nesta Clare; the enigmatic Roundstone and his boat (what did he do, anchored offshore for hours on end. Not fishing.) Robert found it easy to ignore appeals in the agony columns of the London papers, asking him to get in touch.

And then the feeble-minded girl was found murdered, and realities impinged on Robert's retreat – realities connected with Roundstone which Robert could not afford to ignore.

Joan Fleming's fans have come to expect the unexpected, because she is like no other crime writer – in which lies part of her charm. A genuine original, she needs no introduction beyond the announcement: Here is her new book.

### When I Grow Rich
May 1962

*In Turkey convicted murderers are hanged in public.* This thought is uppermost in the minds of some of the characters in this novel, not least Madame Miasma and her accomplices who have good reason to view the processes of law with apprehension.

The story is set in Istanbul; it conveys both the mystery and squalid magnetism of the old Imperial City embraced by the legendary Bosphorus – the dark fast stream between the Black Sea and the Mediterranean, in whose waters inconvenient bodies have been disposed of for century after century; it describes the extraordinary circumstances from which arose the relationship between Nuri bey, a Turkish philosopher and scholar, and Jenny Bolton, an English teenager, both highly individual pawns in a game which is not merely disreputable but criminal.

Once again Joan Fleming achieves a bizarre and exotic tour-de-force, the more seductive because, though told with wit ad restraint, it nevertheless achieves a thrilling climax.

### You Can't Believe Your Eyes
April 1957

A murder took place in a house in Regent's Park. Four people were in the room at the time and a man-servant had been going in and out. Simple enough, one might suppose, to get from those eye-witnesses a coherent account of what had taken place around the time of the murder. But in reality people see things differently from one another – and they may have many reasons for telling what is not quite the truth. The person who *seemed* to see most was Mr. Totterdell, yet it was rumoured that he was really blind. Joan Fleming's brilliant new crime story is told in turn by each of the people involved, seen through their eyes… And in the telling, the character of each narrator is revealed too. By this means the suspense is maintained while the whole pattern of motives surrounding the murder of Richard Rangward is skilfully unfolded. This, her first novel under the Crime Club imprint, makes exciting reading and will add to her growing reputation.

### You Won't Let Me Finish
August 1973

The scene is Helsinki's splendid harbour overlooked by a South American Embassy where the Ambassador carries out his ambassadorial duties. Every human drama in the calendar takes place at some time or another in the small cosmos he surveys, including the one that begins on his own front doorstep in the pale early light of a new day. It involves a kind old Russian who befriends drop-outs; a red-headed cosmetic demonstrator from New England on a business tour of Northern Europe; an English business executive turned street busker with a missing ear; and a wild Lapp reindeer farmer from the Arctic Circle who is becoming Americanized. None of it need have happened if the Lapp had not lost his nerve about the fortune he was carrying in a plastic bag, but why he did so and what the consequences were will provide Joan Fleming's many fans with one of the best and brightest of her scintillating entertainments.

### Young Man, I Think You're Dying
January 1970

This is the story of a young successful criminal, how he became one and how he operated. He lives in a London tower block. It begins at the moment when he has reached the height of his career and becomes careless verging on the bored. During a robbery he not quite accidentally goes too far; the result is murder. This touches off his latent psychopathic tendencies; he murders again.

There's an immature boy who helps him, in trouble too; there's a girl who has run away from home; there are the goodies and the baddies in the way of parents, and glimpses of life in a tower block.

The end is immoral but stunning. Taken as a whole, it is seen to be fitting comment on the Youth Underworld of today.

### FLETCHER, J. S.
**Marrendon Mystery and other Stories of Crime and Detection, The**
February 1931

The difficult art of writing short stories which really mystify and thrill the reader has no more brilliant exponent than J. S. Fletcher. His plots are ingeniously constructed, and

his mysteries are solved in a most convincing manner.

What perhaps gives most pleasure to the reader is the diversity of his characters – railway booking clerks, poachers, fisher-folk, prison-warders, judges – all drawn with the power and subtlety that reveals the hand of a master craftsman.

### FLOWER, PAT
*Cat's Cradle*
April 1973

'They'd been at it all along, his go, her go... It was cat and mouse. No, it was a cat's cradle. A game with string passed backwards and forwards and getting more tangled with every move. Tangled in hatreds and grudges. But it wasn't string they played with, it was their lives,'

That was how Jane, wealthy, ailing English girl, saw her marriage to Simon, undoubtedly Australian and – doubtfully – a sculptor. Simon had followed her half across the world – was it for love? It was certainly not for love that he took her back to Australia, whose climate had precipitated her ill-health. Nor out of consideration for Jane that he insisted that they take their slatternly housekeeper with them, although Jane detested her. But then Jane began to prove herself not exactly defenceless against Simon and more than a match for Mrs. Barnes.

And all the time there was Simon's old friend Monica in the background. Who was Monica and what did she want? As Pat Flower turns the screws of an intolerable situation, a violent climax erupts.

### Cobweb
July 1972

Martin Briggs ought to have been sitting pretty. Part-owner of a successful boutique, living with a loving and beautiful woman who was his partner and right hand in the business and who loyally refused to hear a word against him, he should have had no need for alcohol and sleeping pills and other manifestations of frayed nerves.

Of course Martin had been a widower – a recent widower – when he met Valerie, but Valerie had been his wife's closest friend. And a loyal, loving friend, who liked nothing better than to talk of Ellie – poor Ellie, who fell downstairs and broke her neck.

Naturally Martin could not tell Valerie that he had pushed her, that his idyllic marriage had been a lie. If only his former neighbour would stop hinting. If only that police inspector would not keep pointing out trifling discrepancies in his statement. If only he had never taken up with that girl Marge …

And if only Valerie would be less sweetly understanding. But against such a generous woman, what could any man do? What Martin did, what Valerie wanted him to do and why she wanted it, make an original and engrossing study of the unexpected consequences of a crime.

### Crisscross
January 1976

Edward Piper was an accountant in Sydney who yearned to write film scripts. Sybil, his loving wife, was a slatternly housewife and an enthusiastic do-gooder, whose pet cause was ecology. Lindsay Reid, a client of Edward's, was a scriptwriter engaged on a film on ecology, who proposed to pick Sybil's brains via Edward's artistic aspirations. Inevitably, their conflicting aims crisscrossed.

Pat Flower's story of madness and murder is unfolded through Edward's eyes. Her flair for creating characters who are at one remove from reality and enabling us to share their vision of a world which, below the surface, is infinitely madder than they are, gives an added dimension to her original and absorbing novel, in which each character in turn invites – and sometimes gets – nemesis.

### *Odd Job*
March 1974

If you had been married for upwards of twenty years to a burdensome, bulgy wife and just the right bulgy sofa came your way, you might – if you were Sydney junk-and-antique dealer Ned Paine – get the idea of putting an end to domestic discord by stuffing the one inside the other. Naturally there would have to be a little matter of murder first.

Ned executes the bloody deed – or so he thinks. But in the morning it becomes apparent that his disorientation is greater than he or anyone else had suspected. It is the sofa's remains that have to be disposed of. Of his wife there remains only a note.

From then on Ned flounders in a quicksand. What is real and what is fantasy? Has he killed Norah or has she left him, as she claims, because he will not sell out to property developers? Is the sofa-owner's daughter in love with him? And what about Harry, his assistant and old wartime buddy whom Ned likes to dominate? He too has a demanding wife. Surely he would like to be rid of her? Harry half-heartedly agrees.

And all the time the property developers are leaning on Ned. And then the police start leaning on him too. And notes begin to arrive, ostensibly from Norah, each making more outrageous demands than the last.

Pat Flower, who has rapidly established a reputation as one of the most original crime novelists now writing, once again brilliantly illustrates her distinctive themes that marriage is a fine breeding-ground for murder, and that something as fleeting as a domestic flare-up or a weather change may ultimately tip the scales.

### *Shadow Show*
September 1976

Athol Cosgrove, big, bonhomous and bogus, was sales manager of an export firm. Richard Ross was a junior accountant in the same firm, conscientious, hardworking and unsure of himself. When Ross discovers that Cosgrove is accepting bribes from contractors, he is more than ever uncertain what to do, but eventually he decides to beard the lion in his den and have it out with Cosgrove at his home. By doing so, he involves himself in murder and pits himself against the stronger man.

Like shadow boxers, the two feint and circle, Cosgrove keeping always just out of reach. Meanwhile the police are interested in Ross's movements and his evasiveness when questioned makes them suspicious. His wife too is interested – but she decides his guilt or innocence for herself. Only the head of the firm is not interested when Ross belatedly goes to him with his disclosures: he tells the accountant to grow up or shut up.

And then Ross catches another glimpse of the mysterious stranger, first seen on the night of the murder, whose existence everyone, including the police, has denied … The tension and claustrophobia which Pat Flower creates in all her novels have never been better exploited than in this story of an ordinary man who sees his options eliminated until the only one remaining produces a shockingly unexpected result.

### *Slyboots*
November 1974

Rick Coleman and Emily Sutton were one of the unlikeliest pairs ever to embark on a tour of Europe. Rick was young, English, unmarried and living on his wits. Emily was middle-aged, Australian, married and intent on living for evermore on her husband and his legacy – if she could only catch up with him. But Basil Sutton had left her and had a good start. It was to nose out Basil and the child he was escorting round Europe that Emily engaged Rick. And Rick, who had no interest in Basil or Emily, accepted the arrangement for the financial gains he hoped it would bring.

From Italy to Germany, England, Scotland and back to Italy, the curious chase went on, with Rick becoming bolder and slyer, and Emily slyer and bolder, and Basil remaining always one step ahead. Except that Rick was now in touch with Basil in an effort to outwit Emily, for there was something in Rick's past of which Emily had no inkling. Would it have made any difference if she had?

From its casual beginning in Cremona to its violent climax in the Australian bush, Pat Flower's latest crime novel demonstrates her remarkable talent for creating characters who are already some way round the bend and pushing them still further round it, while unfolding an intriguing mystery in her own inimitable style.

### *Vanishing Point*
May 1975

The safari from Sydney to the Cape York peninsula was not an unqualified success. Geraldine in particular detested it. She had only gone because Noel, her adored husband, had wanted so much to go. Of course Geraldine was too well balanced, too much in love with Noel, to let herself be thrown by the irritations of camp life. It was the others who were unreasonable and edgy, Noel especially so. Geraldine could keep clean and calm and competent in the most trying circumstances, and she made that perfectly plain. Even when Noel pulled out and hotfooted it back to Sydney, she persevered in what she had undertaken, though she inwardly vowed 'Never again'.

But a year later there was another safari to the Cape York peninsula, and Geraldine went along. She had kept her cool through everything that had happened back in Sydney, disturbingly unexpected though it was. The company on this second trip was very different, but Geraldine found she could still cope by recording in her diary those aspects of the trip which seemed to be significant. And then, when she was far from friends and familiar surroundings, the true motive for the second safari began, incredibly, to emerge.

## FOOTNER, HULBERT

### *Almost Perfect Murder and Other Stories, The*
July 1933

Mr. Hulbert Footner's well-known character Madame Storey, is perhaps the most celebrated woman in detective fiction. Her detective ability is aided to some extent by feminine intuition, but she achieves results – amazingly successful results, for the problems here elucidated proved baffling enough to the police. *The Almost Perfect Murder* and the other stories in this volume provide thrilling fare for all readers of detective stories, and Mr. Hulbert Footner writes with his customary verve and ingenuity.

### *Casual Murderer and Other Stories, The*
July 1932

Madame Storey is one of the most interesting as well as one of the most original characters in detective fiction. Her profession, as she would prefer to put it, is solving other people's problems. She is a friend to every troubled soul. She works through her knowledge of the human heart, and her feminine intuition is seldom at fault. In her latest adventures she is at her unsurpassable best, using her woman's wits to solve the strange disappearance of Aline Elder, the mysterious death of Commodore Varick, the multi-millionaire, and other extraordinary occurrences.

### *Dangerous Cargo*
September 1934

If any man ever deserved what was coming to him it was Horace Laghet, multi-millionaire and the worst-hated man in America. It was said that his life had been attempted several times and that he never ventured out without an armed guard. Yet he spent lavishly, boasting that he kept the money in circulation at any rate. He built a luxurious steam yacht and planned to go off with a party of guests for a six-months' cruise to the West Indies in order to escape the Depression. Before leaving, a mysterious voice on the telephone warned him that he would never come back alive. He consulted Madame Storey, the well-known woman detective, and persuaded her to accompany him. The cruise provides a succession of wildly exciting thrills, a startling climax, and an unexpected denouement.

### *Dark Ships, The*
April 1937

Hulbert Footner's hot-paced novels of crime are, as one leading critic has remarked, 'one of the many excellent things that come out of America.' He has got a good dramatic situation for this one. Neil didn't like his girl Janet running round with Fanning, who was crooked, and said so. But Janet would take no notice; and next time he saw her she was in a faint, with a revolver by her side, and Fanning dead at her feet.

### *Dead Man's Hat*
October 1932

Young Dave Westover finds the life of a bank clerk galling to a man of spirit. Calling on a highly desirable young lady for the first time, he discovers the dead body of a man in her clothes-press with a knife sticking in his back. He chivalrously undertakes to dispose of it, and thereafter he is never irked by dullness again. His plans gae agley [go awry]; he falls into the hands of the police, body and all, and with the dead man's hat stuffed inside his waistcoat. However, the body is presently spirited away, and Dave snatched from the hands of the law by means of a motor car smash contrived by the real murderer. Unfortunately for him, he has already extracted the secret of the dead man's hat, consequently his disreputable rescuers quickly turn on him. He is pursued (for different reasons) both by the police and by the most powerful gang in New York. He becomes a pawn in a titanic struggle waged between Jim Mann, the unacknowledged ruler of the town, who coolly issues his orders over the 'phone to judges and bankers, and the Secret Committee of Ten which is sworn to destroy this humiliating state of affairs.

### *Death of a Celebrity*
July 1938

Outside the apartment of Gavin Dordress, the famous playwright, the cameras clicked. It wasn't often he gave a party, and celebrities were to be his guests. The first guest, famous actress Gail Garrett, arrived early, but before long she was shouting at her host '*I could kill you for the way you've used me. I could kill you …*' In their cars and cabs coming to the party other guests were equally outspoken. Said one: '*Gavin has made his way step by step through using women …*' Said another: '*I hate him …*' Another: '*I'm through with him, and I'll tell him so to-night …*' Jealousy, greed, ambition poisoned the minds of the guests that evening – for was not Dordress's new play nearly ready, and did it not spell 'success' to all who were associated with it. The next morning brought the dawn and … the death of a celebrity. Mr. Hulbert Footner has drawn some superb character studies, and the story is rich in suspense and ingenuity.

### *Death of a Saboteur*
January 1944

Lee Mappin is detailed by the Federal Bureau to keep a watchful eye on a certain Prince, Alexis Lenkoran, strongly suspected of anti-Ally activities. Lee employs Jocelyn D'Arcy, a fascinating brunette, to charm her way into the Prince's inner circle. It's a sensation, therefore, when on the very night that Lee had been dining with the Prince, the latter is shot and dies in Jocelyn's arms. This incident marks only the beginning of a succession of nerve shattering escapades which leads Lee from New York to San Francisco. He pursues his investigation with bland and brilliant ingenuity, and is supported by an exceptionally strong cast and a plot of unusual twists and surprises.

### *Easy to Kill*
July 1931

Madame Storey, more alluring and more relentless than ever, discovers in Newport society a criminal worthy of her brilliant detective powers. Old people, RICH old people, are dying strangely. Madame Storey knows they are being murdered, and what is more, she is almost sure of the murderer from the very start. But he leaves no trace. His only weapon is the terror he instils in his aged victims, who, after all, are easy to kill. His plans are devilishly complex, his alibis are wellnigh perfect, and he has no apparent motive, but there is always a weak link somewhere. Madame Storey pits her brains against 'The Leveller's', till that one link is found, and the adventures she encounters in the solving of the ingenious Newport murders are here recorded by her secretary, Miss Brickley, in whom Mr. Footner has created the female counterpart of Dr. Watson.

### *Folded Paper Mystery, The*
September 1930

Nick Peters was a repairer of watches, sole proprietor of a little store in Fourth Street – a strange little man, a bit of a philosopher too, and fond of friendly arguments with Fin Corveth, a free-lance journalist. One day Peters is murdered, and Corveth finds himself involved in a baffling mystery in which a little brass ball plays an important part – for the little brass ball conceals an emerald locket, which in turn conceals a blank square of folded paper, which obviously holds a secret … But what?

### *House With the Blue Door, The*
February 1943

The shabby old house in Henry Street had taken on a new lease of life and a fresh coat of paint. It stood for a great idea, and the latest whim of Sandra Cassells, wealthy New York widow. Henceforth re-named Hope House, it would be a hostel for released convicts, a cheerful home for former residents of Sing Sing and other large establishments. Sandra's friend, Amos Lee Mappin, private investigator, warned her that her interesting but dangerous experiment in social reform was going to mean trouble in plenty, but even he did not foresee the extraordinary murder mystery that he would soon be called upon to elucidate. *The House with the Blue Door* is one of Hulbert Footner's best stories, as entertaining as it is exciting.

### Kidnapping of Madame Storey and Other Stories, The
March 1936

Madame Storey, the famous woman detective created by Hulbert Footner, is a character unique in detective fiction. The present volume consists of five of her most outstanding cases, and in these she proves once again how feminine intuition allied to more than ordinary deductive powers may solve some strange mysteries. The stories offer a rich diversity of scene, moving easily from New York to Monte Carlo, and even to far Peking, but Mr. Hulbert Footner is quite at home in each locale and holds our attention through the unravelling of each baffling problem…

### Murder in the Sun
March 1938

Phil Nevitt, a young American, is sent by his firm to the West Indies to get information about a rival firm of distillers whose headquarters are at Annunziata, a small island seldom visited by tourists. Phil Nevitt duly arrives at the island, but in spite of its sun-drenched atmosphere of scented flowers and tinkling guitars he realises that there is something sinister about the place. Life in the sun there may be … but also Death in the sun.

### Murder of a Bad Man
September 1935

Jack Comerford, newly graduated from Harvard, came down to Washington to talk over his future career with his father, who was an important government official engaged in suppressing the illegal traffic in liquor after the repeal of Prohibition. Jack didn't like his father's suggestions. He didn't want to be a banker, didn't want to go to the bar, didn't think that a year's travel would broaden his mind. But he did want to see life: he craved for excitement and red-blooded adventure, if only for one glorious hour. So his father wisely asked him to lend a hand in cleaning up the liquor racket, and before he quite realised what his new job meant, Jack was swept up in a tornado of crime. Hulbert Footner's latest mystery moves at tremendous pace, and the picture so dramatically presented of the American underworld is startling in its realism.

### Murder Runs in the Family
April 1934

Is murder ever justified? Lance McCrea had thought it all out, and decided that the world would be well rid of the contaminating presence of Jim Beardmore, the wealthy proprietor of Beardmore Linen Mills. Beardmore, in Lance's opinion, was just a skunk – fat, dissipated, lecherous. What right had he to make love to a sweet girl like Freda. Lance certainly would have murdered Beardmore. *But the job was done for him!* An unknown hand struck down Beardmore, and, irony of ironies, Lance is suspected of the crime. Hulbert Footner has excelled himself in this fast-moving thriller, unfolding an absorbing and baffling mystery with a skill that compels our admiration.

### Murder That Had Everything, The
September 1939

The death of René Doria was, in the opinion of the press and public, a murder that had everything – wealth, glamour, mystery, high society, sex appeal. Peggy Brocklin was one of the world's richest young women, but if her bank balance was all that it should be, her stability and characteristics were certainly overdrawn. René Doria was a mystery man who crashed into society with little to commend him but amazing good looks, vitality, and the fact that society women practically swooned every time he looked at them. The engagement of these two people was a sensation in itself, but when René was found murdered it almost paralysed the life of the nation. Lee Mappin was reluctant to take on the case, but when he once agreed to do so, he had to admit it presented one of the most amazing problems of his career. This murder has everything from the reader's point of view, too.

### Murderer's Vanity
June 1941

Hulbert Footner has created an excellent character in Lee Mappin, amateur criminologist, user of snuff, author of books on the psychology of crime, and man-about-town in a quiet way. In this story, Lee receives a series of notes from a Mr. X. about a perfect crime he intends to commit, and which in fact he does commit. The running to earth of Mr. X. makes a grand story, full of startling incidents and dramatic suspense.

### Nation's Missing Guest, The
February 1939

The arrival of His Highness Ahmed bin Said, with his retinue and magnificent jewels was heralded with a fanfare of trumpets. He was greeted by diplomats, sought after by anybody who was Anybody. His visit was the press scoop of the year. Especially as he was keenly interested in the beautiful Diana Morven… . But as suddenly as His Highness was the Nation's guest, he became the Nation's missing guest, for his fat little person, and his jewels, disappeared mysteriously on a train journey. The Nation was in an uproar. Poor Luke Imbrie, who was responsible for His Highness, and in love with Diana Morven, called in his famous detective friend Lee Mappin. And before His Highness was found, the finger of suspicion pointed everywhere. A thrilling, puzzling crime novel this, as ingenious as it is original.

### New Made Grave, The
March 1935

Weir Lambert, a young man fresh from college, had acquired the proprietorship of the *Kent County Witness*, a small country newspaper that had almost ceased to circulate. Weir was proprietor, editor, compositor, and printer, and yet had plenty of time to worry. Nothing ever happened in Kentville; that, to an ambitious newspaper man, was a tragedy. And when at last something did happen, that, too, was a tragedy – a murder mystery that would have got front-page position in any city newspaper. But Weir didn't print it because at the back of his mind was a picture of a beautiful girl and a new made grave, and Weir had promised to help. Hulbert Footner makes a grand job of a dramatic situation and keeps his plot boiling with excitement to the end.

### Orchids to Murder
June 1945

Lee Mappin, the suave bespectacled private detective, was awakened much too early from a morning-after sleep by a visit from a disgruntled and angry Major Dunphy, whose grand-daughter, Mary Stannard, had disappeared an hour before her wedding was scheduled to take place. As Lee takes over, the plot thickens. Three equally implicated suspects appear out of a confusion of evidence and subtle investigations. A myriad of clues – among them two scraps of charred paper, a spray of orchids and an expensive red coupé wrapped around a tree – pile up before Lee Mappin can reach his ingenious and surprising solution. This mystery has all the qualities of a first-rate detective thriller and proves to be an expert and exciting product of Hulbert Footner's skill.

### Ring of Eyes, The
February 1933

Old J. M. Lawrence, commonly known as the lion of Wall Street, one of the biggest financiers – and one of the worst-hated men – in America, had received letters threatening assassination. Much against his will, the old man applied for police protection. From the police point of view there wasn't a worse risk in town. Old 'J. M.' was dogmatic and wilful as a spoiled child, and likely to resent protection. The police selected young Dan Woburn as personal guard, and Dan, with the prospects of a police lieutenancy and the hand of Julia Dormer if he succeeded, grimly settled down to his task. *The Ring of Eyes* is an enjoyable mystery story, with swift action, crisp dialogue, and an ingenious plot which is excitingly solved.

### Sinfully Rich
February 1940

Mrs. Clarence Warrington Ware, a wealthy New York widow, had inherited a fortune at the late age of sixty-seven, and proceeded to have her first taste of life. She hit the high spots, with unfortunate results. One day her body was found trussed up in a beautiful curved Jacobean cabinet in her boudoir. Mike Speedon, a New York columnist, gets busy with his investigations into this sensational story and uncovers some unpleasant facts about Mrs. Ware and her so-called friends. You will like Mike. He seems to know all the answers, and his knowledge of the gay night haunts of New York is peculiar and extensive. Mike puts all his cards on the table and conceals nothing, and yet there will not be many readers who will reach the correct solution of this clever mystery story, which more than maintains Hulbert Footner's high standard.

### Tortuous Trails
July 1937

Police work in the vast spaces of Canada's North-West has a fascination of its own. There is a glamour about the Mounties which never grows dim, and for that reason alone Mr. Footner's new book should be welcome. The four stories included in this book are ingenious and exciting tales of the adventures of Sergeant Brinklow and Trooper MacNab, two typical specimens of this famous corps.

### Unneutral Murder
October 1944

The liner on which Lee Mappin was travelling on what was to be one of his most dangerous and exciting missions, slid unescorted from New York, her sides brilliantly flood-lit to display the neutral flag of Portugal. Among the passengers who crowded every cabin were several in whom Lee took more than a mild interest; the good-looking, smiling young Ronald Franklin, for instance, who said he was an American agent for Swiss watches; John Stanley, going out to the hard-pressed U.S. Legation in Lisbon and his young wife Vera, daughter of a wealthy tobacco nabob; Kate MacDonald, the smartly dressed but slightly pseudo-Scottish woman. Whatever the divers purposes which prompted their voyage to Europe, their immediate activities were going to be very much the concern of Lee Mappin. *Unneutral Murder* is a streamlined story of international espionage, told superbly by Hulbert Footner, and set in the Azores and Lisbon, that glamorous and most intriguing of war-time capitals.

### Viper, The
July 1930

Paris! Paris in June! Paris under a night sky! Dejeuner in the Bois; dinner on Montmartre; ices, and *such* ices, any time of the day or night, at the Café de la Paix, the centre of the world. No wonder Miss Brickley, secretary to the famous woman detective Madame Storey, was thrilled at the prospect of accompanying her employer. It ought to have been a vacation trip, but turned out to be something more strenuous. Almost too strenuous, in fact, but Miss Brickley at any rate came near blessing the little widow who had asked Madame Storey to investigate the mysterious death of her millionaire husband. Here are new exploits of the famous Madame Storey in a new setting, revealing her more fascinating, more ingenious than ever.

### Who Killed the Husband?
January 1942

The murder of the wealthy banker Jules Gartrey in his New York apartment caused a tremendous sensation. Great crowds gathered in the street to gaze up at the windows of the Gartrey apartment; extra editions of the newspapers poured from the presses every half-hour; even Lee Mappin, famous private investigator, was reluctantly forced to abandon his accustomed pose of indifference to murder and take a professional interest in this extraordinary case. Alastair Yohe, a well-known society photographer, was wanted by the police in connection with the murder, although according to Mrs. Gartrey, one of Yohe's countless women admirers, he left the apartment five minutes before she heard the fatal shot. Mr. Hulbert Footner is one of the most accomplished detective story writers, and in Lee Mappin he has created his best character since the famous Madame Storey.

## FORD, FLORENCE

### Ninth Candle, The
April 1960

The letter indicated that old Mrs. Starke, as rich and imperious as ever, was finally sinking; Suzy Fallon was commanded to come, for the first time, to the old woman's island home. Suzy had never met her husband's family. To marry her, Roger had been forced to defy his grandmother, and after that he and his bride had been coldly ignored. Three years earlier he had returned to the island alone. And this trip resulted in the tragic accident which had left Suzy a widow.

Now Suzy had her own reason for wishing to see Roger's grandmother. But after she reached the huge bleak house on the lonely island, and talked to the old woman, she was not allowed to leave. And from the moment she met the other members of his family, she plunged into an atmosphere of greed, suspicion, and hatred. As the hatred turned viciously on her, she began to ask herself a frightening question. Had Roger's death really been an accident?

*The Ninth Candle* has all those qualities of suspense and atmosphere which Florence Ford achieved so successfully in her first book, *Shadow on the House*. Suzy Fallon's desperate struggle to learn the truth about her husband's death was finally to endanger her own life.

### Shadow on the House
January 1958

Something was wrong in the big house perched on a hilltop beside the Ohio River. To Dale Rogers the house was home, and she loved it and the people in it – her cousin Mark, his wife Lois, their small son, and even sharp-tongued old Auntie Birdie. Whenever

Dale had come to the house and been with them, she had been happy.

But this time something was wrong.

At first it seemed almost nothing, just a vague shadow on her usual happiness. A few new misunderstandings, small resentments, and an occasional feeling of discomfort. Then some of the things which were happening began to alarm her.

Becoming frightened, she was forced to realise that one of these people she loved might be hurt – even killed – even as their affection for each other was being killed. The tension mounts, then explodes into real danger. In the end, Dale's courage and determination finally reveal the extraordinary facts behind the mystery of what is actually going on in her beloved household.

This first novel introduces to the Crime Club a writer who takes character seriously, who tells an original story, and who shows a remarkable mastery of atmosphere and suspense.

## FORD, LESLIE

### *Bahamas Murder Case, The*

November 1952

Betsy Dayton thought she would be free from the twelve-year-old scandal of her father's tragic death when she visited Scott Beckwith and his parents in their Bahamas home. Thoughts of the warehouse fire in which Jerome Drayton's secretary had been burned to death and his suicide on the spot had no place in the sun-laden air and brilliant tropic colour of Nassau. But a sequence of frightening events convinced Scott and Betsy that the island held some ink with her father's death. So Betsy sent her thoughts back twelve years and tried to piece together everything she could remember about that terrible day. And finally, when it was almost too late, she dredged up from her childhood the clue to a triple murderer. Leslie Ford has contrived a plot in which the mystery deepens and the suspense heightens until the very last page.

### *Capital Crime, A*

August 1941

The laconic and lynx-eyed Colonel John Primrose, his devoted retainer Sergeant Buck, and the irrepressible Mrs. Grace Latham are the moving spirits in this new mystery by Leslie Ford. Yellowstone Park, America's famous National Park, is the scene, and the man who was found shot to death in a starlit glade was one of the tourist party with which Mrs. Latham was travelling. There were several men and women who had ample motive and opportunity to extinguish George Pelham, and it was Colonel Primrose's difficult job to pierce the dark cloud of suspicion and reveal a subtle and cold-blooded killer. In this he was erratically assisted by Mrs. Latham, whose incorrigible habit of eavesdropping almost brought her to grief. Here is a thoroughly puzzling murder, its impact intensified by the startling events preceding it, told in Leslie Ford's very satisfying manner.

### *Crack of Dawn*

February 1945

From the cross-currents and ambiguities of present-day Washington society, Leslie Ford draws the plot of this her latest adventure involving Mrs. Grace Latham and Colonel John Primrose, with granite-faced Sergeant Buck, as usual, in lumbering and faithful attendance. As always, her characters are completely realised and her situations deftly drawn. A new Leslie Ford mystery is invariably anticipated by her many readers, and this one tops the list for thrilling action and brilliant detection.

### *Devil's Stronghold, The*

December 1948

From the moment that Grace Latham picks up, in a taxi in Washington, a match-book bearing the hurried scrawl 'The Devil's Stronghold', and flies to Hollywood in response to a friend's warning letter to rescue her son Bill from the clutches of a film-struck gold-digger, the die, as they say, is cast. Mrs. Latham liked to think that until she met Colonel Primrose and the formidable Sergeant Buck she knew nothing about murder, violent death and their investigation, but whether it is she or the Colonel who attracts crime as a honey-pot the bees, one can be certain that where they are, there too will be murder, mystery and lively entertainment for all.

### *Girl From the Mimosa Club, The*

November 1957

Kerry O'Keefe, the girl who worked as a hostess in the night spots of Baltimore, was an 'unsuitable match' for Johnny Brayton, son of the old Baltimore family. Kerry's work was not quite what it appeared – but then she couldn't explain that to Johnny, any more than he could persuade his family that a night club "sitter" would make a perfect wife for him.

This was the situation when a murder was committed in the big Brayton home in Mt. Vernon Place. After that nothing could prevent Kerry's profession becoming known; she became involved in the secrets and the scandals that – until the shooting – had been hidden.

A prisoner is tried for the murder in Mt. Vernon Place. Under the searchlights of the public courtroom, amid the stresses of a trial for murder, the characters, including Kerry, are ruthlessly examined; their stories, and the story of the murder, are unfolded.

This is a brilliant and exciting novel in which the tension mounts continuously.

### *Honolulu Murder Story*

April 1947

Leslie Ford presents those popular characters, Colonel Primrose and Mrs. Latham, in another excellent story. It is the story of a black-sheep American whose family had lived in Hawaii for generations, but who went to Japan and came back to play traitor to his country. Mrs. Latham is present when he makes his first appearance in his family's house; she is present when his murdered body is discovered; and she is deeply involved in the circumstances that lead up to a second murder. *Honolulu Murder Story* is told with typical Leslie Ford skill, suspense, deft characterisation and colourful background.

### *Ill Met By Moonlight*

July 1937

Sandra Gould was an inevitable candidate for sudden death by murder. She had been vexing and harassing the entire little community of April Harbour. By nature she was one of those women whom other women and all the men who aren't in love with her would like to murder. Yet the circumstances in which her body was found, huddled in a seat of a car in the Gould's garage, seemed to preclude anything but suicide. Every one in the little town assumed that Sandra Gould killed herself, but gossip and the presence of Colonel Primrose and his faithful Sergeant Buck soon opened up an investigation which led to an amazing tangle of crime and terror.

### *Invitation to Murder*

April 1955

I to M or Invitation to Murder was what the bank called the James V. Maloney Trust. James Maloney's only descendants were his daughter, Dodo, married to her fourth husband, Count Nikki de Gradoff, and his grand-daughter, Jennifer, with whom Fish Finlay, himself an executive of the Maloney Trust, fell in love. The murderer's first difficulty in getting hold of the Maloney fortune was to find out the Trust's secret clauses: to find out whom to marry and whom to kill. The man who risked everything for the Maloney money was clever and unscrupulous. At the mercy of unreliable accomplices, haunted by the lingering traces of another terrible crime committed in the past, driven by the need for immediate cash into a desperate intrigue over a necklace of priceless rubies, he could find one way only to save his skin and forward his plans – by killing, and killing again. The Invitation to Murder was accepted. Against the glittering background of social life at the height of the season in Newport, this story develops excitingly and fast. The deep laid plot comes to a climax as exciting and satisfying as any Leslie Ford has written; not even the staunchest follower of Colonel Primrose will be able to complain about his absence from the book.

### *Lying Jade, The*

August 1953

Rumour is a lying jade, and rumour in Washington was rife. The merest and most private whisper leaked into the public amplifiers with incredible speed. Rumour had all sorts of things to say about the tool king, Rufus Brent, and his wife Lena and his daughter Molly; and Hamilton Vair, who was out to break Brent on a private score and in the process to elevate himself to the Senate, took full advantage of its lying tongue. Grace Latham, who makes so welcome a return in this new Leslie Ford novel, gets drawn into the political dog-fight through her incurable soft-heartedness. As usual she becomes so involved that Colonel Primrose has to come to the rescue, to the great disgust of the granite-face Sergeant Buck!

### *Mr Cromwell is Dead*

June 1939

Boulevard of Broken Dreams, with its clatter and jangle and bars and gambling and all its raggle-taggle tinsel glamour. That is how Reno is described in Leslie Ford's latest book. And it is among the cheap crooks and grafters who infest the celebrated capital of divorce that murder strikes and strikes again. Many people had motives, many had things to conceal, but they were all frightened and they all lied. It took Colonel Primrose and Sergeant Buck quite a time to get on the right track, but the final denouement is as ingenious and thrilling as anything this author has given us in the past.

### *Murder Comes to Eden*

August 1956

The Eden of Spig and Molly O'Leary was a lovely, peaceful place. There the O'Leary's acquired a home largely through the sudden generosity of Miss Celia Fairlie, an odd, vague and unexpectedly shrewd old lady who had take a great liking to small Tip O'Leary. When Spig is already involved in preserving this idyllic spot against industrial encroachment, another, older story begins to unfold: a story that goes back into the past of Miss Celia Fairlie concerning a mysterious death many years before. In both stories – the present crisis and the secret of the past – Spig O'Leary becomes involved; in his bitterness and anger he blunders badly and even his marriage seems threatened. This brilliant new story moves at a dazzling pace. Even the greatest admirers of Colonel Primrose will forgive the author his absence from *Murder Comes to Eden*.

### *Murder Down South*

November 1942

Here are mystery, romance and suspense blended by a master hand in a fascinating story, told against the loveliest of backgrounds, an old town on the Mississippi, drowsing in its old Southern tradition and ablaze with flowers. In this story of modern Montagues and Capulets, and of a young lover who was able not only to win a charming though reluctant bride but also to stop an elusive and determined killer just in time, readers will find Leslie Ford at her best.

### *Murder Is the Pay-off*

November 1951

Everyone in Smithville except the anti-vice leagues had gone mad on fruit machines, and where there are people willing to gamble there is always someone ready to hold the stakes. Doc Wernitz owned all the slot machines in the vicinity, and it was rumoured that he held the cheques of many prominent citizens which he didn't think it politic to redeem. Then he decided to leave town, and turned some cheques into the bank. If he hadn't done that he might never have been found on his cellar floor with his head smashed in. Leslie Ford hits the jackpot in suspense with *Murder is the Payoff*.

### *Philadelphia Murder Story, The*

August 1945

*The Philadelphia Murder Story* concerns the astonishing case of Myron Kane, distinguished columnist and contributor to the *Saturday Evening Post*, in whose palatial offices he is found stabbed to death. It is as baffling a mystery as ever turned a magazine – and Philadelphia society – inside out. Colonel Primrose does a brilliant sleuthing job as usual; Mrs.Latham helps and hinders in her own inimitable fashion; and Sergeant Buck disapproves thoroughly of the whole business. There is a second murder, a romance, plentiful excitement and a great deal of interesting Philadelphia background in this grand story, in which real people under their real names play amusing and exciting roles.

### *Priority Murder*

July 1943

Colonel Primrose does a particularly fine job of detection in *Priority Murder*, a first-rate mystery story set in war-time Washington. The story centres round the strange death of an important official in one of the big Ministries in America's capital, and the solution remains in the dark until the last moment. *Priority Murder* is a grand story sure of an enthusiastic welcome from Leslie Ford's many readers.

### *Road to Folly*

February 1941

All who had known her had had reason to hate and perhaps to kill her – Phyllis Lattimer, the wealthy heiress who is the worthy victim of Leslie Ford's new murder story; but Phyllis Lattimer's death seems somehow linked with the sinister secret that had been sealed for three generations in Strawberry Hill. Here is a story crowded with action and suspense, romance and mystery.

### *Shot in the Dark*

September 1949

Young Dr. Smith, alone but for his dog, is lying on the shore of a creek in Maryland enjoying the last of a peaceful holiday. Suddenly the quiet of the night is shattered by the sound of a car driving up to a neighbouring bungalow, and he unwittingly hears heated words between a girl and her escort. None of my business, thinks the doctor, and retires to bed. But a little while later he is wakened by the sound of a shot, and soon finds that it is all very much his business! He becomes overnight the prime suspect in a case of murder, and finds himself bound to silence by loyalty to a girl with whom he has fallen in love at first sight. Read Leslie Ford and have an enjoyable crime!

### Simple Way of Poison, The
March 1938
Randall Nash lay poisoned in the library, a decanter and glass beside him. Colonel Primrose called the police, put down the telephone and asked quietly of his wife, "Where is the glass he was drinking from?" Her words were scarcely audible as her blanched lips moved: "I washed it and put it away."

### Siren in the Night
March 1944
*Siren in the Night* features Grace Latham and Colonel Primrose, not to mention the latter's granite-visaged, self-appointed guardian Sergeant Buck, in a first-rate mystery set in wartime San Francisco. It was inconceivable on the face of it that anyone would want to murder Loring Kimball, a wealthy citizen with a high reputation as a public benefactor. And yet one person had waited on that eventful night with intent to kill and with what must have been a complete sense of security. Here is a story of lifelong hatred and revenge in which the suspense mounts to an astonishing climax.

### Snow-White Murder
May 1940
Leslie Ford now belongs to the select few writers whose names are synonymous with unfailingly good mystery novels – a startlingly swift accomplishment, for her first stories appeared only a few years ago. Every one will be fascinated by this brilliantly told story of Colonel Primrose and Sergeant Buck hunting a cunning criminal through the charming byways of an old Virginian town.

### Three Bright Pebbles
April 1939
If you know anything about archery, you will know that an arrow describes an arc, so that if you aim at your target you go a long way over it. So you put something on the ground in front to aim at. Rick, the dissolute, was found shot with an arrow, and three bright pebbles lay on the ground nearby. Had they been put there to aim at? That is the problem in a story rich in mystery and entertainment.

### Town Cried Murder, The
November 1939
Four years ago the name of Leslie Ford was known only to a small devoted public as the author of some exceedingly original crime novels. Since then Leslie Ford's audience has grown to millions through serials, and the book sales have quadrupled. *Punch* recommends Leslie Ford books for their entertainment value; the *Spectator* and the *Observer* for their clever detection. Leslie Ford's name is definitely 'on the map'. This new novel, *The Town Cried Murder*, is the tale of a sleepy old town, attractive to tourists, and of the sensational murder that woke it from its long peace.

### Trial From Ambush
June 1962
Mary Melissa Seaton was raped two days before her wedding. This happened just outside her father's house when she was returning alone at night.

Suspicion was to fall on Mary Melissa's friends. And yet the police knew of previous

victims who had been attacked in circumstances that closely resemble the case of Mary Melissa.

A charge is brought, and the case comes to court. The court-room scenes are intensely exciting. Leslie Ford again effectively demonstrates her skill as a crime novelist not least in the startling developments that take place during the trial and its aftermath.

### Woman in Black, The
January 1948
The scene of Leslie Ford's new detective story is Washington, where the shrewd and charming Mrs. Latham sees the first queer indications of peril at an elaborate Georgetown dinner party and shortly afterwards stumbles upon the dead body of the mysterious 'woman in black'. Three people die and several more suffer bitterly before Mrs. Latham, Captain Lamb of the Washington police and, of course, Sergeant Buck, succeed in penetrating the web of mystery surrounding the industrial magnate Enoch B. Stubblefield, and in revealing the significance of the 'woman in black'. Here is Leslie Ford in top form telling a skilfully woven story with real people in it and persuasive atmosphere.

## FORSYTHE, MALCOLM
### Book Lady, The
August 1993
Janet West and Laura Stebbing operated the mobile library that travelled the villages of north-east Essex on a schedule as precise as a railway timetable. When Janet's body was found at a lonely spot on the bank of the River Colne, Chief Inspector Millson wondered why anyone would murder such a respectable and well-liked woman. And where was she going at night by the river? Surely she hadn't been alone?

There was no obvious suspect and as his investigation proceeded he discovered there was more to the friendly librarian than he realized. Then Laura took part in a reconstruction of Janet's movements on the night she was killed and suddenly there were three suspects.

In the end there were three murders too.

### Cousin Removed, A
August 1992
Max Douglas murdered his wife on a pleasant Sunday afternoon in June. He killed her with the easy assurance he did everything else in life and had witnesses on hand to say her death was an accident. Chief Inspector Millson wasn't satisfied Daphne Douglas had drowned by accident. However, he could find no motive for her husband to kill her and turned aside to another case: the disappearance of a man called Boley thirty years earlier. His inquiries uncovered a grim and disturbing story. Meantime, Max Douglas became involved with Poppy Latimer who worked in the florist's that had supplied flowers for his wife's funeral. But Poppy was not at all the kind of girl Max thought she was and when George Millson was confronted with another accident he knew that this time it was definitely murder.

### Without a Trace
November 1991
Eight-year-old Maisie Brown disappeared during Tanniford's annual fete. Chief Inspector Millson suspected Maisie's stepfather. Millson disliked stepfathers. His own daughter had one and he resented having to arrange with him and his ex-wife when he could see her.

Tanniford lay in the bend of a river,

confined there by the railway line. The only road out was over the railway bridge. The local police had closed the road to traffic while the fete was on and no vehicle left the village between two o'clock and six that day. This convinced Millson that Maisie had been abducted by someone in the village and she was still there – dead or alive. The villagers believed a stranger had taken her. In a way, they were both right.

## FRASER, ANTHEA
### April Rainers, The
October 1989
At first, DCI Webb was merely irritated that a local murder should coincide with a visit by Shillingham-born composer Felicity Harwood, since it meant his missing her concert. But as the days passed, it seemed Miss Harwood herself might be in danger. What had caused her inexplicable collapse on stage? And who were the April Rainers, whose death threat, couched in flowery language, seemed to have been carried out?

For Mark Templeton, a music master who had persuaded the composer to play at a fundraising concert at her old school, more personal problems began to emerge as he was suddenly faced with decisions which could change the course of his life, both personal and professional.

Another murder, also foreshadowed by the April Rainers, provided clues which enabled Webb, helped as always by Sergeant Jackson, to probe beneath the green ink and hyperbole and disclose the true identity of the killers.

### Death Speaks Softly
May 1987
When a French girl, Arlene Picard, disappeared from Broadshire University, Chief Inspector Webb found himself with a more complicated case than he'd expected. There were plenty of men, both tutors and postgraduates, who'd been attracted to the girl, as had his young detective-constable.

But not all Webb's unease was caused by suspects. On the fringe of his inquiries was Professor Warwick, a man whose brilliance teetered on the brink of madness, and whom Webb, for reasons he couldn't explain, regarded as 'a walking time-bomb'.

The arrival of the girl's parents from France precipitated town and gown into a further tragedy which had its roots in the past and which Webb had feared but been unable to prevent. He had cause to reflect that love, or the lack of it, often leads to disaster and Death at times speaks softly in the very tones of love.

### Lily-White Boys, The
April 1991
Monica Tovey's initial reaction to the dumping of a disreputable van outside her house is merely annoyance. However, when its gruesome contents are revealed, fear succeeds irritation and a frightening chain of events is set in motion which seems to threaten her life.

DCI Webb finds that murder trails in its wake a net of incongruities – burglary, football hooligans, low-flying aircraft and mysterious phone calls. As usual, his inquiries take him from humble cottages to sumptuous houses as he seeks to dig beneath the evasions, hesitations and denials with which his questions are met.

By the time he has the answer, Monica's life and those of her family and friends have been turned upside down, never again to be the same. And at the root of it all lay the two they called The Lily-White Boys.

### Necessary End, A
April 1985
No one at first connected the body found by a lonely country road with Nancy Pendrick, the career wife of a hotel owner in the village of Frecklemarsh and head of her own London cookery school. After all, Nancy had insisted on returning to London after the New Year holiday, pleading pressure of work, and no one had reported her missing. So what was she doing back in Broadshire?

Her husband Oliver could offer no explanation, though Chief Inspector Webb learned with interest that an old flame of his had recently returned to the village. Rose, his beautiful daughter, knew something but refused to cooperate, while Henry, his son, seemed to have something to hide. Then there was Nancy's ne'er-do-well ex-husband, who disappeared at the time she was killed; the Beresfords, Oliver's in-laws through his first wife, tragically dead; and a little girl who was the last person to see Nancy alive. All of them, whether they realized it or not, held pieces of the jigsaw which, when fitted together, would produce a picture of her killer.

With Sergeant Jackson beside him, Webb set out grimly to assemble those pieces.

### Nine Bright Shiners, The
December 1987
To Jan Coverdale, daughter of one explorer and half-sister of another, the history and legends of Peru had been familiar since childhood. But when her marriage broke down and her half-brother Edward invited her home for Christmas, they became all at once more personal and more threatening.

It began with a body dressed in tramp's clothing, with incongruous green sequins on his lapel. He looked disconcertingly like Edward, whose wallet was in his pocket – but hadn't Edward and his wife flown to Peru?

The discovery that 'the tramp' was an investigative journalist was a development DCI Webb could have done without, since it threw the case wide open. But why was the body dressed so shabbily and what was the meaning of those sequins?

The dead man's notebook was missing, but several of his investigations began to emerge – fraud in the City, minor theft from a squash club, illicit London lunches. And there was still a question-mark hanging over an expedition to Peru made more than thirty years ago. Which of these stories was important enough to kill for, not once but twice?

Only after a long and tortuous trail does Webb discover the truth about The Nine Bright Shiners, and who killed to possess them.

### Pretty Maids All in a Row
April 1986
When Jessica Randal, a West End actress, accompanied her biographer husband to the country for a month's research, she fully expected to be bored, especially since her leg was in plaster following an accident on their honeymoon. Yet within a week of their arrival she'd learned they were renting the house of a murder victim, and that there was an unknown rapist at large, who was obsessed with nursery rhymes.

The different levels of the village, both geographical and social, seemed equally at risk: Carrie Speight the cleaner and her hairdresser sister Della; the Matron and staff of the Old People's Home; the wealthy Markham family; and increasingly Jessica herself apparently singled out by the rapist.

Since she might have met with the man socially, Jessica regarded all her neighbours with growing suspicion. Still worse, there'd been no trouble in the village before they came, and she began to wonder, as others already did, how well she knew her new husband.

Once again, Chief Inspector Webb and Sergeant Jackson pit their wits against a cunning adversary. By the time they unmask him, the innocent world of nursery rhymes has, for the village of Westridge, been contaminated for ever.

### Shroud for Delilah, A
May 1984
Who killed 'Delilah' – again and again, leaving no clue but a lipstick accusation scrawled on a mirror? All the victims in and around the quiet cathedral city had had marital difficulties and all had died at home, apparently waiting meekly in their chairs to be stabbed to the heart. Chief Inspector Webb and his colleagues were baffled. To Kate Romilly, newly separated from her husband and struggling to build a new life for herself and her small son, the deaths posed a personal threat. Who was the watcher on the bench near her home, the silent telephone caller, the sender of unspeakable parcels? Had she too been branded a 'Delilah'?

Cut off from her old friends and unsure of her new ones, against all of whom there was a question-mark, Kate waited in terror as the murders drew ever closer. Who would strike first? The police – or the wielder of the deadly knife?

### Six Proud Walkers
October 1988
The Walker family, manufacturers of world-famous Broadshire Porcelain, seemed a close and loving family, well respected in their home village. But from the day that DCI Webb saw the word 'Murder' spelled out in flowers in their garden, one tragedy followed another, and within a week, two members of the family had died violently. Were their deaths connected with that flowery accusation? Was it a self-fulfilling prophecy?

As Webb and Sergeant Jackson work against time to prevent further killings, a different picture emerges from the public image. Tensions, fears, jealousies, have long been festering under the surface, and the first death proves the catalyst.

There are also those outside the tightly-knit circle who resent the Walkers, among them Dick Ridley, who blames them for his father's death, and Clive Tenby, whose relationship with young Fay was summarily broken off. Did one of them hate enough to strike – and strike again?

Against the background of a peaceful village during a summer heatwave, long-buried truths are unearthed until at last Webb is able to pinpoint the killer, but can he prevent a final tragedy?

### Symbols at Your Door
May 1990
To a casual observer, Beckworth is an idyllic place to live, with its pretty houses, superb views, and the added attraction of a Stately Home in its midst. Yet behind the high hedges some of its residents live lonely, even frightened, lives, and when ugly faces are drawn on several front doors robbery and murder are not far behind. Is it coincidence, DCI Webb wonders, or were the graffiti statements of intent?

His investigations are not helped by the fact that the village itself is divided: old-time residents who grew up there, and newcomers – commuters for the most part – who have brought renovated houses at prices far beyond the villagers' means.

It seems no-one is willing to be completely open with the police, and before Webb can uncover the perpetrator of one killing, another occurs.

Luck, as he acknowledges, plays a part in solving one crime, and the answer to the other has been there for the looking from the very beginning.

### Three, Three, The Rivals
February 1992
What exactly had Sheila Fairchild seen in the middle of the night forty years ago, and could it possibly have a bearing on a recent murder?

This is only one of the problems facing DCI Webb when, against his will, he is assigned to a case in the town where he grew up. Smouldering resentments and old hostilities impede his inquiries as he tries to sort out facts from fancies and the truth from an intricate tissue of lies.

Only after he has faced up to a traumatic incident in this own boyhood does the solution become apparent, and by the end of the case not only Webb but several prominent residents of Erlesborough have been forced to take a long, hard look at themselves.

In her finest novel to date Anthea Fraser digs deep into the wellsprings of human conduct and the confused, often conflicting feelings a man may have about those long since dead whose true relationships he is only now beginning to understand.

## FULLER, TIMOTHY
### J for Jupiter
January 1937
This book has been acclaimed the best first detective novel that has appeared in America last year. It has also been accorded the honour of being the first contemporary mystery story ever serialised in that famous journal, *The Atlantic Monthly*, which sets a very high standard in fiction.

It features Jupiter Jones, eccentric undergraduate and perhaps the most engaging amateur detective that ever muddled the police. Jupiter went to see his professor's room to discuss the Fine Arts, but found himself faced instead with Death.

Mr. Timothy Fuller has not only written an original and refreshing crime novel, but has also set a very baffling mystery.

## GAGNON, MAURICE
### Dark Night Offshore, A
January 1986
The tanker *Kyrios Mercury* blew up and sank off the coast of Newfoundland with the loss of twenty-five lives. To Deirdre O'Hara, Montreal lawyer specializing in marine insurance investigation and retained by the insurers, that was easily the worst aspect of the case – far worse than the $15 million which her clients stood to lose and the perpetrators of the sinking stood to gain. As a lawyer, she was determined to see the guilty prosecuted and punished under the due process of civilized law.

But barratry is a difficult crime to prove at any time, and Deirdre was dealing with a nearly perfect crime. Captain Johnson and the six men rescued with him from the lifeboat were not about to break down and confess in the course of the inquiry into the sinking which opened in St Anthony, and Deirdre could see no way of making them. Even when her patient investigation secured the one piece of incontrovertible evidence she needed, it seemed that those responsible might still escape. Only by risking her life and her career was Deirdre able to see justice done.

### Doubtful Motives
June 1987
Ted Ackroyd, talented Australian electronics engineer and head of the Canadian firm Ackroyd Enterprises, planned a world cruise now that his firm had weathered the financial stresses of extending its operations and his partner could safely be left in charge. To that end he had designed a boat with every device and luxury and insured it heavily, along with himself and crew. At the Royal St Lawrence Yacht Club the boat wins the admiration of Deirdre O'Hara, Montreal lawyer specializing in marine insurance.

Then the boat blows up in the Gulf of St Lawrence and a Lloyd's investigator puts Deirdre on the job to discover whether the insurers will have to pay. How could such a perfect boat explode?

There follows a skilled and knowledgeable investigation as the wreck is raised, the evidence gathered and the legal proofs established. Deirdre returns to Montreal with clear evidence of a premeditated crime and an even clearer idea of who was behind it. But as the investigation proceeds it becomes apparent that nothing in this case is clear, not least Deirdre's view of it.

### Inner Ring, The
July 1985
Deirdre O'Hara, narrator of this finely plotted Canadian mystery, is a Montreal lawyer by profession and a highly specialized marine insurance investigator by what she terms 'accidental avocation'. Early one morning, cycling along the bicycle path on the dyke separating the St Lawrence Waterway canal from the river, she finds a body near the water's edge. Professional training tells her that the girl could not have fallen there: she had been thrown. Murdered.

From then on Deirdre is drawn into an investigation very different from her usual work, for the unknown victim was not struck down on impulse: she had been cold – bloodedly and professionally killed. Working closely with Captain Andre Remillard of the Sûreté du Quebec, Deirdre discovers the victim's identity and penetrates the secret which led to her death, only to realize that if those ultimately responsible are not brought to justice, the lives of many innocent Canadian citizens may be at risk.

In a climax both dramatic and ironic, Deirdre herself is the bait to lure the criminals into revealing their identity – an identity as shocking as it is unexpected.

## GAIR, MALCOLM
### A Long Hard Look
July 1958
The degeneration of Edith Desmond was tragic, embarrassing and pitiable. So was her death. Mark Raeburn had met her not long before her body was found on Wimbledon Common, and it was to Raeburn that her husband turned for help when his career was in jeopardy from the publicity, and later when the hectoring Superintendent Werner seemed too suspicious. Raeburn knew some of the dead woman's friends already: the sleepy-seeming young Michael Evans and his pretty wife; that ageing gallant, Colonel Clayton; Harry Rick, the Anglo-Canadian who had risen to eminence and vast wealth by the pitiless and adroit use of power; and he was to meet more. He knew that somewhere among the men and women that Edith Desmond had used, abused and discarded, there must be a link with the past which would lead logically to her twisted corpse on the grass. Readers of *Sapphires on Wednesday* already know Mark Raeburn's realistic, sophisticated approach

to his work, and that his methods of investigation are forceful and relentless. Malcolm Gair writes fast-moving and enthralling stories which combine the best elements of the detective story and the thriller. *A Long Hard Look* is an exciting and intriguing book.

### Sapphires on Wednesday
May 1957
Mme. Gaia Palatino (like a "white toad") was a tough client for a man just starting on his first assignment as a private detective; it was not long before Mark Raeburn appreciated the justice of the warning a friend had given him about her – 'A formidable woman. One has a feeling there's nothing she mightn't do.' She first commissions Mark to steal some sapphires from a passenger aboard a transatlantic liner. But when he has accomplished this by an impudent piece of deception, he finds that he is only at the beginning of a long and dangerous trail …

It leads him to Long Island, to some surprising discoveries in Milan and finally to an assault on a lakeside villa in the Alps, where a dramatic story comes to a climax in a race along mountain roads.

Malcolm Gair is a new name in crime fiction. Accomplished writing and sympathetic characterisation raise his story to a high level; Mark Raeburn, the young investigator from Scotland, is really credible and as tough as they come. A charming American girl shares his adventures and a delightful romance grows up between them, but 'you don't belong to the ordinary settled world,' she tells him: 'these things – shooting and chasing and crime – for me they're an interlude, but for you they're the real world.' Mark Raeburn certainly enjoys the thrills and dangers of crime investigation. So will the readers of *Sapphires on Wednesday*.

## GARVE, ANDREW
(see also Somers, Paul)
### Ascent of D.13, The
March 1969
The newest, most secret weapon was tested by an RAF plane flying over an airfield in Germany. After the test the plane, with its secret equipment, was ordered to land in Cyprus.

On the way to Cyprus the plane was hi-jacked. Course was set for Russia.

In the upshot it crashed in mountains close to an international frontier between East and West.

This is the story of the men who were sent, as a matter of desperate urgency, to locate that vital, secret equipment in the shell of the crashed aircraft. The wreck lay in fog, snow and blizzards, at some 13,000 feet…

It is the story of the ascent of a major peak by professional climbers, under dramatic conditions and political pressures, and of the return journey…

Nothing more can be said about this ingenious plot without spoiling the reader's enjoyment. Andrew Garve is famous for stories of cliff-hanging suspense – and in *The Ascent of D.13* there is cliff-hanging in the most literal sense, in addition to the absorbing powers of a brilliant story-teller at the top of his exciting form.

### Ashes of Loda, The
April 1965
Lord Quainton is a young British newspaperman stationed in Moscow. On leave in England he falls deeply in love with a girl named Marya Raczinski. He learns that as a small child she was brought to England by her father, whose grim wartime experiences had included a term in the notorious Nazi prison camp of Loda.

Quainton's future looks set and life looks wonderful – until he stumbles on an untold story from Raczinski's past, a story which terribly contradicts the account Raczinski gave his daughter of his wartime years.

Tim Quainton decided that he had to get at the truth – whatever the truth might be. His inquiries began quietly enough in the Lenin Library in Moscow – but before long he was interviewing an alcoholic in a sinister Russian slum, illicitly journeying into former Polish territory, facing death by exposure in a blizzard, hiking across the frozen *steppe*, disguising himself as a Ukrainian peasant, and taking refuge in the labyrinthine catacombs of Odessa.

This is the story, told at a gripping pace, of how a man struggled single-handed and in alien surroundings to uncover events, intrigues and passions long buried in the "ashes of Loda" – and of what he found.

### Boomerang

June 1970

Peter Edward Talbot was a City prodigy. At thirty-three he had built up the Commonwealth Loan Corporation from a name in the telephone directory to a powerful financial organization with wide-ranging interests. His mind was as fast as the Aston-Martin which he owned. Then he was arrested on a charge of reckless, drunken driving. The judge gave him ninety days in gaol and a fine of £100.

This was awkward. Talbot had been fiddling his books, and a shortage of £100,000 had to be made up before the next audit.

In prison he got to know Dawes, an Australian who knew all about mines and explosives. Another cell-mate was Holt, a radio engineer with a talent for mimicry. From Dawes he learnt much about the workings of those fabulous nickel deposits in Australia. And suddenly Talbot knew what he had to do to get his hands on that £100,000 he so desperately needed.

Released from prison, the trio set off for Australia, there to put into effect Talbot's highly ingenious and hazardous plan. It would be unfair to reveal this plan, so closely guarded by the author until the climactic ending. However, any reader familiar with the characteristics of the boomerang will know that it can be as dangerous to the wielder as to the intended victim.

Once again Andrew Garve has turned out an exciting story, rich in fascinating background and local colour.

### Case of Robert Quarry, The

April 1972

*'Morning, Joe,' the Chief Constable said over the telephone. 'I've just had word that Robert Quarry's been murdered. I'd like you to take charge.'*

*For the first time in his professional life Detective Chief Superintendent Joseph Burns demurred at an instruction. 'You haven't forgotten, sir, that I'm being put out to grass in just over a week?'*

*'I know that, Joe – but at least you can make a start on the case. It could be the last big feather in your cap.'*

Instead the industrialist's murder looked as if it was going to be a thorn in Burns's flesh. After visiting his strike-bound factory in the Midlands, where feeling against him was running high, Quarry had telephoned his wife in Hertfordshire, spent the night in an isolated Yorkshire hotel, and was even seen in bed there at 10.45 p.m. Yet next morning his body was found in his car in another country [sic], and he had already been dead for several hours.

Patiently Burns and his sergeant tracked down everyone who might have had a grievance against Quarry – and they were many – but all their alibis seemed watertight. It looked as though Burns must hand the case over unsolved to his successor until a lucky break focused his attention on a curious coincidence. There follows a game of bluff and double bluff and an exercise in deduction which unquestionably puts Andrew Garve among the masters of the craft.

### Counterstroke

May 1978

Life hadn't held much except the bottle for Robert Farran in the months since his beloved wife died. Though a once-celebrated actor and impersonator, he didn't even have a career any more.

Then terrorists kidnapped the young wife of a politician and demanded as ransom the release of one of their number serving a life sentence for killing a security guard. The politician, a wealthy man, offered a quarter of a million as ransom. The gang said they weren't interested, but Robert Farran was.

Could he manage to convince the politician, the police and the Government that his ploy was worth trying? Could he impersonate a man he did not know well enough to fool those who knew him intimately? Farran was prepared to try, but somewhere along the line things went wrong. He still had his life to lose but he no longer stood to gain a fortune.

Andrew Garve wrings the last drop of suspense from this terrifyingly topical novel, which reaffirms his place as an arch-plotter and master of ingenuity.

### Cuckoo Line Affair, The

March 1953

When a highly-respected citizen is accused by a pretty girl of assaulting her in a train, and two unimpeachable witnesses say they saw him do it, his position is serious. This was the astounding thing that happened to Edward Latimer, sixtyish, lovable and slightly quaint, on a journey to the Essex village of Steepleford by the ancient single-track railway known locally as the Cuckoo Line. The incident was only the beginning of his troubles, for a few days later the girl's dead body was found in the lonely nearby saltings and all the evidence pointed to Edward as her killer. It took all the intelligence of his sons, Quentin and Hugh, and the wit of Hugh's fiancée, Cynthia, to produce an alternative theory about the murder – and an alternative suspect. With persistence and unshakable faith, they unravel the plot and in a dramatic reconstruction demonstrate the incredible truth.

Differing greatly in background from *Murder in Moscow*, which was so well received, *The Cuckoo Line Affair* is equally remarkable for its ingenious plot and vivid characterisation.

### Death and the Sky Above

October 1953

Life didn't hold much for Louise Hilary. Middle-aged, drunken, raddled, she was incapable of any genuine emotion except hatred for her husband, Charles. She had been separated from Charles for two years, but by refusing him a divorce she could still torture him by preventing his marrying Kathryn Forrester. In fact, life held very little for Louise Hilary; she was soon to leave it.

Charles found himself accused, tried, convicted and sentenced to hang. A few hours before his execution was due there came a very surprising development. From that moment the pace of this story grows ever faster. Kathyrn, a loyal and courageous ally, plays a big part in the adventure; she helps him to escape from the most formidable and determined pursuer in the world. This is a crime story of tremendous excitement and pace. Readers of *Murder in Moscow* and *The Cuckoo Line Affair* will know the great ingenuity and suspense which Andrew Garve's writing invariably provides.

### End of the Track, The

August 1956

Peter Mallory thought himself the most fortunate of men. Living and working in the calm beauty of the New Forest, it seemed that he had found an oasis of peace for himself, his wife and young family into which no ugliness could penetrate. But ugliness came, and cruelty and malice, in the form in which it could hurt him most – as a threat to the happiness of his family. *The End of the Track* tells of his dire predicament and of his struggles to free himself. When his enemy meets a horrible end, Mallory thinks his problem solved, but instead the net around him draws tighter. This story, of almost intolerable tension, is as exciting as its well-known predecessors, *Murder in Moscow*, *Death and the Sky Above*, and *The Riddle of Samson*. It will add to Andre Garve's reputation as a thrilling storyteller.

### Far Sands, The

February 1961

When you've lost hope you'll try almost anything.

A coroner's verdict of murder faced James Renison with a fateful decision. What hope of happiness had he or Carol if her sister, her identical twin in mind and body, was proved capable of a carefully planned and hideously cruel killing? Carol flatly refused to accept the verdict. Renison saw only one course open to him: assume his sister-in-law's innocence and try to find evidence against the real killer. It was a decision which led him from a manhunt to blackmail and finally to violence and danger. As he pieced together the hidden deeds which had led to death on the Far Sands, he found that he had not only discovered new evidence – he was face to face with the murderer.

Andrew Garve has an outstanding reputation for crime stories which combine reality and cunning plots with action and gripping suspense. *The Far Sands* is vintage Garve.

### File on Lester, The

January 1974

Since Andrew Garve's first crime novel, *No Tears for Hilda*, published in 1950, he has written some 25 books and established a reputation for highly ingenious plots. His novels are sometimes ironic social documents (*Boomerang*), sometimes thrillers behind the scenes of current history (*The Ascent of D.13*), sometimes strict detective stories (*The Case of Robert Quarry*). They are always immensely readable.

The plot of his latest novel reflects both his interest in small boat sailing and his background as a former newspaperman.

James Lester is the new young leader of a political party which seems certain to win the forthcoming general election. At his adoption meeting reporters are delighted when a girl hints at romance. The girl is attractive, Lester a widower. Yet he flatly denies that they have ever met.

Piqued, Shirley Holt gives the Press convincing details of their encounter on the west coast of Scotland, and about Lester's boat on which she spent the night. One of the two is lying and it looks like Lester. Immediately his political career is at stake. The opposition make much of his untrustworthy behaviour. Lester persists in his denials, and his party loses support. Then an old friend, the editor of a national daily, who believes Lester, employs his most experienced staff to dig around. The object is to break Shirley's story, but each successive piece of evidence seems to reverse the one before. And even if Shirley's story can be broken, why did she tell it, and what is in it for her?

Step by step, each skilfully developed and each more dramatic than the last, the reader is embroiled in Lester's dilemma, and ultimately – and unexpectedly – in crime.

### Frame-Up

March 1964

Who killed John Lumsden?

The principal suspects had alibis. Chief Inspector Charles Blair felt quite sure that something was wrong with at least one alibi, yet even a suspicious policeman must face facts: and the facts were that this alibi was unbreakable, the man could not have been in two places at once. Another alibi proved less impervious and yet there *were* elements of corroboration, which didn't add up to proof.

Who killed Lumsden, then, and why? The answer to this question proves once again, and excitingly, that Andrew Garve is among the most ingenious of suspense novelists: *Frame-Up* is different in kind from his last book, *The Sea Monks*, but no less fascinating and gripping.

### Galloway Case, The

May 1958

Peter Rennie's assignment in Jersey looked like being a routine reporting job – before he met Mary. After that it became high romance – until the day she suddenly and mysteriously disappeared.

Spurred by professional curiosity as much as by wounded pride, Rennie sets out to track her down – only to find himself confronted by an even bigger mystery. This time, however, he has help. Like pieces of a fantastic jig-saw puzzle, the facts and motives and deductions which have condemned a man to a living death are reviewed and re-arranged to form a different and startling pattern.

For Peter the prize is Mary; for her it is the rescue of a man – a man she loves. With different motives they pursue the same end, and nearly meet an identical grim fate. Their escape provides a thrilling climax to a highly original story.

Once again Andrew Garve displays the qualities of ingenuity and excitement which have brought him into the front rank of to-day's crime writers.

### Golden Deed, The

February 1960

Frank Roscoe came into the Mellanby's lives dramatically: he saved eight-year-old Tony Mellanby from drowning. Young, kindly, and wealthy, Sally and John naturally did all they could to repay the pleasant young ex-officer for the priceless service he had rendered. But gradually they found they had entangled themselves in a situation which made their lives a nightmare of fear and suspicion – a nightmare which became more terrible after the macabre and violent fate of Frank Roscoe himself.

*The Golden Deed* is a gripping and ingenious book which will add to the unique reputation which Andrew Garve has achieved as a crime novelist of excellence, originality and skill.

### Hero for Leanda, A

May 1959

Mike Conway, an ocean-going yachtsman down on his luck in a tropical port, welcomes the chance to repair his fortunes when he is approached to undertake a dangerous and illegal, but highly-lucrative, mission. For

Victor Metaxas, who planned the enterprise, it is an expensive, millionaire's gesture on behalf of his country. For the hero-worshipping Leanda, who helped him, it is a passionate crusade. That proves to be the biggest obstacle that Conway, a self-styled 'mercenary', has to contend with. When the yacht *Thalia* slips out of Mombasa harbour at the start of the adventure, the prospects seem reasonably good – but there are complications, villainous and romantic, ahead – and the trickiest part of the whole project turns out to be the journey back.

Andrew Garve has once more set a gripping and original story against an unusual background. *A Hero for Leanda* triumphantly achieves the high standards of realism and suspense which this author always sets himself.

### Hole in the Ground, A
October 1952

Andrew Garve has quickly built for himself a reputation as a writer of crime stories that are unconventional. The lively intelligence of his writing alone would take him out of the ordinary run, but he approaches each new story, from his first *No Tears for Hilda* to his recent *Murder in Moscow*, from a fresh and strongly individual angle. *A Hole in the Ground* is no exception. Into this remarkable novel he introduces the little-known art of pot-holing and takes us down to an underground world sometimes frightening, sometimes fantastically beautiful. Laurence Quilter, Labour M.P. for the West Cumbrian Division, finds by chance some underground caves on his property and enlists the help of Peter Anstey, an experienced potholer, in exploring them. Anstey meets his death in their labyrinthine depths, and this tragedy touches off events that can only be explained by an exploration of Quilter's equally tortuous mind. The denouement of this exciting and unusual story has marked topical significance.

### Home to Roost
February 1976

It is one thing to commit a murder, another to confess to it as mystery writer Walter Haines found out, for when Max Ryland was stabbed to death in his cottage on the Essex marshes, Haines was safely in Portugal. The police were perfectly satisfied that he had nothing to do with it, even though he had a first-class motive in that Ryland had run off with his wife.

When Haines, for his own good reasons, chose to confess to the crime, the police were frankly disbelieving; the mystery writer was trying his skills too far. They insisted that Haines re-enact the murder exactly as he alleged that he committed it, and they lay in wait to time him and trap him at every turn. Can Haines convince them of his guilt by breaking a perfect alibi? Was the alibi genuine? When an unexpected twist apparently throws the case open, the reader, like the police, must simply work it out.

This is one of master-plotter Andrew Garve's most original stories. In which the clues, the background, and careful character studies of those involved add up to the right answer. But it will be a shrewd reader who can perceive who really killed Max Ryland in the end.

### House of Soldiers, The
January 1962

On Tara Hill, near Dublin, the site can be traced where 'The House of a Thousand Soldiers' once stood. This gripping novel tells of an archaeologist who becomes involved in a project to rebuild 'The House of Soldiers' and other famous ancient features of Tara

Hill, and to re-people them, for a day, with living images of the soldiers who had once caroused there. But behind the project is a plot; and James Maguire soon finds himself in a predicament from which there seems to be no escape.

Andrew Garve's realism and ingenuity are given full rein in this account of Maguire's desperate but calculated actions to free himself from the trap. Once again Andrew Garve tells a story that is original, compelling and (until the last twist) apparently bound for tragedy.

### Late Bill Smith, The
March 1971

As Francis Iles, writing in the *Guardian* recently remarked: 'It is impossible for Andrew Garve to be anything but supremely readable.' One might justifiably add that Mr Garve in twenty-five novels of suspense has never run out of highly original ideas. He has done it again in this, his twenty-sixth.

We are introduced to a young man as he literally drops onto the balcony of an unknown, pretty young woman. Bill Smith was doing quite all right as a successful sales executive until he happened to be in the wrong place at the wrong time and overheard a conversation he shouldn't have. But Bill Smith didn't know that. All he knew, with growing certitude, was that someone wanted him dead. It was fortunate that the girl on whose balcony Bill Smith landed believed the story for with her help he was able to devise an ingenious plot to evade his pursuers – permanently. And then, on the brink of success, he found he had to do a lot of accounting he hadn't bargained for…

Not the least part of the entertainment of this lively suspense story is Andrew Garve's description of a guided tour to Greece.

### Long Short Cut, The
June 1968

In the gambling club called the Queen of Hearts, Anthony Bliss met a girl who was to become his accomplice. Bliss was a professional con-man, with few nerves and fewer scruples. Corinne Lake was a cool customer too.

As Bliss left the club he witnessed a shooting. From the window of a passing car a gunman mowed down the club proprietor and drove on. Bliss became key witness for the police; the one man who could provide evidence of identity that would at last convict a whole dangerous gang. But now Bliss himself was in peril. Might not the gang see fit to eliminate, or avenge themselves on, such an important witness?

Bliss is just the man to exploit this situation for his own ends, and it is the exotic project he concocts to squeeze the ultimate criminal benefit from it that makes this book so enjoyable and exciting. Bizarre but feasible, dangerous but challenging, Bliss's scheme, as carried out by Corinne and himself, provides gripping reading and a whole sequence of fantastic turns and twists.

Andrew Garve is known as a master of suspense from a number of distinguished novels. *The Long Short Cut* is likely to bring him even greater success and an even larger following.

### Megstone Plot, The
April 1956

How are fortunes made? Clive Easton, D.S.O. – a former submarine commander now at work on a top secret Admiralty project – and his lovely mistress Isobel need a fortune badly; their mutual passion led them to try to find an answer to the question. Honest labour? – too slow. Football pools? – too chancy. Sell your country's secrets to a

foreign Power? – not in Easton's line. Appear to have sold your country's secrets – and claim a staggering sum in damages when the Press denounce you as a traitor? Now that's an idea worth working on! So Easton and Isobel put their clever heads together and devise a plot. An incredibly intricate plot, since every action has to be open to two interpretations, one innocent, one guilty. A plot that demands outstanding physical courage, skill and endurance. Nothing more should be said of the twists that give this unique story its terrific suspense. But readers of Andrew Garve's work may be assured that in *The Megstone Plot* they have the author at the very top of his form.

### Murder in Moscow
November 1951

Foreign correspondent George Verney is sent to Moscow by his newspaper to report on post-war changes there. He feels a nostalgic urge to revisit the city that holds so many memories for him, pleasant and unpleasant, but he isn't so pleased to find himself on the train in company with fellow-travellers in more sense than one – namely eight members of a pro-Soviet delegation from London. His rather aloof attitude towards his 'fellow-travellers' receives a jolt when one of them is murdered in Moscow, and professional zeal as well as humanitarianism prevents him from accepting the official Soviet explanation of the crime. Better versed than most foreigners in Soviet tactics of every kind, he does his own investigation, and in the process gives us a shrewd and often amusing picture of life behind the Iron Curtain.

### Murderer's Fen
April 1966

This is a crime novel of breath-taking ingenuity. Alan Hunt was "bad through and through". When he seduced a very young, very innocent girl in a holiday hotel in Norway, he planned never to meet her again- to disappear so that she would never be able to trace him. Hunt had another quarry in his sights; a plain girl with a lot of money. For her he planned not seduction but marriage.

But events caught up with Hunt. He concluded that only murder would resolve the dilemma in which he found himself. And Ocken Fen – the nature reserve that could so easily become a "murderer's fen" – was on the doorstep of the caravan Hunt lived in.

In this novel things are not what they appear to be; to say more of its content would either mislead, or reveal too much. It is enough to say that one of the most skilled and respected practitioners in the field of suspense is at the very top of his form here. This story, starting on a deceptively quiet note, holds shocks and horrors.

### Narrow Search, The
March 1957

It doesn't take Clare Hunter many years of married life to discover that her husband, Arnold, is ruthless and unscrupulous. But it is not until she attempts to break up their unsatisfactory marriage that she herself becomes the victim of his power-complex.

To prevent her leaving him, Arnold resorts to blackmail – of a highly specialized variety. Ordinary legal methods seem powerless to cope with the situation and Clare is becoming desperate when she finds an ally in a former colleague, Hugh Cameron. With little help to guide them but their own ingenuity, these two find themselves embarked on a series of adventures which take them – and the reader – deep into the heart of a fascinating and little-known aspect of English life.

Readers of *The Megstone Plot, Death and*

*the Sky Above*, and other novels by Andrew Garve will know that they can count on him for a thrilling, realistic and ingenious story.

### No Mask for Murder
September 1950

When young Dr Martin West arrives in the tropical colony of Fontego to take up an important new post, he has no thought but to co-operate with his able chief, Dr. Adrian Garland, in combating a deadly disease. But he is soon caught up in a clash of personalities and a maze of violent events. As the colony throws itself into a brilliant and colourful Fiesta, a masked murderer strikes and Dr. Garland's Negro assistant is killed. A second murder follows. Susan Anstruther, the girl Martin falls in love with, almost becomes the third victim. Then Martin goes on the warpath. For a time he finds himself with a lot of riddles and no answers, until Dr. Garland's glamorous wife, Celeste, gives a dramatic turn to events and precipitates the climax. Martin and Susan succeed in unravelling the mystery for, though the murderer wore a mask, in the long run there is *No Mask for Murder*.

### No Tears for Hilda
March 1950

When Max Easterbrook arrived in London on a month's leave, he was astounded to find George Lambert, his best friend, in prison on a charge of wife-murder. The police were satisfied that here was a clear case of the eternal triangle; no need to look far for the murderer, for George was not exactly weeping tears at his wife's sad demise. But Max was sure George was not the man to murder one woman in order to marry another. He was not nearly so sure that the large and lazy Hilda was not a natural murderee.

Mr. Andrew Garve is a newcomer to the Crime Club list, and in his first story scores a distinct success.

### Press of Suspects, A
March 1951

No one can complain that Andrew Garve's stories lack variety. For his first crime novel, *No Tears for Hilda*, he chose London's suburbia as his setting; for *No Mask for Murder*, his second, a tropical island. For his third, he turns for background to Fleet Street. The Foreign Room of the *Morning Call* was as much a trouble centre as any to which its many correspondents were sent in the course of duty. More personal hatred and professional jealousy existed among the staff than is properly attributed to the world of the theatre. It was an atmosphere in which hates could be intensified and breed murder. This talented new writer goes from strength to strength. Here are good writing, good characterisation and a new angle of approach.

### Prisoner's Friend
August 1962

Of the six convicts Robert Ashe would try to help on his weekly visit to the prison, Terry Booth was the most promising. It seemed that Terry, only twenty-four years old, had gained something positive from Ashe's confidence and friendship; that on his release he might make a new start and confound the consequences of the first terrible crime that had led to his conviction and imprisonment.

Terry was released, and was soon in trouble again – this time very big trouble indeed. This is the story of what happened to Terry Booth after he left prison, and of the relationship between him and Ashe, the 'prisoner's friend', in the ensuing catastrophe. It is told with the realism and ingenuity of which Andrew Garve is a master; it gives the reader an agreeable 'sinking feeling' as it speeds from an initial disaster to an astounding climax.

### *Riddle of Samson, The*
August 1954

A holiday in a tent on Samson, an uninhabited island of the Scillies, should have been peaceful enough. John Lavery's troubles started agreeably when the handsome Olivia Kendrick was stranded on the island and had to shelter in his tent, the only habitation. But this act itself was to prove of major importance when the tangled web of events began to close round Lavery soon afterwards. When that time came he could not tell whether his terrible plight was caused by accident or design; but he could see the shadow of the gallows clearly enough. This exciting, frightening, extraordinary tale will bring the author of *The Cuckoo Line Affair*, *Death and the Sky Above* and *Murder in Moscow*, still more readers.

### *Sea Monks, The*
September 1963

After the murder in the cinema, 'King' Macey and his gang found themselves surrounded by a police cordon. Hiding behind a wall in the harbour they discovered a means of escape in the form of an old cabin cruiser. Soon they were at sea, zig-zagging helplessly through the fog, ignorant of everything nautical. By the time they had holed the boat and it began to sink they were within yards of the Swirlstone Lighthouse; of a fortress where the police would not dream of searching for a murderer and where, if and when they found him, he would be secure from physical arrest…

This fascinating and plausible situation provides the framework for Andrew Garve's most exciting novel. The development of relationships in the light-house is brilliantly handled, as are the sub-plots and diversions in this wonderful story.

Many thousands of readers rely on Andrew Garve's novels for excitement, credibility, ingenuity, and a simple story-line cunningly developed. Here he excels himself in a novel that should appeal to an even wider public.

### *Very Quiet Place, A*
June 1967

From the moment attractive Debbie Sheldon, a 25-year old professional photographer, took a flashlight picture of a carload of men at four o'clock in the morning, her life was in danger. The men were crooks escaping from a scene of robbery and murder, and Debbie's photograph reproduced the unforgettable features of one of them with remarkable clarity.

The gang lost no time in trying to rid themselves of the unexpected witness and her damning evidence, but were frustrated by the intervention of a passer-by, Hugh Freeman, in a terrifying chase. Then, with Hugh still tagging along, the police took over the job of protecting Debbie.

Superintendent Trent knew just the hide-out for her – 'a very quiet place' where he was sure she would be safe. But would she be? Hugh had the gravest doubts. The criminals had laid a trap for Debbie; now the police were preparing a counter-trap for them. But the bait was live, and it was Debbie – and that was an idea Hugh didn't like at all. So he continued to stand by while plot and counter-plot proceeded, until in the wide bleak marshes of an East Anglian estuary, they erupted into unimagined violence.

As in his other celebrated novels, including recently *The Ashes of Loda* and *Murderer's Fen*, Andrew Garve in this gripping story shows himself to be a master of suspense and the surprise ending.

## GASH, JONATHAN
(*see also* **Gaunt, Graham**)

### *Firefly Gadroon*
February 1982

*This story begins where I did something illegal, had two rows with women, one pub fight, and got a police warning, all before mid-afternoon. After that it got worse, but that's the antiques game for you. Trouble.*

The trouble began when what was described as a 'small portable Japanese box. Maybe bamboo' was sold at auction under Lovejoy's nose. He wanted that box, which was a genuine antique firefly cage, but someone else wanted it even more, because an original might provide a clue to the secret of a model, and that secret was worth murdering for. Unfortunately the victim battered to death on the Essex marshes was a friend of Lovejoy's, and though he is not above faking an antique or two (and telling the reader how to do likewise), Lovejoy always ends up on the side of right when the chips are down. So he embarks on a campaign of personal vengeance, culminating in one of the most exciting episodes of his career.

Whether Germoline the donkey is also on the side of right is one of the many things the reader will discover – about antiques and about human (and animal) behaviour – in Lovejoy's latest narrative.

### *Gold from Gemini*
October 1978

Lovejoy – the racy, knowledgeable, irreverent antiques dealer who delighted readers of the award-winning *The Judas Pair* – is back. And broke. Not even a spot of baby-minding and endeavouring to instruct an assistant, whose talents (non-apparent and perhaps non-existent) were never intended for the antiques trade, was going to keep body and soul together much longer. It wouldn't even keep the budgerigars in seed.

So when he learned from a woman – and who else would Lovejoy hear from? – of a skilled faker who had left a series of duplicate clues to an apparently mythical 'find' of Roman treasure, his unfailing instinct told him the find was genuine and he'd better unravel the clues.

Before he could do so, he was pressed into parting with them, the pressure being of a singularly nasty kind. Daunted but determined, Lovejoy set about financing his treasure hunt by faking, and he shares uninhibitedly with the reader the secrets of do-it-yourself instant antiques.

He also shares with the reader his zany but thrilling peregrinations, dogged inescapably by his incompetent assistant, his current lady-love, and of course those who are only waiting for him to lead them to the hoard.

### *Gondola Scam, The*
January 1984

*Nicking antiques lifts the lowest spirits.*

That, at least, is the view of Lovejoy, Jonathan Gash's 'lecherous, crooked, filthy but lovable antique dealer' (Marghanita Laski, *Listener*), who is also a divvie – a diviner. As such, his instincts tell him that a painting auctioned for a high figure is an obvious fake. So why should certain dealers bid themselves almost into poverty for it? And why, later, should antique thieves pull a raid at the expense of friends of Lovejoy's for that same fake?

Before he can find out, Lovejoy, who thought nothing (well, very little) of nicking an antique from the Vatican in *The Vatican Rip*, receives an astonishing offer: will he check the authenticity of the antiques being surreptitiously lifted from Venice (for love, not lucre) by an eccentric, to make sure they are the real thing and not the skilful fakes which should replace them?

It is an offer Lovejoy is in no position to refuse, and it effects an introduction between 'one of the happiest creations of recent crime fiction,' according to Anthony Price in the *Oxford Mail*, and Venice, 'the greatest man-made structure the world has ever known,' according to the preservation-conscious millionaire who is behind the grand scam.

It also introduces Lovejoy to as ugly a bunch of crooks as any he has ever encountered as he battles on La Serenissima's behalf among her squares, her alleyways, her canals and the islands of the lagoon itself.

### *Grail Tree, The*
September 1979

In the world of antiques the Holy Grail is a holy terror. Almost every month someone claims to possess the original – a record equalled only by the lost jewels of King John. So when, during a booze-up on a barge, an inebriated ex-clergyman confided to Lovejoy that he did indeed possess the cup that had once held the Precious Blood, the irrepressible antiques dealer knew just what to make of such a statement. Or thought he did.

The trouble was that someone thought this version of the Grail worth stealing, despite an elaborate security system which the reverend gentleman himself had devised. And now the reverend gentleman was dead amid considerable carnage. In the midst of selecting and training an apprentice, divulging some of the trade's shadier secrets, and coaxing his aged and eccentric motor-car into forward motion and his creditors into reverse, Lovejoy – in true Lovejoy fashion – found time to become involved.

When he at last comes face to face with an unusually cold and callous murderer, the locale and choice of weapons are as unexpected as everything else about this zany and delightful tale. The third chronicle of Lovejoy's amorous and investigative exploits will delight all who have been beguiled by his previous adventures and those who now meet him for the first time.

### *Jade Woman*
October 1988

Even East Anglia becomes too hot for Lovejoy, dodgy antique dealer, when he is forced to flee gangsters, bailiffs, police, bankruptcy… He makes it to Hong Kong, but then things go horribly wrong and he is soon destitute. Wandering the alleys and markets of the colony, he glimpses one of the famous Jade Women, the trained beauties who figurehead the notorious Triads, but by then survival is all he cares about.

Antiques become his lifeline. He manages to contact a fellow passenger for assistance only to see him knifed in Kowloon. On this occasion a garrulous gigolo gets Lovejoy out of trouble, but not before he has met a strangely ubiquitous lame beggar.

Lovejoy becomes enmeshed in the gigolo's sordid lifestyle, the Triads also incorporate him in the antiques scam aimed at acquiring the vast American firm of Bookers Gaiman. When he unwittingly causes the death of another innocent, Lovejoy decides to exact revenge by emulating the exploits of the greatest faker of the nineteenth century…

### *Judas Pair, The*
September 1977

'This story's about greed, desire, love and death – in the world of antiques you get the lot.'

The beguiling and distinctive narrator of this unusual first crime novel knows what he is talking about, for he is an antique dealer himself, handling anything and everything and freely letting fall gems of fascinating information while disseminating his irreverent inside view of the trade. Lovejoy's speciality, however, is flintlock pistols, so when he is approached by a rich but obviously naive collector with the request to obtain for him a pair so rare that the trade even doubts their existence, Lovejoy can only laugh. 'But the Judas Pair do exist,' cries the client. 'I've seen them. They killed my brother.' And a murderer possesses them now.

So now Lovejoy is on the track of both an unsolved crime and of a uniquely valuable pair of pistols, and there is no doubt which interests him most. When a small item comes into his possession which he recognizes as an accessory of the fabled flintlocks, it is as though the dealer had smelt blood. Unfortunately so has the murderer, for this means the precious duellers for which he has killed are incomplete. Yet if he admits to ownership he admits to murder. It is the beginning of a duel to the death.

### *Moonspender*
November 1986

When scruffy antiques dealer Lovejoy achieves instant notoriety by accidentally turning everybody's favourite TV programme on antiques into a shambles, it isn't Lovejoy's fault. Wasn't it the gangster Bill Sykes and his terrible sons who made him do it? And he certainly wasn't to blame for faking that exquisite Roman bronze leopard.

The idea was for Lovejoy to earn the favour of avid antiques collector Sir John Carnforth. It seemed easy, until Lovejoy's friend George was gored to death near the ancient sinister forest. After that, complications set in: Lovejoy's promise to be best man at Big Frank's eighth wedding was one; and the rich and delectable Mrs Ryan's lust to employ Lovejoy as her estate manager was another. Then there was the coven of witches who gathered where risks ran highest; and the dozen writs served on Lovejoy; and the moonspenders, those illicit night seekers after buried archaeological treasures. But it was the death of an unassuming amateur archaeologist which really terrified Lovejoy. He might he next …

Desperately attempting to find a way out, Lovejoy discovers that his allies are enough to hinder anyone. The picturesque wedding should have been a triumph for him, but, beyond the windows of the glittering reception stands the silent wood where he has a midnight appointment with a killer. And in the earth of New Black Field lies his leopard of Roman bronze. And by now it is Hallowe'en …

### *Pearlhanger*
February 1985

*People are stupid: women with money, men with motorbikes, and everybody with pearls. To prove I'm in it too, this story starts in a séance.*

Lovejoy, East Anglia's scruffiest antique dealer and divvie, was unconvinced by the spirit message he received, but accepted the resulting offer of a job and set out to help Donna Vernon find her missing dealer husband. Said spouse had gone on an antiques sweep, yet after losing a luscious piece by a whisker, he didn't even bother to inspect the rest of the stuff on sale. By the time Lovejoy caught up with him on the Essex marshes where the locals still fish for pearls, it was too late.

Freed from arrest by the efforts of his apprentice, Lydia, who wears morality like an erotic gymslip, Lovejoy takes on the killers and proceeds to fake an item of antique pearl jewellery.

Then, harried by crooked police, watched by the Antiques Squad, hated by an insane killer, and increasingly haunted by the medium's prophecy of what lies in store for him 'between the salt water and the sea sand', he awaits the day when he is to be bait at the priciest auction in the district.

Lovejoy's narratives 'fizz with energy', according to the *Times Literary Supplement*. His legion of fans on both sides of the Atlantic will find the ninth no exception.

### *Sleepers of Erin, The*
January 1983

*This story starts where I'm bleeding to death.*

Those who already know Lovejoy, Jonathan Gash's 'delicious antique dealer' (C. H. Hudson, *Oxford Times*), can relax: the haemorrhage will be arrested in the interests of their future enjoyment. But it lands that 'enduring sleuth (and snogger)' (H. R. F. Keating, *The Times*) in hospital, where he engages in a running battle with the Health Service in the person of Sister Sinead Morrison. And when he is discharged, it is into the custody (if that's the word) of a wealthy couple engaged in planting some remarkable discoveries in a Bronze Age tomb in Ireland.

Lovejoy, of course, isn't just an antique dealer: he's a 'divvie' – a diviner, one who can instantly tell true from false, and as such very necessary to this carefully planned operation. It is when Lovejoy discovers that one or two others involved are less than necessary – expendable, even – that he begins to jib. Except that he isn't in a position to do any such thing, with a charge of robbing a church hanging over him, Sister Morrison (with and without relatives) eternally at his side, and the green Irish countryside unrolling endlessly around him …

Lovejoy's admirers will not be surprised when the remarkable discoveries in the Bronze Age tomb prove to be far more remarkable than anyone, including their planters, ever envisaged.

### *Spend Game*
July 1980

*No matter what people say, you can't help getting into trouble. And the antiques game is nothing but trouble – beautiful, lovely trouble. As far as I'm concerned that means being in trouble all the time.*

It is Lovejoy speaking, of course – the antique dealer who is 'tricksy, disreputable, marvellously knowledgeable, engaging and On the Side of Right' *(Oxford Mail)*. In his latest narrative Lovejoy is in trouble up to his ears when, in a compromising position, he witnessed the murder of a fellow dealer whom he had known in the army years before. The dead man had recently purchased some unimportant items belonging to a local doctor recently deceased. Why were the big boys so keen to get them that they were prepared to kill him and then send thugs to dispose of Lovejoy as well?

The clue was a ticket for the first trip on a local railway in 1847. But the railway was never opened. Except as a curiosity the ticket was valueless. Yet in between girls and spotting antiques and imparting his unrivalled knowledge of both, Lovejoy uncovered a story of villainy past and present which climaxed in a long-forgotten railway tunnel with all the attributes of a tomb.

### *Tartan Ringers, The*
February 1986

*This story starts with criminal passion in a shed and descends into sordid corruption. But remember one thing: love and antiques are the same. Hatred and evil are their opposite. I'm an antique dealer, and I should know.*

It was the criminal passion in a shed that saved Lovejoy: he could hardly be responsible for the murder which happened outside it that foggy night. Even so, it seemed wise to leave East Anglia hastily when another dealer drowned and a third vanished. Hitching north on a travelling fair, searching for the source of some missing antiques, Lovejoy soon finds himself in Scotland, masquerading as a distant cousin of the dwindling Clan McGunn.

Lovejoy manages to confirm that the missing antiques originated from the chief's echoingly empty castle at Tachnadray and takes up residence as the clan's forger. But not for nothing does he know every trick of the trade – the antiques trade, of course – and soon he is in over his head in one of the biggest scams of his career.

How 'East Anglia's worst-dressed antique dealer and poorest playboy' (*Scotsman*) makes the running yet again with the goods and the girls, not to mention ending up on the fringe of the Fringe of the Edinburgh Festival, will delight Lovejoy readers everywhere.

### *Vatican Rip, The*
August 1981

*'People say if there's an antique to be got, Lovejoy's the man to get it. 'The big stranger smiled at me as he spoke, but with no warmth. 'Somebody else has got my antique and I want you to get it back.'*

*He'd said 'get'. Not buy, not bid, not collect. Get. As in rob?*

*I swallowed. 'You want me to nick an antique?'*

*He looked pained. 'Not steal, Lovejoy. Think of it as returning it to me, its rightful owner.'*

*'Who has it?' I said.*

*'The Pope.'*

Lovejoy, antique dealer extraordinary, wasn't anxious to do this job, but Signor Arcellano had ways of making him co-operate – even to a crash course in Italian, where he met the delectable Maria. And in Rome there was another delectable damsel. Not to mention the delectable proprietress of the Albanese Antiques Emporium, an anything but delectable murder, hundreds of delectable antiques, most of them genuine, and one in particular. In the very heart of the Vatican. The one he was required to rip.

Lovejoy not only knows how to spot antiques – he knows how to make them, and he doesn't mind spreading his knowledge around. But when the Eternal City threatens to become his eternal resting-place, he manifests other abilities. As the Colosseum witnesses its strangest gladiatorial combat, Lovejoy's skills and thrills are generously shared with the reader in his own inimitable style.

### *Very Last Gambado, The*
October 1989

In the antiques game, there always are those who dream of pulling off that legendary antiques scam which will bring riches and immortality. The greatest of these is robbing the impregnable British Museum. It is the very last gambado.

Lovejoy arrives at his doctor's surgery to establish an alibi, after carrying out a little night robbery. There he recognizes Sam Shrouder, a famous faker. It seems a matter of no consequence, until Sam, is killed and Lovejoy is suspected.

By then, Lovejoy has been hired by movie mogul Ray Meese to advise on antiques used in an epic film. Its story: a robbery at the British Museum.

It seems easy money, until another antiques dealer vanishes, and Lovejoy is battered and his cottage ruined. Lovejoy decides to leave the movie team but is seduced into obedience by the lovely Lorane. Worse, local bad man Big John Sheehan orders him to carry out anther robbery – this time at the Russian Exhibition which Countess Natalia Ruminatzeff and her lovely translator have provided. Maybe worst of all, he is helped throughout by his devoted apprentice, Lydia.

To protect himself from the crooks Lovejoy agrees to join the crew of film extras. On the last day of filming he arrives shakily at the British Museum only to see his one loyal ally defect. Lovejoy is alone, amid the smoke and gunfire of the very last gambado.

## GAUNT, GRAHAM
## (*see also* Gash, Jonathan)
### *Incomer, The*
April 1981

Dr Clare Salford scents trouble in her East Anglian village. Taunton, alleged killer of a girl, has had his conviction quashed on appeal and is coming home. Convinced of his guilt, the villagers are vehemently against his return and attempt to coerce the new young doctor into supporting their petition. She refuses, believing that 'innocence is innocence', but when Taunton arrives, village animosity flares into violence.

Clare's attitude in the conflict is complicated by Ken, her married lover, who is drawn in by reason of being a police inspector. But what really troubles her is to find herself on the same side as the local priest, a man she openly despises for his uselessness in the modern world.

Reluctant allies, priest and doctor are together compelled to oppose the village's assaults on Taunton. Their efforts are vain, and, Clare's sense of impotence grows when Taunton flees from his attackers one night to seek sanctuary in the rectory.

Events lead inexorably towards the night of a party, when a chase begins that draws them all towards the solitude of the ruined church in the woods of the river valley, where once Taunton lay with the murdered girl …

## GIBBINS, JAMES
### *Sudden Death*
September 1983

Is there anything men will not do for money? A dying Chinese millionaire determines to find out by holding a unique golfing tournament. It is a fabulously rich man's ultimate indulgence. It is also his revenge against his own fate and the treachery of his only son, for whom his fortune has been amassed.

The venue is his own private course in a remote part of Borneo.

The participants are one hundred scratch players, chosen because they are among the world's most desperate men, and including professional hit-men, ideological terrorists, arsonists and freedom fighters.

The prize is the tycoon's fortune, estimated at $250 million.

The hazards are deadly. Literally – for the course is mined.

The settings of this suspenseful novel range from St Andrews in Scotland to a small town in Arizona, to Zürich, to CIA headquarters at Langley, to Far Eastern cities, and of course Sabah in north Borneo.

It is a story of crime on many levels. The crime of the tycoon, capriciously exercising his power. The crime of the Zürich bankers, who make his scheme possible. The crimes of the players, who are mercenaries with golf bags over their shoulders. And the 'crime' of the veteran CIA agent who develops a conscience and thereby becomes expendable.

'Golf,' said Winston Churchill, 'is the game of the devil.' *Sudden Death* proves that he had a point.

## GIELGUD, VAL
### *And Died So?*
February 1961

The rural peace of Hares Green was first disturbed by the return of the highly unconventional Humphrey, the Viscount Clymping, to the bosom of his family, and then shattered by the discovery, in the middle of the village, of a corpse with a broken neck. Inspector Gregory Pellew needed all the help which Clymping's local knowledge could give him. Together they unravelled the strange and intriguing network of relationships in a village where the older inhabitants were being crowded out by the new wave of refugees from city life: the luscious starlet Camilla Haze and her husband; the ingratiating and wealthy Oliver Heseltine; the Searles who were opening an 'advanced' school, and Julian Caird, a retired and retiring B.B.C. executive. Somewhere in this strangely ill-assorted group of sophisticates and village leading-lights there was a killer.

Val Gielgud presents an ingenious and fascinating mystery with the urbanity and wit which have earned him a unique place high on the list of the most popular authors in the field of Crime Fiction.

### *CAT*
June 1956

Can murder ever be justified? Charles Trent thought the brutal murder he committed was the rational and only thing to do. He made no defence, and paid the penalty.

From this story we learn what sort of man Trent was; the events in his life that had shaped him; the circumstances of his loves and marriage; the crisis that came on his return from a prison camp in Germany in 1946. Not everyone will agree that Trent was justified. But Val Gielgud's exciting story of murder and the man who committed it, because he thought it the sole remedy for his dilemma, will be read with absorbed interest. It depicts the terrible circumstances that can intrude into a life that could have been happy enough – the circumstances inseparable from a particular man's character and upbringing.

### *Conduct of a Member*
January 1967

This is the story of a scandal in the world of London's West-End Clubland; a scandal leading to violent death. Rule 29 of the Rule book of the Fonthill Club begins as follows:

It shall be within the discretion of the Committee to rule upon any issue arising from a complaint regarding the Conduct of a Member…

In the Club Suggestion Book one member proposes that another should be called upon to resign for 'conduct which renders him unfit to be a member.'

Thus begins a scandal, in which charge is succeeded by counter-charge to stir and muddy the quiet waters of the Fonthill, and to create something of a Nine Days' Wonder in the old-fashioned word of West-End Clubs.

Humphrey (formerly the Viscount) Clymping, and Gregory Pellew (formerly of Scotland Yard), now partners in the Private Enquiry Agency *Prinvest-London*, find a new and singular assignment in investigating just how much scandalous truth lies behind various intemperate and astonishing allegations. And, as usual, Lady Hannnington provides them with considerable assistance.

The setting of the Fonthill Club gives this novel a background both fascinating and unusual.

### *Gallows' Foot*
October 1958
The death of Greta Marais – once so famous among model-girls – was a seven-day sensation to the newspapers. But to the unsuccessful, small-time actor Roger Brand, looking down at the sprawled corpse of his mistress, it implied a terrible and frightening predicament. It was so obvious that he had had the motive, the means and the opportunity to kill her. The alibi which Roger had already fabricated for the benefit of his wife was ready to hand – but he rejected it and chose to face the storm of publicity and notoriety such as only a sensational inquest can produce.

A malignant fate seemed to shadow him even when, with a new name and courage, he endeavoured to build himself a new life. He began to perceive a terrifying pattern which seemed to be repeating the nightmare which he had survived.

In *Gallows' Foot* Val Gielgud tells with skill and insight an absorbing and exciting story of the theatre, and sustains the elements of suspense, surprise and frightening reality which he achieved in such outstandingly successful books as *The High Jump* and *CAT.*

### *Goggle-Box Affair, The*
January 1963
The tycoon who ruled Gargantua Television had undoubtedly committed suicide. There seemed no sense in investigating how or why he had died. And yet – in the very heart of the Establishment – something stirred; with the result that Detective-Inspector Gregory Pellew was secretly seconded from Scotland Yard to learn all he could about the dead man, Simon Hargest, and the people who had been nearest to him in his professional and personal life.

It is the co-operation of Pellew's friend in Gargantua, Humphrey (Viscount) Clymping, and the shrewdness of Humphrey's mother, Lady Hannington, that help him to discover the facts about the extraordinary life of Simon Hargest.

Here is a murder mystery set deep in the fantastic world of Commercial Television, a landscape that Val Gielgud presents in detail and with cool humour. There is more in the death of Simon Hargest than meets the eye – and more goes on behind the scenes of Commercial Television than you ever dreamed of. This is a crime novel with a difference.

### *Necessary End, A*
February 1969
The freighter *Daisy Belle* was bound from Vancouver to London by way of Portland, San Francisco, Los Angeles, the Panama Canal and Rotterdam. She also carried a dozen passengers among whom were Gregory Pellew (of Scotland Yard), Humphrey (formerly the Viscount) Clymping, Humphrey's wife Kate and his mother Lady Hannington. These members of the detective agency, Prinvest London, were cruising for pleasure.

But their fellow passengers appeared to be, as Humphrey remarked, 'a pretty rum lot'.

The story describes the passengers, the crew members and the mounting tensions aboard the *Daisy Belle* as she makes her way down the Western seaboard of the American continent; tensions that culminate in an exceptionally savage murder. The murderer must be one of a small group still on board the ship.

Prinvest finds itself with a job to do. And the story of Pellew's investigation, and of his relationship with the ship's captain, the port authorities, and finally the London C. I. D. is most intriguing; at the end comes a climax and a revelation.

Val Gielgud sets out, as in previous books, to amuse, interest, intrigue and surprise the reader. With wit and professionalism he here holds attention absorbed and brings an odd tale of classical detection to a very satisfactory end.

### *Prinvest London*
June 1965
Prinvest in the name of a new Private Investigation Agency.

Prinvest differs in both personnel and style from other detective agencies we have known; although it is in the able hands of Gregory Pellew, now retired from the C.I.D., he has an occasionally-sleeping partner in the person of Humphrey (Viscount) Clymping; as official supervisor and *eminence grise* the formidable Lady Hannington, Humphrey's mrother.

All three are engaged on Prinvest's first assignment – to ensure the safety of the wife of a millionaire during an Aegean cruise. The delights of the Mediterranean spring are too much for Humphrey, but Pellew knows that among the odd shipmates aboard the *Nereid* are men with designs larger and more sinister than the mere murder of a reputed nymphomaniac.

The many followers of the adventures of Pellew, Clymping and Lady Hannington will be delighted with this exciting account of the first assignment of the private detective agency called Prinvest. It ends with a chase to the death through the mountains of Montenegro – and two murders in which the Prinvest partners are uncomfortably involved.

### *To Bed at Noon*
January 1960
When his doctor advised two months' complete rest, Hugo Bastin went to Sicily to stay in the guest house at Porto Basso started by Rupert Castle and Eva Stallybrass after they left England together, but rather hurriedly. But Hugo found little rest. The personalities of the strangely assorted group of colourful and eccentric guests who are already in residence build up an uneasy and explosive atmosphere which detonates when the knifed body of one of the visitors is discovered on a nearby beach. Murder comes closer still when a second corpse is found in a culvert below the house. As feuds and motives are unravelled against a Mediterranean setting of theatrical beauty, suspicion falls first one way and then another and suspense rises to a climax with the efficient, professional intervention of Inspector Gregory Pellew. *To Bed at Noon* is an exciting and highly entertaining successor to *Cat* and *Gallows' Foot.*

## GILBERT, ANTHONY

### *And Death Came Too*
April 1956
It seems sometimes as though certain people are born under a dark star. Misfortune and tragedy dog them at every step – ships in which they travel come to grief, trains are derailed, hotels go up in flames. Even those near and dear to them are not spared – bereavement, scandal and even death follow them wherever they go. Some people attribute this to certain stars and planets, and declare that so long as a given condition exists it is useless to struggle; the dice are loaded, fate throws with a two-headed penny.

Among these victims of circumstances, Ruth Garside seemed to have her place. As a girl she was accused of a dreadful crime; as a wife she was suspected of responsibility for her husband's death; as a widow she was held guilty of an employer's murder.

*I can't prove her innocence*, cried Thomas Fogg.

*I can't prove my own innocence*, said Ruth.

*She's my client, so she can't be guilty, and by heck, I'll prove it if it means the skies falling*, declared Arthur Crook.

Well – did he?

And was he justified?

Anthony Gilbert leaves the reader to judge the outcome of this exciting and original new crime story.

### *Bell of Death, The*
September 1939
The bell of St. Ethelburga's had stopped ringing. It had pealed out its customary call to the faithful, its gentle reproach to the sluggards; but somehow that morning it did not seem to ring as long as usual. For death had been busy in the belfry, where a startled vicar made an appalling discovery. The murder in the church is the prelude to a highly diverting tale of detection, in which the inimitable Crook and Parsons shine with their usual ingenuity and impudence.

### *Black Stage, The*
December 1945
Among the visitors to the Verekers' family mansion of Four Acres was Lewis Bishop – the perfect victim, whom everyone had reason to hate and fear. When he is suddenly shot dead in the darkness of the library one night, all he leaves behind him is an unpleasant memory and a pretty puzzle for the police, and, of course, for Arthur Crook, that irrepressible and slightly unscrupulous detective, who is in particularly fine form.

### *Body on the Beam, The*
January 1932
During the spring of last year the police were greatly perplexed by a violent death occurring at No. 39 Menzies Street, a disreputable lodging-house tenanted chiefly by single ladies, one of whom, Florence Penny, was found one morning hanged from a beam in her bedroom. The first person to take an intelligent interest in a seemingly commonplace tragedy was Inspector Field, and he slowly pieces together the clues in what proves to be a most absorbing mystery. Mr. Anthony Gilbert has never formulated a more ingenious or enthralling plot, and his characterisation is of the vivid type which marked his previous successes.

### *Case Against Andrew Fane, The*
May 1931
This is the most tensely exciting detective novel the author of *Death at Four Corners* has yet done. He plunges the reader into an atmosphere of suspense by asking the direct question – What would *you* have done? What would you have done if you found yourself, penniless and threatened with five years' penal servitude for unwitting fraud, face to face with the body of the man who had refused to help you and to whose house you had come to get assistance at all costs? Would you have gone to the police with a romantic tale of a mysterious woman whom, having seen for a few moments, you lost by a trick? Or would you have obliterated your tracks, so far as you knew, and gone quietly back the way you came? Would you have faced certain arrest and the knowledge that you could not prove your innocence and every one would assume your guilt? Or would you have taken the mad chance as Andrew Fane did? Well – what WOULD you have done?

### *Case of the Tea-Cosy's Aunt, The*
October 1942
Arthur Crook met T. Kersey, nicknamed the Tea-Cosy, for the first time one night when the absent-minded old man tried to get in to Crook's flat by mistake. The Tea-Cosy lived by himself on the floor below, and Crook went down with him to investigate the mysterious sound of running water. It was there that Crook's eyes lit on that incredible, Victorian, monstrosity of a hat which belonged to the Tea-Cosy's aunt. But of Aunt Clara herself there was no sign, though an unopened letter disclosed the fact that she had proposed to call on her worthy nephew that day. Now that was just the kind of baffling circumstance that whetted the appetite of Arthur Crook, who, with every story in which he appears makes it more evident that in him Anthony Gilbert has created a major character in detective fiction. The story is a grand one, peopled with rich and varied types, and with a wonderfully strong atmosphere of mystery and well-sustained excitement.

### *Clock in the Hatbox, The*
January 1939
Circumstantial evidence was as strong as proof at the trial of Viola Ross. Everything pointed to the conclusion that this beautiful woman had murdered her wisp of a husband. But the twelfth juror, Richard Arnold, would not agree…perhaps he knew something that the others didn't…perhaps he only guessed. Anyhow, a re-trial was ordered and Arnold – haunted by the face of Viola Ross – set out to conduct his own urgent inquiries. Three attempts on his life did not deter him, but before the end of the story he had learned that the police work more surely than the private individual. It is as brilliant a book as any that Anthony Gilbert has written, full of ingenuity, character and refreshing humour.

### *Courtier to Death*
February 1936
Eight years ago the name of René Tessier was notorious. But that was eight years ago. Now times have changed and the once-celebrated film star had sunk to the *demi-monde* of drug-addicts and neurotics who frequent the less reputable of the Parisian cafes. Then at last comes the chance of a return to the limelight and the favour of millions. The brilliant young producer Julian Lane plans to star Tessier in his latest production. A world-weary old man totters from the boat train and reaches with difficulty an obscure hotel in Soho. Next morning Tessier is found dead. Suicide or murder is the query flashed in the headlines of London's newspapers. *Courtier to Death* is an excellent mystery distinguished by clever character drawing and solved in Anthony Gilbert's usual masterly manner.

### *Dear Dead Woman*
March 1940
A night of fog, an evil night, a fearful night – a night when anything could happen and when those safe in their houses sat recalling similar nights and their sometimes dreadful harvest. On such a night the most reassuring of houses may seem full of strange sounds, of ghostly footsteps and voices haunting the stairs and dark corners. On such a night the net of circumstances woven by a strange destiny began to close around Jack Barton. The atmosphere of this story gets you under the skin. Barton's plight is so real that the reader feels that here is a horrifying situation that might suddenly confront any one. Anthony Gilbert's novel is not only a convincing and impressive detective story, but a study of genuine human interest.

### *Death Against the Clock*
February 1958
If the bus hadn't been involved in an accident…if Dinah James hadn't been late …if it

hadn't been for the silver pencil… everything might have happened very differently.

In the event there was a murder, an arrest, a conviction; conclusive evidence, as the prosecution and the jury very reasonably thought.

But that rumbustious lawyer, Arthur Crook, has some very lively opinions of his own as to what sort of evidence he considers conclusive. He charges into the case with all his old bounce and vitality: discrepancies and new suspicions begin to emerge.

Good characterisation, suspense and danger are among the ingredients of Anthony Gilbert's new story; they enhance the excitement of a mystery that leads to a thrilling climax.

### *Death in Fancy Dress*
June 1933

During the last year the Home Office was greatly perplexed by a series of suicides and accidental deaths taking place among two definite sections of the community; on the one hand among men and women of rank and position, and on the other among the more well-to-do professional classes. Their investigations led them to Feltham Abbey, and when suspicion among the authorities was at its height Sir Ralph Feltham himself was found dead in very mysterious circumstances in the abbey grounds during a fancy-dress ball. There are several people who might have reason to wish Feltham out of the way: his cousin Hilary, because she was afraid of him; Arthur Dennis, because he loved Hilary and was jealous of Sir Ralph; Jeremy Freyne for the same reason. The story is told by one of the guests who is present at the abbey at the time, and as blackmail enters into the theme as well as murder, the reader can rely on having full value in this exciting and well-told mystery.

### *Death in the Wrong Room*
February 1947

In the spring of 1946, Lady Bate came to live at the Downs, built by the eccentric Col. Anstruther many years before. War conditions made it necessary for the Colonel's daughter to take in paying guests, but only Lady Bate knew the secret of her past life and the key to her mysterious hermit-like existence. When, in due course, Lady Bate is found dead, a chance remark puts Arthur Crook on the right track, which he follows – but at the risk of his life. In *Death in the Wrong Room* the talented Anthony Gilbert has written a first-rate detective story at once mystifying and well constructed. It is a story which the legion of Crime Club readers will thoroughly enjoy.

### *Death Knocks Three Times*
January 1949

Fashions may change in rather a startling way, but Crime Club readers eagerly look forward each season to the new Crook, and here comes Anthony Gilbert again with a diabolically ingenious crime story featuring our favourite criminal lawyer. Arthur Crook gets caught in a violent storm on the moors while visiting a police-spy client. He demands shelter at an isolated house and is grudgingly given it for the night by an eccentric old man who lives there alone with one servant. On Crook's return to town he reads that this reluctant host has been found dead in his bath. Accident, murder or suicide? Crook is so intrigued that when he hears of the death of two other members of the same family he starts investigations on his own account – even although there is nothing in it for him, which is strictly against his principles, but is in itself eloquent testimony to the originality of Anthony Gilbert's plot.

### *Death Takes a Wife*
July 1959

Would you marry the man you love if he were suspected of shooting his first wife? That was Helen Wayland's problem. Blanch French had died of a gunshot wound, and a jury could not decide if it was accident, suicide or murder.

Helen made her choice, but two years later a second woman died in mysterious circumstances, and once again Paul French's name was involved. It was thanks to Arthur Crook, that intrepid legal champion of lost causes, that the astonishing truth was finally established and innocence vindicated.

The exceptional standards of entertainment and ingenuity for which Anthony Gilbert is famous are fully maintained when *Death Takes a Wife.*

### *Death Wears a Mask*
March 1970

May Forbes, forty plus, single and envying no living creature, came four nights a week to feed the wild birds on Broomstick Common. That was how she happened to glimpse a masked man with an ominous spade. Fearful for her own life, she took the wrong direction and landed up at the Mettlesome Horse, where that remarkable lawyer, Arthur Crook, was drinking at the bar.

He knew Providence had some reason for making him wallow in that Sea of Slops, Crook thought as he listened to her story. When the body of pretty 18-year-old Linda Myers was found buried on the Common, he was convinced of it.

A number of people had good reason for wishing the girl dead, Crook discovered, when he undertook the defence of the man the police accused. He was soon to realise that someone wanted him dead too. And then May Forbes, who had worked contentedly all her life in the local draper's, left work one lunchtime and did not reappear.

*Death Wears a Mask* takes the ubiquitous Mr. Crook from his beloved London to a village community, where he finds that Murder is spelt the same way wherever you come across it.

### *Die in the Dark*
November 1947

Who was Dr. Forrester? Where was the House in the Woods? What happened to Emily Watson when she disappeared from her home? Whose was the unfashionable hat found in the derelict cottage? These are some of the questions Arthur Crook is called upon to answer in his unconventional inquiry into the disappearance of Emily Watson, a rich widow preyed on by an unscrupulous nephew! For once he is almost foiled by superior tactics, but at the eleventh hour he recovers his true form, and once again 'Arthur Crook gets his man.'

### *Don't Open the Door!*
June 1945

That exceptionally gifted detective story writer, Anthony Gilbert, is undoubtedly at his best in this superbly exciting story. It concerns the strange adventure of Nora Deane, a young nurse, who has been instructed to report at 12 Askew Avenue, Charlbury, to look after new patient. Nora stepped out of the station to find herself in an impenetrable blanket of fog. She was glad to accept the escort of an unknown young man to the required address. Then, alone in the darkness, she pressed the bell and waited. She shivered. Suddenly she was frightened. Nothing seemed to matter but that she should get inside, out of the dangers of the dark. And yet some inner voice seemed to warn her insistently not to cross the threshold of that sinister house. *Don't Open the Door!* is a fine detective story, and features, of course, the egregious Mr. Arthur Crook.

### *Fingerprint, The*
April 1964

One of Arthur Crook's favourite maxims was Beware of the Invisible Witness, the man or woman whose presence can't be guarded against because it can't be foreseen. Such a witness was Sara Drew, when, with her four-year-old son, Mike, she saw the two racing cars go flying down the hill to virtually inevitable tragedy and violent death.

This is a story of kidnapping – of a young widowed mother driven to desperation by thugs who have killed and will kill again. In her loneliness and fright Sara finds confidence and encouragement in the cosy and uproarious person of the lawyer/detective, Arthur Crook.

Anthony Gilbert tells an exciting story with wit and conviction, Arthur Crook bounds cheerfully through it, redressing wrongs, and the hardships and hazards of a bitterly cold English winter provides a realistic setting.

### *Footsteps Behind Me*
February 1953

*Your money or your life!* Your money says the blackmailer to his victims, or I take away everything in life that is dear to you. Teddy Lane had sunk to the sordid depths of blackmail. And he was, as he thought, on to a good thing. He knew the dark secrets of four people who had everything to lose by exposure – a young actress, a criminal lawyer, a scientist, an elderly woman with a doctor son. What he hadn't bargained for was that two of them were a good deal more ruthless than himself. It is obvious they will not let him get away with it – even if it means murder, *his* murder. The hunter turns into the hunted, and from that time onwards Teddy sees death at every corner and in every face; fear leans over his shoulder when he sits, and creeps behind him when he walks… This story of blackmail and murder is breathlessly exciting; and, of course, there is the ebullient and resourceful Arthur Crook to prove once again that his client is *always* innocent.

### *Give Death a Name*
May 1957

'Wake up sunshine,' said the young man on Beachampton Parade to the pretty fair-haired girl in the blue coat.

But that was just what she couldn't do.

'I don't know where I'm going, because I don't know who I am; I don't know how I got here and I don't know why. And I can't ask the police to help me, because…'

Well, why couldn't she?

This is the problem confronting the heroine of Anthony Gilbert's new novel.

With no home, no name, no past that she could recall, no future she could anticipate, what was she to do? Her solution was an unconventional one, leading her into a world of suspicion, jealousy and violent death, which in its turn involved the reappearance of a man from the past who could supply the missing links.

Two murders, a daring impersonation, a seeking after identity – these are the mainsprings of the story – with, of course, Arthur Crook, that least conventional of lawyers, to take a hand and unravel as complex a tangle as ever came his way.

Ingenious and exciting, *Give Death a Name* is a fine example of the type of crime story that combines a detective problem with a thrilling story of suspense.

### *He Came by Night*
June 1944

It was sheer luck that caused Arthur Crook, taking an unwanted holiday in November in the little Mereshire village of Bridget St. Mary, to stumble on a body where no body has any right to be. It was Crook who hardily undertook to work for the defence of the old woman arrested for the crime, who followed the trail from King's Fossett to Bishop Cleveland, and thence to London; who unravelled the mystery of that strange girl, Stella Reed; who attacked the murderer with his own weapons and at the eleventh hour, when everything seemed lost, produced the final iota of evidence that brought the criminal to book. And justified his double claim that Crook's clients are always innocent and that he always get his man.

### *Is She Dead Too?*
March 1955

*'Is she dead too?' asked Patsy, in a voice that made Mrs. Derry jump. She'd never heard anything like it in a young child.*

But then Patsy's short experience had already included two mysterious deaths in the dark little rooms over the chemist's shop at Mortcomb where she had lived with her Aunt Alice, Alice's husband, Edwin Poulden, and the strange old woman, Blanche Bannerman, with her pathological terror of cats. But for Patsy there would have been a third victim in the person of her only friend, eighteen-year-old Margaret Reeve, and how should a seven-year-old guess that it was she herself who held the clue to the series of crimes that were eventually to send the killer to the gallows?

It was, first, Patsy and later the indomitable Arthur Crook, who saved Margaret from following the other two women to an untimely grave, though in Crook's case it meant sacrificing his beloved *Scourge,* in a desperate last-minute attempt to foil as macabre a plot as had ever come his way. The climax provides a situation as tense and blood-chilling as any from Anthony Gilbert's pen.

### *Knock, Knock, Who's There?*
October 1964

As I came up the stairs on the afternoon of the murder I could hear the telephone in my furnished flat ringing like mad, and when I lifted the received a voice I'd never heard before cried desperately, 'Listen! Tell him it's no use. I haven't got it. He'll have to wait.'

This is the beginning of Anthony Gilbert's new story of blackmail and murder, which is laid in and around a rather seedy pub called The Admiral Box.

Who was the owner of that desperate voice and why did she ring Simon Crete, the narrator and a man whom she had never seen?

This is one of the questions asked and eventually answered by Arthur Crook (Where there's Crime there's Crook) in Anthony Gilbert's most ingenious story, where nothing is quite what it appears on the surface, and which leads to an astonishing and thoroughly satisfying climax.

### *Lady-Killer*
June 1951

'Being a husband is a whole-time job. That is why so many husbands fail. They cannot give their whole attention to it.' So wrote Arnold Bennett more than thirty years ago. The husband in Anthony Gilbert's new story would have delighted Mr. Bennett's heart. To him being a husband was a vocation, a career. At one time he must have been the most-married man in England, and he showed a skill in ridding himself of superfluous or outmoded wives that Henry VIII himself might have envied. But destiny sometimes hangs on a single hair, and it was the slenderest of chances that put Arthur Crook in contact with the latest of the lady-killer's galaxy of women. *Lady-Killer* is an utterly absorbing crime story, in which Crook is as enterprising and entertaining as ever.

### *Lift Up the Lid*
June 1948
'Chaps who think all the best crimes take place in London don't know their onions,' said Arthur Crook. 'Take this affair down at Hinton St. Luke. The place is so small most country maps don't bother to mention it, but if James East had died in Buckingham Palace there'd hardly have been more fuss. Y'see it's the sort of crime the public like, what I'd call a nice cosy domestic murder. Why, the case has got everything: beautiful young wife, rich curmudgeonly old husband dying at just the right moment for every one but himself, neighbour whose middle name is Galahad, jealous nurse, even the mysterious voice from the past. And, of course, anonymous letters. Now, bear in mind, one of that lot is a murderer. All we've got to find out is which.' That's all the reader has to find out, too!

### *Long Shadow, The*
November 1932
Twenty-five years ago Mlle. Roget had been an actress, the idol of Paris. Something had happened then and for years she had lived alone in a London slum, living in the splendid past and letting the present go by like shadows on a hill at dusk, so light, so swift that they pass unnoticed. And now she was dead! Lying with face upturned, her arms spread wide as for crucifixion, and in her poor breast a knife. An old hag in a tenement! What conceivable motive could any one have for murdering her? Mr. Gilbert skilfully unfolds the extraordinarily interesting story of this woman with a past.

### *Looking Glass Murder, The*
August 1966
'You have been very fortunate,' Solange Peters's lawyer told her when she was waiting to leave Rome under a suspicion of murder. 'If there had been a prosecution you would have had nowhere to hide. As it is, you have a British passport, an air ticket to London that has been provided for you, and upon establishing your identity when you get there a sum of money will be made available to enable you to make your plans for a fresh start in any country except Italy.'

They had even booked a room for her; in short, every contingency had been covered except the one the most astute lawyer couldn't have foreseen.

Into this new contingency bursts Arthur Crook, as buoyant and enterprising as ever, to find himself once more involved in a complicated mystery whose by-product is murder.

A most unusual and ingenious novel begins with a Gothic crime amid scenes of Italian splendour. It pursues its labyrinthine and exciting course through an English household in an English countryside, and comes to a spell-binding climax beside the English sea.

Mr. Gilbert is at his best here.

### *Man in Button Boots, The*
November 1934
The scene of this story is laid in Monte Carlo, where a number of English and American visitors are staying at the Hotel Fantastique. Among them is the man in button boots, who appears something of a mystery to the other guests, and Julian Marks, the well-known diamond merchant, who carries an enormous diamond about with him, on a thin steel chain. On a night of Carnival, Marks is found murdered in a small summer-house in the grounds of the hotel. The motive is presumed to be theft until the discovery of the diamond in an unexpected place causes the French detective, M. Dupuy, to shift his ground and recommence investigations from a fresh angle. Mr. Latimer, the mystery man, gives the police a good deal of unobtrusive assistance, and it is he who, towards the end of the book, outlines the position to the other guests, assuring them that they now have all the necessary facts to discover the murderer. Various speculations arise, but only M. Dupuy actually identifies the criminal and explains the real motive for the crime.

### *Man Who Was Too Clever, The*
July 1935
"Be bloody, bold, and resolute" was the advice of the second apparition to Macbeth, and none better was ever given to a murderer. Had the person responsible for the death of Helen Paget followed it, an innocent man would have been hanged; but a passion for safety brought the real culprit to the gallows. Mrs. Paget was found dead in a private room of the Apsley Hotel, London. Strong suspicion pointed to Denis Paget, the husband of the dead woman. The story develops into an enthralling mystery that will grip and fascinate the reader.

### *Man Who Wasn't There, The*
April 1937
Marjorie Hyde, gifted but unsuccessful actress, was unhappily married. Like many members of her profession she was temperamental, and though not beautiful had that Titian colouring that is supposed to make men mad. Her husband was insanely jealous. He learnt that she was frequently in the company of Philip Clare, a barrister and Parliamentary candidate. Christopher threatened to take divorce proceedings that would ruin his rival's career. The same night he drank his usual glass of after-dinner port and died from hyoscin [sic] poisoning. The unravelling of the mystery surrounding his death makes thrilling reading. Anthony Gilbert's gift for portraying character is seen at its best in this magnificent story of crime and passion.

### *Miss Pinnegar Disappears*
June 1952
Miss Frances Pinnegar and Arthur Crook met by accident at a bus stop. The tough little lawyer and the equally tough spinster, who had been theatre sister at a docklands hospital, took to each other on sight, parting with mutual expressions of esteem and Crook's cordial invitation to Miss Pinnegar to call on him professionally if ever she needed help. Such an eventuality could not have seemed more remote to Miss Pinnegar then, but that was before she had the visit from the female Enoch Arden, the visit that threatened to shake her life to the very foundations. Miss Pinnegar could suddenly see battle, murder and sudden death round the corner, and sent Crook an S. O. S. He came at the double – but it was too late; Miss Pinnegar had disappeared. Where there's Crook there's crime, and where there's Anthony Gilbert there's an ingenious and thoroughly entertaining story.

### *Missing From Her Home*
April 1969
"Missing from her home" is Angela Toni, aged nine. Her terrifying mother, known as "Mumma Toni," is already the bane and scourge of everyone who knows her; now the London police become the victims of her remorseless demands that they find "her Angel" for her.

Angel has vanished in circumstances that are mysterious and ominous. A hair-slide she was wearing is discovered in a car "borrowed" by a young man for a joy ride, which does not auger well for Angel, or for the young man himself, until he becomes the client of Arthur Crook…

Lawyer Crook, exuberant and unconventional as ever, is intrigued by discrepancies in the accounts of the witnesses who last saw Angel. It transpires that there has been a murder – and there are two more to follow before Crook unravels the mystery and at the last moment leads the police to the criminals.

This exciting mystery features some outstanding characters (not least Mumma Toni) and shows Arthur Crook at the top of his form. It is a fine successor to Anthony Gilbert's earlier and celebrated novels, such as *Night Encounter*.

### *Mouse Who Wouldn't Play Ball,The*
March 1943
Everard Hope was dead. Of that there was no doubt. The old man had fallen down the stairs and broken his neck. And there were no mourners; for Everard Hope was singularly unbeloved, a wealthy old miser of unprepossessing habits whose demise was sincerely welcomed by a crowd of needy relatives all eager for the pickings. Anthony Gilbert's characters are drawn with superb craftsmanship, and of course Arthur Crook takes a leading part in patiently piecing together the clues in a mystery which is full of skilfully contrived surprises.

### *Murder By Experts*
June 1936
Fanny Price, a beautiful adventuress, Graham, a dealer in curios, and Curteis, who tells the story, visit the country home of Sampson Rubenstein to see his collection of Chinese antiquities. Fanny is Graham's mistress, Curteis is in love with her, and Lal, Rubenstein's wife, is madly jealous of her. After a scene between Fanny and Lal, Rubenstein motors Fanny to the station to catch the London train, and does not return. Later his car is found at the foot of the cliffs, buried under a fall of rock. But a few days later, when the Chinese room is forced open, Rubenstein is found stabbed to death there. *Murder by Experts* is a most ingenious story, brilliantly narrated.

### *Murder Comes Home*
March 1950
Six little words! – so innocent-seeming, but they were enough to bring a murderer to the gallows! In the problem confronting Arthur Crook in his latest case, he has a further opportunity of exploiting his favourite theory that no matter how carefully a crime is planned it is impossible to exclude the Invisible Witness, the person introduced by fate who provides the one essential detail that destroys the criminal's plan. On a variety of 'ifs' and six little words, a murderer's life hangs in this new and fascinating crime story from the master hand of Anthony Gilbert.

### *Murder Has No Tongue*
October 1937
Flora Horsley, wife of a member of parliament, while overwrought with worry is warned by her palmist that she must leave her husband or she will die. Flora, believing that her husband is attempting to murder her, decides to leave him. The haunting fear of death already holds her in a terrifying and remorseless grip. It is in the exploitation of this fear that Anthony Gilbert strikes a new and original theme, to which his undoubted gifts of style and character drawing give great distinction.

### *Murder's a Waiting Game*
May 1972
Margaret Fielding, married to an eminent QC, is in a seedy pub near Euston Station. Her object: to meet a blackmailer. Ten years before she had been tried for the murder of her first husband and, though innocent, acquitted only for lack of evidence. Now someone unknown is threatening to produce evidence which would have convicted her. What is it? And who possesses it?

Fortunately, in the same pub Margaret also meets Arthur Crook, the ebullient lawyer to whom the innocent never turn in vain. When, some days later, the blackmailer is found murdered shortly after Margaret, in a distraught condition, had been seen leaving the premises, it is to Crook that she tells her tale. And someone knows Crook and knows his reputation, and is more than anxious that he shall not take on Margaret's case.

Anthony Gilbert's many fans will find this latest novel an absorbing study of one woman versus circumstantial evidence in two intriguingly related crimes.

### *Musical Comedy Crime, The*
October 1933
Major John Hillier, a well-known clubman, is found dead in his flat in Upper Paulton Terrace early one morning in rather peculiar circumstances. The discovery is made by a servant, upon whom a certain amount of suspicion falls. Inspector Field traces the dead man's movements on the previous night and learns that, after breaking up a dinner party in a somewhat unconventional fashion, he travelled some distance to a remote suburban theatre to see a leading lady whom he cannot even identify by sight. Following up certain clues and deductions of his own, Field discovers the reason for this strange course of action, and tracing back the dead man's history over a number of years, finds himself entangled in a net of underworld intrigue in England and on the Continent. Dope, blackmail and a crime many years old all play their part in an affair that, starting without sensation, attracts universal attention. The component parts of the mystery are finally put together by Field and Scott Egerton, who, entering the case late in its development, is able to supply the final link.

### *Nice Cup of Tea, A*
December 1950
When Alice Hunter's autocratic old mother died, after grimly clinging to life for eighty odd years, it was enough at first for Alice just to be free: but she began to be lonely when she found her genteel upbringing had left her few points of contact with the sort of people she met in the cheap boarding-houses, which were all she could afford. Then came the news of the legacy, and Alice's soul took wings as she caught the next train to her late aunt's lawyers in Bath. The life that opens before her, however, is not what she expects, and she becomes lost in a miasma of human misunderstanding, hatred and deceit. A nice cup of tea, stirred effectively by Arthur Crook, and now proffered confidently to the reader!

### *Nice Little Killing, A*
March 1974
When the Bankses' [sic] Dutch au pair was stood up by the boy-friend with whom she had arranged to go away secretly while the family were on holiday, she could not have foreseen that it would lead to her meeting

Arthur Crook. She certainly could not have foreseen that she would shortly need the lawyer-detective's services when she sneaked back to the house to find it burgled and a body in the boot cupboard.

Crook was needed more than ever when there was a second murder in the village, and as always he steals the show, though this time young Dawn and Coral Banks run him a pretty close second, both for their engaging personalities (among the best Anthony Gilbert has ever created) and for their effectiveness in thwarting crime.

Anthony Gilbert's many readers need no introduction to the Crook most feared by crooks. Here he is, ebullient and inimitable as ever, with full supporting cast.

### Night Encounter
May 1968

The shades of night were falling fast when Arthur Crook drove the old Superb over the Lakeland Fells and into the valley, to stop at a mysterious house where, though a light burned in an upper window, no one answered the bell.

Only, after he had driven on, the light was dramatically extinguished.

This is the opening of a double murder mystery in which Crook acts in the defence of a young prisoner 'on the run', whose guilt appears to authority to be obvious. Once again the self-confident, red-headed lawyer succeeds in pin-pointing the real criminal by his own unconventional methods.

In a new and dazzling mystery story Anthony Gilbert more than lives up to Edmund Crispin's praise (in the *Sunday Times*) of his last book, *The Visitor*: '*Great verve and wit, notable characterisation and a proper plot properly knitted, Mr Gilbert gets better and better.*'

### No Dust in the Attic
September 1962

On a fast train to London lawyer Arthur Crook meets trouble with a capital T. During the journey one passenger disappears and is subsequently found, dead, of course, beside the line; and it is thanks to Crook's turn of speed that a second corpse isn't found there, too. These events are part of a series of crimes planned by a man who has killed and is preparing to kill again.

This is the gripping story of a girl in desperate circumstances, who finds herself in the hands of a criminal organisation, to whom she herself is a source of danger. Flitting stealthily from one inconspicuous boarding-house to another, she seeks safety in obscurity. Yet, ironically, it is Crook, with his elastic interpretation of the rule of law, to whom obscurity is as unknown as it is undesired, who achieves her salvation after a life-and-death chase.

Again Anthony Gilbert writes a crime novel in his own unique manner – fast-moving, mysterious, rumbustious, and spiced with a worm's-eye view of the oddities of urban life and people.

### Old Lady Dies, An
May 1934

Old Mrs. Wolfe was dying – at last. Nobody seemed really sorry about it. Certainly not her relatives – and legatees. Mrs. Wolfe was wealthy and her periodical indispositions regularly brought her heirs rushing to her bedside. The old lady obviously derived a grim satisfaction from the tragi-comedy, enjoying to the last her sense of power, the will to dominate other people which had become her all-consuming passion. And so, with her various impecunious grandchildren waiting impatiently for the end, the old lady died

– not from natural causes, but by treachery. The mystery of her death provides the most unusual detective story. Mr. Anthony Gilbert writes with commendable restraint. Here are no incredible situations, no absurdly sensational thrills, and, strange to say, no police. But for honest, if unorthodox craftsmanship and the ability to keep the reader guessing, Mr. Gilbert is unrivalled.

### Out for the Kill
May 1960

As Arthur Crook came home to Brandon Street he complained to himself that crime and murder were not what they used to be. He was wrong. At that very moment he was heading straight for a case which was to call for every weapon in his armoury: deduction, quick thinking, guile and fast action. The rumbustious, red-haired solicitor had his curiosity aroused by the death of the milliner's budgerigar. It was but a short step from there to wondering where the bird's owner had gone and, with Arthur Crook, to wonder means to run and find out. The more he found out about the quiet, retiring Miss Chisholm the more suspicious he became about what had happened to her, and why. There was no evidence for the police, at that stage. But there was quite enough for Arthur Crook to get into top gear and to give his army of admirers another fast moving story, told with a light touch and allied to a clever plot, which make *Out For The Kill* a vintage Anthony Gilbert.

### Passenger to Nowhere
August 1965

To Sarah Hollis and her flat-mates a ramshackle villa in the French Pyrenees seemed to offer the perfect holiday: 'romantic, restful, remote' – that was how the advertisement described the Villa Abercrombie.

Sarah went ahead of the others in her own little car. She reached the villa alone. On the way she had met by chance a man called Arthur Crook, though she could hardly believe his assertion, made with hearty and cosy vulgarity, that he was by profession a lawyer. A time would come when Sarah would have need of his services…

The Villa reminded Sarah of the House of Usher, and the events that befell her there revived the terrifying comparison. Sarah proved herself a girl of spirit – and spirit was the quality most needed to save her from the ruthless criminals in whose schemes she became involved.

Set in the deep countryside of France, this exciting story tells of Sarah's dangerous predicament, reveals a complex and wicked plot, and shows Arthur Crook in roaring action to foil the villains.

### Riddle of a Lady
September 1956

'I could have told the narks there was one who'd never die in her bed of old age,' said Crook, when he met the mysterious old woman with the green eyes in the bar of the Nell Gwynne. "Question is, which of them did it? The chap who drove her there, the other chap who drove her back, or our old friend, A. N. Other?"

The rumbustious Arthur Crook, unscrupulous lawyer and unraveller of many mysteries, was on the trail again.

Who was Stella Foster?

Who was the red-haired man in the Nell Gwynne?

Who wrote the postcard found by the police on the morning after Stella's death?

And who (or what) was Henry Greatorex, the charming, indolent, unpredictable dark horse of the firm of Greatorex Brothers, the

sober lawyers of London and Beckfield? Philanderer? Ardent lover? Secret benefactor? Considerate employer? Callous murderer? In Henry, Crook encounters as baffling a client as ever came his way, and the surprising denouement involves as many strange and exciting twists as there are in the splendidly rounded character of Henry himself.

Anthony Gilbert has again achieved a masterly compound of excitement, humour and character.

### Ring for a Noose
March 1963

It was thanks to the fog that Arthur Crook went one evening to the Duck and Daisy instead of his normal resort, The Two Chairmen, and thereby found himself involved with a party of young men and women calling themselves the Peace Brigadiers. Their cause was to aid refugees from Europe. The movement had reached a crisis when it became apparent that one of their number was using the Association for personal, possibly criminal ends, and within a few hours the situation blew up into murder. For once Crook almost tripped over it and in a matter of days he was personally involved, acting for the accused man. His enquiries led him into the oddest quarters until in a dramatic scene he unmasked the traitor.

This ingenious and exciting crime novel depicts a host of convincing characters in a fearful situation. Yet none of these is so dominating as Crook himself, who thunders and almost blunders his way through to prove that once again he only acts for the innocent and always gets his man.

### Scarlet Button, The
October 1944

James Chigwell was a blackmailer, a human spider who fattened on the blood of other men, on their misfortunes, on their mistakes. But retribution came to Chigwell. One of his victims at last rebelled against his devilish iniquity and bludgeoned him to death. But who among Chigwell's many victims had, with the final courage of despair, summoned up the resolution to slay his tormentor? *The Scarlet Button* is at once grim and entertaining, an excellent and unusual detective mystery, featuring, of course, the celebrated Arthur Crook.

### She Shall Die
April 1961

When Arthur Crook's latest client arrived to consult him, unannounced, at eight in the evening, the red-headed rogue among lawyers already had the published facts of the case at his fingertips. No interesting murder case comes to light without Crook keeping an eye on it, and the case against Hatty Savage – young, attractive and with a chip on her shoulder – was making headlines. Some thought she had been lucky to escape a similar charge not long before and feeling was running high in the neighbourhood. Crook attacks the case like a terrier a rat and in his own inimitable and explosive way proves his client's innocence by revealing a cunning killer. *She Shall Die* also shows once again that Anthony Gilbert has an incomparable mastery of the detective story which is both highly ingenious and continuously entertaining.

### Snake in the Grass
April 1954

Con Gardiner had no family: his work and his one-room flat filled most of his solitary existence, until one evening a strange girl in the street asked him for the loan of a pound. Con was attracted to Caro Graves, and, puzzled,

too; he didn't see what would become of a girl who had just left her husband after a bitter quarrel, who had nowhere to go, and whose resources totalled one pound. But he was soon to have greater troubles, for he found out that Toby Graves had been murdered about the time that Caro had left him. He looked like becoming an accessory after the fact. Caro vanished – a disappearance aided by a remarkable old spinster, Emmy Crisp, who was not half so mad as she liked people to suppose. Emmy brought Arthur Crook into the case, and from the time that rumbustious investigator started work some of the facts surrounding Graves' murder began to emerge. Anthony Gilbert has again written a first-rate thriller, full of surprises and humour, and with a problem as baffling as ever.

### Something Nasty in the Woodshed
March 1942

When a middle-aged Gentleman advertises his wish to meet a Gentlewoman of Independent Means with a view to matrimony, various feminine hearts may flutter. Sometimes, too, the roving eye of a detective will momentarily light up with keen anticipation, and the innocent-looking advertisement might even be filed away for future reference. Here, then, is the history of a matrimonial advertisement, an extraordinary and baffling story, written with distinction by Anthony Gilbert, and featuring, of course, that favourite character, Arthur Crook.

### Spinster's Secret, The
July 1946

Miss Martin, a seventy-four-year-old spinster of small means and delicate health, finds her chief interest in sitting in the window of her single room in Kensington and watching the passers-by. One day her attention is caught by a little girl, called Pamela, whom subsequently she gets to know. It is obvious that this child comes from a comfortable home, where she appears to be in the care of a guardian and a charming young governess called Terry. A little later Miss Martin is taken ill, removed to hospital and finally sent to an old ladies' home outside London. Here she is very lonely, but one day, she sees the crocodile of children from the Destitute Children's Orphanage coming down the street, and to her amazement and horror she recognises Pamela. When she tried to make enquiries, however, she is repulsed on all sides and assured that she is mistaken. Profoundly dissatisfied with this explanation, the old lady continues her efforts, hindered by both matron and her unsympathetic niece Doreen Blake. Finally, she takes a leap in the dark and gets in touch with Mr. Crook, to whom she unfolds her story. Crook, feeling that this is a new line of country, makes some enquiries and eventually unearths a most exciting plot involving murder, attempted murder, abduction and fraud.

### Tenant for the Tomb
May 1971

On a quiet country station lawyer Arthur Crook, waiting for the train to London, witnessed a near-fatal accident. Despite the arm of her companion, Miss Imogen Garland, sister of the local MP and known to her family (who considered her eccentric) as Dotty, slipped and almost fell under the train. No harm was done, and Arthur Crook might not have thought anything more about it had not a newspaper item a few weeks later caught his eye. Miss Garland had once again been involved in an accident, this time fatal. Only it was not Miss Garland who had died.

Arthur Crook thus acquired one of his

strangest clients and an exceptionally puzzling case. Someone wanted Dotty dead, but her singular combination of guile and guilelessness proved unexpectedly tough. As usual, Crook digs deep to unearth an ingenious solution, while remaining at the top of his racy form.

### Third Crime Lucky
February 1959
'Let's hope it will be Third Crime Lucky – for the ends of justice,' remarked Arthur Crook, when he found himself involved in the mysterious death of old Mr. Cobb of King's Banbury.

Mr. Cobb was the third elderly invalid to die conveniently, if somewhat unexpectedly, in a household that also contained Fred and Bessie Meadows. And yet – who could suspect this amiable couple, so active, responsible, willing and honest? No trouble too much, no hours too long – wherever they went, Death went, too. But their third crime involved them with Arthur Crook, and that was when the luck turned – against them.

A large and faithful public knows that the irruption of this red-headed and ebullient man of law into a case   means that bustling action and devious cunning of every sort will be employed to ensure the safety of the innocent and the trapping of the guilty. In *Third Crime Lucky* Anthony Gilbert has introduced a chillingly sinister theme into a homely situation and Crook is forced to wage a war of nerves to unravel a baffling and fascinating case which will keep the reader enthralled to the last page.

### Treason in My Breast
April 1938
'Few murderers would go unhung,' said plump, cynical Arthur Crook, 'if people used their eyes more. It's the man selling violets in the gutter, the woman exercising her Pekinese, the chap reading the midday racing news in the Tube who actually have the chance to spot the murderer. They're the people he can't guard against.' On this idea Anthony Gilbert has based his new detective story, and a jolly good one it is. Arthur Crook is a delightful nosey-parker. You will like his blustering humour and bull-dog tenacity, so hurry up and meet him in this first-rate mystery.

### Uncertain Death
September 1961
On the day that Emily Tate vanished, Inspector Marston met her husband on the tow-path of the River Pyle, not far from the weir. The unassuming, quiet, Stephen Tate was on the brink of a nightmare episode which was to make his unhappy marriage, his clandestine and hopeless love affair, and his disappointed hopes, seem positively joyous in comparison. The determination of the girl he loved was the only thing which could save him from the web of circumstances in which he was enmeshed. Anthony Gilbert's legion of admirers will relish again the bounding confidence of the red-haired solicitor who, in his own unique way, is once more able to snatch victory from the jaws of defeat, in a book which is ingenious, realistic and supremely entertaining.

### Vanishing Corpse, The
January 1941
One would have thought that Laura Verity was the last person that things would happen to; a little grey-haired lady with not much money and no past. It was through absolutely no fault of her own that she went in peril of her life, and, indeed, but for Arthur Crook's timely interference would undoubtedly have lost it altogether. The one thing, however, she was never in danger of losing was her head. The police would not believe her? She would

prove them wrong. The reporters would not cease to pester her? She would stay in bed. The wine might be poisoned? She would leave it for Arthur Crook to see. That car might belong to the murderer? She would get in it and see where he went. Someone must know something? She would question them. Nothing deterred Miss Verity. Nothing daunted her. In the body of this middle-aged spinster beat the heart of a lion. Anthony Gilbert's brilliant novel is a story for the times, to defeat the black-out and repel all thoughts of invasion; a really good, exciting, well-told tale.

### Visitor, The
July 1967
"It was odd seeing how undistinguished he looked, that I knew from the first minute he spelt danger"

That was Margaret Ross's instant reaction to the mysterious visitor who called at her flat early one morning, to threaten ruin to her 19-year-old son.

So begins Anthony Gilbert's new novel, intriguing, complex and loaded with suspense. A demand for blackmail leads on to murder, when Margaret finds herself in the position of giving the police information that she believes will clear the accused man only at her son's expense. Surrounded by dangers, unaware from which direction her enemy will strike next, she herself becomes a victim and is only saved at the eleventh hour by the intervention of Arthur Crook, the unconventional lawyer whose boast is that he never loses a client.

Here Anthony Gilbert, one of England's most distinguished crime novelists, writes at top form, exact characterisation adding conviction to a powerful and exciting story.

### Woman in Red, The
July 1941
When Julia Ross rang the bell of the dark forbidding house at 30 Henriques Square, she had made her irrevocable decision. It was too late to retrace her steps, too late to avoid the fateful net that was about to close round her. She could not very well have chosen otherwise. It was two months since she had left Edinburgh to seek work in London, and now all the money she had in the world was two pounds eighteen. An employment agency had sent her there to meet a prospective employer – the strange and sinister Mrs. Ponsonby. On such little things hang our destinies. And so Julia Ross rings the bell and Anthony Gilbert rings up the curtain on a story of truly dramatic suspense.

## GILL, JOSEPHINE
### House That Died, The
January 1956
The Bellamy family considered Anne Chisholm's death to be in the worst taste. As far as they were concerned she was a stranger. She had been living in their large town house in Boston's Back Bay for some six months as a secretary-companion to Elizabeth Bellamy, the ageing dowager of the family. Then, early on an April evening, she had been found lying at the foot of the marble stairs in a broken, untidy heap. One look at the three generations of Bellamys warned Matt Garrick, the *Tribune* reporter, that he was up against the smooth, hard wall of money and influence. Was it pride, a distaste for publicity, or fear that made them unwilling to co-operate with the police investigation? Matt thought it was fear – acute, undisguised fear – and when the family was soon involved in another death, he found he was right. The Crime Club are delighted that this talented author has joined the Crime Club list with her latest book.

## GOLDSBOROUGH, ROBERT
### Bloodied Ivy, The
January 1990
On a tranquil campus in upstate New York, Prescott University's most celebrated and controversial professor falls to an apparently accidental death. Archie Goodwin, curious, begins poking around in the ivy.

Back home in the brownstone, Nero Wolfe professes no interest in the case. But when Archie lands in the local nick, the great man breaks his cardinal rule: he forsakes the comforts of home for the wilds of the larger world, appearing at the scene of the crime to rescue his errant associate and beard the local constabulary in its den. Only Archie is glad to see him, but the reluctant suspects gather at his command: Prescott's ambitious president, feuding colleagues and jealous lovers. Each has a motive – but murder?

Nero Wolfe is not convinced that the professor was murdered until he is back home, safely wedged in his familiar armchair, and a second death bloodies the campus ivy. Then the question of murder becomes more than academic.

### Death on Deadline
February 1989
Nero Wolfe, the orchid-growing gourmet and genius of detection, is back. And, once again, Wolfe and Archie Goodwin are in the confident hands of Robert Goldsborough, author of *Murder in E Minor*.

The first corpse is slated to be a newspaper. If Ian MacLaren, sleazy king of Britain's scandal sheets, succeeds in taking over the *Gazette*, this respectable publication will indeed die. Nero Wolfe decides to stop him.

Archie wonders why the brilliant detective has championed such a cause without a paying client. Yes, their mutual friend, Lon Cohen, has been a *Gazette* reporter for years and Harriet Haverhill, the paper's owner, is a dedicated and noble woman, but what is Wolfe's true motive for butting in?

Yet butt in he does, though when he places a full-page ad in the *New York Times* calling for a united effort to 'Keep New York Clean' of Ian MacLaren's kind, no one, not even Wolfe, suspects that he has advertised for murder.

Naturally he now concentrates on solving it, as Archie lures suspects to the 35th Street brownstone. Despite possible motives running from obsession to greed to revenge, Wolfe soon recognizes the murderer's by-line…and recognizes also that killer is working to a deadline and that the next victim may well be himself.

### Last Coincidence, The
January 1991
Playboy Sparky Linville has a nasty notion of fun and games. But when he picks popular Noreen James as his unwilling playmate the result is murder – and a case that will rock Manhattan's trendy Upper East Side and divide the family of Lily Rowan, Noreen's aunt.

As furore rages in the local press and the police fix their attention on her relatives, Lily turns to her old friend Archie Goodwin for help, hoping he can convey the seriousness of the family's plight to his eminent employer, Nero Wolfe.

Wolfe doesn't enjoy being distracted from his greenhouse and his groaning board. Yet Archie's eloquence – and the prospect of an enormous fee seduce him into accepting the case. It is, of course, understood that since the master detective has no intention of venturing forth from his snug brownstone, Archie will handle the legwork.

But the more shoe leather Archie burns,

the more burning questions arise. There are too many suspects – and every one of them has a strong motive and no alibi. And on top of that, two people have confessed to the crime! Nero Wolfe is left to ponder this bizarre puzzle – and the deadliest coincidence – in the most baffling case of his career.

### Murder in E Minor
May 1987
Nero Wolfe, the brilliant orchid-growing gourmet detective, and his inimitable confidential assistant, Archie Goodwin, are America's most beloved detection team. Now they are back in a splendid new murder mystery that takes us to where Rex Stout left off. In the perfect Stout tradition, author Robert Goldsborough has ingeniously rendered every detail of character and place with such uncanny accuracy that fans will savour every page to the surprising and immensely satisfying conclusion.

Threatening notes have been sent to Milan Stevens, celebrated conductor of the New York Symphony. His niece, Maria, appeals to Nero Wolfe and Archie can barely conceal his surprise when Wolfe agrees to come out of retirement and investigate. But Wolfe has his own reasons for taking the case, for while the world knows Milan Stevens as a brilliant conductor, Wolfe knows him as Milos Stefanovic, the brave freedom fighter who once saved Wolfe's life.

But Maria has come to the big detective too late. Milan Stevens is soon found dead and the juicy public scandal of it all enthrals the city.

With precious little to go on Wolfe and Archie compile a list of suspects, but soon discover that the problem isn't where to start – it's where to stop.

## GRACE, C. L.
### Shrine of Murders, A
September 1993
Geoffrey Chaucer's *Canterbury Tales* forms the backdrop for this ingenious novel, the first in a series of medieval mysteries introducing a unique character: Kathryn Swinbrooke, a physician and chemist practicing in fifteenth century Canterbury, site of the cathedral and the relics that draw pilgrims from across England and Europe. C.L. Grace has based his character on the interesting fact that women doctors played vital roles in English medieval medicine, only to be excluded from the profession in subsequent centuries.

*A Shrine of Murders* revolves around a series of terrible deaths that paralyses Canterbury and threatens the holy shrine. The deaths are announced by bits of doggerel— short poems that may contain clues to the murderer's indentity – pinned to the great cathedral door. Kathryn, a physician with an independent reputation in local affairs, is asked by town officials to investigate, since the murder victims have been poisoned, and a chemist's expertise is needed.

Kathryn is joined by Colum Murtagh, a rough-mannered Irish soldier for the crown. Where Kathryn is skilful, Colum blunders; but Colum is able to open doors that a woman cannot enter. Working together, the two struggle to find a murderer whose tastes are literary, but whose motives are deeply personal.

## GREGSON, J. M.
### Bring Forth Your Dead
January 1991
In darkness and swirling mist, a body is removed from a quiet country cemetery: the body of a murdered man.

Behind the solid walls of his house in a Cotswold village, elderly Edmund Craven had been virtually house-bound. Now it was apparent that he had been killed by one of those closest to him, and by a method both systematic and ruthless.

The conduct of the investigation represents a new challenge even for the experienced Superintendent Lambert and his team: never before has he had to investigate a murder perpetrated over a year earlier, with the scents gone cold and the traces securely covered. Gradually he unearths a network of malice and deceit. Craven's son and daughter, his housekeeper and the American who was his friend for almost fifty years, as well as a young man who is overlooked at first, all had reason to wish Craven dead and the opportunity to kill him.

### *Dead on Course*
November 1991

*The shout came as they were completing the eleventh hole. Away to their left, beneath the shadow of a huge beech, a young greenkeeper waved at them a frantic, unsteady arm…*
The body is that of a man who had been enjoying a few days of golf and relaxation with his friends at the luxurious Wye Castle Hotel and Country Club. Superintendent Lambert and Sergeant Hook establish fairly quickly how he died, but discovering who killed him proves a more difficult challenge. The golf course and hotel are set in spectacular scenery beside one of England's most beautiful rivers, with the square tower of Hereford's ancient Cathedral visible in the distance. In May this incomparable valley is at its best, but it is a bizarre context for the investigation of a brutal murder.

Gradually, over the days of their stay, Lambert unearths the secrets of the group who surrounded the dead man. There is an urgency about his investigation, for even while the suspects play golf and enjoy good food and wine there is more violence abroad within the ivy-clad walls of the old hotel.

### *For Sale – With Corpse*
January 1990

Lydon Hall is a house full of character, as the estate agent's literature claims. But its many interesting features should surely not include a corpse in the elegant drawing-room?

Is this death the suicide it appears to be? The investigation centres upon a tight-knit village community. Both the glamorous French widow of the deceased and the man who lives rough on the moor after a mental breakdown seem to know more about this death than is at first apparent. Moreover, it gradually emerges that the staff of the estate agency he owned all had their different reasons for disliking the dead man.

Superintendent John Lambert and Sergeant Bert Hook bring to the unravelling of the mystery their customary combination of insight, humanity and humour.

J. M. Gregson shows a mastery of pace, as well as his usual skill in revealing the reality beneath appearances and the raw passions that lurk in quiet places.

### *Fox in the Forest, The*
August 1992

A motiveless murder, every policeman's nightmare. It is committed in a stretch of forest between two peaceful villages. Superintendent Lambert and his CID team can find few connections between the people who were around at the time of this death and a victim who seems to have had no enemies.

Before long, it seems that they have a serial killer on their hands, selecting victims at random and dispatching them in a manner which affords few clues to his identity. The press dub the killer The Fox and picture a rural community gripped by fear.

Lambert and Sergeant Hook are on ground they have not trodden before. The village closes in upon itself, preserving its secrets from outsiders. The solution when it comes is complex but satisfying.

### *Murder at the Nineteenth*
March 1989

When there is a violent murder at a historic home counties golf club, Superintendent John Lambert himself discovers the crime. For the first time in a long career, he finds himself conducting a murder inquiry among people he knows well. The victim is the Chairman of the Golf Club and a prominent local businessman, and it is soon clear that the members of the Club Committee are the chief suspects. They are all prominent members of the local community, and Lambert is saddled with a Chief Constable who is uncomfortably aware of the fact. Indeed, he seems more concerned with the media attention which inevitably focuses upon such a sensational murder than with the emerging detail of Lambert's investigation.

Events move quickly in the two days following the murder. Amid further startling developments, Superintendent Lambert, supported by the deceptively stolid Sergeant Hook, moves steadily towards a solution.

### *Stranglehold*
June 1993

When a young girl is raped and murdered and her body left in a deserted house, it is not discovered for two days and there are few clues at the scene of the crime to incriminate her killer.

When a second murder follows, it becomes obvious that the hunt is for a serial killer, who is almost certain to kill again. Moreover the way the bodies are laid out seems to indicate not only a warped mind but a wish to taunt the police. In the quiet country town of Oldford, a whole community is struck with terror as it waits for the nocturnal killer to strike again.

The police machine throws up several suspects, but the fact that there is no obvious motive for the killings makes the investigation more than usually complex – especially when it is suggested that the murderer may come from the ranks of the police themselves.

Superintendent John Lambert feels that strain, as do others around him but aided by Sergeant Bert Hook and the other members of his team he eventually brings the investigation to its thrilling and startling conclusion.

J. M. Gregson's grasp of character and sure ear for dialogue ensure that the search for the killer provides a tense and enthralling read.

## GRIERSON, FRANCIS D.

### *Jackdaw Mystery, The*
May 1931

When young Teddy Gate cheerfully undertook a job as professional guide to English tourists in Paris, he hardly knew the Eiffel Tower from the Moulin Rouge. Teddy blundered gaily on, and had learned many things by the time that mysterious person known as 'The Jackdaw' began to take an interest in his affairs—and those of pretty Betty Draycot Foliat. But when Teddy and Betty vanished—kidnapped by 'The Jackdaw'—things became serious, and that clever detective, Inspector Barraud, found himself faced with a problem that became more and more amazing the more he tried to solve it. How he did it, and what happened to the elusive 'Jackdaw', are told with a pleasant blend of humour and excitement—with some interesting sidelights on the work of the police from behind the scenes.

### *Lady of Despair, The*
June 1930

It was in a sordid Apache case the Geoffrey first saw her – the Lady of Despair, beautiful ward of Paul Daburon, the famous advocate. If he did not actually fall in love with her there and then Geoffrey Barsette was certainly more than a little interested. His luck was in. That very night he made a good friend of Inspector Patras, by rescuing him from a skirmish with two Apaches from the Parisian underworld, into which his duties as detective had led him. M. Patras needed no introduction to Barsette, the author of many thrilling mystery stories. He was able to tell him all about Madelon Marly, the mysterious beauty whose charm had attracted a number of suitors, each of whom had – was it by unhappy coincidence? – met a sudden death in the very moment when their love seemed about to be returned. A few days later the Vicomte de Caramie, the latest aspirant to Madelon's hand, and already a rival of Geoffrey, was found in his apartment murdered, with a fencing foil through his heart.

### *Monkhurst Murder, The*
July 1933

The Honourable Richard Furling is staying at The Black Cygnet, an old-fashioned country inn whose proprietor is an old school and army friend, Major Baxter. They witness a quarrel between the local squire, Vivian Monkhurst, and his brother Jack, and later in the same day are horrified to learn that Monkhurst has been found dead – murdered – on the banks of the stream which flowed through the estate. Suspicion naturally falls on Jack Monkhurst, on whose behalf Furlong investigates the case. The ingenious and puzzling mystery is unravelled with Francis D. Grierson's customary skill, the suspense being well maintained until the end.

### *Murder in Mortimer Square*
April 1932

Supper-time at the gay Everyland Hotel … The famous Jade Room crowded with the usual glittering throng … Bright lights, bright music, dancing and gaiety … and then … A whispered conversation at one of the tables … A young man rises and goes to the manager's room. The Assistant Commissioner is suave but determined. 'It is my duty to detain you on a charge of having murdered – .' The drama begins. Dramatic and entertaining as well as highly ingenious, this new story from the experienced pen of Francis D. Grierson keeps the reader fascinated and thrilled to the last page.

### *Mysterious Mademoiselle, The*
December 1930

'In twelve months time you will have £20,000 to do what you like with!' This was the Great Adventure presented to young Valentine Grey. To prepare him for his new responsibilities, his guardian gave Val £1,500 and a cheque-book, and the young fellow set off to enjoy himself in Paris. He encountered in the train beautiful Gaby Clamart, an ex-actress, whose association with that amazing criminal known as 'The Master', was to provide a perplexing problem for the cleverest brains in the French detective force, aided by the famous British criminologists, Professor Wells and Inspector Sims. A holiday which began with the comedy of Val's friend and ally, cheery 'Marty' Jerrom, was to turn to a sinister tragedy with a startling denouement. This story – although pure fiction – is written with an inside knowledge of the detective services of two nations that enhances the interest of a thrilling plot.

### *Mystery in Red*
October 1931

There was a sort of reptilian fascination about Dr. Bude of Colombo. His suave manners, his wealth and his brilliant reputation in the medical world had gained for him a sure place in London society. He was always there with the best people, and on the evening of Anne Masters' tragic death, Dr. Bude was one of Lord Masters' principal guests. So was Gloria Greshame, and instinctively she sensed a connection between the fire in which Anne lost her life and the presence of Dr Bude. Carefully she sifted the little evidence available, until she had at least enough to justify the suspicion which she confided to her uncle, Sir Andrew Greshame of Scotland Yard. Sir Andrew did not laugh. He had a deep respect for Gloria's brains. Suddenly came a fantastic revelation, which could surely be no more than coincidence! Dr. Bude had been an acquaintance of several women on whom tragedy had suddenly descended – and they had all had red hair! Gloria determined to bring the doctor to justice – Gloria with her lustrous head of red-gold hair! Mr. Grierson has composed a veritable rhapsody of thrills and detection – a Mystery in Red.

### *Mystery of the Golden Angel, The*
January 1933

It was an incredible crime that sent a shudder through the *Courier* office. Picture the feverish activity, the swift action, the marvellous organisation; news being sought, selected, sub-edited. The mighty presses down below preparing for their million run…and the night editor is found murdered. *The Mystery of the Golden Angel*, a cleverly constructed drama with an interesting newspaper setting, is undoubtedly one of the most thrilling and baffling stories that Francis D. Grierson has written.

## HAFFNER, MARGARET

### *Murder of Crows, A*
January 1992

Catherine Edison has everything going for her in the town of Kingsport, Ontario, where she has lived all her life. She has a rewarding career, a loving daughter, an ambitious husband – and John, her lover. She also has good friends, who have formed a close-knit group since childhood.

Then John is found dead on a country road. Hit and run? Maybe. Catherine has her doubts, but no one else seems suspicious, and her husband, campaign manager for another member of her circle who is running for political office, is far too taken up with raising funds for the campaign to take his wife's fears seriously.

Not even when another member of the group is killed and Catherine herself barely escapes the fatal 'accident' does anyone believe her claim that a murderer is on the loose. Staff Sergeant Warshinsky is sympathetic, but that is all.

Alone in a familiar world grown frightening, Catherine must maintain an outward composure in the face of a mounting death-toll among her friends and her own mounting fears. For the murderer can only be one of her circle – and she loves and trusts them all.

### *Snowblind*
January 1993

Simon Hollingford, an Ontario Provincial Police detective, has been suspended while a charge of police brutality against him is investigated. He jumps at the chance to get away from it all by volunteering to be the radio operator for a scientific expedition in Canada's high arctic.

Once in the North, his enjoyment is marred by the information that the previous year's radio man, the scientist Phillip Loew, had been lost in a storm and the body never found. Then a series of potentially fatal accidents sets everyone on edge.

While birdwatching one day, Simon stumbles on the body of the lost man – but he hasn't died of exposure, two bullets in the chest prove the theory that high-velocity lead poisoning can kill faster than sub-zero temperatures.

All the same people are back in the North this year, which means one of them is a murderer. Amid steadily deteriorating weather conditions, Simon searches for the answer and uncovers a web of lies and hatred. Everyone had a motive for wanting Phillip Loew dead, and someone is willing to kill again to keep their secret safe…

## HALL, PATRICIA

### *Coldness of Killers, The*

July 1992

When the body of a young dropout is discovered at a downtown school in a West Yorkshire city, is the motive mindless racism or something more complex but just as brutal?

The ensuing violence and racial tension test loyalties to breaking-point across a mixed community, and no one is more involved than liberal teacher Joanna Robertson, who finds that not only are personal loyalties strained in ways she could never have envisaged, but she is herself suspected of murder. Christmas approaches, and Detective Chief Inspector Harry Huddleston, who had planned to end his police career in his home town on a convivial note, has several suspect killings on his hands and no clues to any of the perpetrators. But as his tenacious investigation gets under way, neither Huddleston nor any-one else foresaw the violent conclusion which was to disrupt so many lives.

### *Poison Pool, The*

September 1991

When they found old Tom Carter dead it looked like a routine mugging gone horribly wrong: a crime which could easily be handled by the relatively junior officer who found himself in charge that night. But when Inspector Alex Sinclair made the quick arrest he had hoped for, he found himself embroiled in a poisonous conspiracy which went right to the heart of his close-knit Yorkshire community, and eventually put his own career on the line.

*The Poison Pool* is set in a realistic small town on the edge of rugged Yorkshire countryside. Suspicion leads from the bleak back alley on a council estate where the old man's body is found, to the more prosperous suburbs, to local business, the town council and the Masonic lodge which Sinclair himself has been urged to join. It is soon clear that the boy Sinclair so confidently arrested could be a convenient scapegoat for far more powerful interests which might have wanted Tom Carter dead.

How far has the poison of corruption spread? As Sinclair and social worker Kate Weston struggle to identify and contain it, they plumb murky depths indeed.

## HAMILTON, BRUCE

### *Hue and Cry*

September 1931

Tom Payton, young, impressionable, good-looking, engaged to the girl he loves, is the reserve goalkeeper of the Swynford Athletic Football Club. He gets his great chance in a big cup-tie. The events of that Saturday afternoon and evening, how a latent antagonism with one of the directors leads him to commit an entirely unpremeditated murder, how he makes his get-away, his coming to London, his hairbreadth escapes and his curious refuges – all these are ingredients of a tale which maintains an atmosphere of suspense and intense excitement to the last page.

## HAMILTON, IAN

### *Thrill Machine, The*

January 1972

She was big, blonde and beautiful, and they called her the Thrill Machine. But when she landed in Sydney, film star Dinah Terry did not realize her name was known to the police because it had been pencilled on the wall by a dying murder victim, a man she had never seen or heard of. All she knew was that she was on the downward path, and that her confidence was descending even faster than she was. Her first appearance at a night-club was a flop.

To Pete Heysen, who has his own factual crime programme on TV, she confides the reason: blackmail. Yet when Heysen puts this out on his programme, she publicly denies it, and his rating, already slipping in face of covert competition from his ambitious assistant, descends another notch.

Then Heysen discovers that a blue film Dinah had made years earlier is now being shown in the Sydney underworld, although she had paid big money to have it suppressed. Someone has made a duplicate and is intent on undermining Dinah. But who? And why? And what connection has it with that mysterious and obscure death?

If Heysen can find out the answers to these questions, even if it means going beyond the law a little, his big TV comeback looks assured. Except that nothing is assured in this wry, fast-moving story of corrupt cops, blue films, and in-fighting on television, set in a world which Australian Ian Hamilton knows well.

## HART, JEANNE

### *Decent Killer, A*

August 1991

Everyone liked Max Follett in the small artistic community of Bay Cove. So when he was fatally electrocuted while taking his morning shower, everyone assumed it was an accident. After all, Max had just posted off to his publisher the manuscript of his long-awaited second novel. There had even been a party for friends and neighbours to celebrate, given by wealthy Leona Morgan. Of course Max had spoiled the party by claiming that an obvious accident was an attempt to kill him, but no one had taken him seriously. That was just Max.

Unfortunately it didn't take Detective Carl Pederson long to conclude that someone hadn't wanted Max to see the publication of his second novel and that among the decent, likeable members of the artistic community lurked a murderer. But who could possibly be guilty in the pleasant neighbourhood where everyone knew everybody else? And where everyone liked Max Follet – or at least they said they did.

### *Lament for Two Ladies*

January 1991

They couldn't have been more different. Ann Koppleman was an attractive, wealthy widow who lived alone in her beautiful California home high on a hillside above the Pacific. Eugenie – just Eugenie – was a bag lady who slept rough and snatched a night's kip when she could in any empty room of the local hospital – something to which most of the staff turned a blind eye. Yet on the same night both women were murdered in identical fashion: by a slender knife efficiently plunged into the heart. What could they have in common, except, presumably, the same killer? Detective Carl Pedersen set to work to find out.

His inquiries took him behind the scenes in Bay Cove Hospital, and into the lives (and secrets) of Ann's seemingly close family. But none of those who might be thought to have a motive for one of the murders had any motive for the other. Everybody was involved with everybody else, but nothing could be made to fit. Until a breakthrough item of evidence turned up and the missing piece of the jigsaw slotted into place.

### *Personal Possession, A*

September 1989

The plan grew out of a joke.

In a small seaside town in Northern California, three women were sitting in a Honda. The three women were friends, but casual ones. Zora Hirsch was the tallest, and a widow. Eileen Brande, also widowed, was slightly built and looked smaller than she was. Sally Robinson had been married and divorced three times and was fiercely optimistic.

They'd been talking about men. Zora said, 'I certainly don't want to marry anybody. I would just like a man to go places with. A weekend lover would be nice.'

The ladies were all in their forties.

Zora said, 'What we need is one man – reasonably attractive. We could share him.'

Sally suggested taking an ad.

So they did, and the responses – pathetic, boastful, demented – flooded in.

And two months later, Sally Robinson was found murdered …

### *Some Die Young*

July 1990

They were intelligent girls, the three friends. Twelve and thirteen years old – not children, not young women. Certainly old enough to know not to go with strange men – and they did know. How, then, did Lisa Margolin's killer manage to persuade her to come with him to a deserted area of the park, in the rain? Because that's what happened to Lisa.

It is soon apparent that the murderer is connected to the arts magazine where Lisa's mother worked, and several of the staff are likely candidates for the role of murderer.

Meanwhile Lisa's two best friends and their parents – their own problems and confusions tied in to yesterday's horror and tomorrow's fear – and especially young Meredith Crane's diary ('it's really a journal, like Anne Frank's') reveal to Detective Carl Pederson that it is now Meredith who is being drawn into a dangerous relationship with the unknown killer. But Meredith refuses to divulge to the adults anything about her mysterious 'friend'…

Can Pederson identify him in time to prevent a final assignation between the smiling killer and the child in jeopardy?

## HAYWOOD, STEVE

### *Murderous Justice*

October 1991

Plucked from the dole queue by the surprise offer of a job, journalist Alan 'Archie' Archibold suddenly finds himself working for a television station reinvestigating a murder. Was the innocuous Terry Frampton really guilty of the grotesque killing for which he was convicted? Or has there been an appalling miscarriage of justice?

Working under the directions of his eccentric boss George Stredwick, Archie starts a search which leads him from the breathtaking heights of the Yorkshire moors to the low-life backstreets of the Midlands.

It is a search that throws up a confusing array of new suspects, and draws him into the passion and violence of their lives.

And it is a search that almost costs him his own life too.

Steve Haywood is currently producer of the BBC's award-winning programme *Rough Justice.*

## HELLER, KEITH

### *Man's Illegal Life: A story of London's Parish Watch, 1722*

April 1984

In the first half of the eighteenth century London was probably the most dangerous city on earth, its streets and alleys frequented by every kind of criminal, its legal system more notorious for brutality than for effectiveness. All that stood between the public and the violence of the age was the Parish Watch.

George Man, who makes his first appearance in this outstandingly original novel, is forty-five years old, honest, shrewd, conscientious and far from infirm. These qualities alone would distinguish him from most of his fellow watchmen, but Man is something more. He is in his own way a detective, and when he learns of the discovery of a body in a house in Drury Lane which has been boarded up in a manner reminiscent of the Great Plague of 1665, his suspicions are aroused. For once again fear of a reappearance of the pestilence is causing a degree of panic, and Drury Lane is where the plague began. Is the aged solitary inhabitant of the house the first victim of a new outbreak – or of murder?

Using only his wits, his knowledge of human nature, and his contacts, who range from Jonathan Wild, king of London's underworld, to Captain Thomas Coram, future founder of the Foundlings Hospital, Man sets about his investigation.

In following it to its conclusion author Keith Heller not only tells an absorbing story with an unfaltering ear for the rhythms of eighteenth-century speech and the felicities of Augustan prose, but demonstrates that police work (and policemen) are much the same in any age.

### *Man's Loving Family: A story of London's Parish Watch, 1727*

May 1986

In October 1727 George II was crowned King of England. But George Man, late of London's Parish Watch, did not share the general celebrations, for he was out of work.

He was therefore glad to take on the job of bodyguard to merchant Abraham Sinclair's son, whose murder on November 20 had been prophesied in an almanac announcement.

He was rather less glad when the prophecy was fulfilled before his very eyes in the course of a tavern brawl. Worse still, the man charged with the crime, and whose hand had indeed held the fatal sword, was Man's friend, the poet Richard Savage, already labouring under his mother's repudiation of him as a bastard.

To clear his friend, to assuage his conscience, Man embarks on his most ambitious investigation yet, which takes him into the bosom of the Sinclair family where a whole nest of vipers is nursed, and introduces him to such characters as the novelist Henry Fielding, here engaged in a somewhat surprising occupation, and young Andrew Millar, the eventual publisher of *Tom Jones*.

This fictionalized re-creation of an actual eighteenth-century murder and the notorious trial of one whom Dr Johnson later vindicated in his *Lives of the Poets*, is the best yet of Keith Heller's brilliantly realized stories of London's Parish Watch.

### Man's Storm: A story of London's Parish Watch, 1703
March 1985

On November 26th 1703 a great gale ravaged England. Daniel Defoe wrote an account of it, which was published the following year. Chimneys and steeples crashed down, ships were driven ashore, slates were torn from roofs and doors form their hinges. Everyone in the City of Westminster had a story to tell; many had had narrow escapes. And at the height of the storm a woman was found dead, battered to death in an ironmonger's shop.

George Man, almost twenty years younger than when first encountered in *Man's Illegal Life*, has just begun his career in London's parish watch. It falls to him to institute inquiries among the petty traders, artisans, and ne'er-do-wells of the district and to trace the network of alliances and antipathies that extends from the murdered woman to a pretty country lass from Tilbury, where Daniel Defoe once owned a brickworks; from a gang of lusty, drunken bullies, to their pleasant-faced victim, a girl named Sarah, whom Man hopes to meet again.

As the stunned inhabitants of Westminster venture forth into the ruin revealed by dawn, Man makes his arrest, and shattered lives, like shattered buildings, can begin to be rebuilt.

Keith Heller's first novel of London's parish watch won high praise. His second establishes him as a gifted historical novelist as well as a skilful crime writer.

## HENDERSON, JAMES

### Copperhead
August 1972

In a secret attack, in an undeclared war – the identity of the aggressor nation unknown – fifteen men and women have been sent into Europe and North America. Each is a deadly 'biological weapon' – each a carrier of a lethal, volatile strain of pneumonic plague. The virus can, within a week of its activation, complete its massive and irreversible chain of infection. Zooming in on Montreal, where by sheer accident the danger is stumbled upon, *Copperhead* races through five days of hidden crisis as the murky and violent world of international espionage explodes into action. High-echelon officers of Canadian, British, and US Intelligence, working with and against each other in uneasy alliance, throw a dragnet across the continent in pursuit of the plague carriers.

At the centre of the chase, moving with nervy agility among spies, counterspies, and double agents, is the sardonic and relentless Sohn. He is a man psychologically stripped for a ruthless task, his feelings virtually anaesthetized by personal tragedy. Assigned to track two women – one a famous scientist, the other a known agent of a possible enemy power – Sohn finds his long-dormant emotions cruelly awakened at the very moment his mission demands of him an ultimate brutality... as he moves closer and closer to the strategic mind at the centre of the conspiracy.

## HILL, REGINALD

### Advancement of Learning, An
January 1972

An academic scandal is brewing at Holm Coultram College, where a lecturer stands accused of falsifying marks in order to fail his former mistress. But this fades into insignificance when a woman's body is found in the staff garden. It has been there at least five years and identification proves difficult. And when her identity is finally established, it only confuses matters further for Superintendent Dalziel and Sergeant Pascoe. Dalziel feels out of place in the college community but he seems to thrive on the antagonism he arouses in both staff and students. Pascoe, more at home, is both aided and confused by the presence of an 'old flame' on the staff. There are two more deaths and both detectives find themselves under attack, physical as well as verbal, before they uncover the truth of what has been going on in this quiet scholastic backwater.

### Another Death in Venice
May 1976

Sarah's heart bleeds for the troubles of the world – its violence, torture, poverty, famine. Michael on the other hand prefers life as seen through the viewfinders of his favourite film-directors. He dislikes suffering humanity in general and the other people on his Italian holiday in particular. But circumstances and Sarah get him involved despite himself – with a battered wife, an Italian boy, a jealous husband, two Florentine whores, and a strange pair of drifters who join the group at Sarah's instigation.

In Venice things get worse with a near-drowning, a botched seduction, an accusation of poisoning, a beating-up, and Michael being questioned by the police about a murder and the films of Fred Astaire. More serious still are the questions Sarah is asking about their marriage. And by the end of the book she at least knows what real blood looks like.

### April Shroud, An
July 1975

After seeing Inspector Pascoe safely married and letting fall a few ill-chosen words, the thoughts of Superintendent Andrew Dalziel turned mournfully to a spring holiday in the rain.

April showers are one thing, April torrents quite another, and Dalziel had gone no distance through the flat Lincolnshire countryside when his car stalled in a flood. From this predicament he was rescued by a water-borne cortege and a group of singularly cheerful mourners. He accompanied them back to Lake House to dry out.

There he was intrigued to discover a half-built medieval banqueting hall, a septuagenarian poet, a hippie film-maker, a deep frozen rat, a cook on the game, and other unusual items. Puzzles like these were hard for a detective to ignore, but Dalziel found it even harder to ignore the mature but still potent charms of Bonnie Fielding, mistress of the house. Regrettably, her two husbands had both died in unfortunate circumstances, so Dalziel had to tread carefully. And by the time Pascoe returned from honeymoon and attended the first banquet in the medieval hall, there were two more corpses and it looked as if the fat superintendent might have finally got out of his depth.

### Blood Sympathy
April 1993

PI can mean many things, from a hi-tec operative working out of a big security firm in downtown NY to a lean, mean, streetwise stud wisecracking his way through high-life, low-life LA.

But can it really mean a balding, middle-aged redundant lathe-operator from a high rise in Luton, Beds.? Joe Sixsmith thinks it can. His Aunt Mirabelle thinks you'd have to be crazy to hire him, and Joe's current clients certainly fit the bill. One seems to be confessing to the brutal murder of his whole family. Another thinks she's a witch. Alongside these, the two heavies who believe Joe is hiding their illicit drugs seem almost normal. And as if mayhem and murder aren't enough, Joe has to deal with the matchmaking ploys of his interfering aunt, and the monocratic rule of his alcoholic cat.

How can Joe survive? Not by hi-tec. Certainly not by being lean, mean or streetwise. But by goodness and mercy and that greatest of PI gifts, serendipity.

Reginald Hill has already brought wit, style and compassion to police investigation. Now he does the same for the private sector. And while he's at it in perhaps his greatest feat of creation, he re-invents Luton!

### Bones and Silence
March 1990

The Mysteries are returning to Mid-Yorkshire, not that to Mid-Yorks CID they ever seem to have been away. Detective-Superintendent Andy Dalziel has witnessed a murder – but it was through a glass darkly and he was being sick at the time. Was he mistaken? What should he make of a string of contradictory statements?

He has other irritations, among them an anonymous letter-writer threatening suicide. Who is she? Why has she picked on him? Peter Pascoe walks into all this on this return from a long convalescence. Uncertain about his job, his marriage, his motives, he must try to divert Dalziel's obsessional pursuit of a probably innocent man; try to make up for the fat man's scornful neglect of the suicidal woman.

And in the background, involving many of the characters and informing much of what they do, are the Mystery Plays themselves as Eileen Chung, their Director, uses and abuses her vast talents to get the cast, the site and the show she wants.

Like the plays, Reginald Hill's novel ranges across much of the Human Comedy, but unlike the plays it stops short of the Divine. For even when Dalziel and Pascoe see solutions to their cases, there remain questions with no answers. Only bones and silence.

### Child's Play
February 1987

Only one thing seems certain to those mentioned in Gwendoline Huby's will: the main beneficiary won't collect as he's been dead for forty years. Or has he? At the funeral an unknown mourner advances hesitantly upon them...

Down at Mid-Yorkshire Police HQ Sergeant Wield finds the past advancing destructively upon him when he picks up the phone and hears a voice calling him 'Mac'. And even Andy Dalziel's solid world is shaken when he comes to believe that a man he has never rated may become the next Chief Constable.

Meanwhile Peter Pascoe tries to concentrate on the work in hand, though distracted by looking up to lofty Eileen Chung, director of the civic theatre, who is the object of racial harassment, and looking down on Lexie Huby, secretary to her great-aunt's solicitor, who has the task of conveying to her irascible father the news of his devastating disappointment and even more displeasing bequest. Other claimants to Mrs Huby's wealth appear, notably PAWS, an animal charity she supported, and WFE, a right-wing women's group she was a member of. But it takes a body in the police car-park to divert Dalziel's attention from his main concerns, which are (a) to scupper the Chief Constable's chances, and (b) to become a 'Gent'.

These and a myriad other apparently unconnected threads are finally woven together in an intricate pattern of brightness and gloom which both is, and isn't, child's play.

### Clubbable Woman, A
September 1970

Connon, keen rugby player and member of a local club, gets knocked out in the second half of a match. Returning home, he retires to sleep off the effects. When he comes down, hours later, it is to find his wife, whom he had left watching TV, lying dead in her chair, the front of her head bashed in.

The police make little progress in uncovering the murderer, but they uncover a great deal about Mary Connon. What sort of woman was this wife and mother who had severed her once-close connection with the rugby club, who apparently enjoyed receiving obscene letters and phone calls, and was not above indulging in something closely akin to blackmail?

Connon is an obvious suspect, particularly when it is hinted that he is having an affair with the rugby captain's wife, but the absence of a weapon puzzles the two well-contrasted investigating officers, whose characters and relationship are skilfully drawn. So are those of the different members of the rugby club and their wives, Connon's student daughter and her boy-friend, and the Connons' friends and neighbours in their Yorkshire town.

An international match at Twickenham provides a fitting finale to this unusual first novel, which is as much concerned with intricacies of character as it is with violent crime.

### Deadheads
November 1983

Life had been roses, roses all the way for Patrick Aldermann ever since Great-Aunt Florence collapsed into her *Madame Louis Lapperierre*, leaving the way clear for Rosemount House and its glorious gardens to come into his possession.

But now here is his employer, 'Dandy' Dick Elgood, suggesting to an incredulous Inspector Pascoe that Patrick had got where he is by killing people. Soon he retracts the accusation, but by then Pascoe and Sergeant Wield have got their teeth into it and Police-Cadet Singh, Mid-Yorkshire's first coloured copper – if he survives the training course – is uncovering some very interesting information about Patrick's elegant wife, Daphne.

Add to this, on the left, Ellie Pascoe, who is trying to radicalize Daphne; and on the right, Superintendent Dalziel, who seems to think that Cadet Singh has been provided as his personal tea-boy; and in the middle an irritating bunch of burglars; and we have a richly colourful did-he-do-it? With a plot that unfolds like the petals of a rose.

### Exit Lines
July 1984

Three old men die on the same stormy November night, one by accident, one by deliberate violence, and the third by cause unknown. Each of them speaks before he dies and these few words plus the slenderest of external clues are all that Inspector Pascoe has to go on in his investigation. Precious little help is forthcoming from Andy Dalziel, his CID boss. He has troubles of his own, namely, the threat of suspension over his suspected involvement in a drunken driving case which in turn leads to other more deadly suspicions, this time of corruption. Peter Pascoe finds himself treading what for him is new ground, the world of the ageing whose special problems make special demands, both personally and professionally. And while Dalziel is wining, dining, and even shooting pheasant with the rich and powerful, Pascoe, aided by the phlegmatic Sergeant Wield, the promising but wayward Detective-Constable Seymour, and even the half-witted Constable Hector, goes exploring the future and finding out how it works.

### *Fairly Dangerous Thing, A*
September 1972

Schoolmaster Joe Askern had made a truce with life. His interests are simple and kept within safe bounds: stately homes; golf; Shelley; big girls. With a bit of luck, they'll see him safely through to the end of his days.

But this end suddenly seems much closer when he encounters Cess Carter, friendly local criminal and dad to one of Joe's more delinquent pupils. Cess and Joe have a common interest – Averingerett, country seat of the terribly old and aristocratic Trevigore family, who have been down-treading the peasants for five or six hundred years. Joe's interest is scholarly, Cess's economic. Cess proposes a merger, and his confederates, the squatly sinister 'Lord' Jim and the squirmingly voluptuous Cynthia Hearth ('Cyn' for short) use their own special talents to persuade Joe to agree.

Everything Joe loves is put at risk; his girlfriend, Maggie; his cat Vardon; his freedom; his thesis on Shelley; even, occasionally, his life. It takes all his agility of body and mind to bring him through his ordeal safely.

Reginald Hill's three previous crime novels have won high praise and established him as one the most up-and-coming writers of the genre. As *The Times* puts it: 'Each new Hill henceforth will evoke the 'Aha' of delight ahead.'

### *Fell of Dark*
May 1971

Reginald Hill's first novel, *A Clubbable Woman*, received fine reviews. In the *Sunday Times*, Edmund Crispin said, 'Unusually well controlled, well written…More from him soon please.'

Crime stories are so often based on a formula [sic] situation that it is a pleasure to encounter a crime writer who is a genuine novelist, who creates scenes and people with conviction. Reginald Hill goes his own independent way, building the story from the nature of the people involved in it.

*Fell of Dark* describes how two men, hiking in the Lake District, are suddenly accused of having raped and killed two girls whom they had seen only casually in their hotel the previous evening. One of the accused is a successful businessman; the other, a friend who is recuperating from a nervous breakdown and whose odd behaviour is responsible for their arrest. Each reacts differently to the police questioning and the circumstantial evidence against them. While one gives way, the other seizes an opportunity to escape. His main hope is to prove the case against him is false, but to do this he must first come to terms with himself and, just as importantly, find a way of surviving among the fells and crags of Cumberland.

### *Killing Kindness, A*
November 1980

One summer night at closing time Mary Dinwoodie said goodnight to her friends and went out into the car park of the Cheshire Cheese.

Next morning she was discovered neatly laid out in a nearby ditch, 'choked', said the farm labourer who found her. And thus began the career of the Yorkshire Choker.

Another little quirk of his was to phone the local paper after each killing with an often ambiguous quotation from Hamlet. This cut little ice with Detective-Superintendent Dalziel, for Fat Andy was indifferent to mysterious phone calls, unappreciative of offers of help from linguists and psychiatrists, and infuriated when it seemed that the inscrutably ugly Sergeant Wield had hired a medium to help with his enquiries.

Inspector Pascoe, on the other hand, though distracted by a not very happily pregnant wife, felt there were more things in heaven and earth than were dreamed of in his superior's philosophy, and struck out on his own.

More girls died. Suspects proliferated: a Heathcliffian gypsy with a record of sexual violence, a disgruntled bank manager, a drop-out schoolmaster 'fingered' by his wife … Finally, modern science, ancient superstition, as well as the Dalziel direct method, all played a part in bringing the Choker to bay. But even then the story was far from ended.

### *One Small Step*
September 1990

It's the crime of the century – but not this century. And there are two hundred and twenty-seven million witnesses – but not one of them can help the investigating officers.

For this is murder on the moon in the year 2010. And when Emile Lemarque keels over on the steps of the space ship *Europa*, he stirs up more than lunar dust as his death threatens to turn into an international incident, requiring the personal intervention of Commissioner Peter Pascoe of the Eurofed Justice Department.

Pascoe, at the peak of his career and facing one of the most baffling and delicate cases , turns for assistance to his old mentor, Andy Dalziel, now deep in gouty retirement. Reunited, though with roles reversed, the old Mid-Yorkshire duo probe deep into space, both inner and outer, as they take one small step after another to a series of surprising truths.

*One Small Step* may be one small book, but readers looking for those elements of style, pace, mystery, humour and characterization they have come to expect from Reginald Hill's novels are in for an out-of-this-world experience.

### *Pascoe's Ghost and Other Brief Chronicles of Crime*
June 1979

Murder is the main ingredient in Reginald Hill's first volume of short stories, but theft, extortion and rape all figure in these brief chronicles of crime, the moods of which range from the merry to the macabre. As usual, the two stories featuring those ill-matched mid-Yorkshire detectives, Inspector Pascoe and Superintendent Dalziel, run the whole gamut.

In *Pascoe's Ghost*, the inspector finds himself in Poe country, investigating the fate of a woman who hasn't been seen by a soul for a year – unless you count her brother, who claims her ghost is haunting him. The trail leads to a storm-racked country churchyard at midnight, with Pascoe convinced the case needs an exorcist as much as a policeman.

In *Dalziel's Ghost*, the fat super who normally wouldn't be seen dead in a graveyard also expresses a hitherto unsuspected interest in the supernatural, though it's Pascoe who gets the Gothic end of the stick.

In both stories things are not always what they seem. Nor are they, for example, in the professor's farewell speech in *The Rio de Janeiro Paper*, nor in the prisoner's diary in *Exit Line*, nor in the padlocked contents of *The Trunk in the Attic*.

The one thing the reader can rely on is the excellence of Reginald Hill's writing, and the entertainment he lavishly provides.

### *Pictures of Perfection*
February 1994

High in the Mid-Yorkshire dales stands the village of Enscombe, pretty as a picture and proud survivor of all that history and nature have been able to throw at it. But now market forces mass at the gates. Developers undermine the Green, the walls of the Hall have been breached by tourists, an estate agent's blazon flies over the Vicarage, and the School is making its last desperate stand.

Against these crimes the Law offers little defence. But when a policeman goes missing, leaving only a handful of bizarre clues, DCI Peter Pascoe gets worried. Andy Dalziel thinks he's just overreacting until the normally phlegmatic Sergeant Wield shows signs of changing his first impressions of village life.

Over two eventful days a new pattern emerges, of lust and lying, of family feuds and ancient injuries, of frustrated desires and unbalanced minds. Finally, inevitably, everything comes to a bloody climax at the Squire's Reckoning, when the villagers gather each Lady Day to feast and gossip and pay old debts. Not even the presence of the Mid-Yorkshire CID trio can change the course of history, though one of them is to find the course of his own personal history changed for ever.

Once more Reginald Hill has found new territory to bring beneath the banner of crime fiction, not by force but by gentle persuasion, showing us that as well as death, deceit and violence, faith, hope and love are native here too.

### *Pinch of Snuff, A*
February 1978

Inspector Pascoe sits and watches and does nothing as the naked girl is struck by a mailed fist and her face collapses in a spume of blood and bone. For it is only a film, and they can fake anything these days, and you can see worse on 'Match of the Day'.

But the image remains with Pascoe even after he seems to have exploded his dentist Jack Shorter's theory that the blow was real; and its two dimensions compete powerfully with all the three-dimensional suffering he comes in contact with: an elderly pervert beaten to death, a middle-aged woman driven towards suicide, a twelve-year-old girl alleging sexual assault. His pursuit of the man or woman who smashed up the Calliope Kinema Club and its owner with it leads him on a curiously circular track, which takes in a twenty-stone female porn producer, a six-stone trampoline stripper, two septuagenarian sisters, eight Siamese cats, a liberated dental hygienist, and a failed Hungarian comic. He is assisted by the splendidly ugly Sergeant Wield and alternately advised and abused by the splendidly gross Superintendent Dalziel, who may know more than he's letting on. But in the end, whoever solves the case, Pascoe must reach his own judgement of those involved, and that includes himself.

### *Recalled to Life*
June 1992

1963. It was the year of the Profumo Scandal, the Great Train Robbery, the Kennedy Assassination – and the Mickledore Hall Murder.

The guests at the Hall that weekend had included a Tory minister keeping his head down, a CIA officer specializing in 'dirty tricks', a British diplomat with royal connections – and Cissy Kohler, a young American nanny who had come to England for love.

And love kept her in England for nearly thirty years.

In jail. For murder.

Now she is out and a full-scale inquiry has been ordered into this seeming miscarriage of justice. The convenient scapegoat is the man in charge of the 1963 investigation, but the present head of Mid-Yorkshire CID, Detective-Superintendent Andrew Dalziel, is convinced his late mentor and friend was straight, which means that Cissy Kohler was – and still is – guilty. But, investigating on his own, Dalziel soon finds his certainties being eroded as he moves from the Old World to the New, from a Golden Age murder mystery to the sleazier killings of the Age of Glitz, from certainties it is dangerous to advertise to truths it is deadly to know.

When *Bones and Silence* won the CWA Gold Dagger Award for the best crime novel of the year, it didn't seem possible for Reginald Hill to get any better, but in *Recalled to Life* he has. It succeeds as a classic mystery, as a riveting thriller, and as a closely observed, deeply felt and stylishly expressed novel of the human comedy.

### *Ruling Passion*
April 1973

Few crime novelists have got off to a more auspicious start than Reginald Hill. From his first book, *A Clubbable Woman*, which *The Times Literary Supplement* described as 'a first work that should be a matter of pride to Mr Hill and a pleasure to readers', to *A Fairly Dangerous Thing*, his last and most lighthearted, which Anthony Price of the *Oxford Mail* finds 'outrageously enjoyable', he has been hailed as a gifted writer. The present novel, more sombre in tone and his most ambitious to date, reintroduces Sergeant Pascoe and Superintendent Dalziel who figured in his first three books.

Sergeant Pascoe has problems – eleven unsolved burglaries and Superintendent Dalziel worried about his health. A weekend in the country seems a very pleasant prospect, especially when it means a reunion with four old friends.

But in the lonely cottage near the Oxfordshire village of Thornton Lacey, only three of his friends await his arrival. And they are dead, blasted with a shotgun.

Pascoe finds himself behaving like the most unco-operative kind of witness as the Oxfordshire police start searching for the missing man. And Dalziel expects a full day's work from him back in Yorkshire where a twelfth break-in has ended in murder.

It's a time of confusion for Pascoe. Nothing is what it seems to be. The two cases overlap and intermingle in his mind till in the end they overlap in reality, bringing together characters and places many miles apart. It's all a matter of finding out what really makes people tick, of grasping the right clue. But Pascoe finds he's not absolutely sure even about himself. And no solution, however ingenious, can bring his friends back to life.

### *There Are No Ghosts in the Soviet Union*
October 1987

Variety is the spice of death in Reginald Hill's six-course feast of brand new short stories. Methods, motives, and milieu range widely – from bayonet to veal pie; from loathing to love; from France to Russia. Time too is not allowed to rest. Here it's 1916, there it's the eighteen-thirties; often it is now, occasionally it is never. And everywhere and everywhen, fascinating questions are being asked: How did Emma's marriage to Mr Knightley turn out? Was it really so terrible in the Bull Ring at Etaples? Why have Superintendent Dalziel and

Sergeant Pascoe not yet appeared on the silver screen? The answers may shock you, they will certainly surprise you, but above all they will leave you replete with gourmet entertainment.

### *Under World*
April 1988

Three years ago little Tracey Pedley went brambling in the woods near the mining village of Burrthorpe and vanished without trace. Deputy Chief Constable Watmough, retiring as he hopes into politics, is convinced that she was a victim of the self-confessed child-killer whose suicide gave him his greatest detective triumph. But in Burrthorpe there were other theories. And to some, the fatal plunge down a disused shaft of the last man known to have seen Tracey alive seemed no more than simple justice.

It was his father's death that brought Colin Farr back home. And it is the dark whispers about its cause that keep him working down the hated pit. A university extra-mural course brings relief one day a week and it's there that Ellie Pascoe meets him and becomes personally involved. Inspector Peter Pascoe sees an emotional as well as an ideological gap opening up between himself and his wife, while Superintendent Andy Dalziel ruminates on the sidelines until a murder in the mine brings him into active and sometimes perilous contact with Farr and the Burrthorpe community.

There is mystery and excitement enough here to satisfy the most exacting crime reader, but there is much more besides as Reginald Hill probes beneath the surface of minds and motives in what is undoubtedly his finest novel yet.

### *Very Good Hater, A*
June 1974

A Tale of Revenge

The two men met every year at their regimental reunion.

Goldsmith was a politician, local at the moment but on the brink of the big time. Templewood was a salesman, extrovert, glib, a compulsive womanizer. They had little in common – except their memories of a man called Hebbel. And their resolve to kill him.

Then, during one of their reunions, the two men encountered a man who strangely resembled Hebbel. Of course there were doubts, hesitations, uncertainties. But the possibility that this was indeed the man they remembered was a very real one. It was a chance that might not come again.

So far, so good. But Reginald Hill, who has been described as 'the best hope of the crime novel' (H. R. F. Keating, *The Times)* can be relied on for an original twist. As his tale of revenge unfolds, layer after layer of the two men's characters is peeled back, revealing that the probity of these two prominent local citizens is not always above suspicion, and affording a fascinating glimpse of the corruption that can exist in public life.

In an attempt to prove that the mysterious man is Hebbel, Goldsmith in particular becomes involved with his family. In addition he arouses the interest of the police, the antagonism of his friends, and deep personal doubts about his own future. By the time he finally stumbles on a body, it is time to ask who is really being revenged on whom?

## HILTON, JOHN BUXTON

### *Anathema Stone, The*
January 1980

The Derbyshire village of Spentlow, where Chief Superintendent Kenworthy and his wife had chosen to spend their autumn holiday, was in the grip of celebrations organised by the Vicar to commemorate a remarkable incumbent of a hundred years ago. It was also in the grip of a long-standing feud between two prominent families, the Allsops and the Brightmores, and of the machinations of Davina Stott, a precocious, pretty adolescent, who had a lead part in the centenary celebration play. One evening Kenworthy walked home with her from rehearsal. Next morning her body was found on the Anathema Stone.

The Anathema Stone, round which superstitions clustered, had originally been part of a Bronze Age barrow, but for the last two hundred years it had lain in Farmer Allsop's yard. Recently a local archaeological society had tried to make him restore it to the original site, and this had sparked off further feuding in the village. In such an atmosphere the local police found it difficult to extract clear and truthful statements about the murder from this closed community. Kenworthy, anxious though he was to help, was made uncomfortably aware that he was an outsider, and worse, the finger of village suspicion was unmistakably pointing at him.

John Buxton Hilton knows his Derbyshire as only the Derbyshire-born can. He also knows how to spin a story remorseless in its unfolding, and alive with vividly drawn characters.

### *Asking Price, The*
August 1983

Kenworthy in retirement is consulted by a special team operating from the Cabinet Office. They need his second opinion on the random kidnapping of a motley collection of customers from a village shop in Bedfordshire. The ransom price is so bizarre that it is kept secret from the public – and on their return the villagers seem none the worse for their experience. But a rougher time is had by all when an entire Norfolk Parish Council is spirited away. Not until they try their hand at abducting a Yorkshire branch of the Women's Institute do the kidnappers meet their match.

In the meantime, Kenworthy has been sorting out the red herrings and finds the answer in the cut-throat power politics of organised crime. The action moves rapidly – and murderously – from the North Country to the Fens, from rural Wiltshire to the hinterland of the Costa del Sol.

John Buxton Hilton is here operating in a new vein. He insists that he never wants to write the same book twice – but for readers, the asking price generated by this title may well prove to be more of the same.

### *Corridors of Guilt*
February 1984

Football hooliganism, violent demos, civil insurrection – what would happen if law and order broke down? One group of men knew. They hoped to be the ones to restore control – in their own way and at their own price. But they were men that Kenworthy knew, too. He last remembered them when corruption at the Yard was being tidied up.

Once again John Buxton Hilton uses the high-powered investigation unit operating direct from the Cabinet Office that he introduced in *The Asking Price.* Called in to help his former colleague Forrester, Kenworthy finds himself disentangling the intrigues of the Duchy of Axholme, a Government department specially established to absorb misfits and failures. Then there is a murder: an academic–minded young lady is saddled with the corpse of an elderly civil servant whom everyone believes to have died while making love to her. Has this anything to do with Peter Paul Whippletree, the drop-out extraordinary and crossword-puzzle compiler with whom she falls in love?

There is pungent oblique comment here on the way things are sometimes managed in high places (the author has been a civil servant). But Kenworthy's main concern is a mystery as obscure as any he has ever tackled. It calls for all the imagination and double dealing he can muster. The reader has every chance to beat him to the solution – though probably not many will.

### *Displaced Person*
September 1987

'Yes,' Kenworthy said. 'I knew Marie-Therese Laniel.'

The retired Superintendent had never envisaged that his wartime Intelligence service would one day enable him to help the French police, now they were holding on unspecified charges a young woman whom he had last seen forty years ago. The Examining Magistrate had requested his assistance. 'You're not subpoenaed. Nobody's pushing you,' they told him. And Kenworthy replied 'Maybe I don't need to be pushed.'

He would never have recognised Marie-Therese in the ageing woman found near a murdered man and with an unexplained three-quarter of a million francs upon her, but he could identify the man. He had been Kenworthy's superior officer in a small advance detachment of British troops during the 1944 thrust through the Low Countries, when Marie-Therese had been something between their camp-follower and mascot. Kenworthy learned that other wartime acquaintances had kept in touch with her. He began to suspect why.

This was not the first time Marie-Therese had been associated with suspected blackmail, but she had never been more than a pawn. Who directed her? Who was their victim? What was their hold over him? In piecing together her life-story, Kenworthy, the Examining Magistrate and the French police uncover a wartime crime.

### *Green Frontier, The*
January 1982

An eminent Lutheran pastor comes to England to take part in an investigative TV documentary called *Crucible* and is caught shop-lifting in the West End. He tries to demand that his case be handled by Superintendent Kenworthy, but Kenworthy has retired and it is decided not to bother him – until Pastor Pagendarm is found murdered on the edge of a Hertfordshire wood. Kenworthy is puzzled, until a meeting with the pastor's widow brings back memories of his days in wartime intelligence.

But this is not a spy story, nor does it repeat the usual clichés about Nazi Germany. It is a patient and sensitive search for the long taproots of evil. The scenes in the ruins of immediate post-war Berlin are among the most atmospheric that John Buxton Hilton has written and, as we have come to expect from this author, there are characters to remember: the foolish, honourable British brigadier, the charming, intelligent, ruthlessly amoral Anna-Maria.

In the tense denouement, Kenworthy uses the shooting script of *Crucible* to break the case, and after all the surprises there is another one still to come…

### *Hobbema Prospect, The*
September 1984

Anne Cossey has a recurring dream of an avenue that reminds her of Hobbema's painting of *The Avenue at Middelarnis.* Beyond that she knows nothing of the place, except that it terrifies her. There is a great deal in her past that she cannot remember. Who is her mother? Who was her father? Who is she?

Then, while she is on honeymoon in Spain, her mother 'commits suicide' in a manner that Anne is the first to recognise as murder. From then on the knots begin to tighten, for Anne is on the civilian payroll of Chief Superintendent Kenworthy, now in his closing years at the Yard, and her husband is a detective-sergeant in the squad of Kenworthy's old winger, Shiner Wright. She unearths various files in the archives that might refer to her mother's elusive past, but then finds herself one chilly dawn abducted under anaesthetic and coming to in the very avenue of her nightmare.

The action grows increasingly sinister, giving Kenworthy one of his most complex cases to date – and John Buxton Hilton the opportunity to introduce a few more to his gallery of memorable characters, including Swanee Foster, a criminal individualist, whom many at the Yard have agreed not to harass.

### *Innocents at Home, The*
September 1986

In this novel we see Kenworthy before his retirement, in the days when it was still not uncommon for regional forces to call in Scotland Yard to help with difficult cases.

Four eleven-year-old girls in the Fenlands of Norfolk have had charges brought against their headmaster. It does not take Kenworthy and his sophisticated Sergeant Parrott long to discover that in the wake of a school puppet play on the Faust theme, they signed their own pact with the Devil, since when they have been doing their best to live up to it. They seem to have become the personification of pure evil, which reaches its climax when their headmaster is murdered.

It is when Kenworthy and Polly Parrott begin to explore the eccentricities and neuroses of the girls' parents that they begin to understand why these children are as nasty as they are. But which of them is really the ring-leader? And who killed Henry Gower?

As always, John Buxton Hilton exploits a macabre location and the private worlds occupied by some if its inhabitants. The story creeps with atmosphere, and calls for Kenworthy's shrewdest detective skills.

### *Moondrop to Murder*
February 1986

When a retired English Colonel plans a nostalgic walking tour in the South of France, his wife engages Kenworthy to mind him. Is this an unpardonable breach of personal privacy? Will the assignment prove a damp squib? Or is Colonel Neville's purpose as sinister as it sometimes seems? Kenworthy finds him in turn eccentric, domineering, secretive and on occasion bumblingly inefficient: then he loses him.

Murder follows, and Kenworthy, helped by Monique Colin, a delectable young private eye from an agency in Nice, traces a trail back to the wartime resistance, a world of pride, passions, jealousies and shame, in which the harshness of reality was sometimes more powerful than the heroism.

This is a story of both adventure and detection. It is also a vivid evocation of a milieu – the lonely uplands of Provence – and a study of the interplay of memorable characters: of Chantal Dupuy, once a ruthless underground leader, now a state prosecutor; of a career French officer who has little to be proud of; of Mesdames Piquemal and Ripault, who seem unable to do anything, except in secrecy.

### *Mr. Fred*
February 1983

The setting of this short, powerful mystery is Edwardian Derbyshire. The story is told by Kathy in her old age, but the events she describes took place when she was still a child at school, living in abysmal poverty but cunning, sensitive and beset by pre-adolescent fears, some imaginary, some all too real.

Kathy secretly encounters the mysterious Mr Fred who is being hidden on her father's farm. But why? Who is Mr Fred? What is the truth behind the scandalous rumours about him? Surely it cannot possibly be true that this kindly man is a pervert and a murderer? And why does her dull-witted brother finally murder him? If he did…

Kathy – who adores Mr Fred – more than once outwits the formidable Inspector Brunt, who has appeared in three of John Buxton Hilton's previous Derbyshire novels. She is a married woman, prospering in the 1920's – and Brunt has already died of old age – before she finally penetrates to the shock of the truth.

This novel, with its haunting evocation of time and place and its keen analysis of emotions, both infantile and adult, will appeal to many who do not usually reckon to care for suspense novels.

### *Passion in the Peak*
August 1985

When Lord Furnival, a left-of-centre dilettante, tries to stage a musical version of the Oberammergau Passion Play in the High Peak of Derbyshire, he does not foresee what strife and tension he is setting in motion. Petty thefts, a peeping Tom, artistic jealousies, a vendetta against Mary Magdalene – the record of crime culminates in the murder of the hyped Rock singer brought out of disgraced retirement to play Christ.

Kenworthy is called in as a private consultant to 'protect the interests of the management' and finds himself involved with a bewildering array of eccentrics: Jimmy Lindop, a sound technician with old scores to settle; Julian Harpur, a neurotic adolescent whose mother believes him a genius; Alfie Tandy, who has confessed to dozens of murders in his time, and who carries his worldly belongings about in an old banjo-case; Freddy Kershaw, a detective-constable who is suspended from duty for telling the truth; and Joan Culver, who is trying to straighten herself out about filial duty, sex and life.

This is as knotty a puzzle as Kenworthy and his readers have ever squared up to, as the case-work takes us out of Derbyshire into the squalid history of the Stalagmites, a failed London rock group. On the way we take a Hiltonian look at more than one level of contemporary society.

### *Playground of Death*
January 1981

The former Mayor of a Lancashire Borough, a County Councillor, Civic Planner and busybody at large, returns home to shoot his wife in her bed after she has telephoned him at the house of his mistress. That is the prosecution's confident contention, which is shaken when the accused man himself is shot in the police station yard on his way to committal proceedings.

Detective-Superintendent Kenworthy, who has appeared in six of the author's novels, is called in from Scotland Yard in view of the dubious local ramifications. Stubbornly patient, devious as ever, he finds himself deeply involved in the past, in the industrial depression of the 1930s, disentangling a story of juvenile delinquency, local government corruption, the ritual loyalties of a depressed community and the inevitable course of sweet-and-sour love. Behind the action, past and present, lies the phantom of a squalid little slag-heap playground, and the denouement, in a small-town bigwigs' social club, brings together threads that transcend the normal divisions of class, breeding and political expediency.

As well as being a satisfying tale of detection in the classical format, this is a vivid, toughly cold and often moving portrayal of injustice and survival against two contrasting settings of modern industrial society.

### *Quiet Stranger, The*
February 1985

In the 1870s, the future Inspector Brunt is a novice detective pulled in opposite directions by Inspector Pickford, to whom the crime statistics are all that matters, and elderly Sergeant Nadin, who has his own interpretation of the functions of the police. On his way home after a reprimand, Brunt has a disturbing encounter with George Ludlam, an enigmatic, taciturn man, strangely intent on reaching one of Derbyshire's more remote villages. Then the news reaches HQ that this man's arrival has terrified some of the villagers. Who is he? More important, who used he to be? And why has he come back?

Brunt is sent to carry out a discreet investigation, thus distracting him from the pursuit of Amelia Pilkington, a fascinating confidence trickster who lives off the hydropathic society of the time, but the affair becomes public when a woman is murdered and George Ludlam is the obvious suspect.

As so often in John Buxton Hilton's stories, the solution lies years back, in the exploitation of child labour in the worst years of the Industrial Revolution. This deeply researched novel has a powerful sting in its tail. Few readers will succeed in beating Sergeant Nadin and Constable Brunt to the solution to the mystery.

### *Slickensides: A Derbyshire Mystery*
March 1987

Slickensides is the name of a farm in the High Peak district of Derbyshire, of a cheese prepared at the farm, and of the old lead mine that lies beneath it. It is also the geological term for a particular rock formation which results in the trapping of energy behind it. Such energy can be dangerously explosive when released.

All this Inspector Brunt has occasion to expound on a visit there in 1911 to investigate a reported break-in at the farm. At the same time a private detective with distinctly Holmesean characteristics (they even include a Watson!) arrives at the local inn. He is there to investigate the alleged disappearance of Barnard Brittlebank, the squire's dissolute son. Before long he informs Squire Brittlebank that his son has left for Canada.

So it is disconcerting when young Brittlebank's body is found in the Slickensides mine. A dense fog descends, cutting off all communication with the outside world, and Brunt is left to answer some tricky questions with no assistance beyond the evidence and that of his own sharp wits.

Although nearing retirement, Brunt is as shrewd as ever. In this beautifully realized story of a closed society three-quarters of a century ago, he demonstrates once again that he is one of the most memorable of fictional detectives, and triggers a denouement as explosive as only Slickensides can produce.

### *Sunset Law, The*
July 1982

Chief Superintendent Kenworthy, now retired, was visiting his married daughter in Florida. The visit was not wholly successful, for to the unsettlement of retirement was added the disorientation of the American scene, anxiety lest his daughter's marriage to a State policeman was in low water, and concern that there might be truth in the allegations of corruption made against his son-in-law.

The scene changed with the murder of the two prostitutes who had preferred the charges. When his son-in-law disappeared, Kenworthy moved into action, contacting the Luther Boones I, II and III, a family who had policed a remote stretch of the Everglades for three generations.

As in other John Buxton Hilton's novels, the roots of the mystery are embedded in the past. Kenworthy found himself listening to tales of the cut-throat land boom of the 1920s when the Everglades were being drained, of the world of gambling and protection, of the massive drug traffic of contemporary South Florida, and of even newer, more ingenious crimes. Two generations of Luther Boones had been outwitted by the man behind the rackets. Could Luther Boone III manage things better? Kenworthy soon had the opportunity to go to work in his most dogged and devious fashion.

### *Surrender Value*
June 1981

Why has John Everard, a gentle-mannered teacher of old-fashioned outlook, surrendered an insurance policy and vanished? Is it really because, as he told his wife, he fears a deterioration in his health and wants to go out 'living it up' in his own way? Have the tensions in a permissive sixth form college got him down? Did other women in his life really matter to him?

Or has he absconded with one of the pupils, prim little Susan Shires, who has also disappeared? Why has Sue dumped her bag and booked a double room at a sleazy London hotel?

Kenworthy, now retired from the Yard, is called in by Mrs Everard and finds himself exploring a world of some strange values. Meanwhile, reports on missing persons all over the country are collated. Are Everard and Sue indulging in love-hate tantrums up and down the Norfolk coast? Or are they in the West Country, being turned away by suspicious landladies?

The mystery is not simplified when a girl's body in Sue's clothes is found in two different places. Kenworthy, working for a change as an official assistant to his former side-kick Shiner Wright, breaks this one by his familiar mixture of leaping imagination, bizarre deception – and by his instinct for the motives behind human eccentricities.

## HINXMAN, MARGARET

### *Boy from Nowhere, The*
October 1985

Harry Riley, brash young reporter on a small Sussex paper, came from Brighton but he might as well have come from nowhere. He had no kin, no sense of community, what he did with his spare time was his secret. Moreover, his sneaky investigations into certain local institutions had aroused local ire. When he was found dead at the foot of a cliff, fellow reporter Sheila Tracy was one of the few to mourn him, but she never suspected his death was anything other than an accident.

Even when her suspicions were aroused, quiet respectable Seahaven seemed an unlikely venue for murder, and Sheila pursued her inquiries into Harry's life and the lives of certain local worthies with no great hopes. Then she unearthed a connection between Harry and a crime some two or three years earlier which convinced her that his death had indeed been deliberately contrived. The rest of what she unearthed was even more unexpected, and – for Sheila – deeply disturbing. Would she ever again have the same view of 'a nice place like Seahaven'?

Margaret Hinxman, former film critic of the *Daily Mail*, puts her knowledge of journalism to good use in this suspenseful story.

### *Corpse Now Arriving, The*
March 1983

Everything seemed normal enough to journalist Kit Morley on the 7.32 pm train from Victoria to Lymhampton on the South Coast. There were the usual delays due to points failure, the regular commuters were drowning their grievances against British Rail in the buffet car. It was just another journey home. Until plump, middle-aged, garrulous Maisie Butler fell to her death from the train as it approached its last station.

The shocking event unnerved the other passengers who knew her well. But Kit was particularly shaken. Only a short while before a befuddled Maisie had come into to her compartment and claimed that someone was trying to kill her. Was the verdict of Accidental Death correct? Was there anyone on the train who might have wanted Maisie dead?

Kit began making enquiries, and soon discovered that Maisie knew a surprising amount about some of her fellow travellers – information which they would not want disclosed. And there were secrets in Maisie's own life. What had she meant, for instance, by that cryptic, drunken remark on her last journey – 'Not Dave'?

As Kit dug deeper and deeper into Maisie's life it became horrifyingly apparent that someone wanted Kit dead too.

Margaret Hinxman, film critic of the *Daily Mail*, commutes regularly between London and the South Coast, like her narrator. The occasional pleasures and frequent frustrations of a commuter's life make a marvellous background to this crime novel of great skill and penetrating characterization, which is guaranteed to make any journey seem half its length.

### *End of a Good Woman*
June 1976

Ruth Brennan, a widow, had lived all her life in the same Shropshire village, and everyone was loud in her praise. Who could have reason to kill such a woman, who was acknowledged to be a loving mother, kind neighbour, loyal friend? Yet Ruth was found mysteriously dead and the police were not satisfied it was the suicide it appeared to be. Suddenly a cloud hung over village life.

No one felt it more than Lydia Manning, Ruth's neighbour. Having lived for ten years in the village, Lydia believed she knew its inhabitants inside out. Now she began seeing them with new eyes: the pinched school-mistress, the amateur dramatics star, the local doctor, Ruth's son and daughter, the niece she had brought up who seldom visited, the man who lived next door. All these people, their lives apparently open, revealed a hidden side. All of them had been powerfully influenced by Ruth in one way or another. One of them might be responsible for the torn scrap of a letter found in her handbag in which Ruth was accused of ruining the writer's life. Did the writer know how Ruth had died? Was Ruth really a good woman? What, if anything, does that expression mean?

Margaret Hinxman leaves the reader to grapple with these questions, and perhaps to answer them. Her deep interest in character and in human relationships is evident in every line of this intriguing mystery, which is concerned as much with people's lives as with a woman's death.

### Night They Murdered Chelsea, The
August 1984

Chelsea Fortune had to be eliminated. They were all agreed on that. She was no longer just a liability – she had become a threat. And with her reputation it was a wonder she hadn't been murdered long ago.

Even so, when the news was leaked to the Press that producer and scriptwriters were planning a gruesome end for one of the major figures in the long-running TV serial *Wild Fortune*, no one could have guessed that on the night they murdered Chelsea, Dame Charlotte Saint-Clair, who played her, would be found murdered in her Sussex home in a manner that precisely paralleled her death on the TV screen.

Inspector Bland, retired but still taking a friendly interest in any case handled by his former assistant, had added reason for his unofficial involvement in this one: all his life he has been one of Charlotte Saint-Clair's fans. Now he discovered that his idol had almost as many enemies as the TV character with which she had become identified; already a man was helping the police with their inquiries…

Patiently Brand set to work to unravel the hidden story of Charlotte's life. In another continent, another era, he uncovered a clue to what really happened on the night they murdered Chelsea.

Margaret Hinxman, film critic of the *Daily Mail*, has drawn on her extensive knowledge of the world of film and TV for the background of what is unquestionably her best crime novel to date.

### Nightmare in Dreamland
June 1991

Anna Sterling, provincial, introverted and self-contained, arrives in Los Angeles to carry out her dying father's last command to find her younger sister Julie, who seems to have disappeared without trace.

Caught in a world of garish and sinister make-believe that both repels and attracts her, she discovers alarming truths about her mother and about her tyrannical father, an acclaimed English author who had once been wooed by Hollywood, as well as being forced to face some of her own inadequacies as a person.

As the search for her sister becomes increasingly labyrinthine, Anna realizes she is becoming enmeshed in a wider conspiracy of secret involving a bizarre cast of Hollywood characters, including the ailing, ageing agent Hilda Klein, her menacing son Bernard, the street-smart Mexican bit player 'Mabel', the James Cagney clone Mick Angelo, and the charming but feckless English actor George Allenby. Too late to draw back, she becomes aware that in searching for Julie she is putting her own life at risk.

Former film critic of the *Daily Mail* and keen observer of the Hollywood scene, Margaret Hinxman draws on her extensive knowledge of the film industry and Los Angeles to create a thriller about deadly human relationships against an intriguing background of the movie and TV dream factory.

### One-Way Cemetery
August 1977

The woman, sprawling half over the driver's seat and half out of the open car door, was unmistakably dead. Even the police were not entirely surprised that the controversial one-way road through the cemetery had claimed a victim at last. Especially when the victim was a woman driving home alone at night after a party, and her blood alcohol content was high.

So there was nothing suspicious about the death of Lesley Salvara, except that so many

people wanted her dead. For Lesley, glamorous, notorious cousin of plain, rich widowed Martha Ransom up at the Hall, was a blackmailer. By chance or design several of her victims had been present at the party Martha gave for Lesley to celebrate her return to the village where she had been born.

Investigation of Lesley's victims led inevitably to investigation of Lesley herself and her relationships past and present. All the loose ends seemed to lead back to Malta in 1968, when Lesley met and married her second husband, and when other, more questionable events took place. Yet Inspector Brand, who visited Malta, returned little wiser than he went. For how was he to prove his suspicion, now certainty, that Lesley had been deliberately killed?

Margaret Hinxman, *Daily Mail* film critic, won high praise for her first crime novel, *End of a Good Woman*. In her second book she reaffirms her conviction that the art of the crime story is to make character destiny. Her second book will also confirm the reader's conviction that Margaret Hinxman is a gifted practitioner of the art.

### Sound of Murder, The
September 1986

Retired from the Sussex police and on holiday in Salzburg to visit his old friend Inspector Leo Kiesler, Ralph Brand found himself staying in the same hotel as the film crew for *The Sound of Murder*. The low-budget film was trading deliberately on *The Sound Of Music* and was designed to give the starring role to Matthew Armstrong, best-known for his portrayal of a police inspector in a popular TV series. Brand had already met Armstrong briefly, now he met Ella, Armstrong's Austrian wife, the aging Austrian actress Lotte Bruckner, and other members of the crew.

It was obvious that there were tensions among them; that Armstrong had something to hide; that the production company was only waiting for a chance to pull out of the whole operation. But none of this explained why Ella Armstrong confided to Brand that she went in fear of her life.

Soon the hotel was alive with the sound of murder, and Brand, far from being retired, found himself assisting Leo Kiesler in what proved to be one of the most complex cases of his career.

Margaret Hinxman, former *Daily Mail* film critic, knows the film world backwards, and readers of her previous crime novels can look forward with confidence to an enjoyable read.

### Suitable Day for Dying, A
June 1989

When actress Paula Denney, a guilt-ridden recluse since her playwright's husband's death, is offered the role of Lisa Lauren in a TV biopic about the deceased superstar of the 1960s it seems the answer to all her problems. The chance to play this plum role transforms her life – but in way she had never anticipated.

As she researched Lisa's background, Paula finds herself identifying with the star who rejected her fame as 'trivial' and devoted herself to controversial causes. Paula begins to suspect that Lisa's death, during a return visit to her Wiltshire home town, was not an accident but murder.

Unravelling the enigmas of Lisa's past, she realizes that many people, including the photographer who discovered her, and rising politician Nicholas Grandage, had reasons to wish her dead. In Lisa's home town Paula meets the friends who knew her when she was plain Lizzie Latch and have now formed

themselves into a sinister fan club. And in discovering the truth about Lisa's life Paula is forced to face another disturbing truth: that her own life is in danger.

Former film critic of the *Daily Mail*, Margaret Hinxman has woven an intricate mystery about the pursuit and punishing consequences of stardom in her most suspenseful and surprising novel yet.

### Telephone Never Tells, The
April 1982

The village of Biderton is tucked away in a crease of the South Downs, by far the greater proportion of its ninety or so inhabitants settled into middle age or older, who cosset their privacy and seldom venture beyond the confines of the village except to visit their solicitors and bank managers.

It would be a mistake, however, to assume that they are not alert to the happenings around them. For kindly Inspector Brand, the visit of two of the ladies to their nearest police station marked the beginning of one of his most disturbing cases. As far as he could see no crime was involved; yet something strange was brewing in Biderton: his callers had certainly witnessed a curious incident, and someone was behind the mysterious telephone calls to a certain house.

Inspector Brand never expected that the roots of the evil he was to uncover would reach far back into the past, never suspected who was behind it, and never anticipated the violence that would erupt. As he pursues his enquiries into the lives of Biderton residents and the tension subtly and steadily builds up, the reader too is involved in the complexities of the human heart and human relationships which Margaret Hinxman lays bare with a novelist's skill.

## HOLT, HENRY
### Calling All Cars
March 1934

*Calling all cars! Calling all cars!* The insistent message was broadcast into the night from Scotland Yard. The cars of the Flying Squad were at work on the greatest comb-out in criminal history. They were clustered in a ring; forming a gigantic trap round about the Yard itself. Eager men, listening through their earphones, knew that at last the net was closing upon that elusive master criminal, The Shadow. In this swift-moving and exciting novel, Henry Holt tells the story of a girl's valiant battle to save her brother, who has been wrongfully convicted of murder. Her desperate efforts to find the real criminal bring her into conflict with The Shadow, who, hurling taunts at Scotland Yard, taxes the ingenuity of the police to the utmost before Detective-Inspector Silver succeeds in solving the most difficult case of his career.

### Murder at the Bookstall
October 1934

The railway termini of London have provided the setting for some of the most sensational mysteries in real life. What more natural and convincing, therefore, than for Mr. Henry Holt to chose a great railway terminus for the opening of his new crime story. Detective Inspector Silver is set the most baffling problem of his career when he is called in to find the murderer of a beautiful girl, whose body is found concealed in the bookstall on the Dover platform at Charing Cross station.

### Murder of a Film Star
September 1940

To one who has been long in city pent [sic] the peace of the countryside in early autumn seems particularly attractive. For that reason

Dale Houston, a rising young dramatist, and his friend Tubby Craig, dashed out of the maddening whirl of London to take refuge and a brief holiday in the comparative tranquility of a Surrey village. That peace, however, was to be rudely shattered. While sitting on the porch of Dale Houston's country bungalow, a scream broke the silence, a scream so poignant, such an outrage upon their relaxed nerves, that they both sprang involuntarily to their feet. That urgent cry in the night sent up the curtain on a tragedy as enthralling as it was mysterious. Mr. Henry Holt has again written a truly engrossing story of detection and mystery.

### Mystery of the Smiling Doll, The
May 1939

When Carl Massey, the famous film producer, was murdered with fiendish cunning by means of a poisoned needle concealed in the clothing of a toy doll, it was the first of a series of murders that was to shake the glamorous film world. Michael Kennedy and Inspector Pope found themselves amongst a strange set of people; undercurrents of love and hatred did not make the investigation easy, and others were to pay the price of their folly before Michael began to make headway with the case. Mr. Henry Holt's unfailing ingenuity makes *The Mystery of the Smiling Doll* a really outstanding detective story.

OR

It was a foolish-looking doll, just a doll with a babyish smiling face. Massey thought it was a joke when he opened the parcel. 'Press my tummy and I will talk' said the label. Idly, Massey pressed it… Soon there was utter stillness in the room. Massey lay dead. Near him lay the doll, still smiling.

### Scarlet Messenger, The
November 1933

Detective-Inspector Silver stooped over something which lay still in a corner on the second floor of the Bramcourt Hotel. It was the body of Lorimer Cranston. A knife had stabbed him clean as a whistle through the heart. Inspector Silver questions the dead man's ward, Auriel Maxwell, and learns that she has been the recipient of several threatening letters, each accompanied by a small scarlet bean. Two of the letters had reached her at Pinelands, her home in Surrey. The second of these messages was accompanied by the dead body of her dog, with a scarlet bean attached to its collar. Auriel had placed the matter in the hands of the local police, but without any result. Cranston had insisted that Auriel should go away, and she had gone on a visit to friends in France, leaving her destination unknown to all but a few of her immediate circle. Nevertheless a third mysterious warning had reached her there, and Cranston had brought her back to London, to the hotel where he himself now lay dead. Inspector Silver investigates the case and soon finds he is up against some mysterious personality who will not stick at Murder – or even one murder. And always the little scarlet bean turns up – scarlet messengers of death.

### There Has Been a Murder
November 1936

The wind howled dismally and rain was falling fast as Richard Seagrave sat in his little Dorset cottage finishing the last act of his new play. Suddenly a face appeared at the window and a moment later a young woman dressed in a man's clothes entered the room. She would not give a satisfactory account of herself except to reveal the fact that her life was in danger. Later, a young woman dressed in a man's clothes was found murdered in a first class railway compartment. Chief Inspector Silver appears on the scene and Seagrave helps him solve the problem; also Andy Collinson with his dry humour has something to contribute. How Seagrave found himself up against a formidable gang known as the Ten Keys and the thrilling adventures he had are ably related by Mr. Holt, who is a born storyteller. Dorset, Paris, Monte Carlo, London, Surrey, Kent, the New Forest – the story moves at incredible speed. There is excitement and a surprise on every page, for the Ten Keys stop at nothing.

### *Tiger of Mayfair*
June 1935

The mysterious disappearance of Dr. John Trafford from his home in a Surrey village brought Chief Inspector Silver and his friend Andy Collinson to the village of Briarhill to investigate what the newspapers referred to as the 'Surrey Mystery'. While there, however, a sensational murder occurred in Mayfair. A well-dressed woman was found stabbed in a motor-car in Clarges Street. Scotland Yard detectives were puzzled by one feature of the crime of a particularly tigerish character – down the side of the woman's face were several distinct scratches as if they had been made by some animal's claw. This crime was followed by another very similar, the body of the second woman also bearing the same marks. It was evident that a' killer' of the worst type was at work. Here is a mystery at once intricate and exciting, one of the most brilliant stories that Mr. Holt has yet written.

### *Unknown Terror*
November 1935

On a foggy November night, Donald Maclean, motoring down from London, lost his way, and his temper, and finally ran out of petrol. Calling at a house in search of assistance, he found it brilliantly lit but apparently empty, save for a corpse and a frightened lady who took the first opportunity of escaping through a convenient window. Maclean, more than puzzled by such events, naturally 'phoned for the police, but could not avoid being involved in the extraordinary adventures that were to follow – adventures entailing the elucidation of a mysterious code, a search for a hoard of valuable pearls, as well as a hunt for a murderer. Mr. Holt's story moves swiftly through a series of dramatic episodes to an exciting climax.

### *Wanted for Murder*
January 1938

Henry Holt has been called 'a born writer of thrillers', and *Wanted for Murder* is one of his finest novels. It is the story of Terry Travers who is sent to Devil's Island, having been found guilty of a murder he had not committed. He escapes, vowing revenge on the man whose lying testimony was instrumental in having him sentenced.

### *Whispering Man, The*
September 1938

It was on Christmas Eve that a man assisted an attractive American girl whose car had broken down in an out-of-the-way country lane. She invited him to a New Year's Eve party at her employer's house – a casual invitation – he could come if he cared to. Her rescuer did care to – and at the party he was in at a death…and later at another death… and later – yet another. Three murders linked up with one another and each more baffling than the last. And the murderer – in the shape of a Whispering Man – could be heard but not seen! Here is a story of detection mixed expertly with mystery and excitement in Mr. Henry Holt's best manner.

## HOWARD, HARTLEY
(*see also* **Carmichael, Harry**)

### *Cry on my Shoulder*
January 1970

At first it looked like an ordinary job that any private enquiry agent could handle without much trouble. Winifred Newell said she only wanted to know if there was any substance in her ex- husband's insistence that he had committed murder or if it were drink that made Ray Durham delude himself into believing he had poisoned his uncle.

But that was only the beginning. That was before ace investigator Glenn Bowman found a dead rat in a beautiful woman's bed… before somebody took a couple of shots at him from out of the fog…before fire disposed of Ray Durham in the holocaust that destroyed his home.

These were the pieces of a murderous jigsaw in which death came to those who knew too much. Behind it all loomed the shadowy figure of a man called Frank McCrea – the man who was the missing player in a deadly game.

*Cry on My Shoulder* – set in Bowman's favourite New York – is a fast, tough story told with the pungent wit that has made Hartley Howard such an outstanding writer in the realm of modern thriller fiction.

### *Dead Drunk*
April 1974

There had been nothing complicated in Andrea Gray's life while she was alive. The complications arose after her presumed death.

She had evidently died as she had lived – an alcoholic. To Glenn Bowman, New York ace investigator, that was not difficult to understand. What presented him with his biggest problem was that she had died twice.

A man called Edwin Craig is prepared to meet a blackmail demand of $100,000 to ensure that she stays dead. Bowman's job is to see that the blackmailer does not come back for more.

As he unravels the tangle of past and present, that first death is followed by another … and then another. Before many days go by, Bowman learns that those who seek to batten on Edwin Craig's wealth meet destruction. That same menace threatens Bowman, too. He realizes he can trust no one associated with Craig … least of all those who live in his palatial home, Bel Air. They are doubly suspect – Craig himself: Judith, mistress of his house: Claire, her blonde and beautiful sister.

*Dead Drunk* is tough and tense in the best Glenn Bowman tradition. It has all the fast storyline technique on which Hartley Howard's reputation is so firmly established.

### *Epitaph for Joanna*
January 1972

The anonymous note read:

*Remember what happened on a June night twenty-three years ago? Joanna may be dead – but now your secret has come alive. What do you think will happen to you if I inform the police?*

It was the first letter of many, the start of a campaign of blackmail with a difference. When Glenn Bowman – New York investigator – gets involved, the difference becomes murder.

*Epitaph for Joanna* begins with a small-time operator who meddles in big-time events and pays for it with his life. From that moment death walks with the ghost of Joanna Priory.

Hartley Howard's latest novel has his usual brand of punch, pace and wry humour, blended with gripping excitement.

### *Highway to Murder*
April 1973

**I could've told Don McGill that I was a private enquiry agent and not a psychiatrist but clients had been kind of thin on the ground of late. I didn't mind playing nurse to a psycho so long as it paid for the groceries.**

And a psycho was what Mrs McGill appeared to be in the eyes of Glenn Bowman. She heard things that nobody else heard – like threatening phone calls telling her what would happen if she told Homicide Bureau she could identify the killer of Vince Portelli.

So Glenn Bowman accepted the retainer and began making enquiries. Then events ran away with him. Wild guesses pointed to not-so-wild answers…just as it was the wrong man who'd been killed for the wrong reason.

This is the story of a crime within a crime – a tough and racy account of violent living told by Glenn Bowman, ace investigator. *Highway to Murder* is Hartley Howard at his best.

### *Last Appointment, The*
January 1951

*The Last Appointment* is a first novel – and an exciting one. Canadian-born Hartley Howard shows at once that he has the authentic touch of a first-rate storyteller. Dr. Cole, successful psychiatrist, consults Glenn Bowman, private investigator, regarding his daughter Helen, who is being blackmailed. The doctor wants to find out who the blackmailer is, and what he can possibly have against Helen. Glenn finds quickly that he is up against thugs who take murder in their stride. The story moves at a fast pace throughout, and is leavened with entertaining quips and wisecracks, and peopled with characters who are really credible.

### *Million Dollar Snapshot*
January 1971

A gigantic theft…an everyday accident… the brutal slaying of two innocent bystanders… these are the ingredients of *Million-Dollar* [sic] *Snapshot*, another breath-taking story from the case-book of Glenn Bowman, New York ace investigator.

It began with the killing of Ben Riley – an alcoholic whose life becomes forfeit the day that chance leads him to Pennsylvania Railroad Station. There he stumbles on a tremendous secret which means nothing to him at the time. When at last he finds the key it is too late.

The price of his knowledge is a bullet in the chest. And that shot lets loose death to shut the mouths of others who might betray the secret of a man called Nelson – a man on the run.

In this, his latest saga, Hartley Howard demonstrates once again his superb mastery of the tough and racy detective story.

### *Murder One*
September 1971

A missing wife, a possessive mother, an unfaithful husband: these are the sides of a triangle enclosing the problems that Glenn Bowman, top-flight New York private detective, is hired to investigate.

Luck leads him to an empty house, long abandoned and almost derelict. But there the trail ends.

Step by step he checks back into the life of Mrs Mary Stowell from the day she was last seen. And soon one fact stands out with frightening significance – directly or indirectly, Mary is worth more dead than alive.

Two people know the answer. A bullet in the back makes sure one of them will never talk.

*Murder One* is a macabre story filled with tense excitement and lightened by flashes of wit. From first page to last it grips the imagination with Hartley Howard's unfailingly relentless hold.

### *Nice Day for a Funeral*
August 1972

Glenn Bowman earns his living the hard way. Life for a private eye in a city like New York is no bed of roses. The only law he can rely on is the law of the jungle.

Frankie Siccola was one of the tigers in that jungle. No sooner was he sewn in a blanket than the scavengers got the scent of rich pickings… and only a fool would have come between them and half a million dollars. Bowman was that kind of fool. And if he'd denied himself the pleasure of watching them plant Siccola in Belleview Cemetery a lot of things wouldn't have happened to a lot of people.

When a pretty lady makes Bowman an interesting proposition he shouldn't have been so keen to accept. But Bowman always asks for trouble, and trouble once again is what he gets.

*Nice Day for a Funeral* is a fast, tough story filled with tension and excitement and tinged with the caustic wit of Glenn Bowman – ace of private investigators.

### *One-Way Ticket*
January 1978

During his career as a private investigator Glenn Bowman had made his share of enemies. In the nature of things that had been inevitable. But when he undertook to trace a man called Danny Faulkner, Bowman found himself in a web of conspiracy where he could trust nobody.

From more than one direction his life was threatened as he followed a treacherous road leading deeper and deeper into a labyrinth of deception. Nothing was what it seemed: death lurked at every twist and turn of the maze.

Before very long he learns that there are overtones of espionage involving the theft of what might be a vital secret. Behind it all lies the greater secret of Danny Faulkner's disappearance.

*One-Way Ticket* is a tale of violent action told as only Glenn Bowman, ace investigator can tell it – the kind of fast-paced story which has made Hartley Howard deservedly well known.

### *Payoff*
June 1976

Dr Wolf Neustadt had an attractive wife, a lucrative practice and an office on Madison Avenue. He also had a problem – one which the New York Police Department had been unable to solve. Somebody in an old Chrysler sedan was intermittently following him from his Riverside Drive home to his office each morning and back to his home each night.

When the police checked out his complaint they found no justification for it. They had to report that he was not followed by anyone while they maintained surveillance on him.

So he hires Glenn Bowman, New York ace investigator. Step by step, Bowman picks up the threads that lead back to Dr Wolf Neustadt's life. As the days go by a tortuous trail becomes revealed – a trail that Bowman learns is flanked by hidden menace.

Soon his own life is in jeopardy. Soon his involvement is complete. He is on a road from which there is no return.

*Payoff* has all the pace and tension which readers have come to expect from Hartley Howard's consistently enjoyable detective thrillers.

### Room 37
July 1970

It began with a legacy for a man called Richard Lindon – a legacy bequeathed by his mother. But someone who had registered at the Star Hotel in Carlsville, Johnson County, had used the name Lindon…and had been found dead in Room 37.

When Glenn Bowman is hired by a New York firm of lawyers they tell him the case is only a matter of establishing a dead man's identity. But then they had no way of knowing that death had come to the man in Room 37 because he knew too much.

This is the story of a secret within a secret – an action-packed story of high adventure told by a master of suspense.

### Sealed Envelope, The
July 1979

Elizabeth Calhoun had everything a beautiful woman could wish for – money, position and a devoted husband. But these things were not enough. And one day in March she left home with no intention of ever coming back. Glenn Bowman, ace private investigator, had no knowledge of what lay ahead of him when he set off from New York that cold wet day on what was apparently a routine assignment. Instead it was the start of a trail with pitfalls every step of the way. And soon death had taken its toll of both innocent and guilty.

*The Sealed Envelope* is a typically Hartley Howard novel in which the pace of events builds up to a crescendo of violence. It is a tough fast story told as only Glenn Bowman can tell it.

### Treble Cross
March 1975

It began with a phone call on a cold wet day in February. The woman on the phone offered a thousand-dollar fee – too large a sum of money for too small a job of work.

But business had not been good of late. Glenn Bowman, New York ace investigator, could not afford to be choosy. That was how he came to meet a pretty woman who looked as if she had everything except peace of mind. And what she was scared of led Bowman straight into trouble.

He finds himself sitting in on a game where the stakes are high. Three players who have drawn the wrong cards play with their lives. And there comes a time when he knows he can win only if he sweetens the jackpot with his own life.

In *Treble Cross* Hartley Howard exploits his old familiar skill to weave the account of a grim adventure laced with Bowman's sardonic wit.

### HULL, HELEN
### Tapping on the Wall, A
August 1961

Richard Macameny had never planned to become a murderer. He was led to contemplate murder because of the predicament in which he found himself: harried by his hypochondriac wife Naomi, he fell in love – or believed he had fallen in love – with Laura Snowden, a young teacher at the University where he worked. Richard was forty-seven – 'the dangerous age' – and a senior lecturer.

Laura had many enemies, the odious Naomi had several friends. Richard's schemes for eliminating the enemies of Laura, his beloved, brewed furiously in his mind and ranged from the possible to the fantastic – until these were rendered superfluous by a chain of events that bore the stamp of miraculous intervention and loaded Richard with a guilt he had barely earned.

This first novel was chosen as the winner

of the 'Red Badge' Mystery competition in America, an event comparable with the 'Dons' Crime Novel Competition' run by the Crime Club in England. It is a penetrating and ingenious story, set against the background of an American university, that poses some enthralling problems and reaches an exciting and surprising climax.

### HULL, RICHARD
### And Death Came Too
June 1939

All connoisseurs of detective fiction know the high quality of work to expect from a Richard Hull novel. He made an immediate name for himself with his brilliantly original first novel *Murder of My Aunt*, ranked by the *Manchester Guardian* among the six best detective novels of the year. His latest book, *Excellent Intentions*, was again picked out (in the *Times Literary Supplement*) as among the six best out of a hundred detective stories. The Crime Club have, therefore, very special pleasure in adding his name to their list of writers. *And Death Came Too* has all the hall-marks (or Hull-marks!) of a first-class detective novel. The opening situation is the night when Arthur Yeldham, a retired housemaster from Finchingfield School, invites four young people to come on to his home after a local dance; and when they get there, Yeldham is found stabbed. The story is told quietly, coolly, and with utter detachment. The treatment is fascinating in itself; the characterization and dialogue are good. Detective story readers will find this novel refreshingly 'different'.

### Invitation to an Inquest
November 1950

Samuel Waterloo Ayres had been a horrid little boy, and had grown progressively nastier until, a nonagenarian, he died. Unfortunately his unpleasantness was quite noticeably visited on the second and third generations. His grandson Meredith was acid-tongued and maliciously cruel, and his great-grandsons were no better, Charles being cynical and selfish, Bill a cadger and a fool. It was because Bill Bowman was drowned that Inspector Yarrow of Scotland Yard was introduced to this unprepossessing family, and, just man though he was, he would cheerfully have pinned murder on to either of the surviving cousins. But he didn't know for certain that it *was* murder, and all he could do was to issue invitations to the inquest and keep an open and enquiring mind. A worth successor to the authors much-praised last novel, *A Matter of Nerves*, this new crime story proves once again the cynical old adage that 'all men are liars'.

### Last First
March 1947

*Last First* is dedicated to those who habitually read the last chapter first, but Mr. Richard Hull's many admirers, even if they do, will not succeed in spotting the man who brought about Mr. Appleyard's death with such ruthless cunning. Only those who follow the story from its first thrilling chapter to the last will know the answer. Set in a hotel in Scotland with a background of lochs, mountains and good fishing, the story is in itself an exciting open-air holiday told with that particular humorous flavour and ingenuity which have justly won for Mr. Hull such a wide and enthusiastic public.

### Left-Handed Death
April 1946

Mr. Richard Hull's writing has its own particular flavour. It is alive with subtle humour

which makes the reader chuckle. He is a master hand at inventing – and solving – a really ingenious mystery. *Left-Handed Death* is an uncommonly good story. The Shergold Engineering Company was in difficulties with one of the ministries. Foster, a government official, was prying into their accounts and asking awkward questions about figures. The activities of Barry Foster had certainly obviously affected the fortunes of the company and they must be stopped once and for all. But the plot to get rid of Foster has ramifications at once intricate and exciting. *Left-Handed Death* is a first-rate story, very enjoyable and very ingenious.

### Martineau Murders, The
January 1953

Murder *isn't* easy. In spite of the countless theories expounded in so many detective stories it isn't just a question of what to do with the body; it isn't easy to arrange an accident: low cunning and high optimism are not enough. Could *you* manufacture from ready-to-hand ingredients a poison that was certain to kill outright? Could you arrange a booby-trap that was sure to be lethal? Could you tamper with a car in such a way that the driver would not realise that anything was wrong and yet have a fatal accident? And if you *could* manage any of these things could you be sure that you were going to get the right victim? This is an absolutely fascinating story which will keep the reader absorbed and guessing to the end. Will the eccentric and really hopelessly incompetent Martineau manage to kill either of his two enemies? Will he, in fact, with the best will in the world, manage to kill anyone at all?

### Matter of Nerves, A
January 1950

When young John Hannan disappeared, his loss was sadly felt in the little East Coast village of Losfield End, because John as a butcher had his contacts and generally managed to supply his customers – if they paid well for it! – with a little bit extra over and above the Sunday joint. Where has John gone? Has he returned to his native Ireland? Has he met with an accident? Is he alive? Or dead? We who read know that he has been murdered, because the murderer tells us so, but we are kept in the dark as to the identity of the killer. This is a most cleverly contrived murder story, told from an unusual angle against the attractive background of an Essex village, where life centres round its church and its inn, and everyone knows not only what everyone else does but what everyone else says. It's guaranteed to please, interest and mystify all Crime Club readers.

### My Own Murderer
February 1940

One does not expect one's friends to drop in in the middle of the night and mention casually that they have committed murder that very evening. And yet that is what happens to Richard Sampson, solicitor and close friend of Alec Renwick, who sought shelter in his flat. Sampson agrees to help him to escape the law's clutches. The extraordinary consequences make a convincing and ingenious story of intense human appeal, seasoned, however, with plenty of humour and irony. Mr. Richard Hull's reputation as a writer of detective stories stands very high; his style is excellent – cool, dry and sardonic. *My Own Murderer* is an exceptionally fine intellectual treat.

### Unfortunate Murderer, The
April 1942

Mr. Richard Hull is a distinguished detective-story writer, and novels such as *Murder*

of *My Aunt* and *My Own Murderer* are gratefully remembered. His new story has a wartime background of munition-making and hush-hush scientific research work. Trench, the unpleasantly efficient managing director at the works, whom every one loathes; Riches, the amiable and easy-going secretary; Findlater, the touchy and resentful chief accountant, are all examples of the author's careful character drawing which adds much to the enjoyment of an extremely clever detective novel.

### Until She Was Dead
May 1949

Nobody but Yvonne de Belmont would have engaged Clara Fison as a companion so recklessly and without proper enquiry. Mrs. de Belmont, a wealthy but slightly eccentric widow who possessed valuable furniture, liked beautiful china and collected the stamps of St. Lucia with intelligence, certainly took a risk there. Clara was a dark horse, and her former employer had died in rather peculiar circumstances – in fact a little too suddenly. Her presence in the house at 17a Elizabeth Square had already resulted in a curiously sinister atmosphere. Mr. Richard Hull has created some excellent characters in this dramatic story of a crime and its solution.

### INCHBALD, PETER
### Or the Bambino Dies
May 1985

Italian banker Silvestro Negroni insures with Lloyd's against kidnapping. Within hours his six-year old son is taken from the garden of the family's Umbrian villa.

Consternation at Lloyd's. Policy-holders are supposed to be anonymous, but this is the fourth such incident in a matter of months. Somewhere there must be a leak.

The underwriter concerned and the head of the security agency call in Franco Corti, formerly a chief inspector at Scotland Yard, now art dealer, restaurateur, security consultant and private eye. His brief is to trace the leak. But once in Italy, in the presence of the distraught parents, the agonizing messages, the cruel game of cat and mouse played by the kidnappers, Corti is drawn inescapably into the mainstream of the action: the locating and attempted recovery of the child.

The scene switches between London, Rome, Florence and the cities and countryside of Umbria. The climax is Peter Inchbald's most thrilling yet. And two important clues are provided by a small brown dog and by Cesare, Corti's own teenage son.

This is the fourth Franco Corti novel. They go from strength to strength.

### Short Break in Venice
September 1983

Restored to his original name, Chief Inspector Franco Corti of Scotland Yard's Art and Antiques Squad is also temporarily restored to the country of his birth, for he and his wife are on a brief holiday in Venice which is blossoming into a second honeymoon.

Then an antique shop is vandalized, and Corti in company with the owner is the first policeman on the scene. After all, the last time he saw Elsa Silverman, wife of his old antagonist Max, she was in Vine Street police station, even though she was released after forty-eight hours.

The thread of consequence shuttles between Venice, haunted by its past, and London, and takes in the Surrey gin-and-Jaguar belt, a dreamy West Country manor, and the 'wild sea moor' of the Venetian lagoon, as it weaves a tapestry of hijack, terror and death.

Old enemies crawl from Latin-American

hideouts. New friends, Italian and English, emerge to help Corti in his fight against a vicious conspiracy. The family continues to cause him pain and joy. And his final deliverance is into a new and independent life.

*Short Break in Venice* completes the trilogy which began with *Tondo for Short* and *The Sweet Short Grass*, but Corti's steadily increasing band of admirers may rest assured that there is more of Franco Corti to come.

### Sweet Short Grass, The
September 1982

The three most dangerous things, in the diplomats' joke, are a quiet bull, a friendly Russian, and an empty gun. Franco Corti, senior detective with the Art and Antiques Squad at Scotland Yard, is a natural for the first, and an old enemy of his the second. But as regards the third...

In *Tondo for Short*, in which he made his first appearance, Corti's Italian jaunt pitched him into a crisis of national identity. By the opening of Peter Inchbald's second novel, the Florentine cockney, art-freak and copper has decided he is English, emigrated from Soho to Acton, and changed his name.

But Italy won't let go. In action for the first time as Chief Inspector Frank Short, he finds himself fighting a vendetta which demands full Machiavellian treatment.

Its origins are diverse: his signature in a visitors' book; accusations of corruption; stolen art treasures; his father's work as a restorer of great skill and perhaps a little too much imagination; and finally murder. All interwoven with a couple of dubious Old Masters too sensitive for the FBI to 'put through channels', and with sorties into the English countryside – Corti never did like the country...

### Tondo for Short
July 1981

'Twenty-five million quid's-worth of artwork's gone missing and a man's dead', said the head of the Art and Antiques Squad at the Yard. 'It's important enough to some.' It was. The artwork was Michelangelo's other tondo, an eight-hundredweight marble relief of Cupid and Psyche, pagan counterpart of the Royal Academy's great Madonna, and it had been stolen from the Royal Gibbonsian Foundation in Pall Mall.

Like the Gibby Tondo, Inspector Franco Corti, the connoisseur built like a battle-tank, came originally from Florence. That was one reason why the crime got under his skin. The other was that two of his children were roughed up because of it. From then on it was war.

The campaign took him to the Italy he had last seen as a small child. The experience (and the vicious power-games he encountered) tore him apart. And back home he had to cope with Special Branch, his tight-knit Soho-Italian family, his bit on the side…

As Franco Corti battled to recover an Italian art treasure it had seemed impossible to steal, he found himself fighting for his life (though not in the usual manner of the fictional detective) and found too that success is not always sweet.

*Tondo for Short* marks the debut of this Florentine cockney, art-freak and copper, and also of his creator, Peter Inchbald.

## INFANTE, ANNE
### Death among the Dunes
August 1990

When popular children's author, Micky Douglas, takes his niece and nephew for a caravan holiday on Queensland's beautiful Sunshine Coast, he's expecting nothing more exciting than three weeks of sun, sand and swimming. And he wouldn't mind getting to know fellow camper Lorraine Marshall a little better, either.

The holiday begins to turn sour when the strangled body of a local teenage girl is uncovered by children digging in a sand dune. The police are confident that, despite an epidemic of summer 'flu, they can solve the murder quickly; until Micky, enjoying an early morning run on the beach, comes across the body of another local teenager.

Micky's friend from Brisbane Homicide, Inspector Reeves, is called in, and it soon becomes clear that a serial killer is at large when two more victims are discovered.

Can the murderer really be one of the seemingly innocent holiday-makers? Micky can't believe it, but he takes up the Inspector's challenge to solve the murders. He has all the clues, yet he's almost too late in putting them together as he becomes involved in a desperate bid to save himself and Lorraine, and bring a dangerous murderer to justice.

### Death in Green
April 1992

Mitchell Island, a rare sand island off the Queensland coast, has become the focus of conflict between timber workers who want to continue to log its abundant forests and conservationists who seek to ban logging. Into this potential battleground comes Damien White, ecologist and presenter of a popular TV series, to film a documentary on the island at the invitation of Hugh Grant, head of the anti-logging campaign.

Before White arrives, there is an attempt on Grant's life, seemingly by someone in Eversleigh, the mainland town which owes its existence to logging, followed by an attack by 'Greenies' on the manager of the timber mill. Then White's scriptwriter is found drowned in suspicious circumstances.

Children's author Micky Douglas agrees to step in to complete the script but is torn between allegiance to White, his friendship with Reeves, who is investigating the scriptwriter's death, his love for Annie Mason, also working for White, and his loyalty to his friend, journalist Duke Jordan, with whom he sets out to investigate the possibility that the warring groups are being secretly manipulated by someone with quite different plans for the island.

### Death Launch
April 1993

When children's author, Micky Douglas, invites Maddy Grey to launch his latest book, he has no idea he's inviting trouble. Maddy, well-known hostess of the successful children's TV show *Kid's World*, isn't as popular with her colleagues as she is with her adoring young audience. In fact, she's managed to alienate quite a number of her acquaintances, some of whom are finding their very livelihood and future happiness threatened by her vindictive behaviour. It seems a lot of people have very good reasons for wishing Maddy Grey dead.

So when her body turns up after the launch, the police have quite a list of suspects. But who killed Maddy Grey? Was it her ex-lover and co-host? Or her own daughter? The *Kids' World* [sic] producer – or his wife? The over-emotional writer of teenage novels whom Maddy threatened to destroy? Or perhaps the journalist whose lover Maddy seduced from her. It might be her agent, or the TV newsreader, or one of the family who runs the bookshop where the launch took place.

The killer is determined to cover any tracks and Micky, realizing that he himself has been responsible for one of the following deaths, is determined to bring a murderer to justice.

### Death on a Hot Summer Night
August 1989

Popular children's author Micky Douglas is in trouble. Either he's incredibly accident-prone or someone is trying to kill him. Returning home one hot and sticky Brisbane afternoon, intent on relaxing in a tub of cold water, he finds his bath already occupied by his illustrator, Owen Pendleton. Except that Owen isn't trying to beat the heat. Owen is very dead.

Micky's old friend Richard Jordan, an investigative journalist, turns up on the trail of a Chinese Triad organization, hoping to link the laundering of drug money to a casino owner, Eric Saunders. Hearing about the spate of accidents, Jordan is instantly suspicious. Not only is Saunders up to his neck in shady deals, he is also having an affair with Micky's ex-wife, and trying to buy Micky's house. Micky has no intention of selling, but that's hardly a motive for attempted murder. After all, there are other houses on the market.

But it's Pendleton's death that is the real bad news for Jordan, for the drug-addict was just about to lift the lid off a major drug racket and give Jordan the biggest story of his life.

As Micky joins forces with Jordan to discover the grim secret of the house the casino boss wants so badly, he finds himself in a desperate race to save his ex-wife and others from a ruthless gang.

### Deathwater
May 1991

Darkwater is a historical home near Brisbane, still owned by the Forrests, the pioneer family whose founder built it in colonial times. Journalist Bob Slater, who is writing an article about the house and family for a local paper, is killed in a car accident on a dark, wet night in the steep and dangerous Kaye Street, so children's author Micky Douglas agrees to finish the article.

But Bob's death bears an uncanny resemblance to that of William, son of the autocratic Eileen Forrest, in the same spot sixteen years previously, and, after finding a cryptic message doodled by Bob Slater shortly before he died, Micky begins to wonder just how 'accidental' both deaths really were.

Driven by curiosity, Micky sets out to investigate and, in spite of being warned by his friend, Inspector Reeves, uncovers a deadly plot to suppress an old scandal of Government and police corruption, the truth about the supposed suicide of Eileen Forrest's husband, a horrific crime against the original native tribe which once inhabited the Darkwater land – and a cunning murderer who is determined to remove Micky before he discovers the truth.

## JACQUEMARD, YVES and SENECAL, JEAN-MICHEL
### Body Vanishes, The
May 1980

In the early hours of Friday morning, the peaceful slumber of the respectable citizens of Strasbourg was shattered by a woman's scream. The body of a beautiful redhead had been spotted in the reeds on the river bank. Then, having made itself the talk of the local inn, the body vanished, leaving Superintendent Dullac with the first of several mysteries.

The body proved to be that of Dyana Pasquier, engaged to the heir of Strasbourg's leading patron of the arts. But Wotan Grun, the most powerful man in more sense than one in the Petite France district, was not going to allow himself to be ruffled by the strange reappearance of the body in his living-room – nor by the burglary that was discovered with it. As the week passed, Dullac made several more discoveries: that the drowning was no accident; that he had a soft spot in his heart for Wotan's daughter; that many people in Wotan's circle had something to hide. But whose alibi was false? Who had a motive for killing Dyana? What was the secret of the House of Grun?

The second death took everyone by surprise – or almost everyone...

The authors of the widely-acclaimed *The Eleventh Little Nigger* have written another intriguing and unusual mystery, set this time in the unique atmosphere of Strasbourg with larger-than-life characters, and picturesque scenery, familiar as the headquarters of the European Parliament.

### Eleventh Little Nigger, The
April 1979

*The play*: an entirely new production of Agatha Christie's *Ten Little Niggers*.

*The scene*: The Theatre Gerard, Paris, under the management of Mme Gerda.

*The producer*: young, talented, and avant-garde.

*The cast*: star-studded

*The plot*: A member of the cast, arriving late at the theatre just before curtain up, finds the rest of the cast dead in their dressing-rooms, and in his own the body of an unknown man: rapidly baptized, the eleventh little nigger, by the Press.

*The detective*: Superintendent Hector Parescot, bright star of the Sûreté and sleuth unparalleled even by Hercule Poirot.

*The authors*: Yves Jacquemard and Jean-Michel Sènècal, actors and playwrights who know the world of the theatre as well as they know the works of Agatha Christie. This novel, their second, closely modelled on the techniques she made famous but with a flavour all its own, is their tribute to her memory.

## JAMES, TERRY
### Sam's Elegy
April 1993

Elegy: *n.* a song of mourning; a poem of serious, pensive or reflective mood. *example*: Gray's *Elegy Written in a Country Churchyard*.

Sam: *m.* proper name, usually dim. Samuel: not uncommon among private detectives.

As he lingers in a Sussex country churchyard before climbing the tower to unblock a water spout, odd job man Sam Bevan has no idea he will soon be sent flying earthwards.

Is it an accident, or a failed murder attempt? And why is Sam suddenly being offered some very odd jobs?

*Sam's Elegy* introduces the not-so-sleepy village of Miston, where a symbolic skull, wild jealousies, threatening mail, an apparent suicide and an almost certain murder interrupt Sam's 'pensive and reflective' rural life.

At the heart of *Sam's Elegy* lies a crime darker perhaps than murder itself. But the tale twists along with much humour, as Sam copes with the vicar's beautiful, unpredictable wife Dora, with young Josie who cheerfully leads him into dangers galore, with Dr Janine Quibbley who might be too clever for her own safety, and with the manipulations of Francis Wyatt, a curiously laid-back policeman. Also on hand, to help or to hinder, is Sam's dog, Eddie.

## JAY, CHARLOTTE
### Arms for Adonis
October 1960

When the bomb exploded in the *suk* Sarah was shaken, deafened and then flung to the ground by panic-stricken Lebanese. It was to be a turning point in her life. The stranger who rescued her in so high-handed a manner made an indelible impression on her mind – and when he was shot down before her eyes in the street a short time later, Sarah found herself involved in a strange and dangerous episode which she neither understood nor liked. It carried her from the lively, cosmopolitan city of Beirut into the interior of Lebanon, to the gigantic ruins of Baalbek, before a crisis was reached in the tiny village of Ain Houssaine.

Charlotte Jay has not only produced a book with a gripping plot and characters who stay in the memory, but the vivid background of present day Lebanon and its inhabitants is brilliantly made part of the story, and this feature alone would make *Arms For Adonis* a worthy successor to *The Man Who Walked Away* and *The Yellow Turban*.

### Man Who Walked Away, The
August 1958

It was a dark, winter afternoon when Helen Graham received two callers. In that gloomy London room she made a choice which she hoped would give her and her child security, reassurance and relief from the bleak world in which she lived. But she was to find that she had stepped into a nightmare, twilight existence where she was forced to fight against enemies as ruthless as they were terrifying.

The strength of old Cedric Crome overshadowed the life of her small son; the weakness of Maurice put her own happiness in jeopardy; and, almost unnoticed at the start, the figure which the child called 'The Grey Lady' grew to dominate and threaten the very fabric of Helen's life, forcing her to turn, at length, and fight back in defence of the two people she loved – and ultimately in defence of her own life.

In *The Man Who Walked Away* Charlotte Jay tells a fascinating story of fear and retribution. It is a macabre and spine-chilling successor to *The Yellow Turban* and *The Fugitive Eye*.

### Yellow Turban, The
April 1955

The story of a man lost to his friends, vanished into Pakistan from Karachi where he was last seen … of his old companion and admirer, Will Brooke, who was sent from London to find him and bring him home.

Will Brooke, the narrator, found in Karachi an unfamiliar world, bustling, colourful, sun-drenched, diseased. Dazed by his first sight of this seething, chaotic city, the beautiful manners and inconsequential thoughts of its people, the bizarre guests at the Grand Hotel where he stayed, he found his waiting role increasingly hard to sustain. There were queer customers at the hotel, among them the English girl, Maggie Hill, who at once attracted and repelled him. Beset by illness and doubt, Will Brooke waited, getting occasional glimpses of the strange machinations in which his friend, Roy Finlay, was involved. And then he found himself implicated in a brutal and savage murder.

Karachi itself, Will's long, uneasy vigil there, his dangerous journey to the hills to find his friend, and the thing that he discovered among those hills, are here described with sympathy and power. The background is detailed, exotic, authentic; the story rises to a climax that cannot be called less than 'horrifying' – the epithet reviewers used to describe Charlotte Jay's earlier books, *The Knife is Feminine*, *Beat Not the Bones* and *The Fugitive Eye*.

## JAY, SIMON
### Death of a Skin-Diver
June 1964

The dead man must have drowned – it was the obvious explanation. But when Dr. Peter Much made post-mortem tests one reaction pointed to carbon monoxide poisoning; which meant that the man's diving cylinders could have been filled with the poisonous gas instead of compressed air. Accidentally, or intentionally?

But the scientific test was inconclusive, and Peter Much's solid reputation did not save him from the scepticism of the coroner. The death was ascribed to accident, and the episode was officially regarded as closed. But a number of unanswered questions remained – such as why the dead man had chosen such an unlikely spot in which to dive for crayfish; there could be no crayfish on such a sandy bottom, as the rascally captain of the skindiver's launch must have known very well…

More awkward questions accumulated – and the next episode of violence clearly could not be ascribed to 'accident'. Gradually it became apparent to the police that there might be a connection between the death of the skin-diver and the mystery of the black-market gin – the current racket which obsessed and baffled the mind of authority in Auckland.

This first novel, set in New Zealand, introduces a new detective-hero, Dr. Peter Much, who is a practising pathologist in that country. It describes the working of a pathologist's laboratory, and the police methods and procedure by which a multiple criminal enterprise is uncovered, piece by piece. It portrays in affectionate and humorous detail the ways of the yachtsmen of Auckland, their sailing grounds, their pleasures and haunts and attitudes. It presents a story that is convincing, exciting and surprising – the first adventure of an entirely new and modern detective, the New Zealander, Dr. Peter Much.

## JEFFRIES, RODERIC
(see also **Ashford, Jeffrey**)
### Almost Murder
March 1986

Inspector Alvarez, who 'endears himself to the reader with each fresh encounter' (*Police*), did not really agree that because one of the two men who had died aboard a motor-cruiser off Mallorca had been a member of the British parliament the investigation was of unusual importance; in his opinion, a dead MP was a source of less trouble than a live one. Nevertheless, he was quite prepared to accept that Spanish honour was at stake and to investigate whether the explosion had been accidental or deliberate, even though Superior Chief Salas demanded that he serve under Comisario Suau, a stickler for discipline and routine, who was convinced that terrorists were responsible for the crime.

Suau soon made clear his contempt for Alvarez's rambling methods of work and his stupid insistence on investigating not just the deaths of those who'd been aboard the boat, but also their lives. Unfortunately for both of them, Alvarez's researches unearthed some awkward facts, though for no one were they more awkward than for Alvarez himself.

### Benefits of Death, The
September 1963

When Mrs. Leithan disappeared her husband behaved very calmly and casually. He assured the police that she'd gone away on a visit, and that there was nothing to worry about. But the police were certain that Charles Leithan knew a lot more than he admitted, and they had good reasons: first, there was a great deal of money involved; and second, Chares Leithan's visits to his mistress became suddenly less furtive after his wife's 'disappearance'.

The disappearance of Mrs. Lethian was made still more mysterious by the fact that her champion dog, Stymie, had disappeared at the same time. At last the police believed that they had solved the mystery; and despite the absence of a body a murder charge was brought before a jury.

But the police were wrong…indeed everyone was wrong. It is not until the very end of this ingenious psychological crime novel that the actions of the characters can be understood, or seen to be inevitable. This grim and exciting story is a fine successor to *Evidence of the Accused* and *Exhibit No. Thirteen*.

### Dead Against the Lawyers
June 1965

In his chambers, and in the daily work of the Bar at Hertonhurst in Kent, Radwick Holter Q.C. was known as a ruthless and determined barrister. Holter was the object of envy – successful and in constant demand, while some of his colleagues struggled to make ends meet. And Holter had a beautiful wife, thirty years younger than himself.

In Holter's office in the Hertonhurst Chambers a man is killed – a solicitor who had business in Hertonhurst, and also enemies …

The police collect their evidence and make an arrest for murder. But when they have this prisoner in the dock, facing a formidable array of evidence, events take a dramatic and extraordinary turn.

Once again Roderic Jeffries has devised a legal predicament of fascinating intricacy. This exciting story grips from the beginning to the startling end.

### Dead Clever
February 1989

After informing Alvarez that he was to help a visiting insurance adjuster from England to investigate more closely the details surrounding the crash of a light aircraft off Mallorca, Superior Chief Salas gave one last, brief, but unambiguous order: on no account was Alvarez to do anything that might compromise a simple and straightforward case.

Alvarez liked a quiet life far too much ever deliberately to complicate anything. But the cases he investigated often had a distressing habit of becoming complicated by the facts. So it proved to be now, the pilot of the aircraft, presumably killed in the crash at sea, had very recently applied to double the amount for which his life was insured; he was known to have been desperately short of money; his estranged wife had been suing him; he had had a girlfriend; it was possible he had owed money to a man who would use force to secure repayments…everything pointed to a false claim. But as Alvarez knew only too well, things did not always point in the right direction.

Few authors are as skilful as Roderic Jeffries at misleading the reader. Here he is at his best.

### Dead Man's Bluff
August 1970

Daniel Knott was a bad farmer and a worse husband. When a poacher heard a shot and shortly afterwards Knott's charred remains were found among the burnt-out farm buildings, the police felt they had not far to seek for the solution to the tragedy, especially when another body was found. It proved to be that of an agricultural salesman running a subsidy swindle in which Knott was deeply involved. And only the local Inspector Clayton was worried by the fact that the salesman had chosen to consume a dinner of boiled beef and dumplings on a sultry August afternoon. Superintendent Akers of the Yard was definitely not.

The poacher's evidence provided alibis for several suspects, but Clayton was not satisfied. When one of the alibis is broken and the suspect sent for trial, his dissatisfaction increases, but the results of his inquiries are unexpected, to say the least.

Roderic Jeffries spins one of his most intriguing mysteries, whose ramifications extend to include the kind of trial scene for which he is justly famous and a legal twist as cunning as any he has ever devised.

### Deadly Marriage, A
July 1967

It was common knowledge that David and Catalina Plesence's marriage was on the verge of collapse and that David was seeing a lot of an attractive widow living nearby. David longed for a divorce, but Catalina was a very vindictive woman and adamantly refused to contemplate the idea: though she was prepared to obtain a judicial separation – provided the alimony was large enough.

When a man died after having had a drink in their house and the police established that he had been poisoned there, Catalina saw her way to a terrible revenge against David. Whether it was true or not, she swore that the poison had been meant for her and that David had tried to kill her.

Tension builds up and there are two exciting court scenes. Roderic Jeffries established a very high reputation for himself in the field of the legal thriller with *Exhibit No. Thirteen* and *Dead Against the Lawyers*. Once again he has used a little known quirk of the law and woven round it an enthralling story of immense intricacy.

### Deadly Petard
January 1983

Barbara was very rich and ten years older than Keir West, who was a philanderer, but when she died with a plastic bag over her head she left a suicide note. The only trouble was that the daily woman accused West of having murdered his wife.

The police uncovered sufficient evidence to make it virtually certain Barbara had been murdered and that the murderer was her husband. But they could not prove him guilty because Gertrude Dean, whom he'd known since both were children, gave him an alibi.

Harassed both by the police, who tried to make her confess she was a liar, and by West, who was desperate that she should continue to lie, Gertrude decided to leave England and find another and happier life for herself.

She found it on the island of Mallorca. That was, until the day Inspector Alvarez, at the request of the English police, questioned her to try to discover the identity of 'Sandra' and West arrived to plead with her not to say who Sandra was …

Roderic Jeffries's ability to twist a plot like a corkscrew has seldom been better demonstrated, and as always, Inspector Alvarez is a delight.

### Death in the Coverts
June 1966

For hundreds of years the Decker family has lived at Hurstley Place in Kent. In to-day's hard times the Deckers are still a great family, though relatively impoverished. Nowadays the coverts of the Decker pheasant shoot are financed and enjoyed by the members of a shooting syndicate: the family retains three guns.

A pheasant drive at Hurstley Place ends in the discovery that a member of the syndicate has been shot dead. This is the first of three tragedies.

There is an arrest for murder and a trial. In the courtroom a fantastic development brings the whole machinery of justice to a halt.

Each book in a distinguished series of crime novels by Roderic Jeffries has hinged on an authentic point of law. Here, as in *Exhibit No. Thirteen* and *Dead Against the Lawyers*, the exploitation of such a legal point has extraordinary consequences.

But this novel is more than the exploitations of a quirk of law. It is an exciting and ingenious whodunit, with rounded characters and a fascinating background of a contemporary pheasant-shooting syndicate.

### *Death Takes Time*
January 1994

Bridget Orr could have fallen accidentally to her death from the patio of her hillside house in France, but she might have been pushed. Asked by the French police to trace a Spanish registered car which had been seen in the village the afternoon of Orr's death, Inspector Alvarez comes to the welcome conclusion that, on the scant information provided, this is an impossible task.

His hope that he has thereby secured for himself a peaceful future is shattered, however, by a suspicious death on his own doorstep. Hugh Robson, a wealthy Englishman with a luxurious lifestyle and a liking for beautiful women, is discovered in a fatal, heroin-induced coma. All the evidence suggests that Robson had never touched drugs in his life…

In next to no time, the investigation has become more than usually labyrinthine. But, as Alvarez tries unsuccessfully to explain to his supercilious Superior Chief, it isn't his fault…even when the multiplying confusions and complications force him to take an unofficial and near-disastrous trip to England. This witty and clever novel is an immensely enjoyable addition to Roderic Jeffries's popular series, and finds Inspector Alvarez on top form.

### *Death Trick*
March 1988

A sense of loyalty was not Pablo Roig's strongest trait. A busy solicitor in Mallorca, he betrayed the trust his clients placed in him whenever there was an advantage to be gained; married, he betrayed his wife as often as possible; in adultery, he betrayed each mistress when he began to tire of her; as an employee he betrayed that too…Small wonder that eventually one of his acts of betrayal should lead to his death. But which?

The murder had occurred outside Inspector Alvarez's territory, as he was very quick to point out. But with typical heavy-handed ill-will, Superior Chief Salas directed him to help with the inquiries, adding a warning that this time he was on no account to complicate what was undoubtedly a straightforward case…

He might as well have saved his breath, but in the skilful hands of Roderic Jeffries the gradually revealed complexities are guaranteed to keep you turning the page.

### *Embarrassing Death, An*
August 1964

Bill Stemple sold the secret photographs of the new Lanfair Model 'for kicks'; he didn't do it for such a simple – if disloyal – reason as making money; he did it to outrage authority, and to annoy the directors of Lanfair Motors. As an employee and publicity representative Bill left almost everything to be desired. His outstanding virtue, albeit a negative one, was that he had not committed murder.

The morning after the office party at Lanfairs a young girl, a member of staff and a friend of Bill's, was found murdered and almost naked. Bill had been with her the last time she had been seen alive and had made a pass at her; he soon found himself under suspicion, and then arrest...

There were to be surprises for all concerned in the legal proceedings that followed. Once again Roderic Jeffries has developed a point of English criminal law as the hinge of a murder story of many qualities and ingredients: the conduct of the staff of a great modern motor-factory, a murder mystery that is sinister and sensational, the detailed work of policemen and lawyers all contribute to a novel even more enthralling and unusual than its predecessors, *Exhibit No. Thirteen* and *Evidence of the Accused*.

### *Evidence of the Accused*
October 1961

It soon became apparent that Linda hadn't just fallen through the banisters into the hall below – someone had killed her. Suspicion was bound to fall on two men, both friends of John Waring, the narrator. One of these was Mark, Linda's husband.

This remarkable crime novel centres on the drastic and ingenious steps that the two main suspects, Mark and Stuart, take to sidetrack the law. There are scenes in the courtroom that are startling in their revelation of the uses that can be made of the law and its processes. It is only after the bizarre and exciting scenes in court have been concluded that the truth about Linda's death is revealed.

Roderic Jeffries has written novels under pseudonyms. This is his first novel under his own name, and his most ambitious one yet. Apart from the originality of the central story it has many virtues: subtlety of characterisation, the impact of a legal drama that is wholly convincing, and twists in the story that constantly raise the tension.

### *Exhibit No. Thirteen*
September 1962

A girl is found raped and murdered in a wood in Kent – the crime, it appears, of a 'case book' sex maniac. Police investigations are widespread and routine since there is no clue which leads to a particular individual. Detective Sergeant Rusk is sent to interview a few men in the area who have a past record of sexual offences; among them he finds Kremayne, who had been at school with him. In those days Kremayne had been a failure, Rusk a successful scholar and athlete. Now Kremayne is a rich farmer, happily married, and Rusk a mere Detective Sergeant…

This is the beginning of a story of extraordinary ingenuity and subtlety, and any further description of it would give hints and spoil the reader's pleasure. As in *Evidence of the Accused* the principal, very dramatic scenes take place in court. *Exhibit No. Thirteen* is a *tour-de-force* of legal ingenuity so startling that it must remind readers of an earlier and famous crime story – *Witness for the Prosecution*.

### *Fatal Fleece, A*
February 1992

To Inés's terror, Walter Miller seemed suddenly to become insane – and when he fell into the swimming pool, his face a contorted mask, she was convinced that she had poisoned him with a love-philtre and he was about to die. However, Dr Llabares, though obnoxiously egotistical, recognized that Miller was suffering from datura poisoning and so was able to treat him in time to save his life.

Inspector Alvarez was not surprised when Inés subsequently denied that she had poisoned her lover; but he was very surprised when Miller agreed that there was not the slightest possibility she could have done so. In the face of these denials, and the lack of any proof, the investigation was at an end – a welcome conclusion since there was nothing more for him to do. That was until two months later when Miller flew to England to stay with his wife, but never arrived at her home …

### *Just Desserts*
September 1980

Miriam Spiller was middle-aged, plain, and resident on Mallorca, where to the English colony's surprise she had just become engaged. Her fiancé was an unsuccessful novelist – so unsuccessful that he risked deportation if he could not put down a lump sum forthwith to satisfy the Spanish authorities. Miriam talked bravely of borrowing the money for him, but instead she went back to her solitary flat and that night drank too much gin, staggered on to the wrought-iron balcony, and crashed through its rusted railing. A clear case of accidental death.

Except that Brenda Stewart, courier with a tour operator and Miriam's nearest approach to a friend, thought otherwise and passed on her suspicions to the police. And the police were represented by Inspector Enrique Alvarez, whose patient investigation into the manners, morals and past histories of those of Mallorca's English residents who knew Miriam led him into a veritable labyrinth of subterfuge.

Alvarez expected to find crime at its heart, but he never expected to uncover a crime which would affect his own life and happiness.

### *Layers of Deceit*
March 1985

The narrow escape of two English visitors to Mallorca when their car brakes failed on a mountain road, the attempted suicide of a Mallorquin girl, the womanizing of wealthy English resident Steven Cullom and the row between him and his brother when one of his women proved unexpectedly resistant; the disappearance of a dog – all these facts seemed to Inspector Alvarez to be connected, though he couldn't decide how, to a death on the island which his instincts told him was murder. Superior Chief Salas disagreed.

Nevertheless, he was obliged to sanction the Inspector's brief visit to England, and what he learned there convinced Alvarez that there was more to that mysterious death than met the eye. But unless fresh evidence came to light, he reported to Salas, it would be impossible to know who was responsible. Or if a crime had been committed at all …

Roderic Jeffries's Spanish detective has won friends on both sides of the Atlantic for his perspicacity, industry and humanity. His latest investigation into the mores of the English expatriates on Mallorca will undoubtedly win him many more.

### *Mistakenly in Mallorca*
September 1974

Elvina Wood's death at her home in Mallorca was sudden and unexpected. Another few days and her great-nephew would have inherited, through her, enough to buy the English farm he craved. So when he returned to the house and found her dead, his first thought was to conceal her death for a short time, his second, how to do it. Only afterwards did he wonder if such action would be wise.

But John Tatham already had reason to despise the law's insistence on the letter rather than the spirit. He planned his deception carefully. Elvina was not exactly popular with the English community or with certain Mallorquins; few would inquire if she were not seen around. And when, later, her body was discovered, her death would be seen to be an accident. Admittedly not the same accident as that which had proved fatal, but differing only in technicalities.

Unfortunately Tatham failed to reckon with Alvarez, the Spanish policeman, with whom he had more in common than he thought. And he failed to reckon with the fact that to a policeman his own role would look highly suspect. Had Tatham in effect framed himself? And had he, in doing so, inadvertently involved himself in another crime? With each fresh twist in Roderick Jeffries's novel, fresh possibilities occur.

### *Murder Begets Murder*
January 1979

The English community on Mallorca were sorry for William Heron. The reclusive, wealthy invalid had come to the island accompanied by his mistress, and now there were indications that while he lay dying, she was carrying on with another man. So no one mourned when it was discovered that instead of leaving the island, as she had planned to do, shortly after his funeral, she had died alone in the house from food poisoning.

Conveniently – too conveniently for Inspector Alvarez – it was no longer possible to determine the poison which had caused her death. If he was right in suspecting it had been deliberately administered, much depended on whether there was any truth in the rumour that she had had another lover, and who the man might be. His enquiries did nothing but arouse hostility among the English residents. Not until he was on a thoroughly unenjoyable professional visit to England did the Mallorquin detective chance to learn something that convinced him that murder could beget murder …

Celebrated alike for their portrayal of a Mallorca very different from the one the tourists annually encounter, and the intricate convolutions of their plots, Roderic Jeffries's crime novels have established themselves steadily, and will do so yet more firmly with this book.

### *Murder Confounded*
February 1993

Two men left Hawdon Hall Rehabilitation Centre on the same day, each with a new identity to enable him to start a fresh life untainted by the past. But the past, with its criminal associations, was not easily lost, even in distant Mallorca where one of the pair settled; nor, as Sir Donald Macadie was later to discover on the same island, was the future easily found. Certainly not when Inspector Alvarez, with that penchant for complications which so infuriated his superiors, decided that there was more to a case of assault than met even the blackest eye.

In his determination not to see an innocent man convicted, Alvarez travelled to England and to Hawdon Hall itself. What he learnt there set in train a vast police operation to avert a terrorist operation which would have altered the course of history, and would for ever have blackened the proud honour of Spain.

### *Murder's Long Memory*
February 1991

When going through his mother's possessions after her death, Steven Armitage is shocked to discover a love-letter written during the war to another woman by his father who had died a hero's death. Surely, only a really vindictive wife would have kept a letter for nearly fifty years? Yet this woman was not the mother he had known. Convinced that the reality of the truth had to be different from its appearance, he determined to try and discover.

It was a quest which took him to Mallorca, officially neutral during World War II, where some curious events had taken place. And it triggered a murder in which Inspector Enrique Alvarez very reluctantly – since it entailed work – became involved …

### *Relatively Dangerous*
February 1987

A tourist car crashed in the mountains, killing the driver and injuring the passenger. Since neither man could be immediately identified, Inspector Alvarez was detailed to find out their names – a task which, as Superior Chief Salas was to say later, should have been simplicity itself. But Alvarez's inquiries raised nothing but unanswered questions. Why had the dead man been travelling on a stolen passport? What connection had there been between him and Muriel Taylor, a woman who believed the rich went to heaven, the poor to another place, and her stepson Mike Taylor, trying to open a restaurant? What had he to do with Robert Reading-Smith, possessed of the morals of an alley cat, and Valerie Swinnerton, who had never overcome her grief at her husband's death? And why were these relationships so important …?

### *Three and One Make Five*
February 1984

Inspector Enrique Alvarez, 'human and humane' (H. R. F. Keating, *The Times*), mourning the death of a close friend, was more than usually kind to Tracey Newcombe, a young New Zealand girl living on Mallorca, who had also suffered bereavement when the man she'd been living with was killed as his car went out of control on a steep bend. Despite his sister's disapproval of the liaison, Alvarez soon found that his sympathy and Tracey's gratitude had blossomed into love.

But even in love Alvarez was still a policeman. He couldn't stop wondering if there might be a connection between the death of Tracey's lover and the death of another English resident, who'd drowned despite being a strong and skilful swimmer. When a third Englishman died in an explosion aboard a motor yacht in Llueso Bay he was convinced of it. And where did that leave the rebellious, unconventional Tracey?

Inspector Alvarez has built up a considerable following since his first appearance seven books ago in *Mistakenly in Mallorca*. His latest adventure will delight existing readers and win him many more.

### *Too Clever By Half*
February 1990

Art expert Justin Burnett was found with a revolver by his side and a note in a nearby typewriter. It seemed a clear case of suicide, and Inspector Alvarez accepted it as such. But then Philippa Burnett began to investigate the life of a man who had become almost a recluse, and sure enough some curious inconsistencies emerged. When a second death, seemingly accidental, also revealed some irreconcilable facts, Alvarez was in no doubt that he was dealing with murder.

The death of Justin Burnett had seemed straightforward. Before long the case had become so complicated that it even astonished Superior Chief Salas, who had always maintained that Alvarez could complicate simplicity itself.

### *Traitor's Crime, A*
May 1968

It was hard for John Keelton, Chief Constable of Flecton Cross, to believe that one of his detectives had turned traitor – he was very proud of the high morale of the force. But the facts suggesting there was a traitor had to be faced, and he wasn't a man to shirk his duty.

In the ensuing investigation, the number one suspect was, inevitably, Robert Elwick, the brash young detective, brought up in the slums, who as a boy had been a hooligan. Elwick, rapidly falling in love with Joanna, Keelton's daughter, was spending a lot of money on her. Where did he get the money? Keelton's sense of duty made him ask that question – which in turn made him appear, in Joanna's eyes, to be deliberately persecuting Elwick for reasons other than those he admitted to.

To tell more would be to spoil the excitement of this gripping and moving story. Roderic Jeffries knows the English Law and its many quirks and foibles and, as in his earlier books, uses it here to construct a crime novel of great complexity and ingenuity. Tense and exciting, *A Traitor's Crime* is impossible to put down until the events in the Flecton Cross police station have been brought to their thrilling conclusion.

### *Troubled Deaths*
October 1977

Geoffrey Freeman was possibly the richest and certainly the most unpopular man on Mallorca, both with fellow English residents and with the Mallorquins. When he died from eating a poisonous fungus, there was only one person who was sorry – and several who were openly glad. Any of them could have slipped the poisonous fungus into the mushrooms he was about to eat. To Inspector Alvarez, however, there was one obvious suspect. It seemed an open and shut case.

The trouble was that as one door shut, another opened. Each time Alvarez built up a case against a suspect, it was demolished by incontrovertible evidence pointing to someone else. Nothing was what it seemed. In particular, Geoffrey Freeman wasn't. In unravelling his English past, Alvarez discovered the perfect motive for murder – except that there were other motives nearer at hand. Indeed, there were too many motives. And one suspect particularly whom Alvarez longed to see proved innocent.

Before he arrived at the final solution, Alvarez was reminded many times of a Mallorquin saying that when a Mallorquin dies, he dies straight-forwardly; when an Englishman dies, he goes out like a corkscrew. Roderic Jeffries's ability as a plotter enables him to straighten the corkscrew of Freeman's death to the reader's entire satisfaction.

### *Two-Faced Death*
September 1976

John Calvin had come to the end of the road. It was a road that had brought him to a luxurious villa in Mallorca, and it was strewn with the currency regulations he had broken or evaded and the other men's wives he had taken and discarded. Now, at the end of it, with the law catching up with him, there seemed only one way out. So no one was altogether surprised when a note was found in his typewriter and his body in one of the island's remoter beauty spots. Shot through the head. An obvious suicide.

Only – there were things that niggled Inspector Alvarez. Was the obvious explanation correct? If it wasn't suicide it must be murder, and discreet enquiry soon produced motives enough for that. A number of English residents and Spanish inhabitants had scores to settle with Calvin. Had someone settled a score? But however hard Alvarez tried to fit the pieces of the puzzle together, there were always one or two left over at the end.

Patient, unspectacular, determined, Alvarez set to work, only to find when at last the puzzle was completed that the picture it presented was very different from what he or anyone else had thought.

### *Unseemly End*
August 1981

Dolly Lund, widow of a scrap-metal merchant, may have been one of the wealthiest women on Mallorca, but she certainly wasn't one of the most popular. No one ever wanted to go to her flauntingly vulgar parties – though those invited always went, if only to ensure their share of the lavish hospitality. Then Dolly died, unregretted, after over-indulging at one of her own extravaganzas. Her impecunious young lover inherited virtually everything, and that was the end of that.

Or would have been, if Inspector Alvarez hadn't discovered that Dolly hadn't died naturally. The principal beneficiary became the number one suspect. Only he happened to have been in England on the night of the party as Dolly's own daughter there could testify. Alvarez's efforts to trace his movements seemed nothing but a waste of time. Like speculating why Dolly had left a battered cigarette case to a young man she hardly knew. Or why her Spanish gardener had it in for her. Or why her daughter's pleas for financial help had been ignored. As always, Alvarez found plenty to interest him in the lives and habits of the English colony in Mallorca. And among them he found the murderer.

## JENKINS, CECIL

### *Message From Sirius*
January 1961

Tony Bayre was the outstanding personality of his time. Singer, wit, racing driver, film star, impresario and composer; the idol of the masses, the darling of the intellectuals. It was strangely appropriate that his death should be as melodramatic as his life: he was shot dead on the stage of his own night club, watched and applauded by an audience of his most eminent and newsworthy contemporaries. Superintendent Marc Ireland set in motion the elaborate machinery of Scotland Yard in a blaze of publicity which hampered every step he took. But it was clear that Bayre's unknown killer was as unusual as his victim. Letters were sent to the press, signed 'Sirius', which stated that he had marked down another victim whose actions he judged a menace to civilisation. Events proved that the threats were not idle. Now Ireland faced the almost impossible task of working against time to break a complex and baffling case.

Cecil Jenkins has given *Message From Sirius* a brilliance and sophistication to match the ingenuity and pace of the plot. Gripping and original, it is his first crime novel and an outstanding achievement.

*Message from Sirius* was chosen by Agatha Christie, Cecil Day Lewis and Julian Symons as one of the joint winners of the Crime Club's Competition for the best crime novel to be written by a University Don.

## JEPSON, SELWYN

### *Black Italian, The*
May 1954

A new Eve Gill adventure is an event in crime fiction. This one begins when that old tough, the Commodore, Eve's father, has just flung Detective-Inspector Christopher Smith off his yacht into the sea. As the old man has taken to smuggling again Eve is not wholly sorry to see the last of Smith, but her anxiety is once more aroused when she spots a secret watcher on the marsh, whose binoculars are trained on the yacht and from time to time on her home, Marsh House. Eve makes friends with the watcher, though she cannot place him; he too, becomes involved in the murder which soon takes Eve to London, then across Europe to Genoa. She finds herself in such jeopardy that all her resource and charm and energy is needed to track the man behind Angel's murder, the Black Italian. Selwyn Jepson is a master of suspense. *The Black Italian* is even more exciting than its well-known predecessors, *Man Running* and *Man Dead*.

### *Man Dead*
August 1951

The man in Sarah Gray's sitting-room was dead. Of that there was no possible doubt. There was danger for Sarah in that fact alone. But he was more than just a man who was dead. Even the question of who had killed and why, even the peril to her own good name that he should have been murdered in her house where she had so carefully and completely isolated herself from him, those were unimportant things against the overwhelming fact of *who* he was. He must *not* be found there. But Sarah was not strong enough physically to move him herself; and that was where she made her big mistake. She telephoned Alan Savage and enlisted his help. From that time forward Fear runs softly, inexorably at her heels. Selwyn Jepson joins the Crime Club list with a story that for sheer breath-taking suspense beats all his previous records.

## JOBSON, HAMILTON

### *Evidence You Will Hear, The*
April 1975

A child is missing from her home. As they conduct a massive but fruitless search, the police are grimly aware that three other children who have gone missing in a neighbouring area have later been found murdered. All the evidence indicates that little Angela Murray will shortly make a fourth.

Patient police work gradually pinpoints a suspect – and in doing so lays bare a number of private lives. But even when the police have succeeded in breaking down the resistance of the one witness who for her own good reasons insists on shielding the suspect, he still has an unbreakable alibi.

In a tense court-room scene the battle between prosecution and defence lawyers swings dramatically to and fro, until an ironic denouement results in a violent climax and the shattering of several lives.

Hamilton Jobson, a former policeman with an established reputation for realistic crime stories, brings to bear all his inside knowledge of court and police procedures in writing about the kind of crime that can and does happen, and about ordinary men and women who for a brief moment find their lives spotlighted by the law.

### *Exit to Violence*
June 1979

The body in the ditch was that of a middle-aged man. He had been throttled, and all marks of identity removed. As the routine police procedures of a murder investigation were set in motion, Chief Superintendent Anders had no idea that it was to be the start of one of the most dangerous and exciting cases of his career.

Discovering the killer proved a dead end – almost literally. The motive for the murder remained unknown. Instead came evidence to link the dead man with German terrorist activities, sophisticated weaponry, and a planned kidnapping on the M4 Motorway.

Not for the first time, police hands were tied when dealing with society's most violent elements by the demands of society itself. Even the terrorists were at first in some disarray when they were forced at the last minute to change their plans.

Few authors can rival Hamilton Jobson when it comes to inside knowledge of police operations. In *Exit to Violence* the ex-inspector has written one of his most gripping stories – tight in plotting, sound in procedures, and with some memorable characters.

### *Judge Me Tomorrow*
January 1978

Trevor Grant, narrator of this original and skilful novel, is a prosperous insurance broker, middle-aged, separated from his wife and living happily enough with Helen, a much younger woman whom he is careful not to ask too much about.

Then one of his clients, a dubious property dealer, is murdered, and the client's son, suspected of the crime, disappears. It is Grant who receives a telephone call from the young man asking for help because he has tangled with a wealthy underworld figure. Inevitably, Grant becomes involved and outwits the underworld king so successfully that those near him become the objects of gangland attentions designed to bring Grant into line. Yet the police persist in saying that they have no evidence that would enable them to make an arrest. Never one to be pushed around, and spurred on by reasons he has not disclosed even to Helen, Grant resolves to act independently and there follows a detailed and fascinating account of his preparations for murder.

Meanwhile the relationship between him and Helen has deepened as he at last learns the secret of her past, and as together they face the fact that the question-mark hanging over his own future has nothing to do with crime.

However, when the police eventually arrest the man responsible for the murder of the property dealer, an ironic and unexpected finale gives the solution an entirely new twist.

### *To Die a Little*
August 1978

When a man saves the life of another, a bond is often created between them. So it is with John Bryant and Tom Hannaford. Hannaford saves Bryant from drowning and Bryant, ready to emerge from a self-imposed exile following a tragedy in his life, is deeply grateful. Gratitude blossoms into friendship. Further, he becomes dazzled by Hannaford's magnetic personality and by his attractive wife.

This leads him to co-operate with Hannaford in ventures he doesn't fully understand. Later he has suspicions. Is his new friend a crook? Is he a Robin Hood figure, as he sometimes claims to be? Is he a murderer prepared to frame someone else for what he has done? Or is he a man who would go to any lengths to help a friend in trouble, even to the extent of falling foul of the law?

All these interpretations are possible and Bryant has to make up his own mind. So has the reader, for Hamilton Jobson weaves a compelling story around this enigmatic figure, peeling back layers of a complex personality with a professional skill. This is a murder mystery with a difference, in which loss, for whatever reason, brings home to several of the characters the old saying that 'to part is to die a little'.

### *Waiting for Thursday*
March 1977

When Paula Richmond left home her friends became worried. There was something odd about the way her husband behaved. It wouldn't be the first time the disappearance of a wife had been followed by the discovery of a woman's body … Someone got in touch with the police.

How wrong Paula's friends were is one of the ironies of Hamilton Jobson's tense story, for if your wife is kidnapped and held to ransom, how are you expected to act? And that was what had happened to Tom Richmond, only for the life of him he couldn't understand why. He was a judge's clerk, neither influential nor wealthy. What did he have that could interest a highly organized gang of criminals? It was the police who painstakingly came up with the answer to that.

But the answer itself posed a dual problem: how to rescue Paula and prevent the commission of a terrible crime. Against a background of time remorselessly running out, the detailed police work and incidental investigations, which for better or worse affect so many lives and for which Hamilton Jobson is already noted, are vividly and suspensefully described.

## JOHNSON, SHEILA

### *Goldilocks*
June 1983

'*Goldilocks, Goldilocks, wilt thou be mine?*' Three blondes in a Midland city had no opportunity to say no when they fell victim to a rapist. As a result, the happy teenager became a neurotic wreck; the cool beautician could no longer endure the long-standing relationship that had brought her such happiness; and for the schoolgirl it wasn't a fate worse than death, bur death itself.

As the police hunt for the attacker steps up, women who want only to forget are forced to remember, and the whole city trembles in the knowledge that the rapist may at any moment strike again.

Sheila Johnson's disturbing crime novel is concerned with the effects of rape on its victims' minds and lives – with the glare of publicity, the gossip of neighbours, the attitude of the police, the doubts that assail even their nearest and dearest. She deals sympathetically with all those unsympathetic clichés which the situation too often calls forth, and makes us understand why the police themselves believe that only one in ten of such crimes is ever reported.

There is nothing cosy about this powerful, haunting novel Sheila Johnson has researched her subject with care and presented it unsparingly. We know rape happens. Our attitude connives at concealment. Can we afford our comfortable indifference when the next victim may be someone we know?

### *Of Wilful Intent*
June 1982

The inhabitants of quiet, residential Lynden Grove were being driven to desperation by sporadic outbursts of teenage vandalism directed against their homes. The police seemed powerless to prevent it and were so anxious to avoid wrongful arrests that they leaned over backwards to be fair to the vandals. By the time Philip Butler's wife looked like losing her baby and perhaps her sanity as a result of the violence, the middle-class backlash was poised to strike.

When it did, the results were unexpected. Worse still, dissension broke out among the inhabitants of Lynden Grove as violence bred violence in an escalation of horror. By the time this brief, powerful novel reaches its stunning climax there are no winners, only losers, in this battle which encapsulates a tragedy of our times.

The realism, compassion and compulsive readability which characterized Sheila Johnson's first novel, *Suffer Little Children*, are abundantly evident in her second. They confirm her position as one of the leading exponents of the crime novel as a novel of social realism.

### *Suffer Little Children*
October 1981

Alice Maxwell is 82 years old, widowed, crippled with arthritis, game, and clinging desperately to the house in a condemned terrace which has been her home for all her married life.

The high spot of her day is when the local children visit her: five of them, ranging in age from eight to fifteen, latchkey kids or those otherwise deprived emotionally, who are only too ready to batten on Alice and her meagre pension when they want the extras in life, which they believe are theirs by right. To Alice they represent company, affection, and when her nights become nights of terror because of sinister sounds in the empty rooms overhead, it never occurs to her that these can have any connection with her daytime visitors. They're only children, after all.

What Alice does not realise is that the children are far advanced on the path of delinquency and are already into organized theft. They stash their loot in her condemned terrace, and they aren't going to see themselves betrayed by an old woman they despise. Despite the well-meant interest of social workers and a kindly taxi-driver, Alice's nights of terror are soon equalled and even surpassed by her days.

Sheila Johnson's first novel, written in a white heat of anger, is a shocker. Unsparing in its honesty, mesmeric in its hold upon the reader, it highlights social evils which most of us prefer not to be aware of, while exposing us to the consequences of our indifference.

## JONES, HAZEL WYNN

### *Death and the Trumpets of Tuscany*
February 1988

The 'fifties were boom years for film-makers in Italy. Rome was Hollywood-on-the-Tiber, and at times it seemed as though the whole peninsula was one vast film studio. To the normal chaos of film-making was added an explosive mixture of different nationalities, and a typically international team had been assembled by producer-director Karl Meiser for *The Trumpets of Tuscany*. His cast list also included a guest star, uninvited and unwelcome, whose name was Death.

The first time Death struck was in Venice, and his victim was one of the stars. By the time he struck again the unit had moved to Lucca, and his victim was a bit-player. Emma Shaw, continuity girl, already struggling with constant changes to the script, could scarcely credit that two of those she worked with had been murdered, and the murderer must be someone she knew.

### *Murder in a Manner of Speaking*
March 1989

Elaine Astolat, a shy and retiring young novelist, is persuaded to embark upon a new career as a speaker to literary societies and luncheon clubs, when she becomes a client of the Crispin Speakers' Agency, whose office is in a quiet riverside warehouse on the edge of London's redeveloped dockland. But Astolat soon discovers that even in the innocent milieu of literary societies there may lurk a thoroughly poisonous serpent. Passion is not far below the surface, people are not what they seem, and before long, she finds herself caught in a spider's web of deception and murder, in a manner of speaking.

Readers of Hazel Wynn Jones's first novel, *Death and the Trumpets of Tuscany*, can look forward to a similar blend of entertainment and excitement as she draws an amusing but affectionate picture of literary societies and luncheon clubs, a world where she is clearly very much at home.

### *Shot on Location*
July 1990

Emma Shaw joins a film unit shooting in the little Italian town of San Biagio, and finds herself working on one of the most famous stories of classical history – the Rape of Lucrece. Admittedly the private life of the film star playing the lead is hardly that of a virtuous Roman matron, but Camilla Cowie is big business at the box-office, and that is what counts. Big business – really BIG Business – also has a part to play, and shock waves from distant boardroom battles add an extra dimension to the normal chaos of film-making.

Then a murder takes place, and handsome polyglot Commissario Spada of the local Questura is soon on the trail, together with his well-meaning assistant who has only a nodding acquaintance with English, gleaned mainly from crime novels. But in the end it is Emma, with her knowledge of film-making and her years of experience as a sharp-eyed script supervisor, who unravels the mystery.

Hazel Wynn Jones writes with the authority of many years in the film business. It shows in her insider's view of film-making and in a certain exasperated affection for even the most outrageous of her characters, which readers will remember from her delightful first novel, also featuring Emma Shaw, *Death and the Trumpets of Tuscany*.

## KALLEN, LUCILLE

### *C. B. Greenfield: A Little Madness*
June 1986

Spring, according to *Sloan's Ford Reporter*'s Maggie Rome, is the season in which the first seductive breezes can wreak more havoc than any winter blizzard. When spring arrives simultaneously with a visiting female violinist, the combination turns the *Reporter*'s morally crusty and Olympian editor C. B. Greenfield into a spellbound stranger, and sends Maggie racing off in wide resentment to join an upstate women's peace camp pitched outside a military base where nuclear missiles are stored.

The British violinist turns up at the camp, Maggie is arrested for sneaking onto the base, a nationally-prominent woman of right-wing persuasion arrives to stage a counter-demonstration, the local townspeople become increasingly hostile to the camp, reinforcement of military police are flown in, tensions escalate, and the result is murder. The suspects number in the hundreds.

Greenfield, drawn to the area by the presence of the woman Maggie calls The Brit, is forced to abandon his lotos-eating [sic] and apply himself to detection when the violinist is implicated in the crime. Maggie's accusing finger points directly at her, and it never wavers.

### *C. B. Greenfield: No Lady in the House*
September 1982

No one answers the doorbell of the expensive house; the lady is out, working – and angry. A cleaning woman fails to show up – and never will. Two respectable men threaten mayhem over flood control. An abandoned school building spells trouble. C. B. Greenfield, publisher of the *Sloan's Ford Reporter*, faced with murder, goes off with his cello to play Schubert. And Maggie Rome, his chief reporter, who plays a reluctant Archie Goodwin to his Nero Wolfe, wears out the tyres on her Honda in pursuit of clues that involve an actress manqué and a best-selling author felled by success.

In their third novel, Lucille Kallen, praised as one of the most promising mystery writers in America, displays all her customary wit and charm, but this time Greenfield and Rome ('among the most engaging yoke-fellows in literate detection' – *Observer*), cut deeper into the fabric of contemporary middle-class life.

### *C. B. Greenfield: The Piano Bird*
November 1984

On the tranquil white sands of the barrier island of Sanibel-Captiva off Florida, five people are engaged in pre-production infighting over the creations of a Broadway musical, additional tensions are contributed by a muscle-flaunting charter-boat captain and a crusading female botanist until the situation explodes in the vast wildlife sanctuary, among the herons, anhingas, and alligators. And Maggie Rome, on temporary leave from C. B. Greenfield's *Sloan's Ford Reporter*, stumbles on the body of a murder victim.

Maggie, caught in the crossfire from the volatile suspects, sends an SOS to Greenfield, who arrives on the island paradise as caustic, rumpled and brilliant as ever, to suffer the slings and arrows of easy living as he unravels the tangled clues that Maggie uncovers.

*The Piano Bird* is the fourth in a series of Greenfield mysteries by an author lauded for her wit, literacy, and unerring delineation of character.

### *C. B. Greenfield: The Tanglewood Murder*
October 1980

Charles Benjamin Greenfield, proprietor and editor of *Sloan's Ford Reporter*, has been known to cut an ego to ribbons while giving an impersonation of a kindly country doctor. Maggie Rome, the housewife who is his chief reporter, is an equally lively character and living proof that life really gets going after forty, as readers of *Introducing C. B. Greenfield* will recall.

When C. B. Greenfield and Maggie visit the famous Tanglewood Festival, their bucolic worship of music is interrupted by a murder: that of the first violinist of the Boston Symphony Orchestra, no less. The crime was cunning and premeditated, as much a matter of 'how' as 'who' and 'why'. But of course no murderer stands a chance against Greenfield's brain and Maggie's leg-work. 'All hail to a literate new twosome', said the *Sunday Times* on their first appearance. Once again civilization wins hands down.

### *Introducing C. B. Greenfield*
September 1979

C. B. (Charles Benjamin) Greenfield had spent twenty-five years as a staff writer for a TV news programme, but had grown increasingly annoyed with the news, the network, the city, and the state of the world. Then he discovered that he had saved enough to indulge his romantic image of himself as a journalistic gadfly, and promptly became owner, editor and king of the *Sloan's Ford Reporter*, a small-town weekly with which he intended to vanquish corruption, greed, injustice, disease, and inferior English teachers in schools.

He made a good gadfly; he was irritating, relentless, stubborn, and waspish, though he walked around in the guise of an immensely calm, soft-spoken man. He also played the cello, and employed one Maggie Rome as his chief reporter (part-time), a middle-aged housewife with two sons flown the nest, a husband often away on business, and corresponding time on her hands.

When a hit-and-run accident involving a member of the *Reporter*'s staff prompts Maggie and C. B. to find the villain, their comfortable local community is turned inside out, so that unsuspected skeletons in cupboards begin to rattle. And a prominent local figure disappears…

Not since Rex Stout gave Nero Wolfe his eyes and legs in the person of Archie Goodwin has a more eccentric detective been teamed with a more observant bloodhound. It's the beginning of a great partnership.

## KEATING, H. R. F.

### *Bats Fly Up for Inspector Ghote*
March 1974

Inspector Ghote is in trouble, worse trouble than ever before. When this adventure of the delightful Bombay CID man (you pronounce his name Go-tay) begins he has already been relegated to anti-pickpocket patrol, where he promptly gets himself into one of those fearful fixes which are equally the product of his faults and his shining virtues. But before long comes a sudden topsy-turvy transfer to the Bats, as the specially selected officers of the Black-money and Allied Transactions Squad proudly call themselves. There Ghote is in even worse straits, under compulsion to suspect every move and every word of his new super-efficient colleagues and soon prey too to black whirling thoughts about even his loved ones at home. Yet Ghote has a way of coming out on top, as readers of the eight other novels that both feature him and light up for us the fascinating world of today's India will know. All one asks here, while the hugely rich traders in Never-accounted-for black money enmesh poor Ghote, is: how on earth can he win now? Or will this turn out to be the end of the ever-engaging inspector?

### *Death of a Fat God*
August 1963

The instant the elegant gold filigree doorknob clicked back into place the chief of police turned to her… The long subtle chase was at its end.

'I have kept my promise.'

He took one step towards her.

She put her head in a gesture which did not deny his claim but insisted on one more tiny delay.

But things are not quite what they seem at the start of this detective novel; and later, when murder is committed on the stage of the Flinwich Opera House, they become extremely complicated and bizarre. For the singers who have come to perform at the Flinwich Festival have large temperaments as well as large voices, and cannot readily be diverted from the furious feuds and obsessive quarrels that are essential to their natures. To detect which of these exotic creatures has committed murder becomes the task of Superintendent Pryde of Scotland Yard C.I.D. Luckily, or unluckily, for him, his work falls under the unsparing scrutiny of Mrs. Craggs, the charlady.

The Crime Club is proud to publish for the first time under its imprint the witty author of *Death and the Visiting Fireman*, *Zen There Was Murder* and *The Dog it was That Died*. *Death of a Fat God*, with its informed and amusing glimpse of what goes on backstage in an opera house, will give pleasure to a large public and add to its author's growing reputation.

### *Filmi, Filmi, Inspector Ghote*
November 1976

They call it Bollywood. It has all the showmanship, all the grandiose vulgarity, all the star worship and more, all the nonsense of Hollywood in its 1920's heyday. But it happens in Bombay. So it has an added very Indian flavour. And there is even a Hindi adjective, specially taken over from English, to describe it – *filmi*.

Into the *filmi* world when a star is murdered on the set goes Inspector Ghote. Diffident and delightful, sensitive yet shrewd, he explores its whole crazy life.

Before his case is over he encounters danger. But, worse, the castles-in-air, sky's-the-limit atmosphere infects even his usually modest and sane self. The battle between Ghote that fans all over the world know and love and a Ghote seeing visions of dazzling success is the story of the book.

Since Inspector Ghote last appeared his creator has actually been to the Bombay he wrote about for some ten years without ever seeing. His visit, and the warm welcome he got from the Bombay police, formed the subject of a BBC-TV film in the World About Us series, *The Search for the Real Inspector Ghote*.

### *Go West, Inspector Ghote*
May 1981

Inspector Ghote meets California. The 'diffident, delightful' detective from Bombay is plunged into super-efficient America at its most dauntingly self-confident. A Sindhi businessman, loaded with that most useful of assets in Indian life, 'influence', has Ghote sent across the world to remove his daughter from a Californian ashram retreat.

And, as if this is not trouble enough, in Los Angeles Ghote encounters first a private eye also hired by his employer, who proves to be dedicated with overwhelming complacency to the American way of life at its most blatant, and then the Swami who dominates the ashram, a man who seems bafflingly part miracle-worker, part charlatan.

And Ghote's troubles have hardly begun. On the very night of his arrival the Swami is found dead in his curious abode, windowless and with only one closely watched way out, and there is no hidden murderer and no weapon beside the body.

Before long Ghote has to pledge himself to solve this mystery in order to free the daughter of his Bombay taskmaster from her self-imposed thrall. How did the weapon that slit the Swami's throat disappear from that sealed chamber?

H. R. F. Keating superimposes this classical 'locked-room mystery' on to a situation that provokes teasing question after teasing question about two very different societies and two seemingly opposed attitudes to life. Not surprising, then, that Len Deighton wrote to him: 'Wonderful! I've always said I'd follow Ghote to the end of the earth and here he is in California: what a truly inspired confrontation!'

### *Inspector Ghote Breaks an Egg*
September 1970

Admirers of Inspector Ghote of the Bombay CID will feel as they embark on his newest adventure all the pleasure of meeting again a friend from the past. He is his same delightful self, yet time has brought out new aspects of his character that are fascinating bit by bit to discover.

This time Ghote finds himself sent to a small provincial town, a setting that comes delightfully alive (it is not for nothing that Mr Keating corresponds regularly with the Superintendent of Police of just such a locality in the State of Maharashtra). Ghote's mandate is to investigate a death fifteen years earlier, but he is not simply to find the murderer. He is told to pin the crime squarely on the town boss, a figure of almost despotic power. Nor is this all. The local holy man has embarked on a fast-to-death against any investigation. So as this Swami (who turns out to be a decidedly unexpected person) sinks nearer his end, Ghote, in face of obstruction of every kind, attempts swiftly to find his answer, experiencing in his own diffident yet resolute person the full extent of the adage 'You cannot make an omelette without breaking an egg.'

### *Inspector Ghote Caught in Meshes*
April 1967

An American visitor to India meets death on the road from Bombay to Poona, and almost as soon as Ghote (Inspector Ganesh Ghote, pronounced 'Go-tay') arrives on the scene to investigate there are hints that everything is by no means as it seems. Soon Ghote is swept into a series of adventures, culminating in a long, tense gun-battle in which the well-known erotic carvings of Indian temple architecture play an unexpected part.

In the void which Ghote finds himself in, all his notions of loyalty and what it is are put to new tests. They reveal more sides of a character which has sent critics on both sides of the Atlantic into a positive orgy of analysis. As the tension grows the pulls of half a dozen different allegiances get Ghote, almost inextricably it seems, caught in meshes.

### *Inspector Ghote Draws a Line*
January 1979

A new task for Inspector Ghote, most delightful of fictional detectives, and one yet more daunting perhaps than any he has hitherto encountered. He is ordered off to a vast old house buried deep in the heat-soaked Indian countryside to protect an aged, unpopular and rigidly obstinate judge of the British Raj era, against whom death threats have been made.

In the old house, itself still run in the routines of the Raj of long ago, Ghote soon finds that his chief opponent is not the unknown who has been leaving Justice Sir Asif Ibrahim threatening letters, but the formidable, iron-principled old judge himself.

### *Inspector Ghote Goes by Train*
November 1971

For anyone, crime addict or not, who has ever travelled by train over a long distance here is a book that at once recalls all the tang and excitement of such a journey, while at the same time introducing what is perhaps the most fascinating transport system in the world, the network of Indian railways.

For anyone who has ever read an adventure of Inspector Ghote – and if you have not, both Violet Grant of the *Daily Telegraph* and the late Francis Iles of the *Guardian* unite to say 'you should' – here is that delightful, diffident detective showing yet another side of a deeply human character.

For anyone, crime addict or not, who has ever stifled an inner doubt, as Ghote so often does, his ups and downs are required reading.

Here as he travels across India, apparently engaged on a routine chore (and, 'apparently' is the word), he shows up that aspect of himself that can best be summed up in the phrase 'resolute for common sense', and from the encounter with perhaps the most monstrous of all Mr Keating's gallery of splendidly monstrous criminals he comes off at last triumphant. But how? There is Mr Keating's secret.

### *Inspector Ghote Hunts the Peacock*

February 1968

Ghote comes to London!

The Indian police inspector (pronounced 'Go-Tay') is sent to attend an international conference on drug smuggling; and in cold, drizzling London he is faced with his first case outside India.

It is a very odd case. The girl Ranee, niece of relatives of Ghote who live in London, has vanished – seduced, kidnapped, murdered, so her relatives allege, by the notorious pop singer Johnny Bull. Ghote is hounded by the relatives into spending his few leisure hours from the conference in trying to find Ranee – known for her brilliance as The Peacock.

Ghote solves his case and the solution is shocking and surprising. The high quality of the Ghote stories is here further enhanced by the study of Ghote in London, his comparison of his dream of the traditional metropolis with the contemporary reality. Because it is the real London that Ghote sees in this fascinating and distinguished story.

### *Inspector Ghote Plays a Joker*

January 1969

If anything could seem odder to Ghote than his recent adventures in London (*Inspector Ghote Hunts the Peacock*), it is surely the beginning of his new case – when he is ordered to prevent a murder, the murder of a flamingo in the Bombay zoo.

Dogged as ever by misfortunes of all sorts – he now gets saddled with a sergeant of alarming waywardness – he finds things going disastrously badly as bit by bit he unearths the traces of a monstrous practical joker who seems to be perpetrating a whole series of hoaxes on a choice selection of respectable Bombay citizens, a phenomenon which outrages all his cherished concepts of responsible behaviour.

And before very long he has on his hands a murder rather more serious than just that of a flamingo.

Inspector Ghote and the record of his cases have received more acclaim from the press than any other recent newcomer to the field of classical detection. On the back of the wrapper will be found a selection from the mass of enthusiastic notices that have greeted H. R. F. Keating's hero. Here again is Ghote at the peak of his form, in a story as odd and funny as it is mystifying.

### *Inspector Ghote Trusts the Heart*

November 1972

There is something new in every adventure of Inspector Ghote, of the Bombay CID. This time he is faced with a kidnapping case with a fearful difference. He is sent to keep contact with the kidnappers at the home of Manibhai Desai, rich manufacturer of Trust-X, 'the tonic you owe to your loved ones'. But it is not the Desai boy's life that is set against a huge ransom: it is that of the son of the tailor who works for the family. It is indicative of the new turn to the deeper aspects of Ghote which the book takes that its story is based on a real case (in Japan some years ago).

But, if there is something new here, there is also much that admirers of Ghote will rejoice to find again. There are, even amid the heart-in-mouth tensions, darts of delightful humour, and there is Bombay, that extraordinary city, vividly evoked from top to bottom (not for nothing does Mr Keating keep up a correspondence with an Indian Superintendent of Police).

Julian Symons in his recent history of the crime novel, *Bloody Murder*, says of Ghote that he 'often teeters on the edge of a totally disastrous mistake without ever actually committing it'. Here he is pushed nearer the brink than ever before. Is he indeed taken over the edge? You need to read to the very last page to decide.

H. R. F. Keating is *The Times* crime reviewer and a past chairman of the Crime Writers' Association.

### *Inspector Ghote's Good Crusade*

February 1966

Hailed by the *Sunday Telegraph* as "a most endearing recruit" and by the *New York Times* as "a genuine addition to the ranks of fictional detectives," Inspector Ghote of the Bombay C.I.D. made his first appearance in *The Perfect Murder*. Ghote (pronounced Go-tay) is no superman; yet for all his very human frailties he is determined that justice shall be done and, if possible, be seen to be done.

*The Perfect Murder* won the accolade of the Crime Writers' Association Award for the best novel published in 1964.

In *Inspector Ghote's Good Crusade* Ghote is charged with solving the murder of Frank Masters, philanthropic head of the Masters Foundation, a Bombay home for young vagrants. Harried from above by unscrupulous superiors, mocked at from below by a witheringly clear-sighted gang of urchins, poor Ghote strives to hold to the narrow path of rightness. His case at first seems all too simple when suspicion falls on a huge Sikh thug, a notorious racketeer hitherto untouched by the law. But before long Ghote is confronted by a very awkward dilemma, much sharpened when he is ordered to get the Sikh convicted with or without evidence.

In its ingenuity, in its convincing and unusual setting, and in the quality of its characterisation, *Inspector Ghote's Good Crusade* will be recognised as a brilliant and highly entertaining latter-day detective story – the best work of an English crime novelist with a mounting reputation.

### *Is Skin-Deep, Is Fatal*

May 1965

In the rough, tough world where predatory young Beauty Queens complete fiercely for money, a murder is committed. Police Constable Peter Lassington is soon enmeshed in a complicated mystery – a mystery made more than usually exotic by the acreage of young feminine flesh that is continuously on show at the Star Bowl ballroom, rehearsing for the contest at which the St. Valentine's prizes will be awarded.

Lassington's superior, the officer in charge of the case, is Superintendent Ironside, Ironside – polite, sophisticated, devious – is somewhat sceptical about the charms of the young ladies: his thoughts roam forward to his imminent retirement, and the prospect of breeding domestic rabbits. He is more or less unmoved even by the charms of Lindylou Twelvetrees, whether partially clothed or not.

This detective novel is carefully plotted and firmly set in a world of bizarre values – values that do not appeal to Ironside, the most striking police detective to appear in fiction for some time. The naked competition of the adolescent Beauty Queens provides the background to a strange and exciting murder novel, with a surprise ending. This is a fine successor to *Death of a Fat God* and *The Perfect Murder*.

### *Murder of the Maharajah, The*

March 1980

In the tradition of Agatha Christie H. R. F. Keating has written as his contribution to the 50th anniversary of Collins Crime Club a murder mystery the way murder mysteries used to be. He has set it in 1930 in one of the truly fabulous places of that world, a princely state in the India of the British Raj.

To Bhopore and its superbly opulent Summer Palace come a handful of visitors to meet its outrageous Maharajah and his entourage. There is pretty Judy Alcott from Wisconsin and her laughably scared mother, there to see the huge new dam Mrs Alcott's tough tempestuous brother, Joe Lloyd, has built. There is handsome Lieutenant James Reeve, Indian Army. There is an American tycoon, Henry Morton III, whose ideas of how business should be done show up all the more the lush extravaganza of Bhopore.

At the palace they meet the Maharajah's heir, the sensual Porgy, and his English chorus-girl mistress, Dolly Brattle. They meet the Maharajah's chief minister, Sir Akhtbar Ali, reserved and enigmatic, and the British Resident, aloof Sir Arthur Pendeverel with his dignified little nine-year-old son. And before long they meet also sudden death.

Five people in the palace become suspects, and District Superintendent of Police, Howard, the imperturbable outsider, is called in. Who does he find guilty of the murder of the maharajah?

### *Perfect Murder, The*

September 1964

Inspector Ghote of the Bombay Police is a passionate believer in the methods and honesty he has learnt from the detective traditions of Western countries. Beset by bureaucracy, incompetence and corruption, he nevertheless struggles to apply his beliefs unwaveringly and conscientiously.

It is just his luck that he should be landed with the Perfect Murder case at the outset of his career. In the cunning, ruthless and overwhelming person of the business tycoon, Lala Arun Varde, he meets the antithesis of all he stands for.

To add to his troubles he finds himself saddled with solving the mysterious theft of one rupee from the desk of the Minister for Police Affairs and the Arts, as well as having to entertain Axel Svensson from Unesco, who, when he might be a pillar of support for the logical methods of the West, betrays a deplorable interest in the mysticism and manifold imperfections which Ghote is so earnestly trying to combat.

This crime novel (by the author of *Death of a Fat God*) offers a moving picture of an honest police inspector surrounded by rogues and bullies. It portrays the teeming street-life of Bombay, and presents with humour and goodwill a curious problem of detection that ends in a surprising and satisfactory revelation.

### *Remarkable Case of Burglary, A*

October 1975

London 1871. The rich man in his castle, or at least in his substantial Bayswater villa; the poor man at his gate, casing the joint. For many of the poor, crime represented the only chance of a start in life, and ostentatious wealth the temptation to crime. In an era when the police force was still emergent and the telephone not thought of, a wave of burglaries terrorized the well-to-do. It was more than enough to put ideas into the head of Val O'Leary, Irish labourer. He lacked the tools, the expertise, the capital, but the Soho underworld, then as now, could provide all those. Only before he could acquire underworld backing Val needed an inside contact. And that was where Janey came in.

Janey was the kitchenmaid, the humblest of the servants, subject to the cook, the butler, and beyond them to the Master and Mistress, whose power to dismiss without a character amounted almost to power of life and death. Through her and Val and a rich range of splendidly realized characters, H. R. F. Keating portrays both the upstairs/downstairs world with its personalities and problems, and the careful underworld preparation of a crime. And in both it is the fallible human element which builds up the suspense to breaking-point and contributes to a totally surprising result.

Temporarily, but only temporarily, deserting Inspector Ghote and India, H. R. F. Keating has applied his talent for making the distant vivid to a time removed rather than a place removed. In doing so he tells a gripping story, recreates a fascinating way of life, and asks some pointed questions about chance and character and the effect of one on the other.

### *Sheriff of Bombay, The*

May 1984

Inspector Ghote (you pronounce it Go-tay) is in worse trouble than ever before. Given a task which at first seems merely embarrassing, to escort an aging British film hero on a tour of Bombay's notorious red-light area, the 'Cages', he is before long confronted with murder.

Yet worse than this, the sole suspect is none other than the Sheriff of Bombay, respected holder of the honorary legal office, an ex-Rajah and former Captain of India's cricket team. And he is a suspect only because Ghote has had one swift glimpse of his face – as he hurriedly left a house of ill-fame.

What should our hero do? If he wants proof, what will he have to do? What humiliations will he have to suffer? What sights will he see? What variety of Bombay's citizens will he encounter in all their rich differences? And what will his wife think of it all?

H.R.F. Keating tells us with that inimitable blend of 'wit, gentleness and expert storytelling' (*Times of India)* which has already won a worldwide readership for what must surely be the world's best-loved policeman.

## KEITH, DAVID

### *Blue Harpsichord*

February 1950

*Blue Harpsichord* is not a conventional murder mystery. There is a murder, but the identity of the murderer is known. Another man is accused, but even the uncertainty of this innocent man's fate is not the main theme of the book. This consists, rather, of quite a different mystery and a series of delights, perplexities and near-disasters in the life of an attractive, even though intellectual, young university professor. The characters include a raddled milliner, a bestial balloon-seller, a trio of glamorous wealthy beauties, a pickle salesman and his spirited old bride, an entrancing harpsichordist and an assortment of opera-goers, singers and professors. There are scenes in the back room of a sordid shop and in splendid apartments, in a low-life bar and in a fashionable night-club, not to mention the Central Park Zoo. As a kind of dividend the reader is twice taken to the opera – to *Rigoletto* and the *The Magic Flute*; he is given seats in a box in the Golden Horseshoe so that he is free to come and go during the performance; and he has some rousing good times in the opera Bar during the entr'actes.

## KELLERMAN, FAYE
### Ritual Bath, The
January 1987

Peter Decker, the detective who takes the call, can hardly believe what he hears: there's been a rape at the yeshiva in the hills of his Los Angeles police district. He knows the place: there have been some unpleasant incidents of Anti-Semitic vandalism – but actual violence? *Rape*?

Worse, this Orthodox Jewish community is isolated, suspicious of outsiders, full of odd customs, fat chance they'll cooperate.

They don't. The police are hamstrung. Rina Lazarus, the young widow who found the victim and summoned the police, tries to explain the religious practices that prevent the detectives from following their necessary investigative procedures. But Decker takes matters into his own hands when there is another victim and it becomes clear that this insular community is protecting their own even though it puts them all at risk.

And it's made even more difficult on a personal basis, when he's attracted to Rina and is himself on the prohibited list. To say nothing of the danger he realizes she is in – and refuses to acknowledge.

*The Ritual Bath* introduces a superb writer whose first novel is not only strikingly original, but a wonderfully authentic and perceptive portrayal of the world of Orthodox Judaism by someone who knows it intimately.

## KELLY, NORA
### Bad Chemistry
July 1993

The death of a brilliant young scientist in the Department of Chemistry at Cambridge shocks both the University and the town. As the police scramble to investigate, Gillian Adams, in Cambridge for the summer, finds herself in the midst of the inquiry. Adams, a historian from Canada, is linked to the victim by old friends and to the Cambridge police by her affair with Scotland Yard Detective Chief Inspector Edward Gisborne. Venomous professional rivalries and a clandestine love-affair are only two of the possible explanations for the murder. When a second body turns up, there appears to be no connection. Yet everyone knows that if the two deaths can be tied, the thread will lead to the murderer. While the police sift the evidence Gillian looks at the crime from a feminist's point of view.

In this compelling story, Nora Kelly, author of *In the Shadow of King's*, takes a new look at town and gown, showing us a Cambridge in which science, contemporary mores and old traditions produce a volatile mixture.

### In the Shadow of Kings
September 1984

'*When Alistair Greenwood died that Monday afternoon, it was not from natural causes. Death came with a sudden violence that no one, least of all himself, expected. It must be said, however, that such a death had been – perhaps frequently – wished upon him.*'

In this novel of Cambridge, Alistair Greenwood, Regius Professor of Modern History, first makes his appearance as host at a luncheon-party. Among his guests is Gillian Adams, historian on a year's Sabbatical from the University of the Pacific Northwest, revisiting Cambridge for the first time since she took her doctorate fifteen years before. Plunged anew into the once-familiar ambience, she is struck as much by the changed as by the unchanging. And the best and worst aspects of both seem crystallized in the person of the cold, brilliant, egotistical, aloof bachelor who is her host.

Twenty-four hours later Greenwood is dramatically dead and Gillian is doubly involved: as a witness, and as friend of Edward Gisborne, the Scotland Yard detective, who, having come to hear her lecture, finds himself seconded to the investigation of Greenwood's death.

Nora Kelly's first novel is outstanding: for its skilful plotting, convincing character portrayal, polished prose, and, above all, for its depiction of Cambridge itself. Some may feel that ancient seat of learning has at last a crime novel which does for it what Dorothy L. Sayers did long ago for Oxford in *Gaudy Night*.

### My Sister's Keeper
March 1992

The headlines called it the Sex War on campus, but no one was supposed to get killed. In the charged atmosphere of the University of the Pacific North-West in 1990, as the battle for equality heats up and every skirmish makes the news, a million-dollar endowment and a prestigious fellowship are at stake.

Gillian Adams, historian and feminist, is head of the History Department. She knows the campus inside out and suspects that the frightening series of incidents adds up to more than random acts of sexual harassment. Even so, she is taken by surprise when Rita Gordon, her most brilliant student, inexplicably fails to get the coveted Carver Fellowship.

Gillian sets out to discover why, never suspecting that she will end up investigating a murder, nor that she herself is running into danger. She needs all the detective skills so dramatically demonstrated in Nora Kelly's memorable first novel, *In the Shadow of King's*.

## KEMP, SARAH
(*see also* **Butterworth, Michael**)
### Goodbye, Pussy
May 1979

She was dazed and wandering when the police found her, apparently suffering from severe nervous strain. It was late, she was alone. And her car had gone out of control and grazed a lamp post near her home in London. Could that alone have brought her to such a pass?

The woman in question was beautiful Kate Hawksmoor, brilliant painter, semi-recluse, and widow of a businessman who had died mysteriously when his car went over a cliff in Cornwall shortly before their child was born. Now three-year old Pussy was missing, and far from being frantic, Kate had not reported it, was determinedly blocking all enquiries, and was even prepared to lie about the child's whereabouts. When the police learn that she had recently made a distressing discovery about her husband, their fears for Pussy and their suspicion of Kate grew.

Bit by bit the case against her built up to a frightening accusation. Then she gave the police the slip...not until the last pages of this unusual and gripping murder mystery is the truth about Pussy revealed.

## KENYON, MICHAEL
### 100,000 Welcomes, The
February 1970

You don't expect an Irish robbery to go without a hitch, particularly when the plan is to lift St Patrick's Cross (all five tons of it) from the Rock of Cashel and hold the Government to ransom. Even so, Finn McQuaid and his companions were unfairly handicapped from the start. To begin with, there was Finn's brother Mickey arriving from the States with $200,000, a gorgeous redhead, and the hoods hard on his heels. Then there was the awkward fact that the Government weren't willing to pay ransom and Finn had to find another bidder for the cross. There was the even more awkward fact that his secretary had had no wages for three weeks and she was a girl of spirit. And there was the little matter of Superintendent O'Malley, a police officer with the disconcerting habit of having premonitory dreams.

Of course the police didn't have it all their own way. They were unexpectedly hampered by the electrical union's strike and a couple of unheralded interventions from the Finance Minister, who felt that more than Ireland's historic cross was at stake.

How the cross was finally restored to the Rock of Cashel, what happened to two ransoms from two different sources, and how Mickey McQuaid became a married man, add up to one of the most hilarious crime stories since Michael Kenyon's previous *May You Die in Ireland*.

### Deep Pocket
January 1978

Inspector Henry Peckover, newly translated from vice squad to fraud squad, was confronted with balance sheets and calculators enough to give a would-be poet a headache. He was also confronted with a mountainous file, part of it missing, relating to suspected municipal corruption and ironically referred to as the Molehill file.

But old habits die hard, and Peckover found it easier to take an interest in the murder of a call girl, especially when it looked as though one of her clients might be the speculator who had been pouring money into a new civic development and tossing in a little extra to grease the palms of certain councillors, builders, even possibly the local MP. Besides, the police investigating the murder were curiously unenthusiastic. Almost as though at Scotland Yard there were one or two who had themselves taken a backhander or two …

Peckover might have been above accepting bribes, but he too lacked enthusiasm for the deep pockets of local government officials. Only when coshed on the head did he develop the kind of personal interest which caused him to move seriously into action.

And he did not just move: he charged, aching head down, hands tearing to pieces the rule book, into a world of bribes, blackmail, sex – and a second murder. Through a London heatwave in pursuit of corrupt, motley characters to a chase across a Northumbrian grouse moor, Peckover found himself matching crime with crime, violence with violence, in Michael Kenyon's inimitable blend of fast action, shrewd observation, delicious absurdity and coruscating wit.

### Free-Range Wife, A
July 1983

For nineteen years Vermont-born Mercy McCluskey had been a faithful wife to Hector, Scottish chef at an exclusive French chateau hotel. Then she decided to roam. A private matter and nothing to do with the British police, one would have thought, especially as they order these things differently in France. But when bodies began to turn up as far afield as Portland, Oregon, and Paris, they were of men known to Mercy, and the killer had made his opinion of them puritanically plain. To Chief Inspector Henry Peckover's superiors at the Yard it seemed providential that their nearest approach to a poet should be holidaying with his wife at the chateau.

Strictly speaking, only Henry was on holiday, while Miriam acted as temporary chef during Hector's absence judging a cookery contest, but that was brushed aside. Would he, English-speaking and on the spot, make a few discreet enquiries? Henry would, and the results of those enquiries put him more than ever on the spot.

They also took him to Lourdes, here viewed from an unusual angle since its crime rate is second only to that of West Berlin, and to Andorra, tax-haven and duty-free Mecca for thousands of motorized French. And they took him into Mercy McCluskey's bed, a point on which Miriam kept discreetly silent, perhaps because it enabled Henry to trap a murderer, perhaps because she had lost her voice.

Michael Kenyon has lived for several years in south-west France, which he portrays with a journalist's sharp eye, a kindly wit, and a gourmet's lyrical pen.

### God Squad Bod, The
October 1982

The Reverend Jody James, American preacher and founder of Arkansas's First Born-Again Church of God, is in Britain, together with his angel-robed choir, stalwart red-coated stewards, smiling accountants and smooth publicity machine. He is for 'creationism' and against evolution, adultery, welfare scrounging and a host of other things. At rallies in London and elsewhere fisticuffs have a way of breaking out, when his opponents attempt to shout him down.

But there is nothing criminal about his pastoral activities – except that reporter Peter Ramsden has reason to suspect that the skeletons in the Reverend's cupboard include murder. If he can prove it, it will be the scoop of the year, and the ambitious Ramsden is prepared to put up with a bit of incidental bruising in his efforts to connect the preacher with the fatal accident that Ramsden alone knows was murder.

Unfortunately for him, Chief Inspector Henry Peckover, Scotland Yard's poetic policeman now idling in the Illegal Immigration Squad, is also taking an interest in the Reverend James. Alerted by his wife to the dangers of the Reverend's born-again, money-making evangelism, Peckover has appointed himself a one-man God Squad. And he's not convinced that a scoop is Ramsden's prime objective. It takes a violent climax in Little Rock, Arkansas, to show hunter and hunted in their true colours. And those colours aren't always what you might expect.

### May You Die in Ireland
July 1965

'A castle in Ireland' was the surprise inheritance that led William Foley to go abroad for the first time. Foley, a professor of mathematics at an American University, was both stimulated and apprehensive at the prospect of exchanging the cosy environment of Chicago for the terrors of the Irish bog, even temporarily; though it was rather a relief to get away from his current girlfriend.

The terrors awaiting Foley in Ireland exceed all possible expectation; for Foley, unwitting, had been chosen as courier by men of wicked designs and these designs in turn, were thwarted by Foley's vagueness and amiability. Scenes of helter-skelter violence, mayhem, and pursuit through the city of Cork and the County of Kerry are part of Foley's experiences in Ireland – as is his romance with Mary Casey.

The climax comes at a 'medieval banquet' for tourists at Bunratty Castle.

This first novel is delightful in its wit and characterisation, and in its 'visitor's view' of the land of saints and scholars. Its pace is fast, its romance gentle and charming. It introduces a young writer hitherto known for his journalism only, and takes its title from a traditional Irish toast: 'Health and long life to you, land without rent to you, a child every year to you, and may you die in Ireland.'

### *Mr Big*
February 1975

Scotland Yard has always insisted there was no single criminal mastermind behind the Great Train Robbery. To admit the possibility of a Mr Big who might have gone undetected would be too much to ask of any police force. So in spite of the suspicions of one copper in particular, Charles Taylor, the West London tearaway who engineered the theft of £2,600,000 from the Glasgow-Euston Royal Mail train on August 8, 1963, is secure. He has used his lion's share of the loot to make more money, legitimately, and to climb the social ladder. Twelve years after the train coup he has homes in Grosvenor Square, Kew and Sussex, a property company, a family, and the OBE.

In a sense it was the OBE that started the trouble – that and the boredom of being rich and respectable. When Taylor is blackballed from an aristocratic London club, he revenges himself by recruiting a crony from the train days to burgle the club chairman's two homes. At once, like an alcoholic who has fallen off the wagon, he can feel the urge coming over him and picture a more glittering prize. What more appropriate target than the Queen herself, the peak of the aristocratic pyramid, and that magnificent 158-carat brooch and pendant which Her Majesty wore when Taylor received his OBE? And what more appropriate moment than during one of her own summer garden parties, to which Taylor can now secure an invitation? All it needs is for Mr Big to pick his team, explode a small bomb by way of diversion – and for cheek and sensation the Great Train Robbery will not begin to complete…

With this book Michael Kenyon forsakes the zany wildness of Ireland for the quieter comedy of the English scene, which he handles with a tongue-in-cheek assurance that will delight existing devotees and win him many more.

### *Out of Season*
July 1968

Otto Haller, a young ex-Bundeswehr officer, makes a tourist trip to Jersey. But simple tourism is not the sole reason for Otto's visit. During the German occupation of Jersey in the war, Otto's father had served in that island and Otto himself had been born there. Otto wants to know more about his father.

It is soon clear to Otto that someone does not welcome him in Jersey. Threats and hostile (though bizarre) actions powerfully suggest that he should remove himself elsewhere. But Otto, though far removed from the Nazi generation before him, is no less determined. He wants to find out about his father, and what is happening.

What Otto discovers is the subject of this novel, and very strange and frightening it is. The background is Jersey, its landmarks, weather, attitudes and mores, with flashbacks to the amazing days of the occupation. The wit that made *May You Die In Ireland* and *The Whole Hog* such distinctive crime novels is no less apparent here, despite the earnestness of the young German hero and the sombre backcloth of the occupation of Jersey during the war.

This novel is racy, gay and exciting, with a freakish and utterly surprising development.

### *Rapist, The*
May 1977

Dungoole is a comatose town in County Cork through which strangers pass without stopping or even noticing. Sophie Hotchkiss and her boy-friend, New Yorkers on a working vacation through Ireland and England, stopped there only because the hotels in Killarney were full.

True to form, nothing happened in Dungoole – except that Sophie, six-foot Women's Lib militant, was raped by someone who wore a Mickey Mouse mask, cursed her in a whisper, and carried a knife.

The local police were uncomfortable, to say the least. Housebreaking, arson and grievous bodily harm they took in their stride. But rape was embarrassing. The Yankee girl was embarrassing. Could she not clear out of it, go home, instead of staying put in Dungoole, complaining and stirring things up? Other women came forward, earlier victims of the Whispering Mickey Mouse, or so they claimed. Then he struck again – and again, adding murder to rape.

Dungoole became a town under siege, as the police uncovered offences they never wanted to know about, from poteen-making to faulty car headlights and banned girlie magazines. But who was the rapist? There were indications that if Sophie insisted on staying in Dungoole she might become his victim a second time – and next time a dead victim.

Readers of Michael Kenyon's hilarious exposé of Irish mores have one great advantage over Sophie Hotchkiss: when rape is inevitable, they can just lie back and enjoy it.

### *Shooting of Dan McGrew, The*
July 1972

When two Canadian prospectors from Ivernia Exploration suddenly disappeared while working on a new site in Ireland, leaving no clue as to what success they had so far had in their researches, Henry Butt, a geologist with the company, was appointed to try and solve the puzzle. So off he set for Ireland – and a series of events so unexpected that he was soon to wish he'd stayed at home.

On his first night at the Kilkelly Castle Hotel – the very place from which McGrew, one of the prospectors, had disappeared – Henry meets husband-hunting Kate Kennedy, eighteen times an aunt and eager to be a wife. But before their romance has had time to flourish, it becomes clear that someone is out to get Henry – and increase the number of missing persons to three. And poor Kate just happens to be on the scene whenever another attempt is made on Henry's life. Like it or not, she finds herself well and truly involved – but in what she is not quite sure!

With shootings and deaths galore, the police don't know which way to turn – even with the added advantage of Superintendent O'Malley's premonitory dreams. And Henry doesn't help matters: despite a police escort, he is unable to avoid trouble.

In this hilarious Irish crime story, Michael Kenyon not only defies readers to guess just who is the villain, but follows Kate and Henry through one of the most accident-prone courtships ever chronicled.

### *Sorry State, A*
February 1974

Superintendent O'Malley's assignment is a straightforward escort duty: to bring back to Dublin from the far side of the world the gun-runner Paddy Byrne. In holiday mood he finds himself on a jetplane to the Philippines, unsure where precisely the Philippines are, but delighted by jet travel and champagne at the taxpayers' expense. These are the honeymoon hours. In Manila he finds that Byrne has been allowed to escape. A guerrilla uprising is rumoured, the city is steamily hot and spooky, and everyone except himself, or so it seems to O'Malley, carries a gun.

Then a gruesome exhibit is delivered to him in a parcel. His assistant, Sergeant Maguire, vanishes. A second parcel arrives, thugs threaten, and an aristocratic beauty attempts seduction. In a holocaust of gunfire the rebellion erupts. For O'Malley, dreaming incomprehensible dreams, the assignment has become a nightmare in which one problem is finding Byrne, the other is staying alive.

Michael Kenyon can always be counted on for the light touch. Here it is allied to sharp first-hand observation of the exotic setting to which O'Malley and Maguire are so unexpectedly translated.

### *Whole Hog, The*
March 1967

In the field of spoof-espionage Michael Kenyon was one of the first and best arrivals with his *May You Die in Ireland*.

*The Whole Hog* is even funnier and more Kenyonesque. Its hero is engaged on the experimental feeding of pigs in Illinois State College Animal Science Laboratory, to his astonishment and alarm he discovers one day that one batch of his pigs – those in Series Three (including Humphrey and Marlon Brandon) – have been stricken with a mad euphoria; they skip about their cage, snuffling and grunting. Into their feed has somehow infiltrated a magic ingredient of critical importance to the conduct of the space race and the cold war. Arthur Appleyeard, 'swine nutritionist', finds himself at the centre of a ruthless clash between authorities and spies who think nothing of murder.

Thus begins a story in which this young novelist's gifts are on brilliant display: American mores are amusingly (though kindly) seen through the eyes of the lad from Yorkshire; the characters are vivid; and the narrative moves with elegance, humour and pace towards a macabre and fantastic climax.

### *Zigzag*
October 1981

The job was a simple escort duty. Heathrow to Dublin, and back with the prisoner, a London stockbroker who had secured custody of his daughter by kidnap and had been caught in Ireland. At the Yard the trip was considered a day out for Chief Inspector Peckover.

But Henry Peckover was very much off Ireland, after a spell in the West End with the anti-terrorist squad. The escort duty was not all that simple, either. As Peckover flew in, writing bitter verses, the prisoner escaped.

Dublin's top detective thought Peckover should stay and lend a hand with the porn which was suddenly flooding Ireland – hadn't he had experiences with the porn in Soho in his Vice Squad days? In return, he, Chief Superintendent O'Malley, would throw himself into the kidnap business, which might tie in with the porn wave, not to mention the visiting Yankees – GAGA (Gael-American Genealogical Association), founded by Paddy Gilhooley, oil billionaire. With these bits and scraps possibly connecting, zigzagging into one another, couldn't the Yard and Dublin work together? Hands across the Irish Sea?

In the event, Peckover had no choice. Saddled with a very young, righteous garda as assistant, menaced, mugged, pursued, shot at, pressed into reading the lesson at a Sunday church service, and held prisoner by a blue-movie queen, he persevered through all perils. Yet the greatest peril remained Ireland's green and boozy charm, which quite as much as its lethal propensities threatened to claim another victim.

## KING, C. DALY

### *Arrogant Alibi*
April 1938

In a room of the magnificent house which her late husband, a keen Egyptologist, had furnished in such luxurious style, Mrs. Timothy lay dead – stabbed to death with a curiously-ornamented dagger. The crime is investigated by Inspector Michael Lord and his friend Dr. Pons, the psychologist; but they have to use all their knowledge of crime and its motives to destroy the many alibis with which they are arrogantly confronted.

### *Bermuda Burial*
May 1940

Bermuda, paradise of the West Indies, where all good Americans go to disport themselves on delectable pleasure beaches, is the attractive setting of Mr. C. Daly King's new story. To Bermuda there come Robert Dunskirk and his little motherless daughter Chloe. Robert has been receiving threatening letters from a gang of kidnappers, for his father-in-law is the immensely wealthy Thaddeus Steel, who has persuaded him to take Chloe to Bermuda for greater safety. Detective-Inspector Michael Lord accompanies Dunskirk to keep an eye on would-be kidnappers. In spite of all possible vigilance, Chloe Dunskirk is kidnapped and later the dead body of her nurse is found shot through the head. The hunt is up, and all possible efforts are made to search the island and all boats leaving the harbours. Mr. Daly King writes with his accustomed ingenuity. The story is very convincingly told, the setting is attractive, and the characters in particular are very well depicted.

### *Careless Corpse*
June 1937

You expect something 'different' in a C. Daly King novel. Here he is at his best; and at his best, as one leading critic has said, 'he combines Agatha Christie's knack for that unexpected, last minute turn of the screw with the pyrotechnic erudition of a Sayers or Van Dine.'

A sensational and brilliantly planned series of crimes is the theme of this story. The victims are all members of a party of celebrities isolated, by the whim of a millionaire scientist, on an island amid the ice-floes of the Hudson River. A dramatic setting for a dramatic tale. Michael Lord (Mr. Daly King's popular investigator) has never had such a baffling problem to solve.

### *Curious Mr Tarrant, The*
October 1935

C. Daly King introduces us to an entirely new character in *The Curious Mr. Tarrant.* The book relates the extraordinary adventures of Trevis Tarrant. He is a gentleman of leisure, living in his New York apartment tended by his valet, really a Japanese doctor who accepts this status since he is a spy, a circumstance of which Tarrant is well aware and which furnishes him with some amusement. Tarrant is not a detective, nor a private investigator. He possesses "a curious and questing intellect" which continually urges him to take part in any strange or bizarre happenings that touch him even indirectly. Thus he involves himself in a series of episodes which he investigates and usually solves. His activities are related by a younger man, Jerry Phelan, who makes his acquaintance in the first episode and subsequently becomes a close friend. The *Episodes* which appear in this book are quite outstanding in the field of detective fiction. Each provides the reader with a real brain-teaser, each in itself represents concentrated excitement, and the ingenuity of the solutions calls forth our warmest admiration.

### Obelists En Route
February 1934

The magnificent Transcontinental Express, last word in super-luxury train travel, was making its first trip from New York to San Francisco. For its record-breaking maiden trip – coast to coast in three days, with no passenger stops – the express carried only invited guests. Among them was the famous banker Sabot Hodges, who was accompanied by his daughter Edvanne, his secretary and his valet, four different brands of psychologists, a full-fledge technocrat, a physician, and a prominent member of the New York City Police Department. When the train is nearing Buffalo early next morning a startling discovery is made. The dead body of Sabot Hodges is found in the swimming pool, which was one of the marvels of the Transcontinental. Had he died from natural causes? Or was his death due to a more sinister cause? The train thunders on, and a praiseworthy effort is made to clear up the mystery before the train comes to a final stop at San Francisco. The situation is one of tense drama. *Obelists en Route* is a truly magnificent detective story. It is a worthy successor to the author's *Obelists at Sea*, which was so enthusiastically received by critics and public.

NOTE. – *An Obelist is one who harbours suspicions.*

### Obelists Fly High
February 1935

'You will die April 13th at noon exactly.' This is the dire threat received on a piece of cheap ruled paper by Dr. Cutter, famous American surgeon. He takes it at once to the Commissioner of Police and asks for protection. The story develops into a truly amazing mystery, a large part of the action taking place on board a transcontinental airplane. Mr. C. Daly King is one of the most original writers of detective stories, and his new novel takes us at a tremendous pace through one of the most exciting mysteries the Crime Club has published.

### KING, PAULINE
#### Snares of the Enemy
January 1985

*'Dom Martin came across the school matron's body at a quarter to six on a fine May morning. She lay in the shadows behind a door giving access from the cloister to the monastery. The very fact that she lay within the Enclosure was proof enough that she had been murdered – for she would never, voluntarily, have invaded the monk's privacy.'*

So begins a murder story with a most unusual setting: that of Ambelhurst, a big monastic school, seemingly the last place to harbour violent death. Now every aspect of this vast institution – monks, boys, lay masters, household staff, even visiting parents – comes under the scrutiny of Inspector Evan Morgan, a devout Wesleyan Methodist, who finds he has much to learn about many matters other than criminal investigation in a society where regard for law and order cannot obscure the fact that its values are not of this world.

Pauline King has been closely associated with schools like Ambelhurst – as parent, teacher and housemistress. In this outstanding first novel she brings beautifully to life their organization, characters, humour, above all their ambience, which affects in one way or another all who enter their gates, even for the briefest of sojourns.

### LE BRETON, AUGUSTE
#### Law of the Streets, The
June 1957

This book, by the author of *Du Rififi Chez Les Hommes*, is le Breton's first publication in the English language.

It is a moving story of the back streets and the petty underworld of Paris. Yves Tréguier, scarcely more than a child, has escaped from the Reformatory School. Lonely, penniless and frightened, his only contact in Paris is another youth, nicknamed La Glace, a social outlaw himself. The only means of survival that offers for these two outcasts is scavenging and petty larceny; they move among the riff-raff, the flotsam and jetsam of the Paris streets, among spivs and crooks.

Le Breton movingly describes the relationship that grows between these scavengers of the streets, and the threats to it that develop with the story. For disaster waits round every corner for those who live outside the law, and yet are faithful to 'the law of the streets'.

Le Breton knows the rough argot and the mixture of kindliness and brutality that may be met in the fierce half-world of the streets. His book will be remembered as much for its humane qualities as for the violence that erupts as the excitement mounts.

### LEWIS, ROY
#### Blood Money
April 1973

Charlie Rutland specialized in scandal-hunting. As a journalist on a smart magazine, his job was to search out anything that could be turned into a good smear story. Then, while carrying out some 'investigations' in Yorkshire, his career came to an abrupt and violent end. Had he this time carried his investigations that bit too far? Had somebody decided that Rutland wasn't going to get his story – at any cost? Or had his affair with the wife of a local licensee been the cause? Inspector Crow, skeletal as ever, arrives from Scotland Yard to find a formidable task awaiting him. He uncovers some strange facts connected with Rutland's death – a Nazi war criminal, an old vagrant of the dales, and in the dead man's diary the number of a stolen car belonging to an attractive and wealthy widow. Yet the solution to the mystery seems no nearer.

In *Blood Money* Inspector Crow is involved in one of his most intriguing cases, one that will baffle and absorb the reader until the very end.

#### Bloodeagle
March 1993

When Arnold Landon is ordered to assist at the excavations of the mediaeval site at Birley Thore he is angry, since it means he is forced to break a promise to Jane Wilson to help her in her research.

At the site he soon becomes aware of tensions among the excavation team. More seriously, he finds himself involved in an inquiry by Detective Chief Inspector Culpeper into ancient Viking practices – the background to an investigation into a series of murders committed as far apart as France, Switzerland, East Anglia and Northumberland.

The horrific nature of these killings is brought home to Arnold when he and Jane discover a member of the excavation team murdered in a similar manner, and he falls foul of Culpeper for what the Chief Inspector sees as interference.

While attempting to assist Jane Wilson in her research into Thomas Becket and his supporter William Fitzstephen, and the police in their investigation of the Birley Thore killings, Arnold is drawn deeper into Viking folklore, the role of the berserkers, and the way in which Nordic names can have modern, murderous meanings.

Unfortunately for Arnold, his attempts to help end by plunging him into a chilling confrontation with the vengeful killer whom the police call Bloodeagle.

#### Blurred Reality, A
June 1985

Investigation of a loan-shark who was preying on some of Tyneside's many unemployed brought Eric Ward, ex-policeman turned solicitor, up against a blank wall. Fear kept the victims silent, and without their help no charges could be brought. The unrelated kidnapping of a rich man's granddaughter from her out of work father's custody seemed at first to have no bearing on the case – until Ward discovered that the child's father was one of the very victims whom he sought – vainly – to protect. But who had carried out the kidnapping? And, since no ransom was demanded – why? It was not only the father who suspected a police cover-up. To Ward's surprise, the man asked him to act for him.

Before long the case had become a murder investigation, and Ward had reason to believe that one of the crime empires of the North-East was involved. But did the connections he thought he perceived exist outside his own irreparably clouded vision? Or was he one of those pulled back from the brink of blindness who, in the words of the eye specialist, 'seem reluctant to accept reality. No – that's not it… their sense of reality is blurred.'

This is the fifth novel to feature Eric Ward, who battles against glaucoma with the same courage and determination that he displays in his battle against crime.

#### Certain Blindness, A
July 1980

Things other than beauty are in the eye of the beholder. In the eyes of solicitor Eric Ward there was something odd about Arthur Egan's life and death. But Ward was a former police inspector, and trained to be suspicious. And he could no longer trust his eyesight, since it was a serious eye condition that had led to his resignation from the Force.

Egan's estate comprises a large sum to go to an heir no one knew he had. To settle the estate Ward has first to trace the offspring of this quiet, lonely bachelor, and the photograph of an unknown tomb-stone his only clue. He made no progress in discovering the grave, but he did discover that Egan had served a term for manslaughter committed during an armed robbery on Lord Morcomb's estate. There were indications that the evidence against him had been planted. So why had he accepted his fate?

Egan's estate was not the only one causing legal problems. The present Lord Morcomb was faced with heavy death duties, and Ward's firm had to advise how these could best be handled for the benefit of his lordship's only daughter.

Despite warnings from the senior partner that he was wasting time on the Egan rather than the Morcomb estate, Ward persisted – and his investigations soon led to murder. By the time Ward realized why, he had also learned that where this case was concerned the defect in his vision was mental, not physical, and his life and career were both at risk.

#### Devil Is Dead, The
April 1989

The Mater used an old, cold language in the murderous rituals…and when planning officer Arnold Landon visited the abandoned church with the sinister reputation while undertaking research for a university acquaintance, he was touched by a sense of evil.

But he had other problems facing him: the failure of a planning appeal, a farming community determined to get rid of a predatory gypsy encampment, veiled threats from an obscure religious body, and a Senior Planning Officer unwilling to accept responsibility. Yet over all hung the menace of an ancient medieval superstition, and when Arnold discovers a body at St. Michael's Church it seems a centuries-old devil worship has been revived.

It is the explosive force of a riot at the gypsy encampment, a kidnapping and a further murder that bring events to a head and finally lead Arnold to the truth – to discover that the Devil is not dead and behind the medieval mists of an ancient superstition the roots of a modern evil can lie hid.

#### Distant Banner, A
October 1976

Henry Jones ought to have been good for something more than working as a scaffolder on a building site. He had a degree, the offer of a job, a girl-friend only too eager to settle down to Welsh respectability. Yet he deliberately turned aside. Instead, he worked with O'Hara, violent and drunken; Davies, a drifter; Thomas, untrustworthy; Tommy Williams, deformed and universally disliked. And all of them in a state of running warfare with the foreman, a tough, hard-working Tynesider with a special down on their group.

When one of them was murdered, it soon became evident that there had been considerable organized pilfering from the site. Willy-nilly, Henry was coerced by Inspector Morgan into unofficially working for the police. What was the nature of the racket that had been going on? Who was behind it? The unscrupulous, lecherous local club-owner, whose receptionist lived with O'Hara but who went nowhere near the site? Was the murder the result of sexual jealousy, or the result of thieves falling out?

The solution, dramatic and unexpected, forced Henry to take a long, hard look at the truth – about himself, about his way of life, his fellow workers. Roy Lewis once again uses his knowledge and understanding of his native Welsh valleys to create a convincing background to his latest book.

#### Double Take
January 1975

Takeover by a big American drug company spelt trouble for Coburn Pharmaceuticals, a small English outfit concentrating mainly on research. Personal tension between the English chairman and the American director responsible for security rose sharply when one or two rivals came out with similar products. Could the formulae have been leaked? The Coburn board called in industrial espionage experts Quarmby and Wood.

While Quarmby worked outside getting the history of employees and checking their references, Hood posed as a management consultant and worked inside. Being an unattached bachelor, he also worked on the attractive girl assigned to him as contact, but she blew unexpectedly hot and cold. Hood narrowed the suspects down to four and identified an Italian drug house as the villain. And then the formula for a secret heart drug – the principal reason for the American takeover – disappeared, and with it an employee who was discovered to have forged references. The case seemed conclusively closed.

But this proved to be only the first step in a round of wheeling-dealing which further divided the board. And then murder stepped in, and with it the police and a consequent enquiry into the firm's business. Quarmby and Hood had more than industrial espionage on their hands.

### Dwell in Danger
May 1982

The opening of solicitor Eric Ward's latest case sounded like an arithmetical text-book problem. A farmer had three sons and three farms. He gave a farm to the eldest; the second son was offered a farm but refused; the youngest was given an option to purchase a farm. But the problem proved to be legal rather than arithmetical when Jack Saxby suddenly discovered that his option had been revoked and blamed Ward's firm for the careless error that had enabled his father to do so.

What had set the dour old man against his youngest son? The past played a part in it, and so did the future and an ambitious scheme to bring sea-bed mining to the North-East. And what about the relationship between the three brothers? There too there were unsuspected complexities.

When a highly suspicious death occurred in the Saxby family it was Eric Ward, for all his failing eyesight, who saw most clearly where the guilt lay.

### Error of Judgement
March 1971

Robert Fanshawe, one of Her Majesty's Inspectors of Schools, was not expecting any trouble on his routine visit to Burton Polytechnic until he drove through the gates and found himself caught up in a student demonstration. Half an hour later, while students milled aimlessly around on the campus, he discovered the body of the Principal's pretty secretary in the lift.

Suspicions immediately fell on several of the Heads of Departments, and Inspector Crow, who was called in, had little doubt where the guilt would prove to lie. But that was before a series of unexpected events and revelations had caused his suspicions to shift like a weather-vane, before there were further attempts at violence, and before the student body's unrest, fanned skilfully by one of its leaders, had blazed into open revolt.

As Crow hunts his man through the labyrinth of the deserted building, a final twist of fate brings yet another situation to his attention, and Crow realizes that the HMI's role of trained observer has its uses when there is a case of murder to be solved.

Roy Lewis, who is himself an HMI (Business Studies in Further Education), has won high praise for his two previous novels, *A Lover Too Many*, which introduced Inspector Crow, and *A Wolf by the Ears*. His third can only enhance his reputation and increase his readership.

### Fenokee Project, The
October 1971

Everything was going well for Ben South and his partner. With the signed contract for the Cornelius hotel chain in their pocket, their future as building contractors looked bright. Then a letter arrived for South from Canada, and overnight everything changed.

Seven years earlier South's young wife had died in the snows of Western Canada when her car skidded on a lonely road. The verdict was accidental death, but now South had cause to wonder: was it murder? He sets of for Canada to find out.

Aided by Rider, an enquiry agent, he discovers that the only witnesses called at the inquest have all come into money and moved away. Several have died in apparently suspect circumstances, and what he learns from the survivors makes him more than ever determined to uncover the truth about his wife.

But when he tangles with tycoon Grant

Sterling and his Fenokee Project, a vast complex of dams, South realizes that he is up against something much bigger than a single murder and that even his own business in England is at stake.

High above the frozen dam, in the icy grip of a Canadian winter, the final drama is played out in one of Roy Lewis's tensest and most compelling crime stories which will lay a cold grip on the reader from the start.

### Fool for a Client, A
November 1972

There's an old saying that the lawyer who defends himself has a fool for a client. Alan Armitage, rising young Q.C., hoped it wasn't true when he decided to defend himself on a murder charge.

It had seemed harmless enough to take Jean Westlake home from a party. Harmless enough, when he discovered she was a struggling law student, to allow her the use of his flat and library while he was in chambers and his beautiful actress wife was in America. And then, on the night of his wife's return, Jean is found dead in compromising circumstances. Worse still, her apparent suicide is quickly shown to be murder.

Horrified, Armitage sees the case build up against him, his most trivial actions made to seem of sinister import as he is interrogated by an obviously hostile police inspector. His friends, even his wife, begin to believe in his guilt.

Only one person is convinced of Alan Armitage's innocence, and that is Alan himself. Hence his decision, against legal advice, to act as his own defence counsel in a trial filled with legal niceties and dramatic, edge-of-the-seat suspense.

Roy Lewis has already made a name for himself with legal crime novels – *A Lover Too Many* and *A Wolf by the Ears*, to name but two. Here his expertise is skilfully deployed in the interests of a compelling and intricate story whose denouement will surprise and satisfy.

### Gathering of Ghosts, A
November 1982

There seemed no reason why the planning application to take over run-down Rampton's Farm and build a leisure complex in its stead should not go through smoothly – until Arnold Landon from the planning department visited the site. For Arnold was a man who understood wood, and the timber-framed building revealed to his discerning eye unmistakable evidence that it was unique in the Northumbrian countryside.

But at the meeting of the planning committee Arnold found himself vigorously opposed by Professor Fisher, a university medievalist who swore the barn was later in date, of a common type, and not worth a preservation order. Revisiting the barn to check on the information it had vouchsafed to him, Arnold found that an interested party had also revisited it – and had not left it alive.

The barn was slow to yield its secrets, but Arnold's persistence in the end won through. The old building revealed not only its history but the secret for which someone had been prepared to kill. As its ghosts gather, it becomes clear to the police and to Arnold Landon who the murderer is.

### Inevitable Fatality, An
September 1978

Mel Chapman was a successful young business consultant, accustomed to operating smoothly and independently in a world of mergers, takeovers, rationalization and dog eating dog. He was also accustomed to the unexpected. But although he anticipated

some boardroom opposition to the proposals, when he was hired by Quarta to advise them on the acquisition of a new television development technology, he hadn't expected the artificially created snags that soon occurred. Nor that his former girl-friend would be a member of the Quarta board, by virtue of having married the chairman as his second wife.

And Chapman certainly hadn't expected the convenient, ostensibly natural death of the chairman, and the disappearance of another director who left only bloodstains behind. Least of all did he expect that the financial attacks on Quarta and an advanced technological development would prove to have their roots deep in the past, and that he himself would have to play detective if his proposals were to be carried through.

Roy Lewis's consistently excellent crime novels are gaining acclaim from the critics and a steadily increasing readership. His latest is an intriguing and knowledgeable glimpse of the world of big business and the passions that can reign behind impersonal corporate facades.

### Kind of Transaction, A
December 1991

The arrival of Malaysian businessman Simon Chan in the North-East brought the prospect of business for Morcomb Estates and an assignment for solicitor Eric Ward: find the missing executive Harry Staughton. At the same time he was given another task by the merchant bank on whose board he sat reluctantly: raise a defence for Artaros SA against an aggressive takeover bid by an American arbitrageur with a shady background.

Neither task was clear-cut: Straughton's complete disappearance, doubtful dealings over the sale and chartering of the *Arctic Queen* to Chan's company, and Eric's own uneasiness over the dirty tricks approach called for by the re-emergence into his affairs of the shady lawyer Charles Davison.

When a body was washed ashore in Spain, the trail led Eric north to Berwick. There he stumbled upon a second murder and had to battle for his life against a professional killer.

But it was in the court-room that the twisted skeins were finally unravelled. Matched against his old legal adversary, Eric discovered just what kind of transaction could go on between three amoral men …

### Limited Vision, A
August 1983

To Eric Ward, solicitor and former police officer recovering from a serious eye operation, the offer of a new, highly paid job seemed unbelievable. A successful entrepreneur, wanting to re-establish himself in the North-East in what he euphemistically called the 'entertainment industry', was anxious to employ Ward to negotiate contracts and planning permission on his behalf. Determined to overcome his own physical limitations, Ward accomplished the journey to London and back on his own, though it was not without mishap.

Then came the phone call. It informed Ward that what had befallen him was no accident and that next time it would be worse. Invariably, Ward's thoughts turned to the threats he had received in his days as a police officer. Was one of his old enemies on his trail?

It took murder to bring it home to him that he was caught up in gangland warfare. And it took one of the most frightening episodes of his life to show him that the limited vision that prevented him from seeing who his enemy really was had nothing to do with his eyes.

### Lover Too Many, A
September 1969

When Peter Marlin discovers his wife strangled in their sitting-room, suspicion falls heavily on him. After all, she had only recently returned home after an unexplained absence of several months; and during that time Peter had taken up with someone else. After the inquest the firm of solicitors in which he works asks Peter to relinquish his partnership. His handling of the Gaines family trust is also criticized, and then Inspector Crow of Scotland Yard arrives to make further enquiries.

Peter's immediate reaction is to show that he was not implicated in his wife's murder. But no sooner has he discovered that she had had a lover, than he finds himself with another corpse on his hands.

Blackmail, and a take-over bid involving the Gaines trust holdings, are only two of the complications that ensue before Inspector Crow finally makes an arrest – and the truth emerges: there is a lover too many somewhere.

### Men of Subtle Craft
September 1987

Asked to assist a historian with research into the movements of a medieval mason in the north-east of England, Arnold Landon, planning officer with a particular interest in ancient buildings, was left in no doubt by his superior that he was to keep his personal activities distinct from his work. That work involved a planning application from Kilgour Estates, owned (although the ownership was disputed) by local magistrate Patrick Yates.

Yates was disliked by many: by his tenant farmers for allowing their farms to fall into disrepair; by some he had sentenced for his harshness; by his housekeeper whom he humiliated; by others as diverse as the historian Arnold was assisting, and the cousin who claimed ownership of the estate. When Yates emerged victorious in the lawsuit, it seemed matters must come to a head. It was Arnold's misfortune to find Yates dead in his own stableyard by means such as a medieval mason might have used.

As Arnold pursued his researches into twelfth-century Ailnoth, the man of subtle craft, he was confronted by a range of clues to Yates's murder. his knowledge of human nature enabled him to discover the killer – but only after himself narrowly escaping death by medieval means.

### Most Cunning Workmen
November 1984

After planning officer Arnold Landon's interest in medieval buildings was so dramatically demonstrated in *A Gathering of Ghosts*, he was requested by a local heritage society to catalogue the papers at a lovely old manor house in Northumbria, a disputed inheritance which was up for sale and on which a US computer firm had already been granted an option.

Landon worked in a difficult atmosphere. Not only did the principals of the computer firm descend on the manor to make immediate plans for its use, but the rival claimant, also an American, put in an unwelcome appearance. Landon's sympathy was with the young woman whose home the manor had been, but he was as powerless to help her as he was to help the aging head of the computer firm, whose position was suddenly threatened by a skilfully plotted coup.

Landon's discovery of a secret – perhaps not so secret – passage was eclipsed by the discovery near the manor of a body, which brought the police on the scene. But the passage ultimately led Landon not only to secrets within the manor's walls, but to secrets within the company boardroom, and to the identity of the murderer.

### *Necessary Dealing, A*
December 1989

It began at a business function attended by Eric Ward, Newcastle solicitor and now part-time director of a London merchant bank. Eric had recently refused to represent his wealthy wife in her dealings with a Tyneside entrepreneur, but when the attractive woman chairman of a company facing a management buy-out approached him for advice, he saw no reason why he should not at least listen.

Eileen O'Hara was suspicious of the bid but her managing director and his allies had financial backing and her board were divided. When there was a rival bid, it was left to Eric to discover that the former company secretary had met a violent end; that O'Hara and a member of her board had until recently been lovers; that the arbitrageur who now entered the lists had his own reasons for discomfiting the rival backer; in short, that all had scores to settle unconnected with the business in hand. And it was left to the police to uncover a murder, with Eric the last known person to see the victim alive.

As tension mounts in the boardroom and between Eric and his wife as she watches him drawn ever deeper into a situation that threatens both their own relationship and his position with the bank, Eric learns bitterly the kind of dealing necessary to win a boardroom battle, to save a marriage – and to uncover a murderer.

### *Nothing But Foxes*
June 1977

A crisp autumn morning and the Hunt in full cry across the Northumbrian countryside. From a view to a death ... And a death it was, when the Master of Foxhounds and several of the Hunt's socially prominent members discovered the body of their most notorious local opponent in a bush.

Investigating the socially prominent can be tricky, and the Chief Constable decided to call in Scotland Yard. Which brought Inspector Crow to the wide, sweeping countryside of Northumbria, and confronted the young, eager, local inspector with an approach to crime he had not met before. But Crow, for all his intuition, was hamstrung by his own preconceived ideas about victim and suspects. Only when patient police work revealed that there were unexpected sides to the do-gooding victim and those who might have killed him did Crow begin to perceive another possible interpretation of events.

With remarkable skill, Roy Lewis builds up a series of cases and allows Crow and the local inspector to demolish each in turn. One case alone resisted demolition, and another murder seemed to clinch it. But Crow had become wary of 'seemed'.

### *Of Singular Purpose*
October 1973

Andrew McDonald had a Highland farm and three sons to inherit it. But the eldest was tragically killed and the second enlisted as a mercenary soldier in the Congo. It was left to the youngest to take over the farm – and to marry attractive Sandra Wise.

For some reason the marriage aroused the disapproval of the family solicitor – something his nephew, Harry, could not understand, especially as he himself was more than half in love with Sandra. And then the second brother, Grant McDonald, returned home.

Soon an act of vengeance for an incident in Grant's mercenary past had shattered the peace of the Highlands and brought tragedy to the farm. Young Harry Wilson, a witness to the horror, was thankful when his own legal work took him abroad. And there in Brussels a chance professional encounter led him to a reassessment of Grant McDonald and his past.

But this only served to deepen the mystery surrounding the farm and the people who lived there – a mystery as impenetrable as Highland mist. Until Harry stumbled on a secret that laid bare the singular and terrifying purpose of all that had puzzled him.

### *Once Dying, Twice Dead*
May 1984

A journalist on the trail of a story about badger-baiting in the North-East accidentally finds himself on the trail of a much bigger story when his scuffle with the hunters uncovers the body of an unknown man.

Eric Ward, solicitor and former police officer, is engaged to represent him in his subsequent action against his attackers, and thus learns of another trail the journalist is interested in: that of Lansley, a crooked Newcastle entrepreneur now living in the South of France. By coincidence, Ward is obliged to visit Lansley in connection with a claim on behalf of his own wife's considerable estates, and events in Marseilles lead him to suspect that while Lansley's Northumbrian activities may be dormant, they are by no means dead.

Ward's inquiries, which include the uneasy task of helping his ex-wife whom he has not seen for twenty years to trace her missing husband, demonstrate that the most disparate events can prove unexpectedly interconnected. He also learns that the making of such connections can be a dangerous business, and that a dead man can die not once, but twice.

### *Part of Virtue, A*
September 1975

Murder seemed grimly out of place amid the peace and beauty of the Cotswolds, but Chuck Lindop was undoubtedly dead, his head bashed in, at the caravan site he ran as manager, and Inspector Crow was there to find out why.

Around the time Chuck died there had been a lot of coming and going at the van site, because young Andrew Keene's wife had decided to bring their first child prematurely into the world. Crow didn't relish the idea that so far as means, motive and opportunity were concerned, Andrew was the prime suspect on his list. But Chuck's ex-girlfriend and her current 'protector' had also been present, and the protector was a violent man. Also present was a worker from the local stone quarries who had a long-standing grudge against Chuck Lindop and was intent on doing whatever damage he could.

There had also been a spate of burglaries in the district in which Chuck might have been involved. He certainly had money, or so his wife believed when she turned up unexpectedly to collect it. And someone – possibly Chuck – had been conspiring with the thieving gipsies, in town for the annual fair.

The case was complex and provided Crow with some challenging human problems, which he solved, as he solved the murder, in his own inimitable way.

### *Premium on Death, A*
July 1986

'The bottom line is,' the accountant said, 'you have by way of disposable assets some £3.5 million. Immediate.'

Eric Ward, Newcastle solicitor, had already discovered that marriage to a wealthy young wife had its pitfalls. Now, with this dramatic increase in Anne's fortune, the pitfalls yawned like chasms. He had always refrained from becoming associated with Anne's financial affairs, but when she bought into a merchant bank he could no longer stand aside if his marriage was to survive.

Reluctantly, he accepted a seat on the board of the bank's Tyneside subsidiary, only to find the company was slated to pay out a vast insurance claim for a ship sunk in Spanish waters. And marine insurance was something Eric knew about. Convinced that the claim was fraudulent, Eric refused to pay. To justify his refusal to his chairman, he was obliged to investigate. The trail took him to Spain, to an encounter with an old opponent, and to one of the most terrifying half-hours of his life, before the truth about the sinking of the *Sea Dawn* and the mysterious deaths that followed was established, and Eric and his chairman were again face to face.

### *Question of Degree, A*
July 1974

The woman whose body was found down a South Wales coal mine was a stranger to those parts. She had come from the north-east in search of a missing husband, and with the help of an enquiry agent had found him. It did not take the local police long to put two and two together, especially when the husband confessed to the crime.

But at the trial an able defence counsel tore the police evidence to shreds and the case was thrown wide open once again much to the relief of Inspector Crow, who had always distrusted that confession. What puzzled him was why it had ever been made.

To find out, Crow travelled to Canada, where the origin of the mystery lay. What he learned there, and how it affected the lives of several members of a close-knit Welsh community, forms the substance of Roy Lewis's suspenseful book.

Himself a Welshman from the Rhondda, Roy Lewis has drawn skilfully on a background he knows to create an unusual and thoughtful crime novel which will win more admirers for the astute and compassionate Inspector Crow.

### *Relative Distance, A*
March 1981

Wolframite had been mined on Dartmoor in the past, though never profitably. Now, its increasing industrial importance had led to an old mine being reopened by an American funded enterprise, with the backing of the local MP.

He it was who was responsible for getting Scotland Yard's Chief Inspector Crow dispatched to Devonshire when Norman, the firm's over-conscientious Environment Coordinator, was found murdered on the site.

Crow soon discovered that there was strong local opposition to the mine because it caused heavy traffic through a village where a girl had recently been knocked down. Ecology and antipollution interests were also opposed, and so was a local land-owner who had unaccountably reneged on a profitable agreement to sell some land and was holding up development by every means in his power. The zealous Norman might have fallen foul of any of these elements. He might even have fallen foul of one of his colleagues, for all records of his activities in the two weeks before his death had vanished, and that seemed to indicate an inside job.

Then all Crow's theories were exploded by a demo which threatened the official opening of the plant, and the detective discovered that the relative distance between events seemingly unconnected could be very deceptive indeed.

### *Salamander Chill, The*
May 1988

'It's not *illegal*, but it's getting borderline,' Eric Ward said. The Newcastle solicitor was still uneasy on the board of Martin & Channing, merchant bankers, and never more so than now when the bank had been called in by the Salamander Corporation to help fight off a hostile takeover bid. The defensive strategy involved a move known as the Salamander chill. If successful, it would preserve Salamander for the American entrepreneur who had founded it; if not, it would breach the City Code. It was Eric's task to point out that uncomfortable fact – and incur the founder's hostility.

But Eric soon had problems nearer home. The acquisition's adviser to his wife's company, Morcomb Estates, was charged with the murder of his fiancée, found strangled in her London flat, and asked Eric to represent him. The case against the young man looked black, but just as Eric was uncovering on Tyneside some interesting facts about the girl's background and associates, the Salamander chill began to fail and he was again summoned to London for a difficult meeting.

Suddenly Eric found his roles intertwining, but not even as he faced his own chairman over the bank's role in the defence could he have foreseen the startling outcome of his involvement in the Salamander chill.

### *Secret Dying, A*
July 1992

Advised to leave the Planning Department as a disruptive influence, Arnold Landon found his new job in the Department of Antiquities and Museums got off to a difficult start: he had to rewrite a brochure on the Northumberland pele towers for a colleague who had mysteriously disappeared.

When he was also asked to help date a medieval painting which had been hidden under a false ceiling his problems increased, for he found both tasks were linked in some way to a double murder at Craster, on the north-eastern coast.

The reappearance of his colleague, now suspected of the murder of his wife and her lover, and hints of occult practices, only drew Arnold further into a network of secrecy and death that involved ancient religious beliefs under the mantle of the Knights Templar.

But the fourteenth-century past was to mingle with the murderous present once more before Arnold discovered the cryptic secret of the de Bohuns. And by that time the murderer had him entombed, and Arnold was in danger of his life.

### *Secret Singing, A*
June 1972

Solicitor Charles Lendon wasn't exactly the most popular person in the small town of Canthorpe. The ruthless pursuit of his career and the local ladies, and the closure of the right of way through his land, had made him many enemies. So when he was found at the Old Mill with a steel skewer in his heart there was no shortage of suspects.

The skeletal Inspector Crow, who has already appeared in *A Lover Too Many* and *Error of Judgment*, arrives from Scotland Yard to find the local police still unsuccessfully investigating another murder—the brutal killing in Kenton Wood of a nine-year-old girl, a direct result of Lendon's closure of the right of way. Could there be a connection between the two killings? Certainly, many people had blamed Lendon for the child's death, and the child's father had sworn revenge.

Gradually Inspector Crow discovers that several of those closest to Lendon had good reason to hate—and perhaps murder—him: his mistress/housekeeper; her mentally unstable brother; a former legal colleague; even the boy-friend of his attractive articled clerk, Cathy Tennant.

Roy Lewis has once again produced a skilfully plotted tale that keeps the reader continually in suspense.

### Seek for Justice
September 1981
Alan Fearnley stood apart from the mourners at his brother's funeral, uncertain of his welcome in the Welsh valley after an absence of fifteen years. Only Jeff's death in an accident had brought Alan back to the restrictive rule of Aunt Matty, from which Jeff had never escaped. Now, a successful accountant, at a crossroads in his professional and personal life, he had returned to his native Wales and found himself, almost immediately, cast in an unfamiliar role. Alan was used to scrutinizing figures; now he was asked to scrutinize facts, for someone was claiming insistently that Jeff's death was no accident.

An unsuspected talent had brought Jeff fame and fortune in the competitive world of professional darts. Greater fortune lay ahead – witness the mysterious cheque for £5,000 among his papers which he had inexplicably left uncashed. But other people's fortunes also depended on Jeff's accuracy and skill in placing his darts. Was that why his game had recently deteriorated? Alan soon learned that the pressures on professional players can go beyond the simple need to win.

It is a new world to Alan Fearnley, but one thing becomes absolutely clear: more than one person had an interest in putting a stop to Jeff 's career.

### Trout in the Milk, A
January 1986
'Arnold,' the Senior Planning Officer intoned, 'we have a problem.'
Arnold London, employed in the Planning Department, sensed what he was in for and his heart sank. In fact, it was not one problem but several. For not only was the owner of a decayed eighteenth-century mansion applying for permission to erect, against the wishes of his heir, a sawmill which would allegedly restore his fortunes, but a consortium of Northumbrian businessmen, intent on profit thinly disguised as a work of community benefit, sought to virtually destroy Penbrook Farm. And the farm, a genuine medieval survival, had a stout defender in the person of the eccentric Mildred Sauvage-Brown.

Much as he sympathized with the lady, Arnold could not approve of her methods, though he approved of the businessmen's still less. When the clash of interests resulted in a violent death he was once again embroiled in an investigation which brought publicity to the Planning Department, and publicity, in the Senior Planning Officers eyes, was a Bad Thing.

If he had known that his assistant was secretly attending an illegal auction on the Holy Island of Lindisfarne, he would have been apoplectic. Yet it was there that a number of disparate clues came together and enabled Arnold to pinpoint who was responsible for that violent death.

### Uncertain Sound, An
February 1978
Crime was the last thing Frank Hales had ever expected to be embroiled in. Partner in a firm of Durham solicitors, and childlessly married to the daughter of a thrustful north-country tycoon, he led a life that was settled, uneventful, and more than a little dull. Yet from the moment he was interrupted in the midst of a party at home with the news that his senior partner had vanished after milking a trust fund, he was plunged into an unfamiliar world.

The first task was to find his missing partner. He traced him to a secret love-nest and there the man was—dead. Moreover, the prostitute he had been associating with had also vanished, and there were indications she might have been murdered too. In an effort to save the firm and with it his career and his marriage, Frank concealed his partner's peculation from the police, hoping his rich father-in-law would lend the money to meet immediate liabilities. But the old man's terms were high and led to a further unacceptable discovery. In desperation, and at his wife's suggestion, Frank engaged a private eye.

His troubles did not diminish. To suspicion of his wife's relationship with the man was added the realization that he was being framed. Roy Lewis's legal training, and his knowledge of the north-east, where he lives, are cleverly combined.

### Violent Death, A
July 1979
Murder is not a subject investigated by Her Majesty's Inspectors of Education in the normal course of their duties. It was certainly not something that Robert Fanshaw, technically retired HMI, was prepared for when he inspected Sinclair School in Northumberland, even though it was what used to be known as an Approved School. Its sixty boys were among the toughest delinquents from the Midlands, and their presence amid the peaceful beauty of the Northumbrian hills was fiercely resented by many local residents who were anxious to see Sinclair closed, or at least in the hands of a more hard line headmaster, a man such as deputy head, Ted James.

The staff were divided on this issue. And then James disappeared, only to reappear with his neck broken – which brought home to Fanshaw what a violent world he was in. The violence seemed epitomized by one boy, a remarkable character, who polarized staff attitudes and seemed a strong contender for the title of School Murderer.

During his week at Sinclair Fanshaw found himself investigating many things outside the brief of an Inspector of Education, including the expression in a woman's eyes and the nature of an old guilt which persistently haunted him.

### Wisp of Smoke, A
May 1991
Vagrant Foxy Fernlea became an obvious suspect when ex-army officer Kenneth Andrews was found shot dead in his remote home. Foxy on his own admission had visited the house, and Chief Superintendent Redvers was only too anxious to wrap up the case. But he had reckoned without those who believed in Foxy's innocence; he had reckoned without the misgivings of his number two, the dedicated Inspector Greybrook; and he had reckoned without planning officer Arnold Landon.

Arnold, whose interest in life was mediaeval architecture, was approached to take on a book Andrews had been writing on the subject. Unfortunately, Andrews had also been engaged on another, less innocuous work, which certain local interests were intent on suppressing. Arnold, deemed guilty by association, found himself falsely accused of fraud and suspended from his job.

Together with Jane Wilson, a historical novelist who shared his interest, Arnold set about clearing his name. He never dreamed that before long he would be involved in a paedophile murder inquiry, the discovery of an old crime, and a flight for life across the Durham moors.

### Witness My Death
March 1976
The murder of a pregnant girl in a Welsh mining valley, and the subsequent arrest in what the police considered an open and shut case, was a double blow to Taliesin Rees, who had been the local doctor for as long as many of the valley's inhabitants could remember. Both accused and victim were his patients.

Rees, a widower, was a dedicated doctor, loved for his humanity. He blamed himself for having failed these two patients, and also for difficulties within his partnership, which a disputed decision was threatening to disrupt. Against this background, he found little comfort in the victory of a small environmentalists' group on two important issues. There was sometimes a smell of corruption about the planning in the valley, where powerful local interests were at work.

Despite the police view that the case was closed, Rees set himself to investigate the death of the girl who had made such a strong impression on him, and who was, he felt certain, no conventional victim of her plight. His inquiries led him into sensitive areas, into confrontation and deadly danger, as the corruption of man and nature in the valley took a dramatic and inexorable revenge.

### Wolf By the Ears, A
May 1970
Roy Lewis's specialized legal knowledge is skilfully but fairly deployed in this cunningly plotted whodunit, which is as full of surprises as the law itself.

After his parents died intestate in a fire, Stephen Kirk stood to inherit a fortune – until doubts were cast on his legitimacy. Davie Centre, a recently qualified solicitor, found himself charged with defending Stephen's claim. Patiently, he set to work to unravel the Kirks' complicated family history. Then, just as he seemed to have succeeded, with the aid of an able enquiry agent, his client was arrested on a far more serious charge.

Was Stephen Kirk telling the truth when he claimed he could remember nothing of his actions on the night his parents died? Putting aside his own very real doubts on this point, Centre set out to prove that he was. In doing so, he discovered that a number of people had had an interest in removing Harry Kirk, whose death opened the way for a big local development scheme, in which another of Centre's clients was head over heels involved. Suddenly there was no shortage of suspects. But the wiles of the law were a match for the murderer among them.

## LITTLE, CONYTH
### Black Coat, The
May 1949
Anne Hillyer was just another small-town girl coming to the big city to make good – wearing the time-honoured flower in the buttonhole for recognition by a friend's boy-friend coming to meet her. But no small-town girl, even as pretty and attractive as Anne, ever met with more fantastic adventures in a gay metropolis. It starts with her being picked up by the wrong young man and deposited at a bizarre private hotel. Shedding artificial roses all the way – not to mention artificial hands and a genuine seal coat – Conyth Little sweeps us along in pursuit of murder on floods of martinis and light-headed laughter.

### Black Corridors
March 1941
Do you remember the [sic] Black Gloves? Conyth Little is even more successful in her latest detective novel, Black Corridors. Blood on a crank for raising a hospital bed, the preference of the murderer for blonde nurses, all lead up to a terrific scene where young Jessie Warren finds herself securely trapped in a hospital room and sees in the mirror – but you must read on for yourself! Not so gruesome as it sounds, for Conyth Little writes of macabre things with unusual gaiety.

### Black Dream, The
February 1953
A cook in the kitchen is only to be expected, but not a cook's corpse! Agatha Benson was horrified to find Em's dead body there. She had a terrible fear that she herself might have done the murder while sleepwalking. In a panic she hides Em in the cupboard under the stairs. Inspector Lewis, called in to investigate Em's disappearance, at once smells, if not precisely the body in the cupboard, certainly a substantial rat! Over Miss Bunson's boarding-house table, and innumerable cups of midnight coffee, he pursues his investigations, adding some barbed comments to the generally crazy conversation of a motley collection of boarders. In the end he unmasks both a ghost and a murderer. Crime with a smile is the Conyth Little Slogan. The Black Dream is excellent entertainment.

### Black Express
May 1945
Murder on a trans-Australian train snaking its way across a vast continent is the theme of this latest mystery by the popular Conyth Little. The girl in the shoddy clothes and ill-fitting red shoes recovered slowly from a bump on the head to find herself in a train compartment with a strange woman who called her "Dearie" and assured her that everything would be all right when she met her relatives in Melbourne. When the girl examined the contents of her handbag she found a driver's licence with the name Cleo Ballister. The name rang no bell of remembrance in her mind. She knew she could not have bought the horrible clothes she wore. Tantalising bits of the past came back to her, but they formed no clues to a sustained memory of who she was or why she was there. Black Express is a well-told murder mystery and should certainly rank as one of Conyth Little's best.

### Black Eye, The
February 1946
Murder in the skilful hands of Conyth Little runs merrily through the pages of this entertaining puzzle as bodies appear and disappear with startling rapidity. It all happens at the Fredons' house near New York which Mary Fredon has kindly lent to some friends, who promptly decided to throw a party – a decision which unfortunately had fatal results. The Black Eye is specially recommended to all who prefer their murders to be not only grim but gay, not only exciting but entertaining.

### Black Gloves, The
October 1940
On the afternoon that the Hammond Vickers with their daughter Lissa returned to their home after a long absence, many peculiar things happened. Lissa heard the sound of coal being shovelled in the cellar, a sound that was to be repeated later with no reason and apparently no human cause. When she also started seeing a light which appeared and disappeared in the attic of the house, Lissa started to investigate these two mysteries.

She found their source certainly, but got herself involved in an ugly tangle of murder and hatred. Conyth Little, a Crime Club discovery, proves herself a master of the mystery story which combines humour and murder, clever dialogue and shrewd characterisation, in just the right proportions to ensure perfect entertainment.

### Black Goatee, The
October 1947
Perhaps you have heard of the housing shortage. America also suffers from that, and one can appreciate the feelings of Aloysius P. Graham when his two cousins Maude and Una refuse to let to him any portion of the huge house which they have inherited from their father. But Aloysius nevertheless moves into the unoccupied premises and straight away offers hospitality to a stranger who calls, an elderly gentleman with a black goatee beard – an unfortunate admission which involves the amiable host in a lot of trouble. Conyth Little not only writes a baffling murder mystery but supplies first rate entertainment. It may help you to forget your own housing problem!

### Black Honeymoon, The
December 1944
The honeymoon of Miriel and Ian Ross turned into a murder investigation when Uncle Richard died of an overdose of feathers. He was not tickled to death but sneezed himself into the hereafter, being highly allergic to feathers. When the said feathers were discovered in the pocket of Miriel's nursing uniform, things looked very bad for the young bride. Whereupon, not being a supine female, she employed a private detective named Kelly to get her out of the mess. He installed himself in the household as a butler who couldn't cook, clean or serve, but was a hound on running down clues. *The Black Honeymoon* has lots of chuckles, some hair-raising scenes, an amusing set-up and a peculiarly evil, cold-blooded murderer. Altogether highly entertaining reading.

### Black House, The
June 1950
Henry Debbon was definitely feeling ruffled that morning. He had been celebrating too freely the night before, the liftboy had cheeked him on his way up to the office and to his mortification he had been unable to think of a suitably crushing retort; and then he found he had arrived an hour too early, which was all against the principles of a short but crowded lifetime. If, however, Henry had not been early that morning he would never have been placed in charge of his boss's stepdaughter, the red-haired Diana, and if it hadn't been for Diana he would never have made the journey to that deserted house in the country where so many strange goings-on were alternately to chill and to thrill him. If you're not quivering with laughter you're shivering with suspense in this latest light-hearted crime story by Conyth Little.

### Black Iris, The
July 1953
The characters which people Conyth Little's crime stories always behave in the oddest possible way, but never have they been more crazily entertaining than in this latest novel, *The Black Iris*. Meet the two batty aunts who live over their brother's grave and who play Russian roulette with deadly – and we mean deadly – purpose every fourth Monday. Be introduced to their handsome nephew Richard, who marries a redhead just to call his mother's bluff! And there's Richard's mother herself, who dashes about in a yellow convertible and is always the first to know everything. Lastly, there's the gardener who makes artificial flowers – among them a black iris… When Conyth Little and a few corpses get together there's no knowing what will happen to the corpses, but you can be sure the reader is going to have a jolly good time!

### Black Lady, The
February 1944
Readers of Miss Conyth Little's very successful stories know how entertaining she can make the grimmest story of murder. There are as many wisecracks as usual in her new book, thumpings in the attic, a small black bottle in the shape of a doll that appears and disappears, and the rustle of the sweeping skirts of the Black Lady herself add an eerie atmosphere to a very enjoyable mystery

### Black Paw, The
October 1941
Callie Drake, charming, bat-brained and trouble-attracting, undertook to assist a friend and was immediately involved in a first-class mess. Callie had intended to do some highly justifiable petty larceny, but the police figured that murder was the motive for her appearance in the Barton household masquerading as a house-maid. Suspense and chills, amusing dialogue and the attractive Callie herself, make this book mystery entertainment of a high quality.

### Black Piano, The
August 1948
Gloria Rouston is pushed off a bridge one dark night. It is only by a miracle that she is not killed, and not unnaturally when she recovers she determines to find out who wanted to murder her. She is suspicious of her husband and his ne'er-do-well family, who have sponged and preyed on her for years, and after drastically altering her appearance she returns to her home town – only to be herself accused of murder! Conyth Little, now favourite with a multitude of readers, seems to have the recipe for blending her crime with the spice of entertainment.

### Black Shrouds, The
May 1942
Diana Prescott leaves her father's house to come to New York with the intention of becoming an actress. Instead she walks into a mess of murder, which draws her irascible father to New York and involves him to his disgust in the same mess. Mrs. Markham's boarding house, where Diana stays, has an oddly assorted group of guests, and why two inoffensive old maid sisters should be murdered is a puzzle to all. But Diana succeeds where the police have failed, an incidentally brings her father's blood pressure to the boiling point. Conyth Little has rapidly risen to the fore as a writer of sprightly murder mysteries which, while stressing plot and suspense, do not ignore a welcome touch of humour.

### Black Smith, The
April 1951
From the moment Judith Onslow arrived at the little country station en route for Smith Hospital and her post as head nurse, everything went haywire. There was only one ancient taxi and she had to fight to share it with an uninhibited lady who introduced herself, unasked, as the new switchboard operator at the hospital. On arrival she found that the doctor under whom she would serve was actually the one man in the world she wanted to avoid. The equipment, moreover, was out of date, and one of the nurses was a faith-healer. There was a crazy patient who kept disappearing and made his final return as a corpse, and there was certainly something very odd indeed about Dr. Smith, the head of the hospital. The Conyth Little stories are as entertaining as they are mystifying, and *The Black Smith* is by no means an exception.

### Black Stocking, The
May 1947
For thrills leavened with laughter and murders not only exciting but entertaining, Conyth Little is well known to Crime Club readers as supplying exactly the right mixture. *The Black Eye* was one such success; *The Black Stocking* is another. Here's a fast-moving story of a girl branded an escaped lunatic. She ends up in a private hospital to become, first, rather more than a handful for her charming doctor, and, finally, a first-class sensation and headache for the local police. Excitement and humour, suspense and a racy atmosphere make Conyth Little's stories a speciality on their own.

### Black Thumb, The
April 1943
For those who prefer their murders mixed with a considerable dash of humour and general gaiety, Conyth Little's stories should have a very definite appeal. Here is the latest – *The Black Thumb* – which is concerned with some strange goings on in a large hospital. Nurse Norma Gale, a very likeable heroine, has to cope with five fever cases in the isolation ward, and loses two of them unexpectedly through a sudden outbreak of murder. It is something with which even the doctors cannot cope, but Norma gives the police very considerable help. The clues at first appear to be slight and even on the surface nonsensical, but in the end by some particularly ingenious detection they add up to a sensational solution. *The Black Thumb* can be recommended as a most entertaining and sometimes terrifying mystery story.

### Blackout, The
March 1952
Continuing a career in pursuit of carefree crime, Conyth Little in *The Blackout* gives us one of her grimmest and gayest. A victim of amnesia trying to remember his past life finally recalls a house where he used to live and finds an agreeable occupation there as companion to Madame Rose, an ex-ballerina endeavouring on a pittance to keep up the luxurious style to which she was once accustomed. In this house gather some bizarre personalities, but in spite of the confusion caused by their eccentricities, Joe gradually remembers all, including the faceless image of a woman named Lily, and, eventually, murder!

## LODER, VERNON

### Button in the Plate, The
February 1938
Colonel Coppe C. V. O., an elderly bachelor, had inherited from his father a quarter of a million pounds. He had inherited from various sisters ten children. He was financially responsible for all these children in some way, and he had made ample provision for them in his will. Everybody was contented until the Colonel met, and desired to marry, a Mrs. Brown. He also decided to change his will, and, gathering all the beneficiaries together, told them his intentions. On that evening a murder was committed which was as baffling as it was unusual.

### Case of the Dead Doctor, The
August 1935
Old Doctor Purton had always been a mystery, and in the manner of his dying he did not disappoint the gossipers in the little town of Lower Plaine. He had lived in a style that was considerably more grandiose than that adopted by the average country doctor. The fact that he kept a butler and lived in Rampole Manor seemed to postulate an income from a source other than the fees from the obstinately healthy inhabitants of a country town. When the doctor was found murdered, his head battered in, rumour got busy. Pages of his case-book were found to be missing. Wild suggestions as to the methods by which the doctor had amassed his fortune were rife. Who had killed him, and why? The tale is told in the first person by Dr. Purton's lawyer, Mr. Gayte, and it is an absorbing and enthralling story.

### Choose Your Weapon
March 1937
Jean Maze thought it rather good fun to be a fortune-teller at the local bazaar. So she dressed the part, acquired a crystal, and called herself 'Sourah the Sorceress." Crowds of people, including wealthy business friends and enemies of her brother-in-law, flocked to her tent. But when rival business interests mix in such surroundings, who could possibly foretell that murder would result? *Choose Your Weapon* sets and ingenious problem that will keep the reader guessing to the very end, and Mr. Loder's clever character studies of sinister people could not be bettered.

### Deaf-Mute Murders, The
March 1936
When a deaf-mute beggar was found murdered in a West End square, the C.I.D. had trouble in finding a motive for the deed. When the body of another deaf-mute, apparently a suicide, was found in the grounds of a Hendon hotel, matters were further complicated. There had been extensive jewel robberies in the squares frequented by the beggar. Had he any connection with them, or the other deaf-mute; and what part did Leonard Grey, photographer and amateur detective, play in the tragedies? This was the problem that confronted Superintendent 'Paddy' Mix of the C.I.D. and his Chief-Inspector Thomson. How they solved it, with the honest aid of hard work, and the dubious assistance of 'psychological' hints supplied to them by a charming young woman, makes a story that for sheer ingenuity must rank as one of the best that this popular author has written.

### Death at the Horse Show
April 1935
Vernon Loder has conceived an absolutely novel idea for his latest detective story – a horse show in the midst of which a man is struck down and killed by the hoofs of a horse. Why should a normally quiet animal suddenly have become a killer? Then a groom discovers a tiny wound, a mere prick in the horse's quarters; the prick is not, of course, accidental, but the police are faced with the question – was the man's death accidental or murder?

### Death at the Wheel
April 1933
The car was parked in an unauthorised place – a contravention of the regulations that called for immediate attention. The policeman dealt with the offender in his best official manner, but the driver, contrary to custom, made no reply. The constable put his hand through the window of the car and shook the occupant. Policemen are generally unemotional, but this one could not refrain from uttering a startled cry as the man crumpled up and fell in a heap against the steering wheel. Simultaneously almost, the constable

pulled open the door and saw the blood that stained the carpet...*Death at the Wheel* is a swift moving mystery story, full of drama and suspense, and satisfying in every respect.

### Death in the Thicket
May 1932
Alexander McDowell, the well-known Labour M. P. and agitator, was found dead in a thicket on the estate of Sir Leonard Craysh, at whose house-party he had been a guest – an exceedingly unpopular guest, for his manner was overbearing and boorish in the extreme. Other members of the house-party had deliberately set out to rag him. Had one of the party gone too far, or was there something even more sinister behind the tragedy? Vernon Loder handles this story in a manner worthy of his previous fine achievements.

### Death of An Editor
April 1931
An ill-assorted party, most of them with axes to grind, have assembled for the week-end at Marsh House, the coastal residence of Sir James Sitheby, the millionaire newspaper proprietor. Sitting at a derby desk at the window of the study, in Sir James's private wing, that Saturday afternoon, Mr. Hay Smith is found dead. His skull has been shattered by a shot, and in his dead fingers are clutched the torn corners of seven or eight sheets of paper. An important document, adumbrating a revolutionary policy for dealing with the Indian North-West frontier troubles, has been stolen from a courier travelling between Marseilles and Paris. It is suspected that the fragments of papers found in Hay Smith's hands came from these documents. Inspector Brews, of the Upperton Police Force, is put on the case, and the lists of suspects grow long. Among them are Sir James himself; Mr. Sape, late editor of Sir James's evening paper; Julius Dunesberg, a mysterious Alsatian; Monsieur Damont, a French journalist, and others. How Damont died a violent death before Hay Smith's inquest took place, and how Inspector Brews methodically sorted his catch, and at last entangled Hay Smith's murderer in the meshes of his net makes an enthralling story.

### Essex Murders, The
October 1930
When Edward Hope, a writer of detective novels, had saved enough to buy Fen Court, a beautiful, neglected Tudor house in the Essex marshes, he took his prospective wife down to see it. In the grounds they found four pieces of ornamental water, and in one of these what appeared to be a dead carp. But closer inspection showed this to be the submerged visage of Mr. Habershon, a London lawyer, and the subsequent dragging operations resulted in two other bodies being recovered from the pond; those of Mr. Habershon's wards, whose wrists were tied together with a silk handkerchief. A despairing note was also pinned to the girl's dress, and the case seemed one of suicide, and death in attempted rescue. Hope was briefed by a newspaper to solve the problem. Inspector Brews, that dry, humorous man, worked hand in hand with Hope. The seemingly simple case proved to be immensely complicated, and death came very near the two solvers before they could find and fit in the last piece of the puzzle.

### Kill in the Ring
October 1938
Tom Martin was the rising star among British heavy-weights. If good looks could kill he would have been a world-beater. A handsome, ex-Public School champion, his physical grace attracted many feminine fans to

the ringside. His terrific right punch not only knocked his opponents horizontal but made his women admirers gasp in admiration. Men of less attractive physique were furiously jealous of the magnificent fighter, and when Martin passed right out in the course of his biggest fight there were rumours that some enemy had at last taken an ingenious revenge. Mr. Vernon Loder in *Kill in the Ring* has written a superb mystery of the boxing world.

### Little Man Murders, The
July 1936
Vernon Loder's characterisation is the most distinctive feature of his excellent novels; furthermore he always achieves what Torquemada (reviewing his *The Deaf Mute Murders* in the *Observer*) called 'the effortless telling of a good Story.' *The Little Man Murders* is perhaps the best he has yet done. In it he describes an extraordinary character who baffled Scotland Yard for years – Mr. Augustus Faynes, a frail-looking little man whose interest in old masters and in tramps had seemed innocent enough, until the discovery of a tramp's body in a lake led to awkward questions.

### Murder From Three Angles
April 1934
The 'County' rather disapproved when Mr. Dansford the financier bought and settled down at 'Colham Gorse', to entertain his business friends, with the late owner, Mr. Colham, and his niece Letty as host and hostess. He had seven guests down to discuss the amalgamation of companies. There were scenes at the conferences, and some strong language was used. But when Dansford was found dead at the side of the lake, all the seven spoke highly of his qualities as a business man. The Chief Constable of the County, scion of a noble house, took the view that the men were afraid to say otherwise, and so provide a motive for murder. Letty Colham, and Hope, Dansford's secretary, took the 'County-cum-Commonsense' view. Inspector Chace of New Scotland Yard viewed the tragedy from the angle of the experienced, impartial detective officer. Three ways of looking at murder. Which was the right angle, and how was it proved to be right?

### Red Stain
November 1931
Inspector Gibbs and the County Detective Force found in the murder of old Farson of Hance House the most ticklish problem of their eventful careers. There was no apparent motive for the crime until it was revealed that old Farson was one and the same as Gilgold and Co., Moneylenders, London. Then all his debtors were possible suspects, but which of them was in Menton at the time of Farson's death, which of them knew that Farson was there that night, and which of them had possessed the medical knowledge that must have directed the death blow? Suspicion at once fell on young Harry Mavish, who 'fitted' the first two of these qualifications at least. But Dr. Kaithe had very good reason for his belief in Harry's innocence. Gibbs, too, was ready to accept Harry's almost unprovable alibi – a superficially imperfect alibi, rather than others less assailable but more imperfect. Mr. Loder holds our undivided interest through an amazingly intricate plot and presents us with a solution as satisfying as it is unexpected.

### Suspicion
October 1933
Vernon Loder's new story is set in the little country town of Martley, where the usual

small-town gossip is retailed over tea-tables and bar-counters. The local gossips were very interested in Mr. Julius Hennessy, who spent a great deal of time on the golf links with the young and pretty wife of Mr. Holt, an elderly solicitor. Suddenly tragedy bursts upon the village, for one morning Hennessy is found murdered on the river bank – a crime for which there seemed to be plenty of motives, but no solution. Mr. Loder cleverly unravels the many intricacies of this absorbing mystery and certainly succeeds in maintaining our interest until the end.

### Two Dead
October 1934
Standing in its own delightfully wooded ground overlooking a lake, the charming, if rather lonely house, called Lakeside provided a peaceful refuge for people who wanted rest, liked orange juice and a change of scene. With considerable professional acumen Dr Sorslie had converted it into a highly successful nursing home mainly for neurasthenic patients, among whom at the start of the story was a financier with a particularly shady past. He was admitted as a patient for a six months' rest cure. His secretary, a Belgian woman, was accommodated in a cottage farther along the lake shore. Some time afterwards she is discovered dead in the cottage. The coroner finds that she had committed suicide, but Mr. Vernon Loder builds up out of these facts a very interesting murder case.

### LORAC, E. C. R.
(*see also* **Carnac, Carol**)
*Accident By Design*
October 1950
No one could call the Vansteads a happy family. Templedean Place had become a house divided against itself. The gracious, well-bred serenity of a fast vanishing mode of life typified by its master, the invalid Sir Charles, and his daughter Judith, clashed violently with the harsher and more realistic outlook on life which Judith's brother Gerald and his Australian wife brought from the prison camps of Malaya. It was not a question of who was right and who was wrong; it was just a question of fundamental incompatibility, aggravated by the knowledge that on Sir Charles's death Templedean and its rich farms would go to Gerald, and Judith would be tolerated where she had reigned, or banished entirely. It was an atmosphere to breed tragedy, and when Gerald and his wife are killed in a car accident, Chief Inspector Macdonald has the uneasy feeling that it *could* have been accident *by design*.

### Ask a Policeman
September 1955
An elderly lady, whose toque and sweeping skirts gave her an Edwardian dignity, reported to the police that her nephew had disappeared. At first it seemed that this was just a matter for routine investigation, but a chance clue reveals that, in fact, the police are faced with a case of murder. The missing nephew, a journalist, had given as his address a rambling, baroque house in St. John's Wood which at one time had enjoyed a sinister reputation in the neighbourhood. The housekeeper denied any knowledge of the journalist, but nevertheless a latent menace seemed to pervade the house, with its eccentric and paralysed owner lying in the basement. When enquiries in Fleet Street were followed by serious accidents to two of the few potential witnesses, it became obvious that the murderer was dangerously active and well-informed. In *Ask a Policeman* action and an atmosphere of mounting

suspense are combined, as E. C. R. Lorac successively casts suspicion on the different characters right up to the moment of the final denouement.

### Bats in the Belfry
February 1937
There seemed to be an atmosphere of disaster about the Attleton family; so many had met with untimely deaths. But Bruce Attleton still continued to joke cynically of the lack of staying power in his unlucky family. It was the whim of the gods that Bruce himself should be the next. He is called away on a mysterious errand to Paris and disappears completely, until eventually his body is found in a ramshackle studio called the Belfry. It is an Inspector Macdonald case, of course, and that detective has a pretty problem to solve. E. C. R. Lorac has written several highly successful detective stones, and *Bats in the Belfry* must surely rank as one of the most outstanding in quality.

### Black Beadle
September 1939
E. C. R. Lorac goes from strength to strength. *Black Beadle* must not be missed on any account, for it is an outstanding detective story, beautifully constructed, the trails of detection alternating so skilfully that the interest never flags for one moment. It is notable too for its excellent characterisation, and there is, of course, Chief Inspector Macdonald, of whom a well-known critic has remarked: 'There is no imaginary inhabitant of Scotland Yard that I would rather see endowed with the breath of actual life.' E. C. R. Lorac's story is a good novel as well as a gripping murder mystery.

### Case in the Clinic
June 1941
E. C. R. Lorac deservedly enjoys a great reputation as a detective writer, and *Case in the Clinic* is a splendid example of this clever author's powers of mystification. It starts with the sudden death of the Rev. Mr. Anderby, who suddenly drops dead in his garden. The small country town gossip that naturally followed Mr. Anderby's death was vastly increased by another sudden death in circumstances which necessitated the police being informed. The case swiftly became a matter for Scotland Yard and Inspector Macdonald quickly takes charge, and in his usual cool and calm way unravels a really amazing mystery.

OR

The story begins with the sudden death of an elderly clergyman named Anderby who drops dead while hosing the garden, a death that is followed by another in circumstances which give rise to suspicion and to the local police calling upon Inspector MacDonald. E. C. R. Lorac's novels are always enjoyable, and Inspector MacDonald is rapidly becoming one of the most popular Crime Club sleuths.

### Checkmate to Murder
February 1944
There are five people in Bruce Manaton's Hampstead studio one foggy day in January. At one end of the fifty-foot studio Bruce Manaton is painting the portrait of an actor, André Delaunier, in the scarlet robes of a cardinal; at the other end Robert Cavenish of the Home Office is playing chess with Ian McKellon a government chemist. Bruce's sister Rosanne is cooking supper in the little kitchen adjoining the studio. To Rosanne, an artist herself, occurred the thought that here was a scene set for a perfect pictorial composition. Actually, had she known, it was set for

high tragedy. Even at that moment the quietness was broken by a knocking at the door… E. C. R. Lorac is a writer with a rare sense of atmosphere and in *Checkmate to Murder* once again thrills us with a grandly exciting story of murder.

### *Crime Counter Crime*
January 1936
E C. R. Lorac, author of *The Organ Speaks* and other excellent detective novels, has written a most ingenious story in *Crime Counter Crime*, which concerns the mysterious death of Laurence Carston, a well-known Communist, while speeding north in his car to an election at Wilbury. The story opens particularly well with the tension of a murder committed on the eve of the poll when feeling is running high, and the author cleverly sustains the interest through all the twists and turns of an amazing plot. The chief characters are drawn with real insight, while the political background adds greatly to the appeal of a first-rate crime story.

### *Crook O'Lune*
August 1953
The beautiful Lancashire fell country which has been the background of previous E. C. R. Lorac novels such as *The Theft of the Iron Dogs* and *Fell Murder* is the setting, too, of this new detective story. Robert Macdonald (Chief Inspector Macdonald when on duty at Scotland Yard) is staying with his friends Kate and Giles Hoggett in Lunesdale, looking for a farm where he can settle down if and when he retires. There have been some cases of sheep stealing reported locally and Macdonald readily agrees to make a few friendly enquiries. He is called on in his official capacity, however, when the more serious crimes of arson, manslaughter and attempted murder follow. Whether or not these are connected with the sheep-stealing is but one of Macdonald's many and knotty problems in this absorbing story.

### *Dangerous Domicile*
September 1957
Keith Merril was positively discouraging about the flat Giles Grantham and his three young friends had just rented in 'North House', in Northern London. Its landlady, Madame Chevreuse, was sinister and formidable; Keith said, 'the whole set-up sounds unpleasant to me.'

But it was an intriguing set-up all the same, presided over by 'La Chevreuse', whose real name, from her fourth marriage, was Mrs. Smith. Giles and his friend thought they were lucky in getting cheap and unusual accommodation – until they found a corpse on the premises...

There was no doubt about whose corpse it should have been, yet Superintendent Macdonald of the C. I. D. was faced with a mass of conflicting evidence and lies. For once it looked as though the police had encountered a criminal with the brains to match theirs. It took another outbreak of violence, a second crime, to resolve the mysterious business at North House.

E. C. R. Lorac has again written an entertaining and masterly detective story. A complex plot, peopled with such imposing characters as Madame Chevreuse, leads to an ingenious problem and an exciting climax.

### *Death at Dyke's Corner*
March 1940
'We've taken the wrong fork. There's a double hairpin bend somewhere'. There was! Immediately in front of them a car was drawn up on the opposite side of the road. As they swung round the wicked curve headlights blazed full at them, blinding them both. A lorry had drawn out to pass the standing car and was coming at them like a battle cruiser. They sensed the rending, tearing scream of metal as the lorry hit them, and darkness came down on them. In that threefold crash it was the occupant of the stationary car who was found dead. Out of the details of a commonplace accident, Inspector Macdonald relentlessly builds up the most amazing elucidation of a murder mystery – a case devised with all E. C. R. Lorac's customary brilliance.

### *Death Before Dinner*
March 1948
One might have run into Elias Trowne anywhere East of Suez. He was a confirmed globe-trotter and had survived the most exciting and incredible adventures. Yet an ironic fate decreed that he should meet his death in a place at once tranquil and law-abiding, a little London restaurant esteemed by epicures, Le Jardin des Olives. One evening eight distinguished travellers and explorers were gathered together to be initiated into that famous and exclusive traveller's club, the Marco Polo. Before dinner it is discovered that the invitation is a hoax, and circumstances lead the disappointed guests to believe that Elias Trowne is the perpetrator. Later his dead body is found on the premises, and Inspector Macdonald, investigating the events of that tragic evening, is faced with a most complicated and baffling mystery.

### *Death Came Softly*
February 1943
Valehead House, standing so serenely in the sunshine among the rich Devonshire meadows, appealed to Mrs. Merrion from the moment she first glimpsed it. To her it was the happy ending to a wearisome home-hunting expedition and she arranged to move in with her father Professor Crewdon. But her happiness, as so often happens, was suddenly snatched from her by the tragic death of her father, whose body was found in a cave on the estate. Chief Inspector Macdonald of Scotland Yard was called in, and was soon looking for motive, method and opportunity. Once again E. C. R. Lorac tells an absorbing and ingenious detective story.

### *Death in Triplicate*
January 1958
'Of course she was mad…For a woman of over sixty, with a good income, a pleasant home and some status in the literary world to marry an adventurer with agreeable manners and nothing else indicates loss of mental stability.' That was Miss Anne Woodhead's very definite opinions of her sister, Elizabeth. Superintendent Kempson was obliged to listen to Anne Woodhead's opinions because she now maintained that Elizabeth's whereabouts needed to be investigated. She succeeded in prodding Kempson into action.

Enquiries soon showed that something was awry, and the finding of a body proved that Anne Woodhead had not been fussing pointlessly. Kempson found himself seeking a murderer who acted with utmost speed and ruthlessness. Two other murders had taken place before the police could disentangle the misleading evidence – and before they could recognise the astounding truth.

E. C. R. Lorac's many readers will forgive the author for the absence of Superintendent Macdonald from this new book. They cannot help but like Superintendent Kempson, and their wits will be fully occupied in trying to detect who is the murderer, before the author reveals it in the exciting climax.

### *Devil and the C. I. D., The*
January 1938
The devil was dead – of that there was no possible doubt – in Inspector Macdonald's own car, too, parked outside Scotland Yard! Hunched together in the car was a man's body clad in the sinister scarlet of Mephistopheles. Dead in the very stronghold of the C. I. D., the corpse in its bizarre fancy dress seemed to mock the guardians of law and order. Here indeed was a challenge from the Devil – even although the victim might just have been a reveller from a fancy-dress ball – a direct challenge, so Inspector Macdonald thought, to the C. I. D. The mystery which E. C. R. Lorac presents with such skill is a formidable challenge to the intelligent reader.

### *Dishonour Among Thieves*
March 1959
When Superintendent Macdonald visited Fellcock Farm, bought against the day of his retirement, he put all thoughts of crime and criminals out of his head. But even there, high in the fell country above Lunesdale, he was forced to face again the fact that a policeman is never off duty. The discovery of a dead body in the deserted house at High Garth set him to unravel a baffling and fascinating case and set him on a trail which led from the fells to Dartmoor and to a figure in prison uniform vanishing into the mist. The Lunesdale setting, which put *Fell Murder*, *Crook O'Lune* and *The Theft of the Iron Dogs* among E. C. R. Lorac's most successful and popular books, gives another opportunity to meet again friends like Giles and Kate Hoggett and that shrewd, indomitable old gentleman Mr. Staple. *Dishonour Among Thieves* combines an exciting and ingenious problem with an unusual and lovely setting. It will maintain E. C. R. Lorac's high reputation.

### *Dog It Was That Died, The*
February 1952
When Rodney Bretton, a lecturer in mathematics, is run down by a lorry and killed, it appears to be merely another tragic road accident and as such of only statistical interest to Scotland Yard. When, however, barely two months later his daughter, Wendy, is found drowned in her bath, Chief-Inspector Macdonald is sent to make a few routine enquiries. Macdonald is immediately struck by two curious facts: Rodney Bretton had been comfortably off and had earned a substantial salary, and yet his widow was forced to take in paying guests. His daughter was not the sort of careless person who would take an opiate just before getting into a hot bath, yet the post-mortem had proved this to be the case. Does the secret of both tragedies lie behind the locked doors of the steel-lined cupboards which Bretton had had specially constructed in the library? That at any rate is the obvious starting-point in one of Macdonald's most difficult investigations.

### *Fell Murder*
September 1944
The Garths had farmed their fertile acres at Garthmere for generations, and fine land it was, lying in a lovely valley of the River Lune, with the towering hills of the Lake Country on the far horizon. Garthmere Hall itself was old before Flodden Field, and here Robert Garth, still hale and hearty at eighty-two and very much an old Tartar, ruled his household with a rod of iron. The peaceful dales and fells of the north country provide the setting for this grim story of murder, a setting in fact which is one of the attractive features of an unusual and distinctive tale of evil passion and murderous hate in a small farming community.

### *Fire in the Thatch*
January 1946
Nicholas Vaughan, invalided out of the navy after an accident to his eyes, had acquired the tenancy of Little Thatch, an old-world Devonshire cottage with a small piece of neglected but cultivable land. Even though the garden was overgrown with weeds and the property was miles away from mains supplies of water and electricity, Little Thatch represented one man's dreams of a post-war heaven. Destiny decreed, however, that these dreams were to come to naught. The story of what happened at Little Thatch makes this one of E. C. R. Lorac's finest detective stories.

### *John Brown's Body*
January 1939
John Brown's Body – and several others

Luckily John Brown had time to speak before his body lay a 'moulderin' in the grave, and it was left for Inspector Macdonald, together with Peter Vernon, journalist, to go marching in the tracks of another dangerous man. The tracks led from the lively bustle of a modern publishing firm to the north coast of Devonshire – no sunny summer resort, but, a bleak winter scene of deserted coombes and cliffs shrouded in mist, and lonely isolated houses. To the man bred in cities, there is a haunting fear in these rocky desolate moors, and it is here that Inspector Macdonald makes his second discovery (this time it is a 'moulderin'), and Peter Vernon gets something less pleasant than a newspaper story. The final drawing-in of the net reveals a totally unexpected haul, and had not Mr. Lorac already established himself as a writer of first-class detective fiction, this book alone would have placed him in the front rank.

### *Let Well Alone*
October 1954
Two young couples, wanting to escape from their drab and squalid London lodgings, are overjoyed to hear of The Old Court House in Devon which can be rented very cheaply. Its isolation, its mystery and sinister past, do not prevent their seeing it as a new and beautiful home, their escape to a freer and happier life. In this holiday mood they move in. They are contemptuous of ghosts and legends, but the real truth is withheld from them; they do not assess correctly the nature of The Old Court House and its past. The finding of the body of a dead man in one of the outbuildings not only shatters their carefree happiness but brings suspicion and doubts they dare hardly consider even to themselves. Can one of *them* be a killer? Superintendent Macdonald (just promoted) and Chief Inspector Reeves find themselves up against one of the most curious, complicated and sinister problems they have ever known. It is finally resolved in a scene of great terror and excitement, when friends and enemies move silently at night over the bleak moorland which surrounds The Old Court House.

### *Murder By Matchlight*
May 1945
It happened in the darkness of a black November evening in Regent's Park. Bruce Mallaig, a young analytical chemist taking a walk in the park, was suddenly attracted by the suspicious behaviour of a man who, obviously believing himself to be unobserved in the black-out, took cover nearby as if waiting in hiding. Soon after, another passer-by stopped to light a cigarette, and beyond that small bright circle of matchlight Bruce glimpsed another face in the darkness – a sullen, dark face. The light went out...there was a dull thud, the sound of a heavy body falling...and then silence. Once again E. C. R.

Lorac casts a spell over us with an extraordinarily good piece of story-telling, a first-class murder mystery that not only grips but mystifies.

### Murder in the Mill-Race
September 1952
When Dr. Raymond Ferens took a practice at Milham in the Moor of North Devon, he and his wife were enchanted with the little hill-top village lying close to moor and sky. At first they saw only charm, but they soon discovered that whenever you get a group of people living together, whether in town or village, you find the same mixed characteristics of humanity – envy, hatred and malice, as well as neighbourliness and honest-to-God goodness. Everyone said Sister Monica, warden of a children's charity home, was wonderful, 'a saint'. But was she? A few months after the Ferens' arrival her body is found drowned in the mill-race and the investigation of Scotland Yard uncovers some surprising facts. Chief Inspector Macdonald has one of his most difficult cases because of the village's determination not to help a stranger.

### Murder in Vienna
May 1956
Supt. Macdonald C. I. D. studied his fellow passengers in the Vienna flight simply because he couldn't help it, because he hadn't conditioned himself to being on holiday. The distinguished industrialist he recognised: the stout man he put down (quite mistakenly) as a traveller in whisky. The fair girl was going to a job (he was right there) and the aggressive young man in the camel coat might be something bookish. Macdonald turned away from his fellow passengers deliberately: they weren't his business, he was on holiday – or so he thought.

Against a background of beautiful Vienna, with its enchanting palaces and gardens, its disenchanted back streets and derelicts of war, E. C. R. Lorac constructs a detective story with all its complexities; an exciting and puzzling new crime story.

### Murder of a Martinet
May 1951
For a long time Muriel Farrington had ruled the lives of her children, gathering them all together, married or single, under the same roof in the old family mansion. She made a fetish of getting her own way, and liked to do it gracefully if possible; but if there was any resistance she could always rely on the subtle effects of the time-honoured heart attack. Self-satisfied, and selfish beyond belief, she did not sense the bitter resentment that burned in the breasts of her family, and was far from realising the point of desperation reached by one of them, a desperation which was leading inexorably to her own destruction. For Chief Inspector Macdonald this was not one of the easy cases, but it is one of E. C. R. Lorac's best.

### Murder on a Monument
September 1958
'So you are having a worthwhile month's holiday in Rome with your brother?' asked the old lady in the plane. 'How delightful for you both.'

Jonet Airdrey was returning to Rome for the first time since she and Nicholas had lived there as children, and she travelled with a light heart and no presentiment of the nightmare which was soon to entangle her.

In broad daylight, and in the most conspicuous place in Rome, a murder was committed which was not only daring and brutal but set off a bewildering and frightening sequence of events. Jonet had one piece of luck.

Superintendent Macdonald of Scotland Yard was in Rome on a case and was intrigued by certain features of the murder, which in his orderly, Scottish way, he felt might have been overlooked.

Murder on a Monument is convincingly set in one of the most exciting cities in the world, and once again the very high standards with which the name E. C. R. Lorac is always associated are achieved.

### Pall for a Painter
September 1936
In Crime Counter Crime E. C. R. Lorac gave us studies of political types and characters; in Post After Post-Mortem a study of intellectuals; and now in this latest book is equally at home among artists. The setting of the amazing crime so graphically portrayed in the present story is Manette's, an art school in St. John's Wood. Chief-Inspector Macdonald, hero of many exploits, is called in to investigate the mysterious death of an artist, and his quiet method of sleuthing is here seen at its best. A Pall for a Painter is a most enjoyable detective story, which will add still further to the reputation of its author.

### Part for a Poisoner
October 1948
A rich and ailing old man, with deserving though expectant relatives – a nurse who ensnares the invalid's affections and looks like disappointing some great expectations – a dose of poison and sudden death – such is the theme of E. C. R. Lorac's new novel, and it is a theme played with fascinating and original variations. As Chief Inspector Macdonald remarks, it seems a homely, old-fashioned crime, quite simple if you only look at it the right way, but nevertheless he comes as near to being completely baffled as he has ever been, which makes the ingenious solution doubly satisfying.

### Picture of Death
February 1957
'It's lovely,' said Shirley Cotton. 'It's the loveliest place I've ever seen.'

Donald Scott said: 'It must be a mistake. Richard Langton's not a millionaire, not by a long chalk.'

It was not until they entered the beautiful Whitescar Hall that they realised its decay, or understood the ties that bound the impoverished Langton to the vast fabric of the dilapidated house.

In the atmosphere of this unusual but realistic 'stately home' there occurs a fatal accident. Or was it an accident? If it was not an accident, how could it possibly have been engineered? Another accident follows, and Superintendent Macdonald of Scotland Yard finds himself investigating a very complicated problem – that leads to a thrilling solution.

This new and brilliantly ingenious story will provide pleasure and suspense to all lovers of detective stories, not least among them E. C. R. Lorac's many admirers.

### Policemen in the Precinct
November 1949
Life in the north-midland town of Paulsborough was dominated by its ancient Norman Abbey. It was a godly town on the surface, with its Abbey hierarchy, its aristocracy of old residents, its traditions of high-mindedness and Christian obligation. But underneath all that simmered a seething brew of gossip and innuendo, suspicion and hatred. The worst scandalmonger of all was Mrs. Mayden, known locally as 'the malicious Mayden', who slandered everyone from the Dean to her best friend. Unfortunately, as somebody remarked, she hit 'at least ten

percent of her nails on the head', and when she dies suddenly, and curiously, and Scotland Yard says it's murder, it is Chief Inspector Macdonald's task to find out if one of that ten per cent killed her to prevent a secret from being divulged. E. C. R. Lorac, accomplished writer of detective novels, has never written a more ingenious story than Policemen in the Precinct.

### Post After Post-Mortem
May 1936
In her sunny bedroom Ruth Surray, well-known writer, lay like a child still and untroubled, her white face smiling the strange, peaceful smile of death. Death had come as she slept, and a sleeping-draught on the table beside her seemed to indicate the manner of her passing. After the inquest, however, her brother Richard reveals to Chief Inspector MacDonald of the Yard that he has a letter from Ruth written shortly before her death – a letter which the Inspector rightly regards as important. E. C. R. Lorac in this ingeniously-woven story displays the most scrupulous craftsmanship, and interest is maintained throughout by the really intelligent sleuthing of Inspector Macdonald, a detective who will appeal as very much the real thing.

### Relative to Poison
July 1947
When Susan Ferriby, lately demobbed from the A. T. S., was offered a job out of the blue by a charming woman in a Regent Street café, she thought that she'd better take her friend Patricia O'Malley along with her – just to make sure! As Pat said: 'A couple of lassies is nobody's idea of a walk-over.' For all that, they did walk into a pretty grim web, and it was just as well that Inspector Macdonald was at hand to track down and corner the spider. A fine story from one of the most popular Crime Club authors.

### Rope's End – Rogue's End
January 1942
Wulfstane Manor, a rambling old country house with many unused rooms, winding staircases and a maze of cellars, had been bequeathed to Veronica Mallowood and her brother Martin. The last time the large family of Mallowoods had all foregathered under the ancestral roof was on the occasion of their father's funeral, and there had been one of those unholy rows which not infrequently follow the reading of a will. That was some years ago, and as Veronica found it increasingly difficult to go on paying for the upkeep of Wolfstane, she summoned another family conference – a conference in which Death took a hand. Rope's End – Rogue's End is, of course, an Inspector Macdonald case, in which that popular detective plays a brilliant part. It is a first-rate story with an enthralling dénouement.

### Shroud of Darkness
March 1954
The fog-bound train from Exeter crawled slowly towards Paddington. Sarah Dillon had made friends with the attractive boy who shared a compartment with herself and the formidable 'writing' lady in the corner. The train made an unscheduled stop at Reading, due to the thick 'London Particular' which had spread out far to the West; there the compartment was invaded by two more men, one a prosperous business man, the other an obvious spiv. The boy Sarah had befriended seemed to become rattled and withdrawn after Reading. Had he something to fear from the newcomers to their compartment? Sarah could not guess, nor did she attach much significance to the boy's words when the

train reached Paddington; when he seemed suddenly to recognise one of his fellow-passengers. Minutes later the boy had his head bashed in while still in the station. His pockets had been emptied to hide his identity, and his assailant had vanished in the swirling fog. From such slender information Chief Inspector Macdonald had to work. Other crimes followed, and his enquiries took him to Devon and to a pub of doubtful reputation in North London. He got his man at last in an exciting and surprising climax on board a Channel steamer. This story will grip you throughout and have you guessing to the end.

### Sixteenth Stair, The
July 1942
The villa in St John's Wood had remained unoccupied for many years, a lovely old house which to Jeremy Hazeley's eyes enshrined the ghosts of dead lovers, and held for him the far-off memories of a child's delight. But the peace of the old house was rudely disturbed when Timothy Broughton Hazeley, an American kinsman of the Hazeleys, went to St John's Wood to see the family ghosts. On entering the villa he finds at the foot of the stairs the body of a man with his neck broken from an obvious fall. Inspector Mcdonald, imperturbable, capable and intelligent as usual, plays a prominent part in this brilliantly told and flawless mystery, which must rank high among E. C. R. Lorac's novels.

### Slippery Staircase
July 1938
E. C. R. Lorac has excelled himself in Slippery Staircase, a novel to which the Crime Club, in 'selecting' it, would like to draw the special attention of all detective-story connoisseurs.

The setting is an old and eerie London house, now converted to flats. In the basement lives the houseman; on the ground floor Martia Vannery; on the second floor a wealthy retired actor; on the third floor Mrs. Thelma Romney, a widow; on the fourth floor two young men interested in flying; and in the attic flat at the top of the house old Miss Fanny Seeley, living alone and lonely, on her modest annuity. It is on the staircase that winds up the old house, linking these people's lives together, that murder takes place.

The atmosphere throughout the book is electrically tense; the description of the terrified Juliet Romney creeping down the stairs after the murder is liable to make anybody's blood run cold; and as to the detection, it represents Inspector Macdonald's greatest triumph.

### Still Waters
May 1949
Chief Inspector Macdonald eyed the quarry pool with foreboding. Its still waters, rain-pocked, surrounded by dripping trees, looked ominous. He noted the treacherous, slippery rocks, the steep fall from the enclosing ridge, the brambles and briars, the creak and whisper of swaying boughs and shivering leaves. Just the place for a sinister crime, a setting made for dark and dangerous deeds. An intriguing problem that is quite different from that posed by the orthodox detective story, with interesting characters that could only be found in the farming district of Lunesdale in the Lancashire fell country, which formed a lovely and fascinating background for Fell Murder and The Theft of the Iron Dogs, two previous E. C. R. Lorac successes.

### Theft of the Iron Dogs, The
September 1946
Giles Hoggett viewed the flooding of his native Lancashire dales that September

morning with secret pleasure. With the rain coming down in sheets, he had a good excuse for abandoning farming for fishing. He had to give some reason to his wife for braving the weather when farming was impossible. So he said he was going to take a look at their summer cottage, and because, although an angler, he was a truthful man, he did so before even glimpsing the river. There he made a discovery that temporarily made him forget all else – he noticed that two iron dogs were missing from the fireplace, as well as a complete reel of salmon line, a strong chain and hook, a clothes-line and a large sack...a significant haul if one imagined someone wanting to sink a heavy article safe and deep in the waters of the Lune. E. C. R. Lorac has again selected as background to a fascinating mystery the beautiful fell county of Lunesdale in Lancashire.

### *These Names Make Clues*
July 1937

When Chief-Inspector Macdonald was invited to attend a party given by Graham Coombe, a publisher of detective stories, he was in two minds whether to accept. Should detectives go to parties? Was it consistent with the dignity of the Yard? The Inspector tossed for it – and went. It was no relaxation, for Macdonald not only had to exercise his wits on a particularly puzzling treasure hunt, but was called upon to solve a much more serious problem. To everyone's horror Andrew Gardien, celebrated author of thrillers, was discovered dead. Heart failure? E. C. R. Lorac presents a real problem in this fascinating new detective story.

### *Tryst for a Tragedy*
November 1940

E. C. R. Lorac is one of the most popular Crime Club authors. *Tryst for a Tragedy* should satisfy the most exacting reader, for it contains some excellent character drawing, is brightly written, and the plot is exceedingly ingenious. What is the reason for the mysterious telephone call that breaks up a bridge party and summons one of the players to a rendezvous with death? Inspector Macdonald is, of course, the detective in the case, and if you enjoy sleuthing in the Cotswolds on a particularly exciting trail you will like this new Lorac story.

## LORAINE, PHILIP

### *Crackpot*
February 1993

In the opening paragraph of Philip Loraine's new novel a murderer describes the process of picking up an unknown girl in a club prior to strangling her, and admits to disposing of nine others in a similar manner. The murderer returns to Crestcote House, a gothic mansion which has been turned into a peaceful retreat for 'artists of recognised stature'.

The community comprises an eccentric composer, a reclusive iron-worker, a beautiful sculptress, a discontented novelist, and three assorted painters, one female, two male. The lord of this remarkable manor is a philanderer, and the place is known locally (and not surprisingly) as Crackpot Castle. No one suspects, however, that one of the denizens is a serial killer.

And no one need ever have suspected if the killer had not elected to play a practical joke on fellow residents which led to a spate of lies, an unsuccessful blackmail attempt – and another killing.

This time Chief Inspector Tom Pennard is very much on the scene. Under his questioning suspicion flickers like a will-o'-the-wisp from one person to the next, while all the time the murderer, anonymous and supposedly secure, offers the reader a first-hand commentary on the unfolding of events, leading to a dramatic unmasking in the final paragraphs of this cunningly plotted story.

### *Death Wishes*
July 1983

Catherine Walden had only met her wealthy American ex-diplomat father once, when she visited him at a chateau in Southern France. At thirteen, she had been too overawed by the Beautiful People with whom he decorated the place to be fully aware of the priceless objects serving the same purpose: works by Degas, Praxiteles, Gainsborough, Faberge, Rembrandt, to name a mere five.

Now, ten years later, Edward Walden is dead (though still omnipresent), and a less ingenuous Catherine has returned to collect her vast inheritance – she is the only child, and all those millions must certainly come to her.

But must they? What about Natalia Beaumont, what about Nicholas Tate – both so decorative and both so very much closer to her father than she ever was? What about Marianne, the housekeeper, who likes to search guest bedrooms, and Abbott, the manservant, who knows too much and won't hesitate to use his knowledge? Come to that, what about those two rather dangerous young men, sexy Pascal and self-centred Jean-Michel?

'Recalls the flavour of Graham Greene in his best entertainment vein', said Marghanita Laski in the *Listener*, reviewing Philip Loraine's last novel, *Sea-Change*. The US *Publisher's Weekly* called it 'an ingenious puzzler…gripping and extremely well done'. His new novel has the same qualities, plus a superbly realized French setting and an ending guaranteed to surprise the reader – except that nothing connected with Edward Walden should surprise anyone, his death wishes least of all.

### *Last Shot*
June 1986

The last shot was so simple – merely a car driving away from Notre-Dame-de-la-Garde, high above Marseille. The unit had been disbanded and the Director had already flown to Hollywood, leaving the camera-crew and pretty Joanna, Production Coordinator (general dosgbody), to take care of it.

Yet within minutes of getting the scene in the can a Mercedes is forcing Joanna's little Renault off the autoroute, men are trying to grab her in the airport, her hotel room is torn apart.

Why? Joanna knows that multi-millionaire Monsieur Laurent has for months been attempting to stop the film –he claims it libels his family. Yet would he go as far as murder? Somebody does. And the only person Joanna can turn to for help in this alien city is charming Marc, with whom she has already had a brief and regrettable affair.

But is Marc the honest young man he seems to be? And why is the last shot so interesting to the lovely mistress of Leo Nogaro, who runs Marseille, inefficiently, on this father's behalf?

The Nogaros can exact the death penalty when and as they wish, and they certainly wish to kill Joanna and Marc, but…but those two have by now hidden the last shot where no one can find it, for it represents not only their Life Insurance but a potential crock of gold.

### *Lion's Ransom*
September 1980

Ask the next person you meet what he knows about the Pegasus Hotel, Heathrow, and he'd probably say, 'Isn't that the place they hijacked?'

If you then asked him the outcome of this event, he'd look puzzled and say, 'Well … it kind of fizzled out, didn't it?' And he'd be wrong.

Far from fizzling out, the Pegasus incident culminated in a number of deafening and disastrous explosions, yet so successful was the confidence trick perpetrated by the government that very few people have any real idea of what actually happened when twelve ruthless men calling themselves 'The Young Lions' seized the top floors of the hotel, paralysed Whitehall and Washington, and threatened to kill a man, woman or child at 3.00 p.m. every day until their seemingly impossible demands were met.

In his new novel, Philip Loraine describes for the first time the massive official cover-up, traces the hijacking back to its African roots, and exposes the three enigmatic figures at the eye of the storm: Tom Connell, who was not exactly the mercenary pilot he pretended to be; Henrik Mannin, Personal Aide and Commander-in-Chief to a President (among other occupations); and Sasha Vanleyden, the fascinating woman whose real relationship with both men remains an open question.

Philip Loraine's previous novels have been highly praised for their excellent characterization and suspense. Both qualities are abundantly evident in his latest thriller.

### *Loaded Questions*
July 1985

Isaac Erter had worked for Peace all his life, but Peace is a dirty word to a lot of people. So, naturally, he was killed. Who by? How? Why was the truth about his death never released? Just three of the questions asked by Tom Wood and David Cameron, the *Follow-Up* team of one of the leading Sunday newspapers.

The questions lead them to Steve Lathan, an American, thought by some to have himself shot Erter. Lathan is ex-CIA. (Why ex? Good question!) His pretty wife, Holly, has a few secrets too: also connected with Isaac Erter.

In London, where the investigation begins, things seem cool enough; but they grow warmer in Paris, and become too hot to handle in Jerusalem – thanks to Anthony Markham, smooth mercenary, arch-manipulator, as much at home in the back rooms of Washington as in Abba Hayil, 40 miles north of the Dead Sea and 400 feet below sea-level.

As he says to Messrs Wood, Cameron and Lathan, when finally forced to pull a gun on them (not at all his style): 'If you go about asking loaded questions you must expect a few loaded answers' – which, plus the kidnapping and possible murder of beautiful Holly, is exactly what they get!

### *Photographs Have Been Sent to Your Wife*
February 1971

'Mr Hardy, 'says the voice on the telephone, 'I have to tell you that I have informed both your employer and your wife of your relationship with Miss Judy Lester. *Photographs have been sent to your wife* – which means, I think, that your career, your marriage, and to a certain extent your life, are at an end.'

Alan Hardy is a top TV personality on both sides of the Atlantic. He is 32 – Judy is under 16. In his few weeks of freedom between indictment and trial, he is determined to find the identity of his hidden destroyer. And the first suspicion that hits him is that he may not be alone. A young gondolier jumps to his death from a bedroom window of a Venetian palazzo. A multi-millionaire keeps his perfectly sane wife shut up in a Swiss 'sanatorium'. In Rome, something very nasty happens to a Harley Street doctor who is hooked on heroin. An elderly Tory MP shoots himself on a beach near Antibes.

Via the painful secrets of a dozen lives, Hardy's dangerous quest leads him at last to an empty flat overlooking the Vieux Port in Marseille – and to a truth which (like the sometimes violent novel of suspense Philip Loraine has woven around it) is both just and frightening.

### *Sea-Change*
June 1982

'Full fathom five thy father lies…'

From the very beginning in Tenerife it is obvious that the accidental drowning of Alex Hunter is not quite what it seems – but then nothing is what it seems in this story full of ambiguous questions.

Catherine Hunter, the beautiful and grieving (?) widow, her desolated schoolgirl daughter, her son David, who is by no means satisfied with the official explanation of his father's death…are they real, or are they inventions living an extraordinary charade? And unaware of the fact?

Alex Hunter's friend and business partner, handsome Patrick MacAlistair, flies out to Tenerife to deal with the formalities (and deals with the Guardia Civil, somewhat curiously, in the process). But why does he lie to the dead man's family? Who are the faceless men five thousand miles away following his every move? Why does he identify the body of a perfect stranger as being that of his friend?

The questions asked on the sunny island in the Atlantic are answered in a stuffy room behind a London art gallery, and reach a deadly conclusion in the streets of Vienna during a snowstorm. Who really 'suffers a sea-change'? Dead Alex Hunter, his wife, his son, his best friend. Or all four of them?

### *Voices in an Empty Room*
October 1973

'No, no! Keep away from me, I can't stand blood! For Christ's sake, it's all over your hands!'

The words come from the mouth of fat Lulu Jenkins (French by birth, English by marriage, and a medium by profession) but the voice is not hers, for Lulu is in deep trance. The rich woman who has hired her claims that her interest in the wealthy Spenser family and their mansion in San Francisco is purely academic – but is it?

And what is the link between the past and Ellie Owen Spenser, the beautiful girl who lies writhing on her bed? To find an answer her brother and the young Englishman who loves her set out on a dangerous quest into an unknown world peopled by shadows and full of more haunting questions. Is Ellie really insane? What happened between the brothers Harold and Owen Spenser? What caused Harold's suicide? And why have so many family papers been locked away in a bank?

Step by step they uncover a story which Lulu Jenkins is already bringing to light in trance. But only two people know that a crime lies at the heart of the mystery, and they are not prepared to let the truth emerge.

Philip Loraine can always be relied upon to tell a good story. This time, as the voices of the dead fill the empty room in the old Spenser mansion, he spins a tale of guilt, expiation and retribution that makes the flesh creep.

## LOW, ONA

### *Murky Shallows: A Story of the Venetian lagoon*
May 1987

The lagoon that surrounds the city of Venice and more than thirty other islands besides, barely covers the mud-flats beneath it, though high tides may flood the city streets. It can be a murky and sinister place in autumn and winter when drifting fog slows water-traffic to a standstill, but no more murky than some of the characters in this novel.

The sensitive Stefano, son of the aristocratic Chiara, has returned with his Finnish wife and two children to make his home on the Lido. Chiara bitterly resents the presence of an alien daughter-in-law and schemes with age-old Venetian cunning to regain sole possession of her son and grandson. Meanwhile her powerful Sicilian husband, reared by the Mafia, is furthering his own unsavoury ends by organizing a publishers' and writers' conference in a prestigious hotel, when matters take a totally unexpected turn. Fortunately Arvo Laurila is already on the scene, the Finnish detective who made his bow in Ona Low's delightful first novel, *To His Just Deserts*. He soon discovers that in a world where polluted air and water are rivalled only by the corruption and decadence of local society, fear, hatred, revenge and sudden death are much at home in the Venice of the Doges.

The author has spent five years on the Lido di Venezia, within hearing of the tolling fog-bells and the sirens of ships making their cautious way up the lagoon.

### To His Just Deserts: A Story of Finland
February 1986

On a summer evening in the Great Courtyard of the castle in Savonlinna in Eastern Finland, audience and cast awaited the start of the final performance of *Don Giovanni* during the annual Opera Festival in the town. Only the singer of the title role was unaccountably missing, but his unpopular understudy was more than ready to take over the part.

During the performance, backstage drama surpassed anything visible to the audience, thanks to the involvement of certain members of the cast in the escape of a reluctant defector from neighbouring Russia and the added tension this entailed. But by the end of the opera it was the understudy who had disappeared. Had he, like the characters he portrayed, been dragged off by one of several persons who had cause to hate him, to what the opera calls 'his just deserts'?

Ona Low lived and taught English in Finland for many years. Her first crime novel sets an unusual story against the little-known background of a snowbound Lapland, bleak winter in a northern city, and Midsummer bonfires along the lake shore.

### LYALL, FRANCIS
#### Croaking of the Raven, The
May 1990

Occasionally guests die in hotel rooms, but the bruised face of one found dead in his bath at a Hydro in the Scottish Highlands arouses the suspicion of a fellow guest, a forensic pathologist. The dead man proves to have a ferocious reputation as an anonymous reviewer for a national journal, a reputation perhaps acquired as compensation for his unsatisfactory professional and marital career. The death looks like suicide, until it begins to seem that it might have been triggered by an anti-depressant drug which should not have been given in the deceased's physical condition.

Then a packet containing a collection of death and other threats arrives at Greyhavens police headquarters. Sent by the dead man's lawyer on his late client's instruction, it indicates the depth of feeling of some of those savagely reviewed. One, resident in the Hydro at the time of his death, has a

prior connection with the dead man. She also writes well about murder…

Superintendent Mason confronts a number of questions, including: Are novelists murderous only on paper?

### Death and the Remembrancer
February 1988

Accidents on grouse moors are not uncommon, but the violent death of a gamekeeper whose dissolute ways have caused distress in a Highland village is a matter which concerns both the police and Edward Williams, the local minister. Others seem less concerned.

Life in a village is always more complex than it appears and it can take a long time before an incomer (even, or especially, the minister or the police) is allowed to know the currents which lie beneath the surface, and in the memories of the inhabitants, past errors are not forgotten, and have their consequences.

How the gamekeeper had died was only too clear. Between them, Williams and his friend, Superintendent Mason come to think they know who shot him, and why.

### Death in the Winter Garden
August 1993

Antoine, a wedding photographer, goes missing during the photo-session at the Greyhavens Winter Garden of a wedding at which Superintendent Alan Mason and his wife happen to be guests. Later that night his premises are firebombed and someone spending the night there is asphyxiated. The portfolio of Antoine's photography proves to be subjects more varied than weddings, and photography is not the extent of his business affairs. But who is Antoine? Who might bear him a grudge?

Sorting out the tangle is the responsibility of Superintendent Mason. Does the onlooker see more of the game, and does the camera never lie?

### Death in Time, A
June 1987

Asked by his former employers in London to keep an eye on a senior academic at a conference at a fishing hotel in Scotland, Jarvis finds that mere watching is easy enough, for Professor Benedict, a refugee from Eastern Europe and a controversial figure, appears to have nothing to hide. But various currents surface among the delegates and the calm of a conference in idyllic surroundings is disrupted, especially when one of the delegates is found in the river in what looks like a nasty accident.

It is not the only death. Soon the police are asking searching questions. Jarvis, his cover blown, is drawn into the investigations and finds that it is not only fish which rise to a skilfully floated fly.

### Flying High
May 1991

Hang-gliding is a dangerous sport. When Ben Turpin, Glasgow art dealer and former colleague of Jarvis, dies in a publicity stunt on Ben Lomond, Jarvis, who is employed on unspecified government service, is asked by his employer to liaise with the police investigation because he had recently re-established contact with Turpin.

Inspector Cohen of the Glasgow Police and Jarvis find that the widow, the ex-wife (a former friend of Jarvis's) and a French art dealer all have more than a normal interest in the death, and Turpin himself may have been involved in the recent deaths of some of those close to him.

With the help of a Parisian salon assistant, an explanation is found, but things are more complicated than they seem. One thing is

clear: those who would fly high should take care not to fall.

### MacDONALD, JOHN D. (Ed.)
#### Lethal Sex, The
August 1962
*The 1959 Anthology of the Mystery Writers of America*

The Editor writes:

'This is an exotic banquet I set before you … Here they are, with their buttons and bows, their silks and scents … and their savage little minds.'

*The Ladies, God bless them* … the ladies whose work appears here are members of the Mystery Writers of America. Among them are names famous in the recent annals of crime writing – Christianna Brand, Ursula Curtiss, Margaret Millar, Margaret Manners, Anthony Gilbert (the pseudonym of a well-known authoress) and others.

This collection of ten short stories is something of a *tour-de-force*. All are written by women and all display the remarkable resourcefulness of the female mind in developing themes that deal with violence, deceit, crime and vice. It is tempting to stress the merits of individual stories; but the standard here is so high that such emphasis will be merely tendentious.

No better, more exciting or more subtle collection of crime stories is to be found to-day than those gathered in *The Lethal Sex*.

### MacDONALD, PHILIP
(*see also* **Porlock, Martin**)
#### Choice, The
April 1931

There were seven people in the Watch House, Polferry, on the night of Eve Hale-Storford's death. Her husband and his two friends made the discovery on their way to bed after an hour together in the smoke-room. It was either all three or none of them. Then there were Dorothy Grey, the housekeeper, Miss Susan Kerr, a friend of Mrs. Hale-Storford, Miss Miriam Rossiter, her sister, and George Anstruther, a young cousin of Hale-Storford – all of whom have retired to bed at the same time as Eve. All possible murderers! But when Colonel Gethryn decided it was time to give Scotland Yard a hand some months later, two of these possibles were dead! – the victims of extraordinary 'accidents'. Mr. MacDonald certainly gets us guessing, and keeps us guessing to the very last chapter.

### Crime Conductor, The
February 1932

Kristania on the screen! Kristania on the hoardings! Kristania in the skylights! Kristania the price of a million hearts! And then Kristania in a murder mystery! What a catch for the press; what a thrill for the world! Willington Sigsbee, the man behind Sigsbee's Revue, has succeeded in engaging and bringing to London Lars Kristania, the idol of the films, to appear in person with Anne Massareen in *Harlequin's Holiday*. There are numerous people who do not like Sigsbee for this, and Sigsbee is found dead in his bath. Anthony R. Gethryn almost apologetically appears on the scene. He has more to do than Mr. MacDonald usually gives him, but he does it even better than he usually does. Mr. MacDonald's characterisation and dialogue are always delightful. This time he has gone into an entirely new world for them, taking with him the inimitable Gethryn.

### Death on My Left
January 1933

In a corner of the ring in the deserted

gymnasium something lay. A man. He lay upon his face. His arms flung wide, one leg twisted beneath him in an attitude impossible in life, 'Kim' Kinnard, the English aspirant for the proud title of heavy-weight champion of the world, was dead – murdered in his training quarters on the eve of his greatest fight. Whose deadly hand had knocked out one of the greatest scrappers the world's ever known in that last contest – Kinnard on my Right; DEATH ON MY LEFT! An amazing mystery of the boxing world told in Philip MacDonald's vivid style, introducing those famous sparring partners, Colonel Anthony Gethryn and Superintendent Pike of Scotland Yard.

### Fingers of Fear and Other Stories
September 1953

Philip MacDonald is no ordinary mystery writer: suspense, horror and humour are only some ingredients of his master touch. Each of the stories in the present volume has its own dramatic atmosphere and intriguing characters. With scenes as divergent as California's glamorous Beverly Hills and the quiet English village of Friar's Wick, Mr. MacDonald captures a multitude of moods and adroitly manipulates a variety of themes. From the wryly humorous story of a 'clairvoyant extraordinaire' who proves that his pipe-line to the 'other world' is direct in a case of fashionable murder, Mr. MacDonald turns to a tale of deduction in which his famous sleuth, Colonel Anthony Gethryn, is challenged by an ominous fog, a sense of evil, and mass murder. In two tales of gripping intensity he depicts the precision of the logical killer and the psychological interplay between murderer and victim, and examines the tragic results when the forces of the abnormal clash with the normal. There is an absorbing study in fear when a San Diego cop winds up a case of child-murder with finesse, and then wonders if he got the right man. Together the tales in this book make up a brilliant *tour de force* by one of to-day's foremost creators of suspense.

### Link, The
July 1930

*The Link* deals with the strange case of Sir Charles Grenville, recorded by one Michael Lawless, as likeable an Englishman as the author has yet created. He was in the saloon of *The Moon* at Samsford on the evening when Sir Charles' body was brought in by a villager. Shot through the head – obviously murdered. Police investigations reveal two possible suspects with weak alibis – Lawless himself and Lady Greville, with whom Lawless is known to be in love. Then an important discovery turns the attention of the police to Dinwater, the landlord of *The Moon*. More discoveries, more suspicions only serve to make the problem more baffling until Colonel Anthony Gethryn takes up the case and unveils one of the most ingeniously constructed crimes in modern detective fiction.

### Maze, The: An Exercise in Detection
April 1932

Maxwell Brunton is found dead in his study… murdered beyond doubt. There are ten people in the house on the night of the murder and at least seven of these have an adequate motive for murdering Brunton. The evidence at the Coroner's inquest gives all the information upon which Anthony Gethryn has to work. In other words, YOU, the reader, and HE, the detective, are upon an equal footing. HE finds out. Could YOU have found out without his help? *The Maze* is an absolutely fair test of the reader's ability as a detective.

Apart from its problem, it is an enthralling story – one of Philip Macdonald's best.

### Murder Gone Mad
February 1931

Mr. MacDonald, who has shown himself in *The Noose* and *The Rasp* to be a master of the crime novel of pure detection, has here told a story of a motiveless crime, or at least a crime prompted only by blood lust. The sure, clear thinking of the individual detective is useless and only wide, cleverly organised investigation can hope to succeed. A long knife with a brilliant but perverted brain directing it is terrorising Holmdale; innocent people are being done to death under the very eyes of the law. Inspector Pyke [sic] of Scotland Yard, whom MacDonald readers will remember in previous cases, is put on the track of the butcher. He has nothing to go on but the evidence of the bodies themselves and the butcher's own bravado. After every murder a business-like letter arrives announcing that another 'removal had been carried out'. But Pyke [sic] gets there with a certainty the very slowness of which will give the reader many breathless moments. In the novelty of its treatment, the humour of its dialogue, and the truth of its characterisation, *Murder Gone Mad* is equal to the best Mr. MacDonald has written.

### Noose, The
May 1930

Detective connoisseurs have already met Anthony Gethryn in *The Rasp* and *The White Crow*. In *The Noose* Gethryn is recalled hurriedly from the weather of Spain to the November fogs of London. He finds that his wife is sheltering Selma Bronson, whose husband, convicted of the murder of a man named Blackatter six months before, is in the condemned cell of a great prison. The Appeal has been rejected; a petition for a Reprieve has been presented and refused – in five days Bronson will hang. But he is not guilty. Anthony knows this – simply because Mrs. Bronson tells him so; which seems absurd – till you know Mrs. Bronson. How does Anthony set about the impossible task of proving a man's innocence and another man's guilt, of a six month's old crime – all in five days?

### Nursemaid Who Disappeared, The
February 1938

This book marks the return of Philip Macdonald to crime fiction after a silence of four years, during which Hollywood has claimed his time, leaving detective connoisseurs to clamour in vain for a new novel from his pen. He made detective-story history with his first novel, *The Rasp*, published in 1924. It was notable, like its distinguished successors, not only for the brilliance of its conception, but also for its high literary quality, and for an unrivalled command of suspense and of the macabre. Six years later he made history again, when *The Noose* was made the first selection of the newly-formed Crime Club.

Now, in *The Nursemaid Who Disappeared*, he gives us a novel which must rank with his best. The detection is really superb, and our old friend, Colonel Anthony Gethryn is in charge. Need we say more?

### R. I. P.
April 1933

Mr. Philip Macdonald is not merely a talented storyteller; he possesses a positive genius for the macabre, and with his vivid imagination and tremendously virile style he has in a comparatively short time gained for himself a very large following. His latest story, *R. I. P.*, must rank as one of his finest achievements. The atmosphere of suspense is cleverly sustained throughout, from the moment that Lady Verity Destrier divulges to her friends that for several years she has received threatening letters from a man who imagines that she had done him a bad turn during the war. That night the last of the series is delivered…Danger is very near, for with Verity Destrier the mysterious correspondent has a long score to settle – *he is the self-appointed avenger of seven hundred men!*

### Rope to Spare
September 1932

The shrill persistence of the bell rang through the house. Anthony Gethryn went to the big oak door, opened it, and stared. Facing him was the figure of a man leaning heavily against the doorway, so that his shoulder kept up a steady pressure upon the button of the bell. Gethryn took a step backwards. Slowly the figure fell, tumbling forward in a head-lolling, ungainly movement, until, with a soft, yielding limpness, it hit the stone floor, seemed to twitch, and lay face downwards at Gethryn's feet. Gethryn knelt. He put a hand upon the tweed-coated shoulder, and knew that he was touching a dead man. Most admirers of Philip Macdonald's work will agree that *Rope to Spare* represents his best work to date. It is a long story—100,000 words of intensely exciting mystery and detection, but there is not a dull page in the whole book. As a grim study of the macabre and an admirably clever detective story *Rope to Spare* would indeed be difficult to surpass.

### Wraith, The
September 1931

Colonel Anthony Gethryn is no longer merely an extremely engaging character, he has become a permanent figure in crime fiction. Since his first appearance in *The Rasp*, he has gradually grown under Mr. MacDonald's pen into the brilliantly outstanding personality he is to-day. Now in *The Wraith* we get a new aspect of the man. The story is that of Gethryn's first case told by him in the first person. We see the debut into detection of a brain that is later to grapple successfully with problems in crime that have baffled and thrilled thousands of MacDonald readers the world over. It was in 1920 – two years after! – that Gethryn was living at the Good Intent at High Fen. He was the guest of the Manxes at Fridays – that strangely named old manor-house – on the evening when John Manx was found with a bullet hole between his eyes. And Gethryn had not gone from High Fen before he had unveiled a crime, a deal less brainless than that ghastly wound had suggested, and until, incidentally, he had taken a very long stride down the road that has brought him to the unique place in detective fiction he now holds.

## MacDONALD, PHILIP and CORRELL, A. BOYD
### Dark Wheel, The
September 1948

Philip MacDonald, famous as the author of many first-rate detective stories, from that classic *The Rasp* to that equally well-remembered *The Nursemaid Who Disappeared*, collaborates with A. Boyd Correll in a novel of great dramatic intensity. The story centres round Cornelius Von Toller, a wealthy New Yorker, whose Jekyll-and-Hyde character is known to few. His obsession for Kay Forrester, the actress, whom he watches night after night from the shadows of his box, sets the stage for a thrilling real-life drama.

## MacDONALD, ROSS
### Black Money
August 1966

In what is perhaps his strangest case Lew Archer, the celebrated private-eye, explores the secret life of a rich Californian residential suburb. A beautiful young woman has jilted her fiancé and taken up with a mysterious character who represents himself as a French political refugee. Hired to investigate this man Archer becomes involved in several murders and a gigantic swindle.

Running through the book, as a central theme, is the corrupting influence of the underworld and its money on modern society.

*Black Money* is the most individual of the brilliant series of novels that have won Ross Macdonald international recognition.

### Blue Hammer, The
September 1976

The theft of a valuable painting. The long-ago disappearance of a famous artist. A murder as deceptive as a magician's illusion. A horrendous – but now buried – explosion of family hatred.

These are the nerve centres of Ross Macdonald's new Lew Archer novel, the richest we have had from the author of 'the best detective novels ever written by an American' (*New York Times*) – a fusion of unfaltering suspense with dramatic revelation of the way lives are shaped and misshaped in the flow of time, in the hidden and dangerous emotional currents beneath the surface of family history.

The time is now: the place, Southern California. The stolen canvas that Archer has been hired to retrieve is reputed to be the work of Richard Chantry, who vanished in 1950 from his home in Santa Teresa. It is the portrait of an unknown woman – and on its trail Archer moves with edgy competence among the intrigues of dealers and collectors. Until suddenly he is drawn into a web of family complications and masked brutalities stretching back fifty years through a world where money talks or buys silence, where social prominence is a murderous weapon, where behind plausible facades of homes not quite broken but badly bent, a heritage of lies and evasions pushes troubled men and women deeper into trouble. And as he pursues the Chantry portrait – and the larger mystery of Richard Chantry – Archer, the solitary traveller, the loner who has through the years deliberately addressed himself to the deciphering of other people's lives, is thrust into an inescapable encounter with a woman who will complicate his own…

From its almost hushed beginning to its violent climax and unexpected – indeed astonishing – resolution, *The Blue Hammer* holds us riveted. This is Ross Macdonald at his incomparable best.

### Chill, The
November 1964

Hired to trace a runaway bride, Lew Archer uncovers a trail of murder that leads half-way across America and twenty years into the past. Beyond that, it need only be said that the story is every bit as exciting, baffling, and ultimately satisfying as would be expected from the author of *The Zebra-Striped Hearse*.

In the direct line of succession that reaches from Dashiell Hammett to Raymond Chandler, Ross Macdonald adds, to the crackling dialogue and narrative tightness of his illustrious predecessors, impressive qualities of his own: a depth of psychological understanding, a sureness in handling a wide variety of social milieus, and a dazzling, unpredictable plot.

### Far Side of the Dollar, The
September 1965

In this new and moving novel, Lew Archer, Macdonald's celebrated California investigator, is hired by the principal of a private reform school to trace a missing boy. What appears to be an ordinary matter of juvenile delinquency is suddenly magnified as Archer plunges into a web of murder and extortion. He ranges all over the Far West, tracking down men and women who are pursuing the fast buck, and hating to be reminded of what is waiting on the far side of the last dollar.

To the hard-boiled story of violence and death, Ross Macdonald has brought substance and depth of characterisation. His novels have a social range and moral dimension that, in combination with a striking prose style and narrative drive, provide the reader with a rewarding experience.

### Ferguson Affair, The
September 1961

The young nurse charged with selling stolen property was to be defended by Bill Gunnarson, a lawyer who had yet to make a name for himself. Bill believed her to be innocent, despite her secretiveness, and her lies. Before the case came to trial a murder had been committed – a murder obviously linked to the multiple burglaries which had led to the girl's arrest. The young lawyer found himself embarked on a tough, complex and dangerous investigation; there were to be several more murders, and some bewildering developments, before Bill Gunnarson could make sense of the Ferguson Case. Very few readers will be ahead of Gunnarson in unravelling the story, or in penetrating the secrets of the film star, Holly May, who was married to the oil magnate called Ferguson.

We are proud to publish this distinguished American crime novelist for the first time in the Crime Club. *The Ferguson Affair*, like Ross Macdonald's previous books, is a novel of quality. Real characters and true observation are worked into a plot that is complex, intriguing and, finally, breathlessly exciting.

### Goodbye Look, The
August 1969

In his new novel, Ross Macdonald's famous non-hero private eye Lew Archer – 'not only the most intelligent of the lot, but civilized and humane as well' (*Daily Telegraph*) – picks his way through the overheated and explosive mazes of a wealthy family's long hidden secrets. A lost heirloom, a murder that breeds murder, a boy's life poisoned by a money-crime committed before he was born – these are the elements of *The Goodbye Look*. It is Ross Macdonald at his unnerving best: a novel at once brilliantly perceptive of the world it atomizes – the freeway culture of Southern California – and from first to last unfaltering in its dramatic excitement and suspense.

Acknowledged master of the 'whipcord thriller' (*Bookman*), Ross Macdonald is increasingly recognized as an author whose books are 'enjoyable on two levels – the straight fascination of a carefully tangled web being unwound for us, and the more complex interest of a portrait of the seamier and corrupted side of a money-rich society' (*Oxford Mail*).

### Instant Enemy, The
August 1968

Davy's note to himself read:
1. DON'T DRIVE CARS
2. DON'T DRINK ALCOHOLIC BEVERAGES
3. DON'T STAY UP TOO LATE – THE NIGHT IS THE BAD TIME

4. DON'T FREQUENT CRUMMY JOINTS
5. DON'T MAKE FRIENDS WITHOUT CAREFUL INVESTIGATION
6. DON'T USE DIRTY LANGUAGE
7. DON'T USE 'AIN'T' AND OTHER VULGARISMS
8. DON'T SIT AROUND AND BROOD ABOUT THE PAST
9. DON'T HIT PEOPLE
10. DON'T GET MAD AND BE AN INSTANT ENEMY

*'You see what kind of boy he is?' Laurel said at my shoulder. 'A real trier.'*

So Davy tried, but his exertions did not result in tranquillity and peaceful order. He was deeply compromised with the young girl, Sandy Sebastian, and with the circumstances that led up to her disappearance.

Lew Archer, the famous detective of all Ross Macdonald's novels, was employed to find Sandy: a commission which led him to Davy, and to a family history loaded with crime and melodrama, starting far back in the past; a long, violent chronicle of betrayals, deceptions and brutality which did not stop at murder.

Lew Archer and Ross Macdonald his creator, now stand head and shoulders above all other contemporary American detective combinations. On both sides of the Atlantic, Macdonald, winner of the English C.W.A.'s 1965 award for the best crime novel of the year, is recognised as a novelist with a social and moral purpose: but also as a craftsman of the thrilling story, the surprise twist, the shock revelation.

### *Sleeping Beauty*
September 1973

The *New York Times Book Review* has called the novels of Ross Macdonald 'the finest series of detective novels ever written by an American.' His new Lew Archer novel – the first since the widely acclaimed *The Underground Man* – plunges Archer into a fascinating and intricate case connected to a disastrous oil spill on the coast of Southern California. It involves him with three generations of the imposing Lennox family whose offshore platform has caused the spill; whose young heiress, glimpsed for a haunting moment on the beach – handsome, angry-eyed, clutching an oil-drenched sea bird in her arms – has disappeared.

On her trail, Archer finds himself journeying into a horrendous past. Into the hidden lives of a family twisted by money, by power, by a ruthless, almost impulsive instinct for infidelity – infidelity between husbands and wives, parents and children, infidelity to friends, dependants, duty and, in a sense, to the earth itself. As Archer moves among these people, among their lives and contradictions; as episodes distant in time are linked – a derelict stranger found dead, a ship destroyed by fire in World War II, a secret case of extortion, a child's long-ago glimpse of violence; as the novel moves to its climactic and complex resolution, the reader is once more held fast by the unique art of Ross Macdonald: crackling suspense rooted in strong perception of reality.

### *Underground Man, The*
October 1971

*The Underground Man* brings Ross Macdonald's cool, pragmatic detective, Lew Archer, to a tragic fire that ravages a hillside community in Southern California. It enmeshes him in the lives of a group of troubled people searching for happy endings but fatally entangled in a web of murder and extortion stretching back through fifteen years – an angry father whose whole life has been a kind of breakdown, a mother using her son as a scapegoat, a pair of alienated adolescents who believe they are rescuing a child from an adult world, and a sad woman living with a dreadful secret. The result is a novel that mingles unfaltering suspense with that extraordinary perception of an American life-style (West Coast Affluent) that is the hallmark of Ross Macdonald.

### *Wycherley Woman, The*
April 1962

Her name was Phoebe Wycherly. Her age was twenty-one.

She was last seen alive at the San Francisco docks, three months before Lew Archer was hired to search for her. The search led him first to her family and her college friends, then far afield from the respectable and monied world where Phoebe had been brought up, into the criminal lower depths where life is valued lightly.

Ross Macdonald's new book has the texture of a good novel; the characters, ranging from an oil millionaire to an unemployed actress writing her 'true confession' autobiography, are freshly seen; and, as always with Ross Macdonald, the narrative is fast-paced, leading up to an explosive climax.

### *Zebra-Striped Hearse, The*
July 1963

Lew Archer was hired by the bride's father to stop a wedding; he was to investigate the mysterious and romantic-looking young painter with whom Harriet was infatuated and show him up as a good-for-nothing. Colonel Blackwell was very proprietary about his daughter although she was twenty-four years old.

Inquiring into the young man's past, Archer soon finds not mere dissipation or minor delinquency – but murder. As his investigation proceeds, this first murder leads to others. The story moves with speed and steadily mounting excitement across the map of California and through its society, from Los Angeles to the floating population of gamblers and their girls at Lake Tahoe.

This is the tenth in this series of celebrated crime novels by Ross Macdonald. Brilliantly written and plotted, its climax comes as a triple shock and an all-too credible revelation.

## MacKENZIE, DONALD

### *Cool Sleeps Balaban*
May 1964

Scott sweated with fear as he stood outside the house, waiting to break in. Usher was an experienced criminal and housebreaker, but Scott, impelled to crime by his desperate need for cash, was a tyro.

The proceeds of at least two robberies was required to save Scott's farm and secure Usher's future. Both projects are described in detail in this story: the reader accompanies Scott and Usher in their planning and execution of the burglaries – is with them when things begin to go wrong, and learns through many hair raising developments the degrees of violence, betrayal and repugnance of which each is capable.

Donald Mackenzie has won a fine reputation as a teller of stories in which professional criminals and their ways are realistically depicted. *Cool Sleeps Balaban* is a powerful successor to *The Genial Stranger* and *Double Exposure* – and its climax is thrilling and nightmarish.

### *Double Exposure*
July 1963

This time Hendry was sentenced to twelve years' imprisonment, and this time he had been framed. But he hadn't been framed the earlier times. Hendry was an experienced jailbird and an expert safe-cracker.

Hendry's conviction came at a moment when one of the Secret Services had urgent need of a professional safe-breaker; of a man known to have skill and nerve – a man who might possibly possess integrity and discretion as well. It was proposed to Hendry that, in exchange for freedom, he should carry out a dangerous assignment; that he should enter into a secret, informal contract with the State – a contract without effective safeguards on either side.

This story tells what happened to Hendry after he had bound himself to this contract. Set mostly in Germany, it describes in detail a theft of exceptional impudence and danger: an undertaking risky enough in itself but made still more precarious and nerve-racking by the nature of the contract, and the breaches in it that stemmed from human frailty.

*Double Exposure* is Donald Mackenzie's most exciting novel, its characters are solidly convincing, the story gripping and original, the climax startling.

### *Genial Stranger, The*
February 1962

Confidence tricksters are operating throughout Europe. Be on your guard against the man wanting to reward you for returning his dropped wallet ... Before parting with money to strangers on ANY pretext, check with your banker or with the local police. Thus read the warning posters.

In this story the reader is introduced to two 'con-men'. He sees every detail of the planning of two confidence swindles, one childishly simple, one elaborate and persuasive. These con-men are professionals, and it is not due to their incompetence or inexperience that events take an extraordinary turn, leading to a situation in which other passions exceed their appetite for stolen money. The action moves from London to Paris, with the danger of exposure to the police never far behind. It reaches a bizarre and complicated climax in Zürich, where at last, after many subtle deceptions and hair-breadth escapes, a crisis occurs which strips the actors of their parts in the confidence charade and reveals the truth. The story moves swiftly; it is absorbing and illuminating in its picture of international 'con-men' at work.

## MacKINNON, ALLAN

### *Danger by my Side*
April 1950

For Ian Douglas, off to the south of France on a business trip, the Golden Arrow means only the first stage of a pleasant journey. But it is also the start of something much more sinister – an adventure that is to lead him from the Pyrenees to London's dockland, from the Sussex Downs to a fighting finish on a Hebridean isle. Mystery, intrigue and violence await him – not to mention a charming and quite unscrupulous girl. Allan MacKinnon's story deals lightly with a very dark conspiracy. Wit and good humour accompany the thrills.

### *Murder, Repeat Murder*
September 1952

Bodies on doorsteps are by no means frequent in the respectable suburbs of South-West London, but on the November night that Detective-Inspector Stanners went to have supper with his superior and friend, Superintendent MacCallum, he found, literally on the doorstep, the body of a young man who had seen strangled with a length of thin wire. It had been a nice night for a murder, with a real London pea-souper descending with the dusk, but that night's fog was nothing to the one the two Scotland Yard men find themselves in before they solve the murder of John Markham, who had been employed by the small film company of Zenith Productions. Allan MacKinnon, author of several first-rate thrillers, in his new crime story uses to great effect the fascinating background of the film world, which through long association he knows so well.

### *Nine Day's Murder*
November 1945

Here is a story you will enjoy. You will like it because it is, above all, highly entertaining, superbly exciting and narrates a mystery that – well, if you can solve it you can give yourself full marks! Moreover there are some grand characters. You will like in particular David Stanners, who tells the story. David, formerly a detective sergeant in the C.I.D., now a wartime captain in the Artillery, while on leave in London is asked by his old chief at Scotland Yard to help tidy up some black market business which has culminated in murder. So David visits a pub or two and a club or two, has a look at the beer and the blondes, and does he get cracking! In *Nine Days' Murder*, incidentally his first novel, Allan MacKinnon takes a big stride towards a first-class reputation.

## MacLEOD, CHARLOTTE

### *Bilbao Looking-Glass, The*
October 1983

*Mirror, mirror on the wall,*
*Where's the axe about to fall?*

That's what Sarah Kelling and her art detective friend Max Bittersohn had to find out when their quiet vacation turned into a rampage of murder.

They were in trouble as soon as they opened the door to Sarah's seaside home at Ireson's Landing, Mass.: on the wall of the seldom-used front entry was a lovely Bilbao looking-glass Sarah had never seen before. Max, mindful of the burglaries around the wealthy summer colony, called the police.

Then Aunt Apple Kelling descended for a visit, and brought with her not only her own special brand of chaos, but Cousin Lionel and his four chips off the old block, their mother having decided (perhaps wisely?) to investigate an alternative lifestyle. As if that weren't enough it was soon grimly apparent that among the well-to-do, intermarried, interrelated summer denizens of Ireson's Landing were thieves, arsonists and killers.

Max and Sarah had to battle their way through a wall of prejudice, a maze of conflicting clues, and some extremely sticky situations before they found out who had taken them on this perilous trip through the looking-glass.

### *Convivial Codfish, The*
November 1984

Jeremy Kelling hadn't thought it would be like this. After years of toiling upward through the ranks, he had finally attained his goal; to preside as Exalted Chowderhead over the Annual Scrooge Day revels of the Comrades of the Convivial Codfish, which had got off to a great start. Then, at the height of the ceremonies, Jeremy discovered that he'd been robbed of his time-hallowed – and extremely valuable – emblem of office. The great Chain of the Convivial Codfish had gone.

Stunned by this catastrophe, Jeremy sent out a distress call to his new nephew-in-law, Max Bittersohn, now married to Sarah and already the nemesis of art thieves. Max was inclined to take the Codfish with a grain of salt, until Jeremy himself fell victim to what might or might not be a particularly vicious practical joke. From then on it was champagne, caviar, and cold-blooded mass mayhem in Bostonian high society.

### *Corpse in Ozark's Pond, The*
November 1986

When staff and students of Balaclava Agricultural College assembled on the gelid banks of Ozark's Pond on February 2 to celebrate Groundhog Day, they were not prepared to find a corpse bobbing among the icecakes. They were even less prepared to find the corpse clad in a suit of clothes a hundred years old, weighted with rocks and bearing an unnerving resemblance to Balaclava Buggins, long-dead founder of the institution that bears his name.

As Professor Shandy struggles to identify the corpse and his wife discovers a similar murder in the Buggins family archives, a fresh calamity hits the College when suit is brought for possession of Ozark's Pond, now vital to the College's power supply.

Worse still, the presumed instigator of the suit and his wife are found dead in their conjugal bed. Their daughter is married to the Security head and their niece to the Library Director. Peter Shandy is soon struggling in a cat's cradle of clues.

Peter Shandy is no stranger to Collins Crime Club readers. His previous adventures include *Rest You Merry*, *The Luck Runs Out*, *Wrack and Rune*, and *Something the Cat Dragged In*.

### *Family Vault, The*
May 1980

Great-uncle Frederick could be counted on to make a nuisance of himself. So when the old gentleman's burial had to be switched at the last minute from his assigned plot to a long-abandoned vault in a historic Beacon Hill cemetery in Boston, his young relative Sarah Kelling was not particularly surprised. But she was as appalled as the rest of her blue-blooded clan when the vault revealed, in Uncle Fred's chosen resting place, the ruby-studded skeleton of a flamboyant night-club queen who had vanished from Boston's equally historic Old Howard some thirty years before.

The Kelling's hadn't even managed to sweep out the rubies and get Uncle Fred decently interred before Sarah began to realize that she and those closest to her were somehow at the vortex of a complex murder plot that reached far back into the past and was moving inexorably and horrifyingly into the present.

### *Gladstone Bag, The*
December 1989

Emma Kelling has a penchant for hurling herself into worthy causes. She's just taken a leap for Ladderman Bechley's widow; now here's dear old Adelaide Sabine, too sick to play hostess to unknown guests at her island retreat. So off Emma goes to Pocapuk Island, her head full of laudable intentions and her Gladstone bag crammed with stage jewellery to repair for her own troupe of Savoyards.

Even before she's off the ferryboat, she's been drugged and temporarily robbed of the Gladstone bag. She's learned that Pocapuk was a pirate and Adelaide's island his ghost ridden lair. She's met the detestable Everard Wont and his odd assortment of henchpersons, who intend to dig up Pocapuk's treasure without having bothered to get Adelaide's permission.

Undaunted, Emma refuses to quail when she spies a pirate on the dock and discovers a vulgarly ostentatious surprise package among her fairy baubles. A mysterious amnesiac in the kitchen is mildly disconcerting but it's the corpse in the cove that puts a real strain on Emma's aplomb. So she does the sensible thing and sends an SOS to niece Sarah and nephew-in-law Max, the Kelling family's only professional sleuths.

As Emma has always maintained, whether you're running a benefit or catching a real-life pirate, success is just a matter of getting things organised and knowing the right people.

### *Luck Runs Out, The*
February 1981

Professor Peter Shandy of the Balaclava Agricultural College, whose Christmas decorations got him into so much trouble in *Rest You Merry*, is in trouble again. On the eve of the local agricultural show, a saboteur has reversed all the horseshoes nailed to the College's stable door as good-luck charms. Shandy predicts dire happenings. His predictions are nowhere dire enough.

As Shandy's wife Helen (nee Marsh) plans a quiet little dinner party, she is taken hostage at gunpoint, while Peter is forced to help steal a vanload of gold and silver that ought to be easily tracked down but isn't. After the party one of their guests is found murdered in the pigpen from which the College's prize sow has been abducted, and the pregnant 900-pound Belinda proves no more easy to trace than the vanload of bullion.

With only twenty-six sunflower seeds and a jar of pickled pig's feet for clues, Shandy faces a series of problems, including solving another murder, getting a distinguished professor out of jail, restoring Belinda, and persuading his old friend and colleague, Timothy Ames, to withdraw from the brink of another disastrous marriage – not to mention restoring serenity to the household of the College President, whose daughter may hold the key to the mystery.

### *Owl Too Many, An*
March 1991

The Annual Owl Count is serious business at Balaclava Agricultural College. But how could a team headed by President Thorkjeld Svenson and containing the redoubtable Professors Shandy, Stott and Binks have saddled itself with an avian ignoramus like Emory Emmerick? And how could Emmerick have had the bad taste to get himself nettled and stabbed to death while in pursuit of a rare owl?

Emmerick had passed himself off as a site engineer for the college's new TV station being funded with money from Professor Winifred Binks's enormous inherited fortune; but nobody from the construction company had ever heard of him. What kind of con game was Emmerick trying to run, and who was the real target? Peter Shandy, the Hercule Poirot of the turnip fields, brings his little grey cells to bear on the enigma; but things get increasingly physical when the perpetrators go so far as to kidnap Winifred Binks. All of a sudden, Peter, the President, and the abducted heiress are being swept in a runaway tugboat down a flood-swollen torrent, facing the dire consequences of what could be the most hostile takeover in corporate history.

Peter and Helen Shandy last appeared in the widely-acclaimed *Vane Pursuit*. Its predecessor, *The Corpse in Ozark's Pond*, won an American Mystery Award and the Nero Wolfe Award for 1987, and was nominated for the Edgar Allan Poe Award, for Best Novel.

### *Palace Guard, The*
June 1982

Sarah knew she shouldn't be there. The Kellings had never been invited back since an unfortunate incident at the opening of Madam Wilkins's palatial Boston museum. But things had been quiet at Sarah's elegant Beacon Hill boarding-house lately, and her lodger Max Bittersohn had free passes for today's concert; which is how Sarah and Max came to be standing on the Palace's second-floor balcony, rejoicing inwardly that the musical fiasco was over, and admiring the flower-filled courtyard below. Suddenly a peacock screamed. A dark something fell past them from the floor above. Serenity turned to pandemonium as the oldest guard sprawled dead among the hyacinths.

It was a case ready-made for Bittersohn, professional tracker of art thieves and forgers, even though the concert impresario tried hard to convince him that there was no case. Then another guard was found poisoned in the locker-room, and Sarah's own Cousin Brooks offered himself as a substitute guard because of his friendship with the lady curator. Before long Bittersohn's investigation became official – and that was in itself one of the most bizarre happenings in a bizarre and puzzling case.

*The Family Vault* and *The Withdrawing Room* have already won many admirers for the Sarah Kelling series. Charlotte MacLeod's latest novel will surely win many more.

### *Plain Old Man, The*
June 1985

*"Oh, you very plain old man, I love you dearly,"* sang Sarah Kelling Bittersohn as she painted scenery for producer Aunt Emma Kelling, whose private troupe of Savoyards were doing *The Sorcerer*. Aunt Emma had always wanted to play Lady Sangazure, but perhaps she had made a less happy choice in casting a well-connected con man in the title role. Certainly it was no mere evil spell that caused a valuable painting to vanish and left Charlie Daventer, as plain an old man as you could find, dead on his bathroom floor.

Cousin Frederick Kelling, almost as plain but not quite so old, was hurled into the breach. Frederick didn't care for certain goings-on among the cast, but what really angered him was the assumption that his good friend Charlie had died by accident. With a homely clue in an exotic container, he convinced Sarah that murder had been committed.

Sarah's art detective husband, Max, was abroad, so she tackled the case herself, even though it involved such perils as lunching at Cousin Mabel's house. Clues weren't hard to find – the problem was to sort them out. Somehow Sarah managed it, but even when the curtain fell, she found the show was far from over.

### *Recycled Citizen, The*
May 1987

Charity begins at home – in this case at the overstuffed mansion now owned by Adolphus Kelling. Dolph and his wife Mary are less interested in Great-Aunt Matilda's beaded footstools than in the Senior Citizen's Center [sic] which they themselves have founded. As they make plans to auction off Dolph's inherited possessions on behalf of their pet charity, their champion recycler is found dead in a part of Boston where he'd vowed never to go. A routine mugging, say the overworked police. If that's the case, say Dolph's cousin Sarah and her detective husband, Max Bittersohn, what are those grains of heroin doing in his collecting bag? So the chase is on, from Beacon Hill to the Back Bay to fashionable Chestnut Hill and back again, with Max and Sarah leading a pack of Kelling uncles and cousins and aunts in full cry after an arrogant criminal who appears to be using the Recycling Center for a purpose Dolph and Sarah never intended, and doesn't care how many senior citizens get recycled in the process.

### *Rest You Merry*
November 1979

For years, Professor Peter Shandy had been badgered in vain by Jemima Ames, Assistant Librarian and Annual Chairwoman, to decorate his campus home for the Grand Christmas Illumination, which was Balaclava Agricultural College's main fund-raising event. Now he could hold out no longer. Goaded to madness, he buried his small brick house under an avalanche of plastic reindeer, flashing lights, and fake Santa Clauses, hooked up to an amplifier blaring 'All I Want for Christmas is My Two Front Teeth', locked the switches at On, and escaped to sea on a tramp steamer.

Shipwrecked and conscience-stricken, he crawled back to face his irate colleagues – and found Jemima Ames dead on his living-room floor. Police and colleague security guards said it was an accident. Shandy said it was murder. And the President of Balaclava Agricultural College said he'd better find out the truth without wrecking the grand Christmas Illumination, or the next corpse would be Shandy's.

### *Resurrection Man., The*
April 1992

This is a red-letter day for art detective Max Bittersohn. His broken leg has mended, he's taking his first solo stroll across Boston Common … and here comes disaster in a hobble skirt and a picture hat. She's Countess Lydia Ouspenska, an expert forger of Byzantine icons and a magnet for catastrophe on the grand scale. When Lydia tells him she's joined a secret guild as a gilder, Max suspects all that glitters may not be gold. Once he's met head guru Bartolo Arbalest, he knows darned well it isn't. Soon the team of Kelling and Bittersohn is embroiled in another all-hands-on-deck adventure as Cousin Percy's wife's parrot is stolen, a very old friend is stabbed to death in his own front hallway, and a weird little man in a red jogging suit trails a crazy thread from one crime to another. It's been a while since Kelling fans have found Sarah, Max, Cousin Brooks and his glamorous Theonia, not to mention henchpersons Mariposa and Charles, together in the historic Kelling brownstone on Beacon Hill. Their various talents are splendidly displayed in the ninth book in Charlotte MacLeod's Kelling family saga, which is guaranteed to delight their ever-growing number of fans.

### *Silver Ghost, The*
December 1987

The New Phantom has vanished. Now the Silver Ghost is gone too.

No, it's not a séance. It's a Renaissance Revel at the estate of Jeremy Kelling's old friends the Billingsgates. Jem's off yachting, but Sarah Kelling Bittersohn is there in hennin and houppelande trying to find out who's stealing her hosts' antique Rolls-Royces. Husband Max has just discovered a corpse near the car shed and the author of *Terpsichore Totters* is pestering her to dance the volta. It's an awkward situation and becomes more so as the incredible legacy of a mad genius comes to light and Aunt Boadicea Kelling disappears, presumably during a stroll through the bee [sic] fields. Is Bodie another victim or is she – preposterous thought! – a car thief? And why is everybody eating all that frumenty?

Aficionados of the Kelling family, who seem to be even more numerous than the

Kellings themselves, will have a splendid time encountering old acquaintances among the Codfish Aristocracy of New England as Sarah and Max find themselves having to toss back some large red herrings before they reel in a most unusual catch.

### Something in the Water
February 1994

How can an innocent helping of chicken pot pie from innkeeper Ellen Bright's impeccable kitchen turn suddenly into a lethal weapon? Having just finished eating the next-to-last piece of that selfsame pie, Professor Peter Shandy has every reason to be concerned when the man at the next table flops over with his face in the gravy, his pulse rate down to nil, and the unmistakable odour of cyanide on his lips.

This is not what Peter's come looking for on the rock bound coast of Pickwance, Maine, to which he's fled from his wife's all-female house party. His objective is to wheedle, buy, or, if necessary, steal seed from the most gorgeous lupin plants he's ever seen, shooting to incredible heights in a spot where theoretically they shouldn't be able to grow.

As head horticulturist at Balaclava Agricultural College, Peter's first duty is to solve the mystery of the leaping lupins. As Balaclava's apology to the shade of Hercule Poirot, Peter can't keep from investigating Pickwance's amazing potpourri of lust, greed, hatred, passion, fraud, embezzlement, murder, and possibly even witchcraft.

### Something the Cat Dragged In
April 1984

Had she but known her cat Edmund had taken to hanging out with Chief Fred Ottermole at the Balaclava Junction Police Station, Mrs Martha Lomax might not have been so dumfounded when Edmund singlehanded (though double-pawed) pulled off a brilliant piece of detection. Acting on Edmund's clue, she discovered the corpse of her aged, unpleasant, but eminently respectable boarder, Professor Herbert Ungley, impaled on a harrow behind the tumble-down clubhouse of the too-exclusive Balaclavian Society. Fred Ottermole was willing to call it misadventure. Mrs. Lomax wasn't, for by that time she and Edmund had found another clue. It led them straight to Balaclava Agricultural College, where Professor Ungley had been emeritized under circumstances even Mrs Lomax didn't know about. Could she have foreseen what a Hallowe'en witches' brew of crime and chicanery she was uncorking, Mrs Lomax might have thought twice before she passed on the clues to Professor Shandy and started what threatened to become a full-scale war between town and gown.

### Vane Pursuit
May 1989

Charlotte Macleod returns to the adventures of Professor Peter Shandy of Balaclava Agricultural College – to the delight of his many fans.

Balaclava County's priceless Praxiteles Lumpkin weathervanes were disappearing fast. This was not due to age or weather but the systematic theft by a gang. The climax came when the Lumpkinton soap works burned down as the result of the gang's activities, killing one man and throwing hundreds out of work.

Of course Professor Shandy could not stand aside from crime on his own doorstep. Moreover, he had a particular interest in the vanes, for Helen, his librarian wife, had been photographing them in preparation

for an article in a learned journal. But when she travelled to Maine to photograph one of the last vanes still in its natural habitat and undertook a whale-watching jaunt by way of sightseeing, neither she nor Peter suspected that she was about to be shanghaied by the vane snatchers.

Peter meanwhile, all unaware, was investigating the activities of a bunch of survivalists on well-named Woeful Ridge who appeared intent on practising for World War III – with Peter and Balaclava's ace reporter Cronkite Swope as the enemy. Rescued by a reclusive naturalist, they are just in time to come to Helen's aid and round up a bunch of the most astonishing and villainous felons in Balaclava County's history.

### Withdrawing Room, The
September 1981

What's the proper way for a Boston landlady to react when her most obnoxious boarder gets squashed by a subway train?

Young Sarah Kelling of the Beacon Hill Kelling's doesn't much mind losing Barnwell Augustus Quiffen. She already has a far nicer applicant for the drawing-room suite, now that money problems, which became acute in *The Family Vault*, have forced her to turn her historic brownstone into a boarding-house. Curmudgeonly Mr Quiffen has been a mistake from the start.

But was he her only mistake? What about her other tenants, especially that statuesque enigma, Mrs Theonia Sorprende? Is dear old Mr Hartler really such a pleasant change? And what about the eye-witness who shows up insisting somebody pushed Mr Quiffen under the train? Or the dreadful tension that builds when she realizes that she is again involved with murder.

This time Sarah need not face her problem alone. She has all too many would-be helpers. Fortunately, they include her basement boarder, Max Bittersohn, and an expert with a very special sort of expertise.

### Wrack and Rune
November 1982

After his efforts in *The Luck Runs Out* and *Rest you Merry*, Professor Peter Shandy ('autocrat of campus breakfast table' – *Observer*) had quite a reputation as a sleuth. So when the hamlet of Lumpkin Corners was visited with a violent and exceedingly unpleasant death, the third call old Timothy Ames made – after the police and the doctor – was to his colleague at the Balaclava Agricultural College.

The cause of Spurge Lumpkin's death was all too clear: quicklime. Whether it had been accidental was not immediately obvious to the shocked farmers, since the Horsefalls' hired man was not necessarily smart enough to keep his nose out of something even as obviously deadly as quicklime.

But, as Shandy soon pointed out, the quicklime had to get to the spreader somehow, and Hengist Horsefall swore there wasn't a lick of it on the farm. Could Spurge's death be a prank gone fatally wrong? Somehow Shandy didn't think so.

And that was before he began to uncover some suspicious connections here, some neat coincidence there; before talk began of the ancient rune stone and its curse; before 102-year old Sven Svenson took up with an older woman…in short, before an awful lot of stir in sleepy little Lumpkin Corners.

### Christmas Stalkings: Tales of Yuletide Murders (Ed.)
November 1992

As the season of goodwill approaches and the short days and cold weather force people

together in cramped quarters, *certain* persons often turn to thoughts of getting rid of all the other people and having the fireside to themselves.

When it becomes necessary to deplete the bank account through the purchase of gifts to disliked neighbours, despised employers, and thoroughly hated relatives, *certain* persons contemplate purchasing instead large economy-sized packages of arsenic.

The enforced gaiety of the Yuletide season only strengthens the belief (again, of *certain* persons) that if only the wife/husband/mother-in-law/doddering aunt could be suddenly electrocuted by the Christmas tree, how much jollier things could be.

The *certain* persons mentioned in the preceding paragraphs are, of course, crime writers. Luckily for the rest of us, their homicidal urges have been channelled into the creation of these delightful new fictions which represent the work of some of the best mystery merchants at work today.

### MALCOLM, JOHN
#### Back Room in Somers Town, A
April 1984

The small painting by a follower of Sickert was not particularly valuable. It dated from the early years of this century and showed a young couple in a back room in Somers Town, a district of north-west London. Some might have found it appealing; no one could have thought it worth robbing an art gallery to possess it, and killing the owner. Yet someone did.

Tim Simpson, young investment specialist, could not forget that the murdered dealer had phoned him just before he died, full of excitement at a discovery he had made in connection with the painting. When Tim's own sortie into what was left of the district of Somers Town proved unhealthy, he became convinced that there was more to the little canvas than met the eye. But before he could pursue his investigation he was whisked off on business to Brazil, never dreaming that it was there, in the midst of financial wheeling and dealing, wealth and luxury, sultry passions and lurking danger, that he was to discover the true value of the painting and why it so desperately mattered to one man.

John Malcolm's first crime novel admirably combines his expertise in both the fine arts and business consultancy. It also marks the debut of Tim Simpson, who is destined to appear again.

#### Burning Ground, The
January 1993

Arriving at a French carpet factory near the Belgian border where he is to have discussions with the firm's technical expert as part of a proposed European merger, Tim Simpson of White's Bank finds the factory destroyed by fire and his prospective contact with it.

The factory was old, so its destruction and the death are suspicious, but the clues are both sparse and strange: a volume of Robert Graves's poetry; the site of his trench before the 1915 battle of Loos; a wartime painting by Nevinson in the Cubist-Futurist style.

The people involved are equally diverse: a brisk Belgian businessman; a Lancashire mill owner and his nephew; a powerful French entrepreneur; a blonde Market-mistress; a French ex-rugby player of Polish extraction; the Whites and the Maucourts, bankers of London and Paris, usually at loggerheads.

Caught in conflicts which are the legacy of terrible wars, Tim faces a tough assignment in locations ranging from Lancashire mills to the inside of French and Belgian police

stations where he is held on a murder charge. The case needs all his penchant for art-biography, the help of his art-expert wife, Sue, his detective skill, and his rugby instincts.

#### Deceptive Appearance, A
February 1992

Why would a distinguished Paris cosmetics house need the advice of art investment specialist Tim Simpson? And why is White's Bank so anxious to send him to help them? A suspicious Tim finds himself drawn into the internal politics of the Bellevie company and the cross-channel power struggle inside White's and Maucourt Frères, their Parisian colleagues, as a series of accidental deaths starts to get closer and closer to him.

Not that Tim is unhappy: he has attractive beauticians and a red herring from the art world to divert him. Moreover, the similarly cross-Channel life of the fashionable nineteenth-century artist James Tissot, 'a Parisian in London and a Londoner in Paris', provides a fascinating sideline for Tim to pursue when his work takes him to Tissot's birth-place, Nantes, where Bellevie has a factory. An agreeable coincidence; or is it?

Then Tim's business investigation takes a lethal turn, and he needs the help of his Tate Gallery curator wife Sue not just for art research but for the defence of his entire career at the Bank. Tim's foray from London to Paris and Nantes provides an entirely new, murderous twist to the challenge of Europe in 1992.

#### Godwin Sideboard, The
November 1984

*He was dead.*

*There were two red holes in the check shirt over his heart, and down the front of it was glistening, sticky red blood. His body had slid downwards, the legs under the well of his pedestal desk, and one arm thrown out across the top, scattering papers.*

*He was dead.*

*Only thirty minutes ago he'd been talking to me on the phone, I couldn't grasp it*

*He really was dead.*

After the first shock of finding the body of his art-dealer friend, Peter Blackwell, art investment specialist Tim Simpson began asking why Blackwell had been killed. Why had he telephoned on his way back from Sussex to London asking Tim to meet him, edgy rather than jubilant over the find he had just made?

Tim had asked him to look for a sideboard by the Victorian designer E.W. Godwin, sometime lover of actress Ellen Terry, but when Tim followed Peter's trail into Sussex there was no evidence that he had ever unearthed such a piece. Instead there was more violence, an old rugger friend of Tim's, now a police inspector – and Marianne.

Marianne was a partner in Appplemore Antiques, San Francisco. Very soon she was Tim Simpson's partner in bed. And in his investigations. And that was when things really hotted up.

#### Gothic Pursuit
March 1987

'I don't know how you do it,' grumbled Chief Inspector Nobby Roberts. 'You're a sort of magnet for corpses. Especially if they're involved in the fine art trade.'

He was addressing his old college chum Tim Simpson, and he had good reason to feel aggrieved. No sooner did Tim, in charge of the Art Investment Fund of White's Bank, set out to acquire a piece of furniture by Richard Norman Shaw, the late nineteenth century's most brilliant domestic architect, than his first informant was murdered. On past experience Nobby feared he might not be the last.

His fears were justified, but it was hardly Tom's fault. In the intervals of negotiating the purchase of a timber business for the Bank he merely charged about the country visiting Shaw houses in quest of the work that had disappeared from under his nose. He claimed he had no responsibility for the unfortunate and unrelated events which happened while he was pursuing information in his own time, but it was increasingly difficult to convince Nobby of that, let alone his superiors at the Bank. And least of all Sue Westerman, who had been involved in his enquiries before and was now positively demanding to be part of them because they were part of his life.

John Malcolm's account of how Tim acquired the Shaw piece, what it was, and who had murdered to stop him getting it, is as racy and knowledgeable as ever. He gets better all the time.

### *Gwen John Sculpture, The*
September 1985

The letter arrived at Tim Simpson's Park Lane office on a bright morning in early June. It was handwritten in a scratchy female script and bore an address in Meudon, a suburb of Paris. It offered a hitherto unknown representation by Rodin of the painter Gwen John. If genuine, it would be a real coup for the Art Investment Fund of White's Bank, of which fund Tim was now head.

Before the day was out it represented a considerable personal coup for Tim also, for the chairman of White's requested him to find a piece of sculpture with British connections to adorn the headquarters of a new company in which White's was to be heavily involved.

And then the troubles began.

For Tim, they included the unwelcome discovery that someone else was in pursuit of the coveted Rodin – someone who would stop at nothing, not even murder, to acquire it. For White's they included the alarming realization that their chairman was hell bent on involving them in a dubious investment, to the risks of which he appeared wilfully blind.

As the unsuspected connection between art and business emerges, and the action shuttles from London to Paris to the Dordogne, Tim makes an even more unwelcome discovery: his own life is at stake.

### *Mortal Ruin*
January 1988

The last thing Tim Simpson expected when he arrived in Chicago, was to be attacked by three men who had apparently singled him out. Tim, ex-Rugby Blue, dealt with them easily enough. What puzzled the director of the Art Fund in White's Bank was why he was of such interest. He was in Chicago on the Bank's business. If he had promised an old friend to check the value of some inherited gold shares, what had that to do with the attack?

Everything, it seemed. The original owner of the now worthless shares was an Englishman, Moreton Frewen, known as Mortal Ruin because investors always lost money on his schemes. Rancher, miner, landowner in Sussex and Ireland, uncle by marriage to Winston Churchill, Frewen was a larger than life figure who came to fascinate Tim and his girlfriend, Sue Westerman. Obviously Frewen had believed the gold shares were valuable, because he had instructed that they were 'to be kept with the sergeant'. By the time Tim and Sue had discovered why, their quest had taken them a dramatic confrontation in Ireland, and Tim had good reason to remember the advice given him by more than one person: 'If you're going to have anything to do with Moreton Frewen and gold shares, keep a sharp eye out. A very sharp eye.'

### *Sheep, Goats and Soap*
March 1991

Tim Simpson, head of the Art Investment Fund at White's Bank, is back in hot water as he and his wife Sue pursue a trail of murder, deception, and violent greed against a brooding background of Pre-Raphaelite artistic inheritance and illusion spun between London, Japan and a Hastings clifftop. Sheep, goats and soap are the last things Tim believes he is seeking, yet the enduring symbolism of the Pre-Raphaelites dogs his every step.

Sheep are innocent creatures needing an attentive shepherd. Holman Hunt painted them in canvases intended as a stern warning to us all. Goats are credited with venal, cunning behaviour, but Holman Hunt's *Scapegoat* is one of the grim sacrificial images of our culture.

When Sir John Millais painted *Bubbles* he never thought that the Pear's Soap Company would like it as an advert for their product. His image needed no laundering.

Now the innocent, the venal and the laundering come together in a deadly trap, baited with a priceless work of art, and with its jaws set to close not only on Tim but on Sue as well.

### *Whistler in the Dark*
May 1986

The Art Investment Fund of White's Bank, now headed by Tim Simpson, is after a Whistler. Very privately, of course, for these days Tim is peacefully ensconced in the City, getting on with his little bit of banking and trying to stay out of trouble.

Unfortunately Tim attracts trouble as a jampot does wasps. Even when he is in the company of the charming Sue Westerman of the Tate Gallery, a quiet expedition in quest of a couple of Whistlers ends in violence. As a result, it looks as though all hope of tracing these unrecorded paintings is lost. But that is to reckon without Tim.

His researches take him deep into the complex relationships of the Whistler family and their problems in building railroads in Russia and the States. Beside these, the dealings of a merchant bank like White's seem simple, though the presence in London of the vice-president of a Chicago bank is a source of some anxiety to Tim: is he perhaps too interested in Whistlers for Tim's good?

Not until he visits a quiet South Coast resort and discovers that it can be a very unhealthy place indeed, does Tim learn the fate of the missing paintings – and who his opponent really is.

Once again John Malcolm, operating within his chosen worlds of merchant banking and the arts, provides his readers with a thrilling mystery which is also 'an information-packed delight' (*The Times*).

### *Wrong Impression, The*
January 1990

It is easy for everyone to get the wrong impression. Especially when a senior police officer on a drugs investigation, various members of the fine art trade and a superb forger have been murdered or subjected to ferocious attacks.

The man trying to make sense of these events is Tim Simpson of White's Bank and its Art Investment Fund, but the resistance to his vengeful investigation of the assault on his now-comatose friend, Nobby Roberts, is widespread; Scotland Yard, his girlfriend Sue Westerman, the art dealer Maurice Goldsworth, and a nurse with a vital clue, all react hostilely.

Even Jeremy White, Tim's chief at the Bank, while keen for the Art Fund to acquire an Impressionist painting by Monet or Pissarro, who both painted some London canvases during their escape from the Franco-Prussian War in 1870-71, seems to have entirely the wrong impression about Tim's motives, especially where the nurse is concerned.

Or has he?

From the pinnacle of the art business in Bond Street, via London's working suburbs to a meeting in Lower Norwood, Tim stalks his lethal opponents through a world where even a dead man's little detective-joke leads to murderous consequences.

## MANN, JESSICA
### *Charitable End, A*
April 1971

Not all crimes are reported to the police – for various reasons. The comfortable Edinburgh citizens who received poison-pen letters thought it more politic to say nothing about them. That way scandal would not break. And one scandal had already broken, when the French-born wife of a judge and chairman of the local ladies' charitable organization received one of the letters and blurted out some details of her husband's not so blameless life.

The matter was discreetly hushed up, but there was a subtle and distressing change of atmosphere. Someone in this small, closed professional circle, filled with domestic problems, good works and social occasions was undoubtedly evilly disposed. Spurred on by a journalist friend, and by the accidental, if oddly convenient, death of her chairman, Diana Drummond, secretary of the charitable organization, begins to investigate.

Everything pointed to a connection with the chairman's French girlhood. On a trip to Paris Diana learns some startling facts. But someone else must already have been aware of them. Was Lady Gossett's timely death indeed an accident?

Jessica Mann fills in the details of her characters' lives and their Edinburgh background to create an absorbing study of the kind of crime we might all know – the crime which makes no headlines, which the police – for lack of evidence – never hear of, but which brings its own retribution in its train.

## MANSFIELD, PAUL
### *Final Exposure*
September 1957

As one of the characters says, 'At any given time you can find two or three families or individuals or even entire cliques in San Rafael who are at loggerheads over something of other. To leave out such warring factions would not only deplete a party, but rob it of all seasoning.'

Vanessa's party had plenty of 'seasoning'. It included Frank Keating, an old boy friend of Vanessa's, and Patricia Leighton who was deeply involved with George Burnley, Vanessa's husband. The ebullient Mrs. Lipton-Crumley and her odious son Peter were there.

It was not surprising that a murder took place at the party.

In the beautiful and exotic island of San Rafael law and order was in the charge of Superintendent Mark Caldwell and his lieutenant, the dark-skinned Sub-Inspector Arrow. They found themselves investigating a murder that was made more mysterious, complex and intriguing by the fact that a photographer had been at work in the room – and at the time – that it occurred.

This unusual detective story, with its affectionate picture of an ocean island and its serious treatment of plot and character, is a first novel by a new writer. Its ingenuity, originality and maturity introduce a new talent to the Crime Club.

## MARCH, MAXWELL
### *Shadow in the House, The*
July 1936

When Mary Coleridge arrived at the seemingly peaceful and pleasant home of the De Liane family she was asked to marry the dying son of the house so that the family fortunes might be secure. An unusual request, but she agreed to do so, though on overhearing a conversation decided it was best to leave her home and husband at once. But escape was impossible for she was part and parcel of the dastardly crime perpetrated by the De Liane family. Outwardly such a very charming family; inwardly so devilish that they stopped at nothing – even if it came to murdering one of their blood relations. Maxwell March imparts a Grand Guignol flavour to her story. It is a book that pulsates with tense drama and excitement and makes splendid reading.

## MARDER, IRVING
### *Paris Bit, The*
August 1967

Humphrey Egalhaft had been killed with a steel knitting needle 'and though it hardly seemed possible, he was as revolting in death as he had been in his heyday.' Who could have killed the pop-singer? 'Almost anybody. Any music lover, any patron of the arts, any public-spirited citizen, any red-blooded American. Or Frenchman, or Micronesian.'

Egalhaft dies in Paris, where this story is set. Max Moritz, reporter for the *Paris Trombone*, gives a good deal of attention to the death of Humphrey which still leaves him time to spare for Natasha, the belly-dancer, and for some considered eating as well. He encounters a variety of characters in the aftermath of Egalhaft's murder, not least Richard Postman, written-out as a novelist but far from faltering as an eccentric. Max Moritz's pursuit of truth is less dedicated than some of his other pursuits, but it leads him to the South of France, into danger, and finally to a bizarre revelation.

A picaresque murder novel – Paris as the tourists do not see it – some witty though disenchanted writing – fine, eccentric characters; those are the main ingredients of Irving Marder's funny and clever first novel.

## MARKHAM, VIRGIL
### *Dead Are Prowling, The*
May 1934

In Murmuring Lodge, her house on a lonely mountainside, a wealthy woman, long a recluse and a believer in spiritualism, lies dead. Just at nightfall, in accordance with the terms of her strange will, music is being played beside her deathbed. Suddenly incredible yet undeniable phenomena begin to occur. Are the terrified onlookers the victims of hallucination? Is some gigantic hoax being perpetrated? Are these visions really flesh and blood? One by one the rationalistic theories are disproved until the conclusion is irresistible that Murmuring Lodge is the abode of spirits. One by one Miss Knoyle's heirs, who with gold for their desire had climbed the hard road to the Lodge, succumb to the terror. These strange creatures with strange names, Wildgen Vincel, Michael Dan MaGehan, [all sic] and the rest, all flee – all but the two, boy and girl, who ultimately penetrate the strange mystery of Murmuring Lodge.

Mr. Virgil Markham, master of the macabre, brings the authentic atmosphere of an Edgar Allan Poe tale to the writing of a modern mystery.

### *Deadly Jest, The*
November 1935
*The Deadly Jest* is as macabre and eerie as anything Virgil Markham has done. There is suspense on the first page and no relief till the last. The setting is an old castle in Wales, occupied by an Earl and Countess, whose peaceful existence is shattered by the appearance of two Americans, who park themselves there and refuse to go. Crooks? And what of the master crook in the background? Shadows lurk; fear treads the ancient halls and stairways. A shot rings out, and death deepens the haunting silence.

### *Devil Drives, The*
February 1932
Frank Holborn, a gangster under sentence of death in an American penitentiary, tells Peters, the warden-in-charge, that he has been framed; how in an attempted last-minute rescue Peters shoots Holborn dead, and how Peters resigns his position and plunges into the underworld of crime and becomes entangled in a web of mystery. This story, exceedingly well-written, with its startling touches of brutality, gruesome humour and convincing revelations of gangsters, is certainly one of the most exciting thrillers ever published.

### *Inspector Rusby's Finale*
April 1933
Inspector Myles Rusby was a man of his word and since he had promised Mrs. Cade-Jack that he would devote a weekend of his holiday to a little problem in her domestic affairs, he duly arrives on the night of his release from duty, at Stoke New Place, her country house, and is cordially welcomed. The next morning when he rises he finds the place absolutely deserted – except for the corpse of an unknown man. Inspector Busby, keen, methodical, is back on the job again, relentlessly applying his trained mind to the unravelling of this extraordinary mystery! Mr. Virgil Markham, author of *Shock!*, *The Song of Doom* and other first-rate mystery stories, has quickly made a name for himself as a writer of detective novels that are peculiarly distinctive in style and method. *Inspector Busby's Finale* is an outstanding example of the author's splendid craftsmanship.

### *Shock!*
May 1930
Here is a super-thriller, with an unusual plot, unusual style and unusual atmosphere! It is the sort of book which one literally cannot put down because of the ingenuity of its plot and because its most incredible passages become convincing through the genius of the author's logic and style. It has for its setting a grim castle in the Welsh mountains – the sort of place where anything might happen. And something does! Sir Anthony has a voice that possesses the spell of the mountains themselves – a hypnotic voice that has conquered the beautiful girl Arthura. There is death in Kestrel's Eyrie, mysterious death that shocks!

### *Snatch*
October 1936
'Snatch' we must enlighten English readers, is the American term for kidnap, and this book of Virgil Markham's, quite his best in our opinion, and up to the highest standard of American detective fiction, is the story of one of the most cleverly devised kidnapping schemes that even America's 'mobsters' could affect. Robert Spring, bookie and tipster, is kidnapped in error for a millionaire playboy and driven off by night, to a lonely farm, among the marshes, vainly protesting his true identity. The whole story is told from the point of view of Edith, his secretary, who was kidnapped with him, with a wealth of detail that makes the activities of both gangsters and police extremely realistic, while the plot is worked out at a tremendous and enthralling speed.

### *Song of Doom*
July 1932
The Song of Doom! At first broad, deep, exultant, like the impassioned utterance of a 'cello string; then rising, throbbing – a mad song in which a frightful joy seemed tempered by embittered grief for what the singer had done, as if the triumphant soul knew that it was sick and sang its own *Dies Irae*… A series of mysterious murders have been committed by an unknown criminal called "the Fox." A characteristic of the murderer is that he always breaks into a song of triumph after the perpetration of each crime. Elsie Ritter, a Parisian actress, receives a message from "the Fox" warning her that she is to be his next victim. The tense story is unfolded by Virgil Markham with that unfailing sense of the *macabre* that makes him unique among writers of mystery stories.

## MARSH, NGAIO
### *Black as He's Painted*
April 1974
The President of Ng'ombwana had been at public school in England, and his best friend had been Chief Superintendent Roderick Alleyn. So when The Boomer, as he was affectionately known, proposed to pay an unofficial visit and dispense with the usual security arrangements, it was natural that Alleyn should be called in to try to persuade him to keep them, and thus ease the task of Special Branch.

Alleyn performed his mission so successfully that on the night of the Ng'ombwanan Embassy's reception the house and grounds were stiff with police. Nevertheless, a murder took place in dramatic circumstances and it seemed clear that it was The Boomer who should have died. Had the attempt been engineered by political rivals in his own country, or by expropriated and disgruntled whites? A happy hunting-ground for suspects was provided by the coterie of ex-colonials residing in the cluster of streets and squares known as the Capricorns, in the very shadow of The Boomer's Embassy. Assisted by Mr Samuel Whippplestone, recently retired from the Foreign Office, who in turn was assisted by Lucy Locket, his cat, Alleyn discovered that each and every member of the coterie had a reason for hating the black race.

But that astonishing and loveable figure, The Boomer, whom Troy Alleyn found such a fascinating figure to paint, had a few surprises up his sleeve and his own idea of justice. Witty, contemporary, civilised this is Ngaio Marsh at her dazzling and delightful best.

### *Clutch of Constables*
October 1968
'He looks upon the murders that he did in fact perform as tiresome and regrettable necessities'.

Thus Chief Superintendent Roderick Alleyn, in a lecture some time after the event, described the international crook known as 'the Jampot'. But it was Alleyn's wife Troy who knew 'the Jampot' best: she had shared close quarters with him in the cruise of the pleasure steamer *Zodiac*, winding its peaceful course along the rivers and canals in the arcadian setting of Tollardwark, Crossdyke, Longminster and Ramsdyke in the 'Constable' country.

Alleyn speaks with hindsight, but Troy was there in person, one of the odd group of passengers in the tiny ship. Troy knew that something was badly wrong with the company she kept. She '...was visited once again by the notion that she was involved in some kind of masquerade, and that the play, if there was a play, moved towards its climax, if there was a climax, that the tension, if indeed there was any tension, among her fellow-passengers, had been exacerbated by the twist of some carefully concealed screw'.

There are two murders aboard the *Zodiac* and it is Roderick Alleyn himself who forces the final showdown and revelations.

Ngaio Marsh and Roderick Alleyn form one of the most famous fiction combinations of our time. All her stories are exotic, witty and characterised in depth, with setting sharply observed. So it is with Troy's fated cruise and the discovery of the master criminal, 'the Jampot'.

### *Colour Scheme*
August 1943
This splendid new novel by the famous Ngaio Marsh promises a rare feast of enjoyment. To begin with it has a refreshingly original setting in the beautiful North Island of New Zealand, Miss Marsh's own country, which she describes with fidelity and affection. There is, too, an unusually interesting set of characters. At the hot springs near Harpoon Inlet, the retired Anglo-Indian Colonel Claire and his wife have opened a thermal spa which attracts a good many visitors desirous of undergoing treatment. At the time of the story, the residents include Dr. Ackrington an irascible retired doctor and the brother of Mrs. Claire; Geoffrey Gaunt, a visiting English actor; Maurice Questing, an unpleasant type of business man suspected also of an unpatriotic interest in the Fifth Column; and Herbert Smith, a remittance man who has imposed on the Claires for many years. Of the crime that so dramatically broke the atmosphere of the spa, and the subsequent hunt for its perpetrator, Miss Ngaio Marsh gives a lively and exciting account.

### *Dead Water*
April 1964
The healing of the warts on Wally Treherne's hands appeared miraculous. He pushed them into the cold waterfall on the hill at Portcarrow, he saw the Green Lady and within a few hours the dreadful warts and shrivelled skin had vanished. Wally was no longer a butt for his schoolmates – but he soon became the focus of a different commotion.

The 'Miracle' at Portcarrow did not pass unnoticed. It was not clear who were the initial movers – the believers looking for a cure or the exploiters with an eye for cash – but soon the rural peninsula was transformed into an expensive spa, renowned for its miraculous healing water. The tills clanged merrily until Miss Emily Pride inherited the celebrated land on which Portcarrow stood.

Miss Pride would have no truck with miracles or the charlatans who exploited them. The ensuing clash of characters and interests involved the leading citizens of Portcarrow, and murder followed. As Miss Pride's guardian angel, Superintendent Roderick Alleyn found himself on the spot in both senses of the word.

Always a brilliant comic writer, Miss Marsh is at her best in describing the attendant pyrotechnics of the 'Miracle' at Portcarrow. Alleyn's civilised manners only veil the astuteness and toughness that enable him to detect a murderer, and Miss Marsh again displays her wonderful gifts for telling a subtle story with life-sized characters – among whom Miss Emily Pride will certainly be remembered.

### *Death and the Dancing Footman*
January 1942
Mr. Jonathan Royal of Highfield Manor, Cloudyfold, Dorset was an artist by temperament. His difficulty was simply that he could not create. His results were pitiable – in paint. That was why there came to him the extraordinary idea that he would use for medium – flesh and blood. Real people would be the characters in the drama that he would devise and play before an audience of one – an intelligent audience – his friend, Aubrey Mandrake, a rising star in the literary firmament. It was lucky for Inspector Alleyn that Thomas, the dancing footman, was at hand when the plot moved to a dramatic climax. Here in large measure are the deft characterisation and sparkling style of Ngaio Marsh, one of the most outstanding detective story writers of the day.

### *Death at the Bar*
January 1940
At the Plume and Feathers in South Devon, one mid-summer evening, eight people are gathered together in the tap-room. They are in the habit of playing darts, but on this occasion an experiment takes the place of the usual game – a fatal experiment which calls for investigation. A distinguished painter, an celebrated actor, a woman graduate, a plump lady from County Clare and a Devonshire farmer all play their parts in the unravelling of the problem. The brilliant Ngaio Marsh is an acknowledged ace writer of detective stories, and in *Death at the Bar* she is at her most ingenious.

### *Death at the Dolphin*
May 1967
'A palace of refined and original entertainment.' Thus the old Dolphin Theatre had once appeared to its erstwhile owner, Mr Adolphous Ruby.

To Peregrine Jay, the young playwright now lusting to own it, it signified something not very different. Down by London's docks, with its decrepit ornaments and fading gilt, it spoke clearly to Peregrine of a contemporary revival of a great English tradition of theatre – and in a most seductive voice.

And Peregrine, through an outlandish train of circumstances, did actually become the master of the Dolphin. The old theatre was renewed, and its stage again became busy with Peregrine's own play about an episode in the life of Shakespeare himself.

This state of bliss was shattered by a murder at the Dolphin. From the murder stems a mystery, which brings Superintendent Alleyn, Inspector Fox and their colleagues, to the old theatre in the role of investigators.

Ngaio Marsh ranks among the greatest of the writers of detective novels. Hers is a household name, and her legion of admirers will be delighted with the humour, the setting, and the tantalising mystery of this exciting new novel.

### *Died in the Wool*
January 1945
*Died in the Wool* is a brilliantly told detective story by that very accomplished writer Ngaio Marsh. Unusual in its richly descriptive setting on a New Zealand sheep station, highly dramatic in its well-conceived plot, and generous in its varied cast of cleverly portrayed characters, *Died in the Wool* is an

outstanding achievement. From the moment when on a summer's day in the wool store of Riven Brothers a strand of metallic gold hair revealed to Alf the foreman the presence of a body in a bale of wool, the story moves dramatically to an exciting denouement.

### *False Scent*
June 1960

Ngaio Marsh's place among the great names of Crime Fiction is assured. This is her 21st book and once again she has given us a story, theatrical in setting and dramatic in plot, which introduces a dazzling and fascinating cast of characters.

The birthday party which Mary Bellamy gave each year had become a theatrical tradition; an occasion when the great names and glittering personalities came to display their affection and pay homage to the brightest star of the British stage. But on this birthday (it was her fiftieth, though few were permitted to know it) everything went wrong. She quarrelled with her husband, her servants and the intimate friends who came with gifts but who also brought news of disloyalty and betrayal. Mary Bellamy needed all her acting ability to disguise the rage in her heart when she greeted her guests. Then the twisted corpse which was discovered upstairs in the course of the evening, brought a disastrous day to its dreadful climax. It also introduced Inspector Roderick Alleyn to a case which makes Ngaio Marsh's newest book rank with *Singing in the Shrouds*, *Opening Night* and *A* [sic] *Surfeit of Lampreys*. It is an outstanding story from a Master Craftsman.

### *Final Curtain*
April 1947

Agatha Troy, world famous portrait painter, eagerly awaiting the return after a long absence of her equally famous husband, Chief Detective-Inspector Roderick Alleyn, is inveigled into accepting a commission to paint the seventy-year-old Sir Henry Ancred, Bart., the Grand Old Man of the stage. Just as she has completed her portrait a tragedy occurs and the old actor dies, making his first bow to death as dramatically as he ever took a final curtain in life – for the circumstances of his death are such that Scotland Yard in the person of Detective-Inspector Alleyn is called in. *Final Curtain* is an outstanding detective story by one of the greatest living practitioners of the art.

### *Grave Mistake*
September 1978

Twice-widowed Sybil Foster was wealthy, silly, sweet and not at all the suicidal type. So her old friend Verity Preston could not believe, when Sybil died amid the luxuries of an expensive private nursing home, that she had taken her own life, as the medical superintendent said. But then, Verity knew too much about the medical superintendent to trust him, even though she had no wish for their past association to become known.

It was true that Sybil had recently behaved out of character, but she was ill, her only daughter had just got engaged to a man Sybil wouldn't have chosen for her, and her ne'er-do-well son had turned up again in her life. These calamities, Verity considered, more than offset the pleasure of having at last found a really good gardener for their beautiful home in a Kentish village, though perhaps not the other, greater joy that had come secretly into Sybil's life.

But now she was dead, her cruelly altered will unsigned, and Chief Superintendent Roderick Alleyn was asking awkward questions in his politest, smoothest voice. Sybil's death was not suicide but murder, and the Empress of Crime once again delights her readers with a magnificent Alleyn and Fox story, in which someone somewhere makes a grave mistake.

### *Hand in Glove*
September 1962

*'My dear: What can I say…I know so well, believe me so* very *well, what a grievous shock this has been for you and how bravely you will have taken it…'*

Thus ran a letter of condolence from Mr. Pyke Period, who was celebrated for his fluency in the contrivance of these mournful epistles.

It was in Mr. Pyke Period's house that a somewhat bizarre company gathered for lunch shortly before violent death (not much softened by the condolences of Mr. Pyke Period) came to Little Coddling. To investigate the murder Superintendent Roderick Alleyn and Inspector Fox of the C.I.D. quickly appeared in the village.

Ngaio Marsh's crime novels are famous; her readers are legion. The craftsmanship that can combine brilliant characterisation, spectacular events and a baffling problem is at work here to the same great effect as in such well-known books as *Artists in Crime*, *Surfeit of Lampreys*, *Off With His Head* and *False Scent*.

### *Last Ditch*
February 1977

Exceptional parents do not always produce exceptional children, but Ricky, only son of Roderick and Troy Alleyn, certainly was. A very young don, he had retired to the Channel Islands during the Easter vacation determined to write a book. Instead, he was soon in the toils of the enchanting , wealthy Pharamond family, and face to face with unnatural death.

Was it murder? Ricky, his father's son, believed so, although it looked like accident. When indications that the peaceful island was a drug-running centre brought Alleyn and Fox on the scene, Ricky was suddenly in mortal danger because he knew too much: about Gil Ferrant, the mysteriously wealthy plumber; about Sidney James, best described as a dabbler in paint; and about Louis Pharamond, his friends" cousin, cool, smooth, enigmatic – and just possibly a murderer.

Ngaio Marsh sets her scene with that amazing sense of the visual which has always invested her settings and atmospheres with something magical. Against this her characters, portrayed with humour, skill and shrewdness, move in yet another of those classically plotted, best-selling stories which have made her deservedly and universally acknowledged as our greatest living Queen of Crime.

### *Light Thickens*
September 1982

Ngaio Marsh's last novel, completed shortly before her death earlier this year at the age of 82, is a testament to her abiding twin interests: drama and detective fiction.

Peregrine Jay, owner of the Dolphin Theatre, the opening of which was marked by murder in *Death at the Dolphin*, is putting on a production of *Macbeth*. Personal tensions among the actors are heightened by the superstitions surrounding the play, and by a series of grisly practical jokes which leave the cast shaken and upset. Someone is intent on reminding all concerned that the play has a reputation for bad luck.

When an additional unscripted murder takes place almost on stage, that reputation seems justified. Fortunately Chief Superintendent Roderick Alleyn was in the audience, and he is soon grappling with a baffling case in which not one of the many suspects with means and motive could conceivably have had opportunity.

Ngaio Marsh here offers her readers a double bill: her thoughts as a distinguished theatrical producer on presenting the bloodiest and most compulsive of Shakespeare's tragedies, and detection of a very high order, as befits the Empress of Crime.

### *Off With His Head*
January 1957

When the versatile Mrs. Bunz arrived at Mardian she said: 'I am a student of the folk-dance…my little monographs on the Abram Circle Bush and the symbolic teapawt have been praised.' She was determined to investigate the rare survival of folk-dancing that was believed to continue to this day at Mardian.

No one in the village, from Dame Alice Mardian ('character out of Surtees') to the five sons of the smith, William Andresen, considered their annual ritual – the Dance of the Five Sons – to be any business of the rest of the world, or of Mrs. Bunz. They did not see the macabre tragedy that was to take place on 'Sword Wednesday' of the winter solstice, amidst the disguises, the dancing, and the torches that lit the ruins of Mardian Castle for the ancient ceremony.

Superintendent Roderick Alleyn found himself faced with a case of great complexity – and also with an impossibility. He made many surprising discoveries in his investigations, which required that he should understand the movements of the dancers in their prehistoric rites.

At a gruesome reconstruction of the night of Sword Wednesday the impossibility is explained and the murderer revealed in an astonishing climax.

This successor to *Scales of Justice* and Ngaio Marsh's other fine detective stories will again delight her many readers.

### *Opening Night*
April 1951

Dreams of stardom had lured Martyn Tarne from far-away New Zealand to make the dreary, soul-destroying round of West-end agents and managers in search of work. The Vulcan theatre had been her last forlorn hope, and now, driven by sheer necessity, she was glad to accept the humble job of dresser to its leading lady, Helena Hamilton. And then came the eagerly awaited Opening Night – words which in the world of the theatre never fail to thrill – fateful words which mean so much to the players. The sweetness of success? The bitterness of failure? To Martyn Tarne the night brought a strange turn of the wheel of fortune, and to one distinguished member of the cast death sudden and unforeseen. *Opening Night* shows Ngaio Marsh at her best, writing of the life of the theatre which she knows so well.

### *Overture to Death*
March 1939

Ngaio Marsh (her name is pronounced 'Nyo') is a detective novelist of the very front rank – a writer of intelligence and style, gifted with a fine sense of character and drama, as well as the ability to devise really ingenious plots. This new novel, with which she joins the Crime Club, is a story that should satisfy the most exacting detective connoisseur.

*Overture to Death* is set in a small village parish which is in the throes of getting up a play to raise money for the Young People's Friendly Circle. The question now under bitter discussion is, who will play the overture: Miss Campanula, the wealthy spinster of the village, or Eleanor Prentice, who keeps house for the squire? Eleanor Prentice wins, but on the night of the performance she is found crying with a bad finger. Miss Campanula steps triumphantly into the breach, plays the first three notes of Rachmaninoff's Prelude, puts her foot on the soft pedal, and dies – shot between the eyes. The problem is astonishingly well worked out.

### *Photo-Finish*
September 1980

Isabella Sommita, world-famous soprano, world-famous temperament – what more fascinating subject for a portrait-painter like Troy Alleyn? So when an invitation arrived from her fabulously wealthy companion for Troy and her husband to be guests at his luxurious lodge on Lake Waihoe where La Sommita was staying, and to paint her portrait, Troy and Rory accepted with alacrity. Especially as Alleyn had already been discreetly approached via Scotland Yard regarding the unflattering photographs of the diva which one 'Stix' was supplying to the world's press. The latest, published shortly before the Alleyns' arrival had caused a ferocious manifestation of the world-famous temperament.

The Alleyns soon found Waihoe Lodge, amid some of New Zealand's most spectacular scenery, to be everything its owner had claimed. Moreover, it was to be the setting for a private first performance of a one-act opera by La Sommita's youthful protégé. A select party of musicians and guests had been invited; the composer was to conduct…At the end of the disaster La Sommita swept from the hall and was shortly afterwards found dead in her bedroom, a stiletto impaling a photograph through her heart.

With a houseful of suspects ranging from servants to serious musicians, now completely isolated by one of the lake's sudden storms, Alleyn faces one of his trickiest cases. And Ngaio Marsh writes one of her best books.

### *Scales of Justice*
May 1955

*Scales of Justice* offers readers an opportunity that comes their way too rarely nowadays, for here is the classical detective novel at its very best. With it Ngaio Marsh returns to the genre in its absolute form: detection arising equally from characters, suspense and a set of extraordinary circumstances.

The village of Chyning [sic] nestles, perhaps a trifle smugly, in the charming valley of the Chyne. Nothing mars the seemliness of the prospect. Even the eccentricities of the inhabitants would appear, on first acquaintance, to follow a time-honoured tradition. We have, for instance, Lady Lacklander's size and she is as vast as she is wily; Commander Syce's inebriated archery; Mr. Danberry-Phinn's cats; Colonel Caterette's angling; his wife's equivocal attitude to the elder male Lacklanders; his daughter's love for the younger. There is Nurse Kettle pedalling briskly about the landscape and finally that monster trout, the Old 'Un in his lurk by Bottom Bridge. It sounds harmless enough yet these are the ingredients which boil up into as pretty a hell-brew, as strange a murder and as ingenious a solution as ever graced the case-book of Mr. Roderick Alleyn

This book, with its particular tang of mounting tension is in the tradition of Ngaio Marsh's other great detective stories, such as *Surfeit of Lampreys*, *Artists in Crime* and *Death and the Dancing Footman*.

### *Singing in the Shrouds*
January 1959

When on a cold February night the cargo ship Cape Farewell sails from the Port of London, she carries nine passengers one of whom is a murderer. At the moment of departure the latest victim of this pathological killer, a girl with flowers, is found dead on the quayside.

Which is why Superintendent Roderick Alleyn joins the ship at Portsmouth on the most difficult assignment of his professional career.

This account of mounting tension among the apparently normal people culminates in the inevitable moment of death. Ngaio Marsh achieves a triumph on a level with such famous detective stories as *Surfeit of Lampreys*, *Scales of Justice*, and *Off With His Head*.

### *Spinsters in Jeopardy*
March 1954

A new novel by Ngaio Marsh is an occasion which all connoisseurs of the detective story will welcome with a cheer. Her last book, *Opening Night*, was chosen to celebrate the Crime Club's coming-of-age. Now, with *Spinsters in Jeopardy* she scores another direct hit. Chief Detective-Inspector Alleyn, C. I. D., with Troy, his wife, and his young son Ricky were all *en route* for a holiday in the Maritime Alps. Alleyn was combining business with pleasure, so for him it was a straight case of killing two birds with one stone. Killing birds, however, was not Alleyn's idea of a happy holiday, and he saw something quite different being killed as the night train on which he and his family were travelling flashed by the cliff-like wall of the Chateau de la Chevre d'Argent. It was precisely then that Miss Truebody, an English spinster who was travelling further down the train, chose to burst her appendix in circumstances of unparalleled confusion and embarrassment. What followed was the most unconventional and in many ways the most fantastic few days that Alleyn and Troy ever endured in the cause of proving the self-evident axiom that English policemen are wonderful.

### *Surfeit of Lampreys*
January 1941

A Surfeit of Lampreys as everyone learnt at school was responsible for the death of an English king. Ngaio Marsh's new story has nothing to do with English history, but it is a brilliant modern detective story – the best this talented New Zealand author has written telling of the strange drama in which Lord Charles Lamprey and his family were to figure so prominently.

### *Swing, Brother, Swing*
September 1949

Gala night at the Metronome, gayest of all the fashionable night-clubs, with Breezy Bellairs and his Boys, slickest of swing bands! Tonight there is a very special attraction, for it is rumoured that the eccentric Lord Pastern is appearing with the Boys as temporary timpanist. Among the after-theatre crowd in the softly-lit, over-heated dance room, Chief-Inspector Alleyn of Scotland Yard and his wife Troy are enjoying a private celebration. While watching the gyrations of the Boys as they put over their latest number in the famous Breezy Bellairs manner, the celebrated detective suddenly realises that he has unwittingly combined business with pleasure; for Carlos Rivera, the piano-accordionist, is murdered before his startled eyes. A superbly written story with fascinating characters, *Swing, Brother, Swing* is a worthy successor to a distinguished line of detective novels by the inimitable Ngaio Marsh.

### *Tied up in Tinsel*
March 1972

Halberd's Manor was a stately home with a difference – a difference that lay in the staff. Every one of the retainers that waited on Hilary Bill-Tasman was a convicted murderer. It was all part of a rehabilitation scheme which the effete but astute Hilary, with the co-operation of the governor of the local prison, had put into operation as much for his benefit as for theirs.

But naturally in such a set-up, when a much-disliked visiting servant disappeared without trace after playing Santa Claus, foul play was at once suspected, and foul play it proved to be. Only – suspicion fell not only on the staff but on the guests, all so unimpeachably respectable that the very thought of murder in connection with any of them seemed almost heresy. Apart from Hilary himself there was his beautiful fiancée; his uncle, a retired Army colonel; his loving but formidable aunt; and Mr Bert Smith, unexpected in such surroundings, who happened to be an authority on antiques. There was also Agatha Troy, distinguished portrait-painter, and equally well-known to Ngaio Marsh's readers as the wife of Superintendent Roderick Alleyn of Scotland Yard. When Alleyn returns unexpectedly from a trip to Australia, it is to find his beloved wife in the thick of an intriguing mystery.

### *When in Rome*
November 1970

The party of tourists which Mr Sebastian Mailer of 'Il Cicerone' Conducted Tours led into the Roman basilica of S. Tommaso in Pallaria seemed much like any other. The members were all apparently well-to-do, strangers to Rome, and eager to hear Barnaby Grant, distinguished novelist and star attraction of the tour, discourse on the basilica. But when one of the party fails to emerge from S. Tommaso and the body of someone unconnected with the tour is found hidden in the basilica's lower depths, Superintendent Alleyn, in Rome, incognito on the track of a drug ring, is forced to show his hand.

The murder hunt, of course, is in the hands of the Roman Questura, but Alleyn takes charge of the members of Mr Mailer's tour and explores with them some of those aspects of *la dolce vita* which the tourist does not normally see. When a second murder occurs, Alleyn joins forces with the Roman police. The result is an unexpected and skilful ending which will both satisfy and surprise.

Neither Ngaio Marsh nor her famous detective Roderick Alleyn need any introduction to their vast and growing public. Here are both of them at their best.

## MARTIN, JAMES E.

### *95 File, The*
July 1973

Written by an American police sergeant, *The 95 File* is a bitingly accurate picture of the investigation by two Homicide detectives into the killing of a policeman.

For months the city has been plagued by a 'Triple Threat Thief'. Each time a squad car is sent out on a burglary call, the thief takes advantage of its assignment to strike twice again in the same neighbourhood, displaying an uncanny knowledge of patrolling habits in the area. Then Detective Murdock and Ashton respond to a routine call, only to discover that a cop has been killed.

As they trace their way through the tangled circumstances surrounding the murder, Roy Murdock and Lester Ashton expose the underside of a typical American city – the corruption, the decay, the racial tension, the disintegration, and the undercurrent of violence that erupts in sudden and savage ways. As the pace of the story accelerates, they are hurtled towards justice, but the triumph achieved is tinged with bitterness.

*The 95 File* includes much factual homicide procedure. It is an insider's portrait of city politics and an intriguing cop's-eye view of the professional and personal lives of a detective.

## MASON, SARAH J.

### *Let's Talk of Wills*
November 1985

Kate Keepdown had thrived on controversy from her first days as a bride in quiet Bardleton village. As a nonagenarian widow, she still revelled in being outrageous. Her anxious friends were quite unable to dissuade her from assembling her relations under one roof to help celebrate her birthday and, most important of all, to learn at last the proposals for the making of her Will. For years until a recent accident, she'd refused even to consider the idea that anyone might be entitled to a share of her estate; but now, the family solicitor tried desperately to warn the childless old lady that the scandalous scheme she'd planned could lead only to trouble. Yet even in his gloomiest moments, he never honestly expected that the weekend would result in violent death – although anyone knowing Kate and her circumstances should have been able to predict it …

When the police eventually arrived at the flood-marooned manor, it was to discover a house full of secrets, of fears, and of motives for murder.

## MATHESON, JEAN

### *So Difficult to Die*
January 1957

'I think I am being murdered' – so Esmond Power wrote in his diary. Power, once a great surgeon, was now in any case dying slowly of a debilitating illness. The diary reviews past incidents, drawing from them deductions and suspicions as to which member of his household is trying to hasten the end of a man who already on the point of death. Who would it be? The enigmatic Saskia, Power's lovely wife? His brother Pierce, a hasty and impatient man with a fondness for Saskia? Willie Brice, the poor little creature on whom Power had once carried out a brilliantly successful operation? Or the dour old housemaid, Emma?

When violent death erupts in this household, there are plenty of causes of suspicion, plenty of motives, plenty of evidence for the conscientious Inspector Newport to act on. Yet few will guess the true nature of the events that led up to that death…

Jean Matheson is well known for her novels, among which *The Island* was a Book Society Choice. In this, her brilliant debut in crime writing, she has achieved a story full of ingenuity and suspense – one that will keep its readers excited and baffled to the end.

## MATTHEWS, LEW

### *Conviction of Guilt, A*
September 1993

The unexplained murder of American private detective Murdoch Finnegan at his flat in Belsize Park poses a heady mystery for Horatio T. Parker chief crime reporter (and secret owner) of the Hampstead Explorer.

Not only is the murder apparently motiveless, but it also emerges that in his will Finnegan has left Parker – already a multi-millionaire – a curious house in Golders Green.

Parker, slightly distracted by the gorgeous Samantha McDuff (a karate expert with an excruciating way of shaking hands), begins a dangerous investigation trail that leads him, via an excursion to New England, back to the horrifying abduction and murder of a little girl in London in 1972.

How is Murdoch Finnegan's death connected to this still unsolved crime, and what dark secret binds him to her wealthy and powerful family?

Parker's investigative methods are amusing, eccentric, sometimes bizarre, and the story is enlivened by a Jewish policeman who is a Talmudic scholar, an habitual burglar and a cheeky Cockney cabby who is Parker's permanent chauffeur.

But there is no humour in the story's climax, which plumbs the dark depths of fury and retribution.

### *Unseen Witness*
September 1992

It seemed at first like an ordinary spring day. But before nightfall local newspaper reporter Horatio Thorpe Parker learns of the murder of Monique Karabekian, sultry film star wife of Hampstead's dashing MP – and learns also that he has inherited a fortune from an elderly lady he had befriended, believing her to be penniless.

While struggling to cope with being a multi-millionaire, Parker becomes ever more deeply enmeshed in the investigation into the film star's death, and in the extraordinary and disturbing activities in which she had become involved. His inquiries bring him into contact with people whose lives were changed for ever by their contact with Monique Karabekian, including the smoothly sinister Eduardo Adolfini, and into situations of violence unheard of in the genteel environs of leafy Hampstead.

Parker's touch is a light one, in which he offers detection with humour and unusual tactics, and the story is enlivened by a beautiful green-eyed reporter called Andy, a Jewish policeman who quotes from the Talmud, and a Cockney taxi-driver who is hired by Parker as a full-time personal chauffeur.

Events nevertheless take a dramatic turn before building to a shattering climax in which the murderer is revealed – in more ways than one.

## MAVITY, NANCY BARR

### *Body on the Floor, The*
September 1930

'Suicide,' said the Chief of Police, and the Coroner agreed with him. So did the great criminological expert engaged by the defence. But Peter Piper, the whistling reporter whose psychological hunches had solved the Tule Marsh murder case, thought differently. The woman who lay dead on the floor could have killed herself – according to the evidence she probably did – but would a woman planning suicide send her dress to the cleaner's? The answer revealed one of the strangest scandals and most amazing crimes of the century.

### *Case of the Missing Sandals, The*
June 1931

The newspapers called it the 'witchcraft murder' – but Peter Piper knew that the famous and beautiful Luna's missing sandals were the clue to a more sinister and terrible power than witchcraft. Luna claimed to worship the devil and had founded the Luna Colony – a witchcraft cult. But Peter found that swindling on a grandiose scale was part of her profession, and when she was found murdered, completely clothed except for her sandals, he scented a mystery that penetrated deeper than the police detectives thought. Fast, thrilling, mysterious, with murder following murder, this tale of detection and crime is easily the best of the Peter Piper stories to date.

### *Fate of Jane Mackenzie, The*
May 1933

She was the famous Jane McKenzie, rich, famous, known everywhere for her fabulous fortune, her eccentric clothes, the power she wielded. But even Jane McKenzie was not proof against the roving hand of death. For one night Jane McKenzie disappeared. The next day it was certain that wherever she had gone she had gone finally and for good. Peter Piper, whose long experience with crime made him suspicious of even the simplest things, was the first to suspect the truth. And then, through a bit of rough paper, a typewriter that should have written one way and actually wrote another, and blood inexplicably on a golf-club head, Peter found a sinister trail to follow. But that was before the second catastrophe occurred, and a man entered a lamp-lit room and said to Peter, 'Have you come to arrest me for the murder of Jane McKenzie?' Nancy Barr Mavity is the author of many distinguished detective stories, but this is probably her most exciting and absorbing novel.

### *He Didn't Mind Hanging*
November 1932

In three short hours the police appeared to have solved the mystery of the death of Gabriel Jeffries, crippled millionaire and philanthropist. But when they announced an open-and-shut case against Sing Wong, Jeffries' Chinese servant, they reckoned without the unusual character of Sing Wong himself, who didn't mind hanging for the crime. Fon Ng Chee, leader of the Chinese colony in San Francisco, first undertook Sing Wong's defence. Then Sam Hardwicke, brilliant and unscrupulous young attorney, took the case – for the publicity. And at last, Peter Piper, the gay young reporter who walks into murder traps and comes out unscathed, and who knows that 'the best story lies with the defence', went after the story. Yet all the while, from his jail cell, the little old Chinese servant with the Ph.D. degree pulled the strings for them all. In three cigarettes, a money-box, a stab wound no expert could explain, a clue that a stethoscope gave, the strange mystery of old Sing Wong and his murdered master rushes to its thrilling conclusion.

### *Other Bullet, The*
January 1931

The story opens with the murder of Don Mortison, a ranch-hand, by Mrs. Everett, whose husband was Mortison's employer. An eye-witness saw her fire twice, point-blank at the dead man, but when Peter Piper reaches the body a short time later, *rigor mortis* has already set in. Peter was holidaying nearby, and in spite of the evidence against Mrs. Everett, determined to take up her defence. It lands him in jail as an accessory, but there he makes a friend of hard-boiled Bill Simpson, clerk, recorder, auditor, and county sheriff, and together they assemble the slender clues that lead to one certain fact – Don Mortison was already dead when Mrs. Everett tired to murder him! In that case, who was the murderer?

## McCANN, THOMAS

### *Come Out, Come Out, Whoever You Are*
April 1971

Jack Coover is an accountant, an ordinary man whose life has been largely uneventful. Married to a wife he no longer cares for, he lives in a suburban house and meets his mistress whenever it happens to be convenient. And then, suddenly, he receives an anonymous letter, it is followed by a threatening telephone call, and then, frighteningly, by a direct attempt on his life.

What has happened? Who would want to kill him? And why? Thrown without warning into a world of fear and suspicion, he finds himself ensnared in a trap of violence and possible death. His only course of action is to flee, as far away as he possibly can. But the assassin's shadow is a long one and Coover finds himself inexorably lured back to the edge of his own destruction.

Set against a background of Brighton in summer, with its holidaymakers and seaside stalls, amusements and bars, *Come Out, Come Out, Whoever You Are* is a chilling story of suspense which will set every reader wondering uneasily. 'What would I do if it happened to me?'

## McGERR, PATRICIA

### *Catch Me if You Can*
April 1949

Pat McGerr does it again! For the third time this unusual writer gives a new twist to the crime story. *Catch Me if You Can* is the fascinating tale of Margot Weatherby, beautiful, blonde and damned, who ruthlessly murders her husband because he stands in the way of the brilliant life she craves. Bur she is not to get away with it as easily as her arrogant vanity leads her to expect. Before his untimely end, Philip Weatherby became suspicious and sent for a detective called Ricky Rhodes. Which one of those in the deserted inn high up in the Colorado Rockies is Rhodes – reporter, travelling salesman, business girl, author? That is Margot Weatherby's problem, and yours. Can you spot the detective?

### *Die Laughing*
May 1952

It was ironic that the only reporter present at a television show where the star was poisoned was Melissa Colvin, who could not make use of the phenomenal scoop, for she was a research journalist for a magazine that was interested only in rather dull economics. The television show that *Enterprise* had chosen for its study of the industry was the popular 'Podge O'Neill and Scottie' programme, and what Melissa learnt behind the scenes was more than *any* magazine could print. She learnt that television, like radio and show business, called for so much ruthlessness in the struggle for advancement that jealousy, and bitter hatred, and even murder, could result. Following the highly successful *Your Loving Victim*, Pat McGerr gives us a tip-top crime story told against the fascinating background of the television studios.

### *Fatal in My Fashion*
June 1955

The scene is the very heart of fashion: St. Pierre, Paris's leading dress designer, is showing the last, and most important and the most secret creation in his new spring collection. It is being displayed by his top model, the tall, magnificent American girl – Sarah-Anne. The guests are dazed by St. Pierre's showmanship. But they leave the Maison St. Pierre under suspicion of *murder*; for murder has been committed while they were assembled, while the collection was being shown. The motive for this murder lies far in the past: in the strange personality of Emily, Sarah-Anne's half-sister, whose ruthless career and domination of others has conjured up hatred all around her. This story is a brilliant study of character and the clash of personalities; its plot is original, its development credible and frightening, its end surprising. It is a *tour-de-force* of story-telling and suspense set against the hard, glittering background of the world of fashion.

### *Is There a Traitor in the House?*
July 1965

Selena Mead was a spy, but now she felt that her employers, Q Section, were asking the impossible ... *"By this time tomorrow I want you to be his closest friend."* Congressman Jeffrey Stone's rabble-rousing speeches had made him one of the best-known men in America, and he was widely tipped as the next Vice-President. How can she become his "closest friend" overnight?

But speed is essential as a top-secret document, vital to the nation's defence programme, has been stolen and must be prevented from leaving the country. Personal feelings and reservations must be ignored. Selena knows this, but it doesn't make things any easier when she finds herself emotionally as well as professionally involved in a dangerous situation.

*Is There a Traitor in the House?* is an exciting book and a welcome return to crime writing by Patricia McGerr. The always busy and often frantic atmosphere of Capitol Hill and the pressures put on those who work there add to the excitement of an espionage tour-de-force.

### *Pick Your Victim*
August 1947

With *Pick Your Victim* the Crime Club introduces a new author who has a first-rate talent for storytelling. This provocative and highly entertaining mystery lets you in on the murderer right away, but keeps you guessing as to which of a group of ten men and women is the victim. Nothing more about the story will be told here, but the Crime Club promises all readers that this really is a breath of fresh air. Written with a satiric touch, Pat McGerr's style is as fresh as the plot, and the characters are drawn with insight and humour.

### *Save the Witness*
May 1950

Nearly every newspaper reporter has a pipe-dream that one day he will be a famous novelist and be able to put his feet up all day, instead of sticking his ears to the ground and his nose to the grindstone. Andy Callahan was different. He was going to be a playwright. The boat trip to Rio was just the job he thought. Plenty of time for wooing the reluctant muse. That's just where he was wrong. Firstly, he meets an old school pal, who puts his not too attractive sister in his charge; then he meets a blonde whom he'd sooner woo than any dry old muse; and, most disturbing of all, a passenger is killed aboard ship. It becomes Andy's self-appointed task to find out who was the witness to the murder, and which person had the strongest motive to be backward in coming forward. This is a fast-moving crime story, with the now famous Pat McGerr 'twist' to the plot.

### *Seven Deadly Sisters, The*
May 1948

Pat McGerr's excellent first novel *Pick Your Victim* set the reader the novel problem of guessing the victim, being given the murderer. Now it's harder. You have to find out who the murderer and the victim are. Sally Bowen, American bride in England, receives a letter from New York expressing sympathy because Sally's aunt had murdered her husband and then committed suicide. Which aunt? Which uncle? Sally had seven aunts and they all had husbands. Sally's husband, however, is able to guess which aunt it is from the description of the deadly seven that Sally gives him. Can you?

### *Your Loving Victim*
February 1951

"It's a long drop to the pavement," Jordan, the former tenant, had said casually to Larry Rock. And when the Rock felt impelled to kill one of the four women in his life, he remembered these words. The dinner party which Rock arranged to celebrate his taking the apartment brought the four women together – ex-wife, wife, mistress, and fiancée. Tension mounted among this ill-assorted group, and you will wonder – as did one of the guests – which of them was to be the Victim. Written with a superb feeling for suspense, timing, and characterisation, *Your Loving Victim* is a gripping story by the author of *Pick Your Victim* and *The Seven Deadly Sisters*.

## McKINLAY, MARGARET

### *Caring Game, The*
October 1993

During a pleasant evening out with his girlfriend in a trendy bar in Edinburgh, accountant and security company owner John Leith meets a stunning young student, Dee, who is there to seek news of her missing flatmate. When he tries to help her in her search, he finds that Dee is not the only person looking for the mysterious Alison; and he soon realizes that these dangerous men are not only looking for the girl, but also for something she has in her possession.

As John investigates the tangle, whilst protecting Dee from almost certain danger, he finds himself up against violent, ruthless men who resent his interference and will stop at nothing. From this time on he is committed to discovering who is behind the organization; and when a murder is unearthed in one of the city's beauty spots, he knows that the faceless man who is the power behind the terror must be drawn out into the open. But will Leith be able to survive the unmasking?

### *Double Entry*
March 1992

John Leith is an easy-going Edinburgh accountant, a widower with a young son, and a long-standing relationship with an attractive woman which neither wants to turn into marriage.

Suddenly his life is disrupted when he is attacked in his office, his flat is searched and vandalized, and his sister's home broken into. John can discern no reason for the incidents, but as the violence against him steps up he begins to feel like a tethered goat and is drawn willy-nilly into the activities of his uncle's detective agency, which seems to offer his best hope of protection, to say nothing of discovering what lies behind these unprovoked attacks.

But when his unknown enemies turn their attention to those who matter to him, John Leith discovers that he too can use violence when necessary, and Margaret McKinlay's first novel reaches a shattering climax as the identity of the villains and their true motives are finally unmasked.

### *Legacy*
January 1993

A phone call from a desperate young woman to John Leith, an Edinburgh accountant, is both intriguing and worrying, and when she disappears he is concerned for her safety. While trying to trace her he is threatened by a man who owns a Harley Davidson motorbike. Is he the girl's boyfriend or simply the reason why she is so frightened? John, using the resource of the Sentinel Agency in an attempt to solve the mystery, is soon involved in an incident where another young girl is injured by a speeding car; but was it an accident?

The biker, who always hides his features behind the visor of his helmet, has a partner and the two become aggressive instead of just using threats. John's car is tampered with, nearly causing a fatal crash, and after other attempts on his life, he begins to piece together the clues that point in only one direction, to the identity of the criminals and the reason for their desperate attempts to make him stop the investigation. John Leith refuses to be put off by their tactics and the tale builds up to a violent confrontation, and a surprising revelation.

## McLARTY, DONALD

### *Deep Blue Seize, The*

November 1989

Romesh Gopal, sitting in the private dining suite of the Ritz, wasn't listening to his diamond-dealing cousin from Amsterdam. He was staring at the antique blue and white porcelain dinner-plate in front of him and dreaming up his next scam.

All he would need was several thousand similar pieces and one eighteenth-century Dutch wreck sunk in two hundred feet of salt water and he would become a truly rich man.

But how to make everything watertight? Foolproof, that is.

Suddenly he saw it clearly. It was all a question of lateral thinking. Applied vertically.

Abandoning property development, he gathers together his fast-driving assistant Nigel Carlton, his nubile daughter Sharmila, and the rest of the deep-sea treasure-hunting team, and heads for the blue-green waters of the Outer Hebrides.

Moving at speed, the Gopal team and their converted trawler cross lines with salmon fishermen, solve the mystery of the sinister White Lodge, and triumph over some murderous rivals, until they present the 'find' at a truly explosive press conference.

All that remains thereafter is to get it (and themselves) back to the London auction rooms and they will become multi-millionaires…

## McMAHON, THOMAS PATRICK

### *Issue of the Bishop's Blood, The*

March 1973

Monday had been a routine day in the offices of 'Peck and Bailey – Investigations'. Until the secretary announced, 'There's a priest outside.' And suddenly Dave Peck's Monday wasn't routine at all.

'I am Bishop Purcell of the Propagation of the Faith.' The little man said. 'I want you to investigate a living saint, and if you believe the person *is* a saint, I want you to kidnap her and turn her over to the Roman Catholic Church.' This might well mean that America would have a new name on the calendar. Besides, as the Bishop carefully pointed out, sainthood happened to be good business. It needed to be in the right hands.

But as if it were not enough to ask a Protestant private eye to commit a crime carrying one of the heaviest penalties in US law, the saint in question was the daughter of none other than Joe Santa Croce, the most feared Mafia Don in Arizona. And Dave had already tangled with Big Nose Joe.

Thus Catholic and Protestant private eye confront each other at the beginning of their first adventure, and Dave Peck confronts a dilemma where the forces of heaven and a very special kind of hell seem to contend, if not for his Protestant soul, at least for his life.

*The Issue of the Bishop's Blood* is a detective novel that is fascinatingly different – one where the term 'saints and sinners' takes on an entirely literal and wholly dangerous meaning.

## McMULLEN, MARY

### *But Nellie Was So Nice*

January 1981

Nellie Hand, pleasant, middle-aged, unmarried, was everybody's friend. Among the people who felt closest to her were Matthew Jones, a television station executive who was reminded by Nellie of his dead sister; worldly Enid, who owned the dress shop in which Nellie worked; Charmian Lyle, a beautiful woman with a neurotically jealous husband; and Lise Kozer, an old friend who for years promised Nellie a fortune from a ship that never seemed to come in.

Nellie was also kind to Enid's niece Lukie, a young girl who was trying to hide from a convict to whom she owed a large sum of money; to Basil, the man downstairs who copied famous paintings; and to Ursula, an artist with whom Nellie was trying to fix up her nephew Jeremy, a famous photographer. So when one of them admitted to Nellie that he had murdered a man in the past, and another that a bundle of cash was hidden in her apartment, and another that a lot of money would be left to one of them in the event of Nellie's death, there were plenty of reasons why one of them might want Nellie permanently silenced.

When she is indeed murdered, Jeremy discovers plenty of skeletons in the closet, and has his hands full trying to find out who killed her, and fulfilling, posthumously, some of Nellie's plans for him.

### *Death of Miss X*

January 1952

The murdered woman was found on Eve Fitzsimmons' second day at the Wade and Wallington Advertising agency. The night before, Eve had stayed late to help on a rush job – she and the other two women copy-writers, and Frieda Lee, who had charge of their group. With Luke Barden, a brilliant, moody art director, they'd been working on the agency's big account, Farmer's Wife. The next morning Eve had gone with the others into the conference room to attend a meeting. When the lights were turned on, there lay the body of an unknown woman, strangled with a tartan tie. For Eve, this is the prelude to a nightmare of suspicion and fear. In her first crime novel Mary McMullen reveals an enviable talent for creating an atmosphere of tension and suspense and for creating colourful and interesting characters.

### *My Cousin Death*

July 1981

Can kindness kill?

Paul Kinsella performed an act of supreme – and secret – kindness for a doomed woman he had once loved. After his own death, the deed returned upon his wife Bel like a boomerang. In the little town of Leam in Connemara, a suspicious figure demanding hush money appeared at the storybook white house where Bel lived. He bore the promise of family ruin and disgrace and the ultimate grief for Bel: that of losing her husband for a second time, and this time for ever.

Into this strange drama came NBC newscaster Conor Niall, who had come to Ireland to win back Sara, a distant cousin, who was all but engaged to Bel's son, Fitz. His ardent pursuit of Sara led him into a tangled web of local deaths, and the possible complication of drug traffic as he and his camera crew moved from castle to rainy graveyard to a crashing, watery finale…

### *Other Shoe, The*

July 1982

Justin Channon is a thirty-eight-year-old writer and illustrator of children's books; Clare Herne is a painter and a distant cousin of Justin's whom he hasn't seen in years.

Imagine his surprise, then, when Clare arrives on his doorstep one evening with a letter accusing her of the murder of her Aunt Lelia four years before – a murder that remains unsolved and one in which Clare looks very much like the most likely suspect.

Lelia, a querulous, spoiled old woman, had been about to marry a much younger man – her doctor – and it looked to most people as though Clare killed her to hang on to her inheritance, although the allegation was never proved.

Justin decides that it's about time to go back to the Maryland farm where it all happened and sort things out once and for all. If his suspicions are correct, the murderer is still in exactly the same place that he was at the time of the crime …

Is there going to be another murder?

### *Something of the Night*

January 1982

*Please, Daddy, don't let them … your son Markie.*

Kells Cavanaugh, prosperous partner in a New York advertising agency, was feeling extremely foolish. In response to a desperately scrawled plea from his small son Mark, he had flown to London on the pretext of visiting the agency's branch there – only to find Master Mark Cavanaugh playing happily in a sunny English garden under the watchful eye of his trusted nanny.

Kells tried to rationalize the boy's plea as an obvious bid for attention from the child of a broken marriage, particularly as his mother, Kells's divorced wife, was planning to marry again. But that line of thinking broke down when someone turned up with a bullet in his back and Kells realized that his son wasn't crying wolf. The six-year-old was all too innocently involved in murder, and before long his father was too – not to mention his involvement with Bridget, that same trusted nanny to whom Mark had already given his heart.

### *Welcome to the Grave*

February 1980

Everything was going splendidly for Harley Ross, a prolific and highly successful novelist. He was rich and famous; he had a beautiful home in an exclusive Connecticut township; and a satisfactory romantic arrangement with a mistress who was both tempestuous and beautiful. Since his wife left him two years before, his creature comforts had been admirably catered for by the perfect housekeeper; and his latest novel was going well. Nothing – but nothing – was allowed to disrupt Harley's work schedule. Until 11.27 on a beautiful April morning, when he looked up to see his wife Marta returning to the fold. The world outside had proved as cold and unfriendly as her lover, so she had returned to take over as a most unwelcome lady of the manor. For Marta had a weapon: she knew Harley's guiltiest secret. It was the kind of information that entitled a woman to a meal-ticket for life. Or death.

## MEEK, M. R. D.

### *Hang the Consequences*

October 1984

People who lead blameless lives rarely consult seedy detective agencies. But was Frances Jessica Moss so blameless? And what had her erring husband to do with the young American woman whose body turned up in a pond in Epping Forest? Lennox Kemp, struck-off solicitor turned inquiry agent, picked his way through a tissue of lies – and found it studded with surprising gemstones.

In the shadow of the past he trod a wary and dangerous path through other people's hidden lives, in pursuit of truth and justice. But one did not necessarily lead to the other, and for Kemp the search drew him back into the sensitive area of his own wrecked career. With a chance of re-enrolment by the Law Society before him, he must risk even that as he tangled with the bitter legacy of murder.

This is an earlier Lennox Kemp than the one encountered in Cornwall in *The Sitting Ducks*, but his inquisitive mind and stubborn tenacity are again in evidence. It remains to be seen whether he will climb back into his honourable profession or continue to work on the seamy side of the law, to which, perversely, his temperament is better suited.

### *In Remembrance of Rose*

June 1986

Had sweet, elderly Rose Amaury only imagined that someone was trying to kill her? Her death a few days later was real enough: brutal murder in the course of a trivial burglary gone wrong. And when the suspected young killer ends up dead in a Dutch canal the police seem only too thankful to put a lid on the case.

But as the old lady's legal executor, Lennox Kemp lifts it and peers inquisitively into the lives of the trio of Newtown families embroiled in the tragedy; the upper-class Warrenders of Castleton House, the impoverished gentry at the Vicarage, and the low-born Rodings grimly hanging on in the Council Estate. Kemp asks too many questions, treads once too often on delicate ground and sets alarm bells ringing in the powerful echelons of the Intelligence Services.

Physically assaulted and professionally impugned, Kemp fights hard as what begins quietly enough as a routine domestic matter in the lawyer's office accelerates into swiftly-moving drama. For the first time in his career, he is up against those formidable forces whose watchword is the interest of the State, and only his own tenacity and sense of justice keep him on the trail.

### *Loose Connection, A*

April 1989

When her friend Amanda dies, Dorothea Copeland is haunted by images from the past, a past she has ruthlessly tried to forget.

Lennox Kemp too is worried by the past. A colleague brings him a story which casts a slur on the integrity of his conveyancing clerk, Dorothea's husband. Should Kemp simply treat it as a spiteful tale-out-of-school and let it go as that? But his curiosity is stirred. It leads him to Edmonton where the shell of a burnt-out building once stood, and to a little house in Balaclava Terrace.

There death strikes swiftly and with so sure a hand that Kemp must question his own responsibility – for had he not felt himself stalked by a malevolent presence down those grey streets?

But as he struggles to find a connection in the yellowed pages of a dead twenty-year old file his speculations remain as insubstantial as the shadows that darken the hyper-sensitive mind of Dorothea Copeland.

It is only when the evil that lurked in those shadows comes out into the open, and Dorothea must fight it on her own home ground, that the past finally catches up with the present in a climax that is as chilling as it is surprising.

### *Mouthful of Sand, A*
September 1988

Wealthy stockbroker Vincent Snape tells solicitor Lennox Kemp that he is happily married, yet shows a curious interest in matrimonial law. To a sceptic like Kemp that can only mean that Snape has been indulging in extra-marital adventure. But when Kemp and Penelope Marsden holiday at the North Cornwall resort of Rocksea where they hope to resolve their own matrimonial intentions, they meet Mirabel Snape, and Kemp must change his view. For Mirabel has a lover, the silver-tongued Robin Adair, an artist with the devil in his eye and a nasty taste in jokes.

Kemp is beguiled by the sunshine and the scenery – and the sea-blue eyes of Snape's wife – but when the severed head of a local fisherman is brought up in the nets and the news sends Mirabel into a catatonic trance, he is forced to ask questions. Is Mirabel the wanton that everyone says she is? Can she really be cured by incarceration in a sinister private hospital run by a psychiatrist with a neat little sideline of his own?

Dangerous currents race across the Doom Bar of the estuary to wreck the plans of those engaged in a dirty trade, but the deeper current running beneath the surface of other lives is malevolent and more damaging in the end. As Kemp observes: 'Leave murder to the hoodlums…there are other ways to snare a rabbit…'

### *Sitting Ducks, The*
March 1984

A series of deaths in a small Cornish town seems adequately mourned and put away until Lennox Kemp with his city-bred suspicions comes to work in a local solicitor's office. Is there a link between them? And does the disreputable hippy colony on the bleak Moor, with its enigmatic leader Crantock, hold the key? Dark forces are unleashed but their source remains uncertain, for there are subtler undertones as conflicts of interests and clashes of cultures lead towards a violent upsurge of popular feeling during a long hot summer.

Each character in the developing drama acts from motives of self-interest, and it is in the disentangling of these that Kemp's investigative powers are involved, as the local community is disrupted by the alien element which in its turn is manipulated – but by whom?

The denouement is as ironic as it is unexpected, but even when Kemp has reached a proper conclusion about the underlying reasons for the deaths, his attitude to the Cornish countryside remains ambivalent: that of an outsider looking in.

### *Split Second, The*
September 1985

Fiona Davison-Maclean was ripe for exploitation. Freed by her domineering mother's death and on holiday alone for the first time, the rich, plain, fortyish spinster fell easy prey to Fergus O'Connell, traveller in hairdressers' sundries and alert to the possibilities of a wealthy wife. After their marriage they settled near Rothesay, and a new life might have begun for Fiona had she not neglected to keep in touch with her aunt.

Worried by her niece's silence, the aunt engaged Lennox Kemp to trace her. Kemp accepted it as a last assignment from the detective agency where he worked, and travelled north. He unearthed a number of unexpected facts about Fergus, Fiona, and her cousin Lindsay, but by the time he traced her to her new home, they were fishing Fiona's body out of the loch.

It was a convenient death for Fergus, but he had a cast-iron alibi, and there was no evidence that anything other than misadventure was involved. Lindsay's refusal to accept the findings seemed unbalanced, and when next Kemp travelled north, it was in answer to an appeal from Lindsay's attractive girlfriend.

Kemp's discoveries this time were so startling that he could hardly believe them true. But they brought a clever murderer to justice and provided him with a memorable case.

The superb Scottish setting, the outstanding characterization, the story unfolded with unforced skill, make this M. R. D. Meek's best crime novel to date and a superb addition to the Crime Club List.

### *This Blessed Plot*
August 1990

Great houses breed history – history and trouble. Courtenay Manor on the outskirts of Newtown is no exception, and solicitor Lennox Kemp should have been wary before getting embroiled in its affairs. But the lady of the Manor is beautiful and in spite of misgivings he succumbs to the heady atmosphere surrounding the Courtenay twins, newly come into their long-awaited inheritance.

He should have kept his eyes on the ground and attended properly to the woman who comes to him for help in finding her errant husband, a poor Italian tomato-picker, but Julie Sorrento is a slatternly wife, careless with her children, living on the Council caravan site – a far cry from Venetia Courtenay's feudal acres – and Kemp gives her scant regard.

Only when the two worlds of Newtown eventually meet and merge in the tiny cell-like room of the Manor where Henry VIII once kept a French prisoner, does Kemp realise how he himself has been manipulated in a monstrous game of deception and cold-blooded murder.

### *Touch and Go*
June 1992

Chance is a fine thing, thought the nurse who had watched wealthy Muriel Probert die in her Fifth Avenue apartment. So she took that chance – along with other fine things – and ran.

To Lennox Kemp, Muriel's ex-husband, the string of gambling casinos in Las Vegas left to him in her will seemed a dubious inheritance, bound to bring out the worst in everyone concerned whether they be prevaricating lawyers or predatory gangsters.

But the slow legal process is undercut when a body is found in the East River, and there will soon be another victim as the hunt for the missing nurse turns murderous. Kemp would prefer the nastiness kept on the far side of the Atlantic, but when the final showdown comes it is on his own home ground of Newtown, where the local police force gets a taste of gun-play, Nevada-style.

### *Worm of Doubt, A*
August 1987

Lawyers, particularly divorce lawyers, get all sorts of clients, not necessarily ones they like, and Lennox Kemp did not like Frelis Lorimer, nor did she seem to like his advice. Why then should she try to trap him into some sort of devious scheme with implications of murder? When her husband's beautiful girlfriend is found drowned in the exotic setting of a Jacuzzi, Kemp suspects that Frelis Lorimer herself may know more about it than she admits.

Another death follows, and this time it is an undoubtedly brutal killing for which David Lorimer is arrested on damning evidence. Reluctantly Kemp agrees to act for the defence, but finds himself baffled by the enigma of Frelis Lorimer's attitude. What deep game is she playing, and is her husband as innocent as he protests he is?

These unanswered questions suddenly become almost irrelevant when a greater peril threatens the Lorimer family. Kemp, with the help of the police must move swiftly to counter danger from an unexpected source.

## MEGGS, BROWN

### *Matter of Paradise, The*
March 1976

Hobie Milne, 42-year-old music critic of a San Francisco paper, didn't want to think about the 25th Reunion of The Mather School's Class of 1950. Hobie didn't really care what had happened to those old classmates of his – until they began to die, one by one.

Like boys everywhere, they had left Dr Knox's prestigious Puritan enclave and gone off into the 'real world' to find their individual destinies: doctor, architect, stockbroker, diplomat, actor, corporate executive, musician, airline pilot, critic.

Now, a quarter of a century later, what had they in common? Nothing but Mather, sudden death – and the 'matter of Paradise'.

Hobie himself is most reluctant to think back on Mather days. He wants only to continue his pointless existence as a psychological drop-out: divorced, isolated from family and friends, trapped professionally on a second-rate newspaper, contentedly dependent on a girl a dozen years his junior with whom he shares a houseboat in Sausalito Bay.

But inevitably, inescapably, Hobie finds himself drawn once again into the 'matter of Paradise', there to face the forbidden secret of his class – and, for the first time in his life, the truth about himself.

### *Saturday Games*
August 1975

Four men in Pasadena, California meet every Saturday for tennis. The game is more than an athletic competition; it has become a vehicle for the relief of tensions, an outlet for emotional pressures that might otherwise exceed the tolerable. Of the four men, three are scientists at Caltech Jet Propulsion Laboratory; the fourth is Baron, their one-time stockbroker.

On this particular Saturday emotional pressures already exceed the tolerable. The night before the three scientists had entertained Baron's sexually voracious wife at a very private swimming party. Now, as play begins, her nude body lies hidden on an abandoned estate in one of Pasadena's most exclusive districts.

Before the first set is finished the body is found and Detective Sergeant Anson Frères comes on the scene. Homicide involving the elite professional elite class is not common in Pasadena, and Anson Frères is no common investigator. Fortyish (like the suspects), a constitutional bachelor, educated at Amherst and Oxford, gourmet cook, accomplished pianist, a man of independent means, Frères is professionally a little too civilised for his own good, but the ideal man to handle this bit of socially sensitive violence.

Reluctantly (it's his day off) Frères gets into the problem. And what he finds is the stuff of present-day psychiatry: four men whose once promising careers have not materialized and whose private lives have led them – inescapably? – to death and destruction.

*Saturday Games*, a first novel, is a sophisticated tale of murder both social and deadly and of compulsive readability, one of the most satisfying and ingenious crime stories of recent years.

## MEYER, LAWRENCE

### *Capitol Crime, A*
October 1977

*'Crime is not my beat. I know some people would disagree and call me more than a shade naive, but I take a philosophical view of these things. I cover the United States Senate.'*

But Tony Jordan, correspondent for the *Washington Journal* and narrator of this outstanding first novel of the higher reaches of politics and journalism, found that crime had become very much his beat when the body of America's top investigative reporter was found stuffed into a manhole in the Capitol. He couldn't sit back and pretend he didn't care when he had known Les Painter, when the police weren't looking very hard for his killer, and when a lot of powerful people were mightily relieved he was dead. They included a Senator with an ambiguous past, a chemicals tycoon with Mob ties, Arab oil lobbyists, and the leading contenders in the forthcoming American presidential primaries.

So Jordan started poking around and asking questions. Then suddenly he was beaten up by an unknown assailant, sources dried up, and one of his informants was killed. After that all pretence of indifference vanished, and Jordan went hot on the trail of Painter's killer – into the inner sanctums of the Capitol, the bedrooms of Georgetown, the arms of a seductive woman Senator, and finally to the most bizarre and revealing press conference ever held.

Witty, even at times comic, this crime novel in the great tradition of Rex Stout and of *The Front Page* has been justly described by Ross Macdonald as 'so intriguing that one hates to see it end'.

### *False Front*
August 1979

You get calls like that when you work for a newspaper. The phone rings. The caller tells you he has a story that will shake the town to its foundations, ruining careers and making people in high places tremble.

Usually the caller is a nut, or a crank. Most often the story evaporates when you check it out. Once in a while it causes a minor sensation.

*And then sometimes you draw a royal flush…*

That was what happened to Paul Silver when a phone call put him on the trail of a senator selling vital military secrets to the Russians. Silver was desperate for a big story – his marriage was shattered and his journalistic career failing – so he disregarded half-hearted warnings, muffled threats, and his own misgivings to gamble everything on this one throw of the dice. If his paper published what he discovered, it would be a journalistic coup beyond his wildest dreams.

Only gradually did he realize that the stakes were higher than he first thought – that 'respectable' people would kill to keep the truth from being revealed. Murder, suicide, corruption, blackmail, and an epic battle within the intelligence bureaucracy of Washington soon swept him into the middle of his own story. He had become the target of ruthless men who must destroy him to save themselves.

Lawrence Meyer's first novel, *A Capitol Crime*, was warmly welcomed. In *False Front* he gives his readers another fast, furious chase down the hidden corridors of Washington power.

## MEYNELL, LAURENCE

### *Death of a Philanderer*

August 1968

*Anthony Langton was commissioned to write a historical monograph of the classy girls' school called Sherrington Abbey. In Sherrington village, at the Black Bull where he was staying, he met the drunken philosopher called Inky … and the middle-aged man called Philip Carver.*

Ostensibly Carver was staying in the village for the fishing. But Langton soon discovered that Carver's days by the river were not devoted to piscatorial exertions. Carver's principal occupation at this time was blackmail. His spare energies were given to the successful seduction of one of the girl pupils from the Abbey.

These are the first, shocking revelations in the story that leads to the death of Philip Carver. Laurence Meynell is in brilliant and dashing form as he develops this story of the hideous crimes that win Carver a violent and final punishment.

### *Die By the Book*

March 1966

The old Duchess of Mexe had inherited the legendary Mexe Book of Hours: an illuminated script produced in the Benedictine Abbey of Luce between 1350 and 1355. The Mexe was one of the six most valuable books in the world, and a handful of rich, acquisitive collectors yearned for it – among them Mr. Leonard Umberton. All these years the treasure had lain unavailable in the Duchess's chateau on the shore of the Lake of Geneva. Now Umberton receives a vital message – the Duchess is willing to sell.

The message leaks to certain other characters who quickly compose a master-plan that will result in the disappearance of 'The Mexe Book of Hours'. They propose to cash in by a secret sale to a collector who is not Umberton.

Their plan requires an impersonation – so enter Robert Craythorne, actor, the narrator and central character of this novel: a man short of money who is led rather easily into a very fishy project.

A series of dramatic, violent and very surprising events unfold at the Duchess's chateau and in the town of Geneva.

Laurence Meynell writes here in a lighter vein than usual. An exciting and original story is told with all the author's gaiety – a story that will hold readers spellbound.

### *Double Fault*

August 1965

The 'Abbey Chase Week-end' was a beacon for social climbers. Under the careful stewardship of Sir Harry and Lady Manby-Bellairs, this annual occasion had become a Mecca of amateur tennis and social ambition.

All the guests were fine tennis players. Among them were the beautiful actress Isadora Costello and the odious tennis professional 'Few' Granville. Of Isadora a witch had predicted that her lovers would include 'an aristocrat, a philosopher and a cad'.

This unusual story describes the circumstances that lead to the gathering of the week-end players at Abbey Chase: the progress of the tournament; and the explosion of a violent death among a group gathered in search of the *dolce vita*.

Laurence Meynell again illuminates the behaviour of a high and brash society with his personal philosophy and humour. The ambitions and aims of each member of this group are convincingly portrayed. When the whole ensemble is gathered for the showdown at Abbey Chase the story comes to a gripping climax.

### *Mauve Front Door, The*

October 1967

'This story starts with me driving a 32 bus for the Corporation Transport Department in a large and popular English seaside town. Let's call the place Sunhaven…'

That the young earl, who had inherited Langley Castle, should be driving a Sunhaven bus was one thing; other possibilities unfolded when an Italian film company, including the glamorous star, Zena Barron, showed signs of renting the ruinous Yorkshire castle for a film set.

Langley abandoned his bus to join the bizarre company of film characters who had invaded the local inn in his native village. To Langley easily the most interesting of these was Zena Barron…

In a quarry outside the village there takes place a violent death, and police enquiries follow.

This is the intriguing and gay account of a strange sequence of events involving some exotic people. Laurence Meynell, in his lighter vein, is a master of the fast, cheerful story spiced with wit, and the tale here races from an odd initial situation to a very startling revelation.

### *More Deadly Than the Male*

October 1964

Charles Wilson, a young barrister, was on the high-road to success and fame. Superbly able at his job, married to the daughter of an influential backwoods peer, he seemed set for the great rewards of this world. Perhaps something was lacking in his marriage – but who could complain about a wife so beautiful and elegant, so influential and ambitious for her husband?

Charles went to Bellings Gambling Club in the course of his work – 'to have a view' as lawyers say. At Bellings he met Kay Kellington. Within hours he fell victim to a fatal obsession; and became irrevocably committed to condoning a crime.

This story tells what became of Charles Wilson. It describes in detail the world he lives in, a high and brassy life in London to-day, where men fight cynically and ruthlessly for position and money. In Charles Wilson's world of M.P.s, press barons, Q.C.s. gamblers, stockbrokers, journalists and jockeys jostle relentlessly for gain; death is regarded casually, he who falters is fast forgotten.

Laurence Meynell's new and moving novel is a tragedy, firmly rooted in character and circumstances. It describes convincingly and with perfect irony the destiny of a contemporary man.

### *Of Malicious Intent*

November 1969

Some crimes are committed physically while others, just as real, are perpetrated in the mind. *Of Malicious Intent* is the fascinating story of a crime which could have been either…

The action is laid in a small English town whose annual Summer festival has achieved international importance. A feature of this festival is the Brains Trust, to which seven members, all intelligent, well-known people, differing greatly in sympathies, outlook and conviction, make their contribution. Desmond Videll, the best-known figure of them all, is now really past his peak; but his vanity and his past reputation still keep him prominently in the public eye.

Then, early in the Festival week Videll meets a violent death. It falls to the lot of a remarkable man – a Roman Catholic priest – to play the part of private investigator and to get at the truth of how he met his end.

*Of Malicious Intent* is a first-rate example of a 'crime novel' – that type of story which sets out to deal with credible characters who find themselves caught up in a tangled human situation at the heart of which, animating it all, lies a crime. Laurence Meynell is in splendid form as he gradually reveals the criminal against the tragi-comic human conceits and up-stagemanship of his microcosmic festival world.

### *Sleep of the Unjust*

October 1963

Richard Young, a free-lance writer, was content at the prospect of spending a month or so in a stately home as a librarian, cataloguing fourteen thousand books. As the house belonged to a Press Baron who supervised his newspapers closely and critically, there promised to be other excitements as well as the library.

It wasn't until His Lordship's mistress, Helena, appeared on the scene that Young recognised a face from the past: a face that had a direct connection with his memories of a wartime parachute drop, of a beloved friend dying from wounds and loss of blood.

There was an old score to be settled as well as the new ones that were generated almost daily at Challens. Young had come to learn a great deal about His Lordship's establishment, and the people who belonged to it, before murder was committed there.

Laurence Meynell writes with the craftsmanship, the gusto and throw-away humour that have coloured his earlier well-known crime novels. The story of *Sleep of the Unjust* is a strange one, told with great skill and gripping the reader with its exciting developments.

### *Virgin Luck*

April 1963

This story is set in the London of today; first in the office of a theatrical agent and then in the central office of a huge bookmaking business. Liz Barton is a modern heroine of great humour, exuberance, candidness and guts; the events set in train by her recklessness, amorality and passion – and by the men who exploit them – come to a climax that is exciting, disastrous and inevitable.

'Childe Roland to the dark tower came' was the quotation that she associated with her emancipation – at the cost only of her virginity – into the glossy and pleasure-devouring life of the metropolis; and with her escape from the stuffy 'zombies' who attended the 'Chapel' and ordered the moral precepts of the humbler community in which she had been brought up.

Later she was to recognise herself in the still more ominous context of another quotation that struck a chord in her: 'By our strange and fatal interview.' For her meeting with John Mannington-Travers was to have fatal consequences indeed.

In its humour, in the detail of its background and in the sweep of its narrative *Virgin Luck* far excels in achievement Laurence Meynell's earlier successful crime novels.

## MILNER, GEORGE

### *Shark Among Herrings*

October 1954

In George Milner's second detective novel the private investigator, Ronald Anglesea, is called on to inquire into the disappearance of the valuable Manders rubies from Deed House, near the north-west coast of Scotland. But one of the guests has vanished, as well as the rubies; to Anglesea it becomes a case of murder. Before it is finished he is to see murder committed in front of his own eyes, and in the sight of other witnesses, but it still remains a problem for the police, Anglesea and, we believe, the reader, to decide who was the *Shark Among Herrings*. This may be one of the queerest fictional murders ever committed. It is not every day that the murderer comes from *under water*. The characters involved are queer enough to match a macabre crime. But the atmosphere at Deed is not only macabre, for Anglesea has cunningly contrived the presence of Diane, his girl friend, and Diane is not one to be disconcerted by a murder, or anything else for that matter. Anglesea himself is quite prepared to mix pleasure with business whenever opportunity affords.

### *Stately Homicide*

June 1953

The floors of the Stately Homes of England have been littered with corpses for many years. Blood has run over library carpets, cyanide has mingled with the vintage port, and the silver fish-knives have seen as much service as stilettos. *Stately Homicide* sees murder once again stalking an ancestral home – but in the year 1952, and with a difference. When the dowager Marchioness of Tranby summons Ronald Anglesea, the private investigator with the impeccable manners and flamboyant tastes, to Tranby Castle, his terms of reference are vague: 'There's something odd going on,' she says, 'something underhand. Find out what it is.' Many odd things happen, but which of them is the one the dowager dislikes so much? Anglesea's casual questioning soon brings some strange things to light, and murder follows. An exciting investigation, which leads to a startling climax, is accompanied by some uproarious moments of farce. George Milner's first essay in murder displays a rare sense of style combined with a wit which makes *Stately Homicide* consistently entertaining.

## MOORE, MARGARET

### *Dangerous Conceits*

March 1988

Assassination is not normally a feature of English political life. So when a prominent MP was fatally shot at the hustings, the ripples spread far and wide, particularly as he was the charismatic leader of the New Radical Party. By comparison, the death a few hours later, from a heart attack, of the candidate he had come to support in a Cambridgeshire by-election made little impact.

To Chief Inspector Richard Baxter the case had obvious political implications, with the IRA as prime suspect. But a compromising photograph of the victim had been splashed across a tabloid's centre spread just hours before his appearance on the platform, and both his actress wife and the girl in the picture might have motives. So had others, political and personal, as Baxter soon found, including some within the University of Cambridge, with which a number of those prominent in his investigations were connected.

As in her first novel, *Forests of the Night*, Margaret Moore unfolds a complex story with understanding and great skill.

### *Forests of the Night*

February 1987

Martin Hobbs, 13, was so disturbed by the break-up of his parents' marriage that he had been receiving therapy at a Cambridgeshire clinic, to the dismay of his attractive mother who resented being involved. She had already suggested that treatment was no longer necessary now that Martin was settled in a new school under the guidance of a wise acting headmaster, but she could not have foreseen that their association with the clinic would have such a dramatic end.

One night, while she was working illicitly on its premises, her son ran out screaming that a tiger had killed her. What prowling beast had he seen? Was it real or the product of his disturbed imagination? Chief Inspector Baxter set himself to find out.

Experience has taught Baxter compassion, as well as thoroughness. He has need of the first quality as he is confronted by the results of the second in an investigation that takes him into the lives of everyone connected with Cheryl Hobbs, and deep into the forests of twentieth-century night.

OR

Martin Hobbs, 13, was so disturbed by the break-up of his parents' marriage that he had been receiving therapy at a Cambridgeshire clinic, to the dismay of his attractive mother who resented being involved. She had already suggested that treatment was no longer necessary now that Martin was settled in a new school under the guidance of a wise acting headmaster, but she could not have foreseen that their association with the clinic would have such a dramatic end.

One night, while she was working illicitly on its premises, her son ran out screaming that a tiger had killed her. What prowling beast had he seen? Was it real or the product of his disturbed imagination? Chief Inspector Baxter set himself to find out.

He soon learned that there were hidden depths to Cheryl Hobbs, who was planning to remarry now that she had amassed money by decidedly doubtful means. But who was the mystery man? What of her ex-husband, anxious to regain custody of Martin? What secret discovered in the confidential files of the clinic could drive someone who knew of her discovery to kill?

### *Fringe Ending*
August 1991

Emma Baxter's path crosses her father's more often than he would like as she directs an amateur musical at the Cambridge festival and he investigates a murder on the fringe of the University community. The elderly victim, Rupert Parsingham, a popular gardening adviser, was the great-grandson of a famous Victorian botanist. Suspects include Rupert's radical activist sister, the Director of The Parsingham Institute for the Scientific Study of the Tropics, his Filipino wife and two members of his staff, a jewel thief, and a playwright with bitter memories of the university city. Detective Chief Inspector Baxter does indeed track down the killer, but not without his daughter's active intervention.

### *Murder in Good Measure*
August 1990

As a Tudor dance course gets under way in Hare Holt Manor, her Cambridgeshire home, Frances Lake worries about the mental health of her young granddaughter. Who better than Dr. Sarah Baxter, family doctor, as well as amateur dancer, to help her elicit the cause of the child's unhappiness? Before long, Frances's problems are compounded by the violent death of a course member, while another – the pretty wife of the Bishop of Fencourt – disappears. Detective Chief Inspector Richard Baxter, Sarah's husband, has a murder case on his hands.

Baxter's contacts in the Metropolitan and City police forces prove useful as his inquiries lead him to London and Cambridge. From encounters with a varied clutch of informants who include financiers, businessmen, a radical woman criminologist and an ex-nark, he pieces together a tale of rejection, obsession and chilling revenge. And when the dancing is done, he confronts his quarry at Hare Holt by moonlight.

## MORROW, SUSAN

### *Murder May Follow*
April 1960

The stranger was always there. Waiting for her to leave her apartment, standing outside the restaurant, loitering, trailing her as she left her interior decorating business. Elizabeth Weller, so attractive and outwardly so calm, didn't strike Lieutenant Condon as a hysterical neurotic, and he had a shrewd idea who her shadow was. But Seth Condon's first investigations seemed to trigger off a sequence of terrifying events which put Elizabeth in danger and which came to a head when the sodden corpse of a man was taken from San Francisco Bay – a man Elizabeth thought she had seen before, though she couldn't remember where or when. Step by step, Seth Condon put together the pieces of the case which was suddenly to come to such a gripping and stormy finish and which make *Murder May Follow*, Susan Morrow's first book, an exciting and fascinating blend of Detective Story and Thriller.

## MOYES, PATRICIA

### *Angel Death*
August 1980

The British Seawards Islands bask in the blue waters of the Caribbean, a still unspoilt yachtsman's paradise. Returning there for a holiday, Superintendent Henry Tibbett and his wife Emmy looked forward to relaxing in the sun. But beneath the calm surface the islands were the centre of a vicious drug ring which aimed at gaining a stranglehold on island life. The drug, PCP, known as Angel Dust, was run in aboard some of those innocent-seeming yachts which put in to little harbours on St Mark's and St Matthew's – and sometimes put out never to be seen again. Lonely beaches, expanses of empty water, were ideal settings for sudden death and loss. When an elderly English spinster vanished on what should have been the first lap of her homeward journey, Henry Tibbett took a hand.

His enquiries had dramatic consequences, including Henry's resignation from Scotland Yard. But all else paled when tropical storms approached the islands, completely disrupting normal life. In the brief period of calm between onslaughts, Henry Tibbett suddenly perceived one single significant fact …

Thereafter events had to move at the speed of the hurricanes if the wrong people were not to end up in control of the Seawards – and in control of Henry himself.

'Some of the problems mentioned in this book are real,' says Patricia Moyes, who now lives in the Caribbean. She makes them as vivid and spellbinding as only a Queen of Crime can.

### *Black Girl, White Girl*
March 1990

When an old friend from the newly independent Caribbean nation of Tampica turns up in London claiming the island has become a haven for the traffic in cocaine – 'white girl' in island argot – and she is afraid for her life, Henry and Emmy Tibbett agree to help her get the goods on the Mafia-corrupted local officials. But amid the deceptive calm of a lush tropic resort, they soon discover that they can trust no one because nothing is what it appears to be and the only reality is that each of them is in the gravest danger.

With the skill which has made her a queen of crime ever since her first Henry Tibbett novel, *Dead Men Don't Ski*, published in 1958 [sic], Patricia Moyes spins a story as suspenseful as it is delightful, set on a Caribbean island very much like the one that is her home. Once again she offers us 'a panoramic piece of detection which is splendid entertainment without any pretensions' – *Yorkshire Post.*

### *Black Widower*
May 1975

*Lady Ironmonger, wife of the newly-appointed Tampican Ambassador, was found dead in her room at the Tampican Embassy here in Washington this evening, following a diplomatic reception …*

The apparent suicide of the Ambassador's beautiful English wife, with her internationally unorthodox reputation, was a potentially disastrous beginning for the newly independent Caribbean island of Tampica and her Ambassador to the United States, Sir Edward Ironmonger. But was Lady Ironmonger's death really suicide? And if not, who was going to question delicately all those diplomats and eminent Washingtonians? For political reasons, the Tampican government was determined to keep the police investigation out of American hands, and fortunately Lady Ironmonger had died in the Embassy, which was technically Tampican territory.

Since Tampica's own small police force was not equipped to deal with so complex and sensitive a case, Sir Edward and his Prime Minister hit on a device whereby Chief Superintendent Henry Tibbett of Scotland Yard could be called in, semi-officially, to assist the Tampican police. Within a few days the affair was cleared up. But the smooth-tongued diplomats had not reckoned with Henry Tibbett and his stubborn determination not to give up until he had dug out the real truth …

The action shuttles between historic Georgetown, the most fashionable quarter of Washington, and the fabulously beautiful Caribbean island of Tampica; between the rarefied atmosphere of jet-set resorts and the down-to-earth lives of hard-working officials.

### *Curious Affair of the Third Dog, The*
August 1973

Patricia Moyes is one of the few women writers who rank as a 'Queen of Crime'. Indeed, she has been described as 'the only true post-was heir to the great tradition of British women detective story writers'. Her Chief Superintendent Henry Tibbett and his wife Emmy have featured in no less than ten novels, whose backgrounds have ranged from behind-the-scenes on a fashion magazine to out-of-season life in a Swiss ski resort. With *The Curious Affair of the Third Dog* she ventures into the world of greyhound racing and romps home with a winner.

The village of Gorsemere was hardly a hotbed of sensational events, so when old Harry Heathfield was sent to prison for Causing Death by Drunken Driving it became a local nine days' wonder, even though it had been an open-and-shut case.

Meanwhile, Harry's troop of stray dogs would have to be cared for, and this chore naturally fell to Jane Spence, the village RSPCA representative. Who ever was going to notice if Jane found only two nondescript mongrels in Harry's backyard, instead of the three she had been led to expect? How could a missing dog possibly be important?

Unfortunately for a ruthless and ingenious murderer, Jane Spence's sister Emmy happened to be the wife of Chief Superintendent Henry Tibbett of Scotland Yard: and the affair of the Third Dog, recounted to Henry as a joke, triggered off an investigation which led him deep into the world of racing greyhounds, trainers, breeders, gamblers and crooks. And brought him uncomfortably close to a violent death.

In a fast-moving and intricate plot, Patricia Moyes weaves together the contrasting strands of English village life, and London's underworld, until the two collide with an explosion of violence at their one point of contact: a greyhound racing stadium.

### *Dead Men Don't Ski*
October 1959

'The whole thing is probably a wild-goose chase,' said Chief-Inspector Henry Tibbett to his wife. 'Heavens know I don't want any trouble. I want to learn to ski. After all we *are* on holiday.' Santa Chiara is high up in the Italian Dolomites and very close to the Austrian border – close enough for the Narcotics Department of Interpol to be suspicious of the activities which seemed to be centred on the Hotel Bella Vista, where Henry and Emmy had in all innocence arranged to spend their holiday. Knowing this the British police had asked him to keep his eyes open while he was there. But Henry's hopes of a wild goose chase died with one of his fellow-guests, who was alive at the top of the ski-lift to the hotel but who had been shot dead before reaching the bottom, having been passed *en route* by seven of the hotel residents who were riding up.

With zest, reality and humour Patricia Moyes writes of a widely assorted and fascinating group of characters engaged in the world's most exhilarating sport. In a setting of breathtaking beauty she has spun a plot worthy of the Masters of Detective fiction. *Dead Men Don't Ski* is a welcome and outstanding addition to the Crime Club.

### *Death and the Dutch Uncle*
August 1968

'Flutter Byers' was a small time crook. He died in hospital after being shot in the lavatory of a shady pub in North London.

But it transpired that the death of Byers was not all that it seemed. And Henry Tibbett was soon listening with awe and amazement to an account of the official proceedings of the Permanent International Frontier Litigation committee – invariably known, so far as it was known at all, as PIFL.

This legal commission had, for some years, been engaged in judicial consideration of an African frontier dispute of the utmost *ennui* and unimportance. Now Henry had to ask himself whether the disputed mountains could be really so valueless...

A most ingenious story, in which the beautiful sisters Madeleine and Yvonne feature large, leads to a tremendous climax by a Dutch waterway; not only Henry, but also Emmy his wife and a very young girl, are trapped by a man who is wholly indifferent to the deaths of others.

Patricia Moyes has been called 'a new Crime Queen' (*Peter Philips*) and this fine and exciting story most successfully extends her record of the investigations of that sympathetic senior police detective, Henry Tibbett.

### *Death on the Agenda*
March 1962

In the Palais des Nations, Geneva, the Intercontinental Narcotics Conference is in progress. Among the senior policemen from

Western countries who are discussing means of countering international drug-pushers, Chief Inspector Henry Tibbett is representing the United Kingdom. His wife Emmy has travelled with him, taking the rare opportunity of a continental holiday.

The sun is shining, the social life is hectic, the secretaries are pretty and Henry Tibbett can even enjoy the sessions of the conference until this brief interlude is violently interrupted. First comes the ominous news that information has leaked from one of the carefully screened members of the conference, information of vital importance to the crooks who traffic in drugs. Next comes murder in the 'closed' suite of the conference room. And then comes suspicion…

The high reputation that Patricia Moyes earned with her first two novels, *Dead Men Don't Ski* and *The Sunken Sailor*, is shown here to be fully justified; this novel brilliantly presents a multiple mystery, made plausible and exciting by its background, its characters, and a very intricate plot.

### Falling Star
August 1964
*Again the whistle shrilled. 'Quiet, now! We're turning this time.'*

*In the dead silence, little Steve, the clapper boy, stepped in front of the camera holding his blackboard.*

'STREET SCENE *Retake One-Nine-Four, Take One.' He announced cheerfully.*

The male star, Bob Meakin, began to run down the steps of the Underground Station; the train – specially hired for the Northern film company – started to roar into the station.

Thus began the most tense and vital of all the many 'takes' that must be shot and assembled before *Street Scene* could be ready for the screen, the critics and the audience.

The work of completing this film was threatened first by bankruptcy, then dogged by disaster and sudden death. Fat Pudge, the rich boy whose money has elected him producer, was beside himself to try and save that money; he found too that he had something even more pressing to cope with in the increasing attentions of an old acquaintance, Chief Inspector Detective Tibbett C.I.D.

The tantrums of the 'film people' provide a contrast with Tibbett's quiet perseverance and the anxieties of poor Pudge about his money. Patricia Moyes's new detective story – like *Murder à la Mode* and *Death on the Agenda* – sets a most ingenious whodunit in an authentic and fascinating contemporary background.

### Johnny Underground
October 1965
**Beau was one of the greatest heroes of the Battle of Britain. He was in Spitfires. His name was Guest, so of course he was nick-named Beau. He was very young then, of course. In 1940, twenty-two. Heaven knows how many German planes he shot down. He won the D.F.C. and a couple of bars, and the miracle was that he survived. He became a sort of legend – he seemed to be indestructible. That was why it was so awful when it happened.**

Thus – in 1965 – Emmy Tibbett describes to her husband, Chief Detective Inspector Tibbett of the C.I.D., the man who had been her first love over twenty years before. 'Beau' Guest, the man she had known at the R.A.F. station in Dymfield in 1943 – and who had died.

A reunion in London reintroduces Emmy to old friends, and to the memory of Beau. And then it transpires that the circumstances of Beau's death might have been different from what had always been supposed. A

murder is committed – and Chief Detective Inspector Tibbett finds himself investigating a case of great complexity stretching over the years – a case involving his wife, Emmy.

Patricia Moyes's brilliant detective novels have been widely praised and read. She will gain more admirers with this clever and nostalgic plot which culminates in a very surprising solution.

### Murder à la Mode
March 1963
The offices of the glossy fashion magazine called *Style* were alight into the early hours of the morning. The paper's team of talented but wayward executives were hard at work preparing lay-outs and comments for the special edition covering the Paris Spring Collections. At least one individual was left alone to work the rest of the night, preparing captions for the printer's messenger who would arrive at 7.30 am.

But the messenger, a young motorcyclist, rang the bell in vain, and it quickly became clear that events had taken a tragic and startling turn inside the building before dawn. Soon Chief Inspector Henry Tibbett of the C. I. D. is installed in the *Style* building; and after much excitement, confusion and mystery Henry demonstrates that he has not been baffled or overwhelmed by the artists, geniuses, executives, neurotics, models designers, or tycoons, of the world of *haute couture*.

Patricia Moyes here again displays a mastery of the classical detective novel. A glamorous contemporary background, described in detail, is the setting for a story in which life-size characters are mixed up with murder, the reader is treated fairly all the way to the surprising and exciting finish.

### Murder Fantastical
February 1967
The Manciple family had lived in Cregwell Grange for two generations. The stories of their eccentricities were legion, though the village liked and admired them for all their wild ways. As the doctor's wife said: 'the Manciples are a lot of fun if you don't have to make sense of them.'

Major Manciple was determined to follow his father's wishes and keep the Grange going as a centre for the family. In order to get the money to do this he sold the Lodge to Raymond Mason, a London bookmaker. Mason, though he tried hard, was cordially disliked by everyone in Cregwell, and their sympathies were strongly behind the Manciples when he was found dying of gunshot wounds in the driveway of the Grange.

Chief Inspector Henry Tibbett is sent from Scotland Yard to investigate Mason's death, and soon finds himself struggling with the unenviable task of 'making sense' of the Manciples, though he quickly succumbs to their terrific gaiety and charm.

This is a tremendously enjoyable light-hearted detective novel, written with all the verve and zest that have placed Patricia Moyes in the front rank of novelists writing in this genre today. Henry Tibbett is in his very best form while dealing with the many and various twists and problems arising from the shooting at Cregwell Grange.

### Night Ferry to Death
November 1985
Chief Superintendent Henry Tibbett and his wife Emmy are looking forward to a relaxing journey home on the Harwich-Hook of Holland ferry after a holiday in Amsterdam. To their disappointment, they find that all cabins have been booked, so they will have to sleep on reclining chairs, known as sleep-seats, in the saloon.

Among the other people besieging the Purser in vain attempts to secure cabins, several are especially persistent: a respected diamond merchant; a young woman accompanied by a tiresome child; a strikingly elegant couple; and Mr Smith, a small nervous man who pleads for a cabin as if his life depended on it.

As indeed it does, for when everyone in the saloon begins to stir next morning, Mr Smith lies still. He has been stabbed to the heart, and the murderer can only be one of the Tibbetts' sleeping partners.

Henry learns that Smith was carrying stolen diamonds, but the jewels have disappeared. It is not until Emmy makes a frightening discovery about the contents of her overnight bag that Henry begins to uncover the sinister web of clandestine relationships that finally explains the murder.

### Season of Snows and Sins
October 1971
'The relentless pressure of a lot of money chasing a good time' – that's how Jane Weston, an English widow living in Switzerland, describes the glittering winter season in the newly-fashionable ski resort of Montarraz. But what happens when the season ends, when the film stars and playboys and political celebrities depart – leaving a host of carelessly strewn problems behind them? How do the villagers grapple with the tensions, the greed, the jealousies, the emotional upheavals scattered in the wake of the rich pleasure-seekers?

The answer is a gathering storm of passion which finally erupts into murder – a classic *crime passionel*. Or so the judge and jury think, and the villagers, too – until Chief Superintendent Henry Tibbett and his wife come to spend a holiday with Jane Weston, and Henry's famous 'nose' begins to detect a sour stench of corruption under the gilded, glistening surface of Montarraz's high season.

Set in the glorious landscape of the Suisse Romande, where the author lived for some years and still has a holiday apartment, the story is not only tensely exciting, but is told with a real knowledge and love of the country and its people, and of the dizzy contrasts of ski-resort life.

### Six-Letter Word for Death, A
May 1983
It all began as a practical joke. Could a real life detective solve a fictional mystery with as much finesse as the heroes of best-selling crime novels? By compiling an intriguing crossword puzzle and sending it anonymously to Chief Superintendent Henry Tibbett of Scotland Yard, a group of mystery writers decided to find out. Then the prank turned deadly.

Henry and Emmy Tibbett had been invited to the annual long weekend of the Guess Who? club. Its members, all pseudonymous, were crime writers published by the firm of Oppenshaw and Trilby and the weekend was held at Sir Robert Oppenshaw's home on the Isle of Wight. There Henry was to reveal his solution to the puzzle.

But when a member of the house party died in an accident just when he was about to reveal the background to one of the clues, Henry found himself following a trail more than twenty years old as he and Emmy began to unravel the loves of the assembled writers. In a gripping story full of surprises, a secret kept for two decades is finally revealed.

### Sunken Sailor, The
May 1961
Their visit to Berrybridge Haven was to be the Tibbett's first experience of sailing.

Henry felt that it would be a doubtful joy for the middle-aged, but Emmy was eager and the Bensons were as enthusiastic about the pleasures of the Berry Bush Inn as they were about *Ariadne*, their boat. Henry was soon lost in a sport which he found fascinating. But blood will tell, and on his first visit to the tiny community on the East Coast he had noticed certain things, almost unconsciously. When tragedy struck these things became important and he faced the task of assuming his professional identity: Chief Inspector Tibbett of New Scotland Yard. Conducting a murder investigation among people who had come to be his friends was a delicate and hateful task, and as he learned more, he realised that the case was not only difficult but that he himself was in deadly danger.

Patricia Moyes scored a notable success with her first crime novel *Dead Men Don't Ski*. In this book she once more succeeds in spinning an intriguing plot, creating a convincing and enjoyable cast of characters and eccentrics, and mixing both against a background of 'messing about in boats' which is as fascinating and authentic as the East Anglian setting.

### To Kill a Coconut
January 1977
Caribbean sea and sun, exotic vegetation, charming people and the most expensive Gold Club in the world – the dreamlike British island of St Matthew's seemed to be blessed with all the ingredients of an earthly paradise. And so it was, until a United States senator was brutally murdered on the golf-course, and a young islander charged with the crime. Then the dream turned into a nightmare, as ugly racial violence broke out, and fear and suspicion began to fragment friendships and tear the economy apart.

So when the Governor of the British Seawards turned to Scotland Yard for help, Chief Superintendent Henry Tibbett and Sergeant Reynolds had more than a murder case on their hands: they had the future of a whole community. It took two more murders and an armed confrontation in the darkness of a tropical rainforest before Henry was able to unravel the complicated tangle of personal, political and economic threads which had brought an idyllic island to the flash-point of self-destruction.

Patricia Moyes now lives in Washington DC, and has travelled extensively in the Caribbean during the last few years. Her new book is a first-class detective novel, with all the plausible ingenuity and incidental charms of characterization and vivid descriptive writing that discriminating readers have come to expect from such an acknowledged Queen of Crime. It also reflects her love of the islands and their people, and her concern for their future.

### Twice in a Blue Moon
August 1993
When Susan Gardiner unexpectedly inherits an old country inn not far from London, she also inherits a long-lost, distant cousin. A few years her senior and infinitely attractive, Cousin James is also very attentive. It isn't long before romance blooms.

Youth and beauty, romance and country inns; a frothy mix if ever there was one – but of course, this is Patricia Moyes and very soon murder enters the picture. When Susan, a skilled restaurateur, reopens the inn as an upmarket gourmet eatery and, against all the odds (and dire predictions of the locals), makes a go of it, customers flock. Things are looking decidedly good until one of the customers, on sampling the chef's *plat du jour*, suddenly keels over, the victim of mushroom poisoning.

Enter Chief Superintendent Henry Tibbett, and once again we are off on another Moyes mystery, which finds Henry Tibbett in top form. And, in Susan Gardiner, it introduces a narrator as fresh and appealing as the menu she oversees. Long-term fans and new readers alike will not be disappointed.

### *Who Is Simon Warwick?*

October 1978

The initial problem wasn't so much 'Who is Simon Warwick?' as 'Where is Simon Warwick?'

When old Lord Charlton knew he was dying, he suddenly decided to alter his will and leave his vast fortune to a long-lost nephew. His family solicitor was instructed to trace the young man.

Orphaned as a boy during the war, the boy had been adopted by an American officer and his English wife and taken to the United States, since when he had completely disappeared. Unfortunately, in answer to the solicitor's advertisement, two claimants turned up, both with impeccable credentials, and 'Who is Simon Warwick?' became a very pertinent question indeed.

Either way a number of people who had expected to inherit under the original will looked like being disappointed, so when one of the claimants was found strangled in the solicitor's waiting-room just before a confrontation, there was no lack of motive and opportunity. Only – was it the true or the false Simon who had been murdered? Was the question even susceptible of proof? Chief Superintendent Henry Tibbett had to find out.

Patricia Moyes's ingenious solution will surprise and delight even the most hardened crime addict. It is tempting to say 'Here is something new'. Except that with every book this Queen of Crime surprises and delights her readers, so that it is only necessary to say, 'Here is the new Patricia Moyes.'

### *Who Saw Her Die?*

June 1970

Six packed suitcases. An elaborately iced cake. Two dozen dark red roses. A case of vintage champagne. All converging on the house known as Foxes' Trot in the county of Surrey…and for the most innocent and pleasant of reasons. Lady Balaclava's three daughters and their husbands were coming to celebrate her seventieth birthday.

So why did Crystal Balaclava go in fear for her life? Why did she use her still-considerable influence in high places to get Chief Superintendent Henry Tibbett of Scotland Yard to join the party as her personal bodyguard? 'The wayward fancies of an elderly woman' – that was the Assistant Commissioner's view, and Henry was inclined to agree.

But his amused scepticism turns to nightmare when Crystal Balaclava literally drops dead at his feet, apparently poisoned – but by a non-existent poison. Was it indeed 'natural causes', as the police doctors and pathologists were forced to conclude? Or was it the perfect murder at last?

Henry, with his professional reputation at stake, determines to find out. But he is involved in a whirlwind trip around the Continent, an encounter with a beautiful woman doctor and a fight for his life before he finds the answer.

Once again Patricia Moyes lives up to her international reputation as a writer who 'puts the who back into who-dunit' (*Chicago Tribune*), and whose name 'can now be mentioned in the same reverent breath as that of Agatha Christie, or Margery Allingham, or Ngaio Marsh' (Peter Phillips, *Sun*).

## MURPHY, HAUGHTON

### *Murder for Lunch*

October 1986

Graham Donovan, senior partner and likely candidate to be the next head of Chase & Ward, a law firm at the apex of Wall Street power, died while at lunch with some of his partners – apparently of a heart attack. But it turns out that death was really due to a slow-acting poison.

Several of Donovan's partners, a young associate lawyer, his devoted long-time secretary and his son are among the suspects with both opportunity and motive. The hallowed halls of Chase and Ward echo with scandal as fresh revelations are made in the tension-filled atmosphere.

Reuben Frost, semi-retired former leader of the firm and a New York establishment figure, becomes the unlikely sleuth – working in unexpected tandem with Luis Bautista, a New York City Police Department homicide detective.

*Murder for Lunch* is not only a spellbinding murder mystery, it is a sophisticated novel of manners, commenting with wit and precision on the upper reaches of power in New York City and the inner workings of a prestigious corporate law firm.

### *Murder Keeps a Secret*

September 1989

The unflappable Reuben Frost, 77-year-old former head of a venerable Wall Street law firm, tackles his most intriguing case to date when his godson, Pulitzer Prize-winning historian and potential presidential speechwriter David Rowan, is shoved from the window of his midtown Manhattan office. Rowan was engaged on his most talked-about work to date, a biography of the late Senator and Supreme Court Justice Garrett Ainslie. When another killing follows Rowan's, Frost is forced to wonder what secrets Rowan had unearthed and who might profit from his silence.

Assisted by his ex-ballerina wife, Cynthia, NYPD homicide detective Luis Bautista, and Bautista's glamorous girlfriend, Frost finds no shortage of people with reason to kill the prickly Rowan, whether among those close to him or those he had encountered in his professional life.

The pseudonymous Haughton Murphy, partner for twenty years in a major Wall Street law firm, recently retired to devote more time to writing. He lives with his wife in Manhattan, and is at work on the fifth Reuben Frost mystery.

### *Murder Saves Face*

August 1991

Chase and Ward, the venerable Wall Street law firm once led by now retired Reuben Frost, has moved to Manhattan's West Side. Its new headquarters is protected from the seedy environs by a complicated security system and all goes smoothly until Juliana Merriman, a talented, beautiful associate, is found strangled in the movable stacks of the law library.

The firm's shaken Executive Partner asks the 77-year-old Frost to investigate – discreetly. Frost, spry and shrewd as ever, finds that the suspects include a disagreeable investment banker involved in a seemingly routine merger; a rough-diamond executive who stands to make a bundle from the deal; a trendy restaurateur who was the dead girl's lover; a moody computer genius out of her past; and a blue-blooded senior partner who may or may not have a scandal to hide.

As the clues mount, former NYPD homicide detective Luis Batista comes to the aid of his old friend Frost. And, as always, Reuben's elegant and charming wife, Cynthia, assists in solving the puzzle.

Haughton Murphy takes the reader inside a busy law 'factory' to observe both the brinksmanship negotiation and the gritty details of a corporate merger. Along the way he provides satiric glimpses of some of New York's most exclusive social events.

### *Murder Takes a Partner*

September 1987

Clifton Holt, famous choreographer and artistic director of the National Ballet Company, is stabbed to death outside the stage door of their New York theatre. A small-time dope-peddler is arrested running from the scene. The murder seems just another senseless, violent crime until the dope-peddler, before being killed in a prison brawl, brags that he was paid to kill Holt.

Reuben Frost, semi-retired former executive partner of a Wall Street law firm, is Chairman of the Board of NatBallet, and he now contacts Luis Bautista, the homicide detective who appeared with him in Haughton Murphy's outstanding first novel, *Murder for Lunch*. Also involved is Cynthia, Reuben's wife and a former ballerina. Together the three develop a list of suspects which seems to get longer rather than shorter – a list, as Cynthia says, about equal in size to the number of dancers in the Company's corps de ballet.

But there is a colourful array of suspects outside the corps de ballet, as the reader learns in the course of an outside tour of the cultural life of New York City. An added bonus is an occasional glance through Haughton Murphy's humorous and observant eye at cultural fund-raising and City politics as they impinge on the pedigreed and wealthy in the New York staked out by Louis Auchincloss.

### *Murder Times Two*

September 1990

Reuben Frost, crusty former Wall Street super-lawyer turned sleuth, faces his most baffling case yet. It begins with the mysterious poisoning of Tobias Vandermeer, eccentric scion of one of New York's wealthy old Dutch families, who has spent his life doing needlepoint, playing jazz piano, drinking prodigiously, and trying to keep his name off the 'Forbes 400' list of America's wealthiest individuals. All this comes to an end when Tobias falls over dead midway through a discussion of Thackery's *Vanity Fair* at a meeting of the fancy reading club started by his socially ambitious wife, Robyn.

Those present at the fatal meeting of the reading club are the most obvious suspects, including the oft-married Robyn, a woman with a past and a potentially rich future; Wayne Givens, a trendy television psychiatrist in need of closer analysis; Pace Padgett, a waiter from a swanky catering outfit who may have been serving more than canapés; Sherman Deybold, an art dealer oilier that the seventeenth-century Dutch paintings he sells; and Reuben Frost himself, a hapless guest at the reading club, whose unfortunate mental lapse arouses police suspicion.

Eager to find the killer and desperate to clear his own name, Frost summons all his resources including the clear-eyed common sense of his wife, Cynthia – and uses his many connections to solve both Tobias's murder and a second killing, even more shocking that the first. The lawyer's adventures offer yet another wry, suspenseful and complex tour through the upper reaches of New York society.

### *Murders and Acquisitions*

October 1988

The mergers and acquisitions game heats up when Jeffrey Gruen, one of Wall Street's most notorious corporate raiders, announces his intention of acquiring the highly profitable Andersen Food Corporation.

Flemming Andersen, Chairman of the Board, opposes the offer. But it is not clear that his family agrees: his publicity-shy wife, Sally; his daughter, eager to sell her shares to support the feminist cause; his son Laurence, anxious for a quick-buck success to help pay his triple alimony; and his nephew Billy O'Neal, nursing a grudge against Flemming's branch of the Andersen family. Amid this disagreement, Flemming is found dead in bizarre circumstances at his Connecticut estate. Then another baffling death follows.

Reuben Frost, urbane retired Wall Street lawyer, returns to solve his most puzzling case yet. Helped by his shrewd wife Cynthia and his friend Luis Bautista of the NYPD Homicide Squad, Frost narrows the circle of suspects to the Andersen family and Casper Robbins, Flemming's hand-picked, possibly restless, successor at AFC; plus, of course, Jeffrey Gruen.

Haughton Murphy once again takes the reader on a suspenseful, authentic and witty guided tour through the upper reaches of Manhattan's financial and social worlds to create a puzzle that will entertain fans of murders – and acquisitions.

## MURRAY, STEPHEN

### *Cool Killing, A*

October 1987

When consultant Dr Geoffrey Swainson goes missing at the local hospital it is merely inconvenient, but when he is discovered dead in the hospital mortuary Detective-Inspector Alec Stainton is pitchforked into a murder inquiry which calls for all his patience and tenacity.

The trouble is, too many people are glad Swainson is dead, and as more of his past is unearthed it becomes plain that the consultant was at the centre of a web of relationships involving his wife, his colleagues, and his lovers, any one of whom had good reason not to mourn his passing.

Indeed, to Alec it seems the dead doctor's influence has tainted the life of everyone he meets…and before the investigation is over, even his own life is not exempt.

Stephen Murray's accomplished first crime novel marks the promising debut of a gifted writer.

### *Fatal Opinions*

September 1991

Strength of character, organizational efficiency, idealistic determination and firmness of principle: Kate Randall, campaigning leader of CAMEX (Campaign Against Medical Experimentation) had them all. Her reward was loneliness, poison-pen letters and a sordid death on a storm-swept common. Was it the latest in a series of attacks on CAMEX, whose well-orchestrated campaign had aroused the wrath of Medisearch, a local laboratory specializing in genetic research, or was it the work of a casual sex-killer? More depended on Kate's death than a million pounds in research grants. Another woman's sanity rested in the balance, and a young boy's future.

Detective Chief Inspector Alec Stainton knew this was a case which would only be solved by sympathetic understanding of his fellow human beings. The question was, had he the necessary insight? But life, it seemed, still had a trick or two up its sleeve …

### *Fetch Out No Shroud*

February 1990

When the weather finally set fair, James

Parker was relieved to start cutting his barley. But work stopped at once when a body was discovered in front of the combine harvester – and was Parker really as surprised as he made out? What had brought Andrew Hunter to the abandoned airfield where he met his death? Why does an embittered old woman sit nursing her memories? And where does a visiting group of South African war veterans fit in?

Chief Inspector Alec Stainton reckons murder usually happens for mundane reasons: people are cheated of their money; spurned by their girl; driven to desperation by the habits of those they live with. So why should anyone wait forty-five years to pull the trigger? Yet every time Alec looks elsewhere, he is drawn back to the airfield and its wartime past, until he becomes convinced that the key to the murder lies in that same windswept spot where so much killing was initiated, and from which so many men set out to their deaths.

So what happened at RAF Hartfield Park in 1944? That is the question Alec must face before he can solve the riddle of Hunter's murder. It is a question to which there is more than one answer…

### *Noose of Time, The*
May 1989

Justin Hamilton was afraid of growing up. The young schoolmaster's attempts to hold back the clock were childish enough; but were they really sufficient reason to kill him with such bizarre ritual? But then, as Detective-Inspector Alec Stainton tells himself, this was not so much a murder as an execution…

There are problems for Alec in returning to his old school to conduct a murder inquiry. Beneath the surface sophistication of pupils and staff, hidden passions and private tragedies fester and grudges are nursed, and Alec's own equanimity is brittle enough, as he is soon forced to acknowledge.

Time is very much on Alec's mind as he pursues the investigation. Time caught up with Justin Hamilton with a vengeance, and threatens too many of the institutions in Alec's own life. It will prove a snare for him also, unless he learns to come to terms with it better than Justin and some of those in his circle ever did.

### *Offences against the Person*
March 1993

It's a war where there can be no winners: a war against corruption. It begins with sordid violence in a public park and ends with ritual child abuse on a smart middle-class estate.

Called in to investigate Trevor Grant, an abrasive officer in a tough northern constabulary, Detective Chief Inspector Alec Stainton and Detective-Sergeant Liz Pink have few illusions about the task ahead. But the deaths of Grant and of a teenage AIDS victim brutally change the rules and force them to ask how high the rottenness goes. Were Alec and Liz really brought in to expose corruption – or to find a scapegoat? Or in a cynical bid to take the media heat off the Chief Constable? And who is the sinister Friend who wields so much influence?

Liz, for one, is out of her depth. She has always met life cheerfully and without asking too many questions. But by the end of her time in Yorkshire, she knows what Trevor Grant's problem really was.

He knew evil when he met it.

Stephen Murray's latest and best crime novel is not only a stunning police procedural but a subtle examination of character under stress and of the nature and existence of evil in our society.

### *Salty Waters*
June 1988

A new career as a glamour model was Tracy Ashford's way of escape from the dullness of the seaside town where she lived: but the local worthies didn't like it, and it cost her her title as a local beauty queen – and her life.

It was Detective-Inspector Alec Swainton's misfortune to be holidaying in the town the day Tracy died. Instead of sunning himself on the sands he finds himself seeing a side of the town which never appeared in the tourist brochures.

The dead girl's picture is before him in more ways than one as he follows her among the seaside crowds and through the shadows of London clubland to her final rendezvous with her killer.

## NABB, MAGDALEN

### *Death in Autumn*
January 1985

A foggy autumn dawn in Florence. Divers have dragged the body of a drowned fifty-year-old woman from the River Arno. It might be just another suicide case but what sort of person would throw herself in the river wearing nothing but jewellery and a fur coat? And who is she, anyway? Marshal Guarnaccia solves that problem but it only serves to deepen the mystery. Everyone who knew Hilde Vogel said she was practically a recluse, but they didn't know about her strange relationship with a hotel porter or about the young boys out at a country villa. They didn't know either about her trips abroad or of her Swiss bank account.

Nobody wants to work on this sordid, unrewarding case, known by the Captain's boys at headquarters as 'that foreigner in a fur coat job', especially not the Marshal who's busy preparing for the arrival of his wife and children from Sicily. Two years pass and two more people die before Captain Maestrangelo, by calling in help from a colleague abroad and from the reluctant but indispensable Marshal at home, identifies the joker in the pack and solves the case. But the Marshal, even after all this time, flies off the handle if anyone so much as mentions the business.

### *Death in Springtime*
December 1983

Snow in March. A thing unheard of in the centre of Florence. Everyone was so distracted by the big wet snowflakes falling slowly into the road that no one noticed what happened right under their noses in the piazza, when two foreign girls were driven away at gunpoint. Marshal Guarnaccia was there, too, but it takes some time before what he saw begins to piece itself together in his mind sufficiently for it to make sense because he is distracted by a dozen other problems. The newly-qualified Sub-lieutenant Bacci does well enough until he is distracted by falling in love, and Captain Maestrangelo, a level-headed man who coolly follows the routine that never fails him normally in such cases, soon finds that nothing is normal about this one. When a body is discovered in a shallow grave and the hunt for a kidnap victim and two villainous Sardinian shepherds turns into a hunt for two fugitives, even the Captain is forced to allow himself to be distracted from routine thinking. The case and its outcome are as weird and unexpected as the capricious spring weather.

### *Death of a Dutchman*
July 1982

'It wasn't her…' The Dutch jeweller's words, as he lay in a gloomy, dust-sheeted flat dying of an overdose of barbiturate, could have meant almost anything, or nothing. Marshal Guarnaccia , at the sweltering height of the tourist season in Florence, has enough to do dealing with lost cameras and stolen cars while trying to keep the ever-present threat of terrorism at bay; but he doesn't like the way the Dutchman died and he doesn't believe it was suicide. Certain plain facts are staring him in the face and he pursues them doggedly, covertly, while the Public Prosecutor applies for the case to be fled and forgotten.

The Marshal's only witnesses are a blind man and a ninety-one-year-old woman given to vicious lying, he has no suspect and no motive, but his persistence leads him to a murderer. And it was true, what the Dutchman said. It wasn't her.

### *Death of an Englishman*
December 1981

It is approaching Christmas in Florence, and the local Carabiniere Marshal, stationed in the Pitti Palace, is looking forward to sending Cadet Officer Bacci back to training school after his two-month 'practical' and getting home to Sicily for the holiday. His peace of mind is shattered when the zealous Bacci finds a retired English bachelor shot dead in his ground-floor flat in a historic palazzo near by.

As the deceased had important family connections in England, two Scotland Yard detectives are sent out to help with the investigation and deal diplomatically with any unpleasant facts that emerge. They interview various members of the English community and discover a very reluctant witness. But it is the fatherly Marshal – in bed with influenza for most of the investigation – who, even more reluctantly, puts a hand on the murderer's shoulder, while his cool-headed, efficient superior looks for a rational explanation of the murder and finds something quite different.

In the labyrinthine streets of a medieval city teeming with twentieth-century traffic, fraud and stolen art treasures come to light, but they are only the backcloth to a more personal tragedy. Fortunately the Marshal is in time to help – and still board the last train on Christmas Eve that will take him home to Syracuse.

### *Marshal and the Madwoman, The*
February 1988

'You keep mastery and strength until the last page,' said Simenon of Magdalen Nabb's last novel, *The Marshal and the Murderer*. The same qualities are apparent in *The Marshal and the Madwoman*.

Florence, deserted by most of its citizens, lies prone beneath the August heat. Only the poorer quarters such as San Frediano are still inhabited. And of course the Carabinieri posts. At the one in Palazzo Pitti Marshal Guarnaccia is drawn into investigating the death of an old madwoman, Clementina, with whom he had had a bizarre encounter only a few days before.

The destitute Clementina was deliberately murdered. But who would want to kill her, and why? And why had she tried in fear to telephone the Marshal on the last night of her life?

Starting with no clues, for nothing is known about Clementina, the Marshal sets out to reconstruct her past. His quest takes him into homes and lives in the San Frediano quarter; to the state mental hospital now officially closed; and as he builds his picture of the dead woman as she was when her life and name were very different, he experiences vicariously the events of a tragic November night in Florence almost twenty-five years ago.

Magdalen Nabb's books are as much portraits of different facets of her adopted city as they are crime novels. Readers of her latest will agree with Simenon: She has struck the bull's eye again.

### *Marshal and the Murderer, The*
April 1987

She had come to report that her friend was missing. They were both Swiss, teachers; they had come to Florence to learn Italian and stayed on, working illegally. The missing girl had worked mornings as a potter in a small local town. No one had seen her since Friday lunch-time. It was now Monday afternoon.

Marshal Guarnaccia contacted his opposite number in the little town and arranged to visit. He found a big, jovial Carabinieri officer from Rome, rather more than life-size, still struggling after a year to understand the complexities of the inbred community around him. When the girl's body is discovered under a heap of potsherds he is completely out of his depth.

It is Marshal Guarnaccia whose gently persistent inquiries at last uncover the truth, not only about the two Swiss girls but about the wartime tragedies which no one wants to talk about. These intertwine strangely with the present and in the end prove strong enough to choke the life out of a girl.

### *Marshal at the Villa Torrini, The*
November 1993

Up at the villa on a muggy February afternoon, a well-known writer lies dead without a mark of violence on her. Her husband snores drunkenly near by.

Down in the city of Florence, Marshal Guarnaccia of the caribinieri struggles in vain with the complications of a new legal system and the hunger pangs of a strict diet. Unnerved by his imminent court appearance, his judgement befuddled by lack of food, the Marshal has to take on board more problems. Those include being bullied by old ladies, and foreign intellectuals, and teased by the most notorious anarchistic prosecutor in town.

He has a suspect, he never wavers on that point, but he has no specialized skill, no confidence in himself and no evidence. He feels out of his depth but help comes from a journalist, a priest and a mother; and from a repressed forty-year-old memory of a ragged child kneeling on grains of rice in the corner of the classroom; Vittorio, the son of the village prostitute, whose long-ago sufferings would lead the Marshal to the solution of the mystery at the Villa Torrini.

### *Marshal Makes His Report, The*
November 1991

Homicide, Suicide or Accident. An HSA Report to fill in as in all cases of sudden death, but when one of the oldest noble families in Florence is involved, the only acceptable version is Accident. Marshal Guarnaccia from the nearby carabinieri station in the Pitti Palace doesn't believe that what happened in the Palazzo Ulderighi was an accident, but he will be risking his career if he says so. The trouble is that the Marshal has a way of making his presence felt without saying anything at all and it isn't long before the accident is acknowledged as a suicide. Still the Marshal isn't satisfied. He claims he isn't accusing the Marchesa of killing her husband, so what, as one witness ventures to ask him, does he believe?

Threatened, afraid and battled, the Marshal paces the colonnaded courtyard inside the palazzo, always in shadow or gloomy half-light, always accompanied by the music of flute or piano and by the conviction that something sinister has happened there. When at last the music stops and the characters silently assume their correct places, the Marshal is proved right and after nine hundred years of survival by bloodshed the Palazzo Ulderighi yields up its latest victim.

*'Whoso foregathers with great people is the last at table and the first at the gallows.' Anonymous chronicler of fifteenth-century Florence.*

### Marshal's Own Case, The
February 1990
Everyone hated Lulu alive, and Lulu dead was even less of an attractive proposition. Nobody wanted this nauseating case, especially not Marshal Guarnaccia, wrenched from his peaceful Station within the Pitti Palace and forced to move in an alien, shadowy Florence of which he knew nothing and understood nothing. There had been other cases of the sort. The files were all marked 'Unsolved'. Nobody expected a solution this time, either, and everyone concerned was both amazed and impressed when an arrest was made after only a few days. Everyone except the Marshal. Despite all the evidence, he couldn't see the hot-tempered, unbalanced Peppina planning and perpetrating such a cold-blooded and complicated murder: the sleeping draught, the deadly blows, the long wait – especially the long, inexplicable wait – and then what had been done to the body…

But if Peppina's version was true, where was the body during the long wait, and where was the witness with no real name? The Marshal had to do battle with his own prejudices, with the Public Prosecutor and with the problems coming to a head within his own family before he found what he was looking for. 'Everybody hated Lulu' – until the Marshal found somebody who didn't.

## NICHOLAS, ROBERT
### White Shroud, The
October 1961
Snow lies round the red-brick university of Granstone. In the austere Chemistry building one of the lecturers is found lying across the desk in his office, his head smashed in. Inspector Stone of the Granstone C. I. D. finds no pleasure in the prospect of searching for a murderer among the staff and students, people whose lives would, he had thought, run gently in the ways of learning and tranquillity. But he soon discovered that many people had good reason to dislike – even to hate – the dead man; and that teachers and scholars, for their different reasons, can lie and behave as desperately as other people.

This first novel powerfully conveys a sense of reality; the reader can believe that this man lived and died in this way; that Inspector Stone's investigation is authentic; and that the north-country university city, lying bleakly under its shroud of snow, is as real as the scenes of passion and violence that animate it.

## NIELSEN, TORBEN
### Gallowsbird's Song, A
November 1976
How do you prove that what looks like an obvious suicide is murder? Superintendent Ancher was determined to find out. He did not believe the handsome young man found hanged in his room had committed suicide. Why should he, when he had everything to live for, even down to an attractive girl-friend who was expecting him to dinner and was already grilling the steak? Yet Kent Berner

had stood on a chair, put his head in a noose, and died from strangulation. And he hadn't been strung up while unconscious. What he'd done, he'd done of his own free will.

Yet only minutes before he had been singing a love song. Did that sound like a prospective suicide? When the 14-year-old who volunteered the information was herself found murdered, Ancher realized she might have had more to reveal. Or did she die simply because a child murderer was on the rampage and she happened to come his way? When the battered body of a second little girl was discovered Ancher found himself in charge of something far removed from a doubtful suicide investigation – except that a connection persisted in his mind. But what was the connection, assuming it existed? And how in a city the size of Copenhagen was it ever going to be found?

One of Denmark's leading crime writers makes an outstanding debut in the Crime Club with a novel in which patient police work, shrewd psychology, logical deduction and skilful misdirection of the reader are brilliantly combined.

### Nineteen Red Roses
August 1978
The exceptionally handsome young man was gazing at a face on the wall. Unframed, and in colour. It was the portrait of a murderer-to-be. And he gazed at it in the mirror that hung over the washbasin.

A year previously his 19-year-old girl-friend had been killed by a car containing four drunken people, one of whom was at the wheel. These were the four the young salesman was intent on destroying. But not by killing them. Oh no. They were going to suffer as he had suffered. In each case he would kill the person – whoever it might be – that they loved most.

So began a bizarre series of murders. Except that at first there seemed no connection between the deaths. Superintendent Ancher investigated patiently, and a terrible battle of wits began. Would the murderer's cunning prove triumphant and all four occupants of the fatal car pay his cruel price? Or would the skill and steadiness of an experienced police officer be in time to save at least one of the innocent victims from death?

Torben Nielsen, a former police inspector, is one of Denmark's leading crime novelists. *19 Red Roses* won the Danish Edgar Allan Poe Award as the best mystery novel of the year when it first appeared in Denmark, and was made into an extremely successful film. Torben Nielsen has since gone on to win the Golden Handcuffs, his country's most prestigious crime fiction award.

## ORDE, A. J.
### Dead on Sunday
March 1993
Denver antique dealer Jason Lynx ('an honest, sensitive version of Lovejoy' – *The Times*), who has recently survived episodes of general mayhem and attempted murder is contemplating adopting a quieter life-style. Though his almost-fiancée, Grace, says he's getting stodgy, Jason acclaims the virtues of a safer and more meditative life. When an old college friend arrives to say his brother has been murdered on an Indian pueblo near Santa Fe however, Jason gets out of his chair and into something more puzzling.

Why was Reverend Ernie Quivada murdered in his church on a Sunday afternoon? Though the church building was leased from the local Pueblo, the Pueblo police do not seem to be greatly concerned. The murder of Reverend Quivada, so everyone hints, was

merely a matter of time. Even so, why are Ernie's wife Margaret and his daughter Felicia taking his death so calmly?

Out of friendship, Jason accepts the challenge of finding out who and why, even though the puzzle extends past the Pueblo into the lives of all those who had known the victim – and those who wished they had not.

### Death and the Dogwalker
December 1990
Jason Lynx, antiques dealer and interior decorator, on an early-morning walk with his dog, is dismayed to come upon the body of a casual acquaintance shot dead and carefully posed on a seat. This startling discovery ensnares him in a tangled web of intrigue, for the murder is linked with an earlier one still unsolved, and it is soon apparent that behind them both is a terrible secret which someone will do anything to keep.

Jason is a lover of puzzles with a taste for solving more than the Sunday crossword. His investigation exposes a storm of illicit passion, greed, betrayal, and a retribution that has a disturbing relevance to his own life and threatens to draw him into its relentless spiral as the list of suspects and motives narrows ominously.

### Death for Old Time's Sake
January 1992
Antique dealer Jason Lynx is faithfully administering his recently deceased foster-father's bequests to various charities when his duties are interrupted by a corpse left on a most inconvenient doorstep: that of a local family planning clinic being blockaded by anti-abortionists.

Jason is piqued, even annoyed, but the dead woman has nothing to do with him or with anyone he knows or cares about. Or so he tells his constant companion, Policewoman Grace Willis, who thinks otherwise and demands that Jason solve the case.

The corpse is soon identified. She is Simonetta Fixe: neighbour, housekeeper, sister, daughter, former parochial school student. Many people knew her, but who knows what she did long ago that brought murder to the clinic's doorstep now, killing her—perhaps trying to kill Jason as well—for old time's sake?

### Little Neighbourhood Murder, A
December 1989
It used to be a good neighbourhood, quiet and friendly, no crime to speak of, but that was before Jason Lynx went over to feed his neighbour's dogs and found a deadly paper-wrapped parcel that would change all that – forever.

An antiques dealer and interior designer, Jason Lynx had moved to the neighbourhood some years back with his attractive young wife Agatha. They got along well with everyone, had a son, and seemed to be thriving in their new environment until Agatha disappeared one day without trace. The couple's car was found at the bottom of a ravine outside town, their severely injured son in the back seat. It's been eight years and Jason, an avid solver of puzzles, has not been able to unearth a single clue as to his wife's whereabouts.

As with all survivors of such tragedies, Jason's life has gone on, but when the neighbour's mysterious parcel is opened, its contents are only the first lead in a series of bizarre events that find Jason embroiled in murder and deception beyond his wildest dreams. As the tangled events are chillingly unravelled, Jason finds himself with the first stunning clue to his beloved Agatha's fate.

An exceptional tale of intrigue, *A Little Neighbourhood Murder* is a masterful debut.

## PAGE, EMMA
### Cold Light of Day
November 1983
Cold light of day revealed Gavin Elliott, successful young stockbroker, lying on his right side in bed, his left arm over his face. The jacket of his pyjamas had been raised, exposing his back, and sticking out from between his shoulder-blades was the long handle of a knife.

Despite a forced window and some missing valuables, Detective Chief Inspector Kelsey quickly discounted burglary and turned his attention to those in family and firm (and the two were closely connected) who had known Elliott would be at home alone that night. In the course of his patient investigation, he discovered that not one of them had a motive and every single one had an alibi.

But he and Sergeant Lambert discovered other things too, some of them far back in the past. Soon Kelsey was asking himself the question first put to him by a retired solicitor's clerk in a town many miles away: in any ordinary group of that size in respectable society in an English provincial town, would you expect to find two separate, totally unconnected individuals, each of them prepared at some time in their lives to stab a man to death?

The answer to the question took Kelsey by surprise. It will take the reader equally by surprise in Emma Page's latest craftily plotted crime novel.

### Dead Lock
June 1991
Anna Conway, rising twenty, had much to live for: a pleasant home, a devoted young husband who put her welfare before all else. Yet she suffered from depression and, just before leaving on a restorative cruise, she was found dead.

Chief Inspector Kelsey and Sergeant Lambert at first accepted Anna's death as suicide, and the more they learned of her childhood, the more understandable suicide became. So it was with shock that they learned that when Anna married David she was already the widow of an elderly man, whose death was not without unusual features.

But when they learned that David Conway too had been a widower, his first wife having also committed suicide, Kelsey developed a gut feeling that this grief-stricken widower was a murderer. Yet there was ample testimony to his devotion to Anna, his alibi was unimpeachable and his motive for her murder non-existent.

Doggedly the Chief Inspector set out to prove David's guilt. But each time he unearthed a suspicious circumstance, David came up with an innocent explanation.

Move, counter-move. Deadlock. Had Kelsey met his match at last? The denouement is swift and shattering. This is Emma Page at her best.

### Element of Chance
July 1975
To be young, attractive, successful, is no bar to making enemies, though Alison Rolt never seemed to care. Her estranged husband and the woman who waited for him had it in for her. So did her jealous assistant in the secretarial agency she ran so efficiently as junior partner, and two of the clients who felt she knew too much about them or was guilty of betraying their trust. So, too, did the strait-laced parents of the adolescent boy she dazzled. And in so far as he had it in for any woman, so did the mysterious prowler on the hills.

Consequently, when Alison died from

unnatural causes, it was not in retrospect a surprise. It was the local police who were due for surprises when they patiently set to work to unravel the several strands of small-town life which all tangled in Alison.

Emma Page has already established herself as a mistress of demure detection in which character drawing plays an important part. Her revelations are nicely timed to give a series of twists to the narrative which will tax the reader's deductive powers to the full.

### *Every Second Thursday*
August 1981

The verdict on Vera Foster was suicide. After all, she'd tried it once before. When the neurotic wife who was still primarily Daddy's pampered daughter was found dead from an overdose, no one suspected a thing. Except Detective Chief Inspector Kelsey. And even his suspicions weren't aroused until after the inquest, when the case was officially closed. What made him change his mind and wonder if Vera's husband and her new nurse-companion had somehow contrived her death? And how could they, when they were virtual strangers and witnesses could testify that on the night in question Gerald Foster was seventy miles from home?

Detective-Sergeant Lambert thought his chief was heading for disaster, though he loyally pursued the enquiries he was asked to make. He turned up some curious information, but nothing to suggest conspiracy. Still less conspiracy to murder. There was an innocent explanation for everything.

Rarely has the reader been offered such a remarkable inside view of a murder investigation carried out unofficially by the police, for of course the two suspects may be completely innocent. Are they? Is there even a case at all?

### *Family and Friends*
February 1972

A number people in the Midland town of Milbourne felt their lives would be happier without Zena Yorke, for Zena, rich, spoilt, once beautiful, diabetic, sat like a spider at the heart of a web of intrigue. There was her husband, initially successful in his garment factory because of her but now grown tired of her; Arnold Pierson, the firm's accountant, over whom she had a mysterious hold; her hard up brother, casting covetous eyes at Zena's money; her beautiful sister-in-law who feared what Zena could disclose. In this situation the arrival in the town of a pretty widow acted as a catalyst. Yet when Zena died, the family doctor was satisfied it was from natural causes. There was no case to investigate.

The reader watches Zena's web spinning, the criss-cross of motive, the random scattering of clues, and gradually perceives that he is assisting at the uncovering of a murder by a remarkably cool and determined hand. Emma Page achieved considerable success with her first crime novel, *In Loving Memory*, which *The Times Literary Supplement* compared to Agatha Christie in her classic days. In her second novel, she once again concentrates on the unfolding of a closely knit plot, involving the lives of a group of well drawn characters.

### *Final Moments*
January 1987

The final moments of Venetia Franklin, attractive divorced mother of two, were a mystery. Instead of going off to spend the weekend with a 'gorgeous guy', as she described him, whom she had only recently met, she had died at home on the Friday, shortly after her ex-husband had collected the children, to whom he had weekend access.

Roy Franklin was an immediate suspect, his second marriage hamstrung by alimony and a business partnership with Venetia which he was legally powerless to dissolve. But Chief Inspector Kelsey could not break his alibi, nor that of the local bank manager who admitted to having loved her all his life. Roy's wife had recently had a row with Venetia, and the 'gorgeous guy' had a history of violence, but their alibis too proved unbreakable. The case reached stalemate.

Then a young man was found dead on a local hillside from an overdose of drugs. He was emotionally disturbed, and in his room were cuttings from national and local papers relating to Venetia's death. The conclusion seemed inescapable, but to Kelsey it seemed too pat. And sure enough, the final moments of Venetia Franklin had been masterminded by a cunning murderer who came within an ace of getting away with it.

### *Fortnight By the Sea, A*
February 1973

At the height of the summer holiday season a number of people converged on Oakfield, now run as a private guest-house by Pauline and Godfrey Barratt, with an old family servant as cook and her recently acquired husband as gardener-handyman. The guest-house was part of the Barratts' bid to keep in the family a house grown too large and expensive for them. Even so, though not even his wife knew it, Godfrey Barratt faced bankruptcy.

The arrivals included Pauline's sister, her businessman husband, and two members of his firm; a police sergeant with his wife and three children; and, unexpectedly, a man who had crossed Godfrey's path years before. Also in the neighbourhood was Pauline's rich and ailing aunt and her African servant, and the solicitor who dealt with her will.

Within this group of people were a number of motives for murder, some reaching far back into the past, but all of them mercilessly exposed when one of the group dies unnaturally and it is clear that among these pleasant, ordinary people is someone prepared to kill.

### *In Loving Memory*
March 1970

A number of people stood to benefit from Henry Mallinson's death and Henry Mallinson was old and sick and very rich. His elder son, who had been estranged from him, needed money for his business. His younger son did not want to see his father's will changed. His pretty daughter-in-law needed money to lay a ghost from her past. His godson was behind with the instalments on a motor-cycle. His nurse needed a few thousands to buy her son a smallholding and his secretary a few hundreds to buy herself expensive clothes. When Henry Mallinson died – not from natural causes – there was no lack of suspects for the police.

In this absorbing, satisfying story, Emma Page subtly lays bare a family situation, the temptations to which members of the household are subject and the means of death to which they have access. It is a tribute to her skill that, as suspicion shifts from one to another, the solution tantalisingly eludes the reader until the end.

### *Last Walk Home*
October 1982

July in Longmead village was idyllic: roses round every doorway, gardens full of lowers, fruit and vegetables, the happy voices of children on holiday from school – it was rural peace personified, except for the flies.

It was the blowflies buzzing within Rose Cottage that alerted the postman to something wrong – food left out while its tenant was on holiday perhaps. The reality was nastier.

Suddenly Longmead had a murder in its midst and every man around the relevant time was a suspect. Ageing widower, bored husband, randy young man, unhappy adolescent and quite a few others were all patiently investigated by the police. Any one of them might have been the killer, yet everyone had an alibi and every alibi held.

Detective Chief Inspector Kelsey and Detective-Sergeant Lambert, who made their bow in Emma Page's last crime novel, *Every Second Thursday*, are up against a brick wall until – unexpectedly – a brick is dislodged.

### *Mortal Remains*
January 1993

There was no reason why anyone should kill Harry Lingard. True, Harry had refused to help his granddaughter and her fiancé financially, and Jill would inherit on his death; true that he had incurred the wrath of local youths by his unofficial vigilante activities; true also that he had had a violent altercation with the owner of the builders' yard where he worked when he had been denied a rise and had gone on to unearth certain dealings that might have been better left buried; but these seemed hardly reasons to kill the old man.

A mugging out of doors during the hours of darkness, with no witness, no weapon found, a lapse of time before the discovery of the body, is always one of the most difficult crimes to solve. But Chief Inspector Kelsey was far from persuaded it had been a mugging. It seemed to him from the start that there was more to it than that.

And Chief Inspector Kelsey was to be proved right. Once again Emma Page spins a complex plot round a single, seemingly simple incident, and once again her readers are spellbound by the revelation of character built up in the unobtrusive, telling, background detail which has become the hallmark of her well-loved novels.

### *Scent of Death*
April 1985

The girl in the green anorak who came into the pub one rainy evening was looking for her sister, who had left home four years before. Now, because an unexpected legacy could not be paid until both girls were accounted for, she was hot on the scent, never suspecting that for her it was a scent of death and that each step she had taken to try to trace her sister Helen would soon be followed by Detective-Inspector Kelsey and Sergeant Lambert.

It was apparent that the vital clue they were seeking lay in Helen's life between the time she left home and the November night when she had vanished without trace. Patiently Kelsey and Lambert followed Helen through various jobs, to the house where she had had a flat, the clinic where she had had an abortion, the young man from whom she had bought a car. At no point could it be proved that Helen was dishonest, yet Kelsey suspected that the hard-working, helpful secretary/book-keeper knew more about her employers and their practices than some of them could have wished. And therein lay the clue to a double murder.

A new Emma Page novel is always eagerly awaited, for her skilfully dovetailed plots, sure delineation of character, and well-realized settings have won her a considerable following among connoisseurs of the classic detective novel, who rightly regard her as one of its most gifted exponents.

### *Violent End, A*
December 1988

Karen Boland's body lay face down in the mud of a winter woodland. She was only sixteen, but her past seemed to have caught up with her. Since her parents' deaths Karen had been a problem to step-parrents and foster-parents alike, until she came to live with a cousin and her husband, where she at last had hopes of settling down. But by then one man had gone to prison because of her and another had seen his marriage on the rocks; and a mature student at the college she attended left town with startling abruptness the day after she was found dead.

To Chief Inspector Kelsey there was no shortage of suspects – and that was before he learned that Karen stood to inherit substantially when she reached the age of twenty-one. Fate and a pretty face and attractive body had taught her far too much about the gentle art of making enemies. Had one of them learned the far from gentle art of making her a corpse? Once again Emma Page offers a solidly convincing plot solved by skilful detection which challenges the reader to match wits with the police.

## PALMER, STUART

### *At One Fell Swoop*
March 1951

It was sheer chance that two speed cops should have been coming out of a roadside café as the car passed, driving at a pace that was strictly beyond the law. Speeding is a more or less minor offence, but the law is inclined to take a more serious view if your passenger is a blonde, beautiful but dead. It looked like an open-and-shut case against the driver, and Oscar Piper, of New York Homicide, was quite content. But Hildegarde Withers, that exasperatingly nosy retired schoolmistress, does not agree, and against Inspector Piper's express orders sets out alone to find the killer.

### *Death in Grease-Paint*
July 1956

James McFarley's death looked like suicide; but his wife Mavis was determined that there should be a full inquiry, and to this end she privately hired an investigator, Howard Rook. Rook soon found that McFarley had a connection with the nearby circus; the killer, he thought, would be found under the 'Big Top'. Rook joined the circus himself.

Stuart Palmer's new book sets a baffling murder problem against the glittering background of a vast travelling circus. Those who like a good murder story, and one set against a strange but authentic background, will find plenty of excitement in *Death in Grease-Paint*.

### *Exit Laughing*
June 1954

*Come and trip it as you go*
*You are going to die, you know,*
*Willy-Nilly fall in line*
*And be in death my valentine*
*Lucy*

This poison-pen doggerel brought along Hildegarde Withers to investigate what was going on in that section of the Miracle-Paradox film studios where the cartoon featuring 'Peter Penguin' were made. On her way to report her first day's work in the studio, Hildegarde found a corpse; someone had fed Larry Reed, a cartoon artist, with a very lethal dose of poison-ivy. Hildegarde was quite capable of taking a murder in her maidenly stride, but her erstwhile collaborator, Inspector Oscar Piper, felt sure the old girl was getting out of her depth: he flew into Los Angeles from New York to help her.

There were to be more poison-pens and more poison-ivy before Hildegarde unveiled the murderer of Miracle-Paradox in a sensational climax. In *Exit Laughing*, Stuart Palmer again mixes frightening and mystifying crime with good characterisation and humour.

### Four Lost Ladies
July 1950

When suddenly asked if he knew how many lonely middle-aged, unattached women disappeared in New York every year, Inspector Piper only said: 'Not enough.' And when Miss Hildegarde Withers, retired schoolma'am in search of a crime, suddenly realised the importance of the Christmas card that hadn't arrived and went rushing off, leaving Inspector Piper with two Italian dinners, he was convinced the old girl was slipping. It was a slip that led to a fall – the plunge of one Harriet Bascom from the thirty-eighth floor of Manhattan's latest luxury hotel – and put Miss Withers on the trail of the four lost ladies and the ruthless, romantic killer she had nicknamed 'Mr. Nemo'…the man she called Mr. Nobody.

### Miss Withers Regrets
January 1948

Miss Hildegarde Withers, who must be the world's most popular school-marm, had promised Inspector Piper that she would stop meddling in police affairs. It looked as if she meant it, too, for when Pat Montague's friends asked her help in clearing Pat of suspicion of murdering the repulsive Huntley Cairns, Hildegarde turned him over to the police. But from then on Hildegarde alternated between investigating suspects, snooping for clues, and watching her tank of tropical fish. Oddly enough, it was the fish that finally gave her one of the most important clues and helped her find the way down a devious trail to the murderer. Hildegarde is as delightful as ever in *Miss Withers Regrets*. And you won't regret that she poked her nose into something that, basically, was none of her business.

### Nipped in the Bud
April 1952

Hildegarde Withers, the retired schoolmistress, who, because of her meddlesome ways had long been a thorn in the flesh of Inspector Oscar Piper of the New York Homicide Squad, returned home from a visit in California to attend a murder trial. Winston H. Gault, Junior, of Gault Foods, had got tired of being guyed on his own programme by Tony Fagan, the radio and television comedian, and apparently did something about it with a blunt instrument. At first Hildegarde's main interest in the affair was that the defence lawyer was an old pupil of hers. But when the trial was postponed because of the disappearance of the prosecution's chief witness, a pretty redhead named Ina Kell, Hildegarde responded to the call like an exiled Scot to the sound of the pipes! With her poodle Talleyrand she pursued the wandering red-head to Mexico, and found plenty of trouble south of the border before the chase ended in unexpected and dramatic fashion.

### No Flowers by Request
February 1937

The telegram, "SUGGEST WE ALL ACCEPT UNCLE JOEL'S XMAS INVITATION THIS YEAR STOP EXCELLENT CHANCE TO DECIDE ABOUT HIS SANITY." brought the Cameron heirs rushing to eccentric Uncle Joel's dilapidated home. Like vultures, the Camerons descended, waiting to pounce on the money that would be theirs if Uncle Joel

could be proved crazy. Openly they discussed ways and means of legally disposing of Uncle Joel, and if Uncle Joel heard them discussing him he never said anything, but continued his wanderings around the eery [sic] house, chuckling evilly. The Camerons get a run for their money – and so does the reader.

### Puzzle of the Blue Banderilla, The
September 1937

After the official opening of the Laredo – Mexico City highway – a number of the delegates travelled by train to the Mexican capital. The journey became interesting when an inoffensive customs officer sniffed the contents of a scent bottle belonging to a delegate's wife and dropped down dead. Inspector Oscar Piper, who was also on the train, wired his friend Miss Hildegarde Withers, who was there to meet him on his arrival at Mexico City. Once there, Miss Withers and Inspector Piper rushed about in the blazing sun saving a woman from certain death. They listened, they questioned, and they followed up clues which brought them back to where they began. But it was at a bull-fight they discovered that other things can be killed besides the bull. This is unquestionably the finest Hildegarde Withers story that Stuart Palmer has ever written. The plot is airtight, the characters are superb, the story is exciting and fast paced, and the typical Stuart Palmer humour and sense of the absurd has never been better displayed.

### Puzzle of the Briar Pipe, The
February 1936

A beautiful girl on a beautiful horse riding at sunrise in the deserted Park… . And then the insistent police radio calling all cars, to proceed towards Central Park. For Violet Feverel, beauty queen and gilded daughter of a great city, lay dead, thrown from her highly-strung thoroughbred. Barely are the police on the job when the redoubtable Miss Hildegarde Withers arrives on the scene to prove that Violet Feverel's death was no accident, but the result of a well-planned and highly ingenious murder. Miss Withers discovers what the men in blue had failed to notice, a well-smoked pipe stuck in the mud, and it is round this tenuous clue that the story turns, twisting its exciting path from horse-track to livery stable, from Inspector Piper's room at police headquarters to Miss Withers' quiet uptown apartment. A thrilling battle of wits ensues, in which Miss Withers ultimately triumphs. Stuart Palmer, the brilliant creator of Miss Hildegarde Withers, has written in *The Puzzle of the Briar Pipe* his most exciting mystery.

### Puzzle of the Happy Hooligan, The
October 1941

Even in Hollywood murder is sometimes real, and Miss Hildegarde Withers, immortalised on the screen by Edna May Oliver, once again appears in her star role of detective and gives a brilliant performance in tracking down the murderer of the Mammoth Studio's ace scenario writer. Despite inexplicable opposition from the Studio she decides to make it her business to find out just how one goes about breaking a man's neck without leaving a mark.

### Puzzle of the Silver Persian, The
January 1935

Mr. Stuart Palmer is a young author new to our list, but he is already well known through his exhilarating detective stories featuring the extraordinary exploits of Miss Hildegarde Withers. The present story presents the most puzzling problem he has yet devised. Why a silver persian should have been a deciding

clue is perhaps the most puzzling question of all.

OR

Miss Hildegarde Withers thought she was embarking on a holiday when she sailed so blithely on *S.S. American Diplomat*. She had no idea then that shortly she would be in acrimonious argument with Chief Inspector Cannon of Scotland Yard, nor that the death of a young girl could burst into such a monstrous flower of evil, catching her in its centre. If it had not been for the clue of the great silver persian cat, stalking so majestically in the shadow of blood and terror, even Miss Withers herself might have fallen a victim to the murderer who recognised no obstacles, who had a debt of fear to pay, and who was determined to pay it.

## PARKES, ROGER
### Abuse of Justice, An
September 1988

When eight-year-old Vicky Bates is sexually molested near her school, Detective-Inspector Taff Roberts knows very well who to arrest. So far as Marlbury CID are concerned, Len Snow is the man responsible for the ten-year reign of terror on the town's children.

But Snow knows his law and the fact that the rules of evidence in child sex cases amount to a virtual Molester's Charter.

*An Abuse of Justice* is about the challenge of beating the Charter – a challenge necessitating the collaboration of doctors and social workers, the police and lawyers of the Crown, in a case where to play it strictly by the book is to lose.

For DI Taff Roberts, first encountered in Roger Parkes's previous crime novel, *Riot*, the case becomes as personal to his moral code as to his career survival. As the final courtroom drama swings to and fro, the reader too is caught up emotionally in a battle ultimately decided by a twist as ironic as it is unexpected.

### Gamelord
October 1990

Judge Vincent Hartington, finalizing his controversial report into the future of the football industry, is lured to a mysterious rendezvous at the Balham United ground and murderously assaulted. Attacked with him is DCI Taff Roberts, recently returned to the Yard to investigate Met corruption. The bedside plea from Isabel Hartington is for Taff to avenge her husband's injuries, which may well prove fatal.

The trail leads from United's manager, players and supporters to the club's Gamelord chairman and his captivating mistress. With the help of an ex-girlfriend, TV Crime Reporter Kate Lewis, Taff's investigation widens to include a giant distilling company, a Cabinet-level politician and Special Branch. All too soon, the detective finds himself in the dog-eat-bloodhound John Stalker dilemma of being investigated by the Met.

Thanks to Kate, a vital witness is found, the action moving to a Munich international match for the first of several arrests, each leading Taff back to the formidable Gamelord. Yet, twist on twist, the dramatic climax to the investigation is radically different from the detective's expectations.

### Riot
September 1986

A riot in the lifers' wing of Brentford Prison results in the death of an IRA prisoner. Chief Superintendent Walsh and Detective-Inspector Roberts are immediately involved in the kind of horror case CID officers always try to

dodge: beset by red tape, staff obstruction, the lies and deceit of the prison subculture. When prison staff are implicated, there is also pressure from unions, from Whitehall administrators, ultimately from politicians.

Walsh, nearing retirement, has no desire to crusade against the Law-and-Order Establishment, yet there are limits to his readiness to compromise and play along with the System. Moreover, the detectives' dilemma is compounded by the resourcefulness of ITN crime reporter Kate Lewis, who, having cultivated a liaison with DI Roberts, learns of a top-level cover-up.

Walsh is soon made aware that his own retirement prospects are at risk; so too, though he does not know it, is Kate's life.

Roger Parkes was a prison visitor at Wormwood Scrubs from 1976-82, and was privy to the massive riot there in 1979. He has also worked as a crime reporter and is a magistrate. He has drawn on all these experiences in *Riot* which, as Robert Kilroy-Silk, MP, says in his Foreword, is 'a dramatic story full of pace and suspense…so true to life, so tellingly descriptive of the cloistered, secret and unnatural world that is a prison, that it could equally well be taken to be an impartial and dispassionate account of a real event.'

### Wages of Sin, The
June 1992

For six years the Free Aristotle Macho Edwards campaign has pulled a variety of exotic publicity stunts. To ITN crime reporter Kate Lewis, FAME is hot news; but to her fiancé, Chief Inspector Taff Roberts, it's a racket. To him, Ari Edwards is a black pimp who fully deserves his life-sentence for the brutal murder of one of his high-society prostitutes.

But then a crucial new witness disappears and the detectives on the original case start pressurizing Taff to get at Kate – who is then grossly assaulted.

Retaliating, Taff eventually gets the murder conviction quashed and Ari Edwards released, but with fatal consequences as those behind the pimp's conviction – senior police and a top City company – close ranks to conceal their involvement.

## PAUL, BARBARA
### But He Was Already Dead When I Got There
August 1986

Miserly Vincent Farwell decided to call in a loan he had made to his family and thereby put their jewellery business at risk. They all had motive and opportunity to kill him, and all of them for one reason or another seemed to have visited the scene of the crime after the murder but before the body was officially discovered. Other people too had been in the study where Uncle Vincent was found, but they all claimed 'he was already dead when I got there'. One of them wasn't telling the truth – but which one?

That was the problem which faced Lieutenant Toomey and Sergeant Rizzuto when they were called in to investigate the death. Every elucidation revealed new complications, and each fresh complication incriminated someone else. The only witness was the cat, and he wasn't telling – or was he?

As this witty send-up of the good old-fashioned mystery gets under way, there are enough twists and turns of plot to make a corkscrew look straightforward and an element of spoof and fun on every page.

### First Gravedigger
February 1982

Earl Sommers, agent with the Speer Galleries,

doesn't know which he enjoys more – cheating Amos Speer out of valuable pieces of furniture, or taking advantage of Speer's wife, Nedda, in them. But when Speer uncovers both illicit activities, it looks as if Earl's little idyll has come to an end.

Then, suddenly, opportunity knocks. When Earl's old friend Charlie Bates turns up in a suicidal mood, Earl agrees to find him a gun … in return for one last trifling favour.

Amos Speer duly shows up in the obituary column, and Earl gets both the directorship of the Galleries and Nedda. What he hasn't counted on, though, is born-loser Charlie changing his mind about killing himself.

And there's the hitch: Charlie never could keep his mouth shut.

Barbara Paul has created a strikingly original situation in this ironic novel, and her handling of it is deft in the extreme.

### Kill Fee
October 1985

If your worst enemy was shot dead while you, quite innocent, were miles away with an unimpeachable alibi, you would hardly be human if you did not feel relief. But what if you then received a note signed Pluto demanding a substantial 'kill fee'?

A number of New Yorkers found themselves in that predicament, and most were willing to pay up, especially when the mysterious Pluto demonstrated what happened to those who did not. For Pluto it represented a very comfortable living. For his carefully selected beneficiaries, it represented a welcome if unlooked-for escape.

But what of Pluto's victims, the men and women he brutally gunned down? They were the concern of Lieutenant Murtaugh of the New York Police Department, who devoted himself to tracking down Pluto, even though it brought him into conflict with his superiors.

And then there was another shooting, and this time it was Murtagh who received a demand for a highly unusual 'kill fee'.

From its beginnings in the world of small magazines, through a series of killings and an ever-tightening police net, up to its electrifying shock ending, Barbara Paul's original and skilfully crafted novel carries the reader along on a rising tide of superb suspense.

### Renewable Virgin, The
March 1984

Kelly Ingram is a rising star who has everything going for her – great looks, a live-wire personality, enough talent to get by one, a new TV series, and a new lover. She also has an agent and a producer who hate each other; but they still manage to work together well enough to keep Kelly's career moving in the right direction.

But then a friend is murdered, a harmless scriptwriter who should have been no threat to anybody. The scriptwriter's mother enters Kelly's life, a history professor named Fiona Benedict who dislikes everything the actress stands for. Mediating between them is Marian Larch of the New York Detective Bureau, assigned to investigate the murder.

What Marian turns up is a tale of ambition and envy and betrayal going back fifteen years. Kelly, Fiona, and Marian – three women who have absolutely nothing in common except the act of murder that brings them together – take turns telling the story, which ultimately demonstrates how friendship can blossom in even the unlikeliest of circumstances.

### Your Eyelids Are Growing Heavy
August 1982

When Megan Phillips came to on the fourteenth-hole fairway of an unfamiliar

golf-course it just wasn't her style. She didn't drink, and lost weekends were not in her repertoire. Yet suddenly the attractive, confident, competent distribution manager of Glickman Pharmaceuticals who was well in line for a vice-presidency, had to confront a thirty-eight-hour blank in her life.

Her neighbour Gus couldn't help her reconstruct the missing day and a half. Even Dr. Henrietta Snooks, psychiatrist, could not draw any memories from her unconscious. It was as if an eraser had wiped out a piece of her past.

When Megan started to get phone-calls, conversations she forgot as soon as she hung up, it became clear that her blackout was no isolated event. She began to realize that during those thirty-eight hours she had been with someone, someone who had hypnotized her and told her to – what?

She couldn't remember – that was the trouble. No matter how hard she racked her brain, she just didn't know. What she did know was that the only way to regain control of her life was to find the mysterious hypnotist…

And kill him.

## PEARCE, MICHAEL
### Mamur Zapt and the Camel of Destruction, The
November 1993

Cairo, 1910, and the end of the boom: half-finished buildings everywhere; banks beleaguered; borrowers in trouble, from the poorest land-working Fellahin to the richest land-owning Pashas – not to mention Gareth Owen, the Mamur Zapt, Head of the Cairo Secret Police.

Then one day a civil servant dies at his desk. Was it pressure of work, or some other, nastier, kind of pressure? The whiff of corruption is in the air, with even the Mamur Zapt seen to live beyond his means, yet he's the one who's supposed to be investigating the affair.

His attempt to do so, aided by such unlikely allies as the local barber, the Grand Mufti, the formidable Widow Shawquat and the monstrous Ali, takes him to the heart of such sinister organizations as the Khedival Agricultural Society – not at all the same sort of thing as the agricultural societies of places such as Maidenhead (and why do the English go in for such distastefully explicit place names anyway?).

Money speaks louder than words in Cairo and the rich are notoriously tricky. To fight them requires particular skills; skills the Mamur Zapt has in abundance. But Owen will need all his wiles if he is to stop the Camel of Destruction running through the city.

### Mamur Zapt and the Donkey-Vous, The
March 1990

'Tourists are quite safe provided they don't do anything stupidly reckless,' Owen assured the Press. 'Like having tea on the terrace at Shepherd's?' asked the man from *Paris-Soir*. Because that was where Monsieur Moulin had been when he was kidnapped. And it was where Mr Colthorpe was when he, too, disappeared. 'About the most conspicuous place in Cairo,' Owen commented bitterly.

Owen, head of Egypt's Political CID in the heyday of British rule, was ultimately responsible for law and order in Cairo. And when they were so openly flouted he had to do something about it. But that was not so easy. To start with, nobody had actually seen the victims go…

And was it just an ordinary kidnapping? Or was it intended as a deliberately symbolic blow at British prestige? Or the start of a

sinister campaign directed particularly at tourism? What lay behind the sudden interest of the Khedive in market gardening? And who was the missing dragoman?

Owen's attempts to solve these puzzles take him into the circle of the Khedive's closest intimates but also to the donkey-vous beneath Shepherd's famous terrace, the basis of Cairo's lowly, but enterprising, donkey-boys. It is there that Owen finds the answer – though perhaps not quite the one he expected.

### Mamur Zapt and the Girl in the Nile, The
January 1992

'What sort of boat do you think this is?' said the eunuch indignantly when Captain Gareth Owen, the Mamur Zapt or Head of Cairo's Political Secret Police, came on board. Well, what sort of boat did he think it was? And for what purpose had Prince Narouz so mysteriously hired it? Surely not just to cruise to Luxor when he had no interest in antiquities? And how had the girl come to fall overboard anyway?

Other people besides Owen would like to know the answers; and other people still would like the answers not to be known. Adrift in the complex political currents of Edwardian Egypt, Owen is in danger of losing sight of the girl at the centre of it all, whose body was glimpsed on a sandbank and then seemed to have vanished into thin air. His attention is sharply focused, however, when some of the most powerful motivation ever seen in the detective novel is brought to bear on the solving or otherwise of the crime.

### Mamur Zapt and the Men Behind, The
February 1991

Riding home on his donkey, Fairclough of Customs is shot at from behind. It is the first of many similar incidents – all seemingly aimed at public servants. The Mamur Zapt himself, British Head of Cairo's Secret Police, nearly becomes a victim. Is this a sinister campaign to undermine British rule in Cromer's Egypt? Who are 'the men behind'? The Mamur Zapt is told to find out: quickly.

His efforts to do so take him into Cairo's student quarter and out to a remote rural estate; involve him in the wily manoeuvrings of the Khedive's court and the no less dubious speculations of a visiting commercial delegation; and require him to handle with equal adroitness an ever-ambitious, fading political Pasha, an over-enthusiastic bomb-juggling Berber bodyguard, and a knife-wielding gipsy girl – whose claims he has to balance against those of his fiery and possessive Egyptian mistress.

One again, Michael Pearce's cultivated pen 'traces colourful arabesques of greed, history and mystery' (*Sunday Times*) as he 'brings the Cairo of yesterday to fly-blown, endearing life.' (*Observer*)

### Mamur Zapt and the Night of the Dog, The
January 1989

The Mamur Zapt, head of Cairo's Political CID in the heyday of British Rule, did not concern himself with routine police matters. Captain Owen, the present incumbent, firmly indicated as much.

But the discovery in a Coptic tomb of the body of a dog, the supreme, Moslem insult, was a delicate matter, not least because the Christian Copts were alleging harassment. If the belief was widely held, any spark could set off an explosion. Owen could not afford to stand aside.

Not could he stand aside from the visit of

a British MP intent on inspecting the British administration's accounts, especially when it affected the Curbash Compensation Fund, on which Owen's police unofficially relied.

And he certainly couldn't stand aside having escorted the MP's niece to see a gathering of dancing dervishes – where one of them was stabbed to death before her eyes.

The incident was part of a pattern which extended up to government level and could mean blood on the streets. It took all the Mamur Zapt's guile to unravel the pattern and in the end avert bloodshed. He was even able to replenish the Curbash Compensation Fund.

Michael Pearce charts Owen's fortunes with the sly humour and keen relish for the idiosyncrasies of Egyptian life which marked his distinguished debut with *The Mamur Zapt and the Return of the Carpet*.

### Mamur Zapt and the Return of the Carpet, The
January 1988

Cairo 1908. As the long period of indirect British rule draws to an end, tensions mount. The attempted assassination of a veteran politician raises the possibility of a major terrorist outrage at the city's principal religious festival, the Return of the Holy Carpet from Mecca.

A grim story? Anything but, as Michael Pearce chronicles the deliciously devious means by which the Mamur Zapt, British head of Cairo's Political CID, tracks down the terrorists in this city of multiple nationalities, three principal languages and four competing legal systems. Helping the Mamur Zapt is Mahmoud, a sharp young Egyptian lawyer from the Parquet, the French-style Ministry of Justice; Nikos, a Copt; and Georgiades, a Greek and one of the Mamur Zapt's best agents. Only at the last minute, as the Holy Carpet is on its way through the streets of Cairo, is disaster averted, and the Mamur Zapt set free to tackle his next assignment.

Here is something different – and how welcome that is in crime fiction! Here is detection with a difference by an author who knows and loves Egypt, has a scholar's approach to his historical material, and a wit's to the humour inherent in the conflicting interests of his multinational characters.

### Mamur Zapt and the Spoils of Egypt, The
December 1992

But what, Captain Owen asked himself, was Miss Skinner doing looking at crocodiles? Especially, mummified ones? It mattered because Miss Skinner was a lady with a habit of asking awkward questions. And because her uncle might, just might, become the next President of the United States, those questions had to be answered. At present they were concentrated on the illegal export of antiquities. And Owen, the Mamur Zapt, or Head of Cairo's Secret Police, had just been given the task of seeing that Egypt's priceless antiquities stayed in Egypt.

But were they priceless? Were they even antiquities? At times it seemed that the whole of Egypt was engaged in one dubious aspect or other of the antiquities business. And what about Miss Skinner herself? When she so narrowly escaped falling under a Cairo tram, was it because she had been nudged by a fat-tailed Passover sheep? Or by something more sinister?

These were minor problems compared to those which later faced Owen. As he fought to halt the flight abroad of Egypt's national treasures he had also to decide whether to ask Zeinhab to marry him. And how to differentiate between archaeology and plunder.

## PENN, JOHN
### Accident Prone
November 1987
The death of Muriel Fayne in her house near Colombury in the English Cotswolds sets off a curious chain of events, mainly affecting her daughter Helen. A tiresome fall, a bolting horse, a possible poisoning, a car crash with which drugs may be associated – do these and other incidents merely suggest that Helen is becoming accident prone, possibly because she drinks a little too much, or are more sinister motives and forces at work?

The whole of Muriel's family, the local vicar, a man who would once have been known as the 'squire' – all are involved, as well as the Drayton Galleries, a nearby riding stables and Coriston College.

Eventually, Dr Band takes a hand in the game, and so does Detective-Superintendent George Thorne of the Thames Valley Police Serious Crime Squad, as incident follows incident in this complex web of motives and deceptions, leading to a denouement as surprising as it is dramatic.

### Barren Revenge
December 1986
Is it coincidence, or is there a connection when glasshouses containing precious orchids are peppered with shot, at the same time as thieves break into Judge Sir Leo Farling's Cotswold home and kill the houseman?

Detective-Superintendent George Thorne and Sergeant Abbot of the Thames Valley Police are called in to find the answer. They soon discover that this is no single crime, but the climax of a series of minor attacks on Sir Leo and his family. Is the motive revenge on the part of some criminal the Judge has sent down?

While Thorne tries to cope with this problem he runs into difficulties in his own life. His wife, Miranda, has disappeared, and all the evidence suggests she went of her own free will. Yet Thorne knows his marriage was not like that; Miranda would never leave him without warning, without even a farewell note. Police officers, like judges, are always at risk from villains they have arrested. Is this another instance of revenge? Is Miranda in danger? The Chief Constable is sceptical and Thorne's colleagues are inclined to snigger.

The Superintendent has to follow a cryptic clue and face a dramatic encounter in a mysterious area outside Oxford before the truth is known.

### Deadly Sickness, A
May 1985
Old Sir Oliver Poston was dying; there was no doubt about that. But the timing of his death would affect the fortunes of his son and his son's wife and their friends and associates.

Was Sir Oliver's death hastened? And was his manservant's accident really accidental? What role did the unexpected Miss Nancy Naury play? These were but a few of the problems that confronted Dr Dick Band, and eventually Detective-Superintendent George Thorne and Sergeant Abbot of the Thames Valley Police Serious Crime squad.

John Penn's readers will find themselves back on familiar ground – near Colombury in the Cotswolds, where the author once again weaves a traditional yet thrilling crime story, in which the characters are human, the situations and locations realistic, and the procedures authentic.

To say more would be to reveal too much of the complex plot, which centres not on a deadly sickness in any clinical sense, but on the expression of greed, sometimes the deadliest sickness of all.

### Death's Long Shadow
October 1991
This time Chief Inspector Tansey and Sergeant Abbot of the Thames Valley Police Force are at work close to home. A relatively unknown but prestigious College in the centre of Oxford is bombed, but there are no known indications that terrorists of the usual kind have been responsible. Instead, Tansey, with his usual acumen, integrates himself into College life and interviews undergraduates and dons, one of whom has faced the most dangerous dilemma of his life.

Indeed, the investigation is fraught with continuing danger, and it is only after shrewd detection and conjecture that Tansey is able to bring the crime home to its perpetrator in a conclusion that is as dramatic as it is unexpected.

John Penn's twelfth novel is his best to date – an Oxford crime story to rival many fine inventions that have gone before. It demonstrates yet again the author's deceptively simple and unambiguous style, and his ability to construct a thrilling plot with realistic setting and characters.

### Deceitful Death
April 1983
Gerald Hinton's eve of wedding stag party at the London Arts and Letters Club was interrupted by a glamorous 'Golden Girl' whom Gerald claimed never to have seen before. But the girl declared herself pregnant and named Gerald as the father of her child. True or false? A hoax in bad taste or a serious attempt to prevent the wedding? No one knew – Gerald least of all. But there was nothing of a hoax about the two deaths that followed; they were all too distressingly real.

John Breland, Harley Street doctor, was both a guest at the party and a member of the club. His friendship with Gerald soon involved him in efforts to solve the mystery, and in a volatile relationship with Chief Superintendent Freeman of Scotland Yard.

### Feast of Death, A
May 1989
The parish church of Fairfield in the Cotswolds was ancient and dedicated to an unusual Saint – St Blaise. Although it lacked a large congregation, and also a vicar, the Parochial Church Council was determined that the Feast of St Blaise should be celebrated in suitable fashion. What the local leaders did not realize was that, though their prayers for a priest were answered, their determination to hold their patronal Festival would lead them into a world of murder, suspicion, and uncertainty.

Once again Detective Chief Inspector Tansey of the Thames Valley Police and Sergeant Hilary Greenway find themselves involved in a fascinating and exciting case, with its roots in the past but its execution very much in the present.

### Haven of Danger, A
April 1993
Detective Chief Inspector Tansey found himself personally involved in his latest case, when a recently widowed family friend went to live in an expensive and select retirement home, run by caring Dr Cassidy and his delightful family. Sadly, Evenlode House soon proved far from the haven it had promised to be.

Petty theft was followed by an outbreak of food poisoning, then murder and attempted murder, and finally arson and another death. But who was to blame? Who, apart from the local reporter, had it in for Evenlode House? And why? Eventually Tansey, with the help of Detective-Sergeant Abbott, managed to fit

together the pieces of the puzzle and reveal what lay behind it all.

This is another of John Penn's intricate, topical and closely-woven stories, with a range of characters from the young to the not so young, all carefully delineated.

### Killing to Hide, A
February 1990
Detective Chief Inspector Dick Tansey of the Thames Valley Police Force has married his erstwhile sergeant, Hilary, and the couple are delighted at the prospect of their first child. Tansey is therefore less than ecstatic when he is told that, as part of an official exchange programme, they are to leave the relative peace of their home patch while he spends six months in the more violent hassle of Central London, attached to the Metropolitan Police, with its reputation for arrogance and inflexibility.

On his arrival in Delta Mike Division, he finds himself immediately embroiled in one of the most intriguing and puzzling cases of his career. What is more, circumstances and staff shortages mean that he remains in charge of the inquiry, under the cynical eyes of the media, and with the assistance of a new detective-sergeant – Sester, a street-wise Met officer of some character.

As one apparently motiveless killing follows another, Tansey and Sester face a curious selection of suspects, mostly centred in the Marylebone area, and the Chief Inspector is forced to rethink his theories many times. As with all John Penn crime novels, the investigation is logical, the clues can eventually be seen to be unambiguous, and the climax is unexpected and dramatic.

### Knife Ill-Used, A
January 1991
Cynthia Faudin was an eminent and well-known scholar – the Principal of an Oxford College and ambitious to become the first woman Vice-Chancellor of the University. Her married life was happy, her husband rich, her twin children now grown-up.

But one morning in Oxford she met an old acquaintance, and this seemingly chance encounter was to change her life and lead to a series of unexpected and dramatic incidents, culminating in two suspicious deaths.

Detective Chief Inspector Tansey of the Thames Valley Police Serious Crime Squad investigates. He misses the accompaniment of his detective-sergeant wife, now confined to a desk job at Headquarters, but is assisted by the shrewd and efficient Sergeant Abbot. At first their inquiries lead nowhere, but a breakthrough leads Tansey to suspect that the roots of the matter lie deep in Mrs Faudin's past – a theory that can only be checked while he is nominally on leave with his wife on two islands: the Isle of Wight, and Jersey.

### Legacy of Death, A
September 1992
Once again, Detective Chief Inspector Richard Tansey and Detective-Sergeant Bill Abbot of the Thames Valley Police are in familiar territory, this time investigating mysterious events at a coeducational day and boarding-school near Colombury in the Cotswolds. A sixteen-year-old girl, Hannah Aston, is facing a desperate dilemma which results in her disappearance on the night of the school's Hallowe'en Party, spirited away like one of the supernatural beings whose costumed embodiments throng the assembly hall. But the mystery of the girl's disappearance is not as inexplicable as it first appears. A surprising number of people turn out to know something about Hannah and her problems.

There is a legacy, of course – a legacy of death – and it is a legacy which leads Tansey and Abbot into a wilderness of contradictory evidence and misleading red herrings. It is only after a dramatic climax that all becomes unambiguous.

### Mortal Term
November 1984
Returning from a conference in Oxford, Hugh Roystone, headmaster of a coeducational boarding-school in the Cotswolds, gave a lift to an unknown girl – only to find himself accused of attempted rape. To which there were witnesses.

It was the climax to a summer term in which Roystone had had to contend with more than his share of unpleasant difficulties, including a fatal traffic accident, pot-smoking among the boys, a girl pregnant, various staff problems, uneasy governors. Worst of all, his new young wife had decided that life in the school's hothouse atmosphere was not for her.

Detective-Superintendent Thorne of the Thames Valley Police regarded investigation of the attempted rape as beneath his dignity. But the Chief Constable requested him to look into it, and he soon discovered unsuspected tensions and rivalries among the school staff which belied the surface calm and might have some bearing on the case.

Then there was a death. Murder? Undoubtedly. Motives? Complex. Suspects? Many. With the help of Sergeant Abbot, Thorne unravelled a crime with its roots in the past, its detection ingenious, and its denouement dramatic.

### Notice of Death
May 1982
'Coming Soon – THE DEATH OF MAJOR CHERYL'. The teaser ad on the book page of a national newspaper did not worry the real Major Cheryl, retired in his Oxfordshire village, apart from the annoying coincidence of name. But when the ads continued to appear and several 'accidents' happened, it no longer seemed coincidence. Urged on by his worried daughter, the Major went to the police.

The police were predictably sceptical – until a violent death occurred. It wasn't Major Cheryl's – but had the victim been the one intended all along and the ads merely an elaborate blind? Chief Inspector David Taylor faced a case in which the answer to each question posed another question, complicated by his growing love for the Major's daughter and his superior's impatience at what he regarded as an investigation needlessly long drawn out. Even when Taylor established that a cold-blooded killer had gone ruthlessly to work, he knew neither the killer's motives nor identity, though there were those who thought it might be Major Cheryl himself. ..

Not until the last piece of the puzzle turned up unexpectedly did the evil design fall into place. But Taylor had still to trap an exceedingly clever villain, who might yet prove too slippery to hold.

### Outrageous Exposures
August 1988
Within the space of a few weeks one October three young women disappeared in and around Oxford. All they had in common were good looks and long hair.

In his latest crime novel John Penn introduces a new member of the Thames Valley Police Force – Detective Inspector Dick Tansey – who, with a woman sergeant, is given the unwelcome task of investigating this sequence of events. Soon, however, it becomes clear that there is a great deal more to the case than the almost routine abduction of young girls. Murder follows murder, an ex-convict is involved, the secret lives of the victims prove important, the relationship between Tansey and his sergeant develops, and disturbing facets of human characters are revealed that are rarely explored.

This book is a new departure for John Penn – a far cry from the eight classic crime stories he has written in the past. His many fans will enjoy it for its complexity, characterization and humanity.

### Unto the Grave
March 1986

Detective-Superintendent George Thorne was delighted when his old friends John and Rose Kempton took over a hotel in the Cotswolds and rapidly advanced it into the luxury class. When one of the guests was found dead in the hotel swimming pool, he was concerned as much for the hotel's reputation as for the dead man, whom no one had particularly liked.

Then a second death followed, and Thorne's concern sharpened to suspicion, though there was no apparent connection between the deaths and at first no evidence to suggest that either victim had been murdered. Nevertheless, Wychwood House's reputation plummeted and ruin stared the Kemptons in the face.

The guests, ranging from a Canon and his family to a woman novelist in search of peace to finish her latest book, dealt with the developing situation in their own ways, and so did some of the staff. Among these people Thorne made his inquiries, and the interplay of character, the reactions to his sometimes unconventional methods, and the need to delve into the past produce a totally unexpected denouement in this variant of the country house mystery – but a variant with a difference.

### Widow's End
November 1993

When Lydia Vail's battered body is found in her secluded house at one end of the Cotswold village of Little Chipping, suspicion inevitably falls on her son, for Oliver has disappeared. But Oliver was said to be devoted to his widowed mother, a possessive woman who still wears widow's weeds ten years after coming to live in the village – where she has made herself far from popular.

Once more it falls to Detective Chief Inspector Dick Tansey, Inspector Whitelaw and Detective-Sergeant Abbot of the Thames Valley Police Force Serious Crime Squad to investigate. Tansey manages to sort out a complex collection of characters, and unearths an old and surprising secret. But by the time he is able to identify the murderer, the killer has struck again.

This is John Penn's sixteenth crime novel, most of them set in and around the imaginary, though closely observed, Cotswold market town of Colombury, where he deploys an intriguing puzzle peopled with a fascinating selection of credible characters.

### Will to Kill, A
November 1983

The Derwents, struggling to retain control of their beautiful Cotswold home, are faced with tragedy when Peter, the head of the family, is found shot. At first sight it seems an accident, but revelations about the Derwents' financial affairs and the details surrounding Peter's will suggest otherwise. Detective-Superintendent Thorne and Sergeant Abbot of the Thames Valley Police, with some assistance from Tim Railton, the Derwents' lawyer, uncover a variety of surprising motives and an array of suspects, any of whom could have had a will to kill.

The action of this deceptively simple story moves rapidly between the market town of Colombury and London. Another fatal shot rings out before a denouement which is both dramatic and unexpected, yet logical enough to satisfy the most demanding devotees of the classic whodunit, their appetites already whetted by John Penn's previous novels, *Notice of Death* and *Deceitful Death*.

## PENNY, RUPERT

### Lucky Policeman, The
May 1938

Rupert Penny's 'Policeman' novels have established themselves, well and truly, as among the most popular books in the Crime Club Calendar. Firstly, because of the excellent and always fair problems they set and, secondly, because of their welcome humour.

The problem he sets now in *The Lucky Policeman* concerns two corpses discovered in the New Forest, each with the left boot missing. The policeman of the title is, of course, Chief Inspector Beale, whose many friends will be delighted to meet him again.

OR

Rupert Penny's 'Policemen' novels have established themselves well and truly among the most popular books in the Crime Club Calendar. The problem he sets in *The Lucky Policeman* concerns an outbreak of murder mania in the New Forest, where not one but several persons are killed in rapid succession. Most extraordinary of all, in each case the victim was robbed of his or her left shoe. The mystery in itself is one of outstanding qualities, and the reader is given every opportunity to solve it. It is an enthralling story, with a startling climax, all worked out with tremendous ingenuity.

### Policeman in Armour
September 1937

Rupert Penny has made his own special niche in detective fiction. For in his novels he makes the time-table of crime as fascinating a problem as Anthony Armstrong made it in his famous play, *Ten Minute Alibi*, which drew London audiences for nearly two years. And like Mr. Armstrong (better known perhaps as 'A. A.' of *Punch*) Mr. Penny has a welcome gift of humour to refresh you when the case seems almost impossible of solution.

In *Policemen in Armour* he once again guides you through the evidence up to a certain point, then turns on you and says: 'Now you ought to know who murdered the man, and how, and why'. But *do* you know? Test your brains and see. You will find it an enthralling-game.

### Policeman's Evidence
October 1938

Detective-story readers nowadays are definitely penny-wise. 'In for a Penny,' they say, 'in for a puzzle.' Here is another first-rate puzzle to tease the brains. The first part of the narrative, setting the stage, comes from Anthony Purdon. The second part, unravelling the mystery, is by Chief-Inspector Beale himself – hence the significance of the title. Readers will enjoy this account by a Scotland Yard detective of the way he set about a case.

### Policeman's Holiday
March 1937

*Cancel reservations pack tails hope you like Dorset letter following await patiently why is policeman like woman because work never done* – Beale. This characteristic wire from Chief-Inspector Beale to his friend Anthony Purdon was definite intimation that his projected holiday was to be of the 'busman's variety. His vacation was spent in unravelling the intricacies of the famous Pomerry case. The dead body of Mr. Bernard Pommery J. P., was found in Dillows Wood, 'depending from a tree', to quote the local paper. There was, however, little reason to suspect suicide, hence Beale's presence. His patient investigation into this mystery deserves to rank as a classic of detection. Here is indeed a detective story which will not disappoint readers; it is brilliantly done, extraordinarily ingenious, and absolutely fair; a worthy successor to Mr. Penny's highly successful story, *The Talkative Policeman*.

### Sealed-Room Murder
May 1941

Rupert Penny excels all his previous form with this highly successful murder mystery. Unlike most 'sealed-room' stories, the problem is perfectly clear-cut and extremely simple in its elements. Where other mysteries try to baffle the reader by their complexity, this one will baffle by its simplicity. The story of Harriet Steele and the family that was forced upon her, is good reading even when considered as a straight novel, the situation is very real, very familiar and always lively and amusing in spite of the undertone of grimness. The thoroughly ingenious and exciting crime is put before the reader with scrupulous fairness so that he has every possible chance of leaping to the solution that will prove completely satisfying.

### She Had to Have Gas
May 1939

The plot of Rupert Penny's new book covers the disappearance of two girls, the unknown Alice West from Craybourne and Philippa Sanders, niece of a well-known detective-story writer from Belling Sands. Two girls missing – one body found. But whose body? The detective story writer is convinced that it is his niece's. The police are convinced that it is Alice West's. One murder or two murders? For a long time Chief-Inspector Beale cannot even be certain how many murders he is investigating. He is accompanied by his friend Anthony Purdon, and Detective-Sergeant Matthews – Tony being more helpful than usual. Colonel Hagshaw, the local Chief Constable, also figures largely in this story.

### Sweet Poison
June 1940

A Penny for your Thoughts! A Rupert Penny detective story makes you think. It will brush up your brains, give your wits an airing, stimulate your grey matter and leave you mentally invigorated, particularly if you succeed in solving the problem presented. Make no mistake, Mr. Penny plays scrupulously fair. No cards are hidden up his sleeve. So join in the hunt for the murderer of little Edwin Weekes, a young preparatory school boy. And who would want to kill little Edwin? There are plenty of suspects – and a rare hunt.

### Talkative Policeman, The
July 1936

*The Talkative Policeman* is a quite exceptionally ingenious detective story. It is frankly a brain-teaser. It takes the reader through the entire routing of a crime investigation, presenting him, as it were, with the complete case-book of a murder and challenging him to make what he can of it. The author says, in effect: 'I am going to give you every possible detail; now it's up to you to sort them out and solve the case.' Undoubtedly what the true detective fan likes to do is to solve the puzzle for himself, and here he is given every chance. There is no trickery, no distraction, simply a case and a challenge to solve it. Mr. Rupert Penny is to be congratulated not only on his daring but on his ingenuity. *The Talkative Policeman* will provide you with plenty of entertainment. Here is excellent fare that is the very food for thought.

## PEREIRA, MICHAEL

### Equal Antagonisms
June 1975

Creek House was a lonely place, standing above the tidal marshes of the Essex coast. It was the home of Sixten Hessenden, VC, famous not merely for his exploits in the war but also for his achievements as a writer. His novels had earned him a worldwide reputation and made him a very rich man, while his autobiography – if he were ever to write it – would make him richer and more famous still. But Hessenden was not tempted by the prospect. Though a celebrity he was a recluse, a prey to bouts of agonizing depression whose cause lay hidden in his past. And it was simply with a view to exorcizing this sense of guilt that he finally wrote the autobiography which everyone had been waiting for. He told his wife it was the last book he would ever write. And it was not for publication. He would destroy the manuscript.

Faced with this crisis Anne Hessenden had to act swiftly. And ruthlessly. Her prime objective was to prevent the destruction of the script, but she took no steps to prevent the self-destruction of its author. Rather, she encouraged it, for a biography by Hessenden's widow, who had powerful though frustrated literary ambitions of her own, would be as certain a bestseller as the autobiography of whose existence no one knew other than herself.

But Anne made a fatal miscalculation. Her daring and cold-blooded scheme failed to take into account that the same jealousy and antagonism which she had long felt towards her husband could be felt by others towards herself.

### Masquerade
March 1973

Set in contemporary London, most of the action takes place in or around the King's Road. *Masquerade* is a frightening but highly believable story of what can happen when a man is tempted to solve an awkward dilemma by a ruse which he knows to be illegal, but which he believes to be both simple and foolproof. John Bower's dilemma is common enough: a mistress whose expensive tastes he can only satisfy by running himself into debt. He is banking on promotion and a large increase in salary, and it is when that promotion fails to materialize that he is forced to seek another way out. The solution he devises is very neat, the only loser being his wife – or so he thinks. It is not until success seems to be actually within his grasp that he realizes that the plan he contrived so cunningly has been given a most unpleasant and unexpected twist: what was to have been mere masquerade has suddenly become murder.

Ingenious in its plot, Mr Pereira's new crime novel is also a subtle study of character and motive. *Masquerade* is concerned not merely with the disguises which people wear, but with the reasons which lead to those disguises. The result is an absorbing crime novel in which the tension mounts steadily as the faces behind the masks are gradually revealed.

### Second Cousin Twice Removed
May 1974

Outwardly, Rose Alton is a successful bachelor girl. She has a good job, a steady boyfriend, a flat of her own, and a car. Beneath the surface, however, she is less satisfied than her manner and way of life suggest. For while now, in her twenties, she apparently has everything she wants, in her childhood she had known the extremes of genteel poverty and loneliness. It was an embittering experience she has never forgotten, and which has never ceased to cause her a nagging feeling of insecurity.

So alone had she been that she had grown up in the belief that she had no relation in the world apart from her mother. It was only on the latter's deathbed that she had learnt otherwise. Then it was that for the first time she had heard of her cousins, the Trees: a brother and sister: elderly: unmarried: and wealthy. Possibly very wealthy. Intrigued, Rose decides to investigate. What she discovers brings out in her all the latent ruthlessness and greed engendered by the harsh world of her childhood.

In his latest crime novel Michael Pereira shows his customary deftness in devising a plot that is exciting without being far-fetched, while his handling of people and his understanding of the complexities of human motivation are as sure as ever.

### *Singing Millionaire, The*
February 1972

A chance meeting between three young people in the streets of Istanbul is the starting-point for a chilling story of murder and blackmail which reaches an exciting climax in the sinister environment of Marseille's dockland. The characters are taken straight from the contemporary scene: John, the idealistic hippie-poet; Maggie, his girl-friend; and Philippe, student drop-out and drug-addict. From a totally different milieu comes Rendel Charles, Philippe's stepfather, wealthy and respected, but ridden by a guilt-complex about his stepson. Force of circumstance and the scheming of Philippe's fertile brain draw these four people together, and the result is as explosive as it is unexpected.

*The Singing Millionaire* is not only a gripping thriller, but a novel of considerable insight into the workings of a warped and vicious mind, written with Mr Pereira's usual mastery of suspense and atmosphere. It makes a timely contribution to an understanding of the motives behind drug addiction in the young in an age when this problem is viewed with increasing alarm.

## PERRY, RITCHIE

### *Bishop's Pawn*
February 1979

'A bishop?' I said.

'A bishop' Pawson agreed.

'But why? What conceivable use is a bishop to anybody?'

Philis had been enjoying himself in Tokyo where job satisfaction had been a girl called Kimi. The bishop was a poor exchange, especially as he had been brought out of East Berlin, a city where Philis had had his problems in the past. As he pointed out to Pawson, a duly constituted court of the German Democratic Republic had already condemned him to death *in absentia*, and affording target practice to an East German firing squad has hardly his idea of fun.

And if Philis was less than enthusiastic about the mission, this was before he had come to know and hate Bishop Mueller, who was hardly a conventional churchman. Not many clerics of Philis's acquaintance boasted a past which included experiments in mass murder. Nor a present which included a strong link with international terrorists.

Then, of course, there was Petrov. If Philis had known the Russian was sitting at the centre of his web in East Berlin, he would have caught the first flight back to Japan. But Philis didn't know, which was why he found himself caught up in an explosive sequence of events leading him across Europe and culminating in a murderous treasure hunt in the Appenines of Italy.

### *Dead End*
August 1977

The Irish Patriotic League wasn't Irish and it wasn't patriotic, but it did have a vested interest in keeping the troubles in Northern Ireland on the boil.

Daley was the head of AmerArmCo, the largest independent arms dealers in the world, and he wanted to impose a total embargo on the flow of arms into Ulster.

These interests were mutually incompatible and, thanks to his boss, Pawson, Philis was the man who found himself bang in the middle.

When he was first given the thankless task of being one of Daley's bodyguards, Philis fully expected the arms king would travel back to the United States in a coffin. That was before he became aware of the IPL's interest in Daley, before he had any idea of their objectives. A dead Daley was no good to them; they wanted something quite different. Only after Daley's daughter had been kidnapped did Philis begin to have an inkling of what the IPL were really after. The disorders in Northern Ireland are only the background to this story, for the action takes place elsewhere. And action there is. It moves from England to Sweden to Holland, before returning to England once again, where Philis finds himself the only obstacle in the way of a successful IPL coup.

### *Dutch Courage*
April 1978

Philis knew all the questions which needed to be asked. The problem was finding somebody who could give him answers. Most of all he wanted to know why an innocuous trip to Amsterdam had led to his capture and torture, and had also resulted in a senseless murder. Before he could sort this out he discovered other problems. The last thing he'd ever wanted was to antagonize Israeli intelligence, but now he learned that his name figured at the top of Mossad's hit list. This made no more sense to him than the knowledge that he had become a subject of interest to the Hashishi, a Palestinian terrorist group who were the modern counterpart of the medieval Assassins.

Philis's boss in the Department, Pawson, was singularly little help. He was more concerned about a threat to his control of departmental finances than about attempts on Philis's life. If Philis wanted answers to his questions, he'd have to find them himself.

As far as Philis could tell, the key to everything was an ex-SAS man called Henry Deventer, and inevitably, his quest for Deventer took him back to Amsterdam. It also plunged him into an explosive situation where the international drug trade, Palestinian terrorism and organized crime were all tied together in a tangle of death, duplicity and deceit.

### *Fall Guy, The*
January 1972

Philis liked to think of himself as a businessman, although it was extremely doubtful whether the Brazilian authorities would have agreed with him. His centre of operations was the red light area of Santos, his self-imposed mission to supply customers with necessities such as Scotch whisky and American cigarettes. To keep his prices down, and to ease the work load of the local officials, he dispensed with much of the routine of modern business, bypassing Customs and making do without office or paperwork.

Pawson was a senior civil servant, the head of SR(2), a small department housed in a building off Queen Victoria Street which took over where Special Branch left off.

The only thing the two men have in common was that they both knew a restaurant proprietor in Porto Allegre, a city which Philis had excellent reasons for avoiding. In fact he had been told in no uncertain terms that any visit there would be to the lasting detriment of his health. However, when their mutual acquaintance disappeared Pawson decided he needed Philis in Porto Allegre and he wasn't over-scrupulous about the means he used to get him there. From the moment Philis set foot in the city he realized his worst fears had been amply justified and it didn't take him long to appreciate that his destined role was the be *The Fall Guy* in this fast-moving story centred on drug-running from Brazilian ports.

### *Fool's Mate*
April 1981

Philis was a practising pessimist. In his experience, once an operation had turned sour, it could only get worse, and this particular assignment had gone bad from the very beginning.

Sir Keith Tenby was one of the country's leading financiers, a man with an international reputation and enough skeletons in various cupboards to stock a cemetery. He wanted somebody escorted safely across France and into England. Philis was assigned by Pawson, his boss at SR(2), to assist Sir Keith's top troubleshooter to perform this service.

The body Philis had been hired to protect was voluptuous and Ugandan, belonging to one of Idi Amin's ex-mistresses. She knew secrets an awful lot of other people hoped to share and it wasn't long before Philis found some formidable adversaries lined up against him. There was a group of Amin's thugs, for whom killing and torture were as natural as breathing. There was Louis Martel, boss of the Marseille underworld, whose network of criminal contacts extended the length and breadth of France. And there was Kironde, whose sole purpose in life was to exact vengeance for what had happened to his family under Amin.

They had in common a fervent desire to seize Philis's charge and a total disregard for Philis's well-being. The mad chase began in the Riviera, moved to the desolate plateau of the Causses, and led to a final explosive confrontation in a Marina on the French coast. It was a game in which whoever held the black queen dictated all the moves, and the first slip would be fatal.

### *Grand Slam*
March 1980

In some ways Philis was old-fashioned: he took the view, for instance, that holidays were for pleasure not work. But pleasure comes expensive, and by the time Pawson, the wily head of SR(2), had finished arranging matters, Philis had only one possible source of funds.

That source was Simon Denny, an oil millionaire to whom Pawson and SR(2) owed several favours. Now his daughter had disappeared, and Philis found himself for the first time working outside the Department, in Simon Denny's employ.

He was required to find out what had happened to Vanessa, why she had vanished from her Oxford college without trace. It seemed straightforward, if slightly outside Philis's usual terms of reference, but he had hardly begun investigations when there was an attempt on his life. Suddenly he found himself with a whole list of questions which needed answering. Why had Vanessa Denny driven over a cliff-top in Norfolk? What was her connection with the gentleman farmer with an apparently unlimited supply of nubile young lady friends? And, most significant of all, how had she become involved with an obscure religious cult which had left a trail of terror and destruction wherever it had gone?

Before he managed to piece the horrific jigsaw together, Philis – 'the latter-day James Bond' as Newgate Callendar called him in the *New York Times Book Review* – had earned every penny Denny was paying him, and come within an inch of losing his own life.

### *Holiday With a Vengeance*
July 1974

Some people might have thought Philis was being unduly cynical but when Pawson offered him a fortnight in the Bahamas with all expenses paid his immediate reaction was to start looking for the snags. Even so, when Pawson chose to reveal his true motives and Philis's holiday came to an abrupt end the assignment seemed to be remarkably straightforward. The British Consul on the small island of Santa Monica had been abducted by local guerillas and was under sentence of death. As the guerilla force was only a dozen strong, had virtually no weapons and had as leader a beautiful young girl who had just left college, Philis didn't anticipate much difficulty.

The real problem was that Philis had visited Santa Monica before. At the time President Dominique had been Chief of Police and he and Philis had failed to see eye to eye. Philis might be returning to the island as a fully accredited representative of the Crown but this didn't afford him any sense of security – Dominique was absolute ruler of Santa Monica and he had a score to settle. This was the reason why what should have been a simple rescue operation soon escalated until Philis found himself at the head of a motley guerilla force which was dedicated to the overthrow of President Dominique. It wasn't quite what Pawson had intended, but then London was a long way away and Philis had never believed in turning the other cheek.

### *Nowhere Man*
January 1973

Schnellinger had been particularly stupid. It was bad enough to have chosen Klemper as his associate, because Heinrich Klemper was a man with a lot of enemies; but it was far worse to have sold out to the CIA. So long as Schnellinger had been neutral, offering an impartial information service to anyone prepared to buy his wares, he had been left well alone; had even been considered a positive asset. Now he had become a marked man. He was scheduled for elimination at the earliest opportunity. To that end, the British and Russians found themselves uneasily allied.

The British contribution was Philis, a less than enthusiastic upholder of democracy, whose only total commitment was to his own well-being. The KGB's offering was John Sutters, a Russian who had lived in England for most of his adult life and who had no more interest in ideology than had Philis himself.

Before they could dispose of Schnellinger, however, they had to find him. This posed certain problems, as he was little more than a name on a file. Klemper was the one person who knew his identity, and the search for Klemper, hampered by the interference of other interested parties, led Philis and Sutters from England to West Berlin and then to Spain, building up to a thrilling and unexpected climax on the island of Ibiza.

### *One Good Death Deserves Another*
May 1976
Cosmetatos was a Greek. He was also a professional killer, an assassin with a reputation which made his services worth a quarter of a million Deutschmarks on the open market. That was why he was at Lisbon airport waiting for a VARIG flight to take him to Sao Paulo. Philis had never met the Greek, in fact he'd never even heard his name. But Philis was in Lisbon as well, with a seat booked on the same plane to Brazil, and this simple coincidence was to have far-reaching consequences for a number of people. Several of them died violently as a direct result, a high-ranking Portuguese general was forced to submit to blackmail from London, and the West German Chancellor found himself the target for a assassin's bullet, his very life depending on how quickly Philis managed to gather all the threads together. Then, of course, there was Philis's chief, Pawson, the head of SR(2), who was in Lisbon playing a complex and dangerous game of his own devising, one in which he was the only player who knew all the rules.

For Philis himself the issue was brutally simple. He wanted to find the men responsible for the three separate attempts to kill him and for the death of the woman he'd once intended to marry. The hunt took him from the Santos docklands to a dead man's apartment in Sao Paolo, back to Lisbon and then to a small town in southern Brazil. From first to last the furious pace never falters, building up to a shattering crescendo when the confrontation between Philis and Cosmetatos finally takes place.

### *Ticket to Ride*
October 1973
There were plenty of things Philis could find fault with in his job. He didn't like the way Pawson had bulldozed him into working for SR(2) in the first place; he had never approved of the physical danger/financial reward ratio; and in particular, he didn't agree with Pawson's reluctance to provide him with more than a bare minimum of pertinent information on any of his missions.

When he found himself masquerading as a private detective assigned as bodyguard to Catherine Zaferelli, a woman who was as good-looking as she was treacherous, Philis suspected he might be involved with the Mafia, although for the life of him he couldn't think why. But by the time his suspicions had hardened into certainty, after he'd learned of the connection with Giuliano Alvano and his New York operations, this problem no longer concerned him. With the kidnapping of the woman he was supposed to be protecting Philis had suddenly become a man of property, the possessor of certain documents which were not only the target of an intensive search by the FBI and Alvano's associates but a guarantee of Philis's future affluence, for, properly handled, they were a ticket to the independence he craved. There was one minor snag, however. A single tactical mistake and these same documents could be Philis's death warrant, whether at the hands of Alvano or those of Pawson.

### *Your Money and Your Wife*
May 1975
Philis had never considered himself to be the marrying kind, then the unexpected happened and he found himself on honeymoon in Norway with a brand new wife. However the course of true love had no chance to run smoothly. Within a few days of their arrival in Norway, Philis's wife was abducted from their lakeside chalet and the honeymoon came to an abrupt end. Nor was this any ordinary kidnapping. There was no ransom demand, as Philis had no money to meet such a payment. All he had were his own slightly tarnished skills. Since Pawson, the head of the security department Philis represented, refused to involve himself, Philis found himself entirely alone, and he was forced to employ the only means at his disposal which might secure the release of his wife, even if this meant betraying his country. Before his quest came to a dramatic and unforeseen conclusion the search had taken him from Norway to Scotland and then to East Germany, with a lot of blood being shed along the way, much of it Philis's own.

## PETERS, ELLIS

### *Black Is the Colour of My True Love's Heart*
August 1967
Young singers and musicians are gathering for a folk music course that will occupy a weekend in the fantastic country mansion called Follymead. Most of them come intent only to sing or listen but one or two have scores to settle that are not musical. Liri Palmer, a young ballad-singer of brilliant vitality and blazing talent, had clearly a message for one of the audience at Follymead when she sings:

'Black, black, black is the colour of my true-love's *heart*!

His tongue is like a poisoned dart

The coldest eyes and the lewdest hands…'

Passions run high and there is murder brewing at Follymead. But the turns of fate are different from what the reader will foresee, though there are clues enough, not least in the high tragedy told in the ballad-history of *Gil Morrice*.

Among the music students are Tossa Barber and her boyfriend Dominic Felse. When disaster strikes Dominic can privately enlist the aid of Detective Superintendent George Felse, his father, who has solved the murder cases reported in Ellis Peter's celebrated novels.

Set excitingly and knowledgeably in the heart of the world of contemporary folk music, most ingeniously designed and skilfully written, this clever crime novel will hold its many readers enthralled – and excite and surprise them by its startling and moving climax.

### *Death and the Joyful Woman*
July 1961
Alfred Armiger had laid his vulgar, clever hands on a beautiful house and turned it into The Jolly Barmaid – the latest addition to his chain of super road-houses. Now someone had laid hands on Armiger. He was found beaten to death on the deserted dance floor. There was no shortage of people who wanted him dead, and the police probed and sifted the suspects and the few shreds of evidence for some time before they finally made an arrest. To Dominic Felse, the young son of the county C.I.D. man in charge of the case, Kitty Norris represented everything that was admirable, desirable and unattainable. His certainty of her innocence drove him to take a line of action which was as heedless as it was shrewd, and which forced him, at sixteen, to measure up to the consequences which were unexpected, frightening – and deadly dangerous.

Ellis Peters once more demonstrates an outstanding ability to involve a fascinating and unusual cast of characters in an ingenious and exciting situation. *Death and the Joyful Woman* will rank with *Death Mask* and *The Will and the Deed* as a gripping and highly entertaining crime novel.

### *Death Mask*
September 1959
The tragic and dramatic death of Bruce Almond during an archaeological expedition in Greece meant that his son, Crispin, was returned instantly to England and the mother he barely remembered. Evelyn Manville became the boy's tutor because he was at a loose end and he was unable to resist Dorothy Almond's appeal for help with this erratic and brilliant stranger who was her son, yet who remained so resolutely withdrawn and coldly sophisticated beyond his sixteen years. It was only when Almond's two assistants, who had been with him when he died, arrived at the house simultaneously and apparently by chance, that Evelyn penetrated the terrible secret which the boy was hiding. Had Bruce Almond's death been only a tragic accident? Evelyn deliberately intervened to protect the boy from his obsession and from a ruthless and unidentified enemy. He found himself in a position of deadly and terrifying danger as events moved to a dramatic climax in an atmosphere of ever mounting tension and suspense.

Ellis Peters, the *nom-de-crime* of an established and successful writer, has combined an outstanding gift for characterisation with a flair for excitement and drama which make *Death Mask* a remarkable debut in Crime Fiction.

### *Flight of a Witch*
July 1964
'Annet Beck. That's a witch's name.'

'Annet is a witch, I shouldn't wonder'

Annet was eighteen and had the kind of beauty that strikes people dumb. Lots of young men fell in love with her but Tom Kenyon was the one to be closely involved in the extraordinary circumstances of her disappearance.

Annet claimed she had been absent only two hours, but everyone else knew she had been missing for five days. Where had she been? She had disappeared and reappeared while walking on the same hill – a historic border site with an uncanny reputation locally….But it became necessary to discover the truth, and none of the investigators believed in witchcraft.

Elli Peters was awarded the 'Edgar' of the Mystery Writers of America for the best crime novel of 1962, *Death and the Joyful Woman* The reputation and public that this novelist has acquired under this pseudonym will be much augmented by *Flight of a Witch*: it is a most unusual crime novel, with characters carefully drawn and a strong and powerful plot.

### *Funeral of Figaro*
November 1962
Rehearsal of Mozart's *Marriage of Figaro* was in full swing when the new baritone – Figaro himself – arrived from Europe to join the cast. He had a fine voice and a fine presence, yet he quickly discovered old enemies – or made new ones – among the friendly company that made up the cast and staff of the small, private opera house called The Leander.

Worse still, he made a dead set at Hero, teenage daughter of the Leander's sponsor and owner, who was playing the part of Cherubino. Tension grew at the Leander and it culminated in a very violent death.

Ellis Peters is the pseudonym of a well-known novelist who has already built a splendid reputation under this name. This detective story is set against the background of Grand Opera and a particular performance of *The Marriage of Figaro*, described in fascinating detail. And there are many ingenious switches of the plot to challenge and baffle the reader.

### *Grass Widow's Tale, The*
April 1968
'Listen to who's talking. I'm not the one who goes hobnobbing with gunmen and such.' This was the way Bunty Felse light-heartedly replied to her husband's parting words of caution as he left for London on urgent police business. Left alone in the house Bunty began to feel depressed. She would be 41 tomorrow, and she felt that now her son had grown up there was nothing left for her to do except grow older.

To shake off this black mood she went to the local pub. There a chance meeting showed her how wrong her farewell words to her husband had been, and also made her realise how much she valued the life that earlier had seemed to stretch out endlessly before her, as she desperately struggled to hang on to it, even if only for a few more hours. The terrifying events following on Bunty's unexpected encounter are excitingly and sympathetically told – the novel is a fine example of Ellis Peters at her very best.

### *House of Green Turf, The*
March 1969
Maggie Tressider, world-famous singer, crashed her car on the way to a concert and woke up in hospital, dazed, in post-operative shock – and haunted. From some secret place in her subconscious arose the awful conviction that somehow, at some time n the past, she had been responsible for a death. Details eluded her, but the nameless spectre would not be laid. The only way to get rid of it was to dig up the lost memory and confront it face to face. A psychiatrist, her doctor suggested. But Maggie chose a very different expert to find her dead for her.

Her commission launched Francis Killian on a hunt across Europe in search of a grave. But the successful end of his search was only the beginning of a long pilgrimage for them both, a journey which led not only back into the past, but far away into a corner of the Continent where many frontiers touched and many trails crossed. And some of them ended – abruptly.

### *Nice Derangement of Epitaphs, A*
February 1965
The epitaphs that Jan and Morwenna Treverra wrote for themselves before their deaths in the eighteenth century were almost gay:

'Shed here no Tears. No Saint could die More Blessed and Comforted than I.'

Dominic Felse made the comment: 'They make the after-life sound like a Christmas sunshine cruise to the Bahamas.'

In 1964 permission has been granted to open the tombs of Jan and Morwenna, in their vault in the abandoned shore graveyard of the little Saxon church near the Cornish village of Maymouth. Detective-Inspector George Felse and his family are on holiday there…and George is present when the tombs are opened, and a macabre and gruesome mystery is discovered. He finds himself investigating acts of violence which stretch across the centuries in Maymouth.

This is a crime novel of a very unusual structure. It follows *Flight of a Witch*, a successful story by the same author who is a well-known novelist writing under the pseudonym Ellis Peters. It fulfils the promise of *Death and the Joyful Woman* (awarded the 'Edgar' of the Mystery Writers of America as the best thriller of 1962) and enriches the canon of English crime novels in which character and literacy contribute to a gripping story.

### *Piper on the Mountain, The*
April 1966

A solitary climber fell to his death from a mountain in Slovakia. Accident, said the local police. Accident, agreed the British authorities. But – hadn't the dead man, an official of a highly secret research institute, worked on the case of a certain renegade scientist? And hadn't that scientist been born in Slovakia? The attaché from Prague said: 'Murder!' And he was indiscreet enough to say it to the young Tossa Barber, the victim's step-daughter.

Tossa felt bound to see justice done. She diverted a student holiday tour into the wild and lovely Tatra mountains to investigate. And there a second death brought her into head-on collision with the Slovak police, and put her own life in peril.

Luckily for Tossa, one of her companions was Dominic Felse, who had the obstinate devotion to justice proper to a policeman's son – not to mention his growing devotion to Tossa herself.

It was Dominic who provoked the crisis that brought the elusive piper down from his mountains at last – and set in motion that final avalanche!

### *Will and the Deed, The*
September 1960

In Vienna Antonia Byrne played her own death scene with all the style and brilliance which had made her the greatest operatic singer of her time. The seven people present had come from a mixture of motives — love and respect; duty and greed. Antonia's last will and testament could be important to all of them for different reasons and they boarded the plane for England with anticipation mingling with their grief. But a forced landing in an isolated part of Austria meant that the will was read under curious circumstances. The terms came as a shock and, to one of the party, they seemed an invitation to murder—an invitation which was accepted.

*The Will and the Deed* skilfully combines an intriguing study of character with suspense and the best traditions of the classic detective story. It will certainly confirm the high reputation which Ellis Peters instantly achieved with *Death Mask*.

## PETERSON, BERNARD

### *Caravaggio Books, The*
October 1992

Welcome to Kingsford, high-powered ivy-covered University and rich commuter town located just off the Washington-New York corridor – where the Chief of Police is Phi Beta Kappa and his Detective-Sergeant has a Master's degree in Sociology. It wakes up one Tuesday morning to find its self-satisfied equilibrium shattered by its first-ever old-fashioned, knife-in-the-throat murder – which has taken place in the bowels of the University library where access is restricted to holders of University ID cards.

While Chief of Police Sam Dawson works on damage control designed to limit the amount of dirty linen exposed, Detective-Sergeant Philip Constanza begins a series of interviews in which he tries, first, to sift through an entire spectrum of motives and, second, to uncover evidence or circumstances that would indicate a likely culprit. His first discovery is something that is not officially taught, but what any small-towner knows instinctively: namely, that gossipers should not be taken lightly. But even though little progress is made initially, a second murder is committed two days later, apparently to suppress evidence that only the killer seems aware of.

Set against the background of town and gown, the trail leads Constanza from surprise to surprise – including some about himself. In the end, it is the library itself that furnishes the vital clues that lead, as inevitably as geometry, to the killer.

## PHILMORE, R.

### *Death in Arms*
July 1939

It was the lock-keeper who found the body in the river. He had seen drowned men before – many of them – but this one was different, for a bullet hole in the forehead showed plainly that the man had been shot. Inspector Garnett of the Yard was called in and found himself involved in an amazing case in which secret agents operating in the shadow factories of Britain's rearmament industry play an important part. The same clever touch which made Mr. Philmore's *Short List* an outstanding success among recent detective novels is again apparent in *Death in Arms*.

### *No Mourning in the Family*
November 1937

Connoisseurs of the detective story will remember with pleasure R. Philmore's previous novels, *The Good Books*, *Riot Act* and *Journey Downstairs*. For Mr. Philmore is that rare thing, a *crime* novelist who is also an exceedingly good *straight* novelist. His wit, his urbanity, his genius for creating character makes his novels enjoyable quite apart from the element of crime; while as to his detective gifts we cannot do better than quote *Punch*: 'Mr. Philmore's close reasoning and powers of deduction call for unqualified praise'. This is the first time that Mr. Philmore has been published by the Crime Club. *No Mourning in the Family* is easily his best book, and will, we are sure, establish him immediately in the front rank of Crime Club favourites.

### *Procession of Two*
December 1940

Ruth Lister, young and attractive secretary to the Principal of a training college for teachers, is found dead in her room one evening, poisoned by cyanide. Suspicion falls on one of the students, Roger Deakin, and the net seems to be closing round him when, through really brilliant detection, Inspector Gregory fastens the guilt securely on the real criminal.

### *Short List*
July 1938

The governors of Radwinter School meet to appoint a successor to the Headmaster. The candidates on the short list include Halliday, Winterton, Fensome and Philmore. At that fateful conference death takes a hand. Here is a brilliantly clever detective story in which every detail dovetails perfectly into place; nothing is hidden from the reader, and yet the mystery is indeed a baffling one. The characters are all compelling figures, and of course there is the shadowy Swan, most modest of all sleuths, but one of the most effective. We like Swan and Swan's way, and recommend this story whole-heartedly.

## PICKARD, NANCY

### *Dead Crazy*
July 1989

Jenny Cain, head of Port Frederick, Massachusetts, Civic Foundation, takes a special interest in the mentally ill. Her mother is a psychiatric patient who will never recover. So when a middle-aged do-gooder begs Jenny for Foundation money to buy a recreation hall for released patients, Jenny feels a natural sympathy.

The proposed hall is a strange-looking, dirt-covered structure that once housed a church, but the land it stands on is valuable. A real estate company plans to erect an apartment high rise there and is prepared to hand over a cheque almost immediately.

Jenny likes the building, the facilities, and the location, but when she canvasses the neighbours, their reactions vary from concerned to frightened to hostile. When a killer begins to stalk the neighbourhood, the project seems impossible. Nevertheless, Jenny searches for a murderer she half hopes she'll never find.

Moving and sensitive, but also witty and entertaining, *Dead Crazy* is a thoughtful appraisal of the world of the mentally ill, the men and women released from psychiatric hospital with nowhere to go.

### *Marriage is Murder*
April 1988

Jenny Cain, director of the Port Frederick, Massachusetts, Civic Foundation, is about to marry her longtime lover, policeman Geof Bushfield. But two weeks before the wedding Jenny and Geof run into trouble.

The husbands and wives of Port Frederick are killing each other off. As any good cop knows, domestic violence is both unpredictable and dangerous. Most murder victims are killed by someone they know. So it's no particular surprise that Port Frederick should have its share of wife-beatings and family homicides.

But Geof is depressed by what he sees. He feels helpless. Should he give up being a cop? Should he and Jenny fly away somewhere and live on their trust funds?

Jenny knows that she must help Geof get through this crisis if they are to have any hope of a good marriage, for police work is what makes his life meaningful. While Geof searches for the answer to past violence, Jenny tries desperately to stop it from occurring again.

### *No Body*
August 1987

As director of the Civic Foundation in the small town of Port Frederick, Massachusetts, Jenny Cain is often called on to decide what is a worthy cause and who is a valid recipient for her charitable fund's largesse.

She has no doubts, however, about pledging her own efforts and the Foundation's money when a landslide reveals, to the distress of many of the town's citizens, that there is no one actually buried in historic Union Hill Cemetery. The cemetery was last used a hundred years ago and the bodies culd have vanished at any time since. Jenny's search may be a long one.

But she has hardly begun her enquiries when she is faced with a much more contemporary corpse. Somebody has murdered an employee of the Harbor Lights Funeral Home and played a macabre joke with the body.

Jenny teams with reporter Lewis Riss to find the answers to an intriguing and dangerous puzzle in this outstanding mystery which offers wit, romance, a complex plot, memorable characters and a delightful detective heroine who promises to become a new star of fictional crime.

## PORLOCK, MARTIN
(*see also* **MacDonald, Philip**)

### *Mystery at Friar's Pardon*
October 1931

This is a first novel by a writer who has, we can safely prophesy, an assured future as a writer of first-class mystery stories. It is well-written, exciting throughout, and carries the reader along to a totally unanticipated solution. Mrs. Lester-Greene, a writer of best-sellers, buys a large country house called Friar's Pardon, reputed to be haunted. The legend runs that for several generations each successive owner of the house has met his death – in the same room and in the same strange and unaccountable manner – by drowning, although no water was present in the room at the time of their death, nor any trace of there having been water there. When the novelist first takes up residence she has a small house-party, but on the second evening after dinner she is found dead in her study – and the manner of her death bears out the ancient legend connected with the house. How Charles Fox-Browne, steward to Mrs. Lester-Greene's estate, forms a theory and eventually proves it, makes dramatic reading, and the denouement cannot fail to thrill the most hardened of mystery fans.

### *Mystery in Kensington Gore*
March 1932

A gentleman down on his luck, reduced, in fact, to burgling a house in Kensington...a beautiful girl who finds him comfortably asleep in the kitchen...an amazing conversation...and they enter the library. At the writing-desk sits an elderly man, dead...stabbed. 'I don't know anything about it, but they'll say I do. They'll say I did it! They're bound to!' And the strange adventure of Peter Craven had begun.

### *X v. Rex*
March 1933

X, symbol of the unknown, against Rex, the symbol of Law and Order and the People. For the perpetrator of a series of appalling murders in the greatest city of the world to defy capture and remain at large, killing, is a blow at the very structure of society; how much more is this so when the victims of his knife are the guardians of the Law themselves. A policeman is killed in amazing circumstances, in a country town near London – and the hunt is up! Another and still another murder in committed until the apparently never-ending series of diabolical crimes engages the serious attention of the whole Cabinet. Distinguished by clever characterisation and good dialogue, *X v. Rex* is a murder story on the truly grand scale – a story in which the excitement rises in dramatic crescendo to a thrilling conclusion.

## POSTGATE, RAYMOND

### *Verdict of Twelve*
January 1940

Raymond Postgate, well-known critic and essayist, and brother of Margaret Cole, writes an unusual, not to say brilliant book around a gripping and unusual murder mystery. In it he gives us some striking cameos of the twelve members of a typical criminal jury. Mr. Postgate knows all about them and he makes them enthralling. Moreover, he shows how their life histories and mental makeups drive them inexorably towards their verdict. There is much merciless probing into the recesses of human nature, yet nothing is forced, nothing over-emphasised. From the first page to the last, the book is a wholly satisfying slice of life.

## POWELL, LESTER

### *Spot the Lady**
February 1950

When Philip Odell, noted criminal investigator, read of the tragic murder of Marguerite, a well-known newspaper columnist, who was found shot in a lonely wood off the Brighton road, he little dreamed that he would be so closely involved in this mysterious case. To his amazement, however, three men come to see him separately and ask him to find out the truth about the death of the lovely Marguerite, and all three claim to be engaged to her. Firstly, comes Sir Alexander Besard, wealthy eccentric night-club owner; secondly, George Burwell, ex-Guardee and nephew of Sir Alexander, and finally Colin Caster, a rugged Scots reporter who was Marguerite's childhood sweetheart. There is no doubt that Lester Powell's story has all the qualities that have made his character Philip Odell so popular on the radio. *Spot the Lady* has many exciting twists, the characterisation is outstanding and the writing witty and pungent.

*This was a title in Collins' *Mystery* series, but was issued with a Crime Club wrapper.

## PUCKETT, ANDREW

### *Bed of Nails*

March 1989

Following a personal tragedy Chris Randall travels around the country in his Dormobile, not caring which hospital employs him next as a locum laboratory worker. He is looking forward to working again in Oxford, however, because of his friendship with John Devlin, a brilliant but anti-social Glaswegian who is working in secret on a cure for AIDS. When Chris arrives in Oxford, John is missing and no one knows where he is. The more he tries to find out what has happened, the more hostile John's erstwhile colleagues become, and Chris begins to wonder whether his disappearance is connected with his recent work. He is threatened, attacked and attempts are made to force him to leave Oxford, but he stays, and with John's ex-girlfriend Sally, tries to solve the mystery. And then he is arrested for murder…

### *Bloodhound*

December 1991

Blood transfusions have saved countless lives over the years; only occasionally have they caused illness or death through accidental contamination with bacteria or viruses.

Now *Leig fa Sgaoil*, a Scottish liberation group, claims that it has deliberately contaminated a hundred blood packs distributed throughout England with lethal bacteria and demands one million pounds in exchange for their identities.

The authorities narrow down the number of Scottish Transfusion Centres from which the blood could have originated and recall Tom Jones from holiday to investigate the most likely of them. Together with Doctor Alan Woodford, a government drug inspector, Tom goes to the West Highland Transfusion Centre in the hope of identifying the culprits before any of the blood can be used, although they are both aware that the terrorists will be able to identify them first.

Matters are complicated when Tom finds an old flame at the Centre who is now having an affair with one of his prime suspects.

Suspicion, however, is not proof, and Tom and Alan are nowhere near that when patients start dying...

### *Bloodstains*

November 1987

A clever DHSS administrator suspects from a discrepancy in the figures that blood is being stolen from the Tamar Blood Transfusion Centre in Devon. His view is supported by the discovery in the blood bank of the body of one of the staff, and the simultaneous disappearance of a night orderly. Tom Jones, ex-police detective now employed by the DHSS , is sent to investigate undercover the possible fraud.

It is the chance Tom needs to prove his worth, but there is one problem: he is terrified by the sight of blood.

As he battles with his own phobia, Tom is aware that nothing is quite what it seems at the Tamar Blood Transfusion Centre and nearly everyone has something to hide. His emotions are soon entangled with the enigmatic Holly, but he has to face violent death in several forms and a threat to his own survival before he can discover the nature of the villainy at the Tamar Centre and the identity of the person behind it.

Andrew Puckett, himself a medical laboratory scientist at a transfusion centre, has written a first crime novel as remarkable for its intriguing information about one of our most vital substances and its glimpse behind the scenes of a little-known aspect of the Health Services, as for its fast action, engrossing plot and credible characters.

### *Desolation Point*

July 1993

All is not well with the Somerset Nuclear Electric power station at Desolation Point. It is being picketed by a women's pressure group, and Liam, the infant son of one of the station's employees, has died of leukaemia, which the women claim was caused by the station.

Then Michael Hempstead, a senior engineer at the station, becomes involved with Sarah Brierly, one of the group's organizers, and things begin to happen.

A colleague of Michael's is found dead. Accident or Murder? There is a radiation leak. Accident or sabotage? A more obvious attempt at sabotage is made by Liam's father, deranged by grief. There is another violent death.

These events are accompanied by a vitriolic media campaign carried out by a suspiciously well-informed local newspaper, and Michael's boss becomes convinced that Sarah is using information gleaned from Michael to help orchestrate this campaign, something that Michael refuses to believe.

Then Michael himself is attacked and nearly killed and the station is hit by an altogether more serious 'mishap'.

Something very sinister is going on at Desolation Point, and the stakes are sky-high.

### *Terminus*

May 1990

The doctors, nurses and other staff who care for the terminally ill in their last few weeks are perhaps the most admired citizens in any community. So it is surely unthinkable that any of them would use their position to steal and market heroin – or is it?

A scatterbrained nurse at St John's Hospice writes to the Department of Health accusing one of her colleagues of just that, but is killed in a gas explosion before she can name the culprit. Her letter lands on the desk of a thoroughly ill-humoured official, who despatches DHSS investigator Tom Jones in the guise of a charity official to find out what's going on.

Tom quickly discovers that St John's is in desperate financial trouble and is liable to be closed unless money can be found quickly – a motive perhaps for even the most honest of men? – and a boot in the ribcage soon persuades him that something is indeed going on. But he can't prove it, let alone find whoever is responsible.

Then his cover begins to break down and time becomes his worst enemy. Unless he can find his villain speedily, he and his boss will be in serious trouble for impersonating a charity official in such a sensitive area…

## QUEEN, ELLERY (Ed.)

### *The Queen's Awards Eighth Series*

August 1955

Ellery Queen is well known as one of the greatest authors and connoisseurs of Crime Stories, and his selection in the Eighth Series, displaying both variety and consistent high quality, will satisfy the most discriminating taste. The anthology is composed of sixteen prize-winning stories chosen from the entries in the *Ellery Queen's Mystery Magazine* annual contest. It is appropriate that these distinguished detective stories should be published in this country as a Crime Club Choice. Steve Frazee is the winner of the first prize with 'My Brother Down There' – an exciting story of a man-hunt in which primitive instincts take possession of the hunters and the hunted. 'The Quality of Mercy' by Eleazar Lipsky challenges its readers with a first class problem, while by way of contrast the detective in 'Mrrrar!' by Edgar Pangborn is a cat! The other authors represented are Roy Vickers, A. H. Z. Carr, Stanley Ellin, Lillian de la Torre, Charlotte Armstrong, Howard Shoenfeld, Thomas Kyd, Dorothy Salisbury Davis, James Yaffe, E. C. Witham, Browning Norton and C. B. Gilford.

### *Ellery Queen's Awards Ninth Series*

June 1956

The Crime Club is again able to present Ellery Queen's selection of the best crime stories of the year. In the brilliant story *Double Image*, Roy Vickers has given a completely new twist to the old situation involving twins: the story develops strangely. There are opportunities for the 'detective' reader to try his wits, but he is likely to be baffled by a story as ingenious as *Anything New on the Strangler* by James Ullman – a story that unfolds in a newspaper office. Among the contributors are Margery Allingham with an 'impossible crime' story, and Philip MacDonald, with a grim story of suspense in a house cut off by foods, of a woman alone with an uninvited stranger…A very high standard is maintained by new and famous writers alike. Anyone who wants exciting reading – and to know what's 'new' in crime – cannot afford to miss this book.

### *Ellery Queen's Awards Tenth Series*

January 1957

Here is the latest – the 1957 – volume containing in the Tenth Series of the Ellery Queen Awards, the best short stories that Ellery Queen, a doyen of great crime writers, has collected from a year's output of crime short stories.

A freakish psychological problem is neatly presented in Stanley Ellin's exciting story, *The Moment of Decision*. Lord Dunsany contributes an ingenious and macabre story in *Near the Back of Beyond*, and in *Once is Once Too Many* Anthony Gilbert shows us the obstreperous Arthur Crook once again on the trail of a murderer. Other famous contributors are Roy Vickers, Charlotte Armstrong, Eleazar Lipsky and James Yaffe. And in his second short story, *The Perfectionist*, a new writer, Donald McNutt Douglass, finds some new and brilliant twists to a story that has something in common with the 'Pygmalion' theme.

Once again Ellery Queen's world-wide search for the work of new and famous writers, and his discrimination in selection, has resulted in a volume that testifies to the very high standard of contemporary writing.

### *Ellery Queen's Awards Eleventh Series*

January 1958

Many of the best short stories ever written have had to do with crime. That writing of high quality is appearing all the time in this field has been well demonstrated in the earlier collections of stories chosen as prize-winners by Ellery Queen, himself a writer of international reputation.

An anthology that contains stories by the following writers carries its own recommendation: Phyllis Bentley, A. H. Z. Carr, Stanley Ellin, Michael Gilbert, Frank Swinnerton, Roy Vickers, James Yaffe. The stories here collected do not conform to any one formula or type. *The Blessington Method* by Stanley Ellin can be recommended as horrid and an entertaining freak. Michael Gilbert's *One-Tenth Man* describes a policeman's dilemma in a clash between his emotions and his duty. *The Customs of the Country* by Thomas Flanagan ends in a splendid climax of Ruritanian double-double-cross. Roy Vickers's realistic story is of a murderer brought to book by his carelessness years after his crime, and in *Miami Papers Please Copy* Rufus King achieves a successful humorous burlesque. This volume contains excitement, humour, some realistic studies of crime and character; it will hold many a reader spellbound.

### *Ellery Queen's Awards Twelfth Series*

January 1959

Ellery Queen keeps a constant and discriminating eye open for the best in Crime Fiction. This is his Twelfth annual selection and the standards are as high, if not higher, then they have even been before. Every type of story is represented from Classic Detection to the Macabre – but in each case they maintain the exacting standards which the connoisseur of crime writing demands.

Stanley Ellin, Rufus King, L. A. G. Strong, Phyllis Bentley and Michael Gilbert are some of the acknowledged masters represented here. There are others who appear in volume form for the first time. Novices or experts, they have one common feature: they have reached Ellery Queen's standards of excellence.

Here are fifteen brilliant stories which will entertain and grip at first sight and which will stand the supreme test of a second and third reading.

### *Ellery Queen's 13th Choice*

March 1960

The twelve stories in this book were chosen by Ellery Queen himself. This selection is an outstanding display of the range of crime-writing today. Here are stories of suspense, excitement, detection and atmosphere. Whether written by newcomers or by established masters of the craft, all the stories maintain the high standard of characterisation, originality and imagination which this anthology has always represented. Each reader will probably have a favourite story, but we are confident that he will find pleasure in all of them.

### *Ellery Queen's 14th Choice*

May 1961

The sixteen stories in this latest volume were selected by Ellery Queen from his own magazine which is published on both sides of the Atlantic. As the choice of one of the outstanding writers of Crime Fiction to-day they maintain those high standards of ingenuity, quality and originality which have always distinguished this anthology in the past. Here are examples of the unconventional, of Queen's encouragement of new writers, as well as stories from Stanley Ellin, Michael Gilbert, Cyril Hare, Rufus King and other crime writers who are internationally famous. The 14th Series of *Ellery Queen's Choice* is another splendid and entertaining selection of stories which will delight the casual reader and the connoisseur alike.

## RAMSAY, DIANA
*Deadly Discretion*
March 1973
When Jennifer Davis was found strangled in her flat and Lieutenant Meredith of the New York Police Department began making enquiries, he soon discovered that Jennifer had led an unusually discreet life. No one knew much about this ballet dancer from California, not even Cassandra Evans, the friend who was drawn into the investigation against her will. Cassandra, becoming more and more deeply involved, decided to make enquiries independently of Meredith, who was chagrined to find his interest in her was taking a personal turn.

Cassandra's enquiries led her to the heart of the bizarre Greenwich Village scene and behind some equally bizarre dance scenes. Between them Meredith and Cassandra ran to ground almost all the people Jennifer ever knew. They discovered that there was good reason for her discreet existence, and that several people had good reason to wish it at an end. But which of them was the murderer? And who was giving Cassandra attention she could well have done without? Diana Ramsay, highly praised for her first crime novel, *A Little Murder Music*, keeps the reader guessing to the end.

*Descent into the Dark*
January 1975
Awakened by shouting in the middle of her first night alone in a New York apartment, Joyce Chandler thought of fire, air raid, disaster, until she realized that the noise emanated from a radio. Only a radio. What a relief. Or was it?

The owner of the radio, all contrition, expressed great willingness to be a good neighbour, but it soon became clear that the good neighbour policy was of a bizarre order, and Joyce, struggling to get her bearings after the collapse of her marriage, found herself being drawn deeper and deeper into a nightmarish situation. There was no refuge in her tedious and frustrating job, or in joining with other women in a conscious-raising group, or even in the sympathy tendered by friends. At last, goaded beyond endurance, Joyce struck back.

The consequences carried her, first as an appalled spectator, then as a reluctant participant, along a course that culminated in violence. It is a course that Diana Ramsay charts rivetingly, readably and with terrifying plausibility.

*Four Steps to Death*
November 1989
While a young dancer celebrates a step forward in her career, a dancer whose career is behind her is murdered. Who killed her? Virtually everyone who knew her had opportunity. Virtually everyone who knew her had reason. But no one better – or so it seems – than Maggie Tremayne, a former dancer and now a teacher of ballet, cruelly betrayed by the dead woman in the past and unable to forget. With mounting horror, Maggie realizes that the killer has deliberately placed her centre stage of the police investigation. As she

tries to find out why, she begins to suspect that being framed for murder may not be all she has to fear.

*Four Steps to Death* goes behind the storybook facade of ballet to explore a world in which bone bruises and pain are more common that bouquets and panegyrics, rewards are seldom commensurate with effort, and memory can become more real than reality.

*Little Murder Music, A*
January 1972
New York's Polyhymnia Hall was full for the concert given by the famous Cantabile Players under their conductor, André Holderlin, and the high point of the programme was a decidedly unorthodox performance of Mendelssohn's music for *A Midsummer Night's Dream*, with specialized lighting effects. But as the wedding march rang out triumphantly, the conductor suddenly fell from the podium, dead. The curtain descended on confusion, as his orchestra realized he had been shot.

Lieutenant Meredith of the New York police department soon discovered that Holderlin had enemies. His wife, his mistress, his ex-mistresses, all had reason to bear him a grudge. Nor did harmony predominate in his relations with his orchestra – professional and personal discord was rife. There was nothing for it but to interview each suspect. And then Holderlin's widow disappeared. Meredith found his job increasingly complicated, as more and more strands from the conductor's past and present were drawn in.

Diana Ramsay's first novel, with its fascinating backstage detail and its insight into musicians and their ways, marks a distinguished debut in the Crime Club.

*No Cause to Kill*
January 1974
Why did she die? No one who had known her could even suggest a reason. Middle-aged, plain, virtually the invisible woman, Pauline Rourke had been the last person in the world to inspire enmity in anyone, by all accounts. And yet someone had killed her – killed her swiftly and viciously, in a public place. Why?

Instead of the usual plethora of suspects, in this case there seem to be none at all, and Lieutenant Meredith of the New York Police Department faces the task of solving an apparently motiveless crime. Patiently, he follows a trail that leads from the rarefied heights inhabited by the very rich to the squalid depths of Hell's Kitchen. The investigation widens in scope, involving more and more people, exposing more and more secrets, but without uncovering the murderer of Pauline Rourke.

Then, just as the trail seems to come to an end, a sudden turn of events has the effect of dialling the combination of a safe, and the murderer is forced once more towards a deed of violence – for motives that are skilfully and dramatically revealed.

This is Diana Ramsay's third crime novel featuring Lieutenant Meredith. Like its predecessors, it scores on three points: sound plotting, excellent characterization, and of course the way she writes.

*You Can't Call It Murder*
July 1977
The young Texan in the ten-gallon hat was brash but engaging, and Dr Judith Walker was glad of his company at the otherwise dull party. Later he escorted her home. The next day he vanished, leaving his hat in her apartment. Judith, worried that something had happened to him, passed on her worry to her good friend, Cassandra Evans. Cassandra's boy-friend, Lieutenant Mike Meredith of the New York City Police Department, didn't

really believe that there was anything to worry about, but, spurred on by Cassandra, he initiated inquiries into the disappearance, just in case.

All of a sudden, Judith was faced with a series of disasters at the hospital where she was completing her residency – disasters for which she was held responsible. Were they connected with her curiosity about the missing Texan? There was no evidence pointing to cause and effect, but Meredith set out to find some. The search was long and frustrating, touching upon totally unexpected places and persons in worlds as far removed from medicine as television and the fight to preserve civil liberties. Before it was over, not only Judith's professional prospects but all the things she cherished – including her life – were in jeopardy.

## RAWSON, CLAYTON
*Death from a Top Hat*
November 1938
Hey, Presto! Death from a Top Hat! The Crime Club presents the amazing conjurer-author, Clayton Rawson, and his magician detective, Merlini.

Here, indeed, is something fresh for crime readers – a mystery with a completely new background, with a weird and wonderful cast of characters that include a card king, an escape artist, a ventriloquist, a second-sight team, a Chinese conjurer, a medium AND *the lady who is sawn in two!* What is more it has a knock-out plot and plays completely fair with the reader. Bodies are found in sealed rooms, suspected murderers vanish into midair, and most of the characters concerned can pull a rabbit, the flags of all nations, a bunch of flowers and a bowl of goldfish out of a top hat quicker than your bank manager can say 'No'.

The first corpse in this highly diverting mystery is that of an unpleasant anthropologist, writer on witchcraft and student of the occult, who is discovered murdered in a sealed room, lying inside a magic pentacle drawn on the floor for the conjuration of a demon.

Under his body is the business card of David Duvallo, escape artist *par excellence*, and on the scene at the time of the discovery are the Mystic La Claires, a second sight team, who manage to give the police some bad moments, even when questioned separately.

But the principal delight of this refreshingly new and original mystery is the Great Merlini, retired prestidigitator, who solves the case for the police. You will find him propounding his theories while fifty-cent pieces vanish from the tips of his agile fingers. You will discover him explaining how a man being watched by the police can calmly disappear into thin air as he steps into a taxi, and chuckling at the bewilderment of his fellow investigators as an apparently perfectly ordinary typewriter taps out a message with no one at the keys.

*Footprints on the Ceiling, The*
November 1939
Meet the Great Merlini! Merlini (just in case you missed *Death from a Top Hat*) is a retired professional conjuror, proprietor of a magic shop and amateur detective extraordinary. Once more, with nimble-fingered sleight of hand, he shakes up a dangerously explosive mixture of Murder, Magic, and Mystery. When Merlini is on a case anything may be expected to happen…even *footprints on the ceiling*. Surprise follows surprise with crackling, rapid-fire action as Merlini sorts out this exciting cast of characters:

SIGRID VERRILL – blonde, lovely, and possibly a damsel in distress.
ARNOLD SKELTON – who has something strangely wrong with his face.
COLONEL WATROUS – authority on ghosts and the dark mysteries of the occult.
MADAME RAPPOURT – medium extraordinary, psychic sensation of two continents.
DR. WILLIAM GAIL – psycho-analyst whose black magic is up-to-date.
IRA BROOKE – inventor and mysteriously reticent about it all.
THE MAN WITH THE BENDS – who was he and how did his body find its way to a hotel room for which no one was registered?
Clayton Rawson's previous book, *Death from a Top Hat*, was outstanding work, but *Footprints on the Ceiling* is easily one of the best thrillers in years. And what a Barnum of a show into the bargain!

*Headless Lady, The*
February 1941
Death cracks the whip as the Great Merlini, magician-detective, matches wits with a ruthless killer beneath the big top of a circus. A mysterious young woman turns up late one afternoon at Merlini's magic shop in New York City. She wants to buy a headless lady – a side-show illusion, we hasten to add, and not a corpse. But why does she use a phoney name and what compels her to steal the apparatus when Merlini refuses to sell it? And why is she being trailed by a detective? Merlini deduces that she is connected with the Mighty Hannum Shows, and that something must be very wrong. Having been born in a circus car and weaned on sawdust, Merlini wants an answer, so he catches up with the Hannum show a few days later. And how right Merlini's deduction is! Major Rutherford Hannum, owner of the show, has been found dead the night before. Automobile accident, says the coroner. Murder, says Merlini. Read *The Headless Lady* and you'll agree that it is Merlini's greatest case to date.

## REZNEK, LAWRIE
*Medicine Men, The*
April 1990
Men of medicine were supposed to be concerned with the welfare of all their patients, even in racist South Africa. So Dr Neal Potter, starting his psychiatry training, believed. Until he came across a suicide in a black patient which his superiors seemed much too keen to keep low-key. His curiosity aroused, he uncovers other suspicious practices that lead him to find irregularities on the part of the white doctors at Durban's Wellington Hospital and on the part of a Zulu witch doctor. But were these irregularities accidents, or were the medicine men, black and white, not what they seemed?

*The Medicine Men* is about the horrors that lie just beneath the surface of ordinary medical practice. Uncovering the truth takes Potter from his hospital duties to black townships and remote asylums on a chase that threatens both his survival and his sanity. Piecing the puzzle together requires all his detective skills and medical technology. But they are not enough to prepare him for the surprise awaiting him – a surprise that will endanger his life.

## RHODE, JOHN
*(see also* **Burton, Miles***)*
*Bloody Tower, The*
November 1938
John Rhode remains supreme – indisputably one of the master minds of detective fiction. He finds continuously, new and subtle ways

of killing people. The construction of his plots is flawless. He is scrupulously fair to the reader; no one could feel cheated by him. Detective-story readers' appreciation of these sterling merits is reflected in his rising sales. His new novel is, for sheer ingenuity, as good a crime novel as it would be possible to find. The setting of the story is Farningcote Priory, the decayed home of the sinister Clapthorne family, whose destiny appeared to be governed by the stone tower that stood in the derelict grounds. The tower was the cause of greed and unhappiness, and of comfort too. The mystery that it held is fully worthy of Dr. Priestley's nimble mind.

### Bricklayer's Arms
April 1945
*Bricklayer's Arms* is a fine new detective story by that favourite Crime Club author, John Rhode. Old Charlie Dalston had been the village carrier at Winghurst for many years, like his father before him. One April afternoon as he approached the railway bridge that spanned the road a short distance from Winghurst he caught sight of a bundle lying by the roadside. Pulling up sharply he got down to investigate, and to his horror discovered that the bundle was the dead body of a man. A few yards farther on a motor-cycle lay on its side. Not quite so simple as it looked, the accident develops into a most intricate and baffling mystery, in which, of course, both Inspector Jimmy Waghorn and Dr. Priestley participate.

### Claverton Mystery, The
June 1933
No. 13 Beaumaris Place was the last remaining private residence in a street long since given up to apartment houses. Dr. Priestley had long been familiar with its rather gloomy interior, for he had been in the habit of calling there to see its owner, his old friend Sir John Claverton. He again visits Sir John while the latter is seriously ill and shortly afterwards receives word of his death. The family physician, however, finds certain circumstances which to him appear suspicious, and after consultation with Dr. Priestley little doubt remains that Sir John Claverton was poisoned. The case presents several baffling aspects, but Dr. Priestley with his ingenious deductions from slender clues, eventually succeeds in finding a satisfactory solution to the case that became famous as The Claverton Mystery.

### Corpse in the Car, The
February 1935
Lady Misterton, out for her usual drive in Windsor Great Park one chilly February afternoon, suddenly ordered her chauffeur to stop. She had forgotten her bag. Being an unreasonable and inconsiderate old lady she coolly asked William to walk back to Clandown Towers – three and a half miles away – to fetch it. The chauffeur departed obediently. The old lady settled down to her needlework to the accompaniment of the music from the car radio. Curious – and prophetic – that she should be listening to the gruesome strains of Saint-Saens' *Danse Macabre*. For in that car an hour or two later Lady Misterton was found dead. Foul play? Well, that was a question for Superintendent Hanslet of the C.I.D., and ultimately for Dr Priestley, who found this strange case developed into one of the most fascinating problems he had ever been called upon to solve.

### Dead Men at the Folly
June 1932
The Inspector threw the rays of his lamp slowly round the room. Something shone

for an instant. He stooped and picked it up – a tiny, glistening metallic tube. Lipstick! So a woman had been here! Had she anything to do with the poor huddled corpse lying out there in the darkness? Clues! the seemingly unimportant trifles that so often form the strongest links in a damning chain of evidence. It certainly looked like a case of suicide! The man had obviously flung himself from the top of Tilling's Folly, that well-known obelisk which dominated the quiet countryside. But the Inspector is not satisfied. And then a second body is found in exactly similar circumstances. So Dr. Priestley, the well-known crime investigator, is called in, and builds up bit by bit the solution to the baffling mystery of the Dead Men at the Folly. Mr. John Rhode, who is undoubtedly one of our most ingenious writers of detective-stories, has surpassed himself in this new thrilling mystery.

### Dead on the Track
April 1943
It was Mr. Maberley, the fussy little station-master at Filmerham, who made the discovery, and immediately the well-ordered routine of his little world was entirely upset. The finding of the body on the railway meant an inquest, the calling-in of the police and a tremendous sensation when it became known that murder was suspected. In fact the case rapidly grew in importance, for there was a mystery that challenged the formidable powers of Superintendent Hanslet and the redoubtable Dr. Priestley himself. Against their combined operations a criminal would have very little chance, but such was the ingenuity of the murderer in this case that he certainly gave them some very good hunting.

### Death at Breakfast
February 1936
At eight o'clock in the morning breakfast was set in the dining-room of 8 Matfield Street, the home of Victor Harleston and his sister Janet. But no sooner had Victor Harleston sipped his coffee than his agonised expression and spasmodic twitching conveyed all too clearly that he had been poisoned. When Dr. Oldland arrived, he saw that the case was hopeless – and called the Yard. Even although, at this early stage, the death of Victor Harleston was surrounded by suspicious circumstances, it was impossible to guess at the extreme ingenuity with which the criminal had carried out his dastardly plan. Once again, however, Dr. Priestley shines in the solving of an extraordinary mystery.

### Death at the Helm
April 1941
White sails in the sunshine; blue skies and placid seas make the harbour of Cauldmouth a perfect picture in the height of the yachting season. But the sensation of that summer was not the outstanding performances of the crack six-metre class at the regatta, but rather the extraordinary discovery of two bodies in the cockpit of the motor-cruiser *Lonicera*. With Dr. Priestley in charge, steering a skilful course amid the shoals and shallows of doubts and difficulties, the reader can be sure of an exciting but very enjoyable voyage of discovery.

### Death in the Hop Fields
January 1937
Kent, garden of England, basked in September sunshine, fragrant with the scent of drying hops, a peaceful picture in spite of the invading host of hop-pickers – such is the colourful background to Mr. John Rhode's new story. It starts with a mysterious burglary at Paddock Court, the residence of Mr. Speight,

a retired city man. The local police seek the assistance of the Yard, and soon it is apparent that there are amazing ramifications in the case. The solution, of course, lies in the hands, or rather in the head, of the brilliant Dr. Priestley.

### Death Invades the Meeting
April 1944
The village of Heringworth was certainly 'invasion-conscious'. It was the job of John Garstairs to see that it was so. He was the Chairman of the village Invasion Committee and had summoned the meeting to discuss how Heringworth should deal with the Hun. How Death itself invaded that meeting and thereby staged a first-rate mystery is the theme of this very fine novel by that ever popular story-teller, John Rhode.

### Death on Sunday
October 1939
An expert forger was worrying Scotland Yard, and Inspector Jimmy Waghorn's investigations took him to a high-class residential hotel near London. Under an assumed name Inspector Waghorn mingled with the guests, and it was difficult for him to realise that among the very respectable-looking visitors in the hotel was the person he was looking for. But worse was to happen. In that peaceful atmosphere a murder was committed so baffling and ingenious that even so brilliant an investigator as Dr. Priestley was for a time stymied in his efforts to solve it. Mr. John Rhode again shows how skilful he is at setting a problem that few will solve.

### Death on the Board
May 1937
John Rhode has set himself a high standard in detective-story writing, and in *Death on the Board*, he gives us another fine example of his art.
…A mysterious explosion occurred at the Beckenham home of Sir Andrew Wiggenhall, chairman of a big firm of chain-store ironmongers. Sir Andrew was in the bath-room at the time, but so great was the force of the explosion that his dismembered body was found in the garden. This was the first of a series of mysteries all of which affected the firm. Even taciturn Dr. Priestley was temporarily embarrassed, but as he reminded Superintendent Hanslet and Inspector Jimmy Waghorn, 'I am a scientist, not a policeman,' and it was left to them to conduct the baffling investigations.

### Death on the Boat Train
April 1940
Fair blew the wind from France, and the Channel steamer *Isle of Jethou* rolled a bit in the stiff south-westerly breeze. But the rough crossing didn't upset the mysterious passenger who had locked himself into his cabin as soon as he boarded the boat at Guernsey. The same desire for seclusion had manifested itself on the boat-train to Waterloo, for the guard had been presented with a pound-note to reserve a compartment for Mr. Mystery. But *did* he travel alone? For at Waterloo the gentleman from Guernsey was a pretty genuine corpse. *Death on the Boat-Train* is a first-rate detective story, once again featuring the coldly clever scientific mind of Dr. Priestley, John Rhode's brilliant creation.

### Death Pays a Dividend
April 1939
Rupert Bayle's body lay at the foot of the stairs. At the top of the staircase was a wire strand over which he must have tripped before crashing headlong to his death. To Inspector Jimmy Waghorn it was obvious

*how* it happened, but not so obvious *why*. Rupert Bayle was a perfect secretary to a not-so-perfect company promoter, and although it had been said of Bayle that he was too honest to live that was no good reason why he should have died. It was Dr. Priestley who found the solution to the problem, but it was probably Inspector Waghorn who found, in his opinion, the most important thing of all. Mr. Rhode presents his many readers with another masterpiece of detection.

### Fourth Bomb, The
April 1942
Yardley Green was not a military objective. It was in fact so small and unimportant that it hadn't even got a siren of its own. But that didn't prevent it from receiving the attentions of the enemy, and one night four bombs were dropped in the village, injuring two of the inhabitants slightly. A third casualty was found in a ditch beside the crater of the fourth bomb. The unfortunate person, subsequently found to be dead, was naturally presumed to be also the victim of enemy action until later evidence suggested that he was alive *after* the bombs dropped. Here is a first-class mystery of topical interest, featuring Jimmy Waghorn and the redoubtable Dr. Priestley and told with that marvellous ingenuity always associated with the name of John Rhode.

### Hanging Woman, The
June 1931
There was something sinister and forbidding about Wargrave House. An atmosphere of mystery hung about its empty rooms, haunted, as the villagers said, by the ghost of a woman who, years before, had hanged herself from a beam in the kitchen. Then one day an astounding discovery was made. The body of a woman was actually found hanging from the same beam! A theory of suicide gives place to a certainty of murder when Scotland Yard takes a hand in the case. The brains behind that hand are those of Dr. Priestley, now famous as a scientific investigator of crime. A curious problem, brilliantly solved.

### Hendon's First Case
June 1935
A number of curious coincidences, seemingly unconnected, provides the background for this enthralling mystery. A research chemist, Mr. Threlfall, dies from ptomaine poisoning. At the same time his laboratory is burgled. He was just about to alter his will. He received a threatening letter from his wife. And his nephew was seen in his company just before his death. Can a motive for murder be found in this most obscure of cases? Superintendent Hanslet and Inspector Jimmy Waghorn, who investigate, represent two different and very interesting types. The former, employing the official method, is direct and efficient once it can be shown that a crime has been committed. The latter, a product of the newly founded Metropolitan Police College at Hendon, has a more exploring mind, and works more by intuition than by rule. But both of them are helped by the ingenious Dr. Priestley, who remains, as ever, discreetly in the background. *Hendon's First Case* is in every respect a truly mystifying mystery.

### In Face of the Verdict
July 1936
The sheer ingenuity of Mr. John Rhode is deservedly a matter for enthusiasm. He is certainly one of our most resourceful providers of puzzles that are real brain-teasers. 'Accidental death by drowning' was the verdict at the inquest on Major Walter Bedworthy. But Sir John Hallatrow, the Major's close friend, suspected murder. His suspicions

were confirmed when some days later Ernest Bedworthy, Walter's brother, was also found drowned. Dr. Priestley, with his uncanny appreciation of the true significance of facts, showed an immediate interest in bicycles, telepathy and wills – all of which have a bearing on this most baffling case. Assisted by Superintendent Hanslet and young Jimmy Waghorn, he succeeds in bringing to justice one of the cleverest of murderers.

### *Invisible Weapons*
April 1938

The murder of Mr. Robert Fransham while he was washing his hands at his niece's house was one of the most amazing problems that ever confronted Scotland Yard. Especially in view of the fact that no weapon could be found and that *there was a policeman in the house when the murder was actually committed*. The combined efforts of Superintendent Hanslet and Inspector Waghorn brought no result and the case was dropped – but not forgotten. It was only after another equally baffling murder had been committed that Dr. Priestley began his investigations. He was as good as told that 'he had a bee in his bonnet', but as the doctor so aptly remarked, it was a bee which might produce the honey of wisdom. And it did, for Dr. Priestley's brilliant deductive powers eventually solved this extraordinary case.

### *Men Die at Cyprus Lodge*
October 1943

Even in these days of acute housing shortage there are some houses that no one seems to want. Cyprus Lodge was one of these. It was the despair of Messrs. Elliot and Frodsham, estate agents in the little town of Troutwich. Yet Cyprus Lodge was an attractive enough residence that suffered unfortunately from a persistent local rumour that it was haunted. And certainly strange things had happened there in the past, and tenants had died in rather mysterious ways. It was the death, however, of Sir Philip Briningham, whose hobby for many years had been investigating haunted houses, which first caused Inspector Jimmy Waghorn to pay particular attention to Cyprus Lodge, and he was followed in due course by Superintendent Hanslet and Dr. Priestley. With that trio of crime investigators the reader is assured of a really brilliant detective story.

### *Motor Rally Mystery, The*
February 1933

Mr. John Rhode's new story is written around the great annual Motor Rally at Torquay. A thousand cars racing on their thousand-mile journey through the night...an accident, or what looks like an accident...The calling in of the local police, and then Scotland Yard, and finally, of course, Dr. Priestley, whose scientific acumen was never more severely tested than in this baffling story. On very slender clues he constructs an elaborate and ingenious piece of deduction which shows Mr. Rhode's clever craftsmanship at its best. *The Motor Rally Mystery*, apart from its novel and topical background of particular interest to motorists, will appeal to all who like a thoroughly honest, straightforward detective story.

### *Murder at Lilac Cottage*
September 1940

Careless Talk may give away Vital Secrets. And sometimes it may happen that tittle-tattle provides the first clue in a murder mystery. The landlord of The Woodcock was definitely of the opinion that you can hear a lot of interesting things in a pub if you keep your ears open. He, for instance, had heard a lot of village gossip about young Mr. Derrington, who lived alone in Lilac Cottage. The villagers thought the young man queer, a bit of a mystery in fact, but they did not anticipate even in their wildest flights of imagination the amazing mystery that surrounded the discovery of his dead body outside Lilac Cottage one evening. But Inspector Jimmy Waghorn of the C. I. D. and the celebrated Dr. Priestley between them do a splendid job of work. Mr. John Rhode fully maintains his reputation as a writer whose ingenuity in devising almost perfect murders is unrivalled.

### *Mystery at Greycombe Farm*
January 1932

The low, graystone buildings of Greycombe Farm were the very embodiment of peace and security. Nothing ever disturbed the general air of tranquillity so typical of a West Country farm until – one memorable night fire broke out in Farmer Jim's cider store. When, as a result of the herculean efforts of the village fire brigade, the flames were finally extinguished, the examination of the building revealed the charred remains of a body. Here was a mystery that immediately engaged the attention of Major Betterton, Chief Constable of Wessex. It was, however only with the calling in of Dr. Priestley, the wealthy but eccentric scientist and crime investigator, that the amazing ramifications of this remarkable mystery were disclosed. This story is certainly one of the best that Mr. John Rhode has written.

### *Mystery at Olympia*
October 1935

A dense crowd surrounded the new Comet car that was fully expected to be the sensation of the great Motor Show at Olympia. Suddenly one of the eager spectators, an elderly man, lurched forward and collapsed in what appeared to be a dead faint on the ground. But Nigel Pershore was dead, and it was his death that provided the real sensation of the show. A post-mortem examination revealed no visible wound, no serious organic disorder, no evidence of poison. Doctors and detectives were equally baffled. Every chapter unfolds a new aspect of an apparently insoluble puzzle. Then a fortunate discovery opens the way for Dr. Priestley's unrivalled deductions and a solution of the mystery that brings to a close a really brilliant story.

### *Night Exercise*
September 1942

*Night Exercise* will deservedly rank as one of John Rhode's best stories. But it is much more than a brilliantly told crime story. *Night Exercise* gives an accurate and intensely interesting picture of Britain's Home Guard at work – preparing for the day when thousands of Nazi paratroops might drop from the skies upon the green fields of England. Mr. Rhode pictures for us a village company of Home Guards on a big night exercise during which Colonel Chalgrove mysteriously disappears. It is soon obvious that a crime has been committed – a murder in which the finding of the body becomes as important as tracking down the murderer.

### *Poison for One*
June 1934

*Poison for One* is the sinister and compelling title of John Rhode's detective story, a story which many of his readers will say is the best he has ever written. For sheer ingenuity and masterly handling of a most difficult and baffling problem this intriguing poison drama, that centres round the mysterious death of Sir Gerald Uppingham at Bucklesbury Park would certainly be hard to surpass. How Dr. Priestley, with very little in the nature of a real clue to work upon, builds up a solution by cool and calculating methods of deduction makes enthralling reading.

### *Proceed With Caution*
November 1937

'Things happen like that,' said Superintendent Hanslet. 'There are times at the Yard when things are as dull as ditch-water. And then suddenly two really important cases are thrust upon us at once.' And so it was that Hanslet searched for the missing Wherwell diamonds whilst Inspector Waghorn went to investigate a death at Fallowchurch and helped to pacify Mr. Wedgwood of the Green Bear, who was very naturally upset at seeing a hearse outside the bar entrance. Hanslet could get no further with his case, and Waghorn, after weeks of investigation, had the doubtful satisfaction of being farther away from the solution of the crime than he was at the beginning. They both took their troubles to Dr Priestley, who, as usual, had some very interesting observations to make. This must surely be the most ingenious crime story that Mr. Rhode, most ingenious of writers, has given us.

### *Robthorne Mystery, The*
January 1934

Dr. Priestley, well-known crime investigator, is called in to solve the mysterious death of Mr. Robthorne, who was found shot in the greenhouse of his country residence. A chain of damning evidence that Dr. Priestley pieces so successfully together forms one of the finest examples of crime detection that Mr. John Rhode has yet produced.

### *Shot at Dawn*
November 1934

The motor-cruiser *Alondra* had come over the harbour bar at Riddinghithe with the last of the flood and dropped anchor for the night. The next morning a boatman putting out to do a bit of fishing noticed the body of a man lying across the cabin top. He put his helm down and steered closer to investigate. And then he saw that the man's head was shattered... The police are baffled, as they cannot discover anything about the dead man beyond his name and the fact that he was a keen yachtsman. It remains for Dr. Priestley to bring about an entirely unexpected denouement providing the biggest surprise in an extremely well-told story.

### *They Watched By Night*
October 1941

John Rhode has beaten his own magnificent record for ingenuity in this splendid new story. An army research camp whose existence is absolutely secret, is bombed three times. Is there a fifth columnist at work? And if so, what are his methods? Inspector Waghorn, now of the Intelligence, and Superintendent Hanslet investigate the matter, but they fail to prevent further attacks and the camp has to be moved elsewhere. Then the chief of the local Special Constabulary is burned to death in his own summerhouse, which happened to be an excellent vantage point for spotting any signallers. This event merely complicates the problem until Dr. Priestley takes a hand and reveals the identity of the traitor and shows how he succeeds in his plans.

### *Tragedy on the Line*
January 1931

Mr. Wickenden and his solicitor finished talking business in the study at Colingrove House. They turned their conversation to books, the new science of the psychic, and finally got on to old Wickenden's favourite subject – crime; and so the night wore on until Mr. Hoddinott was obliged to accept his wealthy client's invitation to postpone his return to London till morning. Two days later Gervase Wickenden was found dead on the railway line near Upton Bishop's station. The shattered head told its own story; but had the unfortunate man planned his own destruction; had he been the victim of an accident; or had some one carried out one of those perfect crimes the contemplation of which had so ironically been Wickenden's great mental recreation? Dr. Kempthorne, his nephew, and the last person to see him alive, was able to rule out the idea of suicide. Old Gervase had actually been on the point of marrying! So the Coroner said – accidental death. But Superintendent Quillan, like you, cannot let it go at that! Here is a "fine art" murder for which Mr. John Rhode deserves the gratitude of every lover of the crime novel and the praise of De Quincey's shade.

### *Vegetable Duck*
November 1944

Of all murders, those perpetrated by the cowardly but cunning hand of the poisoner are perhaps the most baffling, and consequently have provided some of the greatest triumphs of crime detection. The mystery of the flat in Battersea in which the body of Mrs. Fransham was discovered proves no exception. *Vegetable Duck* is certainly one of the most ingenious stories in which Dr. Priestley has figured, and Mr. Rhode is to be congratulated on a very capable and cleverly worked-out detective story.

## RIPLEY, MIKE

### *Angel Hunt*
January 1990

Angel is house-sitting (like baby-sitting but you don't have to keep the noise down) for a relative of his landlord when a body drops in through the bathroom skylight.

Being caught with a corpse, a young lady of brief acquaintance and a suspicious package in the house of a total stranger – no problem. But when the corpse turns out to be an old fellow student trying to cut loose from an Animal Rights splinter group, things get complicated. Especially when the suspicious package disappears (and the owner wants it back – badly) and Angel discovers that Animal Libbers are far from cute and cuddly.

But the time to start worrying (Rule of Life No. 38) is when the policemen get nicer. Helping them *might* put our trumpet-playing, cab-driving hero on the side of the angels, but who's on his? Is it Zaria, who's gone missing along with the suspicious package? The Reverend Bell, a fine example of muscular Christianity in action? Lara, the redheaded ice-maiden? Sunil, a would-be Pakistani gang boss with a growing army of not-too-efficient thugs?

Can even Springsteen, Angel's streetwise black cat, be trusted?

### *Angel Touch*
August 1989

When it comes to financial wheeling and dealing in the big bad City, Fitzroy Maclean Angel is the first to admit he's an innocent. It is just about the only thing he is innocent of; as for streetsmart survival in the real London he's sharp as a pistol.

He needs to be, for when his yuppified (but eminently fanciable) upstairs neighbour Salome is suspected of insider trading on the Stock Exchange, who else can she turn to?

Financial leaks turn into a highly suspicious fatal car accident and a cunning conspiracy masterminded by a disgraced City whizzkid with a chip on his shoulder and a passion for dressing up as a soldier and playing war games.

Finding out who and how is relatively easy; but doing something about it requires Angel's own special 'Touch' – a financial scam designed to lose money!

To pull it off, trumpet-playing Angel needs to recruit his own army of helpers. Even then, the cynical black cat Springsteen has to extend a helping paw and it is Armstrong – Angel's trusty black London cab – who has to come to the rescue when things get really heavy.

### *Angels in Arms*
July 1991

So it seems, for when your name is Werewolf, when you've broken your leg, been kidnapped in a foreign country, are being held for ransom for a consignment of drugs you didn't even know you were carrying, and have five days to live before being executed by a bunch of urban terrorists you've never heard of: who else you gonna call?

And when Angel gets the call from his old and disreputable friend, he just has to get involved in tracking down a shipment of drugs mistakenly smuggled in from France.

On the trail, he encounters Werewolf's brother Gearoid, a wolf in sheep's clothing if ever there was one; a second-rate but very loud Heavy-Metal band; a trendy young Dutchman as well-armed as he is well-dressed; and the mad, bad and definitely dangerous-to-know Lucinda L. Luger.

And then he has to face the bad guys.

Assembling an invasion force of (roughly) 28,002 weird and wonderful allies, Angel lands in France and rides to the rescue.

Will his improvised cavalry arrive in time?

No problem.

### *Just Another Angel*
August 1988

Rule of Life No. 477: When a woman admits that it's difficult for her to ask for something, leave immediately.

Forgetting his own good advice, trumpet-playing Angel (the hero with more street cred than wheel-clamps) agrees to help the enigmatic Jo Scamp, a lady of brief but intimate acquaintance. And what begins with the simple recovery of stolen jewellery develops into violence involving a deranged London gangster and a policeman with a vendetta.

When the nastiness comes unpleasantly close to home, Angel has to go out and try to meet it half way, counting on his wits and his own inimitable Rules of Life to see him through.

But if you've a working knowledge of the seamy underside of London, a trusty black taxi called Armstrong and a cynical black cat called Springsteen to rely on, you can handle it. Can't you?

If you've been christened Fitzroy Maclean Angel by a father with a strange sense of humour, you have to.

## ROBY, MARY LINN
### *Still as the Grave*
July 1965

'The incredible Wakefields' were almost as famous for the success they had made of their marriage as they were for their stage performances; in the theatre they were a triumphant 'husband-and-wife' team.

Kate was beautiful, but also possessive and proud; her pride was savagely hurt when she realised that David was in love with another woman – a girl half his own age. Rather than face the pity and laughter of her friends and public, Kate chose a drastic course: she decided to kill David.

The murder proved easy and the role of sorrowing widow easier still to one who had successfully portrayed so many different characters on the stage. And yet had everything gone so smoothly? Her doubts became realities, and this time she could see no escape from the humiliation inflicted on her.

Mary Linn Roby is a young American authoress who has chosen England as the setting for her first novel. *Still as the Grave* is taut and clever and the climax is as horrifying as it is unexpected.

## RODD, RALPH
### *Midnight Murder*
February 1931

Was the attempt on Wilma Leigh's life made by her husband, bluff, genial, Colonel Leigh, M. F. H.? Why did he disappear on the very night when the attempted murder was discovered? Who else in peaceful little Bullington could have any possible motive for trying to remove the most popular woman in the county? These are some of the questions Giles Egerton, the London specialist who, in answer to a frantic appeal, has fought with death and frustrated the would-be murderer, finds himself trying to answer. His eagerness to do so increases as fresh attempts against Mrs. Leigh's life are made with almost incredible ruthlessness. The hard-bitten, sporting, yet always womanly Wilma Leigh, her overgrown child of a husband, Jaqueline Drury – whom Giles Egerton loves – the dour Professor and his blind girl-wife, the tender-hearted little platitudinarian at the Rectory, and the amazing Anthea Jubb, the inquiry agent's assistant who finally runs the would-be murderer to earth, all play their part in this ingenious detective problem.

## RUSSELL, A. J.
### *Devalino Caper, The*
June 1977

This smooth, fast-paced, suspenseful novel – reminiscent of *The Friends of Eddie Coyle* – introduces an extraordinary operator named Joseph Devalino. Cunning, resourceful, totally amoral, Dev has come to a small Midwestern town to do a job for a relative in trouble. The job: to steal a million dollars in stolen securities secreted by the town's richest man.

An adept manipulator of people, Dev uses whatever help comes his way – three local prostitutes and their black madam – to pull off what appears to be an impossible task. But he is challenging a formidable assemblage: the underworld chief whose beneficence does more for his district than its congressman; a police sergeant who holds up filling stations when broke; a characters known as 'the Indian' who is constitutionally incapable of living as Number Two in the chain of criminal command.

Joe Dev is more than a thief. 'Tell me what you think and I'll tell you what you are,' is his motto. He responds to law enforcement as an insect to DDT. Karate is okay, but psychology backed by mother wit is more effective – and deadlier. Electronic equipment has its advantages, but lip reading is the next best thing to being invisible. Like the insect, Joe Dev adapts and survives.

This is a novel that is remorselessly exciting, filled with suspense

## RUSSELL, MARTIN
### *Advisory Service*
October 1971

The heavy breathing exploded into laughter on the telephone and cut off abruptly. Eddie Mills put down the receiver with a shaking hand. For days he and his wife Pearl had been terrorized by an unknown caller, who seemed to know their movements intimately. The tension was becoming unbearable. It could only be someone they knew. But who in the social and business circles of this ordinary middle-class couple would persecute them like that?

Then their daughter fails to return from school and a mysterious letter arrives offering assistance from 'our Advisory Service', adding meaningly that they 'will be getting in touch'. But no ransom notes follows, only further letters indicating that the child is in their possession. Who are they and what do they want?

Everyone Eddie and Pearl knows comes under suspicion, even Eddie's boss, whose relationship with Pearl before her marriage now assumes a sinister significance. Under the strain and the failure of police enquiries, Pearl breaks down completely, her only comfort a sympathetic woman journalist.

And then, out of the past, the tormentor emerges and the story takes an unexpected turn. As Eddie battles to save his daughter, Martin Russell once again shows himself a master at turning the screw of suspense.

### *All Part of the Service*
September 1982

Celia Sparke was short, plump, fair-haired, bespectacled and faintly glistening. Acceptable enough, you might think for the agony aunt of *Scene 2000*, a Glasgow-based weekly, but – 'Celia Sparke' was a man.

Since journalist Barry Cribb had first moved north of the Border some eight years previously to head the two-man team which handled the Problems Page, he had kept himself to himself. Even his assistant, Ed Lothian, didn't know much about him. He certainly didn't know that Barry had taken to visiting women correspondents as part of the service, nor that he was neurotically sensitive about his lack of height.

When three young women in widely differing circumstances were murdered in Glasgow on three successive days, Ed had no reason to connect the crimes with Barry, not even when the police discovered that two at least of the victims had recently sent a letter to *Scene 2000*, for the attention of Celia Sparke.

Then this gripping story of a psychopathic killer takes a murderous twist nearer home. Can the police catch up with Barry before another death occurs?

### *Backlash*
May 1981

As the senior partner in a successful property conversion company, Steven Cassell saw himself as a man of the world, and his partner, the unfortunately named Albert Hall, as a dependable plodder – like his name, a bit of a joke. So when Albert called Steven's home in the dead of the night, Steven was surprised; and when Albert summoned him urgently to a flat in Finchley, he was astounded. But bigger surprises were in store. For instance, what about Albert's story that he had followed a girl home from a concert and killed her? If that were true, then whose was the corpse in the kitchen of the Finchley flat? Not a girl's – that was for certain.

After these curious events, Steven was further shaken to find that he was being followed and that Albert had disappeared. And when he paid another visit to the Finchley flat, the corpse had turned into someone he recognized. But where was it when the police arrived? By the time matters had been explained, a few of Steven's own secrets were out in the open. The police wouldn't believe his story – but would you?

### *Catspaw*
October 1980

There's nothing new about having troublesome neighbours. That's what Belinda Craig told herself. The quiet, hard-working girl was employed in the local paper's small ads department, and the fact that she lived alone and kept herself to herself meant that she has no one to turn to for help when it seemed as if her upstairs neighbour's noisy all-night record-playing might drive her out of her flat.

Then Adrian Hacker, a journalist at her office, took an interest in her problem. He was writing an article on urban stress, and Belinda's experiences might make a useful contribution. All she had to do was keep a diary.

Almost at once the vendetta became something more sinister, and Adrian and Smokey, his cat, became Belinda's only support in a nightmare ordeal. How would she react? Would she run or freeze – or perhaps become another person altogether? As Belinda became suspicious that she was being used as a catspaw, it seemed to her that there was nothing and no one she could trust: least of all herself.

Martin Russell can be relied upon to tell a chilling, thrilling story. His latest does not disappoint.

### *Censor*
October 1984

Peter Rodgers was riding high. In eight years he had converted the *Planet*, a languishing London tabloid, into a gratifying success. If the hardworking widower from the Midlands had achieved this by pandering unashamedly to his readers' love of sensationalism, who would quibble? Not the proprietor!

It was meat and drink to the paper when a well-known director of horror films was murdered; then the star of a sex/horror movie. Both men were said to have been disturbed shortly before their deaths, possibly by something received through the post, so Rodgers assigned an efficient journalist to try and trace a link between these and other recent killings in the entertainment world.

Then the *Planet*'s proprietor was struck down, and the danger moved nearer home, especially when Rodgers received a covertly threatening letter signed Censor. His daughters were more alert to the danger than he was, especially, Elaine, the actress, who had had a similar note. But those who attended Elaine's preview of a new, very avant-garde play could not have realized the direction from which that danger would come, nor what lay behind Censor's activities.

Martin Russell's enviable talent for smooth dialogue and skilful misdirection has full play in his latest story of suspense.

### *Client, The*
April 1975

The secluded house in Streatham wasn't the usual type of solicitor's office, but nor was the Will to be read the usual type of Will. Seated in his strange room and surveying the three beneficiaries before him, the solicitor reflected that his client would have been only too delighted with how the arrangements were working out.

The Will was that of young and wealthy Susan Bradshaw; the beneficiaries three people who had played a part in her life and perhaps her death. All had come in answer to an advertisement; none could leave before the Will was read in full.

Now the two men and a woman are forced to listen to the solicitor reading Susan's account of her relationship with each of them and comment on her version of events. Gradually a picture of each relationship emerges – but who is telling the truth?

As the tension mounts to a horrifying climax as a diabolically clever crime is revealed. Martin Russell's originality and talent for suspense-building have never been put to better use.

### Concrete Evidence
November 1972

The building of a new community centre is the focus of much criticism and discontent in Lewgate, where slum-dwellers feel that rehousing should have priority. Following the murder of a building inspector, Jim Larkin, the central character in *Deadline*, now a reporter on a Lewgate local paper and married to Bunty, delves into the facts which have been mysteriously suppressed or distorted, and is immediately made unpleasantly aware that his investigations are resented, to the point where his life and that of everyone who helps him are at risk.

Despite the offer of a desk job and better money, Larkin plods on, convinced that there is some link between the building site, the discreetly homosexual club frequented by some of those connected with it, and the drug-peddling which is rife in the town. He is aided in his task by Anne Millett, reporter on a rival paper, and encouraged only by the chairman of the housing committee who is anxious to get the matter cleared up.

When a balcony collapses, killing some children on a neighbouring housing state built by the same contractors, the mood of the tenants turns ugly. Larkin, pursuing his investigations, finds himself in a very tough spot indeed.

What he finally discovers and the identity of the ringleaders provides a splendidly suspenseful finale to a story in which Martin Russell, himself a journalist on a local paper, has made fulllest use of his inside knowledge of local affairs.

### Crime Wave
January 1974

The Green Belt suburb where reporter Jim Larkin and his wife Bunty have now taken up residence has always been free from serious crime. Suddenly a wave of muggings breaks out. Suspicion falls first on members of a local youth club, then on big-time operators from the Smoke, then on those who burgle the Larkins' home.

The Larkins are more directly involved when Jim becomes a victim, and so does the daughter of some friends. And then the muggers turn to murder, and the need to hunt them down becomes imperative.

One by one the suspects have to be ruled out as the leads followed by the police (and Larkin) end in failure. And then Larkin finds himself literally holding the vital clue to the killers, and finds too that he is danger of his life.

Martin Russell, who excels in the unexpected twist, is here seen to advantage. *Crime Wave* is as neatly plotted a yarn as any he has devised.

### Danger Money
January 1968

With its staff underpaid and overworked the local bank was handling larger and larger sums: confusion reigned where order was essential – and security lapsed when enormous sums, often £40,000 odd, were hastily stowed on the premises at night.

Paul Hobbs, a victim of this exploitation, sought promotion: already in danger, after fifteen years, of remaining forever a cashier, he had a wife who expected success and a new

house. The method Hobbs chose of drawing the attention of the bank to his loyalties and abilities was fraught with appalling risk.

There is a theft at the local bank. And the consequences for Hobbs and his associates are here unfolded. The development of the tale is exciting and extraordinary. In a portrait that is almost touching the author of *No Through Road* describes the pathetic and hopeless predicament of the white collar worker struggling to meet the calls made on him in a world of predatory employers and a demanding family: a world itself awash with liquid cash, crying out to be used in a very private and personal context.

### Dangerous Place to Dwell, A
November 1978

The film of the best-selling novel was going to be a screen classic – and it was going to provide Anjelica Browne, its British star, with her great chance to prove that she was not merely a Hollywood sex kitten, but a real actress. At the Hampshire studios all was in readiness to start shooting, and Herb Joseph, renowned California-based producer and Anjelica's staunch friend and protector, was at the helm. For the girl from West Ham, the future looked rosy.

Then, out of the past, came a spectre to menace her in the form of her blackmailing ex-husband. He could destroy her career, Herbie's film, and something even more important. Anjelica was brought to the edge of desperation in her frantic search for a way out.

Against her will, her parents and younger sister, as well as Herbie, were drawn into the struggle. And then Fate took a hand. Anjelica's ex-husband was found murdered, and a new nightmare began.

Was the murderer someone close to her – perhaps a member of her family? With the blackmailer dead, would everything still blow up in her face? When she stumbled upon the answer, she found herself in deadly danger. For Anjelica Browne, the world had indeed become a dangerous place.

### Darker Side of Death, The
May 1985

After twenty-six outstanding crime novels, Martin Russell turns his hand to the short story – with equal success. The talent for neat plotting, sharp characterization and smart dialogue which has stood him in good stead in his novels is here skilfully deployed in shorter compass. Whether he is dealing with skulduggery at the local golf club (*A Slice of Justice*), friction between neighbours (*Kill Before Publication*), a disturbed mental state (*Hard to Live With*), or the rivalries in an old people's home (*Paula's People*), his ability to chill the blood even as the hand mesmerically turns the page is never in doubt.

The short story, often considered one of the most difficult art forms, is safe in Martin Russell's hands. They are those of a master.

### Daylight Robbery
March 1978

The Canary Islands were a holiday paradise and the hotel was excellent, but it was all lost upon Philip Lambert. The young architect was alone – and alone with thoughts which were none too pleasant because they were thoughts of guilt.

No wonder he fell an easy prey to Major Carlisle, jovial, retired, full of anecdotes and bonhomie, and painfully eager to latch on. Before long Lambert was telling him his troubles, only to find that the Major was better acquainted with them than he had thought. And not only the Major...Gradually Lambert was edged into playing a vital part

in a conspiracy designed to divest a trusting woman of her wealth. As guilt for the past was overlaid by guilt for the present, the holiday paradise of the beautiful islands became a holiday hell.

Skilful narrative and taut dialogue distinguish this novel of character and suspense, which marks a new development in Martin Russell's impressive list of successful crime stories, already noted for their versatility.

### Dead Heat
September 1986

What finally tilted it for Marvin Pike were the accounts discrepancies. Until then he had been prepared to accept the adultery of his partner with his wife, but the discovery that he was being cheated both in business and in bed proved sufficient to tip the scales.

All the same, he wasn't contemplating murder and when Arlene's body went limp in his hands in the course of a particularly bitter row, his first reaction was shock. His second: how to cover his tracks. And how better than by involving his partner, Gareth Somers, by burying Arlene in the grounds of his house?

But when the police called next morning it was not in connection with Arlene's disappearance, which Marvin had prudently reported, but to tell him Somers was dead. Stabbed to death on the patio at about the same time that Marvin had been digging Arlene's shallow grave.

Thereafter a nightmare begins for Marvin. Suspected of the murder he has not committed rather than the one he has, his only ally is Gail, his assistant in the shop, who will do anything for him, even lie if need be …

Martin Russell's story is full of twists and turns as Marvin wriggles like an eel to escape detection.

### Deadline
March 1971

'Ever since you came here things have been happening,' a colleague on the local paper remarked to Jim Larkin – the 'things' being a series of increasingly grisly murders which were terrorizing the out-of-season doldrums of the small seaside town. And the maniac, as the police admitted, could be any one of the town's few thousand inhabitants.

As a reporter, Larkin is ideally placed for an overall view of the whole operation, particularly when he is seconded to assist the *Review*'s crime coverage. The personal tragedies, the helplessness of the police, the rising tide of fear, the counter-measures taken by a desperate populace, the corroding suspicion everywhere – all are seen through his eyes and those of the paper's staff. As small-time civic and social items are driven from the *Review*'s pages in favour of banner headlines, feature articles, police appeals and private rewards, as the crisis mounts and special edition follows special edition, the different personal and professional reactions of the staff intensify. And when Larkin realizes that he possesses a clue to the murderer's identity and acts on it, he finds himself in danger of his life.

Martin Russell makes splendid use of his inside knowledge of the workings of local newspapers. Allied to his unfailing inventiveness and imaginative power, this makes *Deadline* his most chilling, gripping thriller to date.

### Death Fuse
February 1980

Somewhere among the city's teeming millions a man was waiting – a man with a sound knowledge of explosives, total self-control, and the need to kill.

What warped mind had used the hideously

effective nail-bomb in a restaurant filled with people enjoying an evening out? It was up to Chief Inspector Harry Cullen, Inspector Bob Royce and the rest of the Squad to find out, but lead after lead turned out to be a false trail for the detectives, and the more they knew the less it made sense.

Were the killer's murderous instincts directed against a newspaper editor or a retired policeman? Was his target a Government Minister or a royal party? Or had the double-pointed nails been intended for someone else altogether?

When the killer struck again, London was gripped by a reign of terror. Theatres were evacuated, people searched, and still the bomber struck. It also seemed that he had acquired a taste for killing at closer range …

Could he be caught? Not until the last minute did the vital clue emerge – but was it too late by then to prevent a new outbreak of violence, this time striking at the heart of the Squad itself?

### Dial Death
July 1977

Twice a week 28-year-old Paula Moss spent an evening a week working for Dial-a-Pal, a voluntary organization to which people with problems could phone in. Paula, responsible, capable secretary to a managing director, was good at handling other people's problems. They helped her forget about her own. One night she took a call from a young man who said he had murdered his father. Before Paula could take any steps to help or to have the call traced, the unknown young man rang off.

The next night he rang again and Paula answered. He repeated his story. Was he telling the truth? Against all the rules of the organization, and well knowing it would cause trouble with her own nagging, tyrannical parent, Paula arranged to meet the 'murderer'. It was beginning of an extraordinary relationship and an extraordinary series of events which will keep the reader taut and guessing, as Martin Russell stays consistently one jump ahead.

Graham Lord in the *Sunday Express* hailed Martin Russell's last novel, *Mr T*, as 'a triumph of trickery, cunning and imagination'. It is now followed by an equally successful tour de force [sic] in which Martin Russell's talent for the bizarre, the suspenseful and the grimly humorous are deployed with customary skill and verve.

### Domestic Affair, A
January 1984

For Colin Fletcher, estate agent, the misery of divorce was as bad as that of the marriage. Not only was his ex-wife a financial drain on him, but she persistently obstructed his legal right of access to their two children. But if he could prove her an unfit person to have control of them, the case would be altered. Fletcher engaged a private investigator to watch his wife.

At first fate seemed to be playing into his hands. Louise inserted an advertisement for suitable companionship in a local paper, and very soon a wealthy companion turned up. When Fletcher and a woman witness arrived at the house late one evening to find that Louise had not come home to her children, it looked as though Fletcher had the evidence he sought.

Unfortunately his ex-wife's disappearance posed more problems than it solved, one of them – and potentially the most serious – being created by Louise herself. Then the private investigator, though sacked by Fletcher, insisted on involving the police. Even the children unexpectedly took a hand in the solution to this ingenious domestic mystery which is both startling and original.

### Double Deal
March 1976

Peter Connors had two mistresses, one married, one not, and a cosy job as travel correspondent for a London paper. He also had a chronic shortage of scruples – and of cash. So when the married Eleanor suggested that he should dispose of her husband and they would split the insurance money, Connors was prepared to try anything – even murder – once. And when Eleanor's husband who was also his colleague, approached him with a similar suggestion regarding Eleanor, Connors was prepared to try anything twice. Unfortunately neither attempt produced the result expected. Nor did it produce the cash.

Still desperate to impress the elusive and unmarried Sarah, Connors tried other ploys. Their results too were unexpected – and highly undesirable. By the time he was confronted with the unpalatable fact that, far from being in control of events, he was at their mercy, Connors could see only one way out. And that way led him, with grim logic, to a situation as neatly inescapable as any Martin Russell's well-known skill has ever contrived.

### Double Hit
May 1973

In comparatively few years Martin Russell has built up an enviable reputation as a master of the tense psychological thriller, often with a splendid surprise twist at the end. He made brilliant use of his experience as a reporter on local papers in such titles as *Deadline* and *Concrete Evidence*, while *Hunt the Killer* [sic] and *Advisory Service* demonstrated to the full his ability to deal with unusual, not to say macabre states of mind. All his novels deal with the irruption of terror into the lives of ordinary men and women. *Double Hit* is no exception.

There was no doubt Nevil West, science teacher in a Midlands comprehensive school, wanted to marry his colleague Jackie Manning as much as she did him. Only one thing held him back: Nevil was being blackmailed.

The blackmailer was none other than the physical education instructor. The nature of this hold might or might not be valid, but he had Nevil scared. Not until he had Jackie to back him was Nevil prepared to go to the police.

But the appointment at the police-station was never kept, for Nevil, returning to the squash-court after a game with his blackmailer, finds the man lying dead, hit over the head with his own steel-shafted racket. Knowing himself to be the obvious suspect, Nevil goes on the run.

What follows is a tense, brilliantly observed, psychological thriller in the vein that Martin Russell has made peculiarly his own. Suspicion darts back and forth with the speed of a ball on the squash-court. The thrilling unexpected twist in the ending is something only Martin Russell could contrive.

### Dummy Run
July 1989

Married to a successful TV chat show presenter, and herself a promising novelist, Rachel Roper seemed to have everything going for her, until one day a telephone call shattered her peace of mind.

The vague threat seemed aimed at her husband, and when Rachel pursued it further, her worst fears were confirmed. A past indiscretion had laid him open to blackmail, and now the sharks were coming back for a second bite…one that only she could avert, by

placing herself in danger of criminal charges.

Loyally she went through with it, obeying the blackmailers' demands, only to find herself at the sharp end of a Customs and police investigation, which threatened her record, her career and her custody of five-year-old Jonathan, the son whom she and her husband adored.

Desperate to keep him, Rachel became locked in a nightmare struggle with those nearest to her – until the moment when chance opened her eyes to the reality of the situation and no longer the dummy, she was able to fight back.

### House Arrest
November 1988

She was old and frail and lived alone, and when they came and told her her roof needed repairing she believed them. She even believed them when they told her it would cost much more than the estimate and they had to have cash down. How could she help believing, when they had taken hostage the most precious thing she had?

It wasn't the end. For her great-niece it was the beginning of a do-it-yourself detective job; dissatisfied with police progress in what had become a murder investigation, the young woman begin making inquiries of her own. Aided by a journalist friend, she uncovered evidence which left her in no doubt of the identity of the criminals, but proof was something else. From do-it-yourself detection to do-it-yourself justice seemed a small step – but it had momentous consequences.

Martin Russell excels at tense domestic situations and ordinary settings for bizarre acts. Here he is at his best, and readers will be riveted by his dramatic unfolding of events.

### Hunt to a Kill
October 1969

Harry Minch is on the run. After he discovers the body of a stabbed girl, the police suspect him, question him, arrest him. Recognizing the blackness of the case against him, Harry makes a break for freedom – and the hunt is up.

From a hide-out of comparative safety, Harry narrates the course of his escape. The mental and physical strain of being an Ishmael with every man's hand against him is graphically portrayed. Only one person believes in him – and to shield her Harry places his own future in jeopardy. With every other encounter – whether with a farmer and his wife, a crowd of teenagers, or his former landlady – Harry finds himself in an even more damning position than before. He is convinced he knows the identity of the mass murderer who is terrorizing the district, but can he prove it before the police net closes in? The final savage psychological twist must be left for the reader to discover. This is Martin Russell's fourth and best thriller yet.

### Leisure Pursuit
July 1993

The funny little couple on holiday in the Mediterranean were obvious targets of a con man – especially as they made no secret of the information that they had just won a huge cash prize in a newspaper contest.

Sure enough, the shark soon rose to the bait. Local 'entrepreneur' Franklin Hooper lost no time in convincing the naïve pair that they should put money into a leisure centre which he claimed to be planning for a site in the Cyprus hills. This worried two of their fellow hotel guests, Giles Badleigh and his new-found friend, Clare Scott, who did their utmost to dissuade the couple from parting with their cash.

What Giles and Clare could not foresee

was that their efforts would lead to an attempt on their lives, and finally to a social expedition that that turned into a nightmare when the ghost of EOKA – the terrorist campaign to secure union with Greece in the 1950s – was invoked in a bid to avenge injustice. In the end, justice was achieved, though not exactly in the manner intended …

### Mr T
January 1977

John Tiverton, senior physicist, returned home from work, opened his own front door – and encountered a wall of blankness. His wife and children did not know him, insisting he had died in a car crash six months before. A neighbour when summoned was equally uncompromising and tried to have him thrown out. Next day, when he sought help from his colleagues in the laboratory, they too insisted Tiverton was dead.

But if he was so anxious to prove his identity as Tiverton, why did he instinctively give the name Charles Thomas when booking into a small hotel? Why did the freelance scientist Charles Thomas seem like an *alter ego*? What if he were really Thomas, hired to investigate the brilliant Tiverton to cover up for something sinister? Was the real Mr T. the one against whom there was a conspiracy to pronounce him dead, or the one who, having assumed another's identity, was unable to regain his own?

Mr T.'s efforts to establish himself as one or other led him into chilling danger and a thrilling across-London chase before he broke through to a convincing explanation. But was it convincing? Martin Russell has achieved a *tour de force* of characterization and a plot of uncanny brilliance which will keep the reader guessing till the last page.

### Murder By the Mile
November 1975

The new road through a Highland glen made necessary by the presence of offshore oil, might bring economic prosperity to the region, but it spelled ruin to the privately owned ferry across the loch which the McCulloch family had profitably operated for years. It would also disrupt an area of great natural beauty, and local conservationists, spearheaded by the Friends of Fur and Feather, were clamorously up in arms. There was plenty of material for the in-depth story that reporter Kim Larkin had travelled north to do.

He arrived just in time to witness an act of sabotage, and learned that it was not the first. Those opposed to the road were prepared to take extreme measures to prevent its completion, and they appeared to have help from within the on-site construction team itself. Soon there was murder, and Larkin, who began asking too many awkward questions, was the area's most unwanted man – except by young Vanessa Lockerbie, a local girl whose determination to become a journalist like him brooked no discouragement, not even that of finding her life at risk.

### Mystery Lady
August 1992

Striving to make a go of a village teashop after his previous career had come to a unscheduled halt, Paul Hunt seemed to be making fair progress – until a series of unwelcome events threw him off track.

Chief among them was his discovery of a murder. The victim was the Mystery Lady of Prior's Farm, who turned out to be something more than an old acquaintance, and while Paul was not exactly heartbroken by her demise, it certainly raised complications for him, especially when the murder weapon was

found in his vehicle, bearing his fingerprints.

Meanwhile, strange noises at his cottage were giving him sleepless nights, and to cap it all, his teashop was raided and vandalised, without apparent motive. Another puzzle hung over the sudden interest in the work of a young local artist whom Paul was trying to promote. Soon he was floundering in a morass of investigation that was finally to threaten his life and unveil the secrets surrounding the Mystery Lady.

### No Return Ticket
September 1966

It is night and Megson is on the Brighton train. In his briefcase he finds banknotes worth £7,000. This is incomprehensible to Megson; but he remembers his job as an accountant to a firm of architects and he remembers his suburban home, his wife Moira and his small daughter Susan. He doesn't know what he's doing on the train with the money.

The circumstances now enfolding Megson develop ever more strangely. Even when he regains his senses, to find himself and his family gravely menaced, it remains impossible to discover what has happened and why. Catastrophe overtakes the Megsons before the end.

In a novel of suspense that is gripping, vivid and very unusual Martin Russell provides a fine successor to his first novel. *No Through Road* was welcomed with widespread and enthusiastic praise from the critics, and extracts from reviews will be found on the back of this wrapper. *No Return Ticket* is equally brilliant and will hold the reader spellbound through the complex ramifications of a plot that is baffling, tense and mysterious.

### No Through Road
November 1965

Arthur Whitlock is driving north. He handles the car with high concentration – desperation almost. His eyes register in magnified detail the sights of the highway: the traffic, the road-signs, the roundabouts and lay-bys, the great articulated lorries, the midland towns. Evidently Whitlock is escaping – is terrified.

What is Whitlock escaping from? Is it a crime? Or does the crime lie in the future, an inevitable concomitant, as Whitlock sees it, to his escape? Or is there perhaps no crime at all? Certainly Whitlock's narrative does not reveal him as a particularly stable character.

The development of this novel is ingenious and subtle. When Whitlock's affairs become the business of a devious police officer (Detective Inspector Noel Kirk of the Edinburgh police) a very unusual battle of wits ensues. The characters are ambitious and credible, the story is convincing and surprising. Martin Russell's first novel establishes him as a crime novelist of high sophistication and promise.

### Phantom Holiday
August 1974

The small Devonshire hotel where reporter Jim Larkin arrived to spend an out-of-season holiday was quiet – too quiet. In perfect order, with beds made up, tables laid, a turkey stuffed ready for the oven but empty of staff and guests. No one in the village knew what had become of the proprietor and his wife and the girl who worked for them. When their disappearance persisted and the nationals got on to it, it was soon headlined as 'the *Marie Celeste* on dry land'.

Was it a publicity stunt, designed to revive a dwindling tourist trade? The local police seemed to think so and implied that Larkin was in on the act. The owners of the rival hotel also seemed suspect. Were they in collusion or had rivalry flared into something worse? It was left to Larkin, with his reporter's instinct, to probe the mystery more deeply – almost to the point of losing his life. Martin Russell's talent for the thrillingly unexpected has seldom been better displayed.

### *Prime Target*
December 1985

Lionel Pitt, advertisement manager of a do-it-yourself magazine, led a quiet life. Separated from his wife, with a divorce pending, he returned at nights to the company of his dog and the meal cooked for him by his daily housekeeper. A pleasant, humdrum routine.

The first time someone addressed him as Spencer, he thought it was a mistake, or due to the caller's eccentricity. But when people in his daily life began doing it – barmaids, business associates, ticket collectors, pub acquaintances – Lionel Pitt became alarmed. He knew no one of the name of Spencer. Nor did he know of any reason why he should be chosen for this insidious disorientation campaign.

Then the campaign stepped up, but Pitt still resisted, clinging to his identity. When he at last discovered the motives behind his victimization, they were no less incredible than the name of the perpetrators and the nature of their prime target.

### *Rainblast*
February 1982

Mike Willoughby, investigative journalist with a national paper, was on the threshold of the greatest exposé of his career. He had uncovered evidence that the death in a car crash of the able and hawkish Minister of Defence was not the accident it appeared.

Then, suddenly, Mike found himself muzzled – and by the most effective means anyone could have devised. More bewildering still, he was told on the highest authority that the Minister was not what he seemed. True, he had successfully negotiated the British purchase of Rainblast, the highly effective American anti-missile system, but his reasons for doing so were as suspect as his death.

Forced to accede to the pressure put upon him, Mike persevered privately none the less in a world where suddenly he could trust nothing and no one – not even his own sanity. Especially when he realized what really lay behind the purchase of Rainblast, and the desperate action he must take.

Martin Russell, former journalist, knows Mike Willoughby's world all too well. In the latest of his expertly crafted crime stories he brings it vividly to life.

### *Search for Sara, The*
July 1983

One summer morning middle-aged Sara Brent walked out of her pleasant suburban home and didn't return. Her husband and two teenage daughters were immediately concerned. So were the police, though their concern was manifestly whether Ralph Brent might know more about his wife's disappearance than he professed. In fact, Ralph had ample motive for wanting his marital freedom, and it may have been preoccupations of this kind that made him fail to recognize a photograph of Sara which his daughters claimed was a good likeness, and to swear that a cut-off telephone message was not her voice. But he continued to protest complete ignorance regarding her whereabouts and the police enquiries seemed to make no headway.

Then, as a direct result of Sara's disappearance, Ralph was involved in what was indisputably murder. Once again he escaped being charged, but suspicion about Sara built up at home and at work.

With dramatic suddenness the picture changed. It looked as though Ralph could again breathe easily. But readers of Martin Russell's suspense novels know better than to anticipate. A series of startling twists brings the story to a violent climax, which once more demonstrates his mastery of the unexpected.

### *Second Time Is Easy, The*
September 1987

Murder is easy – or so Simon Pettifer discovered when he killed the mistress who was threatening to break up his marriage. He even found it surprisingly easy to dispose of her body. As for his wife, all she had to do was keep silent. Polly Gathercole had effectively disappeared.

Of course the police made inquiries, spurred on by Polly's brother, but Simon was ready for them. There was no suspicion in the supermarket where he and Polly worked as manager and till supervisor respectively that their relationship was more than it appeared. Simon agreed that Polly had visited him and his wife socially on the evening of her disappearance, but claimed she had left under her own steam. There was no reason to disbelieve him. Her car was back in her garage; her handbag and its contents unmarked and back in her flat. Even when the police showed interest in the foundations of the home extension the Pettifers were having erected, Simon retained his cool.

It was only later that he lost it, and in circumstances so bizarre that it was understandable if he thought murder the second time was easy. Unfortunately for him, it was not.

### *Touchdown*
August 1979

There was something odd about the airport. Julian Phillips was aware of it from the start. He had arrived early one morning to meet his wife returning from her annual visit to her mother in Boston. And found check-in desks unmanned, flights cancelled, and escalators at a standstill. Questioned about the airport's deserted air, the manager babbled of a sudden walk-out, but Julian knew better than that. And then the plane from Boston was re-routed. And delayed. And delayed again.

Julian was not a journalist for nothing. He soon worked out that this must be because an American VIP was aboard. Threats to kidnap him had been made. But far from avoiding the trap the man was flying straight into it. For the airport was in the hands of terrorists. And at risk with him were all the other passengers, including Julian's wife. Julian had to think fast and act faster, for already the first victim lay dead.

Not since *Mr T*, which Graham Lord in the *Sunday Express* called 'a triumph of trickery, cunning and imagination', has Martin Russell been in such form. Graham Lord found that *Mr T* 'developed with such mounting tension and bewilderment, with a series of shattering twists and surprises, that I found it unputdownable.' Readers of *Touchdown* will find the same.

## RUTHERFORD, DOUGLAS

### *Black Leather Murders, The*
January 1966

The wastes of the *Garrigue* in the South of France are forbidding and inhospitable. Two young men and their girlfriends, touring in an old London taxi, found themselves stranded and set camp in the evening by headlights. Their chosen site was beside a remote Dolmen, a prehistoric monument that dominated the bleak countryside: a place of ill-repute among the locals who knew more of its past than the four campers.

By next morning the whole party, their taxi and all their equipment had vanished completely from the face of the earth.

Deputed later to search for the missing party when the police failed was Jay Delany, a free-lance. Even before Delany could reach the *Garrigue* he became a witness to – and a suspect for – the brutal murder on the Colnbrook by-pass.

But in the *Garrigue* Delany learnt that he was investigating something more than a single savage murder. From his base in the sumptuous, fantastic setting of the Hostelerie de la Fontaine he uncovered a deep-plotted conspiracy involving the fate of nations.

This is an adventure novel with a credible, powerful and original plot. Its setting is authentic and nightmarish. It is even more exciting than Douglas Rutherford's earlier books *Grand Prix Murder* and *The Creeping Flesh*.

### *Clear the Fast Lane*
July 1971

Fasten your seat-belts for the most hair-raising trip of your life – three thousand miles at breakneck speeds over the motorways of Europe.

Racing and rally driver Grant Callaway took the job because the starting money was good and the challenge was one that matched his mood and frustration and despair. All he had to do, he thought, was drive three strangely assorted passengers to Greece – thirty hours out, thirty hours back. No problem about freight – just a plain wooden box a little over two foot square.

But within the confined space of a GT car averaging a hundred miles an hour tensions between three men and a girl can build up to flash-point. As the break-neck journey proceeds, one question begins to hammer at Grant's mind: what does the box in the luggage boot contain?

The answer to that question is enough to cause mayhem in Thessalonika and a marathon car chase in which Grant has to throw off not only the most fanatical of criminals but also the police of five countries. And by this time he's doing it not so much to save his own life and earn the reward as for Sariya, the enchanting and mysterious Arabian girl who has become the key to the whole plot.

This is the story of three men, a woman and – a car. Indeed, the AC 428, with its voluptuous form and spitfire temperament, bids fair to steal the story. Douglas Rutherford, well-known for his expertise on motor-racing, has now surpassed himself in describing racing speeds on open roads.

### *Creeping Flesh, The*
May 1963

Tom Brennan, aged twenty-one, flew from Canada to Paris to try to find his younger brother who had disappeared there. He quickly discovered that Chris had fallen into some very unwholesome company, and had done things that did not make sense to one who had known him well and loved him. The search for Chris leads Tom into an underworld of drug addiction and drug trafficking in Paris. On the one hand Tom meets the customers, fast decaying mentally and physically in the grip of heroin or lesser brews; on the other hand are the dealers and distributors – men to whom heroin only spells money, who cannot afford to be detected or even suspected, who regard murder as a commonplace of their inhuman trade. The trade in narcotics is the source of conflict, suspense and action in many a crime novel – but this one is different. Here a cold realism is used to display all the horrific aspects of addiction to drugs – the squalid details of injection, the crazy euphoria that follows, the degrading and corrupting reaction. And these are not mere back-ground effects but an integral part of a most unusual and unbearably exciting story.

### *Gilt-Edged Cockpit, The*
October 1969

***'Only three people realised it at the time but the takeover battle for Mascot Motors, which as to oust labour disputes, famine and war form the front pages of the British press. Began just a quarter of an hour before the start of the Luxembourg Grand Prix'***

This is a story of conflict, tension and violence on three planes: high finance, motor racing and sex. City men battle for control of the Crawford family firm of Mascot Motors; drivers fight it out on the international racing circuit; two men contend for the love of a beautiful woman. In all three contests no holds are barred. For ace driver Patrick Crawford life suddenly becomes more hazardous, more dangerous, for on his skill and daring depend not only the result of a Formula One Grand Prix, but the lives and fortunes of many men.

At the same time he has to steer his way through the snares of a financier's jungle and grapple with the investigation of two closely linked murders of Mascot stockholders – murders from which he would appear to benefit greatly…

Douglas Rutherford's expertise on the motor-racing scene has led one reviewer to call him 'the Whyte Melville of the open throttle'. In this story he provides an equally authentic close-up of London's 'City', with its ruthless financiers, merchant bankers, and tycoons who will stop at nothing to get what they want.

### *Grand Prix Murder*
February 1955

Here is the authentic atmosphere of continental motor-racing, its danger and menace, its heart-stopping thrills and fabulous spectacle. From the opening, when young Martin Templer is about to drive for the first time in a continental race – the Mondano Grand Prix – until the sensational climax at the end of the Allure Grand Prix the reader will be gripped by this story.

Martin himself, his co-drivers, the other members of the Dayton team and the two young women who accompany it, are put in a terrible position: to the ordinary hazards of Grand Prix racing is added the tension of knowing that a murderer is in their midst, waiting to strike and strike again.

Douglas Rutherford's new novel moves with the speed of the swift machines that play so big a part in it. The murderer is unveiled and the final climax resolved in as strange and exciting a manner as any reader could wish.

### *Kick Start*
September 1973

'Sometimes when I look back on the whole thing I wonder whether the methods I used were nothing more than an excuse. That's what Kareth believed anyway. She maintained that my real motive in stealing the Eiger Diamond lay in the secrecy, the danger and the instruments of speed on which my plan depended.'

The instrument which Kroll chose was the Norton Commando motor-cycle and this is the scorching story of a man and his mount. Kroll thought he had brought off the perfect crime and made a clean getaway. But his plan went wrong and he was forced to barter his freedom and, as an 'agent for Interpol', to attempt the most hair-raising feat ever undertaken on a motor-cycle.

Kroll was a loner with only his bike for company till he met Kareth, 'the most sexually attractive woman outside a harem'. And Kareth made him break the oath he had sworn – never again to trust a woman.

### Long Echo, The
March 1957

In this book Douglas Rutherford ventures into an older world than the one he has described in contemporary thrillers such as *Grand Prix Murder*. In Torrealto, a mountain town in Northern Italy, violence was brewing, born of old feuds, long memories, a savage history and a fierce climate. Andrew Carson believed that it was his destiny to make amends for a wrong done four hundred years earlier, when a beautiful girl had committed suicide after being forsaken by her lover. He felt a strange affinity for this girl as she was portrayed on the central panel of an ancient triptych.

Yet Andrew's every action only precipitated disaster, a brutal murder was committed – a murder for which Andrew himself had a demonstrable motive.

Douglas Rutherford's new novel tells a moving story of love against the brooding atmosphere of Torrealto; and of a crime to which the mountains themselves seemed secret accomplices. From its haunting start till the exciting climax the reader will be gripped by this strange and compelling story.

### Murder Is Incidental
April 1961

The daily ferry-boat was Rio Diana's only link with the rest of Italy. The village had lived at peace with itself and the outer world for centuries. That was why Cary Lassiter had chosen it as a retreat in which he could work and live – and forget. The tentacles of evil arrived with the graceful white yacht *Minerva*, which brought Franco Spadoni on a legal but merciless quest for wealth and power.

*Murder is Incidental* is set against an Italian background of great beauty and has its roots in reality. When the morals and methods of twentieth-century commerce were applied to Rio Diana the results were far-reaching. Greed, fear and bewilderment created an explosive mixture and Cary Lassiter was forced to take part, forced to recognise that his private haven was vulnerable, and to involve himself in a situation which was charged with tension and the threat of public and private violence.

With this book Douglas Rutherford has matched the appeal acclaimed in *The Long Echo*. As the story unfolds, the reader sees the spectre of wickedness emerge in the idyllic Mediterranean port to provide a gripping situation in which murder is incidental. It is a remarkable crime story, written with striking power and insight.

### Mystery Tour
July 1975

The tour was billed as Cities and Lakes of Italy, and the small group of passengers who assembled at Gatwick Airport was as diverse as their pretty courier had come to expect. But when, after a four hours' delay, Flight 327 finally took off for a round of civic and scenic beauties, one of the passengers was missing and the remainder were accompanied by an unseen, unknown additional traveller whose presence was to be felt more than once during the week-long trip to Venice, Padua, Verona, Milan and the Italian Lakes. The unlisted passenger was Death.

Beginning with the violent drama of

an arrest and escape at Gatwick, Douglas Rutherford portrays the tension which builds up among a group of holiday-makers as they come to realise that the disasters which attend their tour are not haphazard. Someone in the group is bent on murder. And only the killer knows whether the victims are struck down at random or whether a terrifying selectivity is at work.

### Perilous Sky, The
January 1956

Two disasters involving the latest type of air liners had jeopardised the future of British Skylines. Within a few hours of his appointment as a roving Security Officer, Barney Finnegan was plunging towards the Mediterranean from 15,000 feet in a burning machine. From that moment on he is whirled into a kaleidoscopic sequence of dangers that switches from the Balearic Islands to the Sahara and back to Algiers. The peril is the more real because the story is set against the authentic background of airline operations and because Barney's growing admiration for Simone, the air hostess, makes him realise that for him more is at stake than the twenty million pound air fleet. The world of commercial flying is here portrayed as vividly as was the business of motor racing in Douglas Rutherford's *Grand Prix Murder*.

### Return Load
February 1977

When Bob Chester set out for the toe of Italy with Sally and Josie in the sleeper cab of his 30-ton lorry it seemed like a family excursion. But Cardona and his associates needed just such a lorry. They also needed its crew. And there was one sure way of getting Bob and Sally's co-operation for a return load, as it was called.

If the life of your only child is at stake, how far will you go? What hardships and exhaustions will you suffer? What degradations will you accept? And when, compared with that one life, nothing else in the world matters, is there anyone you can count as your friend? Bob and Sally learnt the answers to these questions on the next 2000 miles.

The background Douglas Rutherford has chosen for his latest story is the world of the transcontinental lorries, the juggernauts bearing the TIR sign and the warning Long Vehicle. The action thunders along the great motoring highways of Europe, across frontiers, the searchlight headlamps turning night into day. This is a tense and human drama of a man and a woman in the cab of a long-distance lorry whose only thought is to meet the desperate deadline that will keep their child alive.

### Shriek of Tyres, A
April 1958

*The first four cars reached 100 m.p.h. in eight seconds. At the first bend Dan saw a wedge of projectiles leaping towards him, got a confused impression of storming engines, squealing rubber, a kaleidoscope of green, red, silver and blue and then they were past him.'*

Gerry Clinton, in the front rank of racing drivers, and signed to drive with the Romealfa works team, found himself racing under a sinister handicap. Anonymous letters were delivered to him in various ways – written and timed to undermine his confidence and nerve. The notorious and appalling crash during the Grand Prix d'Europe left him to face a grotesque official enquiry – and his most vital evidence had disappeared.

At Silverstone, Le Mans, Monaco and during the Mille Miglia, the story unfolds at racing speed. Readers of *The Chequered*

*Flag* will know that Douglas Rutherford's knowledge and experience of motor racing is first hand and authentic. *Grand Prix Murder* showed how effectively he is able to use his knowledge as a background to his Crime Club books.

*A Shriek of Tyres* will be welcomed as a vivid and exciting addition to his work.

### Skin for Skin
July 1968

'Last year 46,371 cars were unlawfully taken and driven away in the Metropolitan Police area alone. That represents, on an average, one car theft for every ten minutes of the day.'

Linda Campbell was a little too observant for her own good. When a car was stolen from outside the house where she lived, she was enough to be able to identify the thieves. But the car theft was only the prelude to a much more daring crime.

This is the story of that crime, its preparation, its execution and its unpredictable consequences. It is also a brilliant analysis of the effects of tension upon the three main characters – Crispin, the ex-RAF pilot, embittered with society, who believes he has planned the perfect robbery; Jerry, the young accomplice whom Crispin thinks he can mould to his own purposes; and Linda, the girl who must be disposed of because she has seen too much. But Linda is no ordinary girl, and it is her effect, different and dangerous, upon each of the two men that precipitates the tragic conclusion.

Douglas Rutherford is already well known for his novels with motor-racing and Mediterranean background, here for the first time his story is set in England, and in it he achieves a degree of subtlety which, combined with the suspense of a planned crime going wrong, makes this his best novel yet. This is a suspense-packed story with finely-drawn characters, a credible predicament and a totally unexpected ending.

## RYCK, FRANCIS
### Account Rendered
September 1975

Daniel earns a precarious livelihood from cruises aboard the motor-yacht, of which he is skipper and owner. His crew consists of his ten-year-old daughter, Natasha, a none too enthusiastic stewardess, and his friend, Nick, who combines the duties of seaman, engineer, and cook. Daniel's almost obsessional affection for his boat leads him to jump at the offer of an extremely lucrative five-year charter, which will enable him to carry out some badly needed repairs and instal the latest navigational aids, despite Nick's conviction that there is something phoney about the set-up.

Nick's suspicions prove to be well-founded. What promises to be a pleasant cruise to Majorca ends in violence and murder and the ensuing events on land turn out to be even more traumatic for the three members of the crew. The story moves swiftly from Antibes to Paris, Versailles, London, Aix and finally a barren waste in the mountains of southern France. As usual, Francis Ryck can be counted on to provide an ironic and unpredictable denouement.

### Green Light, Red Catch
September 1972

It takes a lot of imagination and ingenuity to plan the abduction of an important Russian scientist holidaying at a Black Sea resort. To carry out the operation in full view of suspicious guards and Soviet naval patrols requires a lot of nerve as well.

Anyone who has read *Loaded Gun* and *Woman Hunt* will have no doubts about

Francis Ryck's ability to handle such a coup and keep the reader on tenterhooks.

The agent entrusted with the task of abducting the Russian scientist is an Englishman. The story opens in London, moves to Russia, Israel, Switzerland and France, gathering momentum all the time.

As a master plotter Francis Ryck has few peers. He is already acknowledged as one of France's leading thriller writers.

### Loaded Gun
September 1971

After Yako, a Russian agent, is caught red-handed by British Intelligence while collecting a message from a 'dead-letter' box in North London, he is offered a deal: freedom, a false passport and £10,000 in return for detailed information about his network – or else… Yako collaborates, but insists on being given a revolver as well.

Yako proceeds to Paris as Henry Forstal, a British travelling salesman. Soon, despite all the elaborate precautions to be expected from a professional agent, the hunt is on. Yako, now joined by a faithful mongrel dog, makes his way across France to Spain, on to Ibiza and back to the mainland – always, quite inexplicably, followed by his pursuers. Ironically, Yako is the last to learn the reason why…

Rarely has there been such an ingeniously plotted manhunt told from the point of view of the hunted.

It is with pleasure that the Crime Club introduces France's leading thriller writer to English readers. Francis Ryck's *Loaded Gun* won the *Grand Prix du Roman Policier* in 1970.

### Sacrificial Pawn
May 1973

What happens when a secret agent becomes contemptuous of his profession and decides the game is not worth the candle? This is the theme of Francis Ryck's latest thriller, which centres on Sern, French counter-espionage agent, who deliberately disobeys orders to kill a KGB agent who is on a mission to France to induce a high official in the Foreign Office to defect.

Flushed with success, Sern boldly sees to it that further missions are aborted in places as far apart as Copenhagen and Leipzig. But it is only a matter of time before his superiors get on to the fact that their trusted agent is in fact playing a lone hand. When the Russians also get on to it, Sern feels the jaws of the pincers closing in.

Only when he discovers that the Russian agent shadowing him feels as he does, does he perceive a chance of escape. The action swings neatly between Sern and his various pursuers. Will he escape before the pincers close?

### Undesirable Company
June 1974

When David and Julia offer the quiet, unassuming stranger the hospitality of their French mountain retreat, they never dream that within forty-eight hours the three of them will be fleeing towards the coast in a desperate effort to evade some mysterious pursuers or alleged pursuers. For if what the stranger said to them was true, they were now in the same deadly jeopardy as he was. Unfortunately for David and Julia there was no safe way of finding out. Even sabotage and a sudden death brought no enlightenment, and nothing could be taken to be what it seemed. When the nightmarish suspense finally grows too much for her, Julia decides to act on her own … producing a denouement as ironical as it is startling.

Once again Francis Ryck displays his virtuosity as the contriver of original and ironical thrillers.

### Woman Hunt
April 1972

When Kola returns to Paris after having expertly handled a job of vital industrial espionage on behalf of a Foreign Power with an extensive network in France, he finds that intense police activity prevents him for 'delivering the goods' and returning home to his wife, Dominique. Instead he has to hole up in the flat of his contact – Francoise. Dominique, who knows nothing of her husband's secret activities, is worried. Worry gives way to suspicion, suspicion to desperation. Feminine intuition, the indiscretion of a friend, and coincidence lead Dominique to her husband's hideout.

As far as the Press is concerned, what follows is just another *crime passionel*. But the Network cannot afford to take chances. Whether Dominique knows or not, she must be eliminated – as are others, ruthlessly. And so the Woman Hunt is on. Foreign agents after Dominique, the police after Dominique and the secret agents, right across France, down to the Mediterranean. In this fast-moving, expertly plotted story in which Francis Ryck describes the new French police system of 'encirclement', he amply defends his title of France's No. 1 crime writer.

## SATTERTHWAIT, WALTER
### At Ease With the Dead
April 1991

When Daniel Begay hires Joshua Croft to find someone, it's not a standard missing-persons case. The silver-haired, distinguished, and more than slightly mysterious Indian wants Joshua to return the lost remains of a Navajo leader, dead nearly one hundred years, to their proper burial site.

Soon Croft is hurtling his trusty Subaru across the South-West, from Santa Fe to El Paso to remote corners of a Navajo reservation, unearthing long-buried hostilities and reviving the mystery of an unsolved, unforgotten murder.

Relying on his unique blend of low-key humour, hard-won street smarts, and a familiarity with bar-room etiquette, Croft uncovers a trail of greed and murder that is as thick as oil and as deeply buried as an archaeological find.

Very different from the author's previous novel, *Miss Lizzie*, which brought a 'rumour-buzzing, small-minded community pungently to life' (*Sunday Times*), Walter Satterthwait's new novel confirms him as a mystery writer of the first rank.

### Death Card, The
March 1994

Quentin Bouvier, a magician and possible reincarnated Egyptian pharaoh, is found hanging from the rafters while attending a New Age healing convention. During the investigations it comes to light that a priceless antique tarot card has been stolen from his room and it seems that the person who holds the card is also the murderer.

When Giacomo Bernardi a tarot reader, is put under arrest, his public defender hires Joshua Croft to prove his innocence. As Croft struggles to find the truth he is brought face to face with the alternative world of healers in Santa Fe. The suspects include: an ageing movie star who acts as a medium for an entity from Alpha Centuri; a Native American shaman who puts accountants in touch with the warrior within; a young hermit involved in 'spiritual alchemy'; a ravishing, mysterious Asian woman who possesses a strange and compelling power and whose fiercely protective brother displays a near-lethal familiarity with martial arts.

The closer Croft comes to a solution the more he risks entering another dimension sooner than he planned.

### Flower in the Desert, A
December 1992

One year ago, Melissa Alonzo accused her ex-husband, television star Roy Alonzo, of sexually abusing their young daughter. Now, after a vicious court battle over custody of the child, mother and child have disappeared, and Roy wants Santa Fe private investigator Joshua Croft to find them both, clear his name, and save his career.

Following a trail from plush Beverly Hills estates to a small farming commune in the remote New Mexico mountains, Croft discovers that Melissa's true identity is as much a mystery as her whereabouts. Is she a courageous, self-denying mother trying to protect her daughter? A dedicated political activist? Or a bored housewife with a taste for kinky sex?

Compelling suspense, taut and entertaining mystery, make *A Flower in the Desert* a complex and totally absorbing tour de force.

### Miss Lizzie
May 1990

Lizzie Borden strikes again. Or does she?

The year is 1921 and a generation has passed since the brutal murders in Fall River of Andrew Borden and his wife – murders for which their daughter, Lizzie, was tried and acquitted, although the entire nation believes her guilty.

During her summer vacation along the Massachusetts shore, young Amanda Burton befriends her elderly next-door neighbour – the notorious Lizzie Borden. But when Amanda finds her stepmother brutally axe-murdered, her secure world is instantly turned upside down. The police are certain they know the culprit: Miss Lizzie, especially as the savage crime bears an uncanny resemblance to the Fall River slayings.

With the inquisitive spirit of a thirteen-year-old, Amanda closely monitors the investigation and looks to Miss Lizzie for support as, with the help of a hard-boiled Pinkerton man and a suave lawyer, Miss Lizzie sets out to clear her name.

Before the novel reaches its climax, Miss Lizzie's search uncovers the secrets that lie beneath the sleepy surface of a small seaside town and, whether she wills it or not, the events of that torrid August day thirty years before.

### Wilde West
February 1992

Midway through his triumphant lecture tour of the American West, the young Oscar Wilde discovers that someone in his entourage has been savagely murdering prostitutes. US Marshal Robert Grigsby – gruff, resolute, and occasionally sober – suspects Oscar. And so the flamboyant aesthete, determined to clear his name, sets out to reveal the madman's identity by what he calls 'a sympathetic application of the poetic imagination'.

Before he finally confronts the killer, Wilde conducts a passionate affair with the fiancée of the most powerful man in Colorado; samples the pleasures of opium; finds himself stalked by a brutal, bearlike buffalo hunter; and shares an occasional drink with the mysterious Doc Holliday, gunman and gambler. A tense mystery, a perverse comedy, *Wilde West* is a brilliant novel that includes, as all books should, murder, sex, insanity, cannibalism, and a herd of goats.

## SCOTT, GAVIN
### Hot Pursuit
June 1977

Being hunted by the CIA is one thing. Being hunted by the KGB is another. Begin hunted by both of them through some of the toughest terrain in the southern hemisphere with no food, maps or anything to shoot back with, looks like one of the surest ways of getting killed.

It was an attempt to bug the office of the chairman of one of Britain's biggest newspaper empires that was indirectly responsible for sending a young freelance reporter twelve thousand miles to New Zealand, where a chief executive had disappeared. Where was the connection between the bugging and the disappearance? Who was behind it? And why were the Kremlin and the White House prepared to co-operate to prevent the astounding truth from getting out – even to the extent of being prepared to silence him permanently?

As the rival forces joined in a hot pursuit raid deep into New Zealand, he and his companion found themselves against the all but impenetrable mountain country of the North Island, as well as the best trained killers the two superpowers could put up.

In his first thriller Gavin Scott builds up a sustained, spectacular and significant chase story in which the endurance and ingenuity of a handful of men are pitted against terrain and technology.

## SCOTT, JACK
### All the Pretty People
September 1983

When Detective-Inspector Alfred Stanley Rosher brought down with a flying tackle the handsome, naked, schizophrenic youth who was intent on going to his Father in Heaven direct from the rooming-house roof, he had no idea that he would meet him again four months later on the thick end of murder. And it was murder. Not a doubt of it … in the unlikely setting of the very pretty village called Hutton Fellows, where all the pretty people lived.

Well – turn the prettiest stone in the prettiest village, and something nasty leers up from underneath. Detective-Inspector Rosher found it so, as he plodded on through more murder; interviewing, eyeing sternly the surprising and often bizarre domestic activities of such well-to-do respectables as the murder victim's pious parents, the farming Wellington twins – 'such good boys,' according to their mother – and the Watson-Harvey's: Daddy, Mumsie and in particular Fiona, spoiled only child and devoted owner of a dog whose activities did not seem to merit attention any more than hers did, but received it just the same.

Rosher, the copper who gets it right in spite of doing it wrong, has built up a steady following on both sides of the Atlantic. Hardly surprising, when 'Mr. Scott adds more depth to his graceless hero with every outing,' as John Coleman said of his last book in the *Sunday Times*.

### Clutch of Vipers, A
March 1979

Detective-Sergeant Alfred Stanley Rosher had been demoted by the Force and deserted by his wife. The result was frustration in a desk job, chaos in the home, and a classified ad for domestic help in the town evening paper.

Oddly enough, on that same July day Mad Frankie Daly, who was setting up a job, also inserted a classified ad in the evening paper, designed to summon those selected for the enterprise and to warn others to stay clear.

The result of this curious coincidence was three deaths and a deal of anguish, for when Mad Frankie saw Rosher's ad, his Irish whimsy was tickled. He decided to provide his old enemy with a housekeeper with two teenage children (they were delinquents but never mind, and they weren't actually her children but never mind that either) and use them to finish off Rosher.

Unfortunately for Frankie, he couldn't foresee the consequences of introducing this highly motivated threesome into the home of a born copper (believed by his superiors to be a bent copper), whose inner man was ready to succumb to the first toothsome steak and kidney pud…

So the reader can enjoy the skilful untangling of cross and double-cross in a crime story that has both style and substance, and a rich vein of irony throughout.

### Death in Irish Town, A
July 1984

They called it Irish Town when PC Alfred Stanley Rosher walked it in his beat copper days with wary fist and beetlecrusher boots. They called it Irish Town still, when Detective Inspector Rosher came back on a sentimental journey in his boxy-toed shoes and was offered a body, all charred from a warehouse fire.

But the ambience had changed. New council estates where the old slum houses used to be, and the canal basin tarted up for tourists. And people he had known grown up, or grown old. Nothing stubs a man's mind so uncouthly against the fact of his own aging. Especially when the charred body, not even born in the old days, is grown nephew to the bolster-bosomed lady whom he remembered as a little girl, her mother the formidable Widow O'Hara, prime battler in an age of battling O'Thises and O'Thats.

He'd have retreated, and never come back; but top brass said: 'You know the area, Mr Rosher – find out about that body. You will team with Superintendent Fisk.' Now there was a man who could bend an elbow.

So Rosher went to work, probing away at the people he knew, the in-come strangers, the publicans and the sinners. And what did he find, down there by the canal? Very dark and scummy water. Very scummy indeed.

### Distant View of Death, A
January 1981

Detective-Sergeant (ex-Detective-Inspector) Alfred Stanley Rosher arrived at the police station in fine fettle: first, because he had just cracked a case, and second, because the grapevine was murmuring that he, bust down in *The Shallow Grave*\*, just might be shoved up again to fill a vacancy caused by retirement. Not even the discovery that he had been assigned to initiate a visiting American patrolman into English police procedure could dismay him for long. It took a distant view (through binoculars) to do that – for what Rosher saw was an act of violence of which no trace remained when police reached the scene. His superiors – one of them, anyway – even doubted the accuracy of his vision. Yet Rosher knew that in his manor three men in a bashed-up car had vanished. And two of them might be dead. Murdered.

Readers of previous adventures of Rosher know what to expect by now: a fast action story packed with memorable characters from high and low life (in the present instance, who could forget Mr Henry Croker, middle-aged, middle-class, devoted husband to his lady wife and receiver of stolen goods?) – all recounted with a blend of exuberance and sardonic observation which has delighted readers on both sides of the Atlantic.

\* Not a Crime Club title

### Gospel Lamb, The
February 1980

Sweltering heat. Thousands of young people converging on a pop festival, and a telephone call to press and police from the man who styles himself 'The Avenger', promising that he will be there. Grimly, the new Chief Constable and all his minions down to Charlie-on-the-beat set about the impossible task of trying to police the festival. The Avenger has kept his word on two occasions, and two girls have already died.

Reinstated thanks to this new and humane top brassman, Detective-Sergeant Alfred Stanley Rosher, his serge suit and black hat, are back in the police ranks. Like his colleagues, he's been told to turn a blind eye to the drugs scene and the sex scene and concentrate on getting The Avenger. Unfortunately, Rosher doesn't have a blind eye. The activities of mincing Donny Marks and his butch boy-friend soon attract his attention. Before long he is back in trouble. There's a dead girl in the shrubbery, the festival is cancelled, a Drugs Squad operation busted, and the local religious, here to urge repentance and respectability to the last chromosome (that goes for The Avenger, too), are being ushered on their way by apologetic police.

Only Rosher could precipitate that kind of situation. Only Rosher could retrieve it. His individual methods – not always according to the rules – have established him as one of crime fiction's 'characters', and his creator, Jack Scott, as one of the leading exponents of the fast, earthy, irreverent spare-no-one crime story.

### Knife Between the Ribs, A
November 1986

When the pleasant town where Inspector Rosher operates is en fête, which it is once a year, you don't expect a little snout to fall over sideways in a crowded pub with a knife between his ribs. Inspector Rosher certainly didn't. It was one of his snouts.

So, black hat riding low on simian brow, he set out after a killer. Being Rosher, he did it his own way. And that was the trouble. This small killing of a small man blew up – and up – until Rosher, at odds yet again with Authority and more and more cognizant of the activities of the Rev. Edgar P. Mitten's Brotherhood of Joy, teeters on the edge of an abyss which threatens to engulf him in matters better suited to Interpol, Scotland Yard, the FBI and other august bodies. Of course it would take more than that to engulf Rosher, but it's enough to get him aboard a runaway coach, along with a group of folk singers in town for the Festival, and no less than three villains, one of them canine.

There we will leave him though no reader will be able to do so. Instead, they can look forward to finding out how Rosher once again proves as durable as his blue serge suit.

### Little Darling, Dead, A
February 1985

She was dead alright, the little darling. Lying, pretty as a picture, in the turbulent water under Lover's Leap. The question was: Did she fall, or was she pushed – murdered on her roundabout way home from school.

It was up to detective Chief Inspector Pete Parsons and his oppo, Sergeant Wammo Wimbush, to find out. We cannot, the Assistant Chief Constable said, treat it as out-and-out murder. Nose about a bit, see what you can pick up.

So they did; and what they turned up

was a tangled web of nastiness spreading far beyond the simple and routine (in police terms) matter of a young girl dead in a wood. She was not so innocent, the little darling.

Nor were her friends; and some of the respectable denizens of the town were nothing to write home about either. But who would have guessed that their small-time aberrations would lead to a second and undoubted murder, and a situation international in its criminal ramifications, big enough to hit the Government where it hurts?

Jack Scott turns aside for a moment from chronicling the deeds and misdeeds of his famous Detective-Inspector Rosher to present a new detective, just as vividly human and with one comfort denied to that gorilla-like man: a plump and comely wife, whom he loves dearly.

### Local Lads, The
December 1982

Detective-Inspector Alfred Stanley Rosher is undoubtedly a man born to trouble as the sparks fly upward, but even he seemed unlikely to get into trouble while lying in a hospital bed. Of course that was before he noticed some decidedly bent-looking characters trying to visit the patient in the ward next door.

These visits were not prompted by unselfish concern. Quite the contrary: the man who lay there was the vital link between the two halves of a carefully planned jewellery heist which had gone badly wrong. The two young men hired as drivers because they had no form had lost no time in acquiring it. Now, having driven the loot to its appointed hiding-place, they had disappeared. And without the aid of the man in intensive care, none of the gang knew where to find them or it.

Failure to deliver the loot brought the big boys from the Smoke on the scene. Nor was that all the frightened locals had to contend with. Detective-Inspector Alfred Stanley Rosher, properly suspicious, had discharged himself from hospital (not without a pang at leaving his attentive nurse), and any trouble Rosher was in for was as nothing compared to what awaited the local lads.

### Uprush of Mayhem, An
January 1982

Detective-Inspector Alfred Stanley Rosher was on the up and up. Newly bounced up again from detective-sergeant (see *A Distant View of Death*), aware of being a legend in the force as the only man ever to come back from downgrading (see *The Shallow Grave\**), he was now out in the woods confronting the body of a murdered girl and preparing to take part in the investigation.

The only fly in the ointment was his new assistant, Detective-Sergeant Boggis, whom Rosher disliked. He saw him as a bombastic, rock-skulled, insensitive, ham-fisted, flat-footed copper. Which was precisely how many people saw Rosher. When Greek meets Greek … well, watch it!

It was soon established that the dead girl was maid at a house the police were interested in. And not only the police. A gang of villains were interested in it too. Or rather, in its contents. Only murder hadn't been any part of their plan, any more than were the deaths that followed. It was when it came to the funeral that they felt they came into their own.

Whether they did the reader will delight in discovering, for Jack Scott is one of the most original writers in the genre. 'The excitement is immediate, continuous and imaginative,' said *The New Yorker*, reviewing a recent Rosher novel. You can say that again. And again.

\* Not a Crime Club title

## SEDLEY, KATE
### Death and the Chapman
October 1991

England 1471, and war between the Yorkist and Lancastrian factions still rages. But for the man in the street, everyday existence goes on: birth, marriage, death – especially death. Roger, a young man who has recently quit monastic life for the freedom of the open road, peddling his wares from town to town, is caught up in the mysterious disappearance of Clement Weaver, only son of a wealthy Bristol merchant. And Clement is not the only person who has vanished without trace from the Crossed Hands Inn in London. There are others …

Roger's interest is aroused and he determines to find out what happened to them; a decision which leads to an extraordinary discovery, linking him with the highest in the land, and puts him in grave danger from an unexpected source.

### Plymouth Cloak, The
September 1992

When, in the autumn of 1473, Philip Underdown, a Royal Messenger carrying an important letter from King Edward IV to Duke Francis of Brittany, is murdered at the Cornish manor of Trenowth, the finger of suspicion points at Roger the Chapman, whose cudgel – or 'Plymouth Cloak' – is the undoubted murder weapon. Worse still, Roger had been entrusted by no less a person than the King's brother, Richard, Duke of Gloucester, with the task of conveying Underdown safely aboard his ship.

Fortunately for Roger, the finger of suspicion points in more than one direction. In faction-torn England, Underdown might have been killed by a Lancastrian or Woodville agent. Or by a jealous husband. Or by an old friend who now bears him a grudge.

In his second tale, Roger must once again use all his deductive powers in order to unmask the culprit and uncover a grotesque evil from the past.

## SEELEY, MABEL
### Beckoning Door, The
August 1950

Mabel Seeley will be remembered as the talented author of *The Listening House*, *The Chuckling Fingers* and *Eleven Come Back*, All fine examples of her craftsmanship. Her new book offers a convincing study of a woman caught in a net and battling to escape. Cathy Kingsman is living in the small American town of Long Meadow, outwardly happy and contented but inwardly seething in revolt at the circumstances which bind her to a life of boredom, bound to a job with no past and no future, bound by debt to her mortgaged house, bound by duty to her crippled mother – and in love with a man she could not hope to marry. What manner of escape was there from all this? A sudden violent death shows Cathy the gateway to freedom, but for a while it looks as if she will exchange one prison for another.

### Chuckling Fingers, The
January 1942

A new book by Mabel Seeley is a great event in the world of mystery fiction. With only three books she has risen to the top as far as both readers and critics are concerned. In *The Chuckling Fingers* she presents the story of the weird and strange events which beset the Heaton family at their remote, pine-grown estate on Lake Superior. But let Mabel Seeley introduce her story herself: 'Other people may think they'd like to live their lives over, but not me – not if this last week is going to

be in it. Out of what has just happened at the Fingers both Jacqueline and I got something worth keeping, but Heaven defend me from ever again having to stand helplessly by while it becomes more and more apparent to almost every one but me that the person I love most in the world is murderously insane … I never again want to know the panic of being up against evil coming out of a mind so much more skilful than mine that even the signs we did see – the acid in a bride's toilet kit, the burned matchsticks under a bed, the word scrawled with a child's blue chalk on a rock – all just bogged us deeper in terror and despair …' Mabel Seeley's story of that 'terror and despair' will be one of the outstanding mysteries of the year.

### Crying Sisters, The
May 1940

Mabel Seeley looks like achieving certain stardom with *The Crying Sisters*, a really superb mystery story that grips right from its opening lines: 'I still pinch myself and say it isn't true. I still wake at night to reach for the tangible proof within touch of my hand. If any one should say to me, "Those things didn't really happen to you last summer; they're just part of some story you've read", I'd probably have dazed moments of wondering if I couldn't distinguish between reality and fiction any more.' This remarkable and dramatic story of a girl librarian's adventures on the first vacation she had taken without her mother is not only an exciting detective story but a splendid piece of writing, with characters and situations that you can't forget.

### Eleven Came Back
September 1943

Mabel Seeley, whose rapid rise to the front rank of American mystery writers has been phenomenal, presents a new novel with the wild and sometimes malevolent beauty of the mountains of Wyoming as a background. The Lady Luck ranch is owned by the wealthy and ambitious Mrs. Parent, who likes to entertain her guests on her vast Western estate. One night, twelve persons set out to enjoy a moonlight ride in the mountains – and the title tells what to expect. Mabel Seeley's story is studded with dramatic incidents, excellent characterisation, lots of suspense, and the definite Seeley mark in style.

### Listening House, The
March 1939

'I am not sure myself,' (says the narrator of this story) 'that I should open the door of Mrs. Garr's house, and let you in. I'm not at all sure that the truth of what happened there is tellable. People keep telling me that the rumours going round are simply ghoulish, and ought to be laid. But I've heard those rumours, some of them at least, and they're not a bit more nightmarish than the truth.

'Finally, or course, I gave in to pressure. Because after all, I'm the one who knows not only everything that went on in Mrs. Garr's house in April, May and June of that year, but also why a lot of it went on.'

'Since agreeing, I have made seventeen entirely separate and different beginnings. I have begun with the cat's swift sneak and hunch under the bookcase of that dark hall. I have begun with those terrifying hands reaching for my throat. I have begun with the opening of a door that was the opening of an unimaginable hell. But with any of these I have to stop too often for explanations. Mrs. Garr's house, I've found, isn't a house into which I can just plump you down. You need introductions. And so I have come round to beginning at the beginning, to telling you the little incidents in which the seeds of the mystery lay – incidents which might easily have meant nothing at all; incidents which, at the time, I considered myself silly for noting and wondering over …'

That is a challenge to you, the reader. Will *you* realise, as you read, the significance of those little incidents that would give you the clue to the mystery?

With *The Listening House*, the Crime Club presents a new author who, on the merits of this first novel, is destined to become one of the most outstanding names in the whole Crime Club list. 'The suspense is piled up,' one critic has said, 'to a surprising and well-built climax. It has excitement, good characterisation – and humour.'

### *Whispering Cup, The*
April 1941

The rise of Mabel Seeley as a mystery story writer has been phenomenal. Her two previous novels *The Listening House* and *The Crying Sisters* have proved extraordinarily successful. The central character of her new story is Solveig Nayes, who came back to her native village wearing the mantle of scandal. There she was confronted with that vicious gossip and animosity which only a small village can bring to its ultimate perfection. There too she was faced with a deadly hatred whose roots went far back into the past. Then murder struck. Not once but twice, and gossiping tongues lost no time in naming Solveig the murderer. Solveig succeeds in clearing herself and uncovering a murderer whose motives were deeper than even she originally suspected.

## SENECAL, JEAN-MICHEL
(*see*: **Jacquemard, Yves**)

## SERAFIN, DAVID
### *Body in Cadiz Bay, The*
April 1985

Superintendent Luis Bernal of the Madrid CID and his devout wife Eugenia are spending Holy Week in Cadiz, where the celebrations are only slightly less colourful than the better-known ones at Seville. Eugenia is doing spiritual exercises at a convent belonging to the recently founded Order of the Palm while she considers the divorce her husband has requested. Bernal, though in Cadiz on private business, is rapidly drawn into a police investigation when the body of an unknown frogman surfaces in a fisherman's net.

The frogman has not drowned – so how did he die? Who is he? Who killed him? And what was he doing in these sensitive waters, once the exclusive preserve of the British Fleet and now shared between the Spaniards at La Carraca naval base and the Americans at Rota?

The answers to these and other questions are bound up with the death of a coastguard, with the strange activities at the Convent of the Palm, with the state of play at one of Spain's new gambling casinos, and with the history of the ancient city of Cadiz itself.

By the time Bernal and his team succeed in exposing the cunning plot involved, the full Spanish Fleet has put to sea and Bernal's health is once again at risk from his wife's cooking.

David Serafin's intricate plots, his vivid descriptions of Spanish life and ceremonies, his meticulous accounts of forensic and police procedures, have ensured the popularity of his crime novels on both sides of the Atlantic and also in Spain – a rare compliment to a foreign author.

### *Christmas Rising*
December 1982

Christmas is coming, and the mysterious MAGOS code messages which seem to threaten the security of the royal palaces are appearing thick and fast in a right-wing daily. Superintendent Luis Bernal is reluctantly persuaded by the royal secretary to act as the King's eyes and ears, though he has to investigate this new military conspiracy to overthrow the Spanish State with the utmost discretion, since a number of VIPs are involved.

As Madrid starts putting up its seasonal decorations, the charred corpse of a young man is discovered under the snow in the grounds of La Granja Palace. A few days later the body of an older man is found floating in the River Tagus at Arunjuez …

In this third Bernal novel the ageing but still acutely observant detective becomes enmeshed in an ingenious and alarming plot, which finally touches upon a member of his own family. His digestion suffers as usual from his wife's appalling cooking, but Eugenia Bernal's religious mania for once proves to be of practical use.

The forensic details and Spanish police procedures are recounted with the meticulousness for which David Serafin is noted and which won the CWA John Creasey Award for his first novel, *Saturday of Glory*, while the delightful Spanish Christmas customs – unfamiliar to most foreign visitors – are fully and lovingly described.

### *Madrid Underground*
April 1982

May, 1977 and Madrid was preparing for the first general election to be held in Spain for forty-one years. Even the tiled walls of the Metro stations were plastered with the election propaganda. It was not surprising that the ticket-clerk scarcely noticed the bearded man supporting a heavily muffled companion. But when the muffled figure killed over, mouth pouring blood, in the moving train, the alarmed passengers noticed that the bearded man had gone.

Three days later a similar incident occurred, but these were only a macabre prologue for what was to follow…TERROR ON THE METRO! MANIAC AT LARGE! screamed the headlines. Inspector Luis Bernal was faced with one of his most difficult and grisly cases.

The Maigret of Madrid had somehow to pinpoint the psychopath at large in the city. Aided by the same team who assisted him in *Saturday of Glory*, he assiduously followed the meagre leads that emerged, and sent his team into Madrid's underworld in a desperate race to save more innocent lives. The tense finale takes place on election day, deep in the Metro network, whose station names head each section of the book.

David Serafin's encyclopaedic knowledge of Madrid and of Spanish forensic methods are happily combined in his second novel, a fitting successor to *Saturday of Glory*, which won the CWA John Creasey Award for the best first crime novel of 1979.

### *Port of Light*
April 1987

The Canary Islands are a Spanish possession but are much nearer to the coast of Africa than that of Spain. There has always been tension between the Islands and the Peninsula, and an official visit to them by the President of the Council of Ministers is more than a little fraught. That is why Superintendent Bernal of the Madrid CID and his team are despatched to Grand Canary to monitor the local criminal and political situation, independent of the Presidents own bodyguard.

The move suits Bernal, whose mistress Consuelo Lozano has discreetly got her bank to post her to Las Palmas, capital of Grand Canary, to await the birth of their child. Now Bernal will be able to be with her for the birth – except that she failed to meet him at the airport as arranged.

Torn between anxiety for Consuelo, who has been kidnapped by unknowns and spirited away to the mountainous interior of the island, and the need to make sense of a series of sinister events beginning with the murder of a blind lottery-ticket seller, Bernal has his work cut out to ensure the President's safety and that of his beloved, for the two are closely linked.

David Serafin's unrivalled knowledge of present-day Spain is once again the effective background for an intricate and enthralling story of high-level skulduggery.

### *Saturday of Glory*
April 1979

Did he fall or was he pushed? That was the question confronting Superintendent Luis Bernal of the Spanish police when, on Palm Sunday, a young journalist fell to death from his top-floor flat in Madrid.

Bernal's conclusion, arrived at by patient forensic investigation, was that this was no suicide. It put his own life at danger. Why? The reason became clear when he stumbled on secret information the journalist has collected – information which had already led to another death. Moreover, it was politically sensitive in a country as delicately balanced as post-Franco Spain. A massive cover-up was mounted, and Bernal received a strong hint from his superiors to lay off the case.

But Bernal, ageing, not in line for promotion, married to the incomparable Eugenia, and trying to come to terms with a police force which now included a woman inspector, was a police officer to his fingertips. It was not in him to leave unsolved a double murder, nor to abandon a case before its end. Saturday of Glory, the old Spanish name for Easter Saturday, was approaching, and he had to prevent a Resurrection of a most unholy kind.

Writing with extensive first-hand knowledge of modern Spain, David Serafin in his first novel has created a classic of detection, carried out by a dedicated Spanish policeman in the teeth of Spanish bureaucrats, which is also a fascinating portrait of contemporary Madrid.

## SHEFFIELD, ROBYN
### *Killing Term, A*
May 1993

There were those who died who should not have died, and those who should – and did.

Detective-Inspector Jones could discover no motive for the suspicious death of the young man who worked in Chalingford's Planning Office. Like others, he could speculate about what went on there, but to his chagrin, there seemed no way his favourite suspect could be involved.

Nevertheless, there was big money and ambition at stake, enough for Jan Ryder to initiate her own kind of killing in a game which was to prove more deadly than she thought.

As for Robert Howick, headmaster of Trelawne School, he was the possessor of dark and damning secrets, and had his own ambitions to satisfy. And having the power to hire and fire his staff and being prepared to use it, he believed he was unassailable.

Who won and who lost in this intricate story of move and counter-move is unfolded with deceptively easy skill.

### *Parting, The*
June 1992

On the spring day when Owen Burgess left his television producer, he was full of optimism. Shortly he was to meet a wealthy Texan who was an avid secret collector of fine art. If Burgess played it right he could see a lifelong ambition realized while also indulging in an overdue act of revenge. In addition there was the provoking memory of Sally Trent, a prospective employee for the Gallery he ran with his partner, his immediate attraction to her confirmed that he was tiring of his present mistress, Dinah Calder. The fact that Sally was happily married would be no bar to his plans.

During the summer, as Burgess developed his schemes, others were taking a long, harsh view of him. Ruth Lyle's loathing was overwhelming: she saw Burgess as responsible for her husband's violent death. Jack Calder knew there would be no reconciliation with his wife while Burgess remained on the scene. And Louise Burgess was being toppled from the neutral stance she had long ago adopted regarding her husband's activities. Now she could not endure seeing her friends being sacrificed one by one to his ambition.

By autumn, Burgess was so well advanced with a fraudulent scheme that he failed to observe the depth of displeasure round him. His judgement seldom failed – but this time he had made a fatal error.

## SMITH, EVELYN E.
### *Miss Melville Regrets*
July 1987

Meet Miss Melville, a middle-aged lady of refinement, impeccable taste and breeding, whose dwindling finances signal a drastic call to action.

Never one to meet a problem other than head-on, Miss Melville decides to take a job and becomes by chance a freelance assassin. Using her patrician air and still-operative female wiles to hold herself above suspicion, she moves freely through upper crust society, knocking off important personages and visiting dignitaries for a most pleasant fee, and, best of all, with firm knowledge that *all* these rascals deserve precisely what they get.

Everything goes well until Miss Melville starts enjoying her job, and developing her own hit list. Things get particularly sticky when the person she next finds in her gunsights demands a new level of expertise. But in an unexpected turn of events Miss Melville recoups with customary grace and élan. Rest assured she will be back!

### *Miss Melville Returns*
May 1988

Now an equally successful artist, Miss Susan Melville, the professional assassin one learned to love in *Miss Melville Regrets*, has the role of amateur sleuth thrust on her when a world-renowned artist is laid low during a knock-dead speech which turns out to be just that.

The death, as Miss Melville quickly discovers, is not from natural causes but is the inevitable result of some shady, dangerous dealings taking place in New York City's art world. Setting out on the investigative path, Miss Melville is greeted along the way by arson, drug-smuggling, and more murder.

Step by step she unravels the mystery with the same acerbic wit and deadly charm that made her initial debut such a resounding success.

### *Miss Melville Rides a Tiger*
May 1992

The impeccable Miss Melville returns in another scintillating adventure.

Enjoying a total immersion in her artistic career, Miss Melville is between jobs, doing what society women do, charitably supporting the Rundle Home for Wayward Girls – and resisting an invitation from the government to assassinate the power-hungry Begum of Gandistan, a ruthless woman whose son has just ascended the throne following the unfortunate deaths of his father and all his siblings.

Miss Melville has her own deeply personal reasons for finally capitulating to official entreaties to undertake this particular covert assignment, and she has also developed a fondness for the young Sultan, realizing that he is an unwitting pawn in his mother's dangerous political games.

As the chase begins, Miss Melville is unaware of the amazing cast of characters who will be drawn into her deadly encounter and its shattering denouement.

## SMITH, SHELLEY
### Afternoon to Kill, An
October 1953

Lancelot Jones was on his way to his first job – as tutor to an Indian Rajah's son. But the Rajah's ancient plane and incompetent pilot decanted him in the middle of the desert, and the wrong desert at that. There, seeking shade, he found, in the only dwelling of any size within miles, a curious old gentlewoman called Alva Hine. Alva Hine buttonholed the prim Mr. Jones as the Ancient Mariner once made a wedding guest his audience. She told him a strange story of a summer fifty years ago in a respectable middle-class Victorian household. Shelley Smith has won high praise for her unusual crime stories. *An Afternoon to Kill* is strikingly original – with a really unexpected 'twist'.

### Come and Be Killed!
January 1946

Shelley Smith can certainly write a crime story that can truthfully be described as enthralling. Following that outstanding success, *This is the House*, comes this quite different type of story, *Come and Be Killed!* which is in essence a psychological study of a murderess. There is nothing of the orthodox mystery in the story and consequently no tiresome red herrings. A novel such as this needs unusual talent, as it depends mainly on its human interest, and in our opinion the author has succeeded brilliantly for it grips the reader from first to last.

### He Died of Murder!
February 1947

In *This is the House* and *Come and Be Killed!* Shelley Smith quickly established a reputation for unusual crime novels in which clever characterisation was one of the salient features. *He Died of Murder!* is another equally fascinating tale. The story opens when Master Titmarsh, head of the old religious community known as 'The Seekers', who devote themselves to farming and the simple life, is found murdered in one of the community's fields. It is only after Detective-Inspector Chaos has moved in to live with the Brotherhood itself that he begins to glimpse the dangerous complexities and grim motives that seethe beneath the apparently placid surface of their lives.

### Man Alone
July 1952

Thomas Bates discovered while still a lad that the one thing he could not *bear* was work. To be compelled to take orders sent him frantic. So he began a life of petty thieving, and from there passed easily to larger, more ambitious crimes in order to provide himself with the

necessities and in particular the luxuries which his inflated ego demanded as its profane right. *Every man by his actions chooses the death he is to die.* At every step of the descent there was one split second when his fate lay in his own thick-fingered butcher's hands. Each time he confidently, unhesitatingly, stepped forward and *down*... Thomas Bates was a creature unworthy of the name of Man, possessed of a mean and squalid mind and a heart of stone. That his story is as fascinating as it is terrible is a triumph of the storyteller's art.

### Man With a Calico Face
January 1951

Shelley Smith's first story since her warmly praised *The Woman in the Sea* is an exceptionally clever study in the psychology of a murderer. In her country home of Hawkswood, young Linda Campion, the mother of four young children, is found spread-eagled and dead at the foot of the stairs by her cousin, Ivor Campion, who is living there. The doctor discovers that she was first killed by a stiletto and then thrown downstairs. Inspector Trevor comes on the scene, and the story soon mounts to a dramatic climax. It is extremely well told, gripping and satisfying.

### Party at No. 5, The
September 1954

Mrs. Rampage lived alone. Adoring her beautiful house and precious *objets d'art*, she had no idea she was lonely until Mrs. Roach come to live with her. But the two women were incompatibles: to Mrs. Roach, Mrs. Rampage was an old miser; to Mrs. Rampage, Mrs. Roach was a pious old humbug. It should have been a simple matter for them to separate if they didn't like one another, but Mrs. Roach didn't wish to leave – she had her reasons – and *nothing* Mrs. Rampage could do would make her go. The friction between them increases, to end in macabre horror. In Mrs. Rampage the author has drawn a character whose every word and action can be believed in as she responds to the situation which is to culminate so catastrophically.

### This Is the House
February 1945

*This is the House* has a most attractive setting on a picturesque isle of the West Indies. The sweltering, ramshackle capital was dominated by the house that Jacques built originally as a commercial venture to attract tourists to the island. And when the tourists did not materialise to any great extent, Jacques did not worry. He was, after all, Chief Justice of the island and was divinely happy with his wife Julia and son Raoul, till Julia was stricken with total paralysis. Now for five years past La Morte, as the people called her, had lain motionless in bed, her lovely, still face crowned by her golden hair. The house itself and its extraordinary occupants reflect the unusual atmosphere of this strikingly original story of murder; for it is murder that invades the tranquillity of this lovely backwater of life. Shelley Smith's story heralds the arrival of a new author of outstanding merit to the Crime Club.

### Woman in the Sea, The
July 1948

The self-satisfied egotism of Zoe Robinson, the fantasies of her husband – a man who preferred memories to real life, the romantic adolescent dreams of Arthur Emery, made up the tawdry household of the Villa Arcadia. But these private dream worlds conflicted with each other and, worse still, with Reality; and this inevitable conflict precipitated

tragedy. Zoe Robinson would have said: 'None was to blame'. But in this story of 'the events leading up to the crime' Shelley Smith skilfully depicts where the guilt lay. This penetrating psychological study has the dramatic intensity of Zola's *Therese Raquin*.

## SMITH, WILLARD K.
### Bowery Murder
May 1930

Something new in detective stories! Screamers from the tabloids, full news stories from the *Times*, scoops from the *World*, scandalous inside gossip from *Broadway Briefs* chronicle the Bowery Bar case from day to day – from Woodward's disappearance to the dramatic accusation of his murderer. Here's a masterpiece of ballyhoo – a murder story as up-to-date as tomorrow's front page.

OR

In *Bowery Murder* Mr Smith has done something unprecedented, for it is the first novel written in newspaper form. He tells the story of a trial of front-page importance in the headlines and news stories of the daily papers. And another unique feature is that the police solve the crime. In large centres such as New York, with a very definite underworld, the police investigation is not so often confronted with an entire lack of clues as he is with a number of them. But these clues mean little because in an area of ten million people the question comes in locating the criminal, not in knowing a lot about his physical and mental makeup. And in *Bowery Murder*, even after the principals are located, the difficulty came in deciding which one of the witnesses was lying the least.

## SOMERS, PAUL
(*see also* **Garve, Andrew**)
### Beginner's Luck
February 1958

When a cannon ball was reported missing from the historic castle of Lodden in Sussex, Hugh Curtis – a very new reporter on the *Daily Record* – was sent to cover the trivial episode by way of punishment, because he'd 'fallen down' badly on a story the previous day. On his mettle, he made up his mind to find the wretched cannon ball at any cost.

In fact, it nearly cost him his life – and Mollie Brown hers, too. Mollie was the beautiful girl reporter of the rival paper – 'the *Courier*'s spoiled darling', according to Hugh. But she proved to be a good companion in a tight spot, for finding the cannon ball was only the prelude to a series of terrifying experiences. Luck, however, was on their side – 'beginner's luck', Hugh modestly called it, when he landed the scoop of the year.

Paul Somers' story has an authentic newspaper background, excellent characterisation, and an exciting plot with a thrilling climax. We are proud to introduce to the Crime Club this new name, the pseudonym of an established writer.

### Operation Piracy
July 1958

PIRATES RAID ATWOOD YACHT
SECRETARY SHOT DEAD
£100,000 JEWEL RAID
So ran the headlines in the *Daily Record*. Hugh Curtis was sent to Falmouth when the story broke – one among dozens of reporters, including the tantalising and lovely Mollie Bourne of the *Courier*. They all wanted a story, but the trail led just so far and then – petered out. But Mollie had a hunch and Hugh, for more reasons than one, was keeping an eye on Mollie.

They were curious about the owner of the vintage Bentley and his girl friend. They were curious about the swimmers in Penlo Cove. They were inquisitive about a walker on Bodmin Moor. They were the last reporters left on the story and they took certain steps to confirm a theory – and suddenly found themselves in a dangerous and terrifying situation. Readers of *Beginner's Luck* will be familiar with Hugh and Mollie, and their affectionate banter and professional bickering. They will know, too, how Paul Somers gives them a story which keeps up a cracking pace from first to last, this book adds to the reputation he achieved with his first book.

## STADLEY, PAT
### Autumn of a Hunter
January 1971

It is late October in the California Sierra country, the hunting season is about to start, and after a long, hot summer the mountains are tinder-dry. Every forest ranger is on the lookout for what may be the fatal spark.

Into this country come three men hired to murder a woman. She is Martha Neilson Cope, head of the Neilson Electronic Works, on a camping trip with her husband. The killer's plan is simple: the gunman will force her to run into the mountains and there shoot her down as though she were the victim of a hunter's bullet.

Then the inevitable autumn thunderstorm strikes and a lightning bolt finds its target. Fire smoulders in the roots of a tree, reaches dry grass, and spreads throughout the canyon. The forest rangers, faced with the hazardous task of quelling a fire which a tragic chain of events has allowed to get out of control, are already stretched to the limit when Martha Cope, on the run from the gunman, is trapped in the forest's fiery heart.

Nor is Martha the only creature to be trapped. The graceful, golden-brown puma, queen of the forest, has also been caught by the fire and plays her part in a finale which demonstrates to the full Pat Stadley's marvellous facility for handling the lore of woods and storms and fires, and the evil ways of man.

## STEWART, DOUGLAS
### Cellars' Market
August 1983

To honour an old-established and exclusive firm of wine-merchants, a select dinner is held at a prestigious London restaurant. But when a famous wine from the cellars is opened in the presence of the assembled connoisseurs, it is not what the label describes. Faced by a crisis of confidence in his firm, the Chairman turns to an old friend, Bart Fraser, a successful London solicitor until his life was shattered by a personal tragedy which has resulted in his expulsion from the partnership.

Bart nevertheless agrees to take his old friend's instructions. He soon discovers that he is investigating more than an act of spite; the wine business is big money and at issue is a multi-million-dollar fraud which stretched from France to the United States mainland and even to the outer Hawaiian island of Maui.

But who is behind it? In his search for the truth Bart Fraser, himself a Master of Wines, is helped – or is he? – by a pretty gossip-column journalist for whom life has always been champagne and fun. As the action moves swiftly from the traditional centres of Beaune and Bordeaux to the East and West Coasts of America, a cunning plot emerges in which, as Bart grimly discovers, human life is cheaper than the cheapest plonk.

## STONE, ZACHARY
### Modigliani Scandal, The
January 1976

The setting of Zachary Stone's impressive first crime novel is the elegant, dignified, international world of art, where fortunes change hands in pursuit of masterpieces and the skullduggery and wheeler-dealering behind the scenes in hushed galleries can be as treacherous and unscrupulous as in any big-money racket.

In *The Modigliani Scandal* it is touched off by three people learning of an unknown masterpiece. They are an ambitious young art historian living in Paris; her uncle, a distinguished London dealer; and a new gallery owner with a financial crisis and a discontented wife. The masterpiece is an undiscovered Modigliani, and no holds are barred in the fight for possession of this prize.

But the art world is due for a shock. A young painter with a chip on his shoulder is planning revenge on its Establishment, and he executes a brilliant forgery whose subsequent authentication is chillingly and convincingly described.

And meanwhile a successful actress, naïvely idealistic and disillusioned by her own success, becomes involved in a Robin Hood-style enterprise designed to benefit the poor by stealing from the rich.

Inexorably the lives of masterpiece hunters, forgers and thieves converge and then collide. Zachary Stone makes an auspicious and unusual début in the Crime Club.

### Paper Money
April 1977

On a spring morning in London a politician wakes up in bed with a beautiful girl, an underworld villain briefs his team of thieves, and a tycoon has breakfast with a Bank of England official. And at the newsdesk of the *Evening Post* it looks like being a quiet day.

Then, one after another, three stories break: the attempted suicide of a public figure, a raid on a currency van, and a takeover bid. At first the *Post* covers them as three separate stories. Later their reporters ask questions, including awkward ones. Why is the Cotton Bank of Jamaica in trouble? Who was the heavily-built man in the grey Rolls-Royce glimpsed near the scene of the raid? How did a character called Deaf Willie end up with gunshot wounds in a hospital car park?

As the day wears on, the *Post* digs deeper, but the answers pose new questions in their turn about the moving and manipulating of paper money. Will the full story of the day's events ever make the headlines? That is the ultimate question-mark.

Zachary Stone was for several years a reporter on a London evening paper, and has made good use of the experience he gained. He has given Fleet Street the same knowledgeable, merciless treatment he gave the art world in his first crime novel, *The Modigliani Scandal*, of which the *Oxford Times* said, 'the author has complicated and entertaining fun at the expense of the art world's sharks and pseudos' without losing what *The Times* praised as 'that essential read-on quality'.

## STOUT, REX
### Alphabet Hicks
September 1942

In *Alphabet Hicks* Rex Stout, ace American writer of mystery stories, creates a brand new detective destined to take his place alongside the famous and beloved Nero Wolfe. But where Wolfe is sedentary, Hicks is a dynamo of energy; where Wolfe is subtle Hicks is brusque and direct; only in one thing are they alike, eccentricity. Hicks is a grand character and the story in which he makes his bow is as clever a mystery as this clever author has written.

### Bad for Business
July 1945

The old fashioned firm of Tingley's Titbits had built up over a number of years a good and solid reputation, which was now in danger of being ruined. Indignant customers were returning jars of liver pate, sandwich spread, spiced anchovies and other such delicacies. Analysts showed that the contents had been adulterated with quinine. Arthur Tingley, the proprietor, was at his wits' end. It was not only bad for business, it looked like being fatal. And it was…for Arthur. Here is a fine new murder story by that most entertaining of all detective writers, Rex Stout, featuring one of his most famous characters, Tecumseh Fox, in the role of detective.

### Before Midnight
May 1956

Nero Wolfe – 'one-seventh of a ton of orchid-loving, beer-drinking genius' – does not much like work. In *Before Midnight* work comes to him in the form of the senior executives of a huge advertising agency, Lippert, Buff & Assa. Their firm has been running a publicity contest involving hundreds of thousands of dollars on behalf of a perfume manufacturer. At the final stage of the contest the man running it – the only man holding the answers to the problems on which so much money depends – is killed. Wolfe is soon deep in a tangle of intrigue and evidence; even his assistant, Archie Goodwin, becomes extremely dissatisfied with the boss's handling of the case. Wolfe makes a slip – but he unravels the mystery out of the threads of information that make up a fascinating, ingenious and surprising story of detection.

### Black Mountain, The
August 1955

Nero Wolfe's great personal friend Marko, owner of Rusterman's, the fashionable New York restaurant for gourmets, is found shot dead. Wolfe, who has undertaken to solve so many murders for such fabulously high prices, in this case sets himself the task of tracking down a murderer for no monetary gain whatever. Marko was not only his friend, and a master of the gastronomic art to dear to Wolfe's heart, but they had been boys together in Montenegro. Never has Nero pursued a murderer with more grim and dedicated purpose than in this latest adventure, which takes him, with Archie Goodwin, from his home – and the United States – across an ocean, a continent and a sea, to penetrate into one of the most dangerous and controversial places on earth. Emerging practically unscathed from the most astounding and sinister encounters, he returns at last to New York – on one of the strangest missions in all detective fiction.

### Black Orchids
July 1943

In all the annals of the great detectives there has never been anyone quite like Nero Wolfe, and certainly no one like the irrepressible Archie Goodwin. If there is any reader who is so unfortunate as not to have made their acquaintance here is his bargain chance, and for Nero's old friends a double treat – two splendid Nero Wolfe mysteries in one book. These two mysteries present Nero and Archie at their brilliant and exciting best, and moreover, set a couple of feathers in the jaunty hat of their creator Rex Stout, who recently added fresh laurels to his fame by appearing as a very transatlantic guest in the Brain's Trust.

### Broken Vase, The
March 1942

Rex Stout, creator of Nero Wolfe, has made a hit with his new character 'Tec' Fox, the private detective who is well named because he is shrewd, wise and wily. And he is as quick on his feet as he is at thinking. Fox was in the audience the night of the debut of Jan Tusar, a promising young violinist, and although he didn't know a lot about music it didn't seem to him that the performance was good. He was talking about it during the interval just before he heard that Tusar had committed suicide. That was the beginning of a really thrilling case for Fox, and for all Rex Stout's readers. In *The Broken Vase* this brilliant author is again at his exciting, skilful and humorous best.

### Champagne for One
September 1959

Within minutes of Faith Usher taking a drink from her glass of champagne she had died a terrible death. Archie Goodwin had been watching her, had actually been given a hint that something might go amiss at the very curious occasion which he was attending: the annual dinner-party, given by Alfred Grantham's widow, to commemorate that millionaire's founding of Grantham House, a home for unmarried mothers. Faith had been one of the four ex-inmates of the institution present at dinner and Archie had good reason to know that she could not have poisoned herself. His hostess, his fellow guests and the police, from different motives and by widely different methods, tried desperately to make him change his mind. Only the intervention of Nero Wolfe released Archie from a delicate and dangerous situation. *Champagne for One* finds that huge, orchid-loving detective on the top of his form, dealing with a baffling and fascinating case in his inimitably successful way. Rex Stout has added another triumph to the long and distinguished list of his successes.

### Crime and Again
May 1959

The seasons of the year mean little enough to Nero Wolfe, apart from the effect on his plants, but in three of these four cases of murder he is forced to realise that the outside world, however abhorrent he finds it, plans its pleasures, displays and celebrations – and often its crimes – by the calendar. Typically, Wolfe only involved himself when he was faced with personal inconvenience. In *Christmas Party* he was genuinely worried about his assistant, Archie Goodwin; in *Easter Parade* Archie attended New York's annual Rite of Spring because Wolfe coveted another man's orchid; in *Fourth of July Picnic* the great man voluntarily left the famous brownstone house on West Thirty-fifth Street, but only to ensure favoured gastronomic treatment for the future – the crime which was committed was alarming and unexpected. In *Murder is no Joke* Wolfe is really on his mettle because someone tried to trick him – a rash move which Wolfe found presumptuous and intolerable. *Crime and Again* maintains the high standards of urbanity, wit and ingenuity which have raised and kept Rex Stout in the ranks of the Masters of Crime Fiction.

### Crime on her Hands
November 1939

(REX) Stout is good for you.

Here is Rex Stout with a new detective. Different in sex and figure from Nero Wolfe, Dol Bonner is just as different in her own way. Her first investigation was a tough one, for it was a strange party that assembled at the Storrs' home for a quiet weekend; seemingly friendly on the surface, there were strange undercurrents of hatred and suspicion and one member of the party at least was guarding a terrible secret about another guest. Then Dol, walking in the garden, finds her host hanged on a tree, and soon realises that it is murder. There were plenty of motives, but as many alibis, and it was not until the strangler had claimed another victim that the chain of evidence was complete.

### Curtains for Three
October 1951

*Curtains For Three* is the latest Nero Wolfe Threesome, featuring the truly great Nero in three first-class crime stories. Here we have the story of the man who should never have gone riding in Central Park; the story of the murderer Archie caught by remembering a casual conversational phrase; and the story of the lethal weapon that wouldn't lie down. *Curtains for Three* is Rex Stout at his best, with Archie Goodwin as inventive as ever and Nero Wolfe as devastatingly brilliant – and both of them even more of an annoyance than usual to ordinary policemen!

### Death of a Doxy
June 1967

Orrie Cather, ablest of Nero Wolfe's occasional employees, has been arrested for the murder of lovely Isabel Kerr. Isabel lived in luxury provided for her by an influential and wealthy man, whose one wish now is not to become involved in any publicity. Nero Wolfe undertakes to prove Orrie's innocence. In itself this doesn't present a very great problem to the great detective genius. But there is an added complication. Isabel's rich protector is prepared to reward Wolfe handsomely if he solves the case without involving the tycoon's name in it in any way. And Wolfe wants this money.

With Archie Goodwin's cheerful and unflagging help he establishes the murderer's identity. But how to clear Orrie and collect the large cheque presents a much greater problem. No one who has followed Wolfe's long and distinguished career will doubt he succeeds – but the brilliant way he manages to get the best of all worlds makes a very exciting and satisfying story.

### Death of a Dude
April 1970

The many admirers of Nero Wolfe are in for a surprise in Rex Stout's latest novel. Nero not only leaves his home on West Thirty-Fifth Street, his cook Fritz and his orchid plants, but he flies across the States to Montana to join Archie Goodwin on a lavish but very private dude ranch.

Here he settles down to solve murder by rifle shot, resigned to the necessity of performing such unWolfean activities as tramping through underbrush, wading in an icy trout stream, eating tinned soups, and attending a Saturday-night hoedown in a cattle town. He also has to deal with a young unmarried mother, some unco-operative cowhands, a highly belligerent sheriff, an off-Broadway actress, and any number of chairs which don't begin to fit his bulk. Yet, throughout, he remains the same inimitable Nero Wolfe.

How does Rex Stout know enough about the Far West to write this novel? Every summer, for a large part of his life, he spent his time riding pack trains, fishing mile-high streams, and enjoying night after night around campfires, yarning with genuine cow-punchers. So there isn't a misplaced piece of harness or an unauthentic Western vista in this, one of the funniest, most engaging, most out-of-doors of all Nero Wolfe adventures.

### *Doorbell Rang, The*
January 1966

A very rich woman comes to Nero Wolfe and Archie Goodwin claiming that she is being harassed by the Federal Bureau of Investigation. She tells of agents following her and members of her family, of wires being tapped and her privacy being otherwise invaded. She demands that Nero compel the F.B.I. to cease these activities and offers him the largest retainer he has ever seen.

After some hesitation, Nero Wolfe takes the case and quickly encounters a murder in which members of the F.B.I. may or may not be involved. He also finds himself in a direct encounter with F.B.I. agents under highly questionable circumstances.

Never before has Rex Stout written a book more perfectly plotted or one with a denouement so skilfully arrived at. The battle between the fat detective genius and the massed uniformed legion of the F.B.I. is an epic in Wolfe's career – and a unique excitement for Wolfe's many enthusiastic fans.

### *Double for Death*
July 1940

The most engaging new detective of the year – *Tecumseh Fox*! Meet him in a neatly dovetailed mystery which is right up to the standard of Rex Stout's best. Two shots in the dark and a silent figure on the floor of Ridley Thorpe's bungalow hideaway start this mystery of a millionaire's death in which passion spins the plot through the lanes and highways of New York's suburbia. You will be hearing a lot more about Tecumseh Fox in the future, so you will do well to make his acquaintance now. Maybe you will agree with the local police officers in the story who think the name most appropriate to the man.

### *Even in the Best Families*
April 1951

Nero Wolfe had in the past had sharp but long-distance encounters with a certain powerful mystery man of crime named Zeck. That Zeck was a blackmailer was obvious. That he was perhaps the most potent and ruthless of all underworld characters seemed more than possible. In this new, full-length novel Zeck plays a leading role. Nero once told Archie that if he ever had to come to grips with Zeck he would disappear first, so as not to endanger Archie, his orchid plants, or his house in lower Manhattan, and Nero is a man of his word. Where Nero went, what happened in his absence, how he came back, and the manner of his coming are as fine a combination of outright drama and downright hilarity as was ever put together in a novel of crime. One of the corollary mysteries of this book is: How on earth is even Rex Stout going to top it?

### *Family Affair, A*
June 1976

What could make Nero Wolfe so determined to solve a crime that he would be willing to work entirely without a fee or client? What would it take to put him, for the first time, at a loss for words? What would make him so angry about a case that he would refuse to speak to the police, even if he had to spend fifty-one hours in jail as a result? Never before in the Nero Wolfe books has Rex Stout shown us the extremes to which his great detective can be pushed, but never before has a bomb blown up in the old brownstone on West 35th Street, murdering someone right under Wolfe's nose. When in October 1974 Pierre Ducos, one of Wolfe's favourite waiters at Rusterman's, Wolfe's favourite restaurant, dies just down the hall from Archie's bedroom, Wolfe is understandably eager to find the perpetrator, but when the murder somehow becomes connected with tape recorders, Washington lawyers, and maybe even a conspiracy to obstruct justice, his fury becomes so intense that even Archie is puzzled.

Sadly, this is Rex Stout's last novel, but it could still capture many new readers and delight (and amaze) the long-standing admirers of Wolfe and Archie.

### *Father Hunt, The*
January 1969

She was twenty-two years old, a Smith graduate, charming, intelligent, appealing. When she buttonholed Archie Goodwin she had a very simple request. She hadn't the faintest idea who her father was, had never seen him or heard of him, and wanted to learn who and where he was. She also, it turned out, had something in excess of a quarter of a million dollars mysteriously received from that father, but she didn't really consider that part of the mystery at all.

Archie, of course, took the problem to Nero, and Nero took the problem on after he discovered that the girl's mother had apparently been murdered and that the possible antecedents of the girl stretched back towards certain men of great power and influence, and into realms as diverse as international banking, national television, and public relations. To solve it, Nero and Archie have to be at the top of their form, and they are.

This is the first new Nero Wolfe in nearly two years – an unusual interval for the productive Rex Stout, who is now 82.

### *Final Deduction, The*
April 1962

Nero Wolfe, the fat detective genius, will do almost anything for money; and the lady who wanted to employ him was very, very rich. On the other hand, Wolfe is not very keen about work, so that when the case became one of murder Archie Goodwin found himself, as usual, making most of the running. And in addition Wolfe had given his client a promise of discretion, a pledge which, if kept, was liable, once the police were investigating a murder, to land both Wolfe and Goodwin in jail. The hope of acquiring big money quickly motivates some other characters in the novel who are less law-abiding than Wolfe. Wolfe picks his way among the clues and suspects with his unique incisiveness and Archie reports as amusingly as always the progress of the investigation. The result is a fascinating addition to the works of Rex Stout, who is the favourite detective writer of many discerning readers.

### *Gambit*
April 1963

In terms of physical bulk Nero Wolfe is without question the "greatest" detective; and in his deductive prowess he is second to few, if any.

He is grumpily engaged in burning page by page a reference book of which he disapproves when a young woman comes to offer him $22,000 for his services: the job – to prove the innocence of her father, held by the police for a murder of which he is obviously guilty.

The murder had taken place at a Chess Demonstration in a private club in New York. The young man who had been playing twelve 'blindfold' simultaneous games against members of the club was poisoned during the course of the evening.

Here then is Rex Stout, a most distinguished exponent of the detective novel, at his very best: it is something of a Chess problem as well as a crime puzzle that has Wolfe (sporadically) cerebrating and Archie Goodwin running round until the truth is cunningly disclosed.

### *Golden Spiders, The*
May 1954

The street urchin reported what he had seen to that famous but slothful detective, Nero Wolfe, instead of to the police because: "I know how you feel about the lousy cops, just like I do." What Pete Drossos had seen, nebulous and improbable as it sounded, in fact led directly to some very solid and dangerous facts. Three murders quickly followed – and the most certain way of getting killed apparently was to come to Wolfe's house and ask for help: his visitors were apt to be hit on the head or run over by cars shortly after leaving. How was the Association for the Aid of Displaced Persons – known as Assadip – being exploited? Who had to commit three murders to cover their tracks? And above all, what was the importance of the golden earrings, shaped like spiders, worn by the lady Pete had seen for a fleeting moment in the Cadillac? Nero Wolfe's cerebral powers, aided possibly by Archie Goodwin's, and certainly by Archie's strong-arm methods, lead to a surprising solution, with a great deal of fun along the way.

### *Homicide Trinity*
February 1963

In the first of these three long stories a woman is strangled *in Nero Wolfe's own house with Nero Wolfe's own necktie*; this is not at all Wolfe's idea of the proper order of things and the fat detective genius is stirred into a moderate display of energy. In the second story a woman comes to show Wolfe a gun saying, 'That's the gun I'm going to shoot my husband with.' In the third Wolfe is extended (if that is the word) not so much by the problem of detecting the murderer as by thwarting the claims of the police on the one hand, and of the Federal Secret Service on the other, to first possession of any corpse, clues or murderers that Wolfe may have under his hand.

This is vintage Rex Stout. Nero Wolfe and Archie Goodwin delve into mysteries in their familiar though different fashions, bringing each to an unexpected and exciting conclusion.

### *If Death Ever Slept*
September 1958

If Otis Jarrell had been a man who could swallow humiliation; if his son had known more about women; if Nero Wolfe and Archie Goodwin had been busy on an important case the morning Otis Jarrell called at the office; if Jarrell had not fired his secretary in a fit of temper; if Wolfe had not been sore at Archie for – as he thought – good and sufficient reason and moved to suggest that Archie join Jarrell's ménage as his secretary; if Archie, also sore, had refused; if Archie's curiosity had not been aroused by certain apparent characteristics of Jarrell's daughter-in-law; if all these things and a couple of others had not happened, this new Nero Wolfe thriller would not have been written. Fortunately for Rex Stout's many admirers – they did!

### *Might as Well be Dead*
August 1957

Nero Wolfe and Archie Goodwin undertake to find a man who has disappeared in New York – a man once accused of theft by his own father and now known to be innocent. The plight the man is in when they locate him – the mystery as to who killed Michael Molloy – the identity of the author of a vast scheme of embezzlement – these are ingredients of a mysterious, ingenious and exciting crime story. Nero Wolfe and Archie have never been in better form; their investigations have never been more complex or enthralling.

### *More Deaths Than One*
February 1949

Nero Wolfe and Archie Goodwin investigate the strange doings of a lady broadcaster, a racetrack tout, and a mathematical wizard. With expert nonchalance they set out to solve a murder which has been broadcast over a great national network, and before they are finished the whole New York police force is working as their assistants. This is one of Nero's neatest tricks and leads to one of his most brilliant successes. *More Deaths Than One* is amusing, fast-paced and completely baffling, a virtuoso performance equal to the pre-War Stout.

### *Mother Hunt, The*
January 1964

It is the fate of the fat misogynist, Nero Wolfe, to be beset by glamorous and seductive women. In this case the service required by the attractive young widow of a famous novelist is specially bizarre and distasteful to Wolfe. Someone has deposited a baby in the hall of her house with a note to the effect that the dead writer had been its father: the widow wants, not unreasonably, to know the mother's name and whether the accusation against her husband can possibly be substantiated.

Archie Goodwin gets busy – with disastrous results; instead of finding 'the mother' he precipitates a murder. Soon Wolfe and Goodwin are caught in an acute predicament of discretion: can they hide the identity of their client if it means withholding from the police material evidence of a murder? This problem – added to the stress of detection – becomes so acute that even Wolfe, the housebound colossus, is obliged to leave the 'old brownstone' and take refuge elsewhere until he can lay hands on the murderer.

This is another brilliant addition to the long canon of Rex Stout's Nero Wolfe stories; the writing is as good, the wit as sharp as ever, and Wolfe's final revelation is both logical and startling.

### *Mountain Cat*
March 1940

'What kind of cartridges,' the girl said, 'should I get for a revolver like this?'

'Depends,' the man behind the counter answered. 'What do you want to use it for?'

'I'm going to shoot a man with it.'

That's how this new mystery begins, and by the time you've gone three pages you'll know it's every bit as good as *Too Many Cooks* and *Some Buried Caesar*. If you like the kind of credible, fast-moving story the one and only Rex Stout can write, don't delay to make the acquaintance of *Mountain Cat*.

### *Murder by the Book*
April 1952

If books could kill! Nero Wolfe finds one that can. It's the manuscript of a novel and it's no safer to handle than a king cobra. Before Nero unearths this manuscript he first has to connect the strange death of the girl in the park – she's a young editor – with the murder of the man in the law office. Archie nearly sees the third killing. He arrives just two minutes too late. Having conquered the worlds of gastronomy and orchid raising, Nero – with Archie – here invades the complex realms of book publishing and the legal profession. Nero baffles five lawyers with his knowledge of law and Archie gets up to his neck in New York's leading publishing houses. Trying to solve this case, Archie has twelve brand-new (to him) girls to examine – one way or another. This is full-length Nero Wolfe at its richest, one of Stout's amplest and headiest mixtures of violence, wit, and puzzlement.

### Murder in Style
August 1960

It was the most distinguished group ever to gather in Nero Wolfe's study: two of America's foremost novelists, a world-famous playwright and the heads of three famous publishing houses.

Somebody, or maybe a league of somebodies, was accusing America's most celebrated living writers of plagiarism, getting away with it and not hesitating to kill to protect themselves. Wolfe has never undertaken a case like it and no other investigator could have cracked it, for the solution required a penetrating eye for literary style to determine who had written what manuscript, as well as brilliant powers of deduction.

With Wolfe tracking down literary nuances while Archie encounters more than his usual quota of cool-looking girls and much cooler corpses and both of them up to their raised eyebrows in the world of best-sellers, smash-hits, and eggheads, *Murder in Style* is one of the freshest, liveliest, wittiest Rex Stout novels ever to challenge a reader.

### Out Goes She
June 1953

Readers who have long followed the adventures of Nero Wolfe will surely agree not only that this is one of the neatest murder puzzles ever set down by Rex Stout, but also that this is the most exciting, adventure-filled, and breathless story he has ever told. Nero Wolfe has represented some pretty unusual clients in his time, but this one, his client – believe it or not – is the fast-talking hard-hitting, skirt-chasing assistant and companion to Nero, Archie Goodwin himself. We'll make three bets with you about this mystery: First – you won't solve it. Second – you'll agree that no author ever played more fair with his readers. Third – when you finish it, you will feel you have been on a forty-eight hour, breath-taking, danger-filled chase up and down the avenues of New York, into some of Manhattan's darkest and more terror- filled alleys.

### Over My Dead Body
October 1940

Rex Stout goes into Nero Wolfe's long buried and jealously guarded past for some of the complications and motives that make *Over My Dead Body* a brilliant and exciting successor to *Some Buried Caesar* and *Too Many Crooks*. It all began one day when two Montenegrin 'females', as Archie called them, arrived in Wolfe's office with a problem Wolfe didn't want to touch. He did touch it though, when there was a murder in the fencing academy in which the girls worked as instructresses, and when the affair began to take on international complications. *Over My Dead Body* is another example of Mr. Stout's skill, thoroughness and accuracy in giving unusual settings to his stories. Fencing is more than a backdrop; it is a fascinating part of this book.

### Please Pass the Guilt
April 1974

A new Nero Wolfe mystery at last – after a gap of four years – and it will be a delight to all Stout fans. The story is set in the summer of 1969, and the mystery involves the explosion of a bomb in the office of a potential candidate for the presidency of a large corporation. The bomb kills another man, however, and no one can figure out whether the actual victim was the intended victim or not, and of course no one knows who set the bomb in the first place.

The unravelling of the mystery, during which Archie encounters his first Women's Liberationist, is full of suspense, humour, orchids, etymology, and good food in the best Stout tradition.

### Red Threads
July 1941

Val Carew was a queer sort of person – very queer. A born gambler, he gravitated from Oklahoma to Wall Street, and made a pile which he laid at the feet of his wife, a beautiful Indian girl of the Cherokee tribe. When she died prematurely, he built a magnificent tomb in her memory, and there one summer morning the wealthy eccentric was found dead, struck by an Indian war club. Carew was undoubtedly one of the strangest victims of a killer's lust – in fact the whole case is one of the most fascinating we have come across, and of course Mr. Rex Stout makes of it a superlatively interesting novel.

### Right to Die, A
April 1965

Twenty-five years ago, in one of Rex Stout's most famous mystery novels, *Too Many Crooks*, Nero Wolfe was aided in the solution of a murder by twenty-year-old negro. Now, in *A Right to Die*, Stout's latest full length novel, this same negro is a man of forty-five and a professor of anthropology. He comes to Nero and to Archie Goodwin with a pressing problem concerning his son and a young, beautiful and wealthy white girl. Both the son and the girl are active in a civil-rights group. Their entanglements with each other and with the group lead to two murders, and Nero and Archie, in their search for the murderer, become fascinatingly involved in America's most immediate domestic problem. They unearth a murder motive unique in mystery fiction, and encounter some of the most interesting people ever invented by the master of the modern mystery, Rex Stout.

### Second Confession, The*
April 1950

The latest adventures of the famous orchid–growing, beer-drinking, self-proclaimed genius, Nero Wolfe, are more exciting, more violent than ever before. This new full length mystery novel not only gives Nero full play for all his egocentricities, but also provides Archie with a satisfying number of opportunities to risk his neck, to fall into what he never calls love, and to be baffled simultaneously by an exceptionally well-concealed murderer and an infuriatingly non-committal Nero. Rex Stout has written a novel in the fine tradition of his *Some Buried Caesar*, *The Silent Speaker*, and *More Deaths Than One*. Probably never before has the reader of a detective story been given quite so full an array of facts; never has the murderer been at the same time so clearly pointed out and yet so bafflingly concealed. We suspect that a lot of people who will presently be talking about *The Second Confession* will be opening the conversation with some such phrase as 'Not since I read Agatha Christie's *The Murder of Roger Ackroyd*…'

* The dust-jacket and page headings read *Second Confession* but the title-page is *The Second Confession*

### Silent Speaker, The
March 1947

The Crime Club sounds a fanfare to welcome the return of Rex Stout in his first full-length Nero Wolfe novel for six years, a war-time shortage we are delighted to remedy. The brilliant detective methods of the fabulous fat man, beloved by so many thousands of readers, are put to another stiff test in solving the murder of Cheney Boon in the Waldorf just before the dinner of the National Industrial Association. *The Silent Speaker* puts a new top to a distinguished career of detective story writing. It is a masterpiece of pace, characterisation and plot.

### Some Buried Caesar
June 1939

Nero Wolfe steps out again, but as he rolls along a country road he finds himself with Archie in the middle of a tangle of death and crime in high places. The murder of a prize bull is a startling innovation in detective fiction. Among millionaire stockbreeders and in the atmosphere of rivalry and hatred in a country community, Nero and Archie triumph in what is Mr. Stout's most original and one of his wittiest and most breathless cases.

### Three at Wolfe's Door
January 1961

Nero Wolfe considers murder slightly illegal – but in the three long stories in this book it is worse: it becomes a personal affront and a grave inconvenience. For murder usually takes place at a decent distance from his presence; but now, in succession, violent death arrived: firstly, during a dinner for gourmets at which Wolfe was present; secondly, when a corpse came, by taxi, to his famous house on West 35th Street; and, thirdly, at another dinner to which Wolfe and Archie had gone especially to sample blue grouse. It was intolerable. Wolfe was forced to work hard. Archie, of course, was expected to work even harder – and a good deal more energetically.

### Three Doors to Death
September 1950

In the casebook of Archie Goodwin the crimes on which each of the three stories in this volume is based must surely have been marked with a star, for each, in its own way, represents something new, not only to Rex Stout fans, but to all readers of crime fiction. There's the case of the couturiere, for instance, in which it turns out to be as important to determine who is alive as it is to find out who is dead, and in which high passion and high fashion march side by side. There's the case of the restaurateur, in which Archie, proving himself as able at deduction as Nero, spots a key clue and master-minds it all by himself. Lastly, there's the case of the horticulturist, in which the lethargic Nero actually goes for a cross-country walk in the snow – and all for the sake of his precious orchids. *Three Doors to Death* – and a Wolfe at every door!

### Three for the Chair
April 1958

The first of these three new detective short stories exercises Nero Wolfe's ingenuity to the full. In the next two he finds his patience sorely tried and his body exercised too, for Wolfe, who has been called 'one-seventh of a ton of orchid-loving, beer-drinking genius' does not care to move out of his own comfortable house; not even to cook trout for a visiting foreign ambassador at a fishing-lodge in the Adirondacks; not even to attend an enquiry among private detectives in connection with a wire-tapping investigation.

Wolfe and Archie find murder on the bank of the beautiful trout stream – murder that has its motives in the great world of high finance and international politics. And in *Too Many Detectives* murder is done right under the noses of a gathering of private detectives.

Wolfe is as resourceful and domineering as ever and Archie is his usual lively self in these three new exciting and ingenious detective stories.

### Three Men Out
January 1955

'A murderer,' says Nero Wolfe, 'is the victim of progressive exigency.' This very Wolfe-ish pronouncement is incontrovertibly proved in the three cases which are narrated in inimitable fashion by Archie Goodwin in this volume. Never has Wolfe been more brilliant in his handling of theses; and never less static. Twice, much to his dislike, he has to leave his house and his orchids. In *Invitation to Murder* he goes to a millionaire's home to rescue Archie, and incidentally to determine if one of three handsome women is a murderess; in *This Won't Kill You* to a baseball game to solve a problem of druggery and skulduggery. To make up for this unaccustomed dashing about, in *The Zero Clue* he not only stays strictly at home but manages to get most of Manhattan's homicide team occupying his house while he tries to decipher the mysterious clue left by a dying mathematical wizard.

### Three Witnesses
October 1956

Here again we get three detective stories in one volume, all featuring the famous fat detective Nero Wolfe, at the top of his form. Wolfe's reluctance to leave his home and his specially-cooked meals is well known to all his admirers, but in 'The Next Witness' he is at first summoned to court to give evidence, and then, in an effort to right an injustice, he undertakes a course of action which makes it impossible for him to return home! 'When a Man Murders' tell of a husband's unexpected return from the dead – but when he really did die the wrong man would have been convicted of his murder had not Wolfe backed a hunch and Archie shown characteristic resource. In the third adventure a Labrador dog is added to the Wolfe household, with most entertaining – and exciting – consequences. Wolfe shows acute penetration in solving this case of the artist's missing model, and indeed each of these cases is likely to keep the reader baffled and enthralled

### Too Many Clients
August 1961

"A bower of carnality" was what Nero Wolfe called the love-nest maintained by a rich businessman whose murder he and Goodwin were investigating. A number of ladies had keys to the secret apartment, and it was not surprising that several people had motives for killing its owner, among them one or two husbands.

This book might have been called any *Too Many Women* had not Archie Goodwin already used that title in his report of an earlier Wolfe investigation. Archie needs to guard his chastity as well as to keep his quick wits about him in the many swift developments that take place before the case is solved – and Wolfe has to move warily amidst the clashing interests of his "too many clients".

*Too Many Clients* is amusing and baffling; it presents the genius Wolfe and his lieutenant Archie at the top of their form in an extraordinary and exciting investigation of murder.

### Too Many Cooks
September 1938

Rex Stout has already been marked down by detective-story connoisseurs as an author for stardom. Every one who has read his earlier novels, *The Red Box*, *The Rubber Band*, *The League of Frightened Men*, and *Fer-de-Lance*, will be eagerly looking forward to his new book. And *Too Many Cooks*, with which for the first time he is published by the Crime Club, is out and away his best. Rex Stout has definitely 'arrived'. From now on we say, with *Scribner's Magazine*, that 'All admirers and despisers of murder stories should read everything ever written by Rex Stout.'

*Too Many Cooks* features once again the ponderous, orchid-fancying Nero Wolfe, one of the best characters ever created for detective fiction. Larding the lean earth when he moves (which is as seldom as possible), Nero Wolfe resembles Falstaff in wit as well as in bulk.

As to the story of *Too Many Cooks*, you must take the title literally and not proverbially. The cooks are ten master chefs from London, Paris, New York, Calcutta, etc., who meet together every five years. After dinner on this particular night there is to be a test. One of the chefs is to make a quantity of Sauce Printemps, for which there are nine seasonings besides salt. Nine dishes are to be prepared, each lacking one of the seasonings. The other chefs and Nero Wolfe are to go into the room in turn and record their guesses as to which seasoning is left out of each dish. While they are waiting they occupy themselves casually, talking and listening to the radio. So it comes to Nero Wolfe's turn. He goes into the room – to find the chef who made the dishes stabbed to the heart!

Here is a story that has everything: good detecting, good characterisation based on sound psychology, humour, imagination, style, a good story, high entertainment value, and – Nero Wolfe.

### *Too Many Women*
April 1948

Archie Goodwin answers an urgent summons from Mr. Jasper Pine, president of a big New York business firm, who has reason to suspect that one of his colleagues, run down by a hit-and-run driver, had in reality been murdered. The case involves on-the-spot investigation in the palatial offices of Naylor-Kerr, Inc., where Archie goes to work as a personnel expert. All Nero Wolfe fans know that the great man never leaves his upholstered, orchid-blooming habitat, so it falls to Archie to do all the big work and quite a lot of the thinking, while Nero sits at home, more Buddha-like than ever but very much in the picture. *Too Many Women* is exciting and highly amusing, and the vast figure of the great Nero, a classic creation in detective fiction, is there for our entertainment – and admiration.

### *Trio for Blunt Instruments*
January 1965

Rex Stout's unique skill with the novelette form has so long been acknowledged that it requires no further proclamation. Here, then, are the three latest demonstrations of his ability to embody full-length story qualities and characterisations in the somewhat shorter form. In 'Kill Now, Pay Later', he gives us the bootblack's beautiful daughter and her involvement with a business executive who might have jumped or fallen from a certain tenth-floor window had not someone bashed his cranium first. 'Murder is Corny' is largely about the story the farmer's daughter told, which nearly put Archie Goodwin on trial for murder. 'Blood Will Tell' is the case of the too curious wife whose final indiscretion led to her being killed with a vodka bottle. Strangely enough, though Nero Wolfe is his ever super-brilliant self in all these affairs, it is only the final one which earns him a fee.

### *Triple Jeopardy*
October 1952

Could you sit in an office on West Thirty-Fifth Street and determine who among six people put a poison pellet into a pill-box that rested on a night club table three days before? Or what a policeman was carrying inside a folded newspaper before he was murdered? Or what sight was witnessed by a gibbering monkey in an over-heated apartment the day before yesterday? Detection never seemed more magical than in these three newest stories by Rex Stout. Each is a gem of mystery narrative. Each finds Nero a little shrewder, a little more intolerant and – probably – even a little fatter. Each finds Archie as indestructible and cynical as ever. Each finds the two of them exactly where they have been for quite some time now, and where every mystery fan who loves good writing, as well as good detection, hope they will stay for long, long while – right at the top of the detective-novel hierarchy.

### *Trouble in Triplicate*
August 1949

Nero Wolfe must be ranked among the great detectives of fiction. The ponderous figure of the corpulent lover of orchids – and beer – has pushed his way forcefully to the very front rank. Nero Wolfe is not only an incomparable investigator of crime; he is a wit, a *bon viveur*, a lovable man of the world, and his running commentary on the crime of the moment is at once intelligent and amusing. Here for the first time are three new Nero Wolfe cases in one rewarding volume, and nowhere among Rex Stout's stories will one find more suspense, or more loving attention to the details of deduction and denouement. Here then is Nero Wolfe, brilliant as he ever was, in all his laziness and all his genius, and in good measure, too, for all his devout followers.

### *Where There's a Will*
March 1941

Nero Wolfe has had some difficult assignments, faithfully reported by his incorrigible assistant, Archie Goodwin, in *Too Many Cooks*, *Some Buried Caesar*, *Over My Dead Body*, etc. But never had there been such a case as this. In the first place the Hawthorne family was eccentric, so there didn't seem to be any reason to call in the most eminent of private detectives because Noel Hawthorne left in his will an apple, a peach, and a pear respectively, to his three sisters. *But*... it was not long before things took a decidedly diabolical turn. Murder and an international intrigue were only two aspects of a case which required all Nero Wolfe's ingenuity and intelligence to unravel, and whose solution forced Nero not only to leave the sanctuary of his office but even flout the workings of justice!

## STRANGE, JOHN STEPHEN

### *Bell in the Fog, The*
January 1937

Having been blown sky high by an explosion, Barney Gantt, staff photographer for a famous newspaper, was shipped off to the isolated Island of Sowback to recuperate. The doctor describing the island said: 'There's no telephone, no boat stops there, nothing ever happens. There's nothing to do but to fish for cod, a soothing occupation.' 'I'd rather die,' replied Barney – but he didn't have time to. On arriving at the Island he was told of a mailbag robbery where only one letter had been stolen, and shortly after he himself discovered the body of a murdered man on the sea shore. News spreads in a small place by some mysterious magic unknown in cities; the gossipy inhabitants of Sowback accused each other of the crime openly and in secret, but as soon as Barney tried to get some sense out of them they shut up like clams. Then a fog descended on the island as well as on the investigation; the uncanny booming of the fog horn every thirty seconds added to the already sinister conditions. Here is an unusual detective story in an unusual setting.

### *Chinese Jar Mystery, The*
March 1934

In the strangely beautiful but sinister Chinese Jar were sealed, so the legend went, the ghosts of evil, and when Hetty Gaunt died and strange tales gathered round her dying, it was to the mystery of the jar that Detective-Sergeant Potter looked for an answer. He found more than he expected, for the background of murder began to spread until it enveloped the whole Gaunt family, closing in first here, then there, until Potter found the one vital clue that ended once and for all the terror of the Gaunts. *The Chinese Jar Mystery* has tense dramatic power and a subtle ingenuity of plot, joined with an expert style and a satisfying story.

### *Come to Judgement*
April 1949

Two shots in the dark; two men running off into the rain to lose themselves in a crowded thoroughfare; a still figure on a wet pavement – so begins a detective story of unusual distinction. On the face of it, there seemed no doubt that Lester Ward, wealthy man-about-town and noted sportsman, shot Andy Newcomb, small garage-owner on that black November night in New York City. Andy twice accused Ward before he died of his wounds. And yet...George Honneger, the efficient, honest and entirely human police officer we first met in the successful *Murder Gives a Lovely Light*, has an uncomfortable feeling that the picture's slightly out of focus. Good characterisation, almost unbearable suspense, and a seemingly insoluble problem, make this a detective story to stand among the great ones.

### *Corpse and the Lady, The*
July 1938

*The Corpse and the Lady* is an excellent detective story, introducing once more that splendid character Barney Gantt, the smart young newspaper photographer with a very pronounced nose for sleuthing. It is also a full-blooded novel with characters whose ultimate fate become a matter of intense interest to the reader. The characterisation of Stella and Giles Redfern is exceptionally well done, from the moment when they are in near panic at the opening of the book, through their growing terror as the evidence against them mounts, to the denouement at the end. *The Corpse and the Lady* should be one of the most popular of this talented writer's books.

### *Dead End*
June 1953

Valentina Abbott, French born, three times married, has been accused and is standing trial for the seventeen-year-old murder of her first husband, Michael Arum. The judge presiding at her trial is, ironically enough, a man who had known and loved her in his youth. The trial is sensational, both in the facts it produces and in the character of the beautiful but enigmatic woman who is accused. It is only after we have seen her through many eyes, and have been swayed for and against her by much conflicting evidence, that she emerges in her true light. *Guilty, or Not Guilty?* Let this utterly absorbing crime story give you the answer.

### *Deadly Beloved*
August 1952

Barney Gantt was through with murder now that he was no longer a crime reporter on the *Globe*. That's what he *thought*. But the old brownstone house in New York where he and his wife Muriel took a third-floor apartment was destined to be the scene of a peculiarly horrible and brutal crime, and Barney was to be for ever mortified by the knowledge that it was committed under his very feet, so to speak. There were so many points of sinister significance he could have noted – for instance, the two different coloured grasses in the small garden at the back of the house ... That well-known couple, Barney and Muriel Gantt, are back again in a story which is a classic example of the macabre.

### *Eye Witness*
March 1962

Joe Perry had been on the point of exposing a call-girl racket when he was murdered. The police nearly broke the Perry case – but there was a leak to the press, the witnesses vanished, and the most important ones were soon found dead. But the 'Eye Witness' remained – an innocent party, an actress who by chance had caught sight of and observed one of the killers; who could make a sure identification. The 'Eye Witness' had to be preserved alive at all costs if the racketeers were to be exposed, a task rendered still more precarious by the growing evidence of corruption among the forces of law and order.

There are many facets to this skilfully told tale of murder, corruption and kidnapping, which culminates in a thrilling, multiple climax.

### *For the Hangman*
April 1935

John Stephen Strange is here seen in the form that made *The Man Who Killed Fortescue* quite outstanding among detective stories. 'Mr. Strange's work will please you by its sound construction and strong detective interest,' wrote Dorothy L. Sayers of his last book, *The Chinese Jar Mystery*. *The Field*, writing of *Murder Game*, said, 'A really first-rate detective story,' and of the same book the *Edinburgh Evening News* said, 'A Crime Club publication which must rank as one of the foremost of its kind.' And the *Daily Dispatch* said, 'Will keep you awake even after a Sunday dinner.' *For the Hangman* will keep you awake too. The author is here concerned with the murder of a thoroughly unpleasant, ratty little man who had occupied himself with finding out details of the skeletons in everybody's cupboards, and afterwards writing them up in a scurrilous newspaper. The murdered man, therefore, had plenty of enemies. The detective had a particularly difficult task in discriminating between many individuals who had ample motive for the murder.

### *Handful of Silver, A*
June 1955

Though years had passed since the war ended, Henri Magritte could not re-shape his life with the thought of his colleagues, who had died in the Resistance, always on his mind. Many of those old friends and companions had been cruelly betrayed to death by torture, among them Henri's beloved brother, Robert. Perhaps it was the thought that Robert's betrayer was still at large that made Henri's life restless and meaningless. And then the arrests began; arrests that unfolded a sordid tale of treachery and treason, that pointed remorselessly to a traitor among the close, affectionate family and friends who were dearest to Henri...In this exciting tale the moods and details of Paris are captured, the war-time terror of the Gestapo is vividly portrayed and the end is startling and horrifying.

### *Look Your Last*
July 1944
Barney Gantt, news photographer and student of the passing show, finds that international oil is a world problem that can at times cast a film over a New York murder investigation. The discovery of a murdered man in an apartment house near Central Park plunges Barney into a fascinating murder case, which forms part of a gigantic international plot engineered in the interests of big business. *Look Your Last* is a first-rate mystery of international intrigue, private wickedness, and sleuthing by capable hands, a story supercharged with excitement.

### *Make My Bed Soon*
May 1948
John Stephen Strange has written a fine novel of suspense and mystery dealing in particular with the effect of murder on normal people, without resorting to the creaking door, wailing banshees, baying bloodhounds and other tried devices. Among the near neighbours of Barney and Muriel Gantt, now living an idyllic existence in a pleasant farmhouse, was Mrs. Webb, an elderly woman who sold eggs, but whose apparent culture hinted at an affluent past. When Mrs. Webb dies, apparently of food poisoning, Barney Gantt hears strange rumours that make him feel fear – fear of the evil man can do!

### *Murder Game*
December 1931
Who murdered the great football coach while thousands looked on from the stands, and two fighting teams played through the climax of a crucial game?

The Yorke team was on the ten-yard line, with three minutes to go. Diederich, the famous coach, sat watching them. There was no sound of a bullet in the turmoil of cheering and excitement, but Diederich slumped suddenly to the ground, a bullet through his heart. It was the first murder that Van Dusen Ormsberry had ever witnessed, but he found that that was no help in his investigations. What had seemed a simple case of homicide was in reality a dark circle of mystery that grew darker and more obscure the more deeply it penetrated. What was Diederich's real past – was Diedrich his real name? Who was the man found dying outside Diederich's rooms? What had Hazen, the man who paid for athletics at Yorke, to do with the killing? Ormsberry sought the answers feverishly, while the killer struck again and again, and the strange shadow across the life of the little college town deepened into terrible tragedy.

### *Murder Gives a Lovely Light*
May 1942
John Stephen Strange, one of the foremost American crime novelists, has written in *Murder Gives a Lovely Light* a superlatively good and off-the-beaten-track story. The death of Simeon Rede, an elderly invalid, came as no surprise to his lovely young wife and his daughter, who had long anticipated a heart attack. However, the combination of a stolen bracelet and a discharged maid, through a strange chain of circumstances, arouses suspicion in Police Inspector Honegger. Further investigation confirmed his suspicion of Rede's murder. Unfortunately, the Rede family was an involved one and its associations many, and Honegger found himself with a surfeit of suspects. Here is one of the most cleverly plotted and ably characterised mystery stories, that will be read and discussed with enthusiasm for many, many months to come.

### *Night of Reckoning*
March 1959
On a sultry August afternoon two women waited tensely to learn whether parole had been granted wealthy Royce Burlingham, convicted of murder eight years before; one was his wife, the other his daughter.

On that same afternoon Police Chief Delahanty had reason to be reminded of the Burlingham case, and his old uneasiness about the original evidence stirred again. But just then he was more concerned over the dark threat of a coastal hurricane which was heading towards the town.

The terrible crisis which boiled up from the Burlingham's past and the havoc of the storm make *Night of Reckoning* a gripping study in suspense and a worthy successor to *A Handful of Silver* and *Deadly Beloved*.

### *Picture of the Victim*
August 1940
When Barney Gantt, news photographer and detective extraordinary, vowed to get a picture of millionaire Jesse Jordan even if he had to shoot him first and prop him against a tree, he was unaware that Fate would save him that trouble. It was not until he had made his way through an unguarded gate in the Long Island estate and found Jordan's dead body slumped on the bench behind the fountain, that he realised that Lady Luck had again played his hand for him. Instead of a photograph of a living malefactor of great wealth, Barney came back with a picture of the victim of a headline-making murder, one that was to fill columns of newsprint for weeks, and provide the most devious and engrossing case that had ever taxed his shrewd and ingenious wits.

### *Reasonable Doubt*
October 1951
One February morning, in New York City, Ruth Purdy went on trial for the murder of her husband. The State contended that George Purdy died of nicotine poisoning, and that the poison was administered wilfully and with malice aforethought by his wife. It was the state's obligation to prove beyond reasonable doubt that she did in fact commit such an act of murder. To Arnold Bricker, the second counsel for the defence, the jury's interpretation of 'reasonable doubt' was literally a matter of life and death, for he was in love with the accused woman. This is a gripping story of intelligent people caught in the shadow of murder, told with skill and an unerring sense of the dramatic.

### *Rope Enough*
March 1939
In *Rope Enough* Barney Gantt, news photographer, solves the mystery surrounding the murder of old Dan Kinney and brings to justice a criminal too powerful to be touched by the law but who, given rope enough, hangs himself. The case demands all Barney's native wit and daring, for the people involved were strong enough to command the indifference of the police and ruthless enough to silence all attempts at opposition. Barney claimed that it was luck that helped him, but this conclusion does less than justice to his own astute reasoning and audacious planning.

### *Strangler Fig, The*
January 1931
You can't convict a vine of murder! And yet the superstitious negroes on World's End, the lovely island home of Stephen Huntington, off the Florida coast, were convinced that the strangler fig – the terrible jungle vine that snares animals and men – had caught and destroyed Huntington when he walked off his lawn into the jungle eight years before and never returned. Of course he might have gone to the mainland in a boat, he might have been devoured by a shark. But no one really *knew* – until one day Bolivar Brown, one of Mrs. Huntington's guests, walking in the jungle after a terrific storm, found a bleached skeleton and under it a cigarette case with the initials S. H. The grisly discovery started in motion a train of death and horror that ringed the island, and the Huntington family, with a terrible strength.

### *Uneasy Is the Grave*
May 1950
Lydia Lowe considered herself a lucky woman. She was not particularly religious – if she had her life over again she would still have done what she did and felt no sense of guilt – but sitting in the firelight with the children's mending, looking at that good and kind man, her husband, the Reverend Gerald Howe, she thanked God for bringing her to so safe and sound a haven. Then came the letter from Ezra Bone, and with it the first faint stirrings of that unquiet grave on the wild and wind-tossed coast of Hawk Island. In this brilliantly-contrived mystery of an old crime that stretched its ghostly fingers through the years to lay their cold touch on the warm and living flesh of a woman, John Stephen Strange has an engrossing tale to unfold and tells it with vigour, imagination and a sure sense of the dramatic.

## STRONG, L. A. G.

### *All Fall Down*
January 1944
Mr. L. A. G. Strong's new story of murder and sudden death has many striking and unusual qualities. It is in essence a novel of high distinction. Mr. Strong concentrates on what is psychologically the most interesting part of every murder case – the circumstances that precede the crime. He shows how murder is the logical outcome of certain mental processes and describes convincingly and dramatically the events that lead – almost inevitably – to the perpetration of the crime. *All Fall Down* is a notable achievement in its lifelike portrayal of character. Paul Gilkison, a young bookseller, slightly prim and rather diffident; Inspector Ellis McKay of Scotland Yard, cockily robust and worldly wise; Matthew Baildon, an old collector of first editions who loves his books better than his own family; the village school teachers Eunice Caunter and David Rattray, caught in a gamut of conflicting emotions; all are characters that live vividly in the reader's memory long after he has finished this absorbing story in which they play their strikingly individual parts.

### *Othello's Occupation*
May 1945
It was the annual matinee of the Kean-Macready Stage School and the curtain had just fallen on the successful performance of *Othello's Occupation*. Now should have been the moment of triumph for Miss Vane, the principal. Students and staff, grouped on either side of the stage, made a lane for the traditional royal entrance. The audience increased their clamour for the principal; she had never been known to mis-time her entrance before. Then abruptly silence fell, a hushed silence. Here was indeed tragedy... Mr. L. A G. Strong's latest story of murder has all this distinguished writer's customary skill at character drawing and is in addition a clever story of detection.

### *Slocombe Dies*
March 1942
Mr. L.A.G. Strong, the distinguished author of *Dewar Rides*, *The Brothers*, and other fine novels, is one of the most versatile of writers. *Slocombe Dies* is Mr. Strong's first venture into the field of crime fiction, and it will undoubtedly bring him fresh laurels. For he tells his story from an unusual angle. The question that intrigues him about the mysterious happenings in a West Country village is not how the murder was done but how it came to be committed at all. How in a sleepy little village did such a hell-broth come to the boil? One minute everything was ordinary, placid and go as you please, the next minute one is plunged bang into the middle of a nightmare. So Mr. Strong takes the advice given to one of his characters, burrows into the lives of the people concerned and lays bare a really fine story of human passion.

### *Treason in the Egg*
August 1958
When Ellis McKay went to Armada House for the course on Modern Art he thought that he had left his official life behind him for a while. But the curious and sinister events which took place there soon found him forced to use his amateur musician's status as a cloak for the activities of his official self – Chief Detective Inspector Ellis McKay of Scotland Yard.

The strange picture of a huge egg, which appeared in the middle of the surrealist film shown to the students on the second evening, causes the audience of neurotic intellectuals, habitual culture vultures and husband-hunting spinsters to react in unexpected and alarming ways. Helped by that amiable West Countryman, Inspector Bradstreet, McKay discloses a deadly and ingenious plot and, in the face of a ruthless opposition, follows the trail to its exciting and dangerous end.

*Treason in the Egg* shows once more that L.A.G. Strong's "police diversions" are as original and distinguished as all this famous author's work.

### *Which I Never*
November 1950
Mr. L. A. G. Strong happily sub-titles his present story, 'A Police Diversion', which fully describes the strange events which for a time provide an exciting diversion for several members of the force. Chief – Detective Inspector McKay, the composer detective, well known through Mr. Strong's previous detective stories, goes down to the country on some highly secret business for Scotland Yard and finds himself working again with his friend Inspector Bradstreet, whose West Country placidity no human meanness or viciousness can shake. But it is the ambitious Constable Hockaday who in the end is to play the most important part in a bewildering case which involves a number of missing girls. Mr. Strong writes detective stories all too seldom, and *Which I Never* will be warmly welcomed by readers who remember *All Fall Down*, *Othello's Occupation*, and *Slocombe Dies*.

## SYMONS, JULIAN

### *Belting Inheritance, The*
March 1965
The heir of Belting had, in a sense, worked for his inheritance; he and his brother had waited, albeit loyally and dutifully, for the day when the big house, the land and the money would belong to them. They were shocked and incredulous when a Claimant announced his existence and his intention of joining the household.

The drama at Belting is recalled years later by young Christopher Barrington, a poor relation who had been brought up there. He had been deeply involved with the sensational advent of the Belting Claimant. The battle for the Belting money occupies the foreground of his narrative, but Christopher also nostalgically recalls his boyhood in the huge house, his first girlfriend, his first taste of Paris in the Spring…

The story is gripping but also comic in the extraordinary scenes where the identity of the Claimant is being questioned. Julian Symons is pre-eminent among crime novelists and famous for novels some of which have been sombre and tragic. The mood of *The Belting Inheritance* is quite different from those. It is gay and touching as well as providing a strong story with several surprising twists to it.

### *Blackheath Poisonings, The: A Victorian Murder Mystery*
July 1978

In Blackheath in the 1890's a close-knit family live in the extraordinary Gothic folly Albert House, built to resemble a church, and the equally strange neo-Palladian Victorian Villa. In Albert House, Harriet, the matriarch, is established with her submissive daughter Charlotte. Victoria Villa houses another daughter, her husband and stepson, and a son and his attractive wife. There is a peaceful routine of Sunday lunch, parlour games, local poetry readings. And then this is interrupted by a death. Gastric fever, says pompous Dr. Porterfield, but young Paul Vandervent, the stepson, is doubtful…

Julian Symons's book is a new departure for him. He calls it 'a Victorian murder mystery', but it is also a delightful period novel, with characters whose talk and behaviour is completely convincing. We see much of what happens through the eyes of the engaging young Paul, who is just leaving school, thinks himself in love with the beautiful Isabel, and writes verses about her. It is Paul who first senses that something is wrong, pursues various trails more or less successfully, and after a trial involving some of the actual legal luminaries of the time, offers a solution to the Blackheath mystery in an epilogue.

This is a fascinating book, whether it is considered as a baffling mystery, or as a story illuminating several unusual facets of Victorian life, and one which is in every way worthy of an acknowledged master of crime.

### *Colour of Murder, The*
June 1957

John Wilkins was a respectable young business man, happily married and living in placid suburban life – on the surface at least – when he met Sheila Morton at the local library. 'Sheila's a sweet girl,' one of the characters says. 'Trouble with her is she can't say no. You say to her come out on the river. Sheila, she won't like to say no if she doesn't want to.' Between his sharp-tongued wife May and the girl who can't say no, respectable John Wilkins finds himself enmeshed in a web of romance and fantasy, a web broken only by murder…

The first half of the book is John Wilkins's story of his actions. The second half describes a trial for murder at Lewes Assizes, with sidelights on the attitudes of everybody concerned, from prosecuting counsel to defence solicitor. The Judge's verdict and the epilogue leave a question mark – or do they? This is for you to decide. This is a remarkable *tour de force* from the author of *The Thirty-First of February* and *The Paper Chase.*

### *End of Solomon Grundy, The*
August 1964

A girl is murdered in a Mayfair mews, the sort of girl who describes herself as a model. Was she a model or was she something less reputable? Superintendent Manners isn't sure, but he slowly becomes convinced that the secret of the crime lies in the affluent suburban housing estate called The Dell. Dell-dwellers, like architect Dick Weldon and wine and food expert Jack Jellifer, think of themselves as living the mid-twentieth century, civilised life, but in The Dell there is one explosive element: red-headed, roughneck Solomon Grundy. Has Grundy killed the girl? Superintendent Manners thinks so.

In a letter to the author, C. P. Snow called his earlier *Progress of a Crime* 'absolutely first class' and said 'I don't think I have ever read a really good English *roman policier* before.' *The End of Solomon Grundy* is a *roman policier* too – there is a splendid series of trial scenes in which the legal antagonists from the earlier book, ascetic Eustace Hardy and red-faced puffing Magnus Newton, Q.C., meet in a battle royal. But there is much else in it, in particular the sharply amusing depiction of life in The Dell. What *was* the end of Solomon Grundy, who was born on Monday? The reader of this tantalising crime novel is kept on edge even after the trial verdict has been reached, and the end of the story is brutal, shocking and moving – and in its own way a surprise.

### *Gigantic Shadow, The*
September 1958

The TV show 'Bill Hunter – Personal Investigator' had become an outstanding success. By careful selection of the celebrities he quizzed and equally careful investigation of their past history, Hunter was often able to promote the unexpected and dramatic rows which put the show into the headlines – until the day he questioned Nicholas Mekles, that fabulous millionaire shipowner whose reputation was as shady as his power was real. Mekles hit back by throwing a searchlight beam on Bill's own past – a past which threw a gigantic shadow, the shadow of murder.

Discredited before a million people, Hunter broke with the network, broke with the lazy and affectionate Anna, cast off his friends and hid. He sulked in a seedy hotel; depressed, bitter and bored. Searching for entertainment he met Anthea Moorhouse and fell headlong for that mercurial and dazzling socialite. With Anthea he hatched the ambitious and daring ploy which was to solve all their problems. For Anthea he turned back into the shadow of the past. Because of Anthea he planned a devious way through the underworld which led him to danger and desperation and fear.

In *The Gigantic Shadow* Julian Symons has told an intriguing and exciting story, in which reality and acute observation blend to make a worthy successor to *The Colour of Murder* and *The Paper Chase.*

### *Killing of Francie Lake, The*
October 1962

The magazine empire known as Plain Man Enterprises was the creation and mouthpiece of the 'plain man' himself, Octavius Gaye, commonly known as 'Ocky'. But the character of Ocky was notably more exotic than plain, and the executives who surrounded him were all the puppets of his magnetism and his influence. One of these executives was called Francie Lake.

This brilliant novel depicts the unscrupulous operations of a tycoon in an imaginary but horribly plausible world of magazine publishing and explains, in time, how and why Francie Lake was killed. It is the work of one of the most celebrated modern crime novelists – author of *The Thirty-First of February* and *The Progress of a Crime.*

### *Man Who Killed Himself, The*
September 1967

When meek, submissive little Arthur Brownjohn decides to murder his dominating wife Clare he consults the best authorities, reading the stories of well-known murderers and trying to avoid their mistakes. But Arthur has been ineffectual all his life, and he is a bungling murderer. When his plans go wrong he seeks the aid of the flamboyant Major Easonby Mellon, who for various reasons needs to disappear from his shady matrimonial agency.

What has timid Arthur Brownjohn to do with dashing Easonby Mellon? That is the heart of a story which is comic, fantastic, and full of surprises, including a neat parody on current fashions in spy stories and sidelights on the incidental benefits of running a matrimonial agency. The meaning of the title? You won't discover that until almost the last page.

Here is one of the world's most distinguished crime novelists writing at the very top of his form. With subtle and ambitious characterisation, with exact and cool observation, with meticulous, elaborate plotting and, a fluent gift for comedy, Julian Symons tells an original story that will bring pleasure to a huge readership; something exciting and new in the field of the crime novel.

### *Man Who Lost His Wife, The*
October 1970

Gilbert Welton had a charming wife and a beautiful house. And although his publishing business was declining it would obviously last his time. He thought of himself as a happy man, and believed that his wife Virginia was happy too. It was a shock when Virginia, without explanation, said that she had to get away, a greater shock when Gilbert made up his mind that she was having an affair with his partner Max. She flew off to Yugoslavia. And then she disappeared.

What has Virginia done, what will Gilbert do, what has really happened? This is a story of suspense and excitement, moving from London to Yugoslavia, where Gilbert goes to search for his wife. It is also a novel about jealousy and about a man who tries to change his way of life, a book which is sharply funny about half a dozen subjects, including publishing, modern art movements and London life in general. It will be a gloomy reader who does not laugh at Jake Bunce's TV interview or Coldharbour's sexual problems. For that matter, Gilbert has his own emotional problems in the form of a love affair with a girl who is not quite what she seems...

Hard to find a label for a book which has so many different elements. We hesitate to call it a new kind of crime story, Mr Symons himself calls it a 'novel of suspicion'. That seems a good description.

### *Man Whose Dreams Came True, The*
November 1968

Tony Scott-Williams had dreams – after all, which of us doesn't dream sometimes, about winning the pools or inheriting a fortune from an unknown relative? But Tony (born Jones, a name which he had rejected) ran into trouble when he tried to put his dreams into practice. There were three dreams. First, marrying a rich woman who would give him a free hand with her money; second, winning a fortune at roulette; third, spending the rest of his life in a foreign country in the company of glamorous girls.

To make his dreams come true Tony gambled, forged, and was led finally to murder. Everything he did went slightly wrong, and to his astonishment he found himself in the dock. Yet in the end Tony's dreams did come true, although the results were far from those he would have chosen.

There is no more distinguished name in the whole field of crime fiction today than that of Julian Symons. Here is a novel, brilliantly plotted, cunningly told and often bitterly funny, that will bring pleasure to the legions who have acquired a taste for Mr. Symons's novels, among which *Progress of a Crime* and *The Man Who Killed Himself* will be well remembered.

### *Paper Chase, The*
March 1956

Charles Applegate took a job at Bramley Hall because he hoped to set his second detective story in a progressive school. But Mr. Pont, the headmaster, took his school very seriously. 'We are co-educational, of course… We use the Brooke-Timla Health Guide.' In the event Applegate, too, was obliged to take Bramley Hall seriously, for a murder took place the first night he was under its roof. Applegate soon found that the practice of detection was different from the theory. For one thing he was embarrassed by the energy of pretty Hedda Pont, who was by no means a docile ally. For another, he discovered that behind the activities of two rival gangs was the mysterious figure of Johnny Bogue, M. D., financier, jailbird and secret agent. Bogue had been killed in an air crash during the war, but his past activities provided twist after twist in the story, like (Applegate thought) the clues in a paper chase. At last the trail of Johnny Bogue led Applegate and Hedda into mortal danger. Julian Symons is famous for crime stories in which the macabre is blended with a dry, ironic humour: *The Thirtyfirst of February* and *The Narrowing Circle* are among them. *The Paper Chase*, quick-moving and light-hearted, is perhaps his most entertaining book.

### *Players and the Game, The*
August 1972

The players are a man who has fantasies about being Count Dracula the vampire, and a woman who imagines that she is Bonnie of *Bonnie and Clyde*. The game is one of let's pretend, rather macabre no doubt, but still nothing more than a game.

And then two girls disappear.

And the game is not pretence any more.

*The Players and the Game* is sometimes horrific, often wryly funny, always sharply realistic. But is this game of murder, who are the players? The background is a journal kept by one of them. In the foreground are the intrigues and jealousies below the smooth surface of life in Timbals Plastics. Bob Lowson, the managing director, pays occasional unmedical visits to Dr. Winstanley; his daughter and her friends, bored with suburban smugness, taste the pleasures discreetly offered in doubtful magazines; and Brian Hartford, his deputy, plots the downfall of the handsome, emotionally erratic personnel director Paul Vane with the same intensity with which he plots the moves in those games of toy soldiers with which he occupies his leisure hours.

As the police (a splendidly varied lot, from Chief Constable through Superintendent and Chief Inspector down to sergeants) close in on the players, the tension rises. Julian Symons has never written anything more powerful, more gripping or more disturbing. His book is a classical puzzle in detection and at the same time an absorbing study of the way in which two people, apparently harmless as individuals, trigger off, when they meet, the terrifying phenomenon known as *folie a deux* which turns them into one single monster of psychopathic crime.

### *Plot Against Roger Rider, The*
July 1973

Roger Rider and Geoffrey Paradine had known each other since childhood. Dashing Roger looked after feeble Geoffrey, and bullied him a bit too. Later Roger became a tycoon, and gave Geoffrey a job. And later still, Geoffrey took a kind of revenge when he went to bed with Roger's beautiful bitchy wife Amanda. So when Roger disappeared on a Spanish holiday had Geoffrey Paradine killed him?

*The Plot Against Roger Rider* finds Julian Symons in sparkling form. The action shuttles between Spain and London, with a stunning climax in Sardinia, there is an attractive young hero who's writing a thesis on crime stories and worrying about whether he's homosexual, a ruthlessly candid heroine who clears up his problem and helps to solve the case, a variety of policemen Spanish and English. And above all, there's a truly baffling puzzle, not solved until the very last chapter. You might – just might – whisper 'Unfair' at the end. But then that's what some readers said when they'd finished *The Murder of Roger Ackroyd*.

### *Progress of a Crime, The*
July 1960

The murder took place on Guy Fawkes' night. There was no doubt about what happened – a group of teddy boys stabbed a man to death round the bonfire on the village green. Hugh Bennett, young reporter on a local paper, saw it happen. But what was it exactly he had seen? Mr. Symon's absorbing book is a mile away from the conventional murder story. The big cast of characters, each exactly etched, includes provincial and London journalists, police, barristers and teddy boys. And at the centre of the story is young, sympathetic Hugh Bennett, who discovers that telling the truth is not as easy as it seems, and that landing a newspaper scoop can involve agonising moral problems. The book can be considered as an attack on newspaper sensationalism, as a criticism of legal procedure or as a novel of human emotions which is far from more exciting that a straight detective story. *The Progress of a Crime* sets an impressive new standard in crime fiction.

### *Sweet Adelaide: A Victorian Puzzle Solved*
April 1980

In 1886 Adelaide Bartlett was tried at the Old Bailey on the charge of poisoning her husband Edwin. In *Sweet Adelaide* Julian Symons offers an imaginative interpretation of this famous case, ending with a solution of an affair which still remains a mystery. Did the adjective 'sweet' apply to Adelaide, or was she a cunning and deliberate poisoner? Was the Weslyan Minister George Dyson just a platonic friend, or something more than that? And if Adelaide committed the crime, how did she do it?

But the book is a novel as much as a crime story. Mr Symons provides a romantic background for Adelaide, an account of her childhood, and the reasons for her strange marriage to Edwin Bartlett, after which she went to school to complete her education. He shows us Adelaide as she was seen by enemies like her father-in-law, and friends like the nurse who attended her confinement. The Victorian background, which counts for much in the story, is flawlessly handled, and at the end Mr Symons has provided answers for the many readers who ask: 'How much is invented and how much is true?' The cunning blending of the two makes a brilliant crime story, which is also a fascinating novel.

### *Three Pipe Problem, A*
February 1975

The life of actor Sheridan Haynes has been transformed by his immense success as TV's Sherlock Holmes. Sher, as his friends call him, has been a passionate Sherlockian from his youth, and he's delighted when the studio suggests that he should live in Baker Street, in rooms that contain many relics of Sherlock's famous cases. And Sher fancies himself as a detective in the Holmesien vein. When some mysterious karate killings take place, he is drawn into a search for the murderer.

Julian Symons's book will delight all lovers of the Holmes stories. Some of Sher's deductions have the authentic flavour of the master, others go disastrously and comically astray. Sher himself, old-fashioned, hating modern life and longing for gas-lit Victorian London, is a bit of a stick but also a most engaging character. And the mystery in which he becomes enmeshed – and eventually solves – is a real mystery set in a vividly realized contemporary London, with a splendid climax in which Sher stalks a killer, and is stalked himself, through a swirling Victorian fog. This is perhaps the most delightfully high-spirited book Mr Symons has written.

## TAPPLY, WILLIAM G.

### *Client Privilege*
April 1991

Boston lawyer Brady Coyne may be no Perry Mason in court, and he'd rather fish for trout than settle estates or negotiate contracts, but his many wealthy clients still value his discretion.

But when his client, the Honourable Chester Y. Popowski, summons Brady to his office, it's not to chat about the judge's nomination to a federal seat. The judge has a letter to show Brady – a letter from a blackmailer.

Brady meets the blackmailer – and later the same night the man is found murdered. Soon Brady finds himself pursued by a pair of dogged cops, a TV journalist, and a newspaper gossip columnist, and quickly realizes that if the murder's to be solved, he'd better get cracking himself. As he investigates, Brady gradually finds himself forced to reconsider his most basic ethical assumptions. How far should client privilege extend? Brady's life, as well as his professional standing, depend on his answer.

### *Dead Meat*
January 1988

Attorney Brady Coyne's discreet service to Boston's wealthier Brahmins is calculated to leave him plenty of time to pursue his real passion: fishing. So when he's called Down East to a reclusive Maine resort hotel to negotiate a land grant with the local Indians, he eagerly – and rather loosely – interprets the trip as an invitation to snare some landlocked salmon. He has no sooner arrived at Raven Lake, snuggled deep inside the nearly impenetrable Maine woods, than he finds the anticipated peaceful idyll shattered.

First, one of the hotel's guests disappears without a trace. Then a mysterious poacher shoots a moose with an old-fashioned crossbow on an ancient Indian burial ground. Then a second guest is killed the same way – and gruesomely scalped. When one of the local Indians is arrested for the murder on flimsy evidence, Brady moves to his defence – and finds himself the next target.

### *Dead Winter*
August 1990

Brady Coyne, the Boston-based lawyer whose clients often need him more than legal advice, is usually deep in the world of wills and contracts. But when his client the Reverend Desmond Winter calls in the middle of the night, it's about something more important: a murder. Maggie, Desmond's daughter-in-law, has just been found bludgeoned to death. Although his son, Marc, has not been arrested, it looks as if he's the chief suspect. Brady has helped the Unitarian minister before his trouble with Marc, and when Brady arrives in Newburyport he learns that Marc cannot substantiate his alibi.

When a man who has left a message on Brady's phone turns up dead in a nearby motel, Coyne wonders if the two crimes are related. As he untangles the intricate web of crime and family secrets he finds more than murder is happening, and more murder than he realized. Ultimately these revelations bring Brady to a confrontation with madness and tragedy.

### *Death at Charity's Point*
January 1985

Death seemed to run rampant in the wealthy Gresham family. First, Dud Gresham blew his brains out. Then his son Winchester was killed in Vietnam. Now George, Win's brother, had been found dead, his body washed ashore after a plummet from Charity's Point, a cliff one hundred feet above the coastline north of Boston. Was it suicide or murder?

The suicide note found in George's pocket seemed to leave no doubt. But Florence Gresham, George's mother and now sole heir to the Gresham fortune, wasn't convinced. Why should the seemingly content, quiet prep school teacher suddenly want to kill himself? There was also the little matter of a life insurance policy Florence had taken out on her son – on which she was due to receive a million dollars if George's death was accidental. Florence strongly suspected that George had been murdered and hired attorney Brady Coyne to investigate.

As Brady probed the life of the shy, unassuming teacher, he discovered that George had his share of enemies at the exclusive school. Aided by drama teacher Rina Prescott, Brady slowly unearthed a deadly secret that climaxed in a dramatic confrontation on Charity's Point.

### *Dutch Blue Error, The*
August 1985

Oliver Hazard Perry Weston had always encouraged the legend of the singular Dutch Blue Error, his prized stamp valued at more than one million dollars. So he was understandably alarmed when a mysterious caller claimed to possess a duplicate, which Weston must purchase in secrecy to safeguard the value of his own stamp. Enter Brady Coyne, lawyer to wealthy Boston Brahmins, as the go-between. But what began as a simple financial transaction quickly turned to murder. Somebody else wanted the duplicate badly enough to kill for it.

As Brady delved into the rarified world of stamp collecting, he found himself simultaneously tracking a cunning murderer, protecting a beautiful young woman whose connection with the Dutch Blue Error had put her life in jeopardy, and defending the prime suspect in the manhunt – his own legal secretary, Xerxes Garrett! As the action rose to a feverish pitch, Brady Coyne discovered just where legend ended and reality began. He also discovered the true nature of the mysterious Dutch Blue Error.

### *Follow the Sharks*
May 1986

Twelve years ago Eddie Donagan was the fastest-rising pitcher the Boston Red Sox ranks had ever seen. But the pressure was too much for him, his red-hot career fizzled, and now the Overnight Sensation is a lonely divorcé selling running shoes at the Burlington Mall. Then his ten-year-old son E.J. is kidnapped and the family turns for help to Eddie's former agent, Boston lawyer Brady Coyne.

It seems the kidnappers are out for more than money – revenge. But why? The FBI is determined to do the investigation by the book; Brady decides to take the matter into his own hands before the trail grows cold. While Brady and hostile FBI agents lock horns, E.J.'s mother despairs over the impending certainty of her little boy's death. Then a critical mistake compounds the kidnapping with a shocking murder, and Brady realizes it's easy to drown when you're following the sharks.

The third appearance of this witty, engaging detective in a mystery enlivened by a rich Boston backdrop, an insider's glimpse of Major League Baseball, and deft characterization will cement the author's fast-growing reputation.

### *Rodent of Doubt, A*
March 1987

It's a routine case for the Boston police: another drunken bum frozen to death on a wintry night. But the bum is really wealthy heir Stuart Carver, masquerading as one of the homeless to gather material for a book – until he is brutally murdered with an icepick in the ear. Was it simply a random act of violence, or has someone penetrated Stu's disguise and found something worth murdering for? Stu's uncle hires Stu's former agent, lawyer Brady Coyne, to find out.

Brady's search begins with the people who knew Stu best – or thought they did. But as he stalks a wily killer who strikes again and again, he delves into the past of a lonely man whose abbreviated life belied all appearances – and stumbles on a truth that almost costs him *his* life.

Attorney Brady Coyne has been hailed as one of the most engaging, likeable sleuths on the crime scene today, and *A Rodent of Doubt*, his fourth investigation, is his most accomplished and exciting showcase yet.

### *Spotted Cats, The*
January 1992

When Brady Coyne gets an urgent request from his old friend Jeff Newton, a former professional big-game hunter, to come and visit on Cape Cod, he knows he can't refuse the invalid. Besides, Jeff's pond is full of trout.

But the weekend results in a very different catch…and for someone else. Daring robbers bind and gag Brady, leave Jeff Newton near death, and take off with seven solid gold pre-Columbian jaguars – a legally questionable gift to Jeff from a Central American chieftain. Searching for the priceless cats and their abductors, Brady follows a trail that leads to Montana, where the air is clear, the fishing great, and the danger greater. Dead ends and the ultimate reversal of hunter becoming quarry force Brady to draw on instinct and intellect before he can bring this adventure to its stunning and unexpected conclusion.

### *Tight Lines*
February 1993

Susan Ames is dying. Her only heir is Mary Ellen, the daughter who ran off with her professor eleven years earlier and hasn't been heard from since. Susan summons her lawyer, Brady Coyne. There is the matter of the estate. And when Susan asks Brady if he ran into the young woman, he senses she would like to hug her daughter one last time.

He tracks down Mary Ellen's expensive Boston apartment, but she's not there. Her answering machine gives Brady some names, but no one will admit to knowing her whereabouts – not the professor who abandoned his family for her; not her ageing coke supplier; not the troubled young superintendent of her apartment buildings; not the suspended Boston cop who thinks she's going to marry him; not even her psychiatrist, Warren McAllister.

Then Mary Ellen is found drowned near her summer cottage at Teal Pond. Dr McAllister rules out suicide. The police conclude it's an accident. Brady suspects murder. But there are too few clues, too many people with murderous motives – and soon there are too many suspects turning up dead.

### *Void in Hearts, A*
June 1989

Boston attorney Brady Coyne spends most days deep in the world of wills and contracts, as befits a lawyer to the old and rich. So it is no surprise that he welcomes a summons from private eye Les Katz who wants to discuss a matter of ethics with him. For a retainer of $10, Brady assures Les he's protected by the lawyer-client relationship: he can tell Brady anything, and it will go no further.

Les's story is long and twisted and comes down to the unsavoury fact that he has cheated a client and blackmailed her husband. Return the blackmail money, advises Brady, and give the wife an honest report that her husband appears to be using his lunch-hour for more than lunch.

Two days later Les is dead, the victim of a 2.00 a.m. hit-and-run driver. It could be an accident, but Brady and Les's widow suspect murder.

Brady finds himself with a new client, the lonely widow. That $10 retainer bought more in the way of legal services than Brady ever intended …

### *Vulgar Boatman, The*
November 1988

'I gotta see you, Brady.' Tom Baron, friend and client of Boston lawyer Brady Coyne and fat-cat Republican candidate for Governor of Massachusetts, had a problem which he wanted to discuss on his home ground, Windsor Harbor on the North Shore.

So, collecting his beautiful Hungarian girlfriend, Brady heads for a night of small-town fun and frolic. He has no intention of joining Tom's campaign, but provided the problem's non-political, he's willing to listen.

The problem is Tom's teenage son, missing after his girlfriend has been found murdered. The girl was attractive and popular, not the kind to get into trouble. Young Buddy may have been with her last night and he hasn't come home. The police, naturally, would like to know his whereabouts. So would his parents. So would Brady.

Tom's problem is both political and personal. He wants to find and help his son, and he wants to salvage his campaign. A scandal could ruin his chances at the polls. And a trial by press could destroy his son. Tom needs Brady's help as he's never needed it before.

Brady sets out to find Buddy and, perhaps, a killer. Before he's done, he will have discovered that little Windsor Harbor is far from the innocent, idyllic spot it seems.

Witty, fast-moving, packed with memorable characters and intriguing insight into the political process, *The Vulgar Boatman* is William G. Tapply's best novel yet.

## TAYLOR, PHOEBE ATWOOD
**(*see also* Tilton, Alice)**

### *Annulet of Gilt, The*
February 1939

Asey Mayo, Phoebe Atwood Taylor's famous detective, has made countless friends. In the present story, he scores another first-class hit. From the beginning of the chilly weekend when he finds himself with a house-party by the sea, Asey scents trouble – and soon finds the first victim, strangled. Tricked by an exotic blonde, decoyed mysteriously on to a yacht, robbed of his car, baffled by a wandering elephant, Asey at last begins to see light, and the story moves quickly to a tremendous climax, with Asey Mayo once again on top.

### *Asey Mayo Trio, The*
November 1946

This Trio brings you the inimitable Asey Mayo again in three of the most thrilling episodes of his adventurous life. In *The Third Murderer* and *Murder Rides the Gale* the ample figure of his talkative cousin Jennie looms large and reassuringly in the tense atmosphere of murder and mystery into which they are both plunged; while in *The Stars Spell Death* Asey has to solve the baffling case alone. The big ultra-modern observatory with its chromium fittings, makes an eerie setting for the corpse he finds. These stories show Phoebe Atwood Taylor at her best – swift, thrilling, grim, light-hearted and entertaining.

### *Banbury Bog*
June 1939

When half the town got poisoned at the church supper they blamed it on Banbury's tarts. Phineas Banbury – big pie and tart man – declared it was a hideous plot to ruin him. Let him get Asey Mayo and he'd prove it right quick! He got Asey Mayo and Asey found the prettiest puzzle ever set before a sleuth. Rich in native humour and with corking characters *Banbury Bog* is a tip-top Asey Mayo and to thousands of readers that means a lot.

### *Criminal C. O. D.*
December 1940

The charms of Phoebe Atwood Taylor's mysteries are too well known to need recounting; the very announcement that a new one is at hand is enough to bring shouts and cheers from fans galore. Her deft touch, the enticing atmosphere of the setting, and the genuine naturalness of her delightful characters have never shone more brightly than in this yarn which offers the two-fold pleasures of down-right detection and first-class fiction.

### *Deadly Sunshade, The*
September 1941

Zing-g-g! The bullet sang past Asey Mayo's ear and whacked into the garage door as he went to get his car for the run to the Yacht Club. Asey didn't pause to investigate but sped to the club to look for Mrs.Newell who had been so anxious to see him. He soon found her. She was lying on the beach, quite lifeless, under her bright umbrella. 'Sunstroke', said the young Dr.Bunting, rather in a hurry with his verdict. But old Dr. Cummings saw a different cause of death, and concluded with Asey that, for someone, Lucia Newell had been too dangerous to live. All the elements that make a perfect Asey Mayo mystery are here in plentiful measure: the spicy wit, the clever invention, a grand crew of characters who are human and amusing, and over it all the careless holiday mood – making hidden terror. *The Deadly Sunshade* is crime fiction and a story you'll go a long way to beat.

### *Diplomatic Corpse*
June 1951

'Buff' Orpington arrived in picturesque Quanomet to find the little Cape Cod town in ferment. A stupendous pageant of American history was being staged, and the inhabitants of Quanomet had time and thought for nothing else. But all was not as it should be in the small community. There had been more curious incidents than could be attributed to the usual petty jealousies and manoeuvrings for the best parts and positions. Quanomet was, in fact, in its modest way, about to make history, and Buff finds himself taking an uncomfortably prominent role when he discovers a newly made corpse in the cemetery. After too long an absence, Asey Mayo, the salty Cape Cod Sherlock, returns in fine form to solve a baffling murder in his own inimitable way.

### *Figure Away*
July 1938

Here is the kind of mystery that has put Phoebe Atwood Taylor in the top flight of detective writers to-day. It's as eerie as Hell Hollow itself, where poor Mary Randall was found dead in her antique shop, killed with a shotgun. But it's gay too, and peopled with as rare a collection of human and engaging characters as ever fell under suspicion. What really matters, however, is that it brings to thousands of delighted readers the incomparable Asey Mayo in what they will have to admit is the most surprising exploit of his entire career.

### *Going, Going, Gone!*
June 1944

Asey Mayo never did like auctions – never went to them no matter how brightly Cousin Jennie painted their attractions. So he ducks when she tells him about the Alden sale, with its alluring rumours of a fortune secreted somewhere among the objects to be knocked down. But Asey should have gone, for the auction that begins as a treasure hunt ends with a murder! It's an incredible discovery that sends Asey off on a hunt for a killer. Phoebe Atwood Taylor's latest story is a fine exciting yarn – mysterious and amusing to boot, as her followers have a right to expect. The likeable characters, the humorous talk, and happy mixture of fun and fright stamp 'Don't miss it' on *Going, Going, Gone!*

### *Octagon House*
March 1938

Asey Mayo has already got countless friends among detective-story readers, but this is the first time that an Asey Mayo novel has been published by the Crime Club. And *Octagon House* is certainly one of his best and most entertaining cases.

The story takes place in the little town of Quanomet, sleepiest place on earth, which has just burst into the headlines with the opening of its new Post Office, complete with pink granite steps, chromium pillars and an amazing mural decorating its walls. And Quanomet stayed in the headlines for some time after, although the Post Office became what the Press called 'The Incredible Backdrop to Those Startling Incidents'. Even Asey Mayo despaired of fitting together all the pieces of the fantastic puzzle of the mysteries at Octagon House. But his uncanny perceptions enable him to avert the final catastrophe and to unmask one of the smoothest villains who ever went unsuspected.

### *Perennial Boarder, The*
February 1942

She had come every summer for twenty-nine years to stay at the Whale Inn. She knew all about the neighbourhood, and the neighbourhood thought it knew all about her. So when Miss Olive Beadle arrives for her thirtieth season there is nothing to hint at disaster; nothing to suggest that death has arrived also; that soon, in circumstances that defy explanation, the quiet figure so long familiar will be found shot through the heart. This new and very entertaining Phoebe Atwood Taylor mystery features, of course, the famous Asey Mayo, 'a detective', Dorothy L Sayers says, 'for whom I have great affection and esteem.'

### *Proof of the Pudding*
February 1946

Asey Mayo switched off the motor and stared unbelievingly at the debris-strewn beach where pieces of lobster-pots and smashed boats rubbed elbows with parts of chairs and tables. The hurricane had utterly wrecked the summer colony at Pogue Neck. Salvage seekers were poking around among the wreckage and Asey decided to join them and hunt up the blinds blown off his house. And then he found the body. He knew at once that the girl was murdered, though the obvious intent was to have the death seem an accident. But a trifling circumstance betrayed the plan. Fresh as paint is this smoothly written story that brings Phoebe Atwood Taylor in top form with her brightest dialogue and a grand set of lively characters. Gruesome and gleeful, *Proof of the Pudding* is a matchless find for the mystery-minded.

### *Punch with Care*
September 1947

Murder is no novelty to Asey Mayo, who is, of course, an established favourite with Crime Club readers. Here, tall, lean, salty Asey encounters the baffling case of Carrie Boone, a summer visitor to quaint Cape Cod whom Asey was in fact about to meet when the news broke that Carrie was dead in mysterious circumstances. It is a strange case in which one meets with some real Cape Cod characters, including Cousin Jennie, old Doc Cummings, the clam diggers and, of course, the Summer Folks. Phoebe Atwood Taylor gets a lot of fun into the telling of a mystery, and this combination of well-knit plot, excitement and comedy is irresistible.

### *Six Iron Spiders, The*
February 1943

It was quiet as a millpond in the little village of Woosset on Cape Cod. The only news stirring was down in the hardware store where Lem Horner sold six iron spiders (Anglice frying pans) all in one day, and after they'd been on his shelves for years too. No one thought much about it until next day when Tubby Wadhams was found dead, felled by a heavy blow – and a brand new iron spider beside him. The trail looked easy to Asey Mayo when he started after the buyers who had made the run on the hardware store. He found them all – but oddly enough, not one could produce a frying pan so recently bought! Then the queer things that happen! Phoebe Atwood Taylor scores again in this masterly job of crime-solving by the ever-likeable Asey Mayo. *The Six Iron Spiders* is a grand thriller of mystery and mirth to enjoy without reservation.

### *Spring Harrowing*
October 1939

To thousands of readers there is nothing to match a new Asey Mayo story, where murder fits thrillingly into an atmosphere of wind-swept dunes and sea, and inimitable characters fall into adventures both grisly and gay. *Spring Harrowing* is not only a fine combination of fun, mental gymnastics and miscellaneous entertainment, but an exciting tale of death and detection, which again proves Phoebe Atwood Taylor to be unsurpassed in the special field she has made her own.

## TELUSHKIN, JOSEPH

### *Eye for An Eye, An*

June 1990

The student daughter of distinguished cardiologist Gerald Braun was murdered by a jealous boyfriend, who promptly gave himself up. That was tragedy enough, but the Brauns then had to endure a trial in which a skilful defence lawyer did not hesitate to blacken their daughter Donna's reputation, while successfully excluding evidence that would have blackened her murderer. As a result the young man received a derisory sentence. Unable to bear this travesty of justice, Gerald Braun took the law into his own hands and shot his child's killer. He was charged with murder.

Rabbi Daniel Winter believed Braun's action was justified and pleaded passionately for his release on bail, even though it meant opposing his own wife Brenda, a psychologist with the Los Angeles Police Department, who feared that Braun might kill again.

The Rabbi prevailed and Braun was released, but when the lawyer who had so successfully defended Donna's killer was also murdered and Braun had no alibi, it looked as if Brenda had been right.

### *Final Analysis of Dr. Stark,*

August 1988

'Return of this rabbi, whose nature belies his name, would be welcome,' said John Coleman in the *Sunday Times* greeting Rabbi Daniel Winter's first appearance. Here is his eagerly awaited second.

Noah Stark had everything going for him. Rich, handsome, popular and one of the most successful psychiatrists in Los Angeles, Dr Stark had just announced his engagement to a beautiful girl – to the delight of his many friends, Rabbi Daniel Winter among them. Yet when Daniel called on him by appointment the next day, he found the psychiatrist dead on his own couch, the victim of a brutal attack.

Angry and grief stricken at the death of his friend, Daniel set out to shock the mourners at the funeral into helping him investigate in parallel with the police. But as the mounting tide of rumour and allegation swept over him, he was grimly reminded of the Talmudic saying that gossip kills three: the gossiper, the one who listens to the gossip, and the victim. What was the real truth about the admired Noah Stark when everyone Daniel spoke to – relatives, friends, patients – had a different view of him, and a different reason for distorting or concealing the truth?

More than one individual or relationship is analysed in this outstanding crime novel by a young rabbi, who blends in the lore of Orthodox Judaism as skilfully as he delineates character and enmeshes the reader in a complex yet credible plot.

### *Unorthodox Murder of Rabbi Moss, The*

July 1986

Rabbi Myra Moss was an aggressive feminist – a woman who made enemies. They include her former lover; the synagogue president; and presumably – after 250,000 people heard her insult him on a radio chat show – Orthodox Rabbi Daniel Winter.

But the chat show audience also heard that Myra Moss, readily identifiable in a green tracksuit, would be jogging home alone after the show. So when she was deliberately run down and killed, the Los Angeles Police Department had no shortage of suspects. To the distress of police psychiatrist Brenda Goldstein who knew and liked him, Daniel Winter was one.

Parallel with the police investigation, Daniel conducts his own, several suspects had no alibi for the vital time, and nor had he, because establishing his alibi would require a breach of trust. This is just one of the dilemmas facing the rabbi as he becomes increasingly involved with the members of Myra's congregation, with her parents, with another murder, and with the charming Ms Goldstein, who may be a stranger to the faith of her fathers but is no stranger to the tragedy that murder brings.

Joseph Telushkin, himself an Orthodox rabbi, has written a first-class mystery which is also a warmly compassionate novel in which the wisdom of Orthodox Judaism helps solve a number of human problems, murder among them.

## TILTON, ALICE

**(*see also* Taylor, Phoebe Atwood)**

### *Beginning With a Bash*

July 1937

A freezing east wind blew through the streets of Boston. To Martin Jones shivering outside Peters' Second-hand Bookstore the printed sign "Come In And Browse – It's Warm Inside" looked very inviting. So in he went; but others too had sought the timely shelter of the store – among them was Professor John North. Sensations were to follow thick and fast in Peters' Store during the next few minutes, for a book thief suddenly rushed out with some precious volumes, and soon after Professor North was found dead amid a sea of books – his head bashed in. Beginning with a bash and ending with a bang, Miss Alice Tilton's story provides a full and satisfying succession of thrills.

### *Cold Steal*

April 1940

Readers of *The Cut Direct* and *Beginning with a Bash* will hail with joy the reappearance of that remarkable scholar and gentleman, Leonidas Witherall, 'the man who looks like Shakespeare' but sleuths like Sherlock Holmes. Peaceful and unassuming, Leonidas finds the dead body of Miss Medora Winthrop. It was embarrassing, to say the least; and he could only agree when Cassie Price said, 'No one must know – we must solve this mystery ourselves!' Through a pell-mell of crises, Leonidas and Cassie hold at bay the combined forces of the Tuesday Club *en masse*, the man who kept trying to switch the refrigerator, Pig-Eyes the lorry-driver, and Miss Chard (Swiss), otherwise known as the mousey woman. Of course they emerge triumphant with assorted plots unearthed and the murderer in the bag.

### *Cut Direct, The*

September 1938

Do you remember Leonidas, the man who was the spitting image of Shakespeare? You must have met him in Alice Tilton's first novel, *Beginning with a Bash*, which went off with a bang. Here he is again in a new story in which he is constantly being run over by cars, and gets into some very tight corners indeed in the course of solving a murder case. Alice Tilton is perhaps the only detective-story writer who gives you a touch of Wodehouse with your corpses. *The Cut Direct* is a distinctive contribution to the worthy cause of gayer detective fiction.

### *Dead Ernest*

April 1945

Deep in finishing his new manuscript, Leonidas Witherall was quite oblivious to his surroundings. He received rather a nasty jar when he found that he had been harbouring a stranger in his house and he had been dead for some time. The seasoned Witherall fan will scent the beginnings of a perfectly wonderful crime and a perfectly wonderful time, for the little man has never been in tighter spots nor improvised so brilliantly to get out of them. In rare form, Leonidas darts after clues, dodges police, innocent bystanders and assorted villains, to achieve a supreme triumph in his highly unorthodox career of detection.

### *File for Record*

March 1944

Alice Tilton has made quite a hit with her inimitable stories of Leonidas Witherall, that amiable and erudite gentleman who somehow can't set out on the most innocuous errand without tripping over a dead body and getting mixed up in murder. His latest adventure, narrated in *File for Record*, is great entertainment. As Leonidas skids from one precarious situation to another, he just manages to keep his wits pinned to the elusive clues that point to the murderer. He never dreamt how it would all come out, and neither will you; but you will find his detecting at top form, and this intriguing mystery the best he has yet solved. Recommended to all victims of the galloping blues!

### *Hollow Chest, The*

August 1942

It's a joy to embark on a new adventure with Leonidas Witherall, the gentle schoolmaster who gets involved with murder and sudden death at the drop of a hat, and whose sleuthing is thoroughly spur-of-the-moment, being inspired chiefly by his desperate desire to get himself out of trouble. Alice Tilton was among the first to sense the new taste for merriment among malefactors, for gaiety rather than gore. In *The Hollow Chest* she has written a sparkling successor to her previous Leonidas Witherall tales – a story that makes rare reading, and piles up the fun and excitement to a new pitch.

### *Iron Hand, The*

December 1947

Though one of Dalton City's leading citizens, a respectable banker and stickler for etiquette, Fenwick Balderston did not mind that three guests arrived for dinner when he had only invited two, nor that his old friend Leonidas Witherall was late. The fact that his two servants were locked up in the pantry and therefore unable to serve up the delicious meal so thoughtfully prepared bothered him not at all; for he had been dead for quite some considerable time before the appointed dinner hour. Leonidas Witherall finds himself for once in the unhappy position of being wanted by the police in a murder chase in which the clues range crazily from dinosaur's footprint to a monkey. All those who like their murders told with élan and an American accent will relish this latest adventure of Leonidas Witherall.

### *Left Leg, The*

April 1941

With his first two cases, Leonidas Witherall, 'the man who looks like Shakespeare', has taken his place as one of the most original detectives. Gentle, unassuming and completely engaging, Leonidas is the last man on earth to seek out crime and embroilment with criminals. But somehow his quiet life is always getting invaded by plot, counter-plot and general villainy, and the first thing he knows he's up to his neck in trouble. How could he know that escaping the unwelcome attentions of the girl on the bus would get him enmeshed in a robbery? That from flying from the scene of the robbery, that he'd stumble right into – murder! For stretched out on the rug was the dead body of his old friend and employer, Marcus Meredith, his head bashed in with a loving cup. No matter how many mysteries you've read, no one like Leonidas has ever crossed your path. His surprising adventures make a rare sort of thriller, gaily exciting, brimming with mirth and mystification.

## TINE, ROBERT

### *State of Grace*

December 1982

When Father Martin Sykes, the papal private secretary, agrees to discuss 'the Church today' with reporter Rafaella Bianchi, daughter of one of Italy's top industrialists, he has little idea of the greed, envy and fanaticism that threaten his patron, the newly elected Pope Anthony. Many within the Vatican consider this half-American pope – the youngest in the Church's history – to be dangerously liberal. But far more disturbing to Martin is the open hostility shown by Gerard Cardinal Van Doorn, head of the Vatican Bank, to the new pope's interest in his management of the Vatican millions.

The young, idealistic American priest and the sophisticated Italian beauty begin to dig deeper into Van Doorn's affairs. Soon they discover disturbing evidence linking the Cardinal with Rafaella's powerful and ruthless father. The implications are frightening, but what they do not suspect is the full extent of the danger menacing the pope – a danger identified only as The Expeditus Plan.

This fast-paced, intelligent drama of power and intrigue is full of startling information about Vatican politics and finances; it marks the introduction of a major talent in suspense fiction.

### *Uneasy Lies the Head*

June 1983

In the 1880's London was terrorized by the notorious Jack the Ripper, who committed five gruesome murders but was never caught. Now, one hundred years later, an unlikely team of Scotland Yard detectives is assigned to a sensational murder case which is a chillingly exact reproduction of Jack the Ripper's crimes. Samuel ('Smudge') Huddleston, a mild-mannered grandfather figure of an officer, and his hot-blooded young colleague Tony Pidgeon are soon involved. The murder's trail is hard to follow by the standard methods – there is a baffling lack of some clues and the sudden appearance of others from unexpected quarters – but the trail seems to lead with embarrassing directness to Buckingham Palace, where young, progressive King George V11 has recently ascended the throne. Or is the trail a false one? And how does the beautiful wife of the American ambassador fit in? Why is Sir Noah Sinclair, Oxford don and murder buff, so helpful to the investigation? And why, just as the net seems to be closing round the murderer, are Smudge and Pidgeon abruptly taken off the case?

An intricate web of treachery and mixed loyalties has been woven, in high places and low. But its creators reckoned without 'the two finest lower-middle-class brains in London'.

The author of *State of Grace* has once more constructed a clever and suspenseful story, set against the veritable institution of the British monarchy and written in the best tradition of entertaining crime fiction.

## TROY, SIMON
### Road to Rhuine
September 1952

It was the insignificant sum of eight pounds and five shillings that sent Lee Vaughan on the road to Rhuine. That was the state of his bank balance when Sheila Fabian put an open cheque for two hundred pounds on his desk and asked for his help. The famous West Country beauty spot and seaside village of Rhuine was Sheila's property left her by her first husband, to be kept in its centuries-old tradition and preserved from exploitation and spoliation. Her second husband, Stuart Fabian, planned to build there half-a-dozen luxury hotels, a pier and an icedrome – and act of vandalism which Sheila wanted Lee to prevent. A miasma of malice and evil as insidious as sea-fog writhed and coiled around the little feudal kingdom as Lee fought his way blindly towards inevitable tragedy. Simon Troy shows a feeling for characters and atmosphere which gives his first crime novel a rare distinction.

## TURNBULL, PETER
### And Did Murder Him
February 1991

The body of a young man is found in a city centre alley. He has been stabbed to death and the murder weapon is lying close by, apparently discarded in panic. The fingerprints found on the knife prove to belong to a known associate of the deceased. It appears to be a motiveless murder, the result of a drunken brawl.

But the officers of Glasgow's P Division do not accept things at face value, and begin to unravel a tale of premeditation and subterfuge. In doing so they follow a trail which leads via the squalid world of the drug addict to the prosperous ambiences of the city's most prominent citizens.

### Big Money
January 1984

The raid on the Maryhill Post Office took place at half past six on an October morning. It was conducted with clockwork precision, minimal violence, extreme professionalism, and netted a quarter of a million pounds in untraceable used notes. From the beginning the officers of Glasgow's P Division knew that for them there would have to be twenty-six hours in the day.

At first luck seemed to be with them: the getaway car was quickly found. But it yielded little in the way of information, apart from the curious coincidence that a former owner was not unconnected with the case – that, and the spore of an extremely rare plant with only one known habitat in Scotland. It was a far cry from the Post Office raid but not from the solution to a mystery which had been on P Division's books for over two years.

As the strands of the investigation come together, as officer after officer is drawn in and Glasgow is laid open as if with a scalpel, Peter Turnbull once again demonstrates the intimate knowledge of the bitch city and her police which has won him a wide readership on both sides of the Atlantic.

### Condition Purple
January 1989

In Glasgow one summer evening a frightened young woman in heels is walking. Click. Click. Click.

The man who will kill her when he sees her is in the city. She knows this because she has seen his car cruising in the grid system, and she knows he knows where to find her because she stands every evening in an alley off Blythswood Street.

The woman is just twenty-one years old. It is her death that will trigger P'Division's latest investigation.

She was found at 10pm, the knife still in her throat. She was a heroin addict and had the words 'I belong to Dino' tattooed on her groin. They were the only clues. Yet as the police interviewed anyone in any way connected with her, combed the area, collated evidence, they began to build up a picture of the dead girl, her associates, her family, lifestyle, which led to the arrest of a vicious murderer who had killed and would kill again. Marked by growing tension and a chilling awareness of the evil that preys on those who inhabit the lower levels of a great city, Peter Turnbull's latest police procedural views with compassion the roles of policemen and victims alike.

### Dead Knock
June 1982

The well-dressed woman who walked into the police station of Glasgow's P Division wanted to report a forthcoming murder: her own. Yet she walked out again without giving so much as her name, claiming that the police couldn't help her. Soon afterwards she was found dead in her home from a massive dose of heroin which was certainly not self-administered. Why didn't she run when she heard the dead knock? What terrible threat had made her submit to her own execution?

The only clues were a coded book and some old photographs. Painstakingly the Glasgow CID set to work, and the vivid characters who policed Peter Turnbull's first crime novel, *Deep and Crisp and Even*, are soon involved with the Dutch police in the person of an inspector from Amsterdam. With drug-trafficking, local government corruption, and some bizarre coincidences that seem to prove that there's no such thing as a clean break.

Peter Turnbull's second novel highlights one of Glasgow's more recent crime problems. It is every bit as gripping and authentic as his first, as the action moves through different districts of the city, each one skilfully portrayed.

### Deep and Crisp and Even
March 1981

Glasgow was under snow. It lay thick on the schemes – the backstreets; thick to the stairways that led up the buildings. And still it fell. It was deep and crisp and even on the pedestrian precinct in Argyle Street when PC Phil Hamilton saw a man fall dead, and, although he had just been knifed, the snow was an accessory after the fact and had already shrouded the killer's tracks.

The police started routine investigations into what seemed the result of a drunken brawl. Then PC Hamilton – unlucky man – found another corpse left by the knifeman with a typewritten note this time: 'This is for Lissu.'

Glaswegians united against the knifeman as they had against the snow; vigilantes patrolled the streets, and everyone was under suspicion. Communication from someone claiming to be 'Slow Tom' who would 'take nine' made things worse; and the people who could help track down the killer were, like the snow, saying nothing.

This first novel is compellingly evocative of the 90% perspiration, 10% inspiration that make up the job of the police, and of the atmosphere pervading the snowbound,

menaced city. Every character, from lowest criminal to Chief Superintendent, is skilfully brought to life by an author who, as a Glasgow social worker, is much involved in the city and its problems.

### Fair Friday
March 1983

On Fair Friday, the start of Glasgow's annual two weeks' July holiday, a middle-aged unambitious journalist was fatally beaten up in a back court in a slum area. Fear of redundancy had driven him to a pathetic attempt at investigative reporting, and with beginner's luck – bad luck, as it happened – he had stumbled on a major scandal which, in the eyes of someone highly placed in the underworld, necessitated his death.

The case was handled by officers of P Division – the same team who have appeared in Peter Turnbull's two previous highly praised novels, *Deep and Crisp and Even* and *Dead Knock*. Their investigation unfolds through the eyes of four policemen with different personalities, ambitions and techniques, whose enquiries take them the length and breadth of the city (and the heights and depths of its social scale) as they follow their only clue: the word 'Gilheaney' muttered by the dying man.

Peter Turnbull, promptly dubbed 'Scotland's answer to Ed McBain' by *The Times Literary Supplement*, once again 'makes down-town Glasgow sound like seamy New York as braw lads of P Division challenge the 87th Precinct' – *Guardian*.

### Long Day Monday
October 1992

For the officers of Glasgow's P Division the routine duty of attending a stolen vehicle which has been abandoned deep in rural Lanarkshire becomes less routine when disturbed topsoil indicates that something far more sinister has also been abandoned. Sergeant Sussock recalls a similar incident some twenty-five years earlier – and to the horror of the investigators, the fields of Lanarkshire begin to give up their dead.

Forensic evidence indicates that the victims unearthed had all endured a period of captivity before being murdered, so when a separate inquiry into the sudden disappearance of a young boy becomes linked to the murder inquiry, the police realize that a serial killer is at work and that they are racing against time…

### Two Way Cut
March 1988

At first PC Phil Hamilton of Glasgow's P Division thought it was a joke. It was April 1st, after all. But it was no joke: a corpse, its severed head resting neatly on its chest, lay before him on the stretch of rain-sodden waste ground where he had gone for a surreptitious smoke. This was murder, no doubt of it. The men and resources of P Division were immediately mobilized.

Forensic evidence revealed that the victim had been killed elsewhere and the body washed and dressed in immaculate new clothing. Three days earlier he had visited a dental hygienist. His last meal had been Chinese, but even after he had been identified as a meticulous, careful, punctual accountant who had been with the same firm for twenty years, some puzzling facts remained about this only son of narrowly religious parents. Who was the oriental lady with whom he had stayed in a Saltcoats hotel? What connection had he with the Zambesi Club? And what connection with the Chinese restaurant which was torched deliberately on the night following his death?

The officers of P Division who Peter Turnbull brings so vividly to life in his fifth outstanding police procedural have their work cut out to nail the murderer. In doing so they once again lay bare different aspects of their bitch city, and a cross-section of its citizens.

## TURNER, J. V.
### Below the Clock
May 1936

Below the Clock – the clock that is famous throughout the world as Big Ben – many highly dramatic and historic scenes have been enacted, but none more sensational than the happenings on that April afternoon when, before the eyes of a House crowded to its utmost capacity for the Budget Speech, the Chancellor fell headlong to the floor with a resounding crash. And when it was definitely established that the Chancellor had been poisoned, one can imagine the sensation that ensued. For the first time a murder had been committed in the House of Commons itself. In *Below the Clock* J. V. Turner, who made a more than promising debut in the Crime Club with *Homicide Haven*, gives Amos Petrie the best case of his career.

### Homicide Haven
September 1935

Mr. and Mrs. Percy Stone regarded with pride the rapid erection of their new house. As it neared completion they discussed methods of furnishing, and argued about an appropriate name. But on the Sunday morning when Percy's father and mother-in-law arrived to inspect the property they discovered that the first item of property had been delivered. A corpse lay on the floor of the dining-room! The melancholy Inspector Ripple of Scotland Yard was sent down. Fortunately for him Amos Petrie, the small, eccentric solicitor from the Public Prosecutor's Department, was spending a fishing holiday in the district. So Ripple inveigled the little man into the case. At first Petrie was not interested. But as enquiries produced one odd fact after another, as clues arose only to collapse, as the trail led from the country town to London's underworld and back again, he became more eager. Mr. Turner has presented no spectacular story of miraculous foresight, uncanny deductions and amazing prescience. Instead the reader is invited to examine each piece of evidence as it arises, every difficulty faced by Petrie and Ripple, to join with them in their moments of triumph and disillusionment until the time when they solve the problem of the murder in 'Homicide Haven'.

## VALIN, JONATHAN
### Day of Wrath
April 1983

Robbie Segal was a perfectly ordinary teenager from a perfectly ordinary street. She lived in a pleasant room in a neat, orderly house. And one afternoon she walked out of the door and never came back.

*Day of Wrath* is the story of what happened to Robbie and to the people around her – to her very proper, very strait-laced mother, to her loyal and adoring boy-friend, and to Harry Stoner, the detective who was hired to find her. It is a powerful story of lust, love and brutal violence, and of one man's heroic attempt to save the life and soul of a girl who didn't know how low she had become.

Deftly plotted, superbly written, *Day of Wrath* is the best Harry Stoner novel to date. Set in the middle class world of colonial homes and fierce morality, it is a mystery with a social conscience and a keen eye for detail, alive with the fascinating characters that readers have come to expect in a novel by Jonathan Valin whom the *Observer* described as 'Raymond Chandler's natural heir'.

## Dead Letter
August 1982

Professor Daryl Lovingwell had lost some secret government papers. He knew where to find them all right – his daughter Sarah had taken them. The Professor's problem was how to get the papers back without turning his beloved daughter over to the FBI.

So instead of going to the police, he called in Harry Stoner, the Cincinnati private eye who has already appeared in Jonathan Valin's two previous novels, *The Lime Pit* and *Final Notice*. 'Just get the documents back within a week of two,' the Professor told Harry, 'without letting Sarah know she's being investigated.'

Almost at once, Harry's logic and a sentimental streak led him into trouble, murder, and a mystery. What began as a search for the missing papers became a desperate hunt for a madman and for the bizarre truth about Sarah Lovingwell and her charming, eccentric father.

*Dead Letter* is a chilling story of evil. It is also the story of a decent man's attempt to understand that evil, and of what the truth costs him. It is a mystery in the best sense – an investigation of the human heart and of its ultimately inexplicable capacity to twist love into something rich and strange.

## Final Notice
November 1981

Someone's been cutting up the Hyde Park Library – cutting up the books, that is. And the head librarian wants the vandal stopped. After all, those art books cost money and the way in which they've been torn up is enough to chill anybody, even hard-nosed Harry Stonor, the tough, amiable detective hero of this exciting new mystery by the author of *The Lime Pit*.

Harry knows at once that this is no ordinary vandal, not after what this one has done to all the pretty pictures in the art books. But what Harry doesn't know is that those pictures aren't the only things the vandal has been cutting up.

With the unlikely help of a little old librarian and a very liberated young woman, Harry picks up a trail that leads to a murdered girl and to a bizarre psychopath who is planning to keep on killing until someone stops him. And with the Hyde Park Ripper that's no easy thing to do.

*Final Notice* is fast-paced, stylish entertainment guaranteed to put you on the edge of your chair and to keep you there until you've turned the last page.

## Lime Pit, The
May 1981

It didn't seem like much of a case when the old man called and said that his 'little girl' was missing. Only the old man turned out to be a dirty old man and his little girl a venal, sixteen-year-old runaway, who had been living in the old man's apartment for more than a year before her mysterious disappearance.

The young couple across the street claimed there was no mystery to it: the old man simply wouldn't face the truth, which was that his little girl had got sick of living with him and had run away with a teenage friend. The old man said they were lying and he could prove it. So what do you do?

If you're Harry Stoner, the detective hero of this explosive new crime novel, you trust your heart as well as your head. And when your head tells you that, appearances notwithstanding, the old man really loved his

little girl, you start taking his accusations seriously. The more you look into the girl's disappearance, the uglier the case becomes, until it turns into an unforgettable nightmare and violence touches the old man, the missing girl, and Harry himself.

*The Lime Pit* is classic, hardboiled detective fiction, filled with vivid and colourful characters, crackling with suspense, and introducing a private eye who is a tough, appealing character in his own right and already hailed in America as the Philip Marlowe of the 'eighties.

## Music Lovers, The
March 1993

In mid-January with business slower than a crawl, private eye Harry Stoner is virtually hibernating. The only problem is that he's been living off credit cards and Christmas cash, and both sources are running dry.

Enter Leon Tubin, collector of vintage LP recordings, who is sure another member of his music-loving group is ripping him off. They're all jealous of his record library, especially his Wagner-loving rival, Sherwood Loeffler. Harry thinks the whole thing's peanuts, but Leon insists that the recordings in question are worth about $10,000. Moreover, he's prepared to offer Harry a cash advance. Harry takes the case.

After interviewing Leo's music-loving cronies, Harry is struck by their obsessive audio compulsions, but finds it hard to believe any of them guilty of grand theft. It's Leon's blonde bombshell of a wife, Sheila, who has Harry doing a double-take. What's a woman like her doing with a wimp like him? Sheila's confession of a past from which Leon saved her doesn't exactly clarify matters, for what has Sheila's past to do with a bunch of stolen records? A bizarre trail of clues emerges, but neither Harry nor anyone else is convinced they'll lead to a solution.

## Natural Causes
January 1984

Quentin Dover was a man who had everything: a beautiful wife; a loving mother; an estate in Ohio; and a job as a TV writer which paid him half a million dollars a year. Then one morning he had an accident – far from his home, his wife, and his friends. *Natural Causes* is the story of what happened on that August morning in Los Angeles. It is the story of Quentin Dover and the world he lived in – the fierce, moneyed world of daytime serial,

*Natural Causes* is the fifth Harry Stoner novel, and, like the other four, it is more than a simple whodunit. It is a mordant, acid-etched depiction of American life and American dreams, as they are portrayed on television and ironically mirrored in reality. *Natural Causes* explores the fault line between the narcotic fantasies of daytime serial and the broken lives of the men and women who bring these fantasies to life.

As always, tough, competent Harry Stoner is your guide to this particular hell and, as always, it is his values that shape the action and bring Quentin Dover and his world into unforgettable focus.

## WAINWRIGHT, JOHN
### Crystallised Carbon Pig, The
July 1966

Crystallised Carbon. In other words, diamonds – the reason for Detective Sergeant Pewter's assignment.

This is the story of Pewter's Mission, after he has been briefed to insinuate himself with a gang who plan a crime four times as big as the Great Train Robbery. It becomes evident

to Pewter that he has not been told the truth – he is a pawn between conspirators engaged in some large, secret and dangerous game. Soon, he is uncertain even where his own loyalties lie.

The only alleviation of his plight is the intermittent company of the charming Annette Fairfield.

The action ranges across Italy and France. It comes to a violent and dramatic climax in the swampy peninsula of Sierra Leone, when the whole truth at last comes to light after a bloody exchange.

## Darkening Glass, The
September 1968

Close to a Northern village a girl of seven is assaulted and murdered. From the village constable to Superintendent Ripley himself, police resources are mobilised to detect the killer.

To the reader the identity of the killer is disclosed; a man not altogether bad but under heavy pressure from the circumstances of his life and the structure of the community of which he is a part.

This is the story of why the police suspect that man, and the methods they employ to obtain what they lack – proof.

Once again John Wainwright breaks new ground in a story that is both original and thrilling.

## Death in a Sleeping City
April 1965

The dominating character of this novel is Detective Chief Superintendent Lewis. His 'patch' is a large northern provincial city.

Into that 'patch' come two Mafia gunmen – executioners. A savage murder is committed with cold efficiency.

Lewis will not hear of the case being handed over to Scotland Yard. Energetic, ruthless, blustering, he is dedicated to 'stretching the necks' of the foreign gunmen who have used his city for a killing. But for all his bull-headed drive, Lewis is not infallible. A further double-killing brings the police force to a pitch of ceaseless, straining endeavour.

This exciting first novel is written by a police officer. It depicts the police force of a provincial city at full stretch and in full detail; and sets out realistically, convincingly and without exaggeration the differences of personality among the senior officers. The plot, strong and simple in itself, is subtle and varied in its development; it ends in a tense and very surprising climax.

## Evil Intent
March 1966

The naked corpse on Dell Rock had been mutilated. Superintendent Ripley was compelled – very reluctantly – to admit the possibility that a witch's coven had gathered at the Rock on Halloween; and that a black fertility ritual had been carried out there.

This is the start of a story which leads to a brilliant feat of pure detection and ends in an extra-ordinary and exciting chase by helicopter.

The author is a serving police officer, and excels in his accounts of the ways and procedures of policemen of all ranks. *Evil Intent* will increase the big following he acquired with his first two novels – *Death in a Sleeping City* and *Ten Steps to the Gallows*.

## Take-Over Men, The
February 1969

Ex-Detective Sergeant Pewter, hero of *The Crystallised Carbon Pig*, is sent for again by the secret, scheming authorities who work above the law. They want Pewter to commit a crime against his own kind – against the

officers of the police force with which he once served. 'Duty' and 'money' are the pressures put on Pewter to accept, but it is the money that interests Pewter most.

The crime goes hideously, shockingly wrong. Pewter finds himself shamed and bound in toils contrived by his employers and by his enemies, the mysterious Take-Over Men. The beautiful Jonnet Lindsey is his solace – and his lead to knowledge of the secret conspirators.

This is a violent story of violent men, to whom bloodshed, murder and treachery are matters of indifference. Pewter, the pawn in their brutal machinations, stumbles and batters his way toward a bloody denouement.

This exciting tale of a great criminal conspiracy in the United Kingdom makes a worthy successor to the earlier Pewter adventures.

## Talent for Murder
June 1967

In a northern city a dissolute young man seeks the help of criminals; he plans to make contact with the underworld through a prostitute.

He finds his criminals. But these men are tougher, more callous, and brutal than anything imaginable to him from his inexperience and youth. They soon concoct a bloody and ruthless variation on the criminal project he suggests to them.

The crime becomes the concern of Detective Chief Superintendent Lewis, who blustered his way through the author's first and very successful novel, *Death in a Sleeping City*. Lewis again brings his bullying, hectoring, explosive methods to the conduct of the murder investigation – and it is Lewis's own furious obsession that leads to the confused and bloody denouement.

Again John Wainwright grips the reader with his narrative power, with his grim detailed picture of crime in the slums of a city, and his exciting, authentic description of a police force gathered for a murder hunt.

## Ten Steps to the Gallows
October 1965

This is the story of a policeman, a Detective Sergeant, who commits murder.

Sergeant Fraser is a weak man but he is also a trained policeman from a family of policemen. His father-in-law and brother-in-law are policemen. He has been brought up and trained to the tremendous high standards of the British Police Service. But Fraser finds himself in a predicament that becomes too much for him.

There are ten steps to take Fraser from his murder to the gallows. In the course of that fatal decline he plunges deep into violence; and veers ever more desperately to escape his pursuers – a police force angered and sickened with the renegade who has stained their uniform and their good name.

The narrative is fast and exciting. The whole kaleidoscope of police activity is authentic in the second novel by a writer who is a serving police officer and the successful author of *Death in a Sleeping City*.

## Web of Silence
February 1968

Ex-Detective Sergeant Pewter, the hero of *The Crystallised Carbon Pig*, is here trapped into an espionage role in the war between East and West. In the company of a young girl, also a Western agent, he finds himself crossing the East German frontier with orders to kill one particular man; behind these orders there lies a somewhat different and more complex intention.

Thereafter Pewter meets a maelstrom of

killing and deceit. Struggling to retrieve from the shambles those elements that seem to him worthwhile, he encounters the ruthless forces of both sides who conduct cold-war espionage regardless of human lives, feelings or interests. It is only through the help of his tough and unscrupulous friend, Dilton-Emmet, that total disaster is avoided.

John Wainwright is well-known for his powerful and authentic narratives. And the violence here excitingly described, and the reasons behind that violence, will add to his growing reputation.

### *Worms Must Wait, The*
October 1967

'It was a dead man, encased within a stalagmite … the petrifying effect of the dripping water held him in his own opaque, unyielding capsule. It had given him a dark green, semi-transparent dunce's cap … a thin icicle-like beard which bridged his chin to chest.'

Pot-holers discovered the body in a Yorkshire cave. In this bizarre and colourful setting Superintendent Ripley of the Beechwood Brook Division sets up his Murder Headquarters. The massive cadres and resources of a Northern Police Division are portrayed in all the details of their activities, and in their motivations.

Ripley himself, a policeman who has investigated earlier crimes recorded in John Wainwright's novels, here meets a situation which is gruesome in itself; and which is made no easier for him by the involvement of individuals who are important to him in his private life. To his aid comes his friend Superintendent Collins from Hallsworth Hill.

The author of *Death in a Sleeping City* and *The Crystallised Carbon Pig* was himself a serving police officer; and here again he adds authentic knowledge to a gift of powerful story-telling, which will hold readers absorbed right up to the startling dénouement.

## WAKEFIELD, H. RUSSELL
### *Belt of Suspicion*
July 1936

Lucy Bault was the possessor of a figure so perfectly marvellous and so marvellously perfect that she was an invaluable asset to the corset business run by her cousin, Stephen Gallin, proprietor of the celebrated Glovfit Products. Not that there was any need for her to work for a living, for she and her brother Arthur had been left a mint of money by their father. The tragic end of the whisky-drinking Arthur was a matter of considerable regret and a splendid case for investigation by Anthony Faraday. *Belt of Suspicion* is an excellent story. It is original, convincing and brilliantly written; modern, almost one might say streamlined. Mr. H. Russell Wakefield is a stylist, his dialogue is full of verve, his situations are tense but natural and convincing, the story as a whole abounds with the sceptical zest of modern life. It is, in brief, first-rate entertainment.

### *Hostess to Death*
May 1938

When that enigmatic young woman, Miss Monnie Douglas, was found shot in the basement of the Wyze-Crax Bottle-Party, Inspector Marlon came to the conclusion that there were three obvious suspects, each with varying degrees of motive and opportunity. But he soon realised there was little chance of making an immediate arrest. A day or two later Roderick Macintosh, roving crime sleuth for a great American daily and brother of one of the suspects, arrived in England on holiday and offered to assist the Yard. His investigations led him to the unearthing of a gang of criminals which had been responsible for many murders in the West End of London. Mr. Wakefield writes with vigour. He knows his London, his characters live, and he can handle a thrilling situation with a keen sense of dramatic values.

## WALLACE, EDGAR
### *Devil Man, The*
July 1931

Mr. Edgar Wallace, who has surely done more than anyone to disprove the old adage, 'Truth is stranger than fiction', has, in *The Devil Man*, gone to truth for his subject. In Charles Peace he had the perfect central character for a novel, so around this weird personality Mr. Wallace has woven a story as thrilling as his most breathless thriller and as mysterious as his most baffling mystery. The name, 'Charles Peace', has become almost a household word; to whisper it after dark is to start a horde of wild imaginings – ill-lit alleys; shrouded figures under misty lamps; footsteps in an empty house – all that makes the flesh creep and the hair stand on end; but of Peace himself we have no clear picture. Edgar Wallace resurrects him in *The Devil Man* and shows us Peace as he was – a repulsive creature to look upon; a colossal braggart; a gifted musician; a murderer – a dwarf in stature and a Samson in strength; the perfect burglar; and a man with an irresistible attraction for women. In this book Mr. Wallace does more than merely thrill, he adds yet another memorable portrait to the picture gallery of crime.

## WALSH, J. M.
### *Lady Incognito*
October 1932

The detective softly opened the door of Ashlin's office. Before the big safe a figure was kneeling. Slade thrust his revolved forward. 'Hands up!' he snapped. The figure before the safe sprang up. The flash of a ring on one finger caught Slade's eye, and his gaze travelled down the hand. He gasped. It was a woman's hand. He was sure of that, though the figure was masked and a long cloak effectively concealed its form. So the leader of the gang that was terrorising London was a woman after all, but who – ? Mr. J. M. Walsh, well-known writer of thrillers that really thrill, has written his most exciting story in *Lady Incognito*.

## WARD, COLIN
### *House Party Murder*
November 1933

This is an extremely clever detective story, the first novel of a schoolmaster at a famous English public school. Most of the principal characters are introduced to us on board a liner *en route* for England. During the voyage one of the messengers mysteriously disappears. The main characters next foregather at a week-end house party where, following the theft of a pearl necklace and a queer game of planchette, one of the party is murdered. One of the most attractive features of this story is the extremely neat solution, which brings to a very satisfactory end a really brilliant story.

## WELCOME, JOHN
### *Painted Devil, A*
July 1988

Mike Ashley, young solicitor with sporting tastes, is dispatched by his firm on a seemingly innocent errand with instructions to ascertain if the claimant to the Dansford Collection of sporting paintings has a genuine case. The claimant turns out to be a beautiful girl with a mysterious, haunted background. When she disappears and he is sent to find her, his suspicions mount that the motives of his employers are not so purely professional as they would like him to believe.

As Mike and the Dansford claimant struggle to escape from those who wish to end forever the girl's claim to a collection valued in millions, they are plunged into a vortex of peril and adventure in which the strange figure of V. C. Malik, self-styled protector of works of art and artifacts [sic] plays an enigmatic role.

The fast action moves from Egypt to London and the complications of legal practice; to an Irish stud farm; to the only foothills of the Apennines above the Tyrrhenian Sea; and to an English racecourse. Only when the sinister mansion in the Welsh hills which houses the Dansford Collection gives up its secrets is the true ownership revealed and a family curse laid to rest.

### *Reasons of Hate*
July 1990

When Charles Hampton, returning from a spell with horses in the Gulf, found that his guardian has been murdered in Ireland, apparently in an abortive raid for arms, he little knew into what maze of violence, mystery and intrigue his appointment as executor to the estate was going to land him. An enigmatic warning of evil to come had been left him by his guardian and pursuit of the clues it contained led him to hairs-breadth escapes and hurried journeys which stretched from Ireland and Gloucester to the Blue Grass country of Kentucky and the Basses-Pyrenees.

His companion in these adventures is his guardian's daughter, Jo, as avid for the truth as he is. As love develops between them, the reader is treated to some fascinating sidelights on the bloodstock industry and certain of its inhabitants, and learns of an old secret from the Second World War, kept but not forgotten.

As in his previous books, John Welcome, keeps up the pace throughout, and his sense of place and knowledge of the world of which he writes makes this an exciting, contemporary and compelling read.

## WEST, CHARLES
### *Funnelweb*
May 1988

A bizarre and brutal killing in lonely Australian bush country…a body, hidden for seven years, covered by an accidental rock-fall… and 600 miles away, in a popular beach resort, a young prostitute found dead from a drugs overdose. These apparently unrelated incidents, happening in different places and at different times, are not seen to be connected in any way: no one even suspects that there is any link between them. Until Tom Grant, working as a stand-in for a famous film-actor, stumbles across the thread that binds them together in a vicious web of deceit, trickery and murder. What Tom does not discover until too late is that guarding the secrets of this web of crime is a swift, deadly and merciless killer – Funnelweb.

Exotic, sub-tropical Queensland is the setting for this fast-moving thriller; and a large and colourful case of characters play out the drama to the very last page.

### *Little Ripper*
November 1991

It is not that Paul Crook looks for trouble. In fact the only thing the youngest and least enthusiastic private eye in the whole of Australasia is actively looking for is an opportunity to shed the intolerable burden of his virginity – but trouble has a knack of seeking him out.

At first sight, his new assignment doesn't look particularly hazardous: the battered remains he is sent to inspect are merely those of an ancient Harley-Davidson motorcycle. ('A really beautiful machine, a little ripper,' according to Crook's client.) The trouble is that Crook's client, Neville Sheen, is as troppo as a headless chook. He also has a shady past and a passion for marijuana; and when the police start their hunt for a multiple murderer, Neville fits neatly into the frame as their chief suspect. Crook alone believes in his friend's innocence.

From motorbikes to mayhem; the search for the Little Ripper leads Paul Crook into the most dangerous episode of his young life.

### *Stage Fright*
October 1993

In the light of recent experience, Paul Crook is understandably reluctant to take on another murder investigation. As he is the first to admit, his heart is not really in the private eye business. But gang-boss Harry Sheiling is a hard man to refuse; and faced with the threat of actual bodily harm, Crook glumly accepts Harry's brief to 'nose around and flush out the murdering bastard' who killed Mary Dean.

As usual, all Crook's dismal forebodings are justified: the case turns out to be quite as messy, dangerous and life-threatening as his previous escapades. 'Nosing around' among theatre folk soon evokes the smells of old greasepaint and musty, faded programmes and – most insidious of all – the ripe whiff of blackmail.

### *Stonefish*
October 1990

The Stonefish is one the deadliest creatures of the Australian Barrier Reef. Its stillness, its perfect camouflage, its patience and the incredible speed of its killing-strike make it a fearsome predator whose thirteen wickedly sharp spines, packed with poison, can kill a man or drive him mad.

A perfect metaphor, Councillor Harvey thought, for the sinister being behind the illegal drugs trade in Sydney: a creature murderous, greedy – and invisible. When Harvey openly said as much, he was brutally murdered in broad daylight.

None of this was Paul Crook's concern. When he left the outback for the big city, his preoccupations were entirely personal. Coping with a surname that no Australian could take seriously, a frustrating love-affair, an Irish-comedian father, and the unexpected inheritance of a detective agency, gave Paul all the hassle he could handle. But circumstances involve him in the Harvey killing. And other murders brought him into violent contact with a side of Sydney life he hadn't known existed; and he learned the hard way that in those murky waters, there are even worse monsters than the Stonefish…

## WHITE, ETHEL LINA
### *Elephant Never Forgets, The*
October 1937

The setting of Ethel Lina White's book – contrary to the suggestion of the title – is far removed from the East. In fact, instead of the heat and dazzling colour, prepare yourself for frozen snow and the grimness of a Russian port on the White Sea. Instead of the humour suggested by the title, prepare yourself for the whispering terror that grips a Soviet town awaiting an Ogpu purge. Miss

White has recently visited Russia – she must have done to make the atmosphere of this book so convincing. She tells the story of an English girl who goes to Russia out of interest in the proletarian experiment. When she has had enough she decides – simply enough – to return to England. But the effect of the country has worked on her nerves. She begins to wonder whether she will get out; when delays actually occur she loses her grip, hysteria threatens her. Ethel Lina White builds up the tension as only this really great writer could, reproducing in full the terrifying atmosphere of suspicion and the maddening delaying tactics of the Russian character. Here is a book to put beside *The Memoirs of a Secret Agent* by Bruce Lockhart, and other outstanding books about the new Russia – a book of which the Crime Club is intensely proud.

OR

In this strange and unusual story one really seems to experience the indefinable terror that grips a Soviet town awaiting an Ogpu purge. It is the story of an English girl who goes to Russia out of interest in the proletarian experiment. When she has had enough she decides – simply enough – to return to England. But the effect of the country has worked on her nerves. She begins to wonder whether she will get out; and when delays actually occur she loses her grip, hysteria threatens her. Ethel Lina White builds up the tension as only this really admirable writer could, reproducing in full the terrifying atmosphere of suspicion and the maddening delaying tactics of the Russian character.

## Man Who Loved Lions, The
November 1943

The roar of a lion is not exactly the kind of music one expects to hear at night in the stillness of the English countryside. Yet in the neighbourhood of Ganges, Sir Benjamin Watson's house, that terrifying jungle noise was not uncommon. Sir Benjamin was rich enough to indulge in the expensive hobby of a private zoo. The first time that Ann Sherborn, walking at night to the gates of Ganges on that strange eventful visit, heard that savage roar, her courage died and she started to run. But that frightening experience was the mere prelude to a night charged with terror, when not only fear but death stalked the strange house of Ganges and played havoc with the guests assembled there. No living writer surpasses Ethel Lina White in sheer ability to tell a story that is at once macabre and entertaining.

## Midnight House
April 1942

The empty house was listed in the postal directory as No. 11 India Crescent, but it was a dead address. Its absentee owner, General Tygarth, and his wife were reported to be living abroad, but it was so long since they had been seen in the town that few people remembered them. Only a few recalled its tragic history of domestic tyranny, ill-starred love and early death; only Mr. Spree, the lawyer, knew that the old General had ordered his house to be closed for a certain number of years and then reopened. And now within a fortnight the house would be open again. To Elizabeth Fetherstonehaugh, the young governess in No. 10, the emptiness of the house next door was fast becoming an obsession. What dire events were to befall are best left to the uncanny pen of Ethel Lina White to describe. It is certain that no other writer can conjure up effectively that haunting atmosphere of mystery and stealthy terror that casts a spell on every reader.

## She Faded into Air
July 1941

At four o'clock on a misty afternoon in London Evelyn Cross vanished into thin air. Evelyn was the daughter of wealthy Raphael Cross. She had been definitely seen entering the flat of Madame Goya, a fortune teller in Mayfair, but in response to Mr. Cross's distracted inquiries, Madame Goya swore emphatically and fervently that his daughter had never entered her flat. Ethel Lina White manages this strange case of the vanishing lady very well indeed, and her very sure and subtle characterisations are sheer joy, while the story admirably maintains that electric atmosphere of dramatic suspense for which this talented writer is famous.

## Step in the Dark
December 1938

On what trivialities the big things in life hang. From the moment when, dining alone in her Brussels hotel, Georgia Yeo, celebrated writer of detective thrillers, opened her cigarette case and the Count came into her life with the polite offer of a match, she realised that here was fate. And in that moment too we surrender ourselves willingly to the strange and inimitable spell of Ethel Lina White. It is an enthralling story, the story of a woman, successful in her career, yet timid and hesitant in making a decision which might have a far-reaching effect on her private life – a veritable step in the dark. Here is a story that no reader will put down until the last page is read.

## They See in Darkness
November 1944

Ethel Lina White's stories are distinguished by a strange macabre quality which she has made peculiarly her own. In her latest novel she presents an eerily fascinating picture of a town plunged in a miasma of fear and superstition. A killer is at work in the town and a series of murders has thrown many of the inhabitants of Oldtown into a blind, unreasoning terror, the fear of darkness and of strange sounds, the pitiless beat of following footsteps. Here is an outstanding story of murder in which the reader is given a rest from clues and time-tables and from cogitating where such and such a suspect was at a particular moment, and is glad to be carried along on the full tide of thrills which the author so lavishly provides.

## Third Eye, The
January 1937

Ethel Lina White achieved a spectacular success with that extraordinary story, *The Wheel Spins*, a book which won her universal recognition as a master of the macabre, a writer worthy of comparison with Edgar Allan Poe. Her new story fully maintains the high standard that she has set herself. From the first page we realise that this astonishing writer holds us once again enthralled, and we are content to give ourselves up to the peculiar fascination of her strange tale. The leading character is Caroline Watts, a very ordinary young person, a school teacher, who at the start of the story has accepted a post as a games mistress at a school in the west of England. Caroline was happy to get the appointment. She did not know that her predecessor had been found dead in bed from heart failure, and that rumour said she had been frightened to death.

## Wheel Spins, The
March 1936

Ethel Lina White stands by herself among writers of thrillers. In the quality of her imagination and in her undoubted power of

creating a truly macabre atmosphere charged with tense drama, she approaches Edgar Allan Poe. In this brilliant story of Iris Carr and her eerie journey on a continental express, Miss White has risen to the full height of her powers. Her book is superbly constructed, with a highly ingenious, subtle and convincing plot, dialogue and atmosphere as modern as the minute, a style that is witty, audacious, deft and powerful. One dare hardly read on – yet one must. Although so much of it is in the mysterious borderland between the known and the unknown, her story remains throughout utterly convincing, the kind of experience that might happen to anybody. A really fine story from start to finish.

## While She Sleeps
January 1940

Miss Loveapple has always been lucky. She had won a fortune in the Calcutta Sweep, she was pretty, sensible, only twenty-eight years old, and lived a tranquil and comfortable existence in her Kentish home with her devoted maid Elsie, her Aberdeen terrier and her cat. She also owned a house in London, and when she decided to take a holiday in Switzerland she arranged to stay there for the week-end. The atmosphere of that empty London house is superbly real. Since Henry James and Edith Wharton, we know of no author who can compare with Ethel Lina White in permeating normal surroundings with such an eerie atmosphere. *While She Sleeps* will not disappoint her countless admirers.

## WHITE, R. J.
### Smartest Grave, The
January 1961

It was near the end of the reign of Queen Victoria when the Captain brought Cecile to the lonely farm in the wilds of East Anglia. She was half French, a brunette of uncertain age and it was her money which bought the Moat House; but her reign there was short. All the Captain had lacked previously was capital. Now, it seemed, he had it, and Moat House had a second mistress, this time a handsome blonde called Henrietta, and the Captain settled down with her to the life of a gentleman farmer, a regular churchgoer, a friend of the vicar, a jolly English squire in Edwardian England. Then, after nearly three years of this apparently exemplary life, the Captain managed to lose Henrietta too. Inspector Brock, who had watched events with a wary eye for a long time, found his interest quickening. The Captain's downward progress became as flamboyant and spectacular as Brock's methods were patient and inconspicuous.

*The Smartest Grave*, the fascinating story of the rise and fall of a splendid rogue, skilfully combines wit, period appeal and a touch of the macabre to make R. J. White's unusual first crime novel a really outstanding achievement.

*The Smartest Grave* was chosen by Agatha Christie, Cecil Day Lewis and Julian Symons as one of the joint winners of the Crime Club's Competition for the best crime novel to be written by a University Don.

## WHITECHURCH, VICTOR L.
### Murder at the College
October 1932

Francis Hatton had gone to the University town of Exbridge to attend a committee meeting at St. Oswald's College. At the luncheon adjournment Hatton remained behind to eat his sandwiches, to read the report of the Society for the Preservation of Ancient Monuments, and to meet his death – for death, swift and unforeseen, struck him down in

that brief hour. This is a story teeming with interest for the reader, who is kept in full touch with every clue, and with every theory which the clues suggest. The conclusion is arrived at by patient inquiry and logical inferences, but the reader will probably be surprised at the denouement.

### Murder at the Pageant
December 1930

This story presents an interesting study of detective methods in solving the problem of a double crime, committed under peculiar circumstances; the crime in question being a tragic sequel to an historical Pageant performed in the grounds of Frimley Manor. The story opens with a scene in the Pageant in which an old Sedan chair plays a prominent part, and the subsequent crime has a curious connection with this chair. The working out of the solution is graphically told, and the logical inferences from the gradually collected evidence are not in any way far-fetched. An astute country police superintendent and a retired secret service agent are prominent characters in bringing about a denouement with a distinct 'thrill'.

## WILLIAMS, DAVID
### Advertise for Treasure
March 1984

The £2m bid for RTB, the young London advertising agency, comes with strings attached. Howard J. Crabtree Inc. of New York needs the deal to go through fast – too fast for Roger Rorch, the agency chairman. His two partners don't agree – and neither does the devious international company broker who has an extra million to offer if necessary, plus an anonymous 'insider' working for him.

The head of the rival Fentley agency gets deeply involved – and not only because he finds out his wife has her own key to Rorch's riverside London penthouse. As for RTB's biggest client, he stands to lose a £40,000 a year 'kickback' through the takeover.

When one of these people dies suddenly banker Mark Treasure doesn't accept the coroner's verdict of accidental death – for reasons that bafflingly involve the Manchester Central Library, St Paul's Cathedral, Wilton House and the Oribi antelope. But after his invaluable secretary, Miss Gaunt, calls him from Greece about an advertising campaign, he makes the right connection, the right deduction – and a difficult decision.

This is the seventh of David William's beautifully contrived Treasure mysteries, conducted at a pace that 'leaves time for humour, clue dropping, labyrinthine complications' (H.R.F Keating, The Times). The US Publishers Weekly described his last novel as an 'uncommonly intelligent, steadily compelling, admirably well written mystery' and concluded it made Treasure 'a plausible candidate for the mantle of the late Ngaio Marsh's detective Roderick Alleyn.'

### Banking on Murder
May 1993

Sir Ray Bims is about to be charged as the principal in a Caribbean bank that's laundering international drug money. Lord Grenwood, octogenarian chairman of Grenwood, Phipps, the London merchant bankers, is appalled. Three years ago he sold the Eel Bridge Rovers Football Club – known as the Eels – to Bims. The club was founded by Grenwood's grandfather and is still associated with the Grenwoods in the public's mind. Now his lordship wants to buy it back to avoid the suggestion of family involvement in Bims's disgrace.

Only hours after refusing Grenwood's

offer for the Eels, Bims commits suicide – except that Detective-Inspector Jeckels of the Fulham CID concludes gradually that it was murder. And he discovers a string of people with motive and opportunity to dispose of Bims – among them the husband of Bims's mistress; the Eels' manager whom Bims had been about to fire; a well-known concert pianist; a curiously religious pest controller; not to mention several Eels players, and Bims's wife and ex-wife.

But the real motive only becomes apparent when the bank's chief executive Mark Treasure takes a hand in the investigation. This leads to the dramatic capture of the murderer – just in time to prevent another slaying. As John Coleman of the *Sunday Times* said of the recent *Treasure by Post\**: 'As always, Williams maintains suspense while keeping the masks of comedy and tragedy spinning like tops.'

\* Not a Crime Club title

### Copper, Gold and Treasure
April 1982

Roderick Cooper (67), retired Major, and Benny Gold (70), London cabbie, apply on the same morning for residential places with the Rudyard Trust for Retired Officers and Gentleman. But its eccentric and drunken Director tells them the Trust is technically bankrupt, its multi-million-pound assets about to be divided between the Founder's descendants – a curious, motley crew.

Banker Mark Treasure is called in when Copper and Gold's bizarre scheme to preserve the charity goes wrong with terrifying consequences – kidnap, stabbing and sudden death – involving one of the bank's clients, ex-President Cuba of Ngonga, exiled in London with his sensuous third wife, his 15-year-old son, and Gerard Opac, his handsome, ambitious aide.

The plot is ingenious, the action fast-moving. The entertaining contrasts range from drama in the Mall to sex in South Kensington, from comedy at Gatwick Airport to tragedy in Victoria and a gripping finish on the Essex marshes.

Major Cooper and Mr Gold are two of the author's best drawn characters. They make this fifth Mark Treasure whodunit another huge helping of what Patrick Cosgrave in the *Daily Telegraph* describes as David William's astonishing command of 'subtlety and assured comic invention'. His last book, *Murder for Treasure*, was shortlisted for CWA Gold Dagger Award.

### Murder for Treasure
August 1980

Could the take-over of Rigley's Patent Footbalm by giant American Hutstacker Chemical Corporation really be scuppered by Mrs Ogmore-Davie's parrot finding a body in Panty Harbour?

It looked like it, but banker sleuth Mark Treasure, British banking's answer to Emma Lathen, took a different view when a second body was discovered the morning after he arrived in the little West Wales sailing village close to St. David's. By then Treasure had already survived a murderous assault aboard the Fishguard Express, a pitched battle on Whitland Station, and the inexplicable disappearance of a battered Australian clergyman. And that was only the start of his exceedingly unquiet weekend. It was to involve his host, the eccentric Judge Henry Nott-Herbert, a T-shirted detective inspector, the high-powered lady-fancying head of Hutstacker's and his understanding wife, a local schemer with a siren spouse, two children, an immense Irish wolfhound, a tone-deaf Welsh vicar, and a pacifist postman.

It also involved the breathtakingly lovely Anna, the young German widow already promised in marriage to someone more than twice her age.

As always, it's a fast-moving, witty and baffling mystery – the first from David Williams set in his native Wales. 'He goes on improving steadily,' said the late Edmund Crispin in the *Sunday Times* of his last novel. He does indeed.

### Planning on Murder
July 1992

The plan to save the Elizabethan stately home Vormer House by selling part of its deer park for a golf and hotel complex has a mixed reception from local politicians and others. Merchant banker Mark Treasure is financial advisor to the property group behind the development. He and his wife Molly drive up to attend the Thatchford town meeting called to air the project. Scandalous accusations are made, but worse is to come when a party in the house where the Treasures are staying is interrupted by the police, come to question the local MP after finding his glamorous secretary ghoulishly murdered.

While the probable suicide of the likeliest suspect promises a swift and easy solution to the case, it's too much so for the conscientious DCI Furlong, especially when another less explicable death occurs. But when Treasure discovers that Furlong is about to arrest someone who [sic] the banker is positive is blameless, he sets up his own investigation to some purpose, solving the mystery and saving the innocent.

### Treasure By Degrees
April 1977

University College, Itchendever, Hants., is long on brains, short on funds, and up for grabs. It seems to be facing a take-over either by the American Funny Farms Foundation or by the calculating Crown Prince of Abu B'yat. Banker sleuth Mark Treasure tries to adjudicate but finds baffling murder on his hands.

Of course the vital question is who did it, not to mention other knotty problems that have a bearing on the case. Who sent the gory sheep's head – and worse – to the eccentric American matron with millions of dollars in her gift? Was her neurotic attorney entirely to be trusted? Was the celebrated Dr Goldstein, senior tutor and TV personality, behind the Arab bomb scare? Why did the Arabs kidnap the lecturer in English literature?

Readers of David Williams's first book, *Unholy Writ*, will not be surprised to find the college housed in a stately home with an impeccable architectural provenance and peopled by a wealth of memorable characters. A tantalizing choice of suspects and a pervading humour make this indeed a Treasure for the connoisseur.

### Treasure Preserved
March 1983

It's action all the way in this classic and witty whodunit centered round the fate of the 19th century Round House whose survival can wreck a multi-million pound development in a South Coast resort. A dozen interested parties are for knocking it down. They include an Arabian oil sheikh, a sexy English Lit. dropout from Sussex University, the head of a construction company, and a romantic novelist. And where does Canon Tring's languorous young wife fit into all this? You may well ask!

Only Louella, Lady Basset, is committed to keeping the Round House standing; she believes it to be the joint creation of two famous architects, Sir John Soane and William Butterfield. But four hours after Treasure promises her a stay of execution on the

house, it's Louella who's blown up – and another death follows. Double accident – or double murder?

David William's new novel offers a twisting plot, red herrings galore, and a tale peppered with delightfully drawn characters, not forgetting Dung the dog. Of course Treasure finds all the answers, but only after doing battle with a monster demolition machine, a bizarre chase through the sleeping town, and a hair-raising confrontation on the windswept pier.

### Treasure Up in Smoke
April 1978

King Charles Island, a drowsily contented British Colony in the West Indies, came dramatically awake through the foul murder of its most influential citizen. Banker sleuth Mark Treasure arrived on business to discover that his accident-prone assistant was the number one suspect.

Treasure quickly volunteered to assist the daunted Chief Inspector Small in finding the real villain from among a bewildering bunch of runners. The list included Glen Dogwall III, President of the Sunfun Hotel Corporation and his nymphomaniac wife; the Chief Inspector, his wife and his mistress; Angus McLush, journalist and part-time spy; the Governor and his Lady; the enigmatic Father Babington; and the victim's scheming brother. A hectic chase aboard the indestructible *Sir Dafydd*, 'the oldest narrow-gauge steam-engine working west of Talyllyn', a narcoleptic pig and a most unusual convent all add to the flavour of this stylish whodunit, which is 'witty, vibrant, and beautifully written', the adjectives applied by Violet Grant of the *Daily Telegraph* to its predecessor, *Treasure by Degrees*.

### Unholy Writ
July 1976

Merchant banker Mark Treasure was unofficially called in to help rescue historic Mitchell Hall from the clutches of the Forward Britain Movement – an organization whose aims were less progressive than its title. But he soon found that there was more involved than the Moonlights' stately home: the ownership of a Shakespearian holograph, no less. There were also some awkward questions demanding to be answered. Was Maggie Edwards frightened to death in the deserted churchyard? Why was the mysteriously dead gravedigger whisked twenty miles downriver to Windsor? Who assaulted the curious antiquarian? No one – certainly not Treasure – could have foreseen that before his quiet weekend was over, the pleasant Thames-side village would have erupted into explosive action involving a swinging vicar, a frightened Filipino, a calculating Member of Parliament, a laconic police inspector, a lovelorn Shakespearian researcher, and an insomniac retriever called Bach.

## WINSLOW, PAULINE GLEN
### Coppergold
August 1978

Superintendent Merle (for Merlin) Capricorn, last encountered in *The Witch Hill Murder*, is faced with the hardest challenge of his career: to prove his friend and assistant, the hardboiled, wisecracking lady's man Inspector Copper – 'Flash' Copper – innocent of murdering the woman he loved. Complicating Capricorn's dilemma is the suspicion that Copper and his lover were involved in a counterfeit currency scheme involving debased coins which had already attracted the attention of the police. Capricorn uses all his strength and cunning, but everyone's

hand seems against him: his superiors at Scotland Yard; his madcap Music Hall aunts, now enjoying a comeback on television, who sneer at his conventionality; the underworld informers he relies on; even his own doubts assail him. The truth when it is revealed is as subtle and ingenious as a Chinese puzzle; just as deceptive, just as surprising, and just as elegant.

### Counsellor Heart, The
May 1980

A Fawn, as waitresses at Soho's Fawn Club are called, has been slashed to death and the hunt is on for the perpetrator of a sordid sex crime. It is a case which Superintendent Merle Capricorn would have found distasteful at any time, but especially now, when his heart and mind, like most of the Yard's senior officers, are centred on the search for Bridey Lawdon, wife of a colleague and loved for a quality of simple goodness which is as rare and lovely in the pages of crime fiction as it is in life.

For Bridey has been kidnapped and is being held as a hostage, the deadline for meeting the outrageous demands of the unknown terrorist organization that holds her rapidly running out. What connection has the death of the Fawn with the fate of Bridey?

By a process of classic detection, involving characters as diverse as his matrimonially troubled show-biz aunt, a sad-eyed love-sick Levantine merchant, and one of the IRA's most wanted leaders, Merle Capricorn finds out.

### Rockefeller Gift, The
March 1982

Like a magician pulling endless wonders from unlikely places, the unfailingly imaginative Pauline Glen Winslow once again confronts Scotland Yard's Superintendent Merle (for Merlin) Capricorn with a remarkable series of adventures. While in New York investigating the apparent suicide of an erratic young diplomat attached to the United Nations, whose building, on land donated by the Rockefellers, gives the book its title, Capricorn encounters unstable socialites, secretive bankers, the son of an old friend Happy Delaney, now a New York cop in Father's footsteps, and – inevitably – his irrepressible aunts. The aunts are fulfilling an engagement on Broadway which may well be the trio's last if Nelly does indeed succumb to the blandishments of a UN diplomat from Sweden – something their nephew is energetically urged to prevent.

Pauline Glen Winslow, a Londoner who has lived in New York for thirty years, paints an ominous picture of the city in detritus, self-wounding and decay. She also spins an exciting story about a plot centred on the United Nations and neighbouring buildings in which the East seeks to undermine and so destroy the West.

### Witch Hill Murder, The
October 1977

A small town at loggerheads with the quasi-religious movement which has taken over the local mansion, and the town clerk, leading opponent of their expansion, found dead on the Witch Hill Road on the eve of his wedding – Superintendent Capricorn was enmeshed in difficult problems, for all his hundreds of prime suspects had cast-iron alibis. Worse still, the bereaved bride-to-be was an old friend, who had asked for his assistance because she was worried by threats against her fiancé's life. In failing to prevent the murder, Capricorn felt bitterly that he had let her down.

But as he probed deeper into the mysteries of the case, he recalled the words of his magician father who had named him Merle: distrust the obvious, always look for misdirection and deception. Some of the misdirection was the result of Merle Capricorn's own flair for it, but even so, he could not ignore the strange village gossip about the town clerk's glamorous stepmother, nor the suspicious inconsistencies in the stories of some very respectable people who seemingly had nothing to hide.

Not until Capricorn was forced to use all his magician's wiles to escape from a fiendish deathtrap, did he finally understand the complex secret of the Witch Hill Murder in a climax as astounding as it is satisfying.

## WOLF, SARAH
### Long Chain of Death
June 1988

Acting Police Chief Phillip Decker had lived in Fairfield all his life and there had never been a murder in the town. Now there were three: Elizabeth Breen, the prettiest girl in town; a high-school cheerleader; and her football hero boyfriend.

At first nothing seems to connect the crimes, except possibly David Brett, husband of one victim and teacher of the other two. But when David, grief-stricken and under suspicion, sets out to find the murderer, he discovers that in the past twenty years three Fairfield men and many members of their families have died in seeming accidents. These men, David's among them, had been close friends as boys and had served together overseas in World War II. The fourth member of the one-time quartet has disappeared.

The killer's pattern accelerates as David's search heats up, menacing him and the few remaining children of the doomed quartet. And meanwhile Lieutenant Phillip Decker plays his own game, every bit as determined as David to find the murderer.

As tension heightens, David realizes how impressive and frightening are the powers of both killer and policeman. Somehow he, in the middle, must match them both.

## WOOD, TED
### Corkscrew
July 1988

Tough but caring Reid Bennett is the one-man police force in Murphy's Harbour. That's one man and one dog – Reid's Alsatian, Sam. They're quite a team.

But even Reid and Sam may have more trouble than they can handle when a squad of bikers zooms into town. Members of the infamous Devil's Brigade, the bikers deal in drugs, pornography and illegal guns. They aren't the kind of visitors a small resort community like Murphy's Harbour seeks.

Reid has a problem: trying to figure out how to get rid of the bikers without violating their civil rights. And he has another problem: a thirteen-year-old boy is missing. Young Kennie Spenser apparently wandered off to take photographs and hasn't been seen since.

One thing's going right for Reid, however. Girlfriend Freda, the red-headed actress, has returned to keep him company. She may even help to solve the case.

With his fifth Reid Bennett adventure, author Ted Wood has never been better. He continues to prove himself a master of the contemporary action-packed mystery.

### Dead Centre
November 1985

Reid Bennett and his Alsatian, Sam, return to Toronto for a refresher course in urban crime in the new mystery by the author of *Dead in the Water* and *The Killing Cold.*

A Toronto security firm hires Bennett to catch two thugs which have been bashing the night watchmen at a construction site they're supposed to be watching. With the help of Sam, he brings in the culprits without much trouble. But the one-night stand turns into a two-week ordeal when Bennett agrees to stay on and find out who is behind the beatings. What with a Mafia loan shark's hired bullies, a bunch of diminutive but deadly martial arts experts, old enemies on the Toronto police force, and a stunning Chinese woman who reminds him too much of bad days in Vietnam, Bennett finds himself overmatched and confused – and begins to suspect that he is as much the hunted as he is the hunter.

Great action scenes, a varied and vivid set of characters, and a satisfying complex plot make this Ted Wood's best yet.

### Dead in the Water
February 1984

When Reid Bennett was offered a job as the one-man police force of tiny Murphy's Harbour, it seemed too good to be true. The bad publicity that had followed the barehanded killing of two men while off duty, trying to prevent a rape, had ruined his career with the Toronto police force and wrecked his marriage. In this peaceful lakeside town he could put together a normal life in a calm setting.

But a corpse turns up at one end of the lake and a New York woman looking for protection at the other, and Bennett's investigation uncovers indications that Murphy's Harbour is not the idyllic haven he had taken it for. Within a day, the discovery of a second corpse – this time that of a local man – and a cache of drugs makes it clear that the resort is the base of a professional crime operation. The pleasure boats on the lake and the woodland surrounding it make a shifting and treacherous battleground, and before long Bennett, assisted only by his Alsatian, Sam, and a crippled World War II veteran, finds that he must once again overstep the traditional bounds of a policeman's role in order to survive.

Tough, fast-paced, original, *Dead in the Water* introduces an important new writer with a fresh voice and a keen eye for action.

### Flashback
March 1992

A teen-gang drives into peaceful Murphy's Harbour and commits mayhem. When a stolen car is found in the lake with a woman's body in the trunk, police chief Reid Bennett suspects they may also have committed murder.

Surprisingly, the car owner identifies the dead woman not as his wife but as his wife's friend. And *her* husband seems to have disappeared …

Reid's investigations soon uncover a link between the gang leader and a woman movie producer summering locally, which leads him to believe the gang's activities may be being cunningly orchestrated to distract him from his inquiries.

He has other distinctions too. His wife is about to give birth to their first child, and a dangerous criminal whom Reid arrested six years earlier has escaped from prison and is hellbent on revenge.

As events develop, and as one link after another is forged, Reid and his Alsatian Sam have their work cut out to keep themselves and Murphy's Harbour safe.

### Fool's Gold
November 1986

One-man police force Reid Bennett enters gold strike territory in this new mystery.

These are boom times in Canada. The

biggest gold strike ever has turned Olympia into an instant mecca for prospectors, chopper pilots, construction workers, and drifters, all eager for a piece of the new mine. Then a geologist is found dead – apparently mauled by a bear – and Bennett is called to the scene.

It starts like an open-and-shut case, but Bennett soon has his suspicions. There hasn't been a mauling in years. In fact, no one has even spotted a bear recently. Could it have been murder? Bennett and his trained Alsatian, Sam, team up with two locals, the small-town police chief ready for one last hurrah before retirement, and a lovely, lonely motel keeper with a sad secret, to investigate a string of brutal murders and an inconveniently resurfacing corpse.

Ted Wood's twists, jolts, and tensions are here in full force, and once again he has a conjured a vivid, unforgettable case [sic] of characters.

### Killing Cold, The
October 1984

Ted Wood, winner of the Scribner Crime Novel Award 1983 for his first novel, *Dead in the Water*, more than lives up to his own high standard in the second major case for Reid Bennett, the one-man police force of Murphy's Harbour, Ontario.

It began with a kidnapping. The newly crowned Queen of the Ice Festival, the Harbour's midwinter highspot, was abducted from the stage during a brief blackout right under Bennett's nose. But a snowstorm made the roads out of Murphy's Harbour impassable, and the kidnappers – members of the feminist Canadian League of Angry Women (CLAW) – were trapped in town.

Soon after Bennett started tracking them on a snowmobile among the empty hotels and summer cottages that surround the Harbour, he found one of the women from CLAW murdered. When he learned that there were men involved in the kidnapping as well, he realized that the women's group was being used as a front by someone with more malevolent intentions than publicizing the feminist cause.

In a complex and exhausting chase through the mounting drifts, Bennett – again assisted only by Sam, his Alsatian – finds himself forced once more to step outside the bounds of the law in order to discover the true purpose of the plot, to prevent the deaths of local residents, and to save his own life.

### On the Inside
November 1990

On temporary (honeymoon) leave from the small Canadian town of Murphy's Harbour, police chief Reid Bennett, his bride Freda, and his Alsatian Sam travel north to the bleak gold-mining community of Elliot, where Reid has accepted a call from the provincial police commission to talk his way on to the local force in order to probe suspected police corruption from the inside.

Elliot is rough, as Reid learns when he and Sam break up a bar-room fight within minutes of their arrival in town. It's the kind of place where justice and punishment don't wait for courts of law.

It's also a place where the police chief may be taking a lucrative cut from the hotel receipts and the travelling hookers who service miners every payday. When the previous hotel manager reported this to the provincial authorities, he met with a fatal accident …

In this town of greed and subterfuge, Reid must first decide which of the citizens he can trust. But as Reid and Sam draw ever closer to a dramatic confrontation with their enemies, Freda cherishes a secret of her own, for Elliot may be a strange and hostile community, but in its way it welcomes Freda and

helps her to face up to what being Reid Bennett's wife may mean.

### Snowjob
July 1993

Reid Bennett, one-man police department of Canadian Murphy's Harbour, heads for Vermont ski country where Doug Ford, a Marine buddy of his in Vietnam and the only black officer in the local force, is charged with the murder of a ski-resort book-keeper.

Reid learns that Ford was working on a case involving the Mafia. He believed there was a money-laundering operation going on and the dead girl, far from being his partner in an affair, as rumoured, was his lead to the facts

Almost at once Reid and his Alsatian, Sam, are involved with threats to Doug's family and with the local rowdies, one of whom is Reid's prime suspect for the murder of the girl. But when he too is murdered and his body dumped on the resort's most challenging run, Reid himself is arrested and Sam threatened with destruction.

Eventually, with the help of a local lawyer who wants to run for judge, Reid succeeds in cracking the case, but not before there have been other deaths.

Along the way he uncovers a lot of guilty secrets in this small town which is nowhere near as snow-white as the hills surrounding it.

### When the Killing Starts
October 1989

Reid Bennett, police chief of tiny Murphy's Harbour in Canada, was looking forward to a month's vacation – until Norma Michaels, wife of a rich businessman, came along with a $25,000 offer: find her twenty-year old son, Jason, who has run off with some mercenaries to train for overseas service.

Reid points out that the young man is of legal age, but his mother says that's not the issue. She wants her son found and she is willing to pay to extract him from the clutches of the mercenary outfit, run by an ex-sergeant in the British paratroopers who had been court-martialled for brutality. Just the type to round up a bunch of kids to risk their lives in foreign parts while he collects their pay.

Such men tend to annoy Reid so he takes the job. He knows he's up against a pro, and he suspects he may encounter a few difficulties – such as some ex-SAS men with automatic weapons – in tracking down young Jason. And once he finds the boy, will he be willing to come home?

With lots of questions left unanswered, Reid and his Alsation, Sam, start north to find their prey.

## WOODS, SARA
### And Shame the Devil
November 1967

Antony Maitland is not the C.I.D.'s favourite barrister; so he is much surprised to receive an urgent, if unofficial, request for help in defending a police sergeant and a constable who have been accused of wrongful arrest in the Yorkshire town of Arkenshaw.

The case intrigues Maitland because it involves a direct conflict of evidence between two seemingly reputable eye witnesses. At the same time, he is uneasy: the plaintiffs – already acquitted of a charge of burglary – are two immigrants from Pakistan, and the suggestion that they may have been victimized is too obvious to ignore. In spite of this, he goes to Arkenshaw, and learns at first hand something about the 'colour problem' as we know it today in England.

This fascinating story differs in setting and manner from Sara Woods's earlier well-known novels. Maitland's persistence gradually discovers the truth of the widespread mystery at Arkenshaw, and some fine court scenes are part of the sequence of events that lead to startling disclosures.

### *Bloody Instructions*
June 1962

Sir Nicholas Harding, the eminent Counsel, was deeply immersed in his brief; he was in no mood for interruptions, and was disposed even to look on murder as an intolerable distraction.

Yet when murder came to Bread Court ('not more than five minutes walk from the Inner Temple') Sir Nicholas soon discovered that there was more here than a brief to be dispassionately studied and professionally executed; this crime came nearer home – even his nephew, Antony Maitland, was a principal witness and possible suspect.

This first novel is a classical detective story. It is written with rare economy and subtlety and with a detailed knowledge of the ways of the law and lawyers. It does not present a mere puzzle, but living characters in the grip of a situation that leads to a battle in court, a scene as original in presentation as are the other elements in this distinguished and absorbing crime novel.

### *Case is Altered, The*
January 1967

The emeralds – more famous now as belonging to the enchanting Giuditta than for their previous history – had been stolen at a party given by the AngIt company to celebrate the completion of their latest film. The case was over, and Roy Bromley had been convicted and sentenced before Jo Marston, herself an actress under contract to the company, persuaded Antony Maitland to take a hand in the affair.

'There is a future for innocence,' said Angelo, the Director and guiding spirit of AngIt Films. But Angelo was an optimist, and Maitland wasn't so sure.

When he started his inquiries, the question seemed more than ever uncertain, especially when a murder confirmed his impression that the theft of the emeralds was not the simple matter that judge and jury had been led to believe.

Antony Maitland, self-effacing yet shrewd and tough, is in his best form in this exciting story – as is Sir Nicholas Harding, Q.C., his ebullient uncle and friend. This is a fine piece of craftsmanship, a multiple mystery with a very surprising outcome.

### *Enter Certain Murderers*
March 1966

A mysterious rendezvous takes place at an A.A. box on a main road. A packet is deposited there – and swiftly collected. But the man who collects it dies – shot by a hidden rifle as he leaves the box with the precious packet.

This is the prologue to a long and complex story that has its source in a murder committed many years earlier. Its central character is a man whose inheritance includes a vulnerability to blackmail and who rashly enlists the help of his fiancée, a young actress, in an effort to establish the blackmailer's identity. It comes to a thrilling and off-beat climax when this man and Antony Maitland fall into the clutches of a villain whose wickedness is unusually convincing.

Maitland, the reticent barrister who is so much tougher and more persistent than he appears, is at his best here. So is Sir Nicholas Harding, Q.C., in his crotchety or zany brief appearances. This is a fine modern detective novel with a strong plot and good characters – a story that will bring yet more recruits to the ranks of Sara Woods's admirers and Maitland's followers.

### *Error of the Moon*
August 1963

The huge Carcroft works of the General Aircraft Company stood on a lonely moor at Mardingley in Yorkshire – an ideal site for the secret missile research and development programme which was its principal business.

A death that looked like an accident, following the suspicion that secret papers had been tampered with, was a serious matter in the Carcroft works, where anything less than complete security would render the whole vast project worse than useless. An agent was required to investigate inside the works while ostensibly engaged in an administrative job there: the choice fell on Antony Maitland, barrister and nephew of Sir Nicholas Harding, Q. C.; Maitland had served as a 'special agent' during the war – and had occasionally been called on in the post-war years.

Maitland could not forestall other killings at Mardingley, and the puzzle that faced him was bewildering and dangerous. *Error of the Moon* is set convincingly in a great modern research factory, depicted in detail from the missile 'Full Moon' itself to the cups of coffee in the secretaries' offices. Maitland, as always deceptively gentle and withdrawn, is searching for a killer and a traitor, a man more dangerous even that his quarry in *Bloody Instructions* or *The Taste of Fears*.

### *Improbable Fiction, An*
April 1970

The Coroner said Cynthia Edison's death was suicide. Her sister said it was murder. What's more, she said it on TV to some two million people and named as murderer a well-known entertainer. In the ensuing libel action Antony Maitland was briefed for the defence.

The only defence was justification, which was tricky, though Maitland soon had reason to think it might be true. But when the case seemed to be going against her and the entertainer was found murdered, his client found herself in deeper waters still.

To clear her of the charge of murder, Maitland began to investigate. In particular he investigated the Hazard Club, the high-class gaming house which the murdered man had owned. Before long he was asking his usual questions. What role was played by the American lawyer who so smoothly materialized whenever Maitland went there? Was the club being used, as the police had already hinted, as a headquarters for organized crime?

The latest Maitland adventure is highly topical, and as skilfully unfolded as Sara Woods's readers have rightly come to expect.

### *Knavish Crows, The*
August 1971

When barrister Antony Maitland and his wife Jenny set off on an eagerly anticipated holiday to the United States, the commission which a solicitor friend asked him to undertake seemed no more than an excuse for a pleasant detour. He was to visit the aged sole heir to an estate worth half a million and get him to claim it within the stipulated six months.

Maitland visits the old man only to find him dying. But he has a long-lost daughter who can claim if she can be found in time. The quest for her takes Antony and Jenny and their American friends to California – and they are not alone in their search. The executors of the will have come over from England and are also anxious to find her, but they are less disinterested: if she does not claim, they inherit. Maitland's anxiety mounts. There have been two suspiciously convenient deaths already. Is there about to be a third?

Sara Woods spins out her web of suspicion from Washington to San Francisco and a denouement which will both surprise and satisfy.

### *Knives Have Edges*
July 1968

It was simply a routine case…until one of the jurors was offered a bribe. But that would have been no more than a passing annoyance to Antony Maitland, who was leading for the defence, if he hadn't used the free afternoon provided by the adjournment to mix himself up in John Kellaway's affairs.

Even so, it was Sir Nicholas Harding's lost passport that was worrying Maitland most when he talked over the day's events with his wife, Jenny. But that was before Kellaway was charged with murder.

'His past is shady', Maitland told his uncle, 'and his friends seem a disreputable lot.' But circumstances seemed to be conspiring to involve Maitland, and he was soon in much deeper water than ever before. By then he was very much on his own. Sir Nicholas was lecturing in America; Maitland's old enemy, Chief Superintendent Briggs, had his own ideas about what was happening; and the press were in full cry.

And last – and worst – of all, Jenny was in danger…but that was something he didn't know until it was almost too late. This most exciting of the novels by Sara Woods featuring Maitland and Sir Nicholas Harding ends in a thrilling denouement and an astonishing revelation.

### *Let's Choose Executors*
September 1966

In the market town of Chedcombe a murder trial is about to begin. A young woman is to be charged with poisoning her godmother. At the eleventh hour Antony Maitland, in Chedcombe on other business, is asked if he will lead for the defence. His first reaction is:

'I should have thought it was too late for anything but a witch doctor.'

But Maitland becomes involved. He is soon convinced of the innocence of the accused, but perceives too that only one type of defence is likely, in the circumstances, to be successful. It was 'not just a matter of deriding the case for the prosecution … But a full scale defence involving a counter-attack … the most difficult and (in a court of law) the most unpopular form of manoeuvre'.

At the very last moment Maitland is in a position to launch his counter-attack. But his investigations in Chedcombe involve him in violent and dangerous events – and the final revelation is entirely surprising.

### *Malice Domestic*
October 1962

Sir Nicholas Harding, eminent counsel, and his nephew Antony Maitland made their first appearance in *Bloody Instructions*, Sara Woods' first novel.

In this, her second book, Sir Nicholas, reluctantly and against his better judgement, is persuaded by Maitland to defend a young man charged with the murder of his great-uncle, William Cassell. Paul Herron had had good reason to kill his grandfather: the police view was that in trying to do so he had killed his grandfather's brother by mistake.

Maitland's enquiries lead far into the past to a tragedy in which three young people had been killed, evidently as the result of a brainstorm. By the meticulous gathering of many and various threads he is able to discover a logical pattern behind the killing of William Cassell…

Like *Bloody Instructions*, this is a classical detective novel. Again it is a crime novel of distinction and authority, with well-observed characters, an intricate plot and – beneath the surface – the compelling qualities of melodrama and surprise.

### *Past Praying For*
November 1968

As junior counsel for the prosecution in the case of Regina versus Barnard (1957) Antony Maitland was not a great success. He developed a feeling of sympathy for the young woman in the dock, and his hesitation may have led to her conviction for manslaughter where a conviction for murder had seemed inevitable.

There the matter should have ended. But many years later a further astonishing development in the Barnard family led to Maitland's being again involved in their affairs. And not only Maitland but his formidable uncle, Sir Nicholas Harding, Q.C.

Sara Woods here presents a story of exceptional fascination and brilliance. Through a series of court scenes that are both humorous and moving, and through the strange interregnums between them when Maitland searches for the truth, the reader is cunningly informed of a most extraordinary situation. *Past Praying For* provides excitement in full, and a sensational ending.

### *Serpent's Tooth*
January 1971

When Antony Maitland returns to Arkenshaw, the scene of his adventures in *And Shame the Devil*, it is to defend 17-year-old Joe Hartley on a murder charge. Joe is one of the thirteen children fostered by Alfred Baker and his wife, and there has never been any hint of serious trouble among them. Yet one Saturday afternoon, on returning from a walk, Joe apparently went berserk and beat Alfred Baker's head in. Before he can hope to defend him, Maitland feels he must know why.

Joe refuses to speak; he insists he will take what's coming to him. Joe's teachers, friends, employers, family, can shed no light. But although the evidence seems to point unerringly to Joe, someone is very determined that Maitland shall not pursue his enquiries. Attempts to put him off, at first innocent, soon escalate to a reckless attempt on his life.

*Serpent's Tooth* introduces the reader to several Arkenshaw characters previously encountered, including the astrologically-minded Grandma Duckett, Inspector Duckett, her son, and her granddaughter Star. It also introduces a story so bizarre that its solution will astound the reader as much as it astounds Antony Maitland's hearers when the secrets of the Baker family are finally brought to light in court.

### *Tarry and Be Hanged*
May 1969

Only one witness could provide Dr. Henry Langton with an alibi for the time of his wife's murder, but that alibi was made of cast iron. Nevertheless, when a year later another body is dug up in the doctor's shrubbery, Antony Maitland finds himself conducting an unusually difficult defence.

Langton's story of blackmail is so damning to his chances that Maitland quixotically believes it. For lack of evidence, Langton is acquitted at the trial. But his career and his second marriage are both in ruins. Maitland finds that his task, far from ending, has only just begun.

Step by step he uncovers a series of

similar murders and a trail of evidence which points inexorably to a ruthless partnership in crime. To clear Langton and prevent further murders, the identity and whereabouts of the killers must be discovered.

*Tarry and Be Hanged* is Sara Woods at her wittiest and most ingenious.

### *Taste of Fears, The*
February 1963

Antony Maitland served as a secret agent in France in the Second World War. Much later, when he became a barrister in the Inner Temple and right-hand man to his eminent uncle, Sir Nicholas Harding, Q.C., the aftermath of those dangerous days caught up with him in the form of present danger…

In this new crime novel there is danger to be countered, and a mystery to be solved. A murder, an arrest, a second murder – all need the explanation that only Maitland can provide, and it is his fate to serve several masters – the law, the secret service and – most demanding and idiosyncratic of all – Sir Nicholas Harding.

Once again Sara Woods, as in *Bloody Instructions* and *Malice Domestic*, shows a mastery that will give heart to all supporters of the detective novel and a new slant on 'the cult of the great detective'. And this again is a contemporary story, written with a subtlety and distinction that will establish Sir Nicholas Harding and Antony Maitland, both lawyers, high among the redressers of criminal wrongs.

### *This Little Measure*
October 1964

The codicil to old Roderick Gaskell's will baffled the family, and worried them too: in it he bequeathed to his son 'the problem of the Velasquez'. The trouble was he hadn't a Velasquez, and, to their knowledge, had never possessed one.

But it seemed the old man had known what he was doing. The problem might have been a simple one – but not for the Gaskells. It wasn't long before Antony Maitland, still at this time at the junior bar, found himself involved in their affairs – and found soon afterwards that he was helping his uncle, Sir Nicholas Harding, to prepare a defence against a charge of murder.

The wide public that delights in and follows the adventures of Antony Maitland and his uncle in and out of the courtroom will be delighted with the skill and subtlety which they bring to their latest case. *This Little Measure* is an exciting addition to the canon of novels that now runs from *Bloody Instructions* to *Trusted Like the Fox*.

### *Though I Know She Lies*
September 1965

'The prisoner's hair was red; the rich, dark shade often described as 'Titian', though the painter never lived who could capture its beauty fully. Now that the dusk was deepening outside, the lights in the courtroom came into their own, and it was as though the brightness of flame was entangled in it.'

'Sir Nicholas Harding, who led for the defence, was uneasily and rather angrily conscious of her impact on judge and jury.'

'Derek Stringer concentrated – eyes and thought alike – on the prisoner…A generous mouth, he thought, she doesn't look like a poisoner, and, of course, she hasn't admitted…But there the evidence was, all neatly docketed.'

Sir Nicholas, in desperation, asks his nephew Antony Maitland to busy himself, at the last moment, in the background of a case that has brought the prisoner close to conviction as a murderess. Antony's discoveries are startling – as is the final revelation of the truth.

This new novel is a fine criminal addition to the canon of Sara Woods's celebrated stories of Sir Nicholas Harding and Antony Maitland.

### *Trusted like a Fox*
February 1964

Antony Maitland is Counsel for the Defence in a case that has become a cause célèbre: a charge of murderous assault and treason is being defended on grounds of identity, a kind of Tichborne case 'in reverse'. Maitland is concerned to prove – though privately he does not altogether believe it – that the prisoner arrested in 1962 is not the same person as the traitor who took secrets to Germany during the war: that the identifications, made first by a police constable strolling down the sea-front and then supported by many witnesses who had known the man well twenty years before, are mistaken.

In this defence Maitland might have succeeded … 'you went into this case with a properly cynical attitude,' said Sir Nicholas … but that was before the shattering and startling developments which were to alter the whole nature of the problem, and the rôle he must play.

By a remarkable feat of narrative ingenuity this dramatic story is told almost entirely in the courtroom. The feelings of the judge, something of the attitude of the jury, the by-play between Prosecuting and Defending Counsel, Maitland's relationship with a highly exasperating client, are presented as parts of the whole; and the sum of all these is the answer to the question – whether a man should live or die.

The very successful author of *Bloody Instructions* and *The Taste of Fears* is at her best in this new novel, as are the subtle Maitland and the boisterous Sir Nicholas Harding.

### *Windy Side of the Law, The*
May 1965

'He didn't know where he was … and hard on that realisation came the further thought with the force of a blow. He didn't know who he was.'

These were Peter Hammond's first bewildering thoughts when he woke up in a strange room. The only clue he could find to his own identity was the name of Antony Maitland scrawled in his diary.

Antony recognised him as an old childhood friend and felt inclined to believe his story – but not so the police when they asked him to explain how the hidden packet got into his suitcase.

Much against the wishes of his wife Jenny and his uncle Sir Nicholas Harding, Q.C., Antony agrees to undertake the defence. But whether Peter is telling the truth or not, the evidence against him is strong and Antony's efforts to extricate him only result in he himself becoming deeply enmeshed in a seemingly indefensible situation.

*The Windy Side of the Law* will delight Sara Wood's [sic] many readers. Antony Maitland meets a ruthless, well organised opponent determined not to have his activities interfered with; but Antony is stubborn too and their clash is tough and exciting.

## WRIGHT, ERIC

### *Body Surrounded By Water, A*
July 1987

Homicide is rare on Prince Edward Island, so rare that when a local historian is killed the Mounties have to create a special unit to investigate the crime. When the officer in charge finds that a Toronto policeman, Inspector Charlie Salter, is holidaying in the neighbourhood he is happy to invite him to join the unit unofficially, especially as the Toronto man's in-laws seem connected to the crime.

When Clive Elton was killed, apparently by a burglar he had disturbed, he had just returned from Toronto with the Island's Great Silver Seal which had reappeared after being missing for two hundred years. The seal had been secretly bought back from a dealer by a group of Island backroom politicians, headed by Salter's father-in-law, and Elton had been acting as their courier. Now Salter becomes the go-between linking his father-in-law and the Mounties as they try to establish a connection between Elton's death and the disappearance, again, of the seal.

Salter is delighted to get out of the house and he makes some crucial contributions towards solving both mysteries. Along the way, a changed relationship with his son and a new discovery (by Salter about his wife Annie), make this the best holiday he has ever spent near his in-laws, even without a couple of homicides.

### *Death by Degrees*
May 1993

Staff Inspector Charlie Salter badly needs something to take his mind off the fact that his father is in hospital and may be dying. Salter's boss suggests that investigating a series of anonymous letters, not normally worth a staff inspector's time, might be just the job.

The letters, from nearby Bathurst College, concern the death of a newly-appointed dean, shot and killed during a break-in at his home. There has been no reason to suspect anyone on campus, and Salter assumes that his presence on the scene will be enough to satisfy the letter-writer, while the homicide unit looks elsewhere for the killer. But by the time a suspect is found, an Ojibway Indian living on the Toronto streets, Salter is convinced that this is not their man.

Because of his new familiarity with the campus, Salter is now allowed to investigate the homicide proper, and he follows a trail beginning with the Indian, which takes him to the truth.

### *Death in the Old Country*
March 1985

When Inspector Charlie Salter of the Metropolitan Toronto Police takes a holiday in England with his wife, Annie, their only problem seems to be to find the good restaurants and hotels that lie hidden in the English countryside. Their first night is a disaster — but this is not typical; nothing in England is, they discover, and when a few nights later, after a minor road accident near the town of Tokesbury Mallett, the local police recommend an inn, it so delights them that they decide to stay for a few days. But their stay is cut short when their landlord is found dead, stabbed in his office.

At first Salter is an interested and wondering observer of the methods of the newly appointed local inspector, but the arrival of a second police officer forces him to concede that it is as dangerous to generalize about English policemen as it is to generalize about English food.

Superintendent Hamilton allows Salter to watch him at work before sending the Canadian on his way. But despite a developing addiction to steeplechasing, Salter cannot resist a little private investigation of his own (especially as it is still raining). The trail leads him to Italy, and back through London to Tokesbury Mallett, where Hamilton has been continuing his own investigation, before the case is satisfactorily resolved. For Salter it has been a real busman's holiday, and Annie has enjoyed it too.

### *Final Cut*
March 1991

There is trouble on the set of a movie being made in Toronto, and Staff Inspector Charlie Salter of the Special Affairs Unit has been assigned to investigate it. The trouble started out as no more than a few incidents of petty vandalism; it soon escalates into assault, arson and murder.

Salter is faced with a truly international cast of suspects, from Hollywood, Romania, Czechoslovakia, Quebec and Newfoundland, and enough personal feuds among them to provide plenty of motives.

In the beginning, before the crimes become serious, Salter enjoys mixing with the actors and crew, watching a movie being made, as does his stage-struck son, Seth, who has wangled his way on to the set. In the end, though, Salter's sympathy with many of these people makes him vulnerable, and his discovery of the identity of the killer puts him in a serious dilemma. How he handles his crisis, with the unwitting help of his old boss, Orliff, provides the story's resolution.

Annie, his wife, is around to help out with Seth's problems, and Constable Ranovic is back, helping (or not impeding) in his favourite undercover guise. But the heart of the story is the conflict in Charlie Salter, the struggle between his humanity and his responsibility as a policeman.

### *Fine Italian Hand, A*
April 1992

When a well-known actor with a taste for gambling is found garrotted in a Toronto motel, the identity of the killers seems obvious. But when a homicide detective says so to the press, the Italian community is outraged. Even the Mafia is annoyed. The police need someone to take the heat, and Staff Inspector Charlie Salter is given the problem.

Salter is not enthusiastic. The case looks obvious to him, too, and probably hopeless. His concentration is not helped by an apparently serendipitous encounter with an old would-be girlfriend, Julie Peters, a lady he knew more than thirty years before, whose appearance reminds him of some unanswered questions left from their past. Since his wife is away visiting her parents, Salter has the time to investigate both mysteries.

A further puzzle develops when a sergeant in the gambling squad who is helping Salter is suddenly suspended on charges of corruption, and refuses to clear himself. But Sergeant Horvath has already helped him enough to set Salter on the right trail, a search that takes him (and sometimes Julie Peters) into the world of bookies, racetracks and the theatre. By the time he has found out what really happened in that motel, he has also found the answers to the other questions.

Once again it is Charlie Salter, 'the most human cop in the entire cop-shop', who is at the heart of the novel. He begins this time in the grip of a powerful nostalgia, but in the end he is policeman enough to have paid attention to all the small details which lead him to the killer.

### *Night the Gods Smiled, The*
March 1983

It is a particularly puzzling murder case that Inspector Charlie Salter of the Metropolitan Toronto Police is assigned to solve: Professor David Summers of Douglas College, Toronto, has been found dead in a Toronto hotel bedroom while attending a conference. The only tangible clues are a lipstick-marked glass and the whisky bottle that was used to crush Summers's skull – clues so banal that they present a challenge in themselves.

From four of the late Professor's academic colleagues who had also attended the conference, and with the aid of one of Montreal's detectives, 'Onree' O'Brien, Slater must try to piece together the pattern of the victim's last hours.

Salter discovers that one of Summers's colleagues hated him with a vengeance but for a reason that comes to light only late in the story. And any of the others, it seems, could have had less obvious motives to murder. As the investigation proceeds Salter becomes aware of the parallels between himself and the dead man, he finds he likes the Professor's friends and dislikes his enemies. He is intrigued by the girl who was his favourite student. In the end is through these similarities in their lives that he discovers the killer.

Charlie Salter is a most engaging detective. Real promotion within the Force has eluded him thus far – a compliment, it might be said, to his personal originality. Mystery fans will be delighted to learn that there are more Charlie Salter stories to come, for in *The Night the Gods Smiled* Eric Wright combines a fine sense of life's small absurdities with a distinct flair for creating a story full of suspense.

### Question of Murder, A
September 1988

The Metropolitan Toronto Police Force is at full stretch: the Princess is coming, and not since Kosygin's visit has there been such a security operation. When some anonymous letters threaten a disturbance along the Princess's route, the Special Affairs Centre is the only unit left to handle the job.

But the Princess isn't Inspector Charlie Salter's only worry. Someone has been forging Canadian art, Salter's son has decided to turn his grandfather into an unwilling welfare project, and Charlie's boss, Superintendent Orliff, is retiring, leaving Salter to wonder if it isn't time for him to quit, too. When a bomb does explode (after the Princess has passed) Salter accepts too easily his Superintendent's opinion that the case is insoluble. As the force returns to normal, it soon begins to look as if he will have to hand over an unsolved, sloppily-handled case to the experts in Homicide.

*A Question of Murder* is the story of a crime, but once again it is Salter's world, a world this time of fashionable retailers, street-traders and art forgers, as well as his family and his new assistant, Constable Ranovic of the undercover squad, that provide as much interest and entertainment as the crime and its solution.

### Sensitive Case, A
January 1990

The case seemed routine enough at first.

A woman, a massage therapist, had been found dead in her bathtub. The janitor discovered her when he called to fix the radiator, and reported that the water was still warm. Except that she had her bathrobe on, she might have just stepped into the tub. But when the investigating team learned that her recent clients included a deputy minister of the provincial government and a well-known TV personality, the case was passed to the Special Affairs Centre, now headed by Staff Inspector Charlie Salter – the proper place for sensitive matters.

Salter shouts for help and is given the services of Mel Pickett, a nearly retired Sergeant from the Bail and Parole Unit, who is soon to have his own problem in the form of a young girl from England, in Canada to look for the man who was her grandmother's lover during the war.

The search for the identity of the killer takes the two men into the worlds of television and the senior civil service, and to the office of a university president. Along the way, Salter (who doesn't get much help form the preoccupied Pickett) learns a lot about the private lives of some eminent and lonely people, and once more it is the reality of these people's lives that creates the fabric of a novel which fully meets the expectations aroused by Charlie Slater's earlier investigations.

### Single Death, A
August 1986

The only thing on the mind of Inspector Charlie Salter of the Toronto Police is what to buy Annie, his wife, for Christmas – until Gerry, his first wife, walks in. She is back to make life difficult for him, as she did twenty years ago.

Some weeks before, a woman was found dead, strangled in her apartment, and Gerry wants to know why the police seem to have done nothing about it. Gerry is an activist and she can get the attention of the media, so the police authorities, wanting to convince her that they are doing their job, assign the case to Salter.

The dead woman has been looking for a male companion through advertisements, at singles club meetings, and in bars, and the number of possible suspects makes the case look hopeless. Salter unpicks the investigation for any flaws his ex-wife might seize on, but then uncovers a fresh lead which, with some help from Gerry herself, leads him eventually to the killer.

Along the way, he learns a lot about the world of single, lonely women. He also realizes, not only why he left Gerry, but why he married her in the first place. And he is guided by both his wives, to learn something about himself.

### Smoke Detector
May 1984

The death of a second-hand furniture dealer seems an unlikely stimulus for the stalled career of lnspector Charlie Salter of the Metropolitan Toronto Police. But the victim had died of smoke inhalation in a fire deliberately set – and that meant arson and murder.

The dealer, Cyril Drecker, had been operating successfully at the shady end of the antique trade and Salter soon discovers plenty of suspects: Drecker's assistant, his mistress, his wife, and any number of other unfortunate people he might have cleverly swindled. All these promising leads seem to go nowhere until chance points Salter back forty years to wartime Vancouver and step by intricate step he works his way towards the truth.

Salter gets his man all right, but it is not an unqualified triumph. His chief satisfaction is the assurance from his boss that his career is due to get rolling again.

Salter is clearly more successful this time with mixing his personal problems: his teenage son clears a path (literally) to a new understanding between them, his wife teaches him to accept her need to break away from the domestic scene, and his house and his health – both of which seemed in precarious shape at one point – are pronounced good for any number of years.

Readers of *The Night the Gods Smiled* will be delighted with this new instalment in the career and times of this most engaging cop.

## WRIGHT, L. R.
### Sleep While I Sing
April 1987

She was a woman travelling alone, with no identification and next to no luggage, a woman who hitched a ride with a stranger on a country road in British Columbia. Now she is dead, killed by the driver of the car that picked her up, and Staff Sergeant Karl Alberg has to find her killer – not an easy task when he does not know her identity or destination, and when his mind is distracted by his on-again, off-again relationship with Cassandra Mitchell, local librarian. For Cassandra has become infatuated with a good-looking actor, Roger Galbraith, staying locally with his mother and flirting outrageously with all the local women.

When it turns out that Galbraith may possibly have known the dead woman, Alberg's distraction deepens: is his distrust for Roger based on his feelings about the murder, or his feelings about Cassandra? As Alberg struggles to separate jealousy from suspicion, the killer stalks the sleepy town of Sechelt, and only another murder can lead Alberg to the horrifying truth.

L. R. Wright's first suspense novel, *The Suspect*, won the Edgar for the best novel of the year from the Mystery Writers of America and was compared to the work of writers like Ruth Rendell and P. D. James. *Sleep While I Sing* has all the rich characterization, the sure sense of place and the silken story-telling of its predecessor.

## WYLIE, PHILIP
(See: **Balmer, Edwin**)

## YASTROW, SHELBY
### Undue Influence
July 1991

If, as Balzac said, behind every great fortune there is a crime, what were the crimes of Benjamin Stillman? A respected but colourless bachelor, Stillman laboured for years as a modestly paid accountant in a prominent Chicago brokerage house; even the young attorney who drafted his will could scarcely connect a face with a name.

Now Benjamin Stillman is dead at eighty-three. And attorney Philip Ogden is stunned to discover that the client he met only once has left an estate worth $8 million! The entire bequest goes to Beth Zion Synagogue, a stipulation almost as startling as the fortune itself – for Benjamin Still was a Catholic, buried with full rites of the Church.

The headlines speculating on this mysterious millionaire are barely dry when a second, very different, will be brought forward. Accusations of embezzlement resound, a search for heirs is launched, and lawyers prepare for a winner-takes-all battle; but the questions about Stillman's wealth remain far from being answered. Ogden is thrust into the biggest case of his career and the pursuit of a truth that had been kept hidden for a lifetime.

Against a background of taut legal intrigue, *Undue Influence* weaves a suspenseful tale of passion, corruption, and the many guises of justice.

# SHORT STORY COLLECTIONS

**ANON**
*Crime Wave: World's Winning Crime Stories 1981* (1981)
Introduction – Desmond Bagley
A Visit With Montezuma – Frank Sisk (1st Prize)
Genesis – Dwight Steward (2nd prize)
The Witch, Yazzie, and the Nine of Clubs – Tony Hillerman (3rd prize)
The Case of the Baker Street Dozen – Arthur Douglas
The Silence Is Rest – Francis King
Wrong Number – Michael Z. Lewin
The Inside Pocket – Michael Gilbert
The Murders in the Alley of the Mad Nun – Janwillem van de Wetering
Last Testament – Grace Hogarth
The Other Eye – Edward D. Hoch
Murder a la Mode – Richard Grayson
The Battered Mailbox – Stanley Cohen
Little Knives – Madelaine Duke
The Last Winter – Thomasina Weber
Some Shall Be Pardon'd, and Some Punished (The Capulet v. Montague Case) – Jaroslav Veis
The Unknown Pillow – Alida Baxter
All in Good Taste – Lawrence Treat
The Price of Murder – John Stevenson

**ANON**
*A Suit of Diamonds: Crime Club Diamond Jubilee Commemorative Volume* (1990)
The Dangling Man – Robert Barnard
Ladies Who Lunch – Gwendoline Butler
An Acquaintance with Mr. Collins – Sarah Caudwell
Custody – Elizabeth Ferrars
Nemesis – Anthea Fraser
A Shameful Eating – Reginald Hill
A Sticky Business – Charlotte MacLeod
The Cisterna – John Malcolm
The Man Who Had Everything – Patricia Moyes
The Mamur Zapt and His House of Doves – Michael Pearce
Smeltdown – Mike Ripley
Diamond and Pearl – Martin Russell
Twins – Eric Wright

**BARNARD, ROBERT**
*Death of a Salesperson and Other Untimely Exits* (1989)
The Woman in the Wardrobe
A Business Partnership
Little Terror
Breakfast Television
What's in a Name?
Sisters
The Injured Party
Just Another Kidnap
Blown Up
A Process of Rehabilitation
Holy Living and Holy Dying
The Oxford Way of Death
Daylight Robbery
Happy Release
Death of a Salesperson
My Last Girlfriend

**CHRISTIE, AGATHA**
*The Adventure of the Christmas Pudding and a Selection of Entrees* (1960)
Foreword by the Author
The Adventure of the Christmas Pudding
The Mystery of the Spanish Chest
The Under Dog
Four-and-Twenty Blackbirds
The Dream
Greenshaw's Folly

*The Labours of Hercules* (1947)
The Nemean Lion
The Lernean Hydra
The Arcadian Deer
The Erymanthian Boar
The Augean Stables
The Stymphalean Birds
The Cretan Bull
The Horses of Diomedes
The Girdle of Hyppolita
The Flock of Geryon
The Apples of the Hesperides
The Capture of Cerberus

*Miss Marple's Final Cases and Two Other Stories* (1979)
Sanctuary
Strange Jest
Tape-Measure Murder
The Case of the Caretaker
The Case of the Perfect Maid
Miss Marple Tells a Story
The Dressmaker's Doll
In a Glass Darkly

*Murder in the Mews* (1937)
Murder in the Mews
The Incredible Theft
Dead Man's Mirror
Triangle at Rhodes

*Poirot's Early Cases* (1974)
The Affair at the Victory Ball
The Adventure of the Clapham Cook
The Cornish Mystery
The Adventure of Johnnie Waverly
The Double Clue
The King of Clubs
The Lemesurier Inheritance
The Lost Mine
The Plymouth Express
The Chocolate Box
The Submarine Plans
The Third Floor Flat
Double Sin
The Market Basing Mystery
Wasps' Nest
The Veiled Lady
Problem at Sea
How Does Your Garden Grow?

*The Thirteen Problems* (1932)
The Tuesday Night Club
The Idol House of Astarte
Ingots of Gold
The Blood-Stained Pavement
Motive v. Opportunity
The Thumb Mark of St. Peter
The Blue Geranium
The Companion
The Four Suspects
A Christmas Tragedy
The Herb of Death
The Affair at the Bungalow
Death by Drowning

**COLE, G. D. H. AND M.**
*A Lesson in Crime and Other Stories* (1933)
A Lesson in Crime
A Question of Coincidence
Mr. Stevens's Insurance Policy
Blackmail in the Village
The Cliff Path Ghost
Sixteen Years' Run
Wilson Calling
Brentwardine Mystery
The Mother of the Detective
A Dose of Cyanide
Superintendent Wakley's Mistake

*Mrs Warrender's Profession* (1938)
The Mother of the Detective
Death in the Sun
The Toys of Death
Fatal Beauty
In Peril of His Life

*Wilson and Some Others* (1940)
**Wilson:**
Death in the Tankard
Murder in Church
The Bone of the Dinosaur
A Tale of Two Suitcases
The Motive
Glass
Murder in Broad Daylight: A Broadcast Story
**Others:**
A Present from the Empire
Strychnine Tonic
The Letters
The Partner
The Strange Adventures of a Chocolate Box
Ye Olde Englysshe Christmasse; or Detection in the Eighteenth Century

**FERRARS, ELIZABETH**
*Designs on Life* (1980)
The Dreadful Bell
After the Deluge
The Truthful Witness
Go, Lovely Rose
Drawn into Error
Safety
A Very Small Thing
Scatter His Ashes
Undue Influence

**FLETCHER, J. S.**
*The Marrendon Mystery and Other Stories of Crime and Detection* (1931)
The Blank Wall
The Dower Chest
The Forgotten Details
Green Wax
Issy and the Widow Pearlmark
The Long Arm
The Marrendon Mystery
The Ninth Green
No Risks Taken
The Opportune Arrival
Other People's Property
The Particular Brand
Prima Facia
Rendezvous Creek
The Thirty Years' Tenant
The Winnowing Machine

**FOOTNER, HULBERT**
*The Almost Perfect Murder* (1933)
The Almost Perfect Murder
Murder in Masquerade
The Death Notice
Taken for a Ride

*The Casual Murderer* (1932)
The Casual Murderer
It Never Got into the Papers
The Blind Front

*The Kidnapping of Madame Storey and Other Stories* (1936)
Madame Storey's Gigolo
The Scent of Almonds
Pink-Eye
The Kidnapping of Madame Storey
The Murder in the Hotel Cathay

*Tortuous Trails* (1933)
The Case of Shem Packer
The Case of Luke Darrow
The Case of Adam Tasker
The Case of Angus Blair

*The Viper* (1930)
The Viper
The Steerers
The Handsome Young Man

**HILL, REGINALD**
*Pascoe's Ghost and Other Brief Chronicles of Crime* (1979)
Pascoe's Ghost
The Trunk in the Attic
The Rio de Janeiro Paper
Threatened Species
Snowball
Exit Line
Dalziel's Ghost

*There Are No Ghosts in the Soviet Union and Other Stories* (1987)
There Are No Ghosts in the Soviet Union
Bring Back the Cat!
The Bull Ring
Auteur Theory
Poor Emma
Crowded Hour

**KING, C. DALY**
*The Curious Mr Tarrant* (1935)
The Episode of the Codex' Curse
The Episode of the Tangible Illusion
The Episode of the Nail and the Requiem
The Episode of the 'Torment IV'
The Episode of the Headless Horrors
The Episode of the Vanishing Harp
The Episode of the Man with Three Eyes
The Episode of the Final Bargain

**MACDONALD, JOHN D. (Ed.)**
*The Lethal Sex: The 1959 Anthology of the Mystery Writers of America* (1962)
Introduction – John D. MacDonald
Dear Mr. MacDonald – Christianna Brand
Snowball – Ursula Curtiss
McGowney's Miracle – Margaret Millar
Two for Tea – Margaret Manners
You'll Be the Death of Me – Anthony Gilbert
The Withered Heart – Jean Potts
To Be Found and Read – Miriam Allen deFord
A Matter of Ethics – Carolyn Thomas
No Trace – Veronica Parker Johns
There Are No Snakes in Hawaii – Juanita Sheridan

**MACDONALD, PHILIP**
*Fingers of Fear* (1953)
The Green-and-Gold String
Something to Hide
The Wood-for-the-Trees
Malice Domestic
Love Lies Bleeding
Fingers of Fear

**MACLEOD, CHARLOTTE (Ed.)**
*Christmas Stalkings* (1992)
Counterfeit Christmas – Charlotte MacLeod
The Running of the Deer – Reginald Hill
Liz Peters, PI – Elizabeth Peters
Angels – Medora Sale
The Only True Unraveller – John Malcolm
The January Sale Stowaway – Dorothy Cannell
The Santa Claus Caper – Bill Crider
Family Christmas – Patricia Moyes
Miss Melville Rejoices – Evelyn E. Smith
Two in the Bush – Eric Wright

The Fabulous Nick – Mickey Friedman
A Political Necessity – Robert Barnard
Fruitcake, Mercy, and Black-Eyed Peas – Margaret Maron

**QUEEN, ELLERY (Ed.)**
Titles of all Queen anthologies have been standardised.

*Ellery Queen's Awards 8* (1955)
My Brother Down There – Steve Frazee
Miss Paisley's Cat – Roy Vickers
If a Body... – A. H. Z. Carr
The Betrayers – Stanley Ellin
The Quality of Mercy – Eleazer Lipsky
The Stroke of Thirteen – Lillian de la Torre
Laugh It Off – Charlotte Armstrong
All of God's Children Got Shoes – Howard Schoenfeld
High Court – Thomas Kyd
Born Killer – Dorothy Salisbury Davis
On the Brink – James Yaffe
The Town Without a Straight Man – Will Stanton
Mrrrar! – Edgar Pangborn
The Silver Spurs – E. C. Witham
The Panther – Browning Norton
Heaven Can Wait – C. B. Gilford

*Ellery Queen's Awards 9* (1956)
Double Image – Roy Vickers
The House Party – Stanley Ellin
The Couple Next Door – Margaret Millar
Wild Goose Chase – John Ross Macdonald
Backward, Turn Backward – Dorothy Salisbury Davis
You Know What, Teacher? – Zenna Henderson
A Case of Catnapping – A. H. Z. Carr
Tall Story – Margery Allingham
The Dipping of the Candlemaker – Hayden Howard
The Pale Sergeant – Henry Myers
Heat Spell – John L. Hayward
Mom in the Spring – James Yaffe
Anything New on the Strangler? – James Michael Ullman
Due Process – Harry Miner
The Man Out of the Rain – Philip MacDonald
Banquet and a Half – Lee Hays
The Day of the Last Rock Fight – Joseph Whitehill

*Ellery Queen's Awards 10* (1957)
The Moment of Decision – Stanley Ellin
Stay Away from My Mother – Joseph Whitehill
What Would You Have Done? – Charlotte Armstrong

Near the Back of Beyond – Lord Dunsany
Once is Once Too Many – Anthony Gilbert
The Perfectionist – Donald McNutt Douglass
A Woman of Principle – Roy Vickers
The Gentleman Caller – Veronica Parker Johns
Tiger in the Night – Eleazar Lipsky
Invitation to an Accident – Wade Miller
The Splinter – Mary Roberts Rinehart
The Man Who Made People Mad – Mark Van Doren
Dodie and the Boogerman – Vinnie Williams
Mom Makes a Wish – James Yaffe

*Ellery Queen's Awards 11* (1958)
The Black Kitten – A. H. Z. Carr
The Blessington Method – Stanley Ellin
A Telegram for Miss Phipps – Phyllis Bentley
The Customs of the Country – Thomas Flanagan
One-Tenth Man – Michael Gilbert
From the Mouse to the Hawk – Dion Henderson
A Toy for Jiffy – Roy Vickers
Miami Papers Please Copy – Rufus King
A Bad Time of Day – Wade Miller
Try It My Way – Frederick Nebel
One of the Family – James Yaffe
Gifts to My People – Michael Forrestier
Compliments of Caliph Bernie – Charles Green
Don't Believe a Word She Says – William Lindsay Gresham
The Waiting Thing Inside – Theodore Sturgeon & Don Ward
Soho Night's Entertainment – Frank Swinnerton

*Ellery Queen's Awards 12* (1959)
The Necessity of His Condition – Avram Davidson
Lilith, Stay Away from the Door – B. J. R. Stolper
The Kachina Dolls – Alvin Pevehouse
The Birdwatcher – L. A. G. Strong
A Matter of Public Notice – Dorothy Salisbury Davis
The Faith of Aaron Menefee – Stanley Ellin
Malice in Wonderland – Rufus King
Snap Shot – Michael Gilbet
Cottage for August – Thomas Kyd
An End to Fear – Hugh Pentecost
The Doe and the Gantlet – Pat Stadley
Driving Lesson – F. L. Wallace
Miss Phipps Goes to School – Phyllis Bentley
The Mayor Calls His Family – Manly Wade Wellman
The Town Is Waiting – Joseph Whitehill

*Ellery Queen's Awards 13* (1960)
The Goldfish Button – Anthony Gilbert
You Bet Your Life – Stuart Palmer
Miracles Do Happen – Ellery Queen
Cop on the Prowl – Thomas Walsh
Sock Finish – Robert Bloch
The Girl on the Beach – William O'Farrell
You Can't Be a Little Girl All Your Life – Stanley Ellin
The $2,000,000 Defense – Harold Q. Masur
The Income Tax Mystery – Michael Gilbert
Hunting Day – Hugh Pentecost
The Women in His Life – Whit Masterson
Carnival Day – Nedra Tyre

*Ellery Queen's Awards 14* (1961)
Unreasonable Doubt – Stanley Ellin
Miracles—All in the Day's Work – Clayton Rawson
Sermon in Bags – Cyril Hare
All Men Make Mistakes – Frances & Richard Lockridge
The Love Connoisseur – John Collier
The Flight of the Bumble Bee – Kem Bennett
The Man with Half a Face – Hugh Pentecost
A Routine Night's Work – George Harmon Coxe
Blonde Beauty Slain – Cornell Woolrich
The Second Skin – Michael Gilbert
Wry Highball – Craig Rice
Murder in a Motel – Lawrence G. Blochman
Then They Come Running – Herbert Brean
The Lady, or the Murderer? – William E. Barrett
The Patron Saint of the Impossible – Rufus King
The Long Black Shadow – Rosemary Gibbons

**RUSSELL, MARTIN**
*The Darker Side of Death* (1985)
A Slice of Justice
Paula's People
The Loss Adjuster
Bye-Bye, Shimmy
Kill Before Publication
Hard to Live With
The Lesson

**STOUT, REX**
*Black Orchids* (1943)
Black Orchids
Cordially Invited to Meet Death

*Crime and Again* (1959)
Christmas Party
Easter Parade
Fourth of July Picnic
Murder is No Joke

*Curtains for Three* (1951)
The Gun with Wings
Bullet for One
Disguise for Murder

*Homicide Trinity* (1963)
Death of a Demon
Eeny Meeny Murder Mo
Counterfeit for Murder

*Three at Wolfe's Door* (1961)
Poison à la Carte
Method Three for Murder
The Rodeo Murder

*Three Doors to Death* (1950)
Man Alive
Omit Flowers
Door to Death

*Three for the Chair* (1958)
Window for Death
Immune to Murder
Too Many Detectives

*Three Men Out* (1955)
This Won't Kill You
Invitation to Murder
The Zero Clue

*Three Witnesses* (1956)
The Next Witness
When a Man Murders…
Die Like a Dog

*Trio for Blunt Instruments* (1965)
Kill Now – Pay Later
Murder is Corny
Blood Will Tell

*Triple Jeopardy* (1952)
The Cop-Killer
The Squirt and the Monkey
Home to Roost

*Trouble in Triplicate* (1949)
Before I Die
Help Wanted, Male
Instead of Evidence

**TAYLOR, PHOEBE ATWOOD**
*The Asey Mayo Trio* (1946)
The Third Murderer
Murder Rides the Gale
The Stars Spell Death

# OMNIBUSES

**VOLUME 1 (1932)**
*The Noose*: Philip MacDonald
*Burglars in Bucks*: G. D. H. and M. Cole
*Q. E. D.*: Lynn Brock
*Sir John Magill's Last Journey*: Freeman Wills Crofts

**VOLUME 2 (1932)**
*The Murder at the Vicarage*: Agatha Christie
*The Wedding Chest Mystery*: A. Fielding
*Murder at the Pageant*: Victor L. Whitechurch
*Tragedy on the Line*: John Rhode

**VOLUME 3 (1932)**
*The Murder of Geraldine Foster*: Anthony Abbott
*Mystery in the Channel*: Freeman Wills Crofts
*The Case against Andrew Fane*: Anthony Gilbert
*The Hanging Woman*: John Rhode

**VOLUME 4 (1934)**
*The Devil Man*: Edgar Wallace
*Mystery at Friar's Pardon*: Martin Porlock
*Death Comes to Perigord*: John Ferguson
*Dead Man's Watch*: G. D. H. and M. Cole

**VOLUME 5 (1934)**
*Peril at End House*: Agatha Christie
*The Crime Conductor*: Philip MacDonald
*The Click of the Gate*: Alice Campbell
*Dead Men at the Folly*: John Rhode

**VOLUME 6 (1934)**
*Rope to Spare*: Philip Macdonald
*Death of a Star*: G. D. H. and M. Cole
*Dead Man's Hat*: Hulbert Footner
*Song of Doom*: Virgil Markham

**THE NICHOLAS BLAKE OMNIBUS (OCTOBER 1966)**
Author's Introduction
*The Beast Must Die*
*A Penknife in My Heart* (not CC originally)
*A Tangled Web* (not CC originally)

**THE JULIAN SYMONS OMNIBUS (JANUARY 1967)**
Author's Introduction
*The 31st of February* (not CC originally)
*The End of Solomon Grundy*
*The Progress of a Crime*

# DUPLICATE TITLES

In a series of 2,012 books some title duplication is inevitable. Not all titles are precisely the same: *Off with His/Her Head* and *A Capitol/Capital Crime*; Smith's and Ferrars' *Come and be Killed* are separated by an exclamation mark; and Stout's and Eberhart's *Family Affair* by an indefinite article. But while almost a third of a century separates MacDonald's and Carmichael's *The Link*, the seven-year gap between Russell's and Eberhart's *Danger Money* looks like carelessness. And a half-century separates the first and final appearance of *Sudden Death*.

*And Death Came Too*: Hull, Richard
*And Death Came Too*: Gilbert, Anthony

*Capital Crime, A*: Ford, Leslie
*Capitol Crime, A*: Meyer, Lawrence

*Cat's Cradle*: Flower, Pat
*Cat's Cradle*: Curzon, Clare

*Child's Play*: Campbell, Alice
*Child's Play*: Hill, Reginald

*Come and Be Killed!*: Smith, Shelley
*Come and Be Killed*: Ferrars, Elizabeth

*Danger Money*: Russell, Martin
*Danger Money*: Eberhart, M. G.

*Dead End*: Strange, John Stephen
*Dead End*: Perry, Ritchie

*Family Affair*: Eberhart, M. G.
*Family Affair, A*: Stout, Rex

*Flashback*: Carmichael, Harry
*Flashback*: Wood, Ted

*Hand in Glove*: Eberhart, M. G.
*Hand in Glove*: Marsh, Ngaio

*Last Will and Testament*: Cole, G. D. H. and M.
*Last Will and Testament*: Ferrars, Elizabeth

*Legacy of Death*: Burton, Miles
*Legacy of Death, A*: Penn, John

*Link, The*: MacDonald, Philip
*Link, The*: Carmichael, Harry

*More Deaths Than One*: Stout, Rex
*More Deaths Than One*: Eccles, Marjorie

*Murder Comes Home*: Child, Nellise
*Murder Comes Home*: Gilbert, Anthony

*Necessary End, A*: Gielgud, Val
*Necessary End, A*: Fraser, Anthea

*Off With Her Head!*: Cole, G. D. H. and M.
*Off With His Head*: Marsh, Ngaio

*Paper Chase, The*: Fielding, A.
*Paper Chase, The*: Symons, Julian

*Sleep of the Unjust*: Meynell, Laurence
*Sleep of the Unjust*: Ferrars, Elizabeth

*Stranglehold*: Carmichael, Harry
*Stranglehold*: Gregson, J. M.

*Sudden Death*: Crofts, Freeman Wills
*Sudden Death*: Delman, David
*Sudden Death*: Gibbins, James

# ABROAD IN CRIME CLUB

Although the UK is by far the most common setting for Crime Club novels, 'foreign' settings featured regularly; the US, France and Ireland appearing in the first few months. This trend continued with some writers 'specialising' in certain countries: Egypt (Pearce), India (Blochman and Keating), Ireland (Fitzgerald), Italy (Inchbald and Nabb), Spain (Serafin). For reasons of space this list does not include UK, US or Canadian settings.

**AFRICA**
Birmingham: *The Heat of the Sun*
Cody: *Rift*
Farjeon: *The House of Shadows*
Ferrars: *The Swaying Pillars*

**AUSTRALIA**
Barnard: *Death of an Old Goat*
Ferrars: *Come and Be Killed*
Ferrars: *The Crime and the Crystal*
Ferrars: *The Small World of Murder*
Garve: *Boomerang*
Hamilton: *The Thrill Machine*
Novels of Charles West
Novels of Pat Flower
Novels of Anne Infante

**AUSTRIA**
Carnac: *Crossed Skis*
Hinxman: *The Sound of Murder*
Lorac: *Murder in Vienna*
Peters: *The House of Green Turf*
Peters: *The Will and the Deed*

**BRAZIL**
Benton: *Twenty-Fourth Level*
Perry: *The Fall Guy*
Perry: *One Good Death Deserves Another*

**CARIBBEAN**
Christie: *A Caribbean Mystery*
Eberhart: *House of Storm*
Mansfield: *Final Exposure*
Moyes: *Black Girl, White Girl*
Moyes: *To Kill a Coconut*
Moyes: *Angel Death*

**CHINA**
Epstein: *Murder in China*

**DENMARK**
Novels of Torben Nielsen

**EGYPT**
Christie: *Death Comes as the End*
Christie: *Death on the Nile*
Novels of Michael Pearce

**FINLAND**
Fleming: *You Won't Let Me Finish*
Low: *To His Just Deserts: A Story of Finland*

**FRANCE**
Arley: *Dead Man's Bay*
Arley: *Ready Revenge*
Butterworth: *The Black Look*
Butterworth: *The Man Who Broke the Bank at Monte Carlo*
Butterworth: *Virgin on the Rocks, A: Variations on a Theme in the Black Manner*
Campbell: *The Click of the Gate*
Campbell: *Desire to Kill*
Campbell: *Keep Away From Water*
Campbell: *No Light Came On*
Farjeon: *Sinister Inn*
Ferrars: *Hunt the Tortoise*
Fleming: *Hell's Belle*
Gilbert: *The Man in Button Boots*
Gilbert: *Passenger to Nowhere*
Grierson: *The Jackdaw Mystery*
Grierson: *The Lady of Despair*
Grierson: *The Mysterious Mademoiselle*
Hilton: *Displaced Person*
Hilton: *Moondrop to Murder*
Jacquemard-Senecal: *The Body Vanishes*
Jacquemard-Senecal: *The Eleventh Little Nigger*
Kenyon: *A Free-Range Wife*
Le Breton: *The Law of the Streets*
Loraine: *Death Wishes*
Loraine: *Last Shot*
Malcolm: *A Deceptive Appearance*
Mander: *The Paris Bit*
Markham: *Song of Doom*
Marsh: *Spinsters in Jeopardy*
McGerr: *Fatal in My Fashion*
Perry: *Fool's Mate*
Rutherford: *The Black Leather Murders*
Rutherford: *The Creeping Flesh*
Ryck: *Sacrificial Pawn*
Ryck: *Undesirable Company*
Ryck: *Woman Hunt*
Strange: *A Handful of Silver*

**GREECE**
Cole: *Greek Tragedy*
Curzon: *The Face in the Stone*
Curzon: *The Quest for K*
Curzon: *Trail of Fire*
Ferrars: *No Peace for the Wicked*
Garve: *The Late Bill Smith*

**INDIA**
Novels of Lawrence Blochman
Novels of H. R. F. Keating

**IRELAND**
Babson: *Untimely Guest*
Blake: *The Private Wound*
Bringle: *Death of an Unknown Man*
Crofts: *Man Overboard*
Crofts: *Sir John Magill's Last Journey*
Garve: *The House of Soldiers*
Gash: *The Sleepers of Erin*
Kenyon: *The 100,000 Welcomes*
Kenyon: *May You Die in Ireland*
Kenyon: *The Rapist*
Kenyon: *The Shooting of Dan McGrew*
McMullen: *My Cousin Death*
Novels of Nigel Fitzgerald

**ITALY**
Benton: *Spy in Chancery*
Brandon: *The Gorgon's Smile*
Butterworth: *Villa on the Shore*
Caudwell: *Thus Was Adonis Murdered*
Donati: *The Paper Tomb*
Ferrars: *Alibi for a Witch*
Fitzgerald: *Imagine a Man*
Gash: *The Gondola Scam*
Gash: *The Vatican Rip*
Gielgud: *To Bed at Noon*
Hill: *Another Death in Venice*
Jones: *Death and the Trumpets of Tuscany*
Jones: *Shot on Location*
Lorac: *Murder on a Monument*
Low: *Murky Shallows: A Story of the Venetian Lagoon*
Marsh: *When in Rome*
Moyes: *Dead Men Don't Ski*
Rutherford: *Grand Prix Murder*
Rutherford: *The Long Echo*
Rutherford: *Murder Is Incidental*
Rutherford: *Mystery Tour*
Rutherford: *Return Load*
Tine: *State of Grace*
Novels of Magdalen Nabb
Novels of Peter Inchbald

**MADEIRA**
Ferrars: *Breath of Suspicion*
Ferrars: *Skeleton Staff*
Ferrars: *Witness Before the Fact*

**MEXICO**
Eberhart: *Wings of Fear*
Palmer: *The Puzzle of the Blue Banderilla*

**NEW ZEALAND**
Jay: *Death of a Skin Diver*
Marsh: *Colour Scheme*
Marsh: *Died in the Wool*
Marsh: *Photo-Finish*
Scott: *Hot Pursuit*

**NORWAY**
Barnard: *Death in a Cold Climate*
Barnard: *Death in Purple Prose*
Perry: *Your Money and Your Wife*

**PORTUGAL**
Benton: *Sole Agent*
Fleming: *Death of a Sardine*
Footner: *Unneutral Murder*

**RUSSIA**
Garve: *The Ashes of Loda*
Garve: *Murder in Moscow*
White: *The Elephant Never Forgets*

**SPAIN**
Ashford: *Presumption of Guilt*
Farjeon: *Peril in the Pyrenees*
Jeffries: *A Fatal Fleece*
Novels of David Serafin

**SWITZERLAND**
Curzon: *Shot Bolt*
Moyes: *Death on the Agenda*
Moyes: *Season of Snows and Sins*

**TURKEY**
Fleming: *Nothing Is the Number When You Die*
Fleming: *When I Grow Rich*
Garve: *The Ascent of D.13*
Pereira: *The Singing Millionaire*

**WEST INDIES**
Eat: *Twenty-Five Sanitary Inspectors*
Footner: *Murder in the Sun*
Garve: *No Mask for Murder*
Smith: *This is the House*
Williams: *Treasure Up in Smoke*

# TOPICS IN CRIME CLUB

Some backgrounds exert a fascination for crime writers and readers. As can be seen, Academia is a particular favourite with settings ranging from Barnard's day school in *Little Victims* to Cambridge in Kelly's *In the Shadow of Kings*. The 'smell of the grease-paint' is strong in the theatre novels of Ngaio Marsh, while Roderic Jeffries and Sara Woods specialise in legal settings. Historical settings were not as common, in the early days of Crime Club, as they later became and Christie's 2000 BC setting for *Death Comes as the End* was, at the time, unique. One title on the Historical list merits mention: Hill's *One Small Step* is still unique – check the blurb and find out why.

## ACADEMIA
Aird: *Parting Breath*
Anthony: T*he Midnight Lady and the Mourning Man*
Barnard: *Death of an Old Goat, Little Victims*
Blake: *The Morning after Death,A Question of Proof*
Carnac: *Murder as a Fine Art*
Christie: *Cat Among the Pigeons*
Clemeau: *The Ariadne Clue: A Classical Mystery*
Cole: *Knife in the Dark*
Cole: *Off With Her Head!*
Cole: *Scandal at School*
Dean: *By Frequent Anguish*
Delman: *Death of a Nymph*
Devine: *Devil at Your Elbow, His Own Appointed Day, Death is My Bridegroom*
Ferrars: *Thy Brother Death*
Fraser: *Death Speaks Softly*
Fuller: *J for Jupiter*
Goldsborough: *The Bloodied Ivy*
Hill: *An Advancement of Learning*
Hilton: *The Innocents at Home, Surrender Value*
Hull: *A Tapping on the Wall*
Kelly: *Bad Chemistry, In the Shadow of Kings, My Sister's Keeper*
King: *Snares of the Enemy*
Lewis: *Error of Judgement, A Violent Death*
Lorac: *Pall for a Painter*
MacLeod: *The Luck Runs Out*
Meynell: *Death of a Philanderer*
Murray: *The Noose of Time*
Nicholas: *The White Shroud*
Penn: *Death's Long Shadow, A Legacy of Death, Mortal Term*
Penny: *Sweet Poison*
Peterson: *The Caravaggio Books*
Philmore: *Procession of Two, Short List*
Strong: *Othello's Occupation, Treason in the Egg*
Symons: *The Paper Chase*
Tapply: *Death at Charity's Point*
White: *The Third Eye*
Whitechurch: *Murder at the College*
Wright: *Death by Degrees*

## CHRISTMAS
Babson: *The Twelve Deaths of Christmas*
Blake: *The Sad Variety, Thou Shell of Death*
Braun: *The Cat Who Turned On and Off*
Cairns: *New Year Resolution*
Caldwell: *The Late Clara Beamee*
Christie: *Four-Fifty from Paddington,*

*Hercule Poirot's Christmas, Adventure of the Christmas Pudding*
Eberhart: *Postmark Murder*
Farjeon: *Mystery in White*
Ferrars: *The Crime and the Crystal, The Small World of Murder, Smoke without Fire, Something Wicked*
Fraser: *Nine Bright Shiners*
Hall: *The Coldness of Killers*
Jenkins: *Message from Sirius*
Macleod: *Rest You Merry, The Convivial Codfish, Christmas Stalkings*
Marsh: *Tied up in Tinsel*
Moyes: *Black Girl White Girl*
Nabb: *Death of an Englishman*
Palmer: *No Flowers by Request*
Peters: *The Will and the Deed*
Serafin: *Christmas Rising*
Stout: *Crime and Again*

## FILM
Babson: *Murder, Murder, Little Star, Reel Murder, Shadows in their Blood*
Edington: *Murder to Music*
Farrar: *Zero in the Gate*
Fitzgerald: *Imagine a Man*
Ford: *The Devil's Stronghold*
Gash: *The Very Last Gambado*
Hill: *A Pinch of Snuff*
Hinxman: *Nightmare in Dreamland*
Holt: *The Mystery of the Smiling Doll*
Jones: *Death and the Trumpets of Tuscany, Shot on Location*
Keating: *Filmi, Filmi, Inspector Ghote*
Loraine: *Last Shot*
MacKinnon: *Murder, Repeat Murder*
Meynell: *The Mauve Front Door*
Moyes: *Falling Star*
Palmer: *Exit Laughing, The Puzzle of the Happy Hooligan*
Russell: *A Dangerous Place to Dwell*

## TV
Babson: *Cover-Up Story*
Dewhurst: *The House That Jack Built*
Gielgud: *The Goggle-Box Affair*
Hamilton: *The Thrill Machine*
Hinxman: *The Night They Murdered Chelsea*
McGerr: *Die Laughing*
Paul: *The Renewable Virgin*
Valin: *Natural Causes*

## HISTORICAL
Armstrong: *Less than Kind, Night's Black Agents*
Barnard: *Out of the Blackout, Skeleton in the Grass*
Baxt: *The Dorothy Parker Murder Case*
Blake: *The Private Wound*
Butler: *Coffin Underground, Coffin in Fashion, Coffin on the Water*
Butterworth: *The Man Who Broke the Bank at Monte Carlo, A Virgin on the Rocks*
Christie: *Death Comes as the End*
Clarke: *The Deathless and the Dead, The Lady in Black, Last Voyage, My Search for Ruth*
Cody: *Rift*
Eberhart: *The Bayou Road, Casa Madrone, The Crime at Honotassa, Enemy in the House*
Fleming: *Every Inch a Lady*
Grace: *A Shrine of Murders*
Heller: *Man's Illegal Life, Man's Loving Family, Man's Storm*

Hill: *One Small Step, Recalled to Life*
Hilton: *The Quiet Stranger, Mr. Fred, Slickensides*
Jones: *Shot on Location, Death and the Trumpets of Tuscany*
Keating: *The Murder of the Maharajah, A Remarkable Case of Burglary*
Satterthwait: *Miss Lizzie, Wilde West*
Sedley: *Death and the Chapman, The Plymouth Cloak*
Smith: *An Afternoon to Kill*
Strange: *A Handful of Silver*
Symons: *The Blackheath Poisonings, Sweet Adelaide*
White: *The Smartest Grave*

## ISLAND
Carmichael: *Noose for a Lady*
Christie: *A Caribbean Mystery, Ten Little Niggers, Evil Under the Sun*
Cork: *Unnatural Hazard*
Eberhart: *House of Storm, Speak No Evil, The White Dress, Witness at Large*
Ferguson: *Terror on the Island*
Ferrars: *No Peace for the Wicked, Skeleton Staff*
Fitzgerald: *The Candles Are All Out*
Footner: *Murder in the Sun*
Ford: *The Ninth Candle*
Ford: *The Bahamas Murder Case*
Garve: *The Riddle of Samson*
Infante: *Death in Green*
Kallen: *C. B. Greenfield: The Piano Bird*
King: *Careless Corpse*
Mansfield: *Final Exposure*
Marsh: *Photo-Finish*
Moyes: *Angel Death, Black Girl, White Girl, To Kill a Coconut*
Rawson: *The Footprints on the Ceiling*
Strange: *The Bell in the Fog, The Strangler Fig*
Williams: *Treasure Up in Smoke*

## LEGAL
Carmichael: *Confession*
Jeffries: *Dead Against the Lawyers, Dead Man's Bluff, A Deadly Marriage, Death in the Coverts, An Embarrassing Death, Evidence of the Accused, Exhibit Number Thirteen*
Jobson: *The Evidence You Will Hear*
Lewis: *A Fool for a Client, A Wolf By the Ears*
Mavity: *He Didn't Mind Hanging*
Murphy: *Murder for Lunch*
Parkes: *Abuse of Justice*
Postgate: *Verdict of Twelve*
Strange: *Dead End, Reasonable Doubt*
Woods: *All titles*

## THEATRE/OPERA/BALLET
Babson: *Nine Lives to Murder*
Dean: *It Can't be My Grave*
Eccles: *More Deaths Than One*
Footner: *Death of a Celebrity*
Gielgud: *Gallows' Foot*
Gilbert: *The Musical Comedy Crime*
Hilton: *Passion in the Peak*
Jacquemard-Senecal: *The Eleventh Little Nigger*
MacDonald: *The Crime Conductor, The Dark Wheel*
MacLeod: *The Plain Old Man*
Marsh: *Death at the Dolphin, False Scent, Light Thickens, Opening Night*

Moore: *Fringe Ending*
Roby: *Still as the Grave*
West: *Stage Fright*

Barnard: *Death and the Chaste Apprentice, Death on the High C's*
Keating: *Death of a Fat God*
Low: *To His Just Deserts: A Story of Finland*
Peters: *Funeral of Figaro*

Murphy: *Murder Takes a Partner*
Ramsay: *Deadly Discretion, Four Steps to Death*

## TRANSPORT: SHIPS/PLANES/TRAINS
Ashford: *Deadly Reunion*
Babson: *The Cruise of a Death Time, Murder Sails at Midnight*
Blake: *The Widow's Cruise*
Burton: *Murder in Absence*
Christie: *Death on the Nile*
Cole: *Greek Tragedy*
Eberhart: *Five Passengers from Lisbon, The Patient in Cabin C*
Farjeon: *Murderer's Trail*
Footner: *Dangerous Cargo*
Garve: *A Hero for Leanda*
Gielgud: *A Necessary End, Prinvest London*
Marsh: *Clutch of Constables, Singing in the Shrouds*
McGerr: *Save the Witness*
Moyes: *Night Ferry to Death*
Palmer: *The Puzzle of the Silver Persian*
Ryck: *Account Rendered*

Christie: *Death in the Clouds*
King: *Obelists Fly High*

Blochman: *Bombay Mail*
Christie: *Murder on the Orient Express*
Keating: *Inspector Ghote Goes by Train*
King: *Obelists En Route*
Little: *Black Express*
White: *The Wheel Spins*

## WRITERS
Blake: *The Beast Must Die*
Brock: *Fourfingers*
Carmichael: *Death Counts Three*
Clarke: *Lady in Black, Poison Parsley*
East: *Murder Rehearsal*
Farjeon: *End of an Author*
Ferguson: *Death of Mr Dodsley*
Ferrars: *The Sleeping Dogs*
Fleming: *Kill or Cure*
Footner: *Murderer's Vanity*
Grierson: *Lady of Despair*
Infante: *All titles*
Loder: *Death of an Editor*
Lorac: *Post after Post-Mortem, These Names Make Clues*
Low: *Murky Shallows*
McMullen: *Welcome to the Grave, The Other Shoe*
Meynell: *Sleep of the Unjust*
Moyes: *A Six-Letter Word for Death*
Nabb: *The Marshal at the Villa Torrini*
Paul: *The Renewable Virgin*
Pereira: *Equal Antagonisms*
Porlock: *Mystery at Friar's Pardon*
Smith: *An Afternoon to Kill*
Valin: *Natural Causes*
White: *Step in the Dark*

# WHITE CIRCLE PAPERBACKS

Numbers ran from 1 (April 1936) to 297c (September 1959). The addition of a 'c' from 100 on indicates a Crime novel. White Circle Westerns began numbering at 101, hence the necessary suffix.

Prices were as follows:

6d April 1936 – August 1941
9d January 1942 –1946
1/- February 1947 –March 1951
1/6d April 1951 – June 1957
2/- January 1958 – September 1959

The original cover design had variations, including:

• A dust-wrapper on early titles
• 'A Crime Club Sixpenny' emblazoned across the shoulders of the Gunmen.
• The inclusion/exclusion of The Hooded Gunman logo/price on the front cover.
• The colour of the Gunmen – one White, one Green on a Black background – was amended, when glossy covers were introduced in 1954. The background changed to Green and one of the Gunmen to Black.

**6d**

1. Christie: *Murder on The Orient Express*
2. Crofts: *Mystery in the Channel*
3. Porlock: *X v. Rex*
4. Macdonald: *The Crime Conductor*
5. Rhode: *Shot at Dawn*
6. Wallace: *The Devil Man*
7. Rhode: *The Corpse in The Car*
8. Macdonald: *R.I.P.*
9. Christie: *Why Didn't They Ask Evans?*
10. Cole: *End of an Ancient Mariner*
11. Abbot: *The Murder of Geraldine Foster*
12. Holt: *Calling All Cars*
13. Christie: *Three Act Tragedy*
14. Macdonald: *The Wraith*
15. Rhode: *Poison for One*
16. Crofts: *Sudden Death*
17. Cole: *Corpse in the Constable's Garden* (Originally *Corpse in Canonicals*)
18. Ferguson: *Death Comes to Perigord*
19. Christie: *The Murder of Roger Ackroyd*
20. Abbot: *The Murder of the Circus Queen*
21. Rhode: *Hendon's First Case*
22. Campbell: *Desire to Kill*
23. Cole: *Death in the Quarry*
24. Ferguson: *Night in Glengyle*
25. Crofts: *The Cask*
26. Campbell: *The Murder of Caroline Bundy*
27. Strange: *The Man Who Killed Fortescue*
28. Holt: *The Scarlet Messenger*
29. Macdonald: *The Rynox Mystery*
30. Porlock: *Mystery in Kensington Gore*
31. Brock: *The Kink*
32. Christie: *The Murder at The Vicarage*
33. Holt: *Murder at The Bookstall*
34. Macdonald: *The Noose*
35. Ferguson: *The Grouse Moor Mystery*
36. Footner: *Murder Runs in the Family*
37. Cole: *Big Business Murder*
38. Rhode: *Mystery at Greycombe Farm*
39. Adams: *A Word of Six Letters*
40. Brock: *The Dagwort Combe Murder*
41. Christie: *Lord Edgware Dies*
42. Porlock: *Mystery at Friar's Pardon*
43. Rhode: *The Motor Rally Mystery*
44. Cole: *Death of a Star*
45. Footner: *Dangerous Cargo*
46. Macdonald: *The Choice*
47. Christie: *The Seven Dials Mystery*
48. Brock: *The Mendip Mystery*

49. Farjeon: *Detective Ben*
50. White: *The Lady Vanishes*
51. Christie: *Death in the Clouds*
52. Eberhart: *The House on the Roof*
53. Rhode: *The Robthorne Mystery*
54. Holt: *Tiger of Mayfair*
55. Footner: *Murder of a Bad Man*
56. Brock: *Murder on the Bridge* (Originally *Q. E. D.*)
57. Cole: *Scandal at School*
58. Farjeon: *Thirteen Guests*
59. Ferguson: *Death of Mr Dodsley*
60. Penny: *Policeman's Holiday*
61. Macdonald: *The Maze*
62. Adams: *Fate Laughs*
63. Christie: *The A B C Murders*
64. Gilbert: *An Old Lady Dies*
65. Campbell: *The Click of The Gate*
66. Cole: *Dead Man's Watch*
67. Burton: *Death of Mr Gantley*
68. Farjeon: *Mountain Mystery*
69. Holt: *Unknown Terror*
70. Strange: *Clue of The Second Murder*
71. Loder: *The Shop Window Murders*
72. Footner: *The Owl Taxi*
73. Rhode: *Mystery at Olympia*
74. Gilbert: *The Musical Comedy Crime*
75. Christie: *The Sittaford Mystery*
76. Footner: *The New Made Grave*
77. Macdonald: *Murder Gone Mad*
78. Rhode: *The Venner Crime*
79. Cole: *Poison in the Garden Suburb*
80. Farjeon: *Holiday at Half Mast*
81. Gilbert: *Death in Fancy Dress*
82. Whitechurch: *Murder at the College*
83. Macdonald: *The Noose*
84. Macdonald: *The Wraith*
85. Cole: *Death in the Quarry*
86. Macdonald: *The Rynox Mystery*
87. Christie: *The Murder at the Vicarage*
88. Christie: *Lord Edgware Dies*
89. Blake: *A Question of Proof*
90. Blake: *There's Trouble Brewing*
91. Brock: *The Slip Carriage Mystery*
92. Brock: *Colonel Gore's Second Case*
93. Burton: *The Platinum Cat*
94. Christie: *Murder in Mesopotamia*
95. Cole: *Last Will and Testament*
96. Cole: *The Missing Aunt*
97. Eberhart: *The Glass Slipper*
98. East: *Detectives in Gum Boots*
99. Farjeon: *Dark Lady*
100c. Farjeon: *Mystery in White*
101c. Fielding: *Black Cats Are Lucky*
102c. Fielding: *The Case of the Two Pearl Necklaces*
103c. Footner: *The Substitute Millionaire*
104c. Footner: *The Dark Ships*
105c. Gilbert: *Courtier to Death*
106c. Gilbert: *The Long Shadow*
107c. Holt: *The Whispering Man*
108c. Holt: *There Has Been a Murder*
109c. Holt: *Wanted for Murder*
110c. Penny: *Policeman's Evidence*
111c. Palmer: *The Puzzle of Blue Banderilla*
112c. Rhode: *Death on the Road*
113c. Rhode: *In Face of the Verdict*
114c. Wakefield: *Belt of Suspicion*
115c. Whitechurch: *Murder at the College*
116c. Footner: *The New Made Grave*
117c. Cole: *Scandal at School*
118c. Farjeon: *Holiday at Half Mast*
119c. Christie: *Appointment with Death*
120c. Gilbert: *Murder Has No Tongue*
121c. Rhode: *Death at Breakfast*
122c. Footner: *Murder in the Sun*
123c. Taylor: *Figure Away*
124c. Fielding: *Mystery at The Rectory*
125c. Crofts: *Crime at Guildford*
126c. Brock: *Two of Diamonds*

127c. Farjeon: *Exit John Horton*
128c. Strange: *Rope Enough*
129c. Christie: *The Murder at The Vicarage*
130c. Crofts: *The Loss of The Jane Vosper*
131c. Gilbert: *Murder by Experts*
132c. Christie: *The Mystery of The Blue Train*
133c. Rhode: *The Bloody Tower*
134c. Cole: *Dr Tancred Begins*
135c. Footner: *Death of a Celebrity*
136c. Eberhart: *Murder of My Patient*

**9d**

137c. Wakefield: *Belt of Suspicion*
138c. Adams: *Black Death*
139c. Holt: *The Mystery of The Smiling Doll*
140c. Farjeon: *End of an Author*
141c. Brock: *The Stoat: Colonel Gore's Queerest Case*
142c. Gilbert: *The Bell of Death*
143c. Cole: *Off with Her Head*
144c. Footner: *The Murder That Had Everything*
145c. Christie: *Murder Is Easy*
146c. Farjeon: *Seven Dead*
147c. Christie: *Sad Cypress*
148c. Rhode: *Murder at Lilac Cottage*
149c. Christie: *Hercule Poirot's Christmas*
150c. Lorac: *Case in the Clinic*
151c. White: *While She Sleeps*
152c. Farjeon: *The Third Victim*
153c. Stout: *Double for Death*
154c. Burton: *The Three Corpse Trick*

**1/-**

155c. Taylor: *Going, Going, Gone!*
156c. Strange: *Look Your Last*
157c. Gilbert: *He Came by Night*
158c. Farjeon: *Black Castle*
159c. Ford: *Siren in the Night*
160c. Christie: *Towards Zero*
161c. White: *The Man Who Loved Lions*
162c. Christie: *N or M?*
163c. Christie: *The Body in the Library*
164c. Christie: *The Moving Finger*
165c. Farjeon: *Greenmask*
166c. Lorac: *Checkmate to Murder*
167c. Campbell: *Ringed with Fire*
168c. Christie: *Five Little Pigs*
169c. Farjeon: *The Judge Sums Up*
170c. Lorac: *The Sixteenth Stair*
171c. Marsh: *Colour Scheme*
172c. Gilbert: *The Case of the Tea-Cosy's Aunt*
173c. Eberhart: *The Man Next Door*
174c. Burton: *Murder M.D.*
175c. Farjeon: *The House of Shadows*
176c. Stout: *Bad for Business*
177c. Lorac: *Rope's End, Rogue's End*
178c. Blake: *The Case of the Abominable Snowman*
179c. Christie: *Sparkling Cyanide*
180c. Gilbert: *The Mouse Who Wouldn't Play Ball*
181c. Lorac: *Death Came Softly*
182c. Christie: *Death Comes as The End*
183c. Burton: *Four-Ply Yarn*
184c. Farjeon: *The Oval Table*

**2/-**

185c. Stout: *The Broken Vase*
186c. Christie: *One, Two, Buckle My Shoe*
187c. Gilbert: *The Scarlet Button*
188c. Eberhart: *Unidentified Woman*
189c. Christie: *Evil Under the Sun*
190c. Ford: *Crack of Dawn*

191c. Lorac: *Fire in the Thatch*
192c. Campbell: *Travelling Butcher*
193c. Burton: *This Undesirable Residence*
194c. Farjeon: *The House of Shadows*
195c. Lorac: *Murder by Matchlight*

**1/6**

196c. Gilbert: *The Black Stage*
197c. Christie: *Five Little Pigs*
198c. Christie: *The Body in the Library*
199c. Farjeon: *Prelude to Crime*
200c. Christie: *Hercule Poirot's Christmas*
201c. Christie: *Three Act Tragedy*
202c. Ferrars: *Murder Among Friends*
203c. Smith: *He Died of Murder*
204c. Ferrars: *The March Hare Murders*
205c. Stout: *Too Many Women*
206c. Christie: *Taken at the Flood*
207c. Smith: *This Is the House*
208c. Stout: *Alphabet Hicks*
209c. Christie: *Appointment with Death*
210c. Farjeon: *Room Number Six*
211c. Ferrars: *With Murder in Mind*
212c. Christie: *The Murder at the Vicarage*
213c. Christie: *N or M?*
214c. Eberhart: *Wings of Fear*
215c. Stout: *The Silent Speaker*
216c. Christie: *Evil Under the Sun*
217c. Christie: *The A B C Murders*
218c. Farjeon: *The Third Victim*
219c. Christie: *Why Didn't They Ask Evans?*
220c. Christie: *Peril at End House*

**GLOSSY COVERS**

221c. Garve: *A Press of Suspects*
222c. Ferrars: *Hunt the Tortoise*
223c. Stout: *More Deaths Than One*
224c. Burton: *Heir to Lucifer*
225c. Lorac: *Relative to Poison*
226c. Christie: *Murder on the Orient Express*
227c. Farjeon: *Peril in the Pyrenees*
228c. Gilbert: *Death Knocks Three Times*
229c. Smith: *The Man with The Calico Face*
230c. Eberhart: *House of Storm*
231c. Christie: *Partners in Crime*
232c. Christie: *Death in the Clouds*
233c. Christie: *Towards Zero*
234c. Lorac: *Death Before Dinner*
235c. Carmichael: *Death Leaves a Diary*
236c. Eberhart: *Another Woman's House*
237c. Christie: *Ten Little Niggers*
238c. Garve: *No Tears for Hilda*
239c. Smith: *Man Alone*
240c. Carnac: *It's Her Own Funeral*
241c. Stout: *The Second Confession*
242c. Ferrars: *The Clock That Wouldn't Stop*
243c. Gilbert: *Lift Up the Lid*
244c. Farjeon: *The Shadow of Thirteen*
245c. Rhode: *Dead on the Track*
246c. Carr: *Death on Milestone Buttress*
247c. Lorac: *Part for a Poisoner*
248c. Christie: *The Sittaford Mystery*
249c. Smith: *An Afternoon to Kill*
250c. Carmichael: *The Vanishing Trick*
251c. Gilbert: *Murder Comes Home*
252c. Eberhart: *The Unknown Quantity*
253c. Burton: *Death in Shallow Water*
254c. Christie: *Taken at the Flood*
255c. Lorac: *Fire in the Thatch*
256c. Lorac: *Still Waters*
257c. Christie: *The Murder at the Vicarage*
258c. Christie: *Five Little Pigs*
259c. Eberhart: *Dead Men's Plans*
260c. Eberhart: *Unidentified Woman*
261c. Ferrars: *Alibi for a Witch*

262c. Ferrars: *Murder Among Friends*
263c. Christie: *Towards Zero*
264c. Burton: *Devil's Reckoning*
265c. Gilbert: *Footsteps Behind Me*
266c. Gilbert: *He Came by Night*
267c. Christie: *Crooked House*
268c. Carmichael: *Deadly Nightcap*
269c. Stout: *Out She Goes*
270c. Stout: *The Broken Vase*
271c. Christie: *The Listerdale Mystery*

272c. Ferrars: *Enough to Kill a Horse*
273c. Stout: *Even in the Best Families*
274c. Christie: *The Moving Finger*

**2/-**
275c. Carmichael: *School for Murder*
276c. Christie: *Murder in the Mews*
277c. Gilbert: *Snake in the Grass*
278c. Lorac: *The Dog It Was That Died*

279c. Carnac: *Murder as a Fine Art*
280c. Ferrars: *The Lying Voices*
281c. Eberhart: *Escape in the Night*
282c. Gilbert: *Miss Pinnegar Disappears*
283c. Lorac: *Murder in the Mill Race*
284c. Christie: *Taken at the Flood*
285c. Lorac: *Let Well Alone*
286c. Christie: *The Mysterious Mr Quin*
287c. Lorac: *Shroud of Darkness*
288c. Christie: *The Labours of Hercules*

289c. Gilbert: *Don't Open the Door*
290c. Carnac: *A Policeman at the Door*
291c. Gilbert: *Death in the Wrong Room*
292c. Christie: *Parker Pyne Investigates*
293c. Ferrars: *Murder Moves In*
294c. Carmichael: *Why Kill Johnny?*
295c. Stout: *Murder by The Book*
296c. Eberhart: *Five Passengers from Lisbon*
297c. Ferrars: *Always Say Die*

# SELECT REFERENCES

Anon: *Stories from HarperCollins Publishers 1817-2017* (HarperCollins 2017)
Anon: *The Author's Handbook* (Methuen 1937)
Burack, A. S. (Ed): *Writing Suspense and Mystery Fiction* (The Writer Inc. 1977)
Canick, Michael: *Clayton Rawson: Magic and Mystery* (Volcanick Press 1999)
Clark, Neil: *Stranger Than Fiction: The Life of Edgar Wallace, the Man Who Created King Kong* (The History Press 2014)
Cole, Margaret: *The Life of G. D. H. Cole* (Macmillan 1971)
Cypert, Rick: *America's Agatha Christie: Mignon Good Eberhart Her Life and Works* (Susquehanna University Press 2005)
Day-Lewis, Sean: *C. Day-Lewis: An English Life* (Weidenfeld and Nicolson 1980)
Edwards, Martin: *Northern Blood 2* (Flambard Press 1995)
Gilbert, Michael (Ed): *Crime in Good Company* (Constable 1959)
Hogarth, Basil: *Writing Thrillers for Profit* (A & C Black 1936)
Hubin, Allen *Crime Fiction IV: A Comprehensive Bibliography* (Addenda to Revised edition 2006)
Keating, H. R. F. (Ed): *Whodunit: A Guide to Crime, Suspense and Spy Fiction* (Windward 1982)
Keating, H. R. F.: *Murder Must Appetize* (Lemon Tree Press 1975)
Keir, David: *The House of Collins* (Collins 1952)
Lachman, Marvin: *A Reader's Guide to The American Novel of Detection* (G. K. Hall and Co. 1993)
Lewis, Margaret: *Edith Pargeter: Ellis Peters* (Seren 1994)
Marsh, Ngaio: *Black Beech and Honeydew* (Collins 1966)
Madden, Cecil: *Meet the Detective* (Allen and Unwin 1935)
McAleer, John: *Rex Stout: A Biography* (Little Brown 1977)
Meredith, Anne: *Three-a-Penny* (Faber 1940)
Ognall, Harry: *A Life of Crime: The Memoirs of a High Court Judge* (HarperCollins 2017)
Oursler, Fulton: *Behold This Dreamer!* (Little Brown 1964)
Reilly, John (Ed): *Twentieth-Century Crime and Mystery Writers*, 2nd Edition (St James Press 1985)
Reilly, John (Ed): *Twentieth-Century Crime and Mystery Writers*, 3rd Edition (St James Press 1991)
Sutro, John (Ed): *Diversion* (Max Parrish 1950)
Symons, Julian: *Bloody Murder: From the Detective Story to the Crime Novel: A History* (Faber 1972)
Williams, Richard (Ed.) *Collins Crime Club: A Checklist of First Editions* compiled by Peter Foord and Richard Williams (Dragonby Press 1999)
Winn, Dilys: *Murder Ink: The Mystery Readers' Companion* (Westridge Books 1977)

Aird, Catherine: *The Religious Body* (Crime Club Famous First 1981)
Bawden, Nina: *The Odd Flamingo* (Crime Club Jubilee reprint 1980)
Baxt, George: *The Bette Davis Murder Case* (St. Martin's Press 1994)
Crofts, Freeman Wills: *The Cask* (Collins Library of Classics 1946)
Ferrars, Elizabeth: *Give Death a Name* (Crime Club Famous First 1981)
Garve, Andrew: *No Tears for Hilda* (Crime Club Famous First 1981)
Kenyon, Michael: *May You Die in Ireland* (Crime Club Famous First 1981)
MacDonald, Philip: Introduction to *Three for Midnight* omnibus (Doubleday 1963)
Macdonald, Ross: *Blue City* (Crime Club Famous First 1981)
Moyes, Patricia: *Dead Men Don't Ski* (Crime Club Famous First 1981)

**PERIODICALS**
Crime and Detective Stories 20: March 1993
Crime and Detective Stories 34: December 1998
Crime and Detective Stories 37: May 2000
Crime and Detective Stories 63: July 2012

*The Armchair Detective* Vol. 26 No. 3: Summer 1991
*The Armchair Detective* Vol. 41 No. 35: October
*The Armchair Detective* Vol. 23 No. 4: Fall 1990
*The Armchair Detective* Vol. 8 No. 1: November 1974
*The Armchair Detective* Vol. 24 No. 4: Fall 1991
*The Armchair Detective* Vol. 30 No. 3
*The Armchair Detective* Vol. 17 No. 3: Summer 1984
Crime Club Newsletter: Autumn 1938

# INDEX OF AUTHORS

Authors' dates are shown where known, and book jacket images are indicated in **bold**.


Abbot, Anthony (1893-1952) **32, 35, 37, 40, 50, 54, 66, 74**, 226
Adam, Paul (1958-) **206, 209**
Adams, Herbert (1874-1958) **45, 47, 48, 50, 51, 53, 55, 57, 59, 60, 65, 66, 67, 69, 70, 72, 74, 75, 76**, 226-7
Aird, Catherine (1930-) **135, 143, 149, 154, 159, 163, 170, 175, 182**, 218, 227-8
Alexander, Colin James *see* Jay, Simon
Alington, Cyril (1872-1955) **59**, 228
Allan, Stella **158, 164, 170**, 228
Allingham, Margery *see* March, Maxwell
Amdrews, John Malcom *see* Malcolm, John
Anonymous **167, 196**, 228, 386
Anson, Lindsay **57, 60, 65**, 229
Anthony, David (1929-) **134, 138, 141, 153, 158**, 229; *see also* Anthony, Michael David
Anthony, Michael David (1929-) **199**, 229; *see also* Anthony, David
Arley, Catherine (1924-) **103, 108, 113**, 229
Armstrong, Charlotte (1905-1969) **136**, 230
Armstrong, David (1946-) **206, 209**, 230
Armstrong, Vivien **201, 204**, 230
Ashford, Jeffrey (1926-2017) **166, 168, 174, 176, 180, 183, 187, 190, 193, 199, 202, 205, 208**, 231; *see also* Jeffries, Roderic
Auswaks, Alex (1934-2013) **163**, 231

Babson, Marian (1929-2017) **138, 140, 142, 145, 147, 148, 149, 151, 152, 154, 156, 157, 159, 163, 164, 166, 168, 169, 172, 173, 175, 177, 178, 180, 184, 187, 191, 193, 198, 202, 205, 209**, 219, 231-4
Bahr, Edith-Jane (1926-) **144, 148**, 234
Balmer, Edwin (1883-1959; 1902-1971) **55**, 234
Barker, Dudley *see* Black, Lionel
Barnard, Robert (1936-2013) **147, 150, 152, 154, 155, 158, 162, 164, 167, 168, 171, 173, 175, 177, 179, 180, 182, 184, 187, 190, 191, 193**, 234-6
Bawden, Nina (1925-2012) **97, 102**, 217, 236
Baxt, George (1923-2003) **180**, 236
Benton, Kenneth (1909-1999) **131, 136, 141**, 236-7
Birmingham, Maisie (1914-) **147, 152, 155**, 237
Black, Gavin (1913-1998) **138, 142, 144, 148, 151, 159, 172, 202**, 218, 237-8
Black, Lionel (1910-1980) **136, 138, 141, 144, 146, 150, 155, 157, 163, 166**, 238-9
Blake, Nicholas (1904-1972) **46, 49, 52, 56, 61, 66, 69, 80, 85, 94, 98, 104, 106, 108, 115, 119, 121, 126, 129**, 216, 218, 239-40
Blochman, Lawrence (1900-1975) **44, 53, 58**, 240
Bodington, Nancy Hermione *see* Smith, Shelley
Booth, Martin (1944-2004) **163**, 240
Bowen-Judd, Sara Hutton *see* Woods, Sara
Brandes, Rhoda *see* Ramsay, Diana
Brandon, Ruth (1943-) **181, 200, 204**, 241
Braun, Lilian Jackson (1913-2011) **127, 128, 131**, 241
Brennan, John Needham Huggard *see* Welcome, John
Bringle, Mary **185**, 241
Brock, Lynn (1877-1943) **32, 55, 58, 60, 66**, 241
Bromley, Gordon (1910-) **141, 143**, 242
Brown, Morna Doris *see* Ferrars, Elizabeth
Brown, Zenith *see* Ford, Leslie
Buchanan, Eileen-Marie Duell *see* Curzon, Clare
Burden, Pat **191, 197, 201, 208**, 242
Burford, Roger D'Este *see* East, Roger
Burgess, Eric (1912-1995) **109, 114**, 242
Burton, Miles (1884-1964) **32, 33, 34, 35, 37, 38, 40, 41, 42, 43, 45, 46, 47, 48, 49, 51, 52, 54, 56, 57, 58, 60, 64, 66, 66, 68, 69, 71, 73, 73, 74, 75, 76, 77, 78, 79, 80, 81, 82, 83, 84, 85, 88, 90, 91, 92, 93, 94, 95, 97, 98, 99, 100, 101, 102, 104, 105, 106, 107, 109, 109, 112, 114**, 242-6; *see also* Rhode, John
Busby, Roger (1941-) **131, 135, 137, 140, 143, 150, 155, 179, 186, 198, 205, 219**, 246-7
Butterworth, John Michael *see* Butterworth, Michael *and* Kemp, Sarah
Butterworth, Michael (1924-1986) **135, 137, 140, 144, 146, 150, 151, 155, 172, 177, 182**, 219, 248-9; *see also* Kemp, Sarah

Cairns, Alison **172, 176**, 249
Caldwell, Taylor (1900-1985) **120**, 249
Campbell, Alice (1887-) **37, 39, 44, 46, 53, 56, 60, 64, 68, 72, 73, 75, 79, 81, 83, 89**, 249-50
Campbell, Harriette (1883-) **65**, 250
Carmichael, Harry (1908-1979) **92, 93, 94, 96, 96, 98, 99, 100, 101, 102, 103, 104, 106, 107, 108, 109, 112, 113, 114, 115, 116, 117, 118, 120, 122, 123, 126, 126, 128, 130, 134, 136, 138, 139, 140, 142, 144, 147, 150, 153, 155**, 250-53; *see also* Howard, Hartley
Carnac, Carol (1894-1958) **91, 93, 94, 96, 98, 99, 100, 102, 104, 106, 109**, 253-4; *see also* Lorac, E. C. R.
Caudwell, Sarah (1939-2000) **165, 176, 192**, 254
Cheyney, Peter (1896-1951) 220-21
Child, Nellise (1901-1981) **41, 45**, 254
Christie, Agatha (1890-1976) **33, 35, 37, 38, 41, 43, 44, 45, 47, 48, 50, 51, 52, 53, 55, 56, 58, 60, 61, 64, 66, 68, 70, 71, 72, 73, 75, 76, 78, 79, 81, 83, 85, 89, 90, 92, 94, 95, 96, 98, 100, 103, 105, 107, 109, 113, 116, 118, 120, 122, 124, 126, 128, 130, 131, 135, 139, 142, 144, 146, 149, 152, 159**, 216, 217, 254-9, 386
Clarke, Anna (1919-2004) **145, 147, 150, 152, 152, 154, 155, 158, 159, 163, 260**
Clarke, Brenda Margaret Lilian Honeyman Clarke *see* Sedley, Kate
Clemeau, Carol (1935-) **171**, 260
Cockburn, Sarah *see* Caudwell, Sarah
Cody, Liza (1944-) **164, 170, 176, 180, 183, 189**, 261
Cole, G. D. H. & M. (1889-1959; 1893-1980) **33, 42, 57, 32, 34, 36, 39, 41, 42, 44, 45, 46, 48, 50, 51, 55, 58, 60, 61, 65, 66, 67, 70, 71**, 219, 261-2, 386
Cole, George Douglas Howard *see* Cole, G. D. H.
Cole, Margaret *see* Cole, M.
Collins, Norman (1907-1982) **93**, 262
Cork, Barry **188, 192, 197, 201, 206**, 263
Craig, Mary (1923-) **157**, 263
Crofts, Freeman Wills (1879-1957) **32, 34, 36, 38, 46, 48, 51**, 217, 263
Culpan, Maurice (1918-1992) **123, 125, 126, 129, 130**, 263-4
Curzon, Clare (1922-2010) **159, 165, 172, 175, 178, 181, 184, 187, 190, 193, 197, 200**, 264-5

Davis, George **121, 129, 137, 146**, 265
Dean, S. F. X. **169, 171, 173**, 265
Dekker, Anthony (1929-) **135**, 266
Delman, David (1943-2012) **144, 149, 154, 181, 186, 191, 199, 206**, 266
Delving, Michael (1914-1978) **134, 136, 140, 148, 151, 156**, 266-7
Devine, D. M. (1920-1980) **116, 121, 123, 125, 127**, 218, 267; *see also* Devine, Dominic
Devine, Dominic (1920-1980) **128, 130, 134, 137, 139, 154, 167**, 268; *see also* Devine, D. M.
Dewhurst, Eileen (1929-) **162, 165, 168, 173, 176, 179, 182, 188**, 268-9
Doherty, Paul C. *see* Grace, C. L.
Doliner, Roy (1932-) **157**, 269
Donati, Sergio (1933-) **106**, 269
Donnelly, Patricia **207**, 269
Du Bois, Theodora (1890-1986) **100**, 269
Duffy, James *see* Murphy, Haughton

East, Roger (1904-1981) **41, 43, 44, 46, 51, 98, 112**, 219, 269-70
Eberhart, M. G. (1899-1996) **47, 51, 53, 54, 58, 59, 60, 64, 67, 69, 71, 73, 74, 76, 77, 78, 79, 80, 82, 85, 90, 91, 95, 96, 98, 103, 107, 112, 115, 117, 119, 121, 122, 125, 127, 129, 131, 138, 141, 145, 149, 153, 156, 158, 163, 167, 171, 175, 179, 184, 189**, 216, 270-74
Eccles, Marjorie (1927-) **191, 197, 200, 204, 207**, 274
Edington, A. C. & Carmen (1890-1953; 1894-1972) **33, 34**, 274
Edmonds, Janet **190, 192, 199, 205, 208**, 274-5
Elkins, Aaron (1935-) **199, 201, 204**, 275
Epstein, Charlotte **184**, 275
Escott, Jonathan *see* Scott, Jack
Esler, Carole Clemeau *see* Clemeau, Carol
Estridge, Robin Phillip Lorraine *see* Loraine, Philip
Everton, Francis (1883-1956) **37, 44, 51**, 275

Farjeon, J. Jefferson (1883-1955) **36, 38, 38, 39, 40, 42, 42, 43, 44, 49, 54, 55, 57, 57, 59, 61, 65, 68, 70, 71, 73, 75, 76, 78, 79, 83, 85, 85, 89, 91, 92, 94, 96, 98**, 219, 275-7
Farrar, Stewart (1916-2000) **106, 112, 119**, 278
Farrer, Katharine (1911-1972) **97**, 216, 278
Ferguson, John (1873-1952) **36, 42, 45, 53, 70**, 278
Ferrars, Elizabeth (1907-1995) **79, 82, 84, 88, 89, 93, 93, 95, 97, 100, 101, 102, 104, 105, 108, 112, 113, 116, 117, 119, 120, 122, 125, 128, 129, 131, 134, 137, 140, 142, 143, 144, 147, 148, 149, 150, 153, 154, 155, 157, 159, 162, 164, 166, 167, 169, 171, 173, 176, 178, 180, 182, 185, 189, 191, 192, 197, 198, 201, 203, 206, 208, 209**, 216, 217, 218, 278-83, 386
Fielding, A. **33, 33, 34, 38, 39, 41, 43, 45, 46, 48, 49, 51, 52, 54, 56, 74**, 283-4
Fitzgerald, Nigel (1906-) **95, 96, 98, 103, 106, 107, 109, 112, 113, 115, 120, 128**, 284-5
Fleming, Anne **199**, 285
Fleming, Joan (1908-1980) **104, 105, 108, 109, 113, 115, 116, 119, 120, 122, 125, 126, 128, 130, 134, 138, 141, 143, 146, 151, 153, 155**, 218, 219, 285-7
Fletcher, J. S. (1863-1935) **34**, 287, 386
Flower, Pat (1914-1978) **141, 143, 145, 147, 148, 150, 152**, 287-8
Follett, Ken (Kenneth Martin) *see* Stone, Zachary
Footner, Hulbert (1879-1944) **32, 32, 35, 38, 39, 40, 41, 44, 45, 46, 47, 49, 53, 53, 56, 57, 59, 61, 64, 68, 70, 72, 74, 75, 77**, 288-9, 386
Ford, Florence **105, 112**, 289
Ford, Leslie (1898-1983) **53, 56, 59, 60, 61, 65, 67, 69, 72, 73, 75, 76, 77, 80, 81, 83, 85, 92, 94, 96, 99, 102, 105, 116**, 290-91
Forsythe, Malcolm **202, 205, 208**, 291
Fraser, Anthea (1930-) **175, 178, 182, 185, 187, 190, 193, 197, 200, 203**, 291-2
Fuller, Timothy (1914-1971) **52**, 292

Gagnon, Maurice **179, 181, 185**, 292
Gair, Malcolm (1917-1980) **104, 106**, 292
Garve, Andrew (1908-2001) **88, 89, 90, 92, 94, 94, 96, 98, 101, 102, 104, 106, 108, 112, 114, 116, 117, 119, 120, 122, 125, 127, 129, 130, 134, 137, 140, 145, 150, 155**, 217, 218, 292-5; *see also* Somers, Paul
Gash, Jonathan (1933-) **154, 156, 159, 163, 166, 168, 171, 174, 177, 181, 183, 190, 193**, 219, 295-6; *see also* Gaunt, Graham
Gaunt, Graham (1933-) **165**, 296; *see also* Gash, Jonathan
Gibbins, James **173**, 296
Gielgud, Val (1900-1981) **102, 107, 112, 114, 118, 123, 126, 130**, 296-7
Gilbert, Anthony (1899-1973) **34, 36, 39, 41, 42, 44, 45, 47, 49, 50, 53, 54, 56, 58, 61, 64, 67, 69, 70, 72, 72, 75, 75, 77, 78, 79, 80, 81, 82, 84, 88, 90, 91, 93, 94, 97, 99, 101, 102, 104, 105, 108, 109, 112, 114, 115, 117, 118, 120, 121, 123, 125, 127, 129, 130, 134, 137, 140, 145**, 216, 219, 297-301
Gill, Josephine (1921-2006) **101**, 301
Goldsborough, Robert (1937-) **185, 191, 196, 199**, 301
Gough, Anna May *see* Stadley, Pat
Grace, C. L. (1946-) **208**, 301
Grant, John *see* Gash, Jonathan *and* Gaunt, Graham
Gregson, J. M. (1934-) **191, 196, 199, 202, 205, 208**, 301-2
Grierson, Francis D. (1888-1972) **32, 33, 34, 36, 37, 39, 41**, 302

Haffner, Margaret **203, 206**, 302
Hall, Patricia **202, 205**, 303
Halls, Geraldine Mary *see* Jay, Charlotte
Hamilton, Bruce (1990-1974) **35**, 303
Hamilton, Ian (1935-) **139**, 303
Harcourt, Palma & Trotman, Jack *see* Penn, John
Harding, Richard *see* Tine, Robert
Hardinge, George Edward *see* Milner, George
Hart, Jeanne **193, 198, 199, 202**, 303
Haywood, Steve **202**, 303
Heller, Keith (1949-) **175, 178, 182**, 303-4
Henderson, James (1934-) **141**, 304
Hill, Reginald (1936-2012) **135, 137, 139, 141, 143, 146, 148, 151, 155, 158, 164, 173, 175, 184, 187, 188, 196, 198, 204, 207, 209**, 219, 304-6, 386
Hilton, John Buxton (1921-1986) **162, 164, 166, 167, 169, 171, 172, 174, 176, 177, 179, 181, 183, 185, 186**, 219, 306-7
Hinxman, Margaret (1924-) **151, 154, 168, 171, 176, 180, 183, 192, 201**, 307-8
Holt, Henry **42, 43, 45, 46, 48, 51, 55, 57, 60, 66**, 308-9
Howard, Hartley (1908-1979) **90, 134, 135, 136, 138, 139, 141, 143, 145, 147, 151, 154, 158**, 309-10; *see also* Carmichael, Harry
Howard, Herbert Edmund *see* Philmore, R.
Hull, Helen (Rose) (1888-1971) **115**, 223, 310
Hull, Richard (1896-1973) **60, 64, 70, 78, 80, 84, 88, 90, 94**, 310

Inchbald, Peter (1919-2004) **166, 170, 173, 178**, 310-11
Infante, Anne **192, 198, 201, 204, 207**, 311

Jacquemard, Yves & Sénécal, Jean-Michel (1943-1980; 1943-) **157**, **162**, 311
James, Terry **207**, 311
Jay, Charlotte (1919-1996) **99**, **107**, **113**, 312
Jay, Simon (1920-2007) **121**, 312
Jeffries, Roderic (1926-2017) **115**, **117**, **119**, **121**, **123**, **125**, **127**, **129**, **135**, **146**, **151**, **154**, **157**, **163**, **166**, **171**, **174**, **178**, **181**, **184**, **188**, **191**, **196**, **200**, **203**, **206**, **209**, 312-14; *see also* Ashford, Jeremy
Jenkins, Cecil (1927-) **114**, 222-3, 314
Jepson, Selwyn (1899-1989) **91**, **97**, 219, 314
Jobson, Hamilton (1914-1981) **148**, **153**, **154**, **156**, **158**, 314-15
Johnson, Sheila **167**, **168**, **172**, 315
Jones, Hazel Wynn **188**, **191**, **197**, 315

Kallen, Lucille (1922-1999) **159**, **164**, **170**, **177**, **182**, 315-16
Kark, Nina Mary Mabey Kark *see* Bawden, Nina
Keating, H. R. F. (1926-2011) **119**, **121**, **122**, **124**, **126**, **128**, **130**, **135**, **139**, **142**, **145**, **149**, **152**, **157**, **162**, **165**, **175**, 218, 316-17
Keith, David (1906-1994) **88**, 317
Kellerman, Faye (1952-) **184**, 318
Kelly, Nora (1945-) **176**, **204**, **208**, 318
Kemp, Sarah (1924-1986) **158**, 318; *see also* Butterworth, Michael
Kenyon, Michael (1931-2005) **123**, **126**, **129**, **134**, **141**, **145**, **147**, **153**, **154**, **167**, **170**, **172**, 218, 318-19
King, C. Daly (1895-1963) **43**, **45**, **47**, **53**, **56**, **65**, 217, 319-20, 386
King, Pauline (1917-2013) **177**, 320

Le Breton, Auguste (1913-1999) **104**, 320
Lewi, Charlotte Armstrong *see* Armstrong, Charlotte
Lewin, Matthew *see* Matthews, Lew
Lewis, Cecil Day *see* Blake, Nicholas
Lewis, Roy (1933-) **131**, **134**, **137**, **138**, **141**, **142**, **143**, **144**, **146**, **147**, **149**, **150**, **152**, **153**, **155**, **156**, **158**, **163**, **165**, **166**, **168**, **170**, **173**, **175**, **176**, **178**, **181**, **182**, **186**, **189**, **192**, **193**, **201**, **203**, **205**, **207**, 219, 320-23
Lieberman, Lilian *see* Child, Nelise
Little, Conyth (1899-1980; 1906-1985) **66**, **67**, **69**, **71**, **73**, **74**, **76**, **77**, **78**, **80**, **81**, **83**, **84**, **89**, **91**, **92**, **94**, **95**, 323-4
Loder, Vernon (1881-1938) **33**, **34**, **36**, **38**, **40**, **42**, **44**, **45**, **46**, **47**, **49**, **51**, **52**, **55**, **58**, 324-5
Lorac, E. C. R. (1895-1958) **48**, **50**, **51**, **52**, **54**, **55**, **57**, **58**, **61**, **64**, **67**, **68**, **70**, **71**, **72**, **74**, **75**, **77**, **78**, **79**, **80**, **82**, **83**, **85**, **85**, **89**, **91**, **92**, **94**, **96**, **97**, **98**, **100**, **101**, **103**, **105**, **105**, **107**, **108**, 219, 325-8; *see also* Carnac, Carol
Loraine, Philip (1920-2002) **137**, **144**, **163**, **169**, **172**, **179**, **182**, **207**, 328-9
Low, Ona **181**, **185**, 328-9
Lyall, Francis **185**, **188**, **197**, **201**, **208**, 329

MacDonald, John D. **117**, 329, 386
MacDonald, Philip (1899-1981) **32**, **32**, **34**, **34**, **35**, **37**, **37**, **38**, **39**, **40**, **55**, **83**, **96**, 217, 219, 329-30; *see also* Porlock, Martin
Macdonald, Ross (1915-1983) **115**, **116**, **119**, **121**, **123**, **126**, **129**, **131**, **138**, **144**, **151**, 218, 330-31
MacKenzie, Donald (1908-1993) **116**, **119**, **120**, 331
MacKinnon, Allan **78**, **88**, **93**, 331
MacLeod, Charlotte (1922-2005) **159**, **162**, **164**, **166**, **169**, **170**, **173**, **175**, **176**, **178**, **183**, **185**, **187**, **192**, **193**, **200**, **204**, **206**, **209**, 331-3, 386
Malcolm, John (1936-) **175**, **176**, **179**, **182**, **185**, **187**, **196**, **200**, **203**, **206**, 333-4
Malleson, Lucy Beatrice *see* Gilbert, Anthony
Mann, Jessica (1937-) **137**, 334
Mansfield, Paul (1922-) **105**, 334
March, Maxwell (1904-1966) **50**, 334
Marder, Irving **127**, 334
Markham, Virgil (1899-1973) **32**, **37**, **38**, **40**, **44**, **48**, **51**, 334-5
Marsh, Edith Ngaio *see* Marsh, Ngaio
Marsh, Ngaio (1895-1982) **59**, **64**, **67**, **70**, **73**, **76**, **80**, **85**, **91**, **97**, **99**, **103**, **108**, **113**, **117**, **120**, **126**, **130**, **136**, **140**, **145**, **152**, **156**, **163**, **170**, 216, 217, 218, 335-7
Martin, James E. **143**, 337
Mason, Sarah J. (1949-) **180**, 337
Matheson, Jean **103**, 337
Matthews, Lew (1944-) **205**, **209**, 337
Mavity, Nancy Barr (1890-1959) **33**, **35**, **39**, **41**, 337-8
McAllister, Alister *see* Brock, Lynn
McCann, Thomas **137**, 338
McConnell, James Douglas Rutherford *see* Rutherford, Douglas
McGerr, Patricia (1917-1985) **81**, **82**, **84**, **89**, **90**, **93**, **99**, **123**, 338
McIntosh, Kinn Hamilton *see* Aird, Catherine
McKinlay, Margaret **204**, **206**, **209**, 338
McLarty, Donald **193**, 339
McMahon, Thomas Patrick **142**, 339
McMullen, Mary (1920-1986) **92**, **162**, **164**, **166**, **167**, **169**, 339
Meek, M. R. D. (1918-2009) **174**, **176**, **179**, **182**, **186**, **190**, **191**, **198**, **204**, 339-40
Meggs, Brown (1930-1997) **149**, **150**, 340
Meyer, Lawrence (1941-) **154**, **159**, 340
Meynell, Laurence (1899-1989) **118**, **119**, **121**, **123**, **124**, **128**, **129**, **131**, 341
Michael, Ian David Lewis *see* Serafin, David
Millar, Kenneth *see* Macdonald, Ross
Milner, George (1921-1997) **95**, **98**, 341
Montfort, Auguste *see* Le Breton, Auguste
Moore, Margaret **184**, **188**, **198**, **202**, 341-2
Morrow, Susan **112**, 342
Moyes, Patricia (1923-2000) **109**, **114**, **116**, **118**, **121**, **124**, **126**, **129**, **134**, **138**, **143**, **148**, **152**, **156**, **163**, **172**, **180**, **196**, **208**, 218, 219, 342-4
Murphy, Haughton (1953-) **183**, **186**, **190**, **193**, **198**, **202**, 344
Murray, Stephen **187**, **189**, **192**, **196**, **202**, **207**, 344-5

Nabb, Magdalen (1947-2007) **167**, **169**, **174**, **177**, **185**, **188**, **196**, **203**, **209**, 345-6
Nassim, Liza *see* Cody, Liza
Nicholas, Robert **115**, 223, 346
Nielsen, Torben (1918-1985) **152**, **156**, 346
North, William *see* Rodd, Ralph
Nuttal, Magdalen *see* Nabb, Magdalen

Ognall, Leopold Horace *see* Carmichael, Harry *and* Hartley, Howard
Orde, A. J. (1929-) **193**, **199**, **203**, **207**, 346
Oursler, Charles Fulton *see* Abbot, Anthony

Page, Emma (1921-) **134**, **140**, **142**, **148**, **166**, **170**, **173**, **178**, **184**, **191**, **201**, **206**, 346-7
Pakenham-Walsh, Patricia *see* Moyes, Patricia
Palmer, Stuart (1905-1968) **45**, **48**, **52**, **54**, **69**, **82**, **89**, **90**, **93**, **98**, **102**, 219, 347-8
Pargeter, Edith Mary *see* Peters, Ellis
Parkes, Roger (1933-2008) **183**, **190**, **199**, **204**, 348
Paul, Barbara (1931-) **168**, **169**, **174**, **180**, **183**, 348-9
Pearce, Michael (1933-) **188**, **191**, **196**, **200**, **203**, **206**, **209**, 349
Penn, John (1917-1999) **168**, **172**, **173**, **177**, **178**, **181**, **184**, **187**, **190**, **192**, **196**, **199**, **202**, **205**, **207**, **209**, 350-51
Penny, Rupert (1909-1970) **50**, **52**, **54**, **56**, **58**, **59**, **65**, **68**, 351
Pereira, Michael (1928-) **140**, **142**, **145**, **148**, 351-2
Pernot, Pierette *see* Arley, Catherine
Perry, Ritchie (1942-) **139**, **142**, **144**, **146**, **148**, **150**, **153**, **155**, **157**, **162**, **165**, 352-3
Peters, Ellis (1913-1995) **109**, **113**, **115**, **118**, **121**, **122**, **125**, **127**, **128**, **130**, 353-4
Peterson, Bernard **205**, 354
Philmore, R. (1900-1963) **55**, **57**, **60**, **67**, 354
Pickard, Nancy (1945-) **186**, **189**, **192**, 354
Porlock, Martin (1899-1981) **36**, **37**, **40**, 216, 354; *see also* MacDonald, Philip
Postgate, Raymond (1896-1971) **64**, 354
Powell, Lester (1912-1993) **88**, 354
Puckett, Andrew **187**, **191**, **197**, **203**, **208**, 355

Queen, Ellery **100**, **102**, **103**, **105**, **107**, **112**, **114**, 355, 387

Ramsay, Diana (1934-2014) **139**, **143**, **144**, **147**, **153**, **193**, 356
Rawson, Clayton (1906-1971) **58**, **61**, **67**, 356
Reznek, Lawrie (1906-1971) **197**, 356
Rhode, John (1884-1964) **34**, **35**, **37**, **38**, **40**, **41**, **43**, **44**, **45**, **46**, **46**, **48**, **49**, **50**, **52**, **53**, **55**, **56**, **58**, **59**, **61**, **65**, **66**, **68**, **69**, **71**, **72**, **73**, **74**, **75**, **76**, **76**, 219, 356-8; *see also* Burton, Miles
Ripley, Mike (1952-) **190**, **192**, **197**, **201**, 358-9
Rivett, Edith Caroline *see* Carnac, Carol *and* Lorac, E. C. R.
Roby, Mary Linn (1930-) **123**, 359
Rodd, Ralph (1869-) **34**, 359
Russell, A. J. **153**, 359
Russell, Martin (1934-) **124**, **126**, **128**, **131**, **137**, **138**, **142**, **143**, **144**, **146**, **148**, **149**, **150**, **152**, **153**, **155**, **157**, **159**, **162**, **164**, **165**, **168**, **169**, **172**, **174**, **176**, **178**, **180**, **183**, **186**, **190**, **192**, **205**, **208**, 219, 359-62, 387
Rutherford, Douglas (1915-1988) **99**, **100**, **103**, **106**, **114**, **119**, **124**, **129**, **131**, **138**, **144**, **149**, **152**, 362-3
Ryck, Francis (1920-1977) **138**, **140**, **141**, **143**, **146**, **149**, 363-4

Sampson, Richard Henry *see* Hull, Richard
Satterthwait, Walter (1946-) **197**, **200**, **203**, **206**, **209**, 364
Scott, Gavin **153**, 364
Scott, Jack (1922-1987) **157**, **162**, **164**, **167**, **171**, **173**, **175**, **177**, **183**, 364-5
Scott, John Dick *see* Gair, Malcolm
Sedley, Kate (1926-) **202**, **205**, 365
Seeley, Mabel (1903-1991) **59**, **65**, **68**, **70**, **73**, **89**, 365
Sénécal, Jean-Michel *see under* Jacquemard, Yves
Serafin, David (1936-) **158**, **168**, **170**, **178**, **185**, 366
Sheffield, Robyn **204**, **207**, 366
Smith, Evelyn E. (1922-2000) **186**, **189**, **204**, 366
Smith, Francis *see* Dean, S. F. X.
Smith, Shelley (1912-1998) **76**, **78**, **80**, **83**, **90**, **93**, **96**, **98**, 217, 367
Smith, Willard K. **32**, 367
Smith, William Dale *see* Anthony, David
Somers, Paul (1908-2001) **106**, 367; *see also* Garve, Andrew
Stadley, Pat (1917-2003) **136**, 367
Steegmuller, Francis *see* Keith, David
Stenstreem, Ruth *see* Babson, Marian
Stewart, Douglas **173**, 367
Stokes, Francis William *see* Everton, Francis
Stone, Zachary (1949-) **150**, **153**, 368
Stout, Rex (1886-1975) **57**, **60**, **61**, **65**, **66**, **66**, **68**, **69**, **70**, **71**, **73**, **77**, **80**, **82**, **84**, **85**, **88**, **89**, **90**, **91**, **93**, **94**, **95**, **97**, **99**, **100**, **101**, **103**, **104**, **106**, **107**, **108**, **109**, **113**, **114**, **115**, **116**, **118**, **118**, **120**, **122**, **122**, **124**, **127**, **130**, **134**, **145**, **151**, 216, 217, 368-71, 387
Strange, John Stephen (1896-1983) **33**, **36**, **43**, **46**, **52**, **57**, **59**, **66**, **71**, **75**, **82**, **84**, **89**, **91**, **93**, **95**, **100**, **108**, **116**, 371-2
Strathern, William *see* Jobson, Hamilton
Street, Cecil John Charles *see* Burton, Miles *and* Rhode, John
Strong, L. A. G. (1896-1958) **70**, **74**, **77**, **90**, **107**, 217, 372
Symons, Julian (1912-1994) **101**, **104**, **107**, **113**, **117**, **121**, **122**, **127**, **130**, **136**, **141**, **143**, **147**, **156**, **162**, 373-4

Tapply, William G. (1940-2009) **177**, **179**, **182**, **185**, **188**, **190**, **192**, **198**, **201**, **203**, **207**, 374-5
Taylor, Phoebe Atwood (1909-1976) **56**, **57**, **59**, **60**, **61**, **67**, **69**, **70**, **72**, **75**, **78**, **79**, **81**, **91**, 375, 387; *see also* Tilton, Alice
Telushkin, Joseph (1948-) **182**, **190**, **197**, 376
Tepper, Sheri Stewart *see* Orde, A. J.
Thornett, Ernest Basil Charles *see* Penny, Rupert
Tillett, Dorothy Stockbridge *see* Strange, John Stephen
Tilton, Alice (1909-1976) **53**, **57**, **65**, **68**, **71**, **75**, **76**, **81**, 219, 376; *see also* Taylor, Phoebe Atwood
Tine, Robert (1955-) **171**, **172**, 376
Tirbutt, Honoria *see* Page, Emma
Troy, Simon (1904-1974) **93**, 377
Turnbull, Peter (1950-) **165**, **169**, **171**, **174**, **188**, **191**, **200**, **206**, 377
Turner, J. V. (1900-1945) **47**, **50**, 377

Vahey, John George Hazlette *see* Loder, Vernon
Valin, Jonathan (1947-) **165**, **167**, **169**, **172**, **174**, **207**, 377-8

Wainwright, John (1921-1995) **122**, **124** **125**, **127**, **128**, **129**, **130**, 378-9
Wakefield, H. Russell (1888-1964) **50**, **56**, 379
Wallace, Edgar (1875-1932) **35**, 379
Walsh, J. M. (1897-1952) **38**, 379
Walsh, James Morgan *see* Walsh, J. M.
Ward, Colin **42**, 379
Warriner, Thurman *see* Troy, Simon
Welcome, John (1914-2010) **189**, **198**, 379
West, Charles (1927-) **189**, **199**, **202**, **209**, 379
White, Ethel Lina (1876-1944) **49**, **52**, **54**, **58**, **64**, **69**, **71**, **74**, **75**, 216, 378-80
White, R. J. (1905-1971) **114**, 222-3, 380
Whitechurch, Victor L. (1868-1933) **33**, **39**, 380
Williams, David (1926-2003) **151**, **153**, **155**, **163**, **168**, **171**, **174**, **205**, **207**, 219, 380-81
Williams, Jay *see* Delving, Michael
Wilson, Mary Reilly *see* McMullen, Mary
Winslow, Pauline Glen **154**, **156**, **162**, **168**, 381
Winterton, Paul *see* Garve, Andrew *and* Somers, Paul
Wolf, Sarah (1931-2019) **189**, 382
Wood, Ted (1931-2019) **174**, **176**, **180**, **184**, **189**, **193**, **199**, **204**, **208**, 382
Woods, Sara (1922-1983) **116**, **118**, **118**, **119**, **120**, **121**, **123**, **123**, **124**, **126**, **126**, **128**, **129**, **130**, **131**, **134**, **137**, **138**, 382-4
Wright, Eric (1929-2015) **171**, **175**, **177**, **182**, **186**, **190**, **196**, **200**, **204**, **207**, 384-5
Wright, L. R. (1939-2001) **185**, 385
Wynd, Oswald Morris *see* Black, Gavin

Yastrow, Shelby **201**, 385
Yves, Delville *see* Ryck, Francis

# INDEX OF TITLES

*A B C Murders, The* (Christie) **48**, 217, 254
*Abuse of Justice, An* (Parkes) **190**, 348
*Accident By Design* (Lorac) **89**, 325
*Accident Prone* (Penn) **187**, 350
*Account Rendered* (Ryck) **149**, 363
*Advancement of Learning, An* (Hill) **139**, 304
*Adventure of the Christmas Pudding and a Selection of Entrees, The* (Christie) **113**, 255, 386
*Advertise for Treasure* (Williams) **174**, 380
*Advisory Service* (Russell) **138**, 359
*Affair at Aliquid, The* (Cole) **42**, 261
*Affairs of Death* (Fitzgerald) **128**, 284
*After the Funeral* (Christie) **95**, 255
*Afternoon to Kill, An* (Smith) **96**, 217, 367
*Alas Poor Father!* (Fleming) **141**, 285
*Alibi* (Carmichael) **114**, 250
*Alibi for a Witch* (Ferrars) **93**, 278
*Alive and Dead* (Ferrars) **147**, 278
*All Fall Down* (Strong) **74**, 372
*All Part of the Service* (Russell) **169**, 359
*All the Pretty People* (Scott) **173**, 364
*Almost Murder* (Jeffries) **181**, 312
*Almost Perfect Murder and Other Stories, The* (Footner) **41**, 288, 386
*Alphabet Hicks* (Stout) **71**, 368
*Alpine Condo Crossfire* (Eberhart) **179**, 270
*Always Say Die* (Ferrars) **101**, 278
*Anathema Stone, The* (Hilton) **162**, 306
*And Death Came Too* (Gilbert) **101**, 297
*And Death Came Too* (Hull) **60**, 310
*And Did Murder Him* (Turnbull) **200**, 377
*And Died So?* (Gielgud) **114**, 296
*And Shame the Devil* (Woods) **128**, 382
*Angel Death* (Moyes) **163**, 342
*Angel Hunt* (Ripley) **197**, 358
*Angel Touch* (Ripley) **192**, 358
*Angels in Arms* (Ripley) **201**, 359
*Annulet of Gilt, The* (Taylor) **59**, 375
*Another Death in Venice* (Hill) **151**, 219, 304
*Another Man's Murder* (Eberhart) **107**, 270
*Another Woman's House* (Eberhart) **82**, 270
*Answer Came There None* (Ferrars) **206**, 279
*Appointment With Death* (Christie) **56**, 255
*April Rainers, The* (Fraser) **193**, 291
*April Shroud, An* (Hill) **148**, 304
*Araway Oath, The* (Adams) **70**, 226
*Ariadne Clue, The: A Classical Mystery* (Clemeau) **171**, 260
*Arms for Adonis* (Jay) **113**, 312
*Arrogant Alibi* (King) **56**, 319
*Arrow in the Dark* (Allan) **170**, 228
*Ascent of D.13, The* (Garve) **130**, 292
*Asey Mayo Trio, The* (Taylor) **79**, 375, 387
*Ashes of Loda, The* (Garve) **122**, 292
*Ask a Policeman* (Lorac) **100**, 325
*Asking Price, The* (Hilton) **172**, 306
*At Bertram's Hotel* (Christie) **124**, 255
*At Death's Door* (Barnard) **190**, 234
*At Ease With the Dead* (Satterthwait) **200**, 364
*At One Fell Swoop* (Palmer) **90**, 347
*Aunt Sunday Sees it Through* (Farjeon) **65**, 275
*Autumn of a Hunter* (Stadley) **136**, 367

*Back Room in Somers Town, A* (Malcolm) **175**, 333
*Backlash* (Russell) **165**, 359
*Bad Chemistry* (Kelly) **208**, 318
*Bad Company* (Cody) **170**, 261
*Bad for Business* (Stout) **77**, 368
*Bad Track, The* (Booth) **163**, 240
*Bahamas Murder Case, The* (Ford) **94**, 290
*Banbury Bog* (Taylor) **60**, 375
*Banking on Murder* (Williams) **207**, 380
*Barren Revenge* (Penn) **184**, 350
*Bat That Flits, The* (Collins) **93**, 262
*Bats Fly Up for Inspector Ghote* (Keating) **145**, 316
*Bats in the Belfry* (Lorac) **52**, 325
*Bayou Road, The* (Eberhart) **158**, 270
*Beast Must Die, The* (Blake) **56**, 239
*Becket Factor, The* (Anthony) **199**, 229
*Beckoning Door, The* (Seeley) **89**, 365
*Bed of Nails* (Puckett) **191**, 355
*Before Midnight* (Stout) **101**, 368
*Beginner's Luck* (Somers) **106**, 367
*Beginning With a Bash* (Tilton) **53**, 219, 376
*Bejewelled Death* (Babson) **166**, 231
*Bell in the Fog, The* (Strange) **52**, 371
*Bell is Answered, The* (East) **44**, 269
*Bell of Death, The* (Gilbert) **61**, 297
*Below the Clock* (Turner) **50**, 377
*Belt of Suspicion* (Wakefield) **50**, 379
*Belting Inheritance, The* (Symons) **122**, 372
*Ben on the Job* (Farjeon) **92**, 219, 275
*Ben Sees It Through* (Farjeon) **39**, 276
*Benefits of Death, The* (Jeffries) **119**, 312
*Bengal Fire* (Blochman) **53**, 240
*Bermuda Burial* (King) **65**, 319
*Beware of the Dog* (Ferrars) **203**, 279
*Beware Your Neighbour* (Burton) **91**, 242
*Big Business Murder* (Cole) **45**, 261
*Big Money* (Turnbull) **174**, 377
*Big Wind for Summer, A* (Black) **148**, 237
*Bilbao Looking-Glass, The* (MacLeod) **173**, 331
*Bishop's Pawn* (Perry) **157**, 352
*Bitter Tea, The* (Black) **142**, 237
*Black as He's Painted* (Marsh) **145**, 335
*Black Beadle* (Lorac) **61**, 325
*Black Castle* (Farjeon) **76**, 276
*Black Cats Are Lucky* (Fielding) **54**, 283
*Black Coat, The* (Little) **84**, 323
*Black Corridors* (Little) **67**, 323
*Black Death* (Adams) **59**, 226
*Black Dream, The* (Little) **94**, 323
*Black Express* (Little) **77**, 323
*Black Eye, The* (Little) **78**, 323
*Black Girl, White Girl* (Moyes) **196**, 342
*Black Gloves, The* (Little) **66**, 323
*Black Goatee, The* (Little) **81**, 324
*Black Honeymoon, The* (Little) **76**, 324
*Black House, The* (Little) **89**, 324
*Black Iris, The* (Little) **95**, 324
*Black Is the Colour of My True Love's Heart* (Peters) **127**, 353
*Black Italian, The* (Jepson) **97**, 219, 314
*Black Lady, The* (Little) **74**, 324
*Black Leather Murders, The* (Rutherford) **124**, 362
*Black Look, The* (Butterworth) **140**, 248
*Black Money* (Macdonald) **126**, 330
*Black Mountain, The* (Stout) **100**, 368
*Black Orchids* (Stout) **73**, 368, 387
*Black Paw, The* (Little) **69**, 324
*Black Piano, The* (Little) **83**, 324
*Black Shrouds, The* (Little) **71**, 324
*Black Smith, The* (Little) **91**, 324
*Black Stage, The* (Gilbert) **78**, 216, 297
*Black Stocking, The* (Little) **80**, 324
*Black Thumb, The* (Little) **73**, 324
*Black Welcome* (Fitzgerald) **115**, 284
*Black Widower* (Moyes) **148**, 342
*Blackheath Poisonings, The: a Victorian Murder Mystery* (Symons) **156**, 373
*Blackout, The* (Little) **92**, 324
*Blood Brotherhood* (Barnard) **154**, 219, 234
*Blood Flies Upwards* (Ferrars) **150**, 279
*Blood Money* (Lewis) **143**, 320
*Blood on a Harvest Moon* (Anthony) **141**, 229
*Blood Sympathy* (Hill) **207**, 304
*Bloodeagle* (Lewis) **207**, 320
*Bloodhound* (Puckett) **203**, 355
*Bloodied Ivy, The* (Goldsborough) **196**, 301
*Bloodstained Toy, The* (Campbell) **83**, 249
*Bloodstains* (Puckett) **187**, 355
*Bloody Instructions* (Woods) **116**, 383
*Bloody Success* (Culpan) **130**, 263
*Bloody Tower, The* (Rhode) **58**, 356
*Blue City* (Macdonald) 218
*Blue Hammer, The* (Macdonald) **151**, 330
*Blue Harpsichord* (Keith) **88**, 317
*Blue-Eyed Boy, The* (Curzon) **197**, 264
*Bluff!, The* (Adams) **55**, 226
*Blurred Reality, A* (Lewis) **178**, 320
*Bodies* (Barnard) **182**, 234
*Body in Cadiz Bay, The* (Serafin) **178**, 366
*Body in the Bunker, The* (Adams) **45**, 226
*Body in the Library, The* (Christie) **71**, 255
*Body on the Beam, The* (Gilbert) **36**, 297
*Body on the Floor, The* (Mavity) **33**, 337
*Body Surrounded By Water, A* (Wright) **186**, 384
*Body Vanishes, The* (Jacquemard-Sénécal) **162**, 311
*Bombay Mail* (Blochman) **44**, 240
*Bones and Silence* (Hill) **196**, 304
*Bones in the Brickfield* (Burton) **106**, 242
*Book Lady, The* (Forsythe) **208**, 291
*Boomerang* (Garve) **134**, 293
*Bowery Murder, The* (Smith) **32**, 367
*Boy from Nowhere, The* (Hinxman) **180**, 307
*Breakaway* (Black) **136**, 238
*Breath of Suspicion* (Ferrars) **140**, 279
*Bricklayer's Arms* (Rhode) **76**, 357
*Brief Return* (Eberhart) **60**, 270
*Bring Forth Your Dead* (Gregson) **199**, 301
*Broken Vase, The* (Stout) **70**, 368
*Brothers Sackville, The* (Cole) **51**, 261
*Burglars in Bucks* (Cole) **32**, 261
*Burning Ground, The* (Malcolm) **206**, 333
*Burning Question, The* (Carnac) **104**, 253
*Bury Him Kindly* (Burden) **201**, 242
*Busy Body, The* (Ferrars) **116**, 279
*But He Was Already Dead When I Got There* (Paul) **183**, 348
*But Nellie Was So Nice* (McMullen) **164**, 339
*Button in the Plate, The* (Loder) **55**, 324
*By Frequent Anguish* (Dean) **169**, 265
*By the Pricking of My Thumbs* (Christie) **130**, 255
*Bye-Bye Baby* (Delman) **206**, 266

*C. B. Greenfield: A Little Madness* (Kalen) **182**, 315
*C. B. Greenfield: No Lady in the House* (Kalen) **170**, 316
*C. B. Greenfield: The Piano Bird* (Kalen) **177**, 316
*C. B. Greenfield: The Tanglewood Murder* (Kalen) **164**, 316
*Call after Midnight* (Eberhart) **122**, 270
*Calling All Cars* (Holt) **43**, 308
*Candidate for Lilies* (East) **43**, 269
*Candles Are All Out, The* (Fitzgerald) **112**, 284
*Candles for the Dead* (Carmichael) **144**, 251
*Capital Crime, A* (Ford) **69**, 290
*Capitol Crime, A* (Meyer) **154**, 340
*Caravaggio Books, The* (Peterson) **205**, 354
*Cards on the Table* (Christie) **51**, 255
*Careless Corpse* (King) **53**, 319
*Caribbean Mystery, A* (Christie) **122**, 255
*Caring Game, The* (McKinlay) **209**, 338
*Casa Madrone* (Eberhart) **163**, 270
*Case Against Andrew Fane, The* (Gilbert) **34**, 297
*Case in the Clinic* (Lorac) **68**, 325
*Case is Altered, The* (Woods) **126**, 383
*Case of Robert Quarry, The* (Garve) **140**, 293
*Case of the Abominable Snowman, The* (Blake) **69**, 239
*Case of the Dead Doctor, The* (Loder) **47**, 324
*Case of the Missing Diary, The* (Fielding) **48**, 283
*Case of the Missing Sandals, The* (Mavity) **35**, 337
*Case of the Stolen Bridegroom, The* (Adams) **65**, 226
*Case of the Tea-Cosy's Aunt, The* (Gilbert) **72**, 297
*Case of the Two Pearl Necklaces, The* (Fielding) **49**, 284
*Castle of Fear* (Farjeon) **98**, 276
*Casual Murderer and Other Stories, The* (Footner) **38**, 288, 386
*Cat* (Gielgud) **102**, 296
*Cat Among the Pigeons* (Christie) **109**, 255
*Cat Jumps, The* (Burton) **78**, 242
*Cat Who Ate Danish Modern, The* (Braun) **128**, 241
*Cat Who Could Read Backwards, The* (Braun) **127**, 241
*Cat Who Turned On and Off, The* (Braun) **131**, 241
*Cat's Cradle* (Curzon) **200**, 264
*Cat's Cradle* (Flower) **143**, 287
*Catch Me if You Can* (McGerr) **84**, 338
*Catspaw* (Russell) **164**, 359
*Cause Unknown* (Farjeon) **89**, 276
*Cautley Conundrum, The* (Fielding) **43**, 284
*Cellars' Market* (Stewart) **173**, 367
*Censor* (Russell) **176**, 359
*Certain Blindness, A* (Lewis) **163**, 320
*Champagne for One* (Stout) **109**, 368
*Chance to Poison, The* (Bromley) **143**, 242
*Charabanc Mystery, The* (Burton) **43**, 242
*Charitable End, A* (Mann) **137**, 334
*Checkmate to Murder* (Lorac) **74**, 325
*Chief Witness, The* (Adams) **66**, 226
*Chiffon Scarf, The* (Eberhart) **64**, 270
*Child's Play* (Hill) **184**, 304
*Child's Play* (Campbell) **81**, 250
*Chill and the Kill, The* (Fleming) **120**, 285
*Chill, The* (Macdonald) **121**, 330
*China Expert, The* (Delving) **151**, 266
*Chinese Jar Mystery, The* (Strange) **43**, 371
*Chinese Puzzle, The* (Burton) **104**, 242
*Choice, The* (MacDonald) **34**, 329
*Choose Your Weapon* (Loder) **52**, 324
*Christmas Rising* (Serafin) **170**, 366
*Christmas Stalkings: Tales of Yuletide Murders* (MacLeod, ed.) **206**, 333, 386
*Chuckling Fingers, The* (Seeley) **70**, 365
*Claverton Mystery, The* (Rhode) **41**, 219, 357
*Clear the Fast Lane* (Rutherford) **138**, 362
*Click of the Gate, The* (Campbell) **37**, 250
*Client Privilege* (Tapply) **201**, 374
*Client, The* (Russell) **148**, 359
*Clock in the Hatbox, The* (Gilbert) **58**, 297
*Clock That Wouldn't Stop, The* (Ferrars) **93**, 279
*Clocks, The* (Christie) **120**, 255
*Clubbable Woman, A* (Hill) **135**, 304
*Clutch of Constables* (Marsh) **130**, 335
*Clutch of Vipers, A* (Scott) **157**, 364
*Cobweb* (Flower) **141**, 287
*Cockroach Sings, The* (Campbell) **79**, 250
*Coffin and the Paper Man* (Butler) **197**, 247
*Coffin for Charley, A* (Butler) **208**, 247
*Coffin in Fashion* (Butler) **186**, 247
*Coffin in the Black Museum* (Butler) **192**, 248
*Coffin on Murder Street* (Butler) **201**, 248
*Coffin on the Water* (Butler) **181**, 248
*Coffin Underground* (Butler) **189**, 248
*Cold Light of Day* (Page) **173**, 346
*Cold Steal* (Tilton) **65**, 376
*Coldness of Killers, The* (Hall) **205**, 303
*Colour of Murder, The* (Symons) **104**, 373
*Colour Scheme* (Marsh) **73**, 335
*Come and Be Killed* (Ferrars) **185**, 279
*Come and Be Killed!* (Smith) **78**, 367
*Come Out, Come Out, Whoever You Are* (McCann) **137**, 338
*Come to Judgement* (Strange) **84**, 371

*Company She Kept, The* (Eccles) **207**, 274
*Concrete Evidence* (Russell) **142**, 360
*Condemned, The* (Carmichael) **128**, 251
*Condition Purple* (Turnbull) **191**, 377
*Conduct of a Member* (Gielgud) **126**, 296
*Confession* (Carmichael) **115**, 251
*Conflict of Interests, A* (Ashford) **193**, 230
*Conviction of Guilt, A* (Matthews) **209**, 337
*Convivial Codfish, The* (MacLeod) **176**, 331
*Cool Killing, A* (Murray) **187**, 344
*Cool Sleeps Balaban* (MacKenzie) **120**, 331
*Copper, Gold and Treasure* (Williams) **168**, 381
*Coppergold* (Winslow) **156**, 381
*Copperhead* (Henderson) **141**, 304
*Corkscrew* (Wood) **189**, 382
*Corpse and the Lady, The* (Strange) **57**, 371
*Corpse Had Red Hair, The* (Campbell) **89**, 250
*Corpse in a Gilded Cage, A* (Barnard) **175**, 234
*Corpse in Canonicals* (Cole) **33**, 261
*Corpse in Ozark's Pond, The* (MacLeod) **183**, 332
*Corpse in the Car, The* (Rhode) **46**, 357
*Corpse Now Arriving, The* (Hinxman) **171**, 307
*Corridors of Guilt* (Hilton) **174**, 306
*Counsellor Heart, The* (Winslow) **162**, 381
*Counterpoint Murder* (Cole) **67**, 261
*Counterstroke* (Garve) **155**, 293
*Courtier to Death* (Gilbert) **49**, 297
*Cousin Removed, A* (Forsythe) **205**, 291
*Cover-Up Story* (Babson) **138**, 231
*Crack of Dawn* (Ford) **76**, 290
*Cracking Open a Coffin* (Butler) **206**, 248
*Crackpot* (Loraine) **207**, 328
*Crackshot* (Busby) **198**, 246
*Craig Poisoning Mystery, The* (Fielding) **33**, 284
*Creeping Flesh, The* (Rutherford) **119**, 362
*Cretan Counterfeit, The* (Farrer) **97**, 216, 278
*Crime and Again* (Stout) **108**, 368, 387
*Crime and the Crystal, The* (Ferrars) **178**, 279
*Crime at Guildford* (Crofts) **46**, 263
*Crime at Honotassa, The* (Eberhart) **117**, 271
*Crime Conductor, The* (MacDonald) **37**, 329
*Crime Counter Crime* (Lorac) **48**, 326
*Crime in Threadneedle Street* (Davis) **129**, 265
*Crime in Time, A* (Burton) **100**, 243
*Crime of the Century, The* (Abbot) **35**, 226
*Crime on her Hands* (Stout) **61**, 368
*Crime on the Kennet* (Alington) **59**, 228
*Crime Remembered, A* (Ashford) **187**, 230
*Crime Wave* (Russell) **144**, 360
*Crime Wave: World's Winning Short Stories 1981* (Anon) **167**, 228, 386
*Criminal C. O. D.* (Taylor) **67**, 375
*Crisscross* (Flower) **150**, 287
*Croaking of the Raven, The* (Lyall) **197**, 329
*Crook O'Lune* (Lorac) **96**, 326
*Crooked House* (Christie) **85**, 255
*Crossed Skis* (Carnac) **93**, 253
*Cruise of a Death Time, The* (Babson) **173**, 231
*Cry on my Shoulder* (Howard) **134**, 309
*Crying Sisters, The* (Seeley) **65**, 365
*Crystallised Carbon Pig, The* (Wainwright) **125**, 378
*Cuckoo Line Affair, The* (Garve) **94**, 293
*Cup and the Lip, The* (Ferrars) **149**, 279
*Curious Affair of the Third Dog, The* (Moyes) **143**, 342
*Curious Mr Tarrant, The* (King) **47**, 319, 386
*Curtain: Poirot's Last Case* (Christie) **149**, 256
*Curtains for Three* (Stout) **91**, 368, 387
*Cut Direct, The* (Tilton) **57**, 376

*Damned Spot, The* (Adams) **57**, 227
*Danger by my Side* (MacKinnon) **88**, 331
*Danger From the Dead* (Ferrars) **201**, 279
*Danger Money* (Eberhart) **149**, 271
*Danger Money* (Russell) **128**, 360
*Dangerous Cargo* (Footner) **45**, 288
*Dangerous Conceits* (Moore) **188**, 341
*Dangerous Domicile* (Lorac) **105**, 326
*Dangerous Place to Dwell, A* (Russell) **157**, 360
*Dangerous to Know* (Babson) **163**, 231
*Dark Lady* (Farjeon) **57**, 276
*Dark Night Offshore, A* (Gagnon) **181**, 292
*Dark Ships, The* (Footner) **53**, 288
*Dark Wheel, The* (MacDonald) **83**, 330
*Darkening Glass, The* (Wainwright) **129**, 378
*Darker Side of Death, The* (Russell) **178**, 360, 387
*Day of the Adder, The* (Fitzgerald) **120**, 285
*Day of the Donkey Derby, The* (Fleming) **155**, 286
*Day of Wrath* (Valin) **172**, 377
*Daylight Robbery* (Russell) **155**, 360
*Dead Against the Lawyers* (Jeffries) **123**, 312
*Dead Are Prowling, The* (Markham) **44**, 334
*Dead Ball* (Cork) **188**, 263
*Dead Centre* (Wood) **180**, 382
*Dead Clever* (Jeffries) **191**, 312
*Dead Crazy* (Pickard) **192**, 354
*Dead Drunk* (Howard) **145**, 309
*Dead End* (Perry) **153**, 352
*Dead End* (Strange) **95**, 371
*Dead Ernest* (Tilton) **76**, 376
*Dead Faces Laughing* (Delman) **186**, 266
*Dead Giveaway, A* (Allan) **164**, 228
*Dead Heat* (Russell) **183**, 360
*Dead in the Water* (Wood) **174**, 382
*Dead Knock* (Turnbull) **169**, 377
*Dead Letter* (Valin) **169**, 378
*Dead Liberty, A* (Aird) **182**, 227
*Dead Lock* (Page) **201**, 346
*Dead Man's Bay* (Arley) **108**, 229
*Dead Man's Bluff* (Jeffries) **135**, 312
*Dead Man's Folly* (Christie) **103**, 256
*Dead Man's Hat* (Footner) **39**, 288
*Dead Man's Heath* (Farjeon) **42**, 276
*Dead Man's Watch* (Cole) **36**, 261
*Dead Meat* (Tapply) **188**, 374
*Dead Men at the Folly* (Rhode) **38**, 357
*Dead Men Don't Ski* (Moyes) **109**, 218, 342
*Dead Men's Plans* (Eberhart) **95**, 271
*Dead of the Night, The* (Carmichael) **101**, 251
*Dead on Course* (Gregson) **202**, 302
*Dead on Sunday* (Orde) **207**, 346
*Dead on the Track* (Rhode) **73**, 357
*Dead Spit* (Edmonds) **192**, 274
*Dead Stop* (Burton) **73**, 243
*Dead Trouble* (Devine) **137**, 268
*Dead Water* (Marsh) **120**, 335
*Dead Winter* (Tapply) **198**, 374
*Deadheads* (Hill) **173**, 304
*Deadline* (Russell) **137**, 360
*Deadlock* (Busby) **137**, 246
*Deadly Beloved* (Strange) **93**, 371
*Deadly Discretion* (Ramsay) **143**, 356
*Deadly Jest, The* (Markham) **48**, 335
*Deadly Joker, The* (Blake) **119**, 239
*Deadly Marriage, A* (Jeffries) **127**, 312
*Deadly Night-Cap* (Carmichael) **94**, 251
*Deadly Petard* (Jeffries) **171**, 312
*Deadly Reunion* (Ashford) **202**, 230
*Deadly Secret* (Abbot) **74**, 226
*Deadly Sickness, A* (Penn) **178**, 350
*Deadly Sunshade, The* (Taylor) **69**, 375
*Deaf-Mute Murders, The* (Loder) **49**, 324
*Dear Dead Woman* (Gilbert) **64**, 297
*Death Against the Clock* (Gilbert) **105**, 297
*Death among the Dunes* (Infante) **198**, 311
*Death and the Chapman* (Sedley) **202**, 365
*Death and the Chaste Aprentice* (Barnard) **193**, 235
*Death and the Dancing Footman* (Marsh) **70**, 335
*Death and the Dogwalker* (Orde) **199**, 346
*Death and the Dutch Uncle* (Moyes) **129**, 342
*Death and the Joyful Woman* (Peters) **115**, 353
*Death and the Princess* (Barnard) **168**, 235
*Death and the Rembrancer* (Lyall) **188**, 329
*Death and the Sky Above* (Garve) **96**, 293
*Death and the Trumpets of Tuscany* (Jones) **188**, 315
*Death at Breakfast* (Rhode) **49**, 357
*Death at Charity's Point* (Tapply) **177**, 374
*Death at Dyke's Corner* (Lorac) **64**, 326
*Death at Low Tide* (Burton) **56**, 243
*Death at the Bar* (Marsh) **64**, 335
*Death at the Club* (Burton) **52**, 243
*Death at the Cross Roads* (Burton) **42**, 243
*Death at the Dolphin* (Marsh) **126**, 335
*Death at the Helm* (Rhode) **68**, 357
*Death at the Horse Show* (Loder) **46**, 324
*Death at the Wheel* (Loder) **40**, 324
*Death Before Dinner* (Lorac) **82**, 326
*Death Beside the Seaside* (Babson) **169**, 231
*Death by Degrees* (Wright) **207**, 384
*Death By Hoax* (Black) **146**, 238
*Death Came Softly* (Lorac) **72**, 326
*Death Card, The* (Satterthwait) **209**, 364
*Death Comes as the End* (Christie) **76**, 256
*Death Comes to Perigord* (Ferguson) **36**, 278
*Death Counts Three* (Carmichael) **98**, 251
*Death for Old Time's Sake* (Orde) **203**, 346
*Death Framed in Silver* (Campbell) **53**, 250
*Death from a Top Hat* (Rawson) **58**, 356
*Death Fuse* (Russell) **162**, 360
*Death Has a Cold Nose* (Edmonds) **208**, 274
*Death Has Green Fingers* (Black) **138**, 238
*Death in a Cold Climate* (Barnard) **162**, 235
*Death in a Duffle Coat* (Burton) **102**, 243
*Death in a Sleeping City* (Wainwright) **122**, 378
*Death in Arms* (Philmore) **60**, 354
*Death in Autumn* (Nabb) **177**, 345
*Death in Fancy Dress* (Gilbert) **41**, 298
*Death in Fashion* (Babson) **178**, 232
*Death in Grease-Paint* (Palmer) **102**, 347
*Death in Green* (Infante) **204**, 311
*Death in Irish Town, A* (Scott) **175**, 364
*Death in Purple Prose* (Barnard) **184**, 235
*Death in Shallow Water* (Burton) **82**, 243
*Death in Springtime* (Nabb) **174**, 345
*Death in the Clouds* (Christie) **47**, 256
*Death in the Coverts* (Jeffries) **125**, 312
*Death in the Hop Fields* (Rhode) **52**, 357
*Death in the Old Country* (Wright) **177**, 384
*Death in the Quarry* (Cole) **44**, 262
*Death in the Thicket* (Loder) **38**, 325
*Death in the Tunnel* (Burton) **48**, 243
*Death in the Winter Garden* (Lyall) **208**, 329
*Death in the Wrong Bed* (Farrar) **119**, 278
*Death in the Wrong Room* (Gilbert) **80**, 298
*Death in Time, A* (Lyall) **185**, 329
*Death in Triplicate* (Lorac) **105**, 326
*Death Invades the Meeting* (Rhode) **75**, 357
*Death is My Bridegroom* (Devine) **130**, 268
*Death Knocks Three Times* (Gilbert) **84**, 298
*Death Launch* (Infante) **207**, 311
*Death Leaves a Diary* (Carmichael) **92**, 251
*Death Leaves No Card* (Burton) **58**, 243
*Death Lives Next Door* (Butler) 219
*Death Mask* (Peters) **109**, 353
*Death of a Celebrity* (Footner) **57**, 288
*Death of a Doxy* (Stout) **127**, 368
*Death of a Dude* (Stout) **134**, 368
*Death of a Dutchman* (Nabb) **169**, 345
*Death of a Fat God* (Keating) **119**, 316
*Death of a Fire-Raiser* (Davis) **146**, 265
*Death of a Good Woman* (Eccles) **191**, 274
*Death of a Lady Killer* (Carnac) **109**, 253
*Death of a Minor Character* (Ferrars) **171**, 279
*Death of a Nymph* (Delman) **181**, 266
*Death of a Philanderer* (Meynell) **129**, 341
*Death of a Saboteur* (Footner) **74**, 288
*Death of a Salesperson and Other Untmely Exits* (Barnard) **191**, 235, 386
*Death of a Sardine* (Fleming) **119**, 286
*Death of a Skin Diver* (Jay) **121**, 312
*Death of a Star* (Cole) **39**, 262
*Death of An Editor* (Loder) **34**, 325
*Death of an Englishman* (Nabb) **167**, 345
*Death of an Old Goat* (Barnard) **147**, 235
*Death of an Unknown Man* (Bringle) **185**, 241
*Death of John Tait* (Fielding) **38**, 284
*Death of Miss X* (McMullen) **92**, 339
*Death of Mr Dodsley* (Ferguson) **53**, 278
*Death of Mr. Gantley* (Burton) **37**, 243
*Death of Two Brothers* (Burton) **68**, 243
*Death off the Fairway* (Adams) **51**, 227
*Death on a Hot Summer Night* (Infante) **192**, 311
*Death on Deadline* (Goldsborough) **191**, 301
*Death on My Left* (MacDonald) **39**, 329
*Death on Sunday* (Rhode) **61**, 357
*Death on the Agenda* (Moyes) **116**, 342
*Death on the Board* (Rhode) **53**, 357
*Death on the Boat-Train* (Rhode) **65**, 357
*Death on the High C's* (Barnard) **152**, 235
*Death on the Nile* (Christie) **55**, 256
*Death on the Way* (Crofts) **38**, 263
*Death Paints a Picture* (Burton) **114**, 243
*Death Pays a Dividend* (Rhode) **59**, 357
*Death Speaks Softly* (Fraser) **185**, 291
*Death Swap* (Babson) **177**, 232
*Death Takes a Detour* (Burton) **107**, 243
*Death Takes a Flat* (Burton) **66**, 243
*Death Takes a Wife* (Gilbert) **109**, 298
*Death Takes the Living* (Burton) **84**, 243
*Death Takes Time* (Jeffries) **209**, 313
*Death Trap* (Carmichael) **136**, 251
*Death Trick* (Jeffries) **188**, 313
*Death Warmed Up* (Babson) **168**, 232
*Death Wears a Mask* (Gilbert) **134**, 298
*Death Wishes* (Loraine) **172**, 328
*Deathless and the Dead, The* (Clarke) **152**, 260
*Death's Long Shadow* (Penn) **202**, 350
*Deathwater* (Infante) **201**, 311
*Deceitful Death* (Penn) **172**, 350
*Decent Killer, A* (Hart) **202**, 303
*Deceptive Appearance, A* (Malcolm) **203**, 333
*Deep and Crisp and Even* (Turnbull) **165**, 377
*Deep Blue Seize, The* (McLarty) **193**, 339
*Deep Pocket* (Kenyon) **154**, 318
*Descent into the Dark* (Ramsay) **147**, 356
*Designs on Life* (Ferrars) **162**, 279, 386
*Desire to Kill* (Campbell) **44**, 250
*Desolation Point* (Puckett) **208**, 355
*Destination Unknown* (Christie) **98**, 256
*Detective Ben* (Farjeon) **49**, 276
*Detectives in Gum Boots* (East) **51**, 269
*Devalino Caper, The* (Russell) **153**, 359
*Devereux Court Mystery, The* (Burton) **46**, 243
*Devil and the C. I. D., The* (Lorac) **55**, 326
*Devil at Your Elbow* (Devine) **125**, 267
*Devil Drives, The* (Markham) **37**, 335
*Devil Finds Work, The* (Delving) **134**, 267
*Devil Is Dead, The* (Lewis) **192**, 320
*Devil Man, The* (Wallace) **35**, 379
*Devil's Reckoning* (Burton) **83**, 243
*Devil's Stronghold, The* (Ford) **83**, 290
*Dial Death* (Russell) **153**, 360
*Diamond Ransom Murders, The* (Child) **45**, 254
*Die By the Book* (Meynell) **124**, 341
*Die in the Dark* (Gilbert) **81**, 298
*Die Laughing* (McGerr) **93**, 338
*Die Like a Man* (Delving) **136**, 267
*Died in the Wool* (Marsh) **76**, 335
*Diplomatic Corpse* (Taylor) **91**, 375
*Disappearances of Uncle David, The* (Farjeon) **85**, 276
*Dishonour Among Thieves* (Lorac) **108**, 326
*Displaced Person* (Hilton) **186**, 306
*Disposal of the Living, The* (Barnard) **179**, 235
*Distant Banner, A* (Lewis) **152**, 320
*Distant View of Death, A* (Scott) **164**, 364

*Divers Diamonds* (Dekker) **135**, 266
*Divided We Fall* (Burgess) **109**, 242
*Doctors Also Die* (Devine) **116**, 267
*Dog It Was That Died, The* (Lorac) **92**, 326
*Dog's Body* (Edmonds) **190**, 275
*Domestic Affair, A* (Russell) **174**, 360
*Don't Open the Door!* (Gilbert) **77**, 298
*Door Closed Softly, A* (Campbell) **60**, 250
*Doorbell Rang, The* (Stout) **124**, 369
*Dorothy Parker Murder Case, The* (Baxt) **180**, 236
*Double Blackmail* (Cole) **60**, 262
*Double Crime, The* (Farjeon) **96**, 276
*Double Deal* (Russell) **150**, 361
*Double Entry* (McKinlay) **204**, 338
*Double Exposure* (MacKenzie) **119**, 331
*Double Fault* (Meynell) **123**, 341
*Double for Death* (Stout) **66**, 369
*Double Hit* (Russell) **143**, 361
*Double Take* (Lewis) **147**, 320
*Double Turn, The* (Carnac) **102**, 253
*Doubly Dead, The* (Ferrars) **119**, 280
*Doubtful Motives* (Gagnon) **185**, 292
*Dr. Tancred Begins* (Cole) **46**, 262
*Dreadful Hollow, The* (Blake) **94**, 239
*Drink This* (Dewhurst) **162**, 268
*Drowned Rat* (Ferrars) **148**, 280
*Dumb Witness* (Christie) **53**, 256
*Dummy Run* (Russell) **192**, 361
*Dupe* (Cody) **164**, 261
*Dutch Blue Error, The* (Tapply) **179**, 374
*Dutch Courage* (Perry) **155**, 352
*Dwell in Danger* (Lewis) **168**, 321

*Early Morning Murder* (Burton) **77**, 244
*Easy to Kill* (Footner) **35**, 288
*El Rancho Rio* (Eberhart) **138**, 271
*Element of Chance* (Page) **148**, 346
*Elephant Never Forgets, The* (White) **54**, 379
*Elephants Can Remember* (Christie) **142**, 256
*Eleven Came Back* (Seeley) **73**, 365
*Eleventh Little Nigger, The* (Jacquemard-Sénécal) **157**, 311
*Ellery Queen's 13th Choice* (Queen, ed.) **112**, 355, 387
*Ellery Queen's 14th Choice* (Queen, ed.) **114**, 355, 387
*Ellery Queen's Awards Eighth Series* (Queen, ed.) **100**, 355, 387
*Ellery Queen's Awards Eleventh Series* (Queen, ed.) **105**, 355, 387
*Ellery Queen's Awards Ninth Series* (Queen, ed.) **102**, 355, 387
*Ellery Queen's Awards Tenth Series* (Queen, ed.) **103**, 355, 387
*Ellery Queen's Awards Twelfth Series* (Queen, ed.) **107**, 355, 387
*Embarrassing Death, An* (Jeffries) **121**, 313
*Emergency Exit* (Carmichael) **104**, 251
*Encore Murder* (Babson) **193**, 232
*End of a Good Woman* (Hinxman) **151**, 307
*End of an Ancient Mariner* (Cole) **42**, 262
*End of an Author* (Farjeon) **57**, 276
*End of Chapter* (Blake) **104**, 239
*End of Solomon Grundy, The* (Symons) **121**, 373
*End of the Track, The* (Garve) **102**, 293
*Endangered Species* (Cork) **206**, 263
*Endless Night* (Christie) **128**, 256
*Enemy in the House* (Eberhart) **119**, 271
*Enough to Kill a Horse* (Ferrars) **100**, 217, 280
*Enter Certain Murderers* (Woods) **124**, 383
*Epitaph for Joanna* (Howard) **139**, 309
*Equal Antagonism* (Pereira) **148**, 351
*Error of Judgement* (Lewis) **137**, 321
*Error of the Moon* (Woods) **119**, 383
*Escape the Night* (Eberhart) **77**, 271
*Essex Murders, The* (Loder) **33**, 325
*Eve of the Wedding, The* (Black) **163**, 238
*Even in the Best Families* (Stout) **90**, 217, 369
*Even Yuppies Die* (Babson) **209**, 232
*Every Inch a Lady: a Murder of the Fifties* (Fleming) **153**, 286
*Every Second Thursday* (Page) **166**, 347
*Evidence of the Accused* (Jeffries) **115**, 313
*Evidence You Will Hear, The* (Jobson) **148**, 314
*Evil Intent* (Wainwright) **125**, 378
*Evil Under the Sun* (Christie) **68**, 256
*Exceptional Corpse, An* (Adam) **206**, 226
*Exhibit Number Thirteen* (Jeffries) **117**, 313
*Exit John Horton* (Farjeon) **61**, 276
*Exit Laughing* (Palmer) **98**, 347
*Exit Lines* (Hill) **175**, 304
*Exit to Violence* (Jobson) **158**, 314
*Experiment With Death* (Ferrars) **166**, 280
*Eye for An Eye, An* (Telushkin) **197**, 376
*Eye Witness* (Strange) **116**, 371

*Face in the Stone, The* (Curzon) **193**, 264
*Fair Friday* (Turnbull) **171**, 377
*Fair Warning* (Eberhart) **51**, 271
*Fairly Dangerous Thing, A* (Hill) **141**, 305
*Fall Guy, The* (Perry) **139**, 352
*Falling Star* (Moyes) **121**, 343
*False Evidence* (Carmichael) **150**, 251
*False Front* (Meyer) **159**, 340
*False Scent* (Marsh) **113**, 336
*Family Affair* (Eberhart) **167**, 271
*Family Affair, A* (Stout) **151**, 369
*Family and Friends* (Page) **140**, 347
*Family Fortune* (Eberhart) **153**, 271
*Family Vault The* (MacLeod) **162**, 332
*Far Sands, The* (Garve) **114**, 293
*Far Side of the Dollar, The* (Macdonald) **123**, 330
*Fatal Fleece, A* (Jeffries) **203**, 313
*Fatal Fortune* (Babson) **187**, 232
*Fatal in My Fashion* (McGerr) **99**, 338
*Fatal Opinions* (Murray) **202**, 344
*Fatal Shadow, A* (Black) **172**, 237
*Fate at the Fair* (Burton) **40**, 244
*Fate Laughs* (Adams) **47**, 227
*Fate of Jane Mackenzie, The* (Mavity) **41**, 338
*Father Hunt, The* (Stout) **130**, 369
*Father, Forgive Me* (Burden) **208**, 242
*Fear the Light* (Ferrars) **112**, 280
*Feast of Death, A* (Penn) **192**, 350
*Feel the Force* (Donnelly) **207**, 269
*Fell Murder* (Lorac) **75**, 326
*Fell of Dark* (Hill) **137**, 305
*Fenokee Project, The* (Lewis) **138**, 321
*Ferguson Affair, The* (Macdonald) **115**, 330
*Festival!* (Butterworth) **151**, 248
*Fetch Out No Shroud* (Murray) **196**, 344
*Fifth Cord, The* (Devine) **127**, 267
*Fighting Chance, A* (Eberhart) **184**, 271
*Figure Away* (Taylor) **57**, 375
*File for Record* (Tilton) **75**, 376
*File on Lester, The* (Garve) **145**, 293
*Filmi, Filmi, Inspector Ghote* (Keating) **152**, 316
*Final Analysis of Dr. Stark, The* (Telushkin) **190**, 376
*Final Curtain* (Marsh) **80**, 336
*Final Cut* (Wright) **200**, 384
*Final Deduction, The* (Stout) **116**, 369
*Final Exposure* (Mansfield) **105**, 334
*Final Moments* (Page) **184**, 347
*Final Notice* (Valin) **167**, 378
*Fine Italian Hand, A* (Wright) **204**, 384
*Fingerprint, The* (Gilbert) **120**, 298
*Fingers of Fear* (MacDonald) **96**, 329, 386
*Fire in the Thatch* (Lorac) **78**, 326
*Firefly Gadroon* (Gash) **168**, 295
*First Gravedigger* (Paul) **168**, 348
*Five Little Pigs* (Christie) **72**, 256
*Five Million Dollar Prince, The* (Butterworth) **182**, 248
*Five Passengers from Lisbon* (Eberhart) **79**, 271
*Flashback* (Carmichael) **122**, 251
*Flashback* (Wood) **204**, 382
*Flight of a Witch* (Peters) **121**, 353
*Flower in the Desert, A* (Satterthwait) **206**, 364
*Flowers for a Dead Witch* (Butterworth) **137**, 248
*Flying Blind* (Campbell) **56**, 250
*Flying High* (Lyall) **201**, 329
*Folded Paper Mystery, The* (Footner) **32**, 288
*Follow the Sharks* (Tapply) **182**, 374
*Fool for a Client, A* (Lewis) **142**, 321
*Fool for Murder,A* (Babson) **172**, 232
*Fool's Gold* (Wood) **184**, 382
*Fool's Mate* (Perry) **165**, 352
*Foot in the Grave* (Ferrars) **142**, 280
*Footprints on the Ceiling, The* (Rawson) **61**, 356
*Footsteps Behind Me* (Gilbert) **94**, 298
*For Sale – With Corpse* (Gregson) **196**, 302
*For the Hangman* (Strange) **46**, 371
*Forests of the Night* (Moore) **184**, 341
*Fortnight By the Sea, A* (Page) **142**, 347
*Found Drowned* (Burton) **101**, 244
*Four Lost Ladies* (Palmer) **89**, 348
*Four Steps to Death* (Ramsay) **193**, 356
*Four Winds* (Adams) **75**, 227
*4.50 from Paddington* (Christie) **105**, 256
*Fourfingers* (Brock) **58**, 241
*Four-Ply Yarn* (Burton) **74**, 244
*Foursome, The* (Black) **155**, 238
*Fourth Bomb, The* (Rhode) **71**, 357
*Fox in the Forest, The* (Gregson) **205**, 302
*Frame-Up* (Garve) **120**, 293
*Free-Range Wife, A* (Kenyon) **172**, 318
*Friday Before Bank Holiday* (Davis) **121**, 265
*Frighteners,The* (Busby) **135**, 246
*Fringe Ending* (Moore) **202**, 342
*Frog in the Throat* (Ferrars) **164**, 280
*Funeral of Figaro* (Peters) **118**, 353
*Funnelweb* (West) **189**, 379
*Furnished for Murder* (Ferrars) **104**, 280

*Galloway Case, The* (Garve) **106**, 293
*Gallows' Foot* (Gielgud) **107**, 297
*Gallowsbird's Song, A* (Nielsen) **152**, 346
*Gambit* (Stout) **118**, 369
*Gamelord* (Parkes) **199**, 348
*Garvey's Code* (Busby) **155**, 246
*Gathering of Ghosts, A* (Lewis) **170**, 321
*Genial Stranger, The* (MacKenzie) **116**, 331
*Ghost in the Making* (Fitzgerald) **113**, 285
*Gigantic Shadow, The* (Symons) **107**, 373
*Gilt-Edged Cockpit, The* (Rutherford) **131**, 362
*Girl From the Mimosa Club, The* (Ford) **105**, 290
*Give a Corpse a Bad Name* (Ferrars) 218
*Give Death a Name* (Gilbert) **104**, 298
*Gladstone Bag, The* (MacLeod) **193**, 332
*Glass Slipper, The* (Eberhart) **58**, 271
*Go West, Inspector Ghote* (Keating) **165**, 316
*God Squad Bod, The* (Kenyon) **170**, 318
*Godwin Sideboard, The* (Malcolm) **176**, 333
*Goggle-Box Affair, The* (Gielgud) **118**, 297
*Going, Going, Gone!* (Taylor) **75**, 375
*Gold from Gemini* (Gash) **156**, 295
*Golden Cockatrice, The* (Black) **144**, 237
*Golden Deed, The* (Garve) **112**, 293
*Golden Spiders, The* (Stout) **97**, 369
*Goldilocks* (Johnson) **172**, 315
*Gondola Scam, The* (Gash) **174**, 295
*Goodbye Look, The* (Macdonald) **131**, 330
*Goodbye, Pussy* (Kemp) **158**, 318
*Gorgon's Smile, The* (Brandon) **204**, 241
*Gospel Lamb, The* (Scott) **162**, 365
*Gothic Pursuit* (Malcolm) **185**, 333
*Grail Tree, The* (Gash) **159**, 295
*Grand Prix Murder* (Rutherford) **99**, 362
*Grand Slam* (Perry) **162**, 352
*Grass Widow's Tale,The* (Peters) **128**, 353
*Grave for Two, A* (Carmichael) **153**, 251
*Grave Mistake* (Marsh) **156**, 336
*Great Southern Mystery, The* (Cole) **34**, 262
*Greek Tragedy* (Cole) **61**, 262
*Green Frontier, The* (Hilton) **167**, 219, 306
*Green Light, Red Catch* (Ryck) **141**, 363
*Greenmask* (Farjeon) **75**, 276
*Grim Death and the Barrow Boys* (Fleming) **138**, 286
*Ground for Suspicion* (Burton) **88**, 244
*Grouse Moor Mystery, The* (Ferguson) **45**, 278
*Guilt with Honour* (Ashford) **168**, 230
*Guilty Party* (Babson) **191**, 232
*Gwen John Sculpture, The* (Malcolm) **179**, 334

*Hallowe'en Party* (Christie) **131**, 257
*Hand in Glove* (Eberhart) **53**, 271
*Hand in Glove* (Marsh) **117**, 336
*Handful of Silver, A* (Strange) **100**, 371
*Hang the Consequences* (Meek) **176**, 339
*Hanged Man's House* (Ferrars) **144**, 280
*Hanging Woman, The* (Rhode) **35**, 357
*Hangman's Whip, The* (Eberhart) **67**, 272
*Hardway Diamonds Mystery,The* (Burton) **32**, 244
*Harm's Way* (Aird) **175**, 227
*Hasty Wedding* (Eberhart) **59**, 272
*Haven of Danger, A* (Penn) **207**, 350
*He Came by Night* (Gilbert) **75**, 298
*He Didn't Mind Hanging* (Mavity) **39**, 338
*He Died of Murder!* (Smith) **80**, 367
*Head Case* (Cody) **180**, 261
*Head of a Traveller* (Blake) **85**, 239
*Headless Lady, The* (Rawson) **67**, 356
*Healthy Way to Die, A* (Black) **150**, 238
*Heat of the Sun, The* (Birmingham) **152**, 237
*Heir to Lucifer* (Burton) **80**, 244
*Heir to Murder* (Burton) **95**, 244
*Hell's Belle* (Fleming) **130**, 286
*Help, Please* (Bahr) **148**, 234
*Hendon's First Case* (Rhode) **46**, 357
*Hercule Poirot's Christmas* (Christie) **58**, 257
*Hero for Leanda, A* (Garve) **108**, 293
*Hickory Dickory Dock* (Christie) **100**, 257
*High Jump* (Busby) **205**, 247
*Highway to Murder* (Howard) **143**, 309
*His Burial Too* (Aird) **143**, 227
*His Own Appointed Day* (Devine) **123**, 267
*Hobbema Prospect, The* (Hilton) **176**, 306
*Hobby of Murder, A* (Ferrars) **209**, 280
*Hole in the Ground, A* (Garve) **94**, 294
*Holiday at Half-Mast* (Farjeon) **54**, 276
*Holiday With a Vengeance* (Perry) **146**, 352
*Hollow Chest, The* (Tilton) **71**, 376
*Hollow, The* (Christie) **79**, 257
*Home to Roost* (Garve) **150**, 294
*Homicide Haven* (Turner) **47**, 377
*Homicide Trinity* (Stout) **118**, 369, 387
*Honey Trap, The* (Armstrong) **204**, 230
*Honolulu Murder Story* (Ford) **80**, 290
*Honourable Detective, The* (Ashford) **190**, 230
*Hostess to Death* (Wakefield) **56**, 379
*Hot Pursuit* (Scott) **153**, 364
*House Arrest* (Russell) **190**, 361
*House Is Falling, The* (Fitzgerald) **98**, 285
*House of Green Turf,The* (Peters) **130**, 353
*House of Shadows, The* (Farjeon) **73**, 276
*House of Soldiers, The* (Garve) **116**, 294
*House of Storm* (Eberhart) **85**, 272
*House on the Roof, The* (Eberhart) **47**, 272
*House Opposite, The* (Farjeon) **34**, 276
*House Over the Tunnel, The* (Farjeon) **91**, 276
*House Party Murder* (Ward) **42**, 379
*House That Died, The* (Gill) **101**, 301
*House That Jack Built, The* (Dewhurst) **173**, 268
*House With the Blue Door, The* (Footner) **72**, 288
*How to Live Dangerously* (Fleming) **146**, 286
*Hue and Cry* (Hamilton) **35**, 303
*Hung by an Eyelash* (Anson) **60**, 229
*Hunt the Tortoise* (Ferrars) **88**, 280
*Hunt to a Kill* (Russell) **131**, 361

*Hunt With the Hounds* (Eberhart) **90**, 272
*Hunter,The* (Busby) **179**, 247

*I Don't Like Cats* (Anson) **65**, 229
*I Give You Five Days* (Curzon) **172**, 264
*I Met Murder* (Ferrars) **180**, 280
*Icy Clutches* (Elkins) **201**, 275
*Ideal Crime, An* (Ashford) **180**, 230
*If Death Ever Slept* (Stout) **107**, 369
*Ill Met By Moonlight* (Ford) **53**, 290
*Illegal Solution, An* (Ashford) **199**, 230
*Illegal Tender* (Devine) **134**, 268
*Imagine a Man* (Fitzgerald) **103**, 285
*Impact of Evidence* (Carnac) **98**, 254
*Improbable Fiction, An* (Woods) **134**, 383
*In a Deadly Vein* (Culpan) **126**, 264
*In at the Kill* (Ferrars) **157**, 281
*In Face of the Verdict* (Rhode) **50**, 357
*In Loving Memory* (Page) **134**, 347
*In Rembrance of Rose* (Meek) **182**, 339
*In the Absence of the Body* (Bromley) **141**, 242
*In the Red* (Fleming) **115**, 286
*In the Shadow of Kings* (Kelly) **176**, 318
*Incomer, The* (Gaunt) **165**, 296
*Inevitable Fatality, An* (Lewis) **156**, 321
*Inner Ring, The* (Gagnon) **179**, 292
*Innocents at Home, The* (Hilton) **183**, 306
*Inside Job, An* (Allan) **157**, 228
*Insoluble* (Everton) **44**, 275
*Inspector Ghote Breaks an Egg* (Keating) **135**, 316
*Inspector Ghote Caught in Meshes* (Keating) **126**, 316
*Inspector Ghote Draws a Line* (Keating) **157**, 316
*Inspector Ghote Goes by Train* (Keating) **139**, 316
*Inspector Ghote Hunts the Peacock* (Keating) **128**, 317
*Inspector Ghote Plays a Joker* (Keating) **130**, 317
*Inspector Ghote Trusts the Heart* (Keating) **142**, 317
*Inspector Ghote's Good Crusade* (Keating) **124**, 317
*Inspector Rusby's Finale* (Markham) **40**, 335
*Instant Enemy, The* (Macdonald) **129**, 330
*Introducing C. B. Greenfield* (Kalen) **159**, 316
*Invisible Weapons* (Rhode) **56**, 358
*Invitation to an Inquest* (Hull) **90**, 310
*Invitation to Murder* (Ford) **99**, 290
*Iron Hand, The* (Tilton) **81**, 376
*Is She Dead Too?* (Gilbert) **99**, 219, 298
*Is Skin-Deep, Is Fatal* (Keating) **122**, 317
*Is There a Traitor in the House?* (McGerr) **123**, 338
*Issue of the Bishop's Blood* (McMahon) **142**, 339
*It Can't be My Grave* (Dean) **173**, 265
*It's Her Own Funeral* (Carnac) **91**, 254

*J for Jupiter* (Fuller) **52**, 292
*Jackdaw Mystery, The* (Grierson) **34**, 302
*Jade Woman* (Gash) **190**, 295
*James Knowland: Deceased* (Carmichael) **106**, 251
*John Brown's Body* (Lorac) **58**, 326
*Johnny Underground* (Moyes) **124**, 343
*Judas Pair, The* (Gash) **154**, 295
*Judge and Be Damned* (Edmonds) **199**, 275
*Judge Me Tomorrow* (Jobson) **154**, 315
*Judge Sums Up, The* (Farjeon) **71**, 276
*Judgement Deferred* (Ashford) **208**, 230
*Jury of One* (Eberhart) **115**, 272
*Just Another Angel* (Ripley) **190**, 359
*Just Deserts* (Jeffries) **163**, 313
*Justice Enough* (Carmichael) **102**, 251

*Keep Away From Water* (Campbell) **46**, 250
*Kick Start* (Rutherford) **144**, 362
*Kidnapping of Madame Storey and other stories, The* (Footner) **49**, 289, 386
*Kill Fee* (Paul) **180**, 349
*Kill in the Ring* (Loder) **58**, 325
*Kill or Cure* (Fleming) **128**, 286
*Killer Grew Tired, The* (Davis) **137**, 265
*Killing Cold, The* (Wood) **176**, 382
*Killing Frost, A* (Burgess) **114**, 242
*Killing Kindness, A* (Hill) **164**, 305
*Killing of Francie Lake, The* (Symons) **117**, 373
*Killing Term, A* (Sheffield) **207**, 366
*Killing to Hide, A* (Penn) **196**, 350
*Kind of Transaction, A* (Lewis) **203**, 321
*Kingston Black* (East) **112**, 270
*Knavish Crows, The* (Woods) **138**, 383
*Knife Between the Ribs, A* (Scott) **183**, 365
*Knife Ill-Used, A* (Penn) **199**, 350
*Knife in the Dark* (Cole) **70**, 262
*Knives Have Edges* (Woods) **129**, 383
*Knock, Knock, Who's There?* (Gilbert) **121**, 298

*Labours of Hercules, The* (Christie) **81**, 257, 386
*Lady in Black, The* (Clarke) **152**, 260
*Lady Incognito* (Walsh) **38**, 379
*Lady of Despair, The* (Grierson) **32**, 302
*Lady-Killer* (Gilbert) **91**, 298
*Laid Dead* (Cork) **197**, 263
*Lament for Two Ladies* (Hart) **199**, 303
*Last Appointment, The* (Howard) **90**, 309
*Last Coincidence, The* (Goldsborough) **199**, 301
*Last Ditch* (Marsh) **152**, 336
*Last First* (Hull) **80**, 310
*Last Gambit, The* (Delman) **199**, 266
*Last Respects* (Aird) **170**, 227
*Last Shot* (Loraine) **182**, 328
*Last Voyage* (Clarke) **163**, 260
*Last Walk Home* (Page) **170**, 347
*Last Will and Testament* (Cole) **50**, 219
*Last Will and Testament* (Ferrars) **155**, 281, 262
*Late Bill Smith, The* (Garve) **137**, 294
*Late Clara Beame, The* (Caldwell) **120**, 249
*Late of This Parish* (Eccles) **204**, 274
*Late Phoenix, A* (Aird) **135**, 228
*Law of the Streets, The* (Le Breton) **104**, 320
*Layers of Deceit* (Jeffries) **178**, 313
*Leaven of Malice, A* (Curzon) **159**, 264
*Left Leg, The* (Tilton) **68**, 376
*Left, Right and Centre* (Brandon) **181**, 241
*Left-Handed Death* (Hull) **78**, 310
*Legacy* (McKinlay) **206**, 338
*Legacy of Death* (Burton) **112**, 244
*Legacy of Death, A* (Penn) **205**, 350
*Legacy of Evil* (Clarke) **150**, 260
*Legal Fiction, A* (Ferrars) **120**, 281
*Leisure Pursuit* (Russell) **208**, 361
*Less than Kind* (Armstrong) **209**, 230
*Lesson in Crime and other stories* (Cole) **41**, 262, 386
*Let Sleeping Dogs Lie* (Edmonds) **205**, 275
*Let Well Alone* (Lorac) **98**, 326
*Lethal Sex, The* (MacDonald, ed.) **117**, 329, 386
*Let's Choose Executors* (Woods) **126**, 383
*Let's Talk of Wills* (Martin) **180**, 337
*Letter From the Dead* (Clarke) **154**, 260
*Liars' League, The* (Delman) **191**, 266
*Life and Death of Peter Wade, The* (Black) **144**, 238
*Life Cycle* (Carmichael) **155**, 251
*Lift Up the Lid* (Gilbert) **82**, 299
*Light Thickens* (Marsh) **170**, 336
*Lily-White Boys, The* (Fraser) **200**, 291
*Lime Pit, The* (Valin) **165**, 378
*Limited Vision, A* (Lewis) **173**, 321
*Link, The* (Carmichael) **116**, 251
*Link, The* (MacDonald) **32**, 329
*Lion's Ransom* (Loraine) **163**, 328
*Listening House, The* (Seeley) **59**, 365
*Little Darling, Dead, A* (Scott) **177**, 365
*Little Local Murder, A* (Barnard) **150**, 235
*Little Man Murders, The* (Loder) **51**, 325
*Little Murder Music, A* (Ramsay) **139**, 356
*Little Neighbourhood Murder, A* (Orde) **193**, 346
*Little Ripper* (West) **202**, 379
*Little Victims* (Barnard) **173**, 235
*Loaded Gun* (Ryck) **138**, 363
*Loaded Questions* (Loraine) **179**, 328
*Local Lads, The* (Scott) **171**, 365
*Long Chain of Death, The* (Wolf) **189**, 382
*Long Day Monday* (Turnbull) **206**, 377
*Long Echo, The* (Rutherford) **103**, 363
*Long Hard Cure, The* (Anthony) **158**, 229
*Long Hard Look, A* (Gair) **106**, 292
*Long Shadow, The* (Gilbert) **39**, 299
*Long Shadows* (Carnac) **106**, 254
*Long Short Cut, The* (Garve) **129**, 294
*Look Alive* (Burton) **85**, 244
*Look Your Last* (Strange) **75**, 372
*Looking Glass Murder, The* (Gilbert) **125**, 299
*Loose Connection, A* (Meek) **191**, 339
*Lord Edgware Dies* (Christie) **41**, 257
*Lord Mayor of Death, The* (Babson) **152**, 232
*Loss of the 'Jane Vosper', The* (Crofts) **48**, 217, 263
*Loss of the Culion, The* (Ashford) **166**, 231
*Lover Too Many, A* (Lewis) **131**, 321
*Luck Runs Out, The* (MacLeod) **164**, 332
*Lucky Policeman, The* (Penny) **56**, 351
*Lying Jade, The* (Ford) **96**, 290
*Lying Voices, The* (Ferrars) **97**, 281

*Madrid Underground* (Serafin) **168**, 366
*Maiden's Prayer* (Fleming) **105**, 286
*Make My Bed Soon* (Strange) **82**, 372
*Make No Bones* (Elkins) **204**, 275
*Malice Domestic* (Woods) **118**, 383
*Malice in Wonderland* (Blake) **66**, 239
*Malice Matrimonial* (Fleming) **108**, 286
*Mamur Zapt and the Camel of Destruction, The* (Pearce) **209**, 349
*Mamur Zapt and the Donkey-Vous, The* (Pearce) **196**, 349
*Mamur Zapt and the Girl in the Nile, The* (Pearce) **203**, 349
*Mamur Zapt and the Men Behind, The* (Pearce) **200**, 349
*Mamur Zapt and the Night of the Dog, The* (Pearce) **191**, 349
*Mamur Zapt and the Return of the Carpet, The* (Pearce) **188**, 349
*Mamur Zapt and the Spoils of Egypt, The* (Pearce) **206**, 349
*Man Alone* (Smith) **93**, 367
*Man Dead* (Jepson) **91**, 314
*Man From Nowhere, The* (Fleming) **113**, 286
*Man in Button Boots, The* (Gilbert) **45**, 299
*Man in the Sopwith Camel, The* (Butterworth) **146**, 248
*Man Lay Dead, A* (Marsh) 218
*Man Missing* (Eberhart) **98**, 272
*Man Next Door, The* (Eberhart) **74**, 272
*Man Overboard* (Crofts) **51**, 263
*Man Who Broke the Bank at Monte Carlo* (Butterworth) **172**, 249
*Man Who Killed Himself, The* (Symons) **127**, 373
*Man Who Lost His Wife, The* (Symons) **136**, 373
*Man Who Loved Lions, The* (White) **74**, 380
*Man Who Walked Away, The* (Jay) **107**, 312
*Man Who Was too Clever, The* (Gilbert) **47**, 299
*Man Who Wasn't There, The* (Gilbert) **53**, 299
*Man Whose Dreams Came True, The* (Symons) **130**, 373
*Man With a Calico Face* (Smith) **90**, 367
*Man's Illegal Life: A story of London's Parish Watch, 1722* (Heller) **175**, 303
*Man's Loving Family: A story of London's Parish Watch, 1727* (Heller) **182**, 303
*Man's Storm: A story of London's Parish Watch, 1703* (Heller) **178**, 304
*March Hare Murders, The* (Ferrars) **84**, 281
*Marrendon Mystery, The* (Fletcher) **34**, 287, 386
*Marriage is Murder* (Pickard) **189**, 354
*Marshal and the Madwoman, The* (Nabb) **188**, 345
*Marshal and the Murderer, The* (Nabb) **185**, 345
*Marshal at the Villa Torrini, The* (Nabb) **209**, 345
*Marshal Makes His Report, The* (Nabb) **203**, 345
*Marshal's Own Case, The* (Nabb) **196**, 346
*Martineau Murders, The* (Hull) **94**, 310
*Masks and Faces* (Curzon) **175**, 264
*Masquerade* (Pereira) **142**, 351
*Matter of Nerves, A* (Hull) **88**, 310
*Matter of Paradise, The* (Meggs) **150**, 340
*Mauve Front Door, The* (Meynell) **128**, 341
*May You Die in Ireland* (Kenyon) **123**, 218, 318
*Maze, The: An Exercise in Detection* (MacDonald) **37**, 217, 329
*Medicine Men, The* (Reznek) **197**, 356
*Megstone Plot, The* (Garve) **101**, 294
*Melora* (Eberhart) **112**, 272
*Men Die at Cyprus Lodge* (Rhode) **74**, 358
*Men of Subtle Ctraft* (Lewis) **186**, 321
*Menace on the Downs,The* (Burton) **35**, 244
*Message From Hong Kong* (Eberhart) **131**, 272
*Message From Sirius* (Jenkins) **114**, 222-3, 314
*Midnight Hag* (Fleming) **125**, 286
*Midnight House* (White) **71**, 380
*Midnight Lady and the Mourning Man, The* (Anthony) **134**, 229
*Midnight Murder* (Rodd) **34**, 359
*Midsummer Malice* (Fitzgerald) **95**, 285
*Might as Well be Dead* (Stout) **104**, 369
*Milk of Human Kindness* (Ferrars) **89**, 281
*Milk-Churn Murder, The* (Burton) **47**, 244
*Million Dollar Snapshot* (Howard) **136**, 309
*Mind Out* (Brandon) **200**, 241
*Minister of Injustice, The* (Culpan) **125**, 264
*Minute for Murder* (Blake) **80**, 217, 239
*Mirror Crack'd from Side to Side, The* (Christie) **118**, 257
*Miss Bones* (Fleming) **109**, 287
*Miss Lizzie* (Satterthwait) **197**, 364
*Miss Marple's Final Cases and two other stories* (Christie) **159**, 257, 386
*Miss Melville Regrets* (Smith) **186**, 366
*Miss Melville Returns* (Smith) **189**, 366
*Miss Melville Rides a Tiger* (Smith) **204**, 366
*Miss Pinnegar Disappears* (Gilbert) **93**, 299
*Miss Withers Regrets* (Palmer) **82**, 348
*Missing Aunt, The* (Cole) **55**, 262
*Missing Bronte, The* (Barnard) **171**, 236
*Missing From Her Home* (Gilbert) **130**, 299
*Mistakenly in Mallorca* (Jeffries) **146**, 313
*Modigliani Scandal, The* (Stone) **150**, 368
*Money for Murder* (Carmichael) **99**, 252
*Monkhurst Murder, The* (Grierson) **41**, 302
*Monkshood Murders, The* (Edington) **34**, 274
*Moon for Killers, A* (Black) **151**, 237
*Moondrop to Murder* (Hilton) **181**, 306
*Moonspender* (Gash) **183**, 295
*More Deadly Than the Male* (Meynell) **121**, 341
*More Deaths Than One* (Eccles) **200**, 274
*More Deaths Than One* (Stout) **84**, 369
*Morning after Death, The* (Blake) **126**, 239
*Mortal Affair, A* (Allan) **158**, 228
*Mortal Remains* (Page) **206**, 347
*Mortal Ruin* (Malcolm) **187**, 334
*Mortal Term* (Penn) **177**, 350
*Most Cunning Workmen* (Lewis) **176**, 321
*Most Deadly Hate* (Carmichael) **138**, 252
*Mother Hunt, The* (Stout) **120**, 369
*Mother's Boys* (Barnard) **164**, 236

*Motive, The* (Carmichael) **147**, 252
*Motor Rally Mystery, The* (Rhode) **40**, 358
*Mountain Cat, The* (Stout) **65**, 369
*Mouse Who Wouldn't Play Ball, The* (Gilbert) **72**, 299
*Mouthful of Sand, A* (Meek) **190**, 340
*Moving Finger, The* (Christie) **73**, 257
*Mr Babbacombe Dies* (Burton) **60**, 244
*Mr Big* (Kenyon) **147**, 319
*Mr Cromwell is Dead* (Ford) **60**, 290
*Mr T* (Russell) **152**, 219, 361
*Mr. Fred* (Hilton) **171**, 306
*Mr. Westerby Missing* (Burton) **66**, 244
*Mrs McGinty's Dead* (Christie) **92**, 257
*Mrs Warrender's Profession* (Cole) **57**, 262, 386
*Murder à la Mode* (Moyes) **118**, 343
*Murder Among Friends* (Ferrars) **79**, 281
*Murder Among Members* (Carnac) **99**, 254
*Murder as a Fine Art* (Carnac) **94**, 254
*Murder at Buzzard's Bay* (Abbot) **66**, 226
*Murder at Lilac Cottage* (Rhode) **66**, 358
*Murder at the Bookstall* (Holt) **45**, 308
*Murder at the College* (Whitechurch) **39**, 380
*Murder at the Moorings* (Burton) **38**, 244
*Murder at the Munition Works* (Cole) **66**, 262
*Murder at the Nineteenth* (Gregson) **191**, 302
*Murder at the Pageant* (Whitechurch) **33**, 380
*Murder at the Vicarage, The* (Christie) **33**, 257
*Murder Begets Murder* (Jeffries) **157**, 313
*Murder By Experts* (Gilbert) **50**, 299
*Murder By Matchlight* (Lorac) **77**, 326
*Murder by Proxy* (Carmichael) **126**, 252
*Murder by the Book* (Stout) **93**, 369
*Murder By the Mile* (Russell) **149**, 361
*Murder Comes Home* (Child) **41**, 254
*Murder Comes Home* (Gilbert) **88**, 299
*Murder Comes to Eden* (Ford) **102**, 290
*Murder Confounded* (Jeffries) **206**, 313
*Murder Down South* (Ford) **72**, 290
*Murder Fantastical* (Moyes) **126**, 343
*Murder for Lunch* (Murphy) **183**, 344
*Murder for Treasure* (Williams) **163**, 381
*Murder From Three Angles* (Loder) **44**, 325
*Murder Game* (Strange) **36**, 372
*Murder Gives a Lovely Light* (Strange) **71**, 372
*Murder Gone Mad* (MacDonald) **34**, 330
*Murder Has No Tongue* (Gilbert) **54**, 299
*Murder in a Manner of Speaking* (Jones) **191**, 315
*Murder in Absence* (Burton) **97**, 244
*Murder in China* (Epstein) **184**, 275
*Murder in Crown Passage* (Burton) **54**, 245
*Murder in E Minor* (Goldsborough) **185**, 301
*Murder in Good Measure* (Moore) **198**, 342
*Murder in Mesopotamia* (Christie) **50**, 216, 257
*Murder in Mortimer Square* (Grierson) **37**, 302
*Murder in Moscow* (Garve) **92**, 294
*Murder in Style* (Stout) **113**, 370
*Murder in Suffolk* (Fielding) **56**, 284
*Murder in the Coalhole* (Burton) **64**, 245
*Murder in the Mews* (Christie) **52**, 257, 386
*Murder in the Mill-Race* (Lorac) **94**, 327
*Murder in the Queen's Armes* (Elkins) **199**, 275
*Murder in the Sun* (Footner) **56**, 289
*Murder in Time* (Ferrars) **95**, 216, 281
*Murder in Vienna* (Lorac) **101**, 327
*Murder in Waiting* (Eberhart) **145**, 272
*Murder is Announced, A* (Christie) **89**, 257
*Murder is Easy* (Christie) **60**, 258
*Murder Is Incidental* (Rutherford) **114**, 363
*Murder Is the Pay-off* (Ford) **92**, 290
*Murder Keeps a Secret* (Murphy) **193**, 344
*Murder M.D.* (Burton) **73**, 245
*Murder May Follow* (Morrow) **112**, 342
*Murder May Pass Unpunished* (Everton) **51**, 275
*Murder Moves In* (Ferrars) **102**, 281
*Murder of a Bad Man* (Footner) **47**, 289
*Murder of a Chemist* (Burton) **49**, 245
*Murder of a Film Star* (Holt) **66**, 308
*Murder of a Man Afraid of Women* (Abbot) **54**, 226
*Murder of a Martinet* (Lorac) **91**, 327
*Murder of a Startled Lady* (Abbot) **50**, 226
*Murder of Caroline Bundy, The* (Campbell) **39**, 250
*Murder of Crows, A* (Haffner) **203**, 302
*Murder of Geraldine Foster, The* (Abbot) **32**, 226
*Murder of the Circus Queen, The* (Abbot) **40**, 226
*Murder of the Maharajah, The* (Keating) **162**, 317
*Murder of the Nightclub Lady, The* (Abbot) **37**, 226
*Murder on a Monument* (Lorac) **107**, 327
*Murder on Duty* (Burton) **93**, 245
*Murder on Show* (Babson) **140**, 232
*Murder on the Orient Express* (Christie) **43**, 258
*Murder One* (Howard) **138**, 309
*Murder Out of School* (Burton) **92**, 245
*Murder Rehearsal* (East) **41**, 270
*Murder Runs in the Family* (Footner) **44**, 289
*Murder Sails at Midnight* (Babson) **148**, 233
*Murder Saves Face* (Murphy) **202**, 344
*Murder Takes a Partner* (Murphy) **186**, 344
*Murder That Had Everything, The* (Footner) **61**, 289
*Murder Times Two* (Murphy) **198**, 344
*Murder to Music* (Edington) **33**, 274
*Murder Too Many, A* (Ferrars) **189**, 281
*Murder Unrecognised* (Burton) **99**, 245
*Murder, Murder, Little Star* (Babson) **154**, 219, 232
*Murder, Repeat Murder* (MacKinnon) **93**, 331
*Murder's Long Memory* (Jeffries) **200**, 314
*Murderer's Trail* (Farjeon) **36**, 277
*Murderer's Fen* (Garve) **125**, 294
*Murderer's Vanity* (Footner) **68**, 289
*Murderous Justice* (Haywood) **202**, 303
*Murder's a Waiting Game* (Gilbert) **140**, 299
*Murders and Acquisitions* (Murphy) **190**, 344
*Murders Anonymous* (Ferrars) **154**, 281
*Murky Shallows: A Story of the Venetian lagoon* (Low) **185**, 328
*Music Lovers, The* (Valin) **207**, 378
*Musical Comedy Crime, The* (Gilbert) **42**, 299
*My Brother's Killer* (Devine) **116**, 218, 267
*My Cousin Death* (McMullen) **166**, 339
*My Own Murderer* (Hull) **64**, 310
*My Search for Ruth* (Clarke) **147**, 260
*My Sister's Keeper* (Kelly) **204**, 318
*Mysterious Mademoiselle, The* (Grierson) **33**, 302
*Mystery at Friar's Pardon* (Porlock) **36**, 354
*Mystery at Greycombe Farm* (Rhode) **37**, 358
*Mystery at Olympia* (Rhode) **48**, 358
*Mystery at the Rectory* (Fielding) **51**, 284
*Mystery in Kensington Gore* (Porlock) **37**, 354
*Mystery in Red* (Grierson) **36**, 302
*Mystery in the Channel* (Crofts) **34**, 263
*Mystery in White* (Farjeon) **55**, 277
*Mystery Lady* (Russell) **205**, 361
*Mystery of the Creek, The* (Farjeon) **40**, 277
*Mystery of the Golden Angel, The* (Grierson) **39**, 302
*Mystery of the Smiling Doll, The* (Holt) **60**, 308
*Mystery on the Moor,The* (Farjeon) **33**, 277
*Mystery Tour* (Rutherford) **149**, 363

*N or M?* (Christie) **70**, 258
*Naked to the Grave* (Carmichael) **140**, 252
*Narrow Search, The* (Garve) **104**, 294
*Nasty Dose of Death, A* (Adam) **209**, 226
*Nation's Missing Guest, The* (Footner) **59**, 289
*Natural Causes* (Valin) **174**, 378
*Necessary Dealing, A* (Lewis) **193**, 322
*Necessary End, A* (Fraser) **178**, 291
*Necessary End, A* (Gielgud) **130**, 297
*Nemesis* (Christie) **139**, 258
*Never Look Back* (Eberhart) **91**, 272
*New Face in Hell* (Busby) **150**, 247
*New Made Grave, The* (Footner) **46**, 289
*New Year Resolution* (Cairns) **176**, 249
*Next of Kin* (Eberhart) **171**, 272
*Nice Cup of Tea, A* (Gilbert) **90**, 299
*Nice Day for a Funeral* (Howard) **141**, 309
*Nice Derangement of Epitaphs, A* (Peters) **122**, 353
*Nice Little Killing, A* (Gilbert) **145**, 299
*Nice Murderers, The* (Delman) **154**, 266
*Nice Neighbourhood, A* (Bahr) **144**, 234
*Nice Place to Die, A* (Culpan) **123**, 264
*Night Encounter* (Gilbert) **129**, 300
*Night Exercise* (Rhode) **72**, 358
*Night Ferry to Death* (Moyes) **180**, 343
*Night in Glengyle* (Ferguson) **42**, 278
*Night of Reckoning* (Strange) **108**, 372
*Night Run From Java* (Black) **159**, 238
*Night the Gods Smiled, The* (Wright) **171**, 384
*Night They Murdered Chelsea, The* (Hinxman) **176**, 308
*Nightmare in Dreamland* (Hinxman) **201**, 308
*Night's Black Agents* (Armstrong) **206**, 230
*Nine Bright Shiners, The* (Fraser) **187**, 291
*Nine Day's Murder* (MacKinnon) **78**, 331
*Nine Lives to Murder* (Babson) **205**, 233
*Nine o'Clock Tide* (Eberhart) **156**, 273
*Nineteen Red Roses* (Nielsen) **156**, 346
*Nineteenth Hole Mystery, The* (Adams) **60**, 227
*95 File, The* (Martin) **143**, 337
*Ninth Candle, The* (Ford) **112**, 289
*Ninth Life* (Ferrars) **122**, 281
*Nipped in the Bud* (Palmer) **93**, 348
*No Body* (Pickard) **186**, 354
*No Bones About It* (Fleming) **126**, 287
*No Cause to Kill* (Ramsay) **144**, 356
*No Dust in the Attic* (Gilbert) **117**, 300

*No Flowers by Request* (Palmer) **52**, 348
*No Light Came On* (Campbell) **72**, 250
*No Mask for Murder* (Garve) **89**, 217, 294
*No Mourning in the Family* (Philmore) **55**, 354
*No Murder of Mine* (Campbell) **68**, 250
*No Peace for the Wicked* (Ferrars) **125**, 282
*No Return Ticket* (Russell) **126**, 361
*No Sign of Life* (Delving) **156**, 267
*No Tears for Hilda* (Garve) **88**, 218, 294
*No Through Road* (Russell) **124**, 361
*Noose for a Lady* (Carmichael) **100**, 252
*Noose of Time, The* (Murray) **192**, 345
*Noose, The* (MacDonald) **32**, 219, 330
*Not a Leg to Stand on* (Burton) **76**, 245
*Nothing But Foxes* (Lewis) **153**, 322
*Nothing Is the Number When You Die* (Fleming) **122**, 287
*Notice of Death* (Penn) **168**, 350
*Nowhere Man* (Perry) **142**, 352
*Number Nineteen* (Farjeon) **94**, 277
*Nursemaid Who Disappeared, The* (MacDonald) **55**, 330

*Obelists En Route* (King) **43**, 320
*Obelists Fly High* (King) **45**, 217, 320
*Octagon House* (Taylor) **56**, 375
*Odd Flamingo, The* (Bawden) **97**, 217, 236
*Odd Job* (Flower) **145**, 288
*Of Malicious Intent* (Meynell) **131**, 341
*Of Singular Purpose* (Lewis) **144**, 322
*Of Unsound Mind* (Carmichael) **117**, 252
*Of Wilful Intent* (Johnson) **168**, 315
*Off With Her Head!* (Cole) **58**, 262
*Off With His Head* (Marsh) **103**, 336
*Offences aginst the Person* (Murray) **207**, 345
*Old Jew Mystery, The* (Adams) **50**, 227
*Old Lady Dies, An* (Gilbert) **44**, 300
*Old Man Mystery* (Farjeon) **42**, 277
*On the Edge* (Doliner) **157**, 269
*On the Inside* (Wood) **199**, 382
*Once Dying, Twice Dead* (Lewis) **175**, 322
*One Good Death Deserves Another* (Perry) **150**, 353
*100,000 Welcomes, The* (Kenyon) **134**, 318
*One Man's Murder* (Delman) **149**, 266
*One of Us Must Die* (Clarke) **155**, 260
*One Small Step* (Hill) **198**, 305
*One, Two, Buckle My Shoe* (Christie) **66**, 258
*One-Way Cemetery* (Hinxman) **154**, 308
*One-Way Ticket* (Howard) **154**, 309
*Opening Night* (Marsh) **91**, 336
*Operation Piracy* (Somers) **106**, 367
*...Or Be He Dead* (Carmichael) **108**, 250
*Or the Bambino Dies* (Inchbald) **178**, 310
*Orchids to Murder* (Footner) **77**, 289
*Ordeal by Innocence* (Christie) **107**, 258
*Organisation, The* (Anthony) **138**, 229
*Othello's Occupation* (Strong) **77**, 372
*Other Bullet, The* (Mavity) **33**, 338
*Other Devil's Name, The* (Ferrars) **182**, 282
*Other Shoe, The* (McMullen) **169**, 339
*Out for the Kill* (Gilbert) **112**, 300
*Out Goes She* (Stout) **95**, 370
*Out of Season* (Kenyon) **129**, 319
*Out of the Blackout* (Barnard) **177**, 236
*Outrageous Exposures* (Penn) **190**, 350
*Oval Table, The* (Farjeon) **78**, 277
*Over My Dead Body* (Stout) **66**, 216, 370
*Overture to Death* (Marsh) **59**, 336
*Owl Too Many, An* (MacLeod) **200**, 332

*Painted Devil, A* (Welcome) **189**, 379
*Palace Guard, The* (MacLeod) **169**, 332
*Pale Horse, The* (Christie) **116**, 258
*Pall for a Painter* (Lorac) **51**, 327
*Paper Chase, The* (Fielding) **45**, 284
*Paper Chase, The* (Symons) **101**, 373
*Paper Money* (Stone) **153**, 368
*Paper Tomb, The* (Donati) **106**, 269
*Paris Bit, The* (Marder) **127**, 334
*Part for a Poisoner* (Lorac) **83**, 327
*Part of Virtue, A* (Lewis) **149**, 322
*Parting Breath* (Aird) **154**, 228
*Parting, The* (Sheffield) **204**, 366
*Party at No. 5, The* (Smith) **98**, 367
*Pascoe's Ghost* (Hill) **158**, 305, 386
*Passenger to Frankfurt* (Christie) **135**, 258
*Passenger to Nowhere* (Gilbert) **123**, 300
*Passing Strange* (Aird) **163**, 228
*Passion in the Peak* (Hilton) **179**, 307
*Past Praying For* (Woods) **130**, 383
*Past Regret* (Babson) **198**, 233
*Path for Serpents, A* (Black) **202**, 238
*Patient in Cabin C, The* (Eberhart) **175**, 273
*Pattern of Violence* (Busby) **143**, 219, 247
*Pattern, The* (Eberhart) **54**, 273
*Payoff* (Howard) **151**, 309
*Pearl Choker* (East) **98**, 270
*Pearlhanger* (Gash) **177**, 295
*Penknife in my Heart, A* (Blake) **106**, 240
*Penny Murders, The* (Black) **157**, 239
*Perennial Boarder, The* (Taylor) **70**, 375
*Perfect Murder, The* (Keating) **121**, 218, 317
*Peril at End House* (Christie) **37**, 258
*Peril in the Pyrenees* (Farjeon) **79**, 277
*Perilous Sky, The* (Rutherford) **100**, 363
*Personal Possession, A* (Hart) **193**, 303
*Phantom Holiday* (Russell) **146**, 361
*Philadelphia Murder Story, The* (Ford) **77**, 290
*Photo-Finish* (Marsh) **163**, 336
*Photographs Have Been Sent to your Wife* (Loraine) **137**, 328

*Pick Your Victim* (McGerr) **81**, 338
*Picture of Death* (Lorac) **103**, 327
*Picture of the Victim* (Strange) **66**, 372
*Pictures of Perfection* (Hill) **209**, 305
*Pinch of Snuff, A* (Hill) **155**, 305
*Piper on the Mountain, The* (Peters) **125**, 354
*Plain Old Man, The* (MacLeod) **178**, 332
*Planning on Murder* (Williams) **205**, 381
*Platinum Cat, The* (Burton) **57**, 245
*Players and the Game, The* (Symons) **141**, 373
*Playground of Death* (Hilton) **164**, 307
*Playing Safe* (Dewhurst) **179**, 269
*Please Pass the Guilt* (Stout) **145**, 370
*Plot Against Roger Rider, The* (Symons) **143**, 374
*Plot Counter-Plot* (Clarke) **145**, 260
*Plymouth Cloak, The* (Sedley) **205**, 365
*Pocket Full of Rye, A* (Christie) **96**, 258
*Pointer to a Crime* (Fielding) **74**, 284
*Poirot's Early Cases* (Christie) **146**, 258, 386
*Poison for One* (Rhode) **44**, 358
*Poison Parsley* (Clarke) **159**, 260
*Poison Pool, The* (Hall) **202**, 303
*Poisoned Web, The* (Clarke) **158**, 260
*Policeman at the Door, A* (Carnac) **96**, 254
*Policeman in Armour* (Penny) **54**, 351
*Policeman's Evidence* (Penny) **58**, 351
*Policeman's Holiday* (Penny) **52**, 351
*Policemen in the Precinct* (Lorac) **85**, 219, 327
*Political Suicide* (Barnard) **180**, 236
*Port of Light* (Serafin) **185**, 366
*Post After Post-Mortem* (Lorac) **50**, 327
*Post Mortem* (Carmichael) **123**, 252
*Postern of Fate* (Christie) **144**, 258
*Posthumous Papers* (Barnard) **158**, 236
*Postmark Murder* (Eberhart) **103**, 273
*Prelude to Crime* (Farjeon) **83**, 277
*Premium on Death, A* (Lewis) **182**, 322
*Press of Suspects, A* (Garve) **90**, 294
*Presumption of Guilt* (Ashford) **176**, 231
*Pretty Lady* (Babson) **142**, 231
*Pretty Maids All in a Row* (Fraser) **182**, 291
*Pretty Pink Shroud, The* (Ferrars) **153**, 282
*Prime Target* (Russell) **180**, 362
*Prinvest London* (Gielgud) **123**, 297
*Priority Murder* (Ford) **73**, 290
*Prisoner's Friend* (Garve) **117**, 294
*Private Prosecution, A* (Dewhurst) **182**, 269
*Private Wound, The* (Blake) **129**, 240
*Proceed With Caution* (Rhode) **55**, 358
*Procession of Two* (Philmore) **67**, 354
*Progress of a Crime, The* (Symons) **113**, 374
*Proof of the Pudding* (Taylor) **78**, 375
*Protégé, The* (Armstrong) **136**, 230
*Punch with Care* (Taylor) **81**, 375
*Put Out That Star* (Carmichael) **103**, 252
*Puzzle of the Blue Banderilla, The* (Palmer) **54**, 348
*Puzzle of the Briar Pipe, The* (Palmer) **48**, 348
*Puzzle of the Happy Hooligan, The* (Palmer) **69**, 348
*Puzzle of the Silver Persian, The* (Palmer) **45**, 219, 348

*Q. E. D.* (Brock) **32**, 241
*Quest for K, The* (Curzon) **181**, 264
*Question of Degree, A* (Lewis) **146**, 219, 322
*Question of Murder, A* (Wright) **190**, 385
*Question of Principle, A* (Ashford) **183**, 231
*Question of Proof, A* (Blake) **46**, 216, 218, 240
*Question of TIme, A* (Carmichael) **107**, 252
*Queue Here for Murder* (Babson) **164**, 233
*Quiet Stranger, The* (Hilton) **177**, 307
*Quiet Woman, The* (Carmichael) **139**, 252

*R. I. P.* (MacDonald) **40**, 330
*R.S.V.P. Murder* (Eberhart) **125**, 273
*Rainblast* (Russell) **168**, 362
*Ransom for a Nude* (Black) **141**, 239
*Rapist, The* (Kenyon) **153**, 319
*Ready Revenge* (Arley) **113**, 229
*Reasonable Doubt* (Strange) **91**, 372
*Reasonable Man, A* (Busby) **140**, 247
*Reasons of Hate* (Welcome) **198**, 379
*Recalled to Life* (Hill) **204**, 305
*Recycled Citizen, The* (MacLeod) **185**, 332
*Red Snow at Darjeeling* (Blochman) **58**, 240
*Red Stain* (Loder) **36**, 325
*Red Threads* (Stout) **69**, 370
*Reel Murder* (Babson) **184**, 233
*Relative Distance, A* (Lewis) **165**, 322
*Relative to Poison* (Lorac) **80**, 327
*Relatively Dangerous* (Jeffries) **184** ,314
*Religious Body, The* (Aird) 218
*Remains to be Seen* (Butterworth) **150**, 219, 249
*Remarkable Case of Burglary, A* (Keating) **149**, 317
*Remote Control* (Carmichael) **134**, 252
*Renewable Virgin, The* (Paul) **174**, 349
*Requiem for a Dove* (Eccles) **197**, 274
*Requiem for Charles* (Carmichael) **113**, 252
*Rest You Merry* (MacLeod) **159**, 332
*Resurrection Man, The* (MacLeod) **204**, 332
*Return From the Dead* (Burton) **109**, 245
*Return Load* (Rutherford) **152**, 363
*Riddle of a Lady* (Gilbert) **102**, 300
*Riddle of Samson, The* (Garve) **98**, 295
*Riddle of the Roost, The* (Brock) **60**, 241
*Rift* (Cody) **189**, 261
*Rigging the Evidence* (Carnac) **100**, 254
*Right to Die, A* (Stout) **122**, 370
*Ring for a Noose* (Gilbert) **118**, 300
*Ring of Eyes, The* (Footner) **40**, 289
*Ringed With Fire* (Campbell) **73**, 250
*Riot* (Parkes) **183**, 348
*Ritual Bath, The* (Kellerman) **184**, 318
*Road to Folly* (Ford) **67**, 290
*Road to Rhuine* (Troy) **93**, 377
*Robbery Blue* (Busby) **131**, 247
*Robthorne Mystery, The* (Rhode) **43**, 358
*Rockefeller Gift, The* (Winslow) **168**, 381
*Rodent of Doubt, A* (Tapply) **185**, 374
*Roger Bennion's Double* (Adams) **69**, 227
*Room 37* (Howard) **135**, 310
*Room Number Six* (Farjeon) **68**, 277
*Root of All Evil* (Ferrars) **176**, 282
*Rope Enough* (Strange) **59**, 372
*Rope to Spare* (MacDonald) **38**, 330
*Rope's End – Rogue's End* (Lorac) **70**, 327
*Rosy Pastor, The* (Fitzgerald) **96**, 285
*Royston Affair, The* (Devine) **121**, 267
*Ruling Passion* (Hill) **143**, 305
*Rumanian Circle, The* (Black) **166**, 239
*Run Scared* (Eberhart) **121**, 273

*Sacrificial Pawn* (Ryck) **143**, 363
*Sad Cypress* (Christie) **64**, 259
*Sad Variety, The* (Blake) **121**, 240
*Safe Secret* (Carmichael) **120**, 253
*Salamander Chill, The* (Lewis) **189**, 322
*Salty Waters* (Murray) **189**, 345
*Sam's Elegy* (James) **207**, 311
*Sapphires on Wednesday* (Gair) **104**, 292
*Saturday Games* (Meggs) **149**, 340
*Saturday of Glory* (Serafin) **158**, 366
*Save the Witness* (McGerr) **89**, 338
*Scales of Justice* (Marsh) **99**, 336
*Scandal at School* (Cole) **48**, 262
*Scarecrow* (Fielding) **52**, 284
*Scarlet Button, The* (Gilbert) **75**, 300
*Scarlet Messenger, The* (Holt) **42**, 308
*Scent of Death* (Page) **178**, 347
*School for Murder* (Carmichael) **96**, 253
*Screaming Bones* (Burden) **191**, 242
*Sea Monks, The* (Garve) **119**, 295
*Sea-Change* (Loraine) **169**, 328
*Sealed Envelope, The* (Howard) **158**, 310
*Sealed-Room Murder* (Penny) **68**, 351
*Search for Sara, The* (Russell) **172**, 362
*Season of Snows and Sins* (Moyes) **138**, 343
*Second Confession, The* (Stout) **88**, 370
*Second Cousin Twice Removed* (Pereira) **145**, 351
*Second Time Is Easy, The* (Russell) **186**, 362
*Secret Dying, A* (Lewis) **205**, 322
*Secret of High Eldersham, The* (Burton) **33**, 245
*Secret Singing, A* (Lewis) **141**, 322
*Seeds of Hate, The* (Carmichael) **112**, 253
*Seeing Red* (Du Bois) **100**, 269
*Seek for Justice* (Lewis) **166**, 323
*Sense of Loyalty, A* (Ashford) **174**, 231
*Sensitive Case, A* (Wright) **196**, 385
*Serpent's Tooth* (Woods) **137**, 383
*Seven Dead* (Farjeon) **59**, 277
*Seven Deadly Sisters, The* (McGerr) **82**, 338
*Seven Sleepers, The* (Ferrars) **134**, 282
*Shadow in the House, The* (March) **50**, 334
*Shadow of Himself, A* (Delving) **140**, 267
*Shadow of Thirteen, The* (Farjeon) **85**, 277
*Shadow on the House* (Ford) **105**, 289
*Shadow Show* (Flower) **152**, 288
*Shadows in their Blood* (Babson) **202**, 233
*Shark Among Herrings* (Milner) **98**, 341
*She Faded into Air* (White) **69**, 380
*She Had to Have Gas* (Penny) **59**, 351
*She Shall Die* (Gilbert) **114**, 300
*Sheep, Goats and Soap* (Malcolm) **200**, 334
*Sheer Torture* (Barnard) **167**, 236
*Sheriff of Bombay, The* (Keating) **175**, 317
*Shield of Silence* (Balmer) **55**, 234
*Shock!* (Markham) **32**, 335
*Shooting of Dan McGrew, The* (Kenyon) **141**, 319
*Short Break in Venice* (Inchbald) **173**, 310
*Short List* (Philmore) **57**, 354
*Shortest Way to Hades, The* (Caudwell) **176**, 254
*Shot at Dawn* (Rhode) **45**, 358
*Shot Bolt* (Curzon) **187**, 264
*Shot in the Dark* (Ford) **85**, 290
*Shot on Location* (Jones) **197**, 315
*Shriek of Tyres, A* (Rutherford) **106**, 363
*Shrine of Murders, A* (Grace) **208**, 301
*Shroud for Delilah, A* (Fraser) **175**, 292
*Shroud of Darkness* (Lorac) **97**, 327
*Signal for Invasion* (Adams) **72**, 227
*Silent Speaker, The* (Stout) **80**, 370
*Silver Ghost, The* (MacLeod) **187**, 332
*Silver Sickle Case, The* (Brock) **55**, 241
*Simple Way of Poison, The* (Ford) **56**, 291
*Sinfully Rich* (Footner) **64**, 289
*Singing in the Shrouds* (Marsh) **108**, 336
*Singing Millionaire, The* (Pereira) **140**, 352
*Single Death, A* (Wright) **182**, 385
*Single Hair, A* (Adams) **53**, 227
*Sinister Inn* (Farjeon) **44**, 277
*Sir John Magill's Last Journey* (Crofts) **32**, 263
*Siren in the Night* (Ford) **75**, 291
*Sirens Sang of Murder, The* (Caudwell) **192**, 254
*Sittaford Mystery, The* (Christie) **35**, 259
*Sitting Ducks, The* (Meek) **174**, 340
*Situation Vacant* (Burton) **79**, 245
*Six Iron Spiders, The* (Taylor) **72**, 375
*Six Proud Walkers* (Fraser) **190**, 292
*Six-Letter Word for Death, A* (Moyes) **172**, 343
*Sixteenth Stair, The* (Lorac) **71**, 327
*Skeleton in Search of a Cupboard* (Ferrars) **169**, 282
*Skeleton in the Grass, The* (Barnard) **187**, 236
*Skeleton Staff* (Ferrars) **131**, 282
*Skin for Skin* (Rutherford) **129**, 363
*Sleep in a Ditch* (Birmingham) **155**, 237
*Sleep of the Unjust* (Ferrars) **198**, 282
*Sleep of the Unjust* (Meynell) **119**, 341
*Sleep While I Sing* (Wright) **185**, 385
*Sleeper, The* (Dewhurst) **188**, 269
*Sleepers of Erin, The* (Gash) **171**, 296
*Sleeping Beauty* (Macdonald) **144**, 331
*Sleeping Dogs, The* (Ferrars) **113**, 282
*Sleeping Murder: Miss Marple's Last Case* (Christie) **152**, 259
*Sleeping Tiger, The* (Devine) **128**, 268
*Sleight of Hand* (Armstrong) **201**, 230
*Slickensides: A Derbyshire Mystery* (Hilton) **185**, 307
*Slight Mourning* (Aird) **149**, 228
*Slightly Bitter Taste, A* (Carmichael) **130**, 253
*Slippery Staircase* (Lorac) **57**, 327
*Slocombe Dies* (Strong) **70**, 372
*Slyboots* (Flower) **147**, 288
*Small World of Murder, The* (Ferrars) **143**, 282
*Smartest Grave, The* (White) **114**, 222-3, 380
*Smell of Smoke, A* (Burton) **109**, 245
*Smiler with the Knife, The* (Blake) **61**, 240
*Smoke Detector* (Wright) **175**, 385
*Smoke Without Fire* (Ferrars) **197**, 282
*Snake in the Grass* (Gilbert) **97**, 300
*Snake on 99, The* (Farrar) **106**, 278
*Snares of the Enemy* (King) **177**, 320
*Snatch* (Markham) **51**, 335
*Snow Man* (Busby) **186**, 247
*Snowblind* (Haffner) **206**, 302
*Snowjob* (Wood) **208**, 382
*Snow-White Murder* (Ford) **65**, 291
*So Difficult to Die* (Matheson) **103**, 337
*So Soon Done For* (Babson) **157**, 233
*Sole Agent* (Benton) **136**, 236
*Solitary Child, The* (Bawden) **102**, 236
*Some Buried Caesar* (Stout) **60**, 370
*Some Die Eloquent* (Aird) **159**, 228
*Some Die Young* (Hart) **198**, 303
*Something in the Water* (MacLeod) **209**, 333
*Something Nasty in the Woodshed* (Gilbert) **70**, 300
*Something of the Night* (McMullen) **167**, 339
*Something the Cat Dragged In* (MacLeod) **175**, 333
*Something to Hide* (Burton) **94**, 245
*Something Wicked* (Ferrars) **173**, 282
*Song of Doom* (Markham) **38**, 335
*Sorry State, A* (Kenyon) **145**, 319
*Sound of Murder, The* (Hinxman) **183**, 308
*Sparkling Cyanide* (Christie) **78**, 259
*Speak No Evil* (Eberhart) **69**, 216, 273
*Special Occasion* (Curzon) **165**, 265
*Spend Game* (Gash) **163**, 296
*Spinsters in Jeopardy* (Marsh) **97**, 217, 337
*Spinster's Secret, The* (Gilbert) **79**, 300
*Split Second, The* (Meek) **179**, 340
*Spot the Lady* (Powell) **88**, 354
*Spotted Cats, The* (Tapply) **203**, 374
*Spring Harrowing* (Taylor) **61**, 375
*Spy in Chancery* (Benton) **141**, 237
*Stab in the Back* (Adams) **67**, 227
*Stage Fright* (West) **209**, 379
*Stalker* (Cody) **176**, 261
*Stalking Lamb, The* (Babson) **145**, 233
*State of Grace* (Tine) **171**, 376
*Stately Homicide* (Milner) **95**, 341
*Step in the Dark* (White) **58**, 380
*Still as the Grave* (Roby) **123**, 359
*Still Waters* (Lorac) **85**, 327
*Stoat, The* (Brock) **66**, 241
*Stonefish* (West) **199**, 379
*Strained Relations* (Cairns) **172**, 249
*Stranger and Afraid, A* (Ferrars) **137**, 283
*Stranglehold* (Carmichael) **109**, 253
*Stranglehold* (Gregson) **208**, 302
*Strangler Fig, The* (Strange) **33**, 372
*Stud Game* (Anthony) **153**, 229
*Student Body, The* (Fitzgerald) **107**, 285
*Such Natural Deaths* (Anson) **57**, 229
*Such Pretty Toys* (Dean) **171**, 265
*Sudden Death* (Crofts) **36**, 263
*Sudden Death* (Delman) **144**, 266
*Sudden Death* (Gibbins) **173**, 296
*Suddenly, at Singapore* (Black) 218
*Suffer a Witch* (Fitzgerald) **106**, 285
*Suffer Little Children* (Johnson) **167**, 315
*Suicide Clause* (Carmichael) **126**, 253
*Suit of Diamonds, A: Crime Club Diamond Commemorative Volume Jubilee* (Anon) **196**, 229, 386

*Suitable Day for Dying, A* (Hinxman) **192**, 308
*Sunk Without Trace* (Devine) **154**, 268
*Sunken Sailor, The* (Moyes) **114**, 343
*Sunset Law, The* (Hilton) **169**, 307
*Surfeit of Lampreys* (Marsh) **67**, 216, 337
*Surrender Value* (Hilton) **166**, 307
*Suspicion* (Loder) **42**, 325
*Swaying Pillars, The* (Ferrars) **129**, 283
*Sweet Adelaide* (Symons) **162**, 374
*Sweet Poison* (Penny) **65**, 351
*Sweet Short Grass, The* (Inchbald) **170**, 311
*Swing, Brother, Swing* (Marsh) **85**, 337
*Symbols at Your Door* (Fraser) **197**, 292

*Taken at the Flood* (Christie) **83**, 259
*Take-Over Men, The* (Wainwright) **130**, 378
*Tale of Two Murders, A* (Ferrars) **108**, 283
*Talent for Murder* (Wainwright) **127**, 378
*Talkative Policeman, The* (Penny) **50**, 351
*Tall House Mystery, The* (Fielding) **41**, 284
*Tapping on the Wall, A* (Hull) **115**, 223, 310
*Tarry and Be Hanged* (Woods) **131**, 383
*Tartan Ringers, The* (Gash) **181**, 296
*Taste of Fears, The* (Woods) **118**, 384
*Telephone Never Tells, The* (Hinxman) **168**, 308
*Ten Little Niggers* (Christie) **61**, 259
*Ten Steps to the Gallows* (Wainwright) **124**, 378
*Tenant for the Tomb* (Gilbert) **137**, 300
*Terminus* (Puckett) **197**, 355
*Terror on the Island* (Ferguson) **70**, 278
*Theft of the Iron Dogs, The* (Lorac) **79**, 327
*There Are No Ghosts in the Soviet Union* (Hill) **187**, 305, 386
*There Goes Charlie; A Rural Murder* (Fleming) **199**, 285
*There Has Been a Murder* (Holt) **51**, 308
*There Must Be Some Mistake* (Babson) **149**, 233
*There Was a Little Girl* (Dewhurst) **176**, 269
*There's Trouble Brewing* (Blake) **52**, 240
*These Names Make Clues* (Lorac) **54**, 328
*They Came to Baghdad* (Christie) **90**, 259
*They Do it with Mirrors* (Christie) **94**, 259
*They Hunted a Fox* (Campbell) **64**, 250
*They See in Darkness* (White) **75**, 380
*They Watched By Night* (Rhode) **69**, 358
*Thinner Than Water* (Ferrars) **167**, 283
*Third Crime Lucky* (Gilbert) **108**, 301
*Third Eye, The* (White) **52**, 380
*Third Girl* (Christie) **126**, 259
*Third Victim, The* (Farjeon) **70**, 277
*Thirteen Problems, The* (Christie) **38**, 259, 386
*This Blessed Plot* (Meek) **198**, 340
*This is the House!* (Smith) **76**, 367
*This is Your Death* (Devine) **167**, 268
*This Little Measure* (Woods) **121**, 384
*This Undesirable Residence* (Burton) **71**, 246
*This Won't Hurt You* (Fitzgerald) **109**, 285
*Thou Shell of Death* (Blake) **49**, 240
*Though I Know She Lies* (Woods) **123**, 384
*Three Act Tragedy* (Christie) **45**, 259
*Three and One Make Five* (Jeffries) **174**, 314
*Three at Wolfe's Door* (Stout) **114**, 370, 387
*Three Bright Pebbles* (Ford) **59**, 291
*Three Corpse Trick,The* (Burton) **75**, 246
*Three Crimes,The* (Burton) **34**, 246
*Three Days for Emeralds* (Eberhart) **189**, 273
*Three Doors to Death* (Stout) **89**, 370, 387
*Three for the Chair* (Stout) **106**, 370, 387
*Three Green Bottles* (Devine) **139**, 268
*Three Men Out* (Stout) **99**, 370, 387
*Three Names for Murder* (Campbell) **65**, 250
*Three Pipe Problem, A* (Symons) **147**, 374
*Three Witnesses* (Stout) **103**, 370, 387
*Three, Three, The Rivals* (Fraser) **203**, 292
*Three-Core Lead* (Curzon) **190**, 265
*Thrill Machine, The* (Hamilton) **139**, 303
*Thus Was Adonis Murdered* (Caudwell) **165**, 254
*Thy Brother Death* (Ferrars) **208**, 283
*Ticket to Ride* (Perry) **144**, 353
*Tied up in Tinsel* (Marsh) **140**, 337
*Tiger of Mayfair* (Holt) **46**, 309
*Tight Lines* (Tapply) **207**, 374
*Tightrope for Three* (Babson) **156**, 233
*Time for Pirates,A* (Black) **138**, 238
*To Bed at Noon* (Gielgud) **112**, 297
*To Catch a Thief* (Burton) **45**, 246
*To Die a Little* (Jobson) **156**, 315
*To His Just Deserts: A Story of Finland* (Low) **181**, 329
*To Kill a Coconut* (Moyes) **152**, 343
*To Make an Underworld* (Fleming) **151**, 287
*Tondo for Short* (Inchbald) **166**, 311
*Too Clever By Half* (Jeffries) **196**, 314
*Too Late for Tears* (Carmichael) **142**, 253
*Too Many Clients* (Stout) **115**, 370
*Too Many Cooks* (Stout) **57**, 370
*Too Many Women* (Stout) **82**, 371
*Toper's End* (Cole) **71**, 262
*Tortuous Trails* (Footner) **53**, 289, 386
*Touch and Go* (Meek) **204**, 340
*Touchdown* (Russell) **159**, 362
*Towards Zero* (Christie) **75**, 259
*Town Cried Murder, The* (Ford) **61**, 291
*Tragedy at Beechcroft* (Fielding) **46**, 284
*Tragedy at the Thirteenth Hole* (Burton) **41**, 246
*Tragedy on the Line* (Rhode) **34**, 358
*Trail of Ashes, A* (Babson) **175**, 234
*Trail of Fire* (Curzon) **184**, 265
*Traitor's Crime, A* (Jeffries) **129**, 314
*Travelling Butcher* (Campbell) **75**, 250
*Treason in My Breast* (Gilbert) **56**, 301
*Treason in the Egg* (Strong) **107**, 372
*Treasure By Degrees* (Williams) **153**, 381
*Treasure Preserved* (Williams) **171**, 381
*Treasure Up in Smoke* (Williams) **155**, 219, 381
*Treble Cross* (Howard) **147**, 310
*Trial by Fury* (Ferrars) **191**, 283
*Trial From Ambush* (Ford) **116**, 291
*Trick of Diamonds, A* (Auswaks) **163**, 231
*Trio for Blunt Instruments* (Stout) **122**, 371, 387
*Trio in Three Flats* (Dewhurst) **165**, 269
*Triple Jeopardy* (Stout) **94**, 371, 387
*Trojan Hearse, The* (Curzon) **178**, 265
*Trouble in Triplicate* (Stout) **85**, 371, 387
*Troubled Deaths* (Jeffries) **154**, 314
*Trout in the Milk, A* (Lewis) **181**, 323
*Trunk Call* (Farjeon) **38**, 277
*Trusted like a Fox* (Woods) **120**, 384
*Tryst for a Tragedy* (Lorac) **67**, 328
*Twelve Deaths of Christmas, The* (Babson) **159**, 234
*Twenty-Five Sanitary Inspectors* (East) **46**, 219, 270
*Twenty-Fourth Level* (Benton) **131**, 237
*Twice in a Blue Moon* (Moyes) **208**, 343
*Twisted Justice* (Ashford) **205**, 231
*Two Dead* (Loder) **45**, 325
*Two Little Rich Girls* (Eberhart) **141**, 273
*Two Lovers Too Many* (Fleming) 218
*Two Way Cut* (Turnbull) **188**, 377
*Two-Faced Death* (Jeffries) **151**, 314

*Uncertain Death* (Gilbert) **115**, 301
*Uncertain Sound, An* (Lewis) **155**, 323
*Under Contract* (Cody) **183**, 261
*Under World* (Hill) **188**, 306
*Underground Man, The* (Macdonald) **138**, 331
*Undesirable Company* (Ryck) **146**, 363
*Undue Influence* (Yastrow) **201**, 385
*Uneasy Is the Grave* (Strange) **89**, 372
*Uneasy Lies the Head* (Tine) **172**, 376
*Unfair Exchange* (Babson) **147**, 234
*Unfortunate Murderer, The* (Hull) **70**, 310
*Unholy Writ* (Williams) **151**, 381
*Unidentified Woman* (Eberhart) **76**, 273
*Unknown Quantity, The* (Eberhart) **96**, 273
*Unknown Terror* (Holt) **48**, 309
*Unnatural Hazard* (Cork) **192**, 263
*Unneutral Murder* (Footner) **75**, 289
*Unorthodox Murder of Rabbi Moss, The* (Telushkin) **182**, 376
*Unreasonable Doubt* (Ferrars) **105**, 283
*Unruly Son* (Barnard) **155**, 236
*Unseemly End* (Jeffries) **166**, 314
*Unseen Witness* (Matthews) **205**, 337
*Until She Was Dead* (Hull) **84**, 310
*Untimely Guest* (Babson) **151**, 234
*Unto the Grave* (Penn) **181**, 351
*Unwanted Corpse,The* (Burton) **98**, 246
*Up the Garden Path* (Burton) **69**, 246
*Upfold Farm Mystery, The* (Fielding) **34**, 284
*Uprush of Mayhem, An* (Scott) **167**, 365

*Vane Pursuit* (MacLeod) **192**, 333
*Vanishing Act* (Butterworth) **135**, 249
*Vanishing Corpse, The* (Gilbert) **67**, 301
*Vanishing Point* (Flower) **148**, 288
*Vanishing Trick, The* (Carmichael) **93**, 253
*Vasiliko Affair, The* (Culpan) **129**, 264
*Vatican Rip, The* (Gash) **166**, 219, 296
*Vegetable Duck* (Rhode) **76**, 358
*Vendetta* (Carmichael) **118**, 253
*Verdict of Twelve* (Postgate) **64**, 354
*Very Good Hater, A* (Hill) **146**, 306
*Very Last Gambado, The* (Gash) **193**, 296
*Very Quiet Place, A* (Garve) **127**, 295
*Victory Song* (Adams) **74**, 227
*Villa on the Shore* (Butterworth) **144**, 249
*Village Afraid, A* (Burton) **90**, 246
*Violent Death, A* (Lewis) **158**, 323
*Violent End, A* (Page) **191**, 347
*Viper, The* (Footner) **32**, 289, 386
*Virgin Luck* (Meynell) **118**, 341
*Virgin on the Rocks, A* (Butterworth) **177**, 249
*Visitor, The* (Gilbert) **127**, 301
*Voices in an Empty Room* (Loraine) **144**, 328
*Void in Hearts, A* (Tapply) **192**, 375
*Vulgar Boatman, The* (Tapply) **190**, 375

*Wages of Sin, The* (Parkes) **204**, 348
*Waiting for Thursday* (Jobson) **153**, 315
*Wandering Widows, The* (Ferrars) **117**, 283
*Wanted for Murder* (Holt) **55**, 309
*Wave of Fatalities, A* (Delving) **148**, 267
*Web of Silence* (Wainwright) **128**, 378
*Wedding-Chest Mystery, The* (Fielding) **33**, 284
*Weekend for Murder* (Babson) **180**, 234
*Welcome to the Grave* (McMullen) **162**, 339
*Were He a Stranger* (Craig) **157**, 263
*Westwood Mystery, The* (Fielding) **39**, 284
*Wheel Spins, The* (White) **49**, 216, 380
*When I Grow Rich* (Fleming) **116**, 219, 287
*When in Rome* (Marsh) **136**, 337
*When the Killing Starts* (Wood) **193**, 382
*Where is Barbara Prentice?* (Burton) **51**, 246
*Where There's a Will* (Stout) **68**, 371
*Which I Never* (Strong) **90**, 217, 372
*While She Sleeps* (White) **64**, 380
*Whisper in the Gloom, The* (Blake) **98**, 240
*Whispering Cup, The* (Seeley) **68**, 366
*Whispering Man, The* (Holt) **57**, 309
*Whistler in the Dark* (Malcolm) **182**, 334
*White Dress, The* (Eberhart) **80**, 273
*White Shroud, The* (Nicholas) **115**, 223, 346
*Who Is Simon Warwick?* (Moyes) **156**, 344
*Who Killed the Husband?* (Footner) **70**, 289
*Who Saw Her Die?* (Moyes) **134**, 219, 344
*Whoever I Am* (Dewhurst) **168**, 269
*Whole Hog, The* (Kenyon) **126**, 319
*Why Didn't They Ask Evans?* (Christie) **44**, 259
*Why Kill Johnny?* (Carmichael) **96**, 253
*Widow's Cruise, The* (Blake) **108**, 240
*Widow's End* (Penn) **209**, 351
*Wilde West* (Satterthwait) **203**, 364
*Will and the Deed,The* (Peters) **113**, 354
*Will in the Way, A* (Burton) **81**, 246
*Will to Kill, A* (Penn) **173**, 351
*Wilson and Some Others* (Cole) **65**, 262, 386
*Windmill Mystery, The* (Farjeon) **43**, 277
*Windy Side of the Law, The* (Woods) **123**, 384
*Wings of Fear* (Eberhart) **78**, 273
*Winter Rules* (Cork) **201**, 263
*Wisp of Smoke, A* (Lewis) **201**, 323
*Witch Hill Murder, The* (Winslow) **154**, 381
*With Murder in Mind* (Ferrars) **82**, 283
*With This Ring* (Eberhart) **71**, 274
*Withdrawing Room, The* (MacLeod) **166**, 333
*Without a Trace* (Forsythe) **202**, 291
*Witness at Large* (Eberhart) **127**, 274
*Witness Before the Fact* (Ferrars) **159**, 283
*Witness My Death* (Lewis) **150**, 323
*Wolf By the Ears, A* (Lewis) **134**, 323
*Wolf in Man's Clothing* (Eberhart) **73**, 274
*Woman Hunt* (Ryck) **140**, 364
*Woman in Black, The* (Ford) **81**, 291
*Woman in Red, The* (Gilbert) **69**, 301
*Woman in the Sea, The* (Smith) **83**, 367
*Woman of Straw* (Arley) **103**, 229
*Woman on the Roof* (Eberhart) **129**, 274
*Woman Slaughter* (Ferrars) **192**, 283
*Word of Six Letters,A* (Adams) **48**, 227
*Worm of Death, The* (Blake) **115**, 240
*Worm of Doubt, A* (Meek) **186**, 340
*Worms Must Wait, The* (Wainwright) **128**, 379
*Wrack and Rune* (MacLeod) **170**, 333
*Wraith, The* (MacDonald) **35**, 330
*Wreath of Honesty* (Burden) **197**, 242
*Writing on the Wall, The* (Adams) **76**, 227
*Wrong Impression, The* (Malcolm) **196**, 334
*Wycherley Woman, The* (Macdonald) **116**, 331

*X Marks the Spot* (Butterworth) **155**, 249
*X v. Rex* (Porlock) **40**, 216, 354

*Yellow Turban, The* (Jay) **99**, 312
*You Can Help Me* (Birmingham) **147**, 237
*You Can't Believe Your Eyes* (Fleming) **104**, 287
*You Can't Call It Murder* (Ramsay) **153**, 356
*You Won't Let Me Finish* (Fleming) **143**, 287
*Young Man, I Think You're Dying* (Fleming) **134**, 287
*Young Vanish, The* (Everton) **37**, 275
*Your Eyelids Are Growing Heavy* (Paul) **169**, 349
*Your Loving Victim* (McGerr) **90**, 338
*Your Money and Your Wife* (Perry) **148**, 353

*'Z' Murders, The* (Farjeon) **38**, 277
*Zebra-Striped Hearse, The* (Macdonald) **119**, 331
*Zero at the Bone* (Ferrars) **128**, 283
*Zero in the Gate* (Farrar) **112**, 278
*Zigzag* (Kenyon) **167**, 319